The New REVISED
Appleton-Cuyás
SPANISH-ENGLISH
ENGLISH-SPANISH
DICTIONARY

PREFACIO

Pocas frases introductorias son necesarias para presentar el *Nuevo Diccionario Appleton-Cuyás*. Es hijo del gran *Diccionario Appleton Español-Inglés Inglés-Español* de Arturo Cuyás, cuyo prestigio está sólidamente establecido en los mundos de habla española e inglesa. Se basa en la Cuarta Edición de esa obra, que contiene las revisiones y adiciones incorporadas a ella por el Profesor Lewis E. Brett y la Srta. Helen S. Eaton. El mismo rigor científico que caracterizó la labor tanto de Don Arturo Cuyás como la de aquellos lexicógrafos ha guiado la larga, minuciosa y cuidada tarea de preparación de este compendio.

Ahora bien, hay muchas gentes cuyas necesidades no justifica la adquisición de un diccionario de carácter tan exhaustivo como el Cuyás grande; tal es el caso de un gran número de las personas que tienen un interés general por el aprendizaje del español o el inglés. Por otra parte, hay también ciertas personas: estudiantes universitarios, traductores, hombres de negocios, viajeros, trabajadores sociales y otros que, a pesar de tal vez poseer ya el Cuyás grande, gustarían de tener una edición factible de llevarse sin estorbo para consulta inmediata y rápida en cualquier lugar donde se presente la necesidad. El objetivo principal que se persiguió a lo largo de toda la preparación de esta obra portátil fue el poder ofrecer en forma concisa y eficaz todo el contenido del diccionario original que fuese compatible con los propósitos y el tamaño del volumen que se proyectaba. Dentro del ámbito de su propósito, este diccionario responde a las necesidades expresivas básicas de todos los campos principales de la actividad humana y abarca todos los niveles del uso aceptado de expresión hablada y escrita de los dos idiomas. Tenemos la convicción de que, a base de la eficiente condensación de las definiciones y el empleo aprovechado del espacio disponible, el *Nuevo Diccionario Appleton-Cuyás* ofrece un número más elevado de vocablos y giros que ningún otro diccionario de tamaño semejante.

En la selección de la materia léxica se han utilizado, dándoles el valor auxiliar que tienen, todos cuantos cómputos de frecuencias y listas de palabras y modismos son accesibles hoy para ambas lenguas. Se han mantenido todos los términos y expresiones de alto índice de incidencia en el lenguaje hablado y escrito que aparecen en la obra original y se han añadido otros de incorporación reciente al uso común. El criterio para la selección de los términos ha sido la norma del uso culto medio que prevalece en ambas lenguas. Para esa norma en el continente americano se ha recurrido a la autoridad de los diccionarios de Santamaría y Malaret, amén de otras fuentes de información. En la parte española, la extensión del empleo de las variedades lingüísticas hispanoamericanas va indicada adecuadamente de la siguiente manera: (Am.) para los vocablos y giros de uso continental y (Mex.), (Arg.) etc., para aquellos que tienen sólo validez regional.

Llamamos la atención del lector hacia ciertas secciones de especial utilidad que este diccionario contiene y que rara vez se encuentran juntas en ninguno de este tamaño, a saber: listas de números cardinales, ordinales y fraccionarios; tablas completas de verbos irregulares; claves de pronunciación, de carácter sencillo y claro; tablas de pesos, medidas y unidades termométricas; abreviaturas de uso común, y listas de nombres propios personales y geográficos.

Tuvimos la fortuna de contar, como colaboradores directos en esta empresa, con el Dr. Alberto Andino, antiguo Catedrático de Lengua y Literatura Españolas de la Universidad de Las Villas, Cuba, el Dr.

Fernando Figueredo, distinguido ex-miembro del Colegio de Abogados de Cuba, y el lexicógrafo Sr. Bernard Witlieb, Licenciado en Artes del Departamento de Inglés de la New York University. Suerte no menor fue el haber contado en todo momento con el sabio y experimentado consejo en materia editorial de la Srta. Catherine B. Avery, funcionaria de la casa Appleton-Century-Crofts.

New York University   E.G.D.
New York

ADVERTENCIAS AL CONSULTANTE

1. *Distribución y orden.* Para ahorrar espacio y poder incluir un mayor número de palabras hemos agrupado en familias todas aquellas que tienen una estrecha relación, ya de origen y significado, ya de ortografía, respetando, sin embargo, siempre, el orden alfabético. Todos los artículos principales van en negritas. Los modismos y giros van en itálica, alfabetizados por la primera palabra de la expresión. En las definiciones, la separación por medio de punto y coma indica áreas diferentes de significado; la coma, términos sinónimos dentro de cada área específica. Para ahorrar más espacio se ha omitido la parte común de las palabras que constituyen una misma familia. Las partes omitidas de las palabras que forman un grupo están referidas siempre al término que lo encabeza. Se llama la atención del consultante hacia el hecho de que el alfabeto inglés y el español no se corresponden exactamente: la ch, y la ll, por ejemplo, no son en aquél letras independientes. Por tanto, esto obliga a habituarse a una ordenación alfabética diferente en la que achievement precede a acid y ally a almanac.

2. Todos los verbos irregulares van indicados por abreviaturas (*vti., vii., vai.*). Los números que van a continuación de las abreviaturas hacen referencia a la *Tablas de Verbos Irregulares*, en la página x.

3. *Adverbios.* Todos los adverbios ingleses terminados en -*ly* se han omitido, excepto aquellos cuyo significado no tiene exacta correspondencia con el de sus equivalentes etimológicos en español.

4. *Abreviaturas.* Todas las abreviaturas empleadas en el texto para indicar limitaciones de uso, geográficas o de otra índole (ex. *Méx.*, México; *aer.*, aeronáutica; *med.*, medicina) se hallarán explicadas en la lista de *Abreviaturas usadas en la parte 1ª* en la página iv.

5. *Pronunciación.* La pronunciación y acentuación de todas las palabras inglesas va indicada entre corchetes por medio de una adaptación simplificada del Alfabeto Fonético Internacional. En las páginas xxix-xxx se incluye una Clave de las equivalencias españolas aproximadas de los sonidos ingleses representados por los símbolos fonéticos.

iii

PRONUNCIACION INGLESA
CLAVE DE LOS SIMBOLOS FONETICOS

I. Vocales

Símbolo	Grafías y Ejemplos	Equivalencia aproximada de sonido
[a]	*a* (father); *e* (sergeant); *ea* (heart); *o* (hot); *ow* (knowledge)	Como la *a* de pecado.
[ǝ]	*a* (legitimacy); *ai* (certain)	Entre *e* y *a*.
[ạ]	*a* (attire); *ea* (pageant)	Entre *a* y *e*.
[ǎ]	*a* (forward, sofa)	Muy cercano a la *a*, pero más cerrado.
[æ]	*a* (man, that); *ai* (plaid); *au* (laugh)	Entre la *a* de caso e la *e* de guerra.
[aị]	*ai* (aisle); *ay* (aye); *ei* (height); *ey* (eye); *i* (life); *ie* (pie); *uy* (buy); *y* (by); *ye* (goodbye)	Como *ai* en vais.
[aụ]	*ou* (house); *ow* (cow)	Como *au* en causa.
[e]	*a* (any); *ae* (aeronautics); *ai* (chair); *ay* (prayer); *e* (let); *ea* (head); *ei* (heifer); *eo* (leopard); *ie* (friend); *u* (bury)	Como la *e* de cerro.
[ě]	*e* (adequate, courtesy)	Muy cercana a la *e*.
[ɛ]	*e* (ardent); *ea* (sergeant)	Como la anterior.
[ei]	*e* (case); *ai* (train); *au* (gauge); *ay* (pay); *e* (fete)	Como *ei* en seis.
[i]	*ae* (alumnae); *ay* (quay); *e* (be); *ea* (clean); *ee* (sleep); *ei* (seize); *eo* (people); *ey* (key); *i* (machine); *ie* (fiend)	Como la *i* de vida.
[ị]	*a* (average); *ay* (Sunday); *e* (subsequent); *ea* (fear); *ee* (cheer); *ei* (sovereign); *ey* (money); *i* (bit); *ie* (sieve); *o* (women); *oi* (chamois); *u* (business); *ui* (guilt); *y* (very)	Como la *i* de sin, pero más breve y abierta.
[iu]	*eau* (beautiful); *eu* (feud); *ew* (few); *iew* (view); *u* (mute); *ue* (cue); *ui* (suit)	Como *iu* en ciudad o *yu* en yugo.
[o]	*o* (obese, notation)	Como la *o* de sola.
[ǫ]	*eo* (dungeon); *io* (nation); *o* (atom)	Entre *o* y *e*.
[œ]	*e* (her); *ea* (earth); *i* (bird); *o* (word); *ou* (courage); *u* (burn); *y* (martyr)	Sonido parecido al de *eu* en francés (peur) o al de *ö* en aleman (schön).
[oụ]	*eau* (beau); *eo* (yeoman); *ew* (sew); *o* (alone); *oa* (road); *oe* (foe); *oo* (brooch); *ou* (dough); *ow* (crow)	Como la *o* de loca seguida de una *u* leve.
[u]	*eu* (maneuver); *ew* (blew); *o* (do); *oe* (shoes); *oo* (food); *ou* (coupon); *u* (rude); *ue* (true); *ui* (juice)	Muy cercana a la *u* de suyo.
[ụ]	*o* (woman); *oo* (good); *ou* (could); *u* (bull)	Como la *u* de suyo, pero más cerrada.
[ų]	*u* (commensurate, corduroy)	Como *iu* en ciudad, pero más atenuado.

Símbolo	Grafías y Ejemplos	Equivalencia aproximada de sonido
[ṷ]	u (censure, natural)	Lo mismo que el anterior, pero más relajado.
[waɪ]	oi (choir); uay (Paraguayan)	Como ua en guapa seguido de una i muy relajada.
[weɪ]	ua (persuade)	Como ue en sueco seguido de una i muy relajada.
[yṷ]	eu (euphemism); ew (ewe); ou (you); u (unite)	Como iu en ciudad o yu en yugo.
[yṷ]	u (regular, secular)	Como iu en ciudad pero bastante más atenuado.
[ɔ]	aᵣ (all); au (launch); aw (law); o (song); oa (broad); ou (fought)	Como la o de sol pero más prolongada.
[ɔi]	oi (oil); oy (toy); uoy (buoy)	Como oy en voy.
[ʌ]	o (come); oe (does); oo (flood); ou (young); u (just)	Sonido entre o y e. Parecido al de la o francesa en homme.

II. CONSONANTES

Símbolo	Grafías y Ejemplos	Equivalencia aproximada de sonido
[b]	baby; robber	Como la b de lumbre.
[ch]	church; furniture; righteous; christian; catch	Como la ch española.
[d]	did; ladder	Como la d de onda.
[dʒ]	arduous; grandeur; budge; adjacent; gem; judge	Sonido semejante al de la y de conyugal o al de g italiana en cortigiani.
[f]	far; rough; philosophy	Como la f española.
[g]	gag; wriggle	Como la g de gana.
[gz]	exact; example	Como la g de gana seguida de la s francesa de maison.
[h]	here; behave; who; whole	Como la j española pero más aspirada y más suave.
[hw]	what; when	Como la j de juez, pero más suave.
[k]	car; account; ache; back; kill; joke; antique	Como la c de calle.
[ks]	excuse; tax	Como la x de flexión.
[kw]	queen; acquaint	Como cu en cual o qu en que.
[l]	lard; lull; small	Como la l de lado.
[m]	man; mammal	Como la m española.
[n]	nun; banner	Como la n española.
[ŋ]	anchor; sink; sing; angle	Semejante al de la n de banco, pero más nasal.
[p]	top; pepper	Como la p española.
[r]	rat; merry	Parecida a la r suave española.
[s]	cent; sister; miss; quartz; façade	Como la s de sala, pero algo más tensa y larga.
[ʃ]	ocean; chagrin; sure; conscience; fish; mission; partial; anxious	Como la ch francesa en chaise.
[t]	fixed; taunt; rattle; thyme	Próxima a la t española de parte.
[v]	of; vivid; over	Parecida a la v española, pero labiodental.
[w]	we; awake	Como la u española.
[y]	onion; year	Semejante a la y de ayer, pero más relajada.
[z]	riches; discern; dessert; desert; anxiety; zeal; dazzle	Como la s francesa de maison. Parecida a la s española de isla.
[ʒ]	mirage; pleasure; vision; azure	Como la g francesa de genre.
[ð]	this; with; mother	Muy semejante a la d de nada.
[θ]	thin; theater; truth	Como la z de Castilla en zorro.

SINOPSIS DE LA GRAMÁTICA INGLESA

I. Consideraciones generales

El idioma inglés no es tan exacto como el español. No hay reglas fijas para la pronunciación ni para la colocación del acento ni acentos ortográficos para ayudar en la pronunciación de una palabra. Consecuentemente, hay que aprender de memoria la pronunciación de un gran número de vocablos. (Véase la sección PRONUNCIACIÓN INGLESA, págs. xxix-xxx.)

Se usan las mayúsculas en inglés como en español, y en los casos siguientes:
a) el pronombre sujeto I (*yo*) se escribe con mayúscula;
b) los nombres de los meses y días se escriben con mayúsculas;

Saturday, July 17   *el sábado, 17 de julio*

c) los gentilicios y todos los adjetivos formados de nombres propios se escriben con mayúsculas;

the Spaniards   *los españoles*

d) los títulos y tratamientos de cortesía se escriben con mayúsculas;

Mr.   *señor*
Mrs.   *señora*
Miss   *señorita*

e) todas las palabras en un título de libro, película, etc. se escriben con mayúsculas, exceptuando las palabras cortas si no van al principio.

From Here to Eternity

II. Las partes de la oración

A. Del artículo

1. El artículo indefinido en inglés carece de género; tiene las formas **a** y **an** (*un, una*). Cuando se antepone a una palabra comenzada en consonante se usa la forma **a**, y cuando se antepone a una palabra comenzada en vocal se usa la forma **an**. El plural de ambas formas es **some** (*unos, unas*).

a book   *un libro*
some books   *unos libros*
an airplane   *un avión*
some airplanes   *unos aviones*
a pen   *una pluma*

Generalmente, se usa el artículo indefinido en inglés como en español, aunque no tan frecuentemente. Algunas diferencias se citan a continuación:
a) no es necesario repetir el artículo indefinido antes de cada nombre;

I have a car, house and television   *Tengo un coche, una casa y una televisión*

b) se usa el artículo indefinido antes de substantivos de cantidad como a half (*medio*), a, one hundred (*cien*), a, one thousand (*mil*);

There are a hundred soldiers here *Hay cien soldados aquí*

c) se usa el artículo indefinido cuando el nombre predicado no está modificado;

John is a doctor *Juan es médico*

d) se usa el artículo indefinido cuando se sobrentiende que la cantidad aludida es uno;

He is wearing a coat *Lleva abrigo*

e) se usa el artículo indefinido cuando se habla de precios.

He sells eggs at twenty cents a dozen *Vende los huevos a veinte centavos la docena*

2. El artículo definido en inglés carece de género; tiene una única forma **the**, que corresponde indistintamente a los artículos definidos españoles *el, los, la, las* y *lo*.

the book	*el libro*
the books	*los libros*
the pen	*la pluma*
the pens	*las plumas*

No es tan corriente su uso en inglés como en español.

Mr. Martin is ill	*El señor Martínez está enfermo*
Love is not enough	*El amor no es suficiente*
Spanish	*El español*
It is one o'clock	*Es la una*
He goes to church on Sundays	*Va a la iglesia los domingos*
This coming year	*El año que viene*
Last Sunday	*El domingo pasado*

Se usa el artículo definido antes del número en un título.

Charles the Fifth *Carlos V*

B. Del nombre

1. El nombre carece de género en el idioma inglés y generalmente sólo cambia para indicar el número. Por eso el artículo definido es siempre el mismo.

the house	*la casa*
the houses	*las casas*
the pencil	*el lápiz*
the pencils	*los lápices*

2. El plural de los nombres ingleses generalmente se forma añadiendo -s al final de la palabra.

SINGULAR		PLURAL	
chair	*silla*	chairs	*sillas*
book	*libro*	books	*libros*

Se forman algunos plurales añadiendo -es después de las terminaciones -s, -sh, -x, -j, -z y -ch.

SINGULAR		PLURAL	
dress	*vestido*	dresses	*vestidos*
bush	*arbusto*	bushes	*arbustos*
box	*caja*	boxes	*cajas*
birch	*abedul*	birches	*abedules*

Se forma el plural de los nombres terminados en -y (después de una consonante o de -qu) cambiando la -y por -i y añadiendo -es.

SINGULAR		PLURAL	
enemy	*enemigo*	enemies	*enemigos*
lady	*señora*	ladies	*señoras*
soliloquy	*soliloquio*	soliloquies	*soliloquios*

Se forma el plural de los nombres que terminan en -y precedida de vocal añadiendo una -s al final de la palabra.

SINGULAR		PLURAL	
donkey	*burro*	donkeys	*burros*

Se forma el plural de los nombres que terminan en -f, -fe, y -ff como sigue.
a) añadiendo -s al final de la palabra;

SINGULAR		PLURAL	
roof	*techo*	roofs	*techos*
chief	*jefe*	chiefs	*jefes*
cuff	*puño de camisa*	cuffs	*puños de camisa*

b) cambiando -f a -v y añadiendo -es.

SINGULAR		PLURAL	
knife	*cuchillo*	knives	*cuchillos*
leaf	*hoja*	leaves	*hojas*

N. B. Staff, scarf y wharf tienen dos formas para el plural. staffs y staves; scarfs y scarves; wharfs y wharves.

Se forma el plural de los nombres que terminan en -o precedida de vocal añadiendo -s al final de la palabra.

SINGULAR		PLURAL	
radio	*radio*	radios	*radios*

Se forma el plural de los nombres que terminan en -o precedida de consonante añadiendo -es al final de la palabra.

SINGULAR		PLURAL	
hero	*héroe*	heroes	*héroes*
potato	*patata*	potatoes	*patatas*

Se forma el plural de los números y letras añadiendo un apóstrofe y una -s.

There are ten 5's in this column *Hay diez cincos en esta columna*
There are two s's in the word *Hay dos eses en la palabra possible*
possible

Algunos nombres, como los nombres de tribus, pueblos, razas y animales, tienen la misma forma para el singular que para el plural.

SINGULAR		PLURAL	
Chinese	*chino*	Chinese	*chinos*
Portuguese	*portugués*	Portuguese	*portugueses*
Norse	*escandinavo*	Norse	*escandinavos*
sheep	*oveja*	sheep	*ovejas*
deer	*ciervo*	deer	*ciervos*

Algunos nombres forman el plural de manera irregular.

SINGULAR		PLURAL	
child	*niño*	children	*niños*
tooth	*diente*	teeth	*dientes*
mouse	*ratón*	mice	*ratones*

En el caso de las palabras compuestas, generalmente se forma el plural de éstas pluralizando a la palabra principal.

SINGULAR		PLURAL	
mother-in-law	*suegra*	mothers-in-law	*suegras*
man-of-war	*buque de guerra*	men-of-war	*buques de guerra*

C. Del adjetivo

1. El adjetivo inglés no tiene ni género ni número; generalmente, se antepone al substantivo que modifica.

the red house	*la casa roja*
the red houses	*las casas rojas*
the white pencil	*el lápiz blanco*
the white pencils	*los lápices blancos*
the beautiful girl	*la muchacha hermosa*
the beautiful girls	*las muchachas hermosas*

2. *La comparación de los adjetivos.* Hay tres grados de comparación en inglés, que son: el positivo, comparativo y superlativo. El positivo de una o dos sílabas forma el comparativo añadiendo el sufijo -er. Los positivos con más de dos sílabas forman el comparativo anteponiendo el adverbio more (*más*). Los positivos de una o dos sílabas forman el superlativo añadiendo el sufijo -est, y los de dos o más sílabas forman el superlativo anteponiendo el adverbio most (*el más*). Se usa el comparativo less para indicar la cualidad de menos, y least para indicar el menos; ambas formas se anteponen al positivo.

POSITIVO		COMPARATIVO		SUPERLATIVO	
hard	*duro*	harder	*más duro*	hardest	*el más duro*
long	*largo*	longer	*más largo*	longest	*el más largo*
bright	*claro*	brighter	*más claro*	brightest	*el más claro*
capable	*capaz*	more capable	*más capaz*	most capable	*el más capaz*
clever	*listo*	less clever	*menos listo*	least clever	*el menos listo*

Se forma el comparativo y el superlativo de los adjetivos que terminan en -y después de una consonante cambiando la -y por -i y añadiendo los sufijos -er y -est respectivamente.

POSITIVO		COMPARATIVO		SUPERLATIVO	
pretty	*bonito*	prettier	*más bonito*	prettiest	*el más bonito*
happy	*feliz*	happier	*más feliz*	happiest	*el más feliz*

En algunos casos es necesario modificar la ortografía del positivo para acomodar a los grados del comparativo y superlativo. Generalmente, cuando el adjetivo de una o dos sílabas termina en consonante precedida de vocal, la consonante se dobla.

POSITIVO		COMPARATIVO		SUPERLATIVO	
drab	*pardo*	drabber	*más pardo*	drabbest	*el más pardo*
fat	*gordo*	fatter	*más gordo*	fattest	*el más gordo*

A continuación se dan algunos adjetivos de comparación irregular:

POSITIVO		COMPARATIVO		SUPERLATIVO	
bad	*mal*	worse	*peor*	worst	*el peor*
ill	*mal*	worse	*peor*	worst	*el peor*
evil	*mal*	worse	*peor*	worst	*el peor*
good	*bueno*	better	*mejor*	best	*el mejor*
many	*muchos*	more	*más*	most	*los más*
much	*mucho*	more	*más*	most	*el más*

D. Del adverbio

1. Se usa el adverbio en inglés, como en español, para modificar un verbo, un adjetivo u otro adverbio.

He ran quickly	*Corrió rápidamente*
The very good man	*El hombre muy bueno*
He ran very quickly	*Corrió rapidísimamente*

2. Generalmente, se forma el adverbio añadiendo el sufijo -ly a un adjetivo. La terminación -ly corresponde a la terminación -*mente* en español. Pero no todas las palabras terminadas en -ly son adverbios; algunas son adjetivos, como: friendly (*amigable*), lovely (*hermoso*), kindly (*bondadoso*), etc.

ADJETIVO		ADVERBIO	
strong	*fuerte*	strongly	*fuertemente*
regular	*regular*	regularly	*regularmente*

3. Algunas veces los adverbios toman la misma forma que los adjetivos.

ADJETIVO		ADVERBIO	
a slow watch	*un reloj atrasado*	go slow	*ve lentamente*
a late train	*un tren tardío*	he arrived late	*él llegó tarde*

4. El adverbio, como el adjetivo, tiene tres grados de comparación, que son: el positivo, comparativo y superlativo. Generalmente, se forma el comparativo y superlativo añadiendo more (*más*) o less (*menos*) para el comparativo, y most (*el más*) o least (*el menos*) para el superlativo, antes del adverbio. No obstante, se forma el comparativo y superlativo de algunos adverbios añadiendo -er y -est respectivamente al final de la forma positiva.

POSITIVO		COMPARATIVO		SUPERLATIVO	
rapidly	*rápida-mente*	more rapidly	*más rápida-mente*	most rapidly	*más rápida-mente*
easily	*fácil-mente*	more easily	*más fácil-mente*	most easily	*más fácil-mente*
soon	*pronto*	sooner	*más pronto*	soonest	*más pronto*
easily	*fácil-mente*	less easily	*menos fácil-mente*	least easily	*menos fácil-mente*

Los siguientes adverbios tienen comparaciones irregulares.

POSITIVO		COMPARATIVO		SUPERLATIVO	
far	*lejos*	farther; further	*más lejos*	farthest; furthest	*el más lejos*
ill, bad	*mal*	worse	*peor*	worst	*el peor*
little	*poco*	less	*menos*	least	*el menos*
much	*mucho*	more	*más*	most	*el más*
well	*bien*	better	*mejor*	best	*el mejor*

E. Del pronombre

1. *Los pronombres personales.* Los pronombres personales se dividen según el caso y son: el sujeto, objeto y posesivo. En inglés, es necesario usar el pronombre sujeto, porque los verbos no indican a la persona gramatical; se usa el mismo pronombre para el objeto directo que para el objeto indirecto. No hay equivalente inglés para las formas españolas usted, Vd. y ustedes, Vds. Se usa la forma del pronombre sujeto de segunda persona you (*tu, vosotros*) siempre, ya sea cuando se hable a una o a varias personas.

He is going tomorrow	*Irá mañana*
I see him now	*Le veo ahora*
I gave it to him	*Se lo di*
Do you speak Spanish?	*¿Habla Vd. español?*

A continuación se citan los pronombres personales que se usan ya como sujeto, ya como objeto directo o indirecto.

SINGULAR

	SUJETO		OBJETO DIRECTO E INDIRECTO	
primera persona	I	*yo*	me	*me*
segunda persona	you	*tú*	you	*te*
tercera persona	he	*él*	him	*lo, le; se*
	she	*ella*	her	*la, le; se*
	it	*ello*	it	*lo*

PLURAL

	SUJETO		OBJETO DIRECTO E INDIRECTO	
primera persona	we	*nosotros*	us	*nos*
segunda persona	you	*vosotros*	you	*vos, os*
tercera persona	they	*ellos*	them	*los, las; les*

Los pronombres posesivos en inglés carecen de género. Se refieren y concuerdan en número con el poseedor y no con la cosa poseída.

This book is mine	*Este libro es el mío*
Those books are mine	*Esos libros son los míos*
That dog is his	*Aquel perro es el suyo*
Are these pencils yours, Peter?	*¿Son estos lápices los tuyos, Pedro?*

PRONOMBRES POSESIVOS

mine	*el mío, la mía, los míos, las mías*
yours	*el tuyo, la tuya, los tuyos, las tuyas; el vuestro, la vuestra, los vuestros, las vuestras*
his	*el suyo, los suyos*
hers	*la suya, las suyas*
ours	*el nuestro, la nuestra, los nuestros, las nuestras*
theirs	*el suyo, la suya, los suyos, las suyas*

Los adjetivos posesivos en inglés carecen de género. Concuerdan en número con el poseedor y no con la cosa poseída y preceden al substantivo que califican.

My books are in the drawer	*Mis libros están en la gaveta*
Our house is white	*Nuestra casa es blanca*

ADJETIVOS POSESIVOS

my	*mi, mis*
your	*tu, tus; vuestro, vuestros*
his	*su, sus*
her	*su sus*
its	*su, sus*
our	*nuestro, nuestros*
their	*su, sus*

2. *Los pronombres relativos.* Los pronombres relativos sirven para referir a un nombre o pronombre que generalmente les precede en una oración. Los pronombres relativos se dividen en simples y compuestos.

a) Los pronombres relativos simples son:

who	*quien, que, cual, el que*
whom	*que, quien, el cual*
whose	*de quien, cuyo, del cual*
that	*que, cual, el que*
which	*que, quien, cual, el que*
what	*que, el que*

The man who came to dinner	*El hombre que vino a comer*
The man whom we saw is my brother	*El hombre que vimos es mi hermano*
The girl with whom he went to the movies is here	*La muchacha con quien fue al cine está aquí*
Give me what books you can	*Déme Vd. los libros que pueda*

b) Los pronombres relativos compuestos se forman añadiendo las terminaciones -ever y -soever a who, which y what (whoever, whichever, whatever) y se usan con carácter enfático.

c) Los pronombres relativos en inglés carecen de género y de número.

John and Charles, who are students, are on vacation	*Juan y Carlos, quienes son estudiantes, están de vacaciones*
Mary is the girl who sings	*María es la muchacha que canta*

d) Generalmente, who se refiere a una o algunas personas, which a una o algunas cosas, y that a ambas. Whom se puede usar tanto como objeto directo que indirecto. Whose se usa como posesivo.

Mary is the girl who sings	*María es la muchacha que canta*
Here is the book of which I spoke to you	*Aquí está el libro del cual te hablé*

Albert is the one that is playing the piano	*Alberto es el que toca el piano*
She is the girl to whom we gave the prize	*Ella es la muchacha a quien dimos el premio*
John, whose uncle is ill, is leaving tonight	*Juan, cuyo tío está enfermo, partirá esta noche*

3. *Los pronombres demostrativos.* Los pronombres demostrativos se usan para mostrar uno o varios objetos, a la vez que indican su proximidad o lejanía respecto a la persona que habla o de aquella a quien se habla. Los pronombres demostrativos en inglés carecen de género. Concuerdan en número con la cosa a la que se refieren.

SINGULAR		PLURAL	
this	*éste, ésta, esto;* cerca de la persona que habla	these	*éstos, éstas*
that	*ése, ésa, eso; aquél, aquélla, aquello;* lejos de la persona que habla	those	*ésos, ésas; aquéllos, aquéllas*

This is the pen	*Ésta es la pluma*
These are the books	*Éstos son los libros*
That is his	*Eso es suyo*
Those are hers	*Aquéllos son de ella*

4. *Los pronombres indefinidos.* Se usan los pronombres indefinidos en inglés como en español. A continuación se dan los pronombres indefinidos más usados en inglés:

all	*todo*	everybody	*todos*	nothing	*nada*
another	*otro*	everyone	*todos*	one	*uno*
any	*cualquier*	everything	*todo*	other	*otro*
anybody	*alguien, cualquiera*	few	*pocos*	some	*algunos*
anyone	*alguien, cualquiera*	many	*muchos*	somebody	*alguien*
anything	*algo, cualquier cosa*	neither	*ni uno ni otro*	someone	*alguien*
both	*ambos*	nobody	*ninguno, nadie*	something	*algo*
each	*cada uno, cada cual*	none	*ninguno, nadie*	such	*tal*
either	*uno u otro*	no one	*ninguno, nadie*		

One (*uno*) y other (*otro*) son los únicos que tienen plural.

| These are the ones I like | *Estos son los que me gustan* |
| The others have already left | *Los otros ya se fueron* |

5. *Los pronombres reflexivos o intensivos.* Los pronombres reflexivos, también llamados intensivos por su carácter enfático, carecen de género. Concuerdan en número con la persona a la que se refieren. Se forman de la unión del pronombre personal o del adjetivo posesivo con la terminación -self para el singular y -selves para el plural.

myself	*yo mismo; mí, mí mismo; me*
yourself	*tú mismo; Vd. mismo; ti, ti mismo; te, se*
himself	*él mismo; sí, sí mismo; se*
herself	*ella misma; sí, sí misma; se*
itself	*mismo; sí, sí mismo; se*
ourselves	*nosotros mismos; nos*
yourselves	*vosotros mismos; Vds. mismos; vos, os*
themselves	*ellos mismos; sí, sí mismos; se*

I did it myself	*Yo mismo lo hice*
It moves by itself	*Eso se mueve por sí mismo*
Did you do it yourself?	*¿Lo hizo Vd. mismo?*

F. Las palabras interrogativas

Las palabras interrogativas en inglés carecen de género y de número. A continuación se dan las de uso más frecuente.

how?	*¿cómo?*	where?	*¿dónde?*
how many?	*¿cuántos?*	which?	*¿cuál?*
how much?	*¿cuánto?*	who?	*¿quién?*
what?	*¿qué?*	why?	*¿por qué?*
when?	*¿cuándo?*		

How do you sell them?	*¿A cómo los vende Vd.?*
How many eggs are in that box?	*¿Cuántos huevos hay en esa caja?*
How much are they?	*¿Cuánto cuestan?*
What time is it?	*¿Qué hora es?*
When did you arrive?	*¿Cuándo llegó Vd.?*
Where are you going?	*¿Dónde va Vd?*
Which sister did he marry?	*¿Con cuál de las hermanas se casó?*
Who goes there?	*¿Quién va?*
Why do you weep?	*¿Por qué llora Vd.?*

G. Del verbo

1. Los verbos en inglés pueden ser regulares o irregulares, según la conjugación. Cada verbo consta de tres partes principales: el presente, el pretérito y el participio pasado.

2. El infinitivo se forma con to y el presente del verbo.

to change	*cambiar*	to play	*jugar*
to look	*mirar*	to use	*usar*

El infinitivo se puede usar como substantivo; también puede hacer oficio de adjetivo o adverbio.

To play in the park is fun	*El jugar en el parque es divertido*
I have plenty of books to read	*Tengo muchos libros que leer*
The student came to learn English	*El alumno vino a aprender inglés*

3. El participio presente o gerundio del verbo generalmente se forma añadiendo -ing al presente.

PRESENTE	PARTICIPIO PRESENTE
look	looking
play	playing

Los verbos que tienen el presente terminado en -e muda generalmente pierden la -e y añaden -ing para formar el participio presente.

PRESENTE	PARTICIPIO PRESENTE
change	changing
use	using

Los verbos que doblan la consonante final para formar el pretérito y el participio pasado también doblan la consonante final para formar el participio presente.

PRESENTE		PARTICIPIO PRESENTE
stop	*parar*	stopping
tip	*ladear*	tipping

El participio presente se puede usar con el verbo auxiliar to be para formar un tiempo progresivo.

I am playing cards	*Estoy jugando a las cartas*
I was playing football last week	*Jugaba al fútbol la semana pasada*

4. El pretérito y el participio pasado generalmente se forman añadiendo -d o -ed al presente.

PRESENTE	PRETÉRITO	PARTICIPIO PASADO
change	changed	changed
look	looked	looked
play	played	played
use	used	used

Sin embargo, muchos vergos en inglés tienen formas irregulares para el pretérito y para el participio pasado. A continuación se da una descripción de algunos verbos que forman el pretérito y el participio pasado de manera irregular. No se incluyen los que forman el pretérito y el participio pasado de manera regular, aunque éstos tengan a la vez una forma alterna, a menso que ésta sea la preferida.
a) Algunos verbos duplican la consonante final del presente para formar el pretérito y el participio pasado.

PRESENTE	PRETÉRITO	PARTICIPIO PASADO
abet	abetted	abetted
abhor	abhorred	abhorred
acquit	acquitted	acquitted

Los verbos de esta clase incluidos en este diccionario, a excepción de sus compuestos, se dan a continuación.

admit	concur	fit	jet	permit	scrap
allot	confer	flag	jig	pet	scrub
aver	control	flap	jot	pin	sham
bag	cop	flat	jut	plan	shin
ban	corral	flit	kid	plod	ship
bar	crab	flog	knot	plot	shop
bed	cram	flop	lag	plug	shrug
beg	crib	fog	lap	pop	shun
blab	crop	fret	log	prefer	sin
blot	dam	fur	lop	prod	skim
blur	defer	gad	lug	prop	skin
bob	deter	gag	man	propel	slam
bog	dim	gap	map	pun	slap
bootleg	din	gem	mar	quip	slip
brag	dip	grab	mob	quiz	slop
brim	dispel	grin	mop	rag	slot
bud	distil	grip	mud	ram	slug
bum	dog	grit	nab	rap	slum
can	don	grub	nag	recur	slur
cap	dot	gum	nap	refer	smut
chap	drag	gun	net	remit	snag
char	drip	gut	nip	rib	snap
chat	drop	handicap	nod	rig	snip
chip	drug	hem	occur	rip	snub
chop	drum	hop	omit	rob	sob
chum	emit	hug	outwit	rot	sod
clap	equip	impel	pad	rub	sop
clip	excel	incur	pan	rut	span
clog	expel	infer	pat	sag	spar
clot	extol	inter	patrol	sap	spat
club	fan	jab	peg	scan	spot
commit	fat	jam	pen	scar	spur
compel	fib	jar	pep	scram	squat

stab	strip	sum	thin	trap	war
star	strop	sun	throb	trim	wed
stem	strut	sup	tin	trot	whet
step	stub	tag	tip	tug	whip
stir	stud	tan	top	up	whir
stop	stun	tap	transfer	wad	whiz
strap	submit	tar	transmit	wag	wrap

b) Algunos verbos cambian la -y final del presente en -ied para formar el pretérito y el participio pasado.

PRESENTE	PRETÉRITO	PARTICIPIO PASADO
accompany	accompanied	accompanied
acetify	acetified	acetified
acidify	acidified	acidified

Los verbos de esta clase incluidos en este diccionario, a excepción de sus compuestos, se dan a continuación:

ally	dignify	hurry	occupy	shy
amnesty	dirty	identify	pacify	signify
amplify	diversify	imply	parry	solidify
apply	dizzy	indemnify	personify	specify
baby	dry	intensify	pillory	spy
beautify	eddy	inventory	pity	steady
belly	edify	jelly	ply	stratify
bloody	electrify	jolly	prophesy	study
body	empty	justify	pry	supply
bully	envy	levy	purify	tally
busy	espy	liquefy	putty	tarry
candy	falsify	lobby	qualify	terrify
carry	fancy	magnify	quarry	testify
certify	ferry	marry	query	tidy
classify	fortify	modify	rally	try
codify	fry	mortify	rectify	typify
comply	glorify	muddy	rely	unify
copy	gratify	multiply	remedy	vary
crucify	gully	mutiny	reply	weary
cry	harry	mystify	sally	worry
defy	horrify	notify	sanctify	
deny	humidify	nullify	satisfy	

c) Algunos verbos no cambian en la formación del pretérito y del participio pasado. Los verbos de esta clase incluidos en este diccionario, a excepción de sus compuestos, se dan a continuación.

PRESENTE	PRETÉRITO	PARTICIPIO PASADO	PRESENTE	PRETÉRITO	PARTICIPIO PASADO
bid (ofrecer)	bid	bid	let	let	let
burst	burst	burst	put	put	put
cast	cast	cast	read	read	read
cost	cost	cost	set	set	set
cut	cut	cut	shed	shed	shed
hit	hit	hit	spread	spread	spread
hurt	hurt	hurt	thrust	thrust	thrust

d) Algunos verbos añaden -ked al presente para formar el pretérito y el participio pasado. Los verbos de esta clase incluidos en este diccionario se dan a continuación.

PRESENTE	PRETÉRITO	PARTICIPIO PASADO	PRESENTE	PRETÉRITO	PARTICIPIO PASADO
frolic	frolicked	frolicked	picnic	picnicked	picnicked
mimic	mimicked	mimicked	shellac	shellacked	shellacked
panic	panicked	panicked	traffic	trafficked	trafficked

e) Algunos verbos irregulares no siguen regla fija en la formación del pretérito y del participio pasado. Los verbos de este grupo incluidos en este diccionario, a excepción de sus compuestos, se dan a continuación.

PRESENTE	PRETÉRITO	PARTICIPIO PASADO	PRESENTE	PRETÉRITO	PARTICIPIO PASADO
abide	abode	abode	forego	forewent	foregone
alight	alighted, alit	alighted, alit	foresee	foresaw	foreseen
arise	arose	arisen	foretell	foretold	foretold
awake	awoke, awaked	awoke, awaked	forget	forgot	forgotten
be	was, were	been	forgive	forgave	forgiven
bear	bore	born, borne	forsake	forsook	forsaken
beat	beat	beaten	forswear	forswore	forsworn
become	became	become	freeze	froze	frozen
begin	began	begun	get	got	got, gotten
behold	beheld	beheld	give	gave	given
bend	bent	bent	go	went	gone
beseech	besought, beseeched	besought, beseeched	grind	ground	ground
			grow	grew	grown
bid (ordenar)	bade	bidden	hang	hung, hanged	hung, hanged
			have	had	had
bind	bound	bound	hear	heard	heard
bite	bit	bitten	hide	hid	hid, hidden
bleed	bled	bled	hold	held	held
blow	blew	blown	keep	kept	kept
break	broke	broken	know	knew	known
breed	bred	bred	lay	laid	laid
bring	brought	brought	lead (dirigir)	led	led
build	built	built			
buy	bought	bought	leave	left	left
can	could		lend	lent	lent
catch	caught	caught	lie (echarse)	lay	lain
			light	lighted, lit	lighted, lit
chide	chide, chided	chid, chidden, chided	lose	lost	lost
			make	made	made
choose	chose	chosen	may	might	
cleave	cleft, cleaved, clove	cleft, cleaved, cloven	mean	meant	meant
			meet	met	met
			mistake	mistook	mistaken
			pass	passed	passed, past
cling	clung	clung	pay	paid	paid
come	came	come	pen (encerrar)	penned	pent
creep	crept	crept			
deal	dealt	dealt	quit	quit	quitted
dig	dug, digged	dug, digged	rend	rent	rent
dive	dove, dived	dove, dived	rid	rid, ridded	rid, ridded
do	did	done	ride	rode	ridden
draw	drew	drawn	ring	rang	rung
drink	drank	drunk	rise	rose	risen
drive	drove	driven	run	ran	run
eat	ate	eaten	say	said	said
fall	fell	fallen	see	saw	seen
feed	fed	fed	seek	sought	sought
feel	felt	felt	sell	sold	sold
fight	fought	fought	send	sent	sent
find	found	found	shake	shook	shaken
flee	fled	fled	shine	shone, shined	shone, shined
fling	flung	flung			
fly	flew	flown	shoe	shod	shod
forbear	forbore	forborne	shoot	shot	shot
forbid	forbade	forbidden	show	showed	shown

PRESENTE	PRETÉRITO	PARTICIPIO PASADO	PRESENTE	PRETÉRITO	PARTICIPIO PASADO
shrink	shrank, shrunk	shrunk, shrunken	swear	swore	sworn
sing	sang	sung	sweep	swept	swept
sink	sank, sunk	sunk, sunken	swell	swelled	swelled, swollen
			swim	swam	swum
sit	sat	sat	swing	swung	swung
slay	slew	slain	take	took	taken
sleep	slept	slept	teach	taught	taught
slide	slid	slid, slidden	tear	tore	torn
sling	slung	slung	tell	told	told
slink	slunk	slunk	think	thought	thought
sow	sowed	sown, sowed	thrive	throve, thrived	thrived, thriven
speak	spoke	spoken			
speed	sped, speeded	sped, speeded	throw	threw	thrown
			tread	trod	trodden, trod
spend	spent	spent			
spin	spun	spun	understand	understood	understood
spit	spat, spit	spat, spit	wake	woke, waked	woken, waked
spring	sprang, sprung	sprung			
			wear	wore	worn
stand	stood	stood	weave	wove	woven, wove
steal	stole	stolen			
stick	stuck	stuck	weep	wept	wept
sting	stung	stung	wet	wet, wetted	wet, wetted
stink	stank, stunk	stunk			
			win	won	won
strike	struck	struck, stricken	wind	winded, wound	winded, wound
string	strung	strung	wit	wist, wiste	wist
strive	strove	striven	wring	wrung	wrung
	strived	strived	write	wrote	written

5. Los tiempos del modo indicativo. Hay seis tiempos principales, que son: el presente, el pretérito, el futuro, el presente perfecto, el pretérito perfecto y el futuro perfecto. Los tiempos se forman de las partes principales del verbo. Obsérvese que el verbo inglés no cambia su terminación para indicar a la persona gramatical, por eso es necesario usar siempre los pronombres personales.

a) *El presente.* El presente se usa para expresar una acción o estado actual, una acción habitual o una verdad.

John works in the garden   *Juan trabaja en el jardín*

	SINGULAR	PLURAL
primera persona	I play	we play
segunda persona	you play	you play
tercera persona	he, she plays	they play

b) *El pretérito.* El pretérito expresa una acción terminada en el pasado.

Columbus discovered America   *Colón descubrió América*

	SINGULAR	PLURAL
primera persona	I played	we played
segunda persona	you played	you played
tercera persona	he, she played	they played

No hay ningún tiempo en inglés que corresponda al imperfecto en español. La idea del imperfecto se expresa por medio del pretérito del verbo auxiliar **to be** y el participio presente del verbo conjugado.

SINGULAR		PLURAL
primera persona	I was playing	we were playing
segunda persona	you were playing	you were playing
tercera persona	he, she was playing	they were playing

c) *El futuro.* El futuro expresa una acción realizada después del momento actual. En inglés es necesario usar el verbo auxiliar will para formar el tiempo futuro.

He will work tomorrow   *El trabajará mañana*

SINGULAR		PLURAL
primera persona	I will play	we will play
segunda persona	you will play	you will play
tercera persona	he, she will play	they will play

En inglés no se usa el futuro para expresar probabilidad.

d) *El presente perfecto.* El presente perfecto expresa una acción pasada que se prolonga hasta el presente. Se forma con el presente del verbo auxiliar **to have** y el participio pasado del verbo conjugado.

I have played football many times   *He jugado al fútbol muchas veces*

SINGULAR		PLURAL
primera persona	I have played	we have played
segunda persona	you have played	you have played
tercera persona	he, she has played	they have played

e) *El pretérito perfecto.* El pretérito perfecto expresa una acción completada antes de algún momento indicado en el pasado. Se forma con el pretérito del verbo auxiliar **to have** y el participio pasado del verbo conjugado.

He had played the year before   *El había jugado el año anterior*

SINGULAR		PLURAL
primera persona	I had played	we had played
segunda persona	you had played	you had played
tercera persona	he, she had played	they had played

f) *El futuro perfecto.* El futuro perfecto expresa una acción que habrá de completarse en algún momento indicado en el futuro. Este tiempo es de escaso uso en inglés.

SINGULAR		PLURAL
primera persona	I will have played	we will have played
segunda persona	you will have played	you will have played
tercera persona	he, she will have played	they will have played

6. Los verbos auxiliares **to be** y **to have.** La conjugación del verbo **to be** es irregular en el presente y en el pretérito.

a) *El presente* de to be y to have

SINGULAR	PLURAL	SINGULAR	PLURAL
I am	we are	I have	we have
you are	you are	you have	you have
he, she, it is	they are	he, she, it has	they have

b) *El pretérito de* to be

I was	we were
you were	you were
he, she, it was	they were

7. *El modo subjuntivo y sus tiempos.* El modo subjuntivo expresa una duda, deseo, reproche, concesión, suposición o una condición contraria a la realidad. El subjuntivo es de escaso uso en inglés. En su lugar se emplean otras construcciones que sirven para expresar la misma idea. Se puede usar el indicativo para expresar la idea del subjuntivo.

He commands that I leave	*Él manda que yo salga*

También se puede expresar la idea del subjuntivo por medio de las palabras should, would, could might, etc.

John should have come	*Juan debiera de haber venido*
He could have taken the train	*Él pudo haber tomado el tren*

Nótese que el modo potencial no existe en inglés. En su lugar se usa **would**, que equivale al presente, futuro o pretérito del subjuntivo, según las circunstancias.

If he had the money he would go	*Si él tuviera el dinero, iría*
Would you like to dance?	*¿Querría Vd. bailar?*

No se usa el subjuntivo en inglés para expresar probabilidad en el pasado.

It was probably three o'clock	*Serían las tres*

8. *El modo imperativo.* El modo imperativo expresa un mandato; sólo tiene el tiempo presente. Se forma con la segunda persona singular del verbo, sin el pronombre sujeto **you**.

go!	¡ve! ¡id!
come!	¡ven! ¡venid!

9. *La voz pasiva.* La voz pasiva se forma con el verbo auxiliar to be y el participio pasado del verbo conjugado.

The earth was seen clearly by the astronauts	*La tierra fue vista claramente por los astronautas*
This play has been performed many times	*Esta pieza teatral ha sido representada muchas veces*

H. De la conjunción

Las conjunciones son una parte invariable de la oración; se usan para enlazar dos o más palabras u oraciones. Las conjunciones se dividen en inglés, como en español, en *copulativas y disyuntivas.* Las conjunciones copulativas principales son: and (*y, e*), but (*pero, mas, sin embargo,* etc.) y or (*o, u*).

It was a black and white cat	*Era un gato negro y blanco*
John can play piano or guitar	*Juan toca piano o guitarra*

Las conjunciones disyuntivas principales son: if (*si, aunque,* etc.), while (*mientras que,* etc.), although (*bien que, aunque,* etc.), though (*bien que, aunque,* etc.), when (*cuando,* etc.), until (*hasta que,* etc.), as (*como; a medida que,* etc.), since (*desde que; puesto que,* etc.), that (*que; para que,* etc.) y because (*porque,* etc.).

I will play if you ask me	*Tocaré si Vd. me lo pide*
He didn't go out while it was raining	*Él no salió mientras que llovía*

I. De la preposición

La preposición sirve para denotar la relación entre dos palabras en una oración. Muchas preposiciones indican dirección o posición (over, *sobre, encima;* behind, *tras, detras de;* from, *de, desde;* to, *a, hasta, para;* above, *sobre, encima;* below, *bajo, debajo de;* out, *fuera de;* in, *en, mientras;* around, *cerca de, alrededor de;* through, *por, a través de;* beyond, *más allá de, tras;* across, *a través de;* beside, *al lado de, junto a,* etc.), y otras representan varios tipos de relación (of, *de;* except, *excepto, con excepción de;* for, *por, para;* besides, *además de, a más de,* etc.).

NUMEROS–NUMERALS

Números Cardinales	Cardinal Numbers	Números Ordinales	Ordinal Numbers	Fracciones	Fractions
1-uno, una	one	primero	first	—	—
2-dos	two	segundo	second	medio	half
3-tres	three	tercero	third	tercio	third
4-cuatro	four	cuarto	fourth	cuarto	fourth, quarter
5-cinco	five	quinto	fifth	quinto	fifth
6-seis	six	sexto	sixth	sexto	sixth
7-siete	seven	séptimo	seventh	séptimo	seventh
8-ocho	eight	octavo	eighth	octavo	eighth
9-nueve	nine	noveno, nono	ninth	noveno	ninth
10-diez	ten	décimo	tenth	décimo	tenth
11-once	eleven	undécimo	eleventh	onceavo	eleventh
12-doce	twelve	duodécimo	twelfth	doceavo	twelfth
13-trece	thirteen	décimotercie, o decimo-tercero	thirteenth	treceavo	thirteenth
14-catorce	fourteen	décimocuarto	fourteenth	catorceavo	fourteenth
15-quince	fifteen	décimoquinto	fifteenth	quinceavo	fifteenth
16-dieciséis, diez y seis	sixteen	décimosexto	sixteenth	dieciseisavo	sixteenth
17-diecisiete, diez y siete	seventeen	décimoséptimo	seventeenth	diecisieteavo	seventeenth
18-dieciocho, diez y ocho	eighteen	décimoctavo	eighteenth	dieciochoavo	eighteenth
19-diecinueve, diez y nueve	nineteen	décimonono, o decimo-noveno	nineteenth	diecinueveavo	nineteenth
20-veinte	twenty	vigésimo	twentieth	veinteavo o vigésimo	twentieth
30-treinta	thirty	trigésimo	thirtieth	treintavo o trigésimo	thirtieth
40-cuarenta	forty	cuadragésimo	fortieth	cuarentavo o cuadragé-simo	fortieth
50-cincuenta	fifty	quincuagé-simo	fiftieth	cincuantavo o quincuagé-simo	fiftieth
60-sesenta	sixty	sexagésimo	sixtieth	sesentavo o sexagésimo	sixtieth
70-setenta	seventy	septuagésimo	seventieth	setentavo o septuagé-simo	seventieth
80-ochenta	eighty	octogésimo	eightieth	ochentavo o octogésimo	eightieth
90-noventa	ninety	nonagésimo	ninetieth	noventavo o nonagésimo	ninetieth
100-cien, ciento	one hundred	centésimo	(one) hun-dredth	centavo céntimo ceatésimo	(one) hun-dredth
101-ciento uno	one hundred and one	centésimo primo o centésimo primero	(one) hundred and first		(one) hun-dred(th) and first

Números Cardinales	Cardinal Numbers	Números Ordinales	Ordinal Numbers	Fracciones	Fractions
200-doscientos	two hundred	ducentésimo	two-hundredth	ducentésimo	two-hundredth
300-trescientos	three hundred	tricentésimo	three-hundredth	tricentésimo	three-hundredth
400-cuatrocientos	four hundred	cuadringentésimo	four-hundredth	cuadringentésimo	four-hundredth
500-quinientos	five hundred	quingentésimo	five-hundredth	quingentésimo	five-hundredth
600-seiscientos	six hundred	sexagentésimo	six-hundredth	sexagentésimo	six-hundredth
700-setecientos	seven hundred	septingentésimo	seven-hundredth	septingentésimo	seven-hundredth
800-ochocientos	eight hundred	octingentésimo	eight-hundredth	octingentésimo	eight-hundredth
900-novecientos	nine hundred	noningentésimo	nine-hundredth	noningentésimo	nine-hundredth
1000-mil	one thousand	milésimo	(one) thousandth	milésimo	(one) thousandth
10,000-diez mil	ten thousand	diezmilésimo	(one) ten thousandth	diezmilésimo	(one) ten thousandth
100,000-cien mil	one hundred thousand	cienmilésimo	(one) hundred thousandth	cienmilésimo	(one) hundred thousandth
1,000,000-un millón	one million	millonésimo	(one) millionth	millonésimo	(one) millionth
1,000,000,000 (000)-un billón	one billion (in Spain, one million millions)	billonésimo	(one) billionth	billonésimo	(one) billionth

TABLAS DE VERBOS IRREGULARES INGLESES

El número que aparece en corchetes a la derecha de un verbo irregular indica la clase a que pertenece en las tablas siguientes.

CLASE 1

Los verbos de esta clase duplican la consonante final del infinitivo para formar el pretérito y el participio pasado. Ejemplos:

Presente	Pretérito	Participio	Presente	Pretérito	Participio
annul	annulled	annulled	quiz	quizzed	quizzed
bag	bagged	bagged	etc.	etc.	etc.
cap	capped	capped			

CLASE 2

Los verbos pertenecientes a esta clase pueden, al formar el pretérito y el participio pasado, duplicar la consonante final del infinitivo o dejarla simple. Ambas formas son aceptadas en el uso. Ejemplos:

Presente	Pretérito	Participio
anvil	anviled, anvilled	anviled, anvilled
bias	biased, biassed	biased, biassed
focus	focused, focussed	focused, focussed
kidnap	kidnaped, kidnapped	kidnaped, kidnapped
patrol	patroled, patrolled	patroled, patrolled
travel	traveled, travelled	traveled, travelled
etc.	etc.	etc.

CLASE 3

Presente	Pretérito	Participio	Presente	Pretérito	Participio
bet	bet, betted	bet, betted	quit	quit, quitted	quit, quitted
dig	dug, digged	dug, digged			
dip	dipped, dipt	dipped, dipt	rid	rid, ridded	rid, ridded
			shred	shredded, shred	shredded, shred
drip	dripped, dript	dripped, dript	wed	wedded	wedded, wed
drop	dropped, dropt	dropped, dropt	wet	wet, wetted	wet, wetted
knit	knitted, knit	knitted, knit	whip	whipped, whipt	whipped, whipt
pen (en-cerrar)	penned, pent	penned, pent	wrap	wrapped, wrapt	wrapped, wrapt

CLASE 4

Presente	Pretérito	Participio
alight	alighted, alit	alighted, alit
awake	awoke, awaked	awoke, awaked
bend	bent, bended	bent, bended
blend	blended, blent	blended, blent
broadcast	broadcast, broadcasted	broadcast, broadcasted
burn	burned, burnt	burned, burnt
chide	chided, chid	chided, chid, chidden
cleave	cleft, cleaved, clove	cleft, cleaved, cloven
clothe	clothed, clad	clothed, clad
dream	dreamed, dreamt	dreamed, dreamt
dress	dressed, drest	dressed, drest
dwell	dwelt, dwelled	dwelt, dwelled
forecast	forecast, forecasted	forecast, forecasted
gild	gilded, gilt	gilded, gilt
gird	girded, girt	girded, girt
grind	ground, grinded	ground, grinded
heave	heaved, hove	heaved, hove
kneel	knelt, kneeled	knelt, kneeled
lean	leaned, leant	leaned, leant
leap	leaped, leapt	leaped, leapt
learn	learned, learnt	learned, learnt
light	lighted, lit	lighted, lit
misspell	misspelled, misspelt	misspelled, misspelt
mix	mixed, mixt	mixed, mixt
outwork	outworked, outwrought	outworked, outwrought
overwork	overworked, overwrought	overworked, overwrought
plead	pleaded, pled, plead	pleaded, pled, plead
smell	smelled, smelt	smelled, smelt
speed	sped, speeded	sped, speeded
spell	spelled, spelt	spelled, spelt
spill	spilled, spilt	spilled, spilt
spoil	spoiled, spoilt	spoiled, spoilt
stave	staved, stove	staved, stove
stay	stayed, staid	stayed, staid
sunburn	sunburned, sunburnt	sunburned, sunburnt
sweat	sweat, sweated	sweat, sweated
thrive	throve, thrived	thrived, thriven
unclothe	unclothed, unclad	unclothed, unclad
work	worked, wrought	worked, wrought

CLASE 5

Presente	Pretérito	Participio	Presente	Pretérito	Participio
bide	bode, bided	bided	dive	dived, dove	dived
crow	crowed, crew	crowed	wake	waked, woke	waked
dare	dared, durst	dared			

CLASE 6

Presente	Pretérito	Participio	Presente	Pretérito	Participio
hew	hewed	hewed, hewn	shave	shaved	shaved, shaven
melt	melted	melted, molten	shear	sheared	sheared, shorn
mow	mowed	mowed, mown	show	showed	showed, shown
pass	passed	passed, past	sow	sowed	sowed, sown
prove	proved	proved, proven	strew	strewed	strewed, strewn
saw	sawed	sawed, sawn	swell	swelled	swelled, swollen
sew	sewed	sewed, sewn	weave	wove	wove, woven

Clase 7

Los verbos pertenecientes a esta clase cambian la *y* final del infinitivo en *ied* para formar el pretérito y el participio pasado. Si la *y* se pronuncia [ai], *ied* se pronuncia [aid]. Cuando se pronuncia [i] el pretérito y el participio se pronuncian [id]. Ejemplos:

bury	buried	buried	fancy	fancied	fancied
certify	certified	certified	worry	worried	worried
dirty	dirtied	dirtied	etc.	etc.	etc.

Clase 8

Todos los verbos pertenecientes a esta clase añaden *ked* al infinitivo para formar el pretérito y el participio pasado. Ejemplos:

frolic	frolicked	frolicked	panic	panicked	panicked
mimic	mimicked	mimicked	etc.	etc.	etc.

Clase 9

Los verbos pertenecientes a esta clase no varian en la formación del pretérito y el participio pasado. Ejemplos:

cut	cut	cut	put	put	put
hit	hit	hit	etc.	etc.	etc.
let	let	let			

Clase 10

abide	abode	abode	eat	ate	eaten
arise	arose	arisen	fall	fell	fallen
backbite	backbit	backbitten, backbit	feed	fed	fed
bear	bore	borne, born	feel	felt	felt
beat	beat	beaten, beat	fight	fought	fought
			find	found	found
			flee	fled	fled
			fling	flung	flung
become	became	become	fly	flew	flown
befall	befell	befallen	forbear	forbore	forborne
begin	began	begun	forbid	forbade, forbad	forbidden, forbid
behold	beheld	beheld			
beseech	besought	besought	forego	forewent	foregone
bid	bade, bid	bidden, bid	foresee	foresaw	foreseen
			foretell	foretold	foretold
bind	bound	bound	forget	forgot	forgotten, forgot
bite	bit	bitten, bit			
bleed	bled	bled	forgive	forgave	forgiven
blow	blew	blown	forsake	forsook	forsaken
break	broke	broken (roto), broke (arruinado)	forswear	forswore	forsworn
			freeze	froze	frozen
			get	got	gotten, got
			give	gave	given
			go	went	gone
breed	bred	bred	grow	grew	grown
bring	brought	brought	hang	hung	hung
build	built	built		(colgar)	
buy	bought	bought	hear	heard	heard
catch	caught	caught	hide	hid	hidden, hid
choose	chose	chosen	hold	held	held
cling	clung	clung	inlay	inlaid	inlaid
come	came	come	keep	kept	kept
creep	crept	crept	know	knew	known
deal	dealt	dealt	lay	laid	laid
draw	drew	drawn	lead	led	led
drink	drank	drunk	leave	left	left
drive	drove	driven	lend	lent	lent

Presente	Pretérito	Participio	Presente	Pretérito	Participio
lie (echarse)	lay	lain	sing	sang, sung	sung
			sink	sank, sunk	sunk, sunken
lose	lost	lost			
make	made	made	sit	sat	sat
make-up	made-up	made-up	slay	slew	slain
mean	meant	meant	sleep	slept	slept
meet	met	met	slide	slid	slid, slidden
mislay	mislaid	mislaid			
mislead	misled	misled	sling	slung	slung
mistake	mistook	mistaken	slink	slunk	slunk
misunderstand	misunderstood	misunderstood	smite	smote	smitten, smit
outbid	outbid	outbidden, outbid	speak	spoke	spoken
			spellbind	spellbound	spellbound
outdo	outdid	outdone	spend	spent	spent
outgo	outwent	outgone	spin	spun	spun
outgrow	outgrew	outgrown	spit	spat, spit	spat, spit
outlay	outlaid	outlaid	spring	sprang, sprung	sprung
outrun	outran	outrun			
outshine	outshone	outshone	stand	stood	stood
overbear	overbore	overborne	steal	stole	stolen
overbid	overbid	overbidden, overbid	stick	stuck	stuck
			sting	stung	stung
overcome	overcame	overcome	stink	stank, stunk	stunk
overdo	overdid	overdone			
overdraw	overdrew	overdrawn	stride	strode	stridden
overeat	overate	overeaten	strike	struck	struck, stricken
overfeed	overfed	overfed			
overgrow	overgrew	overgrown	string	strung	strung
overhang	overhung	overhung	strive	strove	striven
overhear	overheard	overheard	swear	swore	sworn
overlay	overlaid	overlaid	sweep	swept	swept
overrun	overran	overrun	swing	swung	swung
oversee	oversaw	overseen	take	took	taken
overshoot	overshot	overshot	teach	taught	taught
oversleep	overslept	overslept	tear	tore	torn
overtake	overtook	overtaken	tell	told	told
overthrow	overthrew	overthrown	think	thought	thought
partake	partook	partaken	throw	threw	thrown
pay	paid	paid	tread	trod	trodden, trod
prepay	prepaid	prepaid			
rebuild	rebuilt	rebuilt	typewrite	typewrote	typewritten
remake	remade	remade			
rend	rent	rent	undergo	underwent	undergone
repay	repaid	repaid	underpay	underpaid	underpaid
resell	resold	resold	undersell	undersold	undersold
retake	retook	retaken	understand	understood	understood
ride	rode	ridden			
ring	rang	rung	undertake	undertook	undertaken
rise	rose	risen	undo	undid	undone
run	ran	run	uphold	upheld	upheld
say	said	said			
see	saw	seen	waylay	waylaid	waylaid
seek	sought	sought	wear	wore	worn
sell	sold	sold	weep	wept	wept
send	sent	sent	win	won	won
shake	shook	shaken	wind	wound	wound
shine	shone, shined	shone, shined	withdraw	withdrew	withdrawn
			withhold	withheld	withheld
shoe	shod	shod	withstand	withstood	withstood
shoot	shot	shot	wring	wrung	wrung
shrink	shrank, shrunk	shrunk, shrunken	write	wrote	written

CLASE 11 (Verbos auxiliares, anómalos y defectivos)

	Present	Preterit	Past Participle
to be	I am, you are, he is; (pl.) are	I was, you were, he was; (pl.) were	been
can	can	could	—
to do	I, you do, he does; (pl.) do	did	done
to have	I, you have, he has; (pl.) have	had	had

	Present	Preterit	Past Participle
may	may	might	—
must	must	—	—
ought	ought	ought	—
shall	shall	should	—
will	will	would	—

ABREVIATURAS USADAS EN LA PARTE II^a

a.	adjetivo.	*inf.*	infinitivo.
abrev.	abreviatura.	(ing.)	ingeniería.
adv.	adverbio.	*interj.*	interjección.
(aer.)	aeronáutica.	*interrog.*	interrogativo.
(agr.)	agricultura.	(joy.)	joyería.
(alb.)	albañilería.	(lóg.)	lógica.
(álg.)	álgebra.	*m.*	masculino.
(Am.)	América.	(mar.)	marina.
(anat.)	anatomía.	(mat.)	matemáticas.
(ant.)	anticuado.	(mec.)	mecánica.
(apl.)	aplícase.	(med.)	medicina.
(Arg.)	Argentina.	*mf.*	masculino y
(arit.)	aritmética.		femenino.
(arm.)	armería.	(mil.)	milicia.
(arq.)	arquitectura.	(miner.)	minería,
art.	artículo.		minerología.
(arti.)	artillería.	(mús.), (mus.)	música, musical.
(astr.)	astronomía,	(ópt.)	óptica.
	astrología.	(orn.)	ornitología.
(aut.)	automovilismo.	*pers.*	personal.
aux.	auxiliar.	(pert.)	perteneciente (a).
(b.a.)	bellas artes.	*pl.*	plural.
(biol.)	biología.	(poét.)	poética.
(bot.)	botánica.	(pol.)	política.
(carp.)	carpintería.	*pos.*	posesivo.
(carr.)	carruajería.	*pp.*	participio pasado.
(cir.)	cirugía.	*pp. i.*	participio pasado
(coc.)	cocina.		irregular.
(com.)	comercio.	*prep.*	preposición.
comp.	comparativo.	*pret.*	pretérito.
conj.	conjunción.	*pron.*	pronombre.
contr.	contracción.	(quím.), (quim.)	química.
(cost.)	costura.	(rad.)	radiocomunicación.
defect.	defectivo.	*refl.*	reflejo o reflexivo.
(elec.), (eléc.)	electricidad.	*rel.*	relativo (gram.)
(esp.)	especialmente.	(rel.)	relativo a.
(E.U.)	Estados Unidos.	*s.*	substantivo.
f.	femenino.	*sing.*	singular.
(fam.)	familiar.	(sociol.)	sociología.
(farm.)	farmacia.	*subj.*	subjuntivo.
(f.c.)	ferrocarriles.	*super.*	superlativo.
(fig.)	figurado.	(teat.)	teatro.
(filos.)	filosofía.	(técn.)	técnica.
(fís.)	física.	(tej.)	tejidos.
(fisiol.)	fisiología.	(tlf.)	telefonía.
(fon.)	fonética.	(tlg.)	telegrafía.
(for.)	voz forense.	(Ú., ú.)	Úsase, úsase.
(fort.)	fortificación.	(V., v.)	Véa(n)se, véa(n)se.
(fot.)	fotografía.	*va.*	verbo auxiliar.
(gen.)	generalmente.	*vai.*	verbo auxiliar
(geog.)	geografía.		irregular.
(geol.)	geología.	(vg., v.g., v. gr.)	por ejemplo.
(geom.)	geometría.	*vi.*	verbo intransitivo.
ger.	gerundio.	*vii.*	verbo intransitivo
(gram.)	gramática.		irregular.
(heráld.)	heráldica.	*vr.*	verbo reflexivo
(hidr.)	hidráulica.		o recíproco.
(hist.)	historia.	*vrí.*	verbo reflexivo
(hort.)	horticultura.		o recíproco
(ict.)	ictiología.		irregular.
(igl.)	iglesia.	*vt.*	verbo transitivo.
imp.	imperfecto.	*vti.*	verbo transitivo
impers.	impersonal.		irregular.
(impr.)	imprenta.	(vulg.)	vulgarismo.
indic.	indicativo.	(zool.)	zoología.

A

a [a, ei], *art.* un, una.—*from A to Z*, de pe a pa.

aback [ạbǽk], *adv.* detrás, atrás.—*to take a.*, desconcertar, coger de improviso.

abandon [ạbǽndọn], *vt.* abandonar, dejar.—*vr.* entregarse a (la bebida, etc.).—*s.* indiferencia, naturalidad; abandono, abandonamiento.

abase [ạbéis], *vt.* abatir, humillar.

abash [ạbǽṡ], *vt.* avergonzar, turbar; sonrojar.

abate [ạbéit], *vt.* reducir, rebajar; impedir; condonar; anular.—*vr.* disminuirse, calmarse.

abbey [ǽbi], *s.* abadía.—**abbot** [ǽbọt], *s.* abad.

abbreviate [ạbrívieit], *vt.* abreviar, reducir, compendiar.—**abbreviation** [ạbrivjéiṡọn], *s.* abreviatura; cifra; compendio.

abdicate [ǽbdikeit], *vt.* abdicar (al trono).

abdomen [ǽbdomen], *s.* abdomen, vientre.—**abdominal** [æbdámiṇạl], *a.* abdominal.

abduct [ạbdʎkt], *vt.* secuestrar, raptar (a alguien).— **—ion** [æbdʎkṡọn], *s.* robo, secuestro; (anat.) abducción.

aberration [æbẹréiṡọn], *s.* error; desliz; aberración.

abet [ạbét], *vti.* [1] favorecer, apoyar; instigar.

abeyance [ạbéiạns], *s.* expectativa.—*in a.*, suspenso; latente.

abhor [æbhór], *vti.* [1] aborrecer, detestar, abominar.

abide [ạbáid], *vti.* [10] esperar, tolerar, sufrir.—*vii.* habitar, permanecer.—*to a. by*, atenerse a.

ability [ạbíliti], *s.* capacidad, talento.

abject [ǽbdẓekt], *a.* abatido, servil.— **—ion** [æbdẓékṡọn], *s.* abyección; servilismo.

abjure [æbdẓúr], *vt.* abjurar, retractarse de; renunciar solemnemente a.—*vi.* retractarse; hacer renuncia solemne (del reino, etc.).

ablaze [ạbléiz], *adv.* en llamas.

able [éibl], *a.* capaz, apto, capacitado. —*a.-bodied*, robusto.—*to be a.*, poder, saber.

abnormal [æbnórmạl], *a.* anormal, deforme.

aboard [ạbórd], *adv.* a bordo.—*all a.!* ¡viajeros al tren!—*to go a.*, embarcarse.

abode [ạbóud], *s.* morada, residencia.— *pret. y pp.* de TO ABIDE.

abolish [ạbáliṡ], *vt.* abolir, revocar, anular.—**abolition** [æbolíṡọn], *s.* abolición, revocación, anulación.

abominable [ạbámiṇạbl], *a.* abomi-nable; aborrecible.—**abomination** [ạbamiṇéiṡọn], *s.* abominación, odio; maldad.

abortion [ạbórṡọn], *s.* aborto; fracaso.

abound [ạbáund], *vi.* abundar.—*abounding in o with*, nutrido de.

bout [ạbáut], *adv.* casi; poco más o menos; alrededor; por ahí (en el lugar, edificio, etc.).—*a.-face*, media vuelta (voz de mando).—*all a.*, por todas partes.—*prep.* de, acerca de; sobre, con respecto a; alrededor de; a eso de; por, en.—*to be a.*, estar para, al punto de.—*to think a.*, pensar en.— *to walk a. town*, pasear por el pueblo.

above [ạbʎv], *a.* susodicho, precitado; precedente.—*s.* lo anterior, lo precedente.—*adv. y prep.* sobre, arriba (de), superior (a), fuera de, anteriormente.—*a. all*, sobre todo.—*from a.*, de lo alto, del cielo; desde arriba.

abrasion [ạbréiẓọn], *s.* raspadura, desgaste.—**abrasive** [ạbréisiv], *a.* raspante.—*s.* abrasivo.

abreast [ạbrést], *adv.* de frente, en fila. —*four a.*, de cuatro en fondo.—*to keep a. of something*, estar al tanto de algo.

abridge [ạbrídẓ], *vt.* abreviar, condensar.— **—ment** [-mẹnt], *s.* compendio, resumen.

abroad [ạbród], *adv.* en el extranjero, fuera de casa o del país; en público.— *to go a.*, salir del país, ir al extranjero.

abrupt [ạbrʎpt], *a.* brusco, repentino; escarpado; grosero.

abscess [ǽbsẹs], *s.* absceso.

absence [ǽbsẹns], *s.* ausencia, falta.— *in the a. of*, a falta de.—*leave of a.*, licencia, permiso.—**absent** [ǽbsẹnt], *a.* ausente.—*a.-minded*, distraído, abstraído, absorto; en Babia.—*to a. oneself*, retirarse (de), ausentarse.

absolute [ǽbsolut], *a.* absoluto, categórico, positivo.

absolution [æbsolúṡọn], *s.* absolución.

absolve [æbsálv], *vt.* absolver, dispensar, remitir los pecados.

absorb [æbsórb], *vt.* absorber; empapar; ocupar (el ánimo) intensamente.— **—ed** [-d], *a.* absorto, cautivado.— **—ent** [-ẹnt], *s. y a.* absorbente.— **absorption** [æbsórpṡọn], *s.* absorción.

abstain [æbstéin], *vi.* abstenerse, privarse.

abstemious [æbstímiʌs], *a.* sobrio, abstemio.

abstinence [ǽbstịnẹns], *s.* abstinencia, ayuno.

abstract [ǽbstrækt], *s.* término abstracto; abstracción; sumario, extracto.—*a.* abstracto, distraído.—*vt.* [æbstrǽkt], abstraer; resumir, extractar; compendiar; separar.— **—ion** [æbstrǽkṡọn], *s.* abstracción, recogimiento.

absurd [æbsérd], a. absurdo, ridículo, disparatado.— -ity [-iti], s. absurdo, disparate.

abundance [əbándəns], s. abundancia, exuberancia.—abundant [əbándənt], a. abundante, copioso.

abuse [əbiúz], vt. abusar de; insultar; ultrajar, maltratar.—s. [əbiús], abuso; injuria; maltrato; violación.— abusive [əbiúsiv], a. abusivo, insultante, injurioso.

abyss [əbís], s. abismo; sima.

academic(al) [ækədémik(əl)], a. académico; convencional; teórico.— academy [əkǽdemi], s. academia, instituto.

accede [æksíd], vi. acceder; subir o ascender (al trono).

accelerate [æksélereit], vt. acelerar, apresurar.—vi. darse prisa.—acceleration [ækseleréiʃən], s. aceleración.— accelerator [æksélereitọ(r)], s. acelerador.

accent [æksent], s. acento, dejo.—vt. [æksent], acentuar, recalcar.—accentuate [æksénchueit], vt. acentuar; hacer más patente.

accept [æksépt], vt. aceptar, admitir; reconocer.— —able [-əbl], a. aceptable, grato, admisible.— —ance [-əns], s. aceptación; buena acogida.

access [ækses], s. acceso, entrada; aumento; acceso o ataque (de tos, etc.).— —ible [æksésibl], a. accesible, asequible.— —ion [ækséʃən], s. aumento; subida (al trono); accesión; consentimiento.— —ory [æksésọri], a. accesorio; secundario; adicional.—s. dependencia; cómplice.— pl. accesorios, repuestos, enseres, útiles (de cocina, etc.).

accident [æksident], s. accidente, casualidad; percance.— —al [æksidéntal], a. accidental, casual.—s. (mus.) accidente.

acclaim [ækléim], vt. y vi. aclamar, aplaudir, proclamar.—s. aclamación. —acclamation [æklaméiʃən], s. aclamación, aplauso, proclamación.

acclimate [æklájmit], o acclimatize [æklájmɐtajz], vt. y vi. aclimatar(se).

accommodate [əkámodeit], vt. acomodar, ajustar; componer; hacer un favor; alojar.—to a. oneself, conformarse, adaptarse.—accommodation [əkamodéiʃən], s. acomodamiento; favor; adaptación; ajuste; acuerdo.—pl. facilidades, comodidades, alojamiento.

accompaniment [əkámpaniment], s. acompañamiento.—accompanist [əkámpanist], s. acompañante.— accompany [əkámpani], vti. [7] acompañar.

accomplice [əkámplis], s. cómplice.

accomplish [əkámpliʃ], vt. efectuar, cumplir, completar; lograr.— —ment [-ment], s. cumplimiento, enajenación, ejecución; proeza.—pl. conocimientos, habilidades; méritos.

accord [əkórd], s. acuerdo, convenio; concierto; armonía; (mus.) acorde.— in a., de mutuo acuerdo.—of one's own a., espontáneamente.—vt. acordar, conceder, otorgar.—vi. concordar; convenir, avenirse, concertar, estar de acuerdo.— -ance [-əns], —ancy [-ənsi], s. conformidad, armonía, acuerdo.—in accordance with, de acuerdo con.— -ant [-ənt], a. acorde, conforme, propio.— -ing [íŋ], a. conforme, acorde.—a. as, a medida que.—a. to, según.— —ingly [-iŋli], adv. en conformidad, en efecto; de consiguiente; por ende.

accordion [əkórdiən], s. acordeón.

accost [əkóst], vt. dirigirse a, abordar (a alguien en la calle); acosar.

account [əkáunt], vt. tener por, considerar, estimar.—vi. dar cuenta y razón.—to a. for, dar razón o responder de.—s. relato, relación; importancia, valor; explicación, cuenta, razón; cálculo; consideración; aprecio; (com.) cuenta.—a. book, libro de cuentas.—by all accounts, según el decir o la opinión general.—charge a., cuenta abierta o corriente.—of a., de nota, de importancia.—on a. of, a causa de.—on my own a., por mi cuenta, por mi cuenta y riesgo.—on no a., de ninguna manera.— —able [-əbl], a. responsable, explicable.— —ant [-ənt], s. contador; tenedor de libros.— —ing [-iŋ], s. contabilidad, contaduría; estado de cuentas.—to ask an a., pedir rendición de cuentas.

accredit [əkrédit], vt. acreditar; dar credenciales; dar crédito; atribuir a.

accrue [əkrú], vi. crecer, tomar incremento; acumularse.

accumulate [əkiúmjuleit], vt. y vi. acumular(se), amontonar(se), atesorar; crecer.—accumulation [əkiumjuléiʃən], s. acumulación, amontonamiento, hacinamiento.

accuracy [ækyúɾasi], s. exactitud, precisión, esmero.—accurate [ækyúɾit], a. exacto, preciso; certero (en el tiro); exacto (en los cálculos).

accursed [əkúɾst], a. maldito; execrable; perverso, infame.

accusation [ækiuzéiʃən], s. acusación.— accuse [əkiúz], vt. acusar, denunciar, (in)culpar.

accustom [əkástɐm], vt. y vi. acostumbrar(se), habituar(se), hacer(se).

ace [eis], s. as (de naipes o dados); as (el más sobresaliente en su actividad); migaja, partícula.—within an a. of,

por poco, en un tris.—*a.* sobresaliente.

ache [eik], *s.* dolor.—*vi.* doler.

achieve [ǎchv], *vt.* realizar, ejecutar.——**ment** [-mẹnt], *s.* realización, logro; hazaña; proeza.

acid [ǎsịd], *s.* y *a.* ácido.——**ity** [æsị́djtị], *s.* acidez, acedía.

acknowledge [æknálịdẑ], *vt.* reconocer; confesar, admitir; testificar.—*to a. receipt,* acusar recibo.——**acknowledgment** [-mẹnt], *s.* reconocimiento; confesión; admisión; acuse de recibo; testificación.

acolyte [ǎkolajt], *s.* acólito, monaguillo.

acorn [ẹ́jkorn], *s.* bellota.

acoustic [ǎkústịk], *a.* acústico.—*s. pl.* acústica; condiciones acústicas.

acquaint [ǎkwẹ́jnt], *vt.* instruir, familiarizar; enterar, informar, advertir.—*to a. oneself with,* ponerse al corriente de, ponerse al tanto de.——**ance** [-ạns], *s.* conocimiento; familiaridad.

acquiesce [ǎkwịẹ́s], *vi.* asentir; consentir, conformarse.——**nce** [ǎkwịẹ́sẹns], *s.* aquiescencia, asentimiento, resignación.

acquire [ǎkwájr], *vt.* adquirir, obtener, contraer (hábitos, etc.).—**acquisition** [ǎkwịzị́ṣọn], *s.* adquisición, consecución.

acquit [ǎkwít], *vti.* [1] absolver, dispensar; exonerar, relevar; pagar.—*to a. oneself,* quedar bien; exonerarse.——**tal** [-ạl], *s.* absolución.

acre [ẹ́jkœr], *s.* acre (medida de superficie). Ver Tabla.

acrimonious [ǎkrịmóụnjạs], *a.* acre.

acrobat [ǎkrobæt], *s.* acróbata.

across [ǎkrós], *adv.* a o de través; de una parte a otra; al otro lado; en cruz.—*prep.* a través de; al otro lado de; por.—*a. the way,* enfrente.

act [ækt], *s.* acción, acto, hecho; (teat.) acto, número; (for.) ley, decreto, acta.—*a. of God,* fuerza mayor.—*vi.* obrar, actuar, funcionar; representar (en el teatro); simular; portarse.—*to a. as,* servir de, estar de.—*to a. up,* jaranear.—*vt.* hacer o desempeñar el papel de.——**ing** [ǎktịŋ], *s.* acción; (teat.) representación.—*a.* interino.——**ion** [ǎkṣọn], *s.* acción, acto; operación, funcionamiento; movimiento; (teat.) argumento; (mil.) batalla; (mec.) mecanismo; (for.) demanda, proceso.—*to bring an a.,* entablar un pleito.—*to take a.,* proceder (contra).

activate [ǎktịvejt], *vt.* activar.—**active** [ǎktịv], *a.* activo, diligente, ágil, eficaz.—**activity** [ǎktịvịtị], *s.* actividad, vigor.—*pl.* ocupaciones.

actor [ǎktọ(r)], *s.* actor, comediante; (for.) demandante.—**actress** [ǎktrịs], *s.* actriz; (for.) actora, demandante.

actual [ǎkchuạl], *a.* real, verdadero; efectivo; existente.

actuary [ǎkchuẹrị], *s.* actuario (de seguros); escribano, registrador.

acumen [ǎkịúmịn], *s.* cacumen.

acute [ǎkịút], *a.* agudo; ingenioso, perspicaz.

ad [æd], *s.* (fam.) anuncio, aviso.

adamant [ǎdạmænt], *a.* firme, inflexible.

adapt [ǎdǎpt], *vt.* adaptar, ajustar, amoldar; refundir.——**ation** [ædæptéjṣọn], *s.* adaptación, ajuste.

add [æd], *vt.* sumar, adicionar, totalizar, añadir.—*vi.* sumar.

addict [ǎdịkt], *s.* adicto, aficionado.—*drug a.,* narcómano.——**ed** [ǎdị́ktịd], *a.* adicto, entregado o afecto a; partidario de.

addition [ǎdị́ṣọn], *s.* adición, añadidura; aditamento, adjunto, suma.—*in a.,* por añadidura.—*in a. to,* además de.——**al** [-ạl], *a.* adicional.

address [ǎdrés], *vt.* dirigir la palabra, arengar; dirigir o poner el sobre a una carta.—*s.* [ǎdrés, ǎdres], dirección, señas; sobrescrito; membrete; discurso; solicitud; memorial.——**er** [-œ(r)], *s.* remitente (de una carta, etc.).

adept [ǎdépt], *a.* adepto, perito.

adequacy [ǎdẹkwạsị], *s.* adecuación, suficiencia.——**adequate** [ǎdẹkwịt], *a.* adecuado, proporcionado, suficiente.

adhere [ædhír], *vi.* adherirse, unirse; pegarse.——**nce** [ædhírẹns], *s.* adhesión, apego, adherencia.—**adhesion** [ædhíẑọn], *s.* adhesión, adherencia.—**adhesive** [ædhísịv], *a.* adhesivo, sustancia adhesiva.—*a.* adhesivo, pegadizo, engomado (sello).—*a. tape* o *plaster,* esparadrapo.

adjacent [ædẑéjsẹnt], *a.* adyacente, contiguo.

adjective [ǎdẑẹktịv], *s.* adjetivo.

adjoin [ǎdẑój n], *vt.* juntar, unir.—*vi.* (co)lindar con, estar contiguo.——**ing** [-ịŋ], *a.* contiguo, inmediato, adyacente.

adjourn [ǎdẑœ́rn], *vt.* diferir, aplazar, clausurar, suspender o levantar la sesión.—*vi.* levantarse o suspenderse (una sesión).——**ment** [-mẹnt], *s.* aplazamiento, traslación, suspensión, clausura.

adjunct [ǎdẑʌŋkt], *s.* aditamento, adjunto; ayudante; subalterno.—*a.* adjunto, auxiliar, subordinado.

adjust [ǎdẑʌst], *vt.* ajustar, adaptar, acomodar, concertar; dirimir (disputas, etc.); regular.——**ment** [-mẹnt], *s.* arreglo, adaptación, ajuste; regulación.

administer [ædmịnịstœ(r)], *vt.* administrar; desempeñar (un cargo); suminis-

trar; dar; aplicar (remedios, un castigo, etc.).—*to a. an oath*, tomar juramento.—*vi.* servir, auxiliar.—
administration [ædmɪnɪstréɪʃən], *s.* administración; ministerio; gobierno; gerencia; manejo.—**administrative** [ædmínɪstreɪtɪv], *a.* administrativo; gubernativo.—**administrator** [ædmínɪstreɪtə(r)], *s.* administrador; albacea.
admirable [ædmɪrabl], *a.* admirable.
admiral [ædmɪral], *s.* almirante.- —**ty** [-tɪ], *s.* almirantazgo; departamento o ministerio de marina.
admiration [ædmɪréɪʃən], *s.* admiración. —**admire** [ædmáɪr], *vt.* admirar; estimar; contemplar con placer.—*vi.* admirarse de; sentir admiración por.—**admirer** [ædmáɪrœ(r)], *s.* admirador; enamorado, pretendiente.
admission [ædmíʃən], *s.* admisión, entrada; acceso; precio de entrada; concesión, reconocimiento.—*a. fee,* cuota de entrada (en un club, etc.).—**admit** [ædmít], *vti.* [1] admitir, recibir; dar entrada; reconocer.—**admittance** [ædmítans], *s.* admisión; entrada.
admonish [ædmáníʃ], *vt.* amonestar; advertir; prevenir.—**admonition** [ædmoníʃən], *s.* amonestación; advertencia, prevención.
adolescence [ædolésɛns], *s.* adolescencia.—**adolescent** [ædolésɛnt], *s.* y *a.* adolescente.
adopt [ædápt], *vt.* adoptar, prohijar. —**ion** [ædápʃən], *s.* adopción, prohijamiento.
adorable [ædórabl], *a.* adorable—**adoration** [ædoréɪʃən], *s.* adoración; idolatría.—**adore** [ædór], *vt.* adorar; idolatrar.
adorn [ædórn], *vt.* adornar, ornamentar, embellecer, acicalar, aderezar.— —**ment** [-mɛnt], *s.* adorno, atavío, ornamento, aderezo, acicalamiento.
adrenaline [ædrénalɪn], *s.* adrenalina.
adrift [ædríft], *adv.* al garete; abandonado; a la deriva.
adroit [ædróɪt], *a.* diestro, hábil, listo.
adulation [ædʒuléɪʃən], *s.* adulación, lisonja.
adult [ædʌlt], *a.* y *s.* persona mayor; adulto.
adulterate [ædʌltœreɪt], *vt.* adulterar, falsificar, viciar.—*a.* adulterado, falso; adúltero.—**adultery** [ædʌltœrɪ], *s.* adulterio.
advance [ædvǽns], *vt.* avanzar; adelantar, promover; aventajar; acelerar; (com.) anticipar dinero, pagar adelantado, ofrecer; subir el precio de.—*vi.* avanzar, adelantarse; progresar; subir de valor o de precio.—*s.* avance; delantera; adelanto, progresso.—*pl.* propuestas; requerimientos amorosos; (com.) adelanto, anti-

cipo, préstamo; alza; precio adicional, —*a.* previo, anticipado.—*a. guard.* (mil.) avanzada.—*in a.*, anticipadamente; al frente; de antemano; (com.) por adelantado; anticipado.- —**d** [-t], *a.* avanzado, adelantado, desarrollado.—*a. in years,* entrado en años; de edad madura.- —**ment** [-mɛnt], *s.* progreso, adelantamiento; promoción; mejora.
advantage [ædvǽntɪdʒ], *s.* ventaja, beneficio, delantera.—*to one's a.*, con provecho para uno.—*to take a. of,* aprovecharse de, sacar partido de.— *vt.* adelantar, mejorar, favorecer; remunerar.—*vi.* medrar, sacar ventaja.— —**ous** [ædvantéɪdʒʌs], *a.* provechoso, ventajoso, conveniente.
advent [ædvent], *s.* venida, advenimiento.
adventure [ædvénchʊr], *s.* aventura; casualidad; lance.—*vt.* aventurar, arriesgar.—*vi.* aventurarse (a), arriesgarse.- —**r** [-œr)r], *s.* aventurero.— **adventurous** [-ʌs], *a.* aventurero; aventurado, arriesgado; atrevido.
adverb [ædvœrb], *s.* adverbio.
adversary [ædvœrserɪ], *s.* adversario, enemigo, contrario.—**adverse** [ædvœrs], *a.* adverso, contrario, opuesto, enemigo.—**adversity** [ædvœrsɪtɪ], *s.* adversidad, desgracia.
advertise [ædvœrtaɪz], *vt.* anunciar, avisar, hacer propaganda o publicidad.- —**ment** [ædvœrtízmɛnt], *s.* aviso, anuncio, reclamo.- —**r** [ædvœrtaɪzœ(r)], *s.* anunciante.—**advertising** [ædvœrtaɪzɪŋ], *s.* propaganda, publicidad.
advice [ædváɪs], *s.* consejo; aviso, notificación, parecer, advertencia.
advisable [ædváɪzabl], *a.* aconsejable, prudente; conveniente.—**advise** [ædváɪz], *vt.* aconsejar; avisar, notificar, advertir, enmarcar, denunciar; asesorar.—*vi.* consultar, aconsejarse, pedir o tomar consejo.—**adviser** [ædváɪzœ(r)], **advisor** [ædváɪzɔ(r)], *s.* consejero, consultor.—*legal a.*, abogado, asesor.
advocate [ædvokeɪt], *vt.* defender, abogar por, propugnar, interceder.—*s.* abogado; defensor, intercesor, partidario.
aerial [eíɾɪal], *a.* aéreo, elevado; etéreo. —*s.* antena (radio, televisión).
aerodynamics [erodaɪnǽmɪks], *s.* aerodinámica.—**aeronaut** [éronɔt], *s.* aeronauta.—**aeronautics** [eronɔ́tɪks], *s.* aeronáutica.—**aeroplane** [éroplein], *s.* aeroplano.
aesthetic [esθétɪk], *a.* = ESTHETIC.- —**s** [-s], *s.* = ESTHETICS.
afar [afár], *adv.* lejos, distante.—*a. off,* remoto.—*from a.*, desde lejos.

affable [ǽfəbl], *a.* afable, atento.

affair [əfér], *s.* asunto, negocio, lance; cosa.—*a. of honor,* duelo.—*love a.,* amorío.

affect [əfékt], *vt.* afectar, hacer efecto o mella en, conmover; tomar la forma o el carácter de; fingir; tener afición a.— —ion [əfékʃən], *s.* afectación; melindre, remilgo.— —ed [-id], *a.* emocionado; relamido; inclinado, afecto a.— —ion [əfékʃən], *s.* afecto, devoción, ternura; emoción; inclinación; impresión; (med.) afección, dolencia.— —ionate [əfékʃənit], *a.* afectuoso, cariñoso, amoroso.— —ive [əféktiv], *a.* afectivo, conmovedor.

affidavit [æfidéivit], *s.* declaración jurada; testimonio.

affiliate [əfílieit], *vt.* afiliar; prohijar, adoptar; asociar; (for.) legitimar.— *vi.* y *vr.* afiliarse, asociarse, unirse (a un partido, etc.).

affinity [əfíniti], *s.* afinidad, atracción; semejanza; amor; conexión; parentesco matrimonial.

affirm [əfórm], *vt.* afirmar, aseverar.— *vi.* afirmarse en alguna cosa; declarar formalmente ante un juez.— —ation [æfœrméiʃən], *s.* afirmación, aserto.— —ative [əfórmətiv], *a.* afirmativo.— *s.* aserción; afirmativa.

affix [əfíks], *vt.* anexar, fijar, pegar, unir; poner (firma o sello).—*s.* [ǽfiks], añadidura; (gram.) afijo, sufijo, prefijo.

afflict [əflíkt], *vt.* afligir, atormentar; castigar.— —ion [əflíkʃən], *s.* aflicción; angustia, duelo; achaque; desgracia.

affluence [ǽfluəns], *s.* abundancia, opulencia; afluencia.—**affluent** [ǽfluənt], *a.* opulento, afluente, abundante, copioso.—*s.* afluente, tributario.

afford [əfórd], *vt.* dar, proporcionar, proveer; tener medios o recursos para una cosa, permitirse el lujo de.

affray [əfréi], *s.* riña, pendencia.

affront [əfrʌnt], *vt.* afrentar, insultar.— *s.* afrenta, insulto, agravio.

afield [əfíld], *adv.* lejos de casa; descarriado.—*far a.,* muy lejos.

afire [əfáir], *adv.* ardiendo.

aflame [əfléim], *adv.* en llamas.

afloat [əflóut], *a.* y *adv.* a flote, flotante, a nado; inundado.

afoot [əfút], *a.* y *adv.* a pie; en movimiento.

afraid [əfréid], *a.* acobardado, medroso, tímido.—*to be a.,* tener miedo, temer.

afresh [əfréʃ], *adv.* nuevamente, desde el principio.

African [ǽfrikən], *s.* y *a.* africano; negro.

aft [æft], *adv.* a popa o en popa.

after [ǽftœ(r)], *prep.* después de; de-trás de, tras (de); al cabo de; en pos de; por, en busca de; según.—*a. all,* después de todo, de todas maneras.— *the day a.* tomorrow, pasado mañana. —*to be a.* something, buscar algo.— *adv.* después, enseguida, seguidamente.—*soon a.,* poco después.— *conj.* después (de) que, así que.—*a.* posterior, siguiente; subsiguiente, resultante.—*a.-effect,* resultado, consecuencia.— —math [-mæθ], *s.* desenlace, consecuencia.— —noon [-nun], *s.* tarde.— —taste [-teist], *s.* resabio (sabor).— —ward(s) [-wờrd(z)], *adv.* después.

again [əgén], *adv.* otra vez, aún, nuevamente, además; asimismo.—*a. and a.,* muchas veces.—*come a.,* vuelva Ud.

against [əgénst], *prep.* contra; enfrente de; junto a (una pared, etc.); en contraste con; listo para.—*a. the grain,* a contrapelo; de mal grado.— *a. time,* dentro de tiempo limitado.

age [eidʒ], *s.* edad; época, período, era, siglo; vejez, ancianidad; envejecimiento.—*a. old,* secular, milenario.—*full a.,* mayoría de edad.—*of a.,* mayor (de edad).—*under a.,* minoría, menor (de edad).—*vi.* envejecerse; deteriorarse.—*vt.* madurar.— —d [éidʒ(i)d], *a.* anciano, añejo.

agency [éidʒənsi], *s.* agencia; gestión, influencia, medio.—*free a.,* libre albedrío.—**agent** [éidʒənt], *s.* agente; representante, intermediario, apoderado; (for.) mandatario.

aggregate [ǽgrigeit], *a.* agregado; aglomerado; mezclado.—*s.* agregado, suma, conjunto; mezcla.—*in the a.,* en conjunto.—*vt.* y *vi.* agregar, sumar, juntar.

aggression [əgréʃən], *s.* agresión, ataque; acometida.—**aggressive** [əgrésiv], *a.* agresivo, acometedor.— **aggressor** [əgrésɔ(r)], *s.* agresor.

agile [ǽdʒil], *a.* ágil, listo.—**agility** [ədʒíliti], *s.* agilidad, ligereza, soltura.

agitate [ǽdʒiteit], *vt.* agitar, revolver, menear; inquietar, alborotar; maquinar.—*vi.* excitar la opinión pública.— **agitation** [ædʒitéiʃən], *s.* agitación; discusión; perturbación, ajetreo.— **agitator** [ǽdʒiteitɔ(r)], *s.* agitador; perturbador, alborotador; demagogo.

aglow [əglóu], *y a.* resplandeciente, encendido.

ago [əgóu], *a.* y *adv.* pasado, en el pasado.—*a long time a.,* hace mucho tiempo.—*how long a.?* ¿cuánto tiempo hace?—*two years a.,* hace dos años.

agonize [ǽgonaiz], *vt.* angustiar; causar gran pena.—*vi.* agonizar; penar, sufrir intensamente, retorcerse de dolor.

—agony [ǽgoni], *s.* agonía; angustia, tormento, zozobra.

agrarian [agrériạn], *a.* **y** *s.* agrario.— *s.* agrarista.

agree [agrí], *vi.* concordar, coincidir, acordar; entenderse, avenirse; consentir; quedar o convenir en (precio, etc.); sentar (un precedente, etc.); sentarle a uno bien (ropa, clima, etc.); (gram.) concordar.— —**able** [-ạbl], *a.* agradable; satisfactorio; simpático; complaciente.—*a. to*, de acuerdo con.— —**ment** [-mẹnt], *s.* acuerdo, convenio, ajuste, concierto, avenencia; consentimiento; armonía; conformidad; (gram.) concordancia.—*in a. (with)*, acorde con.

agricultural [ægrikálchụrạl], *a.* agrícola, agrario.—**agriculture** [ǽgrikάlchụ(r)], *s.* agricultura.—**agriculturist** [ægrikάlchụrist], *s.* agricultor.

ahead [ạhéd], *adv.* delante, al frente, a la cabeza; adelante; hacia delante.

aid [eid], *vt.* y *vi.* ayudar, socorrer, auxiliar, apoyar.—*s.* ayuda, auxilio, concurso, socorro; subsidio; (mil.) ayudante.—*first a.*, primeros auxilios (médicos).

ail [eil], *vt.* afligir, molestar (algún dolor).—*vi.* estar enfermo o indispuesto.— —**ment** [éilmẹnt], *s.* dolencia, enfermedad.

aim [eim], *vt.* apuntar (con un arma); dirigir, asestar, encarar.—*vi.* (con at) hacer puntería; aspirar a, pretender, proponerse, tirar a.—*to a. high*, picar alto.—*s.* puntería, encaro; blanco; designio, mira, propósito, finalidad.— *accurate a.*, tino.—*to miss one's a.*, errar el tiro.— —**less** [éimlis], *a.* sin objeto, sin rumbo, a la ventura.

air [er], *vt.* airear, ventilar, orear, aventar; secar (al aire o por calor); sacar a relucir, pregonar.—*s.* aire; atmósfera; brisa; semblante, ademán; (mús.) tonada.—*in the a.*, en vilo.— *in the open a.*, al aire libre; a la intemperie.—*to be on the a.*, estar trasmitiendo por radio.—*to put on airs*, darse tono o ínfulas.—*up in the a.*, indeciso; perplejo.—*a.* de aire, neumático; para aire; aéreo; aeronáutico, de aviación.—*a. brakes*, frenos neumáticos.—*a. carrier*, portaaviones.— *a. conditioning*, acondicionamiento del aire.—*a. cooling*, enfriamiento por aire.—*a. drill*, taladro neumático.— *a. duct*, canal de aire.—*a. force*, aviación militar, fuerzas aéreas.—*a. hostess*, aeromoza, azafata.—*a. lane*, vía aérea.—*a. line*, línea o empresa aérea. —*a. liner*, avión de una empresa o línea aérea.—*a. mail*, correo aéreo. *a.-mail service*, servicio aeropostal.— *a. plant*, talleres de aviación.—*a.

pocket*, bache o cajón de aire.—*a. pressure*, presión atmosférica.—*a. proof*, hermético.—*a. raid*, ataque aéreo.—*a.-tight*, hermético.—*a. valve*, válvula (de admisión o salida) de aire.—*by a.-mail*, por vía aérea, por avión.— —**craft** [érkræft], *s.* máquina de volar (aeroplanos, dirigibles, etc.).— —**field** [-fild], *s.* campo de aviación.— —**plane** [-plein], *s.* aeroplano, avión.— —**port** [-port], *s.* aeropuerto; aeródromo.— —**sickness** [-siknjs], *s.* mareo en viaje aéreo.— —**way** [-wei], *s.* ruta de aviación, vía aérea.—*pl.* red aérea.— —**y** [-i], *a.* aéreo, airoso; bien ventilado; etéreo, tenue; ligero; vanidoso, estirado.

aisle [áil], *s.* pasillo (de un teatro); nave (de una iglesia).

ajar [ạdžár], *adv.* y *a.* entreabierto, entornado.—*to set a.*, entornar, entreabrir.

akimbo [ạkímbou], *a.* y *adv.* en jarras.

akin [ạkín], *a.* consanguíneo, emparentado, afín; análogo, semejante.

alabaster [ǽlạbǽstœ(r)], *s.* alabastro.

alarm [ạlárm], *s.* alarma; rebato.—*a. clock*, (reloj) despertador.—*to sound the a.*, dar la alarma, tocar a rebato.— *vt.* alarmar; asustar; inquietar.—*vi.* dar la alarma; asustarse.

Alaskan [ạlǽskạn], *s.* natural de Alaska. —*a.* de o referente a Alaska.

alb [ælb], *s.* (igl.) alba.

Albanian [ælbéiniạn], *s.* y *a.* natural de Albania; lengua albanesa; albanés.

alcohol [ǽlkohol], *s.* alcohol.— —**ic** [ælkohólịk], *a.* alcohólico.— —**ism** [-izm], *s.* alcoholismo.

alcove [ǽlkouv], *s.* alcoba, nicho.

alderman [óldœrmạn], *s.* regidor, concejal.

ale [eil], *s.* cerveza (inglesa).

alert [ạlért], *a.* alerta, vigilante; cuidadoso.—*on the a.*, sobre aviso.—*s.* alarma.—*vt.* poner sobre aviso.

algebra [ǽldžẹbrą], *s.* álgebra.

Algerian [ældžíriạn], *a.* y *s.* argelino.

alibi [ǽlibai], *s.* excusa; coartada.

alien [éilyẹn], *a.* extraño, ajeno; extranjero, forastero.—*s.* extranjero, residente extranjero.— —**ate** [-eit], *vt.* enajenar, traspasar; quitar, indisponer; alejar (a una persona de otra).

alight [ạláit], *vii.* [4] descender, bajar, apearse; (con on) posarse (sobre); (aer.) aterrizar, acuatizar (un hidroavión).—*a.* y *adv.* encendido; iluminado.

align [ạláin], *vt.* alinear(se).— —**ment** [-mẹnt], *s.* alineación.

alike [ạláik], *adv.* igualmente, del mismo modo; a la par.—*a.* semejante; igual.

alimony [ǽlimoni], *s.* (for.) alimentos,

pensión a la mujer en el divorcio o separación.

alive [əláiv], *a.* vivo, viviente; encendido; animado; sensible.

alkali [ǽlkəlai], *s.* (quím.) álcali.

all [ol], *a.* todo, todos; todo (el), todos (los).—*s. y pron.* todo, totalidad, conjunto; todos, todo el mundo; todo lo.—*adv.* completamente, enteramente.—*above a.*, sobre todo, ante todo.—*after a.*, después de todo, al fin y al cabo.—*a. along*, siempre, constantemente, sin cesar, por todo (el camino, tiempo, etc.).—*a. around*, en todo respecto.—*a. at once*, repentinamente; de un golpe; a un tiempo.—*a. but*, todo(s) menos, o sino; casi, por poco.—*s. in*, agotado, rendido de cansancio.—*a. out*, completamente; apagado (el fuego, un incendio).—*a. out!* ¡salgan todos!—*a. out of*, sin; desprovisto de.—*a. over*, terminado, acabado.—*a. right*, ciertamente, está bien, bueno.—*a.-round*, por todas partes; completo; acabado, consumado; de idoneidad general.—*a. set*, listo dispuesto.—*a. that*, todo el (o lo) que, todos los que, cuanto(s).—*a. the better* (*worse*), tanto mejor (peor).—*a. the same*, a pesar de eso; lo mismo.—*a. told*, en (con)junto, por todo.—*not at a.*, de ningún modo, nada de eso; no por cierto; no hay de que.—*once and for a.*, una vez por todas; definitivamente; para siempre.

allay [əléi], *vt.* aliviar; calmar.

allegation [ælɛ̜géišən], *s.* alegación, argumento; (for.) alegato.—**allege** [əlédž], *vt.* alegar; declarar; sostener; pretender; (for.) deducir.

allegiance [əlídžəns], *s.* lealtad, homenaje, fidelidad.

allergic [əlǽrdžik], *a.* alérgico.—**allergy** [ǽlœrdži], *s.* alergia.

alleviate [əlívieit], *vt.* aliviar, mitigar; aligerar.

alley [ǽli], **alley-way** [ǽliwei], *s.* callejuela, callejón.—*blind alley*, callejón sin salida.—*bowling alley*, bolera, boliche.

alliance [əláians], *s.* alianza.—**allied** [əláid], *a.* aliado, unido; relacionado.

alligator [ǽligeitə(r)], *s.* caimán; yacaré.—*a. pear*, aguacate.

allocation [æləkéišən], *s.* colocación; asignación, distribución.

aloe [ǽlou], *s.* (bot.) áloe.—**—s** [-z], (sing. y pl.) áloe o acíbar.

allot [əlát], *vti.* [1] distribuir, repartir, asignar.

allow [əláu], *vt.* permitir, consentir, dejar, conceder; dar, admitir; (com.) rebajar, deducir.—*vi.* (con *for*) tener en cuenta.—**—ance** [-əns], *s.* concesión; asignación; ración; pensión,

mesada; permiso; indulgencia; descuento, bonificación, refacción; (tecn.) tolerancia, discrepancia permitida.—*annual a.*, anualidad.—*monthly a.*, mensualidad.—*retirement a.*, jubilación, retiro.—*to make a. for*, tener en cuenta.

alloy [ǽlói], *s.* mezcla; (fund.) aleación; liga.—*vt.* alear, ligar (los metales).

allude [əliúd], *vi.* aludir, referirse a.

allure [əliúr], *vt.* halagar, atraer, seducir.—*s.* seducción, atractivo.—**alluring** [əliúriŋ], *a.* seductivo, tentador.

allusion [əliúžən], *s.* alusión.

ally [əlái], *vti.* [7] unir.—*vii.* aliarse, coligarse.—*s.* aliado; pariente.

almanac [ólmənæk], *s.* almanaque, calendario.

almighty [olmáiti], *a.* todopoderoso, omnipotente.—*s.* (con the) Dios.

almond [ámənd], *s.* almendra.—*a. tree*, almendro.

almost [ólmoust], *adv.* casi, por poco.

alms [ams], *s.* limosna.

aloft [əlóft], *adv.* arriba, en alto, en los aires.

alone [əlóun], *a. y adv.* solo, solitario; sólo, solamente.—*all a.*, a solas.—*to let a.*, dejar en paz, no molestar.

along [əlóŋ], *prep.* por; a lo largo de; al lado de.—*adv.* a lo largo de; adelante.—*all a.*, todo el tiempo; de un extremo al otro.—*a. these lines*, en este sentido.—*a. with*, con, junto con.—*come a.*, venga conmigo.—*move a.!* ¡largo de aquí!—*to get a. with*, adelantar; ir tirando; llevarse (bien) con.—**—shore** [-šor], *adv.* a la orilla, a lo largo de la costa.—**—side** [-said], *adv. y prep.* a lo largo de, al lado, lado a lado.

aloof [əlúf], *adv.* lejos, apartado, a distancia.—*a.* huraño, reservado.—*to stand o keep a.*, mantenerse apartado; aislarse.—**—ness** [-nis], *s.* alejamiento, aislamiento.

aloud [əláud], *adv.* alto, en voz alta, recio.

alphabet [ǽlfəbet], *s.* alfabeto, abecedario, abecé.—**—ical** [ælfəbétikəl], *a.* alfabético.

already [olrédi], *adv.* ya, antes de ahora.

also [ólsou], *adv.* también, igualmente, además, asimismo.

altar [óltə(r)], *s.* altar, ara.—*a. boy*, monaguillo, acólito.—*a. bread*, pan de la eucaristía, hostia.

alter [óltœ(r)], *vt.* alterar, cambiar, modificar, mudar, variar.—*vi.* alterarse, cambiarse, variar.—**—ation** [-éišən], *s.* alteración, cambio, mudanza; arreglo.

alternate [ǽltœrneit], *vt. y vi.* alternar; turnar; variar.—*a.* [ǽltœrnit], alterno; alternativo.—s. suplente, sustituto.—alternating [ǽltœrneitiŋ], a. alternante, alternativo, alterno.—a. current, corriente alterna.—alternative [œltǽrnǎtiv], s. alternativa.—a. alternativo.

although [olðóu], conj. aunque, si (bien), bien que, no obstante, aun cuando.

altitude [ǽltitiud], s. altura, altitud; elevación.

altogether [oltugéðœ(r)], adv. en conjunto; enteramente, del todo.

alumnus [alʌ́mnʌs], s. (pl. alumni [alʌ́mnai]), f. alumna [alʌ́mnǎ], (pl. alumnae [alʌ́mni]), ex-alumno; antiguo estudiante de una universidad o escuela.

aluminum [œljúminʌm], s. aluminio.

always [ólweiz], adv. siempre.

am [æm], (1ª pers. pres. ind. de TO BE), soy, estoy.

amalgamate [amǽlgameit], vt. y vi. amalgamar, unir, incorporar.

amaranth [ǽmǎranθ], s. bledo.

amass [amǽs], vt. acumular, amasar (riquezas, etc.); apilar.

amateur [ǽmǎtjur], s. y a. aficionado, no profesional.

amaze [amǽiz], vt. asombrar, pasmar, dejar atónito o maravillado.—-ment [-ment], s. asombro, pasmo, aturdimiento.—amazing [améiziŋ], a. asombroso, pasmoso, admirable.

ambassador [æmbǽsǎdǫ(r)], s. embajador.

amber [ǽmbœ(r)], s. ámbar; color de ámbar.—a. ambarino.

ambiguity [æmbigiúiti], s. ambigüedad.—ambiguous [æmbígiuas], a. ambiguo, equívoco; evasivo.

ambition [æmbíʃǫn], s. aspiraciones; ambición, codicia.—ambitious [æmbíʃʌs], a. lleno de aspiraciones; ambicioso, codicioso.

amble [æmbl], vi. andar; vagar.—s. (paso de) andadura.

ambulance [ǽmbiulǎns], s. ambulancia.

ambush [ǽmbuʃ], vt. acechar, poner celada, emboscar.—s. emboscada, celada.

amen [eimén, amén], interj. y s. amén.

amend [aménd], vt. enmendar, rectificar, modificar, corregir, reformar.—vi. enmendarse, reformarse, restablecerse.—-ment [-ment], s. enmienda, reforma.

American [amérikan], s. y a. americano; norteamericano, estadounidense.

amethyst [ǽmeθist], s. amatista; color de amatista.

amiable [éimjabl], a. amable, afable.

amicable [ǽmikabl], a. amigable, amistoso.

amid [amíd], amidst [amídst], prep. entre, en medio de.

amiss [amís], adv. mal, fuera de lugar o de razón; impropiamente; de más. —to take a., tomar a mal.—a. inoportuno, impropio, errado.

amity [ǽmiti], s. amistad, concordia, armonía.

ammonia [amóuniǎ], s. amoníaco.

ammunition [æmyuníʃǫn], s. munición, municiones.

amnesty [ǽmnesti], s. amnistía.—vt. amnistiar.

among [amʌ́ŋ], amongst [amʌ́ŋst], prep. entre, mezclado con, en medio de.

amorous [ǽmoras], a. enamorado, amoroso, enamoradizo.

amortize [amórtaiz], vt. amortizar.

amount [amǽunt], s. cantidad; importe, suma; monto (capital más intereses).—vi. montar, ascender (a), valer; equivaler.

amperage [æmpíridǎ], s. amperaje.—ampere [æmpír], s. amperio.

amphibian [æmfíbjan], s. y a. anfibio.

amphitheater [ǽmfiθiǎtœ(r)], s. anfiteatro.

ample [ǽmpl], a. amplio; lato; abundante.

amplifier [ǽmplifaiœ(r)], s. amplificador, megáfono.—amplify [ǽmplifai], vti. [7] amplificar; ampliar.

amputate [ǽmpiuteit], vt. amputar, desmembrar.

amuse [amiúz], vt. entretener, distraer, divertir.—to a. oneself, divertirse. —-ment [-ment], s. diversión, pasatiempo, entretenimiento.—amusing [amiúziŋ], a. divertido, recreativo; risible, gracioso.

an [æn], art. un, uno, una.

anachronism [ænǽkronizm], s. anacronismo.

analogous [anǽlogas], a. análogo.—analogy [anǽlodǎi], s. analogía.

analysis [anǽlisis], s. análisis.—analyze [ǽnalaiz].—vt. analizar.

anarchist [ǽnǎrkist], s. anarchistic [ænǎrkístik], a. anarquista.—anarchy [ǽnǎrki], s. anarquía; confusión, desorden, caos.

anathema [anǽθemǎ], s. anatema; excomunión; maldición.

anatomy [anǽtomi], s. anatomía, disección.

ancestor [ǽnsestǫ(r)], s. progenitor; antepasado.—ancestral [ænséstral], a. ancestral, hereditario.—ancestry [ǽnsestri], s. ascendencia; linaje, prosapia, alcurnia.

anchor [ǽŋkǫ(r)], vi. anclar; asegurar. —s. ancla, áncora; artificio de sujeción o amarre; escape de reloj.—to drop a., echar el ancla.—to ride at a.,

estar fondeado o anclado.—*to weigh*
a., zarpar.— —**age** [-idž], *s.* ancladero,
fondeadero.

anchovy [ǽnchouvi], *s.* anchoa, an-
chova.

ancient [éinšent], *a.* antiguo, vetusto.—
the Ancients, la Antigüedad.

and [ænd], *conj.* y, e.—*a. so forth*, o *a.
so on*, etcétera, y así sucesivamente.—
ifs, ands or buts, dimes y diretes.

Andalusian [ændaliúžan], *a.* y *s.* anda-
luz.

Andean [ǽndían], *a.* y *s.* andino.

andirons [ǽndaiœrnz], *s. pl.* morillos.

anecdote [ǽnikdout], *s.* anécdota.

anemia [ænímiž], *s.* anemia.—**anemic**
[ænímik], *a.* anémico.

anesthesia [ænesθíziž], *s.* anestesia.—
anesthetic [ænesθétik], *a.* y *s.* anesté-
sico.

anew [anjú], *adv.* nuevamente.

angel [éindžel], *s.* ángel, serafín.— —**ic**
[ændžélik], *a.* angelical, angélico.

anger [ǽngœ(r)], *s.* enfado, enojo, ira,
cólera.—*to provoke to a.*, encolerizar,
enfadar.—*vt.* enfadar, enojar, encolerizar.

angina [ændžáinǝ, ǽndžinǝ], *s.* angina.
—*a. pectoris*, angina de pecho.

angle [ǽngl], *vt.* pescar con caña; intrigar; halagar con fin de lucro.—*s.*
ángulo; esquina, rincón; avíos de pescar; punto de vista.— —**r** [ǽnglœ(r)],
s. pescador (de caña).

angling [ǽnglin], *s.* pesca con caña.

angry [ǽngri], *a.* enojado, enfadado,
encolerizado, bravo.—*to get a.*, enfa-
darse, enojarse, encolerizarse.

anguish [ǽngwiš], *s.* ansia, angustia,
zozobra.

angular [ǽngiulǝ(r)], *a.* angular, anguloso.

aniline [ǽnilin], *s.* anilina.

animal [ǽnimǝl], *s.* y *a.* animal.

animate [ǽnimeit], *vt.* animar.—*a.*
[ǽnimit], animado, viviente.—**ani-
mation** [ænimέišǝn], *s.* animación.—
animism [ǽnimizm], *s.* animismo.—
animosity [ænimásiti], *s.* animosidad,
rencor.—**animus** [ǽnimʌs], *s.* ánimo,
intención; animosidad.

anise [ǽnis], **anisette** [ænizέt], *s.* anís.

ankle [ǽŋkl], *s.* tobillo.— *strap*,
correílla de zapato que cruza el pie
un poco arriba del empeine.

annex [ǽnέks], *vt.* anexar, anexionar.—
s. [ǽneks], anexo; añadidura; dependencia; ala o pabellón (de un edificio).— —**ation** [ænekséišǝn], *s.*
anexión, adición, unión.

annihilate [anáijleit], *vt.* aniquilar; anonadar; demoler.—**annihilation** [anaji-
léišǝn], *s.* aniquilación, anonada-
miento.

anniversary [ænivœrsǝri], *s.* aniversario.
—*a.* anual.

annotate [ǽnoteit], *vt.* anotar; acotar,
apostillar; comentar, glosar.—**anno-
tation** [ænotéišǝn], *s.* anotación,
apunte; nota, notación; acotación,
apostilla.

announce [anáuns], *vt.* anunciar, notificar, avisar; declarar.— —**ment**
[-ment], *s.* aviso o anuncio; declaración, proclama.— —**r** [-œ(r)], *s.* anunciador, avisador.

annoy [anói], *vt.* molestar, incomodar,
fastidiar.— —**ance** [-ans], *s.* molestia,
incomodidad, disgusto, fastidio.—
—**ing** [-in], *a.* fastidioso, molesto, incómodo, importuno, engorroso.

annual [ǽnyuǝl], *a.* anual.—**annuity**
[anjúiti], *s.* anualidad; pensión o
renta vitalicia; retiro.

annul [anʌ́l], *vti.* [1] anular, rescindir;
derogar, revocar.— —**ment** [-ment],
s. anulación, rescisión, cancelación,
revocación, derogación.

anodyne [ǽnodain], *a.* y *s.* (med.) ano-
dino, calmante.

anoint [anóint], *vt.* untar; ungir; administrar la extremaunción.

anonymous [anánimʌs], *a.* anónimo.

another [anʌ́ðœ(r)], *a.* otro; distinto,
diferente.—*pron.* otro, uno más.—*a.
such*, otro que tal.—*one a.*, uno(s) a
otro(s).

answer [ǽnsœ(r)], *vt.* y *vi.* responder,
contestar; refutar; corresponder; obedecer; convenir; comparecer.—*to a.
back*, replicar; refunfuñar.—*to a. for*,
abonar, acreditar; salir fiador de; ser
responsable de; hacer oficio de.—*to a.
to the name of*, tener por nombre,
llamarse.—*s.* respuesta, contestación;
refutación, réplica; defensa; (mat.)
solución, resultado.

ant [ænt], *s.* hormiga.—*a. hill*, hormiguero en forma de montículo.

antagonism [æntǽgonizm], *s.* antagonismo; contienda; oposición.—**antagon-
ist** [æntǽgonist], *s.* antagonista,
adversario.—**antagonize** [æntǽgo-
naiz], *vt.* y *vi.* contender, oponerse;
contrariar; ser antagónico.

antarctic [æntárktik], *a.* antártico.

anteater [æntítœ(r)], *s.* oso hormiguero.

antecedent [æntisídent], *a.* y *s.* antecedente, precedente.

antechamber [ǽntichejmbœ(r)], *s.* ante-
cámara, antesala.

antedate [æntidéit], *vt.* antedatar; retro-
traer.

antelope [ǽnteloup], *s.* antílope; gacela,
gamuza.

antenna [æntέnž], *s.* (zool. y radio)
antena.— —**e** [æntέni], *pl.* (zool.) an-
tenas.

anthem [ǽnθem], *s.* himno; motete.

anthology [ænθálodʒi], *s.* antología, florilegio.

anthropology [ænθropálodʒi], *s.* antropología.

antiaircraft [æntʃérkræft], *a.* antiaéreo.

antibiotic [æntibaiátik], *a.* y *s.* antibiótico.

antibody [ǽntibadi], *s.* anticuerpo.

antic [ǽntik], *s.* zapateta, cabriola.— *pl.* travesuras; actos ridículos.

anticipate [æntísipeit], *vt.* esperar, prever; prevenir, anticipar(se), adelantar(se) a; impedir.—**anticipation** [æntisipéiʃon], *s.* anticipación, previsión; expectación.

anticommunist [æntikámyunist], *s.* y *a.* anticomunista.

antidote [ǽntidout], *s.* antídoto, contraveneno.

antifreeze [ǽntifriz], *s.* y *a.* anticongelante.

antiknock [ǽntinak], *s.* y *a.* antidetonante.

antimony [ǽntimouni], *s.* antimonio.

antinomy [æntínomi], *s.* antinomia; paradoja.

antipathy [æntípaθi], *s.* antipatía.

antipode [ǽntipoud], *s.* antípoda.

antiquarian [æntikwérian], *s.* y *a.* anticuario.—**antiquated** [ǽntikweitid], *a.* anticuado.—**antique** [æntík], *a.* antiguo.—*s.* antigüedad, antigualla.—*a. shop,* tienda de antigüedades.—**antiquity** [æntíkwiti], *s.* antigüedad; ancianidad; la Antigüedad.

anti-Semite [æntisémait], *s.* antisemita.

antiseptic [æntiséptik], *a.* antiséptico, desinfectante.

antiskid [ǽntiskid], *a.* antideslizante.

antler [ǽntlœ(r)], *s.* asta (del ciervo, venado, etc.).

anus [éinas], *s.* ano.

anvil [ǽnvil], *s.* yunque.—*vti.* [2] formar o trabajar sobre el yunque; martillar.

anxiety [æŋgzáieti], *s.* ansiedad, anhelo; desasosiego, zozobra; cuidado; afán, ansia.

anxious [ǽŋkʃas], *a.* inquieto, impaciente, ansioso.

any [éni], *a.* y *pron.* cualquier(a), cualesquier(a); algún, alguno; todo.—*a. longer,* más tiempo, todavía; más.— *a. more,* más, aún; todavía.—*a. way,* de cualquier modo.—*at a. rate,* o *in a. case,* de cualquier modo, de todos modos.—*not a. longer, not a. more,* ya no, no más.—**-body** [-badi], *-one* [-wʌn], *pron.* alguno, alguien, cualquiera; todo el mundo, toda persona.— **-how** [-hau], **-way** [-wei], *adv.* de cualquier modo; en cualquier caso; de todos modos; sea lo que sea; sin embargo.— **-thing** [-θiŋ], *pron.* algo, alguna cosa, cualquier cosa; todo,

todo lo que.—*a. else,* cualquier otra cosa, algo más.—*to be a. but,* ser todo menos, no ser ni con mucho.— **-where** [-hwer], *adv.* donde quiera, en todas partes.—*a. near,* siquiera aproximadamente.—*not a.,* en ninguna parte.

apart [apárt], *adv.* aparte; separadamente; de por sí; además; prescindiendo de; en pedazos, en partes.—*to take a.,* desarmar, desmontar.

apartment [apártment], *s.* apartamento, piso; aposento, cuarto.—*a. building,* casa de apartamentos.

apathy [ǽpaθi], *s.* apatía, flema, dejadez.

aperitif [æperitíf], *s.* aperitivo.

aperture [ǽpœrchʊr], *s.* abertura, paso, rendija.

apex [éipeks], *s.* (*pl.* apices [ǽpisiz]) ápice, cúspide, punta, cima.

apiece [apís], *adv.* por persona, por cabeza; cada uno; sendos.

ape [eip], *s.* simio; imitador.—*vt.* imitar, remedar.

aplomb [aplóm], *s.* aplomo, seguridad; verticalidad.

apogee [ǽpodʒi], *s.* apogeo; auge.

apologetic(al) [apalodʒétik(al)], *a.* contrito; lleno de disculpas.—**apologize** [apálodʒaiz], *vt.* y *vi.* excusar(se), disculpar(se).—**apology** [apálodʒi], *s.* apología, excusa, disculpa, satisfacción.

apostasy [apástasi], *s.* apostasía.

apostle [apásl], *s.* apóstol.—**apostolic(al)** [apostálik(al)], *a.* apostólico.—*Apostolic See,* (igl.) sede apostólica, la Santa Sede.

apostrophe [apástrofi], *s.* apóstrofe; apóstrofo.

apothecary [apáθekeri], *s.* boticario.

appall [apól], *vt.* espantar, aterrar; consternar.— **-ing** [-iŋ], *a.* espantoso, aterrador.

apparatus [æparéitas], *s.* instrumento, aparato; aparejo.

apparel [apérel], *s.* ropa; vestiduras; aparejo y demás accesorios de un barco.—*vti.* [2] vestir; adornar; proveer.

apparent [apérent], *a.* aparente, visible, manifiesto.—*a. horizon,* horizonte sensible.—*a. time,* tiempo solar.— *heir a.,* heredero forzoso.

apparition [æparíʃon], *s.* aparición, aparecimiento; aparecido, fantasma, espectro.

appeal [apíl], *vi.* apelar o recurrir a; pedir o suplicar; mover, excitar; despertar atención o simpatía; poner por testigo; exhortar a.—*vt.* apelar de, llevar a un tribunal superior.—*s.* súplica, instancia; llamamiento, exhortación; apelación, recurso; simpatía, atracción.

appear [apír], *vi.* aparecer(se), mostrarse, personarse; brotar, surgir; semejar; comparecer.—*to a. to be*, aparentar, representar.— **—ance** [-ans], *s.* apariencia, aspecto, facha; aparición, comparecencia.

appease [apíz], *vt.* apaciguar, pacificar; calmar.— **—ment** [-ment], *s.* conciliación, apaciguamiento.— **—r** [-œ(r)], *s.* apaciguador.

appellable [apélabl], *a.* apelable.— **appellancy** [apélansi], *s.* apelación.— **appellation** [æpeléíson], *s.* nombre (apelativo); denominación, título, tratamiento.—**appellative** [apélativ], *s.* sobrenombre; apellido.

append [apénd], *vt.* añadir, anexar; atar, colgar.— **—age** [-idž], *s.* pertenencia, dependencia, accesorio; colgajo, apéndice.— **—ectomy** [æpendéktomi], *s.* apend(ic)ectomía.— **—icitis** [apendisáitis], *s.* apendicitis.— **—ix** [apéndiks], *s.* (*pl.* **appendices** [apéndisiz]) apéndice.

appetite [æpetait], *s.* apetito, hambre, apetencia, gana; deseo, anhelo.— **appetizer** [æpetaizœ(r)], *s.* aperitivo.

applaud [aplódj, *vt.* aplaudir, aclamar.— **—applause** [aplóz], *s.* aplauso, aclamación.

apple [æpl], *s.* manzana, poma.— *Adam's a.*, nuez, bocado de Adán.— *a. of discord*, manzana de la discordia.— *a. of one's eye*, niña del ojo.—*a. orchard*, manzanal, pomal.—*a. pie o tart*, pastel(illo) de manzana.—*a.-pie order*, orden perfecto.—*a. tree*, manzano.— **—jack** [-džæk], *s.* aguardiente de manzana.— **—sauce** [-sos], *s.* compota de manzana.

appliance [apláians], *s.* aparato, instrumento, utensilio.—**applicable** [æplikabl], *a.* aplicable.—**applicant** [æplikant], *s.* solicitante, aspirante, candidato.—**application** [æplikéíson], *s.* aplicación; uso, empleo; instancia, solicitud.—*a. blank, a. form*, formulario, planilla.—**applied** [apláid], *a.* aplicado; adaptado, utilizado.—*a. for*, pedido, encargado.—**apply** [aplái], *vti.* y *vii.* [7] aplicar, poner, fijar; ser aplicable o pertinente.

appoint [apóint], *vt.* nombrar, elegir; comisionar, destinar; asignar; equipar, amueblar.—**ment** [-ment], *s.* nombramiento; puesto, empleo; cita; acuerdo.—*pl.* mobiliario; accesorios.

appraise [apréjz], *vt.* (a)valuar, valorar, justipreciar, aforar, tasar; estimar, apreciar.— **—ment** [-ment], *s.* tasación.— **—r** [-œ(r)], *s.* tasador.

appreciable [aprísiabl], *a.* apreciable.— **appreciate** [aprísieit], *vt.* apreciar,

valuar, tasar.—**appreciation** [aprisiéíson], *s.* valuación, tasa.

apprehend [æprihénd], *vt.* y *vi.* comprender, entender; temer, recelar; aprehender, capturar.—**apprehension** [æprihénson], *s.* aprensión, recelo, desconfianza; aprehensión, captura.— **—apprehensive** [æprihénsiv], *a.* aprensivo, receloso; penetrante, perspicaz.

apprentice [apréntis], *s.* aprendiz, novicio, principiante.—*vt.* contratar como aprendiz.— **—ship** [-šip], *s.* aprendizaje, noviciado.

approach [apróuch], *vt.* y *vi.* aproximar(se), acercar(se); hacer propuesta, insinuación.—*s.* acercamiento; acceso; proximidad.

approbation [æprobéíson], *s.* aprobación.

appropriate [apróuprieit], *vt.* apropiar(se), destinar; posesionarse.—*a.* apropiado, apto, pertinente.—**appropriation** [aprouprííson], *s.* apropiación, suma consignada.

approval [aprúval], *s.* aprobación; visto bueno; consentimiento.—*on a.*, a prueba.—**approve** [aprúv], *vt.* aprobar, sancionar, confirmar.—*vi.* (seguido de *of*), aprobar, sancionar.

approximate [apráksimit], *a.* aproximado, aproximativo.—*vt.* y *vi.* [apráksimeit], aproximar(se), acercar(se).

apricot [éiprikat], *s.* albaricoque, (Am.) chabacano.

April [éipril], *s.* abril.

apron [éipron], *s.* delantal, mandil; plancha de protección; cubierta.— *tied to the a. strings*, dominado por la mujer o la madre.

apt [æpt], *a.* apto, idóneo, capaz; propenso.— **—itude** [æptitjud], **—ness** [æptnis], *s.* aptitud, capacidad; tendencia, disposición.

aquamarine [ækwamarín], *s.* (min.) aguamarina.—**aquarium** [akwériam], *s.* acuario, pecera.—**aquatic** [akwætik], *a.* acuático.—**aqueduct** [ækwidakt], *s.* acueducto.

Arab [ærab], *s.* árabe.— **—ian** [aréibian], *a.* árabe, arábigo.— **—ic** [ærabik], *s.* árabe, lengua arábiga.—*a.* arábigo.

Aragonese [æragoníz], *a.* y *s.* aragonés.

arbiter [árbitœ(r)], *s.* árbitro.—**arbitrary** [árbitreri], *a.* arbitrario, despótico.—**arbitrate** [árbitreit], *vt.* y *vi.* arbitrar, terciar.—**arbitration** [arbitréíson], *s.* arbitraje.—**arbitrator** [árbitreitọ(r)], *s.* árbitro.

arbor [árbọ(r)], *s.* (mec.) árbol, eje; tambor; (bot.) emparrado, glorieta.

arc [ark], *s.* arco.— **—ade** [arkéid], *s.* arcada; arquería.

arch [arch], *vt.* y *vi.* arquear(se), enar-

car(se), encorvar(se); abovedarse.—
s. arco, bóveda.—a. travieso; astuto.
archangel [árkéjndžel], s. arcángel.
archbishop [árchbįšǫp], s. arzobispo.—
—ric [-rįk], s. arzobispado.
archer [árchœ(r)], s. arquero, flechero.—
—y [-į], s. tiro de arco.
archetype [árkįtaįp], s. arquetipo.
arching [árchįŋ], a. arqueado.—s.
arqueo, curvatura.
archipelago [arkįpélagǫu], s. archipié-
lago.
architect [árkįtekt], s. arquitecto, artífice.— —ure [árkįtekchų(r)], s. arqui-
tectura.
archive [árkaįv], s. archivo, documento
archivado.—archivist [árkįvįst], s.
archivista, archivero.
archway [árchweį], s. arcada; pasadizo
bajo un arco.
arctic [árktįk], a. ártico, septentrional;
frígido.—s. región ártica, círculo
ártico.
ardent [árdęnt], a. ardiente; apasionado.—ardor [árdǫ(r)], s. ardor,
calor; pasión, ansia.
arduous [árdžųʌs], a. arduo, difícil;
alto, escabroso, enhiesto.
are [ar], 2da. pers. sing., 1ra., 2da. y
3ra. pl., pres. ind. de TO BE.
area [érįə], s. área; extensión; región,
zona; terreno.
arena [arínə], s. arena, liza, ruedo.
Argentine(an) [ardžéntin, ardžéntín-
įan], s. y a. argentino.
argue [árgįu], vt. y vi. debatir, disputar,
discutir, argüir, argumentar; sostener; demostrar, indicar.—argument
[árgįumęnt], s. controversia, disputa;
alegación.
arid [érįd], a. árido, seco.— —ity [arįd-
įtį], s. aridez, sequedad.
arise [arájz], vii. [10] levantarse, subir;
surgir; proceder, provenir (de); suscitarse; originarse, sobrevenir; resucitar.—arisen [arízen], pp. de TO ARISE.
aristocracy [ærįstákrasį], s. aristocracia.
—aristocrat [ærįstokræt], s. aristó-
crata.—aristocratic(al) [ærįstokrǽtįk-
(ąl)], a. aristocrático.
arithmetic [arįθmętįk], s. aritmética.—
—al [arįθmétįkąl], a. aritmético.—
—ian [arįθmętíšąn], s. aritmético.
ark [ark], s. arca.—A. of the Covenant,
Arca de la Alianza.—Noah's a., Arca
de Noé.
arm [arm], s. brazo; rama, canal; arma.
—pl. armas, blasón.—a. band, brazalete.—a. bone, canilla o caña del
brazo.—a. in a., de bracete, del brazo.
—a.'s reach, alcance del brazo.—vt.
armar; fortalecer; proveer de medios
o elementos.—vi. armarse.
armament [ármamęnt], s. armamento;
equipo.

armchair [ármcher], s. sillón.
armful [ármfųl], s. brazada, brazado.
armistice [ármįstįs], s. armisticio.
armless [ármlįs], a. desarmado; manco.
armor [ármǫ(r)], s. armadura, arnés;
coraza, blindaje.—a.-clad, blindado,
acorazado.—vt. acorazar, blindar.
—ed [-d], a. blindado, acorazado.—
—y [-į], s. cuartel; armería; heráldica.
armpit [ármpįt], s. sobaco.
army [ármį], s. ejército, tropas; multitud, muchedumbre.
aroma [arǫumə], s. aroma, fragancia.-
—tic(al) [ærǫmǽtįk(al)], a. aromático.
arose [arǫuz], pret. de TO ARISE.
around [aráųnd], adv. alrededor o en
derredor; a la redonda; a la vuelta;
allá, por todos lados; de un lado para
otro.—the other way a., al contrario,
viceversa, al revés.—prep. al volver
de, alrededor de, cerca de, en torno
de.—a. here, por aquí.—a. the corner,
a la vuelta de la esquina.
arouse [aráųz], vt. despertar; mover,
excitar, alborotar.
arraign [arejn], vt. procesar criminal-
mente; acusar, denunciar.- —ment
[-męnt], s. proceso, instrucción de
cargos.
arrange [aréjndž], vt. arreglar, acomodar, preparar; colocar, ordenar; convenir, concertar; (mus.) arreglar,
adaptar.—vi. prevenir, hacer arreglos;
concertarse, convenir.- —ment
[-męnt], s. colocación; orden, arreglo,
distribución; preparativo, medida,
providencia, convenio.
array [aréj], s. orden de batalla, formación; pompa, adorno; conjunto,
colección.—vt. poner en orden de
batalla; ataviar, adornar.
arrears [arírz], s. pl. atrasos, cantidades
vencidas y no pagadas.—in a., atrasado en el pago.
arrest [arést], s. prisión, arresto, reclusión; detención; captura.—vt. impedir, detener, atajar, reprimir; arrestar, prender, recluir; atraer; fijar la
atención.- —ing [-įŋ], a. impresionante, llamativo.
arrival [arájvąl], s. arribo, llegada; logro, consecución.—arrive [arájv], vi.
llegar, arribar.
arrogance [érogans], s. arrogancia.—
arrogant [érogant], a. arrogante.
arrow [érǫu], s. flecha, saeta.—a.
wound, flechazo.
arsenal [ársįnąl], s. arsenal.
arsenic [ársįnįk], s. y a. arsénico.
arson [ársǫn], s. incendio premeditado.—
—ist [-įst], s. incendiario.
art [art], s. arte, habilidad, destreza;
artificio; oficio, gremio.—fine arts,
bellas artes.

artery [ártẹri], s. arteria.

artesian [artíẓan], a. artesiano.—a. well, pozo artesiano.

artful [ártful], a. artero, ladino; diestro.

artichoke [ártichoụk], s. alcachofa.

article [ártịkl], s. artículo (gr., lit., leg., com.).—a. of clothing, prenda de vestir.—leading a., artículo de fondo.

articulate [artíkjuleịt], vt. articular, enunciar; enlazar.—vi. articular, enunciar; estar unido por articulación.—a. [artíkjulịt], articulado, claro, de expresión inteligible.—**articulation** [artikjuléịṣọn], s. coyuntura, articulación; pronunciación.

artifice [ártịfịs], s. artificio; ardid.- —r [artífịsœ(r)], s. artífice; inventor; artesano.—**artificial** [artifíṣạl], a. artificial; imitado; ficticio, afectado, artificioso.

artillery [artíllẹri], s. artillería.

artisan [ártịẓan], s. artesano.—**artist** [ártịst], s. artista; artífice; actor.—**artistic** [artíṣtịk], a. artístico.

arum [ɛ́rʌm], s. aro, (Am.) malanga.

Aryan [ɛ́rịan], s. y a. ario (pueblo e idioma).

as [æz], adv., conj. y pron. rel. como; a medida que, mientras (que), según, conforme; cuando, en el momento en que, al; hasta donde va, en lo que contiene.—a. for, en cuanto a, por lo que respecta a.—a. from, a partir de.—a. if, como si.—a. it were, por decirlo así.—a. late a., tan recientemente como, apenas, no más.—a. many a., tantos como, cuantos; hasta.—a. much a. to say, como quien dice.—a. of, con fecha de.—a. per, según, de acuerdo con.—a. soon a. possible, cuanto antes.—a. such, como tal.—a. well, también, además.—a. well a., también como, lo mismo que; así como.—a. yet, todavía, aún, hasta ahora.

asbestic [æsbéstịk], a. incombustible.—**asbestos** [æsbéstọs], s. asbesto, amianto.

ascend [asénd], vt. subir.—vi. ascender, subir.- —ancy [-ạnsị], —ency [-ẹnsị], s. predominio, ascendiente.—**ascension** [asénṣọn], s. ascensión.—**ascent** [asént], s. subida, ascensión; ascenso.

ascertain [æscœrtéịn], vt. averiguar, indagar.—vi. cerciorarse (de).

ascribe [askráịb], vt. atribuir, imputar.

ascetic [asétịk], s. asceta.—a. ascético.— —**ism** [asétiẓịzm], s. ascetismo.

aseptic [aséptịk], a. aséptico.

ash [æṣ], s. ceniza, cenizas.—a. tray, cenicero.—A. Wednesday, miércoles de ceniza.- —es [ǽṣịz], s. restos mortales.

ashamed [aṣéịmd], a. avergonzado,

corrido.—to be a., darle a uno vergüenza.

ashore [aṣór], adv. en tierra, a tierra.—to go a., desembarcar.

Asian [éịẓan], **Asiatic** [eịẓịǽtịk], a. y s. asiático.

aside [asáịd], adv. a un lado; aparte.—s. aparte (en obras teatrales).

ask [æsk], vt. y vi. preguntar; pedir, rogar; invitar, convidar.—to a. one down, in, up, rogar a uno que baje, entre, suba.

askance [askǽns], adv. de soslayo, recelosamente.—to look a., no aprobar; mirar recelosamente.—**askew** [askjú] adv. de lado, de través.

asleep [aslíp], adv. y a. dormido, durmiendo; entumecido.—to fall a., dormirse.

asparagus [æspǽrạgạs], s. espárrago.

aspect [ǽspekt], s. aspecto; apariencia.

asperity [æspérịtị], s. aspereza; rudeza, acrimonia.

asphalt [ǽsfolt], s. asfalto.

aspirant [aspáịrạnt], s. y a. aspirante.—**aspiration** [aspịréịṣọn], s. aspiración; anhelo.—**aspire** [aspáịr], vi. aspirar, ambicionar, pretender.

aspirin [ǽspịrịn], s. aspirina.

ass [æs], s. asno, burro, etc.

assail [aséịl], vt. asaltar, atacar.- —**ant** [-ạnt], —**er** [-œ(r)] s. y a. asaltante, atracador.

assassin [asǽsịn], s. asesino.- —**ate** [-eịt], vt. asesinar.- —**ation** [-éịṣọn], s. asesinato.

assault [asólt], s. asalto, ataque; violación; atraco.—vt. asaltar, atacar, violar.

assay [aséị], vt. ensayar; probar, aquilatar.—s. prueba, contraste, ensayo.

assemble [asémbl], vt. juntar; convocar, congregar; montar maquinaria.—vi. reunirse, juntarse.—**assembly** [asémblị], s. reunión, asamblea.—a. line production, producción en serie.

assent [asént], vi. asentir, convenir.—s. asentimiento.

assert [asœ́rt], vt. afirmar, asegurar; hacer valer.—to a. oneself, hacerse valer.- —**ion** [asœ́rṣọn], s. aserto, afirmación.

assess [asés], vt. tasar, valorar, asignar impuestos.- —**ment** [-mẹnt], s. tasación, avaluación; impuesto.

asset [ǽset], s. cualidad, ventaja.—pl., activo, haber, capital.

assiduous [asídʒuʌs], a. asiduo.

assign [asáịn], vt. asignar, señalar; adscribir; consignar, traspasar.- —**ment** [-mẹnt], s. asignación, señalamiento, cesión.

assimilate [asímịleịt], vt. y vi. asimilar(se); comparar(se).

assist [asíst], vt. asistir, ayudar.—vi.

ayudar; asistir, concurrir.— —ance [-ans], s. auxilio, socorro, asistencia; concurso, ayuda.— —ant [-ant], s. y a. ayudante, auxiliar.

associate [asóusieit], vt. y vi. asociar(se), unir(se).—a. [asóusiit], asociado.—s. compañero; (con)socio, colega; cómplice.—**association** [asousiéisọn], s. asociación; unión; sociedad; conexión, relación.

assort [asórt], vt. surtir con variedad; clasificar.— —ed [-id], a. variado, surtido, mezclado.— —ment [-mẹnt], s. surtido variado, colección.

assume [asúm], vt. tomar, asumir, suponer, dar por sentado.—vi. arrogarse, atribuirse.— —d [-d], a. supuesto; fingido.—**assumption** [asámpṣọn], s. suposición, supuesto.

assurance [aṣúrạns], s. seguridad, certeza; confianza; seguro.—**assure** [aṣúr], vt. afirmar; infundir confianza; asegurar (contra riesgos).—**assured** [aṣúrd], s. y a. asegurado (contra riesgos); cierto, seguro.

asterisk [ásterisk], s. asterisco.

astern [astόern], adv. por la popa, á popa.

asthma [ézmạ], s. asma.

astonish [astániṣ], vt. asombrar.— —ed [-t], a. atónito.— —ing [-iŋ], a. sorprendente, asombroso.— —ment [-mẹnt], s. pasmo, asombro, sorpresa.

astound [astáund], vt. y vi. pasmar; aturdir, confundir.

astraddle [astrédl], adv. y a. á horcajadas.

astray [astréi], adv. y a. desviada ó descarriadamente.—to go a., desviarse, perderse.—to lead a., llevar por el mal camino.

astride [astráid], adv. a horcajadas.

astrologer [astrálodẓœ(r)], s. astrólogo. —**astrology** [astrálodẓi], s. astrología.

astronomer [astránomœ(r)], s. astrónomo.—**astronomic(al)** [æstronámik(ạl)], a. astronómico.—**astronomy** [astránomi], s. astronomía.

Asturian [æstúriạn], s. y a. asturiano, astur.

asylum [asáilʌm], s. asilo, casa de beneficencia; amparo.—insane a., manicomio.

at [æt], prep. a; en; con; de; por.— angry a. me, enfadado conmigo.—a. his command, por orden suya.—a. last, por fin.—a. once, inmediatamente.—a. one stroke, de un golpe.— a. Rome, en Roma.—a. the door, a o en la puerta.—a. work, trabajando.

ate [eit], pret. de TO EAT.

atheism [éiθiizm], s. ateísmo.—**atheist** [éiθiist], s. ateo.—**atheistic(al)** [eiθiistik(ạl)], a. ateo, ateístico.

athlete [æθlit], s. atleta.—**athletic** [æθlétik], a. atlético.—**athletics** [æθlétiks], s. deportes, atletismo; gimnasia.

Atlantic [ætlántik], a. atlántico.—s. el mar Atlántico.

atlas [átlạs], s. atlas.

atmosphere [átmọsfir], s. atmósfera.— **atmospheric(al)** [ætmọsférik(ạl)], a. atmosférico.—**atmospherics** [ætmọsfériks], s. estática (rad.).

atom [átọm], s. átomo.—a. bomb, bomba atómica.—a. splitting, fisión nuclear.— —ic(al) [atámik(ạl)], a. atómico.—atomic fission, fisión atómica.— —ization [ætọmaizéiṣọn], s. pulverización.— —ize [átomaiz], vt. atomizar, pulverizar, rociar.— —izer [átomaizœ(r)], s. pulverizador.

atone [atóụn], vt. y vi. expiar, purgar; reparar.— —ment [-mẹnt], s. expiación, etc.

atop [atáp], adv. y prep. encima (de).

atrocious [atróuṣạs], a. atroz.—**atrocity** [atrásiti], s. atrocidad.

attach [atéch], vt. unir, juntar; atar; pegar; enganchar; prender, coger; sujetar; asignar, atribuir; acompañar; embargar bienes.— —e [ataṣéi], s. agregado (diplomático).— —ed [atécht], a. fijo; anejo; adicto, devoto.— —ment [atéchmẹnt], s. adhesión, apego, devoción; unión; cariño; embargo (de bienes).

attack [atæk], vt. y vi. atacar, acometer, asaltar, embestir.—s. ataque, agresión, atentado; acceso (de tos, etc.).

attain [atéin], vi. lograr, alcanzar, llegar a.— —able [-abl], a. asequible, accesible.— —ment [-mẹnt], s. logro, consecución; dote, cualidad.

attempt [atémpt], vt. y vi. intentar, atentar; aventurar; tentar; procurar; probar, pretender.—s. prueba, ensayo; tentativa; atentado; conato.

attend [aténd], vt. y vi. atender, cuidar; servir; acompañar; asistir o concurrir a; presenciar.—well-attended, muy concurrido (espectáculo, etc.).— —ance [-ạns], s. presencia, asistencia; comparecencia; público, concurrencia.— —ant [-ạnt], s. acompañante; sirviente; asistente.—a. concomitante, acompañante.

attention [aténṣọn], s. atención; cortesía, fineza; agasajo.—to pay o give a., prestar atención; hacer caso.—**attentive** [aténtiv], a. atento, solícito, cortés.—**attentiveness** [aténtivnis], s. cuidado, cortesía; atención.

attest [atést], vt. atestiguar, atestar, certificar; autenticar; dar testimonio ó fe.

attic [átik], s. desván, buhardilla; ático.

attire [ətái(r)], *vt.* vestir, ataviar, adornar.— *s.* atavío, traje, ropa.
attitude [ǽtiṭiud], *s.* actitud, ademán,
postura.
attorney [əṭǿrni], *s.* abogado; apoderado.— *a. general*, fiscal nacional.—
district a., fiscal del distrito.
attract [əṭrǽkt], *vt. y vi.* atraer; cautivar.— —**ion** [əṭrǽksǫn], *s.* atracción;
atractivo, aliciente.- —**ive** [əṭrǽk-
ṭiv], *a.* atractivo; cautivador; simpático.— —**iveness** [əṭrǽkṭivnis], *s.*
atracción, atractivo.
attribute [əṭríbiut], *vt.* atribuir, imputar, achacar.—*s.* [ǽtribiut], atributo,
característica, distintivo.
attrition [ætríṣǫn], *s.* roce, rozadura,
frotación; atrición.
attune [əṭiún], *vt.* armonizar, afinar.
auburn [ǿbœrn], *a.* castaño rojizo.
auction [ǿksǫn], *s.* subasta, almoneda,
remate.—*vt.* subastar, rematar.—
—**eer** [-ír], *s.* subastador; pregonero,
rematador.—*vt.* vender en pública
subasta.
audacious [ǫdéiṣʌs], *a.* audaz, osado;
descarado.—**audacity** [ǫdǽsiṭi], *s.*
audacia, osadía.
audible [ǿdibl], *a.* audible.—**audience**
[ǿdiens], *s.* auditorio, concurso, concurrencia, público; los oyentes o
circunstantes; audición; audiencia o
entrevista.—**audit** [ǿdiṭ], *s.* intervención y ajuste de cuentas.—*vt.* intervenir, revisar una cuenta.—**auditor**
[ǿdiṭǫ(r)], *s.* oyente; interventor.—
auditorium [ǫdiṭóriam], *s.* auditorio,
salón de actos o de espectáculos.
auger [ǿgœ(r)], *s.* barrena; taladro.—*a.
bit*, broca o mecha de taladro.
aught [ǫt], *s.* algo; cero; nada.—*adv.*
absolutamente.
augment [ǫgmént], *vt. y vi.* aumentar,
crecer.- —**ative** [-ǽṭiv], *a.* aumenta-
tivo.
august [ǫgʌ́st], *a.* augusto, majestuoso.
—**A.** [ǿgʌst], *s.* agosto (mes).
aunt [ænt, ant], *s.* tía.
aureola [ǫríolǎ], *s.* aureola, corona.
aureomycin [ǫriǫumáisin], *s.* aureomi-
cina.
auricular [ǫríkyūlǎ(r)], *a.* auricular;
oíble; confidencial, secreto, dicho al
oído.
auspices [ǿspisiz], *s. pl.* auspicios;
dirección.—**auspicious** [ǫspíṣʌs], *a.*
favorable, propicio.
austere [ǫstír], *a.* austero.- —**ness**
[-nis], **austerity** [ǫstériṭi], *s.* austeridad.
Australian [ǫstréilyən], *a. y s.* austra-
liano.
Austrian [ǿstrian], *a. y s.* austríaco.
authentic(al) [ǫθéntik(ạl)], *a.* autén-

tico.— —ity [ǫθentísiṭi], *s.* autentici-
dad.
author [ǿθǫ(r)], *s.* autor.— —**ess** [-is], *s.*
autora.
authoritative [ǫθáriteiṭiv], *a.* autorizado.
—**authority** [ǫθáriṭi], *s.* autoridad.—
authorization [ǫθǫrizéiṣǫn], *s.* autorización.—**authorize** [ǿθǫraiz], *vt.*
autorizar, facultar.
authorship [ǿθǫrṣip], *s.* autoría, paternidad literaria.
auto [ǿtou], *s.* automóvil, auto.
autocracy [ǫtákrasi], *s.* autocracia.—
autocrat [ǿtokræt], *s.* autócrata.
autograph [ǿtogræf], *a. y s.* autógrafo.—
vt. autografiar.
automat [ǿtomæt], *s.* mecanismo automático; restaurante de servicio automático.- —**ic(al)** [otomǽtik(ạl)], *a.*
automático.- —**ism** [otámạṭizm], *s.*
automatismo.- —**on** [otámạtan], *s.*
autómata.
automobile [ǿtomoubil], *s.* automóvil.
autonomous [otánomʌs], *a.* autónomo.
—**autonomy** [otánomi], *s.* autonomía.
autopsy [ǿtapsi], *s.* autopsia.
autumn [ǿtʌm], *s.* otoño.
auxiliary [ǫgzílyạri], *a.* auxiliar.
avail [əvéil], *vt.* aprovechar, beneficiar,
valer.—*vi.* valer, servir, ser útil.—*to
a. oneself of*, aprovecharse de.—*s.*
provecho, utilidad.- —**able** [-abl], *a.*
aprovechable, disponible.
avalanche [ǽvạlænch], *s.* alud.
avarice [ǽvạris], *s.* avaricia, codicia.—
avaricious [ævạríṣʌs], *a.* avaro, avariento.
avenge [əvéndž], *vt. y vi.* vengar(se).
avenue [ǽveniu], *s.* avenida, calzada;
alameda.
aver [əvœ́r], *vt.* asegurar, afirmar.
average [ǽveridž], *s.* promedio; término
medio.—*on an a.*, como promedio.—
a. medio, común, corriente, típico.—
vt. calcular el promedio o término
medio; prorratear.
averse [əvœ́rs], *a.* adverso, contrario;
renuente.—**aversion** [əvœ́ržǫn], *s.*
aversión.
avert [əvœ́rt], *vt.* desviar, apartar;
prevenir, conjurar.
aviary [éivieri], *s.* pajarera.
aviation [eiviéiṣǫn], *s.* aviación.—**avia-
tor** [éivieiṭǫ(r)], *s.* aviador.
avid [ǽvid], *a.* ávido, codicioso; ansioso.
- —**ity** [əvídiṭi], *s.* avidez, codicia;
ansia.
avocado [ævokádou], *s.* aguacate.
avocation [ævokéiṣǫn], *s.* vocación;
distracción, diversión.
avoid [əvóid], *vt.* evitar, eludir, esquivar, evadir; zafarse de.- —**able** [-abl],
a. evitable, eludible.- —**ance** [-ạns],
s. evitación.
await [əwéit], *vt. y vi.* aguardar, esperar

awake [ǝwéjk], *vti.* y *vii.* [4], **awaken** [ǝwéjkǝn], *vt.* y *vi.* despertar(se).— *a.* despierto, desvelado.—**awakening** [ǝwéjkǝniŋ], *s.* despertar, despertamiento.

award [ǝwórd], *vt.* y *vi.* otorgar, conferir; premiar; adjudicar.—*s.* premio; sentencia, adjudicación.

aware [ǝwér], *a.* consciente; enterado, sabedor; sobre aviso.

awash [ǝwáš], *a.* y *adv.* a flor de agua.

away [ǝwéj], *adv.* y *a.* lejos; a lo lejos; ausente, fuera.—*far a.*, muy lejos.— *right a.*, ahorita.—*to go a.*, alejarse.— *to take a.*, quitar.—*interj.* ¡fuera de aquí! ¡lárguese usted!

awe [ɔ], *s.* temor; pasmo; pavor.—*a.- inspiring,* imponente.—*a.-struck,* despavorido, aterrado, espantado.— *to stand in a. of,* temer; reverenciar.— *vt.* aterrar, infundir miedo o respeto.

awful [ɔ́ful], *a.* tremendo; terrible.

awhile [ǝhwájl], *adv.* un rato, algún tiempo.

awkward [ɔ́kwǝrd], *a.* torpe, desmañado, desgarbado; embarazoso.- —**ness** [-nis], *s.* torpeza, desmaña.

awl [ɔl], *s.* lezna; punzón; lengüeta.

awning [ɔ́niŋ], *s.* toldo.

awoke [ǝwóuk], *pret.* y *pp.* de TO AWAKE.

ax(e) [æks], *s.* hacha.

axiom [ǽksiǝm], *s.* axioma, postulado, sentencia.

axis [ǽksis], *s.* (*pl.* axes [ǽksiz]) eje.

axle [ǽksl], *s.* eje, árbol.

aye, ay [aj], *adv.* sí.—*s.* voto afirmativo.

Aztec [ǽztek], *a.* y *s.* azteca.

azure [ǽʒur], *a.* y *s.* azur, azul celeste.

B

babble [bǽbl], *vt.* y *vi.* balbucear; charlar; murmurar (un arroyo).—*s.* charla, balbuceo, charlatanería; susurro, murmullo.— **r** [bǽblœ(r)], *s.* charlatán, hablador; trapalero.—**babbling** [bǽbliŋ], *a.* murmurante, balbuciente.—*s.* cháchara, garrulería, balbucencia.

babe [bejb], *s.* criaturita, nene, bebé.

baboon [bæbún], *s.* mandril.

baby [béjbi], *s.* criatura, crío, nene, nena, pequeñuelo, bebé; (Am.) guagua.—*a.* de niño; de, para o como nene; pequeño; de tierna edad; infantil.—*b. blue,* azul claro.—*b. carriage,* cochecillo de nene.—*b. grand piano,* piano de media cola.—*b. talk,* modo infantil de hablar, media lengua.—*b. tooth,* diente de leche.—*vti.* [7] tratar como niño; mimar.

baccalaureate [bækǝlɔ́rijt], *s.* bachillerato.

bachelor [bǽchǝlǝ(r)], *s.* soltero, célibe; bachiller.

bacilli [bǝsílaj], *s. pl.* bacilos, bacterias.—**bacillus** [bǝsílʌs], *s.* bacilo, bacteria.—**bacillary** [bǽsileri], *a.* bacilar.

back [bæk], *s.* espalda; lomo, espinazo (de un animal); respaldo; dorso, revés (de la mano); reverso; parte posterior o de atrás, trasera; lomo (de un cuchillo, de un libro); (teat.) foro; (dep.) zaguero, defensa.—*behind one's b.,* por detrás, a espaldas de uno.—*in the b. of one's mind,* en lo recóndito del pensamiento.—*on one's b.,* a cuestas, boca arriba, de espaldas.— *to turn one's b.* (*on*), volver la espalda; negar ayuda (a).—*with one's b. to the wall,* entre la espada y la pared.— *a.* trasero, posterior, inferior; dorsal; atrasado, pasado (apl. al tiempo); lejano.—*b. pay,* sueldo atrasado.— *adv.* atrás, detrás; de nuevo; de vuelta.—*b. and forth,* de un lado a otro.—*to come b.,* volver, regresar.— *to give b.,* devolver.—*interj.* ¡atrás!— *vt.* hacer retroceder; apoyar, respaldar; endosar.—*vi.* (a veces con up) recular, retroceder, ciar.—*to b. down, to b. out,* volverse atrás; abandonar una empresa. —**ache** [bǽkejk], *s.* dolor de espalda.—**backbit** [bǽkbjt], *pret.* y *pp.* de TO BACKBITE.—**bite** [-bajt], *vti.* y *vii.* [10] difamar, murmurar; morder.— **biter** [-bajtœ(r)], *s.* murmurador, difamador, detractor.— **biting** [-bajtiŋ], *s.* murmuración, difamación, calumnia.—**backbitten** [bǽkbjtǝn], *pp.* de TO BACKBITE.— **board** [-bɔrd], *s.* respaldo, espaldar. —**bone** [-boun], *s.* espinazo; nervio; fundamento.— **breaking** [-brejkiŋ], *a.* agobiante, abrumador.— **fire** [-fajr], *s.* contracandela; explosión prematura.—*vi.* salir el tiro por la culata.— **ground** [-graund], *s.* trasfondo; antecedentes; base, fondo; lejanía.— **shop** [-šap], *s.* trastienda; rebotica. —**side** [-sajd], *s.* envés, vuelta, espalda; nalgas.— **stitch** [-stjch], *s.* pespunte, punto atrás.—*vt.* y *vi.* pespuntar.— **ward** [-wǝrd], *a.* vuelto o dirigido hacia atrás; retrógrado, atrasado; retraído; tardo, tardío.—*to go b. and forward,* ir y venir.— **wardness** [-wǝrdnis], *s.* atraso; torpeza; retraimiento.— **wards** [-wǝrdz], *adv.* atrás, de espaldas.—*to go b.,* retroceder, ir para atrás.

bacon [béjkǝn], *s.* tocino.

bacteria [bæktíriǝ], *s. pl.* bacterias.— **bacterial** [bæktíriǝl], *a.* bacteriano, bactérico.

bad [bæd], *a.* mal(o), perverso, depravado; dañoso; enfermo, indispuesto; dañado, podrido.—*b. blood,* animosi-

dad, encono.—*b. coin,* moneda falsa.
—*b. time,* mal rato.—*very b.,* pésimo.

bade [bæd], *pret.* de TO BID.

badge [bædź], *s.* condecoración, insignia, placa, distintivo.

badger [bædźœ(r)], *vt.* molestar, cansar, fatigar.—*s.* tejón.

baffle [bǽfl], *vt.* desconcertar; contrariar; frustrar, impedir.—**baffling** [bǽfliŋ], *a.* desconcertante, desconcertador.

bag [bæg], *s.* saco, costal, talega; bolsa, zurrón; presa; saquito de mano.— *to be in the b.,* (fam.) ser cosa segura.— *to hold the b.,* (fam.) pagar los vidrios rotos.—*vti.* [1] ensacar, entalegar; cazar, cobrar (la caza).—*vii.* hacer bolsa o pliegue (la ropa).— —**gage** [bǽgidź], *s.* equipaje, maletas.—*b. check,* contraseña de equipaje.

bail [beil], *s.* caución, fianza; fiador; cubo o vertedor para achicar (agua).— *on b.,* bajo fianza.—*to go b. for,* salir fiador de.—*vt.* dar fianza, caucionar; poner en libertad bajo fianza; achicar.—*vi.—to b. out,* (aer.) arrojarse de un avión.

bailiff [béiljf], *s.* alguacil.

bait [beit], *vt.* cebar; atraer, tentar; molestar, acosar.—*s.* cebo, carnada; anzuelo, señuelo; pienso.—*to take the b.,* tragar el anzuelo, caer en un lazo.

baize [beiz], *s.* bayeta.—*green b.,* tapete verde.

bake [beik], *vt.* cocer o asar al horno; calcinar.—*vi.* hornear (como oficio); cocerse el horno.— —**d** [-t], *a.* horneado; cocido al horno.—*b. eggs,* huevos al plato.— —**r** [béikœ(r)], *s.* panadero, hornero; pastelero.— —**ry** [-œri], *s.* horno, tahona, panadería, pastelería.—**baking** [-iŋ], *s.* hornada; cocción.

balance [bǽlⱥns], *s.* balanza; equilibrio; balance, contrapeso; (com.) balance, saldo.—*b. wheel,* balancín, volante.— *vt.* equilibrar; balancear; contrapesar; (com.) saldar; pesar, considerar.—*vi.* equilibrarse; contrarrestarse; (com.) saldarse; balancearse, mecerse.— **balancing** [bǽlⱥnsiŋ], *s.* equilibrio; balanceo.—*a.* compensador.—*b. flap,* (aer.) alerón.

balcony [bǽlkoni], *s.* balcón; (teat.) galería, anfiteatro.

bald [bold], *a.* calvo; escueto; pelado, desnudo; desabrido.— —**head** [bóldhed], *s.* persona calva.— —**ness** [-njs], *s.* calvicie.

bale [beil], *s.* fardo; tercio (de tabaco); bala, paca (de algodón, de papel).— *vt.* embalar, empaquetar.

Balearic [bæljǽrjk], *a.* balear.

baling [béiliŋ], *s.* embalaje; enfardeladura.

balk [bok], *vt.* frustrar, desbaratar.—*vi.* plantarse, encabritarse (un caballo); resistirse.—*s.* obstáculo, impedimento, fracaso; (carp.) viga.

ball [bol], *s.* bola, pelota, globo; yema (del dedo); baile; bala (de cañón).— *b. bearing,* caja de bolas, cojinete.— *b. game,* juego de pelota, de beisbol.— *b. of yarn,* ovillo.—*to b. up,* embrollar, confundir.

ballad [bǽlⱥd], *s.* balada, romance; copla, canción.

ballast [bǽlⱥst], *s.* lastre; (f.c.) balasto. —*b. bed,* firme (de carretera).— *washed b.,* guijarro.—*vt.* lastrar; (f.c.) balastar.— —**ing** [-iŋ], *s.* lastre; balasto.

balloon [bⱥlún], *s.* globo (aerostático).— —**ist** [-ist], *s.* aeronauta.

ballot [bǽlⱥt], *s.* cédula o boleta para votar; voto; votación.—*b. box,* urna electoral.—*vt.* y *vi.* votar.— —**ing** [-iŋ], *s.* votación.

balm [bam], *s.* bálsamo, ungüento fragante.— —**y** [bámi], *a.* balsámico, fragante; calmante; alocado, tonto.

ban [bæn], *s.* bando, edicto, proclama, pregón; excomunión.—*vti.* [1] prohibir, proscribir; excomulgar.

banal [béinⱥl], *a.* trivial, vulgar.

banana [bⱥnǽnⱥ], *s.* plátano, banano, guineo.—*b. plantation,* platanal, platanar.—*b. tree,* banano, plátano bananero.

band [bænd], *s.* banda, faja, tira; correa, cinta, franja, lista; abrazadera, zuncho; banda, pandilla, cuadrilla; (mús.) banda, charanga.—*vt.* y *vi.* juntar, congregar; fajar, atar.— *to b. together,* asociarse; formar pandilla.

bandage [bǽndjdź], *s.* vendaje, venda, faja.—*vt.* vendar.

bandit [bǽndjt], *s.* bandido, bandolero.— —**ry** [-ri], *s.* bandolerismo, bandidaje.

bane [bein], *s.* ruina, azote, daño.— —**ful** [béinful], *a.* pernicioso, dañino, ponzoñoso, funesto.

bang [bæŋ], *vt.* golpear con ruido, hacer estrépito.—*vi.* dar estampido; saltar. —*s.* golpe; estampido; portazo; ruido de un golpe; flequillo.—*with a b.,* con un golpe violento; con estrépito. De repente.—*interj.* ¡pum!

banish [bǽnjś], *vt.* desterrar, deportar; confinar.— —**ment** [-mⱥnt], *s.* destierro, deportación; confinamiento.

banister [bǽnjstœ(r)], *s.* baranda, pasamano.

bank [bæŋk], *s.* orilla, ribera, margen; loma, cuesta; banco, bajío; (com.) banco, casa de banca.—*b. book,* libreta de banco.—*b. note,* billete de banco.—*vt.* represar, estancar; amontonar, apilar; depositar en un banco.

—*vi.* ocuparse en negocios de banca; ser banquero.—*vt.* y *vi.* (aer.) ladear(se).—*to b. on,* contar con, confiar en.— —**er** [bǽŋkœ(r)], *s.* banquero; cambista.— —**ing** [-iŋ], *s.* banca, operaciones de banco.— *a.* bancario.— —**rupt** [-rʌpt], *s.* y *a.* quebrado, en quiebra, insolvente.—*vt.* quebrar, arruinar.— —**ruptcy** [-rʌptsi], *s.* bancarrota, quiebra.—*to go into b.,* declararse en quiebra.

banner [bǽnɐr], *s.* bandera, estandarte.

banns [bænz], *s. pl.* amonestaciones.

banquet [bǽŋkwit], *s.* banquete, festín.—*vt.* y *vi.* banquetear.

banter [bǽntœ(r)], *vt.* y *vi.* zumbar(se), dar matraca, chotear, embromar.—*s.* zumba, burla, chunga.— —**er** [-œ(r)], *s.* zumbón, burlón.

baptism [bǽptizm], *s.* bautismo, bautizo.— —**al** [bæptízmạl], *a.* bautismal. —*b. name,* nombre de pila.—**baptize** [bǽptaiz], *vt.* bautizar.

bar [bar], *s.* barra; varilla; barra o pastilla (de chocolate, etc.); palanca; impedimento; barrera; cantina, bar, mostrador de taberna; reja, barrote; tribunal; abogacía, foro, cuerpo de abogados; (for.) foro, estrados; recinto de los acusados; (mus.) barra, raya de compás; (metal.) barra, lingote.—*b. association,* colegio de abogados.—*b. bell,* palanqueta de gimnasio.—*to be admitted to the b.,* recibirse de abogado.—*vti.* [1] trancar; estorbar, obstruir; prohibir; excluir.—*prep.* excepto, salvo.—*b. none,* sin excepción.

barb [barb], *s.* púa; lengüeta (de saeta, anzuelo).

barbarian [barbérịạn], *a.* y *s.* bárbaro, barbárico.—**barbarism** [bárbạrizm], *s.* barbarie; barbarismo.—**barbarity** [barbériti], *s.* barbaridad, ferocidad. —**barbarous** [bárbạrʌs], *a.* bárbaro, inculto; cruel.

barbecue [bárbikju], *vt.* hacer barbacoa. —*s.* barbacoa; churrasco.

barbed [barbd], *a.* barbado, armado con lengüetas o púas.—*b. wire,* alambre de púas.

barber [bárbœ(r)], *s.* barbero, peluquero.—*b. shop,* barbería, peluquería.

bard [bard], *s.* bardo, poeta.

bare [ber], *a.* desnudo; raso; pelado; liso; sencillo; desarmado; descarnado; descubierto; público; desamueblado; vacío; mero, solo.—*b. of money,* sin un cuarto, sin un real.—*vt.* desnudar, descubrir, despojar.— —**back** [bér-bæk], *a.* y *adv.* (montado) al pelo, sin silla.— —**boned** [-bound], *a.* muy flaco, descarnado.— —**faced** [-feist], *a.* descarado, insolente, atrevido.— —**facedness** [-feistnịs], *s.* descaro,

desfachatez.— —**foot** [-fut], *a.* descalzo.— —**headed** [-hedịd], *a.* sin sombrero, descubierto.— —**legged** [-legịd], *a.* sin medias.— —**ly** [-li], *adv.* mera, sola, escasamente.— —**necked** [-nekt], *a.* descotado, con escote.— —**ness** [-nịs], *s.* desnudez; flaqueza; miseria.

bargain [bárgịn], *s.* convenio, concierto; ganga; negocio, trato de compra o venta; artículo muy reducido de precio.—*at a b.,* baratísimo; en una ganga.—*b. driver,* regateador.—*to strike a b.,* cerrar un trato; hallar una ganga.—*vt.* y *vi.* concertar, negociar; regatear.—*to b. away,* permutar; vender regalado.— —**ing** [-iŋ], *s.* regateo; trato.

barge [bardʒ], *s.* lanchón, barcaza.

baritone [bǽritoun], *s.* barítono.

bark [bark], *s.* corteza; ladrido; velero. —*vt.* descortezar, raspar, raer; curtir o teñir en una infusión de corteza.— *vi.* ladrar; vociferar.—*to b. up the wrong tree,* tomar el rábano por las hojas, ir descaminado.

barkeeper [bárkipœ(r)], *s.* tabernero cantinero.

barley [bárli], *s.* cebada.

barmaid [bármeid], *s.* cantinera, moza de taberna, (Am.) mesera.

barn [barn], *s.* granero, pajar, troje; henil; establo (para ganado).

barnacle [bárnạkl], *s.* lapa, percebe.

barnyard [bárnyard], *s.* corral.

barometer [bạrámetœ(r)], *s.* barómetro. —**barometrical** [bærométrikạl], *a.* barométrico.

barrack [bǽrạk], *s.* barraca, cabaña.— *pl.* cuartel.—*vt.* y *vi.* acuartelar(se).

barrel [bǽrẹl], *s.* barril, cuba, bocoy, tonel; tambor de reloj; cañón (de arma de fuego).—*vti.* [2] embarrilar.

barren [bǽrẹn], *a.* estéril, árido, infecundo.— —**ness** [-nịs], *s.* esterilidad, infecundidad, aridez.

barricade [bǽrikéid], *s.* barricada, barrera, empalizada.—*vt.* cerrar con barricadas; obstruir el paso.

barrier [bǽrịœ(r)], *s.* barrera; valla; obstáculo, estacada, atasco; límite.

bartender [bártendœ(r)], *s.* cantinero, tabernero.

barter [bártœ(r)], *vt.* permutar, trocar, cambiar.—*s.* permuta, cambio, trueque.— —**er** [-œ(r)], *s.* traficante, cambalachero.

base [beis], *a.* bajo, ruín, villano; básico; (mus.) bajo, grave.—*b. court,* tribunal inferior.—*s.* basa, base, cimiento, fundamento; pedestal; zócalo; (mus.) bajo, grave; (beisbol) base.—*vt.* basar, apoyar, fundamentar.— —**ball** [béisbol], *s.* beisbol o basebol; pelota de beisbol.— —**board** [-bord], *s.* zócalo, plancha que sirve de base; rodapié.— **—born** [-born], *a.* plebeyo; bastardo.— **—less** [-lis], *a.* desfondado; sin fundamento.— **—ment** [-ment], *s.* sótano; basamento.— **—ness** [-nis], *s.* bajeza, vileza; ruindad.

bashful [bǽʃful], *a.* vergonzoso, tímido, corto.— **—ness** [-nis], *s.* vergüenza, timidez, cortedad.

basic [béjsik], *a.* básico, fundamental.

basilica [basílikǎ], *s.* basílica.

basin [béjsin], *s.* (al)jofaina, bacía, palangana; cubeta; pila (de agua bendita); taza, pilón; estanque, represa, dársena; charca; cuenca de un río.

basis [béjsis], *s.* base; fundamento.

bask [bæsk], *vt.* y *vi.* asolearse, calentarse al sol, tomar el sol.

basket [bǽskit], *s.* cesto, canasta; cesta; (aer.) barquilla.— **—ball** [-bɔl], *s.* baloncesto, basketbol.

Basque [bæsk], *a.* y *s.* vasco, vascongado; (lengua) vascuence.

bass [bejs], *a.* (mus.) bajo, grave.—*b. drum,* bombo.—*b. horn,* tuba.—*b. string,* bordón.—*b. viol,* violón, contrabajo.—*s.* [bæs] (ict.) perca; [bejs] bajo (apl. a la voz).

bastard [bǽstard], *s.* bastardo, hijo natural.—*a.* bastardo; falso, espurio.— **—y** [-i], *s.* bastardía.

baste [bejst], *vt.* bilvanar; echar grasa sobre el asado; (fam.) azotar.— **—basting** [béjstiŋ], *s.* hilván; (fam.) paliza.

bastion [bǽschon], *s.* bastión, baluarte.

bat [bæt], *s.* bate de beisbol; garrote; murciélago; guata.—*vti.* y *vii.* [1] golpear; batear; pestañear.

batch [bæch], *s.* hornada; tanda; grupo.

bath [bæθ], *s.* baño, cuarto de baño; bañadera.— **—e** [bejð], *vt.* bañar, lavar.—*vi.* bañarse.— **—er** [béjðœ(r)], *s.* bañista.— **—house** [bǽθhaus], *s.* casa de baño.— **—ing** [béjðiŋ], *s.* baño.—*a.* de baño.—*b. resort,* balneario.—*b. suit,* traje de baño; (Am.) trusa.—*b. trunks,* calzón de baño.— **—robe** [bǽθroub], *s.* bata de baño, albornoz.— **—room** [-rum], *s.* cuarto de baño.— **—tub** [-tʌb], *s.* bañadera, bañera.

baton [bætán], *s.* bastón de mando; (mus.) batuta.

battalion [bætǽlyon], *s.* batallón.

batter [bǽtœ(r)], *vt.* y *vi.* golpear, batir, majar.—*b. down,* demoler.—*s.* batido, masa culinaria; golpeadura.

battery [bǽtœri], *s.* (arti. y mec.) batería; (elec.) pila; batería, acumulador; asalto, agresión.

battle [bǽtl], *s.* batalla, combate; lucha.—*vi.* y *vt.* batallar, combatir; luchar.— **—field** [-fild], **—ground** [-graund], *s.* campo de batalla.— **—ment** [-ment],

s. muralla almenada.— **—ship** [-ʃip], *s.* acorazado.

bawl [bɔl], *vt.* pregonar.—*vi.* gritar, chillar, desgañitarse.—*s.* gritería.— **—er** [bɔ́lœ(r)], *s.* vocinglero, alborotador, chillón.

bay [bej], *a.* bayo.—*vt.* y *vi.* ladrar, aullar.—*s.* bahía, ensenada, cala, rada; ladrido, aullido; caballo bayo; laurel.—*at b.,* acorralado; a raya.—*b. window,* mirador, ventana saliente.

bayonet [béjonit], *s.* bayoneta.—*vt.* cargar o herir con bayoneta.

bazaar [bazár], *s.* bazar, feria.

be [bi], *vii.* [11] ser, existir; estar, encontrarse, hallarse, verse, quedar(se); haber; hacer; tener.—*he is no more,* ya no existe.—*it is cold, hot, etc.,* hace frío, calor, etc.—*there is no one there,* no hay nadie allí.—*to be American, Spanish, etc.,* ser americano, español, etc.—*to be astonished, surprised, etc.,* quedar(se) atónito, sorprendido, etc.—*to be cold, hungry, right, two years old, etc.,* tener frío, hambre, razón, dos años, etc.—*to be healthy, sick, etc.,* estar sano, enfermo, etc.—*to be in a serious situation, without money, etc.,* encontrarse, hallarse, verse en una situación seria, sin un centavo.

beach [bich], *s.* playa, costa, orilla.—*vt.* y *vi.* arrastrar a la playa; varar; encallar en la playa.

beacon [bíkon], *s.* faro; baliza, boya; fanal; señal luminosa.—*vt.* abalizar; iluminar, guiar.

bead [bid], *s.* cuenta (de rosario, collar), abalorio; burbuja; espuma; gota (de sudor); saliente.—*pl.* rosario.—*vt.* adornar con abalorios; redondear los bordes (de un tubo ensanchado).—*vi.* formar espuma; burbujear.— **—ing** [bídiŋ], *s.* abalorio; listón; moldura convexa; pestaña, reborde.

beadle [bídl], *s.* pertiguero o macero, muñidor, bedel, alguacil, ministril.

beak [bik], *s.* pico; hocico; (fam.) rostro; cabo; espolón (de buque).— **—ed** [-t], *a.* picudo.— **—er** [bíkœ(r)], *s.* vaso, copa.

beam [bim], *s.* rayo, destello; viga, tablón; (mar.) bao; manga de un buque; brazo de romana.—*on the b.,* ir bien encaminado.—*radio b.,* radio faro.—*vi.* destellar, fulgurar; rebosar de alegría.—*vt.* enviar; emitir, irradiar; radiar.— **—ing** [bímiŋ], *a.* radiante; brillante; alegre.— **—y** [-i], *a.* radiante; alegre, vivo; macizo; (mar.) ancho de manga.

bean [bin], *s.* frijol, haba, habichuela, alubia, judía; grano, semilla; (fam.) cabeza, chola, cayuca.—*string b.,* habichuela verde, ejote, poroto.

bear [ber], *vti.* [10], sostener, sustentar;

llevar; aguantar, soportar, sobrellevar; sufragar; producir; parir, dar a luz.—*to b. company*, acompañar.—*to b. in mind*, tener en cuenta.—*to b. out*, confirmar, corroborar.—*to b. with*, tener paciencia con.—*to b. witness*, dar testimonio.—*s.* oso; (com.) bajista (en la Bolsa).— —**able** [bérabl], *a.* sufrible, soportable.— —**er** [-œ(r)], *s.* portador; mensajero; soporte.— —**ing** [-iŋ], *s.* cojinete, caja de bolas; paciencia, sufrimiento; porte, presencia; relación, conexión; cosecha; gestación.—*pl.* orientación, rumbo; línea de flotación.—*to find one's b.*, orientarse.—*a.* de apoyo, de contacto; productivo.—*fruit b.*, fructífero.

beard [bird], *s.* barba o barbas; (bot.) arista.

beast [bist], *s.* bestia; animal; cuadrúpedo; hombre brutal.—*b. of burden*, acémila.

beat [bit], *vti.* [10] batir; revolver; sacudir; pegar; golpear; ganar, vencer; aventajar; marcar (el compás); (caz.) dar una batida; sonar (el tambor).—*to b. a retreat*, batirse en retirada.—*vii.* latir, pulsar; batir (el sol, las olas); golpear repetidamente; sonar.—*to b. around the bush*, andar(se) con rodeos.—*to b. it*, (fam.) poner pies en polvorosa.—*s.* golpe; palpitación, latido; toque de tambor; ronda.—*a.* (fam.) fatigado, rendido de cansancio.—*pret.* y *pp.* de TO BEAT.—**beaten** [bíten], *pp.* de TO BEAT.—*a.* trillado; batido, vencido.— —**er** [-œ(r)], *s.* martillo, maza; molinillo; batidor, agitador, sacudidor.— —**ing** [-iŋ], *s.* paliza, zurra, tunda; latido, palpitación, pulsación; golpeo.

beatitude [biétitjud], *s.* beatitud; bienaventuranza.—*the Beatitudes*, las bienaventuranzas.

beau [bou], *s.* pretendiente, acompañante, novio.

beautician [bjutíʃan], *s.* peluquero, peluquera.—**beautiful** [bjútiful], *a.* bello, hermoso, precioso.—**beautify** [bjútifai], *vti.* [7] hermosear, embellecer, acicalar.—*vii.* hermosearse, pulirse, maquillarse.—**beauty** [bjúti], *s.* belleza, beldad, hermosura, preciosidad.—*b. parlor*, salón de belleza.

beaver [bívœ(r)], *s.* castor; piel de castor.— —**board** [-bɔrd], *s.* cartón de fibras para tabiques.

becalm [bikám], *vt.* calmar, sosegar; encalmarse (tiempo o viento).

became [bikéjm], *pret.* de TO BECOME.

because [bikóz], *conj.* y *adv.* porque, pues, que.—*b. of*, a causa de.

beckon [békon], *vt.* llamar o mandar con (o por) señas.—*vi.* hacer señas

o ademanes.—*s.* seña, ademán, llamada.

become [bikÁm], *vii.* [10] devenir; hacerse; llegar a ser; ponerse; volverse; convertirse en; quedarse (cojo, sordo, etc.).—*vti.* sentar bien, caer bien (trajes, vestidos, colores).— *pp.* de TO BECOME.—**becoming** [bikÁmiŋ], *a.* propio, conveniente; favorecedor (vestido, color).

bed [bed], *s.* cama, lecho; (geol.) capa, estrato, yacimiento; cauce (de río); (mec.) asiento, lecho, fondo; armadura, base, cimiento; (ing.) firme.— *double b.*, cama de matrimonio, cama camera.—*to go to b.*, acostarse.—*vti.* [1] acostar.— —**bug** [bédbAg], *s.* chinche.— —**clothes** [-klouðz], *s. pl.* ropa de cama; (Am.) cobijas.

bedlam [bédlam], *s.* casa de orates; bullicio; desbarajuste.

Bedouin [béduin], *s.* beduino; vago.

bedplate [bédplejt], *s.* (mec.) bancaza, platina.

bedraggled [bjdrægld], *a.* enlodado.

bedridden [bédriden], *a.* postrado en cama.—**bedroom** [bédrum], *s.* alcoba, dormitorio; (Mex.) recámara.—**bedside** [bédsajd], *s.* lado de cama; cabecera.—**bedspread** [bédspred], *s.* colcha, cobertor.—**bedspring** [bédspriŋ], *s.* colchón de muelle.—**bedtime** [bédtajm], *s.* hora de acostarse.

bee [bi], *s.* abeja; (fam.) reunión, tertulia.—*b. line*, línea recta.

beech [bich], *s.* (bot.) haya.— —**nut** [bíchnat], *s.* nuez de haya, hayuco.

beef [bif], *s.* carne de res; res; queja.— *vi.* (fam.) jactarse; quejarse.

beehive [bíhajv], *s.* colmena.—**beekeeper** [bíkipœ(r)], *s.* apicultor, colmenero.—**beekeeping** [bíkipiŋ], *s.* apicultura.

been [bin], *pp.* de TO BE.

beer [bir], *s.* cerveza.

beet [bit], *s.* remolacha, (Mex.) betabel.

beetle [bítl], *s.* escarabajo.—**beetling** [bítliŋ], *s.* saliente, colgante; estampación.

before [bifór], *adv.* delante, al frente; antes, con prioridad; (mar.) de proa. —*b.-mentioned*, antemencionado, susodicho.—*prep.* delante de, enfrente de; ante, en presencia de; antes de.— *b. the wind*, viento en popa.—*conj.* antes (de) que, primero.— —**hand** [-hænd], *adv.* de antemano; previamente, con antelación.—*a.* acomodado; con recursos.

befriend [bifrénd], *vt.* favorecer, patrocinar; brindar amistad.

beg [beg], *vii.* [1] mendigar, pordiosear, vivir de limosna.—*vti.* rogar, suplicar, pedir.—*to b. (leave) to*, permitirse.

began [bigén], *pret.* de TO BEGIN.

beggar [bégǎr], *s.* pordiosero, mendigo.—
—**ly** [-li], *a.* pobre, miserable.—*adv.*
pobremente.—**begging** [bégin], *s.*
mendicidad, mendicación, pordioseo.

begin [bigín], *vti. y vii.* [10] comenzar,
principiar, empezar; iniciar; (for.) in-
coar (un pleito).— —**ner** [-œ(r)], *s.*
principiante; novicio, novato; (com.)
meritorio.— —**ning** [-in], *s.* comienzo,
iniciación, principio, origen; génesis.
—*from b. to end*, de cabo a rabo, de
pe a pa.

beguile [bigáil], *vt.* engañar, seducir;
defraudar; pasar el tiempo.

begun [bigán], *pp.* de TO BEGIN.

behalf [bijéef], *s.*—*in o on behalf of*,
por; a favor, en nombre de; en pro de;
de parte de.

behave [bijéiv], *vt. y vi.* proceder, obrar,
conducirse; (com)portarse (bien o
mal).—*b. yourself!* ¡pórtate bien!—
behavior [bijéivyǫr], *s.* conducta,
comportamiento; funcionamiento.

behead [bijéd], *vt.* decapitar, degollar.—
—**ing** [-in], *s.* decapitación, degüello.

beheld [bijéld], *pret. y pp.* de TO
BEHOLD.

behind [bijáind], *adv.* atrás, detrás; en
o a la zaga.—*to fall b.*, atrasarse,
retrasarse.—*prep.* tras; detrás de;
después de.—*b. one's back*, a espaldas
de uno.—*b. the scenes*, entre bastidores.—*b. the time*, atrasado de noticias.—*s.* (coll.) nalgas, trasero.

behold [bijóuld], *vti.* [10] mirar, ver,
contemplar.—*interj.* ¡he aquí! ¡mire
Ud.!— —**er** [-œ(r)], *s.* espectador.

being [bíin], *ger.* de TO BE.—*for the time
b.*, por el momento; por ahora.—*s.*
ser, ente, criatura; existencia, vida.

belch [belch], *vi.* eructar; vomitar.—
vt. arrojar; vomitar.—*s.* eructo.

belfry [bélfri], *s.* campanario.

Belgian [béldʒan], *s. y a.* belga.

belief [bilíf], *s.* fe, creencia, crédito;
confianza; credo; opinión.—**believ-
able** [bilívąbl], *a.* creíble.—**believe**
[bilív], *vt. y vi.* creer; pensar; opinar.
—*to b. in*, creer en; tener fe en.—
believer [bilívœ(r)], *s.* creyente, fiel.

bell [bel], *s.* campana; campanilla; timbre; cencerro; cascabel.—*b. boy*, botones.—*b. clapper*, badajo.—*b. ringer*,
campanero.—*b. tower*, campanario.—
to b. the cat, ponerle el cascabel al gato.

belligerent [bilídʒęrent], *s.* beligerante.
—*a.* belicoso, guerrero.

bellow [bélou], *vi.* bramar, berrear; mugir, rugir; vociferar.—*s.* bufido, bramido, rugido.— —**s** [-z], *s. pl.* fuelle(s).

bellwether [bélweðœ(r)], *s.* (carnero o
morueco) manso.

belly [béli], *s.* vientre; barriga, tripa,
panza; estómago.—*vii.* [7] pandear.—
—**ache** [-eik], *s.* dolor de vientre.—

—**ful** [-fu̟l], *s.* panzada, hartazgo.

belong [bilón], *vi,* pertenecer; tocar;
corresponder.— —**ing** [-in], *a.* perteneciente.—*s.* pertenencia, propiedad.
—*pl.* bienes; efectos; bártulos.

beloved [bilÁv(i)d], *a.* querido, amado.
—*s.* persona amada.

below [bilóu], *adv.* abajo, bajo, debajo,
más abajo.—*prep.* bajo, debajo de;
después de.—*b.-stated*, más adelante,
o más abajo mencionado.

belt [belt], *s.* cinto o cinturón, faja,
cincho; correa; tira; (mec.) correa
de trasmisión; área, perímetro.—*b.
shaft*, árbol de transmisión.—*vt.* fajar;
ceñir; poner correa a (una máquina).

bench [bench], *s.* banco, banca; escaño;
(for.) tribunal.—*b. warrant*, auto de
prisión.

bend [bend], *vti. y vii.* [4] encorvar(se),
curvar(se), doblar(se), plegar(se), tor-
cer(se); inclinar(se); doblegar(se);
someter(se).—*s.* comba(dura), encorvadura, curvatura; curva; recodo;
codillo.—*to b. one's efforts*, redoblar
uno sus esfuerzos.

beneath [biníé], *adv.* abajo, debajo.—
prep. bajo, debajo de; por bajo.

benediction [benidíksǫn], *s.* bendición.

benefactor [bénifæktǫ(r)], *s.* benefactor,
bienhechor.

benefice [bénifis], *s.* beneficio, pre-
benda.— —**nce** [binéfisęns], *s.* beneficencia; caridad.— —**nt** [binéfisęnt],
a. benéfico, caritativo.—**beneficial**
[benifíšąl], *a.* beneficioso, provechoso,
ventajoso.—**benefit** [bénifit], *s.* beneficio; lucro; provecho, ventaja.—*vt.*
beneficiar, aprovechar.—*vi.* sacar
provecho.

benevolence [binévolęns], *s.* benevolencia.—**benevolent** [binévolęnt], *a.*
benévolo.

benign [bináin], *a.* benigno; afable.—
—**ity** [binígniti], *s.* benignidad,
bondad.

bent [bent], *pret. y pp.* de TO BEND.—*a.*
curvo, encorvado, torcido; inclinado.
—*s.* encorvadura, curvatura; inclinación, propensión, tendencia.

bequeath [bikwíð], *vt.* legar, donar (en
testamento).— —**er** [-œ(r)], *s.* el que
lega o dona (en testamento).— **be-
quest** [bikwést], *s.* manda, donación
o legado.

berate [biréit], *vt.* reprender, reñir,
regañar.

beret [beréj], *s.* boina.

berry [béri], *s.* baya (fresa, mora, etc.);
grano (de café, etc.).

berth [bœrθ], *s.* litera, camarote; atra-
cadero, dársena.—*vt. y vi.* atracar,
llevar al puerto; dar camarote, pasaje
o empleo a.

beseech [bisích], *vti.* [10] suplicar, rogar, implorar.

beset [bisét], *vti.* [9] acosar, perseguir; bloquear; rodear.—*pret.* y *pp.* de TO BESET.—*a.* acosado; engastado.

beside [bisáid], *adv.* cerca, al lado, a la mano.—*prep.* al lado de; junto a; en comparación de.—*b. himself*, fuera de sí.—*b. the point*, que no viene al caso.—*s* [-z], *adv.* también, además.—*prep.* además de; sobre, por encima de; excepto.

besiege [bisídž], *vt.* sitiar; asediar, acosar.—*r* [-œ(r)], *s.* sitiador; asediador.

besought [bisót], *pret.* y *pp.* de TO BESEECH.

best [best], *a.* y *adv. super.* de GOOD y WELL: mejor, del mejor modo, óptimo, óptimamente, superior(mente).—*b. man*, padrino de boda.—*b. seller*, el que más se vende, el favorito (apl. a libros).—*the b. part of*, casi todo, la mayor parte de.—*you know b.*, Ud. sabe mejor que nadie.—*s.* [el, lo] mejor, [los] mejores, etc.—*at* (*the*) *b.*, a lo más, cuando más, aun en el mejor caso.—*to do one's b.*, hacer lo posible.—*to make the b. of*, sacar el mejor partido de.—*to the b. of my knowledge*, según mi leal saber y entender.—*vt.* aventajar, vencer, ganar a.

bestial [béschal], *a.* bestial, brutal.—*ity* [beschiéliti], *s.* bestialidad, brutalidad.—*ize* [béschalaiz], *vt.* embrutecer.

bestow [bistóu], *vt.* conceder, conferir; otorgar; agraciar; donar.—*to b. in abundance*, colmar (de).—*al* [-al], *s.* otorgamiento; dádiva, presente.

bet [bet], *s.* apuesta.—*it's a good b.*, es cosa segura.—*vti.* y *vii.* [3] apostar.—*you b.*, (fam.) claro, ya lo creo.—*pret.* y *pp.* de TO BET.

betray [bitréi], *vt.* traicionar, vender; revelar, descubrir; engañar; dejar ver.—*al* [-al], *s.* traición, perfidia; engaño; seducción.—*er* [-œ(r)], *s.* traidor; seductor.

betroth [bitróθ], *vt.* y *vi.* desposar(se), contraer matrimonio o esponsales, comprometerse, dar palabra de casamiento.—*al* [-al], *s.* esponsales, desposorio, compromiso, noviazgo.—*ed* [-t], *s.* prometido, novio, futuro.

better [bétœ(r)], *a.* y *adv. comp.* de GOOD y WELL: mejor, de mejor modo; más bueno o bien; superior(mente).—*b. half*, cara mitad, costilla, media naranja (esposo o esposa).—*the b. part of*, casi todo.—*to be b.*, estar mejor.—*to know b.*, saber que no se deben hacer ciertas cosas.—*s.* superioridad, ventaja; persona superior

(a uno).—*all o so much the b.*, tanto mejor.—*our betters*, nuestros superiores.—*vt.* mejorar; aventajar.—*vi.* mejorarse, progresar.—*ment* [-ment], *s.* mejora; adelantamiento, superación.

betting [bétiŋ], *s.* apuesta. ¶

between [bitwín], *adv.* en medio, de por medio, entre los dos.—*prep.* entre.—*b. now and then*, de acá para allá.

beverage [béviradž], *s.* bebida.

beware [biwér], *vi.* (Ú. sólo en *inf.*) guardarse, cuidarse de, estar alerta contra.—*interj.* ¡cuidado! ¡mucho ojo!

bewilder [biwíldœ(r)], *vt.* aturdir, azorar; desorientar.—*ment* [-ment], *s.* aturdimiento, azoramiento, perplejidad.

bewitch [biwích], *vt.* embrujar, aojar; encantar, hechizar, embelesar.—*er* [-œ(r)], *s.* brujo, encantador.—*ing* [-iŋ], *a.* hechicero, encantador.

beyond [biyánd], *adv.* más allá, más lejos; allende.—*s.* lo que está más allá; la otra vida.—*prep.* más allá de, tras; después de; sobre; superior a; susceptible de.—*b.* (*a*) *doubt*, fuera de duda.—*b. the seas*, ultramarino.

bias [báias], *s.* sesgo, oblicuidad; preferencia; prejuicio.—*a.* sesg(ad)o, diagonal, terciado.—*vti.* [2] influir, predisponer, torcer.—*biased* o *biassed* [báiast], *a.* parcial.

bib [bib], *s.* babero.

Bible [báibl], *s.* Biblia, historia sagrada.—*Biblical* [bíblikal], *a.* bíblico.

bicarbonate [baikárbonit], *s.* bicarbonato.

bicker [bíkœ(r)], *vi.* altercar, reñir, disputar.—*er* [-œ(r)], *s.* camorrista.—*ing* [-iŋ], *s.* altercado o disputa ociosa.

bicycle [báisikl], *s.* bicicleta, velocípedo.—*vi.* andar o montar en bicicleta.

bid [bid], *s.* postura, licitación; oferta; envite.—*vti.* [10] ofrecer, pujar licitar; envidar; mandar; rogar; invitar.—*to b. farewell, good-bye*, despedirse, decir adiós.—*vii.* hacer una oferta.—*pret.* y *pp.* de TO BID.—*der* [-œ(r)], *s.* postor, licitador.—*the highest b.*, el mejor postor.—*ding* [-iŋ], *s.* orden, mandato; invitación; licitación, postura.

bide [baid], *vii.* [5] residir, quedarse; esperar.—*to b. one's time*, reservarse para mejor ocasión.

bidet [bidéi], *s.* bidé, bidel.

bier [bir], *s.* féretro.

big [big], *a.* grande, gordo, grueso; importante, considerable; abultado, fatuo.—*b. brother*, hermano mayor.—*b. game*, caza mayor.—*b. shot*,

(fam.) pez gordo, personaje influyente.

bigamist [bígamist], *s.* bígamo; bígama.— **bigamous** [bígamʌs], *a.* bígamo.— **bigamy** [bígami], *s.* bigamia.

bigness [bígnis], *s.* grandeza; tamaño, volumen.

bigot [bígot], *s.* fanático, persona intolerante.— **—ry** [-ri], *s.* fanatismo, intolerancia.

bile [bail], *s.* bilis, hiel; cólera, mal genio.

bilge [bildż], *vi.* (mar.) abrirse una vía de agua, hacer agua; combar.—*vt.* (mar.) quebrar el pantoque (de un buque); hacer combar.—*s.* (mar.) pantoque, sentina; barriga de barril.

bilingual [bailíngwal], *a.* bilingüe.

bilious [bílyʌs], *a.* bilioso.

bilk [bilk], *vt.* defraudar.

bill [bil], *s.* billete de banco; cuenta, factura; letra; giro; proyecto de ley; ley; certificado, documento; declaración; lista; cartel; pico (de ave); (teat.) programa.—*b. broker*, corredor o agente de cambios.—*b. of exchange*, letra de cambio.—*b. of fare*, menú.—*b. of indictment*, acusación oficial escrita.—*b. of lading*, conocimiento de embarque.—*b. of rights*, declaración de derechos, ley fundamental.—*b. of sale*, escritura de venta.—*vt.* cargar en cuenta; anunciar por carteles; facturar, adeudar.—*vi.* juntar el pico (las aves).— **—board** [bílbord], *s.* cartelera.— **—ed** [-d], *a.* picudo.— **—fold** [-fould], *s.* billetera, cartera para billetes.

billiard [bílyàrd], *s.* carambola.—*pl.* billar.

billow [bílou], *s.* oleada, ola grande; golpe de mar; onda.—*vi.* ondular o hincharse como una ola.— **—y** [-i], *a.* ondeante, ondulante.

billy goat [bíli gout], *s.* chivo, cabrón.

bin [bin], *s.* receptáculo; depósito.—*coal b.*, carbonera.

bind [baind], *vti.* [10] atar; juntar; ligar; ceñir; obligar; vendar; ribetear; encuadernar, empastar; compeler.—*to b. over*, obligar a comparecer ante el juez.— **—er** [báindœr], *s.* encuadernador; portafolio, archivador; atadero.— **—ing** [-iŋ], *s.* atadura; venda, tira, cinta; encuadernación; ribete.—*half b.*, media pasta.—*paper b.*, encuadernación en rústica.—*a.* obligatorio; válido.

binoculars [binákyʊlàrz], *s. pl.* gemelos, binóculos.

biochemical [baioukémikal], *a.*, **biochemist** [baioukémist], *s.*, **biochemistry** [baioukémistri], *s.* bioquímica.

biographer [baiágrafœr], *s.* biógrafo.— **—biographical** [baiográfikal], *a.* bio-gráfico.— **biography** [baiágrafi], *s.* biografía.

biologic(al) [baioládżik(al)], *a.* biológico.— **biologist** [baiálodżist], *s.* biólogo.— **biology** [baiálodżi], *s.* biología.

birch [bœrch], *s.* abedul; disciplina.—*vt.* azotar, fustigar.

bird [bœrd], *s.* ave, pájaro; (fam.) persona, tipo raro o singular.—*b. of prey*, ave de rapiña.—*b.'s eye view*, vista de pájaro.— **—call** [-col], *s.* reclamo.— **—lime** [-laim], *s.* liga (de caza).— **—seed** [-sid], *s.* alpiste.

biretta [birétà], *s.* (igl.) birreta, birrete, bonete.

birth [bœrθ], *s.* nacimiento; origen; parto, alumbramiento; linaje.—*b. certificate*, partida de nacimiento.—*by b.*, de nacimiento.—*to give b. to*, dar a luz, parir.— **—day** [bœrθdei], *s.* cumpleaños, natalicio.— **—place** [-pleis], *s.* suelo natal.

Biscayan [biskéian], *s.* **y** *a.* vizcaíno, vasco.

biscuit [bískit], *s.* galleta; bizcocho.

bishop [bíʃop], *s.* obispo; alfil (en el ajedrez).— **—ric** [-rik], *s.* obispado.

bit [bit], *s.* trozo; pizca; pedacito; poquito; momento; taladro, broca; bocado del freno.—*not a b.*, ni pizca.—*to smash to bits*, hacer añicos.—*pret.* y *pp.* de TO BITE.

bitch [bich], *s.* perra; (vulg.) ramera, zorra.

bite [bait], *vti.* **y** *vii.* [10] morder, mordiscar; picar (un insecto, un pez, la pimienta).—*s.* mordedura, dentellada; mordisco; tentempié; picadura.— **—r** [báitœr], *s.* mordedor.— **—biting** [báitiŋ], *a.* penetrante; mordaz; picante; caústico; mordedor.— **—bitten** [bítən], *pp.* de TO BITE.

bitter [bítœr], *a.* agrio, amargo(so); áspero; agudo, mordaz; encarnizado; cortante.—*s. pl.* amargo.— **—ness** [-nis], *s.* amargor; acíbar, hiel; rencor; encono.

bitumen [bitjúmən], *s.* betún.— **bituminous** [bitjúminʌs], *a.* bituminoso, abetunado.

blab [blæb], *vii.* [1] revelar.—*vti.* chismear.—*b.* o **blabber** [blǽbœr], *s.* hablador; chismorreo.

black [blæk], *s.* negro; luto.—*a.* negro; oscuro; sombrío; tétrico.—*b. and blue*, amoratado.—*in b. and white*, por escrito.— **—berry** [blǽkberi], *s.* (zarza)mora.— **—bird** [-bœrd], *s.* mirlo.— **—board** [-bord], *s.* pizarrón, pizarra.— **—en** [-ən], *vt.* ennegrecer; teñir de negro; embetunar; difamar.—*vi.* ennegrecerse, oscurecerse.— **—head** [-hed], *s.* espinilla.— **—ish** [-iʃ], *a.* negruzco, bruno.— **—mail** [-meil], *s.* chantaje.— **—mailer** [-meil-

œ(r)], *s.* chantajista.— —**ness** [-nḁs]
s. negrura, oscuridad.— —**out** [-aṵt],
s. apagón.— —**smith** [-smḭθ], *s.*
herrero.

blade [bleɪd], *s.* hoja (de navaja,
espada, etc.); hoja (de hierba); pala
(de remo, etc.); paleta (de hélice,
turbina o ventilador).

blame [bleɪm], *vt.* (in)culpar; censurar.
—*s.* (in)culpación; reproche, censura;
culpa.— —**less** [bléɪmlᶖs], *a.* inocente;
inculpado.

blanch [blænch], *vt.* blanquear; hacer palidecer.—*vi.* palidecer.— —**ing**
[blénchɪŋ], *s.* blanqueo.

bland [blænd], *a.* blando, suave.

blank [blæŋk], *a.* en blanco; vacío;
pálido; inexpresivo.—*s.* espacio en
blanco; laguna, hueco; forma o papel
en blanco, planilla; esqueleto.—*b.
verse*, verso libre o suelto.

blanket [blǽŋkɪt], *s.* manta, frazada,
cobija.—*vt.* cubrir con manta.

blaspheme [blæsfím], *vt.* y *vi.* blasfemar;
vilipendiar.—**blasphemy** [blǽsfᶖmɪ],
s. blasfemia.

blast [blæst], *s.* ráfaga, bocanada;
explosión, detonación; onda explo-
siva.—*b. furnace*, alto horno.—*vt.*
volar, hacer saltar; maldecir.

blaze [bleɪz], *s.* llama, llamarada; hoguera; fogata; ardor; arranque (ira,
etc.).—*vt.* templar (acero); encender,
inflamar; proclamar.—*vi.* arder con
llama; resplandecer.

bleach [blich], *vt.* blanquear al sol;
descolorar; aclarar (el pelo).—*vi.*
ponerse blanco; desteñirse; palidecer.
—*s.* blanqueamiento.— —**er** [blích-
œ(r)], *s.* blanqueador.—*pl.* gradería,
gradas o tendido de sol (deportes).

bleak [blik], *a.* desierto, desolado,
yermo; helado.—*b. region*, páramo,
puna.—*s.* dardo.

blear(ed) [blír(d)], **bleary** [blírɪ], *a.*
nublado; bañado en lágrimas; lega-
ñoso, lacrimoso.

bleat [blit], *s.* balido.—*vi.* balar.

bled [bled], *pret.* y *pp.* de TO BLEED.
—**bleed** [blid], *vii.* [10] sangrar, de-
sangrarse.—*vti.* sangrar a (persona,
planta); arrancarle a uno el dinero,
chuparle la sangre.—*to b. white*,
desangrar a, arrancar hasta el último
centavo.

blemish [blémᶖʃ], *vt.* dañar, manchar,
empañar; infamar.—*s.* tacha, defecto,
borrón.

blend [blend], *vti.* [4] mezclar, combinar; templar.—*vti.* mezclarse, fundirse; armonizar.—*s.* mezcla; matiz.—
—**er** [bléndœ(r)], *s.* batidora, licua-
dora.

bless [bles], *vt.* bendecir.— —**ed** [blésᶖd],
a. bendecido, bendito; bienaventu-

rado.— —**ing** [-ɪŋ], *s.* bendición;
gracia, favor.—**blest** [blest], *a.* =
BLESSED.

blew [blu], *pret.* de TO BLOW.

blight [blaɪt], *s.* tizón, pulgón(parásito);
contratiempo, malogro; ruina.—*vt.*
y *vi.* destruir(se), agostar(se), frus-
trar(se).

blind [blaɪnd], *vt.* cegar; deslumbrar;
ofuscar; encubrir; tapar; engañar.—
a. ciego.—*b. alley*, callejón sin salida.
—*b. flying*, vuelo a ciegas.—*b. man*,
ciego (*b. woman*, ciega).—*s.* cualquier
cosa que impide ver o quita la luz

blindage [blǽɪndɪdʒ], *s.* blindaje.

blindfold [blǽɪndfoṵld], *s.* venda para
los ojos.—*a.* con los ojos vendados.
—*vt.* vendar los ojos; ofuscar.—
blinding [blǽɪndɪŋ], *a.* deslumbrador,
cegador.—*s.* acción de cegar.—
blindness [blǽɪndnɪs], *s.* ceguera,
ceguedad.

blink [blɪŋk], *vi.* pestañear, parpadear;
destellar.—*vt.* guiñar; mirar con los
ojos entreabiertos.—*s.* pestañeo,
guiño o guiñada; destello.— —**er**
[blíŋkœ(r)], *s.* pestañeador; aparato
trasmisor de señales luminosas.

bliss [blɪs], *s.* gloria; bienaventuranza,
felicidad; arrobamiento, deleite.—
—**ful** [blísfṵl], *a.* dichoso.

blister [blístœ(r)], *s.* ampolla, vejiga,
burbuja.—*vt.* y *vi.* levantar ampollas;
ampollar(se).

blizzard [blízᶎard], *s.* ventisca, tormenta
de nieve.

bloat [bloṵt], *vi.* hincharse, abotagarse.
—**ed** [blóṵtɪd], *a.* tumefacto, hinchado.

block [blak], *s.* bloque, trozo; obstáculo,
obstrucción; lote; tableta o bloc de
papel; plancha o estampa de impresión; horma; fajo; cuadra, manzana.
—*vt.* bloquear; tapar; estorbar; planchar sobre horma; parar (una pelota,
una jugada).—*to b. out*, esbozar,
bosquejar.—*to b. the way*, impedir el
paso.— —**ade** [-éɪd], *s.* bloqueo, asedio.— —**head** [blákhed], *s.* tonto,
estúpido, mentecato.

blond(e) [bland], *a.* y *s.* rubio, (Am.)
huero, catire.

blood [blʌd], *s.* sangre; linaje o parentesco; savia.—*b. clot*, coágulo.—*b.
count*, análisis cuantitativo de sangre.
—*b.-curdling*, horripilante.—*b. pudding o sausage*, morcilla.—*b. relative*,
pariente, consanguíneo.—*to get one's
b. up*, encendérsele a uno la sangre.—
—**less** [blʌ́dlɪs], *a.* exangüe, de-
sangrado.— —**shed** [ʃed], *s.* efusión o derramamiento de sangre.—
—**shot** [-ʃat], *a.* inyectado de sangre.
—**sucker** [-sʌkœ(r)], *s.* sanguijuela,
usurero.— —**thirsty** [-θœrstɪ], *a.* san-

guinario.— —y [-i], *a.* ensangrentado, sangriento, sanguinario.—*vti.* [7] ensangrentar.

bloom [blum], *s.* flor; floración; florecimiento; lozanía.—*vi.* florecer.— —ing [blúmiŋ], *a.* en flor; floreciente; fresco, lozano.

blossom [blásǫm], *s.* flor; floración.—*vi.* florecer.— —y [-i], *a.* lleno de flores, floreciente.

blot [blat], *s.* borrón; mancha, mancilla; tacha.—*vti.* [1] emborronar; manchar; mancillar; empañar; secar con papel secante.—*to b. out,* tachar, borrar.—*vii.* correrse la tinta; pasarse (el papel).— —ch [-ch], *s.* mancha; borrón; pústula.—*vt.* marcar o cubrir con manchas o ronchas.

blouse [blaus], *s.* blusa.

blow [blou], *s.* golpe; contratiempo; vendaval; (re)soplido; trompada; trompetazo; fanfarrón—*at a b.,* de un solo golpe.—*to come to blows,* venir a las manos.—*without striking a b.,* sin dar un golpe, sin esfuerzo. —*vti.* [10] (re)soplar; hacer sonar (un instrumento de viento); ventear; divulgar; gastar con profusión; fanfarronear, alardear.—*to b. up,* estallar, reventar.—*vt.* inflar; volar con dinamita.—*to b. one's nose,* sonarse las narices.— —er [blóuœ(r)], *s.* soplador; soplete.— —ing [-iŋ], *s.* soplo, soplido.—*a.* soplador.—**blown** [bloun], *pp.* de TO BLOW.—*a.* jadeante, rendido; soplado, inflado.— —out [-aut], *s.* reventón, escape violento de aire, gas, etc.— —pipe [-paip], *s.* soplete.— —torch [-torch], *s.* lámpara de soldar, soplete.— —up [-ʌp], *s.* explosión; acceso de ira.— —y [-i], *a.* ventoso.

bludgeon [blʌ́dʒǫn], *s.* porra, garrote, estaca.

blue [blu], *s.* azul.—*pl.* melancolía.—*a.* azul; triste, melancólico.—*vt.* azular; teñir de azul; añilar.—*vi.* ponerse azul.— —bell [blúbel], *s.* campanilla (flor).— —print [-print], *s.* ferroprusiato (impresión de planos, etc.).

bluff [blʌf], *a.* francote, brusco; escarpado.—*s.* escarpadura; fanfarronada; fanfarrón; farsa; farsante; embaucador.—*vt.* conseguir algo a fuerza de descaro; alardear, baladronar; pretender, simular lo que no se tiene.— —er [blʌ́fœ(r)], *s.* baladrón, fanfarrón, embaucador.

bluing [blúiŋ], *s.* azul o añil para la ropa.—**bluish** [blúiš], *a.* azulado, azulino.

blunder [blʌ́ndœ(r)], *vt.* desatinar, disparatar, meter la pata.—*s.* disparate; patochada.

blunt [blʌnt], *a.* embotado, romo;

brusco, descortés; lerdo.—*vt.* embotar; calmar o mitigar.— —ness [blʌ́ntnis], *s.* embotadura; franqueza.

blur [blœr], *s.* trazo borroso o confuso; borrón, mancha.—*vti.* [1] hacer borroso; embotar, entorpecer; empañar; manchar.—*vii.* ponerse borroso; nublarse; empañarse.

blush [blʌš], *vi.* ruborizarse, sonrojarse; abochornarse.—*s.* rubor; bochorno; sonrojo.

bluster [blʌ́stœ(r)], *s.* ventolera; tumulto; jactancia; fanfarronada.—*vi.* soplar con furia; fanfarronear; enfurecerse.— —er [-œ(r)], *s.* fanfarrón.

boar [bor], *s.* verraco.—*wild b.,* jabalí.

board [bord], *s.* tabla; tablero; mesa; comida(s); hospedaje; tribunal, consejo, junta; cartón; bordo; borda(da). —*pl.* escenario, tablas.—*b. and lodging, o room and b.,* cuarto y comida, pensión completa.—*vt.* abordar; subir (a un tren, etc.); entablar, entarimar; dar manutención por dinero.—*vi.* estar a pupilaje.— —er [bórdœ(r)], *s.* huésped, pupilo.— —ing [-iŋ], *s.* tablazón; tabique de tablas; pupilaje; abordaje.—*b. house,* casa de huéspedes; pupilaje.

boast [boust], *vi.* alardear, cacarear; blasonar; jactarse.—*vt.* decantar, ponderar; ostentar.—*s.* jactancia, ostentación; baladronada; cacareo.— —er [bóustœ(r)], *s.* fanfarrón.— —ful [-ful], *a.* jactancioso.— —fulness [-fulnis], *s.* jactancia.

boat [bout], *s.* buque, navío; bote, lancha, chalupa.—*vt.* poner o llevar a bordo.—*vi.* navegar, remar, ir en bote.— —house [bóuthaus], *s.* cobertizo para botes.— —ing [-iŋ], *s.* ir o pasear en bote; manejo de un bote; transporte en bote.— —man [-man], *s.* barquero, botero, etc.

bob [bab], *vii.* [1] moverse con sacudidas o de arriba abajo; cabecear.—*s.* corcho (en la pesca); meneo; borla; plomo de plomada; disco de un péndulo; melena.

bobbin [bábin], *s.* bobina, canilla, broca.

bobsleigh [bábslei], *s.* trineo.

bode [boud], *vt.* presagiar, pronosticar, presentir.—*vi.* predecir; prometer.— *to b. ill (o well),* ser de mal (o buen) agüero.—*pret.* de TO BIDE.

bodice [bádis], *s.* corpiño, jubón, cuerpo de vestido.

bodily [bádili], *a.* corpóreo, corporal, físico.—*adv.* corporalmente; en persona; en conjunto; en peso.— **body** [bádi], *s.* cuerpo; conjunto; gremio; cadáver; fuselaje; carrocería; parte principal o central; persona.— *vti.* [7] dar cuerpo o forma a;

representar.— —guard [-gard], s. guardaespaldas.

bog [bag], s. pantano, fangal, atolladero; ciénaga.—vti. y vii. [1] hundir(se), atollar(se), atascar(se).

bogey [bóugi], s. espantajo; fantasma; duende, coco.

Bohemian [bouhímiạn], a. y s. bohemio.

boil [bọil], vt. y vi. hervir; cocer, salcochar; agitarse, hervirle a uno la sangre.—s. hervor, ebullición; divieso, tumorcillo.— —er [bóilœ(r)], s. olla; marmita; caldera; caldera de vapor.— —ing [-iŋ], a. hirviente.

boisterous [bóistœrʌs], a. turbulento, ruidoso, revuelto.

bold [bould], a. arrojado, valiente; descarado; escarpado; bien delineado.— —face [bóuldfeis], s. descaro; persona desfachatada; letra negra, negrita o negrilla.— —ness [-nịs], s. arrojo, etc.; descaro.

Bolivian [bolíviạn], s. y a. boliviano.

bolster [bóulstœ(r)], s. travesaño, almohada larga; cabezal; larguero, soporte, refuerzo.—vt. sostener, reforzar, apoyar, auxiliar.

bolt [boult], s. cerrojo, pestillo, falleba; perno; clavija; proyectil; dardo; rayo; suceso repentino; pieza o rollo de paño.—vt. echar el cerrojo; escudriñar; engullir; arrojar, echar.—vi. saltar de repente; lanzarse; desbocarse; resistirse.

bomb [bam], s. bomba; suceso inesperado y perturbador.—b. shelter, refugio contra bombardeos.—vt. bombardear.— —ard [bambárd], vt. bombear, bombardear.— —ardier [bambạrdír], s. bombardero.— —ardment [bambárdmẹnt], s. bombardeo, cañoneo.

bombast [bámbæst], s. ampulosidad.— —ic [bambǽstịk], a. ampuloso, altisonante, campanudo.

bomber [bámœ(r)], s. avión de bombardeo; bombardero (avión o aviador).— —ing [-iŋ], s. bombardeo.— —proof [-pruf], a. a prueba de bombas.— —sight [-sait], s. mira o visor de bombardeo.

bond [band], s. lazo, vínculo; unión, ligazón; bono, obligación; fiador; fianza.—pl. cadenas, cautiverio.—vt. unir; dar fianza; hipotecar; poner mercancías en depósito afianzado.— —age [bándiḍʒ], s. cautiverio, esclavitud; obligación.— —holder [-houldœ(r)], s. accionista; rentista.— —sman [-zmạn], s. fiador, garante.

bone [boụn], s. hueso; espina de pez.— pl. osamenta.—vt. deshuesar.— —ache [bóuneịk], s. dolor de huesos.— —d [-d], a. deshuesado.— —head [-hẹd], s., —headed [-hẹdịd], a. mentecato,

imbécil.— —less [-lịs], a. sin huesos.

boner [bóunœ(r)], s. (fam.) patochada, disparate.

bonfire [bánfaịr], s. hoguera, fogata.

bonito [bonítoụ], s. (ict.) bonito.

bonnet [bánịt], s. gorra, gorro; sombrero de mujer; toca; solideo, bonete.

bonus [bóunʌs], s. bonificación; prima; gratificación.

bony [bóunị], a. huesudo; óseo.

boo [bu], s. abucheo, grita, rechifla. —vt. y vi. dar grita, abuchear.— interj. ¡fuera!, ¡bu!

boob [bub], s., booby [búbị], s. y a. bobo, gaznápiro, papanatas.

book [buk], s. libro.—b. stand o stall, puesto de libros.—b. worm, (fig.) ratón de biblioteca.—vt asentar, inscribir; sacar, comprar o reservar (pasaje, localidades, etc.); contratar o apalabrar (a un artista, conferenciante, etc.).— —binder [búkbaịndœ(r)], s. encuadernador.— —binding [-baịndịŋ], s. encuadernación.— —case [-keịs], s. librero, estante para libros.— —ing [-iŋ], s. registro, asiento; compra o venta de billetes.— —keeper [-kipœ(r)], s. tenedor de libros.— —keeping [-kipịŋ], s. teneduría de libros.— —let [-lịt], s. folleto.— —maker [-meịkœ(r)], s. corredor de apuestas.— —ie [-i], s. corredor de apuestas.— —seller [-selœ(r)], s. librero, vendedor de libros.— —store [-stor], s. librería.

boom [bum], s. estampido; alza en el mercado; auge o prosperidad repentina.—vi. dar estampido; resonar; estar en auge; medrar.—vt. favorecer, fomentar.

boon [bun], s. dádiva, don; gracia; dicha, bendición.—a. jovial, festivo.

boor [bur], s. patán, rústico.— —ish [búrịʃ], a. rústico, agreste; tosco; guajiro, jíbaro.— —ishness [-ịʃnịs], s. rusticidad; grosería.

boost [bust], vt. empujar; levantar; alzar desde abajo; fomentar, promover.—s. alza; ayuda, asistencia.— —er [bústœ(r)], s. impulsador; elevador de potencial o de tensión.

boot [but], vt. y vi. aprovechar, valer, servir; calzarse uno las botas; dar patadas a.—s. bota; ganancia.—to b., por añadidura, de pilón, de contra, de ñapa.— —black [-blæk], s. limpiabotas.

bootee [bútị], s. botín (calzado).

booth [buθ], s. garita, casilla; puesto o mesilla de venta; cabina; reservado (restaurantes, etc.).

bootleg [bútleg], vti. y vii. [1] contrabandear (esp. en licores).—a. de contrabando.

booty [bútị], s. botín, despojo, presa.

border [bórdœ(r)], s. frontera; orilla;

borde; margen; límite, confín; orla, ribete, cenefa.—*vi.* lindar; rayar, acercarse.—*vt.* orlar, ribetear; guarnecer; confinar.

bore [bor], *vt.* taladrar; barrenar, horadar; sondear; aburrir, dar la lata. —*s.* taladro, barreno; agujero hecho con taladro o barreno; calibre; diámetro interior de un cilindro.—*pret.* de TO BEAR.— —**d** [-d], *a.* taladrado; aburrido.— —**dom** [bórdǫm], *s.* fastidio; aburrimiento, tedio.— —**r** [-œ(r)], *s.* horadador; barrena; taladro; perforadora; cualquier animal que horada; pelmazo, latoso.—**boring** [bóriŋ], *a.* pesado, aburrido, latoso.—*s.* perforación; sondeo.—*pl.* partículas que se desprenden al taladrar o barrenar.

born [born], *a.* nacido; de nacimiento; por naturaleza.—*pp.* de TO BEAR. —*to be b.*, nacer.— **borne**[born], *pp.* de TO BEAR.

borough [bárǫu], *s.* barrio; villa; municipio incorporado; distrito administrativo de una ciudad.

borrow [bárǫu], *vt.* pedir o tomar prestado; tomar fiado; apropiarse, copiar.— —**er** [-œ(r)], *s.* prestatario, el que pide o toma prestado.

bosom [búzǫm], *s.* seno, pecho, corazón; buche, pechera; amor, inclinación. —*a.* íntimo, querido; secreto.

boss [bos], *s.* amo, capataz, patrón; jefe, cabecilla; cacique.—*vt.* mandar; dominar; regentear; dirigir.— —**ism** [bósjzm], *s.* caciquismo, caudillismo.— —**y** [-i], *a.* mandón, autoritario.

botany [bátani] *s.* botánica.

both [bouθ], *a.* y *pron.* ambos, entrambos.—*b. my father and his*, tanto mi padre como el suyo.

bother [báðœ(r)], *vt.* y *vi.* incomodar(se), molestar(se); marear.—*s.* molestia, incomodidad; lata, pejiguera.

bottle [bátl], *s.* botella; frasco.—*vt.* embotellar.

bottom [bátǫm], *s.* fondo; suelo; lecho de un río, lago, etc.; parte inferior, lo más bajo; fundamento; trasero, nalgatorio; hez; asiento de una silla; pie (de página).—*vt.* poner fondo o asiento; cimentar, basar.—*vi.* apoyarse.— —**less** [-ljs], *a.* sin asiento; insondable.

bough [bau], *s.* rama, ramo.

bought [bot], *pret.* y *pp.* de TO BUY.

bouillon [búlyan], *s.* caldo.

boulder [bóuldœ(r)], *s.* peña, roca, pedrusco.

bounce [bauns], *vi.* rebotar; brincar, saltar; lanzarse; echar bravatas; fanfarronear.—*vt.* hacer (re)botar; echar a cajas destempladas, despedir.—*s.*

(re)bote; salto, brinco; acto de arrojar a alguien violentamente.— —**r** [báunsœ(r)], *s.* (coll.) guardián fornido a cargo de echar del lugar (cabaret, etc.) a los perturbadores.

bound [baund], *s.* límite, término, lindero; bote, brinco, corcovo.—*vt.* deslindar; parcelar; hacer saltar; confinar.—*vi.* saltar, (re)botar; corvetear.—*pret.* y *pp.* de TO BIND.—*a.* atado, sujeto; confinado; moral o legalmente obligado; encuadernado; destinado; resuelto (a).— —**ary** [báundari], *s.* límite, lindero, frontera; término.—*a.* limítrofe, divisorio.— —**less** [-ljs], *a.* ilimitado, infinito.

bounteous [báuntiʌs], **bountiful** [báuntiful], *a.* liberal, generoso; copioso.— **bounteousness** [báuntiʌsnjs], **bountifulness** [báuntifulnjs], *s.* munificencia, liberalidad, generosidad; copiosidad.—**bounty** [báunti], *s.* generosidad, liberalidad; merced, gracia; subvención; prima.—*b. money* (mil.), enganche.

bouquet [bukéi], *s.* ramo, ramillete; aroma.

bout [baut], *s.* encuentro, combate; asalto de esgrima o boxeo; ataque de enfermedad; vez, turno.

bow [bau], *s.* saludo, reverencia; zalema; proa.—*vi.* inclinarse; hacer una reverencia; agobiarse; ceder, someterse.—*s.* [bou], arco (flecha, violín, etc.); curva; lazada; lazo (de corbata, cinta, etc.).

bowels [báuęlz], *s.* intestinos, tripas; entrañas; mondongo.

bower [báuœ(r)], *s.* glorieta, emparrado, cenador, enramada.

bowl [boul], *s.* escudilla, cuenco; concavidad; tazón de fuente; palangana, jofaina; bola, bocha; ponchera.—*pl.* juego de bolos.—*vi.* bolear, jugar a los bolos, al boliche, etc.

bowman [bóumạn], *s.* arquero.

box [baks], *s.* caja, cajón; estuche; cofre, arca; palco de teatro; apartado (de correos); casilla; compartimento; taquilla; establo; manotazo, revés. —*vt.* encajonar, embalar; abofetear. —*vi.* boxear.— —**er** [báksœ(r)], *s.* boxeador; embalador.— —**ing** [-iŋ], *s.* encajonamiento, empaque; madera para encajonar; boxeo, pugilismo; marco de puerta o de ventana.—**box tree, boxwood** [bákswud], *s.* boj.

boy [boi], *s.* muchacho, niño, chico; hijo varón; mozo; criado; grumete.

boycott [bóikat], *s.* boicot, boicoteo. —*vt.* boicotear.

boyhood [bóihud], *s.* niñez; pubertad, adolescencia.

brace [breis], *vt.* ligar, asegurar; re-

forzar; fortalecer; ensamblar: empatar; atirantar; bracear; cercar,
rodear; encerrar en una llave o
corchete.—*vi.* animarse.—*s.* abrazadera; berbiquí; tirante; corchete,
llave; braguero; ligadura.— *let*
[bréjslit], *s.* brazalete.
bracket [brǽkit], *s.* soporte, brazo o
sostén (de lámpara, candelabro, etc.)
asegurado en la pared; consola,
repisa; ménsula; grupo, clase, nivel,
categoría.—*pl.* corchetes; paréntesis
angulares.—*vt.* poner entre paréntesis; unir; poner en una misma clase.
brackish [brǽkiš], *a.* salobre, salado.
brag [brǽg], *s.* jactancia, fanfarronada;
fanfarrón.—*vii.* [1] jactarse (de);
fanfarronear; alardear; farolear.-
—*gart* [brǽgart], *s.* matasiete.
braid [breid], *vt.* trenzar, entrelazar;
galonear.—*s.* galón, trencilla; trenza.
brain [brein], *s.* cerebro, seso.—*pl.*
sesos; inteligencia, juicio.—*to rack
one's b.*, devanarse los sesos.- —*y*
[bréini], *a.* sesudo, inteligente.
brake [breik], *s.* freno, retranca; grada,
rastra; palanca.—*b. lining*, forro de
freno.—*b. shoe*, zapata de freno.—*vt.*
frenar; gradar.- —*man* [bréikman],
s. guardafrenos, retranquero.
bramble [brǽmbl], *s.* zarza.
bran [brǽn], *s.* salvado, afrecho.
branch [brǽnch], *s.* rama; ramo; dependencia; división o sección; ramal,
brazo; afluente; sucursal; bifurcación, ramal; arma (de las fuerzas
armadas).—*a.* dependiente, tributario.—*vi.* ramificarse; echar astas
o ramas.—*to b. off*, bifurcarse.
brand [brǽnd], *s.* sello o marca de
fábrica; calidad; hierro de marcar
reses; estigma, baldón.—*b. name*,
marca conocida.—*b.-new*, nuevecito,
flamante.—*vt.* herrar, marcar ganado,
calimbar; tildar; infamar.— —*ing*
[brǽndin], *s.* herradero, hierra.—*b.
iron*, hierro de marcar ganado.
brandish [brǽndiš], *vt.* blandir; cimbrar, florear.—*s.* floreo, molinete.
brandy [brǽndi], *s.* coñac; aguardiente.
brass [brǽs], *s.* latón; cualquier objeto
de latón; descaro; calderilla (dinero);
cobres (instrumentos de música).—
b. band, banda, charanga.—*vt.* revestir de latón.
brassière [brazír], *s.* sostén, corpiño,
ajustador.
brat [brǽt], *s.* rapaz, mocoso; niño
travieso y díscolo.
bravado [bravádou], *s.* bravata, baladronada.
brave [breiv], *a.* bravo, valiente;
bizarro.—*vt.* desafiar, arrostrar.— *y*
[bréivęri], *s.* valor; bizarría, heroísmo.
brawl [brol], *s.* alboroto, pendencia,

camorra; quimera; trapisonda.—*vi.*
alborotar, armar camorra.—*vt.* decir
a gritos.
bray [brei], *vi.* rebuznar.—*s.* rebuzno.-
—*ing* [bréiin], *s.* rebuzno.
braze [breiz], *vt.* broncear; soldar; endurecer.- —*n* [bréizen], *a.* (como)
de latón; broncíneo; bronco; descarado.
brazier [bréizœ(r)], *s.* brasero.
Brazilian [brazílian], *a.* y *s.* brasileño,
brasilero.
breach [brich], *s.* brecha, abertura;
rotura, fractura; quebrantamiento;
infracción, violación; rompimiento.—
b. of promise, violación de palabra
de matrimonio.—*vt.* hacer brecha.
bread [bred], *s.* pan.—*b. crumb*, miga
de pan.—*vt.* empanar; empanizar.
—*breaded cutlet*, chuleta empanizada.
breadth [bredθ], *s.* anchura, ancho;
envergadura; latitud; amplitud.—
wise [brédθwaiz], *adv.* a lo ancho.
break [breik], *vti.* [10] romper, quebrantar, partir; infringir, violar (la
ley, etc.); abrir brecha en; domar;
arruinar; interrumpir; cambiar (un
billete, etc.); moderar, amortiguar;
exceder; descomponer.—*to b. away*,
escaparse, fugarse.—*to b. down*, abatirse; (mec.) averiarse.—*to b. in*,
forzar, romper o abrir empujando
hacia adentro; domar (animales);
entrometerse.—*to b. into a house*,
escalar, allanar una casa.—*to b. out*,
estallar.—*to b. up*, dividir en partes.
—*vii.* romperse, quebrarse, frustrarse; descomponerse; rayar el
día; brotar, florecer; dispersarse.—*s.*
rotura, ruptura; abertura, grieta;
comienzo, principio; intervalo, pausa;
interrupción; baja en el mercado;
casualidad, chiripa.— —*able* [bréik-
əbl], *a.* quebradizo, frágil.— —*age*
[-idž], *s.* fractura, rotura; indemnización por daños (tránsito, etc.).-
—*down* [-daun], *s.* derrumbamiento;
trastorno; interrupción o paralización de un servicio; avería; agotamiento.- —*er* [-œ(r)], *s.* rompiente
(ola); infractor.
breakfast [brékfast], *s.* desayuno.—*vi.*
desayunarse.
bream [brim], *s.* (ict.) besugo.
breast [brest], *s.* pecho, seno; teta;
mama; pechuga.—*vt.* amamantar;
arrostrar resueltamente.- —*bone*
[bréstboun], *s.* esternón.
breath [breθ], *s.* aliento, respiración,
resuello; soplo; pausa, respiro; instante.—*b.-taking*, conmovedor, sorprendente.- —*e* [brið], *vi.* y *vt.*
respirar, alentar; vivir; tomar aliento;
soplar; aspirar; exhalar.— —*r* [brið-
œ(r)], *s.* respirador; viviente; inspi-

rador; tregua.— —ing [bríðiŋ], *s.*
respiración; respiro, resuello.— —less
[bréθlịs], *a.* sin resuello; jadeante;
muerto.— —lessness [-lịsnịs], *s.* jadeo,
desaliento; muerte.

bred [bred], *pret.* y *pp.* de TO BREED.

breech [brich], *s.* (arti.) recámara,
culata, cierre.

breeches [bríchịz], *s.pl.* calzones, bra-
gas.

breed [brid], *vti.* [10] engendrar; criar;
empollar; parir; producir; educar.
—*vi.* multiplicarse.—*s.* casta, raza,
progenie; prole.— —er [bríðœ(r)],
s. criador, ganadero; padre, reproductor o semental.— —ing [-iŋ], *s.*
cría, crianza; educación; maneras.

breeze [briz], *s.* brisa, airecillo.—
breezy [brízi], *a.* airoso, ventilado;
animado, vivo.

breviary [brívịerị], *s.* breviario.

brevity [brévịtị], *s.* brevedad; concisión.

brew [bru], *vt.* hacer cerveza; preparar
té; fermentar licores; fraguar, urdir,
tramar.—*vi.* amenazar; formarse,
prepararse.—*s.* cerveza; mezcla.—
—er [brúœ(r)], *s.* cervecero.— —ery
[-œrị], *s.* fábrica de cerveza, cerve-
cería.— —ing [-iŋ], *s.* elaboración de
cerveza; señales de borrasca.

briar [bráịᶟ(r)], *s.* rosal silvestre; zarza;
brezo (para pipas).

bribe [brại̯b], *s.* cohecho, soborno.—*vt.*
sobornar, cohechar.— —ry [bráịberị],
s. cohecho, soborno.

brick [brịk], *s.* ladrillo(s).—*vt.* enla-
drillar.— —bat [brịkbæt], *s.* tejoleta,
pedazo de ladrillo; insulto.— —layer
[-leịœ(r)], *s.* albañil.

bridal [bráịdl], *a.* nupcial.—*s.* boda,
fiesta nupcial.—**bride** [brại̯d], *s.* novia, desposada.—**bridegroom** [bráịd-
grum], *s.* novio.—**bridesmaid** [bráịdz-
meịd], *s.* madrina de boda.

bridge [brịdž], *s.* puente; caballete de
la nariz; juego de naipes.—*b.* toll,
peaje, pontazgo.—*draw b.,* puente
levadizo.—*vt.* tender un puente; atravesar.—*to b. a gap,* llenar un vacío.

bridle [bráịdl], *s.* brida, freno; frenillo.
—*vt.* enfrenar; reprimir; embridar.
—*vi.* erguirse.

brief [brif], *a.* breve, conciso; fugaz.—*s.*
epítome, resumen, memorial, informe;
alegato.—*to hold no b. for,* no estar
defendiendo o no ser defensor de.
—*vt.* abreviar; dar instrucciones bre-
ves.— —case [brífkeịs], *s.* cartera.—
—ing [-iŋ], *s.* órdenes o instrucciones.

brigade [brịgéịd], *s.* brigada.—**brigadier** [brịgạdír], *s.* brigadier, general
de brigada.

bright [brại̯t], *a.* brillante, claro, lus-

troso; subido (colores); eximio; vivo,
inteligente; halagüeño.— —en [bráịt-
ẹn], *vt.* pulir; alegrar, consolar;
ennoblecer; mejorar.—*vi.* aclarar,
despejarse (el cielo); animarse.—
—ness [-nịs], *s.* lustre, lucidez;
resplandor, claridad; agudeza.

brilliance [brílyans], **brilliancy** [bríl-
yạnsị], *s.* brillantez, brillo; resplandor; esplendor.—**brilliant** [brílyạnt],
a. brillante; talentoso; excelente.—
s. brillante; diamante.

brim [brịm], *s.* borde, margen; labio
de un vaso; ala de sombrero.—*vti.* [1]
llenar hasta el borde.—*to b. over,* rebosar; desbordar, derramar.

brimstone [brímstoụn], *s.* azufre.

brine [brại̯n], *s.* salmuera; agua car-
gada de sal.—*vt.* salar.

bring [brịŋ], *vti.* [10] traer; llevar;
conducir; persuadir; aportar; causar,
producir.—*to b. about,* efectuar, poner
por obra; lograr; dar lugar a; causar.
—*to b. forth,* producir; parir; dar
a luz.—*to b. forward,* empujar; llevar
una suma a otra cuenta.—*to b. out,*
presentar; publicar; poner en escena;
descubrir.—*to b. over,* persuadir; convertir; traer.—*to b. up,* criar, educar.

brink [brịŋk], *s.* orilla, margen; extremidad.—*on the b. of,* a pique de,
al borde de.

brisk [brịsk], *a.* vivo, activo; enérgico;
rápido; estimulante.— —ness [brísk-
nịs], *s.* vivacidad, despejo; gallardía.

bristle [brísl], *s.* cerda.—*vt.* erizar,
poner tieso.—*vi.* erizarse.

British [brịtịš], *a.* británico, inglés.
—*the B.,* el pueblo inglés.

brittle [brịtl], *a.* quebradizo; frágil;
vidrioso.— —ness [-nịs], *s.* fragilidad.

broach [broụch], *s.* broca, mecha;
punzón.—*vt.* mencionar por primera
vez; introducir; hacer público; espetar; traer a colación.

broad [brod], *a.* ancho; amplio; claro;
general; tolerante; indelicado; pronunciado, marcado; pleno.

broadcast [bródkæst], *vti.* y *vii.* [4]
transmitir, perifonear; propalar;
esparcir; sembrar a voleo; (radio)-
difundir.—*pret.* y *pp.* de TO BROAD-
CAST.—*s.* (radio)difusión, transmisión; siembra al voleo.—*adv.* por
todas partes.—*a.* radioemitido, radiado; esparcido, difundido.— —er
[-œ(r)], *s.* radiodifusor(a), estación
radiodifusora.— —ing [-iŋ], *s.* (radio)-
difusión; transmisión; siembra al
voleo.—*a.* (radio)difusor(a), (radio)-
emisor(a).

broadcloth [bródkloθ], *s.* paño fino de
lana o algodón.

broaden [bródẹn], *vt.* y *vi.* ensanchar(se).

brocade [brokéid], s. brocado.—vt. decorar con brocado.

broccoli [brákoli], s. bróculi, brécol, brecolera.

brochure [broŝúr], s. folleto.

broil [broil], s. carne, etc. asada al fuego o a la parrilla; calor intenso; pendencia; tumulto; alboroto.—vt. asar sobre las ascuas o en parrillas. —vi. asarse; asarse de calor.—er [brójlœ(r)], s. parrilla(s); pollo propio para asar; camorrista.—ing [-iŋ], a. extremadamente cálido, abrasador.

broke [brouk], pret. de TO BREAK.—a. tronado, sin blanca, sin un real.—**broken** [bróukẹn], pp. de TO BREAK. —a. quebrado, roto; imperfecto; interrumpido; domado; mal pronunciado; debilitado; arruinado.—r [bróukœ(r)], s. corredor, cambista; agente de bolsa.—rage [bróukœridž], s. corretaje, correduría.

bronchial [bráŋkial], a. bronquial.

bronze [branz], s. bronce.—vt. broncear.

brooch [brouch], s. broche, pasador.

brood [brud], a. clueca.—b. mare, yegua madre o paridera.—s. cría; pollada, nidada; camada; melancolía.—vt. empollar, incubar.—vi. preocuparse, ensimismarse.—to b. over, cavilar.

brook [bruk], s. arroyo, riachuelo; cañada, quebrada.—vt. sufrir, aguantar.— —let [brúklit], s. arroyuelo.

broom [brum], s. escoba; retama.— —stick [brúmstik], s. palo de escoba.

broth [broθ], s. caldo.

brothel [bráðẹl], s. burdel, lupanar.

brother [bráðœ(r)], s. hermano.—b.-in-law, cuñado.—vt. hermanar; tratar como a un hermano.—hood [-hụd], s. hermandad; hermanazgo; confraternidad; cofradía.—like [-laik], a. fraternal.—ly [-li], a. fraternal, fraterno.—adv. fraternalmente.

brought [brot], pret. y pp. de TO BRING.

brow [brau], s. ceja; frente; sien; arco superciliar.

brown [braun], a. pardo, castaño, moreno, carmelita.—s. color pardo, castaño o carmelita.—vt. poner moreno o tostado; broncear; quemar (el sol).— —ish [bráuniŝ], a. pardusco.

browse [brauz], vt. y vi. ramonear; tascar; rozar; curiosear; hojear (un libro).

bruise [bruz], vt. magullar; golpear; machacar; machucar; abollar; majar. —s. magulladura, etc.

brunette [brunét], s. y a. morena o trigueña.

brush [braŝ], s. cepillo; escobilla; brocha; pincel; matorral; escaramuza; haz de leña menuda.—vt. (a)cepillar; frotar, restregar; pintar con brocha. —vi. moverse apresuradamente.—to

b. aside, echar a un lado.—to b. away, restregar duro.—to b. up (on), repasar, refrescar; retocar.— —wood [bráŝwụd], s. broza, maleza.

brusk [brask], a. brusco, rudo.

brutal [brútạl], a. brutal.— —ity [brutéliti], s. brutalidad.— —ize [brútalaiz], vt. embrutecer; tratar cruelmente.—vi. embrutecerse.—**brute** [brut], s. bruto, bestia.—a. bruto, brutal.—**brutish** [brútiŝ], a. bruto, brutal; embrutecido.

bubble [bábl], s. burbuja, pompa; ampolla; bagatela; engañifa.—vi. burbujear; hacer espuma; bullir; murmurar el río; ampollarse.—to b. over, rebosar; estar en efervescencia. —to b. up, ampollarse.—**bubbly** [bábli], a. burbujeante, espumoso.

bubo [biúbou], s. bubón.— —nic [biubánik], a. bubónico.

buck [bak], s. gamo; macho cabrío; macho de ciervo, alce, reno, etc.; corveta o respingo; topada.—to pass the b., (coll.) rehuir una responsabilidad.—vi. encabritarse, respingar.

bucket [bákit], s. cubo, pozal, balde; contenido de un balde; excavadora de cucharón.

buckle [bákl], s. hebilla.—vt. abrochar con hebilla.—vi. doblarse, combarse.

bud [bad], s. yema, botón, capullo; brote, retoño.—vii. [1] brotar, retoñar; echar capullos.

buddy [bádi], s. camarada, compañero.

budge [badž], vt. mover.—vi. moverse, menearse; hacer lugar.

budget [bádžit], s. presupuesto.—vt. hacer presupuesto.

buff [baf], s. piel de ante, búfalo, etc.; color crema; pulidor.—a. de ante, de color crema.—vt. pulir, bruñir.

buffer [báfœ(r)], s. pulidor; amortiguador de choques.—b. state, estado o país que sirve de valla entre dos naciones rivales.

buffet [buféi], s. aparador; repostería; ambigú; [báfit], bofetada; (fam.) sopapo; embote.—vt. abofetear; luchar contra.

buffoon [bafún], s. bufón.— —ery [-eri], s. bufonada.

bug [bag], s. insecto; bicho; sabandija; (fam.) microbio.

bugaboo [bágạbu], **bugbear** [bágber], s. coco, espantajo, bu.

buggy [bági], s. coche ligero, calesa; vagón de cola.—a. lleno de chinches u otros insectos.

bugle [biúgl], s. corneta de órdenes; trompeta; clarín.— —r [biúglœr], s. trompetero, corneta.

build [bild], vti. y vii. [10] edificar, construir, fabricar.—s. estructura; forma; figura (de una persona).—

—er [bɨ́ldœ(r)], s. constructor; maestro de obras.— —ing [-iŋ], s. edificio, casa, obra, local.—a. constructor, para construcciones; relativo a casas o edificios.—built [bilt], pret. y pp. de TO BUILD.

bulb [bʌlb], s. bulbo; ampolleta; bomb(ill)a, foco; pera de goma; ensanche, protuberancia.

Bulgarian [bʌlgériạn], s. y a. búlgaro.

bulge [bʌldž], s. pandeo, comba.—vt. y vi. pandear(se); abultar(se).—bulgy [bʌldžị], a. combo, pandeado; saliente.

bulk [bʌlk], s. bulto, volumen; masa; parte principal; la mayor parte; el grueso.—vi. hincharse; aumentar (bulto, peso, importancia).— —y [bʌ́lkị], a. abultado, voluminoso.

bull [bụl], s. toro; bula pontificia; disparate; alcista.—b.'s eye, diana, centro del blanco; tiro perfecto.— —dog [bụ́ldɔg], s. perro dogo.— —dozer [-doụzœ(r)], s. máquina razadora.

bullet [bụ́lịt], s. bala.

bulletin [bụ́lịtịn], s. boletín.—b. board, tablón o tablilla de anuncios.

bullfight [bụ́lfạịt], s. corrida de toros.— —er [-œ(r)], s. torero.— —ing [-iŋ], s. toreo.

bullfrog [bụ́lfrag], s. rana toro.

bullock [bụ́lɔk], s. buey.

bullpen [bụ́lpen], s. toril.—bullring [bụ́lriŋ], s. plaza de toros.

bully [bụ́lị], s. matón, bravucón, valentón.—a. magnífico, excelente.— vti. [7] intimidar.—vii. bravear, fanfarronear.

bulwark [bụ́lwạrk], s. baluarte, bastión; defensa.

bum [bʌm], vti. [1] (fam.) sablear, obtener (algo) graciosamente.—vii. (fam.) holgazanear; vivir parasitariamente.—s. (fam.) vago; golfo; atorrante.—a. (fam.) de calidad ínfima.

bumblebee [bʌ́mblbị], s. abejorro, moscardón.

bump [bʌmp], s. tope(tazo); chichón, protuberancia.—vt. chocar contra.— to b. off, (coll.) matar, despachar.— —er [bʌ́mpœ(r)], s. parachoques, defensa; lo que da golpes.—a. lleno; excelente; abundante.

bumpy [bʌ́mpị], a. desigual, con baches.

bun [bʌn], s. buñuelo; fruturita, bollo.

bunch [bʌnch], s. haz, manojo, atado; mazo, montón; racimo; ramillete; grupo; bulto.—vt. agrupar, juntar.— vi. arracimarse, amacollarse.

bundle [bʌ́ndl], s. atado, lío; haz, mazo; fardo, bulto.—vt. liar, atar; empaquetar, envolver.—to b. up, abrigarse, taparse bien.

bungle [bʌ́ŋgl], vt. chapucear, echar a

perder.—vi. hacer chapucerías.—s. chapucería.— —r [bʌ́ŋglœ(r)], s. chapucero, chambón.—bungling [bʌ́ŋgliŋ], a. chapucero.

bunion [bʌ́nyɔn], s. juanete.

bunk [bʌŋk], s. tarima, litera; embuste; (fam.) baladronada, palabrería.

buoy [bɔ́ị, bụ́ị], s. boya.—vt. aboyar. —vi. aboyarse, flotar, boyar.— —ancy [-ạnsị], s. flotabilidad; flotación; alegría, animación; fuerza ascensional.— —ant [-ạnt], a. boyante.

burden [bœ́rdẹn], s. carga, peso, gravamen; capacidad, tonelaje.—vt. cargar, agobiar, gravar.— —some [-sʌm], a. gravoso, oneroso, molesto.

bureau [bịụ́roụ], s. buró, escritorio; oficina, despacho; agencia, negociado; ramo, división, departamento.— —cracy [bịụrákrạsị], s. burocracia.— —crat [bịụrɔkræt], s. burócrata.— —cratic [bịụrɔkrǽtịk], a. burocrático.

burglar [bœ́rglạr], s. ladrón (de viviendas).— —y [-ị], s. robo con escalo; hurto.

burial [bérịạl], s. entierro, inhumación, sepelio.

burlap [bœ́rlæp], s. arpillera.

burlesque [bœrlésk], s. parodia; (E.U. teat.) espectáculo de variedades de carácter burlesco.—a. burlesco, paródico.—vt. chufar, parodiar.

burly [bœ́rlị], a. corpulento, fornido; nudoso.

Burmese [bœ́rmịz], a. y s. birmano.

burn [bœrn], vti. y vii. [4] quemar(se), abrasar(se), incendiar(se); calcinar(se).—vi. arder.—s. quemadura; marca de hierro candente.— —er [bœ́rnœ(r)], s. quemador, mechero, hornilla.

burnish [bœ́rnịš], vt. bruñir, pulir.—vi. tomar lustre.—s. bruñido.— —er [-œ(r)], s. bruñidor.

burrow [bœ́roụ], s. madriguera, cueva. —vt. hacer cueva(s) en.—vi. encuevarse; minar, horadar.

burst [bœrst], vti. y vii. [9] reventar(se), romper(se); abrir(se) violentamente. —to b. into flames, inflamarse.—to b. into tears, romper a llorar.—pret. y pp. de TO BURST.—s. reventón, estallido; ataque, arrebato.

bury [bérị], vti. [7] enterrar, inhumar; sepultar; ocultar.

bus [bʌs], s. ómnibus, autobús, guagua, camión.

bush [bụš], s. arbusto; matorral; terreno cubierto de malezas, manigua. —to beat around the b., andar(se) con rodeos.

bushel [bụ́šẹl], s. medida de áridos. Ver Tabla.

business [bíznịs], s. negocio(s); cuestion de negocios; oficio, trabajo, profesión;

comercio.—*b.* **man,** negociante, hombre de negocios o de empresas.

bust [bʌst], *s.* busto; pecho (de mujer); parranda, borrachera.

bustle [bʌsl], *vi.* bullir, trajinar, ajetrearse.—*s.* bullicio, trajín; polisón.

busy [bízi], *a.* ocupado; activo; atareado.—*b.* **street,** calle concurrida, de mucho tráfico.—*vti.* [7] ocupar, emplear.— —**body** [-badi], *s.* entremetido; chismoso.

but [bʌt], *conj.*, *prep.* y *adv.* pero, mas; sin embargo; excepto, menos; sólo, solamente, no más que; sino; que no; sin que; sin.—*b.* **for,** a no ser por. —*none b.,* solamente.—*s.* objeción, pero.

butcher [búchœ(r)], *s.* carnicero.—*b.'s* **shop,** carnicería.—*vt.* matar reses; dar muerte cruel, hacer una carnicería.— —**y** [-i], *s.* carnicería, matanza; oficio de carnicero; matadero.

butler [bʌ́tlœ(r)], *s.* mayordomo.

butt [bʌt], *s.* culata (de rifle, etc.); colilla, cabo; mango, cabo; fin, límite; blanco (de las miradas, etc.); topetazo.—*b. of ridicule,* hazmerreir. —*vt.* topar; mochar.—*vi.* embestir.

butter [bʌ́tœ(r)], *s.* mantequilla, manteca (de nata de leche).—*vt.* untar con mantequilla o manteca; adular.

butterfly [bʌ́tœ(r)flai], *s.* mariposa.

buttermilk [bʌ́tœ(r)milk], *s.* suero de mantequilla.—**buttery** [bʌ́tœri], *s.* bodega; despensa.—*a.* mantecoso; adulador.

buttock [bʌ́tǫk], *s.* nalga, trasero.—*pl.* posaderas.

button [bʌ́tǫn], *s.* botón; tirador de puerta.—*vt.* abotonar.—*vi.* abotonarse.— —**hole** [-houl], *s.* ojal, ojera, silla.—*vt.* abrir ojales; importunar.

buy [bai], *vti.* [10] comprar.—*to b. off,* sobornar.—*s.* compra.— —**er** [bái-œ(r)], *s.* comprador, marchante.

buzz [bʌz], *s.* zumbido; susurro.—*b. saw,* sierra circular.—*vi.* zumbar; susurrar.

buzzard [bázg̣ard], *s.* buitre, aura, zopilote, carancho.

buzzing [bázin̩], *s.* zumbido.

by [bai], *prep.* por; a, en; para, por, junto a, cerca de, al lado de; según, de acuerdo con.—*adv.* cerca, al lado; aparte, a un lado.—*b. and b.,* pronto, luego.—*b. day,* de día.—*b. God!* ¡por Dios!—*b. itself,* por sí mismo.—*b. means of,* mediante.—*b. much,* con mucho.—*b. the dozen,* por docenas.— *b. the way,* apropósito, de paso, ya que viene al caso, etc.—*b. then,* para entonces.—*b. this time,* ahora, ya.— *b. way of,* por vía de.—*days gone b.,* días pasados.— —**gone** [báigon], *a.* pasado.—*let bygones be bygones,* olvi-

demos lo pasado; pelillos a la mar.— —**law** [-lǫ], *s.* estatuto o reglamento.— —**path** [-pæθ], *s.* senda.— —**product** [-pradʌkt], *s.* producto accesorio, derivado, residual.— —**stander** [-stændœ(r)], *s.* espectador, circunstante, presente.

C

cab [kæb], *s.* taxi; coche; (f.c.) casilla del maquinista; casilla del chofer de un camión.—*c. stand,* parada de taxis; punto de coches.

cabal [kǫbǽl], *s.* cábala.

cabaret [kæbạréi], *s.* cabaret, café cantante.

cabbage [kǽbiḍẓ], *s.* berza, col, repollo.

cabby [kǽbi], *s.* (fam.), cabdriver [kǽbdraivœ(r)], *s.* cochero; chofer de taxi.

cabin [kǽbin̩], *s.* cabaña, barraca, choza; (mar.) cabina, camarote.

cabinet [kǽbinit], *s.* escaparate, vitrina; armario; (pol.) gabinete; caja o mueble (de radio, T.V.).—*c. council,* consejo de ministros o del gabinete.— *a.* ministerial; secreto, reservado.— —**maker** [-meikœ(r)], *s.* ebanista.— —**making** [-meikin̩], *s.* ebanistería.

cable [kéibl], *s.* cable; (mar.) amarra, maroma; telégrafo submarino; cablegrama.—*c. railroad,* funicular.—*vt.* y *vi.* cable(grafi)ar; proveer de o atar con cables.— —**gram** [-græm], *s.* cablegrama, cable.

cacique [kǫsík], *s.* cacique.

cackle [kǽkl], *vi.* cacarear; chacharear. —*s.* cacareo; cháchara.

cadaver [kǫdǽvœ(r)], *s.* cadáver.— —**ous** [-ʌs], *a.* cadavérico.

cadence [kéidẹns], **cadency** [kéidẹnsi], *s.* cadencia, ritmo.

cadet [kǫdét], *s.* cadete.

cafeteria [kæfẹtíriẹ], *s.* cafetería.

cage [keiḍẓ], *s.* jaula.—*vt.* enjaular.

cajole [kǫdẓóul], *vt.* lisonjear, engatusar.

cake [keik], *s.* torta, bizcocho, pastel, bollo, hojaldre; pastilla o pan de jabón, de cera, etc.; terrón.—*vi.* apelmazarse, formar costra.

calabash [kǽlạbæš], *s.* calabacín; calabaza.

calaboose [kǽlạbus], *s.* (fam.) calabozo.

calamitous [kǫlǽmitʌs], *a.* calamitoso. —**calamity** [kǫlǽmiti], *s.* calamidad.

calcium [kǽlsiʌm], *s.* calcio.

calculate [kǽlkiuleit], *vt.* calcular.—**calculation** [kælkiuléiṣǫn], *s.* cálculo, cómputo.—**calculator** [kǽlkiuleitǫ(r)], *s.* calculista; calculador, (máquina) calculadora.—**calculus** [kǽlkiulʌs], *s.* cálculo.

caldron [kóldrǫn], *s.* caldero, paila.

calendar [kǽlindǧ(r)], *s.* calendario;

almanaque.—*c. year*, año natural; año civil.—*vt.* poner en el calendario o en una lista.

calf [kæf], *s.* becerro, ternero; piel de becerro; pantorrilla.—*c. bound*, encuadernado en piel.— —**skin** [kǽf-skịn], *s.* piel de becerro curtida.

caliber [kǽlibœ(r)], *s.* calibre; diámetro; (fig.) mérito.—**calibrate** [kǽlịbreịt], *vt.* calibrar.—**calibration** [kælịbréị-šǫn], *s.* calibración.

calipers [kǽlịpœrs], *s.* calibrador, calibre.

calk [kok], *vt.* calafatear; rellenar; tapar.— —**er** [kókœ(r)], *s.* calafate, calafateador.— —**ing** [kókịŋ], *s.* calafateo, calafateadura.

call [kol], *vt.* llamar; visitar; denominar; apellidar; citar.—*vi.* gritar.—*to c. again*, volver.—*to c. at*, (mar.) hacer escala, tocar (en un puerto).—*to c. back*, mandar volver; retirar.—*to c. for*, pedir; ir por; ir a buscar.—*to c. forth*, producir.—*to c. in*, hacer entrar. —*to c. names*, insultar.—*to c. off*, suspender; desistir de.—*to c. out*, gritar; hacer salir.—*to c. together*, convocar. —*to c. up*, recordar; llamar por teléfono.—*s.* llamada; llamamiento; citación; reclamo; vocación; señal, aviso; visita; (mil.) toque; (com.) demanda. —*on c.*, disponible; (com.) a solicitud, al pedir.—*to make o pay a c.*, hacer una visita.—*within c.*, al alcance de la voz.— —**er** [kólœ(r)], *s.* visitante.— —**ing** [-ịŋ], *s.* vocación; llamamiento; visita.

callous [kǽlᴧs], *a.* calloso, córneo, encallecido.— (fig.) duro, insensible.— **callus** [kǽlᴧs], *s.* callo, dureza.

calm [kam], *s.* calma, serenidad, tranquilidad.—*a.* calmado, tranquilo, sereno.—*vt.* tranquilizar; apaciguar, calmar; aplacar.—*to c. down*, calmarse, serenarse.— —**ness** [kámnịs], *s.* = CALM.— —**y** [-ị], *a.* tranquilo, apacible.

calorie [kǽlǫrị], *s.* caloría.

calumny [kǽlᴧmnị], *s.* calumnia, difamación.

calves [kævz], *s. pl.* de CALF.

calyx [kéịlịks], *s.* (bot.) cáliz.

cam [kæm], *s.* (mec.) leva.

came [keịm], *pret.* de TO COME.

camel [kǽmẹl], *s.* camello.

camellia [kᴧmíliǎ], *s.* (bot.) camelia.

cameo [kǽmịǫu], *s.* camafeo.

camera [kǽmẹrǎ], *s.* cámara fotográfica.— —**man** [-mæn], *s.* fotógrafo; operador cinematográfico.

camomile [kǽmǫmaịl], *s.* manzanilla.

camouflage [kǽmụflaž], *s.* camuflaje; disfraz de protección.—*vt.* camuflar, disfrazar, encubrir.

camp [kæmp], *s.* campo, campamento. —*vt.* acampar.

campaign [kæmpéịn], *s.* campaña (mil., pol., etc.).—*vi.* hacer campaña o propaganda.

camphor [kǽmfǫ(r)], *s.* alcanfor.—*c. ball*, = MOTH BALL.—*vt.* alcanforar.

campus [kǽmpᴧs], *s.* (E.U.) terreno o campo de un colegio o universidad.

can [kæn], *s.* (envase de) lata.—*c. opener*, abrelatas.—*vti.* [1] enlatar, envasar o conservar en latas; (fam.) despedir (de un empleo).—*v. def. i.* [11] poder, saber.

Canadian [kǎnéịdịǎn], *s. y a.* canadiense.

canal [kǎnǽl], *s.* canal; conducto.—*vti.* [2] canalizar; acanalar.

canary [kǎnérị], *s.* canario; color de canario.

cancel [kǽnsẹl], *vti.* [2] cancelar, revocar, rescindir; tachar; anular; suprimir.— —**lation** [kænsẹléịšǫn], *s.* cancelación, rescisión; supresión.

cancer [kǽnsœ(r)], *s.* cáncer.— —**ous** [-ᴧs], *a.* canceroso.

candid [kǽndịd], *a.* candoroso, sincero.

candidacy [kǽndịdǎsị], *s.* candidatura. —**candidate** [kǽndịdeịt], *s.* candidato.

candied [kǽndịd], *a.* garapiñado.

candle [kǽndl], *s.* vela, bujía; cirio; unidad lumínica.— —**stick** [-stịk], *s.* palmatoria, candelero.

candor [kǽndǫ(r)], *s.* candor, candidez, franqueza; sinceridad.

candy [kǽndị], *s.* confite, caramelo, bombón, dulce.—*vti.* [7] almibarar, confitar, garapiñar.

cane [keịn], *s.* caña; bastón.—*c. field* o *plantation*, cañaveral.—*c. juice*, guarapo.—*sugar c.*, caña de azúcar.— *vt.* bastonear, apalear.

canine [kéịnaịn], *a.* canino; perruno.

canned [kænd], *a.* enlatado.

cannibal [kǽnịbạl], *s.* caníbal, antropófago.— —**ism** [-ịzm], *s.* canibalismo.

cannon [kǽnǫn], *s.* cañón; (billar) carambola.—*c. bone*, canilla, caña.— *c. shot*, cañonazo.—*vt. y vi.* cañonear.— —**ade** [kænǫnéịd], *s.* cañoneo.—*vt.* cañonear.

cannot [kǽnat], *fusión* de CAN (poder) y NOT.

canny [kǽnị], *a.* astuto.

canoe [kǎnú], *s.* canoa, piragua; (Mex.) chalupa.—*vt. y vi.* llevar o pasear en canoa.

canon [kǽnǫn], *s.* canon; regla o precepto; (igl.) canon o cánones; canónigo.— —**ize** [-aịz], *vt.* canonizar.

canopy [kǽnǫpị], *s.* dosel; palio; toldo; pabellón.

can't [kænt], *contr.* de CANNOT.

cant [kænt], *s.* jerga; beatería, gazmoñería.

cantaloupe [kǽntạloup], *s.* variedad de melón.

canteen [kæntín], *s.* cantina, taberna; cantimplora.

canter [kǽntœ(r)], *s.* medio galope.

canticle [kǽntịkl], *s.* cántico, canto.

canton [kǽntọn], *s.* cantón, distrito.

canvas [kǽnvạs], *s.* lona; lienzo, cuadro; vela, velamen.

canvass [kǽnvạs], *s.* examen; investigación; escrutinio; encuesta; pesquisa.

canyon [kǽnyọn], *s.* garganta, cañón, desfiladero.

cap [kæp], *s.* gorro, gorra; birrete; tapa; cima, cumbre; cápsula fulminante; casquillo, coronilla.—*vti.* [1] cubrir con gorra; poner tapa; poner cima o remate.

capability [keipạbịlịtị], *s.* capacidad, idoneidad, aptitud.—capable [kéipạbl], *a.* capaz; apto, idóneo, competente.

capacious [kạpéịʃʌs], *a.* capaz, espacioso.—capacitate [kạpǽsịteịt], *vt.* capacitar.—capacity [kạpǽsịtị], *s.* capacidad, cabida, espacio; inteligencia; disposición, suficiencia; poder.

cape [keip], *s.* (geog.) cabo; promontorio; capa.

caper [kéipœ(r)], *s.* cabriola; voltereta; alcaparra.—*to cut a c.,* hacer una cabriola.—*vi.* dar brincos, retozar.

capillary [kǽpịlerị], *a.* capilar.

capital [kǽpịtạl], *s.* capital; principal; excelente, magnífico.—*c. letter,* mayúscula.—*c. punishment,* pena de muerte.—*s.* capital (ciudad), cabecera (de un territorio o distrito); capitel; (com.) capital; fondos; caudal.—*to make c. (out) of,* sacar partido de.—-ism [-ịzm], *s.* capitalismo.—-ist [-ịst], *s.* capitalista.—-istic [-ịstịk], *a.* capitalista (sistema, teoría, etc.).—-ization [-ịzéịʃọn], *s.* capitalización; empleo de mayúsculas.—-ize [-aịz], *vt.* capitalizar; principiar una palabra con mayúscula.

capitol [kǽpịtọl], *s.* capitolio.

caprice [kạprís], *s.* capricho, antojo; fantasía.—capricious [kạpríʃʌs], *a.* caprichoso.

capsize [kæpsáịz], *vi.* zozobrar, dar la vuelta.—*vt.* hacer zozobrar, volcar.

capsule [kǽpsịul], *s.* cápsula, celdilla, vaina.

captain [kǽptịn], *s.* capitán.—*vt.* capitanear.—-ship [-ʃịp], *s.* capitanía.

captious [kǽpʃʌs], *a.* capcioso; quisquilloso.

captivate [kǽptịveịt], *vt.* cautivar, captar, fascinar.—captivating [kǽptịveịtịŋ], *a.* cautivador, encantador, atractivo, seductor.—captivation [kæptịvéịʃọn], *s.* encanto, fascinación.—captive [kǽptịv], *s.* y *a.* cautivo.—

captivity [kæptívịtị], *s.* cautiverio, cautividad, prisión.—captor [kæptọ(r)], *s.* captor, aprehensor.—capture [kǽpchụ(r)], *s.* captura, apresamiento, prisión; presa.—*vt.* capturar, apresar, prender; (mil.) tomar.

car [kar], *s.* coche, auto, automóvil; carro, vagón (de f.c.); (Am.) ascensor, elevador.

caracole [kárạkoụl], *s.* (equit.) caracoleo.—*vi.* caracolear.

carafe [kạréf], *s.* garrafa, cantimplora.

caramel [kárạmel], *s.* caramelo.

carat [kérạt], *s.* quilate.

carbine [kárbaịn], *s.* carabina.

carbon [kárbọn], *s.* copia de papel carbón; carbono; carbón (de lámpara de arco).—*c. dioxide,* ahidrido carbónico.—*c. paper,* papel carbón.—-ic [karbáŋịk], *a.* carbónico. —-ization [karbọnịzéịʃọn], *s.* carbonización.—-ize [kárbọnaịz], *vt.* carbonizar.

carbuncle [kárbʌŋkl], *s.* (joy.) carbúnculo o carbunclo; (med.) carbunc(l)o.

carburetor [kárbịureịtọ(r)], *s.* carburador.

carcass, carcase [kárkạs], *s.* res muerta; esqueleto; despojo; caparazón (de ave); (mar.) casco o armazón.

card [kard], *s.* tarjeta, papeleta; naipe, carta; postal; ficha.—*to have a c. up one's sleeve,* tener algo (plan, etc.) en reserva.—-board [kárdbọrd], *s.* cartulina, cartón.

cardiac [kárdịæk], *a.* cardíaco.

cardinal [kárdịnạl], *a.* cardinal, fundamental; rojo vivo; cardenalicio.—*s.* cardenal.

care [ker], *s.* cuidado; atención, cautela; esmero; ansiedad; cargo, custodia.—*vi.* tener cuidado, ansiedad o interés por; querer; importarle a uno; estimar, apreciar; hacer caso.

career [kạrír], *s.* carrera, profesión.

carefree [kérfrí], *a.* alegre, sin cuidados.—careful [kérfụl], *a.* cuidadoso, esmerado; cauteloso, prudente.—*to be c.,* tener cuidado.—carefulness [kérfụlnịs], *s.* cuidado, cautela, atención.—careless [kérlịs], *a.* descuidado, negligente, indiferente; desatento.—*to be c.,* descuidar.—carelessness [kérlịsnịs], *s.* descuido, indiferencia; desaliño.

caress [kạrés], *vt.* acariciar, halagar.—*s.* caricia, halago, cariño.

caretaker [kértekœ(r)], *s.* curador, guardián, vigilante.

carfare [kárfer], *s.* dinero para el pasaje (urbano).

cargo [kárgoụ], *s.* carga, flete, cargamento.

Carib [kérịb], *s.* caribe.—-bean [kạríbịạn], *a.* caribe, del mar Caribe.

caricature [kǽrɪkǎchụr], *s.* caricatura. —*vt.* caricaturizar.—**caricaturist** [-ɪst], *s.* caricaturista.

carload [kárloụd], *s.* carga de un furgón o vagón (f.c.)

Carmelite [kármẹlaɪt], *s.* carmelita (monje o monja).

carnal [kárnạl], *a.* carnal; sensual, laseivo.

carnation [karnéɪṣọn], *s.* clavel; color encarnado.

carnival [kárnɪvạl], *s.* carnaval.

carnivore [kárnɪvọr], *s.* carnívoro.— **carnivorous** [karnívọras], *a.* carnívoro, carnicero.

carob [kǽrọb], *s.* algarrobo.

carol [kǽrọl], *s.* villancico de Navidad; canto alegre.—*vti.* [2] cantar villancicos.

carouse [karǎuz], *vi.* jaranear, andar de parranda; (fam.) correrla; embriagarse.—*s.* parranda; juerga; franca-chela.

carp [karp], *s.* (íct.) carpa.

carpenter [kárpentœ(r)], *s.* carpintero. —*vi.* carpintear.—**carpentry** [kár-pentrị], *s.* carpintería.

carpet [kárpit], *s.* alfombra.—*vt.* alfombrar, entapizar.— —**ing** [-ɪŋ], *s.* tela o tejido para alfombras; alfombrado.

carriage [kǽrɪḍʒ], *s.* carruaje, coche; conducción, acarreo, transporte; porte, aire de una persona; tren de aterrizaje.—**carrier** [kǽrɪœ(r)], *s.* (trans)portador; arriero; carretero, cargador; empresa de transporte; mensajero; portaaviones; portador, agente transmisor de gérmenes; (rad.) onda de transmisión.—*c. pigeon,* paloma mensajera o correo.

carrion [kǽrɪọn], *s.* carroña.

carrot [kǽrọt], *s.* zanahoria.

carry [kǽri], *vti.* [7] llevar, conducir, transportar, acarrear; cargar; traer, llevar encima; contener; comprender; entrañar; dirigir; aprobar (una moción); ganar (las elecciones); tomar; aguantar, sostener; portarse.—*to c. away,* llevarse, entusiasmar, arrebatar.—*to c. off,* llevarse, retirar; ganar. —*to c. out,* llevar a cabo; sacar.—*to c. through,* llevar a cabo, completar.— *vii.* portear (como oficio); tener alcance (voz, tiro, etc.).

cart [kart], *s.* carro, carromato, carreta. —*c. load,* carretada.—*vt.* acarrear.— —**er** [-œ(r)], *s.* carretero.

cartilage [kártịlịḍʒ], *s.* cartílago, ternilla.

carton [kártọn], *s.* (caja de) cartón fino.

cartoon [kartún], *s.* (pint.) cartón, boceto; caricatura.—*vt. y vi.* caricaturizar.— **ist** [-ɪst], *s.* caricaturista.

cartridge [kártrɪḍʒ], *s.* (armas) cápsula,

casquillo; cartucho.—*c. belt,* canana, cartuchera.

cartwright [kártraɪt], *s.* carretero.

carve [karv], *vt. y vi.* esculpir; tallar; labrar; trinchar carne.— —**n** [kárvẹn], *a.* esculpido, entallado, grabado.— —**r** [kárvœ(r)], *s.* escultor; grabador, tallista; trinchante.—**carving** [kárvɪŋ], *s.* escultura, talla; arte de trinchar.— *c. knife,* trinchante.

cascade [kæskéɪd], *s.* cascada, catarata.

case [keis], *s.* caso; ejemplo; suceso; situación; causa, pleito, proceso; caja; vaina, funda, cubierta; bastidor. —*c. shot,* metralla.—*in c.,* caso (de) que, por si (aeaso).—*in any c.,* de todos modos.—*in the c. of,* en cuanto a, respecto a.—*such being the c.,* siendo así.—*vt.* embalar, encajonar; enfundar.

cash [kæ̃ʃ], *s.* efectivo, dinero contante y sonante; (cont.) caja.—*c. balance,* saldo (en) efectivo.—*c. on delivery,* (C.O.D.), pago contra entrega.—*c. payment,* pago al contado.—*c. register,* caja registradora; contadora.— *in c.,* en efectivo.—*adv.* al contado.— *vt.* cambiar, cobrar, hacer efectivo (un cheque, etc.).— —**book** [kǽʃbụk], *s.* libro de caja.— —**ier** [kæʃír], *s.* cajero.—*c.'s check,* cheque de caja.

cashmere [kǽʃmir], *s.* (tej.) casimir, cachemir(a).

casing [kéɪsɪŋ], *s.* envoltura, cubierta, funda; forro; marco de ventana o puerta.—*pl.* tripas para embutidos.

cask [kæsk], *s.* barril, tonel, bocoy; cuba.

casket [kǽskịt], *s.* cofrecito, estuche, joyero; ataúd, féretro.

casserole [kǽsẹroụl], *s.* cacerola.

cassock [kǽsọk], *s.* sotana.

cast [kæst], *vti.* [9] tirar, botar, emitir, lanzar; echar; tumbar, derribar; dirigir (la mirada o el pensamiento); vaciar, moldear (metales); calcular; (teat.) repartir (papeles); depositar (una boleta electoral).—*to c. anchor,* anclar, fondear.—*to c. aside,* desechar.—*to c. down,* abatir, descorazonar.—*to c. forth,* exhalar, despedir.— *to c. in one's teeth,* echar en cara.—*to c. in the rôle of,* adjudicar el papel de. —*to c. lots,* echar suerte.—*to c. off,* desamarrar, largar.—*to c. out,* echar fuera, arrojar.—*pret. y pp.* de TO cast.—*a.* vaciado, fundido.—*c. iron,* hierro fundido.—*c. net,* atarraya.—*s.* lanzamiento, tirada; fundición; molde; mascarilla; aspecto, estampa; tinte; (teat.) reparto de papeles; actores (en un drama).

castanets [kæstạnéts], *s. pl.* castañuelas, palillos.

castaway [kǽstạweị], *s.* náufrago.

caste [kæst], *s.* casta.—*to lose c.*, desprestigiarse.

Castilian [kæstɫiǎn], *s. y a.* castellano.

castle [kǽsl], *s.* castillo; torre o roque de ajedrez.—*c. builder*, soñador.

castor [kǽstǫ(r)], *s.* castor; paño o sombrero de castor.—*c. oil*, aceite de ricino.

casual [kǽʒɑl], *a.* casual, fortuito, ocasional; de paso.— **—ness** [-nis], *s.* descuido, inadvertencia; indiferencia. — **—ty** [-ti], *s.* accidente, desastre; víctima (de un accidente); muerte violenta; (mil.) baja; pérdida; (for.) caso fortuito.

cat [kæt], *s.* gato.—*to bell the c.*, poner el cascabel al gato.—*to let the c. out of the bag*, revelar un secreto.—*to rain cats and dogs*, llover a cántaros.

catacombs [kǽtǎkoumz], *s. pl.* catacumbas.

Catalan [kǽtǎlǎn], *s. y a.* catalán.

catalog, **catalogue** [kǽtǎlag], *s.* catálogo.—*vt.* catalogar.

Catalonian [kǽtǎlóunjǎn], *a. y s.* catalán.

cataract [kǽtǎrækt], *s.* catarata.

catarrh [kǎtár], *s.* catarro.

catastrophe [kǎtǽstrofi], *s.* catástrofe; cataclismo.

catcall [kǽtkol], *s.* silbido, rechifla.

catch [kæch], *vti.* [10] coger, agarrar; contraer, atrapar; pescar; sorprender. —*to c. in the act*, pescar in fraganti.— *to c. on*, comprender; popularizarse.— *to c. one's eye*, llamarle a uno la atención.—*vii.* engancharse; engranar; prenderse (fuego).—*to c. hold of*, agarrarse a, asirse de.—*to c. up (with)*, alcanzar a, emparejarse (con); ponerse al día.—*s.* presa, captura; botín; redada; gancho, enganche; pestillo; cogida (de la pelota); trampa. — **—er** [kǽchœ(r)], *s.* cogedor; agarrador; receptor (de beisbol).— **—ing** [-iŋ], *s.* engranaje.—*a.* contagioso, pegadizo; seductor.

catechism [kǽtekizm], *s.* catecismo.— **catechize** [kǽtekaiz], *vt.* catequizar.

category [kǽtegǫri], *s.* categoría, clase.

cater [kéjtœ(r)], *vi. y vt.* abastecer, proveer, surtir (de víveres); complacer o halagar a uno en sus gustos.— **—er** [-œ(r)], *s.* proveedor, abastecedor, surtidor, despensero.

caterpillar [kǽtœrpilǎ(r)], *s.* oruga, gusano.

catgut [kǽtgʌt], *s.* cuerda de tripa.

cathartic [kǎθártik], *a.* purgante.—*s.* purga, purgante.

cathedral [kǎθídrǎl], *s.* catedral.

Catholic [kǽθǫljk], *a. y s.* católico.—*a.* (c.) católico, universal.— **—ism** [kǎθáljsizm], *s.* catolicismo.

catsup [kǽtsʌp], *s.* salsa de tomate.

cattle [kǽtl], *s.* ganado, ganado vacuno, res.—*c. barn*, establo.—*c. bell*, cencerro, esquilón.—*c. raising*, ganadería.—*c. ranch*, hacienda de ganado, ganadería, rancho; (Am.) estancia.— *c. thief*, abigeo, cuatrero.—*c. tick*, garrapata.— **—man** [-mæn], *s.* ganadero.

Caucasian [kokéjʒǎn], *s. y a.* caucásico.

caught [kot], *pret. y pp.* de TO CATCH.

cauliflower [kóljfiauœ(r)], *s.* coliflor.

caulk [kok], *vt.* -. CALK.

cause [koz], *s.* causa, origen, razón; (for.) proceso.—*vt.* causar; motivar; originar.

cauterize [kótœraiz], *vt.* cauterizar.

caution [kóʃǫn], *s.* cautela; cuidado; advertencia.—*vt.* advertir, precaver, prevenir.—**cautious** [kóʃʌs], *a.* cauto, precavido, prudente.

cavalier [kævǎlír], *s.* caballero; jinete; galán.—*a.* caballeresco; altivo, desdeñoso.—**cavalry** [kǽvalri], *s.* caballería; caballos.—**cavalryman** [kǽvǎlrimǎn], *s.* jinete; soldado de caballería.

cave [kejv], *s.* cueva, gruta, caverna.— *c. in*, hundimiento.—*vi.* hundirse, desplomarse.—**cavern** [kǽvœrn], *s.* caverna, gruta.

cavity [kǽviti], *s.* cavidad, hueco; caries.

caw [ko], *s.* graznido.—*vi.* graznar.

cay [kei, ki], *s.* cayo; isleta.

cayman [kéjmǎn], *s.* caimán.

cease [sis], *vi.* cesar (de), desistir o dejar de, parar (de).—*vt.* cesar, parar, suspenderse.—**—less** [síslis], *a.* incesante.

cedar [síd̥(r)], *s.* cedro.

cede [sid], *vt.* ceder, traspasar, transferir.

ceiling [síliŋ], *s.* techo interior, cielo raso; (aer.) altura máxima; límite de visibilidad.

celebrant [sélẹbrǎnt], *s.* celebrante.— **celebrate** [sélẹbrejt], *vt.* celebrar; festejar; alabar.—*vi.* celebrar; echar una cana al aire.—**celebrated** [sélẹbreitid], *a.* célebre, famoso.—**celebration** [selẹbréjʃǫn], *s.* celebración.— **celebrity** [selẹbriti], *s.* celebridad, renombre.

celerity [selériti], *s.* celeridad, prontitud.

celery [sélẹri], *s.* apio.

celestial [seléschǎl], *a.* celeste; celestial.

celibacy [sélẹbǎsi], *s.* celibato, soltería.

cell [sel], *s.* celda, calabozo; célula; pila eléctrica.

cellar [sélǎ(r)], *s.* sótano, bodega.

cello [chélou], *s.* violoncelo.

cellophane [sélofejn], *s.* celofán.

celluloid [séljuloid], *s.* celuloide; película de cinema.

cellulose [séljulous], *s.* celulosa.

Celt [selt], *s.* **Celta.— —ic** [séltik], *a.* céltico.

cement [semént], *s.* cemento.—*vt.* cementar; recubrir con cemento; unir; pegar.—*vi.* pegarse; unirse.

cemetery [sémęteri], *s.* cementerio, necrópolis.

censor [sénsọ(r)], *s.* censor; crítico.—*vt.* censurar, someter a la censura (cartas periódicas, etc.).— —**ship** [-ṣip], *s.* censura.—**censure** [sénṣụ(r)], *s.* censura, reprimenda, crítica.—*vt.* censurar, reprender, criticar.

census [sénsʌs], *s.* censo, empadronamiento, registro; catastro.—*vt.* empadronar, hacer el censo.

cent [sent], *s.* centavo.—*per c.*, por ciento.

center [séntœ(r)], *s.* centro.—*a.* central; céntrico.—*vt.* centrar, centralizar.—*vi.* concentrarse; estar o colocarse en el centro.— —**piece** [-pis], *s.* centro de mesa.

centigrade [séntigrejd], *s.* centígrado.

centipede [séntipid], *s.* ciempiés.

central [séntrạl], *a.* central, céntrico.—*s.* central (de teléfono).— —**ize** [-ajz], —*vt.* centralizar.— —**izer** [-ajzœ(r)], *s.* centralizador.

centrifugal [sentrífjugạl], *a.* centrífugo.

centripetal [sentrípetạl], *a.* centrípeto.

century [sénchụrj], *s.* siglo; centuria.

cereal [síriạl], *s.* cereal, grano.—*a.* cereal.

ceremonial [serẹmóụnjạl], *a.* y *s.* ceremonial; rito.—**ceremonious** [serẹmóụnjʌs], *a.* ceremonial; ceremonioso.—**ceremony** [sérẹmọụnj], *s.* ceremonia, ceremonial; cumplido, etiqueta.

certain [sœ́rtạn], *a.* cierto, alguno; seguro; positivo.—*for c.*, de fijo, con seguridad.— —**ty** [-tj], *s.* certeza, certidumbre; seguridad.

certificate [sœrtífikit], **certification** [sœrtifikéjṣọn], *s.* certificado, testimonio; (for.) atestado, certificación, partida.—*certificate of residence*, carta de vecindad.—*certificate of stock*, bono, obligación.—**certify** [sœ́rtifaj], *vti.* [7] certificar, atestiguar, responder de o por.

cervix [sœ́rviks], *s.* (anat.) cerviz, nuca.

cessation [seséjṣọn], *s.* cese, cesación, paro.

cession [séṣọn], *s.* cesión, traspaso.

cesspool [séspul], *s.* pozo negro, cloaca.

chafe [chejf], *vt.* excoriar, rozar; irritar.—*vi.* irritarse.—*s.* excoriación, rozadura; irritación.

chaff [chæf], *s.* hollejo, cáscara.—*vt.* y *vi.* embromar.

chagrin [ṣagrín], *s.* mortificación, disgusto.—*vt.* mortificar, enfadar.

chain [chejn], *s.* cadena.—*pl.* (fig.) prisiones; esclavitud.—*c. of mountains*, cordillera.—*vt.* encadenar; esclavizar.

chair [cher], *s.* silla; asiento; cátedra; sillón de la presidencia; (por extensión) presidencia, presidente (de una junta, etc.).—*folding c.*, silla de tijeras, silla plegable.—*rocking c.*, mecedora.—*to take the c.*, presidir (una junta).— —**man** [chérmạn], *s.* presidente de una junta, persona que preside.

chalice [chǽlịs], *s.* cáliz.

chalk [chok], *s.* tiza, yeso.—*c. for cheese*, gato por liebre.—*vt.* enyesar; dibujar o marcar con tiza; poner tiza (al taco).— —**y** [chókị], *a.* yesoso; blanco.

challenge [chǽlịndž], *vt.* desafiar, retar; disputar, contradecir; (for.) tachar, recusar; (mil.) dar el quién vive.—*s.* desafío, reto; (for.) recusación, tacha; (mil.) quién vive.— —**r** [-œr], *s.* retador, desafiador; (for.) demandante.

chamber [chéjmbœ(r)], *s.* cámara; gabinete, alcoba, dormitorio; tribunal o sala de justicia; (mec.) depósito, cilindro.— —**lain** [-lịn], *s.* camarero; chambelán.— —**maid** [-mejd], *s.* camarera, doncella de cuarto.

chameleon [kạmíljọn], *s.* (zool.) camaleón.

chamois [ṣǽmj], *s.* gamuza.

champ [chæmp], *s.* (fam.) campeón.

champagne [ṣæmpéjn], *s.* champaña.

champion [chǽmpjọn], *s.* campeón, adalid; defensor.—*vt.* defender.— —**ship** [-ṣip], *s.* campeonato.

chance [chæns], *s.* azar, casualidad; fortuna; ocasión, oportunidad; riesgo; probabilidad.—*by c.*, por casualidad; de chiripa.—*there is no c.*, no hay esperanza.—*to take chances*, correr un albur, aventurarse.—*a.* casual, fortuito.—*vi.* acontecer.—*to c. to have*, tener por casualidad.—*to c. upon*, topar (con).—*vt.* arriesgar.

chancellery [chǽnsẹlẹrj], *s.* cancillería. —**chancellor** [chǽnsẹlọ(r)], *s.* canciller; ministro; magistrado; rector de universidad.

chandelier [ṣændẹlír], *s.* araña o lámpara de techo.

change [chejndž], *vt.* cambiar, alterar, modificar; substituir, reemplazar.—*to c. one's mind*, mudar de parecer.—*vi.* mudar, cambiar, alterarse.—*s.* cambio, alteración, mudanza; substitución, trueque; muda (de ropa, voz, etc.); vuelto; menudo; moneda suelta; novedad.—*c. of life*, menopausia.—*for a c.*, para variar, por cambiar.— —**able** [chéjndžạbl], *a.* variable; inconstante; alterable; (tej.) tornasolado.— —less [-ljs], a. inmutable.

channel [chǽnel], s. canal; cauce; ranura; estría.—vti. [2] acanalar, estriar; conducir.

chant [chænt], vt. y vi. cantar (salmos, etc.).—s. canto llano; salmodia.

chaos [kéjas], s. caos; gran confusión o desorden.—**chaotic** [kejátik], a. caótico.

chap [chæp], vti. [1] rajar, agrietar.—vii. rajarse, cuartearse.—s. grieta, raja, hendidura; (fam.) chico; tipo.

chapel [chǽpel], s. capilla.

chaperon [šǽperoun], s. acompañante, señora de compañía o respeto.—vt. acompañar a una o más señoritas en lugares públicos.

chaplain [chǽplin], s. capellán.—army c., capellán castrense.

chaps [chæps], s. pl. (Am.) chaparreras, zamarros.

chapter [chǽptœ(r)], s. capítulo; cabildo; filial (de una asociación).—c. and verse, con sus pelos y señales.

char [char], vti. y vii. [1] carbonizar(se), chamuscar(se).

character [kǽrjktœ(r)], s. carácter, genio; reputación; sujeto; (lit.) personaje; (teat.) papel; (fam.) tipo raro u original.— —istic [-ístjk], a. característico, propio.—s. característica, rasgo típico.— —ize [-ajz], vt. caracterizar.

charcoal [chárkoul], s. carbón de leña.—c. pencil, carboncillo de dibujo.

charge [chardž], vt. cargar (armas, acumuladores, etc.); instruir; encargar; gravar; cobrar (precio); cargar en cuenta; acusar; atacar; embestir.—vi. pedir (precio); cargarse; cargar (a la bayoneta).—s. carga, embestida; carga (de un acumulador, etc.); cargo, custodia; encargo, encomienda; persona o cosa de que uno está encargado; impuesto; acusación, cargo.—pl. honorarios, gastos.—c. account, cuenta abierta.—to take c. of, encargarse de.

chariot [chǽrjot], s. carro antiguo de guerra o de carreras; cuádriga.

charitable [chǽritabl], a. caritativo, benéfico.—**charity** [chǽriti], s. caridad; limosna.

charlatan [šárlatan], s. charlatán, curandero.

charm [charm], s. encanto, hechizo; embeleso; talismán.—vt. hechizar; encantar, embelesar, prendar.— —ing [chármin], a. encantador; fascinante, atractivo; seductor.

chart [chart], vt. poner en una carta náutica; cartografiar; trazar en un diagrama.—s. carta náutica; mapa; plano; gráfica.

charter [chártœ(r)], s. cédula, título, carta de fuero o privilegio; estatuto; constitución.—vt. estatuir; fletar un barco; alquilar un tren, etc.—c., member, socio fundador.

charwoman [chárwuman], s. fregatriz, mujer de la limpieza.

chase [cheis], vt. cazar; perseguir.—to c. away, ahuyentar, espantar.—s. caza; persecución; ranura, muesca.— —r [chéisœ(r)], s. cazador; perseguidor; (aer.) avión de caza.

chasm [kǽzm], s. abismo, precipicio, sima.

chassis [šǽsi], s. armazón, bastidor; marco; chasis.

chaste [cheist], a. casto; honesto; puro.

chastise [chæstáiz], vt. castigar, corregir.— —ment [-ment], s. castigo, corrección.

chastity [chǽstiti], s. castidad, pureza, honestidad.

chat [chæt], vii. [1] charlar, platicar.—s. charla, plática, palique.

chattels [chǽtelz], s. pl. enseres, bienes muebles.

chatter [chǽtœ(r)], vi. castañetear o rechinar (los dientes); parlotear, charlar, (fam.) hablar por los codos; (mec.) vibrar.—s. charla, cháchara; vibración.

chauffeur [šoufœ́r], s. chófer o chofer, conductor de automóvil.

cheap [chip], a. barato; de pacotilla.—to feel c., avergonzarse, sentirse inferior.— —en [chípen], vt. y vi. abaratar(se), despreciar(se).— —ness [-njs], s. baratura, modicidad; vulgaridad.

cheat [chit], vt. engañar, embaucar; defraudar; timar.—s. trampa, fraude, engaño; timador.— —er [chítœ(r)], s. estafador, embustero; tramposo, fullero.— —ing [-iŋ], s. engaño, fraude.

check [chek], vt. refrenar, reprimir; comprobar, confrontar, cotejar, verificar y marcar; registrar, facturar o depositar (equipajes, etc.); dar a guardar (el sombrero, etc.), recibiendo una contraseña; dar jaque (ajedrez).—to c. out, desocupar (el cuarto de un hotel, etc.).—vi. detenerse; corresponder; rajarse; dar jaque.—s. cheque; póliza; comprobación, prueba; contraseña; talón de reclamo (de equipajes, etc.); cuenta (de restaurante); detención; rechazo; obstáculo; contratiempo; jaque (en el ajedrez); ficha (en el juego); grieta (en el hormigón); muesca.—c. mark, marca, contraseña.—c. up, examen, comprobación.— —book [chékbuk], s. talonario, chequera.— —er [-œ(r)], s. cuadro, casilla; verificador; cada pieza del juego de damas.—pl. juego de damas.— —erboard [-œ(r)bord], s.

tablero de damas.— —ing [-iŋ], **s.** comprobación.—**c.** *account,* cuenta corriente (en un banco).— —**mate** [-meit], **vt.** dar (jaque) mate; desconcertar, derrotar.—**s.** (jaque) mate.— —**room** [-rum], **s.** guardarropa.

cheek [chik], **s.** carrillo, mejilla, cachete; montante, larguero; (fam.) tupé, descaro; jamba (de puerta o ventana).— —**bone** [chíkboun], **s.** pómulo.

cheer [chir], **s.** alegría; jovialidad; consuelo.—*pl.* vivas, aplausos.—*vt.* alentar, alegrar; vitorear, aplaudir.— **vi.** alegrarse.—**c.** *up!* ¡ánimo! ¡valor!— —**ful** [chírful], **a.** alegre, animado, jovial.— —**fulness** [-fulnis], **s.** alegría, jovialidad.

cheese [chiz], **s.** queso.— —**cake** [chízkeik], **s.** quesadilla.— —**cloth** [-klɔθ], **s.** estopilla de algodón.

chemical [kémikal], **a.** químico.—**s.** producto químico.

chemise [šęmíz], **s.** camisa de mujer.

chemist [kémist], **s.** químico; farmacéutico.— —**ry** [-ri], **s.** química.

cherish [chériš], **vt.** apreciar, fomentar; abrigar, acariciar.

cherry [chéri], **s.** cereza; cerezo (árbol y madera).—**a.** hecho de cereza o de cerezo; de color de cereza.

cherub [chérʌb], **s.** querubín.

chess [ches], **s.** ajedrez.— —**board** [chésbord], **s.** tablero de ajedrez.

chest [chest], **s.** pecho, torax; arca, cofre.—**c.** *of drawers,* cómoda, buró.

chestnut [chésnʌt], **s.** (bot.) castaña; castaño (árbol, madera; color).

chevron [šévrɔn], **s.** (mil.) galón, insignia.

chew [chu], **vt. y vi.** mas(ti)car; rumiar; (fig.) meditar.—*to c. the rag,* (fam.) charlar, estar dale que dale.—**s.** mascada; mordisco, bocado.— —**ing** [chúiŋ], **s.** masticación; rumia.—**c.** *gum,* chicle, goma de mascar.

chick [chik], **s.** polluelo, pollito; pajarito; (fam.) chica, pollita.— —**en** [chíkęn], **s.** pollo, gallina (como alimento).—**c.-hearted,** cobarde, gallina.— —**c. pox,** varicela, viruela loca.— —**pea** [-pi], **s.** garbanzo.

chief [chif], **s.** jefe; cabecilla; caudillo; cacique; (com.) principal.—**a.** principal; primero, en jefe.— —**tain** [chíftin], **s.** jefe, comandante; caudillo; capitán; cabeza.

chiffon [šifán], **s.** gasa.

chignon [šíɲan], **s.** moño, castaña.

chilblain [chílblein], **s.** (med.) sabañón.

child [chaild], **s.** niño o niña; hijo o hija; criatura; chiquillo.—*with c.,* embarazada, encinta.— —**birth** [cháildbœrθ], **s.** parto, alumbramiento.— —**hood** [cháildhud], **s.** infancia, niñez.— —**ish**

[-iš], **a.** pueril, frívolo.—**c.** *action,* chiquillada, niñería.— —**less** [-lis], **a.** sin hijos.— —**ren** [chíldręn], **s.** pl. de CHILD.

Chilean [chílian], **s. y a.** chileno.

chili, chilli [chíli], **s.** (bot.) (Am.) chile, ají picante, mole.

chill [chil], **a.** frío, desapacible.—**s.** frío, (es)calofrío; enfriamiento; estremecimiento.—*chills and fever,* fiebre intermitente.—**vt.** enfriar, resfriar, helar; desanimar.—**vi.** dar escalofríos, calofriarse.— —**(i)ness** [chíl(i)nis], **s.** frialdad, calidad de frío.— —**y** [-i], **a.** frío, fresco; friolento.

chime [chaim], **s.** juego de campanas; campaneo, repique; armonía, conformidad.—**vt.** tocar, tañer las campanas.—**vi.** repicar (las campanas); sonar con armonía.

chimney [chímni], **s.** chimenea.—**c.** *corner,* hogar, chimenea.—**c.** *flue,* cañón, tiro de la chimenea.

chimpanzee [chimpænzí], **s.** chimpancé.

chin [chin], **s.** barba, barbilla, mentón.—**c.** *cloth,* babero, babador.—**c.** *strap,* barboquejo.—**c.** *up!* ¡ánimo!

china [cháina], **s.** porcelana, loza fina, vajilla fina.—**c.** *cabinet,* chinero, vitrina.— —**man** [-man], **s.** chino.— —**ware** [-wer], **s.** = CHINA.

chine [chain], **s.** espinazo; lomo.

Chinese [chainíz], **s.** chino (lengua y persona).—**a.** chino.—**C.** *lantern,* farolillo.

chink [chink], **s.** grieta, resquicio.—**vt. y vi.** (hacer) sonar, (hacer) tintinar (copas, monedas, etc.).

chip [chip], **vti.** [1] desmenuzar, picar, astillar.—**vii.** quebrarse, desconcharse.—**s.** fragmento, astilla; desconchadura; viruta; ficha; tanto (en el juego).—**a** *c. off the old block,* de tal palo tal astilla.—*potato chips,* papas a la inglesa, ruedetas de papas.

chipmunk [chípmʌnk], **s.** especie de ardilla.

chiropodist [kairápodist], **s.** pedicuro, callista, quiropedista.

chirp [chœrp], **vi.** chirriar, gorjear, piar.—**s.** chirrido; gorjeo; canto.

chisel [chízęl], **s.** cincel; escoplo; buril.—**vti. y vii.** [2] cincelar; burilar; (fam.) engañar, embaucar.— —**(l)er** [-œ(r)], **s.** (fam.) engañador; ventajista.

chivalrous [šívalrʌs], **a.** caballeroso, cortés, caballeresco.— —**chivalry** [šívalri], **s.** caballerosidad, cortesía, galantería.

chlorine [klórin], **s.** cloro.— —**chloroform** [klórofɔrm], **s.** cloroformo.— —**chlorophyll** [klórofil], **s.** clorofila.

chock [chak], **s.** calzo, cuña; choque.—

vt. afianzar, soportar, calzar.—*c.-full*, colmado, atestado, de bote en bote.

chocolate [chákl̦it], *s.* chocolate; bombón.—*c. pot*, chocolatera.

choice [chois], *s.* elección; selección; preferencia, opción; cosa elegida; lo selecto, lo más escogido; variedad.— *a.* escogido, selecto, exquisito.

choir [kwair], *s.* coro, masa coral.

choke [chouk], *vt.* y *vi.* estrangular(se); ahogar(se); sofocar(se); atragantar(se), atorar(se); obturar(se) (el carburador).—*s.* estrangulación; ahogo; sofoco; estrangulador o ahogador (del automóvil).

cholera [kálr̦a], *s.* cólera; cólera morbo. —**choleric** [kálr̦ik], *a.* colérico, irascible.

choose [chuz], *vti.* [10] escoger, preferir, seleccionar, optar por; desear.

chop [chap], *vti.* [1] tajar, cortar; picar carne; desbastar; hender.—*to c. off*, tronchar.—*vii.* dar cuchilladas.—*s.* proción, parte; tajada; chuleta o costilla.—*pl.* quijadas (de animal).

choral [kór̦al], *s.* y *a.* (mus.) coral.—*c. society*, orfeón, masa coral.

chord [kord], *s.* cordón, cuerda; (mus.) acorde.

chore [chor], *s.* quehacer, faena, tarea.

chorus [kór̦as], *vt.* y *vi.* corear; componer o cantar música coreada; cantar o hablar a coro; hacer coro a.—*s.* (teat.) coro; estribillo.—*c. girl*, corista.—*in c.*, al unísono.

chose [chouz], *pret.* de TO CHOOSE.— **chosen** [chóuz̦en], *pp.* de TO CHOOSE.

chrism [kríz̦m], *s.* (igl.) crisma.

Christ [kraist], *s.* Cristo.—*the C. child*, el niño Jesús.—**christen** [kríșen], *vt.* bautizar.—**Christendom** [kríșend̦om], *s.* cristiandad, cristianismo.—**christening** [kríșen̦iŋ], *s.* bautismo, cristianismo; bautizo.—*a.* bautismal.— **Christian** [kríșchan], *a.* y *s.* cristiano. —*C. name*, nombre de pila o de bautismo.—**Christianism** [kríșchan̦izm], **Christianity** [krișchiän̦iți], *s.* cristianismo, cristianidad.—**Christmas** [kríșmas], *s.* Navidad.—*C. carol*, villancico, cántico de Navidad.—*C. Eve*, nochebuena.

chronic [kránik], *a.* crónico, inveterado.

chronicle [kránik̦l], *s.* crónica.—*vt.* escribir, registrar o narrar en forma de crónica.— **r** [kránik̦l̦oe(r)], *s.* cronista, historiador.

chronologic(al) [kranol̦ád̦žik(al)], *a.* cronológico.

chronometer [kronámețoe(r)], *s.* cronómetro.

chrysalis [kríșal̦is], *s.* (ent.) crisálida.

chrysanthemum [krișén̦θ̦em̦am], *s.* crisantemo.

chubby [chÁbi], *a.* regordete, gordinflón, rechoncho.

chuck [chÁk], *vt.* desechar, tirar lo inútil; acariciar la barbilla.—*s.* mamola; echada, tirada; golpecito, caricia.—*c. hole*, bache.—*c. steak*, bisté de falda.— **le** [chÁkl], *vi.* reir entre dientes.—*s.* risa ahogada, risita.

chum [chÁm], *vii.* [1] (fam.) ser camarada.—*s.* (fam.) camarada, compinche.

chunk [chÁŋk], *s.* pedazo corto y grueso, trozo; (fam.) persona fornida.— **y** [chÁŋki], *a.* trabado, fornido, rechoncho.

church [chœrch], *s.* iglesia; templo; culto público, el clero.—*c. calendar*, santoral.— **man** [chœrchman], *s.* sacerdote, clérigo.— **yard** [chœrchyard], *s.* cementerio (de parroquia).

churn [chœrn], *s.* mantequera.—*vt.* agitar, menear, revolver; batir manteca.—*vi.* agitarse, revolverse.— **ing** [chœrn̦iŋ], *s.* batido; cantidad de manteca batida de una vez.

chute [šut], *s.* conducto; canal; tubo; sumidero; vertedero; paracaídas.

chyle [kail], *s.* (fis.) quilo.

cider [sáid̦oe(r)], *s.* sidra.

cigar [sigár], *s.* cigarro, tabaco, puro, habano.—*c. case*, petaca.—*c. holder*, boquilla.—*c. lighter*, mechero, encendedor.—*c. store*, tabaquería, estanco.— **ette** [sig̦arét], *s.* cigarrillo, pitillo, cigarro.—*c. case*, pitillera, cigarrera.

cinch [sinch], *vt.* cinchar; apretar.—*s.* cincha; (fam.) ganga, cosa fácil o segura.

cinder [síndoe(r)], *s.* ceniza; carbón; brasa; rescoldo.—*pl.* pavesas, cenizas; carbón a medio quemar.—*vt.* reducir a cenizas.

cinema [sín̦em̦a], *s.* cine, cinematógrafo.

cinnamon [sín̦am̦on], *s.* canela; árbol de la canela.

cipher [sáif̦oe(r)], *s.* cifra; (arit.) cero; nulidad.—*vt.* calcular; cifrar con clave.—*vi.* numerar.

circle [sœrkl], *s.* círculo; circunferencia, redondel, esfera; círculo (social); rueda, corro.—*vt.* circundar, cercar, rodear.—*vi.* dar vueltas, remolinear.

circuit [sœrkit], *s.* circuito; vuelta, rodeo; radio; distrito; partido, jurisdicción.—*c. breaker*, interruptor automático.

circular [sœrkiul̦a(r)], *a.* circular; redondo.—*c. letter*, circular.—*c. plate*, disco.—*s.* circular; carta, aviso o folleto circular.—**circulate** [sœrkiuleit], *vt.* propalar, propagar; poner en circulación.—*vi.* circular; propagarse. —**circulation** [sœrkiuléišon], *s.* circulación; propaganda.—**circulatory**

[sœrkjulₐtori], a. circulatorio, circular.

circumcise [sœrkʌmsaiz], vt. circuncidar.—**circumcision** [sœrkʌmsíƺọn], s. circuncisión.

circumference [sœrkʌmfẹrẹns], s. circunferencia, periferia; perímetro.

circumscribe [sœrkʌmskráib], vt. circunscribir, fijar, limitar.

circumspect [sœrkʌmspekt], a. circunspecto, discreto.

circumstance [sœrkʌmstæns], s. circunstancia, incidente, acontecimiento.—*under no circumstances*, jamás; de ningún modo.—*under the circumstances*, en las circunstancias presentes, siendo así las cosas.—**circumstantial** [sœrkʌmstǽnƺạl], a. circunstancial, accidental, incidental.—*c. evidence*, prueba de indicios.

circus [sœrkʌs], s. circo.

cistern [sístœrn], s. cisterna, aljibe.

citadel [sítạdẹl], s. ciudadela.

citation [saitéiƺọn], s. cita, mención; (for.) citación, emplazamiento.—**cite** [sait], vt. citar, referirse a; (for.) citar a juicio.

citizen [sítizẹn], s. ciudadano, vecino.—**ship** [-ṣip], s. ciudadanía; nacionalidad.—*c. papers*, carta de ciudadanía o nacionalidad.

city [síti], s. ciudad, población, urbe; municipio.—a. municipal; citadino, urbano.—*c. council*, ayuntamiento.—*c. district*, barrio.—*c. hall*, ayuntamiento, casa consistorial.

civic [sívjk], a. cívico.—**ism** [sívjsizm], s. civismo.—**s** [sívjks], s. cívica, ciencia del gobierno civil.—**civil** [sívjl], a. civil, ciudadano; cortés, urbano.—*c. procedure*, enjuiciamiento civil.—*c. service*, ramo civil de la administración pública.—**civilian** [sivjl-yạn], s. paisano (no militar), civil.—*pl.* la población civil.—a. civil.—**civility** [sivjlịti], s. civilidad, cortesía, urbanidad.—**civilization** [sivjlizéiƺọn], s. civilización.—**civilize** [sívjlaiz], vt. civilizar.

clad [klæd], a. vestido, aderezado.

claim [kleim], vt. demandar, pedir en juicio; reclamar; denunciar (una mina); sostener, pretender, alegar.—*to c. to be*, echárselas de.—s. demanda; reclamación, petición; pretensión, título, derecho; denuncia minera.—**ant** [kléimạnt], **er** [-œ(r)], s. reclamante.

clairvoyance [klervóiạns], s. videncia, clarividencia.—**clairvoyant** [klervóiạnt], a. clarividente.

clam [klæm], s. almeja.

clamor [klǽmọ(r)], s. clamor(eo), gritería, vocería, algarabía; estruendo.—vi. clam(ore)ar, gritar, vociferar.—**ous** [-ʌs], a. clamoroso, ruidoso, estruendoso.

clamp [klæmp], s. tornillo de banco; grampa; abrazadera; pinzas, tenazas; montón (de mineral, ladrillos, etc.); pisadas recias.—vt. empalmar; afianzar; sujetar.—vi. pisar recio.

clan [klæn], s. clan; tribu; cuerpo o sociedad exclusivista.

clang [klæŋ], s. retintín; campanada; campanillazo.—vt. y vi. (hacer) sonar, resonar o retumbar.

clap [klæp], vti. [1] batir; cerrar de golpe; aplaudir.—*to c. the hands*, batir palmas.—vii. aplaudir, dar palmadas, palm(ot)ear.—s. ruido o golpe seco; palmada, aplauso; (fam.) gonorrea.

claret [klǽrit], s. clarete, vino tinto.

clarinet [klǽrinet], s. clarinete.

clarity [klǽriti], s. claridad.

clash [klæʃ], vi. chocar, entrechocarse, encontrarse; discordar, oponerse.—vt. batir, golpear.—s. choque; encontrón, colisión; antagonismo, discordia.

clasp [klæsp], s. broche, presilla, traba, hebilla, abrazadera; cierre; (mec.) grapa; apretón, abrazo.—vt. abrochar, enganchar; asir, agarrar; asegurar; abrazar, ceñir; apretar (la mano).

class [klæs], s. clase; condición, rango; (mil.) promoción; clase en las escuelas; (fam.) elegancia.—vt. clasificar, calificar, ordenar.

classic [klǽsjk], s. y a. clásico.—**al** [-ạl], a. clásico.

classification [klæsjfikéiƺọn], s. clasificación.—**classify** [klǽsjfai], vti. [7] clasificar, ordenar.

classmate [klǽsmeit], s. condiscípulo.—**classroom** [klǽsrum], s. aula, clase.

clatter [klǽtœ(r)], vi. resonar ruidosamente, matraquear, guachapear; charlar.—s. ruido, estruendo; gritería; alboroto, bulla.

clause [kloz], s. cláusula.

clavicle [klǽvjkl], s. clavícula.

claw [klo], s. garra, zarpa, uña; pinza o tenaza (del cangrejo); gancho, garfio.—*c. hammer*, martillo de orejas.—vt. desgarrar, arañar; rasgar, despedazar.—vi. arañar.

clay [klei], s. arcilla, greda, barro.

clean [klin], a. limpio; puro; despejado; aseado; nítido; simétrico.—*c.-bred*, de pura raza.—*c.-handed*, con las manos limpias, sin culpa.—*to show a c. pair of heels*, tomar las de Villadiego.—vt. limpiar, asear; desengrasar, desenlodar.—vi. (gen. con *up*) limpiar(se), asear(se).—**er** [klín-œ(r)], s. limpiador; mondador; tintorero; quitamanchas; depurador (de aire, etc.).—**ing** [-iŋ], s. aseo, limpieza; desengrase.—**liness** [klénlinis], *s.* limpieza, **aseo**, aliño; compostura; tersura.— **—ly** [klénli], *a.* limpio, aseado; puro, delicado.— **—ness** [-nis], *s.* limpieza, aseo; pureza.—**cleanse** [klenz], *vt.* limpiar, purificar; purgar, depurar.—**cleanser** [klénzœ(r)], *s.* limpiador, purificador.

clear [klir], *a.* claro, lúcido, transparente; despejado, (d)escampado; inocente; (com.) neto; sin deudas; puro; evidente.—*c.-headed*, inteligente, listo.—*c. profit*, beneficio neto.—*c.-sighted*, clarividente, perspicaz.—*c. track*, vía libre.—*s.* claro, espacio entre objetos.—*vt.* despejar, quitar estorbos; aclarar; justificar; salvar (un obstáculo); absolver; desenredar; desmontar, tumbar; obtener una ganancia líquida.—*to c. the table*, levantar la mesa.—*vi.* aclarar(se), serenar(se); liquidar cuentas.—*to c. off o up*, despejarse o escampar (el cielo).—*to c. out*, irse, escabullirse.— **—ance** [klírans], *s.* despejo; despacho de aduana; beneficio líquido; (com.) venta de liquidación; (mec., ing.) juego, espacio libre.—*c. papers*, certificación del pago de derechos de aduana.— **—ing** [-iŋ], *s.* aclaramiento, despejo; desmonte; claro, raso; justificación.—*c. house*, banco de liquidación.— **—ness** [-nis], *s.* claridad; luz; despejo.

cleave [kliv], *vti.* [4] partir, rajar, tajar; penetrar.—*vii.* resquebrar, henderse; pegarse, adherirse.— **—r** [klívœ(r)], *s.* partidor; cuchilla o cortante de carnicero.

clef [klɛf], *s.* (mus.) clave, llave.

cleft [kleft], *pret.* y *pp.* de TO CLEAVE.— *a.* agrietado, partido.—*s.* grieta, fisura, rajadura, rendija.

clemency [klémensi], *s.* clemencia, misericordia.—**clement** [klémɛnt], *a.* clemente, misericordioso.

clench [klench], *vt.* agarrar; apretar o cerrar el puño; remachar.—V. CLINCH.—*s.* agarradera.— **—er** [klénchœ(r)], *s.* agarrador; remachador; (fig.) argumento sin réplica.

clergy [klœrdži], *s.* clero.— **—man** [-man], *s.* clérigo; cura, sacerdote.— **cleric** [klérik], *s.* clérigo.—*a.* clerical. **—clerical** [klérikal], *a.* clerical; eclesiástico; burocrático, oficinesco.—*s.* clérigo.—*pl.* ropa clerical.—**clerk** [klœrk], *s.* oficial de secretaría; escribiente; empleado de oficina; clérigo; escolar; escribano, actuario.

clever [klévœ(r)], *a.* diestro, hábil; avisado, listo; inteligente.— **—ness** [-nis], *s.* talento; destreza, maña, habilidad.

cliché [klišéi], *s.* (impr.) clisé; frase hecha, lugar común.

click [klik], *s.* golpe seco; seguro, gatillo; gatillazo; chasquido de lengua.— *vt.* y *vi.* (hacer) sonar con uno o más golpes secos; hacer tictac; piñonear (un arma de fuego); (fam.) tener buen éxito.

client [kláient], *s.* cliente; parroquiano.— **—ele** [-él], *s.* clientela.

cliff [klif], *s.* farallón, risco, acantilado, precipicio.

climate [kláimit], *s.* clima.

climax [kláimæks], *s.* clímax.

climb [klaim], *vt.* trepar, subir, escalar.— *vi.* trepar, subir, encaramarse, elevarse.—*s.* subida, ascenso.— **—er** [kláimœ(r)], *s.* trepador, escalador; enredadera; oportunista.— **—ing** [-iŋ], *s.* trepa, subida.—*a.* trepante, trepador.

clime [klaim], *s.* clima.

clinch [klinch], *vt.* remachar; agarrar; afianzar.—*vi.* agarrarse; (fam.) abrazarse estrechamente.—*s.* remache; forcejeo, lucha cuerpo a cuerpo (esp. en el boxeo); (fam.) abrazo estrecho.— **—er** [klínchœ(r)], *s.* remachador; clavo remachado; argumento decisivo.

cling [kliŋ], *vii.* [10] asirse, adherirse, pegarse.— **—ing** [klíŋiŋ], *a.* colgante, pendiente; adhesivo.

clinic [klínik], *s.* clínica.— **—al** [-al], *a.* clínico.

clinker [klíŋkœ(r)], *s.* escoria.—*vi.* formar escorias.

clip [klip], *vti.* [1] trasquilar; tijeretear; cercenar; podar; pellizcar; agarrar.— *s.* tijeretazo; recorte; trasquila; cantonera; grapa, pinza, sujetapapeles; pasador o broche (de presión).— **—per** [klípœ(r)], *s.* trasquilador; cercenador, recortador; maquinilla para cortar el pelo.—*pl.* tijeras de trasquilar.— **—ping** [-iŋ], *s.* trasquileo; recorte; cercenadura; tijereteo.—*pl.* recortes.

clique [klik], *s.* camarilla, compadraje.

cloak [klouk], *s.* capa, manto.—*vt.* encapotar; embozar; ocultar.— **—room** [klóukrum], *s.* guardarropa.

clock [klak], *s.* reloj (de mesa o pared).— *c. dial o face*, esfera.—*vt.* medir o contar el tiempo de un acto.— **—maker** [klákmeikœ(r)], *s.* relojero.— **—smith** [-smiθ], *s.* relojero.— **—wise** [-waiz], *a.* y *adv.* en el sentido de las agujas del reloj.— **—work** [-wœrk], *s.* maquinaria del reloj.

clod [klad], *s.* terrón; necio, gaznápiro.

clog [klag], *vti.* [1] embarazar; obstruir, entorpecer; amontonar.—*vii.* apiñarse, atestarse; amontonarse; atorarse; obstruirse; atascarse.—*s.* traba, obstáculo; carga; chanclo, zueco.— *c. dance*, zapateado.

cloister [klóistœ(r)], *s.* claustro; monasterio.—*vt.* enclaustrar.— —ed [-d], *a.* enclaustrado.

close [klouz], *vt.* cerrar; tapar; terminar; levantar (una sesión); finiquitar (una cuenta).—*vi.* cerrar(se); unirse; terminar; fenecer.—*to c. with,* cerrar (con el adversario).—*s.* fin, terminación; caída (de la tarde); clausura; cierre; coto; parcela.—*a.* [klous], cerrado; apretado; justo; íntimo (amistad); sofocante; mal ventilado; cercano, próximo; tupido, compacto; inmediato; sucinto; oculto; reservado; restringido; tacaño; casi empatado; parejo; reñido (combate, etc.).—*at c. range,* a quema ropa, a boca de jarro. —*adv.* cerca, de cerca; estrechamente. —*c. by,* muy cerca.—*c. to,* junto a; arrimado o pegado a; a raíz de.— —d [klouzd], *a.* cerrado; concluso.—*c. chapter,* asunto concluído.— —ness [klóusnis], *s.* contigüidad; estrechez; falta de ventilación; firmeza; soledad; fidelidad (de copia o traducción).— *close-out* [klóuzaut], *s.* (com.) liquidación.—*closet* [klázit], *s.* armario, alacena; excusado, retrete.—*a.* secreto, confidencial.—*vt.* encerrar a uno para conferenciar a puerta cerrada.— *close-up* [klóusap], *s.* fotografía de primer plano.—*closing* [klóuziŋ], *s.* cierre; final, conclusión; clausura; remate (de cuentas).—*a.* de cierre; último; de clausura.—*closure* [klóu-žŋ(r)], *s.* clausura; cierre; fin, conclusión.

clot [klat], *s.* coágulo, grumo.—*vii.* [1] coagularse, engrumecerse.

cloth [kloθ], *s.* tela, paño, género, tejido. —*c. binding,* encuadernación en tela. —*clothe* [klouð], *vti.* [4] vestir; cubrir, arropar; revestir.—*to c. with authority,* investir de autoridad.— *clothed* [klouðd], *pret.* y *pp.* de TO CLOTHE.— —es [klouðz], *s. pl.* vestido, vestuario, indumentaria; ropaje, ropa de toda especie.—*c. chest,* ropero.— *c. hanger,* perchero.—*c. moth,* polilla. —*c. rack,* perchero.— —esline [klóuž-lain], *s.* tendedera.— —espin [klóuž-pin], *s.* pinzas para colgar ropa; (Cuba) palitos de tendedera.— **clothier** [klóuðiœ(r)], *s.* comerciante o fabricante de ropa; pañero, ropero. —*clothing* [klóuðiŋ], *s.* vestidos, ropa; vestuario, indumentaria.

cloud [klaud], *s.* nube; nublado, nubarrón; muchedumbre, multitud.— *under a c.,* desacreditado, sospechoso. —*in the clouds,* abstraído; en las nubes.—*vt.* anublar, nublar; enturbiar; abigarrar; empañar.—*vi.* nublarse, obscurecerse.— —iness [kláud-inis], *s.* nebulosidad, obscuridad.— —less [-lis], *a.* sin nubes, despejado,

claro.— —y [-i], *a.* nublado, encapotado; nebuloso; turbio; obscuro; lóbrego; (fot.) velado.

clove [klouv], *s.* clavo de especia.—*c. of garlic,* diente de ajo.—*pret.* de TO CLEAVE.—*cloven* [klóuvęn], *pp.* de TO CLEAVE.

clover [klóuvœ(r)], *s.* trébol.—*to be o live in c.,* vivir en la abundancia.

clown [klaun], *s.* payaso, bufón; gracioso.— —ish [kláunis], *a.* rudo, zafio, grosero.

cloy [kloi], *vt.* empalagar; hastiar, hartar.

club [klʌb], *s.* porra, garrote, tranca; tolete; club, círculo; centro de reunión; palo o maza de golf.—*pl.* bastos (de baraja).—*c. law,* la ley del más fuerte; gobierno tiránico.—*c. steak,* pequeño biftec.—*vii.* [1] contribuir a gastos comunes; unirse o juntarse para un mismo fin.—*vti.* aporrear, golpear con garrote, apalear.

cluck [klʌk], *vt.* y *vi.* cloquear.—*s.* cloqueo.

clue [klu], *s.* indicio, pista; norte, guía.

clump [klʌmp], *s.* tarugo; terrón; aglutinación, masa, grupo; pisada recia.— *vt.* y *vi.* aglutinar(se); andar torpemente con fuertes pisadas.

clumsy [klʌmzi], *a.* desmañado, chapucero; incómodo; difícil de manejar.

clung [klʌŋ], *pret.* y *pp.* de TO CLING.

cluster [klʌstœ(r)], *s.* racimo; ramillete; grupo; caterva; enjambre.—*vi.* agruparse, arracimarse.—*vt.* apiñar, amontonar.

clutch [klʌch], *vt.* agarrar; apretar; embragar.—*to c. at,* tratar de empuñar.—*s.* agarro, presa; uña, garra; nidada; embrague.

clutter [klʌtœ(r)], *s.* baraúnda, batahola; desorden, confusión.—V. CLATTER.—*vi.* alborotar, hacer ruido o estrépito.—*vt.* poner en desorden, trastornar.

coach [kouch], *s.* coche, carruaje; carroza; automóvil; (f.c.) vagón; maestro particular; (dep.) entrenador.— *vt.* adiestrar; aleccionar; entrenar.— *vi.* (dep.) entrenarse; servir de entrenador.— —er [kóuchœ(r)] *s.* preceptor; entrenador.— —man [-man], *s.* cochero.

coagulate [kouǽgiuleit], *vt.* y *vi.* coagular(se), cuajar(se).

coal [koul], *s.* carbón, hulla, antracita. —*c. bin,* carbonera.—*c. brick,* briqueta, carbón prensado.—*c. dust,* cisco.—*c. tar,* alquitrán de hulla.—*vt.* y *vi.* echar carbón; hacer carbón; proveer(se) de carbón.

coalition [koualíšŋn], *s.* coalición, liga.

coarse [kors], *a.* basto, ordinario; tosco-vulgar; burdo.—*c. file,* lima de desbastar.— —ness [kórsnɪs], s. tosquedad; vulgaridad, grosería, rudeza.

coast [kouṣt], s. costa, litoral.—c. *guard*, guarda de costas, servicio costanero; guardacostas.—*the c. is clear*, no hay moros en la costa.—vt. (mar.) costear.—vi. navegar a lo largo de la costa; deslizarse cuesta abajo.— —er [kóuṣtœ(r)], s. piloto práctico; barco de cabotaje; habitante de la costa; deslizador.— —line [-laɪn], s. costa, litoral.

coat [kout], s. americana, chaqueta, saco; abrigo; pelo, lana, pelaje de los animales; funda, caperuza; revestimiento; capa o mano (de pintura, etc.).—c. *hanger*, perchero.—c. *of arms*, escudo de armas.—*to turn one's c.*, cambiar de casaca.—vt. vestir, revestir; dar una mano o capa de; azogar.— —ing [kóutɪŋ], s. revestimiento, capa, mano de pintura; enlucido.

coax [kouks], vt. y vi. persuadir con halagos, engatusar.

cob [kab], s. tusa o carozo de maíz; jaca.

cobble [kábl], s. guijarro.

cobbler [káblœ(r)], s. zapatero de viejo, remendón; chapucero.

cobweb [kábweb], s. telaraña.

cocaine [koukéin], s. cocaína.

coccyx [káksɪks], s. (anat.) coxis, rabadilla.

cock [kak], s. gallo; macho de ave; espita (de agua, etc.); percusor o martillo de armas de fuego.—c.-*eyed*, bizco; (fam.) extravagante, loco.—c. *robin*, petirrojo.—vt. montar o amartillar (un arma de fuego); ladear (el sombrero).—vi. engreírse, gallear.

cockatoo [kakatú], s. cacatúa.

cockfight(ing) [kákfait(iŋ)], s. riña o pelea de gallos.—**cockfighter** [kákfaitœ(r)], s. gallero.

cockpit [kákpit], s. (aer.) carlinga del avión; parte baja de popa de la cubierta (de un yate); cámara.

cockroach [kákrouch], s. cucaracha.

cockscomb [kákskoum], s. cresta (de gallo); gorro de bufón; (Am.) moco de pavo.—**cockspur** [kákspœ(r)], s. espuela (de gallo), espolón.

cocktail [kákteɪl], s. coctel; aperitivo.—c. *shaker*, coctelera.

cocky [káki], a. arrogante, engreído.

cocoa [kóukou], s. cacao molido o en polvo; bebida de cacao.

coconut [kóukonʌt], s. coco; cocotero.—c. *plantation*, cocal.

cocoon [kokún], s. capullo (del gusano de seda, etc.).

cod [kad], s. bacalao, abadejo.

coddle [kádl], vt. mimar, consentir.

code [koud], s. código; clave.

codeine [kóudin], s. codeína.

codfish [kádfɪṣ], s. = COD.

codify [kádɪfaɪ], vt. codificar, compilar leyes.

coefficient [kouɪfíṣɛnt], s. coeficiente.

coerce [kouœ́rs], vt. forzar, obligar.— **coercion** [kouœ́rṣɒn], s. coerción, coacción.

coexist [kouɪgzíst], vi. coexistir.— —ence [-ɛns], s. coexistencia.

coffee [kófi], s. café.—c. *plantation*, cafetal.—c. *tree*, cafeto, café.— —house [-haus], s. café (establecimiento).— —pot [-pat], s. cafetera.

coffer [kófœ(r)], s. arca, cofre.

coffin [kófɪn], s. ataúd, féretro.

cog [kag], s. (mec.) diente o punto de rueda.— —wheel [kághwil], s. rueda dentada.

cohabitation [kouhæbitéɪṣɒn], s. contubernio, cohabitación.

coherence [kohɛ́rɛns], **coherency** [kohɛ́rɛnsi], s. coherencia.—**coherent** (kohɛ́rɛnt], a. coherente.

cohesion [kouhíʒɒn], s. cohesión, adhesión, unión.—**cohesive** [kouhísɪv], a. cohesivo, coherente, adherente.

ceif [kóif], s. cofia, toca.

coiffure [kwafyúr], s. tocado, peinado.

coil [koɪl], s. bobina, carrete; rosca; rollo; espiral de alambre.—vt. enrollar.—vi. enrollarse; enroscarse.

coin [koɪn], s. moneda acuñada.—vt. acuñar; inventar, forjar (palabras, mentiras).— —age [kóinidʒ], s. acuñación; moneda; sistema monetario; invención.

coincide [kouɪnsáid], vi. coincidir; estar de acuerdo.—**coincidence** [kouɪnsidɛns], s. coincidencia.

coke [kouk], s. cok (carbón).

colander [kʌlandœ(r)], s. colador; espumadera, escurridor.

cold [kould], a. frío; helado; indiferente.—c. *cream*, crema cosmética.—c. *cuts*, fiambres variados.—c.-*hearted*, insensible, impasible.—s. frío, frialdad; enfriamiento; resfriado, catarro, constipado.—*to catch c.*, resfriarse, acatarrarse.— —ness [kóuldnɪs], s. frialdad; tibieza, indiferencia, despego.

colic [kálɪk], s. cólico.

coliseum [kalɪsíam], s. coliseo.

collaborate [kolǽboreɪt], vt. colaborar.—**collaboration** [kolæboréɪṣɒn], s. colaboración.—**collaborator** [kolǽboreɪtɒ(r)], s. colaborador.

collapse [kolǽps], s. derrumbamiento; desplome; fracaso; colapso.—vi. derrumbarse, desplomarse; fracasar; sufrir un colapso.

collar [kálǝ(r)], s. cuello (de camisa, etc.); collar (de perro; collera; aro.—vt. poner cuello, aro; agarrar del cuello, acogotar.

collateral [kǫlǽtęrạl], *a.* colateral.—*s.* garantía, resguardo.

collation [kǫléjṣǫn], *s.* cotejo; (igl.) colación; merienda, colación.

colleague [kálig], *s.* colega.

collect [kǫlékt], *vt.* colectar, recaudar; coleccionar; (re)copilar.—*c. on delivery* (*C.O.D.*), entrega contra reembolso, cóbrese al entregar.—*to c. one's self*, volver en sí, reponerse.—*s.* [kálekt], colecta.— **—ion** [kǫléksǫn], *s.* colección; colecta; montón; recaudación; cobranza; reunión.— **—ive** [kǫléktịv], *s.* (gram.) nombre colectivo.—*a.* colectivo.— **—or** [kǫléktǫ(r)], *s.* coleccionista; colector; recaudador; cobrador.

college [kálịdż], *s.* colegio universitario; escuela o facultad profesional.—*a.* de colegio; estudiantil.

collet [kálịt], *s.* (mec.) collar, mandril; (joy.) engaste.

collide [kǫlájd], *vi.* chocar, topar; contradecir, estar en conflicto.

collision [kǫlíżǫn], *s.* colisión, choque; antagonismo.

colloquial [kǫlóukwịạl], *a.* familiar, dialogal.— **—ism** [-ịzm], *s.* expresión familiar.

Colombian [kǫlámbịạn], *s.* y *a.* colombiano.

colon [kóulǫn], *s.* (gram.) dos puntos (:); (anat.) colon.

colonel [kœrnęl], *s.* coronel.

colonial [kǫlóunịạl], *a.* colonial.— **colonist** [kálǫnịst], *s.* colono.— **colonize** [kálǫnajz], *vt.* colonizar, poblar.—*vi.* establecerse en colonia. —**colony** [kálǫnị], *s.* colonia.

color [kálǫ(r)], *s.* color; colorido; (naipes) palo.—*pl.* colores nacionales. —*c.-blind*, daltoniano.—*vt.* color(e)ar; teñir; iluminar; embellecer.—*vi.* ruborizarse.— **—ed** [-d], *a.* de color; persona negra; engañoso, disfrazado; adornado.— **—ful** [-fụl], *a.* lleno de colorido; pintoresco.— **—ing** [-ịŋ], *s.* colorante, color; coloración; estilo o aire particular; colorido.— **—less** [-lịs], *a.* descolorido; incoloro.

colossal [kǫlásạl], *a.* colosal, descomunal.

colt [koụlt], *s.* potro.

Columbian [kǫlámbịạn], *a.* colombino, relativo a Colón.

column [kálʌm], *s.* columna.— **—ist** [kálʌm(n)ịst], *s.* periodista encargado de una sección permanente.

comb [koụm], *s.* peine; peineta; rastrillo; cresta de ave; panal de miel.— *vt.* peinar; cardar; rastrillar; escudriñar.

combat [kámbæt], *s.* combate.—*vt.* y *vi.* combatir.— **—ant** [kámbạtạnt], *s.* y *a.*

combatiente, luchador.— **—ive** [kʌmbǽtịv], *a.* combativo.

combination [kambịnéjṣǫn], *s.* combinación.—**combine** [kǫmbájn], *vt.* y *vi.* combinar(se); mezclar(se); unir(se).

come [kʌm], *vii.* [10] venir, llegar; ir, acudir; provenir; aparecer, salir; acontecer.—*come in!* ¡entre(n)! ¡adelante!—*to c. about*, suceder.—*to c. across*, topar con.—*to c. back*, volver; retroceder.—*to c. by*, obtener; pasar junto a.—*to c. down*, bajar; descender. —*to c. down with*, enfermar de.—*to c. in*, entrar.—*to c. off*, desaparecer.— *to c. on*, seguir, progresar.—*to c. out*, salir, mostrarse.—*to c. over*, venir, cruzar.—*to c. through*, salir bien.—*to c. upon*, acometer, topar con.—*pp.* de TO COME.— **—back** [kámbæk], *s.* rehabilitación; regreso al puesto u oficio; respuesta aguda; motivo de queja.— **—down** [-daụn], *s.* revés de fortuna; humillación, chasco.

comedian [kǫmídịan], *s.* comediante, actor cómico.—**comedy** [kámędị], *s.* comedia.

comet [kámịt], *s.* cometa.

comfort [kámfǫrt], *s.* comodidad; consuelo; bienestar.—*vt.* confortar; consolar.— **—able** [-ạbl] *a.* cómodo; consolador; adecuado.— **—er** [-œ(r)], *s.* edredón.— **—ing** [-ịŋ], *a.* confortante.

comic [kámịk], *a.* cómico, gracioso, chistoso.—*a.* y *s.* bufo.—*s. pl.* tiras cómicas, historietas.

coming [kámịŋ], *s.* venida, llegada.—*a.* próximo, venidero.

comma [kámạ], *s.* coma (,).

command [kǫmǽnd], *vt.* mandar, ordenar, disponer; acaudillar, capitanear. —*vi.* imperar; imponerse.—*s.* mando; mandato, orden; comandancia; comando.— **—er** [-œ(r)], *s.* comandante, jefe supremo.— **—ment** [-męnt], *s.* mandato, precepto.—*the Commandments*, los Mandamientos.

commemorate [kǫmémorejt], *vt.* conmemorar.—**commemoration** [kǫmemoréjṣǫn], *s.* conmemoración.

commence [kǫméns], *vt.* y *vi.* comenzar, iniciar.— **—ment** [-męnt], *s.* comienzo; inauguración; acto de distribución de diplomas.

commend [kǫménd], *vt.* encomendar, recomendar; alabar.— **—able** [-ạbl], *a.* loable.— **—ation** [kamęndéjṣǫn], *s.* elogio, alabanza.

comment [kámęnt], *vt.* y *vi.* comentar; glosar, anotar.—*s.* comentario.— **—ary** [kámęnterị], *s.* comentario.— **—ator** [kámęntejtǫ(r)], *s.* —**er** [kámęntœ(r)], *s.* comentarista.

commerce [kámœrs], *s.* comercio; trato.

—commercial [kǫmœ́rşạl], *a.* comercial.

commiseration [kǫmizẹréişǫn], *s.* piedad, conmiseración.

commissary [kámiṣẹri], *s.* comisario, delegado.—commission [kǫmíşǫn], *s.* comisión; misión; encargo; nombramiento.—*commissioned officer,* oficial del ejército.—commissioner [kǫmíṣǫnœ(r)], *s.* comisario; comisionado.

commit [kǫmít], *vti.* [1] cometer, perpetrar; encargar, encomendar.—*to c. one's self,* comprometerse.—*to c. to memory,* aprender de memoria.—*to c. to prison,* encarcelar, encerrar.—*to c. to writing,* poner por escrito.—*—ment* [-mẹnt], *s.* compromiso, obligación.

committee [kǫmíti], *s.* comité, comisión, delegación.

commodity [kǫmáditi], *s.* comodidad; artículo de consumo; mercancía, género.

common [kámǫn], *a.* común, corriente; vulgar, trivial; público, general, comunal; inferior.—*c. law,* derecho consuetudinario.—*c. sense,* sentido común.—*c. soldier,* soldado raso.—*s. pl.* ejido; refectorio, campo común.—*—ness* [-nịs], *s.* comunidad; frecuencia; vulgaridad.—*—place* [-plẹis], *a.* común, vulgar.—*s.* lugar común.—*—weal* [-wil], *s.* el bien público.—*—wealth* [-welθ], *s.* estado; nación; comunidad de naciones; cosa pública.

commotion [kǫmóuşǫn], *s.* conmoción.

commune [kǫmjún], *vi.* comulgar; conversar, ponerse en contacto.—communicate [kǫmjúniḳẹit], *vt.* comunicar, dar parte de; contagiar; tomar la comunión.—*vi.* comunicarse; tomar la comunión.—communication [kǫmjuniḳéişǫn], *s.* comunicación.—communion [kǫmjúnyǫn], *s.* comunión.

communism [kámyuniẓm], *s.* comunismo.—communist [kámyunịst], *a.* y *s.* comunista.

community [kǫmjúnịti], *s.* comunidad; vecindad; sociedad.

commuter [kǫmjútœ(r)], *s.* abonado al ferrocarril; (elec.) conmutador.

compact [kámpæk t], *s.* pacto, convenio; polvera de bolsillo; compresa.—*a.* [kǫmpækt], compacto, conciso.

companion [kǫmpǽnyǫn], *s.* compañero; acompañante.—*—ship* [-şịp], *s.* compañerismo; compañía.—company [kámpạni], *s.* compañía; sociedad; visita.—*ship's c.,* tripulación.—*present c. excepted,* mejorando lo presente.

comparable [kámpạrạbl], *a.* comparable.—comparative [kǫmpǽrạtịv], *a.* comparativo, relativo; comparado.—compare [kǫmpér], *vt.* comparar; comprobar, cotejar; equiparar.—*vi.* poderse comparar; ser comparable;

ser igual.—*beyond c.,* sin igual o rival, sin par.—comparison [kǫmpǽriṣǫn], *s.* comparación, cotejo; equiparación; símil; metáfora.

compartment [kǫmpártmẹnt], *s.* compartimiento; departamento; división; sección.

compass [kámpạs], *s.* compás de dibujo; brújula; circunferencia; alcance, ámbito.

compassion [kǫmpǽşǫn], *s.* compasión.—*—ate* [-ịt], *a.* compasivo, misericordioso.—*vt.* [-ẹit], compadecer.

compatible [kǫmpǽtịbl], *a.* compatible.

compatriot [kǫmpéịtrịǫt], *s.* y *a.* compatriota.

compel [kǫmpél], *vti.* [1] compeler, obligar; dominar, someter.

compendium [kǫmpéndiAm], *s.* compendio, resumen.

compensate [kámpenseịt], *vt.* compensar; indemnizar.—*vi.* compensar; (con for) igualar, equivaler.—compensation [kampenséịşǫn], *s.* compensación; remuneración.

compete [kǫmpit], *vi.* competir, rivalizar; (con for) disputarse.—*—nce* [kámpẹtẹns], *—ncy* [kámpẹtẹnsị], *s.* competencia, suficiencia; subsistencia.—*—nt* [kámpẹtẹnt], *a.* competente, adecuado, calificado.—competition [kampẹtíşǫn], *s.* competición; rivalidad; certamen, concurso, oposición.—competitive [kǫmpétịtịv], *a.* competidor, que compite.—competitor [kǫmpétịtǫ(r)], *s.* competidor, rival, opositor.

compilation [kampịléịşǫn], *s.* compilación, recopilación.—compile [kǫmpáịl], *vt.* compilar, recopilar.

complacence [kǫmpléịsẹns], complacency [kǫmpléịsẹnsị], *s.* complacencia; presunción.—complacent [kǫmpléịsẹnt], *a.* complaciente; satisfecho de sí mismo.

complain [kǫmpléịn], *vi.* quejarse, lamentarse; querellarse.—*—t* [-t], *s.* queja; lamento; querella; enfermedad.

complement [kámplẹmẹnt], *s.* complemento; accesorio.—*vt.* complementar, completar.

complete [kǫmplít], *a.* completo.—*vt.* completar, rematar; perfeccionar.—*—ness* [-nịs], *s.* perfección, minuciosidad.—completion [kǫmplíşǫn], *s.* terminación; cumplimiento; completamiento.

complex [kámplẹks], *a.* complejo, complicado.—*s.* complejo; obsesión.

complexion [kǫmplékşǫn], *s.* tez; cutis.

complexity [kǫmplékşịtị], complexness [kǫmpléksnịs], *s.* complejidad.

compliance [kǫmpláịạns], *s.* sumisión; complacencia; acatamiento; anuencia.—*in c. with*, de acuerdo con, accediendo a.—**compliant** [kǫmpláiant], *a.* dócil, obediente; complaciente.

complicate [kámplikeit], *vt.* complicar, enredar.—*a.* complicado.— —**d** [kámplikeitid], *a.* complicado, enredado.—**complication** [kamplikéişǫn], *s.* complicación.

compliment [kámplimęnt], *s.* galantería, lisonja; piropo; fineza; cumplido.— *pl.* recados, memorias.—*vt.* piropear; cumplimentar; obsequiar.—*vi.* hacer cumplimientos.

comply [kǫmplái], *vii.* [7] obedecer a; cumplir con.

component [kǫmpóunęnt], *a.* y *s.* componente.

compose [kǫmpóuz], *vt.* componer; conciliar, sosegar.— —**d** [-d], *a.* sosegado, sereno; compuesto (de).— —**r** [-œ(r)], *s.* autor, compositor.—**composite** [kǫmpázit], *a.* compuesto; mixto.—*s.* compuesto, cosa compuesta; mixtura.—**composition** [kampozíşǫn], *s.* composición; tema; componenda.

composure [kǫmpóuẓụ(r)], *s.* compostura, calma, sangre fría.

compote [kámpout], *s.* compota, dulce.

compound [kámpaund], *s.* compuesto; mezcla; palabra compuesta; cuerpo compuesto.—*a.* compuesto; mezclado.—*vt.* [kámpáund], componer, combinar, mezclar.—*vi.* avenirse, transigir.

comprehend [kamprihénd], *vt.* comprender; abarcar, incluir.—**comprehensible** [kamprihénsibl], *a.* comprensible, inteligible.—**comprehension** [kamprihénşǫn], *s.* comprensión. —**comprehensive** [kamprihénsiv], *a.* compre(he)nsivo, inclusivo; amplio; perspicaz.

compress [kǫmprés], *vt.* comprimir, apretar, condensar.—*s.* [kámpres], compresa.—**ion** [kǫmpréşǫn], *s.* compresión.

comprise [kǫmpráiz], *vt.* incluir, contener, comprender; constar de.

compromise [kámpromaiz], *s.* compromiso, arreglo, avenencia.—*vt.* comprometer.—*vi.* avenirse, transigir, transar.

comptroller [kǫntróulœ(r)], *s.* interventor, contralor.

compulsion [kǫmpálşǫn], *s.* compulsión, apremio.—**compulsive** [kǫmpálsiv], *a.* compulsivo.—**compulsory** [kǫmpálsǫri], *a.* obligatorio.

compunction [kǫmpáŋkşǫn], *s.* compunción, remordimiento, escrúpulo.

computation [kampiutéişǫn], *s.* computación, cálculo.—**compute** [kǫmpiút], *vt.* computar, calcular.—**computer**

[kǫmpiútœ(r)], *s.* calculista; computador; máquina calculadora.

comrade [kámræd], *s.* camarada, compañero.— —**ship** [-şip], *s.* camaradería.

concave [kánkeiv], *a.* cóncavo.—**concavity** [kankǽviti], *s.* concavidad.

conceal [kǫnsíl], *vt.* ocultar, esconder, encubrir.— —**ment** [-męnt], *s.* ocultación; encubrimiento.

concede [kǫnsíd], *vt.* conceder, admitir. —*vi.* asentir; convenir.

conceit [kǫnsít], *s.* presunción, engreimiento, ínfulas; vanagloria; concepto.— —**ed** [-id], *a.* vanidoso, engreído.

conceivable [kǫnsívabl], *a.* concebible. —**conceive** [kǫnsív], *vt.* y *vi.* concebir.

concentrate [kánsęntreit], *vt.* (re)concentrar.—*vi.* reunirse.—*s.* substancia concentrada.— —**d** [kánsęntreitid], *a.* concentrado.—**concentration** [kansęntréişǫn], *s.* (re)concentración; recogimiento.

concept [kánsępt], *s.* concepto.— —**ion** [kǫnsépşǫn], *s.* concepción.

concern [kǫnsœrn], *vt.* concernir; afectar; interesar; inquietar.—*s.* interés; inquietud; asunto; incumbencia; compañía, firma; importancia, consecuencia.—*of what c. is it to you?* ¿qué le importa? ¿qué más le da a Ud.?— —**ed** [-d], *a.* inquieto, preocupado; interesado; comprometido.—*as far as I am c.*, en cuanto a mí.— —**ing** [-iŋ], *prep.* por lo concerniente a, respecto a.

concert [kánsœrt], *s.* concierto.—*vt.* [kǫnsœrt], concertar.

concession [kǫnséşǫn], *s.* concesión, privilegio.— —**ary** [-eri], *s.* concesionario.—*a.* otorgado por concesión.

conch [kaŋk, kanch], *s.* caracol marino; concha; (arq.) concha.

conciliate [kǫnsílieit], *vt.* conciliar; apaciguar.—**conciliation** [kǫnsiliéişǫn], *s.* conciliación.—**conciliatory** [kǫnsíliatǫri], *a.* conciliatorio.

concise [kǫnsáis], *a.* conciso, sucinto.— —**ness** [-nis], *s.* concisión, laconismo.

conclude [kǫnklúd], *vt.* y *vi.* concluir(se).—**conclusion** [kǫnklúžǫn], *s.* conclusión; decisión; deducción.—**conclusive** [kǫnklúsiv], *a.* concluyente; decisivo.

concord [kánkǫrd], *s.* concordia; armonía; concordancia.— —**ance** [kankórdạns], *s.* concordancia, conformidad.

concrete [kánkrit], *a.* fraguado; cuajado; de hormigón.—*s.* concreto; hormigón; cemento.—*c. steel* o *reinforced c.*, hormigón armado.

concur [kǫnkœr], *vii.* [1] concurrir;

convenir con, **estar de acuerdo;** unirse, juntarse.

concussion [kǫnkáṣǫn], *s.* sacudida, golpe, conmoción.

condemn [kǫndém], *vt.* condenar; expropiar.— **—ation** [kandemnéiṣǫn], *s.* condenación; confiscación.— **—atory** [kǫndémnǫtǫri], *a.* condenatorio.

condensation [kandenséiṣǫn], *s.* condensación.—**condense** [kǫndéns], *vt.* y *vi.* condensar(se); reducirse.—**condenser** [kǫndénsœ(r)], *s.* condensador.

condescend [kandiṣénd], *vi.* condescender.—**condescencion** [kandiṣénṣǫn], *s.* condescendencia.

condiment [kándiment], *s.* condimento.

condition [kǫndíṣǫn], *s.* condición; estado; requisito; nota o calificación provisional.—*vt.* estipular; acondicionar; reprobar (en un examen).— **—al** [-ǫl], *a.* condicional.

condole [kǫndóul], *vi.* condolerse, dar el pésame.— **—nce** [kǫndóulens], *s.* condolencia, pésame.

condor [kándǫ(r)], *s.* cóndor.

conduce [kǫndiús], *vi.* conducir a, favorecer, tender a.—**conducive** [kǫndiúsiv], *a.* conducente, conveniente, apropiado.

conduct [kǫndÁkt], *vt.* conducir, guiar; (mus.) dirigir.—*vr.* conducirse, comportarse.—*vi.* ser conductor; llevar la batuta.—*s.* [kándakt], conducta, comportamiento; manejo, conducción.— **—ion** [kǫndÁkṣǫn], conducción.— **—or** [kǫndÁktǫ(r)], *s.* conductor; director de orquesta; revisor o inspector de boletines.—**conduit** [kándit], *s.* conducto, tubería, cañería.

cone [kǫun], *s.* cono; cucurucho; barquillo.—*pine c.,* piña (del pino).

confection [kǫnfékṣǫn], *s.* confección, hechura; confite, confitura.— **—er** [-œ(r)], *s.* confitero.— **—ery** [-eri], *s.* dulces, confites; confitería, repostería.

confederacy [kǫnfédœrǫṣi], *s.* confederación.—**confederate** [kǫnfédœreit], *vt.* y *vi.* confederar(se).—*a.* y *s.* [kǫnfédœrit], confederado.—**confederation** [kǫnfédœréiṣǫn], *s.* confederación.

confer [kǫnfœr], *vii.* [1] conferenciar, tratar.—*vti.* conferir, otorgar.— **—ence** [kánfœrens], *s.* conferencia, deliberación, entrevista; el acto de conferir.

confess [kǫnfés], *vt.* y *vi.* confesar(se).— **—ion** [kǫnféṣǫn], *s.* confesión.— **—ional** [kǫnféṣǫnal].—**ionary** [kǫnféṣǫneri], *s.* confes(i)onario.— **—or** [kǫnféṣǫ(r)], *s.* confesor.

confidant [kanfidént], *s.* confidente.—

confide [kǫnfáid], *vt.* y *vi.* confiar(se), fiar(se).—**confidence** [kánfidens], *s.* confianza; confidencia.—**confident** [kánfident], *a.* cierto, seguro; confiado.—*s.* confidente.—**confidential** [kanfidénṣǫl], *a.* confidencial.

confine [kǫnfáin], *vt.* y *vi.* confinar.—*to be confined in bed,* guardar cama.—*s.* *pl.* [kánfainz], confín, límite.— **—ment** [kǫnfáinment], *s.* confinamiento, encierro; restricción; ahogo.

confirm [kǫnfœrm], *vt.* confirmar.— **—ation** [kanfœrméiṣǫn], *s.* confirmación; ratificación.

confiscate [kánfiskeit], *vt.* confiscar.

conflagration [kanflǫgréiṣǫn], *s.* conflagración.

conflict [kánflikt], *s.* conflicto, choque, oposición.—*vi.* [kǫnflíkt], luchar, estar en pugna.— **—ing** [kǫnflíktiŋ], *a.* antagónico; contradictorio.

confluence [kánfluens], *s.* confluencia.

conform [kǫnfórm], *vt.* y *vi.* conformar(se), ajustar(se).— **—ity** [-iti], *s.* conformidad, concordancia; resignación.

confound [kǫnfáund], *vt.* confundir, aturrullar; trabucar.— **—ed** [-id], *a.* maldito, condenado.

confront [kǫnfrÁnt], *vt.* afrontar; confrontar; carear.

confuse [kǫnfiúz], *vt.* confundir.— **—d** [-d], *a.* confuso; confundido, turbado.—**confusing** [kǫnfiúziŋ], *a.* confuso, desconcertante.—**confusion** [kǫnfiúṣǫn], *s.* confusión, desorden.

congeal [kǫndżíl], *vt.* y *vi.* congelar(se), helar(se); cuajar(se).

congenial [kǫndżínjal], *a.* congenial; agradable, simpático.— **—ity** [kǫndżinjáliti], **—ness** [-nis], *s.* simpatía, congenialidad.

congest [kǫndżést], *vt.* y *vi.* congestionar(se), apiñar(se).— **—ed** [-id], *a.* congestionado, apiñado.— **—ion** [kǫndżéschǫn], *s.* congestión; apiñamiento.

congratulate [kǫngrǽchuleit], *vt.* felicitar, congratular.—*to c. on,* felicitar por.—**congratulation** [kǫngrǽchuléiṣǫn], *s.* felicitación, congratulación.

congregate [kángrigeit], *vt.* y *vi.* congregar(se).—**congregation** [kángrigéiṣǫn], *s.* congregación; asamblea, reunión; grey.

congress [káŋgris], *s.* convención, congreso, asamblea; (C.) Congreso, Parlamento.— **—ional** [kǫngrésiǫnal], *a.* perteneciente o relativo al congreso.— **—man** [káŋgrismǫn], **—woman** [káŋgriswumǫn], *s.* congresista, diputado; miembro de un congreso.

congruent [káŋgruent], *a.* congruente.

conjecture [kǫndżékchŭr], *s.* conjetura.—*vt.* conjeturar.

conjugate [kándzugeit], *vt.* conjugar.—

conjugation [kandzugéjʃən], *s.* conjugación.—**conjunction** [kəndžʎŋk-ʃən], *s.* conjunción; unión, liga.

conjuration [kandžuréjʃən], *s.* conjuro; sortilegio, encantamiento.—**conjure** [kəndžúr], *vt.* rogar o pedir con instancia, conjurar; [kándžu(r)], exorcizar.—*vi.* [kándžu(r)], conjurar; escamotear, hacer juegos de mano.

connect [kənékt], *vt.* y *vi.* conectar(se), unir(se), acoplar(se); relacionar(se); comunicar(se); entroncar(se); empalmar(se).— —**ion** [kənékʃən], *s.* conexión; enlace; relación, parentesco.

connivance [kənáivəns], *s.* connivencia. —**connive** [kənáiv], *vi.* hacer la vista gorda, tolerar.—**conniver** [kənáj-vœ(r)], *s.* consentidor, cómplice.

connoisseur [kanjsǽr], *s.* conocedor, perito.

conquer [kǽŋkœ(r)], *vt.* conquistar; vencer.—*vi.* triunfar.— —**ing** [-iŋ], *a.* conquistador, victorioso.— —**or** [-ǫ(r)], *s.* conquistador, vencedor.— **conquest** [kǽŋkwest], *s.* conquista.

conscience [kánʃəns], *s.* conciencia (moral).—**conscientious** [kanʃénʃʌs], *a.* concienzudo.—**conscious** [kánʃʌs], *a.* consciente.—**consciousness** [kán-ʃʌsnjs], *s.* conocimiento, sentido; conciencia.

conscript [kənskrípt], *vt.* reclutar, alistar.—*a.* y *s.* [kánskript], conscripto, recluta.— —**ion** [kənskrípʃən], *s.* conscripción, reclutamiento.

consecrate [kánsɛkrejt], *vt.* consagrar, santificar; ungir; dedicar; canonizar. —**consecration** [kansɛkréjʃən], *s.* consagración; dedicación; canonización.

consecutive [kənsékyutjv], *a.* consecutivo, sucesivo.

consent [kənsént], *s.* consentimiento, permiso, aquiescencia.—*by common c.*, de común acuerdo.—*vi.* consentir, acceder.

consequence [kánsɛkwens], *s.* consecuencia; importancia.—**consequent** [kánsɛkwent], *a.* y *s.* consecuente, consiguiente.

conservation [kansœrvéjʃən], *s.* conservación, preservación.—**conservative** [kənsœrvạtjv], *s.* y *a.* conservador.—**conservatory** [kənsœrvạtorj], *s.* conservatorio, academia; invernadero.—**conserve** [kənsœrv], *vt.* conservar, preservar; hacer conserva.— *s.* [kánsœrv], conserva, dulce.

consider [kənsídœ(r)], *vt.* considerar; tratar con respeto.—*vi.* pensar, reflexionar.— —**able** [-əbl], *a.* considerable; notable.— —**ate** [-it], *a.* considerado, (muy) mirado.— —**ation** [-éjʃən], *s.* consideración, miramiento;

deliberación.— —**ing** [-iŋ], *prep.* en atención a, considerando que, visto que, etc.

consign [kənsáin], *vt.* consignar; confiar, traspasar; relegar.— —**ment** [-mȩnt], *s.* (com.) consignación, partida, envío.

consist [kənsíst], *vi.* consistir (en), constar (de).— —**ence** [-ȩns], —**ency** [-ȩnsj], *s.* consistencia; consecuencia; firmeza, estabilidad.— —**ent** [-ȩnt], *a.* consecuente, conveniente; armonizable; coherente, consistente, denso.

consistory [kənsístorj], *s.* consistorio; asamblea, congreso.

consolation [kansoléjʃən], *s.* consuelo.— **console** [kənsóul], *vt.* consolar.—*s.* [kánsoul], consola.

consolidate [kənsálidejt], *vt.* y *vi.* consolidar(se); unir(se); fundir(se).— **consolidation** [kənsalidéjʃən], *s.* consolidación; unión; fusión.

consoling [kənsóuljŋ], *a.* consolador.

consonant [kánsonạnt], *s.* y *a.* consonante.

consort [kánsort], *s.* consorte, cónyuge. —*vi.* [kənsórt], asociarse; armonizar. —*vt.* asociar, casar.

conspicuous [kənspíkyuʌs], *a.* conspicuo, eminente, notorio, manifiesto.

conspiracy [kənspírasj], *s.* conspiración, complot.—**conspirator** [kənspírạto(r)], *s.* conspirador.—**conspire** [kənspáir], *vi.* conspirar.—*vt.* maquinar, tramar.

constable [kánstạbl], *s.* alguacil, agente de policía; condestable.

constancy [kánstạnsj], *s.* constancia; lealtad.—**constant** [kánstạnt], *a.* constante.—*s.* (mat.) constante.

constellation [kanstɛléjʃən], *s.* constelación.

consternation [kanstœrnéjʃən], *s.* consternación.

constipate [kánstipejt], *vt.* estreñir.— **constipation** [kanstipéjʃən], *s.* estreñimiento.

constituent [kənstíchuȩnt], *s.* elemento, ingrediente o componente.—*a.* constitutivo; constituyente (asamblea, etc.).—**constitute** [kánstitjut], *vt.* constituir, establecer.—**constitution** [kanstitúʃən], *s.* constitución; complexión, naturaleza (de una persona); estatutos.—**constitutional** [kanstitúʃənạl], *a.* constitucional; constituyente.—*s.* (fam.) paseo higiénico.

constrain [kənstréjn], *vt.* constreñir, compeler, forzar.— —**t** [-t], *s.* fuerza, constreñimiento.

construct [kənstrʌkt], *vt.* construir; fabricar.— —**ion** [kənstrʌ́kʃən], *s.* construcción.— —**ive** [kənstrʌ́ktjv], *a.* constructivo; provechoso, de utilidad positiva.

construe [kǫnstrú], *vt.* interpretar, explicar; inferir; construir, componer.

consul [kánsʌl], *s.* cónsul.— **—ar** [kánsjulǎ(r)], *a.* consular.— **—ate** [kánsjulĭt], *s.* consulado.

consult [kǫnsʌlt], *vt.* consultar.—*vi.* asesorarse, consultarse, aconsejarse (con); conferenciar.— **—ant** [-ạnt], **—er** [-œ(r)], *s.* consultante, consultor.— **—ation** [kansʌltéjṣǫn], *s.* consulta(ción), junta; deliberación.

consume [kǫnsjúm], *vt.* y *vi.* consumir(se).— **—r** [kǫnsjúmœ(r)], *s.* consumidor.

consummate [kánsʌmejt], *vt.* consumar, acabar, completar.—*a.* [kánsʌmĭt], consumado.— **consummation** [kansʌméjṣǫn], *s.* consumación.

consumption [kǫnsʌmpṣǫn], *s.* consunción; consumo, gasto; tisis.— **consumptive** [kǫnsʌmptĭv], *a.* consuntivo, destructivo.—*s.* y *a.* tísico.

contact [kántækt], *s.* contacto.—*pl.* relaciones.—*vt.* y *vi.* tocar(se), poner(se) en contacto.

contagion [kǫntéjdʒǫn], *s.* contagio; infección, peste.— **contagious** [kǫntéjdʒʌs], *a.* contagioso.

contain [kǫntéjn], *vt.* contener, caber, tener cabida para; abarcar; reprimir; ser exactamente divisible.— **—er** [-œ(r)], *s.* recipiente, vasija, envase.

contaminate [kǫntǽmĭnejt], *vt.* contaminar; viciar.— **contamination** [kǫntæmĭnéjṣǫn], *s.* contaminación.

contemplate [kántemplejt], *vt.* contemplar; proyectar, tener la intención de.— **contemplation** [kantempléjṣǫn], *s.* contemplación, especulación; intención, proyecto.

contemporary [kǫntémporerĭ], *a.* y *s.* contemporáneo, coetáneo.

contempt [kǫntémpt], *s.* desprecio, menosprecio, desdén.—*c. of court*, (for.) contumacia; rebeldía.— **—ible** [-ĭbl], *a.* despreciable, desdeñable.— **—uous** [kǫntémpchuʌs], *a.* desdeñoso, despreciativo.

contend [kǫnténd], *vt.* sostener o afirmar.—*vi.* contender.— **—er** [-œ(r)], *s.* contendiente, competidor.

content [kǫntént], *a.* contento, satisfecho.—*vt.* (com)placer, contentar.—*s.* contento, satisfacción; [kántent], cantidad, proporción; volumen.—*pl.* contenido.—*table of contents*, índice general.— **—ed** [kǫnténtĭd], *a.* contento, placentero.

contention [kǫnténṣǫn], *s.* contención, contienda; argumento; aseveración; tema.

contentment [kǫnténtmǫnt], *s.* contentamiento, satisfacción.

contest [kántest], *s.* contienda, debate; certamen, competencia; litigio.—*vt.*

[kǫntést], disputar; discutir; litigar.—*vi.* contender; competir; rivalizar con.— **contestant** [kǫntéstạnt], *s.* contendiente, opositor; litigante.

context [kántekst], *s.* contexto.

contiguous [kǫntígjuʌs], *a.* contiguo.

continent [kántĭnǫnt], *s.* continente.—*a.* casto, continente.— **—al** [kantĭnéntạl], *a.* continental.

contingency [kǫntíndʒensĭ], *s.* contingencia.— **contingent** [kǫntíndʒǫnt], *a.* y *s.* contingente.

continual [kǫntínyuạl], *a.* continuo, incesante.— **continuance** [kǫntínyuạns], *s.* (for.) aplazamiento; continuación.— **continuation** [kǫntínyuéjṣǫn], *s.* continuación, prolongación.— **continue** [kǫntínyu], *vt.* continuar; mantener, prolongar; (for.) aplazar.—*vi.* continuar; durar; proseguir.— **continuity** [kantĭnjúĭtĭ], *s.* continuidad; coherencia.— **continuous** [kǫntínyuʌs], *a.* continuo, ininterrumpido.

contour [kántur], *s.* contorno; curva de nivel.—*vt.* contorn(e)ar, perfilar.

contraband [kántrạbænd], *s.* contrabando.—*a.* prohibido, ilegal.— **—ist** [-ĭst], *s.* contrabandista.

contract [kántrækt], *s.* contrato, convenio, pacto, ajuste; contrata.—*vt.* [kǫntrǽkt], contratar, pactar; contraer (enfermedad, deuda, etc.).—*vi.* contraerse, encogerse; comprometerse por contrato.— **—ion** [kǫntrǽkṣǫn], *s.* contracción, encogimiento, estrechamiento.— **—or** [kǫntrǽktǫ(r)], *s.* contratista.

contradict [kantrạdíkt], *vt.* contradecir, desmentir, llevar la contraria a.— **—ion** [kantrạdíkṣǫn], *s.* contradicción.— **—ory** [kantradíktorĭ], *a.* contradictorio; contrario.

contrary [kántrerĭ], *a.* contrario; testarudo, porfiado.—*c.-minded*, de diversa opinión.—*s.* contrario.—*on the c.*, al contrario.

contrast [kántræst], *s.* contraste, contraposición.—*vt.* y *vi.* [kǫntrést], contrastar.

contribute [kǫntríbjut], *vt.* y *vi.* contribuir.— **contribution** [kantrĭbjúṣǫn], *s.* contribución; colaboración literaria, donativo.— **contributor** [kǫntríbjutǫ(r)], *s.* colaborador, contribuidor.

contrite [kántrajt], *a.* contrito.— **contrition** [kǫntríṣǫn], *s.* contrición.

contrivance [kǫntráivạns], *s.* idea, plan, invención; artefacto, dispositivo; traza, artificio; estratagema.— **contrive** [kǫntráiv], *vt.* idear, inventar; tramar, urdir.—*vi.* darse maña o trazas (de); maquinar.

control [kǫntróul], *s.* mando, dirección, dominio; influencia predominante;

regulación, inspección; restricción.— pl. mandos, controles.—a. regulador; de gobierno; de comprobación.—vti. [1] controlar, gobernar, dirigir, regular; tener a raya; tener predominancia en; reprimir, restringir.— —ler [-œ(r)], s. interventor, registrador, contralor; aparato de manejo y control.

controversy [kántrovœrsi], s. controversia, debate.

contumacy [kántiumasi], s. contumacia, terquedad.

contusion [kontúȝon], s. contusión.

convalesce [kanvalés], vi. convalecer.— —nce [kȯnvályȯns], s. convalecencia.— —nt [kanvalésȯnt], a. y s. convaleciente.

convene [kȯnvín], vt. convocar, citar; emplazar.—vi. reunirse.—convenience [kȯnvínyȯns], conveniency [kȯnvínyȯnsi], s. comodidad, conveniencia.—at one's earliest convenience, en la primera oportunidad que uno tenga, tan pronto como sea posible.—convenient [kȯnvínyȯnt], a. conveniente.

convent [kánvȯnt], s. convento, monasterio.

convention [kȯnvénȝon], s. convención, congreso; convenio; costumbre; convencionalismo.— —al [-al], a. convencional.

conversant [kánvœrsant], a. versado, experto, entendido.—conversation [kanvœrséiȝon], s. conversación, plática.—converse [kȯnvœrs], vi. conversar.—a. [kánvœrs], inverso, contrario.—s. (fam.) conversa; (lóg.) inversa, recíproca.

conversion [kȯnvœrȝon], s. conversión.— —convert [kȯnvœrt], vt. convertir; transmutar; reducir a; cambiar (valores).—vi. convertirse, transformarse.—s. [kánvœrt], neófito, converso.—convertible [kȯnvœrtibl], a. convertible, convertible.

convex [kánveks], a. convexo.

convey [kȯnvéi], vt. conducir, acarrear, transportar; transferir; transmitir, comunicar; dar a entender.— —ance [-ans], s. vehículo, conducción; transmisión; traspaso; escritura de traspaso.

convict [kánvikt], s. reo convicto; presidiario.—vt. [kȯnvíkt], condenar; probar la culpabilidad.— —ion [kȯnvíkȝon], s. convicción; fallo condenatorio.

convince [kȯnvíns], vt. convencer.— convincing [kȯnvínsiȵ], a. convincente.

convocation [kanvokéiȝon], s. convocación, llamamiento.—convoke [kȯnvóuk], vt. convocar, citar.

convoy [kȯnvói], vt. escoltar, convoyar.— s. [kánvoi], convoy, escolta.

convulsion [kȯnvÁlȝon], s. convulsión.— convulsive [kȯnvÁlsiv], a. convulsivo.

coo [ku], s. arrullo.—vi. arrullar, decir ternezas.

cook [kuk], vt. y vi. cocinar, cocer, guisar.—to c. up, tramar, urdir.—what's cooking? (fam.) ¿qué se trama? ¿qué pasa?—s. cocinero, cocinera.— —ery [kúkœri], s. arte de la cocina.— —ie [i], —y [i], s. gallet(it)a, bizcochito.— —ing [iȵ], s. arte culinario; cocción.— —a. de la cocina.—c. pan, cacerola, cazuela.

cool [kul], a. fresco; frío, indiferente; sereno.—c.-headed, sereno.—s. frescura.—vt. enfriar, refrescar.—to c. one's heels, hacer antesala, esperar mucho tiempo.—vi. enfriarse, calmarse.— —er [kúlœ(r)], s. enfriadera; enfriadero; refrigerante; nevera.— —ing [-iȵ], a. refrescante, refrigerante.— s. enfriamiento, refrigeración.— —ness [-nis], s. frialdad; sangre fría; tibieza, despego.

coon [kun], s. mapache o coatí.—old c., viejo marrullero.

coop [kup], s. jaula.—chicken c., gallinero.—vt. (in o up) enjaular, encerrar.

coöperate [koápȯreit], vi. cooperar.— coöperation [koapȯréiȝon], s. cooperación.—coöperative [koápȯrȧtiv], a. cooperativo, cooperante.—s. cooperativa.—coöperator [koápȯreitȯ(r)], s. cooperador.

coördinate [koɔ́rdineit], vt. coordinar.— s. [koɔ́rdinit], igual, semejante; coordenada.—a. coordenado; relativo a las coordenadas.—coördination [koordinéiȝon], s. coordinación.

cop [kap], s. (fam.) polizonte.—vti. [1] hurtar.

copartner [koupártnœ(r)], s. (con)socio; copartícipe.

cope [koup], vi. hacer frente a, habérselas con.—I cannot c. with this, no puedo con esto.

copilot [koupáilȯt], s. copiloto, segundo piloto.

copious [kóupiᴀs], a. copioso, abundante.

copper [kápœ(r)], s. cobre; (fam.) policía.—a. de cobre, cobrizo.— —smith [kápœrsmiθ], s. calderero.

copulation [kapyȯléiȝon], s. cópula o coito; unión.

copy [kápi], s. copia; ejemplar (de una obra); imitación; número de un periódico.—c. book, copiador (para cartas, cuentas, etc.); libreta, cuaderno.—vti. y vii. [7] copiar; imitar.— —right [-rait], s. derechos de propiedad (literaria, etc.).—vt. obtener la propiedad literaria.— **righted** [rai-tid], a. derechos registrados.

cord [kord], s. cordel, cuerda; tendón.

cordial [kórdżal], s. cordial, tónico.—a. cordial, sincero.— **ity** [kərdżæliti], s. cordialidad.

cordovan [kórdovan], s. cordobán.— (C.), a. y s. cordobés.

corduroy [kórduroi], s. pana.

core [kor], s. centro, corazón, parte central; fondo, núcleo.—vt. quitar el corazón o centro; despepitar (fruta).

cork [kork], s. corcho; tapón de corcho. —vt. tapar con corcho.— **screw** [kórkskru], s. tirabuzón, sacacorchos.

corn [korn], s. maíz; grano, cereal; callo (de los pies o manos).—c. cob, mazorca.—vt. salar, curar; granular.— **ed** [-d], a. acecinado, curado.—c. beef, cecina.

corner [kórnœr], s. esquina; rincón; recodo; aprieto o apuro; monopolio. —c. bracket, rinconera.—to cut corners, echar por el atajo, atajar; economizar.—to drive into a c., poner entre la espada y la pared.—vt. arrinconar, acorralar, poner en aprieto; copar; monopolizar.— **ed** [-d], a. anguloso, esquinado; acorralado, en aprietos; copado.— **stone** [-stoun], s. piedra angular; primera piedra.— **wise** [-waiz], adv. diagonalmente.

cornet [kornét], s. corneta; cornetín.

cornice [kórnis], s. cornisa.

corny [kórni], a. de maíz; de trigo; calloso; (coll.) afectado, exageradamente sentimental; inferior, de mala calidad o gusto; manido.

corolla [korálə], s. (bot.) corola.— **ry** [kárəleri], s. corolario.

coronation [karonéişon], s. coronación.

coroner [káronœr], s. médico forense.

corporal [kórporal], a. corporal, corpóreo.—s. (mil.) cabo.

corporation [korporéişon], s. corporación; sociedad mercantil; cuerpo, sociedad, gremio.

corps [kour], s. cuerpo o grupo organizado.—army c., cuerpo de ejército.

corpse [korps], s. cadáver.

corpuscle [kórpasl], s. corpúsculo.

corral [korél], vt. acorralar.—s. corral.

correct [korékt], vt. corregir; reprender, castigar; reparar, remediar.—a. exacto; correcto.— **ion** [korékşon], s. enmienda, corrección.— **ional** [korékşonal], a. correccional, penal. — **ness** [koréktnis], s. corrección.— **or** [-ǫr], s. revisor, corrector.

correlate [kárəleit], vt. correlacionar.— vi. tener correlación.—**correlative** [korélativ], a. y s. correlativo.— **correlation** [karəléişon], s. correlación.

correspond [korɛspánd], vi. corresponder; mantener correspondencia.— **ence** [-ɛns], **ency** [-ɛnsi], s. correspondencia; reciprocidad.— **ent** [-ɛnt], a. correspondiente.—s. corresponsal, correspondiente.

corridor [kárido(r)], s. corredor, galería, pasillo.

corroborate [korábóreit], vt. corroborar, confirmar.— **corroboration** [koraboréişon], s. corroboración.

corrode [koróud], vt. y vi. corroer(se).— **corrosive** [koróusiv], a. corrosivo; mordaz.

corrugation [karugéişon], s. corrugamiento; contracción.

corrupt [korápt], a. corrompido; depravado.—vt. corromper.—vi. corromperse, podrirse.— **ion** [korápşon], s. corrupción.

cortege [kortéż], s. comitiva, séquito.

cortisone [kórtisoun], s. cortisona.

corvette [korvét], s. (mar.) corbeta.

cosmetic [kazmétik], a. y s. cosmético.— cosmical(al) [kázmik(ạl)], a. cósmico.

cosmopolitan [kazmopálitạn], **cosmopolite** [kazmápolait], a. y s. cosmopolita.

cost [kost], s. costo, coste, costa; precio, importe.—at all costs, a toda costa.— vii. [9] costar.—pret. y pp. de to cost.— **liness** [kóstlinis], s. suntuosidad, carestía.— **ly** [-li], a. costoso, caro.

costume [kástium], s. vestuario; disfraz.

cot [kat], s. cabaña, choza; catre, camilla.

coterie [kóuteri], s. camarilla, claque.

cottage [kátidż], s. casita, cabaña, choza; casa de campo.—c. cheese, requesón.

cotton [káton], s. algodón (planta y fibra); ropa o género de algodón.— c. belt, (E.U.), región algodonera.— c. wool, algodón en rama.—c. yarn, hilaza.

couch [kauch], s. diván.

cough [kof], s. tos.—c. drop, pastilla para la tos.—whooping c., tosferina. —vi. toser.—to c. up, expectorar; (fam.) pagar.— **ing** [kófiŋ], s. acceso de tos.

could [kud], pret. de CAN.

council [káunsil], s. concilio; consejo; concejo.—city c., consejo municipal. —c. of war, consejo de guerra.— **man** [-man], s. concejal.— **(l)or** [-ǫr)], s. concejal; consejero.

counsel [káunsel], s. consejo; deliberación; dictamen; abogado consultor.— vti. [2] aconsejar, recomendar; asesorar.— **(l)or** [-ǫ(r)], s. consultor; asesor.—c. at law, abogado.

count [kaunt], vt. contar, numerar, calcular.—vi. valer.—to count on o *upon*, contar con, confiar en.—*s.* cuenta, cómputo; conde; acusación, cargo.

countenance [káuntenans], *s.* semblante, cara; talante, aspecto.—*out of c.*, desconcertado.—*to give c.* apoyar, favorecer.—*vt.* aprobar; apoyar.

counter [káuntœ(r)], *s.* mostrador, tablero; ficha; contador.—*adv.* contra, al contrario, en contra.—*to run c. to*, oponerse, violar.—*a.* contrario. —*vt.* contradecir; rechazar; prevenir. —*vi.* oponerse.

counteract [kauntœrǽkt], *vt.* contrariar; neutralizar, contrarrestar.

counterattack [kauntœratǽk], *vt. y vi.* contraatacar, hacer un contraataque. —*s.* contraataque.

counterbalance [kauntœrbǽlans], *vt.* contrapesar, compensar.—*s.* [káuntœrbælans], contrapeso, equilibrio, compensación.

counterfeit [káuntœrfjt], *vt.* falsificar.— *s.* falsificador, moneda falsa.—*a.* falsificado.—**counterfeiter** [káuntœrfjtœ(r)], *s.* falsificador, monedero falso.

countermand [kauntœrmǽnd], *s.* contraorden.—*vt.* revocar.

countermarch [káuntœrmarch], *s.* contramarcha.

counterpart [káuntœrpart], *s.* contraparte.

counterpoint [káuntœrpojnt], *s.* contrapunto.

counterrevolution [kauntœrrevoljúṣ̌ọn], *s.* contrarrevolución.

counterstroke [káuntœrstrouk], *s.* contragolpe.

countess [káuntjs], *s.* condesa.

countless [káuntljs], *a.* innumerable, sin cuento.

country [kántrj], *s.* país, nación; región, tierra, patria; campo.—*a.* campestre. —*— man* [-mạn], *s.* compatriota, coterráneo; campesino, aldeano.— *—side* [-sạjd], *s.* campo; distrito rural.

county [káuntj], *s.* condado, jurisdicción.—*c. seat*, cabecera de distrito o jurisdicción.

couple [kápl], *s.* pareja, par.—*vt.* acoplar, (a)parear.—*vi.* acoplarse, formar pareja.—**coupling** [kápljŋ], *s.* acoplamiento; cópula; unión, junta.

courage 'kœrjdʒ], *s.* coraje, valor.— *—ous* [kΛréjdʒΛs], *a.* corajudo, valiente, valeroso. —**ousness** [kΛréjdʒΛsnjs], *s.* valor, brío.

courier [kúrjœ(r)], *s.* mensajero, propio.

course [kors], *s.* curso; marcha; rumbo, dirección; progreso.—*in due c.*, a su tiempo.—*matter of c.*, cosa de cajón, de rutina.—*of c.*, por supuesto, desde luego, etc.

court [kort], *s.* tribunal de justicia, juzgado, corte, audiencia; pista, cancha, campo de juego (tenis, etc.); séquito; patio, plazoleta; cortejo, galanteo.—*to pay c. to*, hacer la corte a.—*to put out of c.*, demostrar la falsedad de.—*vt.* cortejar, galantear; atraerse, captar.

courteous [kœrtjΛs], *a.* cortés.—**courtesy** [kœrtẹsj], *s.* cortesía; reverencia.

courtier [kórtjœ(r)], *s.* cortesano; palaciego.

courtship [kórtṣ̌jp], *s.* cortejo, galanteo.

courtyard [kórtyard], *s.* patio, atrio.

cousin [kázjn], *s.* primo o prima.— *first c.*, primo hermano o carnal.

couturier [kutyryé], *s.* modisto.

cove [kouv], *s.* cala, ensenada.

covenant [kávenạnt], *s.* contrato, convenio, pacto; escritura de contrato.

cover [kávœ(r)], *vt.* cubrir; tapar, ocultar; cobijar, proteger; forrar; abarcar; recorrer (distancias, etc.); empollar; ponerse el sombrero; (con *up*) encubrir.—*s.* cubierta, tapa; forro; envoltura; capa, pretexto; albergue; cubierto; funda; cartera, tapete.— *c. charge*, (precio de) cubierto (en restaurantes, etc.).—*to take c.*, buscar abrigo.—*—ing* [-jŋ], *s.* funda, cubierta; envoltura; ropa, abrigo.—*—t* [kávœrt], *a.* encubierto, disimulado.

covet [kávjt], *vt.* codiciar.—*—ous* [-Λs], *a.* codicioso.

cow [kau], *s.* vaca; hembra de otros cuadrúpedos grandes (elefantes, etc.). —*vt.* acobardar, intimidar.

coward [káuạrd], *a. y s.* cobarde.—**—ice** [-js], **—liness** [-ljnjs], *s.* cobardía.

cowbell [káubel], *s.* cencerro.—**cowboy** [káubɔj], *s.* vaquero, montero.

cower [káuœ(r)], *vi.* agacharse; aplastarse de miedo.

cowhide [káuhạjd], *s.* cuero, vaqueta.

cowpox [káupaks], *s.* vacuna.—**cowshed** [káuṣ̌ed], *s.* establo de vacas.

coxcomb [kákskoum], *s.* petimetre.

coy [kɔj], **coyish** [kójjṣ̌], *a.* recatado, modesto; tímido.

cozy, cozey [kóuzj], *a.* cómodo, agradable.

crab [krǽb], *s.* cangrejo; (fig.) cascarrabias.—*c. apple*, manzana silvestre. —*a.* agrio, áspero.—*vii.* [1] regañar, estar de mal humor; pescar crustáceos.

crack [krǽk], *s.* grieta, rajadura; crujido, chasquido; trueno, estampido; chanza.—*at the c. of dawn*, al romper el día.—*a.* de calidad superior.—*c. shot*, tirador certero.—*vt.* romper; rajar; chasquear, restallar; crujir; trastornar.—*to c. jokes*, gastar bromas.—*vi.* agrietarse; rajarse, partirse; traquetear.—*—ed* [-t], *a.* agrietado, cuarteado; chiflado; (voz) cascada, desapacible.— —er [krǽkœ(r)], s. galleta, bizcocho; triquitraque.— —le [krǽkl], vt. hacer crujir.—vi. crujir, crepitar, restallar.—s. crujido, crepitación.

cradle [kréjdl], s. cuna.—vt. acunar.—vi. mecerse en la cuna.

craft [krǽft], s. artificio; maña, habilidad; arte u oficio; gremio; embarcación, embarcaciones.— —sman [krǽftsmąn], s. artífice, artesano.— —y [-i], a. astuto, taimado.

crag [krǽg], s. despeñadero, risco.— —gy [krǽgi], a. escarpado.

cram [krǽm], vti. y vii. [1] rellenar(se), hartar(se), atracar(se); cebar(se); (fig.) preparar(se) rápidamente para un examen.

cramp [krǽmp], s. calambre; grapa.—a. contraído, apretado.—vt. comprimir, apretar; estrechar; sujetar con grapa.

cranberry [krǽnberi], s. arándano agrio de los pantanos.

crane [krejn], s. grulla; grúa.—vt. levantar con la grúa; estirar, extender (el cuello).—vi. estirarse, alargarse.

cranium [kréjnįʌm], s. cráneo.

crank [krǽŋk], s. manija, manubrio; biela; cigüeña, manivela; maniático, caprichoso; capricho, chifladura.—c. axle, cigüeñal.— —case [krǽŋkkejs], s. cárter del cigüeñal.— —shaft [-ṣæft], s. cigüeñal.— —y [-i], a. chiflado.

cranny [krǽnį], s. grieta, resquicio.

crape [krejp], s. = CREPE.

crash [krǽš], vi. romperse, caerse estrepitosamente, estrellarse; estallar; quebrar; aterrizar violentamente.—vt. romper o despedazar estrepitosamente, estrellar; echar a pique.—to c. the gate, colarse.—s. estallido, estampido, estrépito; quiebra; aterrizaje violento; choque, estrellamiento.

crate [krejt], s. canasto, jaula de embalaje; huacal.—vt. embalar (en huacales, etc.).

crater [kréjtœ(r)], s. cráter.

cravat [kravǽt], s. corbata; chalina.

crave [krejv], vt. anhelar, desear; apetecer vehementemente.—vi. pedir o desear con vehemencia, suspirar por.

craven [kréjvįn], a. cobarde.

crawl [krol], vi. arrastrarse, andar a gatas; serpear; humillarse; ir a paso de tortuga.—s. arrastramiento; natación marinera.

crayon [kréjǫn], s. lápiz de color, creyón; tiza; dibujo al pastel.

craze [krejz], vt. y vi. enloquecer(se).—s. locura, manía; moda.— —d [-d], a.

enloquecido, loco.—crazy [kréjzį], a. loco.

creak [krik], vi. crujir, rechinar, chirriar.—s. crujido, rechinamiento.

cream [krim], s. crema, nata.—cold c., crema cosmética.—vi. criar nata.—vt. desnatar.— —ery [krímœri], s. lechería.— —y [-i], a. cremoso.

crease [kris], s. pliegue; arruga; raya (del pantalón, etc.).—vt. y vi. plegar(se); arrugar(se).

create [krįéjt], vt. crear o criar.—creation [krįéjšǫn], s. creación.—creative [krįéjtįv], a. creador.—creativeness [krįéjtįvnįs], s. facultad creadora.—creator [krįéjtǫ(r)], s. creador.—the C., el Creador, Dios.—creature [kríchǫ(r)], s. criatura.

creche [krejš], s. (igl.) belén, nacimiento.

credence [krídęns], s. creencia; crédito.—credentials [krędénšalz], s. pl. cartas credenciales.

credit [krédįt], s. crédito, fe; (com.) activo, haber.—on c., al fiado, a plazos.—vt. creer; atribuir; reconocer; acreditar; abonar en cuenta; dar al fiado.— —able [-ạbl], a. estimable, loable.— —ed [-įd], a. acreditado.— —or [-ǫ(r)], s. acreedor.

credulous [krédjulas], a. crédulo.

creed [krid], s. credo, creencia.

creek [krik], s. cala; riachuelo, arroyo.

creep [krip], vii. [10] arrastrarse; gatear; trepar; moverse cautelosamente; someterse abyectamente.—s. arrastramiento.—pl. hormigueo; pavor.— —er [krípœ(r)], s. reptil; enredadera; trepadora, trepador.

cremate [krímejt], vt. incinerar.

cremation [krįméjšǫn], s. incineración.

creole [kríǫul], s. y a. criollo.

crepe [krejp], s. crespón, cendal.

crept [krept], pret. y pp. de TO CREEP.

crepuscular [krepʌskjulạ(r)], a. crepuscular.—crepuscule [krepʌskjul], s. crepúsculo.

crescent [krésęnt], a. creciente.—s. (cuarto) creciente; media luna.

cress [kres], s. mastuerzo, berro.

crest [krest], s. cresta; penacho; cima; blasón.— —fallen [kréstfolęn], a. cabizbajo, abatido.

cretonne [krítan], s. (tej.) cretona.

crevice [krévįs], s. hendedura, grieta, rendija.

crew [kru], s. tripulación o dotación; marinería; cuadrilla de obreros.—pret. de TO CROW.

crib [krįb], s. pesebre; camita de niño; granero; arcón; cascucha; plagio.—vti. [1] hurtar; plagiar; enjaular; estribar.

cricket [kríkit], s. grillo; cri(c)quet.

crime [krajm], s. crimen, delito.—

criminal [krímiṇaḷ], *a.* y *s.* criminal.

crimp [krimp], *vt.* rizar, encrespar, engrifar.—*a.* rizado.—*s.* rizo.

crimson [krímzọṇ], *a.* y *s.* carmesí.

cripple [krípḷ], *s.* cojo o manco; tullido. —*vt.* lisiar, derrengar, baldar.

crisis [kráịsịs], (*pl.* **crises** [kráịsiz]) *s.* crisis.

crisp [krisp], *a.* quebradizo; tostado; crespo; vivo, animado.—*vt.* encrespar; hacer frágil.— **—y** [kríspị], *a.* crespo, frágil; fresco.

criterion [kraịtíriọṇ], *s.* criterio.

critic [krítịk], *s.* crítico; censor; crítica.— **—al** [-ạḷ], *a.* crítico, criticón; difícil; decisivo.— **—ism** [krítịsịzm], *s.* crítica; juicio crítico; censura.— **—ize**, **—ise** [krítịsaịz], *vi.* criticar.—*vt.* censurar, fiscalizar.

croak [kroụk], *vi.* graznar; croar; gruñir.—*s.* graznido, canto de ranas.

crock [krak], *s.* vasija de barro.— **—ery** [krákœrị], *s.* loza, cacharros.

crocodile [krákodaịl], *s.* cocodrilo; caimán.

crook [kṛụk], *s.* falsario, estafador; fullero; maleante; gancho, curva-(tura).—*vt.* y *vi.* encorvar(se); torcer-(se).— **—ed** [kṛúkịd], *a.* encorvado; torcido; pícaro.

crop [krap], *s.* cosecha; látigo; buche de ave.—*vti.* [1] segar, cosechar.—*vii.* dar frutos.

croquette [kroụkét], *s.* (coc.) croqueta.

crosier [krúʒœ(r)], *s.* báculo pastoral.

cross [kros], *s.* cruz (sentidos recto y figurado); cruce; querella, encuentro; cruzamiento (de razas).—*a.* relativo o perteneciente a la cruz; atravesado, transversal; cruzado; malhumorado. —*c.-eyed*, bizco.—*crossword puzzle*, crucigrama.—*vt.* cruzar, atravesar; marcar con una cruz; cruzar (razas); eliminar tachando; poner el trazo transversal a una letra; santiguarse; hacerse cruces.—*vi.* cruzarse.— **—bar** [krósbar], *s.* travesaño.— **—beam** [-bim], *s.* viga transversal.

crossing [krósịŋ], *s.* cruce, intersección; paso, vado; travesía, acción de cruzar; cruzamiento (razas); santiguamiento.—**crossroad** [krósroụd], *s.* cruce de dos caminos.

crouch [krauch], *vi.* agacharse, agazaparse; rebajarse.

crow [kroụ], *s.* cuervo; canto del gallo. —*c.'s foot*, pata de gallo (arrugas).— *vii.* [5] cantar el gallo.—*vi.* cantar victoria, alardear.— **—bar** [króụbar], *s.* barra o palanca de hierro.

crowd [kraud], *s.* gentío, multitud; apiñamiento.—*vt.* amontonar, apiñar. —*vi.* apiñarse.— **—ed** [kráụdịd], *a.* apiñado; lleno de bote en bote.

crown [kraụn], *s.* corona; diadema;

guirnalda; monarca; soberanía; coronilla; copa de sombrero; cima.—*vt.* coronar.

crucible [krúsịbl], *s.* crisol.

crucifix [krúsịfịks], *s.* crucifijo.—**crucify** [krúsịfaị], *vti.* [7] crucificar.

crude [krud], *a.* crudo; imperfecto; tosco.— **—ness** [krúdnịs], *s.* crudeza, tosquedad.

cruel [krúẹḷ], *a.* cruel.— **—ty** [-tị], *s.* crueldad.

cruet [krúịt], *s.* ampoll(et)a; vinajera; vinagrera.—*c. stand*, convoy de mesa.

cruise [kruz], *vi.* cruzar, viajar de crucero; andar de un lado a otro.—*s.* crucero, viaje.—*cruising speed*, velocidad de crucero.— **—r** [krúzœ(r)], *s.* (mar.) crucero.

crumb [kram], *s.* migaja, migajón; pizca.—*vt.* desmig(aj)ar; desmenuzar. — **—le** [krámbl], *vt.* desmigar, desmenuzar.—*vi.* desmoronarse.

crumple [krámpl], *vt.* arrugar.—*vi.* contraerse, apabullarse.

crunch [kranch], *vi.* crujir; mascullar.— *vt.* tascar; cascar.—*s.* crujido.

crusade [kruséịd], *s.* cruzada.— **—r** [kruséịdœ(r)], *s.* cruzado.

crush [kraš], *vt.* romper por compresión; aplastar, machacar; estrujar; majar; abrumar.—*vi.* aplastarse; romperse o deformarse por compresión.—*s.* estrujamiento o deformación por compresión o choque.

crust [kṛast], *s.* costra; postilla; corteza (pan, queso, etc.); mendrugo; carapacho, concha.—*vt.* encostrar, incrustrar.—*vi.* encostrarse.

crustacean [kṛastéịšiạṇ], *a.* y *s.* crustáceo.

crusty [krástị], *a.* costroso; sarroso; brusco, malhumorado.

crutch [kṛach], *s.* muleta; arrimo; muletilla; horquilla; horcajadura, entrepierna.

cry [kraị], *vti.* y *vii.* [7] gritar; llorar; exclamar; lamentarse; vocear; pregonar.—*s.* grito; lloro, llanto; pregón.— *a far c. from*, muy lejos de.— **—ing** [kráịịŋ], *a.* llorón, gritón; enorme; urgente.

crypt [kript], *s.* gruta, cripta.— **—ic** [kríptịk], *a.* enigmático, oculto.

crystal [krístạḷ], *s.* cristal; cristal de roca; cristal de reloj.—*a.* de cristal. — **—line** [-ịn], *a.* cristalino.— **—lization** [-ịzéịšọṇ], *s.* cristalización.— **—lize** [-aịz], *vt.* y *vi.* cristalizar(se).

cub [kab], *s.* cachorro (de fiera).

Cuban [kiúbạṇ], *a.* y *s.* cubano.

cube [kịub], *s.* cubo.—*c. root*, raíz cúbica.—**cubic** [kịúbịk], *a.* cúbico.

cuckold [kákọld], *s.* marido cornudo, cabrón, cuclillo.—*vt.* encornudar.

cuckoo [kúku], *s.* cuco; cucú (canto).—
a. (fam.) chiflado.
cucumber [kiúkΛmbœ(r)], *s.* pepino.—
cool as a c., fresco como una lechuga.
cud [kΛd], *s.* rumia.—*c.-chewing,* rumiante.—*to chew the c.,* rumiar;
charlar.
cuddle [kΛdl], *vt.* abrazar con ternura;
acariciar, mimar.—*vi.* abrazarse;
estar abrazados.—*s.* abrazo.
cudgel [kΛdżęl], *s.* garrote, estaca,
porra, cachiporra.
cue [kiu], *s.* señal, indicación; (teat.)
pie, apunte; indirecta, sugestión.—
billiard c., taco de billar.
cuff [kΛf], *s.* trompada; puño de camisa;
bocamanga; vuelta del pantalón.—*c.*
buttons o *links,* gemelos.—*pl.* manillas, esposas.—*vt.* abofetear; maniatar.—*vi.* darse puñetazos.
culinary [kiúlineri], *a.* culinario.
culminate [kΛlmineit], *vi.* culminar.—
culmination [kΛlminéişǫn], *s.* culminación.
culprit [kΛlprit], *s.* reo, delincuente,
culpable.
cult [kΛlt], *s.* culto, devoción; secta.
cultivate [kΛltiveit], *vt.* cultivar.—
cultivation [kΛltivéişǫn], *s.* cultivo.—
cultivator [kΛltiveitǫ(r)], *s.* labrador,
cultivador; máquina cultivadora.
culture [kΛlchǫ(r)], *s.* cultura; cultivo
(de bacterias, etc.).—**d** [-d], *a.*
culto, cultivado.
cumbersome [kΛmbœ(r)sΛm], *a.* pesado, engorroso.
cumulus [kiúmyǫlΛs], *s.* montón;
(meteor.) cúmulo.
cunning [kΛniŋ], *a.* astuto; socarrón;
sutil; sagaz; gracioso, mono (aplícase
a los niños).—*s.* astucia; sagacidad.
cup [kΛp], *s.* taza, jícara, pocillo;
cubeta; cáliz; trago; (deportes) copa.
—**board** [kΛbǫrd], *s.* aparador.
cupola [kiúpolǎ], *s.* (arq.) cúpula, domo.
cur [kœr], *s.* perro callejero; canalla,
bellaco.
curate [kiúrit], *s.* cura.—**curator** [kiúreitǫ(r)], *s.* conservador (de museo).
curb [kœrb], *s.* borde o encintado (de
la acera); freno, restricción; barbada;
brocal de pozo.—*vt.* refrenar, contener; poner freno o coto a.
curd [kœrd], *s.* cuajada; requesón.—*vt.*
y vi. cuajar(se), coagular(se).—**le**
[kœrdl], *vt. y vi.* cuajar(se), coagular
(se); helar(se).
cure [kiur], *s.* cura, curación; remedio.
—*vt.* curar; vulcanizar.—*vi.* vulcanizarse; curarse; sanarse.
curfew [kœrfiu], *s.* toque de queda.
curio [kiúriou], *s.* objeto curioso y raro.
— **sity** [kiuriásiti], *s.* curiosidad;
rareza.— **us** [kiúriΛs], *a.* curioso;
entremetido; cuidadoso; raro.

curl [kœrl], *s.* bucle, rizo; ondulación.—
vt. rizar; fruncir.—*vi.* enroscarse;
rizarse.
curlew [kœrliu], *s.* chorlito.
curly [kœrlj], *a.* rizado, crespo.
currant [kœrant], *s.* grosella.
currency [kœrensi], *s.* moneda corriente; dinero en circulación; uso
corriente; valor corriente.—**current**
[kœrent], *a.* corriente, común; actual,
en curso.—*c. account,* cuenta corriente.—*c. events,* asuntos de actualidad.—*s.* corriente (de aire, agua,
etc.).—*direct c.,* corriente continua.
curriculum [kΛríkyǫlΛm], *s.* plan de
estudios.
curse [kœrs], *vt.* maldecir.—*vi.* renegar;
blasfemar.—*s.* maldición; terno.—**d**
[kœrsjd], *a.* maldito.
curt [kœrt], *a.* brusco; conciso.— **ail**
[kœrtéjl], *vt.* cortar; abreviar; restringir.
curtain [kœrtin], *s.* cortina; (teat.)
telón.—*pl.* cortinaje.
curvature [kœrvachǫ(r)], *s.* curvatura,
encorvamiento.—**curve** [kœrv], *vt.*
curvar, combar, encorvar.—*vi.* encorvarse; torcerse.—*s.* curva; curvadura, comba.—**curved** [kœrvd], *a.*
curvo; encorvado; combado.
cushion [kúşǫn], *s.* cojín; almohadilla;
almohadón; amortiguador.—*vt.* acojinar, suavizar, amortiguar.
cusp [kΛsp], *s.* cúspide.
custard [kΛstǎrd], *s.* flan, natillas.—*c.*
apple, guanábana, anona.
custody [kΛstodi], *s.* custodia, guardia.
custom [kΛstǫm], *s.* costumbre; usanza;
clientela o parroquia.—*c.-made,* hecho
especialmente.—*pl.* derechos de
aduana o arancelarios.— **ary** [-eri],
a. habitual, acostumbrado.— **er**
[-œ(r)], *s.* parroquiano, cliente.—
shouse [-shaǫs], *s.* aduana.
cut [kΛt], *vti.* [9] cortar; dividir, partir;
rebanar; grabar; labrar, tallar; segar;
desbastar; recortar; negar el saludo a;
cortar los naipes; rebajar, reducir
(sueldos, gastos, etc.); cortar (trajes).
—*to c. across,* cruzar, atravesar, cortar al través.—*to c. a figure,* descollar;
hacer buen papel.—*to c. asunder,*
separar cortando, despedazar.—*to c.*
away, recortar.—*to c. capers,* hacer
cabriolas.—*to c. down,* tumbar; talar;
mermar, rebajar, cercenar.—*to c. off,*
cercenar; aislar; interceptar (la
comunicación); interrumpir; suspender los abastecimientos; des_heredar.—*to c. up,* trinchar; despedazar.
—*vii.* hacer un corte o incisión; ser
cortante.—*pret. y pp.* de TO CUT.—*s.*
corte; cortadura, incisión; tajo;
ofensa; cosa o palabra hiriente;
ausencia (de una clase, etc.); pedazo,

cosa cortada; atajo; rebaja (sueldos, gastos, etc.); clisé, grabado; talla.—*a.* cortado.—*c. and dried*, preparado, convenido de antemano.

cute [kjut], *a.* lindo, mono, gracioso; listo.

cuticle [kjútjkl], *s.* cutícula; película.

cutler [kátlœ(r)], *s.* cuchillero.— —y [-j], *s.* cuchillería, cuchillos; tienda del cuchillero.

cutlet [kátljt], *s.* chuleta.

cutter [kátœ(r)], *s.* cortador; herramienta o máquina para cortar.— **cutting** [kátjŋ], *a.* cortante; de cortar; incisivo, mordaz.—*s.* cortadura; corte; incisión.

cuttlefish [kátlfjʃ], *s.* (ict.) pulpo.

cycle [sájkl], *s.* ciclo; bicicleta.—*vi.* andar en bicicleta.—**cycling** [sájkljŋ], *s.* ciclismo.

cyclone [sájkloun], *s.* ciclón.

cyclotron [sájklotran], *s.* ciclotrón.

cylinder [síljndœ(r)], *s.* cilindro; rodillo; tambor.

cymbal [símbal], *s.* címbalo, platillo.

cynic [sínjk], *s.* cínico.— —al [-al], *a.* cínico.— —ism [sínjsjzm], *s.* cinismo.

cypress [sájpres], *s.* ciprés.

Czech [chɛk], *s. y a.* checo.— —oslovak-(ian) [-oslovák(jan)], *s. y a.* checo(e)-slovaco.

D

dabble [dæbl], *vt.* rociar; mojar.—*to d. in*, meterse en.— —r [dæblœ(r)], *s.* aficionado, diletante.

dad [dæd], **daddie, daddy** [dædj], *s.* papá, papaíto; (Am.) papacito, tata.

dado [déjdou], *s.* (arq.) rodapié.

daffodil [dæfodjl], *s.* narciso.

dagger [dægœ(r)], *s.* daga, puñal.

daily [déilj], *a.* diario, cotidiano, diurno.—*s.* periódico diario.—*adv.* diariamente.

daintiness [déjntjnjs], *s.* delicadeza, elegancia.—**dainty** [déjntj], *a.* delicado, elegante, refinado; sabroso; melindroso.—*s.* bocado exquisito, golosina.

dairy [dérj], *s.* lechería; quesería; vaquería.

daisy [déjzj], *s.* margarita; (fam.) primor.

dale [deil], *s.* valle; cañada.

dam [dæm], *s.* (re)presa, embalse, dique; central hidroeléctrica.—*vti.* [1] represar, embalsar.

damage [dæmjdʒ], *s.* daño, perjuicio, deterioro; pérdida; avería.—*pl.* daños y perjuicios.—*vt.* dañar, averiar, deteriorar; perjudicar, damnificar.— *vi.* dañarse, averiarse.

dame [déjm], *s.* dama, señora; (col.) tía, fulana.

damn [dæm], *vt.* maldecir; reprobar. —*d. it!* ¡maldito sea!—*vi.* renegar, maldecir.—*s.* maldición.

damp [dæmp], *a.* húmedo, mojado.—*s.* humedad; desaliento.—**d. o dampen** [dæmpen], *vt.* humedecer, mojar; desanimar, desalentar; amortiguar. —*vi.* humedecerse.— —er [-œ(r)], *a.* registro, regulador de tiro de chimenea; sordina; desalentador; amortiguador.— —ness [-njs], *s.* humedad, relente.

damsel [dæmzel], *s.* damisela, doncella.

dance [dæns], *vi.* bailar, danzar.—*s.* danza, baile.— —r [dænsœ(r)], *s.* bailarín(a); bailador(a).

dandelion [dændjlajon], *s.* (bot.) diente de león.

dandruff [dændrʌf], *s.* caspa.

dandy [dændj], *s.* dandi, petimetre, lechuguino.—*a.* (fam.) excelente, magnífico.

Dane [dejn], *s.* danés, dinamarqués. —*great D.*, perro danés.

danger [déjndʒœ(r)], *s.* peligro, riesgo.— —ous [-ʌs], *a.* peligroso, arriesgado; grave, de cuidado.

dangle [dængl], *vt.* colgar, suspender. —*vi.* pender, bambolearse; andar al retortero.

Danish [déjnjʃ], *a.* danés, dinamarqués. —*s.* danés; lengua danesa.

dapple(d) [dæpl(d)], *a.* rodado, tordo, con manchas, salpicado.

dare [der], *vii.* [5] osar, atreverse, arriesgarse.—*vti.* retar, desafiar; provocar.—*s.* reto, desafío.— —**devil** [dérdevjl], *a. y s.* temerario, osado. —**daring** [dérjn], *a.* osado, temerario; denodado.—*s.* osadía, bravura.

dark [dark], *a.* oscuro; trigueño, moreno; sombrío, tenebroso; siniestro. —*to be left in the d.*, dejar en ayunas, en la ignorancia.—*to grow d.*, anochecer, oscurecer.—*to keep it d.*, ocultar algo.—*s.* oscuridad; tinieblas; noche; anochecer; ignorancia, secreto.— —en [dárkn], *vt.* oscurecer, ensombrecer; cegar; nublar; denigrar, manchar.—*vi.* oscurecerse, nublarse.— —ness [-njs], *s.* oscuridad, sombra, tinieblas; ofuscación; ceguera; ignorancia.

darling [dárljŋ], *a.* querido, amado.—*s.* querido, el predilecto.—*my d.*, vida mía, amor mío.—*you are a d.*, eres un encanto.

darn [darn], *vt.* zurcir, remendar; (fam.) maldecir.—*s.* zurcido.—*I don't give a d.*, me importa un bledo.

darnel [dárnel], *s.* (bot.) cizaña.

darning [dárnjŋ], *s.* zurcido, remiendo.

dart [dart], *s.* dardo, saeta; banderilla; movimiento rápido; (cost.) sisa.— *d. thrower*, banderillero.—*vt.* lanzar, flechar.—*vi.* lanzarse, precipitarse.

dash [dæʃ], *vt.* arrojar, tirar, lanzar; estrellar, romper; magullar; frustrar (esperanzas); rociar, salpicar; sazonar.—*to d. out*, tachar.—*to d. to pieces*, hacer añicos.—*vi.* chocar, estrellarse; lanzarse; saltar.—*s.* arremetida; ataque; choque, embate; guión, raya; energía; condimento; poquito, pizca; carrera corta.— **—board** [dǽʃbord], *s.* (aut.) tablero de instrumentos.

data [déitạ, détạ], *s.* (*pl.* de DATUM [déitʌm]) datos, antecedentes.

date [deit], *s.* fecha; cita, compromiso; época; (bot.) dátil.—*d. palm*, palma datilera.—*down to d.*, hasta la fecha, hasta ahora.—*out of d.*, anticuado, pasado de moda.—*up to d.*, hasta ahora; *al día.*—*vt.* datar, fechar; computar; dar cita a uno.—*vi.* (con *from*) datar de (de), remontarse a.

datum [déitʌm], *s.* dato.

daub [dɔb], *vt* embadurnar; untar; pintarrajear.

daughter [dótœ(r)], *s.* hija.—*d.-in-law*, nuera.

dawn [dɔn], *vi.* amanecer, alborear, clarear; asomar, mostrarse.—*to d. (up)on*, ocurrírsele a uno, caer en la cuenta.—*s.* alba, aurora, madrugada; albores.— **—ing** [dónịŋ], *s.* alborada.

day [dei], *s.* día.—*d. after tomorrow*, pasado mañana.—*d. bed*, sofá cama. —*d. before yesterday*, anteayer.—*d. in, d. out*, día tras día, sin cesar.—*d. laborer*, jornalero.—*days of obligation*, fiestas de guardar.—*d.-star*, lucero del alba.—*d. wages*, jornal.—*every other d.*, cada dos días.— **—book** [déibụk], *s.* libro de cuentas diarias.— **—break** [-breik], *s.* amanecer.— **—dream** [-drím], *s.* ensueño, ilusión. —*vi.* soñar despierto.— **—light** [-lait], *s.* luz del día, luz natural.—*d. saving time*, hora de verano (E.U.).

daze [deiz], *vt.* ofuscar, aturdir, trastornar.—*s.* deslumbramiento, ofuscamiento.

dazzle [dǽzl], *vt.* deslumbrar, ofuscar, encandilar; camuflar.—*s.* deslumbramiento.

deacon [díkọn], *s.* diácono.

dead [ded], *a.* muerto; inerte; marchito. —*d. center*, punto muerto.—*d. end*, callejón sin salida.—*d. eye*, tirador certero.—*d. pan* (*face*), (cara) inalterable.—*d. stop*, parada en seco.—*d. weight*, carga onerosa; tara.—*s. pl.* los muertos.—*the d. of night*, lo más profundo de la noche.—*adv.* entera o absolutamente; del todo; repentinamente.—*d. drunk*, borracho perdido.—*d. tired*, agotado.— **—en** [dédn], *vt.* amortiguar; quitar brillo,

sonido, etc.- **—line** [-lain], *s.* línea vedada; término, plazo final.- **—lock** [-lak], *s.* detención, paro, estancamiento.- **—ly** [-li], *a.* mortal; fatal; fulminante; implacable.- **—ness** [-nịs], *s.* inercia; amortiguamiento.

deaf [def], *a.* sordo.—*d.-mute*, sordomudo.- **—en** [défn], *vt.* ensordecer.- **—ening** [-ẹnịŋ], *a.* ensordecedor.- **—ness** [-nịs], *s.* sordera; ensordecimiento

deal [dil], *s.* trato, negocio; pacto o convenio; mano (en el juego de naipes); porción; parte.—*a great d.*, mucho, una gran cantidad.—*vti.* [10] distribuir, repartir; dar (los naipes); asestar (un golpe).—*to d. out*, dispensar.—*vii.* negociar, traficar, gestionar; mediar; dar (en el juego de baraja).- **—er** [dílœ(r)], *s.* comerciante, negociante, agente de comercio; el mano (en el juego de baraja).- **—ing** [-iŋ], *s.* conducta; trato; negocio.—*pl.* negocios; transacciones.- **—dealt** [delt], *pret.* y *pp.* de TO DEAL.

dean [din], *s.* deán; decano.

dear [dir], *a.* querido, amado; costoso, caro.—*s.* persona querida, bien amado.—*d. me!* ¡válgame Dios!—*d. sir(s)*, muy señor(es) mío(s), o nuestro(s).

dearth [dœrθ], *s.* carestía, escasez.

death [deθ], *s.* muerte; defunción, fallecimiento; mortandad.—*d. certificate*, partida de defunción.—*d. dealing*, mortífero.—*d. rate*, mortalidad.— *d. rattle*, estertor.—*d. struggle*, agonía. —*d. wound*, herida mortal.—*to be in the d. house*, estar en capilla.- **—less** [déθlịs], *a.* inmortal.- **—watch** [-wach], *s.* velorio.

debarkation [dịbarkéiʃọn], *s.* = DISEMBARKATION.

debase [dịbéis], *vt.* rebajar, deshonrar.

debatable [dịbéitəbl], *a.* discutible, disputable.—**debate** [dịbéit], *s.* discusión, debate, disputa.—*vt.* disputar, controvertir; considerar.—*vi.* deliberar, discutir.

debenture [dịbénchụ(r)], *s.* bono; obligación; pagaré del gobierno.

debit [débịt], *s.* débito, cargo; egreso; debe (de una cuenta).—*d. balance*, saldo deudor.—*vt.* adeudar, cargar en cuenta.

debris [dịbrí], *s.* escombros, restos, ruinas; despojos.

debt [det], *s.* deuda, débito; obligación. —*to run into d.*, endeudarse, entramparse.- **—or** [détọ(r)], *s.* deudor.

debut [dẹbiú], *s.* estreno; presentación de una señorita en sociedad.

decade [dékeid], *s.* decenio, década.

decadence [dịkéidẹns], *s.* decadencia.

—decadent [dɪkéɪdɛnt], a. decadente, decaído.

decapitate [dɪkǽpɪteɪt], vt. decapitar, degollar.—decapitation [dɪkæpɪtéɪʃǫn], s. decapitación.

decay [dɪkéɪ], vi. decaer, declinar; deteriorarse; carcomerse; cariarse; pudrirse, dañarse; picarse.—s. decaimiento, decadencia; ruina; caries; podredumbre.

decease [dɪsís], s. fallecimiento, defunción.—vi. morir, fallecer.—d [-t], s. y a. difunto, finado.

deceit [dɪsít], s. engaño, fraude, falacia, trampa.—ful [-fʊl], a. engañoso, falso; mentiroso.—deceive [dɪsív], vt. engañar, embaucar, defraudar.

December [dɪsémbœ(r)], s. diciembre.

decency [dísɛnsɪ], s. decencia; pudor.

decennial [dɪsénɪəl], a. decenal.

decent [dísɛnt], a. decente; razonable, módico.

deception [dɪsépʃǫn], s. engaño, fingimiento, impostura.

decide [dɪsáɪd], vt. y vi. decidir, determinar, resolver.—d [-ɪd], a. decidido, resuelto.

decimal [désɪmǫl], s. y a. decimal.—decimate [désɪmeɪt], vt. diezmar.

decipher [dɪsáɪfœ(r)], vt. descifrar, interpretar; aclarar.

decision [dɪsíʒǫn], s. decisión, resolución; entereza; (for.) fallo, auto, providencia.—decisive [dɪsáɪsɪv], a. decisivo; terminante, perentorio.

deck [dɛk], vt. ataviar, engalanar.—s. cubierta (de un buque); baraja.

declaim [dɪkléɪm], vi. declamar, perorar.

declaration [deklaréɪʃǫn], s. declaración; exposición; manifiesto.—declare [dɪklér], vt. y vi. declarar, manifestar; deponer.

declension [dɪklénʃǫn], s. (gram.) declinación.

decline [dɪkláɪn], vt. rehusar; (gram.) declinar.—vi. rehusar, negarse (a); declinar, decaer.—s. declinio; declive.—declivity [dɪklívɪtɪ], s. declive.

dècolletage [deɪkaltáʒ], s. escote; traje escotado.

decompose [dikǫmpóʊz], vt. descomponer; pudrir.—vi. pudrirse, corromperse.—decomposition [dikampozíʃǫn], s. descomposición; corrupción, putrefacción.

decorate [dékoreɪt], vt. decorar, adornar; condecorar.—decoration [dekoréɪʃǫn], s. decoración; adorno, ornamento, condecoración, insignia.—decorative [dékorɑtɪv], a. decorativo, ornamental.—decorator [dékoreɪtǫ(r)], s. decorador.

decorous [dékǫrʌs], a. decoroso.

decorum [dɪkórʌm], s. decoro, honor; corrección.

decoy [dɪkóɪ], vt. atraer con señuelo o añagaza.—s. señuelo, añagaza, reclamo.

decrease [dɪkrís], vi. decrecer.—vi. y vt. disminuir, reducir, mermar.—s. disminución; merma; menguante; decadencia.

decree [dɪkrí], vt. y vi. decretar, mandar.—s. decreto, edicto, mandato, ley.

decrepit [dɪkrépɪt], a. decrépito, caduco.

dedicate [dédɪkeɪt], vt. dedicar; aplicar.—dedication [dedɪkéɪʃǫn], s. dedicación, dedicatoria.

deduce [dɪdjús], vt. deducir, inferir; derivar.

deduct [dɪdʌkt], vt. deducir, restar, su(b)straer, rebajar, descontar.—ion [dɪdʌksǫn], s. deducción; su(b)stracción; descuento, rebaja; conclusión.

deed [did], s. acto, hecho; hazaña; (for.) escritura.

deep [dip], a. profundo, hondo; abstruso, recóndito; intenso (color); (mus.) grave; sagaz.—d. blue, turquí.—d. sea, alta mar.—d.-sea fishing, pesca mayor, pesca de profundidad.—adv. profundamente.—d.-seated, arraigado.—d. in thought, abstraído.—s. profundidad(es); piélago, mar.—en [dípn], vt. profundizar, ahondar; oscurecer; entristecer.—vi. hacerse más hondo, más profundo o más intenso.—ness [-nɪs], s. profundidad, hondura; intensidad.

deer [dɪr], s. venado, ciervo.

deface [dɪféɪs], vt. afear, desfigurar, mutilar.

default [dɪfɔ́lt], s. omisión; incumplimiento de una obligación; insolvencia; falta; (for.) rebeldía.—vt. y vi. faltar; no pagar; (for.) no comparecer.—er [-œ(r)], s. desfalcador; rebelde.

defeat [dɪfít], s. derrota; frustración; (for.) anulación.—vt. derrotar, vencer; frustrar; anular.—ist [-ɪst], s. y a. derrotista.

defect [dɪfékt], s. defecto, falta, tacha.—ion [dɪféksǫn], s. deserción; defección; abandono.—ive [dɪféktɪv], a. defectuoso; falto de inteligencia; (gram.) defectivo.

defend [dɪfénd], vt. defender, proteger.—ant [-ǫnt], a. acusado; que defiende.—s. demandado, acusado, procesado.—er [-œ(r)], s. defensor, protector.—defense [dɪféns], s. defensa, protección.—d. attorney, abogado defensor.—defenseless [dɪfénslɪs], a. indefenso; inerme.—defensive [dɪfénsɪv], a. defensivo.—s. defensiva.

defer [dɪfœr], vti. [1] diferir, aplazar, retrasar; remitir.—vii. demorarse;

(con to) ceder, acatar, consentir.—**—ence** [défęręns], *s.* deferencia, acatamiento, respeto.

defiance [djfáįąns], *s.* desafío, reto; oposición.—**defiant** [djfáįąnt], *a.* retador, provocador.

deficiency [djfíşęnsį], *s.* deficiencia, defecto.—**deficient** [djfíşęnt], *a.* deficiente; defectuoso.

defile [dįfáįl], *vi.* (mil.) desfilar.—*vt.* manchar, profanar, viciar, corromper. —*s.* desfiladero.

define [djfáįn], *vt.* definir; limitar; fijar; determinar.—**definite** [défįnįt], *a.* definido, exacto, categórico, preciso.—**definition** [defįnįşǫn], *s.* definición.—**definitive** [dįfínįtįv], *a.* definitivo, decisivo, terminante.

deflate [dįfléįt], *vt.* desinflar; reducir (valores, etc.).—**deflation** [dįfléįşǫn], *s.* deflación; desinflación.

deflect [dįflékt], *vt. y vi.* desviar(se), apartar(se), ladear(se).

deflower [dįfiáųœ(r)], *vt.* desflorar; violar.

deform [dįfórm], *vt.* deformar, desfigurar, afear.— **—ation** [dįfǫrméįşǫn] *s.* deformación, desfiguración.— **—ed** [dįfórmd], *a.* deformado, desfigurado; deforme, contrahecho.— **—ity** [dįfórmįtį], *s.* deformidad; deformación; fealdad.

defraud [dįfród], *vt.* defraudar, estafar.— **—er** [-œ(r)], *s.* defraudador, estafador.

defray [dįfréį], *vt.* costear, sufragar.

defrost [dįfróst], *vt.* descongelar, deshelar.

deft [deft], *a.* diestro, hábil.— **—ness** [déftnįs], *s.* destreza, habilidad.

defunct [dįfÁŋkt], *a. y s.* difunto.

defy [dįfáį], *vti.* [7] desafiar, retar.

degenerate [dįdźénęręįt], *vi.* degenerar. —*s. y a.* [dįdźénęrįt], degenerado.

degradation [degrǫdéįşǫn], *s.* degradación; degeneración; corrupción.— **degrade** [dįgréįd], *vt.* degradar; rebajar.—*vi.* degenerar; envilecerse.

degree [dįgrí], *s.* grado; título; cuantía. —*by degrees*, gradualmente, poco a poco.—*to take a d.*, graduarse.

deign [deįn], *vt. y vi.* dignarse, condescender.

deity [díįtį], *s.* deidad, divinidad.

dejected [dįdźéktįd], *a.* acongojado, abatido.—**dejection** [dįdźékşǫn], *s.* melancolía, abatimiento, desaliento; deposición.

delay [dįléį], *vt.* dilatar, demorar, retardar; entretener.—*vi.* tardar, demorarse.—*s.* dilación, tardanza, demora.

delectable [dįléktąbl], *a.* delicioso, deleitable.—**delectation** [dįlektéįşǫn], *s.* deleite, deleitación.

delegate [délęgeįt], *vt.* delegar, comisionar.—*a. y s.* delegado, comisario.—**delegation** [delęgéįşǫn], *s.* delegación, comisión.

delete [dįlít], *vt.* tachar, borrar, suprimir.

deliberate [dįlíbęręįt], *vt. y vi.* deliberar, reflexionar.—*a.* [dįlíbęrįt], deliberado, premeditado; cauto. —**deliberation** [dįlibęréįşǫn], *s.* deliberación, reflexión, premeditación.

delicacy [délįkąsį], *s.* delicadeza; suavidad; ternura; fragilidad; manjar, golosina.—**delicate** [délįkįt], *a.* delicado, frágil; suave; fino; tierno; exquisito.—**delicatessen** [delįkątésęn], *s.* manjares delicados, esp. fiambres; tienda donde se venden.

delicious [dįlíşÁs], *a.* delicioso, sabroso, rico.

delight [dįláįt], *s.* deleite, delicia, encanto.—*vt.* deleitar, encantar, recrear.—*vi.* deleitarse, recrearse, complacerse (en). — **—ed** [-įd], *a.* encantado, contentísimo.—*to be d. to*, tener mucho gusto en; alegrarse muchísimo de.— **—ful** [-fųl], *a.* delicioso, encantador.

delineate [dįlínįeįt], *vt.* delinear, trazar, diseñar.—**delineator** [dįlínįeįtǫ(r)], *s.* delineante.

delinquency [dįlíŋkwęnsį], *s.* delincuencia.—**delinquent** [dįlíŋkwęnt], *s. y a.* delincuente.

delirious [dįlíŗįÁs], *a.* delirante, desvariado.—*to be d.*, delirar, desvariar. **—delirium** [dįlíŗįÁm], *s.* delirio, desvarío; devaneo.

deliver [dįlívœ(r)], *vt.* entregar; libertar; pronunciar (conferencia, discurso, etc.); descargar, asestar (un golpe); despachar (un pedido); transmitir (energía, etc.).—*to d. a baby*, dar a luz.— **—ance** [-ąns], *s.* rescate, liberación.— **—er** [-œ(r)], *s.* libertador; repartidor, mensajero.— **—y** [-į], *s.* entrega; distribución o reparto; remesa; liberación; rescate; dicción, forma de expresión; cesión; parto; (mec.) descarga, proyección.—*d. man*, recadero, mensajero.

dell [del], *s.* cañada.

delude [dįliúd], *vt.* engañar, alucinar.

deluge [déliúdź], *s.* diluvio, inundación; calamidad.—*vt.* inundar.

delusion [dįliúźǫn], *s.* error; ilusión; decepción, engaño.

demagogue [démęgąg], *s.* demagogo.— **demagogy** [démągądźį], *s.* demagogia.

demand [dįmǽnd], *vt.* demandar; exigir; reclamar.—*s.* demanda; exigencia.— *on d.*, a la presentación; a solicitud. —*to be in d.*, tener demanda, ser solicitado.— **—ing** [-įŋ], *a.* exigente.

demeanor [dịmínọ(r)], *s.* conducta, comportamiento, proceder; porte; semblante.

demented [dịméntịd], *a.* demente.

demerit [dịmérịt], *s.* demérito, desmerecimiento.

demijohn [démịdžạn], *s.* botellón.

demise [dịmáịz], *s.* defunción, fallecimiento.

demobilize [dimóụbịlạịz], *vt.* desmovilizar.

democracy [dịmákrạsị], *s.* democracia.—**democrat** [démọkræt], *s.* demócrata.—**democratic** [dɛmọkrǽtịk], *a.* democrático.

demolish [dịmálịš], *vt.* demoler, derribar.—**er** [-œ(r)], *s.* demoledor.—**demolition** [demọlíšọn], *s.* demolición, derribo, arrasamiento.

demon [dímọn], *s.* demonio, diablo.

demonstrate [démọnstrejt], *vt.* demostrar, probar.—**demonstration** [demọnstréjšọn], *s.* demostración, muestra; prueba; manifestación pública.—**demonstrative** [dịmánstrạtịv], *a.* demostrativo; efusivo.—**demonstrator** [démọnstrejtọ(r)], *s.* manifestante.

demoralization [dịmạrạlịzéjšọn], *s.* desmoralización.—**demoralize** [dịmárạlạịz], *vt.* desmoralizar.

den [den], *s.* cueva, guarida, cuchitril, pocilga; gabinete (de estudio).

dengue [déngei], *s.* (med.) dengue.

denial [dịnáịạl], *s.* negación, negativa, desmentida; denegación.

denominate [dịnámịnejt], *vt.* denominar, nombrar.—*a.* denominado.—**denomination** [dịnamịnéjšọn], *s.* denominación, título, designación; confesión religiosa.—**denominator** [dịnámịnejtọ(r)], *s.* (arit.) denominador.

denote [dịnóụt], *vt.* denotar, señalar.

denouement [dejnúman], *s.* desenlace.

denounce [dịnáụns], *vt.* denunciar, delatar.

dense [dens], *a.* denso, espeso, tupido; estúpido.—**density** [dénsịtị], *s.* densidad, espesura; estupidez.

dent [dent], *s.* abolladura; mella; hendidura.—*vt.* y *vi.* abollar(se), mellar(se).

dental [déntạl], *a.* dental.—*d. floss,* hilo dental.—*d. plate,* dentadura postiza.—**dentist** [déntịst], *s.* dentista, odontólogo.—**dentistry** [déntịstrị], *s.* odontología.—**denture** [dénchǚ(r)], *s.* dentadura postiza.

denunciation [dịnʌnsịéjšọn], *s.* denuncia, acusación.

deny [dịnáị], *vtí.* [7] negar; denegar; desmentir; negarse a.—*vii.* negar.

deodorant [díóụdọrạnt], *s.* desodorante.

depart [dịpárt], *vi.* irse, partir, salir;

apartarse, desviarse; morir.—*the departed,* los difuntos.

department [dịpártmẹnt], *s.* departamento; compartimiento; sección (en una tienda, etc.); oficina, negociado; ministerio; distrito.—*d. store,* grandes almacenes, bazar.

departure [dịpárchǚ(r)], *s.* partida, salida, ida, marcha; desviación.

depend [dịpénd], *vi.* depender.—*to d. on* o *upon,* depender de; contar con; confiar en; necesitar (de); ser mantenido por.—**able** [-ạbl], *a.* formal, seguro, digno de confianza.—**ence** [-ẹns], *s.* dependencia; confianza; sostén, apoyo.—**ency** [-ẹnsị], *s.* dependencia.—**ent** [-ẹnt], *a.* y *s.* dependiente, subalterno.—*s.* familiar mantenido.

depict [dịpíkt], *vt.* pintar; representar; describir.

deplorable [dịplórạbl], *a.* deplorable; lastimoso.—**deplore** [dịplór], *vt.* deplorar.

deploy [dịplóị], *vt.* y *vi.* (mil.) desplegar(se).—*s.* despliegue.

depopulate [dịpápyulejt], *vt.* y *vi.* despoblar(se).

deport [dịpórt], *vt.* deportar.—*vr.* (com)portarse, conducirse.—**ation** [-éjšọn], *s.* deportación.—**ment** [-mẹnt], *s.* conducta, comportamiento.

depose [dịpóụz], *vt.* deponer; destronar; (for.) declarar, atestiguar.—*vi.* deponer, testificar.

deposit [dịpázịt], *vt.* depositar.—*vi.* depositarse.—*s.* depósito; sedimiento; (geol., min.) yacimiento, filón.—**deposition** [depọzíšọn], *s.* deposición, testimonio; destitución.—**depositor** [dịpázịtọ(r)], *s.* depositante

depot [dípoụ], *s.* depósito, almacén; paradero de tren.

deprave [dịpréjv], *vt.* depravar, pervertir.—**d** [-d], *a.* depravado.—**depravity** [dịprǽvịtị], *s.* depravación.

depreciate [dịpríšẹjt], *vt.* depreciar, abaratar; menospreciar.—*vi.* abaratarse; depreciarse.

depress [dịprés], *vt.* deprimir, abatir; abaratar, rebajar el precio de; hundir.—**ion** [dịpréšọn], *s.* depresión, abatimiento; concavidad; hondonada.

deprivation [deprịvéịšọn], *s.* privación; pérdida.—**deprive** [dịpráịv], *vt.* privar, despojar.

depth [depθ], *s.* profundidad; hondura; fondo; espesor, grueso (de una cosa); viveza (color); gravedad (sonido); penetración.—*d. bomb,* carga de profundidad.

deputy [dépịutị], *s.* diputado; delegado, agente.

derail [dịréjl], *vt.* y *vi.* descarrilar(se).—

—ment [-mẹnt], *s.* descarrilamiento.
derelict [dérẹlikt], *a.* negligente.—*s.* persona sin amparo; golfo, indigente.
deride [diráid], *vt.* ridiculizar, escarnecer, burlarse o mofarse de.— —r [diráidœ(r)], *s.* burlón.—**derision** [dirízọn], *s.* mofa, escarnio.—**derisive** [diráisive], *a.* burlesco.
derive [diráiv], *vt.* deducir (una conclusión); derivar.—*vi.* derivar, provenir, emanar.
derrick [dérịk], *s.* grúa, cabria; armazón de un pozo de petróleo.
descend [disénd], *vt.* y *vi.* descender, bajar; (con **to**) rebajarse a; (con **up** o **upon**) invadir, caer en o sobre.— —ant [-ạnt], *a.* descendiente.— —ent [-ẹnt], *a.* descend(i)ente; originario (de).—**descent** [disént], *s.* descenso, bajada; descendimiento; declive; alcurnia, descendencia, sucesión.
describe [diskráib], *vt.* describir, pintar.—**description** [diskrípṣọn], *s.* descripción; trazado; clase.—**descriptive** [diskríptiv], *a.* descriptivo.
desert [dézœrt], *s.* desierto, yermo; páramo.—*a.* desierto, yermo, desolado.—*vt.* [dizœrt] desamparar, abandonar.—*vt.* y *vi.* desertar.— —er [dizœrtœ(r)], *s.* desertor.— —ion [dizœrṣọn], *s.* deserción, abandono.— —s [dizœrt(s)], *s.* mérito, merecimiento.—*to get one's d.*, llevar su merecido.—**deserve** [dizœrv], *vt.* merecer.—*vi.* tener merecimientos.—**deserving** [dizœrviŋ], *a.* meritorio; merecedor o digno.—*s.* mérito, merecimiento.
design [dizáin], *vt.* diseñar, delinear; concebir; proyectar.—*vi.* hacer proyectos, diseños, planos.—*s.* diseño; proyecto; disposición, arreglo, construcción; plan; propósito, designio; plano.—*by* o *through d.*, adrede, intencionalmente.— —er [-œ(r)], *s.* dibujante; diseñador; proyectista.— *custom d.* figurinista.—*stage d.*, escenógrafo.— —ing [-iŋ], *a.* insidioso, astuto, intrigante.
designate [dézigneit], *vt.* designar, destinar; señalar.—**designation** [dezignéjṣọn], *s.* designación, señalamiento, nombramiento.
desirable [dizáirạbl], *a.* deseable, apetecible, conveniente.—**desire** [dizáir], *s.* deseo, anhelo, ansia, antojo.—*vt.* desear, anhelar, ansiar.—*vi.* sentir deseo.—**desirous** [dizáirʌs], *a.* deseoso, anheloso.
desist [dizíst], *vi.* desistir.
desk [desk], *s.* escritorio, pupitre, buró. —*d. pad*, carpeta.
desolate [désoleit], *vt.* desolar, arrasar; despoblar; desconsolar.—*a.* [désọlit], desolado; solitario; triste.—**desola-**

tion [desoléiṣọn], *s.* desolación; desconsuelo; soledad; aflicción.
despair [dispér], *s.* desesperanza, desesperación.—*vi.* desesperar, perder toda esperanza.— —ing [-iŋ], *a.* desesperante; sin esperanza.
despatch, *s.*, *vt.* = DISPATCH.
desperado [despẹréidou], *s.* foragido; prófugo; malhechor.—**desperate** [déspẹrit], *a.* desesperado; arrojado, arriesgado o temerario.—**desperation** [despẹréjṣọn], *s.* desesperación; furor.
despicable [déspikạbl], *a.* despreciable, vil.—**despise** [dispáiz], *vt.* despreciar, menospreciar.
despite [dispáit], *s.* despecho, inquina. —*prep.* a pesar de, a despecho de.
despoil [dispóil], *vt.* despojar, expoliar.
despondence, despondency [dispándẹns(i)], *s.* desaliento, abatimiento. —**despondent** [dispándẹnt], *a.* desalentado, abatido, desesperanzado.
despot [déspạt], *s.* déspota.— —ic [despátịk], *a.* despótico.— —ism [déspọtizm], *s.* despotismo; absolutismo.
dessert [dizœrt], *s.* postre.
destination [destinéiṣọn], *s.* destino; paradero.—**destine** [déstịn], *vt.* destinar; dedicar.—**destiny** [déstịni], *s.* destino, hado, sino.
destitute [déstịtjut], *a.* destituido, necesitado; (con **of**) falto, desprovisto de.—**destitution** [destịtjúṣọn], *s.* indigencia, privación.
destroy [distrój], *vt.* destruir, destrozar, desbaratar, acabar con.— —er [-œ(r)], *s.* destructor; (mar.) destructor, cazatorpedero.—**destruction** [distrákṣọn], *s.* destrucción, ruina, destrozo.— **destructive** [distráktiv], *a.* destructor; destructivo; dañino.
detach [ditéch], *vt.* separar, despegar o desprender; (mil.) destacar.— —ed [-t], *a.* suelto, separado; imparcial; desinteresado.— —able [-ạbl], *a.* separable, desmontable, de quita y pon.— —ment [-mẹnt], *s.* separación; indiferencia; desinterés, despego; (mil.) destacamento.
detail [ditéil], *vt.* detallar, particularizar, promenorizar.—*s.* detalle, pormenor; (mil.) destacamento.
detain [ditéin], *vt.* detener; retardar, atrasar; retener.
detect [ditékt], *vt.* descubrir; averiguar; (rad.) rectificar.— —ion [ditékṣọn], *s.* averiguación, descubrimiento; rectificación.— —ive [-iv], *s.* detective, agente de policía secreta o particular.— —or [-ọ(r)], *s.* descubridor; indicador de nivel; rectificador; (elec.) detector.
deter [ditœr], *vti.* [1] disuadir; desanimar, acobardar.

detergent [dɪtɶrdʒɛnt], *a.* **y** *s.* detergente.

deteriorate [dɪtɪ́rɪoreɪt], *vt.* **y** *vi.* deteriorar(se), desmejorar(se).—**deterioration** [dɪtɪrɪoréɪʃon], *s.* deterioro, desperfecto, desmejora.

determination [dɪtɶrmɪnéɪʃon], *s.* determinación, decisión.—**determinative** [dɪtɶrmɪnᶏtɪv], *a.* determinativo, determinante.—**determine** [dɪtɶrmɪn], *vt.* determinar, decidir; (for.) definir.—*vi.* resolverse, decidirse.—**determined** [dɪtɶrmɪnd], *a.* determinado, decidido, resuelto.

detest [dɪtést], *vt.* detestar, aborrecer.—**able** [-ᶏbl], *a.* detestable, aborrecible.

detonate [détoneɪt], *vi.* detonar, estallar.—*vt.* hacer estallar.—**detonating** [détoneɪtɪŋ], *a.* detonante.—**detonation** [detonéɪʃon], *s.* detonación.—**detonator** [détoneɪtọ(r)], *s.* detonador.

detour [dɪtúr], *s.* desviación, desvío, rodeo.—*vt.* **y** *vi.* (hacer) desviar o rodear.

detract [dɪtrækt], *vt.* disminuir o quitar.—*vi.* detractar.—**or** [-ọ(r)], *s.* detractor.—**ion** [dɪtrékʃon], *s.* detracción.

detriment [détrɪmɛnt], *s.* detrimento; perjuicio.

deuce [djus], *s.* dos (en naipes o dados); pata (en otros juegos); (fam.) diantre, demontre.

devaluate [dɪvǽlyueɪt], *vt.* depreciar, desvalorizar.—**devaluation** [dɪvǽlyuéɪʃon], *s.* depreciación, desvalorización.—**devalue** [dɪvǽlyu], *vt.* depreciar.

devastate [dévᶏsteɪt], *vt.* devastar, asolar.—**devastating** [dévᶏsteɪtɪŋ], *a.*, **devastator** [dévᶏsteɪtọ(r)], *s.* devastador, asolador.—**devastation** [devᶏstéɪʃon], *s.* devastación, desolación, ruina.

develop [dɪvélọp], *vt.* desenvolver, desarrollar; mejorar; fomentar; explotar (minas, etc.); revelar (fotos).—*vi.* progresar; avanzar; desarrollarse.—**er** [-ɶ(r)], *s.* (fot.) revelador.—**ment** [-mɛnt], *s.* desarrollo, evolución, progreso; fomento; explotación; revelado.

deviate [dívieɪt], *vt.* **y** *vi.* desviar(se), apartar(se).—**deviation** [diviéɪʃon], *s.* desviación; deriva; desvío, extravío.

device [dɪváɪs], *s.* artefacto, artificio; invento; proyecto; expediente, recurso; ardid; dibujo, patrón; lema, divisa.—*pl.* deseo, inclinación.

devil [dévɪl], *s.* diablo; demonio; manjar muy picante.—*between the d. and the deep sea*, entre la espada y la pared.—*the D.*, Satanás.—*the d. take the*

hindmost, el que venga atrás, que arree.— **ish** [-ɪʃ], *a.* diabólico; perverso; travieso.— **try** [-trɪ], **ment** [-mɛnt], *s.* diablura; travesura; maldad.

devious [dívɪᴧs], *a.* desviado, descarriado; tortuoso.

devise [dɪváɪz], *vt.* idear, trazar; proyectar; (for.) legar.—*vi.* urdir, maquinar.

devoid [dɪvóɪd], *a.* libre, exento; desprovisto (de).

devote [dɪvóʊt], *vt.* dedicar; consagrar.—*vr.* dedicarse, consagrarse (a).—**d** [-ɪd], *a.* devoto, ferviente; leal, afecto.—**devotion** [dɪvóʊʃon], *s.* devoción, piedad; dedicación; lealtad, afecto.

devour [dɪváʊr], *vt.* devorar, engullir.

devout [dɪváʊt], *a.* piadoso, devoto.

dew [dju], *s.* rocío; relente, sereno.—*vt.* rociar; refrescar.— **drop** [djúdrap], *s.* gota de rocío.

dewlap [djúlæp], *s.* papada.

dewy [djúi], *a.* lleno de rocío.

dexterity [dekstérɪtɪ], *s.* destreza, habilidad, maña, tino.—**dexterous** [déksterᴧs], *a.* diestro, hábil.

diabolic(al) [daɪᴧbálɪk(ᴧl)], *a.* diabólico.

diagnose [daɪægnóʊs], *vt.* diagnosticar.—**diagnosis** [daɪægnóʊsɪs], *s.* diagnosis.

diagonal [daɪǽgonᴧl], *a.* **y** *s.* diagonal.

diagram [dáɪᴧgræm], *s.* diagrama; gráfico.

dial [dáɪᴧl], *s.* esfera de reloj; cuadrante; disco del teléfono; indicador.—*vt.* sintonizar; marcar (en el disco de llamada), (Am.) discar.—*sun d.*, reloj de sol.

dialect [dáɪᴧlekt], *s.* dialecto.

dialogue [dáɪᴧlag], *s.* diálogo.

diameter [daɪǽmetɶ(r)], *s.* diámetro.

diamond [dáɪmọnd], *s.* diamante; brillante; oros (de baraja); (geom.) rombo.

diaper [dáɪᴧpɶ(r)], *s.* pañal, braguita.

diaphragm [dáɪᴧfræm], *s.* diafragma.

diarrhea [daɪᴧríᴧ], *s.* diarrea.

diary [dáɪᴧrɪ], *s.* diario.

dice [daɪs], *s.* (*pl.* de DIE) dados.—*d. box*, cubilete.—*vt.* cortar en forma de cubos menudos.

dictate [dɪkteɪt], *vt.* **y** *vi.* dictar; mandar, imponer(se).—*s.* dictamen.—**dictation** [dɪktéɪʃon], *s.* dictado; mando arbitrario.—**dictator** [dɪkteɪtọ(r)], *s.* dictador.—**dictatorial** [dɪktᴧtórɪᴧl], *a.* dictatorial.—**dictatorship** [dɪktóɪtọrʃɪp], *s.* dictadura.

diction [dɪkʃon], *s.* dicción; locución.—**ary** [-erɪ], *s.* diccionario.

did [dɪd], *pret.* de TO DO.

die [daɪ], *vi.* morir(se), expirar, fallecer; marchitarse.

die [daɪ], *s.* (*pl.* dice [daɪs]) dado (para

jugar); (*pl.* **dies** [daiz]) cuño, troquel; molde.—*the d. is cast,* la suerte está echada.

diet [dáiet], *s.* dieta, régimen alimenticio; dieta (asamblea).—*vt.* poner a dieta.—*vi.* estar a dieta.

differ [dífœ(r)], *vi.* diferir; diferenciarse, distinguirse.—*to d. from,* o *with,* no estar de acuerdo con.— —**ence** [-ęns], *s.* diferencia; distinción (de personas, etc.); discrepancia; desacuerdo; (arit.) residuo.—*it makes no d.,* no importa.— —**ent** [-ęnt], *a.* diferente, distinto.— —**ential** [-énṣal], *s.* diferencial.— —**entiate** [-énṣiejt], *vt.* y *vi.* diferenciar(se), distinguir(se).

difficult [dífikʌlt], *a.* difícil; penoso.— —**y** [-i], *s.* dificultad; tropiezo; reparo.—*pl.* apuros, apuro.

diffuse [difiúz], *vt.* difundir; desparramar.—*vi.* difundirse; disiparse.— *a.* [difiús] difundido, esparcido; difuso.—**diffusion** [difiúẓon], *s.* difusión; dispersión; prolijidad.

dig [dig], *vti.* [3] cavar, excavar; ahondar; escarbar.—*to d. out,* desentrañar. —*to d. up,* desenterrar.—*vii.* cavar; (fam.) matarse a trabajar.—*s.* empuje; (fam.) observación sarcástica.

digest [dáidẓest], *s.* compendio, resumen; recopilación.—*vt.* [daidẓést], recopilar, abreviar y clasificar; digerir.—*vi.* digerirse; asimilarse.— —**ible** [daidẓéstibl], *a.* digerible, digestible.— —**ion** [daidẓéschǫn], *s.* digestión; asimilación.— —**ive** [daidẓéstiv] *a.* y *s.* digestivo.

dignified [dígnifaid], *a.* serio, grave; digno.—**dignify** [dígnifai], *vti.* [7] dignificar, honrar, exaltar.—**dignitary** [dígniteri], *s.* dignatario.—**dignity** [dígniti], *s.* dignidad; nobleza, majestuosidad; rango o cargo elevado.

digress [daigrés], *vi.* divagar.— —**ion** [daigréṣǫn], *s.* divagación o digresión.

dike [daik], *s.* dique, represa; zanja; malecón.—*vt.* represar; canalizar.

dilapidate [dilǽpideit], *vt.* dilapidar.— —**d** [-id], *a.* destartalado, arruinado.

dilate [dailéit], *vt.* dilatar, ensanchar. —*vi.* dilatarse, extenderse.

dilemma [dilémǡ], *s.* dilema.

diligence [dílidẓęns], *s.* diligencia; coche diligencia.—**diligent** [dílidẓęnt], *a.* diligente, aplicado; activo.

dilute [diliút], *vt.* desleír, diluir; aguar. —*vi.* desleírse, diluirse.—*a.* diluido.

dim [dim], *a.* oscuro; borroso; empañado; deslustrado; (fot.) velado.— *vti.* [1] oscurecer; empañar, deslustrar; amortiguar o reducir la intensidad de una luz.—*vii.* oscurecerse, etc.

dime [daim], *s.* (E.U. y Canadá) moneda de diez centavos.

dimension [diménṣǫn], *s.* dimensión, extensión, tamaño.

diminish [dimíniṣ], *vt.* disminuir, (a)minorar; rebajar, degradar.—*vi.* disminuir(se), menguar, (a)minorarse, decrecer.—**diminution** [diminiúṣǫn], *s.* di(s)minución, rebaja, reducción. —**diminutive** [dimíniu̥tiv], *a.* diminuto; diminutivo.—*s.* (gram.) diminutivo.

dimness [dímnis], *s.* ofuscamiento; penumbra.

dimple [dímpl], *s.* hoyuelo.—*vt.* y *vi.* formar o formarse hoyuelos.

din [din], *s.* estrépito, alboroto.—*vti.* [1] ensordecer; aturdir.—*vii.* alborotar; (re)sonar con estrépito.

dine [dain], *vi.* comer (la comida principal), cenar.— —**r** [dáinœ(r)], *s.* comedor; comensal.—**dining-car** [dáiniŋkar], *s.* coche comedor.—**dining room** [dáiniŋ rúm], *s.* comedor.

dinghy [díngi], *s.* lancha o bote pequeño.

dingy [díndẓi], *a.* empañado, deslustrado; manchado, sucio; oscuro.

dinner [dínœ(r)], *s.* comida (principal), cena; cubierto.—*d. jacket,* smoking, media etiqueta.—*d. set,* vajilla.

diocese [dáiǫsis], *s.* diócesis.

dip [dip], *vti.* [3] sumergir; bañar, humedecer, mojar; zambullir; saludar con la bandera; (mar.) achicar.—*vii.* sumergirse, zambullirse; hundirse; hojear (en un libro, etc.); inclinarse hacia abajo.—*s.* inmersión, zambullida; baño corto; inclinación, caída, pendiente.

diphtheria [difθíriǡ], *s.* difteria.

diphthong [dífθoŋ], *s.* diptongo.

diploma [diplóumǡ], *s.* diploma; título. —**diplomacy** [diplóuměsi], *s.* diplomacia; tacto.—**diplomat** [díplomæt], *s.* diplomático.—**diplomatic** [diplomǽtik], *a.* diplomático.

dipper [dípœ(r)], *s.* cazo, cucharón.

dire [dair], *a.* extremo, angustioso; horrendo; de mal agüero.

direct [dirékt], *a.* directo; derecho; en línea recta (descendencia, sucesión, etc.).—*vt.* dirigir; encaminar; gobernar.—*vi.* dirigir; servir de guía.— —**ion** [diréksǫn], *s.* dirección; rumbo; gobierno, administración; instrucción.—*d. finder,* (rad.) radiogoniómetro.— —**ive** [-iv], *a.* directivo.—*s.* instrucción, mandato.— —**or** [-ǫ(r)], *s.* director; gerente; administrador; vocal de una junta directiva; director de orquesta.—*board of directors,* consejo de administración.— —**y** (mat.) director, directriz.— —**ory** [-ǫri], *s.* directorio; guía comercial.

dirt [dœrt], *s.* basura; mugre; tierra; lodo; polvo; bajeza.—**dirty** [dœrti], *a.* sucio; manchado; enlodado; inde-

cente; puerco; vil.—*d. trick*, (fam.)
perrada.—*vti.* [7] emporcar, ensuciar.

disability [dɪsǝbʃlɪtɪ], *s.* incapacidad; inhabilidad, impotencia.—**disable** [dɪs-éɪbl], *vt.* imposibilitar; inhabilitar; (for.) incapacitar legalmente.

disadvantage [dɪsǝdvǽntɪdʒ], *s.* desventaja, detrimento.—*at a d.*, en situación desventajosa.

disagree [dɪsǝgrí], *vi.* disentir, discrepar, diferir, desavenirse; estar en pugna.—*to d. with*, no estar de acuerdo con; no sentar bien a.—**able** [-ǝbl], *a.* desagradable; descortés, desapacible.—**ment** [-mǝnt], *s.* desacuerdo, desavenencia; discordia; disensión; discrepancia.

disappear [dɪsǝpír], *vi.* desaparecer(se).—**ance** [-ǝns], *s.* desaparición.

disappoint [dɪsǝpʃint], *vt.* chasquear; decepcionar, desilusionar; defraudar una esperanza.—*to be disappointed*, verse contrariado; estar desilusionado o decepcionado.—**ment** [-mǝnt], *s.* desengaño, desilusión, decepción, contratiempo; chasco.

disapproval [dɪsǝprúvǝl], *s.* desaprobación, censura.—**disapprove** [dɪsǝprúv], *vt. y vi.* desaprobar.

disarm [dɪsárm], *vt.* desarmar; (fig.) apaciguar, sosegar.—*vi.* deponer las armas; licenciar tropas.— **ament** [-ǝmǝnt], *s.* desarme.

disarrange [dɪsǝréɪndʒ], *vt.* desarreglar, descomponer, desordenar.— **ment** [-mǝnt], /s.* desarreglo, desorden.

disassemble [dɪsǝsémbl], *vt.* desarmar, desmontar (un reloj, una máquina).

disaster [dɪzǽstǝ(r)], *s.* desastre; siniestro.—**disastrous** [dɪzǽstrʌs], *a.* desastroso, funesto.

disband [dɪsbǽnd], *vt.* licenciar las tropas.—*vi.* dispersarse, desbandarse.

disburse [dɪsbǫ́ǝrs], *vt.* desembolsar, pagar, gastar.— **ment** [-mǝnt], *s.* desembolso; gasto.—*pl.* (com.) egresos.

disc [dɪsk], *s.* (anat.) disco; ⇒ DISK.

discard [dɪskárd], *vt.* descartar; despedir.—*vi.* descartarse (en el juego).—*s.* [dɪskard] descarte (en el juego).

discern [dɪzǫ́ǝrn], *vt. y vi.* discernir, percibir, distinguir.— **ment** [-mǝnt], *s.* discernimiento; criterio.

discharge [dɪschárdʒ], *vt.* descargar; disparar; cumplir, desempeñar, ejecutar; despedir; exonerar, eximir, dispensar; arrojar, vomitar; (mil.) licenciar.—*vi.* descargarse; vaciarse; desaguar.—*s.* descarga; disparo; (com.) descargo; carta de pago; desempeño; remoción, despido; (mil.) licencia absoluta; absolución, exoneración; derrame, desagüe.

disciple [dɪsáɪpl], *s.* discípulo.

discipline [dísiplin], *s.* disciplina; enseñanza; castigo; materia de estudio.—*vt.* disciplinar, instruir; castigar.

disclose [dɪsklóuz], *vt.* descubrir, destapar; revelar, publicar.—**disclosure** [dɪsklóuʒʊ(r)], *s.* descubrimiento, revelación.

discolor [dɪskʌ́lǫ(r)], *vt. y vi.* descolorar(se), desteñir(se).— **ation** [-éɪʃǫn], *s.* descoloramiento.

discomfort [dɪskʌ́mfǫrt], *s.* incomodidad; malestar, molestia.—*vt.* incomodar; molestar.

disconcert [dɪskǫnsǫ́ert], *vt.* desconcertar, confundir.

disconnect [dɪskǫnékt], *vt.* desconectar; desunir o separar.— **ed** [-ɪd], *a.* desconectado; inconexo, incoherente.

disconsolate [dɪskánsǫlɪt], *a.* desconsolado, inconsolable, desolado.

discontent [dɪskǫntént], *s.* descontento, desagrado.—*a.* descontento; quejoso, disgustado.—*vt.* descontentar, desagradar.— **ed** [-ɪd], *a.* descontent(adiz)o; disgustado.— **ment** [-mǝnt], *s.* descontento, mal humor.

discontinue [dɪskǫntínyu], *vt. y vi.* interrumpir, descontinuar; suspender; desabonarse.

discord [dɪskord], *s.* discordia; desacuerdo, (mus.) disonancia.—*to sow d.*, cizañar.—*vi.* [dɪskórd], discordar.—**ance** [dɪskórdǝns], —ancy [dɪskórdǝnsɪ], *s.* discordia; discordancia; disensión.—**ant** [dɪskórdǝnt], *a.* discorde, desconforme; discordante, disonante.

discount [dískaunt], *vt.* descontar; rebajar, deducir; dar poca importancia a.—*s.* descuento, rebaja.—*d. rate*, tipo de descuento.

discourage [dɪskǫ́rɪdʒ], *vt.* desalentar; desaprobar, oponerse a.— **d** [-d], *a.* desanimado, desalentado.— **ment** [-mǝnt], *s.* desaliento, desánimo, obstáculo.

discourse [dískors], *s.* discurso; plática, conversación; disertación.—*vi.* [dɪskórs], discurrir, discursar; disertar; conversar, razonar.—*vt.* hablar de; proferir, expresar.

discourteous [dɪskǫ́ertɪʌs], *a.* descortés, grosero.—**discourtesy** [dɪskǫ́ertǝsɪ], *s.* descortesía.

discover [dɪskʌ́vœ(r)], *vt.* descubrir.— **er** [-œ(r)], *s.* descubridor.— **y** [-ɪ], *s.* descubrimiento, hallazgo.

discredit [dɪskrédɪt], *s.* descrédito, desconfianza; deshonra, oprobio.—*vt.* desacreditar; desautorizar, desvirtuar.

discreet [dɪskrít], *a.* discreto, prudente, juicioso.— **ness** [-nɪs], *s.* ⇒ DIS-CRETION.

discrepancy [diskrépansi], *s.* discrepancia, diferencia; variación.

discretion [diskréşǫn], *s.* discreción, juicio, prudencia.

discriminate [diskrímineit], *vt.* discriminar, prejuzgar; discernir, distinguir.—*a.* [diskríminit], definido, distinguible; discernidor.—**discrimination** [diskrimínéişǫn], *s.* discriminación, prejuicio; discernimiento; distinción, diferencia.

discuss [diskʌs], *vt.* discutir, debatir; tratar.— **ion** [diskʌşǫn], *s.* discusión, debate; exposición, ventilación.

disdain [disdéin], *vt.* desdeñar, despreciar.—*vi.* desdeñarse, esquivarse.— *s.* desdén, desprecio, esquivez.— **ful** [-ful], *a.* desdeñoso; altivo, altanero.

disease [dizíz], *s.* enfermedad, afección, dolencia.—*vt.* enfermar, hacer daño.— **d** [-d], *a.* enfermo; morboso.

disembark [disembárk], *vt.* y *vi.* desembarcar(se).— **ation** [-éişǫn], *s.* desembarco o desembarque.

disembowel [disembáuel], *vti.* [2] destripar, desentrañar, sacar las entrañas.

disengage [disengéidʒ], *vt.* desunir; desasir; (mec.) desembragar; desenganchar.—*vi.* soltarse, desligarse, zafarse.

disentangle [disentǽŋgl], *vt.* desenredar, desenmarañar, desembrollar.

disfigure [disfígyur], *vt.* desfigurar, afear.

disgorge [disgórdʒ], *vt.* desembuchar; vomitar.

disgrace [disgréis], *s.* ignominia, vergüenza; deshonra, estigma.—*vt.* deshonrar; desacreditar.— **ful** [-ful], *a.* vergonzoso, oprobioso.

disguise [disgáiz], *vt.* disfrazar, enmascarar; desfigurar; encubrir.—*s.* disfraz, máscara; embozo.

disgust [disgʌst], *s.* repugnancia; asco, náusea; disgusto.—*vt.* repugnar; fastidiar, hastiar.— **ed** [-id], *a.* disgustado, fastidiado.— **ing** [-iŋ], *a.* repugnante, asqueroso; odioso.

dish [dis], *s.* plato, fuente; manjar.—*pl.* vajilla, loza.—*d. drainer* o *rack*, escurreplatos.

dishearten [dishártȩn], *vt.* desanimar, descorazonar.

dishevel [dishévȩl], *vti.* [2] desgreñar, desmelenar.

dishonest [disánist], *a.* falto de honradez, pícaro; fraudulento, falso.— **y** [-i], *s.* improbidad, picardía; fraude.

dishonor [disánǫr], *s.* deshonor, deshonra; afrenta.—*vt.* deshonrar; afrentar.— **able** [-abl], *a.* deshonroso, ignominioso; deshonrado, infamado.

dishwasher [diswáşœr], *s.* máquina de lavar platos; lavaplatos.

disillusion [disiljúzǫn], *vt.* desilusionar, desengañar.— **ment** [-mȩnt], *s.* desilusión, desengaño, decepción.

disinfect [disinfékt], *vt.* desinfectar.— **ant** [-ant], *a.* y *s.* desinfectante.— **ion** [disinfékşǫn], *s.* desinfección.

disinherit [disinhérit], *vt.* desheredar.

disinterment [disintœrmȩnt], *s.* exhumación, desenterramiento.

disjoin [disdʒóin], *vt.* desunir, apartar, disgregar.— **t** [-t], *vt.* descoyuntar, dislocar.— **ted** [-tid], *a.* dislocado, descoyuntado; sin ilación.

disk [disk], *s.* disco; rodaja.

dislike [disláik], *s.* aversión, antipatía.—*vt.* tener aversión, no gustar de.

dislocate [díslokeit], *vt.* dislocar, descoyuntar.—**dislocation** [dislokéişǫn], *s.* dislocación, luxación.

dislodge [disládʒ], *vt.* desalojar, echar fuera.—*vi.* mudarse.

disloyal [dislóial], *a.* desleal.— **ty** [-ti], *s.* deslealtad.

dismal [dízmal], *a.* lúgubre, triste.—*s.* pantano.

dismantle [dismǽntl], *vt.* desguarnecer; desmantelar; desmontar.

dismay [disméi], *s.* desaliento, desmayo; consternación.—*vt.* desanimar, espantar, aterrar.

dismiss [dismís], *vt.* despedir, destituir; descartar; despachar; dar de baja.— **al** [-al], *s.* despido, remoción, destitución.

dismount [dismáunt], *vt.* desmontar; desarmar.—*vi.* apearse, descabalgar.

disobedience [disobídiȩns], *s.* desobediencia.—**disobedient** [disobídiȩnt], *a.* desobediente.—**disobey** [disobéi], *vt.* y *vi.* desobedecer.

disorder [disórdœr], *s.* desorden, irregularidad; alboroto; enfermedad.—*vt.* desordenar; inquietar, perturbar.— **ly** [-li], *a.* desordenado, desarreglado; escandaloso, perturbador.— *d. house*, burdel.—*adv.* desordenadamente, etc.

disown [disóun], *vt.* repudiar, negar, desconocer; renunciar, renegar de.

disparity [dispáriti], *s.* disparidad.

dispatch [dispǽch], *vt.* despachar, expedir; remitir.—*s.* despacho; mensaje, comunicación.

dispel [dispél], *vti.* [1] dispersar; disipar, desvanecer.

dispensary [dispénsari], *s.* dispensario.—**dispensation** [dispenséişǫn], *s.* dispensa, exención; designio divino.—**dispense** [dispéns], *vt.* distribuir, repartir; administrar (justicia); dispensar, eximir.

dispersal [dispœrsal], *s.* dispersión.—**disperse** [dispœrs], *vt.* dispersar;

esparcir.—*vi.* dispersarse; disiparse.
—*a.* disperso.—**dispersion** [dispér-
sən], *s.* dispersión; esparcimiento;
difusión.

displace [displéis], *vt.* desalojar, des-
plazar, quitar el puesto *a.*—**ment**
[-mənt], *s.* remoción, desalojo, des-
plazamiento.

display [displéi], *vt.* desplegar, extender;
exhibir, lucir.—*s.* despliegue; ostentación, exhibición.—*d. window*, escaparate, vidriera.—*on d.*, en exhibición.

displease [displíz], *vt.* y *vi.* desagradar,
disgustar.—**displeasure** [displéžu(r)],
s. desagrado, disfavor.

disposal [dispóuzal], *s.* disposición;
colocación, arreglo; venta (de bienes);
donación.—**dispose** [dispóuz], *vt.*
arreglar, disponer; inclinar el ánimo;
ordenar, mandar.—*vi.* disponer.—*to
d. of*, acabar con; deshacerse de; dar,
vender, traspasar; disponer de.—
disposition [dispozišən], *s.* disposición; arreglo, ordenación; índole.

dispossess [dispozés], *vt.* desposeer,
desalojar; (for.) desahuciar, lanzar.

disprove [disprúv], *vt.* refutar.

dispute [dispiút], *vt.* refutar, impugnar.
—*vi.* disputar, discutir.—*s.* disputa,
discusión; litigio, pleito.

disqualify [diskwálifai], *vti.* [7] desca-
lificar, inhabilitar.

disregard [disrigárd], *vt.* desatender,
hacer caso omiso de; desairar, despreciar.—*s.* desatención, descuido,
omisión; desprecio, desaire.

disrespect [disrispékt], *s.* desatención,
falta de respeto.—*vt.* desacatar, desairar; faltar el respeto a.—**ful**
[-ful], *a.* irrespetuoso, irreverente.

disrupt [disrápt], *vt.* romper; rajar,
reventar; hacer pedazos; desorga-
nizar, desbaratar.—**ion** [disrápšən],
s. desgarro, rotura; desorganización
o rompimiento.—**ive** [disráptiv], *a.*
destructor, disolvente.

dissatisfaction [disætisfækšən], *s.* descontento, disgusto.—**dissatisfy** [dis-
sætisfai], *vti.* [7] desagradar, descontentar.

dissect [disékt], *vt.* disecar, anatomizar;
analizar.—**ion** [disékšən], *s.* disección, disecación, anatomía; análisis.

dissension [disénšən], *s.* disensión,
discordia.—**dissent** [disént], *vi.* disentir, disidir.—*s.* disensión, desavenencia.

dissertation [discertéišən], *s.* disertación.

dissimulation [disimyulléišən], *s.* disimulo, disfraz; tolerancia afectada.

dissipate [dísipeit], *vt.* y *vi.* disipar(se),
dispersar(se); desintegrar(se), des-
vanecer(se), evaporar(se).—*vt.* desperdiciar, derrochar.—**d** [dísipei-

tid], *a.* disipado, disoluto.—**dissipa-
tion** [disipéišən], *s.* disipación; libertinaje.

dissociate [disóušieit], *vt.* disociar, dividir, separar.

dissolute [dísoliut], *a.* disoluto, libertino, licencioso.—**dissolution** [diso-
liúšən], *s.* disolución.—**dissolve** [di-
zálv], *vt.* disolver; disipar; dispersar;
desleír; derogar, revocar, anular.
—*vi.* disolverse; descomponerse; desvanecerse; languidecer.

dissonance [dísonans], *s.* disonancia;
desconcierto, discordia.—**dissonant**
[dísonant], *a.* disonante, discordante; contrario, discorde.

distaff [dístæf], *s.* rueca.—*d. o d. side*,
sexo débil.

distance [dístans], *s.* distancia; alejamiento; lejanía, lontananza; trecho;
intervalo.—*at a d.*, de lejos.—*in the
d.*, en lontananza, a lo lejos.—*to keep
one's d.*, guardar las distancias.—*vt.*
alejar, apartar; espaciar; tomar la
delantera.—**distant** [dístant], *a.* distante, alejado; esquivo, frío.

distaste [distéist], *s.* fastidio, aversión,
disgusto.—**ful** [-ful], *a.* enfadoso,
desagradable.

distend [disténd], *vt.* y *vi.* tender(se),
ensanchar(se), dilatar(se), hin-
char(se); distender(se).

distill [distíl], *vt.* y *vi.* destilar.—**ation**
[distiléišən], *s.* destilación.—**ery**
[-œri], *s.* destilería.

distinct [dístiŋkt], *a.* distinto, claro,
preciso; diferente.—*d. from*, distinto
a.—**ion** [dístiŋkšən], *s.* distinción;
discernimiento; diferencia; honor.—
ive [dístiŋktiv], *a.* distintivo, característico.—**distinguish** [distiŋgwiš],
vt. distinguir, discernir, diferenciar;
honrar.—**distinguished** [distiŋgwišt],
a. distinguido; prestigioso; especial,
señalado.

distort [distórt], *vt.* (re)torcer; deformar; falsear, tergiversar.—**ion**
[distóršən], *s.* distorsión; esguince;
deformación, tergiversación.

distract [distrákt], *vt.* distraer; perturbar, interrumpir.—**ion** [dis-
trákšən], *s.* distracción; perturbación; diversión, pasatiempo.

distress [distrés], *s.* pena, dolor;
angustia; desgracia, miseria; embargo, secuestro.—*vt.* angustiar, afligir; poner en aprieto; embargar,
secuestrar.

distribute [distríbiut], *vt.* distribuir.
—*vi.* hacer distribución.—**r** [dis-
tríbiutœ(r)], **distributor** [distríbiu-
tə(r)], *s.* distribuidor, repartidor.
—**distribution** [distribiúšən], *s.* distribución, reparto.

district [dístrikt], *s.* distrito, comarca,

territorio; barriada, barrio; región, jurisdicción.

distrust [distrʌ́st], *vt.* desconfiar, recelar.— *s.* desconfianza, recelo; descrédito.— **—ful** [-ful], *a.* desconfiado, receloso; suspicaz.

disturb [distœ́rb], *vt.* alborotar, (per)turbar; distraer, interrumpir; desordenar, revolver.— **—ance** [-ạns], *s.* disturbio, conmoción, alboroto, desorden.— **—er** [œ(r)], *s.* perturbador.

disuse [disyús], *s.* desuso.—*to fall into d.*, caer en desuso, perder vigencia. —*vt.* [disyúz], desusar; cesar de usar; desechar.

ditch [dich], *s.* zanja; cuneta; trinchera; foso; acequia.—*vt.* zanjar; abandonar, desembarazarse de; (fam.) dar calabazas a.

ditto [dítou], *s.* ídem; lo mismo; marca (") o abreviatura (id.); duplicado, copia fiel.—*vt.* duplicar, copiar.—*adv.* como ya se dijo; asimismo.

divan [dáivæn, divǽn], *s.* diván.

dive [daiv], *vii.* [5] za(m)bullirse, echarse o tirarse de cabeza; bucear; enfrascarse, profundizar; (aer.) picar. —*s.* za(m)bullidura, buceo; enfrascamiento; tugurio; (aer.) picada.— **—r** [dáivœ(r)], *s.* buceador, buzo. **—diving** [dáiviŋ], *s.* za(m)bullida, buceo; deporte del salto de palanca y trampolín; (aer.) picada.—*d. board,* trampolín.

diverge [divœ́rdʒ], *vi.* divergir, diferir, desviarse.— **—nce** [divœ́rdʒens], **—ncy** [divœ́rdʒensi], *s.* divergencia.— **—nt** [divœ́rdʒent], *a.* divergente.

divers [dáivœrz], *a.* varios, diversos.

diverse [divœ́rs], *a.* diverso, variado, distinto.—**diversify** [divœ́rsifai], *vti.* [7] diversificar, variar.—**diversion** [divœ́rʒon], *s.* desviación; diversión, entretenimiento.—**diversity** [divœ́rsiti], *s.* diversidad, variedad; diferencia.—**divert** [divœ́rt], *vt.* desviar; divertir.—**diverting** [divœ́rtiŋ], *a.* divertido, entretenido, recreativo.

divide [diváid], *vt.* dividir; desunir, separar; repartir, compartir.—*vi.* dividirse.— **—nd** [dívidend], *s.* dividendo.

divine [diváin], *a.* divino; teólogo.—*vt.* adivinar; vaticinar.—**divinity** [divíniti], *s.* divinidad; deidad; atributo divino; teología.

division [divị́ʒon], *s.* división; distribución, repart(imient)o; ramo, negociado, departamento; sección; desunión, desacuerdo.

divorce [divórs], *s.* divorcio.—*vt.* y *vi.* divorciar(se).— **—e** [divorsí], *s.* persona divorciada.

divulge [divʌ́ldʒ], *vt.* divulgar, propalar.

dizziness [dízinis], *s.* vértigo, vahído; desvanecimiento.—**dizzy** [dízi], *a.* vertiginoso, desvanecido.—*vti.* [7] causar vértigos; aturdir.

do [du], *vti.* [11] hacer; ejecutar; obrar; finalizar; producir; despachar; cumplir; arreglar; cocer, guisar.—*vii.* hacer; comportarse; proceder; hallarse.—*how d. you d.?* ¿cómo está Ud?—*that will d.*, eso basta, bastará.

docile [dásil], *a.* dócil, sumiso.

dock [dak], *s.* dique, dársena; muelle, desembarcadero; banquillo de los acusados.—*vt.* cortar, cercenar; reducir, rebajar; (mar.) poner en dique.—*vt.* y *vi.* atracar, entrar en muelle.— **—er** [dákœ(r)], *s.* estibador, trabajador de muelle.

docket [dákit], *s.* minuta, sumario; rótulo, marbete.

dockyard [dákyard], *s.* astillero, arsenal.

doctor [dáktọ(r)], *s.* médico; doctor. —*vt.* medicinar, tratar; falsificar, adulterar; componer.— **—ate** [-it], *s.* doctorado.

doctrine [dáktrin], *s.* doctrina, dogma; teoría.

document [dákyụment], *s.* documento. —*vt.* [dákyụment], documentar; probar con documentos.— **—al** [dakyụméntal], *a.*, **—ary** [dakyụméntari], *a.* documental.—*s.* (película) documental.— **—ation** [dakyụmentéiʃọn], *s.* documentación.

dodge [dadʒ], *vt.* esquivar, soslayar, evadir.—*vi.* escabullirse; dar un quiebro o esquinazo; hurtar el cuerpo.

doe [dou], *s.* hembra del gamo, de la liebre, del conejo, del canguro y del antílope.— **—skin** [dóuskin], *s.* ante; tejido fino de lana.

dog [dog], *s.* perro; macho de los cánidos (zorro, lobo, chacal, etc.); calavera, tunante.—*d.-cheap,* baratísimo.—*d.-tired,* cansadísimo.—*to put on the d.*, darse ínfulas.—*vti.* [1] seguir los pasos; espiar, perseguir.— **—fight** [dógfait], *s.* riña de perros; combate entre aviones de caza.—**dogged** [dógid], *a.* terco, tenaz.— **—house** [-haus], *s.* caseta de perro.—*in the d.*, en desgracia.

dogma [dógmạ], *s.* dogma.— **—tic** [dogmǽtik], *a.* dogmático.

doily [dóili], *s.* mantelillo individual.

doings [dúiŋs], *s. pl.* acciones, obras; acontecimientos, cosas que ocurren.

dole [doul], *s.* distribución, reparto; porción; sopa boba; limosna; ración.—*vt.* repartir, distribuir, dar (limosna).— **—ful** [dóulful], *a.* dolorido; lúgubre, triste.

doll [dal], *s.* muñeca, muñeco.—*to d. up,* acicalarse, emperifollarse.— **—y**

[dáli], *s.* muñequita; plataforma rodante.

dolphin [dálfin], *s.* delfín.

domain [doméin], *s.* dominio; heredad.

dome [doum], *s.* cúpula.

domestic [doméstik], *a.* doméstico, familiar; del país, nacional; interno, interior.—*s.* doméstico, sirviente.——**ate** [-eit], *vt.* domesticar; hacer adquirir costumbres caseras.

domicile [dámisil], *s.* domicilio.

dominant [dáminant], *a.* dominante.——**dominate** [dámineit], *vt.* y *vi.* dominar.—**domination** [daminéison], *s.* dominación, dominio, imperio.——**domineer** [daminír], *vt.* y *vi.* dominar, tiranizar.—**domineering** [daminíriŋ], *a.* dominante, tiránico, mandón.——**dominion** [domínyon], *s.* dominio; territorio; distrito; posesión, propiedad.

don [dan], *vti.* [1] vestirse, ponerse, calarse.—*s.* caballero; don (título).

donate [dóuneit], *vt.* donar, contribuir.——**donation** [dounéison], *s.* donación, donativo, dádiva.

done [dʌn], *pp.* de TO DO.—*a.* hecho, ejecutado; acabado; bien cocido o asado.—*d. for*, agotado, rendido; perdido.—*d. up*, envuelto; fatigado.

donkey [dáŋki], *s.* asno, burro.

donor [dóuno(r)], *s.* donante, donador.

doom [dum], *vt.* sentenciar a muerte; predestinar a la perdición.—*s.* sentencia, condena; sino, destino; perdición, ruina.——**sday** [dúmzdei], *s.* día del juicio final.

door [dor], *s.* puerta; portezuela; entrada.—*d. mat*, felpudo.——**bell** [dórbel], *s.* timbre o campanilla de llamada.——**keeper** [-kipœ(r)], ——**man** [-man], *s.* portero.——**knob** [-nab], *s.* tirador o perilla de puerta.——**plate** [-pleit], *s.* placa de puerta.——**sill** [-sil], *s.* umbral.——**step** [-step], *s.* escalón de la puerta.——**way** [-wei], *s.* entrada; portal.

dope [doup], *s.* estupefaciente, narcótico; menjurje; (fam.) datos, informes; tonto, estúpido.—*d. addict*, o *fiend*, narcómano.—*d. racket*, tráfico ilícito de drogas.—*vt.* narcotizar; pronosticar; conjeturar.——**dopy** [dóupi], *a.* (fam.) narcotizado, aletargado.

dormitory [dórmitori], *s.* dormitorio (colectivo).

dormouse [dórmaus], *s.* (zool.) lirón.

dorsal [dórsal], *a.* dorsal, espinal.

dosage [dóusidž], *s.* dosificación.——**dose** [dous], *s.* dosis; (fig.) mal trago.—*vt.* administrar una dosis.—*vi.* medicarse con frecuencia.

dot [dat], *s.* punto.—*on the d.*, en punto, a la hora exacta.—*to a d.*, perfecta-

mente, absolutamente.—*vti.* [1] puntear; poner punto (a una letra).

dotage [dóutidž], *s.* chochera; cariño excesivo.—**dote** [dout], *vi.* chochear.

double [dʌbl], *a.* doble, duplicado; falso, engañoso.—*d. bed*, cama de matrimonio.—*d. boiler*, baño María.—*d.-breasted*, (sast.) cruzado, de dos filas.—*d.-cross*, traición hecha a un cómplice.—*d. chin*, papada.—*d. dealer*, falso, traidor.—*d. entry*, partida doble.—*d. meaning*, doble sentido; equívoco; segunda intención.—*adv.* doblemente.—*s.* doble, duplo; (teat., cine) doble.—*vt.* doblar, duplicar.—*vi.* doblarse, duplicarse; volver atrás.

doubt [daut], *vt.* y *vi.* dudar; desconfiar.—*s.* duda.—*if* o *when in d.*, en caso de duda.—**ful** [dáutful], *a.* dudoso.——**less** [-lis], *a.* indudable, cierto; confiado.—*adv.* sin duda, indudablemente, probablemente.

douche [duš], *s.* jeringa o lavado vaginal; ducha, (Am.) regadera.—*vt.* y *vi.* duchar(se).

dough [dou], *s.* pasta, masa; (fam.) plata, dinero.——**nut** [dóunʌt], *s.* buñuelo, rosca.——**y** [-i], *a.* pastoso.

dove [dʌv], *s.* paloma, tórtola.—[douv], *pret.* de TO DIVE.

dowel [dáuel], *s.* clavija, espiga.

down [daun], *adv.* abajo; hacia abajo; al sur.—*d. below*, allá abajo.—*d. from*, desde.—*d. to*, hasta.—*d. to date*, hasta la fecha.—*to reducir la ebullición.—*to cut d.*, recortar, rebajar.—*to go* o *come d.*, bajar.—*to lie d.*, acostarse.—*interj.* ¡abajo!—*d. with the King!* ¡muera el Rey!—*prep.* en sentido descendente; por, al largo de, hacia abajo.—*d. the street*, calle abajo.—*a.* pendiente, descendente; abatido, alicaído; de abajo; atrasado, atrás.—*d. and out*, fuera de combate; vencido; arruinado.—*d. payment*, primer plazo, paga al contado.—*to be d. on*, tener inquina a.—*s.* plumón; bozo; lana fina o pelo suave, pelusa; revés de fortuna, baja, caída; colina, duna.—*d. bed*, colchón de plumas.—*vt.* derribar; vencer; bajar, creer sin previo examen.——**cast** [dáunkæst], *a.* alicaído, cabizbajo.——**fall** [-fol], *s.* caída; ruina.——**grade** [-greid], *a.* y *adv.* cuesta abajo.—*s.* bajada, descenso.——**hearted** [-hartid], *a.* abatido, descorazonado.——**hill** [-hil], *a.* pendiente, en declive.—*s.* declive, bajada.—*adv.* cuesta abajo.——**pour** [-por], *s.* aguacero, chaparrón.——**right** [-rait], *a.* vertical; claro, categórico; absoluto, completo.—*adv.* claramente, completamente.——**stairs**

[-stérz], *adv.* abajo, en el piso de abajo.—*s.* piso inferior, primer piso.— **—town** [-taṳn], *a.* y *adv.* de ɵ en la parte baja de la ciudad; del centro.

dowry [dáṳri], *s.* dote; arras.

doze [douz], *vi.* dormitar, descabezar el sueño.—*s.* sueño ligero; sopor, adormecimiento.

dozen [dázẹn], *s.* docena.

drab [dræb], *a.* pardusco; monótono; ordinario, sin atractivos.—*s.* color entre gris pardo y amarillento.

draft [dræft], *s.* corriente de aire; tiro (de chimenea, etc.); succión; trago; (mar.) calado; tracción; carretada; trazado, dibujo; plan, plano; borrador, minuta; proyecto, propuesta (de ley, reglamento, etc.); letra de cambio, libranza, orden de pago; (mil.) reclutamiento, leva; destacamento.—*d. ale* o *beer,* cerveza de tonel o de barril.—*d. dodger,* emboscado; prófugo del servicio militar. —*vt.* proyectar, bosquejar; hacer un borrador o diseño, esquema, plan; reclutar; redactar.— **—sman** [dræftsmạn], *s.* dibujante, delineante, diseñador.

drag [dræg], *vti.* [1] arrastrar, tirar; rastrear, rastrillar.—*to d. in,* traer por los cabellos.—*to d. on* o *out,* prolongar.—*vii.* arrastrarse por el suelo; ir tirando; atrasarse, ir en zaga; pasar con penosa lentitud, ser interminable.—*s.* rastra; draga; rémora, cosa que retarda o dificulta.

drain [drein], *vt.* drenar, desaguar; desecar; escurrir; colar; achicar; agotar; consumir, disipar.—*to d. off,* vaciar.—*vi.* desaguarse, vaciarse, escurrirse.—*s.* desagüe, escurridor; sumidero, alcantarilla; consumo; agotamiento.—*to de desagüe.* **—age** [dréinjdž], *s.* drenaje, desagüe.— **—er** [-œ(r)] *s.* colador, coladero.

drake [dreik], *s.* pato o ánade macho.

drama [dráma̦], *s.* drama.— **—tic** [drạmétịk], *a.* dramático.— **—tics** [drạmétịks], *s.* dramática.— **—tist** [drémạtịst], *s.* dramaturgo.— **—tize** [drémạtạiz], *vt.* dramatizar.

drank [dræŋk], *pret.* de TO DRINK.

drape [dreip], *vt.* revestir, entapizar; colgar (cortinas, etc.); formar pliegues artísticos.— **—ry** [dréipœri], *s.* cortinaje, ropaje, colgaduras, tapicería, etc.

draught [dræft], *s.*, *vt.* = DRAFT.

draw [dro], *vti.* [10] tirar; atraer; estirar; sacar; inferir, deducir; desenvainar; hacer salir; chupar o mamar; aspirar, respirar; cobrar (un sueldo); sacarse (un premio); echar (suertes); procurarse, proporcionarse; correr o descorrer (cortinas, etc.);

dibujar; trazar; redactar, extender (un cheque, etc.); devengar (intereses, etc.); retirar (fondos); girar, librar; tender (un arco); destripar (aves).—*to d. along,* arrastrar.—*to d. aside,* llevar aparte.—*to d. back,* hacer retroceder.—*to d. in,* atraer, seducir, embaucar.—*to d. up,* redactar.—*vii.* tirar; atraer gente; (dep.) empatar; dibujar.—*to d. away,* alejarse.—*to d. back,* retroceder.—*to d. near,* acercarse.—*to d. up,* pararse, detenerse. —*s.* tracción; atracción; empate; sorteo.— **—back** [dróbæk], *s.* desventaja, inconveniente.— **—bridge** [-bridž], *s.* puente levadizo o giratorio.— **—er** [-œ(r)], *s.* gaveta, cajón. —*pl.* calzoncillos.— **—ing** [-iŋ], *s.* dibujo; sorteo; giro; cobranza; extracción.—*d. account,* cuenta corriente. **—drawn** [dron], *pp.* de TO DRAW.

dread [dred], *s.* miedo, pavor.—*a.* terrible, espantoso.—*vt.* y *vi.* temer, tener miedo a.— **—ful** [drédfụl], *a.* terrible, espantoso.

dream [drim], *s.* sueño, ensueño.—*vti.* y *vii.* [4] soñar; ver en sueños; fantasear, forjar(se).—*to d. of,* soñar con.— **—er** [drímœ(r)], *s.* soñador.— **—y** [-i], *a.* contemplativo, soñador; propio de un sueño.

dreary [dríri], *a.* triste, melancólico; monótono, pesado.

dredge [dredž], *vt.* dragar; rastrear; polvorear.—*s.* draga; rastra.

dregs [dregz], *s. pl.* heces; sedimento; desperdicios; hez, gentuza.

drench [drench], *vt.* empapar; mojar; remojar.—*s.* empapada; mojadura.

dress [dres], *vti.* [4] vestir; ataviar; adornar; curar (heridas); preparar, arreglar; aliñar, aderezar; curtir; amortajar; arreglar (el pelo).—*to d. down,* poner como nuevo (a alguien). —*vii.* vestirse; ataviarse; adornarse; alinearse.—*to d. up,* vestirse de etiqueta, prenderse de veinticinco alfileres.—*s.* vestido; traje; indumentaria.—*d. ball,* baile de etiqueta o de trajes.—*d. suit,* traje de etiqueta.

drew [dru], *pret.* de TO DRAW.

dried [draid], *a.* seco; secado; desecado. **—drier** [dráiœ(r)], *s.* secador, secadora; secadero; secante; desecante.

drift [drift], *s.* rumbo, tendencia; impulso; deriva; montón (de nieve, arena).—*to get the d. of,* comprender lo esencial de algo; enterarse sólo a medias.—*vi.* (aer., mar.) derivar, ir a la deriva; vagar; apilarse, amontonarse o esparcirse con el viento.— **—wood** [dríftwụd], *s.* madera flotante; madera de playa.

drill [dril], *vt.* taladrar, barrenar, horadar; fresar; sembrar, plantar en hileras o surcos; ejercitar, dar instrucción (ejército, etc.), entrenar. —*vi.* (mil.) hacer la instrucción, practicar, ejercitarse.—*s.* taladro, fresa, barrena; práctica, ejercicio; disciplina; adiestramiento; (tela de) dril.

drink [drįŋk], *vti.* y *vii.* [10] beber. —*s.* bebida; trago, copa.—**able** [drįŋkȧbl], *a.* potable.—**er** [-œ(r)], *s.* bebedor; borrachín.

drip [drįp], *vti.* y *vii.* [3] gotear.—*s.* gota; goteo; gotera.

drive [drȧiv], *vti.* [10] guiar, conducir, manejar (automóviles, etc.); impulsar, empujar; echar, arrojar; inducir; forzar (a); arrear; meter, clavar, hincar.—*vii.* andar o ir de paseo (automóvil, etc); saber guiar, manejar o conducir vehículos.—*to d. at,* aspirar a, tender a; querer decir. —*to d. away,* ahuyentar, echar; alejarse (en un vehículo).—*s.* paseo en automóvil; capacidad de mando, energía; calzada para vehículos; presión, exigencia; tendencia, anhelo; campaña pública; conducción de vehículos.—*d.-in,* cine al aire libre para automovilistas; cafetería que sirve directamente en el automóvil.

drivel [drȧvȩl], *vii.* [2] babear; bobear. —*s.* baba; ñoñería; cháchara.

driven [drȧvȩn], *pp.* de TO DRIVE.— **driver** [drȧivœ(r)], *s.* el que conduce, maneja o gobierna un vehículo (chofer, cochero, carretero, etc.); rueda motriz.—*driver's seat,* asiento del chofer.—*pile d.,* martinete.—**driveway** [drȧivwej], *s.* vía de acceso a un garage; calzada.

drizzle [drȧzl], *vi.* lloviznar.—*s.* llovizna.

drone [droun], *s.* zángano; haragán; zumbido.—*vi.* haraganear; zumbar; hablar en tono monótono.

droop [drup], *vi.* inclinarse, caer; colgar; pender; decaer, desanimarse; languidecer, marchitarse.

drop [drap], *s.* gota; zarcillo; caída, declive, pendiente; pastilla; (com.) baja, caída.—*d. curtain,* telón de boca.—*d. hammer,* martinete.—*vti.* [3] verter a gotas; soltar, dejar caer; desprenderse de; renunciar a, desistir de; despedir, echar.—*to d. a letter,* echar una carta en el buzón. —*to d. a line,* escribir unas líneas. —*to d. in,* hacer una visita inesperadamente.—*to d. out,* desaparecer; separarse.—*vii.* gotear; descender; detenerse.—**let** [drȧplįt], *s.* gotita.

drought [drȧut], **drouth** [drȧuθ], *s.* sequía; aridez, sequedad.

drove [drouv], *s.* manada, recua, hato,

piara; gentío.—*pret.* de TO DRIVE.— —**r** [drȯuvœ(r)], *s.* ganadero.

drown [drȧun], *vt.* y *vi.* ahogar(se); anegar(se); sumergir(se).

drowse [drȧuz], *vt.* y *vi.* adormecer(se), amodorrar(se).—**drowsiness** [drȧuzi-nįs], *s.* modorra, somnolencia, pesadez.—**drowsy** [drȧuzį], *a.* soñoliento, amodorrado; soporífero.

drudge [drȧdż], *vi.* afanarse, fatigarse. —*s.* ganapán, esclavo del trabajo.

drug [drȧg], *s.* droga, medicamento; narcótico; artículo de poca venta. —*d. addict* o *fiend,* narcómano.—*d. store,* farmacia, botica, droguería.— *vti.* [1] mezclar con drogas; narcotizar.—*vii.* tomar drogas.—**druggist** [drȧgįst], *s.* droguero, farmacéutico.

drum [drȧm], *s.* tambor; redoblante; cuñete; cuerpo de columna; tímpano (del oído).—*vti.* y *vii.* [1] tocar el tambor; tamborilear; repetir, machacar; teclear.—**drummer** [-œ(r)], *s.* tambor, tamborilero; viajante de comercio.

drunk [drȧŋk], *pp.* de TO DRINK.—*s.* borrachín; parranda, borrachera.— *a.* ebrio, borracho.—**ard** [drȧŋkȧrd], *s.* borracho, borrachín.—**en** [-ȩn], *a.* ebrio, borracho.—**enness** [-ȩnnįs], *s.* embriaguez; ebriedad.

dry [drȧi], *a.* árido, seco.—*d. cell,* pila o elemento seco.—*d. cleaner,* tintorería.—*d. cleaning,* limpieza en seco. —*d. goods,* lencería; víveres.—*vti.* [7] secar, desecar; enjugar; desaguar; dar sed; acecinar.—*vii.* secarse, enjugarse.—*to d. up,* secarse completa y rápidamente.—**er** [drȧiœ(r)], *s.* = DRIER.—**ness** [-nįs], *s.* sequedad, aridez.

dubious [djúbiȧs], *a.* dudoso; incierto; ambiguo.

duchess [dȧchįs], *s.* duquesa.

duck [dȧk], *s.* pato, ánade; acción de agacharse.—*vt.* chapuzar; evitar (un golpe, deber, etc.).—*vi.* agacharse, chapuzar(se).—**ling** [dȧklįŋ], *s.* patito.

ductile [dȧktįl], *a.* dúctil.

dud [dȧd], *s.* (fam.) persona o cosa floja o inútil; fiasco; bomba o granada que no estalla.—*pl.* (fam.) ropa.

dude [djud], *s.* petimetre, lechuguino.

due [dju], *a.* cumplido, vencido; pagadero; apto, propio, conveniente, oportuno; legítimo; esperado, que debe llegar.—*d. bill,* pagaré.—*adv.* exactamente.—*s.* deuda u obligación; derechos, réditos.—*to get one's d.,* llevar su merecido castigo.

duel [djúȩl], *s.* duelo, desafío; certamen.—*vi.* batirse en duelo.

duet [djuét], *s.* dúo, dueto.

dug [dȧg], *pret.* y *pp.* de TO DIG.—*s.*

teta, ubre.- **—out** [-aut], *s.* chabola;
(mar.) piragua.

duke [djuk], *s.* duque.

dull [dʌl], *a.* embotado, obtuso, sin
punta, sin filo; apagado, sordo; lerdo;
insípido, soso, insulso; flojo, perezoso;
lánguido; (colores) desvaído, mate;
insensible; triste; deslustrado, empañado; opaco, nebuloso; soñoliento;
(com.) inactivo, muerto.—*vt.* y *vi.*
embotar(se); entorpecer(se); ofus-
car(se); empañar(se).- **—ard** [dʌl-
ǥrd], *a.* estúpido.- **—ness** [-njs], *s.*
embotamiento; estupidez; aburrimiento; somnolencia, pesadez.

dumb [dʌm], *a.* mudo; callado; estúpido.—*d. motions*, señas.—*d. show*,
pantomima.- **—ness** [dʌmnjs], *s.*
mudez; silencio; estupidez.

dummy [dʌmi], *a.* imitado, fingido,
contrahecho.—*s.* maniquí; testaferro;
figurón; proyecto de formato de una
publicación; objeto simulado; zoquete, estúpido.

dump [damp], *vt.* vaciar de golpe;
descargar; vender a precios inferiores a los corrientes.—*s.* vaciadero;
vaciamiento.—*pl.* melancolía, mo-
rriña.- **—ing** [dʌmpjŋ], *s.* vaciamiento; inundación del mercado con
artículos de precios rebajados; competir comercialmente con precios ínfi-
mos.

dunce [dʌns], *s.* zopenco, tonto.

dune [djun], *s.* duna.

dung [dʌŋ], *s.* estiércol, boñiga.—*d.
heap o yard*, estercolero; muladar.

dungeon [dʌndʒǝn], *s.* calabozo, maz-
morra.

dunghill [dʌŋhjl], *s.* estercolero, muladar.

dunk [dʌŋk], *vt.* (coll.) mojar, ensopar;
tirar al agua.

dupe [djup], *s.* incauto, primo.—*vt.*
engañar, embaucar.

duplicate [djúplikejt], *vt.* duplicar.—*a.*
[djúplikjt], duplicado, copia.—*in d.*,
por duplicado.—*s.* duplicado, doble,
en pares.—**duplicity** [djuplísjti], *s.*
duplicidad, engaño, segunda intención.

durability [djurǝbíljti], *s.* durabilidad,
duración; permanencia.—**duration**
[djuréjšǝn], *s.* duración.—**during**
[djúrjŋ], *prep.* durante, mientras.

dusk [dʌsk], *a.* oscuro (poet.).—*s.*
crepúsculo vespertino; oscuridad.—
d.-to-dawn, del anochecer, a la madrugada.- **—y** [dʌskj], *a.* oscuro;
moreno, pardo.

dust [dʌst], *s.* polvo; cenizas, restos
mortales.—*d. brush*, plumero.—*d.
cloud*, polvareda.—*vt.* sacudir o quitar
el polvo; (es)polvorear.—*to d. one's
jacket*, zurrar a uno.- **—er** [dʌstǝ(r)],

s. paño del polvo; plumero; guarda-
polvos.- **—y** [-j], *a.* empolvado,
polvoriento.

Dutch [dʌch], *s.* y *a.* holandés.—*D.
tile*, azulejo.—*D. treat*, convite a
escote.—*to go D.*, ir a medias.—
—man [dʌchmǝn], *s.* holandés.

duty [djúti], *s.* deber, obligación; incumbencia; impuesto, derechos de
aduana; trabajo, servicio (mec.).—*d.
free*, libre de derechos.—*in d. bound*,
moralmente obligado.—*off d.*, libre,
franco de servicio.—*on d.*, de guardia
o de servicio.

dwell [dwel], *vii.* [4] habitar, morar.

dwarf [dwɔrf], *s.* enano, pigmeo.—*a.*
diminuto, enano.

dwindle [dwjndl], *vi.* menguar, disminuirse; degenerar; decaer; consumirse.—*vt.* mermar.

dye [daj], *vt.* teñir.—*s.* tinte.- **—r**
[dájœ(r)], *s.* tintorero.

dying [dájjŋ], *a.* moribundo; mortecino;
mortal.—*s.* muerte.

dynamic [dajnǽmjk], *a.* dinámico;
enérgico.

dynamite [dájnǝmajt], *s.* dinamita.—*vt.*
volar con dinamita, dinamitar.

dynamo [dájnǝmou], *s.* dínamo, generador.

dynasty [dájnʌsti], *s.* dinastía.

dysentery [djsɛnterj], *s.* disentería.

E

each [ich], *a.* cada, todo.—*pron.* cada
uno, cada cual, todos.—*e. for himself*, cada cual por su cuenta, o por
su lado.—*e. other*, mutuamente; unos
a otros.—*adv.* por persona, por
cabeza, cada cual.

eager [ígœ(r)], *a.* ansioso, anhelante,
deseoso.- **—ness** [-njs], *s.* ansia,
anhelo, afán, ahinco; vehemencia.

eagle [ígl], *s.* águila.- **—t** [ígljt], *s.*
aguilucho.

ear [ir], *s.* oreja; oído; espiga.—*by the
ears*, en pugna abierta.—*e. muff*,
orejera.—*to be all ears*, (fam.) aguzar
los oídos o las orejas.- **—drum** [ir-
dram], *s.* tímpano.

earl [œrl], *s.* conde.

early [œrlj], *a.* primitivo, primero;
tempran(er)o; próximo.—*e. bird*,
(fig.) madrugador.—*the e. part of*,
el principio de.—*adv.* temprano,
pronto, antes de la hora; al principio.
—*as e. as possible*, lo más pronto
posible.

earn [œrn], *vt.* ganar; merecer.

earnest [œrnjst], *a.* serio, formal.—*s.*
seriedad, buena fe; prenda, señal.-
—ness [-njs], *s.* seriedad; sinceridad;
celo.

earnings [ǝ́rniņz], *s. pl.* salario, sueldo, paga, jornal; ganancias.

earphone [ŕfoun], *s.* auricular; audífono.

earring [ŕiņ], *s.* pendiente, arete.

earth [œrθ], *s.* tierra (materia; planeta); mundo; suelo.— —**enware** [œ́rθǝnwɛr], *s.* loza de barro, cacharros.— —**ly** [-li], *a.* terreno; terrenal, mundano.— —**quake** [-kweik], *s.* temblor de tierra, terremoto.— —**ward** [-wǝrd], *s.* y *adv.* hacia la tierra.— —**worm** [-wœrm], *s.* lombriz de tierra.— —**y** [-i], *a.* terroso; mundano, primario.

ease [iz], *s.* tranquilidad; comodidad, alivio, descanso; facilidad, desenvoltura, naturalidad.—*at e.*, descansadamente, a sus anchas.—*with e.*, con facilidad.—*vt.* aliviar, mitigar, aligerar, desembarazar, facilitar.— *vi.* disminuir, apaciguarse, suavizarse.

easel [íząl], *s.* caballete de pintor; atril.

east [ist], *s.* este, levante, oriente.—*a.* oriental; del este.—*E. Indian*, indio, hindú.—*adv.* hacia el este.

Easter [ístœr(r)], *s.* Pascua florida o de Resurrección.—*E. Saturday*, Sábado Santo.—*E. Sunday*, Domingo de Resurrección.

eastern [ístœrn], *a.* oriental.—**Easterner** [ístœrnœr(r)], *s.* oriental; habitante del este (de los E.U.).

easy [ízi], *a.* fácil; cómodo; suelto, libre; tranquilo; aliviado.—*e. chair*, butaca, poltrona.—*e. going*, lento; calmado, sereno.—*adv.* e *interj.* despacio, qued(it)o.

eat [it], *vti.* [10] comer, tomar.—*to e. away, into* o *through*, corroer.—*to e. breakfast, lunch, dinner, supper*, desayunarse, almorzar, comer, cenar. —*to e. one's heart out*, sufrir en silencio.—*to e. one's words*, retractarse. —*to e. up*, devorar, tragar.—*vii.* comer, alimentarse, sustentarse.— **eaten** [ítęn], *pp.* de TO EAT.

eaves [ivz], *s. pl.* alero.— —**drop** [ívzdrap], *vii.* [1] escuchar solapadamente, fisgonear.

ebb [eb], *vi.* menguar la marea; decaer. —*s.* menguante, marea baja, reflujo; decadencia.—*e. of life*, vejez.—*e. tide*, marea menguante.

ebony [ébǝni], *s.* ébano.

eccentric [ikséntrik], *s.* persona excéntrica o rara; (mec.) excéntrica.—*a.* also —*al* [-ąl], *a.* (geom. y mec.) excéntrico; extravagante, estrafalario.

ecclesiastic [iklizįǽstik], *s.* eclesiástico. —*e.*, —*al* [-ąl], *a.* eclesiástico.

echo [ékou], *s.* eco.—*vi.* repercutir, resonar.—*vt.* repetir con aprobación; hacer eco.

eclipse [iklíps], *s.* eclipse.—*vt.* eclipsar.

economic(al) [ikonámik(ąl)], *a.* económico; moderado, módico.—**economics** [ikonámiks], *s.* economía política.—**economist** [ikánomist], *s.* economista.—**economize** [ikánomaiz], *vt.* y *vi.* economizar, ahorrar. —**economy** [ikánomi], *s.* economía, ahorro.

ecstasy [ékstąsi], *s.* éxtasis, arrobamiento.

Ecuadorian [ekwądóriąn], *a.* y *s.* ecuatoriano.

eddy [édi], *s.* remanso; remolino.—*vi.* arremolinarse; remansarse.

edge [edž], *s.* filo; canto; borde, orilla, margen.—*on e.*, de canto; impaciente, ansioso.—*to set the teeth on e.*, dar dentera.—*vt.* afilar; incitar; (cost.) orlar.—*vi.* avanzar de lado, escurrirse.— —**wise** [édžwaiz], *adv.* de filo o de canto.—**edging** [édžiņ], *s.* orla(dura), pestaña.

edible [édibl], *a.* y *s.* comestible.

edict [idikt], *s.* edicto, mandato; bando.

edifice [édifis], *s.* edificio.—**edify** [édifai], *vti.* [7] edificar; instruir moralmente.

edit [édit], *vt.* redactar; editar; dirigir (un periódico); corregir (manuscritos).— —**ion** [idíšon], *s.* edición; tirada.— —**or** [-ǫ(r)], *s.* redactor; director de un periódico o revista; editor.— —**orial** [-óriąl], *a.* editorial. —*e. rooms* o *staff*, redacción.—*s.* editorial, artículo de fondo.

educate [édjukeit], *vt.* educar; instruir. —**education** [edjukéišǫn], *s.* educación; enseñanza, instrucción.—**educational** [edjukéišǫnąl], *a.* docente; educativo.—*e. institution*, plantel, centro docente.—**educator** [édjukeitǫ(r)], *s.* educador.

eel [il], *s.* anguila.

effect [efékt], *s.* efecto; impresión; eficiencia.—*pl.* efectos, bienes.—*in e.*, vigente; en realidad.—*into e.*, en vigor, en práctica.—*of no e.*, sin resultado; vano.—*to the e. that*, de que, en el sentido de que.—*vt.* efectuar, realizar, llevar a cabo.— —**ive** [-iv], *a.* efectivo, eficaz; vigente.

effeminate [efémįnit], *a.* afeminado.

efficacy [éfikąsi], *s.* eficacia.

efficiency [efíšęnsi], *s.* eficiencia; eficacia; (mec.) rendimiento.—**efficient** [efíšęnt], *a.* eficiente; eficaz, competente; (mec.) de gran rendimiento.

effigy [éfidži], *s.* efigie.

effort [éfǫrt], *s.* esfuerzo, empeño.

effrontery [efrántœri], *s.* desfachatez, descaro.

effusion [efiúžǫn], *s.* efusión, derrame; expansión.—**effusive** [efiúsiv], *a.* expansivo, efusivo, comunicativo.

egg [eg], *s.* huevo.—*e. dealer*, huevero.

—e.-laying, postura.—hard boiled e.,
huevo duro.—poached e., huevo
escalfado.—soft-boiled e., huevo pasado por agua.— —nog [égnag], s.
ponche de huevo.— —plant [-plænt],
s. berenjena.

egotism [ígoutjzm], s. egolatría, ego-
tismo.—egotist [ígoutjst], s. ególatra,
egotista.

Egyptian [idʒípʃan], a. y s. egipcio.

either [íðœ(r), áiðœ(r)], a. y pron. uno
u otro, cualquiera de los dos.—conj.
o, ora, ya.—adv. (después de not, nor)
tampoco.

ejaculate [idʒǽkyuleit], vt. exclamar,
proferir; (med.) eyacular.—ejacu-
lation [idʒækyuléiʃọn], s. exclamación; eyaculación; polución.

eject [idʒékt], vt. arrojar, lanzar, expulsar.— —ion [idʒékʃọn], s. expulsión,
evacuación.

elaborate [ilǽboreit], vt. elaborar; explicar detalladamente.—a. [ilǽbọrit],
elaborado, trabajado, detallado,
esmerado; recargado.—elaboration
[ilæboréiʃọn], s. elaboración; obra
acabada.

elapse [iláps], vi. mediar, pasar, transcurrir.

elastic [ilǽstik], a. elástico.—s. cinta
de goma, elástico.— —ity [ilæstísiti],
s. elasticidad.

elate [iléit], vt. exaltar; alborozar;
elevar.— —d [-id], a. exaltado,
alborozado.

elbow [élbou], s. codo; recodo, ángulo;
brazo de sillón.—at one's e., a la
mano, muy cerca.—e. room, espacio
suficiente, holgura.—vt. dar codazos.
—to e. one's way, abrirse paso a codazos.—vi. codear; formar recodos o
ángulos.

elder [éldœ(r)], a. mayor, de más edad;
antiguo, anterior.—s. anciano; señor
mayor; dignatario.—pl. ancianos,
mayores, antepasados.— —ly [-li],
a. mayor, de edad madura o avanzada.—eldest [éldjst], a. mayor de
todos, [el] de más edad.—e. son,
hijo primogénito.

elect [ilékt], vt. elegir, escoger.—a. y
s. electo o elegido.— —ion [ilékʃọn],
s. elección.— —or [-ọ(r)], s. elector.—
—oral [-ọral], a. electoral.— —orate
[-ọrit], s. electorado.

electric(al) [iléktrik(al)], a. eléctrico;
(fig.) supersensible.—e. bulb, bombi-
lla, (Am.) bombillo.—e. eye, célula
fotoeléctrica.—e. fixtures, aparatos
eléctricos.—e. powerhouse, central
eléctrica.—e. tape, cinta aisladora
adhesiva.—e. wiring, instalación eléctrica.—electrician [ilektríʃan], s. elec-
tricista.—electricity [ilektrísiti], s.
electricidad.—electrification [ilektri-

fikéiʃọn], s. electrización; electrifica-
ción.—electrify [iléktrifai], vti. [7]
electrizar; electrificar.—electrocute
[iléktrokiut], vt. electrocutar.—elec-
trocution [ilektrokiúʃọn], s. electro-
cución.—electronics [ilektránjks], s.
electrónica.

elegance [éligans], s. elegancia.—ele-
gant [éligant], a. elegante.

element [éligment], s. elemento; componente.—pl. nociones, rudimentos.—
—al [eliméntal], —ary [eliménteri],
a. elemental, primordial, rudimentario.

elephant [élifant], s. elefante.

elevate [éliveit], vt. elevar; alzar,
exaltar.—elevation [elivéiʃọn], s.
elevación; exaltación; altura; eminencia.—elevator (éliveitọ(r)], s.
ascensor; elevador.—e. shaft, caja
o pozo del ascensor.—grain e., silo.

eligible [élidʒibl], a. elegible.

eliminate [ilímineit], vt. eliminar, suprimir.—elimination [iliminéiʃọn], s.
eliminación, supresión.—eliminatory
[ilíminatọri], a. eliminatorio.

elk [elk], s. alce o ante.

elm [elm], s. olmo.

elocution [elokiúʃọn], s. elocución;
declamación.

elope [ilóup], vi. fugarse, huir con un
amante.— —ment [-ment], s. fuga
amorosa.

eloquence [élokwens], s. elocuencia,
oratoria, (fam.) labia.—eloquent
[élokwent], a. elocuente.

else [els], a. otro, diferente; más.
—anything e., algo más; cualquiera
otra cosa.—nobody e., no one e.,
ningún otro.—adv. y conj. más,
además; en vez de.—how e.?, ¿de
qué otro modo?.—or e., o bien, o en
su lugar, de otro modo, en otro
caso; si no.— —where [élswer], adv.
en, a o de otra parte.

elude [iliúd], vt. eludir, evadir, evitar,
sortear.—elusive [iliúsiv], elusory
[iliúsori], a. evasivo, esquivo, fugaz.

emaciate(d) [iméiʃieit(id)], a. demacrado, macilento, flaco; extenuado.

emancipate [imǽnsipeit], vt. emancipar.
—emancipation [imænsipéiʃọn], s.
emancipación.—emancipator [imæn-
sipeitọ(r)], s. emancipador, libertador.

embalm [embám], vt. embalsamar.—
—ment [-ment], s. embalsamamiento.

embankment [embǽŋkment], s. dique;
terraplén.

embarcation [embarkéiʃọn], s. = EM-
BARKATION.

embargo [embárgou], s. embargo, detención, prohibición.—vt. embargar,
detener.

embark [embárk], vt. y vi. embarcar(se).— —ation, [-éịŝọn], *s.* embarque.

embarrass [embǽrǎs], *vt.* turbar, desconcertar; embarazar.— —ment [-mẹnt], *s.* turbación; embarazo, estorbo; (com.) apuros, dificultades.

embassy [émbǎsị], *s.* embajada.

embed [embéd], *vti.* [1] encajar, empotrar.

embellish [embélịŝ], *vt.* embellecer.— —ment [-mẹnt], *s.* embellecimiento.

ember [émbœ(r)], *s.* ascua, pavesa. —*pl.* rescoldo.

embezzle [embézl], *vt.* desfalcar.— —ment [-mẹnt], *s.* desfalco.— —r [embézlœ(r)], *s.* desfalcador.

embitter [embịtœ(r)], *vt.* emargar.

emblem [émblem], *s.* emblema, símbolo.

embody [embádị], *vti.* [7] dar cuerpo, encarnar; incorporar; incluir, englobar.—*vii.* unirse, incorporarse.

embolus [émbọlʌs], *s.* (med.) émbolo.

emboss [embôs], *vt.* repujar, realzar, estampar en relieve.——ment [-mẹnt], *s.* realce, relieve.

embrace [embréịs], *vt.* abrazar; abarcar, rodear.—*vi.* abrazarse.—*s.* abrazo.

embrasure [embréịźụ(r)], *s.* (fort.) tronera, aspillera; (arq.) alféizar.

embroider [embrôịdœ(r)], *vt.* bordar, recamar.—*vi.* hacer labor de bordado.— —er [-œ(r)], —ess [-ịs], *s.* bordador; bordadora.— —y [-ị], *s.* bordado, bordadura, labor.

embroil [embrôịl], *vt.* embrollar, enredar.— —ment [-mẹnt], *s.* embrollo, intriga.

embryo [émbrịoụ], *s.* embrión.— —nic [embrịánịk], *a.* embrionario.

emendation [imendéịŝọn], *s.* enmienda, corrección.

emerald [émẹrald], *s.* esmeralda.

emerge [imœ̌rdź], *vi.* emerger, brotar, surgir.

emergency [imœ̌rdźẹnsị], *s.* emergencia, aprieto o necesidad urgente.—*e. hospital,* hospital de urgencia, casa de socorros.—*e. landing,* aterrizaje forzoso.—emergent [imœ̌rdźẹnt], *a.* emergente; urgente.

emery [émẹrị], *s.* esmeril.

emigrant [émịgrǎnt], *a.* emigrante. —*s.* emigrante, emigrado.—emigrate [émịgreịt], *vi.* emigrar, expatriarse. —emigration [emịgréịŝọn], *s.* emigración.

eminence [émịnẹns], *s.* altura, cima, eminencia.—eminent [émịnẹnt], *a.* eminente.

emissary [émịserị], *s.* emisario.— emission [imịŝọn], *s.* emisión, salida. —emit [imịt], *vti.* [1] emitir.

emotion [imóụŝọn], *s.* emoción.— —al [-ạl], *a.* emocional, emotivo, sensible; sentimental.

emperor [émpœrọ(r)], *s.* emperador.

emphasis [émfạsịs], *s.* énfasis.—emphasize [émfạsaịz], *vt.* enfatizar, poner énfasis; recalcar, acentuar.

empire [émpaịr], *s.* imperio.

employ [emplôị], *vt.* emplear; usar; dedicar.—*s.* empleo; ocupación, oficio.— —ee [-ị], *s.* empleado.— —er [-œ(r)], *s.* patrón, patrono.— —ment [-mẹnt], *s.* empleo, colocación; uso, aplicación.

empower [empáụœ(r)], *vt.* autorizar, facultar, dar poder.

empress [émprịs], *s.* emperatriz.

empty [émptị], *a.* vacío, desocupado; vacante; vano; vacuo, frívolo. —*e.-headed,* tonto.—*vti.* [7] vaciar, desocupar, evacuar.—*vii.* vaciarse; desaguar, desembocar.

emulsion [imʌlŝọn], *s.* emulsión.

enable [enéịbl], *vt.* habilitar, capacitar, permitir.

enact [enǽkt], *vt.* promulgar, dar (una ley); decretar; (teat.) hacer el papel de.

enamel [enǽmẹl], *vti.* [2] esmaltar.— *s.* esmalte.

encamp [ɛnkémp], *vt.* y *vi.* (mil.) acampar.——ment [-mẹnt], *s.* campamento.

enchant [enchǽnt], *vt.* encantar, hechizar; fascinar, embelesar.— —er [-œ(r)], *s.* encantador, hechicero.— —ment [-mẹnt], *s.* encantamiento, hechicería, hechizo; encanto.— —ress [-rịs], *s.* maga; encantadora, seductora, hechicera.

encircle [ɛnsœ̌rkl], *vt.* cercar, rodear.

enclose [ɛnklôụz], *vt.* cercar; rodear, circundar; encerrar; incluir, adjuntar o enviar adjunta una cosa.—enclosure [ɛnklôụźụ(r)], *s.* vallado, tapia; cercado; recinto; lo adjunto (en carta, etc.), contenido.

encompass [ɛnkʌmpạs], *vt.* circundar, rodear, encerrar; abarcar.

encounter [ɛnkáụntœ(r)], *s.* encuentro, choque; combate.—*vt.* y *vi.* encontrar; salir al encuentro de; topar o tropezar con.

encourage [ɛnkœ̌rịdź], *vt.* animar, alentar; fomentar.— —ment [-mẹnt], *s.* aliento, ánimo; fomento.

encyclopedia [ɛnsaịklopídịǎ], *s.* enciclopedia.

end [end], *s.* fin; extremidad; punta; remate; desenlace, final; fondo; propósito, objeto.—*at loose ends,* en desorden, desarreglado.—*at the e. of,* al cabo de.—*e. line,* línea de límite. —*no e. of,* un sinfín de, muchísimo(s), la mar de.—*to make both ends meet,* pasar con lo que se tiene.—*to no e.,* sin efecto, en vano.—*vt.* y *vi.* acabar, concluir, terminar, finalizar.

endear [endír], vt. hacer(se) querer.

endeavor [endévǫ(r)], s. esfuerzo, conato, empeño, tentativa.—vt. intentar, pretender, tratar de.—vi. esforzarse, hacer un esfuerzo (por).

ending [éndiŋ], s. fin, conclusión; terminación; desenlace.

endive [éndajv], s. (bot.) escarola.

endless [éndlĭs], a. sin fin; interminable, perpetuo.

endorse [endórs], vt. = INDORSE.—endorsement [endórsmẹnt], s. = INDORSEMENT.

endow [endáu], vt. dotar; fundar.—ment [-mẹnt], s. dotación; fundación.

endurance [endiúrạns], s. paciencia; resistencia; duración.—to be beyond o past e., ser insoportable o inaguantable.—endure [endiúr], vt. soportar, sufrir, resistir, tolerar.—vi. durar, perdurar; tener paciencia.

enema [énẹmặ], s. (med.) enema, lavativa.

enemy [énẹmi], s. enemigo, adversario.

energetic(al) [ĕnœrdžétịk(ạl)], a. enérgico, vigoroso.—energy [énœrdži], s. energía, vigor, carácter.

enervate [énœrveit], vt. enervar, debilitar; desvirtuar, embotar.

enfold [enfóuld], vt. = INFOLD.

enforce [enfórs], vt. dar fuerza o vigor; poner en vigor; cumplimentar, observar o ejecutar (una ley); hacer hincapié en.— —ment [-mẹnt], s. ejecución de una ley; observancia forzosa.

engage [engéidž], vt. ajustar, apalabrar, comprometer; contratar; emplear; entretener; atraer; (mil.) librar o trabar batalla o combate, entrar en lucha con; (mec.) engranar con.—vi. obligarse, dar palabra, comprometerse; ocuparse, entregarse a; pelear.— —d [-d], a. ocupado; comprometido; comprometido para casarse; engranado.——ment [-mẹnt], s. contrato; compromiso, noviazgo; cita; engranaje; batalla, acción.

engender [endžéndœ(r)], vt. engendrar, procrear.—vi. engendrarse, producirse.

engine [éndžĭn], s. máquina; locomotora; motor; instrumento.— —er [-ịr], s. ingeniero; maquinista.—vt. manejar, dirigir.—vi. hacer de ingeniero o maquinista.— —ering [-ịriŋ], s. ingeniería; manejo.

English [íŋglĭš], s. y a. inglés.—E. Channel, Canal de la Mancha.—s. idioma inglés.— —man [ˌmạn], s. inglés.— —woman [-wu̯mạn], s. inglesa.

engrave [engréjv], vt. grabar; cincelar, esculpir.— —r [-œ(r)], s. grabador.

—engraving [engréjvịn], s. grabado; lámina, estampa.

enhance [enhǽns], vt. mejorar, acrecentar; realzar.

enigma [inígmặ], s. enigma, intríngulis.

enjoin [endžóin], vt. mandar, ordenar; imponer.—to e. from, (for.) prohibir.

enjoy [endžój], vt. gozar de; gustar de, gustarle a uno; disfrutar de; saborear.—to e. oneself, gozar, divertirse.— —able [-ạbl], a. deleitable, agradable.— —ment [-mẹnt], s. goce, disfrute, placer; usufructo.

enlarge [enlárdž], vt. agrandar, ensanchar; ampliar o amplificar.—vi. ensancharse o agrandarse; explayarse (en).— —ment [-mẹnt], s. agrandamiento, ensanchamiento; ampliación.— —r [-œ(r)], s. (fot.) ampliador(a).

enlighten [enlájtẹn], vt. iluminar, instruir, ilustrar, alumbrar, esclarecer.

enlist [enlíst], vt. alistar; enrolar; reclutar.—vi. enrolarse; sentar plaza.— —ment [-mẹnt], s. alistamiento, enganche, enrolamiento, reclutamiento.

enliven [enlájvẹn], vt. animar, alentar, avivar.

enmity [énmĭti], s. enemistad.

ennoble [enóu̯bl], vt. ennoblecer.

enormity [inórmĭti], s. enormidad; atrocidad.—enormous [inórmʌs], a. enorme; atroz.

enough [inʌ́f], a. bastante, suficiente.—to be e., bastar.—s. lo suficiente.—interj. ¡bastal ¡no más!—adv. bastante, harto.

enquire [enkwáir], vt. = INQUIRE.—enquirer [enkwáirœ(r)], s. = INQUIRER.

enrage [enréjdž], vt. enfurecer, encolerizar.

enrapture [enrǽpchŭ(r)], vt. arrobar, embelesar, extasiar.

enrich [enrích], vt. enriquecer.— —ment [-mẹnt], s. enriquecimiento.

enroll [enróu̯l], vt. y vi. alistar(se), enrolar(se); matricular(se); envolver(se); enrollar(se).—vi. alistarse, enrolarse; inscribirse, matricularse.— —ment [-mẹnt], s. alistamiento, enrolamiento; matrícula, registro.

ensign [énsain], s. bandera, enseña, pabellón; [énsĭn] alférez; subteniente.—e. bearer, abanderado.

enslave [enslájv], vt. esclavizar.

ensue [ensiú], vi. suceder, sobrevenir.

entail [entéil], s. vinculación.—vt. vincular, perpetuar; acarrear, imponer.

entangle [entǽŋgl], vt. enredar, embrollar, enmarañar.— —ment [-mẹnt], s. enredo, embrollo, complicación.

enter [éntœ(r)], vt. entrar a, por o en; penetrar; asentar, registrar; hacerse miembro de, ingresar en.—*vi.* entrar, introducirse; (teat.) salir al escenario, entrar en escena.

enterprise [éntœrpraiz], *s.* empresa. —**enterprising** [éntœrpraiziŋ], *a.* emprendedor.

entertain [entœrtéin], *vt.* entretener, divertir; festejar, agasajar (en casa). —*to* e. hopes, ideas, abrigar o acariciar esperanzas o ideas.— —**er** [-œ(r)], *s.* artista de variedades; anfitrión.— —**ment** [-męnt], *s.* entretenimiento.

enthrone [enθróun], *vt.* entron(iz)ar.

enthusiasm [enθiúziæzm], *s.* entusiasmo.—**enthusiast** [enθiúziæst], *s.* entusiasta.—**enthusiastic(al)** [enθiuziástik(al)], *a.* entusiástico, entusiasta; entusiasmado.

entice [entáis], *vt.* atraer, seducir, halagar; engatusar.

entire [entáir], *a.* entero, cabal, completo, íntegro, todo.— —**ty** [-ti], *s.* entereza, integridad, totalidad; todo.

entitle [entáitl], *vt.* titular; intitular; dar derecho; autorizar.

entity [éntiti], *s.* entidad; ente, ser.

entrails [éntreilz], *s.* entrañas, vísceras, tripas.

entrance [éntrans], *s.* entrada; ingreso; portal, puerta.—*e. hall*, zaguán, vestíbulo.—*no e.*, se prohibe la entrada.

entrance [entréns], *vt.* extasiar, hechizar.

entreat [entrít], *vt.* rogar, suplicar, implorar, instar.— —**y** [-i], *s.* ruego, súplica, instancia.

entree [ántrei], *s.* entrada; privilegio de entrar; (coc.) principio o entrada.

entrench [entrénch], *vt.* **y** *vi.* atrincherar(se).—*e. on* o *upon*, invadir, infringir.— —**ment** [-męnt], *s.* atrincheramiento, trinchera.

entrust [entrÁst], *vt.* (con **to** o **with**) entregar, encargar (de), (con)fiar, depositar.

entry [éntri], *s.* entrada; acceso; ingreso; asiento, anotación; registro; partida; bervete (catálogo, diccionario, etc.).

entwine [entwáin], *vt.* entrelazar, entretejer.

enumerate [injúmęreit], *vt.* enumerar. —**enumeration** [injumęréişǫn], *s.* enumeración; catálogo.

envelop [envélǫp], *vt.* envolver.— —**e** [énvęloup], *s.* envoltura; cubierta; sobre(carta).

enviable [énviabl], *a.* envidiable.— **envious** [énvias], *a.* envidioso.

environment [enváirǫnmęnt], *s.* cercanía; ambiente o medio ambiente. —**environs** [enváirǫns], *s. pl.* alrededores, suburbios, afueras.

envoy [énvoi], *s.* enviado.

envy [énvi], *vti.* [7] envidiar; codiciar. —*s.* envidia.

epaulet [épolet], *s.* (mil.) charretera.

epic [épik], *a.* épico.—*s.* epopeya.

epidemic [epidémik], *a.* epidémico.— *s.* epidemia, peste, plaga.

epigram [épigræm], *s.* epigrama.

epileptic [epiléptik], *a.* **y** *s.* epiléptico.

epilogue [épilag], *s.* epílogo.

Epiphany [ipífani], *s.* (igl.) Epifanía.

episcopal [ipískǫpal], *a.* episcopal.

episode [épisoud], *s.* episodio.

epistle [ipísl], *s.* epístola.—**epistolary** [ipístoleri], *a.* epistolar.

epitaph [épitæf], *s.* epitafio.

epithet [épiθet], *s.* epíteto.

epitome [ipítǫmi], *s.* epítome.—**epitomize** [ipítǫmaiz], *vt.* abreviar, epitomar.

epoch [épǫk], *s.* época, era.—*e.-making*, trascendental, que forma época.

equal [íkwal], *a.* igual; parejo; adecuado.—*s.* igual; cantidad igual.—*vt.* igualar; emparejar; igualarse a, ponerse al nivel de; ser igual a.— —**ity** [ikwáliti], *s.* igualdad; uniformidad; paridad.— —**ization** [ikwalizéişǫn], *s.* igualación, compensación.— —**ize** [íkwalaiz], *vt.* igualar; compensar.

equanimity [ikwanímiti], *s.* ecuanimidad.

equation [ikwéişǫn], *s.* ecuación; igualdad.

equator [ikwéitǫ(r)], *s.* ecuador.— —**ial** [ikwatórial], *a.* ecuatorial.

equilibrium [ikwilíbriʌm], *s.* equilibrio.

equip [ikwíp], *vti.* [1] equipar.— —**ment** [-męnt], *s.* equipo, habilitación; conjunto de aparatos, accesorios, etc.

equitable [ékwitabl], *a.* equitativo.— **equity** [ékwiti], *s.* equidad, justicia.

equivalence [ikwívalęns], *s.* equivalencia.—**equivalent** [ikwívalęnt], *a.* **y** *s.* equivalente.

equivocal [ikwívǫkal], *a.* equívoco, ambiguo.—**equivocate** [ikwívǫkeit], *vi.* usar palabras o frases equívocas.

era [íra], *s.* era, época.

eradicate [irédikeit], *vt.* desarraigar; destruir, extirpar.—**eradication** [irædikéişǫn], *s.* desarraigo, extirpación.

erase [iréis], *vt.* borrar, raspar.— —**r** [-œ(r)], *s.* borrador, goma de borrar; raspador.—**erasure** [iréişŭ(r)], *s.* borradura, raspadura.

erect [irékt], *vt.* erigir, edificar; montar, instalar; erguir, alzar.—*a.* erecto, erguido; vertical.

ermine [œrmin], *s.* armiño.

erosion [iróuʒǫn], *s.* erosión; desgaste; corrosión.

erotic [erátik], *a.* erótico.

err [œr], *vi.* errar; equivocarse; descarriarse, pecar.— —**and** [érand], *s.* recado, mandado, diligencia.—*e. boy,* mandadero, recadero.— —ant [érȧnt], a. errante.—knight e., caballero andante.— -atic [irǽtik], a. irregular; excéntrico; errático.— -oneous [eróu̯niȧs], a. errado, erróneo.— -or [éro(r)], s. error, yerro, equivocación; pecado.

erupt [irḁ́pt], vi. salir con fuerza; hacer erupción.— -ion [irḁ́pṣȯn], s. erupción; irrupción.

escalator [éskȧleito̯(r)], s. escalera móvil.

escapade [eskȧpéid], s. travesura; correría, aventura; fuga.—escape [eskéip], vi. escaparse o librarse de; fugarse, huir.—vt. evadir, evitar, esquivar.—to e. notice, pasar inadvertido.—s. escapada; fuga o escape.

escarpment [eskárpment], s. escarpa, acantilado.

escort [éskȯrt], s. escolta; acompañante. —vt. [eskórt] escoltar; acompañar.

Eskimo [éskimou̯], s. y a. esquimal.

espionage [éspiȯnidž], s. espionaje.

esplanade [esplȧnéid], s. explanada, paseo.

espy [espái], vti. [7] divisar, columbrar. —vii. mirar alrededor, observar.

esquire [eskwái̯r], s. escudero.—Esq., (abrev.) Sr. D.—country e., hacendado.

essay [eséi], vt. ensayar.—s. [ései] ensayo literario; tentativa.— -ist [éseiist], s. ensayista.

essence [éṣȯns], s. esencia.—in e., esencialmente.—essential [eséṇȧl], a. esencial; indispensable.—s. esencial, substancia.—to stick to essentials, ir al grano.

establish [estǽbliṣ], vt. establecer.— vr. establecerse, radicarse.— -ment [-ment], s. establecimiento; fundación; institución; pensión o renta vitalicia.

estate [estéit], s. bienes, propiedades; patrimonio, herencia; finca, hacienda; estado, clase o condición.—country e., finca rústica.—real e., bienes raíces.

esteem [estím], vt. estimar, apreciar; tener en o por, creer.—s. estimación, aprecio; mérito; juicio, opinión.— **estimable** [éstimȧbl], a. estimable; calculable.—estimate [éstimeit], vt. estimar, apreciar, valorar; calcular aproximadamente.—s. [éstimit], estimación, cálculo; opinión; presupuesto aproximado.—estimation [estiméiṣȯn], s. estima, aprecio; opinión; suposición; valuación; presupuesto.

esthetic [esθétik], a. estético.— -s [-s], s. estética.

estrange [estréindž], vt. extrañar, alejar; enajenar.

estuary [éschi̯ueri], s. estuario, estero, ría.

etch [ech], vt. y vi. grabar al agua fuerte.— -er [échœ(r)], s. grabador, aguafortista.— -ing [-iŋ], s. grabado al agua fuerte.

eternal [itǽrnȧl], a. eterno.—**eternity** [itǽrniti], s. eternidad.

ether [íθœ(r)], s. éter.— -eal [iθíriȧl], a. etéreo.

ethical [éθikȧl], a. ético, moral.— ethics [éθiks], s. ética, moral.

Ethiopian [iθióupiȧn], s. y a. etíope.

ethnic [éθnik], a. étnico.

etiquette [étiket], s. etiqueta.

etymology [etimálodži], s. etimología.

eucalyptus [yucȧlíptȧs], s. eucalipto.

eulogy [yúlȯdži], s. elogio, panegírico.

Eurasian [yuréiži̯ȧn], s. y a. eurasio, eurasiático.

European [yuropíȧn], s. y a. europeo.

evacuate [ivǽkyueit], vt. evacuar.— vi. vaciarse; retirarse.—evacuation [ivækyuéiṣȯn], s. evacuación.

evade [ivéid], vt. evadir, eludir, esquivar.

evaluate [ivǽlyueit], vt. evaluar, tasar. —evaluation [ivælyuéiṣȯn], s. evaluación.

evangelic(al) [ivænddžélik(ȧl)], a. evangélico.

evaporate [ivǽporeit], vt. y vi. evaporar(se); desvanecer(se).—evaporation [ivæporéiṣȯn], s. evaporación.

evasion [ivéiẓȯn], s. evasión; evasiva. —evasive [ivéiṣiv], a. evasivo.

eve [iv], s. noche; vigilia; víspera.— Christmas E., Nochebuena.

even [íven], a. llano, plano, nivelado, liso; igual, uniforme, imparcial; apacible; cabal, justo; constante; (número) par; parejo (con).—of e. date, de la misma fecha.—to be e. with, estar en paz, mano a mano con. —to get e. with, desquitarse.—adv. aun, hasta, incluso.—e. as, así como. —e. if, aun cuando, aunque.—e. now, ahora mismo.—e. so, así; aun así.—e. though, aunque.—not e., ni siquiera.—vt. igualar, emparejar, allanar, nivelar; liquidar.

evening [ívniŋ], s. tarde; (primeras horas de la) noche.—last e., anoche. —a. de la tarde; vespertino.

event [ivént], s. acontecimiento, suceso; caso; consecuencia, resultado.—at all events, in any e., sea lo que fuere, en todo caso, de cualquier modo.— -ful [-ful], a. memorable, lleno de acontecimientos.— -ual [ivénchuȧl], a. último, final; consiguiente; eventual, fortuito.— -uality [ivenchuǽliti], s. eventualidad.

ever [évœ(r)], adv. siempre; alguna vez, en cualquier tiempo; nunca. —as e., como siempre.—e. since, desde que; desde entonces.—for e.

and e., por siempre jamás, por los siglos de los siglos.—*hardly e.*, casi nunca.—*nor e.*, ni nunca.— —green [-grin], *a.* siempre verde.—*s.* planta de hoja perenne.— —lasting [-lǽstiŋ], *a.* perpetuo, perdurable, duradero. —*s.* eternidad.— —more [-mɔr], *adv.* eternamente; por siempre jamás.

every [évri], *a.* cada; todo, todos los. —*e. once in a while*, de vez en cuando. —*e. one of them*, todos, todos sin excepción.—*e. other*, cada dos, uno sí y otro no.— —body [-badi], *pron.* todos, todo el mundo; cada uno, cada cual.— —day [-dei], *a.* de cada día, diario, cuotidiano.— —one [-wʌn], *pron.* todo el mundo; todos.— —thing [-θiŋ], *pron.* todo.— —where [-hwer], *adv.* en o por todas partes, dondequiera.

evict [ivíkt], *vt.* desalojar, desahuciar; expulsar.— —ion [ivíkʃɔn], *s.* desalojamiento; desahucio; expulsión.

evidence [évidɛns], *s.* evidencia; demostración; prueba; testimonio.—**evident** [évidɛnt], *a.* evidente, claro, manifiesto.

evil [ívil], *a.* malo; maligno, perverso; nocivo; aciago.—*e. deed*, mal hecho. —*e. eye*, mal de ojo.—*s.* mal; infortunio; maldad.—*the E. One*, el diablo. —*adv.* mal; malignamente.— —doer [-dœ(r)], *s.* malhechor, persona perversa.

evoke [ivóuk], *vt.* evocar.

evolution [evoljúʃɔn], *s.* evolución, desarrollo; maniobra.— —ism [-izm], *s.* evolucionismo.—**evolve** [iválv], *vt.* desenvolver, desarrollar; producir por evolución.—*vi.* desarrollarse; evolucionar.

ewe [yu], *s.* oveja.

exacerbation [egzæsœrbéiʃɔn], *s.* exacerbación; agravación; exasperación.

exact [egzǽkt], *a.* exacto; justo; puntual.—*vt.* exigir, imponer.— —ing [-iŋ], *a.* exigente.

exaggerate [egzǽdʒɛreit], *vt.* y *vi.* exagerar, ponderar.—**exaggeration** [egzædʒɛréiʃɔn], *s.* exageración.

exalt [egzólt], *vt.* exaltar, enaltecer; regocijar; reforzar.— —ation [-éiʃɔn], *s.* exaltación; enaltecimiento; regocijo.

exam [egzǽm], *s.* examen.— —ination [-inéiʃɔn], *s.* examen; investigación; reconocimiento; ensayo, prueba; (for.) interrogatorio.— —ine [-in], *vt.* examinar; indagar; reconocer; preguntar, inquirir; analizar.— —iner [-inœ(r)], *s.* examinador, inspector.

example [egzǽmpl], *s.* ejemplo, ejemplar; lección, escarmiento.

exasperate [egzǽspɛreit], *vt.* exasperar; irritar; agravar.—**exasperation** [egz-** æspɛréiʃɔn], *s.* exasperación; agravación.

excavate [ɛkskaveit], *vt.* excavar, (so)cavar; vaciar, ahondar.—**excavation** [ɛkskavéiʃɔn], *s.* excavación; desmonte; zanja.

exceed [eksíd], *vt.* exceder; aventajar, sobrepujar; (sobre)pasar; rebasar. —*vi.* excederse, propasarse; preponderar.— —ing [-iŋ], *a.* excesivo; extraordinario.

excel [eksél], *vti.* y *vii.* [1] aventajar, superar; ser superior a; sobresalir.— —lence [ɛksɛlɛns], *s.* excelencia.— —lent [ɛksɛlɛnt], *a.* excelente.

except [eksépt], *vt.* exceptuar, excluir, omitir.—*prep.* excepto, con excepción de, fuera de.— —ing [-iŋ], *prep.* a excepción de, salvo, exceptuando.— —ion [eksépʃɔn], *s.* excepción, salvedad; objeción.—*to take e.*, objetar, oponerse, desaprobar.— —ional [eksépʃɔnal], *a.* excepcional.

excess [eksés], *s.* exceso; excedente; inmoderación o destemplanza; desorden; demasía; sobrante.—*a.* excesivo, sobrante; suplemental, de recargo.— —ive [-iv], *a.* excesivo.

exchange [ekschéindʒ], *vt.* cambiar; canjear, permutar; trocar, intercambiar.—*s.* cambio, trueque, permuta; canje; (com.) lonja, bolsa; cambio (de la moneda).—*bill of e.*, letra de cambio.—*e. rate*, tipo de cambio.—*stock e.*, bolsa de cambios.

excite [eksáit], *vt.* excitar; provocar, suscitar, estimular.— —d [-id], *a.* excitado, acalorado.— —ment [-mɛnt], *s.* excitación; estimulación; agitación; acaloramiento.—**exciting** [-iŋ], *a.* excitante, estimulante, incitante; emocionante.

exclaim [ekskléim], *vt.* y *vi.* exclamar, clamar.—**exclamation** [eksklaméiʃɔn], *s.* exclamación.—*e. point*, signo de admiración.

exclude [eksklúd], *vt.* excluir.—**exclusion** [eksklúʒɔn], *s.* exclusión.—**exclusive** [eksklúsiv], *a.* exclusivo; privativo; selecto.—*e. of*, exclusive, sin contar.—**exclusiveness** [eksklúsivnis], *s.* exclusividad; exclusiva.

excommunicate [ekskɔmjúnikeit], *vt.* excomulgar.—*a.* y *s.* excomulgado. —**excommunication** [ekskɔmjunikéiʃɔn], *s.* excomunión.

excrement [ɛkskrimɛnt], *s.* excremento, heces.

excursion [ekskǽrʒɔn], *s.* excursión, romería; expedición.

excusable [ekskjúzabl], *a.* excusable, disculpable.—**excuse** [ekskjúz], *vt.* excusar, disculpar; sincerar, justificar; eximir; paliar; despedir.—*s.* [ekskjús], excusa; pretexto.

execration [eksikréjəṇ], *s.* abominación.

execute [éksikjut], *vt.* ejecutar, llevar a cabo; legalizar, formalizar; ajusticiar.—**execution** [eksikjúṣon], *s.* ejecución, cumplimiento; mandamiento judicial; legalización; ajusticiamiento.—**executioner** [eksikjúṣonœ(r)], *s.* verdugo.—**executive** [egzékyutiv], *a.* ejecutivo.—*s.* poder ejecutivo; funcionario ejecutivo.—**executor** [egzékyutọ(r)], *s.* ejecutor; albacea.

exempt [egzémpt], *vt.* eximir, franquear.—*a.* exento; libre, franco, inmune.—**ion** [egzémpṣon], *s.* exención, franquicia, inmunidad.

exercise [éksœrsaiz], *s.* ejercicio.—*vt.* ejercer; ejercitar; adiestrar; preocupar, causar ansiedad.—*vi.* adiestrarse, ejercitarse; hacer ejercicio.

exert [egzœrt], *vt.* esforzar; ejercer.—*vr.* empeñarse, esforzarse.— **ion** [egzœrṣon], *s.* esfuerzo, empeño, ejercicio.

exhale [ekshéil], *vt.* exhalar, espirar.—*vi.* vah(e)ar; disiparse, desvanecerse.

exhaust [egzóst], *vt.* agotar, vaciar; gastar, consumir; debilitar, cansar.—*s.* vapor de escape; tubo de escape; (fís. y mec.) vacío.— **ion** [egzóschọn], *s.* agotamiento; debilitación, postración; (mec.) vaciamiento.—**ive** [-iv], *a.* exhaustivo; agotador; completo, cabal.

exhibit [egzíbjt], *vt.* exhibir; presentar, manifestar; exponer, mostrar.—*vi.* dar una exhibición.—*s.* exhibición; manifestación; (for.) pruebas en un juicio.— **ion** [eksibíṣon], *s.* exhibición, exposición; manifestación; ostentación.

exhilarate [egzílareit], *vt.* alegrar, regocijar o alborozar; animar, estimular.

exile [égzail], *s.* destierro, expatriación; desterrado, expatriado.—*vt.* desterrar, expatriar.

exist [egzíst], *vi.* existir, subsistir, vivir.— **ence** [-ens], *s.* existencia, vida, subsistencia; ente, ser.— **ent** [-ent], — **ing** [-iŋ], *a.* existente, actual, presente.

exit [éksit], *s.* salida; (teat.) mutis, vase.—*vi.* salir.

exodus [éksodʌs], *s.* éxodo.

exonerate [egzánereit] *vt.* exonerar; relevar.

exorbitance [egzórbitans], *s.* exorbitancia, exceso.—**exorbitant** [egzórbitant], *a.* exorbitante excesivo.

exotic [egzátik], *a.* exótico.

expand [ekspánd], *vt.* y *vi.* extender(se), expandir(se).—**expanse** [ekspǽns], *s.* extensión, espacio.—**expansion** [eks-

pǽnṣon], *s.* expansión, dilatación; desarrollo.—**expansive** [ekspǽnsiv], *a.* expansivo, efusivo.

expatriate [ekspéitrieit], *vt.* y *vr.* expatriar(se), desnaturalizar(se), desterrar(se).—*s.* y *a.* [ekspéitriit] expatriado, desterrado.

expect [ekspékt], *vt.* esperar; contar con.— **ance** [-ans], — **ancy** [-ansi], *s.* expectativa.— **ant** [-ant], *a.* expectante; embarazada, encinta.— **ation** [-éiṣon], *s.* expectación, expectativa, esperanza.

expectorate [ekspéktọreit], *vt.* y *vi.* expectorar, escupir.

expedience [ekspídiens], **expediency** [ekspídiensi], *s.* conveniencia.—**expedient** [ekspídient], *a.* oportuno, conveniente; prudente, propio.—*s.* expediente, medio, recurso.

expedition [ekspidíṣon], *s.* expedición.— **ary** [-eri], *a.* y *s.* expedicionario.

expel [ekspél], *vti.* [1] expeler, expulsar; despedir.

expend [ekspénd], *vt.* gastar, consumir; desembolsar.— **iture** [-ịchọ(r)], *s.* gasto, desembolso.—**expense** [ekspéns], *s.* gasto, coste, costa, costo; desembolso.—*at any e.,* a toda costa.—**expensive** [ekspénsiv], *a.* costoso; caro, dispendioso.

experiment [ekspériment], *s.* experimento.—*vi.* experimentar.— **al** [eksperiméntal], *a.* experimental.—**experience** [ekspíriens], *s.* experiencia; conocimiento; pericia; lance, incidente personal.—*vt.* experimentar; sentir.—**experienced** [ekspírienst], *a.* experimentado, perito; hábil; avezado; amaestrado o aleccionado.—**expert** [ekspœrt], *a.* experto; pericial.—*s.* [ékspœrt], experto, perito.

expiate [ékspieit], *vt.* expiar.

expiration [ekspiréiṣon], *s.* expiración; vencimiento; espiración; muerte.—**expire** [ekspáir], *vt.* espirar, expeler.—*vi.* expirar, terminar; fallecer, morir.

explain [ekspléin], *vt.* explicar.—**explanation** [eksplanéiṣon], *s.* explicación.—**explanatory** [eksplǽnatori], *a.* explicativo.

explode [eksplóụd], *vt.* volar, hacer estallar o explotar; refutar, confundir.—*vi.* estallar, hacer explosión; reventar.

exploit [eksplóit], *s.* hazaña, proeza.—*vt.* [eksplóit], explotar, sacar partido de; abusar.— **ation** [eksplọitéiṣon], *s.* explotación, aprovechamiento.— **er** [eksplóitœ(r)], *s.* explotador.

exploration [eksplọréiṣon], *s.* exploración.—**explorator** [eksplọreitọ(r)], **ex-**

plorer [eksplórœ(r)], *s.* explorador. —**explore** [eksplór], *vt.* explorar; averiguar; sondear.—*vi.* dedicarse a exploraciones.

explosion [eksplóuʒǝn], *s.* explosión, voladura; detonación, reventón.— **explosive** [eksplóusiv], *a.* y *s.* explosivo.

exponent [ekspóunǝnt], *s.* exponente.

export [ekspórt], *vt.* exportar.—*s.* [éksport] exportación.

expose [ekspóuz], *vt.* exponer, exhibir; poner en peligro; revelar, sacar a luz; desenmascarar.—**exposé** [ekspozéi], *s.* revelación comprometedora o escandalosa.—**exposition** [ekspozíʃǝn], *s.* exposición, exhibición.— **exposure** [ekspóuʒü(r)], *s.* exposición; acción de exponer(se); estar expuesto a (la intemperie); orientación, situación; revelación.

expound [ekspáund], *vt.* exponer, explicar.

express [eksprés], *vt.* expresar, manifestar; enviar por expreso.—*vi.* expresarse.—*a.* expreso; claro, explícito; especial; hecho de encargo; llevado por expreso; pronto, rápido. —*adv.* por expreso; expresa o especialmente.—*s.* tren, autobús, ascensor, etc. expreso o exprés; expreso, servicio de transporte de mercancías.—**ion** [ekspréʃǝn], *s.* expresión; semblante, talante; dicción, locución, giro.— —**ive** [eksprésiv], *a.* expresivo.

expropriate [ekspróuprieit], *vt.* enajenar, expropiar.

exquisite [ékskwizit], *a.* exquisito.

extend [eksténd], *vt.* extender; amplificar; prolongar; ampliar.—*vi.* extenderse, prolongarse; dar de sí.— —**ed** [-jd], *a.* extenso, prolongado; diferido.—**extension** [eksténʃǝn], *s.* extensión; dilatación; expansión; prolongación; prórroga.—**extensive** [eksténsiv], *a.* extens(iv)o.—**extent** [ekstént], *s.* extensión; alcance; grado, punto, límite.—*to a certain e.,* hasta cierto punto.—*to a great e.,* en sumo grado, grandemente.—*to the full e.,* en toda su extensión, completamente.

exterior [ekstíri̯ǝ(r)], *a.* exterior, externo; manifiesto.—*s.* exterior; exterioridad, aspecto.

exterminate [ekstǝ́rmineit], *vt.* exterminar.—**extermination** [ekstœrminéiʃǝn], *s.* exterminio.—**exterminator** [ekstǝ́rmineitǝ(r)], *s.* exterminador.

external [ekstǝ́rnǝl], *a.* externo, exterior; extranjero.—*s.* exterior; exterioridad.

extinct [ekstíŋkt], *a.* extinto; extinguido, apagado.— —**ion** [ekstíŋkʃǝn],

s. extinción.—**extinguish** [ekstíŋgwiʃ], *vt.* extinguir; apagar; sofocar; suprimir, destruir; oscurecer.—**extinguisher** [ekstíŋgwiʃœ(r)], *s.* extintor de incendios; apagador; matacandelas.

extol [ekstóul], *vti.* [1] ensalzar, enaltecer, elogiar.

extort [ekstórt], *vt.* extorsionar; sacar u obtener por fuerza; arrebatar; exigir dinero sin derecho.— —**ion** [ekstórʃǝn], *s.* extorsión; exacción.

extra [ékstrǝ], *a.* extraordinario; suplementario; de repuesto o de reserva. —*e. charge,* recargo.—*s.* exceso; recargo, sobreprecio; gasto extraordinario.—*adv.* excepcionalmente, en exceso.

extract [ekstrǽkt], *vt.* extraer; extractar.—*s.* [ékstrækt], extracto; resumen.

extradite [ékstrǝdait], *vt.* entregar o reclamar por extradición—**extradition** [ekstrǝdíʃǝn], *s.* extradición.

extraordinary [ekstrórdineri], *a.* extraordinario.

extravagance [ekstrǽvǝgǝns], **extravagancy** [ekstrǽvǝgǝnsi], *s.* lujo desmedido, derroche; extravagancia; disparate.—**extravagant** [ekstrǽvǝgǝnt], *a.* extravagante.

extreme [ekstrím], *a.* extremo, extremado; riguroso, estricto.—**extremity** [ekstrémiti], *s.* extremidad; rigor; necesidad, apuro.—*pl.* medidas extremas; extremidades.

exult [egzált], *vi.* saltar de alegría, regocijarse.— —**ant** [-ǝnt], *a.* regocijado, alborozado; triunfante.— —**ation** [-éiʃǝn], *s.* regocijo, transporte; triunfo.

eye [ai], *s.* ojo.—*before one's eyes,* en presencia de uno, a la vista. —*by e.,* a ojo.—*e. shade,* visera, guardavista.—*e. socket,* órbita o cuenca del ojo.—*half an e.,* ojeada, vistazo.—*to keep an e. on,* vigilar. —*to make eyes at,* mirar amorosamente o con codicia; comerse con los ojos.—*to see e. to e.,* ser del mismo parecer.—*to shut one's eyes to,* hacer la vista gorda.—*with an e. to,* con la intención de, pensando en, con vistas a.—*vt.* mirar de hito en hito; clavar la mirada a; hacer ojos o agujeros a.— —**ball** [áibol], *s.* globo del ojo.— —**brow** [-brau], *s.* ceja.— —**glass** [-glæs], *s.* ocular; anteojo. —*pl.* lentes, espejuelos, gafas, anteojos.— —**lash** [-læʃ], *s.* pestaña.— —**lid** [-lid], *s.* párpado.— —**sight** [-sait], *s.* vista; alcance de la vista.— —**sore** [-sor], *s.* cosa que ofende la vista.— —**strain** [-strein], *s.* vista fatigada.— —**tooth** [-tuθ], *s.* colmillo.—

—wash [-waš], *s.* colirio, loción para los ojos; (fam.) patraña.–
—witness [-wítnįs], *s.* testigo presencial.

F

fable [féjbl], *s.* fábula, ficción.
fabric [fǽbrįk], *s.* tejido, género; fábrica, edificio; textura.– —ate [-ejt], *vt.* fabricar; construir; inventar, mentir.– —ation [-éjšǫn], *s.* fabricación; edificio; invención, mentira.
fabulous [fǽbyųлʌs], *a.* fabuloso, ficticio.
façade [fʌsád], *s.* (arq.) fachada.
face [fejs], *s.* cara, rostro; faz; lado; superficie; fachada, frente; aspecto; apariencias; prestigio; esfera (de reloj); descaro; mueca.—*f.* card, figura (en la baraja).—*f.* down(ward), boca abajo.—*f.* powder, polvos de arroz o de tocador.—*f.* value, (com.) valor nominal; significado literal.—*in the f.* of, ante; luchando contra, a pesar de.—*to lose f.*, desprestigiarse.—*vt.* volverse o mirar hacia; arrostrar, afrontar, enfrentarse o encararse con; (for.) responder (a un cargo); cubrir, forrar.—*to f.* out, persistir en o sostener descaradamente.—*to f.* the music, (fam.) hacer frente a las consecuencias.—*vi.* volver la cara; dar o mirar (a, hacia).—*to f.* about, voltear la cara; cambiar de frente.– —t [fǽsįt], *s.* faceta.
facetious [fʌsíšʌs], *a.* jocoso, chistoso, humorístico.
facial [féjšʌl], *a.* facial.
facilitate [fʌsílįtejt], *vt.* facilitar, allanar, expedir.—**facility** [fʌsílįtį], *s.* facilidad; destreza.—*pl.* medios (de transporte, etc.).
fact [fækt], *s.* hecho; realidad.—*in f.*, en efecto, en realidad; de hecho.—*in the very f.*, en el mero hecho.—*matter of f.*, hecho positivo.—*the f.* remains that, ello es que, es un hecho, a pesar de todo.
faction [fǽkšǫn], *s.* facción, bando; alboroto.—**factious** [fǽkšʌs], *a.* faccioso, sedicioso, revoltoso.
factor [fǽktǫ(r)], *s.* elemento, factor; agente comisionado.
factory [fǽktorį], *s.* fábrica, taller, manufactura.
factual [fǽkchųʌl], *s.* exacto; real.
faculty [fǽkʌltį], *s.* facultad; aptitud; claustro de profesores.
fad [fæd], *s.* novedad, moda; manía.
fade [fejd], *vt.* marchitar; desteñir.—*vi.* desteñirse, descolorarse; marchitarse; (rad.) apagarse la intensidad.—*f.-out*, desaparición u oscurecimiento gradual.—*to f.* away, desvanecerse, desa-

parecer.—**fading** [féjdįŋ], *s.* pérdida gradual de intensidad, sonido, etc.; (rad.) fluctuación en la intensidad de las señales.
faggot, fagot [fǽgǫt], *s.* haz, manojo, gavilla de leña; (fam.) marica.
fail [fejl], *vt.* abandonar, dejar; frustrar; (fam.) reprobar, suspender (en los estudios).—*vi.* faltar; fallar; fracasar; frustrarse; consumirse, decaer; (com.) quebrar; salir mal, ser reprobado (en examen, etc.).—*s.* falta; defecto; fracaso.—*without f.*, sin falta.– —ure [féjlyǫ(r)], *s.* fracaso, malogro; suspenso (en un examen); falta, omisión, descuido; (com.) quiebra, bancarrota; (mec.) avería, defecto (de motor, etc.).
faint [fejnt], *vi.* desmayarse; desfallecer.—*a.* lánguido, abatido; indistinto, tenue; desfallecido.—*f.-hearted*, medroso, pusilánime.—*s.* desmayo, desfallecimiento.—*fainting fit* o spell, síncope, desmayo.—*in a f.*, desmayado.– —ness [féjntnįs], *s.* falta de claridad; languidez, desaliento.
fair [fer], *a.* claro, despejado; rubio; limpio; favorable, próspero; bello; justo, imparcial; razonable; regular, pasable.—*f.* and square, honrado a carta cabal.—*f.* complexion, tez blanca.—*f.* name, nombre honrado, sin tacha.—*f.* play, proceder leal, juego limpio.—*f.* sex, bello sexo.—*f.* trade, comercio recíproco.—*f.* weather, buen tiempo, bonanza.—*f.* wind, viento favorable.—*to give f.* warning, prevenir, avisar de antemano.—*to make a f.* copy, poner en limpio.—*adv.* justamente, honradamente; claramente; bien.—*f.-minded*, imparcial, justo.—*s.* feria; exposición.– —ness [férnįs], *s.* hermosura, belleza; honradez; justicia, imparcialidad.– —y [-į], *s.* hada, duende; (fam.) afeminado.—*a.* de hadas, de duendes.—*f.* tale, cuento de hadas.– —yland [-įlænd], *s.* país de las hadas.
faith [fejθ], *s.* fe; confianza; creencia, religión; fidelidad.—*to break f.* with, faltar a la palabra dada a.—*upon my f.*, a fe mía.– —ful [féjθful], *a.* fiel; leal; exacto; justo, recto.– —fully [-fųlį], *adv.* fielmente, firmemente; puntualmente.– —fulness [-fʊlnįs], *s.* fidelidad; honradez; exactitud.– —less [-lįs], *a.* infiel, desleal, pérfido.
fake [fejk], *s.* (fam.) falsificación, fraude, impostura; imitación, copia; patraña, farsa. V. FAKER.—*vt.* y *vi.* (fam.) falsificar; fingir, contrahacer.—*a.* falso, fraudulento.– —r [féjkœ(r)], *s.* (fam.) farsante; falsario, imitador; embustero.
falcon [fólkǫn], *s.* halcón.

fall [fol], *vti.* [10] caer(se); bajar, decrecer, disminuir; decaer.—*to f. asleep,* dormirse.—*to f. back,* retroceder, retirarse.—*to f. back on,* o *upon,* recurrir a, echar mano de.—*to f. behind,* rezagarse.—*to f. down,* postrarse; caerse.—*to f. due,* (com.) vencer(se).—*to f. for,* (fam.) prendarse de; ser engañado por.—*to f. in,* (mil.) alinearse; expirar, caducar.—*to f. in line,* formar cola; seguir la corriente.—*to f, in love,* enamorarse.—*to f. in price,* abaratarse.—*to f. in with,* convenir, estar de acuerdo con.—*to f. out,* desavenirse, reñir.—*to f. short,* faltar; errar el tiro.—*to f. sick,* enfermar.—*to f. through,* fracasar, malograrse.—*s.* caída, bajada, descenso; salto de agua; otoño; ruina; desnivel; desembocadura de un río; (com.) baja de precios; (mús.) cadencia; disminución del sonido.—*a.* otoñal.—**fallen** [fólęn], *pp.* de TO FALL.

fallow [félou], *a.* descuidado, abandonado.—*s.* barbecho.—*vt.* barbechar.

false [fols], *a.* falso, fingido, engañoso; postizo; (mus.) desafinado, discordante.—*f. bottom,* fondo doble.—*f. claim,* pretensión infundada.—*f.-faced,* hipócrita, falso.—*f.-hearted,* pérfido.—*f. step,* desliz; imprudencia.—*f. teeth,* dentadura postiza.—**-hood** [fólshud], *s.* falsedad, embuste.—**-ness** [-nis], *s.* falsedad, perfidia.—**-tto** [-étou], *s.* (mús.) falsete.—**falsification** [folsifikéʃǫn], *s.* falsificación.—**falsify** [fólsifai], *vti.* [7] falsificar; falsear.—*vii.* mentir.

falter [fóltœ(r)], *vt.* balbucear.—*vi.* vacilar; tartamudear.—*s.* vacilación, temblor.

fame [feim], *s.* fama.—*vt.* afamar; celebrar.—**-d** [-d], *a.* afamado, famoso, renombrado; célebre.

familiar [fəmílyā(r)], *a.* familiar, íntimo; confianzudo.—*f. with,* acostumbrado a; versado o ducho en, conocedor de, al tanto de.—*s.* familiar.—**-ity** [fəmiliériti], *s.* familiaridad, intimidad; confianza, llaneza; (con *with*) conocimiento (de).—**family** [fémili], *s.* familia.—*a.* familiar, casero, de la familia.—*f. man,* padre de familia.—*f. name,* apellido.—*f. tree,* árbol genealógico.—*in the f. way,* (fam.) encinta, embarazada.

famine [fémin], *s.* hambre, carestía.—**famished** [fémiʃt], *a.* famélico, hambriento.

famous [féimʌs], *a.* famoso, afamado, célebre; (fam.) excelente.

fan [fæn], *s.* abanico; ventilador; aventador; aficionado, entusiasta,

admirador.—*vti.* [1] abanicar; ventilar; aventar.

fanatic [fənétik], *s.* y *a.* fanático.—**-(al)** [-(ǎl)], *a.* fanático.- **-ism** [fǎnétisizm], *s.* fanatismo.

fanciful [fénsiful], *a.* imaginativo, caprichoso; fantástico.—**fancy** [fénci], *s.* fantasía, imaginación, antojo, capricho; afición, afecto.—*to take a f. to,* aficionarse a; coger cariño a.—*a.* fantástico de fantasía; elegante; de lujo, costoso.—*f. ball,* baile de trajes.—*f. dress,* disfraz.—*vti.* [7] imaginar; gustar de, aficionarse a; antojarse, fantasear.—*vii.* tener un antojo o capricho; creer o imaginar algo sin prueba.

fang [fæŋ], *s.* colmillo (de animal, fiera); diente (de serpiente, del tenedor).—**-ed** [-d], *a.* colmilludo.

fantastic [fæntéstik], *a.* fantástico; caprichoso; ilusorio, imaginario.—**fantasy** [féntasi], *s.* fantasía.

far [far], *adv.* lejos; a lo lejos; en alto grado.—*as f. as, so f. as,* hasta; en la medida que, en cuanto a, según.—*by f.,* con mucho.—*f. and wide,* por todas partes.—*f. away,* muy lejos.—*f. flung,* vasto, extenso.—*f. from,* ni con mucho.—*f. off,* a lo lejos; muy lejos; distante, remoto.—*so f.,* thus *f.,* hasta ahora; hasta aquí; hasta ahí.—*a.* lejano, distante, remoto.—*a f. cry (from),* muy lejos de.

faraway [fárawei], *a.* lejano, alejado, abstraído, distraído.

farce [fars], *s.* (teat.) farsa; comedia, engaño.

fare [fer], *vi.* pasarlo, irle a uno (bien o mal); acontecer.—*s.* pasaje o tarifa (precio); pasajero; comida, plato.—*bill of f.,* menú.—**-well** [férwel], *interj.* ¡adiós! ¡vaya con Dios!—*a.* de despedida.—*f. performance,* función de despedida.—*s.* despedida, adiós.

farm [farm], *s.* finca de labor, granja; (Am.) chácara.—*f. hand,* peón o mozo de labranza, bracero.—**-er** [fármœ(r)], *s.* labrador, granjero, agricultor.—*tenant f.,* colono.—**-house** [-haus], *s.* granja.—**-ing** [-iŋ], *s.* cultivo, labranza; agricultura.—*a.* agrícola; de labranza.—**-stead** [-sted], *s.* granja, alquería.

farther [fárðœ(r)], *adv.* más lejos, a mayor distancia; además de, demás de.—*f. on,* más adelante.—*a.* más lejano; ulterior.—**-most** [-moust], *a.* más lejano o remoto.—**farthest** [fárðist], *a.* más lejano o remoto; más largo o extendido.—*adv.* lo más lejos, a la mayor distancia.

fascinate [fésineit], *vt.* fascinar, hechizar.—**fascinating** [fésineitiŋ], *a.*

fascinador, hechicero.—**fascination** [fæsɪnéɪʃən], s. fascinación, hechizo.

fashion [fǽʃən], s. moda, estilo; elegancia; manera.—*f. plate*, figurín.—*f. shop*, tienda de modas.—*in f.*, de moda.—*out of f.*, pasado de moda.—*to be the f.*, ser (de) moda.—*vt.* adaptar; formar; idear.— —**able** [-ǝbl], a. de moda; elegante, de buen tono.

fast [fæst], vi. ayunar, hacer abstinencia.—*s.* ayuno, abstinencia, vigilia.—*a.* firme, seguro, fuerte; fijo, indeleble; apretado; constante, fiel; profundo (sueño); veloz, ligero, rápido; adelantado (reloj); derrochador; disoluto.—*adv.* fuertemente, firmemente; estrechamente; para siempre; aprisa, rápidamente.—*f. by*, cerca de, junto a.— —en [fǽsn], vt. afirmar, asegurar, sujetar; pegar; atar, amarrar, trabar, unir; abrochar.—*vi.* fijarse; agarrarse, pegarse.

fastidious [fæstídɪʌs], a. escrupuloso, melindroso; descontentadizo; quisquilloso.

fasting [fǽstɪŋ], s. ayuno, abstinencia.

fat [fæt], a. gordo; obeso; graso, mantecoso; opulento, rico; lucrativo.—*s.* gordura; grasa, manteca, sebo.—*vti.* y *vii.* [1] engordar.

fatal [féɪtʌl], a. fatal; mortal; inevitable.— —**ism** [-izm], s. fatalismo.— —**ist** [-ɪst], s. fatalista.— —**ity** [feɪtǽlɪtɪ], s. fatalidad; desgracia; muerte.

fate [feɪt], s. hado, destino, sino; suerte, fortuna; parca.— —**d** [féɪtɪd], a. predestinado; fatal, aciago.

father [fáðœ(r)], s. padre.—*f.-in-law*, suegro.—*vt.* engendrar; prohijar; tratar como hijo.—*to f. on* o *upon*, achacar, atribuir a.— —**hood** [-hud], s. paternidad.— —**land** [-lænd], s. (madre)patria, suelo natal.— —**less** [-lɪs], a. huérfano de padre; bastardo.— —**ly** [-lɪ], a. paternal, paterno.—*adv.* paternalmente.

fathom [fǽðɵm], s. braza.—*vt.* sondar, sondear; profundizar.— —**less** [-lɪs], a. insondable, impenetrable.

fatigue [fatíg], s. fatiga, cansancio; (mil.) faena.—*pl.* (mil.) traje de faena.—*vt.* y *vi.* fatigar(se), cansar(se).

fatness [fǽtnɪs], s. gordura.—**fatten** [fǽtn], vt. engordar, cebar.—*vi.* engordar, echar carnes.—**fattening** [fǽtnɪŋ], s. ceba, engorde (del ganado).—*a.* engordador.

faucet [fɔ́sɪt], s. grifo, llave, espita.

fault [fɔlt], s. falta, culpa; defecto, tacha; (geol.) falla; (elec.) fuga de corriente.—*at f.* o *in f.*, culpable, responsable.—*to a f.*, excesivamente, con exceso.—*to find f. with*, culpar; hallar defecto en.— —**finder** [fɔ́ltfaɪndœ(r)], s. censurador, criticón.—

—**less** [-lɪs], a. sin tacha, impecable.— —**y** [-ɪ], a. defectuoso, imperfecto.

favor [féɪvɵ(r)], vt. hacer un favor; agraciar, favorecer; patrocinar, sufragar.—*s.* favor; fineza, cortesía; auspicio, apoyo; (com.) carta, grata, atenta.—*in f. of*, a favor de; (com.) pagadero a.—*to be in f. with*, disfrutar del favor de.—*to lose f.*, caer en desgracia.— —**able** [-ǝbl], a. favorable, propicio.— —**ed** [-d], a. favorecido; valido.—*well (ill)-f.*, bien (mal) parecido.— —**ite** [-ɪt], a. favorito, preferido.—*s.* favorito, protegido.— —**itism** [-ɪtɪzm], s. favoritismo.

fawn [fɔn], s. cervato, cervatillo; color de cervato.—*vi.* halagar, adular.

fear [fɪr], s. temor, miedo, pavor, recelo.—*vt.* y *vi.* temer, recelar.— —**ful** [fɪ́rfʊl], a. miedoso; tímido, temeroso; horrendo, espantoso, terrible.— —**less** [-lɪs], a. intrépido; sin temor, arrojado.— —**lessness** [-lɪsnɪs], s. intrepidez, arrojo.

feasible [fízɪbl], a. factible, hacedero, practicable, viable.—*adv.* de modo factible.

feast [fist], s. fiesta; festejo, función; (fam.) comilona.—*vt.* festejar, agasajar.—*vi.* comer opíparamente

feat [fit], s. acción; hazaña, proeza; juego de manos.—*pl.* suertes.

feather [féðœ(r)], s. pluma; plumaje; (carp.) lengüeta, barbilla.—*a f. in one's cap*, un triunfo, un timbre de orgullo para uno.—*f. duster*, plumero.—*to show the white f.*, volver las espaldas, huir.—*vt.* emplumar.—*to f. one's nest*, hacer su agosto; sacar tajada.— —**brain** [-breɪn], s. imbécil, tonto.— —**less** [-lɪs], a. desplumado; implume.— —**weight** [-weɪt], a. y s. ligero de peso; (dep.) peso pluma.— —**y** [-ɪ], a. plumado; ligero.

feature [fíchɵ(r)], s. rasgo, carácter distintivo; (teat.) pieza o película principal.—*pl.* facciones, fisonomía.—*vt.* destacar, poner en primer plano; exhibir, mostrar (como lo más importante).

February [fébrueri], s. febrero.

fecund [fíkʌnd], a. fecundo, fértil.— —**ity** [fɪkʌ́ndɪtɪ], s. fecundidad; fertilidad, abundancia.

fed [fed], pret. y pp. DE TO FEED.

federal [fédœrʌl], a. federal.—**federate** [fédœreɪt], vt. y vi. (con)federar(se).— —**federation** [fedœréɪʃən], s. (con)federación, liga.

fee [fi], s. honorarios; derechos; cuota.

feeble [fíbl], a. débil; enfermizo; flojo, endeble; delicado.

feed [fid], vti. [10] alimentar, mantener, dar de comer a; dar pienso.—*vii.* comer, alimentarse; pacer, pastar.—

s. forraje, pienso, comida.—**f.** bag, morral.—**f.** cock o tap, grifo de alimentación.—**f.** pump, bomba de alimentación.—**f.** rack, pesebre, comedero.— —er [fídœ(r)], **s.** alimentador; cebador (de ganado).— —ing [-iŋ], **s.** alimentación; forraje, pasto.—**a.** alimenticio, de alimentación.—**f.** bottle, biberón.

feel [fíl], **vti.** [10] sentir; experimentar; tocar, palpar; percibir.—**to f.** one's way, ir a tientas.—**to f.** the effects of, resentirse de.—**vii.** sentirse, encontrarse.—**to f.** angry, happy, etc., estar enfadado, contento, etc.—**to f.** ashamed, joyous, etc., avergonzarse, alegrarse, etc.—**to f.** bad, sentirse mal; estar triste, entristecerse.—**to f.** cold, warm, hungry, thirsty, tener frío, calor, hambre, sed.—**to f.** for, condolerse de.—**to f.** like (having o doing), sentir deseos de, tener gana(s) de, querer.—**s.** tacto; sensación, percepción.— —er [fílœ(r)], **s.** el que toca o palpa; tentativa; tentáculo, antena.— —ing [-iŋ], **s.** tacto; sensación; sentimiento, sentido, emoción, sensibilidad; ternura, compasión; presentimiento, sospecha.—**to** hurt one's feelings, herir el amor propio, tocar en lo vivo.—**a.** sensible, tierno, conmovedor.

feet [fit], **s. pl.** de FOOT.

felicitate [fil[s]itejt], **vt.** felicitar, cumplimentar.—**felicitation** [filisitéjŝǫn], **s.** felicitación, enhorabuena.—**felicity** [fíl[s]iti], **s.** felicidad, bienaventuranza, dicha; ocurrencia oportuna.

fell [fel], **pret.** de TO FALL.—**vt.** derribar, tumbar, cortar (un árbol); (cost.) sobrecoser.

fellow [félou], **a.** asociado; compañero de o en.—**f.** boarder, compañero de pupilaje.—**f.** citizen, conciudadano.— **f.** countryman, compatriota.—**f.** man, being o creature, prójimo, semejante. —**f.** member, compañero, colega.—**f.** partner, consocio.—**f.** scholar, **f.** student, condiscípulo.—**f.** traveler, compañero de viaje; (pol.) simpatizante. —**s.** compañero, camarada; socio o individuo de un colegio, sociedad, etc.; (fam.) hombre, sujeto, tipo.—**a** good f., (fam.) buen chico.—**a** young f., un joven, un muchacho.— —ship [-ŝip], **s.** confraternidad, compañerismo; asociación; sociedad; colegiatura; beca.—**f.** holder, becario, becado.

felony [félǫni], **s.** crimen, delito, felonía.

felt [felt], **s.** fieltro.—**pp. y pret.** de TO FEEL.—**a.** de fieltro.

female [fímejl], **s.** hembra (mujer, animal, o planta).—**a.** hembra;

femenino.—**f.** dog, donkey, etc., perra, burra, etc.

feminine [féminin], **a.** femenino, femenil; afeminado.—**s.** (gram.) (género) femenino.—**femininity** [feminíniti], **s.** feminidad.

femur [fímœ(r)], **s.** fémur.

fence [fens], **s.** cerca, cerc(ad)o, valla, vallado; estacada; seto; (fam.) comprador de efectos robados; (mec.) resguardo.—**f.** season, tiempo de veda.—**to be on the f.,** estar indeciso. —**vt.** (gen. con in) cercar, vallar.—**vi.** esgrimir.— —r [fénsœ(r)], **s.** esgrimista.—**fencing** [fénsiŋ], **s.** esgrima; materiales para cercar; valladar.—**f.** foil, florete.

fender [féndœ(r)], **s.** guardafango, guardabarros; guardafuegos de chimenea; (mar.) defensas.

fennel [fénel], **s.** (bot.) hinojo.

ferment [fœrmént], **vt.** (hacer) fermentar.—**vi.** fermentar.—**s.** [fœrment] fermento; levadura; fermentación. —**ation** [-éjŝǫn], **s.** fermentación.

fern [fœrn], **s.** helecho.

ferocious [firóuŝas], **a.** feroz, brutal, fiero.—**ferocity** [firásiti], **s.** ferocidad, ensañamiento, fiereza salvaje.

ferret [férit], **s.** (zool.) hurón; (cost.) listón, ribete.—**vt.** (con out) indagar, averiguar; escudriñar.

ferry [féri], **vti. y vii.** [7] transportar de una a otra orilla; cruzar una vía de agua en embarcación.—(aer.) transportar (tropas, etc.) por avión. —**s.** medio de transporte a través de una vía de agua; embarcadero.— **ferryboat** [féribout], **s.** barca chata; transbordador, barco de transbordo.

fertile [fœrtil], **a.** fértil, fecundo.— **fertility** [fœrtíliti], **s.** fertilidad.— **fertilization** [fœrtilizéjŝǫn], **s.** fertilización, abono; (biol.) fecundación.— **fertilize** [fœrtilajz], **vt.** fertilizar, fecundar; abonar.—**fertilizer** [fœrtilajzœ(r)], **s.** abono, fertilizador.

fervent [fœrvent], **a.** ferviente, fervoroso; ardiente.—**fervor** [fœrvǫ(r)], **s.** fervor, devoción; ardor, calor.

fester [féstœ(r)], **vi.** enconarse, ulcerarse, supurar.—**s.** llaga, úlcera.

festival [féstival], **s.** fiesta, festival, festividad.—**festive** [féstiv], **a.** festivo, regocijado.—**festivity** [festíviti], **s.** regocijo, júbilo; fiesta, festividad.

fetch [fech], **vt.** ir a buscar; traer; coger; aportar.—**vi.** moverse, menearse.—**s.** tirada, alcance; estratagema; aparición.

fete [fejt], **vt.** festejar.—**s.** fiesta.

fetter [fétœ(r)], **vt.** engrillar, encadenar; impedir.— —**s.** traba, grillete.—**pl.** grillos, prisiones.

fetus [fítas], **s.** feto.

feud [fjud], *s.* contienda, enemistad entre familias, tribus, etc.; feudo.

fever [fívœ(r)], *s.* fiebre; calentura.— **-ish** [-iš], *a.* febril, calenturiento.

few [fju], *a., pron.* o *s.* pocos; no muchos, contados.—*a f.*, (alg)unos, unos cuantos, unos pocos.

fiancé [fjanséi], *s.* prometido, novio.— **-e** [fjanséi], *s.* prometida, novia.

fib [fjb], *s.* embuste, filfa, bola.—*vii.* [1] contar embustes.

fiber [fáibœ(r)], *s.* fibra, filamento.— **fibrous** [fáibʀas], *a.* fibroso.

fickle [fjkl], *a.* voluble, inconstante, veleidoso.

fiction [fíkšǫn], *s.* ficción; literatura novelesca; novela.—**fictitious** [fjktí-šas], *a.* ficticio.

fiddle [fjdl], *s.* (fam.) violín.—*fit as a f.*, en buena condición física.—*vi.* (fam.) tocar el violín.—*to f. away*, malgastar el tiempo.—*-r* [-œ(r)], *s.* (fam.) violinista.

fidelity [fjdéljtj], *s.* fidelidad; veracidad.

fidget [fjdžjt], *vt.* inquietar.—*vi.* ajetrearse, afanarse; moverse nerviosamente.—*s.* (gen. *pl.*) afán, agitación, inquietud, impaciencia.— **-y** [-j], *a.* inquieto, agitado.

field [fild], *s.* campo (en todas sus acepciones).—*f. artillery*, artillería de campaña.—*f. glass*, gemelos de campaña, anteojo de largo alcance.—*f. hospital*, hospital de sangre.—*f. kitchen*, cocina de campaña.

fiend [find], *s.* demonio, diablo; monstruo.—*dope f.*, narcómano.— **-ish** [fíndjš], *a.* diabólico, malvado.

fierce [firs], *a.* fiero, feroz; bárbaro; furioso; vehemente.— **-ness** [fírsnjs], *s.* fiereza, ferocidad; vehemencia.

fiery [fáirj], *a.* ardiente, vehemente; feroz, furibundo.

fig [fjg], *s.* higo.—*f. tree*, higuera.

fight [fajt], *vii.* [10] pelear, combatir o luchar con (contra); librar (una batalla); lidiar (toros).—*to f. off*, rechazar.—*to f. out*, llevar la lucha hasta lo último.—*vii.* batallar, luchar, pelear, torear, lidiar.—*to f. against odds*, luchar con desventaja.—*s.* batalla, lucha, combate, lidia; pelea, riña.— **-er** [fáitœ(r)], *s.* guerrero; peleador; lidiador, luchador, combatiente.—*f. plane*, avión de combate o de caza.— **-ing** [-jŋ], *a.* combatiente; agresivo; luchador.—*s.* combate, riña, pelea.

figure [fígyṳ(r)], *s.* figura; forma; talle; representación; personaje; (arit.) cifra, número; (com.) precio, valor.—*f. of speech*, tropo; metáfora.—*f. skating*, patinaje artístico.—*to cut a f.*, descollar.—*vt.* figurar, delinear; representar; calcular.—*to f. out*,

hallar por cálculo, resolver.—*to f. up*, computar, calcular.—*vi.* figurar; (fam.) figurarse, imaginarse; calcular; (mús.) florear.

filament [fíljamęnt], *s.* filamento; hilacha.

file [fajl], *s.* lima; escofina; archivo; carpeta o cubierta (para archivar papeles); legajo; actas; protocolo (de notario, etc.); fila, hilera.—*f. case*, archivador; fichero.—*f. card*, ficha o tarjeta (de fichero).—*vt.* limar; archivar; acumular; presentar, registrar, anotar; protocolar.—*vi.* marchar en filas.—*to f. past*, desfilar.

filial [fíljal], *a.* filial.—**filiation** [fjljéi-šǫn], *s.* filiación.

filibuster [fjlibastœ(r)], *vi.* (E.U.) hacer obstrucción en un cuerpo legislativo prolongando el debate.—*s.* obstruccionista u obstrucción parlamentaria; filibustero, pirata.

filigree [fíljgri], *s.* filigrana.

filing [fáiljŋ], *s.* limado, acción de limar; acción de archivar; (gen. *pl.*) limaduras, limalla.—*f. card*, ficha, tarjeta para archivo.

Filipino [fjljpínou], *s.* y *a.* filipino.

fill [fjl], *vt.* llenar; rellenar; desempeñar, ocupar (un puesto); preparar (una receta); despachar (un pedido); hinchar, inflar; empastar (un diente).— *to f. in*, terraplenar; rellenar; insertar. —*to f. out*, completar; llevar a cabo. —*to f. up*, colmar; llenar un impreso; tapar.—*to f. up the time*, emplear el tiempo.—*vi.* (a menudo con **up**) llenarse, henchirse; saciarse.—*s.* terraplén; hartura; abundancia.

fillet [fjlet], *s.* filete; solomillo; cinta o tira de adorno.

filling [fjljŋ], *s.* relleno; envase; empaquetadura; terraplén; empaste dental. —*f. station*, estación de gasolina.

film [fjlm], *s.* película; telilla, velo; membrana; nube en el ojo.—*vt.* cubrir con película; rodar una película, fotografiar.

filter [fjltœ(r)], *vt.* filtrar, colar.—*vi.* (in)filtrarse.—*s.* filtro.

filth [fjlθ], *s.* suciedad, inmundicia, porquería, mugre.— **-y** [fjlθj], *a.* sucio, puerco, asqueroso; inmundo.

fin [fjn], *s.* aleta (de pez); barba de ballena.

final [fáinạl], *a.* final, terminante, definitivo, decisivo.— **-ist** [-jst], *s.* finalista en un torneo deportivo.— **-ity** [fajnéljtj], *s.* finalidad; decisión, determinación.— **-ly** [fáinạlj], *adv.* finalmente, en fin, en conclusión, por último.

finance [fjnǽns], *s.* finanza.—*pl.* finanzas; fondos.—*vt.* financiar.— **financial** [fjnǽnšạl], *a.* financiero,

monetario.—**financier** [finǽnsᵣr], *s.*
financiero, financista, hacendista.—
financing [finǽnsiŋ], *s.* financia-
miento, (Am.) refacción.

find [faind], *vti.* [10] encontrar, hallar.
—*to f. fault with*, censurar o criticar a.
—*to f. out*, descubrir; averiguar,
enterarse (de).—*vii.* (for.) juzgar,
fallar.—*s.* hallazgo, descubrimiento;
encuentro.— **-er** [fáindœ(r)], *s.* el
que encuentra; (fot.) visor, enfocador.
— **-ing** [-iŋ], *s.* descubrimiento;
hallazgo; (for.) fallo, sentencia.

fine [fain], *a.* fino; refinado; excelente,
admirable; primoroso; guapo, ga-
llardo; claro; agradable.—*f. arts*,
bellas artes.—*f. weather*, tiempo
despejado.—*s.* multa.—*vt.* afinar,
refinar; multar.—*to be fined*, incurrir
en multa.—*adv.* finamente; (fam.) de
primera; muy bien (apl. a la salud).
—*f.-tongued*, zalamero.—*interj.* ¡bien!
¡magnifico!.— **-ness** [fáinnis], *s.*
fineza, delicadeza; primor, excelencia;
perfección; finura (de arena, cemento,
etc.).— **-ry** [fáinœri], *s.* gala, adorno,
atavío.

finger [fiŋgœ(r)], *s.* dedo (de las manos).
—*little f.*, (dedo) meñique.—*middle f.*,
dedo (del) corazón.—*to have a f. in
the pie*, meter la cuchara; tener
participación en un asunto.—*to have
at one's fingers' ends* o *f. tips*, tener o
saber al dedillo.—*vt.* tocar, manosear;
hurtar; (mus.) pulsar, teclear.—
-nail [-neil], *s.* uña del dedo.—
-print [-print], *s.* huella dactilar;
impresión digital.—*vt.* tomar las
impresiones digitales de.— **-printing**
[-printiŋ], *s.* dactiloscopía.

finish [fíniš], *vt.* acabar, terminar, rematar; pulir, retocar, perfeccionar.—*to
f. off*, rematar.—*to f. up*, darle la
última mano a; retocar; terminar.—
vi. acabar, finalizar; fenecer.—*s.* fin,
término, remate; pulimento, última
mano, acabado.—*f. line*, (dep.) meta.
— **-ed** [-t], *a.* acabado, perfeccionado,
pulido.— **-ing** [-iŋ], *s.* consumación;
perfección; última mano, repaso.—*a.*
último, de remate; de acabar.—*f.
blow*, golpe de gracia.—*f. coat*, (pint.)
última mano.

Finn [fin], *s.* finlandés, finlandesa.—
-ish [fíniš], *a. y s.* finlandés.

fir [fœr], *s.* abeto; pino.

fire [fair], *s.* fuego; lumbre; incendio,
quema; chispa; ardor, pasión.—*f.
alarm*, alarma de incendios.—*f. department*, servicio de bomberos.—*f.
engine*, bomba de incendios.—*f.
escape*, escalera de incendios.—*f.
extinguisher*, matafuego.—*f. works*,
fuegos de artificio.—*to catch f.*,
encenderse, inflamarse.—*to set f.*, to

set on f., pegar fuego a, incendiar.—
to take f., encenderse; acalorarse.—
under f., (mil., fig.) expuesto al fuego;
atacado; censurado.—*vt.* incendiar;
encender· disparar; enardecer; (fam.)
despedir, echar (empleados).—*to f.
up*, encender.—*vi.* encenderse; inflamarse; disparar, hacer fuego; enardecerse.—*to f. up*, enfurecerse.— **-arm**
[fáirarm], *s.* arma de fuego.— **-brand**
[-brænd], *s.* tea tizón; incendiario.—
-bug [-bʌg], *s.* (fam.) incendiario.—
-cracker [-krækœ(r)], *s.* triquitraque, buscapiés, cohete.— **-fly**
[-flai], *s.* luciérnaga.— **-house**
[-haus], *s.* estación o cuartel de
bomberos.— **-man** [-man], *s.* bom-
bero; fogonero.— **-place** [-pleis], *s.*
hogar, chimenea.— **-proof** [-pruf], *a.*
incombustible, a prueba de fuego,
refractario.—*vt.* hacer refractario o
incombustible.— **-side** [-said], *s.*
hogar, fogón; vida doméstica.—*a.*
casero, íntimo.— **-wood** [-wud], *s.*
leña.— **-works** [-wœrks], *s.* fuegos
artificiales.— **-firing** [fáiriŋ], *s.* descarga, tiroteo.—*f. squad*, (mil.)
pelotón o piquete de fusilamiento.

firm [fœrm], *a.* firme; fijo, estable;
sólido; persistente; tenaz, inflexible.
—*s.* (com.) casa o empresa de comercio; firma, razón social.

firmament [fœrmament], *s.* firmamento.

firmness [fœrmnis], *s.* firmeza; estabilidad, fijeza, solidez; entereza, tesón.

first [fœrst], *a.* primero; primario;
primitivo.—*f.-aid kit*, botiquín de
urgencia o de primeros auxilios.—*f.-
born*, primogénito.—*f. cousin*, primo
hermano.—*f. floor*, planta baja.—*f.-
hand*, de primera mano.—*f. lady*,
primera dama.—*f. name*, nombre de
pila.—*adv.* primero; en primer lugar;
al principio; antes; por, o la, primera
vez.—*at f.*, al principio, al pronto.—
f. of all, en primer lugar, ante todo.—
f. or last, tarde o temprano.—*f.-rate*,
de primera clase.

fiscal [fískal], *a.* fiscal.

fish [fiš], *s.* pez; pescado.—*f. bait*, cebo
o carnada.—*f. hatchery*, vivero,
criadero.—*f. market*, pescadería.—*f.
pole*, caña de pescar.—*f. story*, cuento
increíble.—*f. tank*, pecera.—*neither
f. nor fowl*, ni carne ni pescado.—
shell-f., marisco.—*vt. y vi.* pescar.—
-bone [-boun], *s.* espina de pescado.— **-erman** [-œrman], *s.* pescador.— **-ery** [-œri], *s.* industria pes-
quera; pesquero.— **-hook** [-huk], *s.*
anzuelo; garfio; bichero.— **-ing** [-iŋ],
s. pesca, pesquería.—*a.* de pescar;
pesquero (barco, industria).—*f. line*,
sedal o tanza de pescar.—*f. reel*,
carrete.—*f. rod*, caña o vara de pes-

car.—*f.* tackle, avíos de pescar.—
—monger [-mʌngœ(r)], *s.* pescadero.
- —worm [-wœrm], *s.* lombriz para
pescar.— —y [-i], *a.* que huele o sabe
a pescado; abundante en peces;
(fam.) sospechoso.

fissure [fíṣŋ(r)], *s.* fisura, grieta, rajadura.—*vi.* agrietararse.

fist [fist], *s.* puño; (impr.) llamada,
manecilla, ▨▧▧.—icuffs [fístᴉkʌfs],
s. puñetazos; riña a puñetazos.

fit [fit], *s.* ataque, convulsión; arranque,
arrebato; corte, talle; ajuste, encaje;
conveniencia, adaptación.—*by fits
(and starts)*, a tontas y a locas.—*a.*
apto, idóneo, a propósito, adecuado,
conveniente; capaz; apropiado; en
buena salud, bien.—*f. to be tied*,
(fam.) loco de atar.—*vti.* [1] ajustar,
encajar, acomodar; adaptar; surtir,
equipar; preparar; (cost.) entallar
un vestido, probar.—*to f. out*, equipar;
armar.—*to f. up*, ajustar, componer;
ataviar; amueblar.—*vii.* convenir;
ajustarse, entallarse, venir, sentar o
caer bien o mal.—*to f. into*, encajar
en.— —ness [fítnjs], *s.* aptitud,
idoneidad, disposición; conveniencia;
adaptabilidad.— —ting [-iŋ], *a.*
propio, adecuado, conveniente.—*s.*
ajuste; unión o conexión de tubería;
(cost.) corte, prueba.—*pl.* guarniciones; accesorios; avíos o herrajes.

fix [fiks], *vt.* fijar; asegurar; señalar
(una fecha); arreglar; reparar, componer; (fam.) ajustar las cuentas.—
to f. up, componer, arreglar; equipar.
—*s.* apuro, aprieto.— —ed [-t], *a.* fijo,
estable, permanente.— —ture [fíks-
chŋ(r)], *s.* cosa fija o enclavada en
un sitio; adorno; empleado inamovible.—*pl.* muebles y enseres; aparatos y accesorios eléctricos.

flabby [flǽbj], *a.* flojo, fofo, blando.

flag [flǽg], *s.* bandera; pabellón; banderola.—*vti.* [1] izar bandera; hacer
señales con banderola; enlosar.—*vii.*
flaquear; decaer, debilitarse.

flagpole [flǽgpoul], *s.* asta de bandera.

flagrant [flǽigrant], *a.* notorio, escandaloso; flagrante.

flagship [flǽgṣip], *s.* nave capitana.—
—flagstaff [flǽgstæf], *s.* asta de bandera.—flagstone [flǽgstoun], *s.* losa
grande de embaldosar; laja.

flair [fler], *s.* sagacidad; aptitud,
propensión.

flake [fleik], *s.* escama; copo de nieve;
hojuela, laminilla.—*f. of ice*, carámbano.—*vt.* y *vi.* formar hojuelas o
escamas.—flaky [flǽik], *a.* escamoso.

flame [fleim], *s.* llama(rada), fiama;
ardor, pasión.—*f. thrower*, lanza-
llamas.—*vt.* quemar, chamuscar.—*vi.*
arder, flamear, llamear; brillar,

fulgurar; inflamarse.— —less [flǽjm-
ljs], *a.* sin llama.—flaming [fiéjmiŋ],
a. flamante, llameante; encendido,
inflamado; apasionado.

flamingo [flamíŋgou], *s.* (orn.) flamenco.

flange [flǽndʒ], *s.* borde, reborde,
pestaña, oreja.—*f. joint*, junta de
pestañas.—*f. nut*, tuerca de reborde.
—*vt.* rebordear, poner pestaña o
reborde.—*vi.* sobresalir, hacer reborde.

flank [flǽŋk], *s.* ijar, ijada; flanco,
costado.—*a.* de lado, de costado o
por el flanco.—*vt.* estar a cada lado
de; (mil.) flanquear.—*vi.* (con on)
lindar con.

flannel [flǽnəl], *s.* franela, bayeta.

flap [flǽp], *s.* (sast.) cartera; faldeta;
faldón; aleta; ala de sombrero; hoja
plegadiza de mesa; oreja de zapato;
revés, cachete; (cir.) colgajo.—*f.
door*, trampa.—*f.-eared*, orejudo.—*f.-
mouthed*, hocicudo, morrudo.—*vti.*
[1] batir (las alas), sacudir, pegar;
agitar.—*to f. the wings*, aletear.—*vii.*
batir; colgar.

flare [fler], *vt.* chamuscar; acampanar.
—*vi.* brillar; fulgurar; resplandecer.
—*to f. up*, encenderse; encolerizarse.
—*s.* llama, llamarada, fulgor; luz de
Bengala; cohete de señales; brillantez.—*f. up*, llamarada; arrebato
de cólera; jarana.

flash [flǽsh], *s.* llamarada, destello, resplandor; fogonazo; (period.) breve
despacho telegráfico; (cine) incidencia.—*f. of lightning*, relámpago.—*f. of
the eye*, ojeada, vistazo.—*f. of wit*,
agudeza, ingenio.—*vt.* encender;
enviar o despedir con celeridad;
hacer brillar.—*vi.* relampaguear;
brillar, fulgurar, destellar; pasar o
cruzar como un relámpago.— —ing
[flǽṣiŋ], *a.* centelleante; relampa-
gueante.—*s.* centelleo; relampagueo.—
—light [-lait], *s.* linterna eléctrica de
bolsillo o partátil; reflector de luz
intermitente (de un faro); (fot.) luz
instantánea.— —y [-i], *a.* charro,
llamativo.

flask [flǽsk], *s.* frasco grande; matraz;
caneca.

flat [flǽt], *s.* apartamento, piso; (mús.)
bemol.—*f. of the hand*, palma de la
mano.—*a.* plano, llano, liso; chato,
aplastado; extendido; categórico;
insulso, insípido; (mús.) bemol;
desafinado; monótono; menor o
disminuído.—*f.-bottomed*, de fondo
plano.—*f.-footed*, de pies planos;
(fam.) resuelto, determinado.—*f.-
nosed*, chato, ñato.—*f. rate*, tipo o
tarifa fijos; precio alzado.—*f. tire*,
pinchazo; neumático desinflado.—
adv. terminantemente; resueltamente;

(com.) sin interés.—*vti.* [1] (mús.) bemol(iz)ar; achatar.—*vii.* (mús.) desafinar por lo bajo; aplastarse.- —**boat** [flǽtbout]. *s.* bote o barco de fondo plano.- —**car** [-kar], *s.* (f.c.) (vagón de) plataforma.- —**iron** [-aiœrn], *s.* plancha (de planchar).- —**ly** [-li], *adv.* categóricamente, rotundamente.- —**ness** [-nis], *s.* llanura, lisura, insipidez, insulsez.- —**ten** [-n], *vt.* aplastar, achatar, aplanar; deprimir; enderezar (un avión).—*vi.* aplanarse; (aer.) enderezarse.

flatter [flǽtœ(r)], *vt.* y *vi.* adular, lisonjear.- —**er** [-œ(r)], *s.* adulador; lisonjero, zalamero.- —**y** [-i], *s.* adulación, lisonja, halago.

flattop [flǽttap], *s.* (fam.) portaaviones.

flaunt [flont], *vt.* y *vi.* ostentar, lucir; desplegar, ondear.—*s.* ostentación.

flavor [fléivo(r)], *s.* sabor; sazón.—*vt.* saborear; sazonar.

flaw [flo], *s.* defecto, falta, mancha; grieta, pelo, paño, paja; ráfaga, racha.—*vt.* afear; estropear; agrietar.—*vi.* agrietarse; estropearse.- —**less** [flólis], *a.* entero; intachable, irreprochable; perfecto.

flax [flæks], *s.* lino.

flay [flei], *vt.* desollar, despellejar.

flea [fli], *s.* pulga.

fled [fled], *pret.* y *pp.* de TO FLEE.—**flee** [fli], *vti.* [10] huir de, evitar.—*vii.* huir; fugarse; desaparecer.

fleece [flis], *s.* vellón, lana.—*Golden F.,* Toisón de Oro.—*vt.* esquilar; despojar, esquilmar.—**fleecy** [flisi], *a.* lanudo.

fleet [flit], *s.* armada, escuadra; flota, flotilla.—*a.* veloz, rápido.- —**ing** [flitiŋ], *a.* fugaz, efímero.

Flemish [flémiš], *a.* y *s.* flamenco.—*s.* idioma flamenco.

flesh [fleš], *s.* carne; pulpa (de las frutas).—*f. and blood,* carne y hueso; sangre, parentela, progenie.—*f wound,* herida superficial.—*in the f.,* vivo; en persona.—*to put on f.,* echar carnes.- —**y** [fléši], *a.* gordo, carnoso; pulposo; suculento.

flew [flu], *pret.* de TO FLY.

flexibility [fleksibíliti], *s.* flexibilidad.— **flexible** [fléksibl], *a.* flexible.—**flexion** [fékšon], *s.* flexión.

flick [flik], *vt.* golpear o sacudir levemente.—*vi.* revolotear.—*s.* golpecito. - —**er** [flíkœ(r)], *vi.* flamear; fluctuar, vacilar; aletear; revolotear.—*s.* llama vacilante; pestañeo, parpadeo.

flier [fláiœ(r)], *s.* volador; aviador; fugitivo; (mec.) volante; hoja o papel volante; cosa veloz.

flight [flait], *s.* vuelo; escuadrilla aérea; bandada de pájaros; ímpetu, arran-

que; huída, evasión.—*f. of stairs,* tramo de escalera.

flimsy [flímzi], *a.* débil, endeble; baladí, frívolo.

flinch [flinch], *vi.* vacilar; acobardarse; retroceder.—*s.* titubeo.

fling [fliŋ], *vti.* [10] arrojar, tirar, lanzar, echar.—*to f. about,* desparramar, esparcir.—*to f. away,* desechar.—*to f. open,* abrir de repente.—*to f. out,* arrojar con fuerza; hablar violentamente, echar chispas.—*to f. up,* abandonar, dejar.—*vii.* lanzarse.—*s.* tiro; lanzamiento; indirecta; tentativa.—*to go on a f.,* echar una cana al aire.

flint [flint], *s.* pedernal.

flirt [flœrt], *vi.* coquetear, (neol.) flirtear; dejarse tentar (por una idea, etc.).- —**ation** [-éišon], *s.* coqueteo, galanteo.

flit [flit], *vii.* [1] revolotear; volar; deslizarse velozmente.

float [flout], *vt.* poner, mantener o llevar a flote; (com.) emitir, poner en circulación.—*vi.* flotar, sobrenadar.— *s.* flotador; boya; balsa salvavidas; corcho de una caña de pescar; carroza.—*a.* de flotador.

flock [flak], *s.* hato, manada, rebaño; grey; bandada; congregación; multitud; pelusilla.—*vi.* congregarse.

flog [flag], *vti.* [1] azotar.- —**ging** [flágiŋ], *s.* azotaina, paliza.

flood [flad], *s.* diluvio; avenida, creciente, inundación; torrente; plétora.—*f. light,* reflector.—*f. tide,* pleamar.—*vt.* inundar; anegar; abarrotar.—*vi.* desbordar.- —**gate** [fládgeit], *s.* compuerta.

floor [flor], *s.* suelo; piso; pavimento.—*boarded f.,* entarimado.—*first f.,* ground f.,* planta baja.—*to have the f.,* tener la palabra.—*vt.* derribar, tirar al suelo; entarimar; echar el piso; derrotar; dejar turulato.

flop [flap], *vti.* [1] batir, sacudir.—*vii.* aletear; caer flojamente; colgar; caerse, venir abajo.—*to f. down,* tumbarse, dejarse caer.—*to f. up,* voltear(se).—*s.* fracaso, fiasco.

florist [flórist], *s.* florista.

floss [flos], *s.* seda floja; penacho del maíz.—*dental f.,* hilo dental.

flounce [flauns], *s.* volante, fleco, cairel.

flounder [fláundœ(r)], *s.* (ict.) lenguado.—*vi.* forcejar torpemente; tropezar y caer; revolcarse.

flour [flaur], *s.* harina.—*vt.* enharinar.—*vi.* pulverizarse.

flourish [flœriš], *vt.* florear, blandir; embellecer.—*vi.* florecer; medrar, prosperar; (mus.) florear.—*s.* rasgo; rúbrica; floreo, adorno; (esgr.) molinete.

floury [fláuri], *a.* harinoso.

flout [fláut], *vt.* burlarse de, mofarse de.

flow [flou], *vi.* fluir, manar; correr; seguirse; ondear, flotar; abundar; crecer (la marea).—*to f. away*, deslizarse, pasar.—*to f. from* o *out*, brotar, salir, nacer, manar de.—*to f. into*, desembocar.—*to f. with*, rebosar de. —*vt.* inundar; derramar; hacer fluir. —*s.* corriente; torrente; flujo; desagüe; abundancia.

flower [fláuœ(r)], *s.* flor; planta en flor; flor y nata.—*f. pot*, tiesto.—*f. vase*, florero, búcaro.—*vi.* florecer.— *y* [-i], *a.* florido, ornado.

flowing [flóuiŋ], *a.* corriente, fluente, fluido; suelto; colgante.—*s.* derrame; salida; corriente; flujo; fluidez.

flown [floun], *pp.* de TO FLY.—*a.* vidriado.

flu [flu], *s.* (fam.) influenza, gripe.

fluctuate [flʌkchueit], *vi.* fluctuar; oscilar, ondear.—**fluctuation** [flʌkchuéiʃǝn], *s.* fluctuación.

flue [flu], *s.* cañón de chimenea; tubo de caldera; pelusa, borra; conducto; cañón de órgano.

fluency [flúɛnsi], *s.* fluidez; afluencia; labia.—**fluent** [flúɛnt], *a.* facundo; suelto, corriente; copioso; fluido.

fluff [flʌf], *s.* pelusa, lanilla, vello, plumón.—*vt.* mullir, esponjar.— *y* [flʌfi], *a.* cubierto de plumón o vello; mullido, esponjoso.

fluid [flúid], *s.* fluido; líquido; gas.—*a.* fluido; líquido; gaseoso.—*ity* [fluíditi], —*ness* [flúidnis], *s.* fluidez.

flung [flʌŋ], *pret.* y *pp.* de TO FLING.

flunk [flʌŋk], *s.* fracaso.—*vt.* reprobar, suspender; fracasar en un examen.— *(e)y* [flʌŋki], *s.* lacayo; adulón.

fluorescence [fluǫrésɛns], *s.* fluorescencia.—**fluorescent** [fluǫrésɛnt], *a.* fluorescente.

flush [flʌʃ], *vi.* sonrojarse, abochornarse; inundarse; nivelar(se).—*vt.* limpiar con un chorro de agua.—*a.* nivelado, parejo; copioso.—*s.* rubor; animación; flujo rápido; abundancia; flux (de naipes).

flute [flut], *s.* flauta; estria de una columna; rizado, pliegue.—*vt.* estriar, acanalar; rizar, plegar.

flutter [flʌtœ(r)], *vt.* agitar, menear, sacudir; aturdir.—*vi.* agitarse, menearse; aletear, revolotear; flamear, ondular.—*s.* agitación; vibración; palpitación; aleteo; ondulación.

flux [flʌks], *s.* flujo; diarrea.

fly [flai], *vti.* [10] hacer volar; elevar (una cometa, etc.); enarbolar; evitar, huir de; dirigir (un avión); cruzar o atravesar en avión.—*vii.* volar; lanzarse, precipitarse; pasar rápidamente; escaparse; desaparecer, des-

vanecerse.—*to f. around*, ir de un lado a otro.—*to f. at*, arrojarse o lanzarse sobre.—*to f. away*, irse volando, escaparse.—*to f. from*, huir de.—*to f. into a passion* o *rage*, montar en cólera; irse del seguro.—*to f. off*, desprenderse súbitamente; separarse, sublevarse.—*to f. open*, abrirse repentinamente.—*to f. out*, dispararse, salir a espetaperros.—*s.* mosca; vuelo; bragueta.- —*away* [fláiǫwei], *a.* tremolante; inconstante.- —*er* [-œ(r)], *s.* = FLIER.—*ing* [-iŋ], *a.* volante, volador, volátil; flameante, ondeante; rápido, veloz; breve.—*s.* aviación; vuelo.—*leaf* [-lif], *s.* guarda de un libro.

foam [foum], *s.* espuma.—*vt.* hacer espuma.—*vi.* espumar, echar espuma(-rajos).- —*y* [fóumi], *a.* espumoso.

focus [fóukʌs], *s.* foco; distancia focal. —*out of f.*, desenfocado.—*vti.* y *vii.* [2] enfocar(se); concentrar(se).

fodder [fádœ(r)], *s.* forraje, pienso.— *vt.* dar forraje a.

foe [fou], *s.* enemigo.

fog [fag], *s.* niebla, neblina, bruma; velo; confusión, perplejidad.—*vti.* [1] oscurecer; velar.—*vii.* ponerse brumoso; velarse.- —*gy* [fági], *a.* brumoso, neblinoso; velado.

foil [foil], *vt.* frustrar, contrarrestar.—*s.* hoja delgada de metal; oropel; chapa; hoja de oro o plata; florete; rastro; contraste.

fold [fould], *s.* doblez, pliegue; redil; hato, rebaño.—*vt.* doblar, plegar; encerrar, envolver; meter en redil.— *to f. the arms*, cruzar los brazos.—*vi.* doblarse, plegarse.—*er* [fóuldœ(r)], *s.* plegador, plegadera; carpeta; cuadernillo, circular.- —*ing* [-iŋ], *a.* plegadizo.—*f. bed*, catre de tijera.— *f. chair*, silla plegadiza.—*f. screen*, biombo.—*s.* plegado, doblamiento; repliegue.

foliage [fóuliidʒ], *s.* follaje, frondosidad, fronda.

folk [fouk], *s.* gente; nación, raza, pueblo.—*pl.* parientes, parentela.—*a.* de o perteneciente al pueblo; que tiene fuentes populares.—*f. music*, música tradicional del pueblo.—*f. tale*, conseja.

follow [fálou], *vt.* seguir; venir después de; perseguir; ejecutar, poner por obra; resultar de; ejercer.—*to f. out*, llevar hasta el fin.—*to f. suit*, jugar el mismo palo (en los naipes); seguir el ejemplo; seguir la corriente.—*to f. up*, llevar hasta el fin; continuar.—*vi.* ir detrás; seguirse.—*to f. on*, perseverar.- —*er* [-œ(r)], *s.* seguidor; acompañante; secuaz.—*pl.* comitiva, séquito. - —*ing* [-iŋ], *a.* siguiente; próximo.—

s. adhesión; séquito; oficio, profesión.

folly [fáli], *s.* tontería, locura, desatino.

foment [fomént], *vt.* fomentar.

fond [fand], *a.* aficionado, enamorado; tierno, cariñoso; querido, acariciado. —*to be f. of*, ser amigo de o aficionado a; ser afecto a, estar encariñado con.— **—le** [fándl], *vt.* mimar, acariciar, hacer fiestas a.— **—ness** [fándnis], *s.* afecto, ternura; apego, inclinación.

font [fant], *s.* pila de bautismo o de agua bendita; fuente; (impr.) fundición, torta.

food [fud], *s.* alimento, comida, sustento. **— —stuff** [fúdstʌf], *s.* producto o sustancia alimenticia.—*pl.* víveres, comestibles.

fool [ful], *s.* tonto, necio; inocente, bobo; badulaque; (teat.) gracioso; bufón.—*to f. away*, malbaratar; perder el tiempo.—*vi.* tontear, divertirse, chancear.— **—ery** [fúlœri], *s.* tontería.— **—ish** [-iš], *a.* tonto; disparatado; badulaque; bobo.— **—ish-ness** [-išnis], *s.* simpleza, tontería, disparate.

foot [fut], *s.* (*pl.* **feet** [fit]) pie; pata; base.—*by f.*, a pie.—*f. by f.*, paso a paso.—*f.-loose*, sin trabas y obligaciones, andariego.—*f. soldier*, soldado de infantería.—*on f.*, de pie; a pie; progresando.—*to put one's f. in it*, meter la pata.— **—ball** [fútbol], *s.* football, balompié, balón.— **—ing** [-iŋ], *s.* base, fundamento; cimiento; posición firme.—*on the same f.*, en pie de igualdad.— **—lights** [-laits], *s.* candilejas; el teatro, las tablas.— **—man** [-man], *s.* lacayo.— **—note** [-nout], *s.* nota al pie de una página.— **—pace** [-peis], *s.* descanso de escaleras; paso lento.— **—path** [-pæθ], *s.* senda para peatones.— **—print** [-print], *s.* pisada, rastro.— **—step** [-step], *s.* huella, pisada, paso.— **—stool** [-stul], *s.* escabel, taburete.— **—walk** [-wok], **—way** [-wei], *s.* senda de peatones; acera.— **—wear** [-wer], *s.* calzado.— **—work** [-wœrk], *s.* juego o manejo de los pies (boxeo, baile, etc.)

fop [fap], *s.* petimetre, pisaverde, lechuguino.

for [for], *prep.* por; para; durante, por espacio de; de; con, a pesar de, no obstante.—*as f.*, en cuanto a.—*as f. me*, por mi parte.—*but f.*, a no ser, sin.—*f. all that*, no obstante, con todo, a pesar de eso.—*f. good*, para siempre.—*what f.?* ¿para qué?—*conj.* porque, puesto que, pues; en efecto.

forage [fáridž], *vt.* y *vi.* forrajear, proveer(se) de forraje; apacentar(se); saquear.—*s.* forraje.

forbad o **forbade** [forbǽd], *pret.* de TO FORBID.

forbear [forbér], *s.* antepasado, antecesor.—*vti.* y *vii.* [10] abstenerse de, tener paciencia; reprimirse.

forbid [forbíd], *vti.* [10] prohibir; impedir, estorbar; excluir de.— **forbidden** [forbídęn], *pp.* de TO FORBID. —*a.* prohibido, vedado, ilícito.— **—ding** [-iŋ], *a.* prohibitivo; repulsivo, aborrecible, repugnante.

forbore [forbór], *pret.* de TO FORBEAR. —**forborne** [forbórn], *pp.* de TO FORBEAR.

force [fors], *s.* fuerza; necesidad; personal; cuerpo (de tropas, de policía, etc.).—*pl.* fuerzas (militares o navales).—*by f. of*, a fuerza de.—*in f.*, vigente, en vigor.—*vt.* forzar, obligar; violar; impulsar; embutir.—*to f. along*, hacer avanzar o adelantar.— *to f. away*, obligar a alejarse.—*to f. back*, rechazar, hacer retroceder.—*to f. the issue*, hacer que el asunto se discuta o decida pronto, que se vaya al grano sin demora.— **—ed** [-t], *a.* forzado, forzoso; fingido.— **—ful** [fórsful], *a.* enérgico, potente, violento.— **—forcible** [fórsibl], *a.* fuerte, enérgico; violento; de peso.

ford [ford], *s.* vado.—*vt.* vadear.

fore [for], *a.* anterior, delantero; proel. —*adv.* delante, hacia delante; de proa.—*s.* delantero, frente.— **—arm** [fórarm], *s.* antebrazo.—*vt.* [forárm], armar de antemano.— **—bode** [-bóud], *vt.* y *vi.* pronosticar, presagiar; presentir.— **—boding** [-bóudiŋ], *s.* presentimiento, corazonada.—*a.* agorero.— **—cast** [fórkæst], *vti.* y *vii.* [4] pronosticar, prever, predecir; proyectar, trazar.—*pret.* y *pp.* de TO FORECAST. —*s.* pronóstico, predicción; proyecto, plan.— **—doom** [-dum], *s.* predestinación, sino.— **—father** [-faðœ(r)], *s.* ascendiente, antepasado.— **—finger** [-fiŋgœ(r)], *s.* dedo índice.— **—foot** [-fut], *s.* mano o pata delantera.— **—front** [-frʌnt], *s.* vanguardia, primera fila.— **—go** [-góu], *vii.* [10] privarse de, renunciar a; ceder, abandonar.— **—gone** [-gón], *a.* predeterminado; inevitable, seguro.—*pp.* de TO FOREGO.— **—ground** [-graund], *s.* primer plano.— **—head** [-id], *s.* frente; parte delantera.

foreign [fárin], *a.* extranjero; exterior; extraño; advenedizo; remoto.—*f. commerce*, comercio exterior.—*f. exchange*, cambio extranjero.—*f. to the case*, ajeno al caso.— **—er** [-œ(r)], *s.* extranjero, extraño, forastero.

forelock [fórlak], *s.* guedeja.

foreman [fórman], *s.* capataz; encargado; mayoral; presidente del jurado.

foremost [fórmoʊst], *a.* delantero, primero; principal, más notable.

forenoon [fórnun], *s.* [la] mañana.

forerunner [fɔrrʌ́nœ(r)], *s.* precursor; presagio, pronóstico.

foresaid [fórsɛd], *a.* antedicho, susodicho.

foresaw [fɔrsɔ́], *pret.* y *pp.* de TO FORESEE.—**foresee** [fɔrsí], *vti.* [10] prever.—*vii.* tener previsión.—**foreseen** [fɔrsín], *pp.* de TO FORESEE.—**foresight** [fórsaɪt], *s.* previsión, perspicacia.

forest [fárɪst], *s.* selva, bosque, floresta.—*f. ranger*, guardabosques.—*vt.* arbolar.

forester [fárɪstœ(r)], *s.* silvicultor; guardamonte; habitante del bosque.—**forestry** [fárɪstrɪ], *s.* silvicultura, ingeniería forestal.

foretell [fɔrtél], *vti.* y *vii.* [10] predecir, adivinar.— **—er** [-œ(r)], *s.* profeta.—**foretold** [fɔrtóʊld], *pret.* y *pp.* de TO FORETELL.

forever [fɔrévœ(r)], *adv.* siempre; para o por siempre; a perpetuidad.—*f. and a day,* o *f. and ever,* eternamente, por siempre jamás.

forewarn [fɔrwórn], *vt.* prevenir, advertir, avisar.

forewent [fɔrwént], *pret.* de TO FOREGO.

foreword [fórwœrd], *s.* prefacio.

forfeit [fórfɪt], *s.* prenda perdida; multa; decomiso; pérdida legal de cosa o derecho por incumplimiento de obligaciones.—*pl.* juego de prendas. —*a.* confiscado, perdido por incumplimiento.—*vt.* perder algo por incumplimiento de obligaciones.

forgave [fɔrgéɪv], *pret.* de TO FORGIVE.

forge [fɔrdʒ], *s.* fragua; forja; herrería. —*vt.* forjar, fraguar; falsificar, falsear; inventar; tramar.—*to f. ahead,* abrirse paso, avanzar.— **—ry** [fórdʒœrɪ], *s.* falsificación.

forget [fɔrgét], *vti.* y *vii.* [10] olvidar(se de).—*f. it,* no piense más en eso; no se preocupe, descuide Ud.—*to f. one-self,* excederse, propasarse; ser distraído; ser abnegado.— **—ful** [-fʊl], *a.* olvidadizo.— **—fulness** [-fʊlnɪs], *s.* olvido, descuido; calidad de olvidadizo.—*f.-me-not* [-mɪnat], *s.* (bot.) nomeolvides.

forgive [fɔrgív], *vti.* [10] perdonar, dispensar, condonar.—**forgiven** [fɔrgívɛn], *pp.* de TO FORGIVE.— **—ness** [-nɪs], *s.* perdón; clemencia, misericordia.—**forgiving** [fɔrgívɪŋ], *a.* magnánimo, clemente, de buen corazón, perdonador.

forgot [fɔrgát], *pret.* de TO FORGET.—**forgotten** [fɔrgátɛn], *pp.* de TO FORGET.

fork [fɔrk], *s.* tenedor; horquilla; bifurcación; confluencia de un río.—*vt.* cargar heno con la horquilla.—*vi.* bifurcarse.

forlorn [fɔrlórn], *a.* abandonado; infeliz, desdichado.—*f. hope,* empresa desesperada.

form [fɔrm], *s.* forma; figura; hechura; hoja, modelo que ha de llenarse; condición; estado; práctica, ritual, formalidad; estilo; horma, matriz, patrón; porte, modales.—*vt.* formar, construir, labrar, modelar; idear, concebir; constituir, integrar.—*vi.* formarse.— **—al** [fórmạl], *a.* formal.—**—ality** [-ǽlɪtɪ], *s.* formalidad, etiqueta, cumplimiento.— **—alize** [-ạlaɪz], *vt.* formalizar.— **—at** [-æt], *s.* formato.— **—ation** [-éɪʃɔn], *s.* formación; desarrollo; arreglo.

former [fórmœ(r)], *a.* primero; precedente, anterior; antiguo; ex-, que fue. —*the f.,* aquél, aquélla, aquéllos, etc.— **—ly** [-lɪ], *adv.* antiguamente, antes, en tiempos pasados.

formula [fórmyulạ], *s.* fórmula, receta.—**—te** [fórmyuleɪt], *vt.* formular.

forsake [fɔrséɪk], *vti.* [10] abandonar, desamparar; separarse de; renegar de; desechar; dar de mano a.—**forsaken** [fɔrséɪkɛn], *pp.* de TO FORSAKE.—*a.* abandonado.—**forsook** [fɔrsúk], *pret.* de TO FORSAKE.

forswear [fɔrswér], *vti.* [10] abjurar; renunciar o negar solemnemente.—*vii.* perjurar(se).—**forswore** [fɔrswór], *pret.* de TO FORSWEAR.—**forsworn** [fɔrswórn], *pp.* de TO FORSWEAR.

fort [fɔrt], *s.* fuerte, fortaleza, fortín.

forth [fɔrθ], *adv.* delante; adelante; fuera, afuera; a la vista, públicamente; hasta lo último.—*and so f.,* y así sucesivamente; etcétera.— **—coming** [-kámɪŋ], *a.* venidero, futuro, próximo.—*s.* aparición, acercamiento, proximidad.— **—with** [-wɪθ], *adv.* inmediatamente.

fortification [fɔrtɪfɪkéɪʃɔn], *s.* fortificación; fortalecimiento; fortaleza.—**fortify** [fórtɪfaɪ], *vti.* [7] fortificar; fortalecer; reforzar; corroborar.—*vii.* construir defensas.

fortitude [fórtɪtjud], *s.* fortaleza, fuerza, ánimo.

fortnight [fórtnaɪt], *s.* quincena, dos semanas.— **—ly** [-lɪ], *a.* quincenal, bisemanal.—*adv.* quincenalmente.— *s.* revista bisemanal.

fortress [fórtrɪs], *s.* fortaleza, plaza fuerte.

fortunate [fórchʊnɪt], *a.* afortunado, dichoso.—**fortune** [fórchʊn], *s.* fortuna; dicha; sino; caudal, bienes.—*f. teller,* adivino.—*vt.* dotar con una fortuna.

forum [fórʌm], *s.* plaza; foro; tribunal; reunión para debatir un asunto.

forward [fórwặrd], *adv.* adelante, en adelante, hacia adelante, más allá.—*a.* delantero; adelantado; precoz; anterior; activo; desenvuelto; emprendedor; radical.—*s.* delantero.—*vt.* reenviar; trasmitir, remitir; activar; fomentar.

foster [fástœ(r)], *vt.* criar, nutrir; dar alas, alentar.—*a.* putativo, adoptivo.

fought [fot], *pret. y pp.* de TO FIGHT.

foul [faụl], *a.* sucio, impuro; fétido; viciado (aire); detestable, vil; injusto, sin derecho; contrario, desagradable; obsceno; lleno de errores y correcciones.—*f.-dealing*, dolo, mala fe.—*f. language*, lenguaje soez.—*f.-mouthed*, mal hablado.—*f. play*, juego sucio o desleal.—*f. weather*, mal tiempo.—*s.* acción de ensuciar; violación de las reglas establecidas.—*vt.* ensuciar; trabar; violar las reglas.—*vi.* ensuciarse; trabarse; chocar.

found [faụnd], *pret. y pp.* de TO FIND.—*vt.* cimentar, fundamentar; fundar, instituir; apoyar en; fundir, derretir.—**-ation** [-éịṣọn], *s.* fundación, establecimiento; fundamento, base; dotación; cimiento.—*f. stone*, primera piedra.—**-er** [fáụndœ(r)], *s.* fundador; fundidor.—*vt.* (mar.) hacer zozobrar.—*vi.* irse a pique, zozobrar; fracasar.—**-ry** [-rị], *s.* fundición (fábrica).

fountain [fáụntịn], *s.* fuente; manantial; fontanar; pila.—*f. pen*, pluma estilográfica.—**-head** [-hed], *s.* fuente, origen.

fowl [faụl], *s.* gallo, gallina; pollo; aves en general.—*pl.* aves de corral.

fox [faks], *s.* zorra, raposa; zorro, taimado.—**-hole** [fákshoụl], *s.* trinchera individual.—**-y** [-ị], *a.* taimado, astuto.

foyer [fóịœ(r)], *s.* recibidor; salón de descanso.

fraction [frékṣọn], *s.* fracción, quebrado; fragmento.—*vt.* fraccionar.—**-al** [-ạl], *a.* fraccionario; fraccionado.

fracture [frékchụ(r)], *s.* fractura, rotura, ruptura, quiebra.—*vt. y vi.* fracturar(se), quebrar(se).

fragile [frédʒịl], *a.* frágil.—**-ness** [-nịs], **fragility** [frạdʒílịtị], *s.* fragilidad.

fragment [frégmẹnt], *s.* fragmento; trozo.—**-ary** [-ɛrị], *a.* fragmentario.

fragrance [fréịgrạns], *s.* fragancia.—**fragrant** [fréịgrạnt], *a.* fragante.

frail [freịl], *a.* frágil; endeble.—*s.* canasta, espuerta.—**-ty** [fréịltị], *s.* fragilidad; debilidad.

frame [freịm], *vt.* enmarcar, encuadrar; formar, construir; armar; forjar; idear; arreglar clandestinamente (el

resultado de un juego, etc.); acusar o hacer condenar con falsas pruebas.—*s.* marco; armazón; estructura; figura; armadura, esqueleto; bastidor.—*f. of mind*, estado de ánimo.— —**up** [fréịmʌp], *s.* conspiración, fraude.

franc [frænk], *s.* franco (moneda).

franchise [frénchaịz], *s.* derecho político; franquicia, privilegio; concesión; exención.

frank [frænk], *a.* franco, sincero; francote, campechano.—*s.* franquicia postal.—*vt.* franquear (una carta).

frankfurter [frénkfœrtœ(r)], *s.* salchicha alemana.

frankness [frénknịs], *s.* franqueza.

frantic [fréntịk], *a.* frenético, furioso.

fraternal [frạtœ́rnạl], *a.* fraternal, fraterno.—**fraternity** [frạtœ́rnịtị], *s.* (con)fraternidad; hermandad; gremio estudiantil.—**fraternize** [frétœrnaịz], *vi. y vt.* (con)fraternizar, hermanar(se).

fraud [frod], *s.* fraude; farsante, trampista.— —**ulent** [fródʒụlẹnt], *a.* fraudulento.

fray [freị], *s.* riña, refriega; raedura, desgaste.—*vt.* ludir, raer.—*vi.* deshilacharse.

freak [frik], *s.* capricho, antojo; rareza; monstruo, fenómeno.—*f. of nature*, aborto de la naturaleza.—*a.* raro; anormal.— —**ish** [fríkịṣ], *a.* caprichoso, antojadizo; raro.

freckle [frékl], *s.* peca.—*f.-faced*, pecoso.—*vt.* motear.—*vi.* ponerse pecoso.—**-d** [-d], *a.* pecoso; moteado.

free [fri], *a.* libre; franco; vacante; exento; gratuito; desocupado; liberal, generoso.—*f. of charge*, gratis.—*f. on board*, franco a bordo, libre a bordo.—*vt.* librar, libertar; eximir; desembarazar.—*adv.* libremente, gratis.—**-dom** [frídọm], *s.* libertad; exención, inmunidad; libre uso.

Freemason [fríméịṣọn], *s.* masón.

freeze [friz], *vti.* [10] congelar, helar.—*vii.* helarse; helar, escarchar.—*s.* helada.—*r* [frízœ(r)], *s.* congelador, refrigerador; heladora, sorbetera.—**freezing** [frízịŋ], *a.* congelante, frigorífico; glacial.—*s.* helamiento, congelación.

freight [freịt], *vt.* fletar; cargar.—*s.* carga, cargazón; flete.—*by f.*, como carga.—*f. car o train*, carro, tren de mercancías.—*f. elevator*, montacargas.— —**er** [fréịtœ(r)], *s.* buque de carga.

French [french], *a. y s.* francés.—idioma francés.—**man** [frénchmạn], *s.* francés.— —**woman** [-wụmạn], *s.* francesa.

frenzy [frénzị], *s.* frenesí.

frequency [fríkwẹnsị], *s.* frecuencia.—*f.*

modulation, frecuencia modulada, modulación de frecuencia.—**frequent** [fríkwęnt], *a.* frecuente.—*vt.* [frikwént], frecuentar; concurrir a.

fresh [freš], *a.* fresco; reciente; nuevo; refrescante; desahogado, entremetido. —*f. air,* aire puro; aire libre.—*f. from,* acabado de llegar, sacar, etc.—*f. hand,* novicio.—*f. water,* agua dulce.— —**en** [fréšęn], *vt.* refrescar, refrigerar. —*vi.* refrescarse, avivarse.— —**ly** [-li], *adv.* frescamente, con frescura; nuevamente, recientemente.— —**man** [-man], *s.* estudiante de primer año; novato, novicio.— —**ness** [-nis], *s.* frescura, frescor; lozanía, verdor; descaro.

fret [fret], *vti.* [1] rozar, raer; desgastar; enojar, irritar; adornar con calados.— *vii.* apurarse, inquietarse; incomodarse, impacientarse; agitarse.—*s.* roce; raedura; desgaste; irritación, enojo; hervor; relieve, realce; traste de guitarra.—*f. saw,* segueta, sierra caladora.— —**ful** [frétful], *a.* displicente, irritable, enojadizo; inquieto; incómodo, molesto.

friar [fráiǝ(r)], *s.* fraile.

fricassee [frikasí], *s.* fricasé.—*vt.* hacer fricasé.

friction [fríkšǫn], *s.* fricción; frotación; roce; desavenencia.—*f. tape,* (elec.) cinta aisladora adherente.

Friday [fráidi], *s.* viernes.

friend [frend], *s.* amigo, amiga.— —**less** [fréndlis], *a.* desamparado, desvalido, sin amigos.— —**liness** [-lįnįs], *s.* amistad.— —**ly** [-li], *a.* amistoso, amigable, cordial.—*adv.* amistosamente.— —**ship** [-šįp], *s.* amistad.

fright [frait], *s.* susto, espanto, pavor; espantajo.— —**en** [fráitęn], *vt.* espantar, asustar, amilanar.—*to f. away,* ahuyentar.— —**ful** [-ful], *a.* espantoso, terrible.— —**fulness** [-fulnis], *s.* espanto, terror.

frigid [frídžid], *a.* frío, frígido; indiferente.— —**ity** [frídžídįti], *s.* frialdad, frigidez; indiferencia.

fringe [frindž], *s.* fleco, pestaña; orla, borde.—*vt.* guarnecer con flecos; orlar.

frisk [frisk], *vi.* saltar, brincar, retozar. —*vt.* registrar los bolsillos, cachear.— *s.* retozo; brinco, salto.— —**y** [fríski], *a.* retozón, vivaracho.

fritter [frítǝ(r)], *s.* fritura, fruta de sartén.—*to f. away,* desperdiciar o malgastar a poquitos.

frivolity [frivályti], *s.* frivolidad.— **frivolous** [frívǫlas], *a.* frívolo.

fro [frou], *adv.* atrás, hacia atrás.—*to and f.,* de una parte a otra, de acá y allá.

frock [frak], *s.* vestido (de mujer).—*f. coat,* levita.

frog [frag], *s.* rana; alamar.—*f. in the throat,* carraspera.

frolic [frálik], *s.* juego, retozo, travesura.—*a.* alegre, juguetón, travieso. —*vii.* [8] juguetear, retozar, triscar. —**frolicked** [frálikt], *pret.* y *pp.* de TO FROLIC.— —**some** [-sʌm], *a.* retozón, travieso.

from [fram], *prep.* de; desde; de parte de; a fuerza de; a partir de; a causa de.—*f. memory,* de memoria.—*f. now on,* de ahora en adelante, en lo sucesivo.—*f. nature,* del natural.

frond [frand], *s.* fronda.— —**age** [-idž], *s.* frondosidad, follaje, frondas.

front [frʌnt], *s.* frente (*m.*); frontispicio, fachada, portada.—*in f.,* delante, enfrente.—*in f. of,* delante de, ante.— *shirt f.,* pechera.—*a.* anterior, delantero; frontero; frontal.—*f. door,* puerta principal.—*f. row,* delantera, primera fila.—*vt.* hacer frente a.—*to f. towards,* mirar hacia; dar o caer a. —*vi.* estar al frente de.

frontier [frʌntír], *s.* frontera.—*a.* fronterizo.

frost [frost], *s.* escarcha; helada.—*f. -bitten,* helado.—*vt.* cubrir de escarcha.—*vi.* escarchar, helar, congelarse. — —**y** [frósti], *a.* escarchado; helado.

froth [froθ], *s.* espuma; bambolla.—*vi.* espumar, hacer espuma; echar espuma.— —**y** [fróθi], *a.* espumoso; frívolo, vano.

frown [fraun], *s.* ceño, entrecejo.—*vi.* fruncir el entrecejo.—*to f. at, on,* o *upon,* desaprobar, mirar con ceño.— —**ing** [fráunįŋ], *a.* ceñudo.

froze [frouz], *pret.* de TO FREEZE.— **frozen** [fróuzęn], *pp.* de TO FREEZE.

fructification [frʌktifikéišǫn], *s.* fructificación; fruto.

frugal [frúgal], *a.* frugal.— —**ity** [frugǽliti], *s.* frugalidad.

fruit [frut], *s.* fruta; fruto; provecho; resultado.—*f. tree,* árbol frutal.— —**ful** [frútful], *a.* fructífero, feraz; productivo; prolífico, fecundo; fructuoso, provechoso.— —**ion** [fruíšǫn], *s.* fruición.— —**less** [-lis], *a.* infructuoso, estéril, vano.

frustrate [frʌstreit], *vt.* frustrar.— **frustration** [frʌstréišǫn], *s.* frustración.

fry [frai], *s.* fritada; brete, sofocón; cría, pececillos recién nacidos; enjambre, muchedumbre.—*small f.,* chiquillería, gente menuda.—*vti.* y *vii.* [7] freír(se), achicharrar(se).—*frying pan,* sartén.

fudge [fʌdž], *s.* jarabe o dulce de chocolate; embuste, cuento.

fuel [fiúęl], *s.* combustible; pábulo,

aliciente.—*vt.* y *vi.* abastecer(se) de combustible.

fugitive [fiúdȝitiv], *a.* y *s.* fugitivo.

fulfill [fulfíl], *vt.* colmar, llenar; realizar. — —**ment** [-ment], *s.* cumplimiento, desempeño, ejecución, realización; colmo.

full [ful], *a.* lleno; completo, cabal, repleto; pleno; cumplido; amplio; rotundo; harto, ahito; maduro, perfecto.—*f. age,* mayoría de edad.—*f.-blooded,* de sangre pura, pura raza.— *f.-length,* de cuerpo entero.—*f. name,* nombre y apellido.—*f. scope,* carta blanca, rienda suelta.—*f. speed,* a toda velocidad.—*f. stop,* punto final; detención total de un vehículo.—*f. time,* tiempo o período completo, horas normales de trabajo.—*adv.* enteramente, del todo; de lleno; totalmente, en pleno; derechamente. —*f.-blown,* abierta del todo (una flor).—*f.-grown,* maduro, crecido; completamente desarrollado.—**ness** [fúlnis], *s.* plenitud, abundancia; hartura, saciedad; complemento.

fume [fium], *s.* tufo, gas, emanación; vapores, gases, emanaciones deletéreas.—*vt.* fumigar, sahumar, exhalar. —*vi.* exhalar vapores; encolerizarse.

fumigate [fiúmigeit], *vt.* fumigar, sahumar.—**fumigation** [fiumigéiȝọn], *s.* fumigación; sahumerio.

fun [fʌn], *s.* broma, chanza, burla; diversión.

function [fʌ́ŋkȝọn], *s.* función, ejercicio, ocupación; ceremonia, acto; potencia, facultad.—*vi.* funcionar.— —**al** [-ạl], *a.* funcional.—**ary** [-eri], *s.* funcionario.

fund [fʌnd], *s.* fondo (dinero).—*pl.* fondos.—*vt.* consolidar (una deuda).

fundament [fʌ́ndạment], *s.* fundamento.— —**al** [fʌndạméntạl], *a.* fundamental.—*s.* fundamento.

funeral [fiúnerạl], *a.* funeral, funerario, fúnebre.—*f. home o parlor,* funeraria. —*f. procession,* cortejo fúnebre.—*s.* funeral(es), exequias; entierro; duelo. —**funereal** [fiunírial], *a.* fúnebre.

fungus [fʌ́ŋgʌs], *s.* (*pl.* fungi [fʌ́ndȝai]) hongo.

funnel [fʌ́nl], *s.* embudo; cañón de chimenea.—*vti.* y *vii.* [2] encauzar(se); concentrar(se).

funny [fʌ́ni], *a.* cómico, divertido, gracioso, ocurrente, chusco; (fam.) extraño, curioso.—*f. business,* treta, picardía, fraude.

fur [fœr], *s.* piel, pelo (de los animales); sarro.—*vt.* [1] cubrir, forrar o adornar con pieles.—*vii.* formarse incrustaciones.

furious [fiúriʌs], *a.* furioso, enfurecido.

furl [fœrl], *vt.* plegar, recoger.

furlough [fœrlou], *s.* (mil.) licencia.—*vt.* licenciar.

furnace [fœrnis], *s.* horno (industrial).— *blast f.,* alto horno.

furnish [fœrniȝ], *vt.* surtir, suministrar; aparejar, equipar; amueblar.

furniture [fœrnichụr], *s.* mobiliario; muebles; ajuar; adornos, accesorios; avíos.

furrow [fœrou], *s.* surco; zanja; arruga; muesca; mediacaña.—*vt.* surcar; estriar; arar.

further [fœrðœ(r)], *a.* ulterior, más distante; más amplio; nuevo, adicional.—*adv.* más; más lejos, más allá; además; además de eso.—*vt.* fomentar, adelantar, promover.— —**ance** [-ạns], *s.* adelantamiento, promoción.— —**more** [-mór], *adv.* además; otrosí.—**furthest** [fœrðist], *a.* y *adv.* (el) más lejano, (el) más remoto; (lo) más lejos.

furtive [fœrtiv], *a.* furtivo, secreto.

fury [fiúri], *s.* furia; frenesí.

fuse [fiuz], *vt.* y *vi.* fundir(se).—*s.* espoleta; mecha; fusible.

fuselage [fiúzẹlidȝ], *s.* fuselaje.

fusion [fiúȝọn], *s.* fusión, fundición; unión.

fuss [fʌs], *s.* bulla, bullicio; melindre; agitación o actividad inútil.—*f. budget,* persona exigente o fastidiosa. —*vi.* inquietarse por pequeñeces; hacer melindres.— —**y** [fʌ́si], *a.* inquieto; remilgado, exigente.

futile [fiútil], *a.* fútil.—**futility** [fiutȷ́liti], *s.* futilidad.

future [fiúchụ(r)], *a.* futuro.—*s.* futuro, porvenir.—*in f.,* en lo sucesivo; de aquí en adelante.—*in the near f.,* en fecha próxima.

fuzz [fʌz], *vi.* soltar pelusa o borra.—*s.* pelusa, borra, vello.— —**y** [fʌ́zi], *a.* velloso, cubierto de pelusa; crespo.

G

gabardine [gæbạrdín], *s.* gabardina (tejido y sobretodo).

gabble [gæbl], *vt.* y *vi.* charlar; graznar (los gansos).—*s.* algarabía; charla; graznido.

gable [géibl], *s.* (arq.) aguilón, remate triangular de edificio o pared; pared lateral.—*g. end,* alero.—*g. roof,* tejado de dos aguas.

gad [gæd], *vii.* [1] callejear.— —**about** [gǽdạbaut], *a.* callejero.—*vi.* corretear, callejear.—*s.* placero, persona callejera.—**fly** [-flai], *s.* tábano.

gadget [gǽdȝit], *s.* (fam.) dispositivo, artefacto, artificio.

gaff [gæf], *s.* arpón o garfio; (mar.) botavara.

gag [gæg], *vti.* [1] amordazar; hacer

callar; provocar náuseas; (teat.)
meter morcilla.—*vii.* arquear, dar
náuseas.—*s.* mordaza; asco; (teat.)
morcilla; (fam.) chuscada; payasada;
chiste.

gage, *s.* **y** *vt.* = GAUGE.—**gager,** *s.* =
GAUGER.

gaiety [géiẹti], *s.* jovialidad, alegría,
alborozo; viveza.—**gaily** [géili], *adv.*
alegremente, jovialmente.

gain [geịn], *s.* ganancia, beneficio,
provecho.—*vt.* ganar, adquirir; lograr,
conseguir.—*vi.* ganar.—*to g. weight*,
echar carnes, engordar.— —**ful** [géịn-
fụl], *a.* lucrativo, ventajoso.— —**ings**
[-iŋz], *s. pl.* ganancias.

gait [geịt], *s.* marcha, paso, andadura.
—*at a good g.*, a buen paso.

gale [geịl], *s.* ventarrón, viento fuerte;
(fig.) algazara.

Galician [galíṣạn], *s.* **y** *a.* gallego.

gall [gol], *s.* hiel, bilis; amargura; odio,
rencor; (fam.) descaro.—*g. bladder*,
vesícula biliar.—*vt.* **y** *vi.* irritar,
hostigar.

gallant [gǽlạnt], *a.* galante, cortés;
galanteador; gallardo, bizarro; valeroso, valiente.—*s.* galán.- —**ry**
[-ri], *s.* valentía, gallardía, valor;
galantería.

gallery [gǽlẹri], *s.* galería; tribuna;
pasadizo; (teat.) paraíso, cazuela,
gallinero; público que ocupa el
paraíso.

galley [gǽli], *s.* (mar.) galera; (mar.)
cocina; (imp.) galera.—*g. slave*,
galeote.

gallon [gǽlọn], *s.* galón. Ver Tabla.

gallop [gǽlọp], *s.* galope.—*vi.* galopar.
—*vt.* hacer galopar.

gallows [gǽloụz], *s.* horca; patíbulo.

galore [galór], *adv.* en abundancia.

galosh [galáṣ], *s.* galocha, choclo,
chanclo, zueco.

galvanize [gǽlvạnaịz], *vt.* galvanizar.

gamble [gǽmbl], *vt.* jugar, aventurar
o perder una cosa en el juego.—*vi.*
jugar por dinero.—*s.* (fam.) jugada.-
—**r** [gǽmblœ(r)], *s.* jugador, tahur.
—**gambling** [gǽmbliŋ], *s.* juego (por
dinero).—*g. house*, garito, casa de
juego.

gambol [gǽmbọl], *vi.* brincar, saltar;
cabriolar; juguetear.—*s.* cabriola,
brinco, travesura.

game [geịm], *s.* juego; pasatiempo;
partido o partida de juego; caza
(piezas, vivas o muertas).—*g. warden*,
guardabosque.—*to make g. of*,
burlarse de, mofarse de.—*vt.* **y** *vi.*
jugar; jugar fuerte.—*a.* relativo a la
caza o al juego; dispuesto a pelear;
valeroso.—*to die g.*, morir peleando.-
—**cock** [géịmkak], *s.* gallo de pelea.-

—**keeper** [-kipœ(r)], *s.* guardamonte,
guardabosque.

gander [gǽndœ(r)], *s.* ánsar, ganso.

gang [gǽŋ], *s.* cuadrilla, pandilla; juego
(de herramientas, etc.); grupo.—*vt.*
y *vi.* formar cuadrilla.

gangplank [gǽŋplæŋk], *s.* pasarela,
pasamano, plancha.

gangrene [gǽŋgrin], *vt.* **y** *vi*, gan-
grenar(se).—*s.* gangrena.

gangster [gǽŋstœ(r)], *s.* pandillero,
pistolero.

gangway [gǽŋwei], *s.* (mar.) pasamano,
portalón, tilla.

gap [gǽp], *s.* portillo, abertura, brecha;
vacío, laguna; barranca, hondonada.
—*vti.* [1] hacer una brecha en.

gape [geịp], *vi.* quedarse boquiabierto;
embobarse; bostezar.—*s.* bostezo;
boqueada; brecha, abertura.

garage [garáž], *s.* garaje; taller mecánico
o de reparaciones.

garb [garb], *s.* vestido, vestidura;
apariencia exterior, aspecto.—*vt.* vestir, ataviar.

garbage [gárbiḍž], *s.* basura, desperdicios.

garden [gárdn], *s.* jardín; huerta,
huerto.—*g. of Eden*, paraíso terrenal.
—*g. stuff*, hortalizas, legumbres,
verduras.—*vt.* **y** *vi.* cultivar jardines
o huertos.— —**er** [-œ(r)], *s.* jardinero;
hortelano.— —**ing** [-iŋ], *s.* jardinería;
horticultura.

gargle [gárgl], *vt.* **y** *vi.* gargarizar, hacer
gárgaras.—*s.* gárgara, gargarismo.

garland [gárlạnd], *s.* guirnalda.

garlic [gárlik], *s.* ajo.

garment [gármẹnt], *s.* prenda de vestir;
vestido.—*pl.* ropa, vestimenta.

garnish [gárniṣ], *vt.* (coc.) aderezar;
guarnecer, ataviar; (for.) prevenir,
notificar; aprestar.—*s.* (coc.) aderezo;
guarnición, adorno.

garnet [gárnit], *s.* granate.

garret [gǽrit], *s.* buhardilla, desván.

garrison [gǽriṣọn], *s.* (mil.) guarnición.
—*vt.* (mil.) guarnecer; guarnicionar.

garrote [garóụt], *s.* garrote.—*vt.* agarro-
tar, dar garrote a; estrangular para
robar.

garter [gártœ(r)], *s.* liga (para las
medias).

gas [gǽs], *s.* gas; gasolina.—*g. burner*,
mechero de gas.—*g. meter*, contador
de gas.—*g. range*, o *g. stove*, fogón
o cocina de gas.—*g. station*, estación
o puesto de gasolina.—*tear g.*, gas
lacrimógeno.—*vti.* [1] (mil.) asfixiar,
envenenar o atacar con gas.- —**eous**
[gæsias], *a.* gaseoso; aeriforme.

gash [gǽṣ], *vt.* dar una cuchillada.—*s.*
cuchillada; incisión grande.

gasket [gǽskịt], *s.* (mec.) relleno,
empaquetadura.

gaslight [gǽslajt], *s*. luz de gas; mechero de gas.—**gasoline** [gǽsolin], *s*. gasolina.

gasp [gæsp], *vt*. jadear, boquear; emitir sonidos entrecortados.—*s*. boqueada, jadeo.

gate [gejt], *s*. portón; entrada; puerta; (f.c.) barrera; cancela; compuertas de esclusa; garganta, paso.— **—keeper** [géjtkipœ(r)], *s*. portero; (f.c.) guardabarrera.— **—way** [-wej], *s*. entrada, paso (con portillo).

gather [gǽðœ(r)], *vt*. reunir, recoger; coger; acumular; recolectar; juntar, congregar; (cost.) fruncir; colegir, deducir.—*to g. breath*, tomar aliento. —*vi*. unirse, reunirse, juntarse, congregarse; amontonarse, acumularse; concentrarse.—*s*. (cost.) pliegue, frunce.— **—ing** [-iŋ], *s*. asamblea; reunión; agrupación; (re)colección, acopio; fruncimiento; (cost.) fruncido.

Gaucho [gáuchou], *s*. gaucho.

gaudy [gódi], *a*. vistoso; llamativo, chillón.

gauge [gejdž], *s*. medida; calibre; calibrador; indicador; (mar.) calado; (m.v.) manómetro; (f.c.) ancho de vía; aforo, arqueo.—*g. pressure*, presión manométrica.—*vt*. calibrar; medir; estimar, apreciar.

gaunt [gɔnt], *a*. flaco, delgado, demacrado.

gauntlet [góntlit], *s*. manopla; guantelete.

gauze [gɔz], *s*. gasa, cendal.

gave [gejv], *pret*. de TO GIVE.

gavel [gǽvel], *s*. mazo; (agr.) haz, gavilla.

gawk [gɔk], *vi*. (fam.) bobear, cometer torpezas.—*s*. bobo, torpe.— **—y** [góki], *s*. papanatas.—*a*. bobo, tonto, torpe, desgarbado.

gay [gej], *a*. alegre, festivo, ufano, llamativo; ligero de cascos, calavera. —**gayety**, *s*. = GAIETY.

gaze [gejz], *vi*. mirar con fijeza, clavar la mirada.—*s*. contemplación, mirada fija o penetrante.

gazette [gazét], *s*. gaceta.

gazelle [gazél], *s*. gacela.

gear [gir], *s*. engranaje; mecanismo de tra(n)smisión, de distribución o de gobierno; juego; rueda dentada; (mar.) aparejo; equipo, pertrechos, aperos; atavíos.—*g. box* o *case*, caja de engranajes; (aut.) caja de velocidades.—*g. shifting*, cambio de velocidad o de marcha.—*g. wheel*, rueda dentada.—*in g*., engranado. —*landing g*., tren de aterrizaje.—*out of g*., desengranado.—*to put in g*., relacionar; engranar, embragar.—*to throw out of g*., desengranar, des-

embragar.—*vt*. aparejar; equipar; montar, armar; engranar, embragar. —*vi*. engranar.

geese [gis], *s. pl*. de GOOSE.

gelatin(e) [džélatin], *s*. gelatina.

gem [džem], *s*. gema; alhaja.—*vti*. [1] adornar con piedras preciosas.

gendarme [žándarm], *s*. gendarme, polizonte armado.

gender [džéndœ(r)], *s*. (gram.) género.

general [džénœral], *a*. general, frecuente. —*g. delivery*, lista de correos.—*s*. (mil.) general.—*in g*., en general, por regla general.— **—ity** [dženœréliti], *s*. generalidad.— **—ize** [džénœralajz], *vt*. generalizar.

generate [džénœrejt], *vt*. engendrar; producir, causar.—**generation** [dženœréjšǫn], *s*. generación; reproducción. —**generator** [džénœrejtǫ(r)], *s*. generador, dínamo.

generosity [dženœrásiti], *s*. generosidad, largueza.—**generous** [dženœras], *a*. generoso; noble, magnánimo; amplio.

genial [džínjal], *a*. genial, afable, alegre.— **—ity** [džinjéliti], *s*. afabilidad.

genital [dženital], *a*. genital.—*pl*. genitales, partes pudendas.

genius [džínyʌs], *s*. genio; prototipo.

genteel [dzentíl], *a*. cortés, gentil; gallardo, airoso, elegante; cursi.

gentile [džéntajl], *s. y a*. gentil, pagano.

gentle [džéntl], *a*. suave, dulce, benévolo; dócil, manso; bien nacido.— **—man** [-man], *s*. caballero; señor.— **—manliness** [-manlinjs], *s*. caballerosidad, hidalguía.— **—manly** [-manli], *a*. caballeroso.— **—men** [-men], *s. pl*. de GENTLEMAN; señores; (en cartas) muy señores míos (nuestros).—*g.'s agreement*, pacto de caballeros.— **—ness** [-njs], *s*. dulzura, suavidad; docilidad, mansedumbre; urbanidad. —**gently** [džéntli], *adv*. dulcemente, suavemente; poco a poco, despacio.

genuine [dženyujn], *a*. genuino, auténtico; sincero.

geographer [džiágrafœ(r)], *s*. geógrafo. —**geographic(al)** [džiográfjk(al)], *a*. geográfico.—**geography** [džiágrafi], *s*. geografía.—**geologist** [džiálodžist], *s*. geólogo.—**geology** [džiálodž], *s*. geología.—**geometric(al)** [džiométrjk(al)], *a*. geométrico.—**geometry** [džiámetri], *s*. geometría.

geranium [džœréjnjʌm], *s*. geranio.

German [džœrman], *s. y a*. alemán.—*s*. lengua alemana.—*G. measles*, roseola.

germ [džœrm], *s*. germen; microbio.— **—icide** [džœrmjsajd], *s*. germicida.

germinate [džœrmjnejt], *vi*. germinar. —**germination** [džœrmjnéjšǫn], *s*. germinación.

gerund [džérʌnd], *s*. (gram.) gerundio.

gestation [dźestéjŝǫn], *s.* gestación.

gesture [dźéschǔ(r)], *s.* gesto, ademán, signo.—*vi.* accionar; gesticular o hacer gestos.

get [get], *vti.* [10] conseguir, obtener, adquirir; agarrar, atrapar; ganar; llevar (premio, ventaja, etc.); recibir; procrear; hacer que; incitar; procurar, lograr; ir por, traer; entender.—*to g. back*, recobrar.—*to g. down*, descolgar, bajar; tragar.—*to g. on*, ponerse (ropa).—*to g. out*, publicar, editar, sacar.—*to g. the worse o the worst*, llevar la peor parte, quedar mal parado.—*to g. wind of*, recibir aviso de, tener noticia de.—*vii.* ganar dinero; llegar; ponerse o volverse; hacerse, ser; hallarse, estar; introducirse, meterse.—*g. out!* ¡fuera! ¡largo de aquí!—*g. up!* ¡arre!—*to g. along*, ir pasando.—*to g. along well (badly) with*, llevarse bien (mal) con.—*to g. married*, casarse.—*to g. off*, salir de un asunto; escapar; salir; bajar(se), apearse.—*to g. on*, adelantar; ponerse encima de; subir; montar; entrar en un coche.—*to g. out*, salir, salirse.—*to g. out of order*, desajustarse, descomponerse.—*to g. out of the way*, apartarse o hacerse a un lado.—*to g. ready*, disponerse, aprestarse.—*to g. rid of*, zafarse o librarse de, acabar con, quitar de encima.—*to g. through*, pasar, entrar; terminar.—*to g. together*, juntarse, reunirse; cooperar.—*to g. up*, levantarse; subir.—*to g. well*, curar, sanar, ponerse bueno.— —**away** [gétawej], *s.* ida, partida; escape; arranque (de un auto).— —**ter** [-œ(r)], *s.* persona que consigue o logra.— —**up** [-ʌp], *s.* arreglo, disposición; atavío; traje.

ghastly [gǽstli], *a.* lívido, cadavérico; horrible, espantoso.—*adv.* horriblemente; mortalmente.

ghost [gǫst], *s.* fantasma, espectro, sombra; espíritu.—*the Holy G.*, el Espíritu Santo.—*not a g. of a doubt*, ni sombra de duda.—*to give up the g.*, entregar el espíritu, morir(se).— —**ly** [góŋstli], *a.* espectral, fantástico, de duendes o aparecidos.

giant [dźáiạnt], *a.* gigantesco, gigante. —*s.* gigante.

giblets [dźiblịts], *s. pl.* menudillos.

giddiness [gídịnịs], *s.* vértigo, vahído; desvarío.—**giddy** [gídị], *a.* vertiginoso; voluble, inconstante; atolondrado.

gift [gift], *s.* regalo, dádiva; donación; don, dote, talento.- —**ed** [gíftịd], *a.* talentoso, genial; agraciado.

gigantic [dźạigǽntịk], *a.* gigantesco.

giggle [gịgl], *vi.* reírse sin motivo; reírse por nada.—*s.* risa nerviosa, risita.

gild [gịld], *vti.* [4] dorar.

gill [gịl], *s.* agalla, branquia.

gilt [gịlt], *pret. y pp.* de TO GILD.—*a.* dorado, áureo.—*s.* dorado; oropel; falso brillo.

gin [dźịn], *s.* ginebra (licor de enebro).

ginger [dźíndźœ(r)], *s.* jengibre.—*g. ale*, cerveza de jengibre.- —**bread** [-bred], *s.* pan de jengibre.—*a.* recargado, de mal gusto.

gipsy [dźípsị], *s.* = GYPSY.

giraffe [dźịrǽf], *s.* jirafa.

gird [gœrd], *vti.* [4] ceñir; rodear.- —**le** [gœrdl], *s.* faja; ceñidor; cinto.—*vt.* ceñir, cercar, fajar, circundar.

girl [gœrl], *s.* muchacha, niña; (fam.) sirvienta, criada.- —**hood** [gœrlhụd], *s.* doncellez; vida o edad de muchacha; la juventud femenina.- —**ish** [-iŝ], *a.* juvenil; propio de niña o joven.

girt [gœrt], *pret. y pp.* de TO GIRD.—*a.* (mar.) amarrado.

girth [gœrθ], *s.* cincha; faja, cinto; gordura; circunferencia, periferia.—*vt.* cinchar, ceñir.

gist [dźịst], *s.* substancia, quid.

give [gịv], *vti.* [10] dar, donar; conceder, otorgar.—*to g. advice*, dar consejo; asesorar.—*to g. a lift to one*, ayudar a uno a levantarse o a levantar algo; llevarle (en coche, etc.).—*to g. a piece of one's mind to*, decir las verdades del barquero, decir cuántas son cinco.—*to g. away*, regalar; deshacerse de; vender regalado; divulgar un secreto.—*to g. back*, restituir, devolver.—*to g. birth*, dar a luz, parir; producir.—*to g. chase*, perseguir.—*to g. ear to*, prestar oídos a.—*to g. forth*, publicar, divulgar. —*to g. oneself away*, (fam.) enseñar la oreja.—*to g. oneself up*, rendirse; abandonarse, desesperarse.—*to g. out*, publicar, divulgar; proclamar.—*to g. over*, abandonar; desistir de; desahuciar.—*to g. pause*, dar en qué pensar; hacer pensar.—*to g. place*, dejar el puesto (a).—*to g. rise to*, dar lugar a, ocasionar.—*to g. the slip*, dar esquinazo; echar.—*to g. up*, renunciar a; entregar; resignar.—*to g. up the ghost*, morir; darse por vencido. —*to g. voice to*, decir, expresar.—*to g. warning*, prevenir, advertir.—*to g. way*, ceder, retroceder; ceder su puesto.—*vi.* dar libremente, ser dadivoso; dar de sí, aflojarse; ceder. —*to g. in*, ceder; acceder; asentir. —*to g. up*, desistir, cejar; darse por vencido; perder la esperanza.—*s.* acción de dar de sí o ceder físicamente (como una cuerda); elasticidad.

—**g.-and-take** [gívₐntejk], *s.* concesiones mutuas, componenda.— **given** [gívₑn], *pp.* de TO GIVE.—*a.* dado; citado, especificado; (mat.) conocido.—*g. name*, nombre bautismal.—*g. that*, suponiendo que, sabiendo que.—*g. to*, adicto o aficionado a.—**giver** [gívœ(r)], *s.* donante, donador.

gizzard [gízₐrd], *s.* molleja (de ave).

glacial [gléjṣịₐl], *a.* glacial; (geol.) glaciario.—**glacier** [gléjṣœ(r)], *s.* glaciar, ventisquero.

glad [glæd], *a.* alegre, contento, gozoso. —*to be g.*, alegrarse, tener gusto.— —**den** [glǽdn], *vt.* alegrar, regocijar, recrear.

glade [glejd], *s.* claro, raso o pradera (en un bosque).

gladiolus [glædjóʉlʌs], *s.* (bot.) gladiolo, espadaña.

gladness [glǽdnịs], *s.* alegría, placer, gozo.

glamor [glǽmₒ(r)], *s.* encanto, hechizo, embrujo; embeleso.—*vt.* encantar, hechizar.—**ous** [-ʌs], *a.* encantador, hechicero.

glance [glæns], *s.* mirada, ojeada, vistazo; vislumbre; fulgor.—*at first g.*, a primera vista.—*vt.* mirar de o al soslayo, o de refilón.—*vi.* dar un vistazo o una ojeada; centellear· tocar o herir oblicuamente.

gland [glænd], *s.* glándula.

glare [gler], *vi.* relumbrar, brillar; tener colores chillones; (con at) mirar echando fuego por los ojos.—*s.* resplandor; resol; mirada feroz y penetrante.—*a.* liso, lustroso y resbaladizo.—**glaring** [glérịn], *a.* deslumbrador; evidente, notorio; penetrante, furioso.

glass [glæs], *s.* vidrio; cristal; vaso; copa; espejo; lente, catalejo.—*pl.* anteojos, gafas, espejuelos, lentes. —*g. blower*, soplador de vidrio.—*g. cutter*, diamante de vidriero.—*a.* de vidrio.—*g. window*, vidriera, escaparate.— —**ful** [glǽsful], *s.* vaso (su contenido).— —**ware** [-wer], *s.* vajilla de cristal, cristalería— —**wort** [-wœrt], *s.* (bot.) sosa, matojo.— —**y** [-i], *a.* vítreo, vidrioso.—**glaze** [glejz], *vt.* poner vidrios a una ventana; vidriar; glasear; (cerá.) esmaltar.—*s.* superficie lisa y lustrosa; lustre; capa de hielo. —**glazier** [gléjẑœ(r)], *s.* vidriero.

gleam [glim], *s.* destello, fulgor, viso, centelleo.—*vi.* centellear, fulgurar, destellar.

glean [glin], *vt.* espigar; recoger, juntar.

glee [gli], *s.* alegría, gozo, júbilo; (mús.) canción para voces solas. —*g. club*, cantoría, coro; orfeón.

glib [glib], *a.* suelto de lengua, locuaz.

glide [glajd], *vi.* resbalar, deslizarse; (aer.) planear.—*s.* deslizamiento; (aer.) planeo.— —**r** [glájdœ(r)], *s.* el o lo que se desliza; (aer.) planeador, deslizador.

glimmer [glímœ(r)], *vi.* rielar, centellear.—*s.* luz trémula; vislumbre, viso.

glimpse [glimps], *s.* ojeada, vistazo; vislumbre.—*vt.* vislumbrar.—*vi.* ojear.

glint [glint], *vi.* brillar, destellar.—*s.* destello, relumbre.

glisten [glisn], *vi.* brillar, resplandecer.

glitter [glítœ(r)], *vi.* resplandecer, centellear, rutilar, brillar.—*s.* brillo, resplandor, centelleo.

global [glóʉbₐl], *a.* global; esférico. —**globe** [gloʉb], *s.* esfera, globo. —**globetrotter** [glóʉbtratœ(r)], *s.* trotamundos.—**globular** [glᴀbyulₐ(r)], *a.* globular, esférico.—**globule** [glábyul], *s.* glóbulo.

gloom [glum], *s.* oscuridad, lobreguez, tenebrosidad, tinieblas; melancolía, tristeza.— **gloomy** [glúmi], *a.* tenebroso, sombrío, lóbrego; nublado, triste, melancólico.

glorify [glórịfaj], *vti.* [7] glorificar, exaltar, alabar.—**glorious** [glórịₐs], *a.* glorioso; (fam.) excelente, magnífico. —**glory** [glóri], *s.* gloria.—*vii.* [7] gloriarse, vanagloriarse, jactarse.

gloss [glɔs], *s.* lustre, brillo; pulimento; apariencia; glosa; comentario.—*vt.* pulir, pulimentar, satinar.—*vt. y vi.* glosar, comentar.— —**ary** [glásạri], *s.* glosario.— —**y** [glɔ́si], *a.* lustroso, satinado; (fot.) brillante.

glove [glʌv], *s.* guante.—*to be hand and g.*, ser uña y carne.—*to handle with gloves*, tratar con mucho miramiento.—*to handle without gloves*, tratar sin contemplaciones.—*vt.* enguantar.

glow [gloʉ], *vi.* brillar o lucir suavemente; fosforecer; ponerse incandescente; enardecerse.—*s.* brillo sin llama; incandescencia; calor intenso; vehemencia.— —**ing** [glóʉịn], *a.* incandescente, encendido; ardiente. —**worm** [-wœrm], *s.* luciérnaga, (Am.) cocuyo.

glue [glu], *s.* cola, engrudo o goma de pegar.—*vt.* encolar; engomar.— —**y** [glúi], *a.* pegajoso, viscoso.

glutton [glátₒn], *s.* glotón, tragón, comelón.— —**ous** [-ʌs], *a.* glotón; goloso.— —**y** [-i], *s.* glotonería, gula.

gnash [næʃ], *vt.* rechinar o crujir los dientes.

gnat [næt], *s.* (Am.) jején; mosquito.

gnaw [nɔ], *vt.* roer; carcomer; corroer.— —**er** [nɔ́œ(r)], *s.* roedor.

go [gou], *vii*. [10] ir, irse; andar; marcharse, partir; (mec.) funcionar; acudir; sentar, caer bien.—*to g. abroad*, ir al extranjero.—*to g. across*, cruzar.—*to g. after*, seguir a.—*to g. ahead*, adelantar, proseguir.—*to g. along*, seguir, proseguir; irse, marcharse.—*to g. around*, alcanzar para todos.—*to g. astray*, extraviarse.—*to g. away*, desaparecer; irse, marcharse. —*to g. back*, regresar; volverse atrás. —*to g. in for*, dedicarse a.—*to g. into*, entrar en.—*to g. near*, acercarse. —*to g. off*, irse, largarse; dispararse. —*to g. on*, avanzar, continuar; proseguir.—*to g. out*, salir; apagarse. —*to g. to pot*, arruinarse.—*to g. under*, quedar arruinado; hundirse; ser vencido; pasar por debajo de.—*to g. up*, subir, ascender.—*to g. without saying*, sobreentenderse.—*s*. usanza; energía, empuje; buen éxito.—*is it a g.?* ¿está resuelto? ¿estamos convenidos?—*it is no g.*, es inútil, esto no marcha.—*on the g.*, en actividad.

goad [goud], *s*. aguijón, puya.—*g. spur*, acicate.—*g. stick*, garrocha, rejo.—*vt*. aguijonear; estimular.

goal [goul], *s*. meta, fin, objeto, objetivo, propósito; (dep.) gol, tanto.

goat [gout], *s*. cabra; chiva.—*billy o male g.*, cabrón, chivo, macho cabrío.—*to be the g.*, cargar con la culpa ajena.—*ee* [gouti], *s*. pera, perilla.

gobble [gábl], *vt*. engullir, tragar.—*vi*. hacer ruido con la garganta como los pavos.—*s*. voz del pavo.—*r* [gáblœ(r)], *s*. glotón, tragón; pavo.

go-between [góubitwin], *s*. mediador; alcahuete.

goblet [gáblit], *s*. copa de mesa, vaso de pie.

goblin [gáblin], *s*. trasgo, duende.

gocart [góukart], *s*. carretilla.

god, God [gad], *s*. dios, Dios.—*G. be with you*, vaya usted con Dios. —*G. forbid*, no lo quiera Dios. —*G. willing*, Dios mediante, si Dios quiere.—*—child* [gádchaild], *s*. ahijado, ahijada.—*—dess* [-is], *s*. diosa.—*—father* [-faðœ(r)], *s*. padrino.—*—less* [-lis], *a*. ateo, impío.—*—lessness* [-lisnis], *s*. impiedad, ateísmo.—*—like* [-laik], *a*. divino.—*—liness* [-linis], *s*. piedad, santidad.—*—ly* [-li], *a*. divino; devoto, piadoso.—*—mother* [-mʌðœ(r)], *s*. madrina.—*—parents* [-perents], *s*. padrinos.—*—ship* [-šip], *s*. divinidad.—*—son* [-sʌn], *s*. ahijado.

go-getter [góugétœ(r)], *s*. buscavidas.

going [góuiŋ], *a*. y *ger*. de TO GO; activo,

que funciona.—*a g. concern*, una empresa que funciona o marcha.—*s*. paso, andar; marcha, ida; partida; estado del camine.—*g. out*, salida.

goiter [góitœ(r)], *s*. bocio, papera, (Am.) buche.

gold [gould], *s*. oro; color de oro.—*g. standard*, patrón de oro.—*g. work*, orfebrería.—*—en* [góulden], *a*. áureo, de oro, dorado; rubio, amarillento.— *—finch* [-finch], *s*. cardelina; jilguero amarillo.—*—fish* [-fiš], *s*. pececillo(s) de colores; carpa dorada.—*—smith* [-smiθ], *s*. orfebre.

gondola [gándolǝ], *s*. góndola; (aer.) barquilla o cabina; (f.c.) vagón de mercancías.—**gondolier** [gandolír], *s*. gondolero.

gone [gɔn], *pp*. de TO GO.—*a*. ido; perdido, arruinado; pasado; apagado.

gong [gaŋ], *s*. batintín, gong.

gonorrhea [ganoríǝ], *s*. gonorrea.

good [gud], *a*. bueno; apto, conveniente; genuino, válido, valedero; digno. —*a g. deal*, mucho, bastante.—*a g. turn*, un favor, una gracia.—*as g. as*, casi.—*g. afternoon*, buenas tardes. —*g. enough*, suficientemente bueno, pasadero, suficiente.—*g. evening*, buenas tardes; buenas noches.—*G. Friday*, Viernes Santo.—*g. for nothing*, inútil, sin valor; haragán. —*g.-looking*, guapo, bien parecido.— *g. morning*, buenos días.—*g. nature*, bondad, buen corazón.—*g. night*, buenas noches.—*s*. bien; provecho, ventaja.—*pl*. géneros, mercancías, efectos.—*for g.*, para siempre.—*for g. and all*, terminantemente, una vez por todas.—*it's no g.*, no vale, es inútil.—*interj*. ¡bueno! ¡muy bien!— *—by*, *—bye* [gudbái], *s*. e *interj*. adiós; hasta la vista; vaya usted con Dios.—*—liness* [gúdlinis], *s*. belleza, gracia, elegancia.—*—ness* [-nis], *s*. bondad, benevolencia; fineza.—*interj*. ¡Ave María! ¡Dios mío!—*—y* [-i], *a*. y *s*. bonachón, Juan Lanas.— *—y-y*, santurrón, beato.—*pl*. dulces.

goose [gus], *s*. ganso, oca; necio.— *g. flesh*, carne de gallina (aplicado a la piel humana).—*—berry* [gúzberi], *s*. grosella.

gore [gor], *s*. cuajarón de sangre; (cost.) cuchillo, nesga; pedazo triangular de terreno.—*vt*. herir con los cuernos; poner nesga o cuchillo.

gorge [gordž], *s*. garganta, barranco, desfiladero; cuello de un vestido; trago, bocado; asco.—*vt*. engullir, tragar; atiborrar; hartar, saciar.—*vi*. hartarse, saciarse.

gorgeous [górdžʌs], *a*. vistoso, magnífico, suntuoso.

gorilla [goríǝ], *s*. gorila.

gory [góri], *a.* sangriento, sanguinolento.

gospel [gáspɛl], *s.* evangelio; cosa cierta e indudable.—*g. truth,* verdad palmaria.— **-(l)er** [-œ(r)], *s.* evangelista.

gossip [gásip], *s.* chismografía, murmuración; chismoso; chisme.—*vi.* chismear, murmurar.— **-ing** [-iŋ], **-y** [-i], *a.* chismoso, murmurador.

got [gat], *pret.* y *pp.* de TO GET.

goth [gaθ], *s.* godo.—**Gothic** [gáθik], *a.* gótico.—*s.* lengua goda.

gotten [gátn], *pp.* de TO GET.

gouge [gaudʒ], *s.* gubia; ranura, canal, estría.—*vt.* escoplar; arrancar, sacar, vaciar; engañar.

gourd [gord], *s.* calabaza; (Am.) güiro.

gout [gaut], *s.* gota, artritis.— **-y** [gáuti], *a.* gotoso.

govern [gávœrn], *vt.* y *vi.* gobernar; regir.— **-ess** [-is], *s.* institutriz.— **-ment** [-mɛnt], *s.* gobierno, gobernación; administración, dirección; régimen.— **-or** [-ɒ(r)], *s.* gobernador; regulador.

gown [gaun], *s.* traje de mujer; túnica; toga; vestidura talar.—*dressing g.,* bata. *-vt.* y *vi.* togar(se).

grab [græb], *vti.* [1] asir, agarrar; arrebatar, posesionarse.—*s.* agarrón, toma, asimiento; presa; arrebatiña; copo; gancho, garfio; (fam.) robo.

grace [greis], *s.* gracia, garbo; favor, concesión, privilegio; talante.—*good graces,* favor, amistad, bienquerencia. —*to say g.,* bendecir la mesa.—*with a bad (good) g.,* de mala (buena) gana.— **-ful** [gréisful], *a.* gracioso, agraciado; garboso; fácil, natural; decoroso.— **-fulness** [-fulnis], *s.* donosura, garbo, elegancia.

gracious [gréisas], *a.* bondadoso, benigno; afable; gracioso, grato.— *g. me!* o *good(ness) g.!* ¡válgame Dios! ¡caramba!

gradation [greidéisən], *s.* graduación; grado; serie; escalonamiento; (mus. y pint.) gradación.—**grade** [greid], *s.* grado; clase; nota o calificación; declive.—*at g.,* a nivel.—*down g.,* cuesta abajo.—*g. crossing,* paso a nivel.—*g. school,* escuela primaria.—*highest g.,* de primera clase o calidad. —*up g.,* cuesta arriba.—*vt.* clasificar u ordenar; graduar; (ing.) nivelar. —**gradual** [gréd̨ual], *a.* gradual; graduado.—**graduate** [gréd̨ueit], *vt.* graduar.—*vi.* graduarse, (Am.) recibirse de bachiller.—*a.* [gréd̨uit], graduado, (Am.) que ha recibido el grado.—*s.* el que ha recibido un grado académico.—**graduation** [græd̨uéisən], *s.* graduación, obtención del grado.

graft [græft], *s.* injerto; tejido injertado;

parte donde se hace el injerto; malversación; (Am.) peculado; latrocinio; soborno político.—*vt.* y *vi.* injertar; malversar; traficar con puestos públicos; cometer peculado.

grain [grein], *s.* grano; fibra o veta de la madera, el mármol, etc.—*pl.* cereales, granos en general.—*across the g.,* transversalmente a la fibra.

gram [græm], *s.* gramo.

grammar [græmə(r)], *s.* gramática; elementos de una ciencia.—*g. school,* escuela pública de enseñanza elemental.— **-ian** [græmrian], *s.* gramático.—**grammatical** [græmætikal], *a.* gramatical.

granary [grǽnəri], *s.* granero.

grand [grænd], *a.* grande, grandioso; magnífico; ilustre, augusto.— **-aunt** [grǽndænt], *s.* tía abuela.— **-child** [-chaild], *s.* nieto, nieta.— **-daughter** [-dotœ(r)], *s.* nieta.— **-ee** [grǽndi], *s.* noble, grande.— **-father** [-faðœ(r)], *s.* abuelo.— **-ma** [-ma], *s.* (fam.) abuelita.— **-mother** [-mʌðœ(r)], *s.* abuela.— **-nephew** [-nefiu], *s.* sobrino nieto.— **-ness** [-nis], *s.* grandiosidad.— **-niece** [-nis], *s.* sobrina nieta.— **-pa** [-pa], *s.* (fam.) abuelito.— **-parent** [-pɛrɛnt], *s.* abuelo, abuela.— **-sire** [-saìr], *s.* antepasado.— **-son** [-sʌn], *s.* nieto.— **-stand** [-stænd], *s.* tribuna, tendido, gradería de asientos para espectadores.— **-uncle** [-ʌŋkl], *s.* tío abuelo.

grange [greindʒ], *s.* granja, cortijo, alquería, hacienda; asociación de agricultores.— **-r** [gréindzœ(r)], *s.* granjero.

granite [grǽnit], *s.* granito.

granny [grǽni], *s.* (fam.) abuelita; comadre; viejecita.

grant [grænt], *vt.* conceder; permitir; ceder, transferir; asentir, convenir en. —*to take for granted,* dar por supuesto. —*s.* concesión, donación; otorgamiento, subvención, franquicia, asentimiento; documento que confiere un privilegio o concesión.—*granting that,* dado que, supuesto que.

granulate [grǽnyuleit], *vt.* granular; granear.—*vi.* granularse; (med.) encarnar.—**granule** [grǽnyul], *s.* granito, gránulo.

grape [greip], *s.* uva; vid.— **-fruit** [gréipfrut], *s.* toronja.— **-shot** [-ʃat], *s.* (art.) metralla.— **-vine** [-vain], *s.* vid, parra; noticia que circula por vías secretas.

graph [græf], *s.* gráfica; diagrama.—*vt.* construir la gráfica de, representar gráficamente.— **-ic(al)** [grǽfik(al)], *a.* gráfico.— **-ite** [-ait], *s.* grafito.

grapple [grǽpl], *vt.* agarrar, asir; amarrar.—*vi.* agarrarse; (mar.)

atracarse, abordarse.—s. lucha, riña.

grasp [græsp], *vt.* empuñar, asir; apresar, apoderarse de, usurpar; ver, entender.—*vi.* agarrarse fuertemente. —*s.* asimiento; presa; usurpación; puñado; garras; comprensión.

grass [græs], *s.* hierba; pasto, césped. —*g.* grown, cubierto de hierba.—*vt.* cubrir de hierba; apacentar.—*vi.* pacer; cubrirse de hierba.— **—hopper** [græshɒpœ(r)], *s.* saltamontes, langosta.— **—y** [-i], *a.* herboroso; herbáceo.

grate [greit], *s.* reja, verja, enrejado; parrilla.—*vt.* enrejar, poner enrejado; (coc.) rallar; raspar; frotar, hacer rechinar; emparrillar.—*vi.* rozar; raer; rechinar, chirriar.—*to g.* on, molestar, irritar.

grateful [gréitful], *a.* agradecido; grato, gustoso.— **—ness** [-njs], *s.* gratitud, agrado.

grater [gréitœ(r)], *s.* rallador, rallo, raspador.

gratify [grǽtifai], *vti.* [7] satisfacer, complacer, dar gusto; gratificar.

grating [gréitin], *a.* rechinante, chirriante, discordante; irritante, áspero. —*s.* reja, rejilla, verja, enrejado; emparrillado; escurridero; chirrido, rechinamiento; retícula (de microscopio, etc.); ralladura.

gratis [gréitjs], *adv.* gratis.—*a.* gratuito.

gratitude [grǽtitjud], *s.* gratitud, reconocimiento.

gratuitous [grʌtjúitʌs], *a.* gratuito; injustificado.—**gratuity** [grʌtjúiti], *s.* gratificación; propina.

grave [greiv], *s.* sepultura, sepulcro, tumba; acento grave.—*a.* grave, serio; solemne; (mus.) bajo, profundo.— **—clothes** [gréivklouɒz], *s. pl.* mortaja.— **—digger** [-digœ(r)], *s.* sepulturero, enterrador.

gravel [grǽvel], *s.* cascajo, grava; (med.) cálculos.

graveyard [gréivyard], *s.* cementerio.

gravitate [grǽvjteit], *vi.* gravitar.— **gravitation** [grævjtéiʃɒn], *s.* gravitación.—**gravity** [grǽvjti], *s.* gravedad; seriedad; importancia.

gravy [gréivi], *s.* salsa o caldillo de un guiso de carne.

gray [grei], *vt.* y *vi.* ponerse gris o cano; encanecer.—*a.* gris, pardo; tordo, rucio; cano, encanecido.—*g.-haired,* o *-headed,* canoso; envejecido.—*s.* color gris; animal gris.— **—ish** [gréijʃ], *a.* pardusco, grisáceo; entrecano; tordillo.

graze [greiz], *vt.* apacentar, pastorear; rozar.—*vi.* pacer, pastar; rozarse.

grease [gris], *s.* grasa; pringue; lubrificante.—*vt.* engrasar; ensuciar con grasa; lubrificar; sobornar;

(fam.) untar la mano.— **—r** [grísœ(r)], *s.* engrasador; lubricante, lubrificante. **—greasy** [grísi], *a.* grasiento, pringoso.

great [greit], *a.* gran, grande; magno; admirable; excelente; espléndido. —*a g.* deal, mucho, gran cantidad. —*a g.* many, muchos.—*a g.* way off, muy lejos.—*a g.* while, un largo rato. **—g.-grandchild** [-grǽndchaild], *s.* biznieto.— **—g.-grandfather** [-grǽndfaɒœ(r)], *s.* bisabuelo.—**g.-grandmother** [-grǽndmaɒœ(r)], *s.* bisabuela.— **—ness** [gréitnjs], *s.* grandeza; grandiosidad; magnitud, extensión; fausto.

Grecian [gríʃɒn], *s.* y *a.* griego.

greed [grid], *s.* voracidad, gula; codicia, avidez.— **—ily** [grídjli], *adv.* vorazmente; codiciosamente; vehementemente, con ansia.— **—y** [-i], *a.* voraz; anhelante, ávido, codicioso.

Greek [grik], *s.* griego; (fam.) lenguaje o cosa ininteligible.—*a.* griego.

green [grin], *a.* verde (de color y de sazón); fresco; inexperto, bisoño. —*g.* corn, maíz tierno; trigo nuevo. —*g.-eyed,* ojiverde, celoso.—*g.* goods, verduras.—*g.* hand, novicio.—*s.* color verde; verdor, verdura; prado o pradera; césped.—*pl.* verduras, hortalizas.—*vt.* pintar o teñir de verde.—*vi.* verdear.— **—house** [grínhaus], *s.* invernadero.— **—ish** [-jʃ], *a.* verdoso, verdusco.— **—ly** [-li], *adv.* nuevamente, recientemente; sin madurez.— **—ness** [-njs], *s.* verdor; vigor, frescura; falta de experiencia; novedad.

greet [grit], *vt.* saludar, dar la bienvenida.—*vi.* encontrarse y saludarse.— **—ing** [grítin], *s.* salutación, saludo.—*pl.* ¡salud! ¡saludos!

grenade [grenéid], *s.* (mil.) granada.

grew [gru], *pret.* de TO GROW.

grey [grei], *a.* gris; pardo; canoso.— v. GRAY.— **—hound** [gréihaund], *s.* galgo; lebrel.— **—ish** [-jʃ], *a.* v. GRAYISH.

grid [grid], *s.* red; parrilla; reja, rejilla.— **—dle** [grídl], *s.* tapadera de fogón; tortera.— **—iron** [grídaiœrn], *s.* parrillas; andamiaje; (dep.) campo marcado para el futbol americano.

grief [grif], *s.* pesar, aflicción, dolor, sentimiento.—*g.-stricken,* desconsolado, apesadumbrado.—*to come to g.,* pasarlo mal; malograrse.

grievance [grívʌns], *s.* injusticia, perjuicio; motivo de queja, agravio. **—grieve** [griv], *vt.* afligir, lastimar; apesadumbrar.—*vi.* apesadumbrarse, dolerse, penar.—**grievous** [grívʌs], *a.* penoso, doloroso, oneroso; fiero, atroz, cruel.

griffin [grífin], **griffon** [grífon], *s.* (mit. griega) grifo.

grill [gríl], *vt.* asar en parrillas; atormentar con fuego o calor; interrogar severamente y sin tregua. —*s.* parrilla; manjar asado en parrilla; restaurante.— **—room** [grílrum], *s.* restaurante especializado en asados a la parrilla.

grim [grim], *a.* torvo, ceñudo; horrendo; inflexible; formidable.

grimace [griméis], *s.* mueca, gesto, mohín, visaje.—*vi.* hacer muecas, hacer visajes.

grime [graim], *s.* tizne, mugre, porquería.—*vt.* ensuciar, tiznar.— **grimy** [gráimi], *a.* tiznado, sucio, manchado.

grimness [grímnis], *s.* horror, espanto, grima.

grin [grin], *vii.* [1] hacer muecas mostrando los dientes; sonreír satisfecha, aprobativa o sarcásticamente. —*s.* mueca (de ira, dolor, etc.); sonrisa expresiva (de satisfacción, etc.).

grind [graind], *vti.* [4] moler, quebrantar, triturar; pulverizar; picar carne; hacer crujir o rechinar (los dientes); afilar, amolar; vaciar; rallar, estregar; pulir, esmerilar; mascar; dar vueltas a un manubrio; acosar, oprimir; (fam.) dar lata o matraca.—*vii.* hacer molienda; rozar; pulirse o deslustrarse con el roce. —*s.* molienda; (fam.) trabajo pesado.— **—er** [gráindœ(r)], *s.* molinero; moledor; esmerilador; piedra de molino o de amolar; molino; amolador; muela.— **—ing** [-iŋ], *s.* molienda; afilamiento; esmerilado; pulimento; rechinamiento.—*a.* opresivo.

grip [grip], *s.* apretón de mano; agarrón, asimiento; presa; saco de mano; mango, puño, agarradera; capacidad de agarrar, comprender o retener. —*to be at grips,* estar en un cuerpo a cuerpo.—*vti.* [1] agarrar, empuñar. —*vii.* agarrarse con fuerza.

gripe [graip], *vt.* agarrar, empuñar; pellizcar; (mec.) morder; dar cólico; afligir.—*vi.* agarrar fuertemente; padecer cólico; quejarse, refunfuñar de vicio.—*s.* grapa, abrazadera; puño, mango, manija, agarradera; aprieto.—*pl.* retortijón, cólico.

grippe [grip], *s.* gripe, influenza.

grisly [grízli], *a.* espantoso, terrible.

gristle [grísl], *s.* cartílago, ternilla.

grit [grit], *s.* arena, cascajo; firmeza; entereza; valor.—*pl.* sémola.—*vti.* y *vii.* [1] (hacer) rechinar o crujir (los dientes, etc.).

grizzle [grízl], *s.* color gris; mezclilla.

—grizzly [grízli], *a.* grisáceo, pardusco.—*g. bear,* oso gris.

groan [groun], *vi.* gemir; lanzar quejidos.—*s.* gemido, quejido.

grocer [gróusœ(r)], *s.* especiero, abacero, bodeguero.— **—y** [-i], *s.* abacería, especiería, tienda de comestibles, bodega.—*pl.* especierías, víveres, comestibles.

groom [grum], *s.* novio (en el acto de la boda); mozo de mulas; lacayo. —*vt.* cuidar, almohazar los caballos; peinar y vestir, acicalar.— **—sman** [grúmzman], *s.* padrino de boda.

groove [gruv], *s.* muesca, ranura, estría; surco; rutina.—*g. and tongue,* (carp.) ranura y lengüeta, unión machihembrada; machihembrar.

grope [group], *vt.* y *vi.* tentar, andar a tientas; buscar tentando.

gross [grous], *a.* craso; grueso; espeso, denso; indecoroso, obsceno; tosco, grosero; estúpido; (com.) bruto. —*g. profit,* ganancia bruta.—*g. weight,* peso bruto.—*s.* gruesa (doce docenas); grueso, la mayor parte; la totalidad, el conjunto.

grotto [grátou], *s.* gruta; antro, covacha.

grouch [grauch], *s.* gruñón, descontento. —*to have a g.,* estar de mal humor.

ground [graund], *pret.* y *pp.* de TO GRIND.—*g. glass,* vidrio esmerilado.—*g. meat,* carne picada (molida).—*s.* tierra, terreno, suelo; territorio; base, fundamento; razón, motivo, causa; (pint.) fondo o campo; baño, capa; (elec. y radio) toma de tierra; (mil.) campo de batalla.—*pl.* poso, sedimento, heces; jardín, parque, terrenos; cancha.—*g. floor,* planta baja.—*to break g.,* desmontar, roturar; empezar un trabajo.—*to come o fall to the g.,* caer al suelo; fracasar.—*to gain g.,* ganar terreno. —*to give o to lose g.,* perder terreno, retroceder, atrasar.—*to take the g.,* (mar.) encallar.—*vt.* fundar, apoyar, establecer; poner en tierra; (elec. y rad.) conectar con tierra.—*vi.* encallar, varar.— **—less** [gráundlis], *a.* infundado.

group [grup], *s.* grupo, agrupación, conjunto.—*vt.* y *vi.* agrupar(se), reunir(se).

grouse [graus], *s.* (orn.) chocha; (Am.) guaco.—*vi.* (fam.) quejarse.

grove [grouv], *s.* arboleda, bosquecillo, enramada.

grow [grou], *vti.* [10] cultivar; criar. —*vii.* crecer; aumentar; desarrollarse; nacer, darse o criarse frutas, plantas, etc.). —*to g. crazy,* volverse loco.—*to g. dark,* anochecer, oscurecer.—*to g. late,* hacerse tarde.—*to g. less,* disminuir. —*to g. old,* envejecer.—*to g. on o* *upon*, ir apoderándose de; **ganar o aventajar a;** hacerse cada vez más querido, admirable, etc.—*to g. up*, crecer, hacerse hombre.—*to g. young again*, remozarse.

growl [graṷl], *vi.* gruñir, rezongar.—*vt.* decir gruñendo.—*s.* gruñido, rezongo.

grown [groṷn], *pp.* de TO GROW.—*a.* crecido, espigado; cubierto o lleno de hierbas, malezas, etc.—*g.-up*, crecido, adulto.—**growth** [groṷθ], *s.* crecimiento, desarrollo; aumento; producto, producción; tumor, excrecencia.

grub [grʌb], *s.* (ent.) gorgojo; larva; (fam.) manducatoria.—*vti.* y *vii.* [1] rozar; cavar; emplearse en oficios bajos; (fam.) manducar.

grudge [grʌdʒ], *vt.* envidiar, codiciar; escatimar, dar de mala gana.—*s.* rencor, inquina; renuencia, mal grado.

gruesome [grúsʌm], *a.* macabro; horripilante.

gruff [grʌf], *a.* ceñudo, áspero; grosero; (b)ronco (voz).— **-ness** [grʌ́fnis], *s.* aspereza, mal humor.

grumble [grʌ́mbl], *vi.* refunfuñar, rezongar, quejarse.—*s.* regaño, refunfuñadura.— **-r** [grʌ́mbloe(r)], *s.* refunfuñador, rezongador, malcontento.

grunt [grʌnt], *vi.* gruñir; refunfuñar. —*s.* gruñido.

guano [gwánoṷ], *s.* guano.

Guarani [gwaraní], *s.* guaraní.

guarantee [gærantí], *vt.* garantizar; afianzar, responder de o por; dar fianza.—*s.* garantía, fianza; persona de quien otra sale fiadora.

guard [gard], *vt.* y *vi.* guardar, custodiar; vigilar; estar prevenido; guardarse. —*to g. against*, guardarse de.—*s.* guarda, guardia; guardián, custodio; protección, defensa; vigilancia; centinela; cautela; estado de defensa; guarnición de un vestido o de una espada; conductor de tren.—*on g.*, alerta; en guardia.—*a.* de guardia, de protección.— **-ian** [gárdjan], *s.* guardián, custodio; tutor.—*a.* que guarda, tutelar.—*g. angel*, ángel de la guarda.— **-ianship** [-iạnṣip], *s.* tutela; protección, custodia.

Guatemalan [gwatemálạn], *a.* and *s.* guatemalteco.

guava [gwávə̆], *s.* guayaba; guayabo.

guerrilla [gerílə̆], *s.* guerrilla; guerrillero.

guess [ges], *vt.* y *vi.* conjeturar, suponer; adivinar, acertar.—*s.* conjetura, suposición; adivinación.

guest [gest], *s.* huésped, invitado; forastero, visita; pensionista.

guffaw [gʌfɔ́], *s.* carcajada, risotada. —*vi.* reír a carcajadas.

guidance [gáidạns], *s.* guía, dirección,

conducta.—**guide** [gaid], *vt.* guiar, dirigir, encaminar; adiestrar; arreglar, gobernar.—*guided missile*, proyectil dirigido.—*s.* guía, mentor; baquiano; (mec.) corredera; (impr.) mordante. —**guidebook** [gáidbụk], *s.* guía del viajero.

guild [gild], *s.* gremio; cofradía, hermandad; corporación; colegio profesional (de médicos, abogados, etc.); sociedad benéfica.

guile [gail], *s.* dolo o engaño; estratagema.

guilt [gilt], *s.* delito; culpa, culpabilidad; pecado.— **-less** [gíltlis], *a.* inocente, libre de culpa.— **-y** [-i], *a.* reo; culpable.

guinea pig [gíni píg], *s.* conejillo de Indias.

guitar [gitár], *s.* guitarra.— **-ist** [-ist], *s.* guitarrista.

gulch [gʌlch], *s.* quebrada, cañada.

gulf [gʌlf], *s.* golfo; seno; sima, vorágine.—*G. Stream*, corriente del golfo (de México).

gull [gʌl], *vt.* engañar, timar, estafar. —*s.* gaviota; bobo, primo.

gullet [gʌ́lit], *s.* fauces; gaznate; zanja, trinchera profunda.

gullible [gʌ́libl], *a.* crédulo, simple.

gully [gʌ́li], *vti.* [7] formar canal.— *s.* zanja honda; barranco, barranca; hondonada.

gulp [gʌlp], *vt.* engullir, tragar; sofocar (un sollozo).—*vi.* entrecortar el resuello.—*s.* trago, sorbo.

gum [gʌm], *s.* goma; encía.—*chewing g.*, chicle, goma de mascar.—*vti.* [1] engomar; pegar con goma.

gumbo [gʌ́mboṷ], *s.* (Am.) quimbombó.

gummy [gʌ́mi], *a.* gomoso, engomado.

gun [gʌn], *s.* arma de fuego (cañón; fusil; escopeta; pistola o revólver); disparo de arma de fuego.—*vti.* [1] hacer fuego.—*vii.* cazar con escopeta o rifle.— **-boat** [gʌ́nboṷt], *s.* cañonero. — **-man** [-mạn], *s.* pistolero, bandido armado.— **-ner** [-œ(r)], *s.* artillero; ametrallador.— **-powder** [-paṷdœ(r)], *s.* pólvora.— **-smith** [-smiθ], *s.* armero.

gurgle [gœ́rgl], *vi.* borbotar, gorgotear. —*s.* gorgoteo; borbotón; gluglú.

gush [gʌʃ], *vt.* derramar, verter.—*vi.* brotar, fluir, manar a borbotones, chorrear; (fam.) ser extremoso.—*s.* chorro, borbotón; (fam.) efusión, extremo.

gust [gʌst], *s.* ráfaga, bocanada; acceso, arrebato.

gusto [gʌ́stoṷ], *s.* entusiasmo, satisfacción, celo.

gut [gʌt], *s.* intestino, tripa; cuerda de tripa; (mar.) estrecho.—*pl.*

(fam.) entrañas; valor ánimo.—*vti.* [1] destripar; desentrañar.

gutter [gʌtœ(r)], *s.* canal, canalón; gotera; cuneta; arroyo de la calle; albañal; acequia; estría, canal de ebanistería.—*vt.* acanalar, estriar; construir albañales, etc.—*vi.* acanalarse; manar, gotear.

guy [gaj], *s.* cable de retén, tirante, viento; (fam.) tipo, sujeto, tío; adefesio, mamarracho.—*vt.* sujetar con vientos; hacer burla o mofa.

gymnasium [dʒimnéjziʌm], *s.* gimnasio. —**gymnast** [dʒímnæst], *s.* gimnasta. —**gymnastic(al)** [dʒimnǽstik(ạl)], *a.* gimnástico.—**gymnastics** [dʒimnǽstiks], *s.* gimnasia, gimnástica.

gynecology [gajnękálọdʒị], *s.* ginecología.

H

haberdasher [hǽbœrdǽsœ(r)], *s.* camisero, mercero, tendero.— **y** [-ị], *s.* camisería, mercería.

habit [hǽbịt], *s.* hábito, costumbre; vicio; vestido.—*by* o *from* (*force of*) *h.*, de vicio.—*to be in the h. of*, soler, acostumbrar.

habitable [hǽbịtabl], *a.* habitable.— **habitation** [hæbịtéjšǫn], *s.* habitación, domicilio, morada.—**habitat** [hǽbịtæt], *s.* (biol.) ámbito natural de un animal o planta.

habitual [habíchuạl], *a.* habitual, acostumbrado.—**habituate** [habíchueịt], *vt.* y *vi.* habituar(se).

hack [hæk], *s.* caballo de alquiler, rocín; tos seca; plumífero, autor mercenario; taxi.—*h. stand*, punto o parada de taxis.—*h. saw*, sierra para cortar metal.—*vt.* tajar, picar. —*vi.* cortar; toser con tos seca; alquilarse.

hackle [hǽkl], *s.* rastrillo; plumas de cuello de ciertas aves; mosca para pescar.—*vt.* rastrillar; tajar; mutilar.

hackneyed [hǽknịd], *a.* trillado, gastado.

had [hæd], *pret.* de TO HAVE.

haggard [hǽgærd], *a.* trasnochado, macilento, ojeroso, flaco.

haggle [hǽgl], *vt.* tajar.—*vi.* regatear.

hail [heịl], *s.* granizo; saludo; grito, llamada.—*H. Mary*, Ave María.— *within h.*, al habla, al alcance de la voz.—*interj.* ¡salve! ¡salud!—*vt.* saludar; aclamar; llamar.—*vi.* granizar; vocear.—*to h. from*, ser oriundo de.— *storm* [héjlstorm], *s.* granizada.

hair [her], *s.* pelo; vello; cabello, cabellera; cerda; hebra, filamento; pelusa.—*against the h.*, a contrapelo. —*h. net*, redecilla.—*h.-raising*, espeluznante, horripilante.—*h. remover*,

depilatorio.—*h. stroke*, rasgo muy fino.—*to a h.*, exactamente, perfectamente.— **brush** [hérbrʌš], *s.* cepillo de cabeza.— **cloth** [-kloθ], *s.* tela de erin.— **cut** [-kʌt], *s.* pelado, corte de pelo.— **do** [-du], *s.* peinado.— **dresser** [-drèsœ(r)], *s.* peluquero, peluquera, peinador o peinadora.— **dressing** [-dresịŋ], *s.* peinado.— **less** [-lịs], *a.* pelón; sin pelo, lampiño.— **pin** [-pịn], *s.* horquilla, (Am.) gancho del pelo. —**y** [-ị], *a.* peludo, velludo.

Haitian [héịtịan], *a.* y *s.* haitiano.

hake [heịk], *s.* (ict.) merluza.

hale [heịl], *a.* sano, robusto, fuerte. —*vt.* tirar de, arrastrar; llevar por la fuerza.

half [hæf], *s.* mitad; medio.—*h. and h.*, mitad y mitad; de medio a medio; en partes iguales.—*a.* y *adv.* medio; semi.—*h.-baked*, a medio cocer, asar, etc.—*h. binding*, (enc.) media pasta. —*h.-blood* o *h.-breed*, mestizo, (Am.) cholo.—*h.-closed*, entornado. —*h. hour*, media hora; de media hora.—*h.-mast*, media asta (la bandera); poner a media asta.—*h.-open(ed)*, entreabierto.—*h.-past one, two, etc.*, la una, las dos, etc. y media. —*h.-witted*, tonto, imbécil.—*to h.-open*, entreabrir.— **way** [hǽfweị], *a.* y *adv.* equidistante, a medio camino; parcial(mente).

halibut [hǽlịbʌt], *s.* (ict.) mero.

hall [hɔl], *s.* pasillo, corredor; vestíbulo, zaguán; salón (para reuniones, funciones, etc.); edificio (de un colegio u universidad).—*city h.*, o *town h.*, ayuntamiento, alcaldía.

hallo [halóu], *interj.* ¡hola! ¡oiga!

hallow [hǽlou], *vt.* consagrar; reverenciar.

Hallowe'en [hǽlouịn], *s.* víspera de Todos los Santos.

hallucination [hælịusịnéjšǫn], *s.* alucinación.

halo [héịlou], *s.* halo, nimbo, aureola.

halt [hɔlt], *vi.* vacilar; parar, hacer alto.—*vt.* parar, detener.—*s.* parada, alto.—*interj.* ¡alto!

halter [hɔ́ltœ(r)], *s.* cabestro, ronzal, jáquima; dogal.

halve [hæv], *vt.* dividir o partir en dos partes iguales; (carp.) machihembrar.— **s** [-z], *s.* pl. de HALF

ham [hæm], *s.* jamón, pernil; corva. —*pl.* (fam.) nalgas.

hamburger [hǽmbœrgœ(r)], *s.* emparedado de carne picada, (Am.) hamburguesa, frita.

hamlet [hǽmlịt], *s.* aldea, caserío, villorrio.

hammer [hǽmœ(r)], *s.* martillo; martinete.—*vt.* martillar; machacar; clavar; forjar.—*to h.* one's *brains*, devanarse los sesos.—*vi.* martillar, dar golpes; repiquetear.— **head** [-hɛd], *s.* pez martillo, cornuda.

hammock [hǽmǫk], *s.* hamaca.

hamper [hǽmpœ(r)], *s.* canasta, cesto, cuévano.—*vt.* embarazar, estorbar; encestar, encanastar.

hand [hænd], *s.* mano; palmo; ejecución; mano de obra; manecilla o aguja del reloj; operario, obrero, bracero; carácter de letra; firma; mano (en los naipes).—*at h.*, o *near at h.*, a la mano, cerca.—*by h.*, a mano; con biberón.—*h. and glove*, uña y carne.—*h. in h.*, parejas; junto; de acuerdo.—*h. over head*, inconsideradamente.—*hands off*, no tocar; no meterse.—*hands off policy*, política de no intervención.—*h. to h.*, cuerpo a cuerpo, a brazo partido.—*in h.*, de contado.—*on the one h.*, por una parte.—*on the other h.*, por otra parte; en cambio; al contrario.—*to h.*, a la mano; listo.—*to set the h. to*, emprender; firmar.—*vt.* dar, entregar, poner en manos (de alguien).—*to h. down*, transmitir; entregar; dictar (un fallo).—*to h. over*, entregar, alargar.—*a.* de mano; hecho a mano; manual.—*h. glass*, lente de aumento, lupa.— —**ball** [hǽndbɔl], *s.* pelota, juego de pelota.— —**bag** [-bæg], *s.* maletín; bolsa de mano.— —**bill** [-bil], *s.* volante.— —**book** [-buk], *s.* manual; prontuario; guía.— —**cuff** [-kʌf], *s.* manilla.— *pl.* esposas.—*vt.* maniatar, esposar.— —**ful** [-ful], *s.* puñado, manojo.

handicap [hǽndikæp], *vti.* [1] (dep.) emparejar ventajas entre competidores; poner obstáculos.—*s.* (dep.) ventaja en carreras o torneos; desventaja, impedimento, obstáculo.— **handicapped** [hǽndikæpt], *a.* impedido; que sufre de algún impedimento físico o mental.

handiwork [hǽndiwœrk], *s.* artefacto; trabajo manual.

handkerchief [hǽŋkœrchif], *s.* pañuelo.

handle [hǽndl], *vt.* tocar, manosear; manipular, manejar; tratar; dirigir; comerciar en; poner mango a.—*vi.* usar las manos o trabajar con ellas; ser manejado.—*s.* mango, puño, asa, manigueta, manubrio, tirador; (Am.) cacha (de arma).—**handling** [hǽndliŋ], *s.* manejo; manoseo; maniobra; manipulación.

handmade [hǽndméjd], *a.* hecho a mano.—**handmaid** [hǽndmejd], *s.* criada de mano, asistenta.—**handrail** [hǽndrejl], *s.* pasamano, baranda, barandilla.—**handsaw** [hǽndsɔ], *s.* serrucho, sierra de mano.—**hand-**

shake [hǽndšejk], *s.* apretón de manos.

handsome [hǽndsʌm], *a.* hermoso; guapo; bien parecido; generoso.

handwriting [hǽndrajtiŋ], *s.* carácter de letra; escritura cursiva, caligrafía.

handy [hǽndi], *a.* manuable, fácil de manejar; próximo, a la mano; cómodo; diestro, hábil.—*h.-man*, factótum.—*to come in h.*, venir al pelo, caer bien.

hang [hæŋ], *vt.* ahorcar.—*vi.* ser ahorcado.—*vti.* [10] colgar, suspender; fijar (en la pared); empapelar; poner colgaduras.—*to h. out*, enarbolar; colgar.—*to h. up*, levantar; colgar.—*vii.* colgar, pender, caer.— *to h. around*, rondar, haraganear.—*to h. up*, colgar el auricular.—*s.* caída (de un vestido, cortina, etc.); (fam.) maña, destreza; quid.

hangar [hǽŋa(r)], *s.* hangar.

hanger [hǽŋœ(r)], *s.* perchero, colgadero.—**hanging** [hǽŋiŋ], *s.* muerte en la horca.—*pl.* colgaduras, tapices, cortinaje.—*a.* colgante.—**hangman** [hǽŋman], *s.* verdugo.—**hangover** [hǽŋǫuvœ(r)], *s.* malestar que sigue a una borrachera, (Am.) goma, cruda, ratón.

hank [hæŋk], *s.* madeja.

happen [hǽpn], *vi.* acontecer, suceder, pasar, acaecer, sobrevenir; hallarse por casualidad en.—*to h. on*, encontrarse o tropezar con.—*whatever happens*, suceda lo que suceda.— —**ing** [-iŋ], *s.* suceso, acontecimiento.

happily [hǽpili], *adv.* feliz o dichosamente; afortunadamente.—**happiness** [hǽpinis], *s.* felicidad, dicha, alegría.—**happy** [hǽpi], *a.* feliz, dichoso, alegre, contento; afortunado.

harangue [haræŋ], *s.* arenga, perorata. —*vt.* arengar a.

harass [hǽras], *vt.* acosar, atosigar; (mil.) hostigar, hostilizar.

harbinger [hárbindžœ(r)], *s.* heraldo.

harbor [hárbǫ(r)], *s.* puerto; asilo, abrigo, albergue.—*h. master*, capitán del puerto.—*h. pilot*, práctico.—*vt.* abrigar; hospedar.—*vi.* ampararse, refugiarse.

hard [hard], *a.* duro, endurecido; difícil, arduo; penoso; fuerte, recio; riguroso, severo; inflexible.—*h. drink*, bebida fuertemente alcohólica; licor.—*h. labor*, trabajo forzado.—*h. luck*, mala suerte.—*h. of hearing*, duro de oído. —*h. rubber*, ebonita, vulcanita.— *h. sausage*, salchichón.—*h. to deal with*, intratable.—*h. water*, agua cruda.—*h. words*, palabras injuriosas. —*adv.* mucho; con ahinco, con impaciencia; difícilmente; con fuerza, fuertemente; duramente.—*h.-bitten*, (fam.) endurecido, aguerrido.—*h.- boiled*, duro, insensible.—*h.-boiled egg*, huevo duro.—*h. by*, inmediato, muy cerca.—*h.-hearted*, empedernido. —*to rain h.*, llover a cántaros.— —en [hárdn], *vt.* y *vi.* endurecerse.— —ening [-niŋ], *s.* endurecimiento.— —ly [-li], *adv.* difícilmente, apenas, a duras penas, escasamente; duramente.— —ness [-nis], *s.* dureza, endurecimiento; crudeza (del agua).— —ship [-ŝip], *s.* penalidad, trabajo; privaciones.— —ware [-wer], *s.* ferretería, quincallería; herraje, conjunto de accesorios metálicos.—*h. store*, ferretería, quincallería.— —wareman [-wermən], *s.* ferretero, quincallero.— —y [-i], *a.* fuerte, robusto; bravo, intrépido.

hare [ber], *s.* liebre.— **—brained** [hérbreind], *a.* cabeza de chorlito, ligero de cascos.— *—lip* [-lip], *s.* labio leporino.

harlot [hárlot], *s.* ramera, prostituta.

harm [harm], *s.* daño, perjuicio, mal. —*vt.* dañar, perjudicar; ofender, herir.— **—ful** [hármful], *a.* dañoso, dañino, nocivo, perjudicial.— **—less** [-lis], *a.* inocuo; inofensivo; ileso; sano y salvo.

harmonic [barmánik], *s.* (mús.) armónico, tono secundario.—*pl.* armonía. —*a.* armónico— **—a** [-ə], *s.* (mús.) armónica.—**harmonious** [harmóuni̯Λs], *a.* armónico; armonioso; proporcionado.—**harmonize** [hármonaiz],*vi.* armonizar, concertar.—*vi.* armonizarse, congeniar; armonizar, convenir, corresponder.—**harmony** [hármoni], *s.* armonía, acuerdo.

harness [hárnis], *s.* arreos, guarniciones (de caballerías); arnés; (mec.) aparejo; (fig.) servicio activo.—*vt.* enjaezar; poner los arreos.

harp [harp], *s.* arpa.—*vi.* tocar el arpa. —*to h. on* o *upon*, repetir, machacar; porfiar.

harpoon [harpún], *s.* arpón.

harpy [hárpi], *s.* arpía.

harrow [hérou], *s.* grada, rastrillo; rodillo para desterronar.—*vt.* gradar, rastrillar; perturbar, atormentar.

harry [héri], *vti.* [7] asolar, saquear; acosar, molestar.

harsh [harŝ], *a.* áspero; tosco.— **—ness** [hárŝnis], *s.* aspereza; severidad.

harvest [hárvist], *s.* cosecha; siega, agosto; fruto, recolección.—*h. fly*, cigarra, chicharra.—*h. time*, mies.— *vt.* recoger la cosecha, segar; cosechar.— **—er** [-œ(r)], *s.* cosechero, segador; segadora, máquina de segar.

hash [heŝ], *s.* picadillo, jigote.—*vt.* picar, hacer picadillo.

haste [heist], *s.* prisa.—*in h.*, de prisa.—

—n [héisn], *vt.* apresurar, activar; precipitar.—*vi.* darse prisa, apresurarse.—**hasty** [héisti], *a.* apresurado; precipitado.

hat [hæt], *s.* sombrero.—*bowler h.,* sombrero hongo.—*h. box*, sombrerera. —*h. rack*, perchero.—*Panama h.,* jipijapa.—*silk h.* o *top h.,* sombrero de copa.—*soft h.,* sombrero flexible.

hatch [hæch], *vt.* criar, empollar, incubar; fraguar, tramar, maquinar.—*s.* cría; nidada; pollada; compuerta; portezuela; trampa; escotilla.— **—ery** [héchœri], *s.* incubadora; vivero.

hatchet [héchit], *s.* hacha pequeña, hachuela.—*to bury the h.,* hacer las paces.

hatchway [héchwei], *s.* escotilla.

hate [heit], *vt.* odiar, aborrecer.—*s.* odio, aborrecimiento.— **—ful** [héitful], *a.* aborrecible, odioso.—**hatred** [héitrid], *s.* odio, aborrecimiento.

hatter [hétœ(r)], *s.* sombrerero.

haughtiness [hótinis], *s.* arrogancia, altanería, altivez; ínfulas, humos. —**haughty** [hóti], *a.* arrogante; altivo, altanero.

haul [hol], *vt.* tirar de, arrastrar; transportar; (mar.) halar.—*to h. down the colors*, arriar la bandera.— *to h. the wind*, (mar.) ceñir el viento. —*s.* tirón o estirón, arrastre, transporte; redada; (fam.) buena pesca; botín, ganancia.

haunch [honch], *s.* anca; pernil, pierna, pata.

haunt [hont], *vt.* frecuentar; rondar, vagar por; perseguir, causar obsesión; molestar.—*s.* guarida, nidal; lugar que uno frecuenta.— **—ed** [hóntid], *a.* embrujado, encantado.

have [hæv], *vai.* [11] haber.—*vti.* tener; contener; tomar (comer, beber); recibir (carta, noticia, etc.).—*to h. in hand*, estar ocupado en, tener entre manos.—*to h. on*, tener puesto (traje, etc.).—*to h. one's way*, salirse uno con la suya.—*to h. something done*, mandar hacer algo.—*to h. to*, tener que.

haven [héivn], *s.* puerto, fondeadero, abra; abrigo, asilo.

haversack [hævœrsæk], *s.* mochila.

havoc [hévok], *s.* estrago, ruina.—*to play h. with*, hacer estragos.

Hawaiian [hawái̯ən], *a.* y *s.* hawaiano.

hawk [hok], *s.* halcón; gavilán.—*h.- nosed*, de nariz aguileña.—*vt.* y *vi.* pregonar mercancías; cazar con halcón.— **—sbill** [hóksbil], *s.* carey.

hawthorn [hóθorn], *s.* espino, oxiacanta.

hay [hei], *s.* heno; paja de heno u otras hierbas para forraje.— **—fork** [héi- fork], *s.* horca, tridente.— **—loft**

[-lɔft], *s.* henil, pajar.— —stack [-stæk], *s.* almiar; montón de heno.

hazard [hǽzạrd], *s.* azar, albur; peligro, riesgo; obstáculo (en el golf, etc.).— —*vt.* arriesgar, aventurar.— —ous [-ʌs], *a.* arriesgado, peligroso.

haze [heiz], *s.* niebla, bruma.—*vi.* abrumarse la atmósfera.—*vt.* dar novatadas (en los colegios).

hazel [héjzl], *s.* avellano.—*a.* castaño claro, avellanado; de avellano.— —nut [-nʌt], *s.* avellana.

hazing [héjziŋ], *s.* novatada (en los colegios).—hazy [héjzi], *a.* nublado, brumoso; confuso, vago.

he [hi], *pron. pers.* él.—*h.-bear,* oso (macho).—*h.-goat,* macho cabrío.— *h.-man,* (fam.) hombre cabal, todo un hombre.—*h. who, h. that,* el que, aquel que, quien.

head [hed], *s.* cabeza; cima; parte superior o principal; cabecera (de cama, mesa, río); jefe, caudillo; director; punta (de flecha, etc.); puño (de bastón).—*a h.,* por barba, por persona.—*at the h.* (of), al frente (de).—*h. over heels,* precipitadamente.— *heads or tails,* cara o cruz.—*to bring to a h.,* ultimar.—*to come to a h.,* llegar a un estado definitivo o a una crisis; (med.) madurar.—*a.* principal; de o para la cabeza; de frente; (mar.) de proa.—*h. cold,* romadizo, coriza.—*vt.* encabezar; dirigir, presidir; descabezar; poner título; podar.—*to h. off,* detener, prevenir.—*vi.* (con for) dirigirse a.— —ache [hédejk], *s.* jaqueca, dolor de cabeza.— —board [-bɔrd], *s.* cabecera de cama.— —dress [-dres], *s.* cofia, tocado, redecilla.— —first [-fǝ́rst], *adv.* de cabeza.— —iness [-inis], *s.* terquedad, obstinación; encabezamiento del vino.— —ing [-iŋ], *s.* título, encabezamiento; membrete.— —less [-lis], *a.* descabezado, degollado; acéfalo.— —light [-lajt], *s.* (aut.) faro o farol delantero; (f.c.) farol, fanal.— —line [-lajn], *s.* titular, cintillo; título, encabezamiento.— —long [-lɔŋ], *a.* temerario, arrojado, precipitado.—*adv.* de cabeza, precipitadamente, irreflexivamente.— —master [-mǽstœ(r)], *s.* director de escuela.— —mistress [-místris], *s.* directora.— —quarters [-kwɔrtœrz], *s.* (mil.) cuartel general; jefatura (de policía, etc.); oficina principal de operaciones.— —stone [-stoŋn], *s.* lápida mortuoria.— —strong [-strɔŋ], *a.* terco, testarudo, obstinado.— —way [-wej], *s.* (mar.) salida, marcha de un buque; avance; progreso; adelanto, ventaja.—*to make h.,* adelantar, progresar.— —y [-i], *a.*

temerario, arrojado; violento, impetuoso.

heal [hil], *vt.* curar; componer.—*vi.* sanar; recobrar la salud.—*to h. up,* cicatrizarse.— —ing [híliŋ], *a.* sanativo, curativo.—*s.* cura, curación, cicatrización.

health [helθ], *s.* salud; sanidad.— —ful [hélθful], *a.* sano, saludable, salubre.— —iness [-inis], *s.* salubridad, sanidad.— —y [-i], *a.* sano; saludable.

heap [hip], *s.* montón, pila, acumulación; multitud.—*in heaps,* a montones.—*vt.* amontonar, apilar, acumular.—*h. up,* colmar.

hear [hir], *vti.* [10] oír; oír decir; escuchar; tener noticia de.—*to h. from someone,* saber de, tener noticias de alguien.—heard [hœrd], *pret.* y *pp.* de TO HEAR.— —er [hírœ(r)], *s.* oyente.— —ing [-iŋ], *s.* sentido del oído; audiencia; (for.) vista (de un pleito o causa); examen de testigos; audición.— —say [-sei], *s.* rumor, fama.—*by h.,* de oídas.

hearse [hœrs], *s.* coche o carroza fúnebre.

heart [hart], *s.* corazón; ánimo; (fig.) entraña(s).—*at h.,* en el fondo, esencialmente; en verdad.—*by h.,* de memoria.—*from one's h.,* de todo corazón, con sinceridad.—*h. and soul,* en cuerpo y alma.—*h.-rending,* doloroso, desgarrador.—*to take h.,* cobrar ánimo.—*to take to h.,* tomar a pechos.— —ache [hártejk], *s.* dolor de corazón; angustia, congoja, pesar.— —beat [-bit], *s.* latido del corazón, palpitación; profunda emoción.— —broken [-broųkn], *a.* acongojado, transido de dolor, (fig.) muerto de pesar; desengañado.— —burn [-bœrn], *s.* (med.) acedía, acidez.— —en [-n], *vt.* animar, confortar.— —felt [-felt], *a.* cordial, sincero; sentido.

hearth [harθ], *s.* hogar, fogón, chimenea.

heartily [hártili], *adv.* cordialmente, de corazón.—heartless [hártlis], *a.* sin corazón; cruel; pusilánime.—hearty [hárti], *a.* cordial, sentido, sincero; sano, vigoroso; gustoso, grato.

heat [hit], *s.* calor; ardor, vehemencia; celo (de los animales); hornada; colada; (dep.) carrera o corrida eliminatoria.—*vt.* y *vi.* calentar(se), caldear(se); acalorar(se).— —er [hítœ(r)], *s.* calentador; aparato de calefacción.

heathen [híðɛn], *s.* y *a.* gentil, pagano, idólatra.

heating [hítiŋ], *s.* calefacción.—*a.* caluroso; de calefacción (superficie, área, etc.).—*h. pad,* almohadilla o bolsa eléctrica.

heave [hiv], *vti.* [4] alzar, levantar

(con esfuerzo); (mar.) izar; lanzar, arrojar; exhalar, prorrumpir.—*vii.* levantarse y bajarse alternativamente; suspirar hondo; palpitar; jadear, trabajar penosamente; tener náuseas; (mar.) virar.—*to h. in sight,* (mar.) aparecer, asomar.—*s.* alzadura, levantamiento; náusea, arqueada.

heaven [hévn], *s.* cielo, paraíso.—*pl.* firmamento, las alturas.—*for h.'s sake!* ¡por Dios!— **—ly** [-li], *a.* celeste; celestial.—*adv.* celestialmente.— **—ward** [-wărd], *adv.* hacia el cielo, hacia las alturas.

heaviness [hévinis], *s.* pesantez, pesadez, peso; abatimiento; opresión, carga.—**heavily** [hévili], *adv.* pesadamente; lentamente; tristemente; excesivamente.—**heavy** [hévi], *a.* pesado; grueso; opresivo; molesto; denso, espeso; pesaroso; indigesto. —*h. duty,* servicio o trabajo fuerte (de una máquina).—*h. rain,* chaparrón, aguacero.—**heavyweight** [héviweit], *a.* (dep.) de peso pesado o máximo.—*s.* (boxeo) peso completo.

Hebrew [híbru], *a.* y *s.* hebreo; israelita; judío.—*s.* lengua hebrea.

hedge [hedʒ], *s.* seto, vallado.—*vt.* cercar con seto, vallar; circundar; rodear.— **—hog** [hédʒhag], *s.* (zool.) erizo.

heed [hid], *vt.* atender.—*vi.* prestar atención, hacer caso.—*s.* cuidado, atención.

heel [hil], *s.* talón o calcañar; tacón; talón de una media.—*heels over head,* patas arriba.—*vt.* poner talón a (zapatos y medias).—*to be well heeled,* (fam.) estar bien provisto de dinero.—*vi.* escorarse.—*to h. over,* zozobrar.

heifer [héfœ(r)], *s.* vaquilla, novilla.

height [hajt], *s.* altura, elevación; estatura, talla.—*the h. of folly,* el colmo de la locura.— **—en** [hájtn], *vt.* realzar, elevar; exaltar; avivar.

heinous [héjnʌs], *a.* atroz, nefando, horrible.

heir [er], *s.* heredero.—*h. apparent,* heredero forzoso.— **—ess** [érjs], *s.* heredera.— **—loom** [-lum], *s.* reliquia de familia.

held [held], *pret. y pp.* de TO HOLD.

helicopter [hélikaptœ(r)], *s.* helicóptero.

helium [híljʌm], *s.* (quim.) helio.

hell [hel], *s.* infierno.— **—ish** [hélįš], *a.* infernal.

hello [helóu], *interj.* ¡hola!; (al teléfono) ¡diga! (Am.) ¡bueno!

helm [helm], *s.* (mar.) timón; yelmo.

helmet [hélmit], *s.* casco, yelmo.

help [help], *vt.* ayudar, auxiliar, socorrer; aliviar; remediar.—*I can't h.*

it, no puedo evitarlo.—*to h. one to,* servir a uno (carne, sopa, etc.); proporcionar.—*vi.* ayudar, contribuir; servir (en la mesa).—*I can't h. saying,* no puedo (por) menos de decir.—*s.* ayuda, auxilio, socorro; remedio; fuerza de trabajo (criados, obreros, empleados, dependientes).— *there is no h. for it,* eso no tiene remedio.— **—er** [hélpœ(r)], *s.* asistente, ayudante.— **—ful** [-ful], *a.* útil, servicial; provechoso; saludable.— **—ing** [-iŋ], *s.* ayuda; porción (de comida) que uno se sirve o le sirven.— **—less** [-ljs], *a.* desvalido; imposibilitado; inútil; irremediable.— **—lessness** [-ljsnjs], *s.* desamparo; impotencia.

hem [hem], *s.* (cost.) dobladillo, jaretón, borde.—*vti.* [1] dobladillar, bastillar; (gen. con in) rodear, encerrar.—*vii.* fingir tos.—*interj.* ¡ejem!

hemisphere [hémisfir], *s.* hemisferio.— **hemispheric(al)** [hemisférik(ʌl)], *a.* hemisférico.

hemlock [hémlak], *s.* (bot.) abeto; cicuta.

hemorrhage [hémoridʒ], *s.* hemorragia. —**hemorrhagic** [hemorédʒik], *a.* hemorrágico.

hemorrhoids [hémoroidz], *s. pl.* hemorroides, almorranas.

hemp [hemp], *s.* (bot.) cáñamo.—*h. cord,* bramante.—*h. sandal,* alpargata.

hen [hen], *s.* gallina; hembra de ave. —*h.-pecked,* dominado por su mujer.

hence [hens], *adv.* de aquí; desde aquí; de ahí que, por tanto, en consecuencia.— **—forth** [hénsforθ], *adv.* (de aquí) en adelante, en lo sucesivo.

henchman [hénchmʌn], *s.* secuaz, paniaguado.

her [hœr], *pron.* la, le, a ella, (después de *prep.*) ella.—*a.* su, de ella.

herald [hérʌld], *s.* heraldo.—*vt.* anunciar, pregonar, proclamar.— **—ry** [-ri], *s.* heráldica, blasón.

herb [(h)œrb], *s.* hierba, yerba.

herd [hœrd], *s.* manada, rebaño, hato; piara; multitud.—*vi.* ir en manadas. —*vt.* reunir el ganado en rebaños.— **—sman** [hœrdzmʌn], *s.* pastor.

here [hir], *adv.* aquí, acá; por aquí; ahora, en este momento, en este punto; ¡presente!—*h. it is,* he aquí; aquí tiene Ud.—*h.'s to you!,* ¡a la salud de Ud!—*that is neither h. nor there,* eso no viene al caso.— **—abouts** [-ʌbáuts], *adv.* por aquí, por aquí cerca.— **—after** [-éftœ(r)], *adv.* (de aquí) en adelante, en lo sucesivo, en lo futuro.—*s.* el más allá.— **—by** [-bái], *adv.* por éstas, por la presente, por este medio.

hereditary [hɪrédɪterɪ], *a.* hereditario.
—**heredity** [hɪrédɪtɪ], *s.* (biol.) herencia.

heresy [héresɪ], *s.* herejía.—**heretic** [héretɪk], *s.* hereje.—*a.* herético.

heritage [hérɪtɪdʒ], *s.* herencia.

hermit [hɜ́rmɪt], *s.* ermitaño.— —**age** [-ɪdʒ], *s.* ermita.

hernia [hɜ́rnɪə], *s.* hernia.

hero [hɪ́rou]. *s.* héroe; protagonista.- —**ic(al)** [hɪróuɪk(əl)], *a.* heroico, épico.- —**ine** [héroɪn], *s.* heroína, protagonista.- —**ism** [héroɪzm], *s.* heroísmo, heroicidad; proeza.

heron [hérɒn], *s.* garza.

herring [hérɪŋ], *s.* arenque.

hers [hɜrz]. *pron. pos.* suyo, suya, (de ella); el suyo, la suya, los suyos, las suyas (de ella).- —**elf** [hɜrsélf], *pron.* ella misma. ella, sí misma.

hesitant [hézɪtənt]. *a.* vacilante, indeciso.—**hesitate** [hézɪteɪt], *vi.* vacilar, titubear.—**hesitation** [hezɪtéɪʃɒn], *s.* titubeo, vacilación.

heterogeneous [hetərɒdʒínɪəs], *a.* heterogéneo.

hew [hju], *vti.* [6] tajar, cortar, picar piedra; desbastar; labrar.—*to h. in pieces,* destrozar, destroncar.—*vii.* golpear.—*to h. right and left,* acuchillar a diestra y siniestra.

hey [heɪ], *interj.* ¡eh! ¡oiga! ¡digo!

hi [haɪ], *interj.* ¡hola!

hibernate [háɪbɜrneɪt], *vi.* invernar.— **hibernation** [haɪbɜrnéɪʃɒn], *s.* invernada.

hiccough, hiccup [híkʌp], *s.* hipo.—*vi.* hipar, tener hipo.

hickory [híkɒrɪ], *s.* nogal americano.

hid [hɪd], *pret. y pp.* de TO HIDE.

hidden [hídn], *pp.* de TO HIDE.—*a.* oculto, escondido, secreto.—**hide** [haɪd], *vti.* [10] esconder, ocultar. —*vii.* esconderse, ocultarse; (con out) estarse escondido.—*s.* esconditе; cuero, piel, pellejo.—**hideaway** [háɪdəweɪ], *s.* escondite, escondrijo; fugitivo.

hideous [hídɪəs], *a.* horrible, espantoso, feo.

hierarchy [háɪerarkɪ], *s.* jerarquía.

hieroglyphic [haɪerɒɡlífɪk], *s. y a.* jeroglífico.

high [haɪ], *a.* alto; de alto; elevado; encumbrado o eminente, superior; solemne; supremo, sumo; vivo, intenso; arrogante; poderoso.—*h. altar,* altar mayor.—*h. and dry,* en seco.—*h. blood pressure,* hipertensión arterial.—*h.-brow,* intelectual.— *h. hat,* sombrero de copa.—*H. Mass,* misa cantada o mayor.—*h. priest,* sumo sacerdote.—*h. rank,* categoría, alto rango.—*h. school,* escuela se-

cundaria.—*h. sea,* mar gruesa.—*h. seas,* alta mar.—*h. words.* palabras ofensivas o ásperas.—*in h. gear,* (aut.) en directa.—*in h. terms,* en términos lisonjeros.—*it is h. time to.* ya es hora de.—*adv.* alto; en lo alto; altamente; muy, sumamente; a grande altura; arrogantemente; a precio elevado; lujosamente.—*h. and low,* de arriba abajo; por doquiera. —*h.-handed,* despótico, arbitrario.— *h.-minded,* magnánimo, noble, idealista.—*h.-priced,* caro.—*h.-seasoned,* picante.—*h.-sounding,* altisonante.— *s.* alza, subida; punto o lugar alto; valor o precio máximo. —**ball** [háɪbɒl], *s.* whiskey, ron, etc., mezclado con soda y hielo.— **land** [-lənd], *s.* región montañosa.—*pl.* tierras altas, montañas.- —**lander** [-lǽndə(r)], *s.* montañés de Escocia.— **landish** [-lǽndɪʃ], *a.* montañés.— **light** [-laɪt], *vt.* realzar, hacer destacar, subrayar.—*s.* punto de destaque, o de resalto.- —**ly** [-lɪ], *adv.* altamente; levantadamente, elevadamente; sumamente; arrogantemente; ambiciosamente; encarecidamente. —**ness** [-nɪs], *s.* altura, elevación; celsitud; Alteza (título).- —**way** [-weɪ], *s.* carretera, calzada; camino real; vía pública.

hike [haɪk], *s.* (fam.) caminata; marcha; excursión.—*vi.* dar una caminata o paseo largo; ir de excursión.—*vt.* levantar, arrastrar; aumentar de pronto.- —**r** [háɪkœ(r)], *s.* excursionista.

hill [hɪl], *s.* collado, colina, cerro, cuesta, otero, altozano.—*vt.* aporcar. —*vi.* amontonarse.- —**man** [híljmən], *s.* serrano, arribeño.- —**ock** [-ɒk], *s.* altillo, loma, montecillo, otero.— —**side** [-saɪd], *s.* ladera, flanco de una colina.- —**top** [-tap], *s.* cima, cumbre de una colina.- —**y** [-ɪ], *a.* montañoso, montuoso.

hilt [hɪlt], *s.* puño, empuñadura.—*up to the h.,* a fondo; por completo.

him [hɪm], *pron.* le, (a, para, con, etc.) él.- —**self** [hɪmsélf], *pron.* él, él mismo, se, sí, sí mismo.—*by h.,* solo, por sí, por su cuenta.—*for h.,* por su cuenta, por cuenta propia.—*he h.,* él mismo; en persona.—*he said to h.,* se dijo a sí mismo.

hind [haɪnd], *a.* trasero, zaguero, posterior.—*h. foremost,* lo de atrás delante.—*s.* cierva.- —**brain** [háɪndbreɪn], *s.* cerebelo; parte posterior del encéfalo.- —**er** [híndœ(r)], *vt.* impedir, estorbar, obstaculizar; oponerse.—*a.* [háɪndœ(r)], posterior, trasero.- —**ermost** [-œrmoʊst], —**most** [-moʊst], *a.* postrero, último.

hindrance [híndrans], *s.* impedimento, obstáculo, estorbo.

Hindu [híndu], *s.* y *a.* hindú, indostánico.

hinge [hindʒ], *s.* gozne, gonce, bisagra; punto principal o capital.—*vt.* engoznar, poner goznes.—*vi.* girar sobre goznes.—*to h. on*, depender de.

hint [hint], *vt.* insinuar, indicar, sugerir.—*vi.* echar una indirecta.—*to h. at*, aludir a.—*s.* indirecta, sugestión, insinuación.

hip [hip], *s.* cadera.

hire [hair], *vt.* alquilar, dar o tomar en arriendo; arrendar; emplear; contratar; sobornar.—*to h. out*, alquilar(se).—*s.* alquiler, arriendo; salario; paga; jornal; soborno.

his [hiz], *a.* y *pron.* su, sus (de él); suyo, etc.; el suyo, la suya, los suyos, las suyas (de él).

Hispanic [hispǽnik], *a.* hispánico, hispano.

hiss [his], *vt.* y *vi.* silbar, (re)chiflar; sisear.—*s.* silbido, silba; siseo.

historian [histórian], *s.* historiador.— **historic(al)** [histárik(al)], *a.* histórico.—**history** [hístori], *s.* historia.

hit [hit], *vti.* [9] dar, pegar, golpear; atinar, acertar; encontrar, dar con o en; denunciar.—*to h. it off*, avenirse, simpatizar, hacer buenas migas. —*vi.* rozar, chocar; acaecer o acontecer felizmente, salir bien; encontrar por casualidad; acertar.—*h. or miss*, al azar; atolondradamente.—*to h. against*, dar contra alguna cosa, chocar.—*to h. on o upon*, dar con, hallar; ocurrírsele a uno; acordarse de.—*pret.* y *pp.* de TO HIT.—*s.* golpe, choque, coscorrón; rasgo de ingenio.

hitch [hich], *vt.* atar, ligar; enganchar; mover a tirones.—*vi.* moverse a saltos; enredarse; congeniar, llevarse bien con otro.—*s.* alto, parada; tropiezo, dificultad; tirón.—**hike** [híchhaik], *vi.* (fam.) viajar a pie pidiendo pasaje gratuito a los vehículos que pasan.

hither [híðœr)r], *adv.* acá, hacia acá. —*a.* citerior.— **most** [-moust], *a.* más cercano o próximo.—**to** [-tu], *adv.* hasta ahora, hasta aquí.

hive [haiv], *s.* colmena; enjambre; emporio.—*pl.* urticaria.—*vt.* enjambrar; atesorar, acumular.—*vi.* vivir juntos como en colmena.

hoard [hord], *vt.* y *vi.* acaparar; atesorar, acumular y guardar.—*s.* provisión; montón; acumulación; tesoro escondido.— **er** [hórdœr)r], *s.* acaparador; atesorador.

hoarse [hors], *a.* ronco.— **ness** [hórsnis], *s.* ronquera, carraspera.

hoary [hóri], *a.* blanco, blanquecino;

cano, canoso; escarchado; venerable.

hobble [hábl], *vt.* poner trabas.—*vi.* cojear.—*s.* cojera, traba; dificultad, atolladero.

hobby [hábi], *s.* chifladura, afición, pasatiempo; trabajo que se hace por afición.

hobgoblin [hábgablin], *s.* duende, trasgo.

hock [hak], *s.* vino del Rin; corvejón, jarrete (del caballo, etc.); (anat.) corva.—*in h.*, (E.U., fam.) empeñado. —*vt.* (E.U., fam.) empeñar, dar en prenda.

hodgepodge [hádʒpadʒ], *s.* mezcolanza, baturrillo.

hoe [hou], *s.* azada, azadón, escardillo. —*vt.* azadonar.

hog [hag], *s.* cochino, cerdo; (fam.) persona sucia, tragona o egoísta; (aer.) vuelta hacia abajo.— **gish** [hágish], *a.* porcino; egoísta; comilón.— **gishness** [-ishnis], *s.* porquería, cochinada; glotonería; egoísmo.— **shead** [hágzhed], *s.* pipa, tonel.

hoist [hoist], *vt.* alzar, elevar; izar, enarbolar.—*s.* cabria, pescante, grúa, montacargas; levantamiento, ascensión.—*h. bridge*, puente levadizo.

hold [hould], *vti.* [10] tener, asir, coger, agarrar; retener, reservar; detener, contener; sostener, apoyar; tener de reserva; restringir; encerrar; mantener; tener cabida o capacidad para; opinar, juzgar, reputar; entender; poseer, ocupar, disfrutar; celebrar (sesión, reunión); continuar, seguir; conservar; guardar, observar; obligar; hacer (responsable, etc.).— *to h. a bet o wager*, apostar.—*to h. a candle to*, (fam.) poder compararse con.—*to h. at bay*, tener a raya. —*to h. back*, retener; contener.— *to h. down*, oprimir, tener sujeto; conservar, no perder.—*to h. forth*, expresar, publicar; mostrar.—*to h. in*, sujetar, refrenar, contener.—*to h. off*, apartar, alejar.—*to h. out*, ofrecer, proponer; extender.—*to h. over*, tener suspendido o en suspenso; diferir, aplazar; prolongar una nota musical.—*to h. sway*, gobernar, mandar.—*to h. up*, levantar, alzar; apoyar, sostener; asaltar para robar, atracar.—*vii.* valer, ser válido, estar en vigor; mantenerse firme, sostenerse, aguantar; seguir, proseguir; estar en posesión; refrenarse, abstenerse; aplicarse, ser aplicable.—*s.* presa, asimiento; asa, mango; influencia, dominio; freno; refugio; posesión; custodio; celda; (mus.) calderón.— **er** [hóuldœr)r], *s.* tenedor, posesor; mantenedor; asidero, mango, asa; porta-(*lamp h.,* portalámpara, etc.); **sostén;** pro- pietario; arrendatario; inquilino.— *h. of a* bill, tenedor de una letra. —*h. of a* share, accionista.— —up [-ʌp], s. atraco, asalto.

hole [houl], s. agujero, orificio; cavidad, hueco, hoyo; bache; perforación; pozo, charco (de un río, arroyo, etc.); cueva, madriguera, guarida (de animales); (fam.) atolladero, aprieto, brete.—*vt.* agujerear, taladrar, per- forar; meter una bola de billar en la tronera.—*vi.* encuevarse; hacer un agujero u hoyo.

holiday [hálidei], s. día festivo, festi- vidad.—*pl.* vacaciones, asueto.—*a.* alegre, festivo.

holiness [hóulinis], s. santidad, bea- titud.—*His H.*, Su Santidad.

hollow [hálou], a. hueco, vacío; cón- cavo; hundido; sordo (ruido); falso, insincero.—*h.-chested*, de pe- cho hundido.—*h.-hearted*, solapado. —*h. punch*, sacabocados.—*h. ware*, ollas, pucheros, marmitas.—*s.* ca- vidad, depresión, concavidad; canal, ranura; hueco, hoyo; valle; cañada. —*vt.* excavar; ahondar; ahuecar.— —*ness* [-nis], s. cavidad, oquedad, vaciedad; doblez, falsía.

holly [háli], s. acebo; agrifolio.— —hock [-hak], s. malva loca u hortense.

holster [hóulstœr], s. pistolera, funda (de pistola).

holy [hóuli], a. santo, pío; puro, inmaculado; sacro, sagrado; consa- grado, santificado; bendito.—*h. cross*, santa cruz.—*h. cup*, cáliz.—*h. orders*, órdenes sacerdotales.—*H. Ghost*, Espíritu Santo.—*h. rood*, crucifijo; santa cruz.—*h. water*, agua bendita. —*H. Week*, Semana Santa.—*H. Writ*, la Sagrada Escritura.

homage [hámidʒ], s. homenaje, reve- rencia, culto.—*to do* o *pay h.*, acatar, rendir homenaje.

home [houm], s. hogar, casa; morada; domicilio, residencia, habitación; asilo, albergue, refugio; (dep.) meta, límite o término.—*at h.*, en casa; en el país de uno; con toda como- didad; en su elemento.—*to hit* o *strike h.*, llegar al alma, herir en lo vivo.—*a.* doméstico, de casa, casero; nativo, natal; regional, del país; certero, que llega a la meta.—*adv.* a casa; en casa; al país o en la tierra de uno; en su lugar.— —land [hóum- lænd], s. patria, tierra natal.— —less [-lis], a. sin casa ni hogar; mos- trenco.— —like [-laik], a. como en casa; sosegado y cómodo.— —liness [-linis], s. simpleza, sencillez; fealdad, mal aspecto.— —ly [-li], a. casero, doméstico; sencillo, llano; feo; rús-

tico, inculto, **vulgar.**— —made [-méid], a. casero, hecho en casa; fabricado en el país.— —sick [-sik], a. nostálgico.— —sickness [-siknis], s. nostalgia, añoranza.— —stead [-sted], s. casa de habitación y sus terrenos; heredad; hogar.— —ward [-wərd], adv. hacia casa, hacia su país; de vuelta.—*h.-bound*, de regreso.— —work [-wœrk], s. trabajo, tarea, estudio, etc. para hacer en la casa.

homicidal [hámisaidəl], a. homicida. —homicide [hámisaid], s. homicidio; homicida.

homogeneity [houmodʒenéiti], s. homo- geneidad.—homogeneous [houmodʒí- niəs], a. homogéneo.—homogenize [homádʒenaiz], vt. homogenizar.

homosexual [homəséksuəl], a. homo- sexual, por el propio sexo, por indi- viduos del mismo sexo.—s. homo- sexual; marica.

Honduran [handúran], a. y s. hon- dureño.

hone [houn], s. piedra de afilar.—*vt.* afilar, asentar, pulir, esmerilar.

honest [ánist], a. honrado, probo, recto; sincero; equitativo; honesta (mujer).— —ly [-li], adv. honrada- mente; de veras; francamente; ho- nestamente.— —y [-i], s. honradez, probidad; franqueza; honestidad; bonhomía.

honey [háni], s. miel de abejas; dulzura; querido, querida, mi cariño, etc.— —comb [-koum], s. panal de miel.— —ed [-d], a. dulce, meloso, melifluo.— —moon [-mun], s. luna de miel.— —suckle [-sʌkl], s. ma- dreselva.

honk [haŋk], s. pitazo, bocinazo (auto- móvil); graznido.—*vt.* y *vi.* pitar o sonar la bocina; graznar.

honor [ánər], s. honor, honra; hon- radez, rectitud; cargo, dignidad; lauro.—*pl.* distinción (en estudios, etc.).—*h. bright*, (fam.) de veras, a fe de caballero.—*on* o *upon my h.*, por mi fe, por mi palabra.—*your H.*, usía, vuestra señoría.—*vt.* honrar; laurear, condecorar; respetar.— —able [-əbl], a. honorable; pundonoroso; honrado; honorífico, honroso, **(H.)** honorable (tratamiento).— —ary [-eri], a. honorario, honorífico; honroso.

hood [hud], s. capucha, capucho, ca- peruza; muceta; fuelle de carruaje; (aut.) cubierta del motor; cubierta, tapa; campana del hogar.—*vt.* cubrir con caperuza, capucha, etc.; tapar, ocultar.

hoodoo [húdu], s. mal de ojo.—*vt.* hacer mal de ojo; traer mala suerte.

hoof [huf], s. casco, uña (del caballo,

etc.); pezuña; animal ungulado.— *on the h.*, en pie (ganado), vivo.

hook [huk], *s.* gancho, garabato, garfio; anzuelo; grapón; garra; corchete; atractivo; aliciente; (mús.) rabo de una corchea.—*vt.* enganchar; atraer, engatusar; dar una cornada, coger; pescar; encorvar.—*h. up*, conectar; enganchar.—*—ed* [-t], *a.* enganchado; encorvado, ganchudo, ganchoso.—*—up* [húkʌp], *s.* (rad.) trasmisión en cadena; cadena de emisoras.—*—y* [-i], *a.* ganchudo.— *to play h.*, hacer novillos o rabona; no ir a la escuela o a la clase.

hooligan [húligan], *s.* rufián, truhán.— *a.* de rufianes, truhanesco.—*—ism* [-izm], *s.* truhanería, rufianismo.

hoop [hup], *s.* aro; fleje, zuncho; (mec.) collar(ín); anilla, argolla; sortija; miriñaque; grito.—*vt.* poner aro a; enzunchar; ceñir.—*vi.* gritar; ojear.

hoot [hut], *vi.* gritar, ulular, huchear; dar grita; sonar la bocina o el pito.— *vt.* ridiculizar, recibir con risotada, abuchear.—*s.* grita, ruido, clamor, chillido.—*—ing* [hútiŋ], *s.* grita, rechifla, abucheo.

hop [hap], *vti.* [1] saltar, brincar; (fam.) alzar el vuelo en (un avión), poner en marcha.—*vii.* saltar en un pie, andar a saltitos; cojear.—*s.* salto, brinco; (fam.) baile; lúpulo; (aer.) trayecto de vuelo; (fam.) vuelo.—*pl.* (com.) lúpulo.

hope [houp], *s.* esperanza; expectativa. —*in hopes*, en o con la esperanza.—*vt.* y *vi.* esperar, tener esperanza.—*to h. against h.*, esperar lo imposible.— *—ful* [hóupful], *a.* esperanzado, confiado; que da esperanza o promete. —*s.* (fam.) joven que promete.— *—fully* [-fuli], *adv.* con esperanza.— *—less* [-lis], *a.* desahuciado; desesperante, desespera(nza)do; incurable; irremediable.—*—lessness* [-lisnis], *s.* desesperanza; falta de esperanza o remedio.

horde [hord], *s.* horda; enjambre; hato o manada; muchedumbre.

horizon [horáizən], *s.* horizonte.—*—tal* [harizántal], *a.* y *s.* horizontal.— *—tality* [harizantǽliti], *s.* horizontalidad.

hormone [hórmoun], *s.* hormona.

horn [hɔrn], *s.* cuerno, asta; tentáculo; palpo o antena; (mus.) trompa; corneta de monte o cuerno de caza; bocina.—*pl.* cornamenta.—*vt.* poner cuernos; dar una cornada; dar una cencerrada.

hornet [hórnit], *s.* avispón, moscardón.

horrible [hárib1], *a.* horrible, horroroso.—**horrid** [hárid], *a.* horrible,

hórrido; ofensivo, dañoso.—**horrify** [hárifai], *vti.* [7] horrorizar.—**horrifying** [hárifaiiŋ], *a.* horripilante. —**horror** [hárə(r)], *s.* horror.—*h. -stricken*, horrorizado.

horse [hɔrs], *s.* caballo; (mil.) caballería; potro (de carpintero, gimnasia, etc.); caballete, burro, banco. —*h. breaker*, domador de caballos. —*h. dealer*, chalán.—*h. race*, carrera de caballos.—*h. sense*, (fam.) gramática parda, sentido común.—*h. show*, concurso hípico.—*h. thief*, cuatrero. —*—back* [hórsbæk], *s.* lomo de caballo o asiento del jimete.—*to ride h.*, montar a caballo.—*—fly* [-flai], *s.* tábano.—*—hide* [-haid], *s.* piel de caballo.—*—laugh*(ter) [-læf(tœ(r))], *s.* risotada, carcajada.—*—man* [-mæn], *s.* jinete.—*—manship* [-mænʃip], *s.* equitación.—*—power* [-pauœ(r)], *s.* caballo de fuerza.—*—radish* [-rædiʃ], *s.* rábano picante o rústico.—*—shoe* [-ʃu], *s.* herradura.—*—tail* [-teil], *s.* cola de caballo.—*—whip* [-hwip], *s.* látigo, fuete, fusta.—*vti.* [1] dar fuetazos, azotar con el látigo, etc.— *—woman* [-wuman], *s.* amazona. —*—iness* [hórsinis], *s.* afición a los caballos.—*—y* [hórsi], *a.* caballar, caballuno; hípico, aficionado a caballos.

hose [houz], *s.* calceta; medias o calzas; manguera, manga de bomba o de riego; tubo flexible de goma.— *h. reel*, carretel de manguera.—

hosiery [hóuʒœri], *s.* calcetería.

hospice [háspis], *s.* hospicio.

hospitable [háspitabl], *a.* hospitalario. —*—ness* [-nis], *s.* hospitalidad.— **hospital** [háspital], *s.* hospital.— **hospitality** [haspitǽliti], *s.* hospitalidad.

host [houst], *s.* hospedero, huésped; anfitrión; hueste; multitud; (H.) (igl.) hostia.

hostage [hástidʒ], *s.* rehén.

hostess [hóustis], *s.* posadera, mesonera; anfitriona; (aer.) azafata.

hostile [hástil], *a.* hostil, enemigo, adverso.—**hostility** [hastíliti], *s.* hostilidad.—*pl.* (actos de) guerra.

hot [hat], *a.* caliente, cálido; caluroso; ardiente, fogoso; picante; acre; violento, furioso; (fam.) intolerable; en caliente; (fam.) cercano (de algo que se busca).—*h.-blooded*, apasionado.—*h. dog*, (fam.) = FRANKFURTER.—*h.-headed*, fogoso, exaltado.

hotel [hotél], *s.* hotel.—*h. keeper* o *manager*, hotelero, fondista.

hothouse [háthous], *s.* estufa, invernadero.

hound [haund], *s.* sabueso, podenco;

hombre vil.—*vt.* cazar con perros; soltar los perros; seguir la pista; perseguir; azuzar.

hour [aʊr], *s.* hora.—*pl.* horas (rezos). —*h. hand*, horario (del reloj).— —**ly** [áʊrlɪ], *adv.* a cada hora; por horas; frecuentemente.—*a.* frecuente, por horas.

house [haʊs], *s.* casa, domicilio, vivienda; familia, linaje; casilla (tablero de damas y ajedrez); casa comercial, razón social; cámara de un cuerpo legislativo; (teat.) sala, público; (mec.) caja, cubierta.—*H. of Commons*, (*Lords, Peers, Representatives*), Cámara de los Comunes, (Lores, Pares, Cámara de Representantes). —*vt.* albergar, alojar; poner a cubierto; almacenar.— —**breaker** [háʊsbrejkœ(r)], *s.* ladrón que escala una casa o la violenta para entrar.— —**hold** [-hoʊld], *s.* casa, familia.— —**keeper** [-kipœ(r)], *s.* ama de gobierno o de llaves; mujer de casa.— —**keeping** [-kipɪŋ], *s.* manejo de casa, incluyendo la cocina.—*a.* doméstico, casero, provisto de facilidades para cocinar.— —**top** [-tap], *s.* tejado, techo, azotea.— —**wife** [-wajf], *s.* ama de casa; madre de familia.— —**work** [-wœrk], *s.* tareas domésticas. —**housing** [háʊzɪŋ], *s.* alojamiento, vivienda; almacenaje.

hove [hoʊv], *pret.* y *pp.* de TO HEAVE.

hovel [hável], *s.* cobertizo, choza, cabaña, casucha, tugurio.

hover [hávœ(r)], *vt.* cubrir con las alas.—*vi.* revolotear; cernerse (las aves, y fig.), rondar; estar suspenso; dudar.— —**ing** [-ɪŋ], *s.* revoloteo.

how [haʊ], *adv.* cómo; cuán, cuánto; a cómo.—*h. about it?* ¿qué le parece? ¿y si lo hiciéramos?—*h. do you do?* ¿cómo le va? ¿cómo está usted?—*h. early?* ¿cuándo, a más tardar?—*h. far?* ¿a qué distancia? ¿hasta dónde?—*h. late?* ¿a qué hora? ¿hasta qué hora? ¿cuándo?—*h. long?* ¿cuánto tiempo? ¿cuánto demorará?—*h. many?* ¿cuántos?—*h. much?* ¿cuánto? —*h. now?* ¿y bien? ¿pues qué? ¿qué significa eso?—*h. often?* ¿con qué frecuencia? ¿cuántas veces?—*h. pretty!* ¡qué bonito!—*h. so?* ¿cómo así? —*h. soon?* ¿cuándo? ¿con qué rapidez¿—*h. well!* ¡qué bien!—*s.* cómo, modo, manera.— —**beit** [haʊbíjt], *adv.* sea como fuere, así como así; no obstante.— —**ever** [haʊévœ(r)], *adv.* como quiera que, de cualquier modo; por muy.—*conj.* no obstante, sin embargo.

howitzer [háʊjtsœ(r)], *s.* (arti.) obús.

howl [haʊl], *vi.* aullar, dar alaridos; ulular; rugir; bramar.—*vt.* gritar; condenar o echar a gritos.—*s.* aullido; alarido; gemido; rugido; bramido.

hub [hab], *s.* cubo de la rueda; por extensión, centro, eje; calzo.— —**bub** [hábab], *s.* grita, alboroto, bulla.

huckster [hákstœ(r)], *s.* vendedor ambulante; sujeto ruin.

huddle [hádl], *vt.* amontonar desordenadamente; atrabancar.—*vi.* acurrucarse; apiñarse.—*s.* tropel, confusión; (fam.) junta o reunión secreta.

hue [hju], *s.* matiz, tinte; grita, clamor. —*h. and cry*, alarma, vocerío.— *many-hued*, matizado.

hug [hag], *vti.* [1] abrazar; abrazarse a; navegar muy cerca de la costa.— *to h. one's self*, congratularse.—*s.* abrazo apretado.

huge [hjudʒ], *a.* inmenso, enorme, vasto, colosal.— —**ness** [hjúdʒnɪs], *s.* enormidad, inmensidad.

hulk [halk], *s.* casco de barco; barco viejo; armatoste.— —**ing** [hálkɪŋ], *a.* tosco, grueso.

hull [hal], *s.* cáscara, corteza; vaina de legumbre; casco (de un buque); flotador (de aeroplano); armazón.—*vt.* mondar, descascarar; desvainar; deshollejar.

hum [ham], *vti.* [1] canturrear, tararear.—*vii.* zumbar; susurrar.—*s.* zumbido; susurro; voz inarticulada (¡hum!); (fam.) engaño, filfa, chasco.

human [hjúman], *a.* humano.—*h. race*, género humano.—*s.* mortal, ser humano.— —**e** [hjuméjn], *a.* humano, benévolo, compasivo; humanitario. —**itarian** [hjumænjtérjan], *a.* humanitario.—*s.* filántropo. —**itarianism** [hjumænjtérjanjzm], *s.* humanitarismo.— —**ity** [hjuménjtj], *s.* humanidad.—*pl.* humanidades.— —**ize** [hjúmanajz], *vt.* y *vi.* humanizar(se).— —**kind** [hjúmankajnd], *s.* humanidad, género humano.

humble [hámbl], *a.* humilde, modesto. —*vt.* humillar, someter.—*vi.* bajar o doblar la cerviz.— —**ness** [-nɪs], *s.* humildad.

humbug [hámbag], *s.* farsa, patraña, fraude; farsante.

humdrum [hámdram], *a.* monótono, pesado, cansado.—*s.* fastidio, lata, aburrimiento; posma.

humid [hjúmjd], *a.* húmedo.—**humidify** [hjumídjfaj], *vti.* [7] humedecer.— —**ity** [hjumídjtj], *s.* humedad.

humiliate [hjumíljejt], *vt.* humillar.— **humiliation** [hjumjljéjṣon], *s.* humillación.—**humility** [hjumíljtj], *s.* humildad, sumisión.

humming [hámjŋ], *s.* zumbido; susurro; canturreo, tarareo.—*a.* zumbador; (fam.) muy activo, intenso, grande, etc.—**hummingbird** [hámjŋ bœrd], *s.* colibrí, pájaro mosca, tominejo.

humor [hjúmǫ(r)], *s.* humor, carácter, índole; humorada, fantasía, capricho; humorismo; agudeza, chiste, jocosidad; (med.) humor.—*to be in a bad h. o out of h.*, estar de mal humor.—*vt.* contemporizar, seguir el humor, dar gusto; consentir, mimar.— —ous [-ʌs], *a.* humorístico.

hump [hʌmp], *s.* giba, joroba.—*vi.* encorvarse, doblar la espalda.— —back [hʌmpbæk], *s.* giba, joroba; jorobado.— —backed [-bækt], *a.* jorobado, giboso, corcovado.— —y [-i], *a.* giboso.

hunch [hʌnch], *vt.* empujar, dar empellones; doblar la espalda.—*vi.* moverse o avanzar a tirones o a sacudidas; abalanzarse.—*s.* giba, corcova; pedazo o trozo grueso; (fam.) corazonada, presentimiento.— —back [hʌnchbæk], *s.* joroba; jorobado.— —backed [-bækt], *a.* jorobado.

hundred [hʌndrɛd], *a.* cien(to).—*s.* ciento; (arit.) centena, centenar.— *by hundreds*, a (o por) centenares.— *by the h.*, por ciento(s); por centenares.— —fold [-fould], *s.* céntuplo.— —th [-θ], *a. y s.* centésimo, céntimo; ciento (ordinal).— —weight [-weit], *s.* quintal. Ver Tabla.

hung [hʌŋ], *pret. y pp.* de TO HANG (colgar).

Hungarian [hʌŋgériən], *a. y s.* húngaro. —*s.* lengua húngara.

hunger [hʌŋgǝ(r)], *s.* hambre.—*h. strike*, huelga de hambre.—*vt.* hambrear.—*vi.* hambrear, tener hambre. —*to h. for*, anhelar, tener hambre de. —**hungry** [hʌŋgri], *a.* hambriento; deseoso; estéril, pobre.—*to be o feel h.*, tener hambre, estar hambriento.

hunk [hʌŋk], *s.* (fam.) buen pedazo; rebanada gruesa.

hunt [hʌnt], *vt.* cazar; perseguir, seguir; recorrer buscando.—*to h. up*, buscar.—*to h. up and down*, buscar por todas partes.—*vi.* cazar; hacer un registro minucioso; buscar.—*to h. after*, buscar, anhelar.—*to h. counter*, ir contra la pista.—*s.* caza, cacería; acosamiento. — —er [hʌntœ(r)], *s.* cazador, montero; podenco; caballo de caza.— —ing [-iŋ], *s.* montería, caza, cacería.—*h.-box*, pabellón de caza.— —ress [-ris], *s.* cazadora.— —sman [-smǝn], *s.* montero, cazador.

hurdle [hœrdl], *s.* valla (portátil); (fig.) obstáculo.—*pl.* (dep.) carrera de obstáculos.

hurdy-gurdy [hœrdi gœrdi], *s.* organillo; zanfona.

hurl [hœrl], *vt.* tirar, lanzar, arrojar;

echar; proferir.—*vr.* lanzarse, abalanzarse.—*s.* tiro, lanzamiento.

hurrah [hurá], *interj.* ¡viva! ¡hurra! ¡hurra!—*vt. y vi.* aclamar, vitorear.

hurricane [hœrikein], *s.* huracán, ciclón.

hurried [hœrid], *a.* precipitado, apresurado, hecho de prisa.—**hurry** [hœri], *vti. y vii.* [7] apresurar(se); dar(se) prisa; obrar a la carrera o con precipitación.—*to h. after*, correr detrás o en pos de.—*to h. away*, salir precipitadamente.—*to h. back*, volver de prisa; apresurarse a volver.—*to h. off*, huir, salir o hacer marchar de prisa.—*to h. on*, apresurar, precipitar; impulsar; precipitarse, apresurarse.—*to h. over*, (hacer) pasar rápidamente; despachar, expedir.—*to h. up*, apresurarse, darse prisa.—*s.* prisa, premura, precipitación, apuro.—*there is no h. about it*, no corre prisa.—*to be in a h.*, tener prisa.

hurt [hœrt], *vti.* [9] dañar, hacer mal o daño, lastimar, herir; injuriar, ofender; perjudicar.—*to h. one's feelings*, herirle a uno el amor propio, ofenderlo.—*vii.* doler.—*pret. y pp.* de TO HURT.—*s.* lesión, herida, contusión; mal, daño, perjuicio, detrimento.—*a.* lastimado, herido, perjudicado.

husband [hʌzbǝnd], *s.* marido, esposo.— —ry [-ri], *s.* labranza, agricultura.

hush [hʌʃ], *vt.* apaciguar, aquietar; hacer callar.—*to h. up*, tapar, ocultar, mantener secreto.—*vi.* estar quieto, callar, enmudecer, estar callado.—*s.* silencio, quietud.—*h. money*, dinero para soborno o cohecho.—*very h.-h.*, muy secreto.

husk [hʌsk], *s.* cáscara, vaina, pellejo, hollejo; bagazo; desperdicio.—*vt.* descascarar, desvainar, pelar, mondar, despellejar, deshollejar.— —y [hʌski], *a.* cascarudo; ronco.—*a. y s.* (fam.) fuerte, fornido.—*s.* perro esquimal; un dialecto esquimal.

hussy [hʌsi], *s.* sota, mujerzuela.

hustle [hʌsl], *vt.* mezclar, confundir; empujar, atropellar, sacudir.—*vi.* andar a empellones; (fam.) patear, moverse con actividad.—*h. and bustle*, vaivén.

hut [hʌt], *s.* choza, cabaña, barraca; cobertizo; (Am.) bohío.

hyacinth [háiǝsinθ], *s.* jacinto.

hybrid [háibrid], *a. y s.* híbrido.

hyena [haiínǝ], *s.* hiena.

hydrant [háidrǝnt], *s.* boca de riego.— **hydraulic(al)** [haidrólik(ǝl)], *a.* hidráulico.—**hydrocarbon** [haidrocárbon], *s.* hidrocarburo.—**hydrogen** [háidrodȝin], *s.* hidrógeno.—**hydroplane** [-plein], *s.* hidroplano.

hygiene [háidźin], hygienics [haidźiénjks], s. higiene.

hymen [háimɛn], s. himeneo; himen.

hymn [hjm], s. himne.

hyphen [háifɛn], s. raya, guión.

hypocrisy [hjpákrjsj], s. hipocresía.—
hypocrite [hípokrjt], s. hipócrita.—
hypocritical [hipokrítjkąl], a. hipócrita.

hypothesis [haipáθesjs], s. hipótesis, supuesto.

hysteria [hjstírją], s. histeria.—hysteric(al) [hjstérjk(ąl)], a. histérico.—
hysterics [hjstérjks], s. = HYSTERIA.

I

I [aj], pron. pers. yo.

Iberian [ajbírją̆n], a. ibérico.—a. y s. ibero.

ice [ajs], s. hielo; sorbete.—i. box, nevera, refrigerador.—i. breaker, buque rompehielos.—i. cream, helado, mantecado.—i. water, agua helada.—vt. helar; cubrir con escarcha (un pastel); enfriar con hielo.—berg [ájsbœrg], s. témpano flotante de hielo.—d [-t], a. congelado; enfriado con hielo.

Icelander [ájslandœ(r)], s. islandés.—
Icelandic [ajslǽndjk], a. y s. islandés.
—s. lengua islandesa.

iceman [ájsmæn], s. nevero, vendedor de hielo.—icicle [ájsjkl], s. carámbano.—iciness [ájsjnjs], s. frigidez; calidad de glacial.—icing [ájsjŋ], s. (dulcería) alcorza, adorno de azúcar.
—icy [ájsj], a. helado, frío, álgido.

idea [ajdíǎ], s. idea.—l [ajdíǎl], s. y a. ideal; prototipo.—lism [ajdíǎljzm], s. idealismo.—list [ajdíǎljst], s. idealista.—lize [ajdíǎlajz], vt. idealizar.

identical [ajdéntjkąl], a. idéntico.—
identification [ajdentjfjkéjśǫn], s. identificación.—identify [ajdéntjfaj], vti. [7] identificar.—identity [ajdéntjtj], s. identidad.

ideological [ajdjoládźjkąl], a. ideológico.
—ideology [ajdjálodźj], s. ideología.

idiocy [ídjǫsj], s. idiotez; imbecilidad.

idiom [ídjǫm], s. modismo, idiotismo; habla, lenguaje.

idiot [ídjǫt], s. idiota.—ic [idjátjk], a. idiota.

idle [ájdl], a. ocioso; sin colocación (dinero, etc.); perezoso, haragán; inútil, vano, frívolo.—i. pulley, polea de guía; polea de tensión.—i. wheel, rueda de transmisión.—vi. holgazanear o haraganear; holgar, estar ocioso; (aut.) funcionar el motor sin embragar.—vt. (generalmente con away) gastar ociosamente; dejar sin trabajo.—ness [-njs], s. ocio-

sidad, ocio; pereza, holgazanería, haraganería; inutilidad.— r [ájdlœ(r)], s. holgazán, perezoso.—idly [ájdlj], adv. ociosamente; desidiosamente; inútilmente.

idol [ájdǫl], s. ídolo.— ater [ajdálatœ(r)], s. idólatra.— atry [ajdálatrj], s. idolatría.— ize [ájdǫlajz], vt. idolatrar.

if [if], conj. si; supuesto que; con tal que; aunque; aun cuando.—as i., como si.—s. hipótesis, suposición; condición.

ignite [ignájt], vt. encender, pegar fuego.—vi. encenderse, inflamarse.
—ignition [igníśǫn], s. ignición; encendido (del motor).

ignoble [ignóubl], a. innoble, indigno; bajo.

ignorance [ígnorąns], s. ignorancia; falta de cultura.—ignorant [ígnorąnt], a. ignorante.—ignore [ignór], vt. desconocer, pasar por alto, no hacer caso de; desairar; ignorar.

illegal [ilígąl], a. ilegal, ilícito.— ity [iljgǽljtj], s. ilegalidad.

illegible [ilédźjbl], a. ilegible.

illegitimacy [ilidźítjmąsj], s. ilegitimidad.—illegitimate [iljdźítjmjt], a. ilegítimo.

ill [jl], a. enfermo; malo; dañino.—i. breeding, grosería, mala educación.—i. nature, mala disposición; malevolencia.—i. turn, mala jugada.—i. will, mala voluntad, malquerencia, ojeriza.—s. calamidad; mal.—adv. mal, malamente.—i. at ease, intranquilo, ansioso, inquieto; confundido.—i.-bred, malcriado, descortés.—i.-contrived, mal pensado, mal dispuesto.—i.-disposed, descontento; malintencionado.—i.-favored, feo, repulsivo.—i.-natured, avieso.—i.-shaped, malhecho.—i.-spoken of, de mala reputación.—i.-tempered, de malas pulgas, de mal genio.—i.-will, rencor, malquerencia.—to i.-treat, maltratar.— to take (it) i., tomar a mal.

illicit [ilísjt], a. ilícito; ilegal.

illiteracy [ilítȩrąsj], s. analfabetismo; ignorancia.—illiterate [ilítȩrjt], a. y s. analfabeto; ignorante.

illness [ílnjs], s. enfermedad, mal.

illogical [iládźjkąl], a. ilógico.

illuminate [iljúmjnejt], vt. iluminar, alumbrar; aclarar, esclarecer.—illumination [iljumjnéjśǫn], s. iluminación, alumbrado; (b.a.) iluminación en colores.

illusion [iljúźǫn], s. ilusión.—to cause i., ilusionar.—illusive [iljúsjv], a. ilusorio, ilusivo.—illusory [iljúsorj], a. ilusorio; engañoso.

illustrate [ílȧstrejt], vt. ilustrar, explicar, esclarecer con ejemplos.—illus-

tration [ilʌstréiʃọn], *s.* ejemplo, aclaración; (b.a.) grabado, ilustración, lámina.—**illustrator** [ilʌstreitọ(r)], *s.* ilustrador.—**illustrious** [ilʌstriʌs], *a.* ilustre, preclaro.

image [ímidʒ], *s.* imagen.—**—ry** [-ri], *s.* fantasía; conjunto de imágenes.—**imaginable** [imǽdʒiṇabl], *a.* imaginable.—**imaginary** [imǽdʒiṇeri], *a.* imaginario.—**imagination** [imædʒiṇéiʃọn], *s.* imaginación; inventiva. —**imaginative** [imǽdʒiṇeitiv], *a.* imaginativo; imaginario.—**imagine** [imǽdʒiṇ], *vt.* imaginarse, figurarse. —*vi.* imaginar.

imbecile [ímbisil], *a.* y *s.* imbécil.— **imbecility** [imbisíliti], *s.* imbecilidad.

imbibe [imbáib], *vt.* embeber, absorber; empapar(se), saturarse de.

imitate [ímiteit], *vt.* imitar, remedar.— **imitation** [imitéiʃọn], *s.* imitación.— *a.* de imitación.—**imitator** [ímiteitọ(r)], *s.* imitador.

immaculate [imǽkyulit], *a.* inmaculado, sin mancha; impecable.

immaterial [imatíriạl], *a.* inmaterial, incorpóreo.—*to be i.*, no importar, ser indiferente.

immature [imachúr], *a.* inmaturo, verde; prematuro.

immediate [imídiit], *a.* inmediato, cercano; próximo.—**—ly** [-li], *adv.* inmediatamente, en seguida, en el acto.

immense [iméns], *a.* inmenso, vasto.— **immensity** [ménsiti], *s.* inmensidad.

immerse [imə́rs], *vt.* sumergir; anegar, sumir.—**immersion** [imə́rʃọn], *s.* inmersión, sumersión; bautismo por inmersión.

immigrant [ímigraṇt], *a.* y *s.* inmigrante.—**immigrate** [ímigreit], *vi.* inmigrar.—**immigration** [imigréiʃọn], *s.* inmigración.

imminent [íminẹnt], *a.* inminente.

immobile [imóubil], *a.* inmóvil, inmovible.—**immobility** [imoubíliti], *s.* inmovilidad.—**immobilize** [imóubilaiz], *vt.* inmovilizar.

immodest [imádist], *a.* inmodesto; indecoroso, indecente; atrevido.—**—y** [-i], *s.* inmodestia; indecencia, impudicia.

immoral [imáral], *a.* inmoral, licencioso, depravado.—**—ity** [imorǽliti], *s.* inmoralidad.

immortal [imórtal], *a.* y *s.* inmortal.— **—ity** [imortǽliti], *s.* inmortalidad.— **—ize** [imórtalaiz], *vt.* inmortalizar.

immovable [imúvabl], *a.* inmóvil, inmovible, inamovible, impasible; inmutable; (for.) inmueble.—*s. pl.* inmuebles, bienes raíces.

immune [imiún], *a.* y *s.* inmune.— **immunity** [imiúniti], *s.* inmunidad.

—immunization [imiunizéiʃọn], *s.* inmunización.—**immunize** [ímiunaiz], *vt.* inmunizar.

imp [imp], *s.* diablillo, trasgo.

impact [ímpækt], *s.* impacto, choque.

impair [impér], *vt.* empeorar, dañar, perjudicar, menoscabar, deteriorar.— **—ment** [-mẹnt], *s.* empeoramiento, deterioro, menoscabo.

impart [impárt], *vt* impartir, comunicar, dar.

impartial [impárʃal], *a.* imparcial.— **—ity** [imparʃiéliti], *s.* imparcialidad.

impassable [impǽsabl], *a.* intransitable, impracticable; insuperable.

impassion [impǽʃọn], *vt.* apasionar; conmover o afectar fuertemente.— **—ed** [-d], *a.* apasionado, vehemente, impetuoso.

impassive [impǽsiv], *a.* impasible.

impatience [impéiʃẹns], *s.* impaciencia. —**impatient** [impéiʃẹnt], *a.* impaciente.

impeach [impích], *vt.* acusar (a un funcionario ante un tribunal); poner en tela de juicio; interpelar, residenciar.—**—ment** [-mẹnt], *s.* acusación; imputación, residencia.

impeccable [impékabl], *a.* impecable.

impede [impíd], *vt.* impedir, estorbar, dificultar.—**impediment** [impédimẹnt], *s.* impedimento; obstrucción, traba, cortapisa.

impel [impél], *vti.* [1] impeler, impulsar; abalanzar.

impending [impéndiṇ], *a.* inminente; pendiente; amenazante.

impenetrable [impéṇitrabl], *a.* impenetrable.

impenitent [impéṇitẹnt], *a.* impenitente.

imperative [impérạtiv], *a.* imperativo, imperioso, imprescindible.—*s.* mandato perentorio; (gram.) imperativo.

imperceptible [impọrséptibl], *a.* imperceptible.

imperfect [impọ́rfikt], *a.* imperfecto, defectuoso.—**—ion** [impọrfékʃọn], *s.* imperfección, defecto.

imperial [impíriạl], *a.* imperial.—**—ism** [-izm], *s.* imperialismo.—**—ist** [-ist], *s.* imperialista.

imperious [impíriʌs], *a.* imperioso.

impersonal [impə́rsọnal], *a.* impersonal.

impersonate [impə́rsọneit], *vt.* personificar; (teat.) representar; imitar.— **impersonation** [impọrsọnéiʃọn], *s.* personificación; (teat.) representación, papel; imitación.

impertinence [impə́rtinẹns], **impertinency** [impə́rtinẹnsi], *s.* impertinencia; insolencia.—**impertinent** [impə́rtinẹnt], *a.* impertinente; insolente, atrevido.

imperturbable [impœrtœ́rbabl], *a.* imperturbable.

impervious [impœ́rvi̯ʌs], *a.* impermeable, impenetrable, refractario.

impetuosity [impechu̯ásiti], *s.* ímpetu, impetuosidad.—**impetuous** [impéchu̯ʌs], *a.* impetuoso.—**impetus** [ímpi̯tʌs], *s.* ímpetu.

impiety [impái̯eti], *s.* impiedad, irreligiosidad.—**impious** [ímpi̯ʌs], *a.* impío.

implacable [impléi̯kabl], *a.* implacable, inexorable.

implement [ímplimẹnt], *s.* herramienta, utensilio; instrumento (de guerra, etc.).—*pl.* utensilios, útiles, aperos, enseres.—*vt.* poner por obra, poner en ejecución, cumplir.

implicate [ímplikei̯t], *vt.* implicar, envolver; enredar.—**implication** [implikéi̯šọn], *s.* deducción; complicación.

implicit [implísit], *a.* implícito, sobrentendido, tácito.—*i. faith,* fe ciega.

implore [implór], *vt.* implorar, suplicar, rogar.

imply [implái̯], *vti.* [7] querer decir; significar, denotar, importar.

impolite [impolái̯t], *a.* descortés; grosero.

import [impórt], *vt.* (com.) importar; denotar, significar; interesar.—*vi.* convenir, tener importancia.—*s.* [ímpọrt], sentido, significación; importancia, valor.—*pl.* (com.) artículos importados.—**ance** [impórtạns], *s.* importancia.—**ant** [impórtạnt], *a.* importante.—**ation** [importéi̯šọn], *s.* (com.) importación; artículo importado.—**er** [impórtœ(r)], *s.* importador.

importune [importi̯ún], *vt.* y *vi.* importunar, instar, porfiar, machacar.

impose [impóu̯z], *vt.* imponer; obligar a aceptar.—*o . on o upon,* abusar de; engañar.—**imposing** [impóu̯ziṇ], *a.* imponente; solemne, tremendo.—**imposition** [impozíšọn], *s.* imposición; impuesto, carga.

impossibility [impasibíliti], *s.* imposibilidad.—**impossible** [impásibl], *a.* imposible.

impostor [impástọ(r)], *s.* impostor, embaucador.—**imposture** [impáschu̯(r)], *s.* impostura.

impotence [ímpotẹns], *s.* impotencia.—**impotent** [ímpotẹnt], *a.* impotente.

impoverish [impávœriš], *vt.* empobrecer, depauperar.— **ment** [-mẹnt], *s.* empobrecimiento, depauperación.

impracticable [impráektikabl], *a.* impracticable, intransitable; intratable, irrazonable.

impregnate [ímprẹgnei̯t], *vt.* impregnar;

fecundizar, empreñar.—*a.* impregnado; embarazada, preñada.

impress [imprés], *vt.* imprimir, grabar, estampar; marcar; impresionar.—*s.* [ímpres], impresión, señal, huella.— **ion** [impréšọn], *s.* impresión; marca, señal.— **ionable** [impréšọnạbl], *a.* impresionable, susceptible.— **ive** [imprésiv], *a.* impresionante; grandioso, imponente.

imprint [imprínt], *vt.* imprimir, estampar.—*s.* [ímprịnt], impresión, marca, huella; pie de imprenta.

imprison [impríz̧ọn], *vt.* encarcelar, aprisionar.— **ment** [-mẹnt], *s.* prisión, encarcelación.

improbable [imprábạbl], *a.* improbable.

improper [imprápœ(r)], *a.* impropio, incorrecto.

improve [imprúv], *vt.* mejorar; perfeccionar.—*vi.* mejorarse; mejorar.— **ment** [-mẹnt], *s.* mejora; mejoramiento; adelanto, progreso; mejoría.

improvisation [impravizéi̯šọn], *s.* improvisación.—**improvise** [improvái̯z], *vt.* improvisar.

imprudence [imprúdẹns], *s.* imprudencia, indiscreción.—**imprudent** [imprúdẹnt], *a.* imprudente.

impudence [ímpi̯udẹns], *s.* desfachatez, descaro; impudicia.—**impudent** [ímpi̯udẹnt], *a.* descarado; impúdico.

impulse [ímpʌls], *s.* impulso; estímulo.—**impulsive** [impʌ́lsiv], *a.* impulsivo.

impure [impi̯úr], *a.* impuro.—**impurity** [impi̯úriti], *s.* impureza.

in [in], *prep.* en, de, por, con, mientras, dentro de.—*i. haste,* de prisa.—*i. so far as,* o *insofar as,* en cuanto (a), hasta donde.—*adv.* dentro, adentro; en casa.—*i. here, there, etc.,* aquí dentro, allí dentro, etc.—*to be all i.,* estar rendido, agotado.—*to be i.,* haber llegado; estar (en casa, en la oficina, etc.).—*to be i. with someone,* gozar del favor de alguien.

inability [inabíliti], *s.* inhabilidad, incapacidad, ineptitud.

inaccessible [inæksésibl], *a.* inaccesible.

inaccurate [inǽkyu̯rit], *a.* inexacto, erróneo.

inactive [inǽktiv], *a.* inactivo, inerte.— **inactivity** [inæktíviti], *s.* inactividad, ociosidad.

inadequate [inǽdikwit], *a.* inadecuado.

inadmissible [inædmísibl], *a.* inadmisible.

inadvertence [inædvœ́rtẹns], *s.* inadvertencia.—**inadvertent** [inædvœ́rtẹnt], *a.* inadvertido, accidental; descuidado.

inalienable [inéi̯lyẹnạbl], *a.* inalienable.

inanimate [inǽnimit], *a.* inanimado; exánime.

inasmuch as [inạzmʌ́ch ạz], *adv.* en

cuanto; tanto como; como quiera que, puesto que, visto que, por cuanto.

inaugural [inógiural], *a.* inaugural. —**inaugurate** [inógiureit], *vt.* inaugurar; investir.—**inauguration** [inogiuréişon], *s.* inauguración, estreno; toma de posesión.

inborn [ínborn], *a.* innato, ingénito.

Inca [ínkạ], *s.* inca.—*a.* inca, incaico.

incalculable [ínkælkiuạbl], *a.* incalculable.

incandescent [inkændésẹnt], *a.* incandescente, candente.

incapable [inkéipạbl], *a.* incapaz.—**incapacitate** [inkạpǽsiteit], *vt.* incapacitar, inhabilitar.—**incapacity** [inkạpǽsiti], *s.* incapacidad.

incarnate [inkárneit], *vt.* encarnar.—*a.* [inkárnit], encarnado; personificado.—**incarnation** [inkarnéişọn], *s.* encarnación.

incendiary [inséndieri], *a.* y *s.* incendiario.

incense [ínsens], *s.* incienso.—*vt.* [inséns], exasperar, irritar; incensar.

incentive [inséntiv], *s.* incentivo, estímulo, aliciente.—*a.* incitativo.

incessant [insésạnt], *a.* incesante.

inch [inch], *s.* pulgada.—*by inches,* paso a paso, con gran lentitud.—*every i.,* cabal, en todo respecto.—*i. by i.,* palmo a palmo, pulgada por pulgada.—*within an i. of,* a dos dedos de.—*a.* de una pulgada.—*vi.* (con *along*) avanzar poquito a poquito.

incident [ínsịdẹnt], *s.* incidente; acontecimiento, episodio.—**al** [insịdéntạl], *a.* incidental, incidente, contingente; concomitante.—*s. pl.* gastos imprevistos; circunstancias imprevistas.

incinerator [insínẹreitọ(r)], *s.* incinerador, crematorio.

incision [insíẓọn], *s.* incisión; muesca.—**incisor** [insáiẓọ(r)], *a.* y *s.* (diente) incisivo.

incite [insáit], *vt.* incitar, instigar.

inclination [inklịnéişọn], *s.* inclinación; pendiente, declive.—**incline** [inkláin], *vt.* inclinar, ladear.—*vi.* inclinarse, ladearse; hacer reverencia; sentir inclinación o predilección.—*s.* [ínklain], declive, pendiente, cuesta, rampa.

inclose [inklóuz], *vt.* = ENCLOSE.—**inclosure** [inklóuẓụ(r)], *s.* = ENCLOSURE.

include [inklúd], *vt.* incluir, encerrar; comprender, abarcar.—**inclusion** [inklúẓọn], *s.* inclusión, contenido.—**inclusive** [inklúsiv], *a.* inclusivo.

incoherent [inkohírẹnt], *a.* incoherente, inconexo.

income [ínkʌm], *s.* renta, entrada, ingreso, rédito.—*i. tax return,* declaración del impuesto sobre la renta.

incomparable [inkámpạrạbl], *a.* incomparable, sin igual.

incompetence [inkámpịtẹns], *s.* incompetencia.—**incompetent** [inkámpịtẹnt], *a.* incompetente.

incomplete [inkọmplít], *a.* incompleto.

incomprehensible [inkamprịhénsibl], *a.* incomprensible.

incongruous [inkángruʌs], *a.* incongruente, discordante, mal adaptado; inconsecuente.

inconsiderate [iakọnsídœrịt], *a.* desconsiderado; desatento.

inconsistency [inkọnsístẹnsi], *s.* incompatibilidad, contradicción, inconsecuencia.—**inconsistent** [inkọnsístẹnt], *a.* incompatible, contradictorio, inconsecuente.

inconstancy [inkánstạnsi], *s.* inconstancia.—**inconstant** [inkánstạnt], *a.* inconstante, vario.

inconvenience [inkọnvíniẹns], *s.* inconveniencia, inconveniente; incomodidad, molestia.—*vt.* incomodar, estorbar, molestar.—**inconvenient** [inkọnvíniẹnt], *a.* inconveniente, inoportuno, molesto, incómodo.

incorporate [inkórporeit], *vt.* incorporar; formar corporación.—*vi.* incorporarse, unirse, asociarse.—*a.* [inkórporịt], incorporado; inmaterial.

incorrect [inkọrékt], *a.* incorrecto.

increase [inkrís], *vt.* y *vi.* aumentar(se); acrecentar(se); incrementar; arreciar (en intensidad, sonido, etc.).—*s.* [ínkris], aumento, incremento, crecimiento, acrecentamiento.—**increasingly** [inkrísinli], *adv.* crecientemente; con creces; cada vez más.

incredible [inkrédibl], *a.* increíble.—**incredulity** [inkridiúliti], *s.* incredulidad.—**incredulous** [inkrédẓụlʌs], *a.* incrédulo.

increment [ínkrịmẹnt], *s.* incremento, aumento, crecimiento.

incriminate [inkrímịneit], *vt.* incriminar, acusar.

incubation [inkịubéişọn], *s.* incubación.—**incubator** [ínkịubeitọ(r)], *s.* incubadora; empolladora.

incumbency [inkámbẹnsi], *s.* posesión o goce de un empleo; duración del mismo; incumbencia.—**incumbent** [inkámbẹnt], *a.* obligatorio; sostenido por, colocado sobre, apoyado en.

incur [inkœr], *vti.* [1] incurrir (en); atraerse.—*to i. a debt,* contraer una deuda.

incurable [inkiúrạbl], *a.* incurable, irremediable.—*s.* incurable.

incursion [inkœrẓọn], *s.* incursión, correría.

indebted [indétịd], *a.* adeudado, endeudado o en deuda; (fam.) entrampado; obligado, reconocido.—

—ness [-nis], *s.* deuda; pasivo; obligación.

Indecency [indísensi], *s.* indecencia.—**indecent** [indísent], *a.* indecente, indecoroso.

Indecision [indisízon], *s.* indecisión, irresolución.

Indecorous [indékoras], *a.* indecoroso.

Indeed [indíd], *adv.* verdaderamente, realmente, de veras, a la verdad, claro está.—*interrog.* ¿de veras? ¿es posible?

Indefatigable [indifætigabl], *a.* incansable.

Indefensible [indifénsibl], *a.* indefendible, insostenible.

Indefinite [indéfinit], *a.* indefinido, vago.

Indelible [indélibl], *a.* indeleble.

Indelicate [indélikit], *a.* indecoroso, falto de delicadeza.

Idemnify [indémnifai], *vti.* [7] indemnizar.—**indemnity** [indémniti], *s.* indemnización.

Indent [indént], *vt.* dentar, endentar; (impr.) sangrar.—*s.* mella, diente, muesca.

Independence [indipéndens], *s.* independencia.—**independent** [indipéndent], *a.* independiente.

Indescribable [indiskráibabl], *a.* indescriptible.

Indeterminate [inditérminit], *a.* indeterminado, vago.

Index [índeks], *s.* índice; elenco.—*i. card*, tarjeta o ficha para archivos.—*vt.* ordenar o clasificar alfabéticamente; poner en un índice; indicar.

Indian [índian], *a.* indio; indígena.—*I. ink*, tinta china.—*I. Ocean*, Océano Índico.—*I. summer*, veranillo de San Martín.—*s.* indio, indo; piel roja.

Indicate [índikeit], *vt.* indicar, significar.—**indication** [indikéishon], *s.* indicación, indicio.—**indicative** [indíkativ], *a.* y *s.* indicativo.

Indict [indáit], *vt.* (for.) acusar ante el juez; procesar, encausar, enjuiciar.—**ment** [-ment], *s.* (for.) sumario; denuncia, acusación; proces(amient)o.

Indifference [indíferens], *s.* indiferencia; apatía, despego.—**indifferent** [indíferent], *a.* indiferente; apático.

Indigenous [indídzenas], *a.* indígena, nativo.

Indigestion [indidzéschon], *s.* indigestión.

Indignant [indígnant], *a.* indignado.—**ly** [-li], *adv.* con indignación.—**indignation** [indignéishon], *s.* indignación.—**indignity** [indígniti], *s.* indignidad, ultraje o afrenta, improperio.

Indigo [índigou], *s.* añil, índigo.

Indirect [indirékt], *a.* indirecto.

Indiscreet [indiskrít], *a.* indiscreto.—**indiscretion** [indiskréshon], *s.* indiscreción.

Indispensable [indispénsabl], *a.* indispensable, inprescindible; de rigor.

Indispose [indispóuz], *vt.* indisponer.—**d** [-d], *a.* indispuesto; ligeramente enfermo.—**indisposition** [indispozíshon], *s.* indisposición; malestar.

Indistinct [indistínkt], *a.* indistinto.

Individual [indivídzual], *a.* individual.—*s.* individuo, particular, persona, sujeto.—**ity** [indivídzuéliti], *s.* individualidad, personalidad.

Indivisible [indivízibl], *a.* indivisible.

Indo-Chinese [índou chainíz], *a.* y *s.* indochino.

Indoctrinate [indáktrineit], *vt.* adoctrinar.

Indolence [índolens], *s.* indolencia, desidia.—**indolent** [índolent], *a.* indolente, desidioso.

Indomitable [indámitabl], *a.* indomable.

Indoor [índor], *a.* interno, interior, de casa.—*s* [indórz], *adv.* (a)dentro; en casa; bajo techo.

Indorse [indórs], *vt.* (com.) endosar; respaldar; garantizar; apoyar.—**e** [-í], *s.* endosatario.—**ment** [-ment], *s.* endoso; respaldo; aval, garantía.—**r** [indórse(r)], *s.* endosante.

Induce [indjús], *vt.* inducir, persuadir.—**ment** [-ment], *s.* inducción; aliciente; persuasión.

Induct [indákt], *vt.* instalar; iniciar.—**ion** [indákshon], *s.* (elec. y lóg.) inducción.—*i. valve*, válvula de admisión.

Indulge [indáldz], *vt.* mimar, consentir; gratificar; conceder indulgencia a; (com.) dar plazo o prorrogar el plazo a.—*vi.* (con *in*) entregarse a; gustar de.—**nce** [indáldzens], *s.* indulgencia; exceso, complacencia, favor; (com.) prórroga.—**nt** [indáldzent], *a.* indulgente.

Industrial [indástrial], *a.* industrial.—**ist** [-ist], *s.* industrial.—**ization** [-izéishon], *s.* industrialización.—**ize** [-aiz], *vt.* industrializar.—**industrious** [indástrias], *a.* industrioso, diligente, aplicado, laborioso.—**industry** [índastri], *s.* industria; laboriosidad.

Ineffective [ineféktiv], *a.* ineficaz, inefectivo.—**ineffectual** [inefékchual], *a.* ineficaz; fútil.—**inefficacy** [inéfikasi], *s.* inefficiency [inefísensi], *s.* ineficacia; futilidad.—**inefficient** [inefísent], *a.* ineficaz.

Ineligible [inélidzibl], *a.* inelegible.

Inept [inépt], *a.* inepto.—**itude** [-itjud], *s.* ineptitud, inhabilidad.

Inequality [inikwáliti], *s.* desigualdad, disparidad.

inert [inə́rt], *a.* inerte.— **—ia** [inə́rṣiə̱], *s.* inercia.

inestimable [iné̱stimabl], *a.* inestimable, inapreciable.

inevitable [iné̱vitabl], *a.* inevitable, ineludible.

inexpensive [ineksⱷé̱nsiv], *a.* barato, poco costoso.

inexperience [inekspíriəns], *s.* inexperiencia, impericia.— **—d** [-t], **inexpert** [ineksⱷə́rt], *a.* inexperto, bisoño, novel.—**inexpertness** [ineksⱷə́rtnis], *s.* impericia.

inexplicable [iné̱ksplikabl], *a.* inexplicable.

inexpressible [inekspré̱sibl], *a.* indecible, inexpresable, inenarrable.

infallibility [infælibíliti], *s.* infalibilidad.—**infallible** [infé̱libl], *a.* infalible.

infamous [ínfamas], *a.* infame; infamante.—**infamy** [ínfami], *s.* infamia, ignominia.

infancy [ínfansi], *s.* infancia.—**infant** [ínfant], *s.* infante, niñito, criatura, nene.—*a.* infantil; menor de edad; de niños; naciente.—**infantile** [ínfantil], *a.* infantil.

infantry [ínfantri], *s.* infantería.— **—man** [-man], *s.* soldado de infantería.

infect [infé̱kt], *vt.* infectar, contagiar.—**—ion** [infé̱kṣon], *s.* infección, contagio.— **—ious** [infé̱kṣas], *a.* contagioso, infeccioso.

infelicity [infilísiti], *s.* infelicidad, infortunio; falto de tino.

infer [infə́r], *vti.* [1] inferir, colegir.—*vii.* sacar consecuencias o inferencias.— **—ence** [ínfərəns], *s.* inferencia.— **—entially** [infərénṣali], *adv.* por inferencia.

inferior [infíriə(r)], *s.* and *a.* inferior; subordinado, subalterno.— **—ity** [infiriáriti], *s.* inferioridad.

infernal [infə́rnal], *a.* infernal.—**inferno** [infə́rnou], *s.* infierno.

infest [infé̱st], *vt.* infestar, plagar.

infidel [ínfidel], *s.* infiel; pagano; librepensador.—*a.* infiel; librepensador; de infieles, de los infieles.— **—ity** [infidé̱liti], *s.* infidelidad, descreimiento; infidelidad conyugal.

infield [ínfild], *s.* campo y jugadores situados dentro del cuadro (baseball); campos inmediatos a los edificios (en una granja, etc.).

infighting [ínfaitiŋ], *s.* boxeo cuerpo a cuerpo.

infiltrate [infíltreit], *vt.* y *vi.* infiltrar(se); meter(se); introducir(se) en pequeño número por varias partes.—**infiltration** [infiltréiṣon], *s.* infiltración.

infinite [ínfinit], *a.* infinito; innumerable; perfecto.—*s.* infinito.—**infinitive** [infínitiv], *s.* y *a.* infinitivo.—

infinity [infíniti], *s.* infinidad, inmensidad; (mat.) infinito; sinfín.

infirm [infə́rm], *a.* enfermizo, achacoso; poco firme; (for.) anulable.— **—ary** [-ari], *s.* hospital, enfermería, casa de salud.— **—ity** [-iti], *s.* enfermedad, dolencia, achaque; flaqueza, fragilidad.— **—ly** [-li], *adv.* débilmente.

inflame [infléim], *vt.* inflamar, encender; enardecer; provocar, irritar.—*vi.* arder; inflamarse, hincharse.—**inflammable** [inflǽmabl], *a.* inflamable.—**inflammation** [inflaméiṣon], *s.* inflamación.

inflate [infléit], *vt.* inflar, hinchar.—**inflation** [infléiṣon], *s.* inflación monetaria; hinchazón; inflación.

inflect [inflé̱kt], *vt.* torcer, doblar; modular; (gram.) declinar, conjugar.—**—ion** [inflé̱kṣon], *s.* inflexión, dobladura; acento, modulación; flexión, conjugación, declinación, desinencia.

inflexibility [infleksibíliti], *s.* inflexibilidad.—**inflexible** [inflé̱ksibl], *a.* inflexible.

inflict [inflí̱kt], *vt.* infligir, imponer.—**—ion** [inflí̱kṣon], *s.* imposición, aplicación; pena, castigo.

influence [ínfluens], *s.* influencia, valimiento, influjo; ascendiente.—*vt.* influir; inducir; ejercer presión sobre.—**influential** [influénṣal], *a.* influyente.

influenza [influé̱nzə̱], *s.* influenza, trancazo, gripe.

influx [ínflʌks], *s.* (in)flujo; afluencia; instilación, intromisión; desembocadura, entrada.

infold [infóuld], *vt.* envolver; incluir; abrazar; abarcar.

inform [infə́rm], *vt.* informar, comunicar; poner al corriente; instruir; dar forma a, modelar; animar.—*vi.* soplar, delatar.—*to i. against*, denunciar a, delatar a.— **—al** [-al], *a.* de confianza, sin ceremonia.— **—ality** [informǽliti], *s.* informalidad, irregularidad.— **—ation** [informéiṣon], *s.* informe, información, aviso; conocimiento(s); (for.) acusación, delación.— **—er** [informó̱e(r)], *s.* delator; denunciante; (fam.) soplón, chivato.

infraction [infrǽkṣon], *s.* infracción, transgresión; fractura incompleta.

infrequent [infrí̱kwent], *a.* raro, poco frecuente.

infringe [infríndž], *vt.* infringir, violar.—*to i. upon*, violar.—**—ment** [-ment], *s.* infracción, violación.

infuriate [infiúrieit], *vt.* enfurecer, irritar.

ingenious [indžínjʌs], *a.* ingenioso, hábil.— **—ness** [-nis], *s.* ingeniosidad, ingenio.—**ingenuity** [indžinjúiti], *s.* ingeniosidad, inventiva.

ingenuous [indžényu̧ʌs], *a.* ingenuo, cándido.——**ness** [-nis], *s.* ingenuidad, candidez.

ingoing [íngou̧iŋ], *a.* entrante, que entra.——*s.* entrada, ingreso.

ingot [íŋgot], *s.* lingote; barra.

ingrained [ingréind], *a.* inculcado, arraigado, inveterado.

ingratiate [ingréišieit], *vt.* hacer aceptable.—*to i. oneself with,* insinuarse, hacerse a la buena voluntad de, conquistarse el favor de.—**ingratiating** [ingréišieitiŋ], *a.* insinuante.

ingratitude [ingrǽtitiud], *s.* ingratitud.

ingredient [ingrídient], *s.* ingrediente.

inhabit [inhǽbit], *vt.* habitar, poblar.—*vi.* residir.——**able** [-ᴀbl], *a.* habitable.——**ant** [-ᴀnt], *s.* habitante, poblador, residente.

inhalation [inhᴀléišȯn], *s.* inspiración; (med.) inhalación.—**inhale** [inhéil], *vt.* inspirar, inhalar, aspirar.

inhere [inhír], *vi.* ser inherente.——**nt** [inhírent], *a.* inherente, inmanente; innato, esencial.

inherit [inhérit], *vt.* heredar.—*vi.* suceder como heredero.——**ance** [-ᴀns], *s.* herencia, patrimonio.——**or** [-o̧(r)], *s.* heredero.——**ress** [-ris],——**rix** [-riks], *s.* heredera.

inhibit [inhíbit], *vt.* inhibir, prohibir.——**ion** [inhibíšȯn], *s.* inhibición, prohibición.

inhospitable [inháspitᴀbl], *a.* inhospitalario, inhóspito.

inhuman [inhiúmᴀn], *a.* inhumano.——**e** [inhiuméin], *a.* inhumanitario.——**ity** [inhiumǽniti], *s.* inhumanidad.

inimical [inímikal], *a.* hostil, enemigo.

inimitable [inímitᴀbl], *a.* inimitable.

initial [[iníšᴀl], *a.* inicial, incipiente.——*s.* (letra) inicial.—*vt.* [2] poner las iniciales, firmar con iniciales.——**ly** [-i], *adv.* en primer lugar; en los comienzos; por modo inicial.—**initiate** [iníšieit], *vt.* iniciar, entablar.—*a. y s.* adepto, iniciado.—**initiation** [iníšiéišȯn], *s.* iniciación.—**initiative** [iníšiᵫtiv], *a.* iniciative.—*s.* iniciativa, originalidad.

inject [indžékt], *vt.* inyectar; introducir.——**ion** [indžékšȯn], *s.* inyección; enema, lavativa.

injunction [indžʌ́ŋkšȯn], *s.* mandato, mandamiento; requerimiento; prohibición; embargo.

injure [índžur], *vt.* injuriar; perjudicar; averiar, lastimar, lesionar.— **injurious** [indžúriᴀs], *a.* injurioso; perjudicial; lesivo.—**injury** [índžuri], *s.* daño, avería, desperfecto; perjuicio, detrimento, menoscabo; lesión.

injustice [indžʌ́stis], *s.* injusticia.

ink [iŋk], *s.* tinta.—*vt.* entintar, dar tinta, pasar o linear en tinta.— **ling**

[íŋkliŋ], *s.* insinuación; sospecha; vislumbre, indicio, noción vaga.——**stand** [-stænd], *s.* escribanía; tintero.— **well** [-wel], *s.* tintero; frasco de tintero.

inland [ínlᴀnd], *a.* interior; del país, nacional, regional.—*s.* el interior de un país.—*adv.* tierra adentro.——**er** [-œ(r)], *s.* el que habita tierra adentro.

in-law [ínlᴐ], *s.* (fam.) pariente político.

inlay [inléi], *vti.* [10] embutir; incrustar; hacer ataujía o mosaico.—*s.* [ínlei], taracea, embutido.

inlet [ínlet], *s.* entrada; abra, caleta, ensenada; estero, estuario; boca de entrada.

inmate [ínmeit], *s.* enfermo hospitalizado; recluso; presidiario.

inmost [ínmoust], *a.* más íntimo, recóndito, profundo.

inn [in], *s.* fonda, mesón, posada.

innate [inéit], *a.* innato, ingénito, connatural.

inner [ínœ(r)], *a.* interno, interior.—*i. spring mattress,* colchón de muelles.—*i. tube* o *tire,* cámara de rueda de automóvil.

inning [íniŋ], *s.* entrada, turno (baseball y otros juegos).—*pl.* tierras ganadas al mar.

innkeeper [ínkipœ(r)], *s.* posadero, mesonero, fondista.

innocence [ínosens], *s.* inocencia.— **innocent** [ínosent], *s. y a.* inocente.

innovate [ínoveit], *vt.* innovar.—**innovation** [inovéišȯn], *s.* innovación; novedad.

innuendo [iniuéndou], *s.* indirecta, insinuación.

innumerable [iniúmerᴀbl], *a.* innumerable.

inoculate [inákiuleit], *vt. y vi.* inocular; fertilizar (el suelo) con bacterias; infundir; infectar, inficionar.—**inoculation** [inakiuléišȯn], *s.* inoculación; contaminación, infección; fertilización con bacterias.

inoffensive [inofénsiv], *a.* inofensivo.

inopportune [inapȯrtiún], *a.* inoportuno, intempestivo; inconveniente.

inorganic [inȯrgǽnik], *a.* inorgánico.

inquire [inkwáir], *vt. y vi.* inquirir, preguntar, averiguar.—*to i. into,* investigar, examinar, informarse.—*to i. of,* dirigirse a.—**inquiry** [inkwáiri], *s.* pregunta, indagación, investigación, estudio.

inquisition [inkwizíšȯn], *s.* escudriñamiento, investigación; (I.) (igl.) Inquisición, Santo Oficio.—**inquisitive** [inkwízitiv], *a.* curioso, preguntón.——**inquisitiveness** [inkwízitivnis], *s.* curiosidad, manía de preguntar.

insane [inséin], *a.* loco, demente; de o para locos.—**insanity** [insǽniti], *s.* locura, insania, demencia.

inscribe [inskráib], *vt.* inscribir; grabar; dedicar; apuntar.—**inscription** [inskrípʃən], *s.* inscripción; rótulo; registro; dedicatoria.

inscrutable [inskrútəbl], *a.* inescrutable, insondable.

insect [insekt], *s.* insecto, bicho.— **—icide** [inséktisaid], *s.* insecticida.

insecure [insikiúr], *a.* inseguro.—**security** [insikiúriti], *s.* inseguridad, incertidumbre; riesgo.

insensibility [insensibíliti], *s.* insensibilidad.—**insensible** [insénsibl], *a.* insensible; imperceptible; impasible.

inseparable [insépərəbl], *a.* inseparable.

insert [insœrt], *s.* cosa insertada, intercalada, etc.—*vt.* [insœrt], insertar; introducir, encajar; intercalar.— **—ion** [insœrʃən], *s.* inserción; (cost.) entredós.

inshore [inʃór], *a.* cercano a la orilla. —*adv.* hacia la orilla o cerca de ella.

inside [insáid], *a.* interior, interno.—*s.* el interior; contenido; forro.—*pl.* (fam.) entrañas, interioridades.— *adv.* dentro, adentro, en el interior. —*i. out*, de dentro afuera; al revés.— *prep.* dentro de.— **—r** [insáidœ(r)], *s.* individuo bien informado o con información de primera mano.

insidious [insídiʌs], *a.* insidioso, solapado, capcioso.

insight [insait], *s.* discernimiento, perspicacia; comprensión; conocimiento, idea; penetración.

insignia [insígniə], *s. pl.* insignias.

insignificance [insignifikans], *s.* insignificancia.—**insignificant** [ʌnsignifikənt], *a.* insignificante.

insinuate [insínyueit], *vt.* insinuar, sugerir.—*to i. oneself*, insinuarse, introducirse, congraciarse.—*vi.* echar pullas o indirectas.—**insinuation** [insinyuéiʃən], *s.* insinuación; sugestión; indirecta, pulla.

insipid [insípid], *a.* insípido.

insist [insíst], *vi.* insistir; persistir; hacer hincapié.— **—ence** [-ɛns], *s.* insistencia, porfía.— **—ent** [-ɛnt], *a.* insistente, persistente; porfiado.

insolence [insolens], *s.* insolencia.— **insolent** [insolent], *a.* insolente.

insomnia [insómniə], *s.* insomnio.

inspect [inspékt], *vt.* inspeccionar, reconocer, registrar, revis(t)ar.— **—ion** [inspékʃən], *s.* inspección; reconocimiento, registro.— **—or** [inspéktɒ(r)], *s.* inspector, registrador, interventor, revisor.

inspiration [inspiréiʃən], *s.* inspiración; estro, numen.—**inspire** [inspáir], *vt.* inspirar; animar, alentar; autorizar

(por funcionario público); sugerir, insinuar.—*vi.* inspirar.

instability [instəbíliti], *s.* inestabilidad.

install [instól], *vt.* instalar, montar; colocar.— **—ation** [-éiʃən], *s.* instalación; montaje.— **—er** [-œ(r)], *s.* montador.—**instal(l)ment** [instólmɛnt], *s.* instalación; entrega; plazo. —*i. plan*, pago por cuotas o plazos.

instance [instəns], *s.* ejemplo; caso; instancia, ruego, solicitación; ocasión, lugar.—*for i.*, por ejemplo... *in the first i.*, desde el principio.—*vt.* poner por caso; ejemplificar; citar, mencionar.

instant [instənt], *a.* inminente, inmediato, perentorio; corriente, presente, actual.—*s.* instante, momento, (fam.) santiamén.— **—aneous** [-éiniʌs], *a.* instantáneo.

instead [instéd], *adv.* en lugar, en vez, en cambio (de); en lugar de eso, ello, él, etc.

instep [instep], *s.* empeine o garganta del pie; parte anterior de la pata trasera.

instigate [instigeit], *vt.* instigar, fomentar, incitar, provocar.—**instigation** [instigéiʃən], *s.* instigación.

instinct [instiŋkt], *s.* instinto.— **—ive** [instíŋktiv], *a.* instintivo.

institute [institjut], *vt.* instituir, fundar; iniciar.—*s.* instituto.—**institution** [institjúʃən], *s.* institución; comienzo, establecimiento.

instruct [instrákt], *vt.* instruir; dar instrucciones.— **—ion** [instrákʃən], *s.* instrucción; conocimiento, saber.— *pl.* instrucciones; órdenes; consigna.— **—ive** [-iv], *a.* instructivo, aleccionador.— **—or** [-ɒ(r)], *s.* instructor.

instrument [instrument], *s.* instrumento; agente.— **—al** [instruméntəl], *a.* instrumental; influyente, servicial; conducente.—*to be i.*, contribuir a.

insubordinate [insʌbórdinit], *a.* insubordinado, refractario.—**insubordination** [insʌbordinéiʃən], *s.* insubordinación.

insufficiency [insʌfíʃɛnsi], *s.* insuficiencia.—**insufficient** [insʌfíʃɛnt], *a.* insuficiente; incapaz, inepto.

insulate [ínsjuleit], *vt.* aislar.—**insulation** [insjuléiʃən], *s.* aislamiento.— **insulator** [insjuleitɒ(r)], *s.* aislador.

insult [insʌlt], *s.* insulto.—*vt.* [insʌlt], insultar.

insuperable [insjúpərəbl], *a.* insuperable.

insurance [inʃúrəns], *s.* aseguramiento, seguro; prima o premio del seguro. —*i. agent*, agente de seguros.—*i. company*, compañía de seguros.— *i. policy*, póliza de seguro.—**insure** [inʃúr], *vt.* (com.) asegurar; afianzar;

dar o tener seguridad de; lograr.—
vi. asegurarse.

insurgence [insœ́rdʒęns], *s.* insurrección, rebelión.—**insurgent** [insœ́r-
dʒęnt], *a.* y *s.* insurgente, insurrecto.

insurrection [insœrékʃọn], *s.* insurrección.

intact [intǽkt], *a.* intacto, íntegro,
entero.

intake [íntejk], *s.* entrada, recaudación.

integral [íntigrạl], *a.* íntegro; integrante, inherente; (mat.) entero
(número, función, etc.).—**integrity**
[intégriti], *s.* integridad, entereza.

intellect [íntelekt], *s.* intelecto; persona
o gente de talento.—**ual** [intelék-
chụạl], *s.* y *a.* intelectual.—**intelligence** [intéliḍʒęns], *s.* inteligencia;
información, noticia; correspondencia
mutua; policía secreta.—**intelligent**
[intéliḍʒęnt], *a.* inteligente.

intemperance [intémpœrạns], *s.* in-
temperancia; destemplanza.—**intem-
perate** [intémpœrit], *s.* destemplado;
intemperante; desmedido.

intend [inténd], *vt.* intentar, proponerse;
destinar; aplicar, determinar; querer
decir; tener por objeto.

intendancy [inténdạnsi], *s.* intendencia.
—**intendant** [inténdạnt], *s.* intendente, procurante.

intense [inténs], *a.* intenso; extremado,
sumo; esforzado.—**intensification** [in-
tensifikéjʃọn], *s.* intensificación.—
intensify [inténsifaj], *vti.* y *vii.* [7]
intensificar(se).—**intensity** [intén-
siti], *s.* intensidad.—**intensive** [in-
ténsiv], *a.* intenso, intensivo.

intent [intént], *a.* atento; asiduo;
decidido, resuelto a, empeñado en.
—*s.* intento, designio, intención,
propósito.—*to all intents and pur-
poses*, en realidad, en el fondo.
—**ion** [inténʃọn], *s.* intención; designio, fin, propósito deliberado;
(cir.) procedimiento de curación.—
ional [inténʃọnạl], *a.* intencional.

inter [intœ́r], *vti.* [1] enterrar, sepultar.

intercede [intœrsíd], *vi.* interceder.

intercept [intœrsépt], *vt.* interceptar;
atajar.— **ion** [intœrsépʃọn], *s.*
atajo.

intercession [intœrséʃọn], *s.* intercesión.

interchange [intœrchéjndʒ], *vt.* alternar; cambiar, trocar; permutar.—
vi. alternarse, trocarse.—*s.* [íntœr-
chejndʒ], intercambio; comercio, tráfico.

intercourse [íntœrkors], *s.* comercio,
tráfico; intercambio; correspondencia,
trato; coito, trato sexual.

interdict [intœrdi̯kt], **interdiction**
[intœrdíkʃọn], *s.* veto, veda, pro-

hibición; interdicción, interdicto,
entredicho.

interest [íntœrịst], *vt.* interesar.—*s.*
interés; provecho; simpatía; rédito;
participación en una empresa.—
the interests, las grandes empresas,
los intereses creados, los capitalistas.—
ed [-id], *a.* interesado.— **ing**
[-iŋ], *a.* interesante, atractivo.—*in
an i. condition*, en estado interesante,
encinta.

interfere [intœrfír], *vi.* inmiscuirse,
interponerse, meterse; intervenir;
impedir, estorbar; (fis.) interferir;
(vet.) tropezar un pie con otro (los
caballos),— **nce** [intœrfírẹns], *s.*
ingerencia, intromisión; obstáculo,
impedimento; (fis., rad.) interferencia.

interim [íntœrịm], *a.* interino, intermedio, interin.

interior [intíri̯o(r)], *a.* interior, interno.
—*s.* parte de adentro, interior.

interjection [intœrdʒékʃọn], *s.* inter-
jección; interposición.

interlace [intœrléjs], *vt.* entrelazar.

interlock [intœrlák], *vt.* y *vi.* trabar,
engranar; unirse, entrelazarse; co-
rrar.—*s.* traba, trabazón; (cine)
sincronización; sincronizador.

interlude [íntœrljud], *s.* intervalo;
entreacto, intermedio, entremés;
(mus.) interludio.

intermediary [intœrmídjeri], *a.* y *s.*
intermediario.—**intermediate** [intœr-
mídjit], *a.* medianero, intermedio.—
vi. [intœrmídjejt], mediar, intervenir,
intermediar.

interminable [intœrmi̯nạbl], *a.* interminable.

intermingle [intœrmi̯ŋgl], *vt.* entremezclar.—*vi.* mezclarse.

intermission [intœrmi̯ʃọn], *s.* interrupción, tregua; intermitencia; intermedio, entreacto.

intermittent [intœrmi̯tẹnt], *a.* intermitente.

intermix [intœrmi̯ks], *vt.* entremezclar,
entreverar, interpolar.—*vi.* entremez-
clarse, compenetrarse.

intern [intœ́rn], *vt.* encerrar, poner a
buen recaudo; internar; meter en
un campo de concentración.—*s.*
[íntœrn], interno, practicante de
hospital.— **al** [intœ́rnạl], *a.* interno,
interior; doméstico; íntimo.

international [intœrnǽʃọnạl], *a.* internacional.— **ize** [-ajz], *vt.* interna-
cionalizar.

interne [íntœrn], *s.* = INTERN.

interposal [intœrpóụzạl], *s.* interposición, mediación, intervención.—
interpose [intœrpóụz], *vt.* interponer;
(cine) reemplazar gradualmente una

figura por otra, o cambiar la una en la otra.—*vi.* interponerse.

interpret [intœrprɪt], *vt.* interpretar, descifrar; representar, ilustrar.— **—ation** [-éjŝǫn], *s.* interpretación.— **—er** [-œ(r)], *s.* intérprete, traductor.

interrogate [intérǫgeit], *vt.* interrogar, preguntar.—*vi.* hacer preguntas.— **interrogation** [interǫgéjŝǫn], *s.* interrogatorio, pesquisa.—*i. point*, signo de interrogación (?), interrogante. **—interrogative** [intérágǫtiv], *a.* interrogative.—*s.* palabra interrogativa.

interrupt [intęrápt], *vt.* interrumpir.— **—ion** [intęrápŝǫn], *s.* interrupción.— **—or** [-ǫ(r)], *s.* interruptor, disyuntor.

intersect [intęrsékt], *vt.* cortar.—*vi.* (geom.) cortarse.— **—ion** [intęrsékŝǫn], *s.* intersección; cruce, bocacalle.

intertwine [intœrtwáin], **intertwist** [intœrtwíst], *vt.* entretejer, entrelazar.

interval [íntœrval], *s.* intervalo; blanco, claro, hueco; (mus.) intervalo.

intervene [intœrvín], *vi.* intervenir; interponerse; sobrevenir.—**intervention** [intœrvénŝǫn], *s.* intervención; mediación; interposición.

interview [íntœrvju], *s.* entrevista.—*vt.* entrevistar(se con).— **—er** [-œ(r)], *s.* entrevistador; reportero que hace entrevistas.

intestine [intéstɪn], *a.* interior, intestino, doméstico; interno.—*s.* (anat.) intestino, tripa.

intimacy [íntɪmǫsɪ], *s.* intimidad, confianza.—**intimate** [íntɪmɪt], *a.* íntimo; familiar; profundo (conocimiento).—*s.* amigo íntimo, confidente.—*vt.* [íntɪmeit], insinuar, intimar.—**intimation** [intɪméjŝǫn], *s.* insinuación, indirecta, pulla; indicio.

into [íntu], *prep.* en, dentro, adentro. hacia el interior.—*i. the bargain*, por añadidura.

intolerable [intálęrǫbl], *a.* intolerable, insufrible.—**intolerance** [intálęrǫns], *s.* intolerancia.—**intolerant** [intálęrǫnt], *a.* intolerante.

intonation [intonéjŝǫn], *s.* entonación.

intoxicate [intáksɪkeit], *vt.* embriagar. **—intoxication** [intaksɪkéjŝǫn], *s.* embriaguez, beodez; (med.) intoxicación, envenenamiento.

intransitive [intrǽnsɪtiv], *a.* (gram.) intransitivo.

intrepid [intrépɪd], *a.* intrépido, impávido.

intricate [íntrɪkɪt], *a.* intrincado, enredado.

intrigue [intríg], *s.* intriga; galanteo, lío amoroso.—*vi.* intrigar; tener intrigas amorosas.— **—r** [intrígœ(r)], *s.* intrigante.

introduce [introdiús], *vt.* introducir; implantar; presentar (una persona a otra); poner en uso.—*to i. a bill*, presentar un proyecto de ley,— **introduction** [introdÁkŝǫn], *s.* introducción; prefacio; implantación; presentación.

intrude [intrúd], *vi.* intrusarse, entremeterse, inmiscuirse.—*vt.* meter, forzar.— **—r** [intrúdœ(r)], *s.* intruso, entremetido.—**intrusion** [intrúʒǫn], *s.* intrusión, entremetimiento.—**intrusive** [intrúsiv], *a.* intruso; (geol.) de intrusión; intrusivo.

intrust [intrÁst], *vt.* = ENTRUST.

intuition [intjuíŝǫn], *s.* intuición.— **intuitive** [intjúitiv], *a.* intuitivo.

inundate [ínᴧndeit], *vt.* inundar, anegar.

invade [invéid], *vt.* invadir.— **—r** [invéidœ(r)], *s.* invasor.

invalid [invǽlid], *a.* inválido, nulo.— *a.* y *s.* [ínvalid], inválido, lisiado.— *vt.* lisiar, incapacitar.— **—ate** [invélideit], *vt.* invalidar, anular.

invaluable [invǽlyųabl], *a.* inestimable, inapreciable.

invariable [invériabl], *a.* invariable.

invasion [invéiʒǫn], *s.* invasión.

invective [invéktiv], *s.* invectiva, vituperio.—*a.* ultrajante, injurioso.

invent [invént], *vt.* inventar; idear.— **—ion** [invénŝǫn], *s.* invención, invento.— **—ive** [-iv], *a.* inventivo.— **—or** [-ǫ(r)], *s.* inventor.

inventory [ínventǫri], *s.* inventario.— *vti.* [7] inventariar.

inverse [invœrs], *a.* inverso, invertido. **—invert** [invœrt], *vt.* invertir; volver al revés; trastocar; trasponer.— *inverted commas*, comillas.

invest [invést], *vt.* (com.) invertir, emplear o imponer dinero; (re)vestir; investir, conferir; (mil.) sitiar, cercar. **—investigate** [invéstigeit], *vt.* investigar. **—investigation** [investigéjŝǫn], *s.* investigación.—**investigator** [invéstigeitǫ(r)], *s.* investigador.

investment [invéstment], *s.* (com.) inversión; (mil.) sitio, cerco; investidura; cubierta; envoltura.—**investor** [invéstǫ(r)], *s.* (com.) inversionista.

inveterate [invétęrit], *a.* inveterado, empedernido.

invigorate [invígǫreit], *vt.* vigorizar, fortificar.

invincible [invínsibl], *a.* invencible.

invisibility [invɪzɪbílɪti], *s.* invisibilidad. **—invisible** [invízibl], *a.* invisible.

invitation [invɪtéjŝǫn], *s.* invitación, convite.—**invite** [inváit], *vt.* convidar, invitar; atraer; provocar, tentar; instar.—**inviting** [inváitiŋ], *a.* atractivo; incitante.

invocation [invokéjŝǫn], *s.* invocación; (for.) mandamiento.

invoice [ínvois], *s.* (com.) factura.—*vt.* facturar.

invoke [invóuk], *vt.* invocar; (for.) expedir suplicatorio, exhorto o mandamiento.

involuntary [inválʌnteri], *a.* involuntario.

involve [inválv], *vt.* envolver, enrollar; implicar; entrañar, comprender; complicar, enredar; involucrar; (mat.) elevar a una potencia, hallar una potencia de.

inward(s) [ínw̃rd(z)], *adv.* hacia adentro, hacia lo interior; adentro. —**inward**, *a.* interior, interno.—*s.* el interior.—*pl.* entrañas.

iodin(e) [áiodain], *s.* yodo o iodo.

iota [aióutʌ], *s.* jota, punto, tilde.

irascible [airǽsibl], *a.* irascible.

irate [áireit], *a.* airado, iracundo.—**ire** [air], *s.* ira, furia.

iridescent [iridésent], *a.* iridiscente, tornasolado.

iris [áiris], *s.* (anat.) iris; arco iris; flor de lis.

Irish [áiriș], *a.* y *s.* irlandés.—*s.* lengua irlandesa.

irk [œrk], *vt.* fastidiar, molestar.— **some** [œrksʌm], *a.* fastidioso, enfadoso.

iron [áiœrn], *s.* hierro; plancha (de planchar); herramienta.—*a.* férreo, de hierro; relativo al hierro.—*vt.* planchar; aherrojar.

ironic(al) [airánik(ʌl)], *a.* irónico.

ironing [áiœrniŋ], *s.* planchado, acción de planchar; ropa por planchar.—*a.* de planchar.

irony [áironi], *s.* ironía.

irradiate [iréidieit], *vt.* irradiar; inspirar; esparcir.—*vi.* lucir, brillar.—**irradiation** [ireidiéișon], *s.* irradiación.

irrational [irǽșonʌl], *a.* irracional; absurdo, ilógico; (álg.) irracional.

irregular [irégyʌlʌ(r)], *a.* irregular.— **ity** [iregyʌlériti], *s.* irregularidad.

irrelevancy [irélevʌnsi], *s.* inaplicabilidad.—**irrelevant** [irélevʌnt], *a.* inaplicable, impertinente.

irreligious [irilídżʌs], *a.* irreligioso.

irresponsible [irispánsibl], *a.* irresponsable.

irreverence [iréverens], *s;* irreverencia. —**irreverent** [iréverent], *a.* irreverente.

irrevocable [irévokʌbl], *a.* irrevocable; inapelable.

irrigate [írigeit], *vt.* regar.—**irrigation** [irigéișon], *s.* riego, irrigación.

irritable [íritʌbl], *a.* irritable.— **ness** [-nis], *s.* irritabilidad.—**irritate** [íriteit], *vt.* irritar, exacerbar.—**irritation** [iritéișon], *s.* irritación.

island [áilʌnd], *s.* isla, ínsula.— **er** [-œ(r)], *s.* isleño.—**isle** [ail], *s.* isla,

ínsula.—**islet** [áilit], *s.* isleta, cayo.

isolate [áisoleit], *vt.* aislar, apartar; incomunicar.—**isolation** [aisoléișon], *s.* aislamiento; incomunicación.— **isolationism** [aisoléișonizm], *s.* aislacionismo.

Israeli [izréili], *a.* y *s.* israelita.— **te** [ízrielait], *s.* israelita.

issue [íșu], *s.* (impr.) edición, tirada, impresión; número (de una revista, etc.); prole; (com.) emisión de valores; (for.) beneficios, rentas; salida, egreso; (med.) flujo; fuente, nacimiento; evento, consecuencia; decisión; tema de discusión.—*vt.* echar, arrojar; dar; dictar, expedir; (com.) librar, emitir; dar a luz, publicar.—*vi.* salir, fluir, provenir; nacer; resultar; resolverse.

isthmus [ísmas], *s.* istmo.

it [it], *pron. neutro* él, ella, eso, ello, lo, la, le.—*s. is late*, es tarde.—*i. rains*, llueve.—*what time is i.?* ¿qué hora es?

Italian [itélyʌn], *a.* y *s.* italiano.—*s.* lengua italiana.—**italic** [itélik], *a.* (impr.) bastardilla, itálica (letra); (I.) itálico, italiano.—**italicize** [itélisaiz], *vt.* poner en letra itálica o bastardilla; subrayar, dar énfasis.—**italics** [itéliks], *s. pl.* (impr.) letra itálica, bastardilla o cursiva.

itch [ich], *s.* comezón, picazón; prurito. —*vi.* picar, sentir picazón o comezón; antojarse; desear vehementemente.— **y** [íchi], *a.* sarnoso; picante.

item [áitem], *adv.* ítem; otrosí, aun más.—*s.* partida; artículo; párrafo; detalle; renglón.—**ize** [-aiz], *vt.* detallar, especificar, particularizar, pormenorizar.

itinerary [aitínereri], *s.* itinerario, ruta; relación de un viaje; guía de viajeros. —*a.* itinerario, hecho en viaje.

its [its], *a. posesivo neutro* su, sus (de él, de ella, de ello).— **elf** [itsélf], *pron.* (él) mismo, (ella) misma; sí mismo, sí misma; sí; se.—*it moves of i.*, eso se mueve por sí mismo.

ivory [áivori], *s.* marfil.—*pl.* cosas hechas de marfil.—*a.* ebúrneo.

ivy [áivi], *s.* hiedra o yedra; cazuz.

J

jab [dżæb], *vti.* [1] pinchar, punzar.—*s.* punzada, pinchazo.

jack [dżæk], *s.* macho del burro y otros animales; (mec.) gato, cric; sota de la baraja; (mar.) bandera de proa.—*j.- of-all-trades*, aprendiz de todo y oficial de nada.—*j.-o'-lantern*, fuego fatuo; linterna hecha de una calabaza, con cara grotesca.—*j. plane*, (carp.) garlopa.—*j.-pot*, premio gordo, premio

mayor.—*j. rabbit,* liebre americana.—
vt. alzar un objeto con el gato.

jackal [dʒǽkal], *s.* chacal.

jackass [dʒǽkæs], *s.* asno, borrico,
burro; (fig.) estúpido, necio.

jackdaw [dʒǽkdɔ], *s.* grajo.

jacket [dʒǽkịt], *s.* chaqueta, chamarra;
envoltura; forro; sobrecubierta.

jackknife [dʒǽknajf], *s.* navaja de
bolsillo.

jade [dʒejd], *s.* (min.) jade; rocín,
jamelgo; mujerzuela, sota.—*vt.* cansar.—*vi.* desalentarse.

jagged [dʒǽgịd], *a.* mellado, dentado,
serrado.

jail [dʒejl], *s.* cárcel.—*vt.* encarcelar.—
—er [dʒéjlœ(r)], *s.* carcelero.

jam [dʒæm], *s.* compota, conserva;
agolpamiento; atascamiento; atasca-
dero; situación peliaguda.—*vti.* [1]
apiñar; apretar, apachurrar, estrujar;
atorar; (rad.) causar interferencia en.
—*vii.* atorarse, trabarse, agolparse.

Jamaican [dʒaméjkan], *a.* y *s.* jamai-
quino.

jamb [dʒæm], *s.* montante, batiente (de
puerta, etc.).

jammed [dʒǽmd], *a.* atorado, trabado;
de bote en bote, repleto.

janitor [dʒǽnịtǫ(r)], *s.* portero; conserje.

January [dʒǽnyuęrị], *s.* enero.

Jap [dʒæp], (fam.), **Japanese** [dʒæpa-
níz], *a.* y *s.* japonés, nipón.

jar [dʒar], *vti.* [1] sacudir, agitar, hacer
vibrar o trepidar.—*vii.* chirriar, hacer
ruido desagradable; vibrar, trepidar.
—*s.* jarro o jarra; pote, tarro; vibración; sacudida; chirrido.

jargon [dʒárgǫn], *s.* jerga, jerigonza;
caló.

jasmin(e) [dʒǽsmịn], *s.* jazmín.

jasper [dʒǽspœ(r)], *s.* (min.) jaspe.

jaundice [dʒɔ́ndịs], *s.* ictericia; predisposición.—*vt.* causar ictericia; predisponer.— —d [-t], *a.* ictérico, cetrino.

jaunt [dʒɔnt], *vi.* corretear, ir y venir.—
s. excursión, caminata.— —iness
[dʒɔ́ntịnịs], *s.* ligereza, garbo.— —y
[-ị], *a.* airoso, garboso.

Javanese [dʒávanịs], *a.* y *s.* javanés.

javelin [dʒǽvlịn], *s.* jabalina, venablo.

jaw [dʒɔ], *s.* quijada, mandíbula; (mec.)
mordaza.—*a.* de las quijadas; de
mordaza.— —bone [dʒɔ́bọụn], *s.*
maxilar, quijada, mandíbula (esp. la
inferior).

jay [dʒej], *s.* (fam.) rústico; simplón;
(orn.) grajo.— —walker [dʒéjwok-
œ(r)], *s.* (fam.) peatón descuidado o
imprudente.

jazz [dʒæz], *s.* música popular sincopada.—*vt.* (frecuentemente con up)
animar, alegrar, tocar o bailar el jazz.
— —y [dʒǽzị], *a.* chillón; de última
moda.

jealous [dʒɛ́lʌs], *a.* celoso, envidioso.—
to be j., tener celos.—*to become j.,*
encelarse, ponerse celoso.— —y [-ị], *s.*
celos; envidia.

jean [dʒin], *s.* (tej.) sarga, mezclilla.—
pl. ropa, esp. pantalones, hecha de
esta tela.

jeer [dʒịr], *vt.* y *vi.* mofar, befar, escarnecer, burlarse.—*s.* befa, mofa, burla,
escarnio, choteo.

jelly [dʒɛ́lị], *s.* jalea; gelatina.—*vti.*
y *vii.* [7] convertir(se) en jalea o
gelatina.—**jellyfish** [dʒɛ́lịfịš], *s.*
medusa, aguamala.

jeopardize [dʒɛ́pạrdajz], *vt.* arriesgar,
exponer.—**jeopardy** [dʒɛ́pạrdị], *s.*
riesgo, peligro.

jerk [dʒœrk], *s.* tirón, sacudida;
espasmo muscular; (fam.) estúpido,
idiota.—*vt.* dar un tirón; sacudir;
traquetear; hacer tasajo.—*vi.* moverse a tirones.—*jerked beef,* tasajo.—
—y [dʒœ́rkị], *a.* espasmódico; (fam.)
estúpido, atontado.

jersey [dʒœ́rzị], *s.* tejido de punto.

jest [dʒɛst], *vi.* bromear, chancearse.—
s. chanza, broma, guasa.— —er
[dʒɛ́stœ(r)], *s.* bufón; burlón, guasón.

Jesuit [dʒɛ́žụịt], *s.* jesuita.

jet [dʒɛt], *s.* chorro; surtidor; (min.)
azabache.—*j. plane,* avión de chorro
o de retropropulsión.—*j. propulsion
engine,* motor de retropropulsión o de
chorro.—*vii.* [1] salir en chorro.

jetty [dʒɛ́tị], *s.* malecón, rompeolas;
muelle, espolón.—*a.* de azabache;
negro.

Jew [dʒu], *s.* judío, israelita.

jewel [dʒúẹl], *s.* joya, alhaja; gema,
piedra preciosa.—*j. box,* joyero.—*vti.*
[2] enjoyar; adornar con piedras
preciosas.

Jewish [dʒúịš], *a.* judaico, judío.

jiffy [dʒífị], *s.* (fam.) instante, peri-
quete.—*in a j.,* en un santiamén.

jig [dʒig], *s.* jiga (música y danza).—*j.
saw,* sierra de vaivén o de marquetería.—*vti.* [1] cantar o tocar una
jiga; sacudir de abajo hacia arriba.—
vii. bailar una jiga.

jilt [dʒịlt], *vt.* despedir o dar calabazas;
(fam.) plantar, dejar plantado.—*vi.*
coquetear.

jingle [dʒíŋgl], *vt.* y *vi.* sonar o resonar.
—*s.* retintín, sonido metálico; (rad.,
T.V., etc.) anuncio musical.—*j. bell,*
cascabel.

job [dʒab], *s.* tarea, faena; empleo,
ocupación, trabajo; empresa.—*by
the j.,* a destajo.— —ber [dʒábœ(r)], *s.*
corredor o comisionista al por mayor.

jockey [dʒákị], *s.* jinete (en las carreras
de caballos).—*vt.* y *vi.* trampear,
engañar; maniobrar hábilmente para
sacar alguna ventaja.

jocose [dӡokóᴜs], *a.* **jocoso.**

join [dӡoin], *vt.* **juntar, unir, ensamblar, acoplar; asociar; afiliarse o unirse a.—** *to j. battle,* **librar batalla.—to j. company, incorporarse.—to j. the colors,** (fam.) **alistarse, enrolarse.—vi. asociarse, unirse.— —t** [-t], *s.* **juntura, junta, unión, empalme, ensambladura, acopladura; conexión, enganche; coyuntura, articulación; nudillo; gozne, bisagra; charnela; cuarto de un animal; encuentro de un ave.— out of j.,** **dislocado, descoyuntado.—a. unido, agrupado, colectivo; copartícipe; asociado; mixto; conjunto.— j. property,** **propiedad mancomunada. —j. stock company,** **sociedad anónima.**

joke [dӡoᴜk], *s.* **broma, burla, chanza, chiste, chuscada.—in j.,** **en chanza, de broma.—vi. bromear, chancear- (se), gastar bromas.— —r** [dӡóᴜk- œ(r)], *s.* **burlón, bromista, guasón;** (naipes) **comodín; equívoco o falla de ley o contrato a cuyo amparo pueden ser burlados legalmente.—jokingly** [dӡóᴜkiŋli], *adv.* **por burla, en chanza.**

jolly [dӡáli], *a.* **alegre, festivo, jovial; jaranero; divertido;** (fam.) **excelente, magnífico.—adv.** (fam.) **muy, sumamente.—vt. y vii.** [7] (fam.) **engatusar, lisonjear; seguir el humor (a).**

jolt [dӡoᴜlt], *vt.* **y vi. traquetear, sacudir, dar sacudidas.—s. sacudida, traqueteo.**

jonquil [dӡáŋkwil], *s.* (bot.) **junquillo.**

jostle [dӡásl], *vt.* **y vi. empujar, empellar, codear.—s. empellón, empujón.**

jot [dӡat], *s.* **pizca, jota (cosa mínima). —I don't care a j.** (about), **me importa un bledo.—vti.** [1] (con **down**) **tomar notas, apuntar.**

journal [dӡérnal], *s.* **diario, periódico diario; revista (publicación); acta; diario (apuntes personales);** (com.) **diario (libro).— —ism** [-izm], *s.* **periodismo, diarismo, la prensa.— —ist** [-ist], *s.* **periodista.— —istic** [-istik], *a.* **periodístico.— —ize** [-aiz], *vt.* (com.) **pasar al diario.—vi. apuntar en un diario.**

journey [dӡérni], *s.* **jornada; viaje por tierra; camino, tránsito, pasaje.—vi. viajar, recorrer un trayecto.**

joust [dӡast, dӡaᴜst], *s.* **justa, torneo.— vi. justar.**

jovial [dӡóᴜvial], *a.* **jovial.**

jowl [dӡaᴜl], *s.* **carrillo; quijada; papada.**

joy [dӡoi], *s.* **alegría, júbilo, regocijo; felicidad.— —ful** [dӡóiful], *a.* **alegre, gozoso; placentero.— —ous** [-ᴀs], *a.* **alegre, gozoso.**

jubilant [dӡúbilant], *a.* **jubiloso, alborozado, regocijado, alegre.—jubilee** [dӡúbili], *s.* **jubileo.**

Judaic(al) [dӡᴜdéiik(al)], *a.* **judaico.— Judaism** [dӡúdiizm], *s.* **judaísmo.**

judge [dӡadӡ], *s.* **juez; magistrado; perito.—vt. juzgar; sentenciar, fallar. —vi. juzgar.—judgment** [dӡádӡment], *s.* **juicio, criterio, discernimiento; sentir, opinión, dictamen;** (for.) **fallo; sentencia; ejecutoria.**

judicial [dӡᴜdíʃal], *a.* **judicial.—judiciary** [dӡᴜdíʃieri], *a.* **judiciario; judicial.—s. administración de justicia; judicatura; magistratura; poder judicial.—judicious** [dӡᴜdíʃᴀs], *a.* **juicioso, cuerdo, sensato, sesudo, atinado.**

jug [dӡag], *s.* **botijo; jarro, cacharro, cántaro, porrón; reclamo del ruiseñor;** (fam.) **chirona (cárcel).**

juggle [dӡágl], *vi.* **hacer juegos de manos, escamotear; engañar, hacer trampas.—s. juego de manos, escamoteo; impostura, engaño.— —r** [dӡáglœ(r)], *s.* **prestidigitador; malabarista; impostor.— —ry** [dӡáglœri], *s.* **prestidigitación; juegos malabares; engaño, trampa.**

Jugoslav [yúgosláv], *s.* **= YUGOSLAV. —Jugoslavian** [yúgoslávian], **Jugoslavic** [yúgoslávik], *a.* **= YUGOSLAVIAN, YUGOSLAVIC.**

jugular [dӡágyᴜglᴀ(r)], *a.* **and s. yugular.**

juice [dӡus], *s.* **zumo; jugo, substancia. —juiciness** [dӡúsinis], *s.* **jugosidad, suculencia.—juicy** [dӡúsi], *a.* **jugoso, suculento.**

July [dӡᴜlái], *s.* **julio.**

jumble [dӡámbl], *vt.* **arrebujar,** (fam.) **emburujar; confundir.—vi. mezclarse, revolverse, confundirse.—s. mezcla, revoltillo, embrollo, mezcolanza; bollito delgado y dulce.**

jumbo [dӡámbou], *s.* (fam.) **coloso, cosa o animal enorme.—a. colosal, gigantesco.**

jump [dӡamp], *vt.* **saltar por encima de o al otro lado de; hacer saltar; saltarse, omitir; comer un peón (en el juego de damas).—to j. the track,** **descarrilar.—vi. saltar, brincar; cabriolar; subir rápidamente (precios, etc.); (con with) convenir, concordar.—to j. at,** **apresurarse a aprovechar.—to j. on,** **arremeter;** (fam.) **poner como nuevo.—to j. over,** **saltar por encima de.—to j. to a conclusion,** **sacar precipitadamente una conclusión.—s. salto, cabriola, brinco;** (dep.) **pista de saltos** (esquí); (fam.) **ventaja.—on the j.,** **de un salto, al vuelo.—to get o have the j. on,** **tomar la delantera a, adelantársele a uno.— —er** [dӡámp- œ(r)], *s.* **saltador; blusa de obrero o de mujer; zamarra de pieles; narria, rastra.— —y** [-i], *a.* **nervioso o excitable en exceso.**

junction [dʒʎŋkʂǫn], *s.* conexión; junta; unión; acopladura; bifurcación; entronque, empalme, confluencia de vías.—**juncture** [dʒʎŋkchᴜ(r)], *s.* junta, juntura; coyuntura, articulación; ocasión, oportunidad; trance, momento o circunstancia críticos; exigencia.

June [dʒun], *s.* junio.

jungle [dʒʎŋgl], *s.* jungla, selva, bosque virgen, (Am.) manigua; maraña, matorral.

junior [dʒúnyǫ(r)], *s.* joven; estudiante de tercer año (en escuela superior, colegio o universidad).—*a.* más joven; hijo (Jr.); menor; más nuevo o reciente.—*j. college*, colegio para los dos primeros años universitarios.—*j. high school*, escuela secundaria inferior (intermedia entre la elemental y la secundaria).—*j. partner*, socio menos antiguo o socio menor.

junk [dʒʎŋk], *s.* (mar.) junco; chicote; hierro viejo, chatarra; cecina; (fam.) basura, hojarasca.—*vt.* (fam.) descartar por inservible.

juridic(al) [dʒᴜrídik(ᵊl)], *a.* jurídico, judicial.—**jurisdiction** [dʒᴜrisdíkʂǫn], *s.* jurisdicción; potestad; fuero; competencia.—**jurisprudence** [dʒᴜrisprúdᵊns], *s.* jurisprudencia.—**jurist** [dʒúrist], *s.* jurista, jurisconsulto.—**juristic** [dʒᴜrístik], *a.* jurídico.—**juror** [dʒúrǫ(r)], *s.* (for.) jurado (individuo).—**jury** [dʒúri], *s.* (for.) jurado (cuerpo o institución).

just [dʒʎst], *a.* justo, honrado, recto, justiciero; justificado; legal; legítimo; exacto, cabal.—*adv.* justamente, exactamente; casi; sólo, no más que; apenas; simplemente; hace un momento.—*j. about*, poco más o menos; o poco menos.—*j. as*, al momento que; cuando; no bien; lo mismo que, semejante a.—*j. beyond*, un poco más allá.—*j. by*, al lado, al canto, aquí cerca.—*j. now*, ahora mismo, hace poco.—*j. so*, ni más ni menos.—*to have j. time enough*, tener el tiempo preciso.—*to have j. arrived*, acabar de llegar.—**ice** [dʒʎstis], *s.* justicia; razón, derecho; (for.) juez; magistrado.—**ifiable** [-ifaiᵊbl], *a.* justificable.—**ification** [-ifikéiʂǫn], *s.* justificación; descargo, defensa; razón de ser.—**justify** [-ifai], *vti.* [7] justificar.

jut [dʒʎt], *vii.* [1] sobresalir, resaltar; combarse; proyectar.—*s.* salidizo, proyección.

jute [dʒut], *s.* yute, cáñamo de Indias.

juvenile [dʒúvᵊnil], *a.* juvenil, joven.—*s.* mocito, joven; (teat.) galancete.

juxtapose [dʒʎkstᵊpóus], *vt.* yuxta- poner.—**juxtaposition** [dʒʎkstᵊpouzíʂǫn], *s.* yuxtaposición.

K

kaleidoscope [kᵊláidoskoup], *s.* calidoscopio.

kangaroo [kæŋgarú], *s.* canguro.

karat [kǽrᵊt], *s.* (joy.) quilate.

keel [kil], *s.* quilla.—*vt.* volcar una embarcación poniéndola quilla arriba; volcar.—*vi.* (naut.) dar de quilla; volcarse.—*to k. over*, (fam.) volcarse, zozobrar; desplomarse; desmayarse.

keen [kin], *a.* afilado; aguzado; agudo; sutil; perspicaz; ansioso; mordaz.—**ness** [kínnis], *s.* agudeza; sutileza, perspicacia; anhelo.

keep [kip], *vti.* [10] conservar; quedarse con; guardar; tener (criados, secretario, un perro); llevar (cuentas, libros); cumplir (la palabra, una promesa); detener, mantener.—*to k. an eye on*, vigilar.—*to k. back*, detener; ocultar; impedir.—*to k. down*, sujetar.—*to k. from*, mantener lejos de; impedir (cambiando el giro).—*to k. in*, mantener dentro; no dejar salir.—*to k. in mind*, recordar; tener en cuenta.—*to k. informed (of)*, tener al corriente o al tanto (de).—*to k. on*, mantener; continuar.—*to k. one's distance*, mantenerse dentro de propios límites, no tomarse libertades.—*to k. one's hands off*, no tocar, no meterse en.—*to k. one's temper*, contenerse; obrar con calma.—*to k. one's word*, cumplir su palabra, tener palabra.—*to k. out*, no dejar entrar; excluir.—*to k. up*, mantener, conservar.—*vii.* mantenerse, sostenerse; continuar; permanecer.—*to k. along*, continuar, proseguir.—*to k. at home*, quedarse en casa.—*to k. away*, mantenerse apartado, no acercarse.—*to k. from*, abstenerse de; no meterse en.—*to k. in*, permanecer dentro; estarse en casa.—*to k. off*, no entrar a; no tocar; mantenerse fuera o lejos de.—*to k. on*, seguir, proseguir.—*to k. out of*, no meterse en, evitar.—*to k. out of the way*, estarse o hacerse a un lado.—*to k. up*, mantenerse firme; persistir; no cejar.—*s.* manutención, subsistencia.—*for keeps*, para siempre; para guardar, para quedarse con ello.—**er** [kípœ(r)], *s.* guarda, guardián, custodio; carcelero.—**ing** [-iŋ], *s.* custodia, mantenimiento; cuidado, preservación.—*in k. with*, en armonía con, al mismo tenor que.—**sake** [-seik], *s.* regalo, recuerdo.

keg [kɛg], *s.* cuñete, barrilito, pipote.

kennel [kénᵊl], *s.* perrera.

kept [kept], *pret.* y *pp.* de TO KEEP.

kerchief [kérchif], *s.* pañuelo.

kernel [kérnel], *s.* grano de cereal; médula, núcleo.

kerosene [kérosin], *s.* petróleo destilado, querosén, (Am.) kerosina.

kettle [kétl], *s.* caldera, marmita, olla.——**drum** [-dram], *s.* (mús.) timbal, atabal.

key [ki], *s.* llave; clave; fundamento; tono (de la voz); (mec.) llave; (elec.) conmutador; tecla (del piano, de máquina de escribir, etc.); (mar.) cayo, isleta.—*in k.*, templado, de acuerdo, en armonía.—*k. ring*, llavero.—*pass k.*, llave maestra.—*a.* principal; fundamental; estratégico.—*vt.* poner llaves; afinar.——**board** [kíbord], *s.* teclado.——**hole** [-houl], *s.* ojo de la cerradura.——**note** [-nout], *s.* (mus.) nota tónica; principio fundamental, piedra angular.——**stone** [-stoun], *s.* clave, llave de arco.

khaki [kéki], *s.* kaki, caqui (tela y color).

kibitzer [kíbitsœ(r)], *s.* (fam.) mirón, espectador molesto en los juegos de naipes; entremetido.

kick [kik], *vt.* acocear, dar patadas a.—*to k. the bucket*, (fam.) estirar la pata, irse para el otro mundo.—*vi.* cocear, patear, dar o tirar coces; oponerse; quejarse.—*s.* patada, coz; puntapié; oposición; queja; estímulo, aliento.

kid [kid], *s.* cabrito, chivato; cabritilla (piel); (fam.) niño; muchachito; chico, chica.—*vti. y vii.* [1] (fam.) embromar, tomar el pelo; bromear.

kidnap [kídnæp], *vti.* [2] secuestrar, raptar, (Am.) plagiar.——(p)er [-œ(r)], *s.* secuestrador, raptor, (Am.) plagiario.——(p)ing [-iŋ], *s.* secuestro, rapto, (Am.) plagio.

kidney [kídni], *s.* riñón.—*k. bean*, judía, alubia, habichuela.

kill [kil], *vt.* matar; destruir; amortiguar; suprimir.—*s.* acción de matar; (caza) pieza muerta.—*k.-joy*, aguafiestas.——er [kílœ(r)], *s.* matador, homicida; (fam.) matón.——ing [-iŋ], *a.* matador, destructivo; irresistible.—*s.* acto de matar, matanza.

kiln [kil], *s.* horno, estufa; horno de cerámica.

kilogram [kílougræm], *s.* kilo(gramo). Ver Tabla.—**kilometer** [kílomitœ(r)], *s.* kilómetro.—**kilowatt** [kílowat], *s.* kilovatio.

kimono [kimóunou], *s.* quimono, bata.

kin [kin], *s.* parentesco; parentela, familia.—*the next of k.*, los parientes (más) próximos.—*a.* pariente, allegado.

dial saludo; sentimientos de consideración.—*s.* género, clase, casta, índole, calidad.—*nothing of the k.*, nada de eso; no hay tal.

kindergarten [kíndœrgartin], *s.* escuela de párvulos, jardín de la infancia.

kindle [kíndl], *vt.* encender; inflamar, enardecer.—*vi.* prender; inflamarse.—**kindling** [kíndliŋ], *s.* inflamación; encendimiento.—*k. wood*, leña menuda.

kindly [káindli], *adv.* amable o bondadosamente; cordialmente.—*tell me k.*, tenga la amabilidad de decirme.—*a.* bondadoso, benévolo; favorable.—**kindness** [káindnis], *s.* bondad, benevolencia, amabilidad, atención, favor.

kindred [kíndrid], *s.* parentesco, consanguinidad; parentela.—*a.* emparentado, deudo, consanguíneo, afín; congénere.

king [kiŋ], *s.* rey; rey (en el ajedrez); dama (en el juego de damas).——**dom** [kíŋdom], *s.* reino.——**ly** [-li], *a.* real, regio; majestuoso.—*adv.* regiamente, majestuosamente.——**ship** [-šip], *s.* majestad; monarquía; reinado.

kinky [kíŋki], *a.* ensortijado, crespo; (fam.) chiflado.

kinsfolk [kínzfouk], *s.* parentela.—**kinship** [kínšip], *s.* parentesco.—**kinsman** [kínzmən], *s.* pariente, deudo.—**kinswoman** [kínzwumən], *s.* parienta.

kiosk [kiásk], *s.* kiosco o quiosco.

kiss [kis], *vt.* besar.—*to k. the rod*, someterse a un castigo.—*s.* beso, ósculo.

kit [kit], *s.* tineta; cubo; equipo, avíos, juego o caja de herramientas, medicinas, piezas componentes de un mecanismo, etc.; gatito.—*soldier's k.*, mochila.

kitchen [kíchen], *s.* cocina.—*k. boy*, pinche.—*k. garden*, huerta.—*k. range* o *stove*, cocina económica.——**ette** [-ét], *s.* cocina reducida o pequeña.——**ware** [-wer], *s.* utensilios de cocina, batería de cocina.

kite [kait], *s.* cometa, papalote; milano.

kitten [kítn], *s.* gatito.—*vi.* parir la gata.——**ish** [-iš], *a.* retozón.—**kitty** [kíti], *s.* gatito, minino; (en el juego) puesta.

knack [næk], *s.* tino, don, destreza, acierto, arte; treta; chuchería.

knapsack [népsæk], *s.* mochila; alforja, morral.

knave [neiv], *s.* bribón, bellaco; sota de los naipes.——**ry** [néivœri], *s.* picardía, bribonada, bellaquería.

knead [nid], *vt.* amasar, sobar.—*k. trough*, artesa, amasadura.

knee [ni], *s.* rodilla; codillo (de cuadrúpedo); (mec.) codo, angular, escuadra; (mar.) curva.—*k. deep*, metido hasta la rodilla.—*k. high*, hasta la rodilla.—**kneel** [nil], *vii.* [4] arrodillarse, ponerse de hinojos, hincar la rodilla, postrarse.

knell [nel], *s.* doble, toque de difuntos; clamoreo; mal agüero.—*vt.* y *vi.* doblar, tocar a muerto.

knew [nju], *pret.* de TO KNOW.

knicknack [níknæk], *s.* chuchería, baratija, juguete.

knife [najf], *s.* cuchillo; navaja; bisturí. —*vt.* acuchillar; (fam.) frustrar o arruinar por intrigas.

knight [najt], *s.* caballero (medieval o de las órdenes militares); campeón; caballo (del ajedrez).—*k. commander*, comendador.—*k. errant*, caballero andante.—*k. errantry*, caballería andante.—*vt.* armar caballero; conferir el título de Sir.— **—hood** [nájthụd], *s.* caballería, rango o dignidad de caballero.— **—ly** [-li], *a.* caballeresco.—*adv.* caballerosamente.

knit [nit], *vti.* y *vii.* [3] hacer malla, media o calceta; atar, enlazar, entretejer; contraer; unirse, trabarse; soldarse (un hueso); tejer a punto de aguja.—*to k. one's brow*, fruncir las cejas, arrugar el entrecejo.—**knitting** [nítiŋ], *s.* labor o trabajo de punto. —**knitwear** [nítwer], *s.* artículo(s) de punto.

knives [najvz], *s. pl.* de KNIFE.

knob [nab], *s.* prominencia, bulto, protuberancia; nudo en la madera; borlita o borilla; perilla, tirador (de puerta, gaveta, etc.).

knock [nak], *vt.* y *vi.* golpear; tocar, llamar a una puerta; (fam.) criticar, hablar mal de.—*to k. down*, derribar, tumbar; atropellar (con un auto, etc.); (mec.) desarmar, desmontar.— *to k. out*, hacer salir a golpes; acogotar; destruir; dejar o poner fuera de combate.—*s.* golpe; aldabonazo, llamada; (fam.) crítica.— **—er** [nákœ(r)], *s.* golpeador; llamador, aldaba, aldabón.

knoll [noụl], *s.* loma, otero; cumbre o cima; doble de campanas.

knot [nat], *s.* nudo; lazo, vínculo.—*vti.* y *vii.* [1] anudar(se).— **—ty** [-i], *a.* nudoso; duro, áspero; intrincado, difícil.

know [noụ], *vti.* [10] conocer; saber; discernir.—*to k. how to* (*swim, sing, etc.*), saber (nadar, cantar, etc.).—*to k. the ropes*, conocer los detalles, estar al tanto, (fig.) saber el juego.—*vii.* saber.—*as far as I k.*, que yo sepa.— *to be in the k.*, estar informado o en el secreto.—*to k. best*, ser el mejor juez, saber lo que más conviene.—*to k. better*, saber que no es así; saber lo que debe hacerse o como debe uno por-

tarse.—*to k. of*, saber de, tener noticia o conocimiento de; conocer de oídas.— **—ingly** [nóụiŋli], *adv.* hábilmente, sabiamente; a sabiendas, con conocimiento de causa.— **—ledge** [nálidž], *s.* conocimiento, saber, sapiencia; ciencia, erudición.—*to the best of my k.*, según mi leal saber y entender.—**known** [noụn], *pp.* de TO KNOW.

knuckle [nákl], *s.* nudillo, artejo, articulación de los dedos; jarrete de ternero o cerdo; (mec.) charnela.— *to k. down*, o *to*, consagrarse o emprender con vehemencia.—*to k. (under) to*, doblegarse ante; ceder a.

Korean [koríạn], *a.* y *s.* coreano.

L

label [léjbẹl], *s.* marbete, rótulo, etiqueta; marca.—*vti.* [1] rotular o marcar; apodar; designar, clasificar.

labial [léjbịal], *a.* labial.

labor [léjbọ(r)], *s.* trabajo; [el] obrerismo; mano de obra; labor; obra.— *l. union*, sindicato o gremio obrero.— *vi.* trabajar; estar de parto.—*vt.* elaborar; hacer trabajar, activar.

laboratory [læb(o)rạtọri], *s.* laboratorio.

labored [léjbọrd], *a.* hecho con dificultad; forzado.—**laborer** [léjbọrœ(r)], *s.* peón, jornalero, bracero; obrero, operario, trabajador.—**laborious** [lạbórịas], *a.* laborioso, trabajoso, ímprobo; diligente, industrioso.

labyrinth [læbirịnθ], *s.* laberinto.

lace [lejs], *s.* encaje; cordón, cinta; cordón del corsé o del zapato.—*vt.* atar, abrochar (corsé, zapatos, vestidos, etc.) con lazos o cordones; enlazar; galonear; entrelazar.

lack [læk], *vt.* y *vi.* carecer, necesitar, faltar.—*s.* falta, carencia, escasez, necesidad.— **—ing** [lǽkiŋ], *a.* falto, carente, defectuoso.—*to be l. in*, hacerle falta a uno; carecer de.

lackey [lǽki], *s.* lacayo.—*vt.* y *vi.* servir como lacayo; ser criado.

laconic [lạkánik], *a.* lacónico.

lacquer [lǽkœ(r)], *vt.* dar laca; barnizar. —*s.* laca, barniz.

lacy [léjsi], *a.* de o parecido al encaje.

lad [læd], *s.* mozo, mozalbete, chico.

ladder [lǽdœ(r)], *s.* escalera o escala (de mano).

laden [léjdn], *a.* cargado, abrumado, oprimido.

ladle [léjdl], *s.* cucharón, cazo; (fund.) caldero.—*vt.* sacar o servir con cucharón.

lady [léjdi], *s.* señora, dama.—*l.-killer*, tenorio, conquistador.— **—like** [-lajk], *a.* delicado, tierno, elegante; afeminado.— **—love** [-lʌv], *s.* amada, mujer querida.

lag [læg], *s.* retraso; retardación de movimiento.—*vii.* [1] retrasarse, rezagarse, quedarse atrás.— **—gard** [lǽgărd], *a.* tardo, perezoso, holgazán.—*s.* rezagado, holgazán.

lagoon [lagún], *s.* laguna, charca.

laic [léįįk], *a.* laico, lego, secular, seglar. —*s.* lego, seglar.

laid [leįd], *pret.* y *pp.* de to LAY.

lain [leįn], *pp.* de to LIE (echarse).

lair [ler], *s.* cubil, guarida.

lake [leįk], *s.* lago.

lamb [læm], *s.* cordero, borrego.— **—kin** [lǽmkįn], *s.* corderito.

lame [leįm], *a.* cojo, renco; lisiado, estropeado.—*vt.* lisiar, estropear.— **—ness** [léįmnįs], *s.* cojera; defecto, imperfección.

lament [lamént], *vt.* y *vi.* lamentar(se). —*s.* lamento.— **—able** [lǽmęntabl], *a.* lamentable, deplorable, desconsolador.— **—ation** [læmęntéįȿǫn], *s.* lamento, lamentación.

laminate [lǽmįneįt], *vt.* y *vi.* (metal.) laminar.

lamp [læmp], *s.* lámpara; farol; linterna. —*l. burner,* mechero.—*l. post,* farola de la calle.— *l. shade,* pantalla de lámpara.— **—black** [lǽmpblæk], *s.* negro de humo.

lampoon [læmpún], *s.* pasquín, sátira.— *vt.* pasquinar, satirizar.

lance [læns], *s.* lanza; pica.—*vt.* lancear, dar una lanzada; abrir con bisturí.— **—r** [lǽnsœ(r)], *s.* lancero.— **—t** [lǽnsįt], *s.* (cir.) lanceta.

land [lænd], *s.* tierra; terreno; suelo; país, nación; región, territorio.—*l. breeze,* terral.—*l. surveying,* agrimensura.—*l. surveyor,* agrimensor.—*vt.* desembarcar; echar en tierra.—*vi.* desembarcar; tomar tierra; (aer.) aterrizar; amarar (un avión).— **—holder** [lǽndhoųldœ(r)], *s.* hacendado, terrateniente.— **—ing** [-įŋ], *s.* descanso, rellano de escalera; desembarco, desembarque; desembarcadero; aterrizaje; amaraje.—*a.* de desembarque, de aterrizaje.—*l. craft,* barcaza militar de desembarque.—*l. forces,* tropas de desembarco.—*l. gear,* tren de aterrizaje.— **—lady** [-leįdį], *s.* casera, ama, patrona; arrendadora, propietaria.— **—lord** [-lord], *s.* propietario o dueño de tierras o casas; arrendador; casero, patrón.— **—mark** [-mark], *s.* mojón, señal; (mar.) marca; punto o acontecimiento culminante.— **—owner** [-oųnœ(r)], *s.* hacendado, terrateniente, propietario.—**—scape** [-skeįp], *s.* paisaje.— **—slide** [-slaįd], *s.* derrumbamiento, derrumbe.—*l. victory,*

victoria aplastante (esp. en elecciones).

lane [leįn], *s.* senda, vereda; calle, callejuela; ruta; pista o carrilera (de tránsito).

language [lǽŋgwįdȝ], *s.* lengua, idioma; lenguaje.

languette [lǽŋgwet], *s.* (mus.) lengüeta.

languid [lǽŋgwįd], *a.* lánguido.—**languish** [lǽŋgwįȿ], *vi.* languidecer, consumirse.—**languishing** [lǽŋgwįȿįŋ], *s.* languidez.—*a.* lánguido, decaído.— **languor** [lǽŋgǫ(r)], *s.* desfallecimiento, languidez, debilidad.

lank [læŋk], *a.* flaco, seco; alto y delgado.—*l. hair,* cabellos largos y lacios.— **—y** [lǽŋkį], *a.* larguirucho, langaruto, delgaducho.

lantern [lǽntœrn], *s.* linterna, farol; (mar.) faro, fanal.—*l. jack,* fuego fatuo.

lap [læp], *s.* falda; regazo; (dep.) vuelta completa de la pista; lamedura.—*l. dog,* perrillo faldero.—*vti.* [1] lamer; envolver; sobreponer, solapar.

lapel [lapél], *s.* (sast.) solapa.

Laplander [lǽplændœ(r)], *s.* lapón.

lapse [læps], *s.* lapso; intervalo de tiempo, transcurso; desliz, equivocación, falta; (for.) prescripción, caducidad de la instancia.—*in the l. of time,* con el transcurso del tiempo, andando el tiempo.—*vi.* pasar, transcurrir; decaer, deslizarse; caer en desliz o error; (for.) prescribir, caducar.

larceny [lársęnį], *s.* ratería, hurto.

lard [lard], *s.* manteca (de cerdo), (tocino) gordo.—*vt.* mechar.— **—er** [lárdœ(r)], *s.* despensa.

large [lardȝ], *a.* grande; amplio.—*at l.,* en libertad, suelto; extensamente; sin limitación, libre.— **—ly** [lárdȝlį], *adv.* grandemente; ampliamente; en gran manera.— **—ness** [-nįs], *s.* grandor, gran tamaño; extensión, amplitud.

lariat [lǽrįąt], *s.* lazo, reata, mangana.

lark [lark], *s.* alondra, calandria; (fam.) francachela, parranda, holgorio.

larva [lárvȧ], *s.* (*pl.* larvae [lárvi]) larva.

laryngitis [lærįndȝáįtįs], *s.* laringitis, afonía, ronquera.—**larynx** [lǽrįŋks], *s.* laringe.

lascivious [ląsívįʌs], *a.* lascivo.

lash [læȿ], *s.* látigo, flagelo; azote, latigazo; chasquido; pestaña (del ojo).—*vt.* dar latigazos; azotar, flagelar; reprochar; atar; (mar.) amarrar, trincar.—*vi.* chasquear el látigo.

lass [læs], *s.* doncella, moza, muchacha, chica.

lassitude [lǽsįtjud], *s.* lasitud, languidez.

lasso [lǽsoų], *vt.* (en)lazar.—*s.* lazo, mangana, (Am.) guaso.

last [læst], *a.* último; final, supremo; pasado.—*l. evening*, ayer por la noche, anoche.—*l. night*, anoche.—*l. word*, palabra o decisión final; (fam.) última moda.—*next to the l.*, penúltimo.—*adv.* por la última vez, por último, al fin.—*at l.*, por fin, al cabo. —*s.* fin, término; (lo, el) último; (zap.) horma.—*to the l.*, hasta el fin, hasta lo último.—*vi.* durar, perdurar, permanecer, subsistir.—*vt.* (zap.) ahormar, poner en la horma.— —**ing** [lǽstįn], *a.* duradero, perdurable.— —**ly** [-lį], *adv.* en conclusión, por fin, finalmente, por último.

latch [læch], *s.* aldaba, pestillo, cerrojo, picaporte.—*l. key*, llavín.—*vt.* cerrar con aldaba o pestillo.

late [lejt], *a.* tardío; tardo; último, postrero; reciente; difunto.—*l. arrival*, recién llegado.—*adv.* tarde; poco ha, últimamente.—*l. in the year*, al fin del año.—*to be l.*, llegar tarde, retrasarse, estar atrasado; ser tarde.—*too l.*, (demasiado) tarde.— —**ly** [léjtlį], *adv.* poco ha, no ha mucho; recientemente, últimamente.

latent [léjtent], *a.* latente.

later [léjtœ(r)], *adv.* y *a.* (*comp.* de LATE) más tarde; luego, después, posterior. —*l. on*, más trade, después.

lateral [lǽteṛal], *a.* lateral.

latest [léjtįst], *a.* y *adv.* (*superl.* de LATE) último; novísimo.—*at the l.*, a más tardar.

lathe [lejð], *s.* torno.—*l. bed*, banco del torno.

lather [lǽðœ(r)], *vt.* enjabonar (para afeitar).—*vi.* hacer espuma.—*s.* jabonadura, espuma de jabón.

Latin [lǽtįn], *a.* y *s.* latino.—*s.* latín.

latitude [lǽtįtjud], *s.* latitud; amplitud; libertad.

latrine [latrín], *s.* letrina.

latter [lǽtœ(r)], *a.* posterior, más reciente, moderno.—*the l.*, éste, ésta, esto.

lattice [lǽtįs], *s.* enrejado, celosía.

laud [lǫd], *s.* (canto de) alabanza; loa. —*vt.* alabar, loar, elogiar.— —**able** [lǫ́dạbl], *a.* laudable, loable.

laugh [læf], *vi.* reír(se).—*to l. loudly*, reírse a carcajadas.—*vt.* ahogar en o con risa.—*s.* risa; risotada.— —**able** [lǽfạbl], *a.* risible, irrisorio; divertido. — —**ing** [-įn], *s.* risa, reír.— —**ter** [-tœ(r)], *s.* risa.

launch [lǫnch], *vt.* botar o echar al agua (un barco); dar principio a, acometer; lanzar.—*vi.* lanzarse.—*s.* lancha,

chalupa.— —**ing** [lǫ́nchįn], *s.* lanzamiento; (mar.) botadura.

launder [lǫ́ndœ(r)], *vt.* lavar y planchar la ropa.—**laundress** [lǫ́ndrįs], *s.* lavandera.—**laundry** [lǫ́ndrį], *s.* lavadero; lavandería; tren de lavado; ropa lavada o para lavar.—**laundryman** [lǫ́ndrįmạn], *s.* lavandero.

laureate [lǫ́rįįt], *a.* laureado.—**laurel** [lǫ́rel], *s.* laurel, lauro; honor, distinción.

lava [lávǥ], *s.* lava.

lavatory [lǽvạtorį], *s.* lavatorio, lavabo, lavamanos; lavadero.

lavender [lǽvendœ(r)], *s.* espliego, lavanda.

lavish [lǽvįš], *a.* pródigo, gastador; profuso.—*vt.* disipar, malbaratar, prodigar.— —**ness** [-nįs], *s.* prodigalidad, profusión.

law [lǫ], *s.* ley; derecho; leyes (en general); justicia, jurisprudencia.—*l. abiding*, observante de la ley.—*l. of nations*, derecho internacional; derecho de gentes.—*l. school*, Facultad de Derecho.— —**breaker** [lǫ́brejkœ(r)], *s.* transgresor, infractor.— —**ful** [-fųl], *a.* legal, lícito; permitido, válido.— —**less** [-lįs], *a.* ilegal; desaforado, desmandado, de mal vivir.— —**maker** [-mejkœ(r)], *s.* legislador.— —**making** [-mejkįn], *s.* legislación.—*a.* legislativo.

lawn [lǫn], *s.* césped, prado.—*l. mower*, cortadora de césped.

lawsuit [lǫ́sjut], *s.* pleito, litigio, juicio. —**lawyer** [lǫ́yœ(r)], *s.* abogado, letrado.—*l.'s bill*, minuta.—*l.'s office*, bufete.

lax [læks], *a.* suelto, flojo; laxo, relajado.— —**ative** [lǽksạtįv], *a.* y *s.* laxante, purgante suave.— —**ity** [-įtį], —**ness** [-nįs], *s.* aflojamiento, flojedad; relajamiento; relajación.

lay [lej], *pret.* de TO LIE (echarse).

lay [lej], *vti.* [10] poner, colocar; tender (tuberías, rieles, etc.), instalar; derribar; poner (un huevo, la mesa, etc.); enterrar; calmar; imponer (cargas, tributos).—*to l. against*, acusar de, achacar a.—*to l. apart* reservar, poner aparte.—*to l. aside*, desechar; arrinconar; ahorrar.—*to l. off*, trazar, delinear; despedir.—*to l. out*, gastar, emplear; exhibir; trazar; proyectar.—*vii.* poner (las gallinas, etc.); apostar; (mar.) situarse, colocarse.—*to l. off*, parar (en el trabajo). —*to l. over*, demorarse, detenerse; sobrepasar.—*a.* laico, lego, seglar; profano, incompetente.—*s.* caída; contorno; (fam.) oficio, ocupación; canción, balada.— —**er** [léjœ(r)], *s.* capa, estrato, mano; gallina ponedora.— —**ing** [-įn], *s.* colocación; pos-

tura (del huevo).— —man [-maṇ], *s.*
lego, seglar.— —off [-ɔf], *s.* despedida
o despido (de obreros).— —out [-aut],
s. plan, disposición, arreglo, trazado.—
—over [-ouvœ(r)], *s.* parada temporal en un lugar.

lazily [léjẕili], *adv.* perezosamente.—
laziness [léjẕiṇjṣ], *s.* pereza, holgazanería.—**lazy** [léjẕi], *a.* perezoso,
holgazán; pesado.—*l. bones,* perezoso,
dormilón.

lead [lid], *s.* primacía, primer lugar;
dirección, mando; delantera; (teat.)
papel principal, protagonista; [led],
plomo; mina o grafito del lápiz; (mar.)
sonda, escandallo; plomada.—*l.
poisoning,* (med.) cólico saturnino.—
vti. [10] [lid], llevar de la mano;
guiar, dirigir; mandar, acaudillar; ir
a la cabeza de; enseñar, amaestrar;
llevar (buena, mala vida); inducir.—
to l. a new life, enmendarse.—*to l.
astray,* descarriar, seducir.—*to l. off* o
out, desviar; principiar.—*vii.* guiar,
enseñar el camino; sobresalir; ir
adelante; conducir; dominar; ser
mano en el juego de naipes.—*to l.
(up) to,* conducir a, dar a.— —**en**
[lédn], *a.* plomizo; aplomado; pesado.

leader [lídœ(r)], *s.* jefe, (neol.) líder;
guía, conductor; guión; caballo
delantero; (imp.) puntos suspensivos.
— —**ship** [-ṣip], *s.* jefatura, (neol.)
liderato; dirección, primacía.—**leading** [lídiṇ], *a.* director; principal;
dominante, sobresaliente.—*l. edge,*
(aer.) borde de ataque.—*l. lady,*
(teat.) primera actriz.—*l. man,* jefe,
cabecilla; (teat.) galán, protagonista.

leaf [lif], *s.* hoja.—*l. tobacco,* tabaco en
rama.—*vi.* echar hojas; hacerse
frondoso.—*vt.* hojear (un libro).—
—**less** [lífjṣ], *a.* deshojado.— —**let**
[-lit], *s.* (impr.) folleto, volante,
circular; (bot.) hojuela.— —**y** [-i], *a.*
frondoso; de forma de hoja.

league [lig], *s.* liga, confederación,
alianza; sociedad o asociación; legua
(unas 3 millas).—*vt.* y *vi.* aliar(se);
asociar(se), confederar(se).

leak [lik], *s.* gotera en un techo; fuga o
escape de gas, vapor, etc.; (mar.) vía
de agua.—*vi.* gotear; (mar.) hacer
agua; salirse; dejar escapar (el agua,
vapor, etc.), escurrirse.—*to l. out,*
(fig.) divulgarse, saberse, traslucirse.—
—**age** [líkiḏẕ], *s.* goteo, escape, fuga,
salida; (com.) avería, merma,
derrame.

lean [lin], *vii.* [4] apoyarse, recostarse,
inclinarse; ladearse, encorvarse.— *vti.*
apoyar, reclinar; inclinar; encorvar.
—*a.* flaco; magro; enjuto, delgado.

leap [lip], *vii.* [4] saltar, brincar, dar un
salto o brinco.—*vti.* (hacer) saltar,

cubrir el macho a la hembra.—*s.*
salto, brinco; cabriola, zapateta.—
by leaps and bounds, a saltos; a pasos
agigantados.—*l. year,* año bisiesto.

learn [lœrn], *vti.* y *vii.* [4] aprender;
enterarse de, saber; instruirse.— —**ed**
[lœrnid], *a.* docto, erudito, sabio.—
—**ing** [-iṇ], *s.* saber, ciencia; instrucción; aprendizaje.

lease [lis], *s.* arriendo, contrato de
arrendamiento.—*l. holder,* arrendatario.—*vt.* arrendar, alquilar, dar o
tomar en arriendo.

leash [liṣ], *s.* trailla, correa.

least [list], *a.* (*super.* de **LITTLE**)
mínimo, ínfimo; (el) más pequeño.—
not in the l., de ninguna manera, bajo
ningún concepto.—*adv.* menos.—*s.*
(lo) menos.—*at l.,* al menos, por lo
menos.

leather [léðœ(r)], *s.* cuero, piel, curtido.
—*a.* de cuero.—*l. belt,* correa, cinturón.—*l. strap,* correa.— —**n** [-n], *a.*
de cuero.

leave [liv], *s.* licencia, permiso, venia.—
l.-taking, despedida.—*on l.,* (mil.)
con licencia.—*vti.* [10] dejar; abandonar; salir o partir de; separarse de.—
to l. alone, dejar quieto o en paz; no
meterse con.—*to l. off,* cesar, suspender; dejar (un vicio, una costumbre).
—*to l. out,* omitir, excluir.—*to l. word,*
dejar dicho.—*vii.* irse, marcharse,
salir, partir.

leaven [lévn], *s.* levadura, fermento.—
vt. fermentar.— —**ing** [-iṇ], *s.* fermento.

leaves [livz], *s. pl.* de **LEAF**.

leaving [líviṇ], *s.* partida, marcha.—*pl.*
sobras, desechos, desperdicios.

lecherous [léchœras], *a.* lujurioso,
lascivo.—**lechery** [léchœri], *s.* lujuria,
lascivia.

lecture [lékchṵ(r)], *s.* disertación, conferencia; lectura, instrucción; sermoneo, reprensión.—*l. hall* o *room,* aula,
cátedra, salón de conferencias.—*vi.*
reprender, (fam.) sermonear, regañar.
— —**r** [lékchṵrœ(r)], *s.* conferenciante,
conferencista; lector (de universidad
o iglesia).

led [led], *pp.* y *pret.* de **TO LEAD**.

ledge [ledẕ], *s.* borde; repisa, saledizo.

ledger [ledẕœ(r)], *s.* (com.) libro mayor;
traviesa de andamio.

lee [li], *s.* sotavento, socaire.—*l. side,*
banda de sotavento.—*under the l.,* a
sotavento.

leech [lich], *s.* sanguijuela.

leer [lir], *s.* mirada de soslayo o de
reojo.—*vi.* mirar de soslayo, maliciosa o lascivamente.—**ingly** [líriṇli],
adv. de soslayo.— —**y** [-i], *a.* (fam.)
astuto; receloso.

leeward [líwₐrd, (mar.) lúₐrd], *a.* sotavento.

left [left], *pret. y pp. de* TO LEAVE.—*l. behind*, rezagado.—*l. off*, desechado. —*to be l.*, quedar(se).—*a.* izquierdo.— *l. hand*, izquierdo (lado, etc.); con la mano izquierda.—*l.-handed*, zurdo; torpe, desmañado; insincero, malicioso.—*l. wing*, (pol.) bando izquierdista o radical, las izquierdas.—*s.* mano izquierda, lado izquierdo; (pol.) izquierda(s).—*at, on, o to the l.*, a la izquierda.—*ist* [léftjst], *a. y s.* izquierdista.—*over* [-ouvœ(r)], *s.* sobrante, sobra, rezago.—*a.* sobrante, sobrado.

leg [leg], *s.* pierna; pata o pie (animales y objetos); trayecto, jornada.—*not to have a l. to stand on*, no tener razón o argumento válidos.—*on o upon its legs*, en pie, firmemente establecido.— *on one's last legs*, acabándose; agonizante; sin recursos.—*to pull someone's leg*, tomarle el pelo a uno.

legacy [légₐsi], *s.* legado, manda.

legal [lígₐl], *a.* legal, legítimo, lícito.—*l. tender*, moneda de curso legal.— —*ity* [ligǽliti], *s.* legalidad, legitimidad.— —*ization* [-izéjₐṇ], *s.* legalización.— —*ize* [-aiz], *vt.* legalizar; refrendar.

legate [légit], *s.* legado, enviado.— **legation** [ligéiṣₐṇ]. *s.* legación, misión, embajada.

legend [lédₑₑnd], *s.* leyenda; letrero, inscripción.— —*ary* [-eri], *a.* legendario.

legerdemain [ledₐœrdjméjn], *s.* juego de manos, prestidigitación.

legging [légiṇ], *s.* polaina.

legible [lédₑibl], *a.* legible.

legion [lídₐṇ], *s.* legión.— —*ary* [-eri], *a. y s.* legionario.

legislate [lédₑisleit], *vi.* legislar.—**legislation** [ledₑisléiṣₐṇ], *s.* legislación.— **legislative** [lédₑisleitiv], *a.* legislativo. —**legislator** [lédₑisleitₒ(r)], *s.* legislador.—**legislature** [lédₑisleichₒ(r)], *s.* legislatura, asamblea, cuerpo legislativo.

legitimate [lidₑítimit], *a.* legítimo.—*vt.* [lidₑítimeit], legitimar; legalizar.

leisure [líₑ̣ₒ(r)], *s.* ocio, ociosidad; comodidad.—*l. hours*, horas libres o desocupadas, ratos perdidos.—*to be at l.*, estar desocupado.— —*ly* [-li], *a.* pausado, deliberado.—*adv.* despacio; cómoda o desocupadamente; a sus anchas.

lemon [lémₒṇ], *s.* limón.—*l. tree*, limonero, limón.— —*ade* [-éjd], *s.* limonada.

lend [lend], *vti.* [10] prestar, dar prestado.—*to l. a hand*, dar una mano, ayudar.— —*er* [léndœ(r)], *s.* prestador, prestamista.

length [leṇθ], *s.* longitud, largo(r); extensión, distancia; duración de tiempo; alcance (de un tiro, etc.); (mar.) eslora.—*at full l.*, a lo largo, de todo el largo.—*at l.*, al fin, finalmente; extensamente.— —*en* [léṇₐṇ], *vt. y vi.* alargar(se), prolongar(se).— —*ways* [-wejz], —*wise* [-wajz], *adv.* longitudinalmente; a lo largo; de largo a largo.— —*y* [-i], *a.* largo; larguísimo.

leniency [línjₑṇsi], *s.* indulgencia, lenidad.—**lenient** [línjₑnt], *a.* indulgente, clemente.

lens [lenz], *s.* lente; cristalino (del ojo).

lent [lent], *pret. y pp. de* TO LEND.— (L.), *s.* cuaresma.

lentil [léntil], *s.* (bot.) lenteja.

leopard [lépₐrd], *s.* leopardo.

leper [lépœ(r)], *s.* leproso.—**leprosy** [léprₒsi], *s.* lepra.—**leprous** [léprₐs], *a.* leproso, lazarino.

lesion [líₑ̣ₒṇ], *s.* lesión.

less [les], *a.* (*comp. de* LITTLE) menor, menos, inferior.—*adv.* menos; en grado más bajo.—*l. and l.*, cada vez menos.—*s.* (el o lo) menos.—*prep.* menos; sin.

lessee [lesí], *s.* arrendatario, inquilino.

lessen [lésn], *vt.* aminorar, disminuir, mermar; rebajar.—*vi.* mermar, disminuirse; rebajarse, degradarse.— **lesser** [lésœ(r)], *a.* (*comp. de* LITTLE) menor, más pequeño.

lesson [lésₒṇ], *s.* lección.

lessor [lésₒ(r)], *s.* arrendador.

lest [lest], *conj.* para que no, por miedo de, no sea que.

let [let], *vti.* [9] dejar, permitir; arrendar, alquilar.—*l. alone*, cuanto más; ni mucho menos.—*l. us go!* ¡vamos! ¡vámonos!—*to l. alone*, dejar en paz. —*to l. be*, no molestar; no meterse con.—*to l. down*, dejar caer; bajar; abandonar.—*to l. go*, soltar.—*to l. in*, dejar entrar, admitir.—*to l. know*, hacer saber, avisar.—*to l. off*, disparar, descargar; dispensar, indultar.—*to l. out*, dejar salir, soltar; arrendar; divulgar (un secreto).—*to l. the cat out of the bag*, revelar un secreto.—*vii.* alquilarse o arrendarse.—*pret. y pp. de* TO LET.

lethal [líθₐl], *a.* mortal, mortífero.

lethargic [liθárdₑik], *a.* letárgico.— **lethargy** [léθₐrdₑi], *s.* letargo, apatía.

letter [létœ(r)], *s.* letra; carta.—*l. box*, buzón; apartado.—*l. carrier*, cartero. —*l. of license*, moratoria, espera.—*to the l.*, al pie de la letra, a la letra.—*vt.* rotular; poner letras, título o letreros a.— —*head* [-hed], *s.* membrete.— —*ing* [-iṇ], *s.* letrero, inscripción, rótulo.

lettuce [létis], *s.* lechuga.

leukemia [ljukímɪə], *s.* leucemia.

Levant [livǽnt], *s.* Levante, Oriente.—
—ine [-in], *a.* y *s.* levantino.

level [lévɭ], *a.* plano, llano, igual,
parejo; a nivel.—*l. crossing*, (f.c.)
paso a nivel.—*l.-headed*, juicioso,
discreto.—*s.* nivel (instrumento,
altura); puntería.—*on the l.*, abiertamente, sin dolo.—*adv.* a nivel, a ras.
—*vti.* [2] igualar, allanar; nivelar;
apuntar; emparejar.—*vii.* apuntar
(un arma); nivelar, hacer nivela-
ciones.

lever [lívœ(r)], *s.* palanca; escape de
reloj.—*control l.*, palanca de mando.—
—age [-idʒ], *s.* apalancamiento;
(fig.) ventaja.

Levite [lívait], *s.* levita.

levity [lévɪtɪ], *s.* liviandad; veleidad.

levy [lévɪ], *s.* leva, reclutamiento;
impuesto, recaudación; (for.) embargo.—*vti.* [7] imponer, recaudar;
reclutar; (for.) embargar.

lewd [ljud], *a.* lujurioso, lascivo.—
—ness [ljúdnis], *s.* lujuria, lascivia.

lexicography [leksikágrafi], *s.* lexico-
grafía.—**lexicon** [léksikɔn], *s.* léxico,
vocabulario, diccionario.

liability [laiəbílitɪ], *s.* riesgo; obligación,
responsabilidad.—*pl.* (com.) pasivo,
obligaciones a pagar.—**liable** [láiəbl],
a. sujeto, expuesto; obligado, responsable; propenso.

liar [láiə(r], *s.* embustero, mentiroso.

libel [láibɭ], *s.* libelo; difamación.—*vti.*
[2] difamar.— **—(l)ous** [-ʌs], *a.* difamatorio.

liberal [líbərɑl], *a.* liberal, generoso;
(pol.) liberal.—**—ism** [-izm], *s.* libera-
lismo.—**—ity** [libərǽlitɪ], *s.* liberalidad.

liberate [líbəreit], *vt.* libertar, librar.—
liberation [libəréiʃən], *s.* liberación.—
liberator [líbəreitɔ(r)], *s.* libertador.

libertine [líbœrtin], *a.* y *s.* libertino,
disoluto.

liberty [líbœrtɪ], *s.* libertad; liberación
de presos o cautivos; licencia, permiso.—*to take undue liberties*, propasarse.

librarian [laibrérian], *s.* bibliotecario.—
library [láibrərɪ], *s.* biblioteca.

libretto [librétou], *s.* libreto.

Libyan [líbiən], *s.* y *a.* libio; líbico.

lice [lais], *s. pl.* de LOUSE.

license, licence [láisəns], *s.* licencia,
permiso; título (universitario); licencia, libertinaje.—*driver's l.*, licencia
de conducción (de automóviles).—*l.
plate*, (aut., etc.) placa, matrícula o
chapa.—*vt.* licenciar, dar licencia o
permiso; autorizar.—**licentiate** [lai-
sénʃiit], *s.* licenciado.—**licentious**
[laisénθʌs], *a.* licencioso, desenfrenado, disoluto.

licit [líʃit], *a.* lícito.

lick [lik], *vt.* lamer; (fam.) cascar, dar
una tunda o zurra; vencer.—*to l. the
dust*, morder el polvo.—*vi.* flamear.—
s. lamedura, lengüetada; lamedero;
(fam.) mojicón, bofetón.— **—ing**
[líkiŋ], *s.* tunda, paliza; derrota.

licorice [líkɔris], *s.* anís.

lid [lid], *s.* tapa, tapadera; párpado.

lie [lai], *s.* mentira, embuste.—*to give
the l. to*, desmentir, dar un mentís.—
white l., mentira inocente, mentirilla.
—*vi.* mentir.—*vii.* [10] echarse, estar
tendido; yacer; descansar, hallarse
(sobre una superficie); estar ubicado,
radicar.

lien [lin], *s.* (for.) embargo; derecho de
retención.

lieutenant [ljuténant], *s.* teniente;
lugarteniente.—*l. commander*, capitán
de fragata.

life [laif], *s.* vida; modo de vivir; vivacidad, animación.—*for l.*, de por vida;
vitalicio.—*from l.*, del natural.—*still
l.*, naturaleza muerta, bodegón.—*a.*
de la vida; vitalicio.—*l. annuity*,
renta vitalicia.—*l. belt*, cinturón
salvavidas.—*l. imprisonment*, cadena
perpetua.—*l. preserver*, salvavidas.—
l. sentence, cadena perpetua.—*l.-size*,
de tamaño natural.—*boat* [láifbout],
s. bote o lancha salvavidas, o de
salvamento.— **—guard** [-gard], *s.*
salvavidas (persona).— **—less** [-lis],
a. sin vida, muerto, inanimado; deshabitado.— **—lessness** [-lisnis], *s.*
falta de vida; falta de animación o
vigor.— **—like** [-laik], *a.* que parece
vivo, natural.— **—long** [-lɔŋ], *a.* de
toda la vida, perpetuo.— **—saver**
[-seivœ(r)], *s.* bañero, salvavidas
(persona).— **—time** [-taim], *s.* curso
de la vida; toda la vida.—*a.* vitalicio,
de por vida.

lift [lift], *vt.* alzar, levantar, elevar;
(fam.) hurtar; plagiar.—*to l. up*,
alzar, soliviar.—*to l. (up) the hand*,
prestar juramento levantando la
mano; orar; hacer un esfuerzo.—*vi.*
disiparse (la niebla).—*s.* elevación;
alza; aparejo o gancho de alzar;
ascensión.—*to give one a l.*, ayudar a
uno; alentar o animar a uno; llevar a
uno gratis en un vehículo.

ligament [lígamɛnt], (anat.) ligamento.

light [lait], *s.* luz; claridad, resplandor;
lumbre; alumbrado; día, alba.—*in
this l.*, desde este punto de vista.—*a.*
ligero, leve; sutil; llevadero, fácil;
fútil, frívolo, superficial; ágil, liviano;
inconstante, mudable; alegre, vivo;
incontinente; claro (colores; piel).—
l.-haired, pelirrubio.—*l.-headed*, ligero
de cascos; atolondrado.—*l.-headed-
ness*, atolondramiento, aturdimiento.

—l.-hearted, alegre, festivo.—*l.-witted*, chalado, cascabelero.—*vti.* [4] encender, alumbrar, iluminar.—*vii.* encenderse; iluminarse; descender, posarse; apearse.— *—en* [láįtn], *vt.* iluminar, alumbrar; aclarar; aligerar; aliviar; regocijar.—*vi.* ponerse ligero; relampaguear, centellear.— *—er* [-œ(r)], *a.* (comp. de LIGHT).—*s.* encendedor.—*—house* [-haųs], *s.* faro.— *—ing* [-ịŋ], *s.* alumbrado, luz; iluminación.— *—ness* [-nįs], *s.* levedad, ligereza; agilidad; frivolidad, liviandad.— *—ning* [-nịŋ], *s.* relámpago; relampagueo.

likable [láįkạbl], *a.* amable, simpático, agradable.—**like** [lạįk], *a.* semejante; análogo, igual; lo mismo que, equivalente.—*it looks l. rain*, parece que va a llover.—*to feel l. going*, tener ganas de ir.—*s.* semejanza; semejante, igual.—*pl.* gustos, simpatías, aficiones.—*adv.* y *prep.* como, semejante a; a (la) manera de, a guisa de, en son de; al igual que, del mismo modo que, a semejanza de; (fam.) probablemente.—*l. as*, como, así como.—*l. mad*, como loco, furiosamente.—*l. this*, así, de este modo.—*that is (just) l. him*, eso es muy propio de él.—*what are they l.?* ¿cómo son ellos?—*vt.* gustarle a uno; gustar de; tener gusto en o afición a; aprobar; querer, simpatizar con.—*to l. best, better*, gustarle (a uno) más.—*vi.* gustar, agradar.—*as you l.*, como usted quiera, como a usted guste.—*if you l.*, si le parece (bien).—*she had l. to die* o *have died*, (fam.) por poco se muere.—**likelihood** [láįklihụd], *s.* probabilidad; verosimilitud; apariencia.—**likely** [láįklị], *a.* probable, verosímil, fácil; prometedor; apto, idóneo, a propósito.—*adv.* probablemente.—*l. enough*, no sería extraño.—**liken** [láįkn], *vt.* asemejar, comparar.—**likeness** [láįknịs], *s.* semejanza, parecido; igualdad; apariencia, aire; retrato.—**likewise** [láįkwạįz], *adv.* también, asimismo, además, igualmente; otrosí.—**liking** [láįkịŋ], *s.* afición, gusto, agrado, inclinación; simpatía; preferencia.

lilac [láįlạk], *s.* (bot.) lila.—*a.* de color de lila.

Lilliputian [lịlipiúšạn], *a.* y *s.* liliputiense, enano.

lily [lílị], *s.* (bot.) lirio, azucena; flor de lis.—*l.-livered*, cobarde, ruin.

limb [lịm], *s.* miembro (del cuerpo); rama (de árbol); miembro, individuo; limbo; borde, orilla.—*vt.* desmembrar.— *—er* [límbœ(r)], *a.* flexible, blando.—*vi.* (up) ponerse flexible.— *—erness* [límbœrnịs], *s.* flexibilidad.

lime [lạįm], *s.* cal; liga (para cazar);

(bot.) lima.— *—light* [lájmlạįt], *s.* luz de calcio; proscenio.

limit [lịmịt], *s.* límite, fin; frontera, lindero; ámbito; limitación, restricción; colmo.—*vt.* limitar.— *—ation* [-éįšọn], *s.* limitación.— *—less* [-lịs], *a.* ilimitado.

limp [lịmp], *s.* cojera.—*a.* débil, flojo; fláccido.—*vi.* cojear, renquear.— *—er* [límpœ(r)], *s.* cojo.

limpid [límpịd], *a.* limpio, cristalino, límpido.— *—ity* [limpídịtị], *—ness* [límpịdnịs], *s.* limpidez, diafanidad.

line [lạįn], *s.* línea; tubería, cañería; raya; veta; renglón; sedal (de pescar); frontera, límite; (com.) renglón, ramo, clase; surtido, artículos; (f.c., etc.) recorrido, trayecto; método, plan; línea de conducta; hilera, fila; verso; especialidad.—*along these lines*, en este sentido.—*in a l.*, en línea.—*in l.*, alineado; de acuerdo; dispuesto.—*in one's line*, dentro de la especialidad o conocimientos de uno.—*on the lines of*, conforme a, a tenor de.—*out of one's line*, ajeno a la especialidad o tarea de uno; asunto de que uno no entiende.—*vt.* trazar líneas, rayar; alinear; ir a lo largo o en los bordes u orillas de.—*to l. out*, marcar con rayas.—*to l. up*, alinear.—*vi.* alinearse; estar alineado; (up) formar fila, estar en fila o haciendo cola; formar, ponerse en formación.— *—age* [líŋịdž], *s.* linaje, alcurnia.— *—ar* [líníạ(r)], *a.* lineal; longitudinal; (zool. y bot.) linear.— *—d* [lạįnd], *a.* rayado; forrado.

linen [línẹn], *s.* lienzo, lino; holanda; género de lino; lencería, ropa blanca.

liner [láįnœ(r)], *s.* barco o avión de una línea establecida; delineador; rayador; forrador; forro.

linger [líŋgœ(r)], *vi.* demorarse, ir despacio; subsistir, persistir.—*vt.* (out o away) prolongar, demorar.

linguist [líŋgwịst], *s.* lingüista; políglota.— *—ic* [lịŋgwístịk], *a.* lingüístico.— *—ics* [lịŋgwístịks], *s.* lingüística.

lining [láįnịŋ], *s.* forro; revestimiento; material para forros; (aut.) forro o banda de frenos; encofrado.

link [lịŋk], *s.* eslabón; vínculo; enganche; cada una de las partes de un sistema articulado.—*pl.* cancha de golf.—*vt.* y *vi.* eslabonar(se), enlazar(se).— *—age* [líŋkịdž], *s.* eslabonamiento, encadenamiento; sistema articulado.

linnet [línịt], *s.* jilguero, pardillo.

linoleum [linóųliạm], *s.* linóleo.

linotype [láįnotạįp], *s.* linotipo; **linotipia**.—**linotypist** [-ịst], *s.* linotipista.

linseed [línsid], *s.* linaza.—*l. oil*, aceite de linaza.

lint [lint], *s.* hilas; pelusilla de la ropa.

lion [láiǫn], *s.* león.— **ess** [-is], *s.* leona.— **ize** [-aiz], *vt.* poner por las nubes.

lip [lip], *s.* labio.—*to give l.-service*, defender de dientes a fuera, de boquilla. — **stick** [lípstik], *s.* creyón o lápiz de los labios.

liquefy [líkwifai], *vti. y vii.* [7] liquidar, liquidarse; derretir, fundirse.

liqueur [likǿ(r)], *s.* licor; bebida cordial.

liquid [líkwid], *s.* líquido.—*a.* líquido; (com.) realizable.—**liquidate** [líkwideit], *vt.* liquidar.—**liquidation** [likwidéišǫn], *s.* liquidación.

liquor [líkǫ(r)], *s.* bebida alcohólica.

lisp [lisp], *vt. y vi.* cecear; balbucir o balbucear.—*s.* ceceo; balbuceo, balbucencia.

list [list], *s.* lista; nómina; registro; matrícula; (tej.) orilla, borde; lista, tira; filete, orla; tabloncillo; (mar.) escora, inclinación.—*pl.* liza, palestra.—*vt.* registrar, matricular, inscribir; poner en lista; catalogar; (com.) cotizar, facturar; (mil.) alistar; guarnecer con listones o cenefas.—*vi.* (mar.) escorar.

listen [lísn], *vi.* escuchar, oir; atender, prestar oídos a.—*to l. in*, ser radioyente, escuchar en el radio; oir subrepticiamente o arreglar un instrumento (radio, teléfono, etc.) con ese fin.— **er** [-œ(r)], *s.* oyente.— *radio l.*, radioyente.

listless [lístlis], *a.* desatento; indiferente, descuidado.— **ness** [-nis], *s.* descuido, indiferencia.

litany [lítǫni], *s.* (igl.) letanía.

liter [lítœ(r)], *s.* litro. Ver Tabla.

literacy [lítǫrǎsi], *s.* capacidad de leer y escribir.—**literal** [lítǫrǎl], *a.* literal.—**literalism** [lítǫrǎlizm], *s.* exactitud literal; realismo extremo.—**literally** [lítǫrǎli], *adv.* literalmente.—**literary** [lítǫrǎri], *a.* literario.—**literate** [lítǫrit], *a.* que sabe leer y escribir.—**literature** [lítǫrǎchur], *s.* literatura.

lithography [liθǿgrǎfi], *s.* litografía.

litigate [lítigeit], *vt. y vi.* litigar.—**litigation** [litigéišǫn], *s.* litigio.

litre [lítœ(r)], *s.* = LITER.

litter [lítœ(r)], *s.* litera; camilla, parihuela, andas; camada, cría; yacija (para animales); tendalera, cosas esparcidas desordenadamente por el suelo; desechos, residuos.—*vt.* esparcir (colillas, desechos, etc.); desordenar, desaliñar; preparar una yacija (para un animal).—*vi.* parir (los animales).

little [lítl], *a.* pequeño; poco.—*a. l.* (*bit*), un poco, un poquito.—*a l. sugar*, un poquito de azúcar.—*a l. while*, un rato, un ratico.—*adv.* poco.—*l. by l.*, poco a poco.—*s.* poco; porción o parte pequeña.

live [liv], *vt.* vivir, llevar (tal o cual vida).—*vi.* vivir, existir; habitar, morar, residir; mantenerse, subsistir. —*a.* [laiv], vivo, viviente; de la vida, vital; encendido, en ascua; activo, listo; de interés actual.—**lihood** [láivlihud], *s.* vida, subsistencia.—**liness** [láivlinis], *s.* vida, vivacidad, viveza, animación; agilidad, actividad.— **ly** [láivli], *a.* vivo, vivaz, vivaracho; gallardo, airoso; rápido; animado.—*adv.* enérgicamente; vivamente; aprisa.— **r** [lívœ(r)], *s.* (anat., zool.) hígado; vividor.

livery [lívœri], *s.* librea.

lives [laivz], *s. pl.* de LIFE.

livestock [láivstak], *s.* ganado, ganadería.

livid [lívid], *a.* lívido.

living [lívin], *s.* vida; modo de vivir; subsistencia, mantenimiento; vida, potencia vital.—*the l.*, los vivos, los seres vivientes.—*a.* vivo, viviente, con vida; animado; contemporáneo. —*l. room*, sala.—*l. wage*, salario decoroso.

lizard [lízǎrd], *s.* lagarto; lagartija; saurio.

llama [lámǎ], *s.* (zool.) llama.

load [loud], *s.* carga; peso; (o)presión.—*loads of*, (fam.) montones de, gran cantidad o número.—*vt. y vi.* cargar; recargar.

loaf [louf], *s.* (of bread), pan en sus diversas formas (hogaza, caña, flauta, panecillo, etc.).—*l. of sugar*, pilón de azúcar.—*vi.* haraganear, holgazanear. — **er** [lóufœ(r)], *s.* holgazán, vago, zángano; zapato deportivo (sin cordones).

loan [loun], *s.* préstamo; (com.) empréstito.—*l. shark*, (fam.) usurero, garrotero.—*vt.* prestar (dinero).

loath [louθ], *a.* poco dispuesto, renuente. — **e** [louð], *vt.* detestar, abominar.— *vi.* tener hastío, sentir fastidio, disgusto o aborrecimiento.— **some** [lóuðsam], *a.* aborrecible, repugnante, asqueroso.

leaves [louvz], *s. pl.* de LOAF.

lobby [lábi], *s.* vestíbulo; salón de entrada; paso, pasillo; pórtico; camarilla (política).—*vti. y vii.* [7] politiquear.

lobster [lábstœ(r)], *s.* langosta (de mar), bogavante.

local [lóukǎl], *a.* local; vecinal; regional. —*l. horizon*, horizonte sensible o visible.—*l. train*, tren ordinario o de escalas.— **ity** [lokǎlíti], *s.* situación; localidad; lugar.— **ization** [-izéišǫn],

s. localización.— **—ize** [-aįz], **vt.** localizar.—**locate** [lóukeįt], **vt.** y **vi.** ubicar(se).—**location** [lokéįȿǫn], **s.** ubicación; sitio, localidad; situación, posición.

lock [lak], **s.** cerradura; llave o pestillo (de las armas de fuego); chaveta; esclusa, compuerta; abrazo estrecho y apretado; bucle, guedeja.—**l.** *nut*, (mec.) contratuerca.—**l.** *stitch*, punto de cadeneta.—**l.** *washer*, (mec.) arandela de seguridad.—*under l. and key,* bajo llave.—**vt.** cerrar con llave; poner cerradura; juntar, entrelazar, atar, trabar; abrazar; fijar, trincar; cerrar. —*to l. in*, encerrar, poner bajo llave. —*to l. (one) out*, cerrar la puerta a uno; dejar en la calle o sin trabajo.— *to l. up*, encerrar, encarcelar.—**vi.** cerrarse con llave; unirse; trabarse; sujetarse.— **—et** [lákįt], **s.** relicario, medallón, guardapelo.— **—jaw** [-dʒɔ], **s.** tétano(s).— **—out** [-aųt], **s.** cierre de una fábrica, paro forzoso patronal.— **—smith** [-smįθ], **s.** cerrajero.— **—up** [-ʌp], **s.** calabozo; cárcel; encarcelamiento.

locomotive [loųkomóųtįv], **s.** locomotora.—**l.** *engineer*, maquinista.

locust [lóųkʌst], **s.** langosta, langostón, saltamontes; cigarra.

locution [lokįúȿǫn], **s.** locución.

lodge [ladʒ], **vt.** alojar, albergar; colocar; plantar, introducir, fijar; dar a guardar.—*to l. a complaint*, dar una queja.—**vi.** hospedarse; tenderse, echarse.—**s.** casa de guarda; pabellón; portería; logia.— **—r** [ládʒœ(r)], **s.** inquilino, huésped.—**lodging** [ládʒįŋ], **s.** posada, hospedería; hospedaje, alojamiento; morada, residencia.

loft [lɔft], **s.** ático, sobrado, desván; almacén.— **—iness** [lɔftįnįs], **s.** altura; nobleza; altanería.— **—y** [-į], **a.** alto, encumbrado; noble, elevado; sublime; eminente; altivo, soberbio.

log [lɔg], **s.** leño, palo; tronco, madero; (mar.) corredera.—**l.** *book*, cuaderno de bitácora.—**l.** *cabin, l. hut*, cabaña rústica.—**vti.** [1] cortar (madera) y transportarla; apuntar en el cuaderno de bitácora; indicar en la corredera.— **vii.** cortar, aserrar y transportar trozas; extraer madera.

loge [loųʒ], **s.** palco; anfiteatro.

logic [ládʒįk], **s.** lógica.— **—al** [-ąl], **a.** lógico.— **—ian** [lodʒíȿąn], **s.** lógico.

loin [lɔįn], **s.** lomo; ijada; ijar.

loiter [lóįtœ(r)], **vi.** remolonear, holgazanear.—**vt.** **(away)** malgastar (tiempo).— **—er** [-œ(r)], **s.** vagabundo, holgazán.

loll [lal], **vi.** apoyarse, recostarse, tenderse; pender, colgar (la lengua de

un animal).—**vt.** dejar colgar (la lengua).

lollipop [lálįpap], **s.** caramelo en palito, pirulí.

lone [loųn], **a.** solitario, solo; soltero.— **—liness** [lóųnlįnįs], **s.** soledad; tristeza del aislamiento.— **—ly** [-lį], **a.** solitario; triste, desamparado.— **—some** [-sʌm], **a.** solitario, desierto; triste.

long [lɔŋ], **a.** largo; de largo; extenso, prolongado; tardío, dilatorio; excesivo, de más; distante; (com.) recargado, esperando alza de precios.— *how l.?* ¿de qué largo (medida)?— *in the l. run*, a la larga.—*it is a l. way,* dista mucho, está muy lejos.—*l. dozen*, docena de fraile, trece.—*l. hundred*, ciento veinte.—*l.-suffering*, paciencia, resignación, aguante.—*l. suit*, fuerte, especialidad de una persona.—*l. time*, mucho tiempo, largo rato.—*adv.* a gran distancia; mucho; (durante) mucho tiempo.—*all o the whole day, year, etc. l.*, todo el santo día, todo el año, etc.—*as l. as*, mientras.—*before o ere l.*, en breve, antes de mucho.—*how l.?* ¿cuánto tiempo?—*how l. is it since?* ¿cuánto (tiempo) hace que?—*l. after*, mucho (tiempo) después.—*l. ago*, hace mucho (tiempo).—*l.-drawn*, lento, pesado, prolongado.—*l. live!* ¡viva! *l.-lived*, longevo.—*l.-range*, de largo alcance.—*l.-sighted*, sagaz, previsor. —*l.-standing*, de larga duración.— *l.-term*, (com.) a largo plazo.—*not l. ago o since*, no hace mucho.—*not l. before*, poco tiempo antes.—*so l. as*, mientras que, en tanto que.—**s.** longitud, largo.—*pl.* (com.) los que guardan acciones en espera de alza.—**vi.** (**for**, o **to**) anhelar, suspirar (por), codiciar, apetecer, ansiar; añorar.— **—er** [lɔŋgœ(r)], **a.** más largo.—*adv.* más tiempo, más rato.—*how much l.?* ¿cuánto tiempo más?—*no l.*, ya no, no más.— **—evity** [lɔndʒévįį], **s.** longevidad.— **—ing** [lɔŋįŋ], **s.** deseo vehemente, anhelo, ansia, ansiedad. —**a.** anhelante, ansioso, vehemente.— **—itude** [lándʒįtįud], **s.** longitud.

longshoreman [lɔŋȿormąn], **s.** estibador, cargador del muelle.

look [lųk], **vt.** mirar, pasar la vista a; causar o expresar con la mirada o el ademán.—*to l. daggers*, echar chispas; **(at)** mirar echando chispas.—*to l. in the face*, mirar cara a cara, sin vergüenza.—*to l. one's age*, representar uno los años que tiene.—*to l. over*, mirar ligeramente por encima.—*to l. up*, buscar, averiguar; (fam.) visitar a uno.—**vi.** mirar, ver; parecer, aparentar; poner cuidado o tener cuidado; lucir (bien, mal); tener cara de.—*as it looks to me*, a mi ver.—*to l. about*, observar, mirar alrededor.—*to l. about one*, estar alerta, vigilar.— *to l. after*, cuidar, atender a, mirar por; prestar atención; inquirir, investigar.—*to l. alike*, parecerse.—*to l. alive*, darse prisa.—*to l. at*, mirar; tender la vista a; considerar.—*to l. back*, reflexionar; mirar atrás.—*to l. bad*, tomar mal cariz; parecer feo; tener mala cara.—*to l. down upon*, despreciar.—*to l. for*, buscar; esperar.—*to l. into*, estudiar, examinar, averiguar.—*to l. like*, parecerse a; tener cara o traza de; dar o haber señales de.—*to l. on*, considerar; estimar, juzgar; mirar, ver; ser espectador.— *to l. out of*, asomarse a.—*to l. sharp*, tener ojo avizor.—*to l. through*, examinar, inspeccionar, hacer un registro de.—*to l. to*, cuidar de, velar por; atender a; hacer responsable; esperar de; acudir a.—*to l. up to*, respetar, estimar.—*s.* mirada, ojeada, vistazo.—*pl.* aspecto, apariencia, semblante, traza.—*to have a l. at*, mirar, echar una ojeada a.—*—ing* [lúkiŋ], *s.* miramiento; busca; examen.—*a.* de o para mirar.—*good (bad)-l.*, bien (mal) parecido.—*—out* [-aut], *s.* vigía, vigilancia; observación; mirador; centinela.—*that's his l.*, (fam.) eso le concierne (a él); allá él, con su pan se lo coma.—*to be on the l.*, estar a la mira.

loom [lum], *s.* telar; arte de tejer; presencia, aparición—*vi.* asomar, aparecer exageradamente; destacarse, descollar; (re)lucir.— *—ing* [lúmiŋ], *s.* espejismo.

loon [lun], *s.* bobo, tonto.— *—y* [lúni], *s.* y *a.* (fam.) bobo, loco rematado.

loop [lup], *s.* gaza, lazo, bucle; ojal, presilla, alamar; onda; punto; curva, vuelta; (mec.) abrazadera, anilla; (aer.) rizo.—*vt.* asegurar con presilla; hacer gazas en; formar festones o curvas en.—*to l. in*, (elec.) intercalar (en un circuito).—*to l. the l.*, (aer.) rizar el rizo, dar una vuelta vertical. —*vi.* andar haciendo curvas; formar gaza.— *—hole* [lúphoul], *s.* abertura, mirador; aspillera, tronera; escapatoria, excusa.

loose [lus], *vt.* desatar, desprender; aflojar; aliviar; soltar, libertar, librar; desenredar; desocupar.—*to l. one's hold*, soltar.—*a.* suelto; desatado; flojo, holgado; vago, indefinido; libre, disoluto; negligente.—*s.* libertad, soltura.—*on the l.*, (fam.) libre; sin trabas; de parranda.— *—n* [lúsn], *vt.* aflojar, soltar, desunir; laxar, relajar; librar.—*vi.* desunirse, aflojarse, desa-

tarse.— *—ness* [-nis], *s.* aflojamiento, flojedad, holgura; relajamiento; soltura; flujo de vientre; vaguedad.

loot [lut], *vt.* y *vi.* saquear.—*s.* botín; saqueo, pillaje.

lop [lap], *vti.* [1] (des)mochar, podar; cercenar.—*vii.* colgar, pender, caer flojamente.—*s.* desmochadura; ramas podadas.—*l.-eared*, de orejas gachas.

loquacious [lokwéjšʌs], *a.* locuaz.— **loquacity** [lokwǽsiti], *s.* locuacidad.

lord [lɔrd], *s.* señor; dueño, amo; lord (*pl.* lores).—*L.'s Prayer*, Padrenuestro.—*Our L.*, Nuestro Señor.—*vt.* y *vi.* gobernar, señorear, mandar imperiosamente.—*to l. it over*, dominar (en), señorear, imponerse a.— *—ly* [lɔ́rdli], *a.* señoril; imperioso.—*adv.* señorilmente; altiva o imperiosamente.— *—ship* [-šip], *s.* señorío, dominio, poder; señoría, excelencia. —*your l.*, usía, vuecencia.

lore [lɔr], *s.* erudición, saber, ciencia.

lorgnette [lɔrnyét], *s.* impertinentes; gemelos de teatro con mango.

lose [luz], *vti.* [10] perder.—*to l. face*, desprestigiarse.—*to l. heart*, descorazonarse.—*to l. oneself*, perderse, extraviarse.—*to l. one's temper*, encolerizarse.—*to l. sight of*, perder de vista.—*vii.* perder, tener una pérdida; atrasar (un reloj).—*to l. out*, (fam.) llevarse chasco, ser derrotado.— *—r* [lúzœ(r)], *s.* perdedor.—**losing** [lúziŋ], *a.* perdedor, perdidoso; vencido.—**loss** [lɔs], *s.* pérdida; perjuicio, daño; privación.—*at a l.*, perdiendo, con pérdida; perplejo, indeciso, en duda.—*at a l. to*, sin acertar a.—*it's your l.*, (fam.) usted se lo pierde.— **lost** [lɔst], *pret.* y *pp.* de TO LOSE.—*a.* perdido, extraviado, descarriado; desorientado; perplejo; malogrado; desperdiciado.—*l. and found* (*office*), departamento de objetos perdidos.

lot [lat], *s.* solar; terreno; lote, porción, parte; grupo (de personas); suerte, hado, sino.—*a l.*, (fam.) mucho.—*a l. of*, (fam.) gran número de, gran cantidad de.—*by lots*, echando suertes, a la suerte.—*lots of*, (fam.) mucho, muchos.—*to draw* o *to cast lots*, echar suertes.—*to fall to one's l.*, tocarle a uno en suerte.

lotion [lóušən], *s.* loción.

lottery [látœri], *s.* lotería, rifa.— **lotto** [látou], *s.* lotería.

loud [laud], *a.* ruidoso; recio, fuerte; chillón; (fam.) urgente; llamativo, subido de color.—*l. laugh*, risotada, carcajada.—*l.-voiced*, estentóreo.— *adv.* ruidosamente; en alta voz; a gritos.— *—ness* [láudnis], *s.* ruido, sonoridad; (fam.) vulgaridad, mal gusto.

—**loud-speaker** [láụd spíkœ(r)], *s.* altavoz, altoparlante; megáfono.

lounge [laụndʒ], *vi.* holgazanear; repatingarse; ponerse uno a sus anchas.— *s.* salón de fumar o descansar; sofá, canapé.

louse [laụs], *s.* piojo.—**lousy** [láụzi], *a.* piojoso.

lovable [lávạbl], *a.* amable.—**love** [lʌv], *vt.* amar, querer; (fam.) gustar mucho de, tener gran afición a.—*vi.* amar; gustarle a uno mucho.—*s.* amor, cariño, afecto, devoción; pasión amatoria o sexual; el ser amado.— *for l. or money*, por buenas o por malas; a cualquier precio.—*in l. with*, enamorado de.—*l. affair*, intriga amorosa, amorío.—*l. bird*, periquito. —*not l. or money*, por nada del mundo.—*to make l. to*, enamorar, galantear, cortejar.—**loveliness** [lávlịnịs], *s.* amabilidad, agrado, encanto; belleza.—**lovely** [lávlị], *a.* amable, cariñoso; hermoso, bello; (fam.) agradable, atractivo; ameno.—**lover** [lávœ(r)], *s.* amante; galán; aficionado.—**lovesick** [lávsịk], *a.* enamorado, herido de amor.—**loving** [lávịŋ], *a.* amante, amoroso, cariñoso; afectuoso; aficionado; apacible.

low [loụ], *a.* bajo; abatido; gravemente enfermo; malo (dieta, opinión, etc.); módico (precio); muerto, grosero, vil, rastrero; pobre, humilde; debilitado.—*in l. gear*, (aut.) en primera. —*l. comedy*, farsa, sainete.—*l.-down*, (fam.) bajo, vil.—*l. spirits*, abatimiento.—*l. tide*, bajamar.—*l. trick*, mala pasada.—*l. water*, marea baja. —*adv.* bajo; en la parte inferior; a precio bajo; vilmente; sumisamente; en voz baja; en tono profundo.— *l.-minded*, ruin.—*vi.* mugir, berrear. —*s.* mugido, berrido; punto o lugar bajo; valor o precio mínimo; (aut.) primera velocidad.—*l.-down*, (fam.) información confidencial o de primera mano; los hechos verdaderos.— —**born** [lóụbɔrn], *a.* de humilde cuna.— —**bred** [-bred], *a.* malcriado; vulgar.— —**brow** [-braụ], *a.* poco intelectual.— —**er** [-œ(r)], *vt.* humillar, abatir, deprimir; bajar, poner más bajo; rebajar, disminuir; [láụœ(r)], mirar amenazadoramente. —*to l. the flag*, abatir la bandera.—*vi.* menguar, disminuirse.—*a.* más bajo; inferior.— —**erclassman** [lóụœrkláɛsmạn], *s.* estudiante de primero o segundo año.— —**ering** [lóụœrịŋ], *a.* encapotado, nebuloso; amenazador.— —**land** [lóụlạnd], *s.* tierra baja.— —**liness** [-lịnịs], *s.* humildad; bajeza, vileza.— —**ly** [-lị], *a.* humilde; vil, bajo.—*adv.* humildemente; vilmente.

loyal [lóịạl], *a.* leal, fiel, constante.—**ty** [-tị], *s.* lealtad, fidelidad.

lozenge [lázẹndʒ], *s.* pastilla; rombo.

lubricant [liúbrịkạnt], *s.* y *a.* lubri(fi)cante.—**lubricate** [liúbrịkeịt], *vt.* lubri(fi)car, engrasar.

lucid [liúsịd], *a.* luciente; diáfano; brillante; lúcido; cuerdo.— —**ity** [liusíditị], —**ness** [liúsịdnịs], *s.* lucidez; claridad mental; transparencia; brillantez; cordura.

luck [lʌk], *s.* azar, casualidad; suerte, dicha.—*to be in l.*, estar de buena suerte.—*to be out of l.*, estar de malas. — —**ily** [lʌkịlị], *adv.* por fortuna, afortunadamente, por dicha.— —**y** [-ị], *a.* afortunado, dichoso; propicio. — *l. break*, (fam.) chiripa, coyuntura favorable.

lucrative [liúkrạtịv], *a.* lucrativo.

ludicrous [liúdịkrʌs], *a.* ridículo, risible.

lug [lʌg], *s.* (fam.) tirón, estirón; cosa tirada; cosa lenta y pesada; (mec.) oreja, argolla; saliente; agarradera.— *vt.* tirar de, halar.

luggage [lágịdʒ], *s.* equipaje; (fam.) trastos.

lukewarm [liúkwɔrm], *a.* tibio, templado; indiferente, frío.

lull [lʌl], *vt.* arrullar; aquietar.—*vi.* calmarse, sosegarse.—*s.* momento de calma o de silencio.— —**aby** [lálạbaị], *s.* arrullo; canción de cuna, nana.

lumber [lámbœ(r)], *s.* madera aserrada; maderaje; armatoste; trastos o muebles viejos.—*vt.* amontonar trastos viejos.—*vi.* andar pesadamente; avanzar con ruido sordo.— —**ing** [-ịŋ], *a.* pesado; hachero.— —**jack** [-dʒæk], *s.* leñador, hachero.

luminary [liúmịnerị], *s.* astro; lumbrera.

lump [lʌmp], *s.* masa, bulto, burujón; protuberancia, chichón; hinchazón; pitón; terrón.—*a l. in the throat*, un nudo en la garganta.—*by the l.*, a bulto, en globo, a ojo, por junto.— *in a o in the l.*, todos juntos, sin distinción.—*l. of sugar*, terrón de azúcar.—*l. sum*, suma redonda.—*vt.* amontonar; comprar a bulto, en globo.—*to l. it*, (fam.) soportarlo, tragar saliva.—*vi.* trabajar como estibador; apelotonarse, aterronarse.— —**y** [lámpị], *a.* aterronado.

lunacy [liúnạsị], *s.* locura.—**lunar** [liúnạ(r)], *a.* lunar; lunario; lunado; lunático.—**lunatic** [liúnạtịk], *s.* y *a.* loco, lunático.

lunch [lʌnch], **luncheon** [lánchọn], *s.* almuerzo, comida ligera del mediodía; merienda, refrigerio.—*vi.* almorzar; merendar.

lung [lʌŋ], *s.* pulmón.

lunge [lʌndʒ], *s.* estocada; arremetida.

—*vi.* dar una estocada, tirarse a fondo; arremeter, abalanzarse.

lurch [lœrch], *s.* sacudida, vaivén; bandazo, guiñada.—*to leave in the l.*, plantar, dejar en las astas del toro o en la estacada.—*vi.* andar tambaleando; dar bandazos.

lure [ljur], *s.* añagaza, señuelo; cebo.—*vt.* atraer, inducir, tentar.

lurid [ljúrid], *a.* cárdeno; espeluznante, siniestro.

lurk [lœrk], *vi.* acechar; moverse furtivamente; emboscarse.

luscious [lÁsᴧs], *a.* sabroso, delicioso; meloso; empalagoso.

lush [lᴧs], *a.* suculento, jugoso; fresco y lozano; exuberante.

lust [lᴧst], *s.* lujuria, concupiscencia; codicia; anhelo vehemente.—*vi.* (for o after) codiciar.

luster [lÁstœ(r)], *s.* lustre, brillo.—*pl.* realce, lucimiento; araña de cristal; lustro.—*vt.* lustrar.—**lustrous** [lÁstrᴧs], *a.* lustroso, brillante.

lusty [lÁsti], *a.* lozano, vigoroso.

lute [ljut], *s.* laúd.

Lutheran [ljúθœrᴧn], *s.* y *a.* luterano.

luxuriant [lᴧksúriᴧnt], *a.* exuberante; superfluo; frondoso; lujuriante.— **luxurious** [lᴧksúriᴧs], *a.* lujoso; sibarítico; exuberante; frondoso.—**luxury** [lÁksuri], *s.* lujo; gastos superfluos; cosa que deleita los sentidos.

lye [lai], *s.* lejía.

lying [láiiŋ], *a.* falso, mentiroso; echado, yacente; sito, situado.—*l. down*, acostado.—*l.-in*, parto.—*l.-in hospital*, hospital de maternidad.—*l.-in woman*, mujer parida.—*s.* mentira, embuste.

lynch [linch], *vt.* linchar.

lynx [links], *s.* lince.

lyre [lair], *s.* (mus.) lira.—**lyric(al)** [lírik(ᴧl)], *a.* lírico.—**lyric** [lírik], *s.* poema lírico.—**lyricism** [lírisizm], *s.* lirismo.—**lyrist** [láirist], *s.* tocador de lira; poeta lírico.

M

ma [ma], *s.* (fam.) mamá.

ma'am [mæm], *s. contr.* de MADAM, señora.

macabre [mᴧkábr], *a.* macabro.

macaroni [mækᴧróuni], *s. pl.* macarrones.

macaroon [mækᴧrún], *s.* almendrado.

macaw [mᴧkó], *s.* guacamayo.

mace [meis], *s.* maza, porra.—*m. bearer*, macero.

macerate [mǽsᴧreit], *vt.* macerar.— **maceration** [mæsᴧréiᴧn], *s.* maceración.

machinate [mǽkineit], *vt.* y *vi.* maquinar.—**machination** [mækinéi-

ᴧn], *s.* maquinación, intriga. —**machine** [mᴧsín], *s.* máquina, aparato; vehículo, automóvil, avión, etc.—*m. gun*, ametralladora.—*to m.-gun*, ametrallar, atacar con ametralladora.—*m.-made*, hecho a máquina.—**machinery** [mᴧsínœri], *s.* maquinaria; mecanismo, aparato; organización, sistema.—**machinist** [mᴧsínist], *s.* maquinista, mecánico; tramoyista.

mackerel [mǽkᴧrᴧl], *s.* caballa, (Am.) macarela, pintada.

mad [mæd], *a.* loco, demente; furioso, rabioso; insensato; enojado, encolerizado.—*to go m.*, enloquecerse, volverse loco.

madam [mǽdᴧm], *s.* celestina; dueña de un burdel; señora.

madame [mǽdᴧm, mædǽm], *s.* señora.

madbrain [mǽdbrein], **madcap** [mǽdkæp], *a.* y *s.* fogoso; temerario; calavera, tarambana.—**madden** [mǽdn], *vt.* y *vi.* enloquecer(se), enfurecer(se).

made [meid], *pret.* y *pp.* de TO MAKE.—*a.* hecho, fabricado.— *m.-over*, rehecho; reformado.—**made-up** [méidᴧp], *a.* artificial; ficticio; maquillado, pintado; (con of) compuesto (de).

madhouse [mǽdhaus], *s.* manicomio. —**madman** [mǽdman], *s.* loco, orate. —**madness** [mǽdnis], *s.* locura, demencia; furia, rabia.

Madrilenian [mædrilíniᴧn], *a.* y *s.* madrileño.

magazine [mægᴧzín], *s.* revista; (arti.) cámara o depósito para los cartuchos en las armas de repetición; almacén militar.—*m. rifle*, rifle de repetición. —*powder m.*, polvorín; santabárbara.

magic [mǽdȝik], *s.* magia; prestidigitación.—*a.* mágico, encantador.—*m. wand*, varita mágica, varita de virtud. ––**ian** [mᴧdȝíᴧn], *s.* mago, mágico, prestidigitador.

magistrate [mǽdȝistreit], *s.* magistrado; juez.

magnanimous [mægnǽnimᴧs], *a.* magnánimo.

magnate [mǽgneit], *s.* magnate.

magnet [mǽgnit], *s.* imán, magneto.— **-ic** [mægnétik], *a.* magnético; atractivo.– **-ism** [mǽgnitizm], *s.* magnetismo.– **-ize** [mǽgnitaiz], *vt.* magnetizar, imantar.—*vi.* imantarse.

magnificence [mægnífisᴧns], *s.* magnificencia.—**magnificent** [mægnífisᴧnt], *a.* magnífico.

magnify [mǽgnifai], *vti.* [7] aumentar, amplificar, ampliar.—*magnifying glass*, vidrio de aumento, lupa.

magnitude [mǽgnitjud], *s.* magnitud.

magpie [mǽgpai], *s.* urraca; (fig.) hablador, cotorra.

mahogany [mǝhágǝni], *s.* caoba, caobo.
Mahometan [mǝhámitǝn], *s.* **y** *a.* mahometano.
maid [meid], *s.* doncella, soltera; criada, sirvienta, doméstica; (Am.) mucama. —*m. of honor*, dama de honor.—**en** [méidn], *s.* doncella, virgen, joven soltera.—*a.* soltera.—*m. name*, apellido de soltera.
mail [meil], *s.* correo; correspondencia; cota de malla.—*m. bag*, valija.—*m. carrier*, cartero.—*vt.* echar al correo; enviar por correo.— **box** [méilbaks], *s.* buzón.— **man** [-mæn], *s.* cartero.
maim [meim], *vt.* estropear, lisiar, tullir.
main [mein], *a.* principal; esencial; de mayor importancia.—*m. floor*, planta baja.—*m. office*, (com.) casa matriz. —*m. street*, calle principal, calle mayor.—*m. wall*, pared maestra. —*the m. thing*, lo principal, lo esencial. —*s.* cañería maestra, conducto; océano, alta mar.—*in the m.*, mayor o principalmente, en conjunto.— **land** [méinlǝnd], *s.* continente, tierra firme.— **stay** [-stej], *s.* sostén, apoyo.
maintain [meintéjn], *vt.* mantener, guardar; sostener, afirmar.—**maintenance** [méintǝnǝns] *s.* mantenimiento; manutención; sostén, sustento, sostenimiento; conservación (de vía, máquina, camino, etc.).
maize [meiz], *s.* maíz.
majestic [mǝdžéstik], *a.* majestuoso.— **majesty** [mædžisti], *s.* majestad; majestuosidad.
major [méidžǝ(r)], *a.* mayor, más grande; principal.—*s.* comandante, mayor; mayor de edad; curso de especialización (en universidad o colegio).—*m.-domo*, mayordomo.— *m. general*, general de división.—*vi.* (con in) especializarse en un estudio o asignatura.— **ity** [mǝdžáriti], *s.* mayoría, el mayor número (de); (for.) mayoría, mayor edad.
make [meik], *vti.* [10] hacer; confeccionar; formar; poner (triste, alegre) decir, pronunciar (un discurso, etc.); dar, prestar (excusas, juramento); cometer (error, equivocación).—*to m. a clean breast of*, confesar, admitir francamente un error.—*to m. a fool of*, engañar; poner en ridículo.—*to m. a hit*, (fam.) causar buena impresión. —*to m. fun of*, burlarse de.—*to m. good*, abonar, subsanar.—*to m. haste*, darse prisa.—*to m. known*, hacer saber; dar a conocer.—*to m. love to*, enamorar, cortejar, hacer el amor a. —*to m. money*, ganar dinero.—*to m. no difference*, no importar, ser indiferente.—*to m. off with*, llevarse,

arrebatar.—*to m. one's way*, avanzar; progresar; abrirse paso; salir bien. —*to m. room for*, dar paso a; dejar campo, lugar o puesto para; dar lugar o puesto a.—*to m. sense*, tener sentido (una frase); parecer acertado; (con **of**) comprender.—*to m. sure*, cerciorar, asegurar.—*to m. the most of*, aprovecharse de.—*to m. up*, inventar (cuentos); conciliar, apaciguar; saldar, ajustar.—*to m. up for*, compensar, indemnizar.—*to m. up one's mind*, resolverse, determinar.—*to m. way*, abrir paso.—*vii.* (con **at**, **for**, o **toward**) dirigirse o encaminarse a, abalanzarse a; (con **for** o **to**) contribuir a, servir para.—*to m. merry*, divertirse; regodearse.—*to m. sure*, asegurarse, cerciorarse.—*s.* hechura, forma, figura; fabricación, manufactura; marca, nombre de fábrica.— **believe** [-bilív], *a.* fingido, falso, de mentirijillas.—*s.* artificio, fingimiento.—*vt.* fingir.— **r** [méikœ(r)], *s.* hacedor; artífice; fabricante; autor; librador (de cheque, pagaré, etc.); otorgante (de escritura). — **up** [-ʌp], *s.* conjunto; carácter, modo de ser; (teat.) caracterización; afeite, maquillaje.—*vti.* **y** *vii.* [10] maquillar(se).
malady [mælǝdi], *s.* mal, enfermedad.
maladjustment [mælǝdžástmǝnt], *s.* ajuste defectuoso; inadaptación; discordancia.
malaria [mǝlériǝ], *s.* malaria, paludismo.
Malay(an) [mǝléi(ǝn)], *a.* **y** *s.* malayo, de Malaca.
male [meil], *a.* masculino; macho; varonil.—*s.* varón, hombre; animal macho.
malediction [mælidíkšǝn, *s.* maldición.
malefactor [mælifæktǝ(r)], *s.* malhechor.
malevolent [mǝlévǝlǝnt], *a.* malévolo, maligno.
malice [mælis], *s.* malicia, malignidad. —*m. aforethought*, (for.) premeditación.—**malicious** [mǝlíšǝs], *a.* malicioso, maligno, maléfico.—**malign** [mǝláin], *a.* maligno; pernicioso; perjudicial.—*vt.* difamar; calumniar. —**malignant** [mǝlígnǝnt], *a.* maligno; malévolo; perverso; (med.) maligno, pernicioso.
malinger [mǝlíŋgœ(r)], *vi.* fingirse enfermo.— **er** [-œ(r)], *s.* remolón; (fam.) maula.
malleable [mæliǝbl], *a.* maleable; dúctil; dócil.
mallet [mælit], *s.* mazo, maceta.
malt [molt], *s.* malta.—*malted milk*, leche malteada.
mam(m)a [mámǝ, mǝmá], *s.* mamá.
mammal [mæmǝl], *s.* mamífero.

mammoth [mǽmoɵ], a. enorme, gigantesco.—s. mamut.

mammy [mǽmi], s. mamita, mamá; (E.U.) niñera o criada negra.

man [mæn], s. hombre; varón; peón (de ajedrez o damas).—m. and wife, marido y mujer.—m. Friday, auxiliar competente.—m. of all work, (fam.) factótum.—m. of straw, testaferro.—m. of war, buque de guerra.—to a m., hasta el último hombre.—vti. [1] tripular, dotar; armar; poner guarnición a.

manacle [mǽnakl], s. manilla.—pl. esposas.—vt. maniatar, poner esposas a.

manage [mǽnidʒ], vt. manejar, dirigir, administrar; gestionar, procurar; manipular.—vi. arreglarse, componérselas; darse uno maña.—-able [-abl], a. manejable, dócil, tratable.—-ment [-ment], s. manejo, gobierno, dirección, administración; (com.) gerencia; proceder, conducta; empresa (de teatro, etc.).— -r [mǽnidʒœ(r)], s. administrador, director; empresario; superintendente; (com.) gerente.

manatee [mænatí], s. manatí, vaca marina.

mandate [mǽndeit], s. mandato; mandado, encargo.—vt. asignar por mandato.—mandatory [mǽndatori], a. (for.) preceptivo, obligatorio.—s. mandatario.

mane [mein], s. crin o crines; melena (de león).

maneuver [manúvœ(r)], s. maniobra.—vt. y vi. maniobrar.

manful [mǽnful], a. viril, varonil; resuelto.

manganese [mængœnís], s. manganeso.

mange [meindʒ], s. sarna, roña.

manger [méindʒœ(r)], s. pesebre.

mangle [mǽŋgl], vt. mutilar, destrozar, estropear, lacerar; planchar con máquina.—s. planchadora mecánica.

mango [mǽŋgou], s. (bot.) mango.

mangrove [mǽŋgrouv], s. mangle.

mangy [méindʒi], a. sarnoso, roñoso.

manhood [mǽnhud], s. hombría; edad viril; virilidad; masculinidad; los hombres.

mania [méiniɵ], s. manía.—-c [méiniæk], a. y s. maníaco, maniático, loco.

manicure [mǽnikjur], s. manicura.—vi. hacer la manicura.—manicurist [mǽnikjurist], s. manicuro, manicura, manicurista.

manifest [mǽnifest], a. manifiesto, claro.—s. (com.) manifiesto.—vt. manifestar; poner o declarar en el manifiesto.—vi. hacer una manifestación o demostración pública.—-ation [-éishɵn], s. manifestación.— -o [mæniféstou], s. manifiesto, proclama.

manifold [mǽnifould], a. múltiple, numeroso; diverso.—s. copia o duplicado; (aut.) tubo múltiple, agregado.

manikin [mǽnikin], s. maniquí; muñeco; hombre pequeño.

manipulate [mœnípyuleit], vt. manipular; manejar.—manipulation [mœnipyuléishɵn], s. manipulación.

mankind [mænkáind], s. (la) humanidad, (el) género humano; [mǽnkaind], los hombres, el sexo masculino.—manliness [mǽnlinis], s. virilidad, hombría; valentía, ánimo.—manly [mǽnli], a. varonil; viril; animoso.

manner [mǽnœ(r)], s. manera, modo; modo de ser; suerte, jaez, género, especie; aire, ademán, porte.—pl. modales; costumbres; educación.—after the m. of, como, a la manera de, a la, a lo.—by no m. of means, de ningún modo.—in a m., en cierto modo, hasta cierto punto.—in a m. of speaking, como quien dice, por decirlo así.—-ism [-izm], s. amaneramiento, manerismo.

mannish [mǽnish], a. hombruno, machuno.—m. woman, virago, (fam.) marimacho.

manor [mǽnɵ(r)], s. feudo; finca o casa solariega.

mansion [mǽnshɵn], s. mansión; morada, residencia.

manslaughter [mǽnslɵtœ(r)], s. homicidio sin premeditación, o culposo.

mantel(piece) [mǽntl(pis)], s. repisa o tablero de chimenea; manto de la chimenea.

mantilla [mæntílɵ], s. mantilla; mantón.

mantle [mǽntl], s. manto, capa; palio.

manual [mǽnyual], a. manual; manuable.—s. manual.

manufacture [mænyufǽkchɵr(r)], s. fabricación, elaboración; manufactura.—vt. manufacturar, fabricar.—vi. manufacturar, ser fabricante.—-r [-œ(r)], s. fabricante, industrial.—manufacturing [-iŋ], a. manufacturero, industrial, fabril.—s. fabricación, manufactura, elaboración.

manure [mœnjúr], vt. abonar, estercolar.—s. abono, estiércol.

manuscript [mǽnyuskript], a. y s. manuscrito.

many [méni], a., pron. y s. muchos, muchas.—a great m., muchos, muchísimos.—as m., igual número, otros tantos.—as m. as, tantos como; cuantos; más que; hasta.—how m.? ¿cuántos?—one, two, etc., too m., uno, dos, etc., de más o de sobra.—so m., tantos.—the m., la mayoría, la mayor parte de la gente; las masas, la muchedumbre.—*too m.*, demasiados.—*twice as m.*, dos veces más.

map [mæp], *s.* mapa, carta geográfica; plano (de una ciudad).—*m. maker*, cartógrafo.—*vti.* [1] delinear mapas; (a veces con **out**) proyectar, hacer planes.

maple [méjpl], *s.* arce, (Am.) meple.

mar [mar], *vti.* [1] echar a perder, estropear, desfigurar.

marauder [məródœ(r)], *s.* merodeador. —**marauding** [məródiŋ], *s.* merodeo, pillaje.

marble [márbl], *s.* mármol; canica o bolita de vidrio o mármol.—*pl.* juego de canicas o bolitas.—*a.* marmóreo, de mármol.

march [march], *vt.* poner en marcha, hacer marchar.—*vi.* marchar, caminar.—*to m. in*, entrar.—*to m. off*, irse, marcharse.—*to m. out*, salir o hacer salir.—*s.* marcha; progreso, adelanto; (mil. mús.) marcha, pasodoble; (M.) marzo.

marchioness [márʃǫnįs], *s.* marquesa.

mare [mer], *s.* yegua.

margarine [márdźarin], *s.* margarina, mantequilla artificial.

margin [márdźįn], *s.* margen, borde, orilla; reserva; sobrante.—*vt.* marginar, apostillar; poner borde o margen.—**al** [-al], *a.* marginal.

marigold [mérįgoųld], *s.* (bot.) caléndula, maravilla.

marine [mərín], *a.* marino, marítimo, naval.—*M. Corps*, Infantería de Marina.—**r** [mærįnœ(r)], *s.* marinero, nauta.

marital [mérįtal], *a.* marital, matrimonial.

maritime [mérįtaim], *a.* marítimo.

marjoram [márdźǫram], *s.* mejorana.

mark [mark], *s.* marca; signo; seña o señal; huella, impresión; nota; calificación; marco (moneda); blanco o diana.—*birth m.*, antojo, lunar.—*question m.*, punto de interrogación (?).—*up to the m.*, (fam.) enteramente satisfactorio, perfectamente bueno o bien.—*vt.* marcar, señalar; acotar; advertir, notar.—*to m. down*, poner por escrito, anotar; marcar a un precio más bajo.—*to m. out*, elegir o escoger; cancelar, borrar.— **er** [márkœ(r)], *s.* marcador; marca; jalón.

market [márkįt], *s.* mercado; plaza; feria.—*m. price*, precio corriente.—*m. woman*, verdulera.—*on the m.*, de o en venta.—*vt.* llevar al, o vender en el mercado; hallar mercado para.—*vi.* comprar o vender en un mercado; hacer compras en un mercado

o tienda de víveres.— **ing** [-iŋ], *s.* gasto de plaza; compra o venta en el mercado.

marksman [márksmạn], *s.* buen tirador. — **ship** [-ʃįp], *s.* buena puntería.

marmalade [mármạlejd], *s.* mermelada o conserva de naranja.

marmot [mármǫt], *s.* (zool.) marmota.

maroon [mạrún], *s.* y *a.* castaño o rojo oscuro.—*vt.* abandonar a uno en una costa desierta.

marquee [markí], *s.* marquesina.

marquetry [márkẹtrį], *s.* marquetería.

marquis [márkwįs], *s.* marqués.— **e** [markíz], *s.* marquesa.

marriage [mérįdź], *s.* matrimonio; casamiento, boda, nupcias; enlace. —*m. articles*, capitulaciones matrimoniales.—**married** [mérįd], *a.* casado; matrimonial, conyugal.—*m. couple*, cónyuges, marido y mujer.—*to get m.*, casarse.

marrow [mérou], *s.* tuétano, médula, meollo; substancia, esencia.

marry [mérį], *vti.* [7] casar, desposar, unir en matrimonio; casarse con. —*vii.* casarse, contraer matrimonio.

marsh [marʃ], *s.* pantano, ciénaga, marisma.

marshal [márʃạl], *s.* mariscal; (E.U.) alguacil; jefe de policía en algunas ciudades.—*vti.* [2] ordenar, poner en orden; mandar, guiar.

marshmallow [márʃmælou], *s.* altea; pastilla de altea.

marshy [márʃį], *a.* pantanoso, cenagoso.

mart [mart], *s.* mercado; emporio.

martial [márʃạl], *a.* marcial.

martyr [mártœ(r)], *s.* mártir.—*vt.* martirizar; atormentar.— **dom** [-dǫm], *s.* martirio.— **ize** [-ajz], *vt.* martirizar.

marvel [márvẹl], *s.* maravilla, prodigio. —*vii.* [2] maravillarse, admirarse.— **(l)ous** [-ʌs], *a.* maravilloso, prodigioso; milagroso; increíble; (fam.) excelente.

mascot [mæskat], *s.* mascota, amuleto.

masculine [méskjulįn], *a.* masculino; varonil.—**masculinity** [mæskjulínįtį], *s.* masculinidad.

mash [mæʃ], *s.* amasijo, masa.—*vt.* amasar, majar.—*mashed potatoes*, puré de papas o patatas.

mask [mæsk], *s.* máscara, careta, antifaz; disfraz.—*death m.*, mascarilla. —*masked ball*, baile de máscaras.—*vt.* enmascarar, disfrazar; encubrir.—*vi.* andar disfrazado.

mason [méjsǫn], *s.* albañil; (M.) masón. — **ry** [-rį], *s.* albañilería; mampostería; (M.) masonería.

masquerade [mæskẹréjd], *s.* mascarada, comparsa de máscaras; máscara, disfraz.—*vi.* enmascararse, disfrazarse.

mass [mæs], *s.* masa, montón, mole; bulto, volumen; (M.) misa.—*M. book,* libro de misa; misal.—*m. meeting,* reunión en masa, mitin popular. —*m. production,* producción o fabricación en serie.—*the masses,* el pueblo, las masas.—*vt.* juntar, reunir en masa, amasar.

massacre [mǽsəkœ(r)], *s.* masacre, matanza, carnicería.—*vt.* matar atrozmente, destrozar, hacer una carnicería.

massage [mæsáʒ], *s.* masaje, fricción. —*vt.* dar masaje.—**massagist** [mæsáʒist], *s.* masajista.—**masseur** [mæsœ́r], *s.* masajista (hombre).— **masseuse** [mæsœ́z], *s.* masajista (mujer).

massif [mǽsif], *s.* macizo.—**massive** [mǽsiv], *a.* macizo, abultado, sólido.

mast [mæst], *s.* mástil, palo mayor.—*pl.* arboladura.

master [mǽstœ(r)], *s.* amo, dueño, señor; maestro; director; señorito; perito, experto.—*m. builder,* maestro de obras; contratista.—*M. of Arts,* licenciado, maestro en artes.—*a.* maestro, superior.—*vt.* amaestrar, domar; dominar; conocer a fondo.— —**ful** [-ful], *a.* dominante; experto; excelente.— —**ly** [-li], *a.* magistral; maestro.—*adv.* con maestría; magistralmente.— —**piece** [-pis], *s.* obra maestra.— —**y** [-i], *s.* dominio, poder; maestría, destreza; conocimiento.

mastiff [mǽstif], *s.* mastín.

mat [mæt], *s.* estera, esterilla, felpudo; rejilla; colchón gimnástico; orla, diafragma.—*a.* mate, sin lustre.

match [mæch], *s.* fósforo, cerilla; pareja; igual, semejante; (dep.) partido, juego, contienda; concurso, certamen. —*drawn m.,* empate.—*m. point,* (dep.) tanto o punto decisivo.—*to meet one's m.,* encontrar la horma de su zapato.—*vt.* hermanar, aparear; igualar a, equiparar; competir con. —*vi.* armonizar, hacer juego, casar.— —**less** [mǽchlis], *a.* incomparable, sin igual, sin par.— —**maker** [-meikœ(r)], *s.* casamentero; organizador de encuentros deportivos.

mate [meit], *s.* consorte, cónyuge; compañero, compañera; macho o hembra entre los animales; mate (ajedrez); (mar.) piloto.—*vt.* casar; aparear (animales).—*vi.* aparearse, copular (los animales).

material [mətíriəl], *a.* material; sustancial, esencial.—*s.* material o ingrediente; materia o asunto; género, tejido.— —**ize** [-aiz], *vt.* materializar; dar cuerpo, exteriorizar.—*vi.* hacerse visible o corpóreo; realizarse o

verificarse (planes, etc.); cuajar; tomar forma; aparecer.

maternal [mətœ́rnəl], *a.* maternal, materno.—**maternity** [mətœ́rniti], *s.* maternidad.

mathematic(al) [mæθimǽtik(əl)], *a.* matemático.—**mathematician** [mæθimətíʃən], *s.* matemático.—**mathematics** [mæθimǽtiks], *s.* matemática(s).

matinée [mætinéi], *s.* matiné, función de tarde.

mating [méitiŋ], *s.* apareamiento; casamiento.—*m. season,* época de celo (de los animales).

matriculate [mətríkyuleit], *vt.* y *vi.* matricular(se).—*s.* y *a.* matriculado. —**matriculation** [mətrikyuléiʃən], *s.* matrícula, matriculación.

matrimonial [mætrimóuniəl], *a.* matrimonial; conyugal, marital.—**matrimony** [mǽtrimoni], *s.* matrimonio.

matrix [méitriks], *s.* (*pl.* **matrices** [méitrisiz]) matriz; molde.

matron [méitron], *s.* matrona; ama de llaves; vigilante, celadora (de asilo, cárcel de mujeres, etc.); enfermera jefe; acomodadora.

matter [mǽtœ(r)], *s.* materia; substancia; asunto, cuestión; material; cosa, negocio; importancia; pus.—*as a m. of fact,* a decir verdad; de hecho; en realidad.—*m. of course,* cosa natural, de rutina.—*m. of fact,* realidad, hecho cierto.—*m.-of-fact,* positivista, práctico, prosaico; sensato.—*(it is) no m.,* no importa.—*no m. how (much, good, etc.),* por (bueno, mucho, muy bueno, etc.) que.—*small m.,* cosa sin importancia; menudencia.—*to make matters worse,* para colmo de desdichas.—*what is the matter?* ¿qué pasa? ¿qué ocurre?—*vi.* importar; convenir, hacer al caso.—*what does it m.?* ¿qué importa?

matting [mǽtiŋ], *s.* estera; orla o marco de cartón (para cuadros, grabados, etc.).

mattress [mǽtris], *s.* colchón; jergón.

mature [mətiúr], *a.* maduro; (com.) vencido, pagadero.—*vt.* madurar, sazonar.—*vi.* madurar(se), sazonarse; (com.) vencer, cumplirse un plazo. —**maturity** [-iti], *s.* madurez; (com.) vencimiento.

maul [mol], *vt.* apalear, aporrear; maltratar.—*s.* mazo.

maxim [mǽksim], *s.* máxima, adagio, axioma.

maximum [mǽksiməm], *s.* y *a.* máximo.

may [mei], *vai.* [11] poder, tener facultad o permiso, ser posible o permitido. —*m. I come in?* ¿se puede entrar?— *m. you have a good trip,* que tenga Ud.

buen viaje.—s. (M.) mes de mayo.
—*M. day*, el primero de mayo.

Mayan [máyan], a. y s. maya, de los mayas.

maybe [méibi], adv. acaso, quizá, tal vez.

mayonnaise [meionéiz], s. mayonesa.

mayor [méio(r)], s. alcalde.— **ess [-is], s.** alcaldesa.

maze [meiz], s. laberinto; perplejidad, confusión.—*to be in a m.*, estar perplejo.

me [mi], pron. pers. me, mí.—*do me the favor*, hágame Ud. el favor.—*for me*, para mí.—*with me*, conmigo.

meadow [médou], s. pradera, vega, prado.

meager [míga(r)], a. escaso, pobre, insuficiente; magro, flaco.—**ness [-nis], s.** escasez; delgadez; pobreza.

meal [mil], s. comida; harina.—*m. time*, hora de comer.— **ly [míli], a.** harinoso.

mean [min], a. humilde; mediano; inferior; bajo, vil; malo, desconsiderado; de mal humor; despreciable; tacaño, mezquino; insignificante; medio; intermedio.—*m.-spirited*, ruin, bajo.—*s.* medio; mediocridad, medianía; término medio.—*pl.* modos; fondos, medios, recursos.—*by all means*, sin duda, por supuesto; por todos los medios posibles.—*by means of*, por medio de; mediante. —*by no means*, de ningún modo. —*to live on one's means*, vivir de sus rentas.—*vti.* [10] significar, querer decir; pensar, proponerse, pretender; destinar a; envolver, encerrar; decir de veras.—*I didn't m. to do it*, lo hice sin pensar, o sin querer.—*I m. it*, hablo en serio o formalmente.—*what do you m.?* ¿qué quiere Ud. decir? ¿qué se propone Ud.?—*you don't m. it!* ¡calla!— **ing [minin], a.** significativo.—*well-m.*, de buena fe, bien intencionado.—*s.* intención; sentido; significado, significación.— **ingless [minulis], a.** sin sentido, vacío.— **ness [mínnis], s.** bajeza; vileza; miseria, mezquindad; mal genio.— **meant [ment], pret. y pp.** de **TO MEAN**. —*to be m. for*, o *to*, servir para; haber nacido para; tener por objeto.—*who is m.?* ¿de quién se trata?— **time [mintaim],** —**while [mínhwail], adv.** mientras tanto, entretanto, por de (o lo) pronto.—*s.* ínterin.—*in the m.*, mientras tanto, en el ínterin, hasta entonces.

measles [mízlz], s. pl. sarampión.

measurable [mézurabl], a. mensurable; apreciable; moderado.—**measurably [mézurabli], adv.** perceptiblemente, hasta cierto grado; con moderación.

—measure [mézu(r), s. medida; compás, cadencia; proyecto de ley; (mús.) compás.—*pl.* medios—*beyond m.*, con exceso, sobremanera.—*in a great m.*, en gran manera; en gran parte.—*in some m.*, hasta cierto punto, en cierto modo.—*vt.* medir; calibrar, graduar; (mar.) arquear, cubicar (un barco).—*vi.* medir, tener tal o cual dimensión.—**measured [mézurd], a.** acompasado, medido; moderado; rítmico.—**measurement [mézurment], s.** medición; dimensión; medida; (mar.) arqueo, cubicación.

meat [mit], s. carne; sustento (en general); substancia, jugo.—*cold meats*, fiambres.—*m. ball*, albóndiga. —*m. market*, carnicería.— **y [míti], a.** carnoso; jugoso, substancioso.

mechanic [mikénik], a. y s mecánico.— **al [-al], a.** mecánico, maquinal. —*m. pencil*, lapicero.— **s [-s], s.** mecánica.—**mechanism [mékanizm], s.** mecanismo; maquinaria.—**mechanization [mekanizéishon], s.** mecanización; maquinismo; (mil.) motorización.—**mechanize [mékanaiz], vt.** mecanizar; (mil.) motorizar.

medal [médal], s. medalla; condecoración.— **lion [midélyon], s.** medallón.

meddle [médl], vi. (gen. con **with** o **in**) meterse, entremeterse.— **r [médlœ(r)], s.** entremetido.— **some [médlsam], a.** entremetido, oficioso.

median [mídian], a. mediano, del medio.

mediate [mídieit], vt. y vi. mediar, intervenir, intermediar.—*a.* [mídiit], mediato, medio; interpuesto.—**mediation [midiéishon], s.** mediación, intercesión; intervención; tercería.—**mediator [mídieito(r)], s.** mediador, intercesor, medianero.

medical [médikal], a. médico, medicinal. —*m. corps*, cuerpo de sanidad.— *m. kit*, botiquín.—**medicate [médikeit], vt.** medicinar.—**medication [medikéishon], s.** medicación; medicamento.—**medicine [médisin], s.** medicina, medicamento, remedio; medicina (arte o ciencia).—*m man*, exorcista; curandero (indio).— **medicinal [midísinal], s.** medicinal.

medieval [midível], a. medi(o)eval.

mediocre [mídiokœ(r)], a. mediocre, mediano; vulgar, trivial.—**mediocrity [midiákriti], s.** mediocridad; medianía.

meditate [méditeit], vt. y vi. meditar, reflexionar.—**meditation [meditéishon], s.** meditación, reflexión.— **meditative [méditeitiv], a.** meditativo, meditabundo.

Mediterranean [mediteréinian], a. mediterráneo.

medium [mídiʌm], *s.* medio, instrumento; médium o medio (en el espiritismo); medio ambiente.—*at a m.*, uno con otro, por término medio.—*a.* mediano, intermedio; (coc.) no muy cocido, término medio.

medley [médli], *s.* miscelánea, mezcla, mezcolanza; (mus.) popurrí.

meek [mik], *a.* manso, humilde, dócil.—**ness** [míknis], *s.* mansedumbre, humildad, docilidad.

meet [mit], *vti.* [10] encontrarse con; encontrar, topar o chocar con; satisfacer, llenar (requisitos); pagar, saldar (un pagaré, etc.); sufragar (los gastos, etc.); ir a esperar (un tren, vapor, persona, etc.); combatir o pelear con; conocer o ser presentado.—*to m. a charge,* refutar, responder a una acusación.—*to m. the eye,* saltar a la vista.—*vii.* encontrarse, verse; reunirse, chocarse, tocarse; confluir.—*till we m. again,* hasta la vista, hasta más ver(nos).—*to m. halfway,* partir la diferencia.—**ing** [mítiŋ], *s.* mitin; reunión, sesión; junta, asamblea; entrevista; encuentro, duelo o desafío.—*to call a m.,* convocar a junta.

megaphone [mégáfoun], *s.* megáfono, portavoz, bocina.

melancholy [mélʌnkali], *s.* melancolía, tristeza.—*a.* melancólico.

mellow [mélou], *a.* maduro; sazonado; meloso; tierno, blando, suave.—*vt.* y *vi.* sazonar(se); madurar(se); ablandar(se), suavizar(se).

melodious [melóudiʌs], *a.* melodioso.—**melody** [mélodi], *s.* melodía.

melon [mélon], *s.* melón.

melt [melt], *vti.* y *vii.* [6] derretir(se), fundir(se); deshelar(se); disolver(se).—*to m. into tears,* deshacerse en lágrimas.

member [mémbœ(r)], *s.* miembro; socio, asociado.— **ship** [-ȿip], *s.* asociación, calidad de miembro o socio; número de socios o miembros; personal.—*m. dues,* cuota.

membrane [mémbrein], *s.* membrana.

memento [miméntou], *s.* recordatorio, memoria, recuerdo.—**memo** [mémou], *s. abrev.* de MEMORANDUM.—**memoir** [mémwar], *s.* memoria, informe, relación.—*pl.* memorias; (auto)biografía.—**memorable** [mémorabl], *a.* memorable.—**memorandum** [memoréndam], *s.* memorándum, memoria, nota, apuntación.—*m. book,* memorándum, libreta, prontuario.—**memorial** [mimórial], *a.* conmemorativo.—*s.* monumento conmemorativo; memorial, instancia, petición; (for.) nota, apuntamiento.—**memorize** [mémoraiz], *vt.* aprender

de memoria, memorizar.—**memory** [mémori], *s.* memoria, recuerdo; memoria, retentiva.—*from m.,* de memoria.

men [men], *s. pl.* de MAN.

menace [ménis], *vt.* y *vi.* amenazar.—*s.* amenaza, reto.

mend [mend], *vt.* remendar; repasar, zurcir; arreglar, componer; enmendar.—*vi.* enmendarse, reformarse.—*s.* remiendo; reparación; reforma.—*on the m.,* mejorando(se).

menial [mínial], *a.* y *s.* servil, bajo.

menstruate [ménstrueit], *vi.* menstruar.—**menstruation** [menstruéiȿon], *s.* menstruación.

mental [méntal], *a.* mental.—*m. test,* examen de capacidad mental.—**mentality** [mentéliti], *s.* mentalidad.

mention [ménȿon], *s.* mención, alusión.—*vt.* mencionar, mentar, aludir a.—*don't m. it!* ¡no hay de qué! ¡de nada!—*not to m.,* por no decir nada de; además.

menu [ményu], *s.* menú.

meow [miáu], *s.* y *vi.* = MEW.

mercantile [mérkantil], *a.* mercantil, comercial.—**mercantilism** [mérkantilizm], *s.* mercantilismo.

mercenary [mérseneri], *a.* interesado, mercenario.—*s.* mercenario.

merchandise [mérchandaiz], *s.* mercancía(s), mercadería.—**merchant** [mérchant], *s.* mercader, comerciante; tendero.—*a.* mercante, mercantil.—*m. marine,* marina mercante.

merciful [mérsiful], *a.* misericordioso, compasivo.—**merciless** [mérsilis], *a.* despiadado, desalmado, inhumano.

mercurial [mœrkjúrial], *a.* mercurial; (fig.) vivo, volátil.—**mercury** [mérkjuri], *s.* mercurio, azogue.

mercy [mérsi], *s.* misericordia, clemencia, compasión; merced, gracia, perdón.—*m. killing,* eutanasia.—*m. stroke,* golpe de gracia.

merge [mœrdž], *vt.* y *vi.* unir(se), fundir(se), fusionar(se).—**r** [mœrdžœ(r)], *s.* unión, consolidación, fusión comercial.

meridian [mirídian], *s.* meridiano; mediodía; (fig.) cenit.—*a.* meridiano.

meringue [meréŋ], *s.* merengue.

merit [mérit], *s.* mérito; merecimiento.—*on its (his, etc.) own merits,* por sí mismo.—*vt.* merecer, ser digno de.—**orious** [-órias], *a.* meritorio, benemérito.

mermaid [mérmeid], *s.* sirena.—**merman** [mérmæn], *s.* tritón.

merrily [mérili], *adv.* alegremente, con júbilo.—**merriment** [mériment], *s.* alegría, júbilo, gozo, regocijo; diversión.—**merry** [méri], *a.* alegre, festivo, divertido; feliz; gozoso; risueño.—*m.-go-round*, tiovivo, caballitos.—*m. Christmas*, felices Pascuas. —*to make m.*, divertirse, ir de parranda.—merrymaker [mérimejkœ(r)], *s.* fiestero, parrandero.— merrymaking [mérimejkiŋ], *s.* fiesta, parranda, holgorio.—*a.* regocijado, parrandero.

mesh [meʃ], *s.* malla; punto u obra de malla; redecilla; (mec.) engranaje. —*pl.* red, trampas, lazos.—*vt.* enredar, coger con red; (mec.) endentar. —*vi.* enredarse; (mec.) endentar, engranar.

mess [mes], *s.* ración; rancho (comida); (fam.) lío, confusión.—*vt.* dar rancho; (a veces con up) desarreglar, desordenar, confundir; ensuciar.—*vi.* comer en rancho o hacer rancho; arrancharse; hacer un revoltijo.—*to m. about o around*, ocuparse en fruslerías, entrometerse.

message [mésjdż], *s.* mensaje; recado, parte, aviso.—messenger [mésendżœ(r)], *s.* mensajero, mandadero, propio, recadero.

messy [mési], *a.* sucio, puerco; desordenado, revuelto.

met [met], *pret.* y *pp.* de TO MEET.

metal [métḁl], *s.* metal.—*a.* metálico, de metal.- —lic [métǽlik], *a.* metálico.- —lize [métḁlajz], *vt.* metalizar.- —lurgic(al) [metalœ̈rdżik(ḁl)], *a.* metalúrgico.— —lurgy [métḁlœrdżi], *s.* metalurgia.

metamorphose [metamórfouz], *vt.* metamorfosear.—metamorphosis [metamórfǫsis], *s.* metamorfosis.

metaphor [métḁfǫ(r)], *s.* metáfora.

meteor [mítiǫ(r)], *s.* meteoro; estrella fugaz.- —ological [-olǽdżikḁl], *a.* meteorológico.- —ologist [-álodżist], *s.* meteorólogo.- —ology [-álodżi], *s.* meteorología.

method [méθǫd], *s.* método, procedimiento; orden, regularidad; técnica.- —ic(al) [meθádjk(ḁl)], *a.* metódico, sistemático.

meticulous [mitʃkyulʌs], *a.* meticuloso.

metre [mítœ(r)], *s.* = METER.

metric(al) [métrik(ḁl)], *a.* métrico.

metro [métrou], *s.* medida (poética y de longitud. Ver Tabla.); contador (de gas, agua, etc.).

metronome [métronoum], *s.* metrónomo.

metropolis [metrápolis], *s.* metrópoli; urbe.—metropolitan [metropálitḁn], *a.* metropolitano, de la capital.—*s.* ciudadano de una metrópoli.

mettle [métl], *s.* temple, brío, coraje; vivacidad, fuego.- —some [-sʌm], *a.* brioso, vivo, fogoso.

mew [mju], *s.* maullido; gaviota.—*pl.*

establo, caballeriza.—*vi.* maullar, mayar.- —ing [mjújŋ], *s.* maullido; muda (de las aves).—*a.* maullador; que está en la muda.

Mexican [méksjkḁn], *a.* y *s.* mejicano.

mezzanine [mézḁnin], *s.* entresuelo.

mice [majs], *s. pl.* de MOUSE.

microbe [májkroub], *s.* microbio.

microphone [májkrofoun], *s.* micrófono.

microscope [májkroskoup], *s.* microscopio.—microscopic(al) [majkroskápjk(ḁl)], *a.* microscópico.

mid [mjd], *a.* medio.—*(in) m. air*, (en) el aire.—*m.-course*, media carrera o medio camino.—*m.-sea*, alta mar.- —day [míddej], *s.* mediodía.—*a.* del mediodía.- —dle [mídl], *a.* medio, intermedio, mediano; de en medio. —*M.-Age*, medieval.—*m.-aged*, de edad madura.—*M. Ages*, Edad Media.—*m.-class*, de la clase media. —*m. class*, clase media, burguesía. —*m. finger*, dedo del corazón.—*m. ground*, posición intermedia.—*m.-sized*, de mediana estatura o tamaño. —*s.* centro, medio, mitad.—*about o towards the m. of*, a mediados de. —*m. of*, mediados de.—*m. of the road*, posición intermedia.—*m.-of-the-road*, moderado, enemigo de extremos.— —dleman [mídlmæn], *s.* intermediario; (com.) corredor; revendedor; agente de negocios.- —dlemost [mídlmoust], *a.* del medio; en el medio o más cercano a él.- —dleweight [mídlwejt], *a.* (dep.) de peso medio (hasta 160 lbs.).—*s.* peso medio.- —dling [mídliŋ], *a.* mediano, regular, pasadero.

middy [mídi], *s.* (fam.) guardiamarina; blusa marinera.

midget [mídżit], *s.* enanillo, liliputiense; chiquillo vivaracho.

midnight [mídnajt], *s.* medianoche. —*a.* nocturno; negro.

midriff [mídrif], *s.* (anat.) diafragma; parte media del cuerpo.

midshipman [mídʃipmḁn], *s.* guardiamarina.

midst [mjdst], *s.* medio, centro; (fig.) seno; presión, rigor.—*in our, their, your m.*, en medio de nosotros, ellos, ustedes.—*in the m. of*, en medio de, entre; rodeado de; en lo más (reñido, agitado, etc.).—*adv.* en medio.—*prep.* (poét.) entre.

midstream [mídstrím], *s.* el medio de una corriente.

midsummer [mídsʌmœ(r)], *s.* la mitad del verano, pleno verano.

midway [mídwej], *s.* mitad del camino, medio camino.—*a.* situado a mitad del camino.—*adv.* en medio del camino; a mitad del camino.

midwife [mídwaif], *s.* partera, comadrona.

mien [min], *s.* semblante, aire, talante, facha.

might [mait], *pret. y pres. opcional* de MAY.—*s.* poder, poderío, fuerza. —*with m. and main,* con todas sus fuerzas, a más no poder.— —*ily* [máitili], *adv.* poderosamente.— —*y* [-i], *a.* potente, poderoso; fuerte, vigoroso; enorme; eficaz, importante.

migraine [máigrein], *s.* jaqueca, migraña.

migrant [máigrant], *s.* emigrante; ave migratoria o de paso.—*a.* nómada; (e)migratorio.—**migrate** [máigreit], *vi.* emigrar; trasplantarse.—**migration** [maigréişon], *s.* (e)migración; trasplante.—**migratory** [máigratori], *a.* (e)migratorio; nómada.

mike [maik], *s.* (fam.) micrófono = MICROPHONE.

milch [milch], *a.* lechera.—*m. cow,* vaca lechera.

mild [maild], *a.* suave, moderado, manso; benigno, blando, indulgente; leve, ligero.

mildew [míldiu], *s.* moho; tizón (de las plantas).—*vi.* enmohecerse; atizonarse.

mildness [máildnis], *s.* suavidad, lenidad; apacibilidad; mansedumbre, indulgencia.

mile [mail], *s.* milla. Ver Tabla.— —**age** [máilidž], *s.* longitud en millas; peaje por milla; número de millas (millaje) recorridas o recorribles.

militant [mílitant], *a.* militante, combatiente; belicoso, guerrero.—**military** [mílitari], *a.* militar; guerrero, marcial; castrense; soldadesco; de guerra.—*m. coup o uprising,* pronunciamiento, cuartelazo.—*s.* ejército, milicia, soldadesca, tropa(s), los militares.—**militia** [milíşä], *s.* milicia. —**militiaman** [milíşäman], *s.* miliciano.

milk [milk], *s.* leche.—*m. diet,* dieta o régimen lácteo.—*vt.* ordeñar; (fam.) extraer de.— —**er** [mílkœ(r)], *s.* ordeñador; vaca (etc.) de leche.— —**maid** [-meid], *s.* lechera.— —**man** [-mæn], *s.* lechero.— —**y** [-i], *a.* lácteo; lechoso; blando, tierno, tímido.—*M. Way,* Vía Láctea.

mill [mil], *s.* molino; taller, fábrica; milésimo de un dólar; milésima parte; (fam.) pugilato.—*to go through the m.,* saber una cosa por experiencia. —*vt.* moler, desmenuzar; aserrar; fabricar; acordonar (moneda), estriar; fresar.—*to m. around,* arremolinarse.

miller [mílœ(r)], *s.* molinero; mariposa con manchas blancas.

milliner [mílinœ(r)], *s.* modista de sombreros.— —**y** [mílineri], *s.* artículos para sombreros femeninos; sombrerería femenina; ocupación en este sector; tienda de sombreros femeninos.

milling [mílin], *s.* molienda; acordonamiento, acuñación (moneda); cordoncillo de la moneda; fresado.—*m. around,* remolino.—*a.* de moler, fresar, etc.—*m. cutter o tool,* fresa. —*m. machine,* fresadora.—*m. saw,* sierra.

million [mílyon], *s.* millón.— —**aire** [-ér], *s. y a.* millonario.

millpond [mílpand], *s.* represa de molino.—**millstone** [mílstoun], *s.* muela, rueda de molino.

milt [milt], *s.* (anat.) bazo.

mime [maim], *s.* mimo; truhán; pantomima, farsa.

mimic [mímik], *vti.* [8] remedar.—*s.* imitador, remedador.—*a.* mímico, imitativo, burlesco.—**mimicked** [mímikt], *pret. y pp.* de TO MIMIC.— —**ry** [-ri], *s.* mímica; bufonería; monería, remedo; mimetismo.

mince [mins], *vt.* desmenuzar; picar (carne), hacer picadillo; medir (las palabras); atenuar.—*minced oath,* eufemismo.—*vi.* ser afectado al hablar, andar, etc.—*not to m. words,* hablar sin rodeos.— —**meat** [mínsmit], *s.* relleno de carne para pasteles.— *to make m. of,* destruir, aniquilar. —**mincingly** [mínsinli], *adv.* a pedacitos; a pasitos; con afectación.

mind [maind], *s.* mente, entendimiento, pensamiento, inteligencia; espíritu, ánimo; gusto, inclinación, afecto; memoria; voluntad, gana; intención, resolución; opinión, criterio.—*of one m.,* unánimes.—*of sound m.,* en su cabal juicio.—*out of m.,* olvidado. —*out of one's m.,* loco; fuera de juicio.—*to bear in m.,* tener en cuenta, tener presente.—*to call to m.,* recordar, traer a la memoria.—*to change one's m.,* mudar de parecer.—*to give someone a piece of one's m.,* decirle a alguien cuántas son cinco, ponerlo como nuevo.—*to have a m. to,* tener gana de, querer; proponerse.—*to have in m.,* recordar; tener en consideración; pensar en.—*to keep in m.,* tener presente o en cuenta.—*to make up one's m.,* decidirse.—*to my m.,* a mi juicio, a mi ver.—*with one m.,* unánimemente.—*vt.* notar, observar; atender a; cuidar; cuidarse de; tener inconveniente en; hacer caso a, o de. —*to m. one's business,* meterse uno en lo que le importa.—*vi.* atender,

obedecer, hacer caso; tener cuidado.
—*I don't m.*, no me importa.—
never m., no importa; no se moleste,
no se preocupe.— —**ful** [májndful],
a. atento, cuidadoso.

mine [main], *pron. pos.* mío, mía, míos,
mías; el mío, etc.; lo mío.—*of m.*,
mío, mía.

mine [main], *s.* mina (en todas sus
acepciones).—*vt.* minar; destruir;
zapar; extraer mineral.— —**r**
[májnœ(r)], *s.* minero; zapador.—
—**ral** [mínɛral], *s.* y *a.* mineral.—
—**alogy** [mínɛrálɒdᶎi], *s.* mineralogía.

mingle [míŋgl], *vt.* mezclar; confundir.
—*vi.* mezclarse, incorporarse.

miniature [mínjaçhur], *s.* miniatura.—
a. en miniatura; diminuto.

minimize [mínimaiz], *vt.* atenuar, quitar
importancia; reducir al mínimo;
achicar; menospreciar.—**minimum**
[mínimᴀm], *s.* y *a.* mínimo.

mining [máiniŋ], *s.* minería; acto de
sembrar minas explosivas.—*a.* minero, de mina.

minister [mínistœ(r)], *s.* ministro;
clérigo, pastor.—*vt.* y *vi.* dar,
ministrar, suministrar.—*vi.* atender,
auxiliar; socorrer.—**ministry** [mín-
istri], *s.* ministerio; sacerdocio; clero.

mink [miŋk], *s.* visón; piel de visón.

minnow [mínou], *s.* pececillo de agua
dulce usado como cebo.

minor [máinɒ(r)], *a.* menor; secundario,
inferior; leve.—*m. key*, tono menor.
—*s.* menor de edad.— —**ity**
[maináriti], *s.* minoridad, menoría
(de edad); minoría.

minstrel [mínstrɛl], *s.* juglar, trovador,
cantor; bardo.

mint [mint], *s.* casa de moneda; menta,
hierbabuena; pastilla de menta.—
a m. of money, un dineral.—*vt.* acuñar.

minus [máinʌs], *prep.* menos; falto de;
sin.—*a.* (mat. y elec.) negativo;
deficiente.—*m. sign*, signo de restar
(—).—*to be, come out, etc. m.
(something)*, salir perdiendo (algo).
—*s.* cantidad negativa; deficiencia;
signo menos.

minute [mainjút], *a.* menudo, minúsculo; nimio, minucioso.—*s.* [mínit],
minuto, momento, instante; (geom.
etc.) minuto; minuta, nota, apunte.
—*pl.* actas, minutas; memoria autén-
tica.—*m. book*, minutario, libro de
actas.—*m. hand*, minutero.—*this
(very) m.*, ahora mismito.

miracle [mírakl], *s.* milagro; maravilla.
—**miraculous** [mirǽkyulʌs], *a.* milagroso.

mirage [miráᶎ], *s.* espejismo.

mire [mair], *s.* lodo, cieno, fango;
lodazal.—*vt.* enlodar.—*vi.* atascarse.

mirror [mírɒ(r)], *s.* espejo; ejemplar,
modelo.—*vt.* reflejar.

mirth [mœrθ], *s.* alegría, regocijo.—
—**ful** [mœrθful], *a.* alegre, gozoso.—
—**less** [-lis], *a.* triste, abatido;
sardónico.

miry [máiri], *a.* cenagoso, fangoso.

misadventure [misadvénchɒ(r)], *s.*
desventura, desgracia.

miscarriage [miskǽridᶎ], *s.* aborto,
malparto; fracaso, malogro; extravío,
desmán.—**miscarry** [miskǽri], *vii.*
[7] frustrarse, malograrse; abortar,
malparir; extraviarse.

miscellaneous [misélḗinjᴀs], *a.* mis-
celáneo, mezclado; diverso.

mischief [míschif], *s.* mal, daño; injuria,
agravio; diablura, barrabasada; persona traviesa.—**mischievous** [mís-
chivᴀs], *a.* dañino; malicioso o
malévolo; chismoso o enredador;
travieso.

misdeed [misdíd], *s.* fechoría, delito.

misdemeanor [misdimínɒ(r)], *s.* mala
conducta; (for.) falta, delito de menor
cuantía.

miser [máizœ(r)], *s.* avaro, tacaño.—
—**able** [mízɛrabl], *a.* miserable;
pobre; sin valor; despreciable; lastimero.— —**ly** [májzœrli], *a.* avariento,
tacaño, mezquino.— —**y** [mízɛri], *s.*
miseria, desgracia; aflicción; calamidad.

misfortune [misfórchun], *s.* desgracia,
desdicha, contratiempo, percance,
infortunio, revés.

misgiving [misgívin], *s.* recelo, duda,
presentimiento; desconfianza, temor.

mishap [mishǽp], *s.* desgracia, accidente, contratiempo.

misinterpret [misintérprit], *vt.* y *vi.*
interpretar mal, tergiversar.— —**ation**
[-éjšɒn], *s.* tergiversación.

misjudge [misdᶎádᶎ], *vt.* y *vi.* errar,
juzgar mal.

mislead [mislíd], *vti.* [10] extraviar,
descaminar, descarriar, despistar;
conducir a conclusiones erróneas;
alucinar, engañar, seducir, pervertir.—
—**ing** [-in], *a.* engañoso; de falsas
apariencias.—**misled** [misléd], *pret.*
y *pp.* de TO MISLEAD.—*a.* engañado,
seducido, etc.

mismanagement [mismǽnidᶎmɛnt], *s.*
mal manejo, mala administración,
desconcierto.

misplace [mispléis], *vt.* colocar mal o
fuera de sitio; trastocar, traspapelar.

misprint [mísprint], *vt.* imprimir con
erratas.—*s.* error de imprenta, errata.

mispronounce [mispronáuns], *vt.* y *vi.*
pronunciar mal.—**mispronunciation**
[mispronʌnsiéjšɒn], *s.* pronunciación
incorrecta.

misrepresent [misreprizént], *vt.* desfigurar, tergiversar, disfrazar, falsificar.— —ation [-éįşǫn], *s.* falsedad, noticia o relación falsa, tergiversación.

miss [mįs], *s.* señorita; (abrev.) Srta., Sta.

miss [mįs], *vt.* errar (el tiro, el golpe, etc.); no acertar con, no comprender; equivocar; perder (el tren, la función, etc.); echar de menos; pasar sin, abstenerse, carecer de; pasar por alto, dejar de hacer.—*to m. the mark,* errar el blanco o el tiro.—*vi.* frustrarse, salir mal; marrar, errar, faltar; fallar.—*to m. out,* (fam.) llevarse chasco; llegar tarde.—*s.* malogro, fracaso; tiro fallido.

misshapen [mįsséįpn], *a.* disforme, deformado.

missile [mįsįl], *a.* arrojadizo.—*s.* proyectil; arma arrojadiza.

missing [mįsįŋ], *a.* extraviado, perdido; desaparecido; ausente.

mission [mįşǫn], *s.* misión.— —ary [-erį], *s.* misionario, misionero.—*a.* misional.—*m. station,* (igl.) misión.

missive [mįsįv], *s.* misiva, carta, comunicación escrita.

misspell [mįsspél], *vti.* [4] deletrear mal, escribir con mala ortografía.

mist [mįst], *s.* niebla, neblina, bruma; vapor, vaho; llovizna.—*vt.* empañar.—*vi.* lloviznar.

mistake [mįstéįk], *vti.* [10] equivocar, comprender mal; trabucar, tomar una cosa por otra.—*vii.* errar, equivocarse.—*s.* equivocación, yerro, desacierto; errata.—**mistaken** [mįstéįkn], *pp.* de TO MISTAKE.—*a.* erróneo, incorrecto, desacertado.

mister [mįstœ(r)], *s.* señor.—*Mister* (Mr.), Sr.

mistletoe [mįsltou], *s.* muérdago.

mistook [mįstúk], *pret.* de TO MISTAKE.

mistress [mįstrįs], *s.* señora, dueña, ama; querida.—*Mistress* (Mrs.) [mįsįz], Sra.

mistrust [mįstrʌst], *s.* desconfianza.—*vt.* desconfiar de, dudar de; sospechar, recelar.— —**ful** [-fųl], *a.* desconfiado, receloso.

misty [mįstį], *a.* brumoso; nublado; empañado; vago, impreciso.

misunderstand [mįsʌndœrstǽnd], *vti.* [10] entender mal, tomar en sentido erróneo.—**misunderstood** [mįsʌndœrstúd], *pret. y pp.* de TO MISUNDERSTAND.—*a.* mal entendido o comprendido.

misuse [mįsyús], *s.* mal uso; abuso, maltrato.—*vt.* [mįsyúz], abusar de; maltratar; estropear; usar mal o impropiamente.

mite [maįt], *s.* pizca, triza, mota; óbolo; gorgojo.

miter [máįtœ(r)], *s.* mitra; tiara del Papa; dignidad de obispo.

mitigate [mįtįgeįt], *vt.* mitigar, calmar.—*vi.* calmarse, mitigarse.

mitt [mįt], *s.* mitón; guante de beisbol.

mitten [mįtn], *s.* mitón.—*pl.* (fam.) guantes de boxeo; (fam.) las manos.

mix [mįks], *vti.* y *vii.* [4] mezclar(se), unir(se).—*to m. up,* incorporar, asociar; confundir; envolver.—*s.* mezcla; proporciones de los ingredientes de una mezcla.—*m.-up,* (fam.) lío, confusión; agarrada.— —**ture** [mįkschų(r)], *s.* mezcla; mixtura; mezcolanza.

moan [moun], *s.* quejido, gemido, lamento.—*vt.* lamentar, llorar, deplorar.—*vi.* gemir, quejarse; lamentarse.

moat [mout], *s.* foso.—*vt.* rodear con fosos.

mob [mab], *s.* chusma, populacho, gentuza; (fam.) turbamulta; multitud.—*vti.* [1] atropellar.—*vii.* formar tropel, tumulto, alboroto.

mobile [móųbįl], *a.* movedizo, movible, móvil; inconstante, variable.— **mobility** [mobįlįtį], *s.* movilidad; volubilidad.—**mobilization** [mobįlįzéįşǫn], *s.* movilización.—**mobilize** [móųbįlaįz], *vt.* movilizar, poner en pie de guerra; poner en movimiento.

moccasin [mákąsįn], *s* mocasín o mocasina (calzado); mocasín (serpiente).

mock [mak], *vt.* mofar, escarnecer; remedar; engañar, burlar.—*to m. at,* burlarse o mofarse de, hacer mofa de.—*s.* mofa, burla, befa; remedo.—*a.* ficticio falso, imitado; cómico, burlesco.— —**ery** [mákœrį], *s.* mofa, burla, irrisión; remedo; parodia.— —**ing** [-įŋ], *a.* burlón.— —**ingbird** [-įŋbœrd], *s.* (Am.) sinsonte.

mode [moud], *s.* modo, manera, procedimiento; moda; uso, costumbre; (gram. fil. mús.) modo; (mús.) modalidad.— —**l** [mádęl], *s.* modelo, ejemplar o patrón; prototipo; muestra; horma; patrón, figurín; modelo vivo.—*a.* modelo, ejemplar.—*vti.* [2] modelar; moldear.—*vii.* servir de modelo, modelar.— —**l(l)ing** [mádęlįŋ], *s.* modelado.—*a.* modelador.

moderate [mádęrįt], *a.* moderado; regular, ordinario; razonable, sobrio; módico (en precio).—*s.* moderado.—*vt.* y *vi.* [mádęreįt], moderar(se), calmar(se); presidir.—**moderation** [mádęréįşǫn], *s.* moderación; sobriedad; presidencia, acto de presidir.

modern [mádœrn], *a.* moderno.— —**ize** [-aįz], *vt.* modernizar.

modest [mádįst], *a.* modesto; recatado,

pudoroso.— —y [-į], **s.** modestia; recato, pudor.

modification [madįfįkéįʃ**ə**n], **s.** modificación.—**modifier** [mádįfaįœ(r)], **s.** modificador.—**modify** [mádįfaį], **vti.** [7] modificar, cambiar.

modiste [mouḍíst], **s.** modista.

modulate [mádʒųleįt], **vt.** y **vi.** modular.

Mogul [móų**g**al], **s.** mogol; (m.) capitán de industria.

mohair [móųher], **s.** pelo de la cabra de Angora; tela de este material.

Mohammedan [mouhǽmedən], **s.** y **a.** mahometano.

moist [mojst], **a.** húmedo; lloroso; lluvioso.— —**en** [mójsn], **vt.** humedecer, mojar ligeramente.— —**ure** [mójschǫ(r)], **s.** humedad.

molar [móų**l**ə(r)], **s.** molar.—**s.** muela.

molasses [mol**ǽ**sįz], **s.** melaza, miel de purga.—**m.** candy, (Am.) melcocha.

mold [mouḷd], **s.** molde, matriz; moho; tierra vegetal.—**vt.** moldear, vaciar, amoldar.—**vi.** enmohecerse.— —**er** [móuḷdœ(r)], **vi.** convertirse en polvo, desmoronarse, consumirse.—**vt.** convertir en polvo, consumir, desgastar.— —**ing** [-įŋ], **s.** moldura; amoldamiento; moldeamiento, vaciado.— —**y** [-į], **a.** mohoso, enmohecido.

mole [mouḷ], **s.** lunar o mancha en la piel; muelle, malecón, espolón; topo.—**m.**-eyed, cegato.

molecule [málįkjuḷ], **s.** molécula.

molest [mol** é**st], **vt.** molestar, vejar; faltar al respeto (a una mujer); meterse con, dañar.

mollusk [málask], **s.** molusco.

molt [mouḷt], **vi.** mudar la pluma.— —**ing** [móuḷtįŋ], **s.** muda.

molten [móuḷtən], **pp.** de **TO MELT.**—**a.** fundido, derretido (metales).

moment [móų**m**ənt], **s.** momento, instante; importancia, peso.— —**ary** [-erį], **a.** momentáneo.— —**ly** [-lį], **adv.** por momentos.— —**ous** [momént**a**s], **a.** importante, grave, trascendental.— —**um** [moméntⱭm], **s.** impulso, ímpetu; (mech.) cantidad de movimiento.

monarch [mán**ə**rk], **s.** monarca.— —**y** [-į], **s.** monarquía.

monastery [mánasterį], **s.** monasterio, convento.—**monastic** [mon**ǽ**stįk], **a.** monástico.

Monday [mándį], **s.** lunes.

monetary [mánįterį], **a.** monetario, pecuniario.—**money** [mánį], **s.** dinero; moneda; sistema monetario.— **m.** changer, dealer, o jobber, cambista. —**m.**-exchange house, casa de cambio. —**m.** lender, prestamista, usurero. —**m.**-maker, cosa con que se gana dinero; persona que gana y acumula

dinero, acaudalada; persona metalizada.—**m.** order, giro postal.

Mongol [m**ǽ**ŋ**g**ol], **s.** mongol.— —**ian** [maŋg**ó**uljan], **a.** mongólico.—**s.** mongol.— —**ic** [maŋgálįk], **a.** = **MONGOLIAN.**

mongrel [m**ǽ**ŋgr**ə**l], **s.** y **s.** mixto, mestizo.—**s.** (perro) de raza indefinida.

monk [mⱭŋk], **s.** monje, fraile.

monkey [mⱭ́ŋkį], **s.** mono, macaco, mico.—**m.** wrench, llave inglesa.— **to play the m.,** hacer monadas.—**vt.** y **vi.** (fam.) remedar; hacer payasadas o monerías.—**to m. with,** meterse con; bregar con.— —**shine** [-ʃaįn], **s.** (fam.) monería.

monogram [mánog**ræ**m], **s.** monograma.

monologue [mánolag], **s.** monólogo, soliloquio.

monopolize [monápolaįz], **vt.** monopolizar, acaparar.—**monopoly** [monápolį], **s.** monopolio, estanco.

monosyllable [manosį́labl], **s.** monosílabo.

monotonous [monátⱭn**ə**s], **a.** monótono, machacón.—**monotony** [monátⱭnį], **s.** monotonía.

monster [mánstœ(r)], **s.** monstruo.—**a.** enorme, prodigioso, extraordinario. —**monstrosity** [manstrásįtį], **s.** monstruo; monstruosidad.—**monstrous** [mánstras], **a.** monstruoso; descomunal.

month [manθ], **s.** mes.— —**ly** [mⱭ́nθlį], **a.** mensual.—**adv.** mensualmente.—**s.** publicación mensual.—**pl.** las reglas, menstruo.

monument [mányų**m**ənt], **s.** monumento; memoria, recuerdo; hito.— —**al** [manyuméntⱭl], **a.** monumental; conmemorativo; grandioso.

moo [mu], **vi.** mugir.—**s.** mu, mugido.

mood [mud], **s.** disposición de ánimo, talante, genio, humor; (gram.) modo.— —**y** [múdį], **a.** caprichoso; irritable, de mal humor; caviloso; triste, taciturno.

moon [mun], **s.** luna; satélite; mes lunar.—**m.**-blind, cegato, corto de vista.—**m.**-mad, **m.**-struck, lunático, loco.— —**light** [múnlaįt], **s.** luz de la luna.—**a.** iluminado por la luna.— —**lit** [-lįt], **a.** iluminado por la luna.— —**rise** [-raįz], **s.** salida de la luna.— —**set** [-set], **s.** puesta de la luna.— —**shine** [-ʃaįn], **s.** claridad de la luna; desatino; (fam.) música celestial; licor destilado ilegalmente.— —**y** [-į], **a.** claro como la luna; lunático; simplón; soñador.

moor [mur], **s.** páramo; brezal; (M.) moro, marroquí, sarraceno.—**vt.** (mar.) amarrar, aferrar, afirmar con anclas.—**vi.** (mar.) anclar, atracar;

estar anclado.— —ish [múriʃ], *a.*
pantanoso, cenagoso; árido; (M.)
moro; morisco.

moose [mus], *s.* alce, ante.

mop [map], *s.* (Am.) trapeador; greña,
mechón, cabellera revuelta; mueca.
—*vti.* [1] limpiar el piso, trapear.—
to m. up, acabar con el resto del
enemigo.—*mopping-up,* (mil.) operación de limpieza.

mope [moup], *vt.* abatir.—*vi.* abatirse,
desanimarse, estar tétrico, taciturno
o apático.—*s.* hombre abatido o
desanimado.—*pl.* apatía, murria.

moral [máṛạl], *a.* moral, ético; virtuoso;
honrado, recto.—*s.* moralidad, moraleja.—*pl.* costumbres, conducta;
moral social.— —e [morél], *s.* moral,
estado de ánimo, espíritu.— —ism
[máṛạlizm], *s.* enseñanza moral.
—ist [máṛạlist], *s.* moralista.— —ity
[moréliti], *s.* ética, moral; moralidad;
moraleja.— —ize [máṛạlaiz], *vt.* y *vi.*
moralizar.

morbid [mórbid], *a.* mórbido, morboso,
malsano.

more [mor], *a.* más, adicional.—*adv.*
más, en mayor grado; además.—*s.*
mayor cantidad o número.—*m. and
m.,* cada vez más.—*m. or less,* poco
más o menos.—*no m.,* no más; ya no;
se acabó.—*so much the m.,* tanto más,
cuanto más.—*the m.,* tanto más.—
—over [-óuvœ(r)], *adv.* además, por
otra parte.

morning [mórniŋ], *s.* mañana (primera
parte del día).—*good m.!* ¡buenos
días!—*a.* matutino, matinal, de
mañana.

Moroccan [morákạn], *a.* y *s.* marroquí.

morphine [mórfin], *s.* morfina.

morsel [mórsẹl], *s.* bocado, manjar;
presa.

mortal [mórtạl], *s.* mortal, ser humano.
—*a.* mortal; fatal, letal.— —ity [mor-
téliti], *s.* mortalidad; mortandad; humanidad.—*m. rate,* mortalidad.

mortar [mórtạ(r)], *s.* mortero, almirez;
(arti.) mortero, obús.—*m. piece,*
(alb.) mortero, mezcla.

mortgage [mórgidʒ], *s.* hipoteca,
gravamen.—*m. loan,* préstamo hipo-
tecario.—*vt.* hipotecar, gravar.

mortify [mórtifai], *vti.* [7] mortificar,
humillar, abochornar.

mortuary [mórchuẹri], *s.* depósito de
cadáveres.—*a.* mortuorio.

mosaic [mozéiịk], *a.* y *s.* mosaico.

Moslem [mázlem], *s.* y *a.* musulmán.

mosque [mask], *s.* mezquita.

mosquito [mǫskítou], *s.* mosquito.—*m.
net,* mosquitero.

moss [mǫs], *s.* musgo, moho; tremedal,
ciénaga.—*vt.* cubrir de musgo.— —y
[mósi], *a.* musgoso.

most [moust], *a.* más; lo más, los más,
el mayor número (de); casi todo(s);
la mayor parte (de).—*for the m. part,*
principalmente, generalmente.—*adv.*
más, lo más, sumamente, muy; (fam.)
casi.—*s.* lo principal, la mayor parte,
el mayor número, lo más, el mayor
valor.—*at (the) m.,* a lo más, a lo
sumo, cuando más.— —ly [móustli],
adv. en su mayor parte, casi todo(s),
principalmente.

mote [mout], *s.* mota (de polvo).

moth [moθ], *s.* polilla.—*m. ball,* bola de
alcanfor u otra sustancia contra la
polilla.—*m.-eaten,* apolillado.

mother [máðœ(r)], *s.* madre.—*m.
country,* madre patria, metrópoli.
—*m.-in-law,* suegra.—*m.-of-pearl,*
nácar, madreperla.—*a.* materno,
maternal; nativo, natal; vernáculo,
nacional; metropolitano.—*M. Superior,* madre superiora (monjas).—
m. tongue, lengua materna.—*vt.* servir
de madre a.—*vi.* criar madre (vino,
etc.).— —hood [-hud], *s.* maternidad.—
—less [-lis], *a.* huérfano de madre.—
—ly [-li], *a.* maternal, materno.—*adv.*
maternalmente.

motif [motíf], *s.* motivo, asunto, tema.

motility [motíliti], *s.* movilidad.—
motion [móuʃọn], *s.* movimiento;
signo, señal, seña; moción, proposición; (for.) pedimento.—*m. picture,*
cine; fotografía cinematográfica;
película.—*on the m. of,* a propuesta
de.—*to set in m.,* poner en marcha.
—*vi.* hacer señas.—**motionless** [móu-
ʃọnlis], *a.* inmóvil; yerto.

motivate [móutiveit], *vt.* motivar.—
motive [móutiv], *a.* motor, motriz.
—*m. power,* fuerza motriz.—*s.* motivo,
móvil, porqué; pie, tema, idea.

motley [mátli], *a.* abigarrado; mezclado,
variado, diverso; vestido de colorines.
—*s.* traje de payaso; mezcla de
colores; mezcolanza.

motor [móutọ(r)], *s.* motor.—*a.* motriz,
motor; de motor.—*m. boat* o *launch,*
gasolinera, lancha automóvil.—*vi.* ir
en automóvil.— —car [-kar], *s.* automóvil, auto.— —coach [-kouch], *s.*
autobús, ómnibus.— —cycle [-saikl],
s. motocicleta.— —ist [-ist], *s.*
automovilista, motorista.— —ization
[moutọrizéiʃọn], *s.* motorización.—
—ize [-aiz], *vt.* motorizar.— —man
[-man], *s.* motorista, conductor (de
tranvía o tren eléctrico).

mottle [mátl], *vt.* motear, vetear,
manchar.—*s.* mota, veta, mancha.

motto [mátou], *s.* mote, lema, divisa.

mould [mould], *s., vt.* y *vi.* = MOLD.—
moulder [móuldœ(r)], *vi.* y *vt.* =
MOLDER.—**moulding** [móuldiŋ], *s.* =

MOLDING.—**mouldy** [móųldį], *a.* = MOLDY.

moult [moųlt], *vi.* = MOLT.—**moulting** [móųltįṇ], *s.* = MOLTING.

mound [maųnd], *s.* montón de tierra; montículo; baluarte; túmulo.—*vt.* amontonar; atrincherar, fortalecer.

mount [maųnt], *s.* monte, montaña; baluarte, terraplén; montadura; caballería; montura; apeadero; (mil.) monta, toque de clarín.—*vt.* cabalgar; armar, montar; subir, alzar, elevar; enaltecer; engastar, montar (joyas); (teat.) poner en escena; preparar una cosa para usarla o exhibirla.—*vi.* ascender, elevarse; montar a caballo; subir, montar, ascender (una cuenta, etc.).—**-ain** [máųntįn], *s.* monte, montaña.—*a.* montés, montañés; de montaña.—*m. chain,* sierra, cordillera, cadena de montañas.—*m. climber,* alpinista.—*m. climbing,* alpinismo.—**-aineer** [-įnír], *s.* montañés, serrano.—**-ainous** [-įnʌs], *a.* montañoso.

mourn [moųrn, mɔrn], *vt.* lamentar, llorar, sentir.—*vi.* lamentarse, dolerse; vestir o llevar luto.—*to m. for,* llevar luto por; lamentar, llorar.—**-ful** [mórnfųl], *a.* triste, plañidero, apesadumbrado; fúnebre, lúgubre.—**-ing** [-įṇ], *s.* luto; duelo; dolor, aflicción.—*in m.,* de luto, de duelo; fúnebre.—*m. band,* brazal de luto.

mouse [maųs], *s.* ratón.—**-trap** [máųstræp], *s.* ratonera.

moustache [mʌstáḙš], *s.* = MUSTACHE.

mouth [maųθ], *s.* boca; abertura; embocadura o desembocadura de un río.—**-ful** [máųθfųl], *s.* bocado; buchada; migaja, pizca.—**-piece** [-pis], *s.* boquilla, embocadura; vocero, portavoz.

movability [muvabílįtį], *s.* movilidad.—**movable** [múvabl], *a.* movible; móvil; movedizo.—*s. pl.* muebles, menaje, mobiliario, efectos.—**move** [muv], *s.* movimiento; paso; jugada, lance, turno de jugar.—*on the m.,* en marcha, en movimiento; de viaje.—*to get a m. on,* (fam.) darse prisa, empezarse a mover.—*to make a m.,* dar un paso; hacer una jugada.—*vt.* mover; remover; trasladar, mudar; hacer una moción; conmover; persuadir.—*to m. to,* causar (cólera, etc.), poner (colérico, etc.).—*vi.* moverse; mudarse; ir, andar, caminar; ponerse en marcha; obrar, entrar en acción; avanzar, progresar; mover el vientre; hacer una jugada.—*to m. away,* alejarse; irse; trasladarse; mudar de casa.—*to m. in,* entrar; entrar a habitar una casa.—**-ment** [múvmęnt], *s.* movimiento;

moción; maniobra; paso, acto, acción, incidente; defecación, evacuación.—**movie** [múvį], *s.* (fam.) función de cine; película.—*pl.* cine.—**moving** [múvįṇ], *a.* conmovedor, emocionante, patético.—*m. parts,* piezas que se mueven (en un mecanismo).—*s.* movimiento, moción; traslado, mudanza.

mow [moų], *vti.* [6] segar, guadañar, cortar la hierba.—**-er** [móųœ(r)], *s.* segador; segadora mecánica.

Mr. [místœ(r)], *s.* = MISTER.—**Mrs.** [mísįz], *s.* = MISTRESS.

much [mʌch], *a.* mucho, abundante, copioso.—*adv.* mucho; muy; con mucho, en gran manera.—*as m. as,* tanto como.—*as m. more,* otro tanto más.—*how m.?* ¿cuánto?—*m. as,* por más que, a pesar de.—*m. the same,* casi lo mismo.—*m. too,* demasiado.—*not so m. as,* no tanto como; ni siquiera.—*so m.,* tanto.—*this m. more,* esto más, tanto así más.—*s.* mucho.

muck [mʌk], *s.* abono, estiércol; cieno; porquería, basura.

mucous [mjúkʌs], *a.* mucoso, mocoso.—**-mucus** [mjúkʌs], *s.* moco, mocosidad.

mud [mʌd], *s.* fango, lodo, barro.—*m. wall,* tapia.—*vt.* enlodar, embarrar; ensuciar, enturbiar.—**-dle** [mádl], *vt.* embrollar, confundir; revolver; atontar.—*to m. through,* hacer algo malamente, salir del paso a duras penas.—*s.* embrollo, confusión.—**-dy** [mádį], *a.* lodoso, sucio, turbio; tonto, confuso.—*vti.* [7] enturbiar, ensuciar; entontecer, turbar.

muff [mʌf], *s.* manguito (para las manos); chabacanería, torpeza; (baseball) fallar la bola.—*vt.* desperdiciar (una ocasión); dejar escapar (la pelota); (fam.) hacer algo torpemente.

muffin [máfįn], *s.* panecillo, bollito.

muffle [máfl], *vt.* embozar; encubrir; apagar o atenuar un sonido.—*to m. up,* embozarse.—**-d** [-d], *a.* apagado, sordo.—**-r** [máflœ(r)], *s.* bufanda; (aut.) silenciador; (mús.) sordina.

mug [mʌg], *s.* tarro (para cerveza); (fam.) cara, boca; mueca; vaso con asa.

mulatto [mųlétoų], *a. y s.* mulato.

mulberry [málberį], *s.* mora.—*m. tree,* moral.

mule [mjul], *s.* mulo, mula.—**-teer** [mjulętír], *s.* arriero.

mull [mʌl], *s.* muselina clara; cabo, promontorio.—*vi.* rumiar, cavilar; afanarse mucho sin resultado.

multilingual [mʌltįlíṇgwạl], *a.* políglota.

multiple [máltįpl], *s.* múltiplo.—*a.* múltiple; (mat.) múltiplo.—**multipli-**

cation [mʌltiplikéiʃən], *s.* multiplicación.—*m. table,* tabla de multiplicar.—**multiplicity** [mʌltiplísiti], *s.* multiplicidad, sinnúmero.—**multiply,** *vti.* y *vii.* [7] multiplicar(se).

multitude [mʌltitjud], *s.* multitud; vulgo.

mum [mʌm], *interj.* ¡chitón! ¡silencio! —*a.* callado, silencioso.—*m.'s the word,* punto en boca.—*to keep m.,* callarse.

mumble [mʌmbl], *vt.* y *vi.* rezongar, musitar, hablar o decir entre dientes; murmurar, refunfuñar; (fam.) mascullar.

mummy [mʌmi], *s.* momia.

mumps [mʌmps], *s.* (med.) paperas, parótidas.

munch [mʌnch], *vt.* mascar enérgicamente, mascullar.

municipal [mjunísipəl], *a.* municipal.—**-ity** [mjunisipǽliti], *s.* municipio; municipalidad.

munificence [mjunífisəns], *s.* munificencia.—**munificent** [mjunífisənt], *a.* munífico, generoso, liberal.

munitions [mjunísʃənz], *s. pl.* municiones, pertrechos; equipo.

mural [mjúrəl], *a.* mural; escarpado, vertical.—*s.* cuadro mural.

murmur [mə́rmœ(r)], *s.* murmullo, susurro; murmuración.—*vi.* murmurar, susurrar; refunfuñar.

murder [mə́rdœ(r)], *s.* asesinato, homicidio.—*vt.* asesinar; estropear.—*vi.* cometer homicidio.— **-er** [-œ(r)], *s.* asesino, homicida.— **-ess** [-is], *s.* asesina.— **-ous** [-ʌs], *a.* asesino, sanguinario.

murky [mə́rki], *a.* oscuro, lóbrego.

muscat [mʌ́skət], *s.* moscatel (uva y pasa).—**muscatel** [mʌskətél], *s.* moscatel (vino y uva).

muscle [mʌ́sl], *s.* músculo; fuerza muscular.—**muscular** [mʌ́skjulə(r)], *a.* muscular; musculoso; atlético.

Muse [mjuz], *s.* musa; (m.) meditación o abstracción profunda; estro, numen. —(m.) *vi.* meditar, reflexionar, estar absorto.—*to m. on, over* o *upon,* meditar en.

museum [mjuzíʌm], *s.* museo.

mush [mʌʃ], *s.* masa blanda y espesa; masa espesa de harina de maíz; (fam.) sentimentalismo exagerado; (rad.) ruido como de chisporroteo.

mushroom [mʌ́ʃrum], *s.* seta, hongo. —*a.* hecho con setas u hongos; efímero.—*vi.* recoger setas; (fig.) desarrollarse y extenderse rápidamente.

mushy [mʌ́ʃi], *a.* pastoso; exageradamente sentimental.

music [mjúzik], *s.* música.—*m. hall,* salón de conciertos; café cantante.

—*m. stand,* atril; tablado para una orquesta.— **-al** [-əl], *a.* musical. —*m. comedy,* zarzuela, comedia musical.— **-ian** [mjuzísʃən], *s.* músico.

musk [mʌsk], *s.* almizcle.—*a.* almizclero.

muskmelon [mʌ́skmelən], *s.* melón. —**muskrat** [mʌ́skrǣt], *s.* rata almizclera.

Muslim [mʌ́zlim], *s.* y *a.* = **MOSLEM.**

muslin [mʌ́zlin], *s.* muselina; percal; percalina.—*a.* de muselina; de percal.

muss [mʌs], *s.* (fam.) desorden, confusión; arrebatiña.—*vt.* (fam.) desordenar, manosear, arrugar; ensuciar.

mussel [mʌ́sel], *s.* mejillón.

must [mʌst], *vai.* [11] deber, tener que; haber que; deber (de).—*he m. have gone,* debió ir, debe (de) haber ido. —*it m. be very late,* será muy tarde. —*she m. have missed the train,* habrá perdido el tren.—*s.* mosto; moho.

mustache [mʌstǣʃ], *s.* bigote, mostacho.

mustard [mʌ́stərd], *s.* mostaza.

muster [mʌ́stœ(r)], *vt.* reunir; (mil.) juntar para pasar lista, revista, etc. —*to m. in* o *into service,* (mil.) alistar. —*to m. up,* tomar (valor, fuerza, etc.). —*vi.* (mil.) juntarse; pasar lista.—*s.* (mil.) revista; lista, reseña; alarde, muestra.—*to pass m.,* llenar los requisitos.

musty [mʌ́sti], *a.* mohoso; añejo; rancio; pasado; mustio, triste.

mutability [mjutəbíliti], *s.* inconstancia, veleidad.—**mutable** [mjútəbl], *a.* inconstante, veleidoso.—**mutation** [mjutéiʃən], *s.* mutación.

mute [mjut], *a.* mudo; callado, silencioso; sordo.—*s.* mudo; letra muda; (mus.) sordina.

mutilate [mjútileit], *vt.* mutilar; truncar.—**mutilation** [mjutiléiʃən], *s.* mutilación.

mutinous [mjútinʌs], *a.* amotinado, sedicioso, turbulento.—**mutiny** [mjútini], *vii.* [7] amotinarse.—*s.* motín, amotinamiento.

mutter [mʌ́tœ(r)], *vt.* y *vi.* murmurar, rezongar, gruñir; bisbisar, decir entre dientes.—*s.* refunfuñadura, gruñido.— **-er** [-œ(r)], *s.* rezongador, gruñón.

mutton [mʌ́tən], *s.* carne de carnero. —*m. broth,* caldo de carnero.—*m. chop,* chuleta de carnero.

mutual [mjúchuəl], *a.* mutuo, recíproco. —*m. friend,* amigo común.

muzzle [mʌ́zl], *s.* morro, hocico; bozal; boca de arma de fuego.—*vt.* abozalar, poner bozal; amordazar.—*vi.* hocicar.

my [mai], *a. pos.* mi, mis.

myopia [maióupiə], *s.* miopía.—**myopic** [maiápik], *a.* miope, corto de vista.

myriad [mírɪəd], *s.* miríada; diez mil; millares, un gran número.—*a.* innumerable, numeroso.

myrrh [mœr], *s.* mirra, goma resinosa.

myrtle [mœrtl], *s.* mirto, arrayán.

myself [maisélf], *pron.* yo mismo; me, mí, mí mismo.—*I myself did it*, yo mismo lo hice.—*I said to myself*, me dije a mí mismo o para mí.

mysterious [mistíəriəs], *a.* misterioso. —**mystery** [místəri], *s.* misterio; arcano.

mystic [místik], *a.* y *s.* místico.— **mystify** [místifai], *vti.* [7] confundir, desconcertar; intrigar; mixtificar.

myth [miθ], *s.* mito; fábula; ficción.— **—ical** [míθikəl], *a.* mítico; fabuloso; imaginario.—**ological** [miθolád́źi-kəl], *a.* mitológico.—**ology** [miθálodźi], *s.* mitología.

N

nab [næb], *vti.* [1] (fam.) prender, atrapar, agarrar, echar mano a, echar el guante a.

nag [næg], *s.* jaco, rocín, caballejo; (fam.) penco, jamelgo.—*vti.* y *vti.* [1] (a veces con at) regañar, machacar, sermonear.

nail [neil], *s.* uña.—*n. file*, lima para las uñas.—*n. polish*, esmalte de uñas.— *n. scratch*, arañazo.—*vt.* clavar, clavetear.—**brush** [néilbrʌs], *s.* cepillo para las uñas.

naive [naív], *a.* ingenuo, cándido.

naked [néikid], *a.* desnudo; descubierto; descamisado; patente.—*stark n.*, en cueros, (fam.) en pelota.—*the n. truth*, la verdad pura y simple.—*(with the) n. eye*, (a) simple vista.— **—ness** [-nis], *s.* desnudez.

name [neim], *s.* nombre; apellido; (fam.) gracia; fama, renombre.—*by u of the n. of*, llamado, nombrado.— *Christian n.*, nombre de pila.—*in God's name*, por el amor de Dios.—*in n.*, de nombre.—*n. day*, día del santo, onomástico.—*to call names*, injuriar. —*what is your n.?* ¿cómo se llama usted?—*vt.* nombrar, apellidar; designar; llamar, poner nombre; mentar, mencionar; fijar.—**less** [néimlis], *a.* sin nombre, anónimo.— **—ly** [-li], *adv.* especialmente; a saber, o sea, es decir.— **—sake** [-seik], *s.* tocayo; homónimo.

nap [næp], *s.* siesta; (tej.) lanilla, pelusa.—*vii.* [1] dormitar, echar una siesta, descabezar el sueño; estar desprevenido.

nape [neip], *s.* nuca, cogote; testuz.

naphtha [næfθə], *s.* nafta.—**lene** [-lin], *s.* naftalina.

napkin [næpkin], *s.* servilleta.

narcissus [narsísʌs], *s.* narciso.

narcotic [narkátik], *s.* y *a.* narcótico.

narrate [næréit], *vt.* y *vi.* narrar, relatar. —**narration** [næréiʃən], *s.* narración, relato.—**narrative** [næratjv], *a.* narrativo.—*s.* narración, narrativa, relato.—**narrator** [næréito(r)], *s.* narrador.

narrow [nérou], *a.* angosto, estrecho; limitado; tacaño, mezquino; próximo, cercano, intolerante.—*n. gauge*, (f.c.) de vía estrecha.—*n.-minded*, estrecho de miras.—*n. pass*, desfiladero.—*to have a n. escape*, salvarse en una tabla.—*s. pl.* pasaje angosto; desfiladero; estrecho.—*vt.* estrechar, contraer, encoger; limitar.—*vi.* estrecharse, encogerse, reducirse.— **—ly** [-li], *adv.* estrechamente; por poco, escasamente. **—ness** [-nis], *s.* angostura; estrechez, pobreza.

nastiness [nástinis], *s.* mala intención, malevolencia; suciedad, porquería; obscenidad.

nasty [násti], *a.* malévolo; sucio, asqueroso; ofensivo; obsceno, indecente; (tiempo) inclemente.

natal [néital], *a.* nativo; natal.

nation [néiʃən], *s.* nación; pueblo, gente.—**al** [náʃənəl], *a.* nacional.— *n. debt*, deuda pública.—*s.* ciudadano; súbdito.—**alism** [náʃənəlizm], *s.* nacionalismo.— **—ality** [náʃənǽliti], *s.* nacionalidad; origen, tradición.— **alization** [náʃənalizéiʃən], *s.* nacionalización; naturalización.— **alize** [náʃənalaiz], *vt.* nacionalizar; naturalizar.

native [néitiv], *a.* nativo, natal, natural, oriundo; indígena; del país, patrio.— *n. country o land*, patria, país natal, terruño.—*s.* natural, nativo, indígena.—**nativity** [neitíviti], *s.* nacimiento, natividad; (N.) Navidad.

natural [nǽchʊrəl], *a.* natural; nativo; sencillo, sin afectación; normal, ordinario; ilegítimo, bastardo.—*s.* (mús.) becuadro; tecla blanca.— **ism** [-izm], *s.* naturalismo.— **ist** [-ist], *s.* naturalista.— **ization** [-izéiʃən], *s.* naturalización; nacionalización.—*n. papers*, carta de naturaleza.— **ize** [-aiz], *vt.* naturalizar; nacionalizar.— **—ly** [-li], *adv.* naturalmente; desde luego.— **—ness** [-nis], *s.* naturalidad; sencillez.—**nature** [néichehu(r)], *s.* naturaleza; natural, índole, genio; especie, género, clase; naturalidad.

naught [nat], *s.* nada; cero.—*to set at n.*, hacer tabla rasa de.

naughtiness [nátinis], *s.* maldad, perversidad; picardía, travesura.— **naughty** [náti], *a.* desobediente,

díscolo; pícaro, travieso; libre, pica-resco.

nausea [nɔ́ʃị̯ə̯], *s.* náusea, asco.— —**te** [nɔ́ʃị̯eịt], *vt.* dar asco o disgusto, apestar.— —**ting** [nɔ́ʃị̯eịtịn], *a.* nause-abundo, asqueroso, apestoso.

nautical [nɔ́tịkạl], *a.* náutico, marino.

naval [néịvạl], *a.* naval; de marina.— *n.* base o *station*, base o apostadero naval.

nave [neịv], *s.* (arq.) nave.

navel [néịvẹl], *s.* ombligo.

navigable [nǽvịgạbl], *a.* navegable.— **navigate** [nǽvịgeịt], *vt.* y *vi.* navegar. —**navigation** [nævịgéịʃən], *s.* nave-gación; náutica.—**navigator** [nǽvị-geịtọ(r)], *s.* navegante; piloto; tra-tado de náutica.—**navy** [néịvị], *s.* armada, marina de guerra, flota.—*n. blue,* azul marino.—*n. yard,* astillero; arsenal.

nay [neị], *adv.* no; de ningún modo; más aún, y aún.—*s.* voto negativo; negación.

near [nịr], *prep.* cerca de, junto a, próximo a, por, hacia.—*adv.* cerca; proximamente; (fam.) casi.—*n. at hand,* a (la) mano, cerca.—*a.* cercano, próximo, inmediato; allegado; íntimo, estrecho; a punto de, por poco.—*vt.* y *vi.* acercar(se).— —**by** o n.-**by** [nírbaị], *prep.* cerca de.—*adv.* cerca, a (la) mano.—*a.* cercano, contiguo, próximo.— —**ly** [-lị], *adv.* cerca, cerca de; estrechamente; casi; de cerca; próximamente, aproximada-mente.— —**ness** [-nịs], *s.* proximidad, cercanía.— —**sighted** [-sáịtịd], *a.* miope, corto de vista.— —**sightedness** [-sáịtịdnịs], *s.* miopía.

neat [nịt], *a.* limpio, aseado, pulcro; pulido; mondo, lirondo; nítido, claro; esmerado.— —**ness** [nítnịs], *s.* aseo, pulcritud, nitidez, limpieza; elegan-cia, delicadeza.

nebula [nébyụlạ̯], *s.* (astr.) nebulosa; nube en el ojo.—**nebulous** [nébyụlʌs], *a.* nebuloso.

necessarily [néseserịlị], *adv.* necesaria-mente.—**necessary** [néseserị], *a.* necesario, preciso, forzoso.—*to be n.,* ser menester, hacer falta.—*s.* lo necesario.—*pl.* necesidades, cosas necesarias o imprescindibles.—**neces-sitate** [nịsésịteịt], *vt.* hacer necesario. —**necessity** [nịsésịtị], *s.* necesidad; indigencia.—*pl.* artículos de primera necesidad, requisitos indispensables.

neck [nek], *s.* cuello, garganta; pes-cuezo; gollete (de botella); (cost.) escote; istmo, cabo, península; des-filadero.—*n. and n.* (dep.) parejos en una carrera.—*n. of land,* lengua de tierra.—*in* u *on the n. of,* a raíz de.—

—**lace** [néklịs], *s.* collar, gargantilla.— —**tie** [-taị], *s.* corbata.

nectarine [nektạrin], *s.* abridor (varie-dad de durazno).

need [nịd], *s.* necesidad; carencia, falta; pobreza, miseria.—*if n. be,* si hubiere necesidad, si fuere necesario.—*vt.* necesitar; hacer falta.—*vi.* ser necesa-rio; estar en la necesidad, carecer de lo necesario.— —**ful** [nídfụl], *a.* necesario; necesitado.

needle [nídl], *s.* aguja.—*n. case,* alfiletero.

needless [nídlịs], *a.* inútil, innecesario, superfluo.—*n. to say,* excusado es decir.

needlework [nídlwœrk], *s.* costura; labor, bordado de aguja.

needy [nídị], *a.* necesitado, meneste-roso.

ne'er [ner], *adv. contr.* de NEVER.— **n.-do-well** [nérduwel], *s.* haragán, perdulario.

nefarious [nịférịʌs], *a.* nefando, mal-vado.

negation [nịgéịʃən], *s.* negación, nega-tiva.—**negative** [négạtịv], *a.* nega-tivo.—*s.* negativa; denegación; veto; negación; (foto.) negativo.

neglect [nịglékt], *s.* descuido, negligen-cia; abandono, dejadez.—*vt.* descui-dar, desatender; abandonar.— —**ful** [-fụl], *a.* negligente, descuidado.— **negligence** [néglịdẓẹns], *s.* negligen-cia.—**negligent** [néglịdẓẹnt], *a.* negli-gente.

negotiable [nịgóụʃị̯ạbl], *a.* negociable.— **negotiate** [nịgóụʃị̯eịt], *vt.* negociar; gestionar, agenciar; (fam.) vencer, superar.—*vi.* negociar.—**negotiation** [nịgoụʃị̯éịʃən], *s.* negociación; nego-cio, gestión.

Negro [nígroụ], *s.* y *a.* negro.

neigh [neị], *vi.* relinchar.—*s.* relincho.

neighbor [néịbọ(r)], *s.* vecino; prójimo. — —**hood** [-hụd], *s.* vecindad; vecin-dario; barrio; cercanías, alrededores. —*in the n. of,* (fam.) casi, como, aproximadamente.— —**ing** [-ịn], *a.* vecino, vecinal, colindante, próximo o cercano.

neither [níðœ(r), náịðœ(r)], *a.* ningún, ninguno de los dos.—*conj.* ni; tam-poco, ni siquiera.—*n. he nor she,* ni él ni ella.—*pron.* ninguno, ni uno ni otro, ni el uno ni el otro.

Neo-Latin [nioúlǽtịn], *s.* y *a.* neolatino.

neologism [nịálgdẓịzm], *s.* neologismo.

nephew [néfịu], *s.* sobrino.

nerve [nœrv], *s.* nervio; vigor, fibra; valor, ánimo; (fam.) desfachatez, descaro.—*pl.* excitabilidad nerviosa. —*n.-racking,* horripilante.—**nervous** [nœ́rvʌs], *a.* nervioso.—*n. breakdown,* crisis neurótica.—**nervousness** [nœrvʌsnịs], *s.* nerviosidad; estado nervioso o irritable.

nest [nɛst], *s.* nido; nidada; madriguera.—*vi.* anidar; anidarse.

nestle [nɛsl], *vt.* abrigar, poner en un nido.—*vi.* anidar(se).

net [nɛt], *s.* red; redecilla; malla; (fig.) trampa; (tej.) tul.—*vti.* [1] enredar o coger con red; cubrir con redes o mallas; coger; obtener; producir una ganancia líquida.—*a.* (com.) neto, líquido; de punto de malla.—*n. amount,* importe neto.—*n. balance,* saldo líquido o neto.—*n. profit,* ganancia o utilidad líquida, beneficio líquido.— —**ting** [-ịŋ], *s.* red; tejido de malla.

nettle [nɛtl], *s.* (bot.) ortiga.—*vt.* picar; irritar, provocar.

network [nɛ́twœrk], *s.* red, malla; (rad., T.V., f.c., etc.) cadena, red, sistema.

neurasthenia [njurạsθḗnịạ], *s.* neurastenia.

neurosis [njuróusịs], *s.* neurosis.—**neurotic** [njurátịk], *a.* neurótico.

neuter [njútœ(r)], *a.* neutro; neutral.—**neutral** [njútrạl], *a.* neutral; neutro; indiferente.—*s.* neutral.—*in n.,* (aut.) en punto muerto.—**neutrality** [njutrǽlịtị], *s.* neutralidad.—**neutralize** [njútrạlạịz], *vt.* neutralizar.

never [névœ(r)], *adv.* nunca, jamás; no, de ningún modo.—*n. again,* nunca más, otra vez no.—*n. ending,* interminable, sin fin.—*n. fear,* no hay cuidado, no hay miedo.—*n. mind,* no importa.— —**more** [nevœrmɔ́r], *adv.* jamás, nunca más.— —**theless** [nevœrðẹlés], *adv.* y *conj.* no obstante, con todo, sin embargo, a pesar de eso.

new [nju], *a.* nuevo; moderno; fresco, reciente, recién; distinto.—*what's n.?* ¿qué hay de nuevo?— —**born** [njúbórn], *a.* recién nacido.— —**comer** [njúkʌmœ(r)], *s.* recién llegado.— —**fangled** [njúfǽŋgld], *a.* recién inventado.— —**ly** [njúlị], *adv.* nuevamente, recientemente, recién.—*n. arrived,* recién llegado; advenedizo.— —**lywed** [-ljwed], *a.* recién casado.— —**ness** [-nịs], *s.* novedad; innovación.— —**s** [-z], *s.* noticia, nueva; noticias; noticia fresca.—*no n. is good n.,* la falta de noticias es buena noticia.—*what's the n.?* ¿qué hay de nuevo? ¿qué noticias hay?— —**sboy** [-zbɔị], *s.* chiquillo vendedor de periódicos.— —**smonger** [-zmʌŋgœ(r)], *s.* gacetista, noticiero.— —**spaper** [-zpęịpœ(r)], *s.* periódico, diario.—*n. man,* periodista; reportero, repórter.—*n. serial,* folletín.— —**sreel** [-zril], *s.* noticiario cinematográfico.— —**sstand** [-zstænd], *s.*

quiosco o puesto de periódicos, revistas, etc.

New Zealander [njú zílạndœ(r)], *s.* neozelandés.

next [nɛkst], *a.* siguiente; entrante; próximo, contiguo, inmediato; subsiguiente, futuro, venidero.—*n. door,* la puerta (o casa) al lado.—*n. month,* (week, year), el mes (la semana, el año) entrante, próximo o que viene.—*n. time,* otra vez, la próxima vez.—*the n. life,* la otra vida.—*to be n.,* seguir en turno, tocarle a uno.—*adv.* luego, después, inmediatamente después, en seguida, a renglón seguido.—*n. best,* lo mejor a falta de eso.—*n. to,* junto a, al lado de; después de; casi.—*n. to impossible,* punto menos que imposible.—*what n.?* ¿y ahora (o luego) qué?

nibble [nịbl], *vt.* mordiscar, mordisquear; pacer.—*vi.* picar, morder (como el pez); (at) criticar.—*s.* mordisco, bocadito.

Nicaraguan [nịkạrágwạn], *a.* y *s.* nicaragüense.

nice [naịs], *a.* fino, sutil; delicado; diligente, solícito; esmerado, pulcro, refinado; agradable, lindo; simpático, gentil, amable.— —**ly** [náịslị], *adv.* muy bien, con delicadeza, finamente.—*to get along n. with,* llevarse bien con.— —**ness** [-nịs], *s.* finura, delicadeza, amabilidad; esmero; refinamiento; sutileza.— —**ty** [náịsẹtị], *s.* primor, cuidado; finura, delicadeza; remilgo; pormenor.

niche [nịch], *s.* nicho.

nick [nịk], *s.* muesca, mella, corte, picadura; momento oportuno; jugada favorable.—*in the n. of time,* en el momento justo.

nickel [nịkẹl], *s.* níquel; (fam.) moneda de cinco centavos (E.U.).—*n. steel,* acero níquel.—*to n.-plate,* niquelar.

nickname [nịkneịm], *s.* mote, apodo.—*vt.* motejar, apodar.

nicotine [nịkotin], *s.* nicotina.

niece [nis], *s.* sobrina.

niggard [nịgạrd], *a.* y *s.* tacaño, mezquino.— —**ly** [-lị], *a.* = NIGGARD.—*adv.* mezquinamente, etc.

night [naịt], *s.* noche.—*last n.,* anoche.—*n. before last,* anteanoche.—*tomorrow n.,* mañana por la noche.—*a. nocturno; de noche.—*n. clothes,* ropa de dormir.—*n. club,* café cantante, cabaret.—*n. owl,* buho, lechuza, mochuelo; (fam.) trasnochador.—*n. shift,* turno de noche.—*n. watch,* sereno, guardia nocturno; guardia nocturna; acción de trasnochar.—*n. watchman,* sereno.— —**cap** [náịtkæp], *s.* gorro de dormir.— —**fall** [-fɔl], *s.* anochecida, anochecer, caída de la tarde.— —gown [-gaμn], **s.** camisa de dormir.— —hawk [-hɔk], **s.** chotacabras; (fam.) trasnochador.— —ingale [-iŋgeil], **s.** ruiseñor.— —ly [-li], **adv.** por las noches, todas las noches.—**a.** nocturno, de noche.— —mare [-mɛr], **s.** pesadilla.— —shirt [-ʃœrt], **s.** camisa de dormir.— —time [-taim], **s.** noche.—**in the n.**, de noche.

nimble [nimbl], **a.** vivo, listo, ágil, veloz, expedito.—**n.**-witted, despierto, inteligente.—**nimbly** [nimbli], **adv.** ligeramente, ágilmente.

nip [nip], **vt.** [1] pellizcar; asir, sujetar; recortar, desmochar; helar, escarchar; marchitar.—**to n. in the bud**, cortar en flor.—**to n. off**, desmochar.—**s.** pellizco; pedacito; trago, traguito; dentellada; helada, escarcha; cogida; daño repentino (plantas y sembrados).—**n. and tuck**, (dep.) empate.

nipple [nipl], **s.** pezón; tetilla; mamadera; (mec.) tubo roscado de unión.

Nipponese [nipaníz], **s. y a.** nipón, japonés.

nit [nit], **s.** liendre.

nitrate [náitreit], **s.** nitrato.—**nitric** [náitrik], **a.** nítrico, azoico.—**nitrogen** [náitrɔdʒin], **s.** nitrógeno, ázoe.

no [noμ], **adv.** no.—**no longer**, ya no.—**n. more**, nada más.—**n. sooner**, no bien.—**a.** ninguno, ningún.—**n.**-account, (fam.) sin valor, deleznable.—**n.** fooling, sin broma, fuera de broma.—**n. matter**, no importa.—**n. matter how much**, por mucho que.—**n. one**, nadie, ninguno.—**n. payment**, no delivery, sin pago no hay (o habrá) entrega.—**n. smoking**, se prohibe fumar.—**to n. purpose**, sin objeto.—**with n. money**, sin dinero.—**s.** no, voto negativo.

nobility [nobíliti], **s.** nobleza; hidalguía.—**noble** [noμbl], **a. y s.** noble; hidalgo.—**nobleman** [noμblman], **s.** noble, hidalgo.—**nobleness** [noμblnis], **s.** nobleza, caballerosidad.—**noblesse** [noblés], **s.** nobleza.—**nobly** [noμbli], **adv.** noblemente.

nobody [noμbadi], **pron.** nadie, ninguno.—**n. else**, nadie más, ningún otro.—**s.** persona insignificante, (fam.) quídam.

nocturnal [naktœrnal], **a.** nocturno, nocturnal.—**nocturne** [náktœrn], **s.** nocturno.

nod [nad], **vti.** [1] hacer una seña afirmativa o llamativa con la cabeza; inclinar (una rama, etc.).—**vii.** cabecear, inclinar la cabeza; descabezar un sueño, dormitar.—**s.** cabeceo; cabezada; señal afirmativa con la cabeza; inclinación de cabeza.—**to get the n.**, recibir el visto bueno.

node [noμd], **s.** bulto, protuberancia,

chichón; nudo; tumor, dureza, nódulo; nodo.

noise [nɔiz], **s.** ruido; sonido; estrépito; bullicio, gritería.—**it's being noised about that**, corre el rumor de que, se rumora que.— —less [nɔizlis], **a.** silencioso, sin ruido.—**noisily** [nɔizili], **adv.** ruidosamente.—**noisy** [nɔizi], **a.** ruidoso, turbulento, estrepitoso.

nomad [noμmæd], **a.** nómada; trashumante.—**s.** nómada.—**ic** [nomædik], **a. =** NOMAD.

nominal [náminal], **a.** nominal.—**nominate** [námineit], **vt.** nombrar o nominar como candidato, designar; señalar.—**nomination** [namInéiʃɔn], **s.** nombramiento, nominación; propuesta.—**nominative** [náminativ], **a. y s.** (gram.) nominativo.

nonchalance [nánʃalans], **s.** indiferencia.—**nonchalant** [nánʃalant], **a.** indiferente, impasible.

noncommittal [nankɔmítal], **a.** reservado, evasivo.

nondescript [nándiskript], **a.** indefinido, inclasificable.

none [nʌn], **pron.** nadie, ninguno; nada; nada de.—**adv.** no, de ninguna manera, absolutamente no.—**n. the less**, no obstante, sin embargo; no menos.—**to be n. the better** (worse), no hallarse mejor (peor), no salir o quedar mejor (peor) librado, no ganar (perder).

nonexistent [nanigzístent], **a.** inexistente.

nonrusting [nanrʌstiŋ], **a.** inoxidable.

nonsense [nánsens], **s.** disparate, desatino; tontería, absurdo; (fam.) música celestial.—**interj.** ¡qué disparate! ¡bah! —**nonsensical** [nansénsikal], **a.** disparatado, destinado.

nonunion [nanyúnyɔn], **a.** no agremiado u opuesto a los sindicatos obreros; de fuera de los sindicatos obreros.

noodle [núdl], **s.** tallarín, fideo, pasta alimenticia; tonto, mentecato; (fam.) cabeza.

nook [nuk], **s.** rincón; escondrijo.

noon [nun], **s.** mediodía; las doce del día; (poét.) medianoche; (fig.) culminación, apogeo.—**a.** meridional. —**day** [núndei], **s.** mediodía (mitad del día).—**a.** meridional, de mediodía.

noose [nus], **s.** lazo corredizo, dogal.—**n. snare**, trampa.—**vt.** lazar; coger con lazo corredizo o trampa; ahorcar.

nor [nɔr], **conj.** ni.—**n. I**, yo tampoco.

Nordic [nɔ́rdik], **a. y s.** nórdico.

norm [nɔrm], **s.** norma, modelo, tipo.— —al [nɔ́rmal], **a.** normal, regular, corriente; típico, ejemplar; perpendicular.—**s.** norma, estado normal.— —alize [-alaiz], **vt.** normalizar, regularizar.

north [nɔrθ], **s.** norte, septentrión.—**a**

septentrional.—*N. American*, norteamericano.—*adv.* al norte, hacia el norte.– **—east** [nɔrθíst], *s.* y *a.* nordeste.– **—erly** [nɔ́rðœrli], **—ern** [nɔ́rðœrn], *a.* septentrional, norteño, nórtico; nordista; del norte o hacia el norte.—*northern lights*, aurora boreal.– **—erner** [nɔ́rðœrnœ(r)], *s.* habitante del norte.– **—land** [nɔ́rθlænd], *s.* tierra o región del norte.– **—west** [nɔrθwést], *s.* y *a.* noroeste o norueste.– **—western** [nɔrθwéstœrn], *a.* del noroeste.

Norwegian [nɔrwídžian], *s.* y *a.* noruego.

nose [nouz], *s.* nariz; (animal) hocico; olfato; sagacidad.—*n. dive*, (aer.) picada.—*vt.* y *vi.* oler, olfatear; entremeterse.—*to n. about*, husmear, curiosear.—*to n.-dive*, (aer.) picar.—*to n. out*, descubrir; vencer por poco.

nostalgia [nastáldžă], *s.* nostalgia.—**nostalgic** [nastáldžik], *a.* nostálgico.

nostril [nástril], *s.* ventana de la nariz; nariz.

not [nat], *adv.* no; ni, ni siquiera.—*is it n.?* ¿no es así? ¿no es eso? ¿verdad?—*n. a little*, no poco, bastante.—*n. any*, ninguno.—*n. at all*, nada; de ningún modo; de nada (contestación a *thank you*).—*n. even*, ni siquiera.—*n. one*, ni uno (sólo).—*n. so much as*, ni siquiera.—*n. to*, sin, por no.

notability [nóutabíliti], *s.* notabilidad.—**notable** [nóutabl], *a.* notable.—*s.* notabilidad, personaje eminente.

notary (public) [nóutari (pʌ́blik)], *s.* notario (público).—**notation** [notéišon], *s.* notación; anotación; numeración escrita.

notch [nach], *s.* muesca, corte; ranura; mella.—*vt.* hacer muescas; dentar, mellar.

note [nout], *s.* nota; marca, señal; anotación, apunte; comunicación, nota diplomática; esquela; aviso, conocimiento; distinción, importancia; (mus.) nota; (com.) billete; letra; vale, pagaré.—*vt.* marcar, distinguir; observar, advertir; apuntar, anotar, asentar, registrar.– **—book** [nóutbuk], *s.* libreta, cuaderno.– **—d** [nóutid], *a.* notable, afamado, insigne.– **—worthy** [-wœrði], *a.* notable, digno de atención.

nothing [nʌ́θiŋ], *s.* nada; cero; nadería, friolera.—*for n.*, gratis; inútilmente, sin provecho.—*good for n.*, inservible; despreciable.—*n. but*, sólo, no más que.—*n. else*, ninguna otra cosa; nada más.—*n. less than*, lo mismo que, no menos que.—*n. much*, no mucho, poca cosa.—*(there is) n. to* o *in it*, eso no vale nada, no asciende a nada.—*sweet nothings*, ternezas.—*that is n. to me*, eso nada me importa.—*there is n. else to do* o *n. for it but*, no hay más remedio (que).—*adv.* de ningún modo, en nada.

notice [nóutis], *s.* nota, observación; atención; aviso, anuncio, noticia, informe, notificación; mención; artículo, suelto; llamada; consideración, cortesía.—*at the shortest n.*, al momento, tan pronto como sea posible.—*on short n.*, con poco plazo o tiempo, con poco tiempo de aviso.—*to take n.*, prestar atención; hacer caso; notar, observar.—*until further n.*, hasta más aviso.—*vt.* notar, reparar en, caer en la cuenta de; atender a, cuidar de; hacer mención de.– **—able** [-abl], *a.* digno de atención, notable; perceptible.—**notification** [noutifikéišon], *s.* notificación; cita.—**notify** [nóutifai], *vti.* [7] notificar, avisar; prevenir; requerir, citar.

notion [nóušon], *s.* noción; idea; parecer, opinión; preocupación; intención, inclinación.—*pl.* mercería, novedades, baratijas.—*notions counter*, sección de mercería (en una tienda).

notoriety [noutoráieti], *s.* notoriedad, mala reputación.—**notorious** [notóriʌs], *a.* notorio; escandaloso, sensacional; de mala fama.—**notoriousness** [notóriʌsnis], *s.* notoriedad, mala reputación.

notwithstanding [natwiðstǽndiŋ], *adv.* no obstante, sin embargo.—*prep.* a pesar de, a despecho de.—*conj.* aun cuando, aunque, bien que; por más que.—*n. that*, aunque.

nought [nɔt], *s.* nada; cero; la cifra 0.

noun [naun], *s.* (gram.) nombre, sustantivo.

nourish [nœ́riš], *vt.* nutrir, alimentar; alentar, fomentar.– **—ment** [-ment], *s.* alimento; nutrición, alimentación; pábulo, fomento.

novel [nável], *a.* novel, original; reciente, moderno.—*s.* novela.– **—ist** [-ist], *s.* novelista.– **—ty** [-ti], *s.* novedad; innovación.—*pl.* novedades, artículos de fantasía.

November [novémbœ(r)], *s.* noviembre.

novice [návis], *s.* novicio, novato, aprendiz.—**novitiate** [novíšieit], *s.* (igl.) noviciado.

now [nau], *adv.* ahora; ya; hoy día, actualmente; al instante; después de esto; ahora bien, esto supuesto.—*from n. on*, de aquí en adelante.—*just n.*, ahora mismo, poco ha.—*n. and again* o *then*, de vez en cuando.—*n. rich, n. poor*, ya rico, ya pobre; tan pronto rico como pobre; ora rico, ora pobre.—*n. then*, y bien, ahora bien, bien, pues bien.—*conj.* (con

that) ya que, ahora que, puesto que.
—**s.** actualidad, momento presente.—
—**adays** [náuǝdeįz], *adv.* hoy (en) día.

nowhere [nóųhwɛr], *adv.* en ninguna parte.—*n. else,* en ninguna otra parte.—*n. near,* ni con mucho.—
nowise [nóųwaįz], *adv.* de ningún modo, de ninguna manera, de modo alguno.

noxious [nákѕʌs], *a.* nocivo.

nozzle [názl], *s.* pitón, pulverizador (de manguera); pico (de cafetera); hocico, nariz; (fam.) nariz de persona.

nucleus [nįúkliʌs], *s.* núcleo.

nude [nįud], *a.* desnudo; escueto.—*s.* (b.a.) desnudo, figura humana desnuda.

nudge [nʌdʒ], *vt.* tocar ligera o disimuladamente con el codo.—*s.* codazo ligero.

nudism [nįúdįzm], *s.* nudismo, desnudismo (culto o práctica).—**nudist** [nįúdįst], *s.* y *a.* desnudista.—**nudity** [nįúdįtį], *s.* desnudez.

nugget [nʌ́gįt], *s.* (min.) pepita.

nuisance [nįúsᵻns], *s.* incomodidad, molestia, estorbo, lata, fastidio; (for.) perjuicio o incomodidad causado a tercero; persona fastidiosa, pelmazo.

null [nʌl], *a.* nulo, sin fuerza legal.—
—**ification** [-įfįkéįѕᵻn], *s.* anulación, invalidación.—**nullify** [nʌ́lįfaį], *vti.* [7] anular, invalidar.

numb [nʌm], *a.* aterido, entumecido, entorpecido; torpe.—*vt.* entumecer, entorpecer, adormecer.

number [nʌ́mbœ(r)], *vt.* numerar, contar; computar; incluir, ascender a.—*s.* número, cifra, guarismo; porción, cantidad, multitud; (gram.) número; número o ejemplar (de periódico).—
—**less** [-lįs], *a.* innumerable, sin número.

numbness [nʌ́mnįs], *s.* entumecimiento, adormecimiento.

numeral [nįúmɛrᵻl], *a.* numeral, numérico, numerario.—*s.* número, cifra, guarismo; nombre o adjetivo numeral.—**numeric(al)** [nįumɛ́rįk(ᵻl)], *a.* numérico.—**numerous** [nįúmɛrʌs], *a.* numeroso; muchos.

nun [nʌn], *s.* monja.

nunnery [nʌ́nœrį], *s.* convento de monjas.

nuptial [nʌ́pѕᵻl], *a.* nupcial.—*n. song,* epitalamio.—*pl.* nupcias, bodas.

nurse [nœrs], *s.* enfermera, enfermero; aya, nana.—*wet n.,* ama de cría, nodriza.—*vt.* criar, amamantar; cuidar o asistir enfermos; cultivar (una planta).— —**maid** [nœ́rsmeįd], *s.* niñera, (Am.) manejadora.— —**ry** [nœ́rsœrį], *s.* cuarto de los niños; institución o lugar para párvulos o

lactantes; semillero; vivero (de plantas).—*n. school,* escuela de párvulos (previa al kindergarten).—*n. tales,* cuentos infantiles o de hadas.— —**rymaid** [nœ́rsœrįmeįd], *s.* = NURSEMAID.—**nursing** [nœ́rsįŋ], *s.* crianza, lactancia; asistencia, profesión de enfermera.—*n. bottle,* biberón.—*n. home,* clínica; sanatorio o asilo (de ancianos).

nurture [nœ́rchǝ(r)], *s.* nutrición, alimentación; educación, crianza; fomento.—*vt.* nutrir, alimentar; criar; educar; fomentar, promover.

nut [nʌt], *s.* nuez; tuerca; cejilla de violín o guitarra; (fam.) chiflado, loco; maniático; (fam.) cabeza.—
—**meg** [nʌ́tmɛg], *s.* nuez moscada.

nutrient [nįútrįɛnt], *a.* nutritivo.—
nutriment [nįútrįmɛnt], *s.* alimento.
—**nutrition** [nįutrȋѕᵻn], *s.* nutrición, alimentación.—**nutritious** [nįutrȋѕʌs], **nutritive** [nįútrįtįv], *a.* nutricio, nutritivo, sustancioso.

nutshell [nʌ́tѕɛl], *s.* cáscara de nuez o avellana.—*in a n.,* en sustancia, en pocas palabras.

nutty [nʌ́tį], *a.* abundante en nueces; con sabor a nueces; (fam.) loco, chiflado.

nymph [nįmf], *s.* ninfa.

O

oak [oųk], *s.* roble, encina.—*o. grove,* encinar, robledo.

oar [or], *s.* remo.—*vt.* y *vi.* remar, bogar.— —**sman** [órzmᵻn], *s.* remero.

oasis [oéįsįs], *s.* oasis.

oat(s) [out(s)], *s.* avena.

oath [ouθ], *s.* juramento; blasfemia, terno.—*on o.* o *upon o.,* bajo juramento.—*to take* o *make an o.,* jurar, prestar juramento.

oatmeal [óųtmil], *s.* harina de avena; gachas de avena.

obedience [obídįɛns], *s.* obediencia.—
obedient [obídįɛnt], *a.* obediente.

obeisance [obéįsᵻns], *s.* cortesía, reverencia; homenaje; deferencia.

obelisk [ábɛlįsk], *s.* obelisco; (impr.) cruz.

obese [obís], *a.* obeso, gordo.—**obesity** [obísįtį], *s.* obesidad, gordura.

obey [obéį], *vt.* obedecer.—*vi.* ser obediente.

obituary [obȋchųerį], *a.* y *s.* obituario, necrología.

object [ábdʒɛkt], *s.* objeto, cosa; objeto, propósito; blanco, punto; (gram.) complemento.—*o. ball,* mingo (en el billar).—*vt.* [ǝbdʒɛ́kt], objetar, poner reparos.—*vi.* oponerse, poner objeción, tener inconveniente.— —**ion** [ǝbdʒɛ́kѕᵻn], *s.* objeción, reparo; in-

conveniente.— **—ive** [ɒbdžéktiv], *a.* objetivo.—*o.* caso, (gram.) caso complementario.—*s.* (ópt., mil.) objetivo; objeto, propósito.

obligate [ábligeit], *vt.* obligar, comprometer, empeñar; constreñir.—**obligation** [abligéišɒn], *s.* obligación, compromiso, deber.—*pl.* (com.) obligaciones y compromisos; pasivo.—*to be under o. to one,* deber favores a uno.—**obligatory** [ɒblígatori], *a.* obligatorio, forzoso.—**oblige** [ɒbláidž], *vt.* obligar, constreñir; complacer, servir, hacer un favor.—*I am very much obliged to you,* muchas gracias, le quedo muy agradecido.—*much obliged,* muchas gracias.—**obliging** [ɒbláidžiŋ], *a.* servicial, obsequioso, condescendiente, cortés.

oblique [ɒblík], *a.* oblicuo.

obliterate [ɒblítereit], *vt.* borrar, tachar; destruir, arrasar.

oblivion [ɒblíviɒn], *s.* olvido.—**oblivious** [ɒblíviʌs], *a.* olvidadizo, desmemoriado; abstraído, absorto.

obnoxious [ɒbnákšʌs], *a.* ofensivo, odioso, detestable.

obscene [ɒbsín], *a.* obsceno, indecente, pornográfico.—**obscenity** [ɒbséniti], *s.* obscenidad, indecencia.

obscure [ɒbskiúr], *a.* oscuro.—*vt.* oscurecer; ocultar.—**obscurity** [ɒbskiúriti], *s.* oscuridad.

obsequies [ábsikwiz], *s. pl.* exequias, funeral(es), honras fúnebres.

obsequious [ɒbsíkwiʌs], *a.* obsequioso, zalamero; servil.

observance [ɒbzœ́rvʌns], *s.* observancia, cumplimiento; rito o ceremonia.—**observant** [ɒbzœ́rvʌnt], *a.* observador; observante.—**observation** [abzœrvéišɒn], *s.* observación.—**observatory** [ɒbzœ́rvatori], *s.* observatorio; atalaya, mirador.—**observe** [ɒbzœ́rv], *vt.* observar; notar, reparar; velar, vigilar; guardar (una fiesta).—**observer** [ɒbzœ́rvœ(r)], *s.* observador.

obsolete [ábsolit], *a.* anticuado; desusado.— **—ness** [-nis], *s.* desuso.

obstacle [ábstakl], *s.* obstáculo; traba, tropiezo.

obstetrician [abstetríšɒn], *s.* tocólogo, especialista en obstetricia, partero, comadrón.—**obstetrics** [ɒbstétriks], *s.* obstetricia, tocología.

obstinacy [ábstinasi], *s.* obstinación, porfía, terquedad, tozudez.—**obstinate** [ábstinit], *a.* obstinado, terco, porfiado.

obstruct [ɒbstrákt], *vt.* obstruir, impedir, estorbar.—**obstruction** [ɒbstrákšɒn], *s.* obstrucción, impedimento, estorbo.

obtain [ɒbtéin], *vt.* obtener, adquirir,

conseguir, alcanzar, lograr.—*vt.* prevalecer, reinar.— **—able** [-ąbl], *a.* obtenible, asequible.

obtuse [ɒbtiús], *a.* obtuso (ángulo, etc.); romo, sin punta; lerdo, torpe.

obviate [ábvieit], *vt.* obviar, evitar.—**obvious** [ábviʌs], *a.* obvio, evidente, claro.

occasion [ɒkéižɒn], *s.* ocasión; acontecimiento; oportunidad, lugar, coyuntura; causa.—*as o. requires,* en caso necesario, cuando llegue la ocasión.—*on o.,* en su oportunidad o a su debido tiempo.—*on the o. of,* con motivo de.—*to give o.,* dar pie.—*vt.* ocasionar, causar, acarrear.— **—al** [-ąl], *a.* ocasional, casual; alguno que otro; poco frecuente.— **—ally** [-ąli], *adv.* a veces, de vez en cuando, ocasionalmente.

occident [áksidɛnt], *s.* occidente, ocaso, oeste; (O.) Europa y América, hemisferio occidental.— **—al** [aksidéntąl], *a.* occidental.

occlusion [ɒklúžɒn], *s.* obstrucción; (med.) oclusión.

occult [ɒkált], *a.* oculto, secreto, arcano.

occupancy [ákyɒpansi], *s.* ocupación, tenencia, inquilinato.—**occupant** [ákyɒpant], *s.* ocupante; inquilino.—**occupation** [akyɒpéišɒn], *s.* ocupación, trabajo; oficio, empleo.—**occupy** [ákyɒpai], *vti.* [7] ocupar, llenar, emplear (tiempo); dar empleo, ocupación o trabajo a.

occur [ɒkœ́r], *vii.* [1] ocurrir; suceder, acontecer, acaecer; ocurrirse, venir a la imaginación o a la memoria.— **—rence** [-ɛns], *s.* ocurrencia; suceso, caso, acontecimiento.

ocean [óušan], *s.* océano.—*o. liner,* transatlántico.—**oceanic** [oušiǽnik], *a.* oceánico.

o'clock [ɒklák], *contr.* de OF THE CLOCK.—*it is eight o.,* son las ocho.

octave [áktiv], *s.* (mús.) octava.

October [aktóubœ(r)], *s.* octubre.

octopus [áktɒpas], *s.* (zool.) pulpo.

ocular [ákyɒlą(r)], *a.* ocular, visual.—**oculist** [ákyɒlist], *s.* oculista, oftalmólogo.

odd [ad], *a.* impar; non; suelto; casual, accidental; extraordinario, singular, raro; extraño.—*twenty o.,* veinte y tantos, veinte y pico.— **—ity** [áditi], *s.* singularidad, rareza.— **—s** [adz], *s. pl.* desigualdad, diferencia, disparidad; partido o apuesta desigual; ventaja, exceso; disputa.—*by all o.,* con mucho; sin duda.—*o. and ends,* retazos.—*the o. are that,* las probabilidades son, es lo más probable que.

ode [oud], *s.* oda.

odious [óudiʌs], *a.* odioso, abominable.

odor [óudɒ(r)], *s.* olor.—*bad o.,* mal

olor, hedor.— —ous [-ʌs], a. oloroso.

odyssey [ádiṣi], s. odisea, viaje largo y accidentado.

o'er [our], contr. de OVER.

of [av], prep. de; a; en.—it tastes o. wine, sabe a vino.—o. course, por supuesto, desde luego.—o. late, últimamente.— o. mine, mío, mía.—to dream o., soñar con.—to think o., pensar en.

off [of], adv. lejos, a distancia, fuera; de menos.—day o., día libre.—far o., lejos (de).—hands o., no tocar.—o. and on, de vez en cuando, algunas veces; a intervalos.—six miles o., a seis millas de distancia.—to be badly (o well) o., andar mal (bien) de dinero.—to be o., irse, marcharse, salir.—to put o., diferir, aplazar.—to see someone o., despedir a alguien.— to turn o. the water (the light, the gas), cortar el agua (la luz, el gas).—two dollars o., un descuento de dos dólares.—prep. lejos de; fuera de; de; desde; frente a, cerca de.—an o. day, un día libre; un día desafortunado.— o. the track, (fam.) despistado, por los cerros de Úbeda.

offend [o[énd], vt. ofender, agraviar.— vi. pecar.—to o. against, faltar a.— —er [-œ(r)], s. delincuente, transgresor, reo, pecador.—offense [oféns], s. ofensa; agravio, injuria, falta; delito. —no o., sin ofender a usted; no lo dije por tanto.—to take o., sentirse, agraviarse, ofenderse.—offensive [ofénsjv], a. ofensivo.—s. ofensiva, ataque.

offer [óføœ(r)], vt. y vi. ofrecer(se).—s. oferta, ofrecimiento, promesa; declaración de amor; propuesta.— —ing [-iŋ], s. ofrecimiento, oferta; ofrenda.

offhand [ófhǽnd], a. y adv. improvisado, de repente; sin pensarlo, de improviso.

office [ófjs], s. oficio; ministerio o cargo; oficina, despacho; negociado, departamento.—pl. servicio, favor; buenos oficios.—doctor's o., consultorio médico.—lawyer's o., bufete.—o. boy, mandadero, mensajero (de oficina).— —holder [-hou̯ldœ(r)], s. empleado público, funcionario, burócrata.— —r [ófiscœ(r)], s. oficial; funcionario; guardia, agente de policía.—vt. mandar (como oficial o jefe); proveer de oficiales y jefes.—official [ofíṣal], a. oficial.—s. oficial público; funcionario autorizado o ejecutivo.—officiate [ofíṣieit], vi. oficiar, celebrar (la misa); ejercer o desempeñar un cargo. —officious [ofíṣʌs], a. oficioso, entremetido, intruso.

offset [ófset], s. balance, compensación, equivalencia.—a. fuera de su lugar; desalineado; (impr.) calcado en

láminas de caucho.—vti. [9] [ofsét], compensar, contrapesar; terraplenar. —vii. [ófset], (impr.) repetir; emplear el procedimiento offset.—pret. y pp. de TO OFFSET.

offspring [ófspriŋ], s. hijo(s), vástago(s), prole, progenie o descendencia.

often [ófn], adv. frecuentemente, a menudo, muchas veces.—as o. as, siempre que, tantas veces (o tan a menudo) como.—how o.? ¿cuántas veces? ¿con qué frecuencia?—not o., rara vez.—so o., tantas veces.—too o., con demasiada frecuencia.

ogre [óugœ(r)], s. ogro, monstruo.

oil [oil], s. aceite; petróleo; óleo.—o. can, bidón o lata de aceite.—o. cup, (mec.) lubri(fi)cadora, copilla.—o. painting, pintura o cuadro al óleo; arte de pintar al óleo.—o. tanker, barco petrolero.—vt. aceitar, engrasar, lubri(fi)car; (fam.) untar (la mano), sobornar.— —cloth [ójlkləθ], s. encerado, hule.— —y [-i], a. aceitoso, oleoso, oleaginoso; grasiento.

ointment [óintmęnt], s. ungüento, untura.

O.K., OK, okay [óukéi], a. (fam.) correcto; conforme; bueno, que sirve.— adv. bien.—it is O.K., está bien.— s. (V°.B°.) visto bueno.—vt. aprobar; dar o poner el visto bueno a.

okra [óukrạ], s. (bot.) (Am.) quimbombó.

old [ou̯ld], a. viejo, anciano; antiguo; añejo.—how o. is he? ¿cuántos años tiene?—of o., de antiguo, de atrás.— o. age, vejez, ancianidad.—o. bachelor, solterón.—o. boy, (fam.) chico, (Am.) viejo (expresión de amistad).—o. fashioned, chapado a la antigua; anticuado.—o. lady, anciana; (fam.) madre, esposa.—o. maid, solterona.— o. man, anciano, viejo; (fam.) padre, marido.—o.-timer, antiguo residente.

olive [áljv], s. (bot.) olivo, aceituno; aceituna, oliva.—o.-colored, aceitunado.—o. grove, olivar.—o. oil, aceite de oliva.—a. aceitunado; verde olivo.

Olympic [olímpjk], a. olímpico.—O. games, olimpíadas, juegos olímpicos.

omelet [ámljt], s. tortilla (de huevos).

omen [óumin], s. agüero, augurio, presagio.—vt. presagiar, augurar.— ominous [ámjnʌs], a. ominoso, siniestro, nefasto, de mal agüero.

omission [omíṣọn], s. omisión.—omit [omít], vti. [1] omitir; prescindir de; pasar por alto, olvidar.

omnibus [ámnjbʌs], s. ómnibus; (Mex.) camión, (Arg.) colectivo, (Cuba) guagua.

omnipotent [amnípotęnt], a. omnipotente.

on [an], prep. sobre, encima de; en;

a, al; bajo; por; contra.—*o. account (of)*, a cuenta (de).—*o. an average*, por término medio.—*o. a sudden*, de golpe, de repente.—*o. hand*, entre manos.—*o. leaving*, al salir.—*o. my part*, por mi parte.—*o. my responsibility*, bajo mi responsabilidad.—*o. purpose*, a propósito, adrede.—*o. record*, registrado; que consta.—*o. the contrary*, por el contrario.—*o. the road*, de viaje, viajando.—*o. the table*, sobre la mesa.—*to draw o. my bank*, girar contra mi banco.—*a. y adv.* puesto; encendido; funcionando; en contacto.—*and so o.*, y así sucesivamente; etcétera.—*o. and off*, a intervalos, de vez en cuando.—*o. and o.*, continuamente, sin cesar.—*to have one's hat o.*, tener el sombrero puesto.—*to turn o. the light (the radio, etc.)*, encender la luz (el radio, etc.).

once [wʌns], *adv. y s.* una vez; en otro tiempo.—*at o.*, en seguida, al instante, inmediatamente; a un mismo tiempo, simultáneamente.—*o. and again*, varias veces.—*o. for all*, por última vez, de una vez para siempre.—*o. in a while*, de cuando en cuando.—*o. upon a time*, había una vez, érase que se era.—*this o.*, (siquiera) esta vez.—*a.* de otro tiempo, pasado, que fue.—*conj.* una vez que, tan pronto como.

one [wʌn], *a.* un, uno, una; solo, único; cierto; igual.—*it is all o. to me*, lo mismo me da; me es lo mismo.—*o. day*, cierto día, un día; algún día, un día de éstos.—*o.-eyed*, tuerto.—*o.-handed*, manco; con una sola mano.—*o.-sided*, parcial, injusto, (for.) leonino; unilateral; de un solo lado; desigual.—*o. way*, de una sola dirección; (f.c., avión, etc.) billete o boleto de ida o sencillo.—*s. y pron.* uno.—*a better o.*, uno mejor.—*all o.*, lo mismo.—*o. and all*, todos, todos sin excepción.—*o. and the same*, idéntico.—*another*, uno(s) a otros.—*o. by o.*, uno a uno, uno(s) por uno.—*o. (for) each*, sendos, uno para cada uno.—*o. or two*, unos pocos.—*o.'s*, de uno, su.—*that o.*, ése; aquél.—*the white o.*, el blanco.—*this o.*, éste.

onerous [ánɛrʌs], *a.* oneroso, gravoso, molesto, cargoso.

oneself [wʌnsélf], *pron.* se, sí, sí mismo, (a) uno mismo.—*by o.*, solo, por sí solo.—*with o.*, consigo.

onion [ányɒn], *s.* cebolla.— **—skin** [-skɪn], *s.* papel cebolla.

onlooker [ánlʊkɛ(r)], *s.* espectador, observador; (fam.) mirón.

only [óunli], *a.* único, sólo.—*adv.* (tan) sólo, solamente, únicamente; no más que (o de).—*if o.*, ojalá, si.—*not o.*

. . . *but also*, no sólo . . . sino también.—*conj.* sólo que, pero.

onset [ánset], *s.* embestida, arremetida, carga; arranque.

onto [ántu], *prep. a;* encima de, sobre, en.

onward [ánwǝrd], *a.* avanzado; progresivo.— **—(s)** [-(z)], *adv.* adelante, hacia adelante; en adelante.

ooze [uz], *vt. y vi.* escurrir(se); exudar(se), rezumar(se); manar, fluir.—*s.* cieno, limo.

opal [óupǝl], *s.* ópalo.

opaque [opéjk], *a.* opaco; sin brillo, mate.

open [óupn], *vt.* abrir; destapar; desplegar; empezar, iniciar; entablar.—*vi.* (a veces con **out**) abrirse, entreabrirse; desplegarse; empezar.—*to o. on o upon*, caer, dar o mirar a.—*to o. with*, empezar con.—*a.* abierto; sincero, franco; descubierto; expuesto a un ataque; público; descampado.—*in the o. air*, al aire libre, a la intemperie.—*in the o. field*, a campo raso.—*o.-minded*, razonable, liberal.—*o.-mouthed*, boquiabierto.—*o. port*, puerto franco.—*o. question*, cuestión discutible; asunto en duda.—*o. sea*, alta mar.—*o. season*, temporada de caza, pesca.—*o. secret*, secreto a voces.—*o. winter*, invierno templado.—*wide o.*, de par en par.—*s.* claro, raso, lugar abierto.—*can opener*, abrelatas.—*in the o.*, a campo raso; al aire libre, a la intemperie; al descubierto, abiertamente.— **—ing** [-iɳ], *s.* abertura, brecha; boca, orificio; salida; claro, campo abierto; inauguración, apertura; empleo vacante.—*a.* preliminar, inicial; inaugural.—*o. performance*, (teat.) estreno.

opera [ápɛrǝ], *s.* ópera.—*o. house*, teatro de la ópera.

operable [ápɛrǝbl], *a.* operable.— **operate** [ápɛrejt], *vt.* operar, hacer funcionar, mover; (min.) explotar; manejar.—*vi.* (con **in**, **on** o **upon**) obrar, operar; producir efecto; funcionar; (cir.) operar; (com.) operar, especular; (mil.) operar, maniobrar.—*operated by*, (mec.) accionado por.— **operating** [ápɛrejtiɳ], *a.* operante, actuante; operatorio.—*o. room*, quirófano.— **operation** [apɛréjʂɒn], *s.* operación; funcionamiento; manejo, manipulación.— **operator** [ápɛrejtɒ(r)], *s.* operario; maquinista; telegrafista; telefonista; ascensorista; cirujano; empresario de minas; (fam.) manipulador.

operetta [apɛrétǝ], *s.* opereta, zarzuela.

opiate [óupijit], *s.* narcótico.— **opium** [óupijʌm], *s.* opio.—*o. den*, fumadero de opio.

opinion [ɒpínyɒn], *s.* opinión, concepto, parecer; dictamen.— —**ated** [-éitid], *a.* terco, porfiado, obstinado.

opossum [ɒpásʌm], *s.* zarigüeya, oposúm.

opponent [ɒpóunɛnt], *s.* antagonista, contrincante, contrario; opositor.—*a.* antagónico; opuesto, contrario; oponente.

opportune [apɒrtjún], *a.* oportuno, a propósito, conveniente.—**opportunity** [apɒrtjúniti], *s.* oportunidad; ocasión.

oppose [ɒpóuz], *vt.* oponer; hacer frente a, oponerse a; objetar; resistir.— *vi.* oponerse.—**opposite** [ápɒzit], *a.* opuesto, contrario; frontero, adverso, de cara, de enfrente, al otro lado.— *prep.* del otro lado de; enfrente de, frente a.—*s.* contrario.—*the o.*, lo opuesto, lo contrario.—**opposition** [apɒzíʃɒn], *s.* oposición.

oppress [ɒprés], *vt.* oprimir, agobiar; tiranizar.— —**ion** [ɒpréʃɒn], *s.* opresión; tiranía; agobio, ahogo.— —**ive** [ɒprésiv], *a.* opresivo, opresor; agobiador, abrumador; sofocante.— —**or** [ɒprésɒr], *s.* opresor, tirano.

optic(al) [áptik(al)], *a.* óptico.—**optician** [aptíʃan], *s.* óptico.—**optics** [áptiks], *s.* óptica.

optimism [áptimizm], *s.* optimismo.— **optimist** [áptimist], *s.,* **optimistic** [aptimístik], *a.* optimista.

option [ápʃɒn], *s.* opción, facultad de escoger; alternativa; (com.) opción, plazo para determinar.— —**al** [-al], *a.* opcional, optativo, discrecional.

opulence [ápyulɛns], *s.* opulencia, abundancia.—**opulent** [ápyulɛnt], *a.* opulento.

or [ɒr], *conj.* o, u; si no, de lo contrario.—*o. else,* o bien.

oracle [árakl], *s.* oráculo.

oral [óral], *a.* oral; verbal, hablado; bucal.—*s.* examen oral.

orange [árandʒ], *s.* naranja; color naranja, anaranjado.—*o. blossom,* azahar.—*o. grove,* naranjal.—*o. pekoe,* té negro de Ceilán.—*o. tree,* naranjo. —*a.* perteneciente a las naranjas; anaranjado.— —**ade** [-éid], *s.* naranjada.

orang-utan [oráŋutæn], *s.* orangután.

oration [oréiʃɒn], *s.* oración, discurso.— **orator** [áratɒr], *s.* orador.—**oratory** [áratɒri], *s.* oratoria, elocuencia; oratorio, capilla.

orb [ɒrb], *s.* orbe.

orbit [órbit], *s.* órbita.

orchard [órchard], *s.* huerto, vergel.

orchestra [órkistrə], *s.* orquesta; (teat.) patio de butacas, (Am.) platea.—*o. seat,* luneta, butaca de platea.

orchid [órkid], *s.* orquídea.

ordain [ɒrdéin], *vt.* ordenar, mandar;

decretar; (igl.) conferir órdenes sagradas.

ordeal [ɒrdíl], *s.* prueba muy difícil; ordalía.

order [órdœ(r)], *s.* orden; (com.) orden, pedido.—*pl.* órdenes sagradas o sacerdotales; sacramento.—*in (good) o.,* en regla, en orden, en buen estado.— *in o. to o that,* para, a fin de que, para que, porque, con (el) objeto de. —*in working o.,* en buen estado.— *money o.,* giro postal.—*on the o. of,* de la clase de.—*o. of knighthood,* orden de caballería.—*out of o.,* descompuesto; que no funciona; desordenado, desarreglado.—*to give o place an o.,* hacer un pedido.—*to o.,* a propósito, especialmente; (com.) a la orden, por encargo especial, según se pida, a la medida.—*vi.* dar órdenes. —*vt.* ordenar, mandar; poner en orden; mandar hacer; encargar, pedir (mercancías, un coche, el almuerzo, etc.).—*to o. away,* despedir a uno, decirle que se vaya.—*to o. in,* mandar entrar; mandar traer.—*to o. out,* mandar salir; mandar llevar; echar. — **ly** [-li], *a.* ordenado, metódico; bien arreglado; obediente, disciplinado; tranquilo.—*s.* ordenanza, asistente.— *adv.* ordenadamente, metódicamente, en orden.—**ordinal** [órdinal], *a.* ordinal.—*s.* numeral ordinal; (igl.) libro ritual.—**ordinance** [órdinans], *s.* ordenanza, ley, reglamento; rito, ceremonial; ordenación, disposición.

ordinary [órdineri], *a.* ordinario, común, corriente; tosco, burdo; mediano.

ordnance [órdnans], *s.* (mil.) artillería, cañones.—*o. stores o supplies,* pertrechos de guerra.

ore [oyr], *s.* mineral en bruto, ganga.

organ [órgan], *s.* órgano.—*barrel o.,* organillo.— —**ic(al)** [ɒrgénik(al)], *a.* orgánico; organizado; sistematizado; constitutivo o fundamental.— —**ism** [-izm], *s.* organismo.— —**ist** [-ist], *s.* (mus.) organista.— —**ization** [-izéiʃɒn], *s.* organización; estructura orgánica; constitución; organismo; cuerpo, entidad, compañía, corporación.— —**ize** [-aiz], *vt.* organizar.— *vi.* organizarse, constituirse.— —**izer** [-aizœ(r)], *s.,* —**izing** [-aiziŋ], *a.* organizador.

organdy [órgandi], *s.* organdí.

orgasm [órgæzm], *s.* orgasmo.

orgy [órdʒi], *s.* orgía.

orient [óuriɛnt], *s.* oriente, este, levante.—*the O.,* el Oriente.—*vt.* orientar.— —**al** [oriéntal], *a.* y *s.* oriental.— —**ate** [óuriɛnteit], *vt.* orientar.— —**ation** [orientéiʃɒn], *s.* orientación.

orifice [árifis], *s.* orificio, abertura.

origin [óridʒin], *s.* origen.— —**al** [orídȝinạl], *a.* original; primitivo, primero, originario.— —s. original; prototipo.— —ality [ọrịdȝinélịtị], *s.* originalidad.— —ally [ọrídȝinạli], *adv.* originariamente, en el principio; originalmente.— —ate [ọrídȝineịt], *vt.* originar.—*vi.* originarse, dimanar.— —ator [ọrídȝineịtọ(r)], *s.* originador, iniciador.

oriole [óụrịoụl], *s.* oropéndola.

ornament [órnạment], *s.* ornamento, adorno.—*vt.* [órnạment], ornamentar, adornar.— —al [ọrnạméntạl], *a.* ornamental, decorativo.—*s.* cosa, planta, etc. de adorno.—**ornate** [ọrnéịt], *a.* ornado, ornamentado, adornado; recargado.

ornithology [ọrnịθálọdȝị], *s.* ornitología.

orphan [órfạn], *a.* y *s.* huérfano.—*vt.* dejar huérfano a.— —age [-ịdȝ], *s.* orfandad; orfanato(rio).

orthodox [órθọdạks], *a.* ortodoxo; convencional.— —y [-ị], *s.* ortodoxia.

orthographic(al) [ọrθọgréfịk(ạl)], *a.* ortográfico.—**orthography** [ọrθágrạfị], *s.* ortografía.

oscillate [ásịleịt], *vt.* balancear, hacer oscilar.—*vi.* oscilar, fluctuar.—**oscillation** [asịléịṣọn], *s.* oscilación, fluctuación, vaivén.

osier [óụzœ(r)], *s.* sauce; mimbre.—*a.* de mimbre.

osmosis [asmóụsịs], *s.* ósmosis.

ostensible [asténsịbl], *a.* aparente; pretendido.—**ostentation** [astentéịṣọn], *s.* ostentación, jactancia, alarde.—**ostentatious** [astentéịṣʌs], *a.* ostentoso, fastuoso; jactancioso.

ostracism [ástrạsịzm], *s.* ostracismo.—**ostracize** [ástrạsaịz], *vt.* aislar; desterrar, condenar al ostracismo.

ostrich [ástrịch], *s.* avestruz; (Am.) ñandú, suri.

other [Áðœ(r)], *a.* y *pron.* otro, otra (otros, otras).—*each o.*, uno a otro, el uno al otro, unos a otros.—*every o. day*, en días alternos, un día sí y otro no.—*o. than*, otra cosa que; más que.—*some o. day*, cualquier otro día.— —wise [-waịz], *adv.* de otra manera, de otro modo; de lo contrario, si no; o bien.—*a.* otro, diferente.

otter [átœ(r)], *s.* nutria; piel de nutria.

ought [ɔt], *vai.* [11] deber; convenir.—*it o. to be so,* así debería (o debiera) ser.—*you o. not to go,* usted no debe (debiera, debería) ir.—*you o. to know,* usted debería saberlo.—*pret.* de OUGHT.

ought [ɔt], *s.* y *adv.* algo, alguna cosa; nada; cero.—*for o. I know,* por lo que yo puedo comprender, en cuanto yo sé.

ounce [auns], *s.* onza. Ver Tabla.

our(s) [aụr(z)], *a.* y *pron. pos.* (el, los)

nuestro(s), (la, las) nuestra(s).—*a friend of ours,* un amigo nuestro.—**ourselves** [aụrsélvz], *pron.* nosotros mismos, nosotras mismas; a nosotros mismos; nos (reflexivo).

oust [aụst], *vt.* desposeer, desanuciar, desalojar, echar fuera, despedir.

out [aụt], *adv.* fuera, afuera; hacia fuera.—*prep.* fuera de; más allá de.—*a.* exterior; ausente; fuera de moda; errado (cálculos, etc.); cesante; (declarado) en huelga.—*a way o.*, escapatoria.—*four o. of five*, de cada cinco, cuatro.—*o. and away*, con mucho.—*o. and o.*, cabal, completo; declarado; redomado.—*o. at interest*, puesto a interés.—*o. at the elbows*, andrajoso, roto por los codos.—*o. loud*, en voz alta.—*o. of*, fuera de; más allá de; sin; por.—*o. of fear*, por miedo.—*o. of money*, sin dinero.—*o. of print*, agotado (libros).—*time is o.*, el tiempo (la hora) ha pasado; el plazo ha expirado.—*to be o.*, estar fuera o ausente; no estar en boga; quedar cesante; quedarse cortado; salir perdiendo; estar apagado o extinguido; haberse agotado o acabado; haberse publicado, haber salido (libro, periódico, etc.); estar reñidos.—*to be o. of,* no tener más, habérsele acabado a uno.—*to run o. of,* acabársele a uno, quedarse sin.—*interj.* ¡fuera!—*o. with it!* ¡fuera con ello! hable sin rodeos.—*s.* exterior, parte de afuera; esquina, lugar exterior; exterioridad; cesante; dimisionario; (fam.) pero, defecto; (impr.) olvido, omisión.—*pl.* (pol.) la oposición.

outbalance [aụtbǽlạns], *vt.* sobrepujar, exceder.

outbid [aụtbíd], *vti.* [10] mejorar, pujar, ofrecer más dinero (en subasta, etc.).—*pret.* y *pp.* de TO OUTBID.—**outbidden** [aụtbídn], *pp.* de TO OUTBID.

outbreak [aụtbreịk], *s.* erupción, brote; ataque violento; pasión; tumulto, disturbio; principio (de una guerra, epidemia, etc.).

outburst [aụtbœrst], *s.* explosión, erupción, estallido; acceso; arranque.

outcast [aụtkæst], *a.* desechado, inútil; proscripto; perdido.—*s.* paria.

outcome [aụtkʌm], *s.* resultado.

outcry [aụtkraị], *s.* clamor(eo); grita; alboroto, gritería; protesta.

outdid [aụtdíd], *pret.* de TO OUTDO.

outdistance [aụtdístạns], *vt.* dejar atrás, adelantarse a.

outdo [aụtdú], *vti.* [10] exceder, sobrepujar, descollar, eclipsar, vencer.—*to o. oneself,* superarse, excederse a sí mismo.—**outdone** [aụtdʌ́n], *pp.* de TO OUTDO.

outdoor [aụtdọr], *a.* externo, fuera de la

casa, al aire libre.— —s [-z], s. el campo raso, el mundo de puertas afuera.—*adv.* fuera de casa, a la intemperie.

outer [áųtœ(r)], *a.* exterior, externo.— —most [-moųst], *a.* extremo; [lo] más exterior.

outfit [áųtfịt], *s.* equipo, apresto, tren; ropa, vestido, traje; habilitación; pertrechos; avíos.—*vti.* [1] equipar, habilitar, pertrechar.

outgo [aųtgóų], *vti.* [10] aventajar, vencer.—s. [aųtgoų], gasto, expendio.— —ing [áųtgoųịŋ], *s.* ida, salida, partida.—*a.* saliente, que cesa; que sale, de salida; extrovertido.—**outgone** [aųtgón], *pp.* de TO OUTGO.

outgrew [aųtgrú], *pret.* de TO OUTGROW. —**outgrow** [aųtgróų], *vti.* [10] crecer más que; pasar de la edad de, ser ya viejo para, ser demasiado grande para; curarse de con la edad o con el tiempo.—**outgrown** [aųtgróųn], *pp.* de TO OUTGROW.—*he has o. his crib*, la cuna ya le queda pequeña.—**outgrowth** [áųtgroųθ], *s.* excrecencia; resultado, consecuencia.

outhouse [áųthaųs], *s.* accesoria; retrete situado fuera de la casa.

outing [áųtịŋ], *s.* salida; paseo, caminata, excursión.

outlaid [aųtléịd], *pret.* y *pp.* de TO OUTLAY.

outlandish [aųtléndịš], *a.* extraño, ridículo; de aspecto extranjero o exótico; remoto.

outlast [aųtlést], *vt.* durar más que; sobrevivir a.

outlaw [áųtlọ], *s.* forajido, facineroso; proscrito; fuera de la ley; rebelde.— *vt.* proscribir; declarar fuera de la ley.

outlay [áųtleị], *s.* desembolso, gasto, salida.—*vti.* [10] [aųtléị], gastar; desplegar.

outlet [áųtlet], *s.* salida; orificio de salida; escape; desagüe; sangrador; toma (de agua, corriente eléctrica, etc.).

outline [áųtlaịn], *s.* contorno, perfil; croquis, esbozo, bosquejo, plan general, reseña.—*vt.* bosquejar, delinear, esbozar, reseñar, trazar.

outlive [aųtlív], *vt.* sobrevivir a, durar más que.

outlook [áųtlụk], *s.* vista, perspectiva, aspecto; punto de vista; probabilidades.—*pl.* actitud; atalaya, vigía, garita; centinela.

outlying [áųtlaịịŋ], *a.* distante, remoto; lejos del centro; exterior, exterior.

outnumber [aųtnámbœ(r)], *vt.* exceder en número, ser más que.

outpatient [áųtpeịşẹnt], *s.* enfermo externo.

outpost [áųtpoųst], *s.* (mil.) avanzada, avanzadilla.

outpouring [áųtpọrịŋ], *s.* chorro, chorreo, efusión; desahogo.

output [áųtpụt], *s.* producción total, rendimiento; capacidad, fuerza; (mec., elec.) potencia neta o útil.

outrage [áųtreịdž], *vt.* ultrajar; maltratar; violar, desflorar.—*s.* ultraje; desafuero; atrocidad; violación, rapto.— —ous [aųtréịdžʌs], *a.* ultrajante, injurioso; atroz; desaforado.

outran [aųtrén], *pret.* de TO OUTRUN.

outright [áųtraịt], *a.* completo; directo; sincero, franco.—*adv.* [áųtráịt], completamente; abiertamente; sin reserva; sin tardanza, al momento.

outrun [aųtrán], *vti.* [10] correr más que; pasar, ganar, exceder.—*pp.* de TO OUTRUN.

outset [áųtset], *s.* principio; salida; estreno.

outshine [aųtšáịn], *vti.* [10] dejar deslucido, eclipsar.—**outshone** [aųtšóųn], *pret.* y *pp.* de TO OUTSHINE.

outside [aųtsáịd], *a.* exterior, externo; superficial; extremo; ajeno, neutral. —s. exterior, parte de afuera, superficie; apariencia; extremo.—*at the o.*, (fam.) a lo sumo, a más tirar.—*adv.* afuera, fuera.—*o. of*, (fam.) con excepción de.—*prep.* fuera de; (fam.) excepto.— —r [áųtsáịdœ(r)], *s.* forastero, extraño; intruso.

outsize [áųtsaịz], *s.* prenda de vestir de tamaño fuera de lo común.—*a.* de tamaño extraordinario; (fam.) inmenso.

outskirt [áųtskœrt], *s.* borde, linde.— *pl.* afueras, suburbios, arrabales, inmediaciones.

outspoken [aųtspóųkn], *a.* abierto, franco(te).—*to be o.*, (fam.) no tener pelos en la lengua.

outspread [aųtspréd], *vti.* y *vii.* [9] extender(se), difundir(se); desplegar(se).—*pret.* y *pp.* de TO OUTSPREAD.—*a.* [áųtspred], (ex)tendido; desplegado.—*s.* extensión; despliegue; expansión.

outstanding [aųtsténdịŋ], *a.* saliente; destacado, descollante, sobresaliente, prominente; que resiste; (com.) pendiente, no pagado.

outstretch [aųtstréch], *vt.* extender, alargar, estirar.

outstrip [aųtstríp], *vti.* [1] pasar, rezagar; aventajar, ganar.

outward [áųtwǎrd], *a.* exterior, visible; aparente, superficial; extraño; extrínseco; corpóreo.—*adv.* fuera, afuera, exteriormente; superficialmente; (mar.) de ida; para el extranjero.

outweigh [aųtwéị], *vt.* preponderar;

pesar más que; **exceder en valor o importancia.**

outwent [aụtwént], *pret.* de TO OUTGO.

outwit [aụtwít], *vti.* [1] ser más listo que; llevar ventaja a; engañar con habilidad.

outwork [aụtwœ́rk], *vti.* [4] trabajar más que; acabar.—*s.* (mil.) obra exterior.

outworn [aụtwórn], *a.* ajado, gastado, usado; anticuado.

oval [óuvạl], *s.* óvalo.—*a.* oval, ovalado.

ovary [óuvạri], *s.* ovario.

ovation [ovéişọn], *s.* ovación.

oven [Λvn], *s.* horno.

overall [óuvœroːl], *a.* global, total, de conjunto.—*s.* *pl.* traje de mecánico, mono(s); (Am.) overol, overoles.

over [óuvœ(r)], *prep.* sobre, encima, por encima de; allende, al otro lado de; a causa o por motivo de; a pesar de; más de; mientras, durante; por, en.—*o. all*, total, de extremo a extremo.—*o. night*, durante la noche, hasta el otro día.—*adv.* al otro lado; al lado, parte o partido contrario; enfrente; encima; al revés; más, de más, de sobra; otra vez, de nuevo; demasiado, excesivamente; acabado, terminado; a la vuelta, al dorso.—*to be* (*all*) *o.*, haber pasado; haberse acabado, terminar(se).—*to be left o.*, quedar, sobrar.—*to be o. and above*, sobrar.—*a.* acabado, terminado; demasiado; sobrante, en exceso de; superior; exterior.—*it is all o.*, ya pasó; se acabó.

overate [ouvœréjt], *pret.* de TO OVEREAT.

overbear [ouvœbér], *vti.* [10] sojuzgar; oprimir, subyugar; agobiar, vencer.—*vti.* llevar demasiado fruto.—*-ing* [-iŋ], *a.* despótico, imperioso, dominante, arrogante.

overbid [ouvœbjd], *vti.* [10] ofrecer más que, pujar.—*vti.* ofrecer demasiado.—*pret. y pp.* de TO OVERBID.—*s.* [óuvœbjd], puja.—**overbidden** [ouvœbjdn], *pp.* de TO OVERBID.

overboard [óuvœbord], *adv.* (mar.) al mar, al agua.—*man o.!* ¡hombre al agua!

overbore [ouvœbór], *pret.* de TO OVERBEAR.—**overborne** [ouvœbórn], *pp.* de TO OVERBEAR.

overburden [ouvœbœ́rdẹn], *vt.* sobrecargar; oprimir.

overcame [ouvœkéjm], *pret.* de TO OVERCOME.

overcast [ouvœkǽst], *vti.* [9] anublar, oscurecer; entristecer; cicatrizar; sobrehilar.—*vti.* anublarse.—*pret. y pp.* de TO OVERCAST.—*a.* [óuvœkǽst], nublado, encapotado; sombrío.

overcharge [ouvœchárdẹ], *vt.* cobrar demasiado; recargar el precio; sobrecargar.—*s.* [óuvœchardẹ], cargo excesivo; cargo adicional; recargo; carga eléctrica excesiva.

overcoat [óuvœkout], *s.* sobretodo, gabán, abrigo.

overcome [ouvœkΛm], *vti.* [10] vencer, rendir; sojuzgar, subyugar; superar, vencer, salvar (obstáculos).—*vii.* sobreponerse; ganar, vencer; hacerse superior.—*pp.* de TO OVERCOME.—*a.* agobiado, confundido.

overconfidence [ouvœkánfidẹns], *s.* presunción, excesiva confianza.—**overconfident** [ouvœkánfidẹnt], *a.* demasiado confiado.

overcrowd [ouvœkráud], *vt.* apiñar, atestar.

overdid [ouvœdjd], *pret.* de TO OVERDO.—**overdo** [ouvœdú], *vti.* [10] hacer más de lo necesario; extralimitarse.—*vti.* agobiar, abrumar de trabajo; exagerar; (coc.) recocer, requemar.—**overdone** [ouvœdΛn], *a.* demasiado trabajado; (coc.) recocido, requemado, demasiado asado.—*pp.* de TO OVERDO.

overdose [óuvœdous], *s.* dosis excesiva.

overdraft [óuvœdræft], *s.* descubierto bancario, giro en exceso.—**overdraw** [ouvœdró], *vti.* [10] girar en descubierto; exagerar (en el dibujo, la descripción, etc.).—**overdrawn** [ouvœdrón], *pp.* de TO OVERDRAW.

overdress [ouvœdrés], *vt.* adornar con exceso.—*vi.* vestirse con exceso.—*s.* [óuvœdres], sobreprenda.

overdrew [ouvœdrú], *pret.* de TO OVERDRAW.

overdue [óuvœdjú], *a.* vencido y no pagado, retrasado en el pago.

overeat [ouvœrít], *vii.* [10] comer con exceso, hartarse.—**overeaten** [ouvœrítn], *pp.* de TO OVEREAT.

overestimate [ouvœréstimejt], *vt.* presuponer; estimar en valor excesivo; tener en más de lo justo.—*s.* [ouvœréstimjt], estimación exagerada.

overexcite [ouvœríksáit], *vt.* sobreexcitar.— —*ment* [-mẹnt], *s.* sobreexcitación.

overexposure [ouvœríkspóuẓŭ(r)], *s.* (fot.) exceso de exposición.

overfed [ouvœféd], *pret. y pp.* de TO OVERFEED.—**overfeed** [ouvœfíd], *vti.* [10] sobrealimentar.

overflow [ouvœflóu], *vi.* rebosar, desbordarse.—*vt.* inundar.—*s.* [óuvœflou], inundación; rebosamiento, derrame; exceso, superabundancia; escape, sumidero.

overgrew [ouvœgrú], *pret.* de TO OVERGROW.—**overgrow** [ouvœgróu], *vti.* [10] cubrir con plantas o hierbas; crecer más que.—*vii.* crecer o desa-

rollarse con exceso.—**overgrown**
[ouvœrgróun], *pp.* de TO OVERGROW.
—*a.* grandullón.

overhang [ouvœrhǽŋ], *vti.* [10] sobresalir horizontalmente por encima de;
colgar, suspender; mirar a, dar a,
caer a; ser inminente, amenazar.—
vii. colgar o estar pendiente.—*s.*
[óuvœrhæŋ], (arq.) alero; vuelo.

overhaul [ouvœrhól], *vt.* repasar, registrar, recorrer; componer, remendar;
desarmar y componer; alcanzar.—*s.*
[óuvœrhol], recorrido, revisión, reparación; alcance.

overhead [ouvœrhéd], *adv.* arriba, en
lo alto; más, o hasta más, arriba de
la cabeza.—*a.* [óuvœrhed], de arriba;
de término medio; de techo.—*o.
charges*, gastos generales fijos (alquiler, etc.).—*s.* gastos generales.

overhear [ouvœrhír], *vti.* [10] alcanzar
a oír; oír por casualidad o espiando.—
overheard [ouvœrhœrd], *pret.* y *pp.* de
TO OVERHEAR.

overheat [ouvœrhít], *vt.* recalentar;
abochornar; acalorar, achicharrar.

overhung [óuvœrhʌŋ], *pret.* y *pp.* de
TO OVERHANG.—*a.* colgado e suspendido por arriba.

overjoy [ouvœrdźói], *vt.* alborozar, regocijar.

overlaid [ouvœrléid], *pret.* y *pp.* de
TO OVERLAY.

overland [óuvœrlænd], *a.* y *adv.* por
tierra.

overlap [ouvœrlǽp], *vti.* [1] sobreponer,
sobremontar, superponer.—*vii.* su-
perponerse.—*s.* [óuvœrlæp], superposición.

overlay [ouvœrléi], *vti.* [10] cubrir,
extender sobre; dar una capa e mano
(pintura, etc.); echar un puente
sobre.—*s.* [óuvœrlei], capa o mano.

overload [ouvœrlóud], *vt.* sobrecargar,
recargar.—*s.* [óuvœrloud], sobre-
carga.

overlook [ouvœrlúk], *vt.* mirar desde lo
alto; tener vista a, dar, o caer a;
dominar (con la vista); examinar;
cuidar de; pasar por alto, disimular,
tolerar; hacer la vista gorda; no hacer
caso de; no notar.

overnight [ouvœrnáit], *adv.* durante la
noche; toda la noche; de la noche a
la mañana.—*a.* [óuvœrnait], de una
noche; de la noche anterior.

overpower [ouvœrpáuœ(r)], *vt.* sobreponerse a, vencer, superar; sujetar;
embargar (los sentidos).

overproduction [ouvœrprodákşọn], *s.*
exceso de producción, superproduc-
ción.

overran [ouvœrrǽn], *pret.* de TO OVER-
RUN.

overrate [ouvœrréit], *vt.* encarecer;
exagerar el valor de.

overreach [ouvœrrích], *vt.* ser más listo
que; engañar; alargar demasiado;
tirar alto.—*to o. oneself*, excederse,
ir más allá de lo necesario.

overrule [ouvœrrúl], *vt.* (for.) denegar,
no admitir; predominar, dominar;
gobernar.

overrun [ouvœrrʌn], *vti.* [10] invadir,
infestar; saquear; excederse; desbordarse.—*vii.* rebosar, estar muy abundante.—*pp.* de TO OVERRUN.

oversaw [ouvœrsó], *pret.* de TO OVER-
SEE.

oversea(s) [óuvœrsí(z)], *adv.* allende
los mares.—*a.* de ultramar, ultramarino; extranjero.

oversee [ouvœrsí], *vti.* [10] inspeccionar, vigilar; descuidar, pasar por
alto.—**overseen** [ouvœrsín], *pp.* de
TO OVERSEE.—*r* [óuvœrsiœ(r)], *s.*
sobrestante, capataz; superintendente, veedor, inspector; mayoral.

overset [ouvœrsét], *vti.* [9] volcar,
voltear, derribar; trastornar, arruinar.—*vii.* volcarse, caerse; desarreglarse.—*pret.* y *pp.* de TO OVERSET.

overshoe [óuvœrşu], *s.* chanclo; zapato
de goma.

oversight [óuvœrsait], *s.* inadvertencia,
descuido; vigilancia, cuidado.

oversleep [ouvœrslíp], *vii.* [10] dormir
demasiado; no despertarse a tiempo.

oversleeve [óuvœrsliv], *s.* manguito.

overslept [ouvœrslépt], *pret.* y *pp.* de
TO OVERSLEEP.

overstate [ouvœrstéit], *vt.* exagerar.

overstep [ouvœrstép], *vti.* [1] traspasar,
transgredir, excederse, extralimitarse,
propasarse.

overstock [ouvœrsták], *vt.* abarrotar.—
s. [óuvœrstak], surtido excesivo.

overt [óuvœrt], *a.* abierto, público,
patente, evidente.—*o. act*, (for.) acción premeditada; acto hostil.

overtake [ouvœrtéik], *vti.* [10] dar
alcance, alcanzar; atajar; (fam.) atrapar.—**overtaken** [ouvœrtéikn], *pp.* de
TO OVERTAKE.

overthrew [ouvœrθrú], *pret.* de TO
OVERTHROW.—**overthrow** [ouvœr-
θróu], *vti.* [10] echar abajo, abatir,
demoler, derribar; derrocar, destronar; vencer.—*s.* [óuvœrθrou], derribo,
derrocamiento; caída; derrota, ruina;
subversión; destronamiento; (dep.)
lanzamiento o boleo demasiado alto.
—**overthrown** [ouvœrθróun], *pp.* de
TO OVERTHROW.

overtime [óuvœrtaim], *s.* horas extra-
ordinarias de trabajo; tiempo suplementario; pago por trabajo hecho
fuera de las horas regulares.—*adv.*
fuera del tiempo estipulado.—*a.* en

exceso de las horas regulares de trabajo.

overtook [oụvœrtúk], *pret.* de TO OVERTAKE.

overture [óụvœrchụr], *s.* insinuación, proposición o propuesta formal; (mús.) obertura.

overturn [oụvœrtǽrn], *vt.* volcar; echar abajo; trastornar.—*vi.* volcarse; (mar.) zozobrar.—*s.* [óụvœrtœrn], vuelco, volteo; trastorno.

overweight [óụvœrweịt], *s.* exceso de peso; sobrepeso.—*a.* [oụvœrwéịt], que pesa demasiado.

overwhelm [oụvœrhwélm], *vt.* abrumar, agobiar, anonadar; sumergir, hundir. — **—ing** [-ịŋ], *a.* abrumador, (fam.) aplastante.—*s.* abrumamiento, anonadación.

overwork [oụvœrwǽrk], *vti.* [4] hacer trabajar excesivamente, esclavizar.—*vii.* trabajar demasiado.—*s.* [óụvœrwœrk], trabajo excesivo o hecho fuera de las horas reglamentarias.— **overworked** [oụvœrwǽrkt], *a.* recargado, muy elaborado; agobiado de trabajo.

owe [oụ], *vt.* deber, adeudar; **(to)** ser deudor de; estar obligado a.—*owing to*, debido a, con motivo de, por causa de.—*to be owing to*, ser debido, imputable o atribuible a.—*vi.* estar endeudado, deber.

owl [aụl], *s.* lechuza, buho, mochuelo.

own [oụn], *a.* propio, particular, de mí, su, etc. propiedad.—*a house of his o.*, una casa de su propiedad.—*to be on one's o.*, no depender de otro, trabajar por su (propic) cuenta.—*to hold one's o.*, mantenerse firme.—*vt.* poseer, ser dueño de, tener; reconocer, confesar.—*owned by*, propiedad de.—*to o. up*, confesar de plano.— **—er** [óụnœ(r)], *s.* propietario, amo, dueño.— **—ership** [-œrsịp], *s.* propiedad, pertenencia.

ox [aks], *s.* (*pl.* **oxen** [áksn]) buey.—*o. driver*, boyero.

oxidation [aksịdéịṣọn], *s.* oxidación.— **oxygen** [áksịdẓen], *s.* oxígeno.

oyster [óịstœ(r)], *s.* ostra, (Am.) ostión.

ozone [óụzoụn], *s.* ozono.

P

pa [pa], *s.* (fam.) papá,

pace [peịs], *s.* paso; modo de andar.—*vt.* recorrer o medir a pasos; marcar el paso.—*vi.* pasear, andar, marchar.— **—maker** [péịsmeịkœ(r)], *s.* el que marca el paso o da el ejemplo.

pacific [pasífịk], *a.* pacífico.— **pacifier** [pǽsịfaịœ(r)], *s.* pacificador, apaciguador; chupete (para niños).— **pacify** [pǽsịfaị], *vti.* [7] pacificar, apaciguar, calmar.

pack [pæk], *s.* lío, fardo; paquete; cajetilla o paquete de cigarrillos; jauría; manada; cuadrilla (de pícaros).—*p. animal*, acémila, animal de carga.—*p. cloth*, arpillera.—*p. train*, recua, reata.—*vt.* empacar, empaquetar; embalar, envasar; apretar; cargar (una acémila).—*to p. off*, o *to send packing*, enviar, despedir, despachar; poner de patitas en la calle.—*vi.* empaquetar; hacer el baúl, arreglar el equipaje.—*to p. away* u *off*, largarse.— **—age** [pǽkịdẓ], *s.* fardo, bulto, lío; paquete.—*vt.* empacar, empaquetar.— **—er** [-œ(r)], *s.* embalador, empaquetador, empacador, envasador.— **—et** [-ịt], *s.* paquete, cajetilla; fardo pequeño.— **—ing** [-ịŋ], *s.* embalaje; envase; (mec.) empaquetadura, relleno.—*p. plant*, planta empacadora; frigorífico.

packsaddle [pǽksædl], *s.* albarda.

pact [pækt], *s.* pacto, convenio, tratado.

pad [pæd], *s.* cojinete o cojincillo, almohadilla; (sast.) hombrera, relleno; bloc (de papel); pata (de ciertos animales).—*vti.* [1] forrar, rellenar.—*vii.* caminar (penosa o cansadamente).— **—ding** [-ịŋ], *s.* (cost.) relleno, almohadilla; algodón guata; ripio (en un escrito).

paddle [pǽdl], *vt.* y *vi.* bogar o remar con canalete; chapotear.—*s.* canalete, remo corto.—*p. wheel*, rueda de paletas.

padlock [pǽdlak], *s.* candado.—*vt.* echar el candado, cerrar con candado.

pagan [péịgan], *s.* pagano.— **—ism** [-ịzm], *s.* paganismo.

page [peịdẓ], *s.* página, plana; paje, criado.—*vt.* paginar; vocear, buscar llamando (en los hoteles).

pageant [pǽdẓạnt], *s.* procesión, manifestación imponente; pompa, celebridad; (teat.) espectáculo.

paginate [pǽdẓịneịt], *vt.* paginar, foliar.

paid [peịd], *pret.* y *pp.* de TO PAY.

pail [peịl], *s.* cubo, balde.

pain [peịn], *vt.* doler; causar dolor; apenar, afligir.—*vi.* doler.—*s.* dolor.—*on p. of*, so pena de.—*to be in p.*, tener dolor, estar con dolor.— **—ful** [péịnful], *a.* penoso; doloroso; arduo, laborioso.—*to be p.*, doler.— **—less** [-lịs], *a.* sin pena, sin dolor.— **—s** [-z], *s. pl.* trabajo; esmero, cuidado; ansiedad; dolores de(l) parto.— **—staking** [-zteịkịŋ], *a.* cuidadoso, industrioso; esmerado.—*s.* esmero.

paint [peịnt], *vt.* pintar; pintarse el rostro.—*to p. the town red*, (fam.) ir de parranda, correrla.—*vi.* pintar, ser pintor; pintarse, maquillarse, darse colorete.—*s.* pintura; color; colorete, arrebol.— **—brush** [péịntbrʌʃ], s. brocha, pincel.—**-er** [-œ(r)], s. pintor (artista y obrero).— **-ing** [-iŋ], s. pintura, arte pictórica; cuadro.

pair [per], s. par; pareja.—vt. y vi. (a)parear(se), hermanar(se).

pajamas [padʒáməz], s. pl. pijama; (Am.) piyama.

pal [pæl], s. (fam.) compañero, compinche.

palace [pǽlis], s. palacio.

palatable [pǽlətəbl], a. sabroso, apetitoso; agradable.—**palatal** [pǽlətəl], a. y s. palatal.—**palate** [pǽlit], s. paladar, cielo de la boca.

palaver [pəlǽvœ(r)], s. palabrería, labia; embustes.

pale [peil], a. pálido; descolorido.—to grow p., ponerse pálido.—vi. palidecer; perder el color.— **-ness** [péilnis], s. palidez, descoloramiento.

palette [pǽlit], s. (pint.) paleta.—p. knife, espátula.

palisade [pæliséjd], s. (em)palizada, estacada.—pl. risco.

pall [pɔl], s. paño mortuorio; (igl.) palio.—vt. quitar el sabor; hartar, empalagar.—vi. hacerse insípido, perder el sabor.—**-bearer** [pólberœ(r)], s. portaféretro.

pallet [pǽlit], s. jergón, cama pobre.

pallid [pǽlid], a. pálido, descolorido.

pallium [pǽliʌm], s. (igl.) palio.

pallor [pǽlœ(r)], s. palidez.

palm [pam], s. palma, palmera; palma de la mano.—p. grove, palmar.—P. Sunday, domingo de Ramos.—vt. escamotear; (con off, on o upon) engañar, defraudar con.— **-ist** [pámist], s. quiromántico.—**-istry** [-istri], s. quiromancia.— **-y** [-i], a. floreciente, próspero.

palpable [pǽlpəbl], a. palpable, evidente.

palpate [pǽlpeit], vt. palpar.

palpitate [pǽlpiteit], vi. palpitar, latir. —**palpitation** [pælpitéjʃən], s. palpitación, latido.

pamper [pǽmpœ(r)], vt. mimar, consentir.

pamphlet [pǽmflit], s. folleto, panfleto; impreso.

pan [pæn], s. cacerola, cazuela; perol; caldero.—frying p., sartén.—vii. [1] (con out) (fam.) dar buen resultado o provecho.—vti. (fam.) criticar o poner como nuevo.

Panamanian [pænəméjniən], s. y a. panameño.

Pan-American [pænəmérikən], a. panamericano.

pancake [pǽnkeik], s. hojuela, torta delgada, (Am.) panqué o panqueque.

pane [pein], s. hoja de vidrio o cristal de ventana o vidriera; entrepaño de puerta, etc.

panel [pǽnel], s. panel; entrepaño, tablero; (cost.) paño en un vestido; (for.) jurado.—vti. [2] artesonar, formar tableros.

pang [pæŋ], s. angustia, congoja, dolor, tormento.—pl. ansias.

panic [pǽnik], s. y s. pánico.—p.-stricken, sobrecogido de terror, preso de pánico.—vti. [8] consternar, sobrecoger de terror.—**panicked** [pǽnikt], pret. y pp. de TO PANIC.— **-ky** [pǽniki], a. aterrorizado.

pansy [pǽnzi], s. (bot.) pensamiento; (fam.) marica.

pant [pænt], vi. jadear, resollar; palpitar.—to p. for o after, suspirar por, desear con ansia.

panther [pǽnθœ(r)], s. pantera, leopardo; (Am.) puma.

panties [pǽntiz], s. pl. (fam.) pantalones de mujer, (Am.) pantaletas, pantaloncitos.

panting [pǽntiŋ], a. jadeante.—s. jadeo; (med.) disnea.

pantomime [pǽntomaim], s. pantomima; mímica.

pantry [pǽntri], s. despensa.

pants [pænts], s. pl. (fam.) pantalones; calzoncillos.

pap [pæp], s. (coc.) papilla; gachas.

papa [pápə, papá], s. (fam.) papá.

papacy [péipəsi], s. papado, pontificado. —**papal** [péipəl], a. papal, pontifical.

papaya [pəpáyə], s. (Am.) lechosa, papaya.

paper [péipœ(r)], s. papel; memoria; disertación, ensayo; diario, periódico; (com.) valor negociable.—pl. papeles, documentos, credenciales.—on p., escrito; por escrito; en teoría.—p. clip, grapa, sujetapapeles.—p. currency o money, papel moneda.—p. hanger, empapelador.—p. knife, plegadera.—a. de papel; para papel; escrito.—vt. empapelar.—**-back** [-bæk], s. libro de bolsillo.— **-weight** [-weit], s. pisapapeles.

paprika [pǽprikə], s. pimentón.

par [par], s. equivalencia, paridad; (com.) par.—p. value, valor a la par, valor nominal.—to be on a p. with, ser igual a, correr parejas con.

parable [pǽrəbl], s. parábola.

parachute [pǽrəʃut], s. paracaídas. —**parachutist** [pǽrəʃutist], s. paracaidista.

parade [paréjd], s. (mil.) parada; desfile, procesión; paseo público.—p. ground, plaza de armas.—vt. y vi. formar en parada; pasar revista; desfilar; pasear; ostentar.

paradise [pǽrədais], s. paraíso.

paradox [pǽrədaks], s. paradoja.

paraffin [pǽrafin], *s.* parafina.
paragraph [pǽragræf], *s.* párrafo.—*vt.* dividir en párrafos.
Paraguayan [pærəgwéiən, pærəgwáiən], *a.* y *s.* paraguayo.
parakeet [pǽrəkit], *s.* periquito, perico.
parallel [pǽrəlel], *a.* paralelo.—*p. bars,* paralelas (gimnasia).—*s.* línea paralela; (geog.) paralelo.—*vti.* [2] ser paralelo o igual a; cotejar.
paralysis [pərǽlisis], *s.* parálisis.—**paralytic** [pærəlítik], *s.* y *a.* paralítico.—**paralyzation** [pærəlizéiʃən], *s.* parálisis; paralización.—**paralyze** [pǽrəlaiz], *vt.* paralizar.—**paralyzed** [pǽrəlaizd], *a.* paralítico.
paramount [pǽrəmaunt], *a.* superior, supremo, principalísimo.
paramour [pǽrəmur], *s.* amante, querido; manceba.
parapet [pǽrəpet], *s.* parapeto, baluarte.
paraphernalia [pærəfœrnéiliə], *s. pl.* avíos, trastos.
parasite [pǽrəsait], *s.* parásito; (fam.) gorrista, gorrón.—**parasitic(al)** [pærəsítik(əl)], *a.* parásito.
parasol [pǽrəsol], *s.* parasol, quitasol.
paratrooper [pǽrətrupœ(r)], *s.* soldado paracaidista.—**paratroops** [pǽrətrups], *s. pl.* tropas de paracaídas.
parcel [pársel], *s.* paquete; bulto; partida.—*p. of ground* o *land,* parcela o lote de terreno, solar.—*p. post,* servicio de paquetes postales.—*vti.* [2] (con *out* o *into*) partir, dividir; empaquetar; parcelar, dividir en parcelas.
parch [parch], *vt.* y *vi.* (re)secar(se); tostar(se), quemar(se).—*to be parched with thirst,* morirse de sed.
parchment [párchment], *s.* pergamino.
pardon [párdon], *vt.* perdonar; indultar; disculpar, dispensar.—*p. me!* ¡perdone Ud.! ¡Ud. dispense!—*s.* perdón, absolución, indulto.—*I beg your p.!* ¡Ud. dispense! ¡perdone Ud.!; ¿cómo decía Ud.?
pare [per], *vt.* cortar, recortar; mondar, pelar.
parent [pérent], *s.* padre o madre; autor, origen.—*pl.* padres.— **—age** [-idź], *s.* ascendencia, alcurnia, origen.— **—al** [pǽréntəl], *a.* paternal o maternal.
parenthesis [parénθesis], *s.* paréntesis.—**parenthetical** [pærɛnθétikəl], *a.* entre paréntesis.
paring [périŋ], *s.* peladura, mondadura; recorte.
parish [pǽriʃ], *s.* parroquia.—*p. priest,* (cura) párroco.— **—ioner** [pəríʃənœ(r)], *s.* feligrés.
parity [pǽriti], *s.* paridad, semejanza,

igualdad; (com.) paridad, cambio a la par.
park [park], *s.* parque.—*vt.* y *vi.* estacionar(se) (un coche), (Am.) parquear.— **—ing** [párkiŋ], *s.* estacionamiento (de un vehículo).—*no p.,* prohibido estacionarse.—*p. place,* plaza de estacionamiento, (Am.) parqueo.
parley [párli], *vi.* (mil.) parlamentar; discutir; conferenciar.—*s.* (mil.) parlamento; conferencia.
parliament [párliment], *s.* parlamento.— **—ary** [parliméntəri], *a.* parlamentario.
parlor [párlo(r)], *s.* sala de recibo; salón.
parochial [pəróukiəl], *a.* parroquial; de criterio estrecho, limitado.
parole [pəróul], *s.* libertad bajo palabra de un prisionero.—*vt.* poner en libertad bajo palabra.
parotid [pərátid], *a.* parotídeo.—*s.* parótida.
parricide [pǽrisaid], *s.* parricida; parricidio.
parrot [pǽrot], *s.* cotorra, loro.—*p. fever,* psitacosis.—*vt.* y *vi.* repetir o hablar como loro.
parry [pǽri], *vti.* y *vii.* [7] (esgr.) parar, rechazar, quitar.—*s.* parada, quite.
parsley [pársli], *s.* perejil.
parsnip [pársnip], *s.* chirivía.
parson [párson], *s.* clérigo; pastor, cura (igl. protestante).
part [part], *s.* parte; pedazo, trozo; región, lugar; (teat.) papel; raya del cabello.—*pl.* prendas, cualidades.—*p. and parcel,* parte integrante; uña y carne, carne y hueso.—*p. owner,* condueño.—*p.-time,* por horas, parcial (trabajo).—*to do one's p.,* cumplir uno con su obligación; hacer cuanto pueda.—*to take p. (in),* participar o tomar parte (en).—*vt.* separar, dividir.—*to p. company,* separarse.—*to p. one's hair,* hacerse la raya.—*to p. with,* deshacerse de.—*vi.* separarse; despedirse.—*to p. with,* desprenderse o deshacerse de.
partial [párʃəl], *a.* parcial; amigo; aficionado.— **—ity** [parʃ(i)ǽliti], *s.* parcialidad; afición.— **—ly** [párʃəli], *adv.* parcialmente, en parte; parcialmente, con parcialidad.
participant [partísipant], *a.* y *s.* participante, (co)partícipe.—**participate** [partísipeit], *vt.* y *vi.* participar.—**participation** [partisipéiʃən], *s.* participación.
participle [pártisipl], *s.* participio.
particle [pártikl], *s.* partícula; pizca.
particular [partíkyulǽ(r)], *a.* particular, peculiar; preciso, exacto; delicado, escrupuloso; detallado; exigente, quis-

quilloso.—*s.* particular, particularidad, detalle, pormenor.—*in p.*, particularmente, en particular, específicamente.—*to go into particulars*, entrar en detalles.

parting [pártịŋ], *s.* separación; partida; despedida; bifurcación (de una vía o camino); raya del pelo.—*to be at the p. of the roads* u *of the ways*, haber llegado el tiempo de decidir o de tomar cada uno su camino.—*a.* divisorio; de despedida; último, al partir.

partisan [pártịzạn], *a.* y *s.* partidario; adepto.—*s.* (mil.) guerrillero.

partition [partíʃọn], *s.* partición, repartimiento, división, separación; demarcación; (alb.) tabique; (carp.) mampara.—*p. wall*, tabique; pared medianera.—*vt.* partir, dividir; repartir, distribuir.

partly [pártlị], *adv.* en parte, en cierto modo.

partner [pártnœ(r)], *s.* socio; compañero; pareja (de baile, tenis, etc.).—-ship [-ʃịp], *s.* (com.) compañía; sociedad; consorcio.—*to enter into a p. with*, asociarse con.

partridge [pártrịdẓ], *s.* perdiz.

party [pártị], *s.* partido político; reunión o fiesta privada; partida (de campo, teatro, etc.); (for.) parte, parte interesada; partida, facción; cómplice.

pass [pæs], *vti.* [6] pasar; pasar de; pasar por; aprobar (un proyecto, a un alumno); promulgar (una ley); traspasar (un negocio); ser aprobado (en un examen, una materia); admitir, dar entrada.—*to p. by*, pasar por; pasar de largo.—*to p. each other*, o *one another*, cruzarse.—*to p. over*, atravesar, cruzar, salvar; traspasar; omitir, pasar por alto; excusar.—*to p. sentence*, dictar o pronunciar sentencia.—*to p. the buck*, (fam.) echarle la carga o el muerto a otro.—*to p. the time away*, gastar o pasar el tiempo.—*vii.* pasar; correr, transcurrir (el tiempo, etc.); ser aprobado (un proyecto, un alumno); ser admitido; (esgr.) dar una estocada, hacer un pase.—*to p. away*, fallecer.—*to p. through*, pasar por; atravesar; colarse.—*s.* paso; desfiladero; pase (billete, permiso; de manos, de esgrima, en el juego); (mil.) licencia, salvoconducto; aprobación (en un examen).—-able [pǽsạbl], *a.* pasable, transitable; pasadero, regular.—-age [-ịdẓ], *s.* pasaje; paso, tránsito; travesía; pasillo, pasadizo; callejón; pasaje (de un libro, etc.); trámite y aprobación de un proyecto de ley.—

—ageway [-ịdzwej], *s.* pasadizo, pasaje.

passbook [pǽsbụk], *s.* libro de cuenta y razón; libreta de banco.

passenger [pǽsẹndẓœ(r)], *s.* pasajero.—*pl.* pasajeros, el pasaje.—**passer(-by)** [pǽsœ(r) báj], *s.* transeúnte, viandante.

passion [pǽʃọn], *s.* pasión; cólera.—*p. flower*, pasionaria.—*P. Week*, semana de Pasión, semana santa.—-ate [-ịt], *a.* apasionado.

passive [pǽsịv], *a.* pasivo; inerte.—*s.* (gram.) voz pasiva.—-ness [-nịs], **passivity** [pæsívịtị], *s.* pasividad; inercia.

passkey [pǽski], *s.* llave maestra; llavín.

Passover [pǽsoụvœ(r)], *s.* pascua (de los hebreos).

passport [pǽsport], *s.* pasaporte.—**password** [pǽswœrd], *s.* contraseña; (mil.) santo y seña.

past [pæst], *pp.* de TO PASS.—*a.* pasado, último; ex, que fue (presidente, director, etc.).—*p. master of*, experto o sobresaliente en.—*p. participle*, participio pasivo.—*p. tense*, pretérito.—*s.* (lo) pasado; antecedentes, historia; (gram.) pretérito; pasado.—*in the p.*, antes, en tiempos pasados.—*prep.* más de, después de (tiempo); más allá de, fuera de (lugar).—*half (quarter, etc.) p. two*, las dos y media (cuarto, etc.).—*p. remedy*, irremediable.

paste [pejst], *s.* pasta; engrudo.—*vt.* empastar, pegar con engrudo.—-board [péjstbord], *s.* cartón.

pastel [pǽstél], *s.* (b.a.) pastel; pintura al pastel.

pasteurization [pæstœrịzéjʃọn], *s.* paste(u)rización.—**pasteurize** [pǽstœraịz], *vt.* paste(u)rizar.

pastille [pǽstil], *s.* pastilla, tableta.

pastime [pǽstajm], *s.* pasatiempo, distracción.

pastor [pǽstọ(r)], *s.* pastor espiritual, cura, párroco, clérigo.—-al [-ạl], *a.* pastoril, pastoral; (igl.) pastoral.—*s.* pastoral; idilio; (igl.) (carta) pastoral.

pastry [péjstrị], *s.* pastelería, pasteles, pastas.—*p. cook*, pastelero.—*p. shop*, pastelería, repostería.

pasture [pǽschụ(r)], *s.* pasto, pastura.—*p. ground* o *lands*, pradera, dehesa, prado, pastizal.—*vt.* pastar, apacentar, pastorear.—*vi.* pastar, pacer.

pasty [péjstị], *a.* pastoso; pálido.

pat [pæt], *a.* oportuno, propio, (fam.) pintiparado, al pelo; fijo, firme.—*to have* o *know p.*, (fam.) saber al dedillo.—*adv.* justamente, convenientemente, a propósito.—*s.* golpecito,

palmadita; caricia; porción pequeña
de mantequilla.—*p. on the back*,
(fam.) felicitación, enhorabuena.—
vti. [1] dar palmaditas a, acariciar,
pasar la mano sobre.

patch [pæch], *vt.* remendar.—*vi.* echar
remiendos.—*s.* parche; remiendo;
material para remiendos; sembrado
(de trigo, etc.).—*p. of land* o *ground*,
pedazo de terreno.

pate [peit], *s.* coronilla.

patent [pǽtənt], *a.* patente, palmario,
manifiesto; de patente, patentado.—
p. leather, charol.—*s.* patente.—
p. pending, patente solicitada.—*vt.*
patentar.

paternal [pətǽrnəl], *a.* paternal, paterno.—**paternity** [pətǽrniti], *s.* paternidad; linaje.

path [pæθ], *s.* senda, sendero; vereda;
camino; trayectoria.

pathetic [pəθétik], *a.* patético, conmovedor.

pathological [pæθəlǽdʒikəl], *a.* patoló-
gico.—**pathology** [pəθǽlədʒi], *s.* pato-
logía.—**pathos** [péiθas], *s.* rasgo
conmovedor; sentimiento; patetismo.

pathway [pǽθwei], *s.* senda, vereda.

patience [péiʃəns], *s.* paciencia.—**pa-
tient** [péiʃənt], *a.* paciente.—*s.*
paciente, enfermo.

patriot [péitriət], *s.* patriota.—**-ic**
[peitriátik], *a.* patriótico.—**-ism**
[péitriətizm], *s.* patriotismo.

patrol [pətróul], *s.* patrulla; ronda.
—*vti.* y *vii.* [2] patrullar; hacer la
ronda.

patron [péitrən], *s.* patrón, patrocinador, protector; padrino; cliente, parroquiano.—**-age** [-idʒ], *s.* (igl.)
patronato; patrocinio; clientela habitual; (pol.) control de nombra-
mientos por el partido de gobierno.—
-ess [-is], *s.* patrona, protectora;
patrocinadora, madrina.—**-ize** [-aiz],
vt. patrocinar, apadrinar; tratar con
condescendencia; ser parroquiano
habitual de.

pattern [pǽtərn], *s.* modelo, norma;
patrón, molde, plantilla, diseño.—
vt. copiar, imitar.—*to p. oneself after*,
tomar como modelo a, seguir el
ejemplo de.

paunch [ponch], *s.* panza, barriga,
vientre.—**-y** [pónchi], *a.* barrigón,
panzudo.

pauper [pópœ(r)], *s.* indigente, pobre
de solemnidad.

pause [poz], *s.* pausa.—*vi.* pausar,
cesar, parar, detenerse.

pave [peiv], *vt.* pavimentar, adoquinar,
enlosar, embaldosar.—*paved road*,
carretera pavimentada, camino asfal-
tado.—*to p. the way*, facilitar, preparar el terreno, abrir el camino.—

—ment [péivmənt], *s.* pavimento,
adoquinado, piso; pavimentación.

pavilion [pəvílyən], *s.* pabellón; glorieta; cenador.

paving [péiviŋ], *s.* pavimento; pavimentación; materiales de pavimentación.

paw [po], *s.* garra, zarpa.—*vt.* y *vi.*
patear, piafar; (fam.) manosear.

pawn [pon], *vt.* empeñar, pignorar,
dar en prenda.—*s.* prenda, empeño;
peón de ajedrez.—**—broker** [pón-
broukœ(r)], *s.* prestamista, pren-
dero.—**—shop** [-ʃap], *s.* casa de
empeños.

pay [pei], *vti.* [10] pagar, remunerar;
costear; abonar, saldar; producir
ganancia o provecho a.—*to p. a call*
o *a visit*, hacer una visita.—*to p. a
compliment*, hacer un cumplido;
(fam.) piropear.—*to p. attention*,
prestar atención; fijarse o reparar
(en), hacer caso (de).—*to p. back*,
devolver, reembolsar; pagar en la
misma moneda.—*to p. court*, hacer
la corte, enamorar.—*to p. for*, pagar,
costear.—*to p. off*, pagar; pagar por
completo; vengarse de, ajustarle a
uno las cuentas.—*to p. one's respects*,
presentar u ofrecer sus respetos.—*to
p. up*, pagar por completo.—*to p.
the piper*, pagar el pato, pagar los
vidrios rotos.—*vii.* pagar (a veces
con **off**) compensar, tener cuenta,
ser provechoso; valer la pena.—*to p.
dearly*, costarle a uno caro.—*s.* paga,
sueldo, salario, jornal; recompensa.
—*bad* (*good*) *p.*, mal (buen) pagador,
(fam.) mala (buena) paga.—*p. roll*,
nómina, lista de jornales.—**—able**
[péiəbl], *a.* pagadero; reembolsable.—
—ee [peií], *s.* (com.) tenedor,
persona a quien se paga o debe
pagarse una letra, cheque.—**—master**
[-mæstœ(r)], *s.* pagador.—*p.'s office*, pagaduría.—**—ment** [-mənt],
s. pago, paga.—*p. in advance*,
anticipo, pago adelantado.—*p. in
full*, pago total.

pea [pi], *s.* guisante, chícharo.—*p. gun*
o *shooter*, cerbatana.—*sweet p.*,
guisante de olor.

peace [pis], *s.* paz.—*public p.*, orden
público.—**-able** [písəbl], *a.* pacífico,
tranquilo.—**-ful** [-ful], *a.* tranquilo,
pacífico, apacible.

peach [pich], *s.* melocotón, durazno;
(fam.) persona o cosa admirable.—*p.
tree*, melocotonero; duraznero.

peacock [píkak], *s.* pavo real.

peak [pik], *s.* cima, cumbre, pico,
picacho; cúspide.—*s.* y *a.* máximo.

peal [pil], *s.* repique de campanas;
estruendo, estrépito.—*p. of laughter*,
carcajada, estrepitosa.—*p.-ringing*,

repiqueteo.—*vt.* **y** *vi.* repicar, repiquetear.

peanut [pínʌt], *s.* cacahuete, (Am.) maní.—*p. vendor,* manisero.

pearl [pœrl], *s.* perla.—*p. button,* botón de nácar.—*p.-colored,* perlino.— —**ly** [pœrli], *a.* perlino; nacarado.

peasant [pézʌnt], *s.* **y** *a.* labrador, campesino; rústico, aldeano; (Am.) guajiro, jíbaro.

pebble [pébl], *s.* guijarro, china.

pecan [pikán], *s.* (bot.) pacana (árbol y nuez).

peck [pek], *s.* medida de áridos, celemín; picotazo, picotada.—*vt.* picotear, picar.—*vi.* picotear.

peculiar [pikiúlyə(r)], *a.* peculiar; singular, raro.— —**ity** [pikiulérіti], *s.* peculiaridad, particularidad.

pedagogue [pédagag], *s.* pedagogo.— **pedagogy** [pédagoudʒi], *s.* pedagogía.

pedal [pédʌl], *a.* pedal.—*vii.* [2] pedalear.

peddle [pédl], *vt.* vender de puerta en puerta.—*vi.* ser vendedor ambulante. — —**r** [pédlœ(r)], *s.* baratillero, vendedor ambulante.

pedestal [pédestal], *s.* pedestal, peana.

pedestrian [pidéstrian], *s.* peatón, transeúnte.—*a.* pedestre.

pedigree [pédigri], *s.* genealogía; linaje, estirpe; raza, casta.

peek [pik], *vi.* atisbar.—*s.* atisbo.

peel [pil], *vt.* (a veces con off) descortezar, pelar, mondar.—*vi.* desconcharse, descascararse, pelarse.—*s.* corteza, cáscara; piel.— —**ing** [píliŋ], *s.* peladura, mondadura; desconchado.

peep [pip], *vi.* atisbar, mirar a hurtadillas; asomar; piar.—*not to p.,* (fam.) no chistar.—*s.* atisbo; mirada, ojeada; pío, piada.— —**hole** [píphoul], *s.* mirilla.

peer [pir], *vi.* atisbar, husmear; escudriñar; asomar, aparecer.—*s.* par, igual; Par del Reino.— —**less** [pírlis], *a.* sin par, incomparable.

peg [peg], *s.* espiga, taco; tarugo; (mar.) cabilla; (mus.) clavija; (coll.) (beisbol) tiro.—*p. leg,* pierna o pata de palo.—*to take someone down a p.,* humillar, bajarle a uno los humos. —*vti.* [1] estaquillar, clavar; estacar, jalonear; tirar o lanzar (la pelota). —*vii.* (gen. con **away**) afanarse, trabajar con ahinco.

pelican [pélikan], *s.* pelícano, alcatraz.

pellet [pélit], *s.* píldora, pelotilla; bola, bolita; perdigón.

pelt [pelt], *s.* pellejo, piel, cuero; trastazo.—*vt.* apedrear, llover (piedras o algo análogo) sobre.—*vi.* arrojar alguna cosa; caer con fuerza (la lluvia, etc.).

pen [pen], *s.* pluma (para escribir); corral.—*p. name,* seudónimo.—*p. stroke,* plumazo.—*vti.* [1] escribir con pluma; [3] (a veces con **up**) encerrar, acorralar, enjaular.

penal [pínʌl], *a.* penal.— —**ize** [-aiz], *vt.* penalizar, castigar; perjudicar.— —**ty** [pénʌlti], *s.* pena, castigo; sanción, multa.

penance [pénʌns], *s.* penitencia.

pencil [pénsil], *s.* lápiz.—*mechanical p.,* lapicero.—*p. sharpener,* sacapuntas. —*vti.* [2] dibujar o escribir con lápiz.

pendant [péndant], *s.* medallón, colgante; pendiente; araña (de luces). —*a.* = PENDENT.

pending [péndiŋ], *a.* pendiente.—*prep.* durante; hasta.

pendulum [péndʒülʌm], *s.* péndulo.

penetrate [pénętreit], *vt.* **y** *vi.* penetrar. —**penetrating** [pénętreitiŋ], *a.* penetrante.—**penetration** [penętréişɐn], *s.* penetración.

penguin [péngwin], *s.* pingüino.

penicillin [penisílin], *s.* penicilina.

peninsula [pinínşülɐ], *s.* península.— —**r** [-(r)], *a.* peninsular.

penis [pínis], *s.* pene, miembro viril.

penitence [pénițens], *s.* penitencia; contrición.—**penitent** [pénițent], *a.* **y** *s.* penitente.—**penitentiary** [penițénşari], *a.* penitenciario; de castigo, penal.—*s.* penitenciaría, presidio.

penknife [pénnaif], *s.* cortaplumas.

penmanship [pénmanşip], *s.* escritura, caligrafía.

pennant [pénant], *s.* gallardete, banderola; (fig.) campeonato.

penniless [pénilis], *s.* sin un real; en la miseria; sin dinero.—**penny** [péni], *s.* (E.U.) centavo.

pension [pénşɐn], *s.* pensión; jubilación; retiro.—*vt.* (a veces con **off**) pensionar, jubilar.

pensive [pénsiv], *a.* pensativo, meditabundo.

Pentecost [péntikost], *s.* (pascua de) Pentecostés.

penthouse [pénthaus], *s.* terraza, apartamento en la azotea; cobertizo.

peony [píoni], *s.* peonía.

people [pípl], *s.* pueblo; gente; personas; los habitantes (de un país). —*p. say,* dicen, se dice, dice la gente.—*the common p.,* el pueblo, el vulgo, la plebe.—*the p.,* el público, la gente.—*vt.* poblar.

pep [pep], *s.* (fam.) brío; energía, vigor.—*vti.* [1] (con **up**) (fam.) animar, estimular.

pepper [pépœ(r)], *s.* (bot.) pimienta; pimiento.—*green p.,* ají, pimiento. —*p.-and-salt cloth,* tejido de mezclilla. —*red p.,* chile, pimentón.—*vt.* sazonar con pimienta; acribillar.— —**mint**

[-mint], *s.* menta.— —y [-i], *a.* picante; mordaz; irascible.

per [pœr], *prep.* por.—*p. annum,* al año.—*p. cent,* por ciento.

perambulator [pœræmbjuleitǫ(r)], *s.* cochecito de niño.

percale [pœrkéil], *s.* percal.

perceive [pœrsív], *vt.* percibir; percatar(se) (de); comprender, entender.

percentage [pœrséntidʒ], *s.* (com.) tanto por ciento, porcentaje.

perceptible [pœrséptibl], *a.* perceptible, sensible.—perception [pœrsépʃǫn], *s.* percepción.

perch [pœrch], *s.* (ict.) perca; percha (para las aves).—*vi.* posarse, encaramarse.

perchance [pœrchǽns], *adv.* acaso, tal vez, quizá, por ventura.

percolate [pœrkǫleit], *vt. y vi.* (tras)colar, (in)filtrar, pasar, rezumarse.—percolator [pœrkǫleitǫ(r)], *s.* cafetera filtro.

percussion [pœrkʌ́ʃǫn], *s.* percusión.

peremptory [pœrémptǫri], *a.* perentorio; terminante, definitivo.

perennial [pœrénjɐl], *a.* perenne; continuo, incesante, perpetuo.—*s.* planta de hoja perenne.

perfect [pœ́rfikt], *a.* perfecto; completo.—*s.* (gram.) tiempo perfecto.—*vt.* [pœrfékt], perfeccionar, mejorar.— —ion [[pœrfékʃǫn], *s.* perfección.

perforate [pœ́rforeit], *vt.* perforar.—perforation [pœrforéiʃǫn], *s.* perforación.

perform [pœrfórm], *vt.* ejecutar, hacer, realizar; desempeñar, cumplir.—*vi.* (teat.) desempeñar un papel, representar.— —ance [-ǝns], *s.* ejecución; desempeño, cumplimiento; actuación; funcionamiento; obra, hecho, hazaña; (teat.) función, representación.—*first p.,* (teat.) estreno.— —er [-œ(r)], *s.* ejecutor, ejecutante; actor, actriz.

perfume [pœ́rfjum], *s.* perfume; aroma.— —r [pœrfjúmœ(r)], *s.* perfumador, perfumista.

perhaps [pœrhǽps], *adv.* tal vez, quizá(s), acaso, por ventura.

peril [péril], *s.* peligro, riesgo.—*vti.* [2] poner en peligro.—*vii.* peligrar; correr peligro.— —ous [-ʌs], *a.* peligroso, arriesgado.

perimeter [pœrímetœ(r)], *s.* perímetro.

period [píriǫd], *s.* período; época, tiempo; término, fin, conclusión; (impr.) punto; menstruación.—ic(al) [piriádik(ɐl)], *a.* periódico.—ical [piriádikɐl], *s.* periódico, publicación periódica.

periscope [périskoup], *s.* periscopio.

perish [périʃ], *vi.* perecer, sucumbir.— —able [-ɐbl], *a.* perecedero.—*pl.*

mercancías de fácil descomposición.

perjure [pœ́rdʒur], *vt.* perjurar.—perjury [pœ́rdʒuri], *s.* perjurio.—*to commit p.,* jurar en falso.

perk [pœrk], *vt.* erguir, levantar (la cabeza, la oreja).—*vi.* (con up) animarse, avivarse, levantar la cabeza.— —y [pœ́rki], *a.* animado, despabilado.

permanence [pœ́rmɐnɐns], *s.* permanencia.—permanent [pœ́rmɐnɐnt], *a.* permane(cie)nte, duradero; indeleble.—*s.* ondulado permanente.

permeate [pœ́rmieit], *vt.* penetrar; estar difundido en.

permissible [pœrmísibl], *a.* permisible, lícito.—permission [pœrmíʃǫn], *s.* permiso, licencia.—permit [pœrmít], *vti.* [1] permitir, autorizar.—*s.* [pœ́rmit], permiso, licencia, pase.

pernicious [pœrníʃʌs], *a.* pernicioso, nocivo.

peroration [perǫréiʃǫn], *s.* peroración.

perpendicular [pœrpendíkyulǎ(r)], *a.* perpendicular; vertical.—*s.* perpendicular.

perpetrate [pœ́rpɐtreit], *vt.* perpetrar, cometer.—perpetrator [pœ́rpɐtreitǫ(r)], *s.* perpetrador; el que comete un delito.

perpetual [pœrpéchuɐl], *a.* perpetuo.—perpetuate [pœrpéchueit], *vt.* perpetuar.—perpetuity [pœrpɐtúiti], *s.* perpetuidad.

perplex [pœrpléks], *vt.* confundir, aturdir.— —ed [-t], *a.* perplejo, confuso.— —ity [-iti], *s.* perplejidad, confusión, duda.

persecute [pœ́rsɐkiut], *vt.* perseguir; acosar.—persecution [pœrsɐkiúʃǫn], *s.* persecución.—persecutor [pœrsɐkiutǫ(r)], *s.* perseguidor.

perseverance [pœrsɐvírɐns], *s.* perseverancia; persistencia.—persevere [pœrsɐvír], *vi.* perseverar; persistir.

Persian [pœ́rʒɐn], *s. y a.* persa.

persist [pœrsíst], *vi.* persistir, insistir.— —ence [-ɐns], *s.* persistencia, insistencia.— —ent [-ɐnt], —ing [-iŋ], *a.* persistente, insistente.

person [pœ́rsǫn], *s.* persona.— —age [-idʒ], *s.* personaje.— —al [-ɐl], *a.* personal; en persona (acción, comparecencia, etc.).— —ality [pœrsǫnéliti], *s.* personalidad; alusión personal; personaje.—personify [pœrsánifai], *vti.* [7] personificar.— —nel [pœrsǫnél], *s.* personal.

perspective [pœrspéktiv], *s.* perspectiva.

perspicacious [pœrspikéiʃʌs], *a.* perspicaz, sagaz.—perspicacity [pœrspikǽsiti], *s.* perspicacia, penetración.

perspiration [pœrspiréiʃǫn], *s.* sudor, transpiración.—perspire [pœrspáir], *vt.* y *vi.* sudar, transpirar.—**perspiring** [pœrspáiriŋ], *a.* sudoroso.

persuade [pœrswéid], *vt.* persuadir, inducir.—**persuasion** [pœrswéiʒ̣ọn], *s.* persuasión; creencia, opinión.—**persuasive** [pœrswéisiv], *a.* persuasivo.

pert [pœrt], *a.* atrevido, descarado, insolente; listo, despierto.

pertain [pœrtéin], *vi.* pertenecer; atañer.—*pertaining to,* perteneciente, tocante a.

pertinent [pœrtinẹnt], *a.* pertinente, a propósito, atinado.

perturb [pœrtœrb], *vt.* perturbar, inquietar.

perusal [pẹrúʒạl], *s.* lectura cuidadosa. —**peruse** [pẹrúz], *vt.* leer con cuidado; examinar, escudriñar.

Peruvian [pẹrúviạn], *s.* y *a.* peruano.

pervade [pœrvéid], *vt.* penetrar, llenar. —**pervasive** [pœrvéisiv], *a.* penetrante.

perverse [pœrvœrs], *a.* perverso.— **pervert** [pœrvœrt], *vt.* pervertir, corromper; falsear.—*s.* [pœrvœrt], perverso, depravado; desviado sexual.

pessimism [pésịmịzm], *s.* pesimismo. —**pessimist** [pésịmịst], *s.*, **pessimistic** [pesịmịstịk], *a.* pesimista.

pest [pest], *s.* peste, plaga; persona o cosa molesta o nociva; molestia; (fam.) lata.— —**er** [péstœ(r)], *vt.* molestar, incomodar, importunar.— —**ilence** [-ilẹns], *s.* plaga, pestilencia.— —**ilent** [-ilẹnt], *a.* pestilente.

pet [pet], *s.* cualquier animal domesticado y mimado; favorito; niño mimado.—*a.* mimado; favorito.—*p. name,* diminutivo o epíteto cariñoso. —*vti.* [1] mimar, acariciar.—*vii.* acariciarse (los amantes).

petal [pétạl], *s.* pétalo.

petard [pitárd], *s.* petardo; especie de triquitraque.—*hoist on one's own p.,* cogido en las propias redes.

petition [pẹtíʃọn], *s.* petición, demanda, súplica; instancia, solicitud.—*vt.* suplicar, rogar; pedir.

petroleum [pịtróuljẠm], *s.* petróleo.

petticoat [pétịkọut], *s.* refajo; enagua(s).

pettiness [pétinịs], *s.* pequeñez, mezquindad.—**petty** [pétị], *a.* insignificante, mezquino, despreciable; subordinado, inferior.—*p. cash,* (com.) caja chica.—*p. larceny,* hurto, ratería.—*p. officer,* suboficial, oficial subalterno de marina.

petulance [péchulạns], *s.* mal genio, impaciencia; petulancia.—**petulant** [péchulạnt], *a.* quisquilloso, enojadizo; petulante.

petunia [pịtjúnịạ], *s.* petunia.

pew [pju], *s.* reclinatorio; banco de iglesia.

phalanx [féịlænks], *s.* falange.

phantom [fǽntọm], *s.* fantasma.

pharmacist [fármạsịst], *s.* farmacéutico, boticario.—**pharmacy** [fármạsị], *s.* farmacia, botica.

pharynx [fǽriŋks], *s.* faringe.

phase [feiz], *s.* fase.

pheasant [fézạnt], *s.* faisán.

phenomena [finámẹnạ], *s. pl.* de PHENOMENON.— —**l** [finámẹnạl], *a.* fenomenal.—**phenomenon** [finámẹnan], *s.* fenómeno.

philanthropist [fịlǽnθropịst], *s.* filántropo.—**philanthropy** [fịlǽnθropị], *s.* filantropía.

philharmonic [fịlharmánịk], *a.* filarmónico.

philosopher [fịlásofœ(r)], *s.* filósofo.— **philosophic(al)** [fịlosáfịk(ạl)], *a.* filosófico.—**philosophy** [fịlásofị], *s.* filosofía.

phone [foun], *s.* teléfono.—*vt.* y *vi.* telefonear.

phonetics [fonétịks], *s.* fonética.

phonograph [fóunogræf], *s.* fonógrafo, gramófono.

phony [fóunị], *a.* (fam.) falso, falsificado.

phosphate [fásfeịt], *s.* fosfato.—**phosphorus** [fásfọras], *s.* (quím.) fósforo.

photo [fóutou], *s.* retrato, foto, fotografía.— —**graph** [fóutọgræf], *vt.* fotografiar, retratar.—*s.* fotografía, retrato.— —**grapher** [fọtágrafœ(r)], *s.* fotógrafo.— —**graphic** [fotọgrǽfịk], *a.* fotográfico.— —**graphy** [fọtágrafị], *s.* fotografía (arte).— —**meter** [fotámẹtœ(r)], *s.* fotómetro.— —**stat** [fóutọstæt], *s.* fotocopia.

phrase [freịz], *s.* frase; expresión o locución.—*vt.* frasear; expresar, formular.

physic [fízịk], *s.* purgante; medicina.— —**al** [-ạl], *a.* físico.— —**ian** [fịzíʃạn], *s.* médico, facultativo.— —**ist** [fízịsịst], *s.* físico.— —**s** [fízịks], *s.* física.

physiologic(al) [fịzịoládʒịk(ạl)], *a.* fisiológico.—**physiology** [fịzịálodʒị], *s.* fisiología.

physique [fịzík], *s.* físico, figura, presencia.

pianist [pịǽnịst], *s.* pianista.—**piano** [pịǽnou], *s.* piano.—*p. stool,* banqueta de piano.—*p. tuner,* afinador.

piccolo [píkolou], *s.* flautín.

pick [pịk], *vt.* picar, picotear; abrir (una cerradura) con ganzúa; escoger, elegir; coger, recoger; mondar o limpiar; descañonar (un ave).—*to p. out,* escoger, entresacar.—*to p. pockets,* robar carteras.—*to p. up,* alzar, recoger; coger; recobrar (el ánimo, las carnes).—*to p. up speed,* acelerar la marcha, aumentar la velocidad. —*vi.* picar, comer bocaditos.—*to p.*

up, restablecerse, recobrar la salud; cobrar carnes; desarrollar velocidad. —*s.* (zapa)pico (herramienta); ganzúa; lo más escogido, la flor y nata; cosecha.— **-ax(e)** [pík̯æks], *s.* zapapico, piqueta.— **-et** [-it], *s.* piquete; estaca.—*p. fence*, cerca de estacas puntiagudas.—*vt.* y *vi.* cercar con estacas; (mil.) colocar de guardia; estacionar o poner piquetes de vigilancia y propaganda.

pickle [píkl], *s.* escabeche; salmuera; encurtido; (fam.) lío, enredo, brete, apuro.—*vt.* escabechar; encurtir.— *pickled fish*, pescado en escabeche.

pickpocket [píkpakit], *s.* carterista. ratero.—**pickup** [píkʌp], *s.* (aut.) aceleración; camioneta; (radio) reproductor de tono.

picnic [píknik], *s.* jira campestre, romería.—*vii.* [8] ir de romería.— **picnicked** [píknikt], *pret.* y *pp.* de TO PICNIC.

picture [píkchȳ(r)], *s.* pintura, cuadro; retrato, fotografía; (fig.) estampa, imagen; lámina, grabado; película, film.—*pl.* (fam.) cine.—*p. frame*, marco, cuadro.—*to be out of the p.*, no figurar ya en el asunto.—*vt.* pintar, dibujar; describir; imaginar.— **-sque** [pikchȳrésk], *a.* pintoresco.

pie [pai], *s.* pastel; empanada.—*to have a finger in the p.*, tener parte en el asunto; meter cuchara.

piece [pis], *s.* pieza, pedazo, trozo; sección, parte; cualquier moneda; (teat.) pieza: ficha (del dominó o de las damas).—*of a p.*, de la misma clase, del mismo tenor.—*p. of advice*, consejo.—*p. of furniture*, mueble.—*p. of ground* o *land*, parcela, solar.—*p. work*, destajo.—*to go to pieces*, desarmarse, desbaratarse.—*vt.* remendar. —*to p. on*, pegar o poner a.

pier [pir], *s.* muelle, embarcadero; espigón; (arq.) pila, machón; entrepaño de pared.

pierce [pirs], *vt.* agujerear, taladrar; acribillar; atravesar, traspasar.— *pierced with holes*, acribillado.—*vi.* penetrar, internarse, entrar a la fuerza.—*piercing* [pírsiŋ], *a.* penetrante, cortante.

piety [páiȩti], *s.* piedad, devoción, religiosidad.

pig [pig], *s.* cochino, cerdo, puerco, marrano.—*a p. in a poke*, trato a ciegas.—*p.-headed*, terco, cabezudo.

pigeon [pídẓȩn], *s.* paloma, palomo; pichón.— **-hole** [-houl], *s.* casilla, casillero.—*vt.* encasillar, poner en una casilla; (fig.) archivar; dar carpetazo (a un proyecto de ley, etc.).

piggy [pígi], *s.* lechón, cochinito, cochinillo.—*p. bank*, alcancía.

pigment [pígmȩnt], *s.* pigmento, color.

pigmy [pígmi], *s.* = PYGMY.

pigpen [pígpen], *s.* zahurda, pocilga, chiquero, (coll.) cochiquero.—**pigskin** [pígskin], *s.* piel de cochino o de cerdo; pelota de fútbol.—**pigsty** [pígstai], *s.* = PIGPEN.—**pigtail** [pígteil], *s.* cola de cerdo; trenza, coleta.

pike [paik], *s.* pica, garrocha; (ict.) especie de lucio o sollo; (fam.) carretera; camino o carretera por peaje.

pile [pail], *s.* pila, montón, rimero; pilote; pelillo, pelusa.—*pl.* hemorroides, almorranas.—*p. driver*, *p. engine*, martinete para clavar pilotes. —*vt.* hincar pilotes en; amontonar, apilar; acumular.—*vi.* amontonarse, acumularse.

pilfer [pílfœ(r)], *vt.* y *vi.* ratear, hurtar, birlar, sisar.

pilgrim [pílgrim], *s.* peregrino.— **-age** [-idẓ], *s.* peregrinación.

pill [pil], *s.* píldora; sinsabor, mal trago; (fam.) posma, persona fastidiosa.

pillage [pílidẓ], *s.* pillaje, saqueo.—*vt.* pillar, saquear.—*vi.* rapiñar.

pillar [píla̯(r)], *s.* columna, pilar.—*from p. to post*, de la Ceca a la Meca.

pillbox [pílbaks], *s.* caja para píldoras; (mil.) fortín de ametralladoras.

pillory [pílȯri], *s.* cepo, picota.—*vti.* [7] empicotar; exponer a la vergüenza pública.

pillow [pílou], *s.* almohada; almohadón; cojín.—*vt.* poner sobre una almohada. —**-case** [-keis], *s.* funda de almohada.

pilot [páilȯt], *vt.* pilotear, timonear; dirigir, guiar.—*s.* piloto; práctico (de puerto); guía.

pimp [pimp], *s.* chulo, alcahuete.—*vi.* alcahuetear.

pimple [pímpl], *s.* grano, barro.

pin [pin], *s.* alfiler; prendedor, broche; (mec.) perno, pasador, espiga; bolo; (mar.) cabilla; (mus.) clavija.—*I don't care a p.*, no se me da un bledo, no me importa un pito.—*p. money*, (dinero para) alfileres.—*vti.* [1] prender con alfileres; fijar, clavar; enclavijar.—*to p. one's faith to* u *on*, confiar absolutamente en.—*to p. up*, asegurar o prender con alfileres o tachuelas.

pincers [pínsœrz], *s. pl.* pinzas, tenacillas; alicates, tenazas.

pinch [pinch], *vt.* pellizcar; apretar con pinzas o tenazas; estrechar; escatimar; (fam.) prender, arrestar. —*vi.* pellizcar; apretar.—*my shoes p. me*, me aprietan los zapatos.—*s.* pellizco; pizca; aprieto, apuro; dolor, punzada.—**pinch-hit** [pínch hit], *vii.* [9] batear por otro, batear de emergente; (fig.) servir en lugar de otro en caso de necesidad.—*pret.* y *pp.* de TO PINCH-HIT.—pinch-hitter [pínch hítœ(r)], *s.* bateador emergente.

pincushion [pínkûşọn], *s.* acerico, alfiletero.

pine [pajn], *s.* pino y su madera.— *p.* cone, piña (de pino).—*p.* grove, pinar.—*p.* kernel o nut, piñón.—*vi.* (con away) desfallecer, languidecer, consumirse; (con for) anhelar.— —apple [pájnæpl], *s.* piña, ananá(s).

ping [piŋ], *s.* silbido o zumbido de una bala.—*p.-pong*, pin-pón, tenis de mesa.

pining [pájniŋ], *s.* languidez, nostalgia.

pinion [pínyọn], *s.* (mec.) piñón; ala de ave.—*p.* drive, transmisión por engranajes.—*vt.* atar las alas; atar los brazos.

pink [piŋk], *s.* clavel; color de rosa, rosado.—*in the p.* (of condition), en el apogeo, en el mejor estado posible.—*a.* (son)rosado; (pol. fam.) radical, algo rojo.

pinking [pínkiŋ], *s.* (cost.) picadura.

pinnacle [pínąkl], *s.* (arq.) pináculo, remate; cima, cumbre.

pint [pajnt], *s.* cuartillo, pinta (medida de líquidos).Ver Tabla.

pinto [píntoų], *a.* pintado, pinto.—*s.* caballo o frijol pinto.

pinwheel [pínhwil], *s.* molinete (juguete).

pioneer [pajọnír], *s.* pionero, colonizador; precursor.—*vt.* y *vi.* colonizar; promover.

pious [pájąs], *a.* pío, piadoso, devoto.

pipe [pajp], *s.* tubo, caño; tubería; cañería; pipa de fumar, cachimba; (mús.) cañón (de órgano); (mús.) caramillo, flauta.—*pl.* gaita: tubería.—*p.* line, tubería, cañería; oleoducto.—*p.* stock, tarraja.—*vt.* conducir por medio de cañerías o tubos; instalar cañerías en.—*vi.* pitar; gritar.—*to p. down*, (fam.) callarse.— —r [pájpœ(r)], *s.* flautista; gaitero.—piping [pájpiŋ], *a.* agudo.—*p.* hot, en (o muy) caliente, hirviendo.—*s.* (fam.) llanto, gemido; cañería, tubería; (cost.) vivo, cordoncillo.

pippin [pípiŋ], *s.* camuesa.

pique [pik], *s.* pique, resentimiento, rencilla.—*vt.* picar, irritar; excitar (interés, curiosidad, etc.).—*vi.* (aer.) picar, descender en picada.—*vr.* (gen. con on o upon) preciarse, jactarse; picarse, ofenderse.

piracy [pájrąşi], *s.* piratería.—pirate [pájrịt], *s.* pirata.—*vt.* y *vi.* piratear.

pistil [pístįl], *s.* pistilo.

pistol [pístọl], *s.* pistola; revólver.— *p.* holster, funda, cartuchera.

piston [pístọn], *s.* pistón, émbolo.— *p.* ring, aro del pistón.—*p.* rod, vástago del émbolo.—*p.* travel, carrera del émbolo.

pit [pit], *s.* hoyo; hoya; foso; abisme; hueso de ciertas frutas; (teat.) platea.

pitch [pich], *s.* grado de inclinación, pendiente, declive; paso (de tornillo, hélice, etc.); (mús.) tono; diapasón; (beisbol) lanzamiento, tiro; pez, betún, brea, alquitrán; resina.—*p.* dark, oscuro como boca de lobo.— *p.* pine, pino tea.—*vt.* tirar, arrojar; (beisbol) lanzar la pelota al bateador; armar (tienda, etc.); embrear, embetunar; graduar el tono, dar el diapasón.—*to p. tents*, (mil.) acampar.—*vi.* caerse de cabeza; establecerse; cabecear (el buque).—*to p. in*, (fam.) poner manos a la obra.—*to p. into*, (fam.) arremeter a, embestir; sermonear.—*to p. (up)on*, escoger.— —er [píchœ(r)], *s.* jarro, cántaro; (beisbol) el lanzador.- —fork [-fork], *s.* (agr.) horca, horquilla; tridente.

piteous [pítįas], *a.* lastimero, lastimoso.

pitfall [pítfọl], *s.* trampa, hoyo cubierto; peligro latente.

pith [piθ], *s.* meollo, médula; tuétano; (fig.) fuerza, vigor; substancia, la parte esencial, el quid.

pitiful [pítịful], *a.* lastimoso, enternecedor; pobre, despreciable.—piti-less [pítịlịs], *a.* despiadado, cruel.

pittance [pítạns], *s.* pitanza, ración, porción.

pity [pítị], *s.* piedad, lástima, compasión.—*for p.'s sake*, por piedad.— *it is a p.*, es lástima, es de sentirse.— *vti.* [7] compadecer.—*vti.* apiadarse, tener piedad o compadecerse de.

pivot [pívọt], *s.* espiga, pivote, muñón.—*p.* chair, silla giratoria.—*vt.* colocar sobre un eje, o por medio de un pivote.—*vi.* girar sobre un pivote.

pixie [píksị], *s.* duendecillo.

placard [plǽkard], *s.* cartel, letrero, rótulo.—*vt.* publicar por medio de carteles; fijar (cartel o aviso).

place [plejs], *s.* lugar, sitio; puesto; posición, empleo, colocación; grado; espacio, asiento; cubierto (en la mesa).—*in p. of*, en lugar de, en vez de.—*in that p.*, allí, allá.—*in the first p.*, en primer lugar.—*in the next p.*, luego, después.—*out of p.*, fuera de lugar; impropio, indebido.—*vt.* colocar, poner, situar; dar colocación o empleo a; dar salida a.— *to p. across*, atravesar.—*to p. before*, anteponer.

placid [plǽsịd], *a.* plácido, apacible, sereno.

placket [plǽkịt], *s.* abertura en la

parte superior de una saya; bolsillo
o manera (de falda).

plagiarism [pléjdž(i)ạrizm], *s.* plagio.
—**plagiarist** [pléjdž(i)ạrist], *a.* y *s.*
plagiario.—**plagiarize** [pléjdž(i)ạrajz],
vt. y *vi.* plagiar.

plague [plejg], *s.* plaga, peste; miseria,
calamidad.—*vt.* importunar, fastidiar; infestar, plagar.

plaid [plæd], *s.* manta escocesa; género
escocés.—*a.* a cuadros escoceses.

plain [plejn], *a.* llano, simple, sencillo;
franco; corriente, ordinario; puro,
sin mezcla; claro.—*in p.* English,
sin rodeos, en plata.—*p.-clothes man*,
detective, policía secreta.—*p. speaking*, franqueza.—*p.-spoken*, claro,
franco(te).—*p. truth*, pura verdad.
—*adv.* llanamente, sencillamente;
claramente.—*s.* llano, llanura, pla-
nicie; vega; (Am.) pampa, sabana.

plaintiff [pléjntif], *s.* (for.) demandante,
demandador.

plait [plejt], *s.* pliegue, doblez, alforza;
trenza.—*vt.* plegar; tejer, trenzar.

plaintive [pléjntiv], *a.* dolorido, que-
jumbroso.

plan [plæn], *s.* plan, proyecto, programa; plano, dibujo.—*vti.* [1] idear,
proyectar, planear, proponerse; pensar, resolver.—*vii.* hacer planes.

plane [plejn], *s.* superficie plana; plano;
(carp.) cepillo, garlopa; aeroplano.
—*a.* plano, llano.—*p. tree*, plátano
falso.—*vt.* cepillar; desbastar; alisar.
—*vi.* alisar, cepillar; (aer.) planear.

planet [plǽnit], *s.* planeta.

plank [plæŋk], *s.* tablón, tabla gruesa;
tablazón; (pol.) postulados en el
programa de un partido.—*vt.* entablar, enmaderar; (min.) encofrar.
—**ing** [plǽŋkiŋ], *s.* tablaje, tablazón,
forro; encofrado.

plant [plænt], *s.* planta, mata; fábrica.
—*vt.* plantar, sembrar; instalar;
fundar, establecer.—**ation** [-éjšọn],
s. plantación; (Am.) ingenio; siembra,
plantío; criadero de árboles.— —**er**
[plǽntœ(r)], *s.* plantador, sembrador,
cultivador.

plaque [plæk], *s.* placa.

plasma [plǽzmạ], *s.* plasma; protoplasma.

plaster [plǽstœ(r)], *s.* yeso; argamasa,
mezcla; parche, emplasto.—*mustard
p.*, sinapismo.—*vt.* enyesar, enlucir;
(fig.) embarrar, embadurnar; cubrir
(paredes, etc.) con carteles o anuncios; poner emplastos, emplastar.—
—**ing** [-iŋ], *s.* enyesado, enlucido;
(med.) emplastadura.

plastic [plǽstik], *s.* y *a.* plástico.— *p.
surgery*, cirugía estética.

plate [plejt], *s.* plato; plancha, chapa,
lámina; placa; (dent.) dentadura

postiza.—*p. armor*, blindaje.—*vt.*
platear, dorar, niquelar, platinar;
unir con planchas de metal; blindar.

plateau [plætóµ], *s.* meseta, mesa,
altiplanicie, altiplano.

plateful [pléjtfµl], *s.* un plato lleno;
ración.

platform [plǽtfɔrm], *s.* plataforma,
tablado; tarima; terraplén; andén;
(pol.) programa de un partido.

platinum [plǽtinµm], *s.* platino.

platitude [plǽtitjud], *s.* perogrullada,
trivialidad, lugar común.

Platonic [plẹtóník], *a.* platónico.
(p. o P.) platónico.

platoon [plạtún], *s.* (mil.) pelotón.

platter [plǽtœ(r)], *s.* fuente, platón.

plausible [plóžibl], *a.* plausible, razonable; verosímil.

play [plej], *vt.* jugar (algún juego);
practicar (un deporte); (teat.) representar; desempeñar (un papel);
(mus.) ejecutar, tocar; manipular.
—*to p. a joke on*, hacer una burla a,
dar una broma a.—*to p. one a (bad,
dirty, mean) trick*, jugarle una mala
pasada.—*to p. the fool*, hacerse el
tonto, hacer el papel de bobo.—*to
p. tricks*, hacer suertes; hacer travesuras.—*vi.* jugar, juguetear; entretenerse; burlarse, bromear; (mus.)
tocar; (teat.) representar.—*s.* juego;
jugada; recreo, diversión; (teat.)
drama, comedia, pieza; representación; (teat.) ejecución, desempeño.—
at p., jugando.—*in p.*, chanza, de
burlas.—*p. actor*, actor cómico.—*p.
upon words*, equívoco, juego de
palabras.- —**bill** [pléjbil], *s.* cartel,
programa.- —**boy** [-bɔj], *s.* joven
rico y ocioso; calavera.- —**er** [-œ(r)],
s. jugador; actor, actriz, cómico,
comediante; (mus.) ejecutante, músico.—*piano* (p.), pianista.- —**ful**
[-fµl], *a.* jugetón, retozón, travieso.—
—**ground** [-grạµnd], *s.* campo o patio
de recreo; campo de deportes.-
—**house** [-hạµs], *s.* teatro.- —**mate**
[-mejt], *s.* compañero de juego.-
—**thing** [-θiŋ], *s.* juguete, niñería.-
—**wright** [-rạjt], *s.* dramaturgo, autor
dramático, comediógrafo.

plea [pli], *s.* ruego, súplica; disculpa,
pretexto; (for.) alegato, defensa.—
plead [plid], *vti.* [4] defender (un
pleito, una causa); alegar; aducir
como razón, motivo o excusa.—*vii.*
suplicar, implorar; abogar (por).—
to p. guilty, confesarse culpable.—*to
p. not guilty*, declararse inocente.

pleasant [pléząnt], *a.* grato, agradable,
ameno; simpático, afable.—*p. journey
o trip!* ¡feliz viaje!—*p. weather*, buen
tiempo.—**ry** [-ri], *s.* broma, humorada, chanza.—**please** [pliz], *vt.*

agradar; complacer, dar gusto, satisfacer, complacer.—*to be pleased to*, tener gusto en, o el gusto de; alegrarse de, complacerse en.—*to be pleased with*, estar satisfecho o contento de o con.—*vi.* querer, servirse, ser gustoso en, placerle a uno.—*if you please*, por favor, si usted tiene la bondad, si usted me hace el favor.—*to speak as one pleases*, hablar como a uno le da la gana.—**pleasing** [plízin], *a.* complaciente; agradable, ameno.—*to be p.*, gustar, dar gusto; caer bien.— **pleasure** [plézŭ(r)], *s.* placer, gusto, deleite; complacencia.—*at one's (own) p.*, como uno quiera, como le plazca.

pleat [plit], *vt.* (cost.) plegar, hacer pliegues, plisar.—*s.* pliegue.— *—ing* [plítin], *s.* (cost.) plegado, plisado.

plebeian [plĭbían], *a.* y *s.* plebeyo.

plebiscite [plébĭsait], *s.* plebiscito.

pledge [pledž], *s.* prenda, señal; empeño, fianza; rehén; promesa.— *vt.* pignorar, empeñar, dar en prenda; dar fianza; comprometerse a, dar (la palabra).

plenary [plínari], *a.* plenario; entero, completo; absoluto.

plenipotentiary [plenipǫténšieri], *s.* y *a.* plenipotenciario.

plenitude [plénĭtjud], *s.* plenitud.

plentiful [pléntiful], *a.* copioso, abundante; fértil, feraz.—*plenty* [plénti], *s.* abundancia, profusión, afluencia. —*the Horn of P.*, el Cuerno de la Abundancia.—*a.* (fam.) copioso, abundante.

pleurisy [plúrisi], *s.* pleuresía.

pliable [pláiabl], *a.* flexible; plegable; dócil.—*pliancy* [pláiansi], *s.* flexibilidad, docilidad, blandura.—*pliant* [pláiant], *a.* flexible, cimbreño; dócil, blando, tratable, manual.

pliers [pláiœrz], *s. pl.* alicates, tenacillas, tenazas.

plight [plait], *s.* apuro, aprieto; promesa (de matrimonio).—*vt.* empeñar o dar (palabra).

plod [plad], *vii.* [1] avanzar con lentitud; afanarse, ajetrearse, trabajar con ahínco.

plot [plat], *s.* solar, parcela; plano de un terreno; conspiración, complot; trama o argumento (de drama o novela).—*vti.* [1] tramar, urdir, fraguar; hacer el plano, la gráfica o el diagrama.—*vii.* conspirar, maquinar.

plow [plau], *s.* arado.—*vt.* arar, labrar, surcar; (mar. y fig.) surcar.— *—man* [pláumạn], *s.* labrador; yuguero; patán.—*—share* [-šer], *s.* reja de arado.

pluck [plʌk], *vt.* arrancar; pelar; des-

plumar; (mus.) puntear, pulsar; (fam.) robar, estafar, dejar sin un cuarto.—*to p. up*, arrancar.—*to p. up courage*, cobrar ánimo; hacer de tripas corazón, sacar fuerzas de flaqueza.—*vi.* (at) tirar de, dar un tirón.—*s.* valor, ánimo, resolución; arranque, tirón.— *—y* [plʌki], *a.* animoso, resuelto.

plug [plʌg], *s.* tapón, tarugo, taco; cuña; espita; (dent.) empaste o empastadura; porción de tabaco comprimido; cala (frutas); cierre (de válvula); (elec.) enchufe, adaptador, tomacorriente; conectador; tapón o fusible; (aut.) bujía; (fam.) rocín, penco.—*vti.* [1] atarugar, obturar; (dent.) empastar, orificar; (elec.) *(in)* enchufar, conectar; calar (melones), etc.).

plum [plʌm], *s.* ciruela; golosina, gollería; lo mejor; la nata; puesto muy ventajoso; dividendo jugoso.— *p. pudding*, pudín inglés con pasas. —*p. tree*, ciruelo.

plumage [plúmĭdž], *s.* plumaje.

plumb [plʌm], *a.* vertical, a plomo.— *p. level*, nivel de albañil.—*s.* plomada; sonda.—*off p.*, *out of p.*, desviado de la vertical.—*adv.* a plomo, verticalmente; (fam.) completa o rematadamente.—*vt.* sondear; aplomar; emplomar, sellar con plomo; instalar cañerías.— *—er* [plʌmœ(r)], *s.* plomero.— *—ing* [-in], *s.* plomería; oficio de plomero; sistema de cañerías interiores; instalación de cañerías; acción de sond(e)ar o aplomar.

plume [plum], *s.* pluma; plumaje, penacho.—*vt.* adornar con plumas; desplumar.

plummet [plʌmit], *s.* plomo, plomada; sonda.

plump [plʌmp], *a.* rollizo, regordete; gordinflón.—*adv.* de golpe; a plomo; directamente.—*vt.* soltar, dejar caer; engordar, hinchar.—*vi.* caer a plomo; hincharse, engordar, llenarse.

plunder [plʌndœ(r)], *vt.* despojar, saquear, entrar a saco; expoliar.—*s.* pillaje, saqueo, rapiña; botín.

plunge [plʌndž], *vt.* zambullir, sumergir, chapuzar; hundir; precipitar; sumir. —*vi.* sumergirse, zambullirse; precipitarse, arrojarse, lanzarse.—*s.* sumersión, zambullida; salto, arrojo, embestida; tanque para bañarse.— *—r* [plʌndœœ(r)], *s.* buzo; (mec.) émbolo; jugador o bolsista desenfrenado.

plural [plúral], *a.* y *s.* plural.— *—ity* [plúréliti], *s.* pluralidad; mayoría relativa (de votos); multitud.— *—ize* [plúralaiz], *vt.* pluralizar.

plus [plʌs], *prep.* más; además de,

con, con la añadidura de.—*a.* (mat. y elec.) positivo; (fam.) y más, con algo de sobra; más otras cosas.— *to be, come out,* etc. *p. (something),* (fam.) salir ganando (algo).—*s.* signo más (+); cantidad positiva.

plush [plʌš], *s.* felpa; pana.—*a.* afelpado.

ply [plaj], *vti.* [7] trabajar en con ahinco; ejercer, practicar; emplear, ocupar; manejar (la aguja, el remo); importunar, acosar (con preguntas, etc.); convidar a beber varias veces; atacar tenazmente; plegar.—*vi.* ir y venir regularmente; estar constantemente ocupado o funcionando; solicitar o aguardar compradores; (mar.) hacer la travesía.—*s.* pliegue, doblez; propensión; capa (de tejido, goma, etc.).

pneumatic [njumætjk], *a.* neumático. —*p. tire,* neumático, llanta neumática.—**pneumonia** [njumóunjə], *s.* pulmonía, neumonía.

poach [pouč], *vt.* escalfar; cazar o pescar en vedado; invadir.—*vi.* encenagarse; atollarse o meterse en un fangal.— **er** [póučœ(r)], *s.* cazador furtivo.

pock [pak], *s.* pústula, postilla, viruela. —*p.-marked,* picado de viruelas.

pocket [pákjt], *s.* bolsillo, faltriquera; cavidad, bolsón; bolsa; nasa; hoyo; hondonada, depresión; callejón sin salida; tronera.—*in p.,* con ganancia. —*out of p.,* con pérdida.—*p. clip,* sujetador (de lápiz, etc.).—*p. money,* dinero para alfileres o gastos particulares.—*p. picking,* ratería de carterista.—*p. veto,* veto presidencial tácito.—*vt.* embolsar, meter en el bolsillo; tomar, apropiarse; tragarse (una injuria).- **book** [-buk], *s.* portamonedas, bolsa; cartera, billetera; (fig.) dinero, recursos; libro que cabe en el bolsillo. — **knife** [-najf], *s.* cortaplumas.

pod [pad], *s.* vaina (de frijol, etc.); capullo (de gusano de seda).—*vi.* llenarse, hincharse; criar vainas.

poem [póujm], *s.* poema, composición poética.—*pl.* versos, rimas.—**poet** [póujt], *s.* poeta.—**poetess** [póujtjs], *s.* poëtisa.—**poeti(cal)** [pouétjk(ə)l], *a.* poético.—**poetics** [pouétjks], *s.* (arte) poética.—**poetry** [póujtrj], *s.* poética, poesía.

poignant [pójn(y)ənt], *a.* acerbo, punzante; conmovedor, patético.

point [pojnt], *s.* punto; punta; fin, objeto; peculiaridad; grado (de una escala); momento crítico; instante. —*to be beside the p.,* no venir al caso.—*to get the p.,* caer en la cuenta, verle la gracia.—*to get to the p.,* venir

o ir al grano.—*what's the p.?* ¿a qué viene eso? ¿de o para qué sirve?— *vt.* aguzar, afilar (lápiz, arma, etc.); (con *at,* to o *toward*) apuntar, señalar, indicar; encarar, dirigir, asestar.— *to p. out,* apuntar, señalar, mostrar. —*vi.* apuntar; propender, inclinarse a; dar, mirar hacia; (med.) madurarse (un absceso).- **blank** [pójntblǽŋk], *a.* horizontal; directo, claro, categórico.—*adv.* a quema ropa, a boca de jarro; sin ambages.- **ed** [pójntjd], *a.* puntiagudo; en punta; picante, satírico; directo, acentuado, enfático. - **er** [-œ(r)], *s.* indicador, índice; manecilla, aguja; fiel (de balanza); apuntador, puntero; buril; perro de caza; (fam.) indicación o consejo útil.- **less** [-ljs], *a.* inútil, vano; sin objeto.

poise [pojz], *s.* equilibrio; estabilidad; aplomo, serenidad; porte, talante. —*vt.* equilibrar, estabilizar.—*vi.* quedar en equilibrio.

poison [pójzən], *s.* veneno, ponzoña.— *p.-pen letter,* (fam.) carta anónima ofensiva.—*vt.* envenenar; (fig.) corromper, inficionar.- **er** [-œ(r)], *s.* envenenador.- **ing** [-iŋ], *s.* envenenamiento.- **ous** [-ʌs], *a.* venenoso, ponzoñoso.

poke [pouk], *s.* empuje, empujón; persona indolente; saquito; vejiga de aire.—*vt.* picar, aguijonear; atizar, hurgonear; asomar, sacar (la cabeza, etc.).—*to p. fun at,* mofarse de.—*to p. one's nose into,* meter las narices en; entremeterse, curiosear.—*vi.* rezagarse; andar a tientas.- **r** [póukœ(r)], *s.* atizador; entremetido; juego de naipes.

pok(e)y [póukj], *a.* (fam.) flojo, pesado, lento; apretado, ahogado (cuarto); desaliñado (vestido).—*s.* (fam.) chirona.

polar [póulə(r)], *a.* polar.—*p. bear,* oso blanco.—*p. lights,* aurora boreal o austral.

polarity [polǽrjtj], *s.* polaridad.

pole [poul], *s.* (geog. y elec.) polo; pértiga, palo largo, asta, estaca; poste; jalón; (P.) polaco.—*p. vault,* salto con garrocha.

police [polís], *s.* (cuerpo de) policía.— *p. officer,* agente de policía, vigilante. —*a.* policíaco, policial.—*vt.* vigilar, mantener el orden (con la policía).- **man** [-mən], *s.* (agente de) policía, vigilante.

policy [páljsj], *s.* sagacidad; curso o plan de acción; política; regla, sistema, costumbre; póliza de seguro. —*p. holder,* asegurado, tenedor de póliza.

polish [páljš], *vt.* pulir, pulimentar;

lustrar; educar; civilizar.—*vi.* recibir
lustre o pulimento.—*s.* pulimento,
tersura, lustre; urbanidad, cultura;
betún o bola para zapatos; embolada,
acción de lustrar (zapatos).—**Polish**
[póuḷiš], *a.* polaco, polonés.—*s.*
polaco (idioma).

polite [poláit], *a.* cortés, bien educado,
atento.- —**ness** [-nịs], *s.* cortesía,
u-banidad, buena crianza, buena
educación.—*for* p.'*sake,* por cortesía.

politic [páḷitịk], *a.* político: sagaz,
astuto, hábil; apropiado, atinado.-
—**al** [poḷítịḳạl], *a.* político; (desp.)
politiquero.- —**ian** [paḷịtíšạn], *s.*
político, estadista; (desp.) politi-
castro, politiquero.- —**s** [páḷitịks],
s. política; asuntos, métodos o
intereses políticos; (desp.) politiquería; rivalidades o maniobras de
partido o facción.

poll [poул], *s.* lista electoral; votación;
escrutinio; encuesta.—*pl.* lugar donde
se vota; urnas electorales; elecciones.
—*p. tax,* capitación, impuesto sobre
el voto.—*vt.* dar o recibir votos;
contar los votos, escrutar; someter a
votación.—*vi.* votar en las elecciones.

pollen [páḷẹn], *s.* polen.

pollute [poḷút], *vt.* contaminar; mancillar; profanar.—**pollution** [poḷúšọn],
s. contaminación, corrupción; mancilla, mancha; polución.

polo [póuḷou], *s.* (dep.) polo.—*water p.*,
polo acuático.

poltroon [paltrún], *s.* cobarde.

polygon [páḷigan], *s.* polígono.

Polynesian [paḷịnížạn], *s.* **y** *a.* poli-
nesi(an)o.

pomade [poméid], *s.* pomada.

pomegranate [pámgrænịt], *s.* (bot.)
granada.

pommel [pʌ́mẹl], *s.* pomo (de espada);
perilla (de arzón).

pomp [pamp], *s.* pompa, fausto.-
—**osity** [-ásịtị], —**ousness** [pámpʌs-
nịs], *s.* pomposidad, fausto, ostentación; afectación, altisonancia (de
estilo).- —**ous** [-ʌs], *a.* pomposo,
ostentoso.

poncho [pánchou], *s.* (Am.) poncho,
manta.

pond [pand], *s.* charca, laguito, estanque; vivero (de peces).

ponder [pándœ(r)], *vt.* examinar,
estudiar, pesar, (fig.) rumiar.—*vi.*
(con u over) considerar, deliberar,
reflexionar (acerca de).- —**ous** [-ʌs],
a. pesado; voluminoso; tedioso.

poniard [pányạrd], *s.* puñal.

pontiff [pántịf], *s.* pontífice.—**pontifical**
[pantífịḳạl], *a.* pontifical; papal.

pontoon [pantún], *s.* pontón; barcaza;
(aer.) flotador.

pony [póunị], *s.* jaca; caballito; copa

o vaso pequeño, o el licor que se
sirve en ellos.

poodle [púdl], *s.* perro de lanas o de
aguas.

pool [pul], *vt.* formar una puesta (en
ciertos juegos); pagar a escote;
mancomunar intereses.—*vi.* formar
un charco; resbalarse.—*s.* charco;
alberca; estanque; piscina; puesta;
fusión de intereses o de empresas,
piña; combinación para especular.

poop [pup], *s.* (mar.) popa.—*to be
pooped,* (fam.) estar hecho polvo.

poor [pur], *a.* pobre, necesitado, indigente; deficiente, falto, escaso; en
mal estado; de poco mérito; malo,
de mala calidad; estéril (tierra);
enfermizo.—*s.* (con the) los pobres.-
—**house** [púrhaus], *s.* hospicio, asilo,
casa de beneficencia.- —**ly** [-lị], *a.*
(fam.) indispuesto, enfermizo.—*adv.*
pobremente; malamente.—*p. off,*
escaso de dinero.

pop [pap], *s.* chasquido, ruido seco,
detonación; pistoletazo; taponazo;
bebida gaseosa; (fam.) papá; (fam.)
concierto popular.—*vi.* [1] soltar,
espetar, disparar; chasquear; hacer
saltar un tapón.—*vii.* entrar o salir
de sopetón; saltar un tapón; dar
chasquidos o estallidos; detonar;
reventar.—*to p. off,* (fam.) morir;
dormirse.—*to p. up,* (fam.) aparecer
de repente.—**corn** [pápkorn], *s.*
maíz reventón; rosetas, flores o
palomitas de maíz.

Pope [poup], *s.* papa, sumo pontífice.

poplar [pápḷạ(r)], *s.* álamo.—*black p.*,
chopo.—*p. grove,* alameda.

poplin [pápḷịn], *s.* popelina.

poppy [pápị], *s.* amapola.

populace [pápyọḷịs], *s.* pueblo, plebe;
populacho, chusma.—**popular** [páp-
yọḷạ(r)], *a.* popular, democrático;
populachero; en boga, de moda.—
popularity [papyọḷǽrịtị], *s.* populari-
dad, prestigio, buena acogida general.—**popularization** [papyọḷạrịzéi-
šọn], *s.* popularización, vulgarización.
—**popularize** [pápyọḷạraịz], *vt.* popu-
larizar, divulgar, hacer popular.—
populate [pápyọḷeịt], *vt.* poblar.—
population [papyọḷéišọn], *s.* población, vecindario.—**populous** [páp-
yọḷʌs], *a.* populoso.

porcelain [pórsẹlịn], *s.* porcelana, china,
loza fina.

porch [porch], *s.* pórtico, porche,
entrada; corredor, galería (frontal
o lateral de una casa).

porcupine [pórkyọpaịn], *s.* puerco
espín.

pore [por], *s.* poro.—*vi.* (con on, upon,
over) escudriñar, estudiar escrupulo-
samente.

pork [pɔrk], *s.* carne de puerco.—*p. chop,* chuleta o costilla de cerdo.

porous [pórʌs], *a.* poroso, esponjoso, permeable.

porpoise [pórpʌs], *s.* delfín, marsopa.

porridge [páridž], *s.* gachas de avena.

port [pɔrt], *s.* puerto; babor, lado izquierdo de una embarcación; porte, talante; oporto (vino).

portable [pórtʌbl], *a.* portátil.

portal [pórtạl], *s.* portal, portada; vestíbulo.

portent [pórtɛnt], *s.* portento, prodigio; presagio, augurio.—**ous** [pɑrtɛ́ntạs], *a.* portentoso, prodigioso; de mal agüero.

porter [pórtœ(r)], *s.* mozo de cuerda, maletero; camarero, mozo de servicio (trenes, hoteles, etc.); portero.

portfolio [pɔrtfóul̦iou], *s.* cartera, carpeta, portapliegos; (fig.) ministerio.

porthole [pórthoul], *s.* (mar.) portilla, ojo de buey.

portiere [pɔrtjér], *s.* dosel, cortina de puerta.

portion [pórʃọn], *s.* porción, parte; cuota; dote.—*vt.* dividir, (re)partir; dotar.

portly [pórtli], *a.* corpulento, grueso; majestuoso, serio, grave.

Porto Rican [pórto rikạn], *a.* **y** *s.* puertorriqueño, portorriqueño.

portrait [pórtrịt], *s.* retrato.—*p. painter,* retratista.—*to sit for a p.,* posar para un retrato.—**portray** [pɔrtréi], *vt.* retratar, pintar.—**portrayal** [pɔrtréiạl], *s.* representación gráfica, dibujo, pintura; descripción.

Portuguese [pórchn̦giz], *a.* **y** *s.* portugués.—*s.* lengua portuguesa.

pose [pouz], *vt.* (b.a.) posar; proponer, afirmar; plantear (un problema); confundir con preguntas difíciles.—*vi.* colocarse en cierta postura; tomar posturas afectadas.—*to p. as,* pretender ser; hacerse pasar por; echárselas de.—*s.* postura, posición, actitud.

position [pɔzíʃọn], *s.* posición, situación, ubicación; puesto, empleo, colocación; actitud; proposición.

positive [pázịtịv], *a.* positivo; real, verdadero; categórico, rotundo; afirmativo.—*s.* realidad, certeza; (foto.) positivo; (gram.) grado positivo; (elec.) polo positivo.

posse [pási], *s.* patrulla o fuerza civil armada.

possess [pozés], *vt.* poseer; gozar, disponer (de); señorear, dominar; posesionar.—**ion** [pozéʃọn], *s.* posesión, dominio, goce; apoderamiento.—*pl.* patrimonio, propiedades, bienes.—**ive** [-ịv], *s.* **y** *a.* posesivo.—*a.*

posesorio; posesional.- —**or** [-ọ(r)], *s.* poseedor, posesor.

possibility [pasịbílịtị], *s.* posibilidad; contingencia; potencialidad; oportunidad.—**possible** [pásịbl], *a.* posible, potencial, dable.—*as far as o as much as p.,* en lo posible.—*as soon as p.,* cuanto antes.—*to render p.,* posibilitar.

post [poust], *s.* poste, pilar; (mil.) puesto, plaza, guarnición, avanzada; empleo, cargo; correo, estafeta, propio.—*p.-free,* franco de porte.—*p. office,* correo, casa de correos, administración de correos, estafeta.—*p.-office box,* apartado de correos.—*vt.* pegar o fijar carteles; anunciar; poner en lista; apostar, situar; echar al correo; prohibir la entrada a (un terreno, etc.); estigmatizar; (com.) pasar los asientos al libro mayor; (fam.) informar, tener al corriente, poner al tanto de.—*p. no bills,* se prohibe fijar carteles.- —**age** [póustịdž], *s.* franqueo, porte de correos.—**al** [-ạl], *a.* postal.- —**box** [-baks], *s.* buzón; apartado.- —**card** [-kard], *s.* tarjeta postal.- —**dated** [-déịtịd], *a.* con fecha adelantada.

poster [póustœ(r)], *s.* cartel, cartelón, letrero, rótulo.

posterior [pastírị́o(r)], *a.* posterior.—*pl.* nalgas.—**posterity** [pastérịtị], *s.* posterioridad.

postman [póustmạn], *s.* cartero.—**postmark** [póustmark], *s.* matasellos.—**postmaster** [póustmæstœ(r)], *s.* administrador de correos.

postmeridian [poustmɛ́rịdiạn], *a.* postmeridiano, de la tarde.

postpaid [póustpéịd], *a.* porte pagado, franco de porte.

postpone [poustpóun], *vt.* diferir, aplazar; postergar; posponer.- —**ment** [-mɛnt], *s.* aplazamiento; postergación; posposición.

postcript [póustskrịpt], *s.* pos(t)data.

postulate [páschū̦leịt], *vt.* postular, pedir, solicitar.—*s.* [páschū̦lịt], postulado.

posture [páschū̦(r)], *s.* postura, actitud.—*vt.* **y** *vi.* poner(se) en alguna postura.

postwar [póustwór], *a.* de pos(t)guerra.—*p. period,* pos(t)guerra.

posy [póuzi], *s.* ramillete de flores; flor.

pot [pat], *s.* marmita, olla; pote; cacharro; tiesto (para flores); orinal; cantidad contenida en una olla; crisol; (en el juego) puesta.—*p.-bellied,* panzudo, barrigón.—*to go to p.,* (fam.) arruinarse, desbaratarse, (fig.) irse a pique.

potable [póutạbl], *a.* potable.

potash [pátæš], s. potasa.—**potassium** [potǽsiam], s. potasio.

potato [potéitou], s. patata, papa.— *sweet p.*, batata, boniato, (Am.) camote.

potency [póutẹnsi], s. potencia; actividad (de un veneno); poder, influjo, autoridad.—**potent** [póutẹnt], a. potente, poderoso, eficaz.—**potentate** [póutẹnteit], s. potentado; potestad. —**potential** [poténšạl], a. potencial, posible; virtual; (fis. y gram.) potencial.—s. modo potencial; (fis.) potencial.—**potentiality** [potẹnšiǽliti], s. potencialidad, capacidad.

pothole [páthoul], s. bache.

potion [póušọn], s. poción, pócima.

potpourri [poupurí, patpúri], s. baturrillo, miscelánea, popurrí.

pottage [pátidž], s. potaje, menestra.

potter [pátœ(r)], s. alfarero. —y [-i], s. alfarería; alfar (taller); cacharros (de barro).

pouch [pauch], s. saquito, bolsa; zurrón, morral; valija; (anat. y zool.) bolsa, saco.—vt. embolsar; tragar, engullir.—vi. formar bolsas.

poultice [póultis], s. cataplasma, emplasto.

poultry [póultri], s. aves de corral.— *p. yard*, corral, gallinero.

pounce [pauns], s. zarpada; salto; zarpa, garra.—vt. y vi. saltar o abalanzarse sobre; dar una zarpada; saltar, etc. de repente.

pound [paund], s. libra. Ver Tabla; golpazo.—*p. sterling*, libra esterlina. —vt. golpear; machacar, majar, aporrear; poner a buen recaudo.—vi. golpear; batir con violencia (el corazón); andar pesadamente; avanzar continua o enérgicamente.

pour [por], vt. derramar; verter, vaciar; trasegar; escanciar; gastar pródigamente.—vi. fluir, caer copiosa o rápidamente; llover a cántaros; salir a borbotones.

pout [paut], s. pucherito; berrinche. —vi. hacer pucheros; enfurruñarse, poner mal gesto.

poverty [pávœrti], s. pobreza, indigencia; falta, carencia.—p.-*stricken*, muy pobre.

powder [páudœ(r)], s. pólvora; polvo; polvos de tocador.—*p. magazine*, polvorín, santabárbara.—*p. puff*, borla de polvos, (Am.) mota, cisne. —vt. pulverizar; empolvar; polvorear, espolvorear.—vi. pulverizarse; ponerse polvos.—y [-i], a. polvoriento; empolvado; deleznable, quebradizo.

power [páuœ(r)], s. fuerza, pujanza; poder, poderío, potestad; facultad, atribución; ascendiente, influjo; potencia (nación); (mat. y mec.)

potencia.—*p. of attorney*, (for.) poder. —*p. plant*, planta de fuerza motriz.— **-ful** [-ful], a. poderoso, potente, fuerte; influyente.— **-less** [-lis], a. impotente; ineficaz.

pox [paks], s. cualquier enfermedad que causa erupciones pustulosas.—*chicken p.*, varicela.—*small p.*, viruela.

practicable [prǽktikạbl], a. practicable, factible, viable; accesible, transitable. —**practical** [prǽktikạl], a. práctico; de hecho, real; positivo, prosaico.— *p. joke*, broma pesada.—*p. politics*, política de realidades; politiquería.— **practice** [prǽktis], s. práctica, uso, costumbre; ejercicio; experiencia; sistema, regla, método; clientela.— *in p.*, en la práctica.—vt. y vi. practicar, ensayar(se), adiestrar(se), ejercitar(se); ejercer (una profesión).

prairie [préri], s. llanura, pradera, pampa, sabana.—*p. wolf*, coyote.

praise [preiz], s. alabanza, loa, elogio; fama, renombre.—vt. alabar, encomiar, ensalzar.— **-worthy** [préizwœrði], a. digno de alabanza, laudable.

prance [præns], vi. cabriolar, corvetear, gambetear (el caballo); cabalgar o andar garboso u orgullosamente; bailar.—s. cabriola, corveta.

prank [prænk], s. travesura; jugarreta. —*to play pranks*, hacer diabluras.— **-ish** [prǽnkiš], a. travieso, retozón, revoltoso.

prate [preit], vi. charlar, parlotear.—s. charla.—**prattle** [prǽtl], vi. parlotear, (fam.) chacharear; balbucear; murmurar (un arroyo).—s. parloteo, (fam.) cháchara.

prawn [pron], s. camarón.

pray [prei], vt. rogar, suplicar; implorar. —vi. rezar, orar; (for) hacer votos por.— **-er** [prer], s. oración, rezo, plegaria; súplica, ruego.—*the Lord's P.*, el Padrenuestro.—*p. beads*, rosario.—*p. book*, devocionario.—*p. desk*, reclinatorio.

preach [prich], vt. y vi. predicar; sermonear.— **-er** [príchœ(r)], s. predicador.— **-ing** [-iŋ], s. predicación; sermón.

preamble [príæmbl], s. preámbulo.

prearrange [priarréindž], vt. arreglar de antemano, predisponer, prevenir.

precarious [prikérias], a. precario, inseguro; peligroso, arriesgado.

precaution [prikóšọn], s. precaución.

precede [prisíd], vt. anteceder, preceder. —vi. preceder; ir delante; tener la primacía; sobresalir.— **-nce** [prisídẹns, présẹdẹns], s. prioridad, anterioridad, antelación; precedencia, superioridad.— **-nt** [présẹdẹnt], s.

precedente; antecedente.—*a.* precedente.

precept [prísept], *s.* precepto; ley.— —or [-ǫ(r)], *s.* preceptor.

precinct [prísiŋkt], *s.* recinto; distrito, barriada.—*police p.,* comisaría, delegación o puesto de policía.

precious [préšas], *a.* precioso; preciado; de gran valor; caro, querido.—*adv.* (fam.) muy.

precipice [présipis], *s.* precipicio, despeñadero.—**precipitate** [prisípiteit], *vt.* precipitar, despeñar, derrumbar, arrojar; acelerar, apresurar; (quím.) precipitar.—*vi.* precipitarse.—*a.* precipitado, atropellado.—*s.* (quím.) precipitado.—**precipitation** [prisipítéišǫn], *s.* precipitación; derrumbamiento; rocío; cantidad de lluvia; (quím.) precipitación.—**precipitous** [prisípitas], *a.* escarpado; arrojado; precipitado.

precise [prisáis], *a.* preciso, exacto; justo, ni más ni menos; estricto, escrupuloso; propio, mismísimo, idéntico.—**precision** [prisížǫn], *s.* precisión, exactitud, limitación exacta; escrupulosidad.

predatory [prédatori], *a.* rapaz, de presa, de rapiña.

predecessor [prédisesǫ(r)], *s.* predecesor, antecesor; antepasado.

predesignate [pridézigneit], *vt.* prefijar.

predestination [pridestinéišǫn], *s.* predestinación.—**predestine** [pridéstin], *vt.* predestinar.

predetermine [priditǣrmin], *vt.* predeterminar, prefijar.

predicament [pridíkament], *s.* dificultad, apuro, brete, compromiso; clase, categoría, situación, circunstancias; (log.) predicamento.—**predicate** [prédikeit], *vt.* proclamar; predicar; basar o fundar en algo; afirmar un predicado.—*vi.* afirmarse. —*s.* [prédikit], (gram. y log.) predicado, atributo.

predict [pridíkt], *vt.* predecir, pronosticar, vaticinar.—**ion** [pridíkšǫn], *s.* predicción; pronóstico, profecía.

predilection [predilékšǫn], *s.* predilección.

predispose [pridispóuz], *vt.* predisponer, prevenir.—**predisposition** [pridispozíšǫn], *s.* predisposición.

predominance [pridáminans], *s.* predominio; ascendiente, influencia.—**predominant** [pridáminant], *a.* predominante, prepotente.—**predominate** [pridámineit], *vi.* predominar, prevalecer.

prefabricate [prifébrikeit], *vt.* fabricar de antemano (casa, etc.).—**d** [-id], *a.* prefabricado.

preface [préfis], *s.* prefacio, preámbulo,

prólogo.—*vt.* prologar; hacer un exordio.

prefer [prifǣr], *vti.* [1] preferir; exaltar; presentar, ofrecer; dar preferencia. —*to p. a charge,* presentar una denuncia.—*to p. a claim,* presentar una demanda.— —**able** [préfrabl], *a.* preferible, preferente.— —**ence** [préfrens], *s.* preferencia, predilección; prioridad, prelación; ventaja.

prefix [prifíks], *vt.* prefijar, anteponer. —*s.* [prífiks], prefijo.

pregnancy [prégnansi], *s.* preñez, embarazo, gravidez; gestación; (fig.) fertilidad, fecundidad.—**pregnant** [prégnant], *a.* encinta, grávida, preñada, embarazada; fértil, copioso, fecundo. —*p. with,* repleto, lleno de.

prejudge [pridžádž], *vt.* prejuzgar.

prejudice [prédžudis], *s.* prevención, prejuicio; parcialidad; daño, detrimento.—*vt.* predisponer, prevenir; perjudicar.

prelate [prélit], *s.* prelado.

preliminary [prilímineri], *a.* preliminar; preparatorio.—*s.* preliminar; *pl.* exámenes preliminares; pruebas eliminatorias.

prelude [préljud], *s.* preludio; presagio.

premature [primachúr], *a.* prematuro. —*p. baby,* niño sietemesino.

premeditate [priméditeit], *vt.* y *vi.* premeditar.—**premeditation** [primeditéišǫn], *s.* premeditación.

premier [prímiœ(r)], *s.* primer ministro, jefe de gobierno.—*a.* primero, principal.

premiere [primír], *s.* estreno (de un drama. etc.).

premise [prémis], *s.* premisa.—*pl.* (for.) aserciones anteriores; terrenos, casa, posesiones; local.

premium [prímiam], *s.* premio; remuneración; (com.) prima; interés. —*at a p.,* muy escaso, de gran valor, muy solicitado.

premonition [primoníšǫn], *s.* advertencia; presentimiento, corazonada.

preoccupation [priakyǫpéišǫn], *s.* preocupación.

prepaid [pripéid], *a.* porte pagado; pagado por adelantado.—*pret.* y *pp.* de TO PREPAY.

preparation [preparéišǫn], *s.* preparación; preparativo; (farm.) preparado. —**preparatory** [pripératori], *a.* preparatorio; previo, preliminar.—**prepare** [pripér], *vt.* preparar, apercibir; disponer, prevenir; aderezar, adobar, confeccionar.—*vi.* prepararse, disponerse, hacer preparativos.—**preparedness** [pripéridnas], *s.* preparación, prevención, apercibimiento.

prepay [pripéi], *vti.* [10] pagar por adelantado; franquear (una carta).

preponderance [pripándẹrạns], *s.* preponderancia.—**preponderate** [pripándẹreịt], *vi.* preponderar.

prepossess [pripọzẹ́s], *vt.* predisponer, causar buena impresión.— **-ing** [-iɳ], *a.* simpático, atractivo.— **-ion** [pripozẹ́śọn], *s.* impresión favorable; simpatía, predisposición favorable.

preposition [prepozíśọn], *s.* preposición.

preposterous [pripástẹrạs], *a.* absurdo, ridículo, descabellado.

prerequisite [prirékwịzịt], *a.* previamente necesario.—*s.* requisito previo.

prerogative [prirágạtịv], *s.* prerrogativa.

presage [présịdż], *s.* presagio.—*vt.* presagiar.

Presbyterian [prezbịtíriạn], *a.* y *s.* presbiteriano.

prescribe [priskráịb], *vt.* y *vi.* prescribir; dar leyes o reglas; recetar; caducar. —**prescription** [priskrípśọn], *s.* prescripción, precepto, regla; receta.

presence [prézẹns], *s.* presencia; aspecto, porte; asistencia.—*p. of mind*, presencia de ánimo, aplomo, serenidad.—**present** [prézẹnt], *a.* presente; actual, corriente (mes, semana, etc.).—*at the p. time*, hoy (por hoy), en la actualidad.—*p. company excepted*, mejorando lo presente.—*p. day*, actual, (del día) de hoy.—*p. participle*, participio activo o de presente, gerundio.—*to be p. (at)*, asistir (a); presenciar; concurrir.—*s.* el presente, la actualidad; (gram.) tiempo presente; regalo, obsequio, presente.—*at p.*, al presente, actualmente, (por) ahora.—*for the p.*, por ahora, por el (o lo) presente.—*vt.* [prịzént], presentar, introducir, dar a conocer; dar, regalar, obsequiar; manifestar, mostrar, exponer; representar, poner en escena; (for.) denunciar, acusar.—**presentation** [prezẹntéịśọn], *s.* presentación; introducción; entrega ceremoniosa de un obsequio; (teat.) exhibición, representación.

presentiment [prịzéntịmẹnt], *s.* presentimiento.

presently [prézẹntlị], *adv.* luego, ya, dentro de poco, pronto.

preservation [prezœrvéịśọn], *s.* preservación, conservación.—**preservative** [prịzœ́rvạtịv], *a.* preservativo.— *s.* preservativo, salvaguardia.—**preserve** [prịzœ́rv], *vt.* preservar; proteger; reservar; conservar, mantener; salar, curar; confitar, almibarar.— *vi.* hacer conservas de fruta.—*s.* (gen. *pl.*) conserva, dulce, compota, confitura; vedado, coto.—**preserved** [prịzœ́rvd], *a.* conservado, en conserva.

preside [prịzáịd], *vi.* and *vt.* presidir.— *to p. at o over a meeting*, presidir

una reunión o asamblea.—**presidency** [prézịdẹnsị], *s.* presidencia.—**president** [prézịdẹnt], *s.* presidente.— **presidential** [prezịdénśạl], *a.* presidencial.

press [pres], *vt.* prensar; comprimir; exprimir; pisar (el acelerador, la uva, el pedal, etc.); oprimir (el botón); planchar (ropa); abrumar, oprimir; presionar, obligar, apremiar; acosar; hostigar; abrazar, dar un apretón.—*pressed for money*, apurado de dinero.—*vi.* pesar, ejercer presión; urgir, apremiar; apiñarse; ser importuno; influir en el ánimo. —*tò p. forward* or *on*, avanzar, adelantarse; arremeter, embestir.— *s.* muchedumbre; apiñamiento; empujón, apretón; prisa, presión, urgencia; cúmulo de negocios; (mec.) prensa; imprenta; prensa (periódica); escaparate, armario; (mil.) leva, enganche.—*p. agent*, agente de publicidad.—*p. box*, tribuna de la prensa.—*p. clipping*, *p. cutting*, recorte de periódico.—*p. conference*, entrevista de prensa.—*p. gang*, (mil.) patrulla de reclutamiento.—*p. proof*, (impr.) prueba de prensa.—**-ing** [présiɳ], *a.* urgente, apremiante, importuno.—*s.* prensado, prensadura; compresión, presión.— **-ure** [préśụ(r)], *s.* presión; urgencia; apretón; opresión; fuerza electromotriz.

prestige [prestíż], *s.* prestigio, fama.

prestidigitator [prẹstịdịdżíteịtọ(r)], *s.* prestidigitador.

presumable [prịzịúmạbl], *a.* presumible. —**presume** [prịzịúm], *vt.* presumir, suponer; (con to) atreverse a.—*vi.* jactarse, presumir; obrar presuntuosamente; (con on o upon) abusar de.—**presumption** [prịzámpśọn], *s.* presunción, conjetura; suposición; engreimiento, soberbia.—**presumptuous** [prịzámpchuạs], *a.* presuntuoso, presumido; insolente; atrevido.

presuppose [prisʌpóụz], *vt.* presuponer. —**presupposition** [prisʌpozíśọn], *s.* conjetura.

pretend [prịténd], *vt.* aparentar, fingir, simular; alegar o afirmar falsamente.—*vi.* fingir; presumir, alardear.—*to p. to*, pretender, reclamar, aspirar a.—*to p. to be*, echárselas de, darse por, hacerse el.— **-er** [-œ(r)], *s.* pretendiente (a la corona o trono); el que finge.—**pretense** [prịténs, prịtens], *s.* fingimiento; pretexto, excusa; máscara, capa, velo; pretensión; ostentación; afectación, simulación.—*under false pretenses*, con falsas apariencias, con dolo.—*under p. of*, so pretexto de, a título de.—**pre-**

tentious [pritɛ́nɸʌs], *a.* presuntuoso, presumido, de o con pretensiones.

preterit(e) [prɛ́tɛrit], *a.* y *s.* pretérito.

pretext [prítekst], *s.* pretexto, excusa.

prettily [prítili], *adv.* lindamente, bonitamente.—**prettiness** [prítinis], *s.* lindeza, galanura.—**pretty** [príti], *a.* lindo, bonito, (fam.) mono; bello, bueno, grande.—*a p. mess you made*, buena la hizo usted.—*a p. penny*, (fam.) una buena suma.—*adv.* algo; un poco, bastante.—*p. good*, bastante bueno.—*p. much*, bastante; casi.—*p. well*, medianamente, así así.

prevail [privéil], *vi.* prevalecer, preponderar; ser muy frecuente; estar en boga; (con **over** o **against**) vencer a, triunfar de; sobresalir, predominar.—*to p. on, upon* o *with*, persuadir, inducir, convencer.—**prevalence** [prévɑlɛns], *s.* predominio, preponderancia; frecuencia.—**prevalent** [prévɑlɛnt], *a.* prevaleciente, común, muy generalizado.

prevent [privɛ́nt], *vt.* prevenir, precaver, evitar, impedir, desbaratar.—*vi.* obviar.—**ion** [privɛ́nɸɔn], *s.* prevención; obstáculo, estorbo.—**ive** [privɛ́ntiv], *a.* preventivo.—*s.* preservativo, profiláctico.

previous [prívjʌs], *a.* previo, anterior.

prey [prei], *s.* presa; pillaje, rapiña; víctima.—*vi.* (con **on** o **upon**), devorar (la presa); rapiñar, robar; consumir, oprimir, agobiar.

price [prais], *s.* precio; importe, valor. —*vt.* valuar, fijar o poner precio a.— **less** [práislis], *a.* inapreciable; sin precio.

prick [prik], *vt.* punzar, picar, pinchar; marcar, indicar o calcar con agujerillos; causar una punzada (dolor punzante); puntear (marcar con puntos).—*to p. on* o *forward*, aguijonear, incitar.—*to p. up one's ears*, aguzar, erguir o enderezar las orejas. —*vi.* sentir una punzada (dolor punzante); erguirse o estar erguido; picarse (el vino).—*s.* aguijón; acicate; garrocha; puntura, picadura, punzadura, pinchazo; agujerillo; (fig.) escozor, espina, remordimiento.—**le** [prikl], *s.* pincho, púa, espina.—*vt.* y *vi.* producir o sentir picazón.—**ly** [príklj], *a.* lleno de púas o puntas, espinoso.—*p. heat*, salpullido.—*p. pear*, higo chumbo; (Am.) tuna.

pride [praid], *s.* orgullo; engreimiento, vanidad; altivez, arrogancia; dignidad, amor propio; brío; persona o cosa predilecta, la flor y nata, causa de satisfacción.—*to take p. in*, ufanarse o preciarse de.—*vr.* enorgullecerse o jactarse (de).— **ful**

[práidful], *a.* orgulloso, arrogante, vanidoso.

priest [prist], *s.* sacerdote; cura, clérigo.— **hood** [prísthud], *s.* sacerdocio; casta sacerdotal.

prig [prig], *s.* persona pedante, mojigata o melindrosa.— **gish** [prígiʃ], *a.* pedantesco; gazmoño.

prim [prim], *a.* afectadamente formal o pudoroso; remilgado; etiquetero, relamido, estirado, (fam.) almidonado.

primacy [práiməsi], *s.* primacía; supremacía; precedencia.—**primal** [práiml], *a.* primordial; principal.

primarily [práimerili], *adv.* primariamente, en primer lugar; originalmente; principalmente.—**primary** [práimeri], *a.* primario, primero; primitivo; fundamental, principal; elemental.—*s.* (lo) primero; comicios preliminares; circuito primario; ala de un insecto.

prime [praim], *s.* la flor (de la vida, edad, etc.); albor, principio; alba, aurora, amanecer; la flor y nata, lo mejor; (igl.) (Hora) prima; número primo; (esgr.) primera; (impr.) virgulilla, signo (').—*a.* primero, principal; primoroso, de primera clase; selecto; original, prístino; (mat.) primo; (impr.) marcado con el signo (').—*p. mover*, fuente natural de energía o fuerza motriz; máquina generadora de energía; móvil primero; alma, palanca (de una empresa).—*vt.* informar, instruir previamente; cebar (un carburador, arma, etc.); dar la primera capa de pintura; poner el signo (').

primer [prímœ(r)], *s.* cartilla, libro primero de lectura; devocionario.

primitive [prímitiv], *a.* primitivo, original; (biol.) rudimentario.—*s.* y *a.* (b.a.) primitivo (artista u obra).

primp [primp], *vt.* y *vi.* vestir(se) con afectación; acicalar(se); portarse afectadamente.

primrose [prímrouz], *s.* (bot.) primavera; color amarillo claro.—*a.* florido, gayo.—*p. path*, vida sensual.

prince [prins], *s.* príncipe.—*p. of the royal blood*, infante.— **ly** [prínsli], *a.* principesco, regio.—*adv.* principescamente.— **ss** [prínsis], *s.* princesa.

principal [prínsipəl], *a.* principal, esencial, capital; máximo; (arq.) maestro. —*s.* principal, jefe; director o rector (de escuela o colegio primarios o secundarios); (for.) causante, constituyente; (com.) capital o principal (puesto a interés); (arq.) jamba de fuerza.—**principle** [prínsipl], *s.* principio, origen; fundamento, motivo, razón; principio (regla, ley); (quim.) principio activo.

print [prɪnt], *vt.* estampar, imprimir; tirar, hacer una tirada; publicar; escribir imitando letra de molde.— *s.* impresión, estampa; tipo o letra de molde; impreso, folleto, volante, periódico, etc.; grabado; estampado; molde.—*pl.* estampados.—*in p.*, impreso, publicado; en letra de molde.—*out of p.*, (edición) agotada.— **-er** [prɪ́ntœ(r)], *s.* impresor, tipógrafo.— **-ing** [-ɪŋ], *s.* imprenta, tipografía; impresión; tirada; impreso; estampado.—*a.* de imprenta, de imprimir.

prior [práɪə(r)], *a.* anterior, precedente.—*p. to*, antes de.—*s.* prior.— **-ity** [praɪári̯ti̯], *s.* prioridad.

prism [prɪ́zm], *s.* prisma; espectro solar.

prison [prɪ́zən], *s.* prisión, encierro, cárcel.—*p. term*, duración de la condena.— **-er** [-œ(r)], *s.* prisionero, recluso.

pristine [prɪ́stɪn], *a.* prístino.

privacy [práɪvə̯si̯], *s.* retiro, aislamiento, retraimiento; independencia de la vida privada; el derecho a esa independencia; reserva, secreto.— **private** [práɪvɪt], *a.* privado; particular; personal, confidencial; secreto, oculto; reservado, excusado.—*s.* soldado raso.—*pl.* partes pudendas.— **privation** [praɪvéɪʃən], *s.* privación; carencia; falta de bienestar, estrechez.— **privative** [prɪ́vəti̯v], *a.* privativo.—*s.* negación.

privilege [prɪ́vɪli̯dʒ], *s.* privilegio.—*vt.* privilegiar; (from) eximir.— **-d** [-d], *a.* privilegiado, exento.

privy [prɪ́vi̯], *a.* (con to) informado, enterado (en); particular, propio, personal; (ant.) privado, secreto, excusado.—*s.* retrete, letrina.

prize [praɪz], *s.* premio, galardón; presa, botín; adquisición, ganancia, ventaja.—*vt.* apreciar, estimar; valuar, tasar.

pro [prou], *adv.* en favor; por.—*s.* voto afirmativo; (dep. fam.) profesional.—*p. and con*, en pro y en contra.

probability [prabəbíli̯ti̯], *s.* probabilidad.—**probable** [prábəbl], *a.* probable, verosímil; fácil, regular.

probation [probéɪʃən], *s.* prueba, ensayo; noviciado; meritoriado.—*on p.*, a prueba.

probe [proub], *s.* (cir.) sonda, cánula; prueba, ensayo; indagación.—*vt.* (cir.) sondear, explorar; indagar.

probity [próubi̯ti̯], *s.* probidad, hombría de bien.

problem [práblem], *s.* problema; cuestión.— **-atic(al)** [prablemǽti̯k(əl)], *a.* problemático.

procedure [prosíi̯dʒu̯(r)], *s.* proceder, procedimiento, conducta; (for.) procedimiento(s) judicial(es).—**proceed** [prosíd], *vi.* seguir (adelante), proseguir; marchar, adelantar, avanzar; proceder, obrar.—*to p. to business*, ir a lo que importa; poner manos a la obra; entrar en materia.—**proceeding** [prosíi̯dɪŋ], *s.* procedimiento, conducta, proceder; transacción; trámite; proceso.—*pl.* actas; (for.) actuaciones, autos.—**proceeds** [próusidz], *s.* producto, réditos; ingresos.

process [práses], *s.* procedimiento, método, sistema; proceso (conjunto o serie de fenómenos naturales); progreso, continuación; curso, serie, sucesión; (for.) causa, proceso, expediente, autos.—*vt.* someter a procedimiento especial, tratar, industrializar, elaborar; (for.) procesar.

procession [proséʃən], *s.* procesión; desfile; cortejo.

proclaim [prokléɪm], *vt.* proclamar; promulgar; pregonar, vocear.—**proclamation** [praklǝméɪʃən], *s.* proclamación; proclama, edicto, bando.

proclivity [proklívi̯ti̯], *s.* propensión, tendencia, inclinación.

procrastinate [prokrǽsti̯neɪt], *vt. y vi.* diferir, aplazar, dejar para mañana; ser moroso.

procreate [próukri̯eɪt], *vt.* procrear, engendrar.

procure [prokiu̯(r)], *vt.* procurar, obtener, conseguir; causar, ocasionar.—*vt. y vi.* alcahuetear.— **-r** [-œ(r)], *s.* alcahuete.— **-ss** [-i̯s], *s.* alcahueta.

prod [prad], *vti.* [1] punzar, picar, aguijonear.—*s.* pincho; picadura, pinchazo.

prodigal [prádi̯gəl], *a.* pródigo.—*s.* pródigo, manirroto, derrochador.— **-ity** [pradi̯gǽli̯ti̯], *s.* prodigalidad.

prodigious [prodídʒʌs], *a.* prodigioso; ingente.—**prodigy** [prádi̯dʒi̯], *s.* prodigio; portento.

produce [prodiús], *vt.* producir; causar; mostrar, presentar; (com.) rendir, rentar; (teat.) montar o poner en escena una obra; (geom.) prolongar.—*vi.* producir; fructificar.—*s.* [prádi̯us], producto, producción, fruto; productos agrícolas, provisiones.— **-r** [prodiúsœ(r)], *s.* productor; (teat.) empresario; generador, gasógeno.— **product** [prádʌkt], *s.* producto; resultado, efecto, fruto; (com.) rendimiento, renta; (mat.) producto.— **production** [prodʌ́kʃən], *s.* producción; presentación; (teat.) representación.— **productive** [prodʌ́kti̯v], *a.* productivo; generador; fecundo.— **productiveness** [prodʌ́kti̯vni̯s], pro-

ductivity [proʊdʌktíviti], s. productividad; fecundidad.

profanation [prafənéiʃən], s. profanación.—**profane** [proféin], a. profano; secular; impío, blasfemo, irreverente. —vt. profanar; desacatar.

profess [profés], vt. profesar, creer en; declarar, manifestar; fingir, aparentar; enseñar (como profesor); ejercer una profesión.— **ion** [proféʃən], s. profesión.— **ional** [proféʃɔnal], a. profesional, facultativo; de profesión. —s. profesional; deportista de profesión.— **or** [-ɔ(r)], s. profesor, catedrático.— **orship** [-ɔrʃip], s. profesorado, cátedra.

proffer [práfœ(r)], vt. proponer, ofrecer, brindar.—s. oferta, propuesta, ofrecimiento.

proficiency [profíʃɛnsi], s. aprovechamiento, adelanto; pericia, habilidad. —**proficient** [profíʃɛnt], a. proficiente; experto, perito.

profile [próufail], s. contorno; perfil. —in p., de perfil.—vt. perfilar; recortar.

profit [práfit], s. provecho, beneficio, ventaja; fruto; beneficio; lucro, ganancia, utilidad.—clear p., beneficio neto.—p.-sharing system, sistema cooperativo.—vt. aprovechar a, servir.—vi. sacar utilidad o provecho, ganar.—to p. by, sacar partido de, beneficiarse de.— **able** [-əbl], a. provechoso, útil, beneficioso, ventajoso; productivo, lucrativo.— **eer** [prafitír], vi. usurear, explotar con agio.—s. usurero, explotador.

profound [profáund], a. profundo; hondo; intenso; recóndito; pesado (sueño).— **ness** [-nis], profundity [profánditi], s. profundidad, hondura.

profuse [profíús], a. profuso; pródigo. —**ness** [-nis], **profusion** [profíúʒən], s. profusión, abundancia; prodigalidad.

progenitor [prodʒénitɔ(r)], s. progenitor.

progeny [prádʒeni], s. progenie, prole, linaje.

program [próugræm], s. programa, agenda; plan.

progress [prágres], s. progreso, adelanto; progresos, aprovechamiento; desarrollo, mejoramiento; marcha, curso.—vt. [progrés], adelantar, llevar adelante.—vi. progresar, hacer progresos.— **ive** [progrésiv], a. progresivo; progresista.—s. progresista.

prohibit [prouhíbit], vt. prohibir, vedar; impedir.— **ion** [prou(h)ibíʃən], s. prohibición, veda; veto.— **ive** [prouhíbitiv], a. prohibitivo.

project [prodʒékt], vt. proyectar; trazar, dibujar; idear; echar, arrojar, despedir.—vi. resaltar, sobresalir, destacarse.—s. [prádʒekt], proyecto; plano; empresa; (educ.) tema (en que el alumno tiene que investigar).— **ile** [prodʒéktil], s. proyectil.—a. proyectante, arrojadizo.— **ion** [prodʒékʃən], s. lanzamiento, echamiento; resalte; (arq.) vuelo, saliente; plan, proyecto; (geom.) proyección.— **or** [prodʒéktɔ(r)], s. proyectista, proyector (de cine, etc.); aparato de proyección.

proletarian [prouletériən], a. y s. proletario.—**proletariat** [prouletériət], s. proletariado.

prolific [prolífik], a. prolífico, fecundo, fértil.

prologue [próulag], s. prólogo.—vt. prologar.

prolong [prolóŋ], vt. prolongar, extender.— **ation** [proloŋgéiʃən], s. prolongación.

promenade [pramenád], vi. pasear(se). —s. paseo (lugar y acto); caminata, vuelta.

prominence [práminɛns], s. eminencia, altura, relieve, distinción; prominencia, protuberancia; apófisis.—**prominent** [prámiŋɛnt], a. prominente.

promiscuous [promískyuʌs], a. promiscuo.

promise [prámis], s. promesa; cosa comprometida; esperanza.—vt. y vi. prometer, ofrecer; dar o hacer concebir esperanzas.—**promising** [prámisiŋ], a. que promete, prometedor, halagüeño.—**promissory** [prámisori], a. promisorio.—p. note, pagaré, vale.

promontory [prámontori], s. (geog.) promontorio, punta, cabo; (anat.) promontorio, eminencia.

promote [promóut], vt. promover, fomentar; provocar, suscitar; alentar, estimular; mejorar, ascender; (com.) agenciar, gestionar; capitalizar y organizar (una empresa).— **r** [-œ(r)], s. promotor; gestor; agente de negocios.—**promotion** [promóuʃən], s. promoción, ascenso; fomento.

prompt [prampt], a. pronto, listo, expedito; puntual.—vt. impulsar, mover, incitar; (teat.) apuntar; indicar, sugerir; (fam.) soplar, decirle a otro en voz baja lo que debe contestar.— **er** [prámptœ(r)], s. (teat.) apuntador, traspunte; incitador.— **ness** [-nis], s. prontitud; puntualidad.

prone [proun], a. postrado; inclinado, pendiente; dispuesto, propenso.— **ness** [próunis], s. postración; propensión.

prong [praŋ], s. púa, diente, punta

(de tenedor, horquilla, etc.); pitón de asta; punta de colmillo.

pronoun [próynaun], s. pronombre.

pronounce [pronáuns], vt. pronunciar. —vi. pronunciar; hablar magistralmente.— —d [-t], a. pronunciado, marcado, fuerte, subido.— —ment [-ment], s. pronunciamiento, declaración.—**pronunciation** [pronᴧnsiéi̯ʃən], s. pronunciación.

proof [pruf], s. prueba; impenetrabilidad; comprobación.—to be p. against, ser o estar a prueba de.—to put to the p., poner a prueba.—a. impenetrable, resistente; de prueba.—p. sheet, prueba de imprenta.— —read [prúfrid], vti. y vii. [9] leer y corregir pruebas.—[prúfred], pret. y pp. de TO PROOFREAD.— —reader [-rídœ(r)], s. corrector de pruebas.— —reading [-ridiŋ], s. corrección de pruebas.

prop [prap], vti. [1] sostener, apuntalar, afianzar; (fig.) mantener, sustentar. —s. apoyo, puntal; (fig.) apoyo, báculo.—pl. (fam.) piernas.

propaganda [prapagǽndǎ], s. propaganda.—**propagandist** [prapagǽndist], s. y a. propagandista.—**propagate** [prápageit], vt. propagar; diseminar; propalar.—vi. propagarse, reproducirse; cundir.—**propagation** [prapagéi̯ʃən], s. propagación, generalización, reproducción, diseminación; difusión.

propel [propél], vti. [1] propulsar, impeler, empujar.— —er [-œ(r)], s. impulsor, propulsor; hélice.—p. shaft, (aut.) eje cardán.

proper [prápœ(r)], a. propio, conveniente; decoroso, formal; justo, exacto; propiamente dicho; (her.) natural.— —ty [-ti], s. propiedad; hacienda, caudal, bienes inmuebles; posesión, dominio, pertenencia.— personal p., bienes muebles.—pl. (teat.) guardarropía, (Am.) utilería.

prophecy [práfesi], s. profecía, predicción.—**prophesy** [práfesai], vti. y vii. [7] profetizar, predecir.—**prophet** [práfit], s. profeta.—**prophetic(al)** [profétik(al)], a. profético.

prophylactic [proufilǽktik], a. y s. profiláctico.

propitiate [propíʃieit], vt. propiciar, conciliar.—**propitious** [propíʃᴧs], a. propicio; oportuno.

proportion [propórʃən], s. proporción; simetría; armonía.—pl. tamaño, dimensiones.—in p. as, a medida que. —out of p., desproporcionado.—vt. proporcionar, armonizar.— —al [-al], a. proporcional.—s. (mat.) número o cantidad proporcional.

proposal [propóuzal], s. propuesta, proposición, oferta; declaración de

amor.—**propose** [propóuz], vt. proponer; proponerse, pensar, tener intención de.—vi. declararse (a una mujer).—**proposition** [prapozíʃən], s. proposición, propuesta; (log. y mat.) proposición; (mus.) tema; (fam.) cosa, asunto, problema, etc.

propound [propáund], vt. proponer; presentar.

proprietary [propráieteri], a. propietario; patentado (medicinas).—s. propietario; hacendados, propietarios; propiedad; remedio de patente.

proprietor [propráietǫ(r)], s. propietario, dueño, amo.—**propriety** [propráieti], s. propiedad, corrección; decoro, decencia.—pl. normas o cánones (del arte, sociales, etc.).

propulsion [propᴧ́lʃən], s. propulsión; impulso, impulsión.

pro rata [prou réitǎ], a prorrata.— **prorate** [prouréit], vt. prorratear.

prosaic [prozéik], a. prosaico; insulso, trivial.

proscribe [proskráib], vt. proscribir; encartar; prohibir; condenar, reprobar.

prose [prouz], s. prosa.—a. de prosa, en prosa; insulso, pesado.

prosecute [prásikiut], vt. continuar, (pro)seguir, llevar adelante; (for.) acusar, encausar, enjuiciar, procesar. —vi. querellarse ante el juez; seguir un pleito; fiscalizar.—**prosecution** [prasikiúʃən], s. prosecución, (pro)seguimiento; (for.) procesamiento; acusación; ministerio fiscal.—**prosecutor** [prásikiutǫ(r)], s. (for.) acusador; fiscal.

prosody [prásodi], s. prosodia; métrica.

prospect [práspekt], vt. y vi. (min.) explorar, buscar.—s. perspectiva, panorama; probabilidad; expectativa; situación, orientación; (min.) indicación o señal de veta; cata, muestra; (com.) comprador o parroquiano probable.— —ive [prospéktiv], a. anticipado, venidero, en perspectiva; presunto.—s. perspectiva, vista.— —or [práspektǫ(r)], s. explorador o buscador de minas, petróleo, etc.— —us [prospéktᴧs], s. prospecto, programa.

prosper [práspœ(r)], vi. prosperar, medrar.— —ity [praspériti], s. prosperidad.— —ous [-ᴧs], a. próspero, floreciente; favorable o propicio.

prostitute [prástitiut], vt. y vi. prostituir(se).—s. prostituta, ramera. — **prostitution** [prastitiúʃən], s. prostitución.

prostrate [prástreit], a. postrado, prosternado, humillado.—vt. tender, postrar; demoler, derribar; arruinar; (med.) postrar, debilitar.—vi.

postrarse, prosternarse.—**prostration** [prastréjṣǫn], **s.** postración, abatimiento, depresión.

protagonist [prǫtǽgǫnjst], **s.** protagonista.

protect [protékt], **vt.** proteger.— —**ion** [protékṣǫn], **s.** protección.— —**ive** [-jv], **a.** protector; (e.p.) proteccionista.— —**or** [-ǫ(r)], **s.** protector.— —**orate** [-ǫrjt], **s.** protectorado.

protégé [próutǎ̹žei], **s.** protegido, paniaguado.

protein [próuti(j)n], **s.** proteína.

protest [protést], **vt.** protestar, declarar; (com.) protestar (una letra).—**vi.** protestar.—**s.** [próutest], protesta-(ción); (com.) protesto.— —**ant** [prátjṣtant], **a.** y **s.** (P.) (igl.) protestante.— —**antism** [prátjṣtantjzm], **s.** (P.) protestantismo.— —**ation** [pratestéjṣǫn], **s.** protesta(ción); declaración.

protocol [próutokal], **s.** protocolo, registro.

protoplasm [próutoplæzm], **s.** protoplasma.

prototype [próutotajp], **s.** prototipo.

protract [protrǽkt], **vt.** alargar, prolongar; trazar con el transportador (en un plano).

protrude [protrúd], **vt.** empujar hacia afuera, hacer sobresalir.—**vi.** sobresalir, resaltar.

protuberance [protjúbǝrans], **s.** protuberancia, prominencia.—**protuberant** [protjúbǝrant], **a.** protuberante, prominente, saliente.

proud [praud], **a.** orgulloso; soberbio, arrogante, altanero; majestuoso; (poét.) brioso, pujante.—**to be p. of,** enorgullecerse de, ufanarse de.

prove [pruv], **vti.** [6] probar, demostrar; comprobar; acreditar, evidenciar; poner a prueba; (for.) abrir y hacer público (un testamento); (imp.) sacar prueba de.—**vii.** resultar, venir a parar, salir (bien o mal); demostrar, dar prueba de.

proverb [právœrb], **s.** proverbio; adagio, refrán.— —**ial** [provǿrbjal], **a.** proverbial.

provide [provájd], **vt.** proveer, proporcionar, surtir, abastecer, suministrar; estipular.—**vi.** (con **for**) mantener, proveer lo necesario, sufragar gastos, abastecer de víveres; encargarse de; tener en cuenta; precaverse, tener cuidado; dar disposiciones para, sobre o con respecto.—**provided** (that), con tal que, a condición de que, siempre que.

providence [právidǝns], **s.** providencia; prudencia; frugalidad; (P.) la Providencia.—**providential** [pravidénṣạl], **a.** providencial.

provider [provájdœ(r)], **s.** proveedor, abastecedor.—**providing** [provájdjǫ], **conj.** con tal que.

province [právjns], **s.** provincia, región; obligación, incumbencia; esfera, competencia.—**that is not my p.,** eso no me toca, no es de mi incumbencia.—**provincial** [provínṣạl], **a.** provincial; provinciano; rudo, grosero.—**s.** provinciano; (igl.) provincial.

provision [provížǫn], **s.** provisión, aprovisionamiento; medida, disposición, estipulación.—**pl.** provisiones, comestibles.— —**al** [-ạl], **a.** provisional, interino.—**provisory** [provájzorj], **a.** provisional; condicional, que lleva estipulación.

provocation [pravokéjṣǫn], **s.** provocación; excitación, estímulo.—**provocative** [provǽkǎtjv], **a.** provocativo, provocador.—**s.** estimulante.—**provoke** [provóuk], **vt.** provocar, irritar, encolerizar; excitar, incitar; causar, promover.—**vi.** causar enojo, excitar cólera.

prow [prau], **s.** proa.

prowess [práujs], **s.** valentía; proeza, hazaña.

prowl [praul], **vt.** y **vi.** rondar (para robar o vigilar); merodear; andar acechando; vagar.— —**er** [práulœ(r)], **s.** merodeador.

proximity [praksímjtj], **s.** proximidad, inmediación.

proxy [práksj], **s.** apoderado, delegado; procuración, poder.—**by p.,** por poder.

prude [prud], **s.** mojigato, remilgado, gazmoño.

prudence [prúdǝns], **s.** prudencia, cordura, circunspección.—**prudent** [prúdǝnt], **a.** prudente, juicioso, circunspecto.

prudery [prúdœrj], **s.** melindre, mojigatería, remilgo, gazmoñería.—**prudish** [prúdjṣ], **a.** gazmoño, remilgado, melindroso.

prune [prun], **vt.** y **vi.** podar; expurgar.—**s.** ciruela pasa.

Prussian [prúṣạn], **a.** y **s.** prusiano.

pry [praj], **vti.** y **vii.** [7] espiar, acechar, atisbar, observar, registrar o escudriñar.—**to p. into,** fisgar, fiscalizar, curiosear, entremeterse, (fam.) husmear.—**to p. off,** despegar.—**s.** inspección, reconocimiento o registro escrupuloso; persona curiosa o entremetida; palanca, barra.— —**ing** [prájjǫ], **a.** fisgón, entremetido.

psalm [sam], **s.** salmo, himno.

pseudo [súdou], **a.** seudo, falso.— —**nym** [súdonjm], **s.** seudónimo.

psyche [sájkj], **s.** psique; mente.— **psychiatric(al)** [sajkjǽtrjk(ạl)], **a.** psiquiátrico.—**psychiatrist** [sajkájǎtrjst], **s.** psiquiatra.—**psychiatry** [sajkái̯atri], **s.** psiquiatría.—**psychoanalysis** [sai̯ko̱ə̯nǽli̯si̱s], **s.** psicoanálisis.—**psychoanalyst** [sai̯ko̱ǽnǽli̱st], **s.** psicoanalista.—**psychoanalyze** [sai̯ko̱ǽnǽlai̯z], **vt.** psicoanalizar.—**psychologic(al)** [sai̯koládʒi̱k(ǝl)], **a.** psicológico.—**psychologist** [sai̯kálo̱dʒi̱st], **s.** psicólogo.—**psychology** [sai̯kálodʒi̱], **s.** psicología—**psychopath** [sái̯ko̱pæθ], **s.** psicópata.—**psychosis** [sai̯kóu̯si̱s], **s.** psicosis.—**psychotherapy** [sai̯ko̱ǽθ̱ǝrǝpi̱], **s.** psicoterapia.—**psychotic** [sai̯kátik], **s. y a.** psicótico, psicopático.

puberty [pi̱úbœrti̱], **s.** pubertad.

public [pʌ́bli̱k], **a.** público; común; notorio.—**p.** prosecutor, fiscal.—**s.** público.——**ation** [-éi̯ʃǝn], **s.** publicación; divulgación; promulgación; proclama(ción).——**ist** [pʌ́bli̱si̱st], **s.** publicista.——**ity** [pʌbli̱si̱ti̱], **s.** publicidad.—**publish** [pʌ́bli̱ʃ], **vt.** publicar; promulgar; editar.—**to p. the banns**, amonestar, correr las amonestaciones.—**publisher** [pʌ́bli̱ʃœ(r)], **s.** editor.—**publishing** [pʌ́bli̱ʃi̱ŋ], **a.** editorial, de publicaciones.—**p. house**, casa editora, editorial.

puck [pʌk], **s.** duende travieso; disco de goma (en el hockey sobre hielo).

pucker [pʌ́kœ(r)], **vt.** (cost.) fruncir, plegar, recoger, arrugar.—**vi.** arrugarse.—**s.** (cost.) fruncido, pliegue, fuelle, arruga; (fam.) agitación.

pudding [pú̱di̱ŋ], **s.** budín, pudín.—**p. dish** o **pan**, flanera, tortera.

puddle [pʌ́dl], **s.** charco, poza.

pudgy [pʌ́dʒi̱], **a.** (fam.) regordete, gordinflón.

puerile [pi̱úǝri̱l], **a.** pueril.

Puerto Rican [pwértọ ríkạn], **a. y s.** = PORTO RICAN.

puff [pʌf], **s.** resoplido; soplo, bufido; bocanada, fumada; elogio exagerado; (cost.) bullón; especie de buñuelo.—**powder p.**, polvera, borla de polvos.—**p. adder**, víbora venenosa.—**p. box**, polvera, caja de polvos.—**p. of wind**, ráfaga, soplo, racha; ventolera.—**vt.** inflar; engreír; dar bombo; (cost.) abollonar; dar chupadas (pipa, tabaco, etc.).—**vi.** inflarse; engreírse; bufar; resoplar; jadear, hipar; echar bocanadas; fumar.—**p. up**, hincharse, henchirse.——**y** [pʌ́fi̱], **a.** hinchado, inflado.

pug [pʌg], **s.** moño (del pelo); (alb.) torta.—**p. nose**, nariz respingada.

pugilist [pi̱údʒi̱li̱st], **s.** pugilista, púgil, boxeador.

pugnacious [pʌgnéi̱ʃʌs], **a.** belicoso, peleador, discutidor.—**pugnacity** [pʌgnǽsi̱ti̱], **s.** pugnacidad.

puke [pi̱uk], **vt. y vi.** vomitar.

pull [pu̱l], **vt.** tirar de; halar; estirar; sacar, arrancar (un diente, etc.); pelar, desplumar; bogar, remar; (fam.) sorprender, copar (un garito, etc.); prender (a uno); sacar (un arma).—**to p. a face**, hacer una mueca.—**to p. asunder** o **away**, arrancar o quitar con violencia.—**to p. back**, tirar hacia atrás; hacer recular o cejar.—**to p. down**, derribar, demoler; degradar; humillar, abatir.—**to p. in**, tirar hacia dentro; contener, refrenar.—**to p. in** o **to pieces**, hacer trizas, despedazar.—**to p. one's leg**, (fam.) tomarle el pelo a uno.—**to p. oneself together**, recobrar la calma; arreglarse, componerse.—**to p. out**, sacar, arrancar.—**to p. the trigger**, apretar el gatillo.—**to p. through**, sacar de dificultades o de un aprieto.—**to p. together**, llevarse bien; obrar de acuerdo.—**to p. up**, extirpar, desarraigar; contener, refrenar (un caballo); arrimar (una silla); subir (las persianas).—**vi.** tirar con esfuerzo; tironear, dar un tirón; ejercer tracción.—**to p. apart**, romperse por tracción.—**to p. for**, abogar por (una persona).—**to p. in**, llegar (un tren); contenerse, refrenarse.—**to p. through**, salir de un a̱puro.—**s.** tirón, estirón; tirador (de puerta, etc.); tracción; (fam.) influjo, influencia; (impr.) impresión con la prensa de mano; (dep.) ejercicio de remos, boga.——**er** [pú̱lœ(r)], **s.** el o lo que tira, saca o arranca; extractor.

pullet [pú̱li̱t], **s.** polla, gallina a medio crecer.

pulley [pú̱li̱], **s.** polea, trocla, garrucha; motón; (anat.) tróclea.—**p. block**, aparejo (de poleas).—**p. wheel** roldana.

pullman [pú̱lmạn], **s.** (f.c.) coche salón; coche cama.

pullover [pú̱lou̯vœ(r)], **s.** jersey, chaleco de lana.

pulmonary [pʌ́lmo̱ne̱ri̱], **a.** pulmonar.

pulp [pʌlp], **s.** pulpa.

pulpit [pú̱lpi̱t], **s.** púlpito.

pulsate [pʌ́lseịt], **vi.** pulsar, latir rítmicamente.—**pulsation** [pʌlséi̯ʃǝn], **s.** pulsación, latido.—**pulse** [pʌls], **s.** pulso; pulsación; (bot.) legumbres colectivamente.—**to feel the p.**, tomar el pulso.

pulverize [pʌ́lvǝrai̯z], **vt.** reducir a polvo, pulverizar.

pumice [pʌ́mi̱s], **s.** piedra pómez.

pump [pʌmp], **s.** bomba (de agua, aire, etc.); zapatilla, escarpín.—**p. water**, agua de pozo.—**vt. y vi.** dar a la bomba, (Am.) bombear.—**to p. in**, inyectar (aire, etc.).—**to p. out**, achicar, sacar a bomba.—*to p. up*, inflar (un neumático, etc.).

pumpkin [pʌ́mpkin, pʌ́ŋkin], *s.* calabaza (planta y fruto).

pun [pʌn], *s.* equívoco, retruécano, juego de vocablos.—*vii.* [1] decir retruécanos o equívocos, jugar del vocablo.

punch [pʌnch], *vt.* punzar, taladrar, horadar con punzón; aguijar o conducir ganado; dar puñetazos.—*s.* punzón, sacabocado(s), máquina o aparato de taladrar; ponche (bebida); puñetazo; (fam.) energía, actividad.

punctual [pʌ́ŋkchual], *a.* puntual, exacto.—**punctuality** [pʌŋkchuǽliti], *s.* puntualidad.

punctuate [pʌ́ŋkchueit], *vt.* y *vi.* puntuar.—**punctuation** [pʌŋkchuéiṣən], *s.* (gram.) puntuación.

puncture [pʌ́ŋkchu(r)], *s.* pinchazo, perforación; puntura, punzadura, picad(ur)a; punción.—*vt.* punzar; pinchar, perforar, agujerear, picar. —*punctured wound*, herida hecha con un instrumento puntiagudo.

pungency [pʌ́ndžənsi], *s.* sabor picante; acerbidad, acrimonia, mordacidad.—**pungent** [pʌ́ndžənt], *a.* picante; punzante; acre, mordaz.

punish [pʌ́niṣ], *vt.* castigar.— **ment** [-mənt], *s.* castigo; pena, corrección.

puny [pjúni], *a.* encanijado; diminuto; mezquino.

pup [pʌp], *s.* cachorro, perrillo.—*p. tent*, (fam.) tienda de campaña pequeña.

pupil [pjúpil], *s.* (anat.) pupila; (for.) pupilo; discípulo, alumno.

puppet [pʌ́pit], *s.* títere, muñeco, monigote, maniquí, marioneta; (fig.) títere, que sirve de instrumento a otro.—*p. show*, función de títeres o marionetas.

puppy [pʌ́pi], *s.* cachorro, perrillo; (desp.) fatuo, petimetre.

purchase [pə́rchis], *vt.* comprar; adquirir.—*s.* compra; adquisición; (mec.) palanca, aparejo, maniobra.— **r** [-œ(r)], *s.* comprador, marchante.

pure [pjur], *a.* puro; neto; castizo.

purgative [pə́rgativ], *a.* purgativo, purgante.—*s.* (med.) purga, purgante.—**purgatory** [pə́rgatori], *s.* purgatorio.—**purge** [pœrdž], *vt.* purgar, purificar; depurar.—*vi.* purificarse.—*s.* (med.) purgante; purgación; depuración.

purification [pjurifikéiṣən], *s.* purificación, depuración; expiación.—**purify** [pjúrifai], *vti.* [7] purificar; purgar, limpiar, refinar; expiar; expurgar, depurar.—*vii.* purificarse.—**Puritan** [pjúritan], *s.* y *a.* puritano.—**puritan-**

ical [pjuritǽnikal], *a.* puritano, riguroso, rígido, severo.—**purity** [pjúriti], *s.* pureza; casticidad; limpieza (de sangre).

purple [pœrpl], *a.* purpúreo, purpurino, morado; imperial, regio; brillante, vistoso.—*s.* púrpura; dignidad real o cardenalicia.

purport [pœrport], *s.* significado; tenor, sustancia.—*vt.* y *vi.* [pœrpórt], significar, querer decir, implicar, dar a entender.

purpose [pœrpɒs], *s.* propósito, fin, objeto, intención, mira; resultado, utilidad; voluntad, determinación; uso, caso.—*on p.*, de propósito, aposta.—*to come to the p.*, venir a cuento.—*to no p.*, inútilmente.—*vt.* y *vi.* proponer(se), intentar.— **ful** [-ful], *a.* determinado, tenaz.

purr [pœr], *s.* ronroneo del gato; zumbido del motor.—*vi.* ronronear (el gato).

purse [pœrs], *s.* bolsa, bolso de bolsillo; portamonedas; talega, bolsa de dinero; (fig.) peculio, riqueza; colecta. —*p. bearer*, tesorero.— **r** [pœrsœ(r)], *s.* sobrecargo, comisario de a bordo.

pursue [pœrsiú], *vt.* y *vi.* perseguir, dar caza, acosar; (pro)seguir, continuar; seguir (una carrera), dedicarse a, ejercer; (for.) demandar, poner pleito, procesar.— **r** [-œ(r)], *s.* perseguidor.—**pursuit** [pœrsiút], *s.* perseguimiento, persecución, caza; práctica, ejercicio; prosecución; busca; ocupación; pretensión; empeño.—*pl.* ocupaciones, estudios, investigaciones, actividades.

purvey [pœrvéi], *vt.* proveer, abastecer, suministrar.— **or** [-ɒ(r)], *s.* proveedor, abastecedor.

pus [pʌs], *s.* pus, podre.

push [puṣ], *vt.* empujar; propugnar, promover, activar; oprimir, pulsar; apremiar, obligar; importunar, molestar.—*to p. ahead o through*, pujar. —*to p. in*, encajar, hacer entrar.— *to p. off*, apartar con la mano; desalojar.—*to p. on*, incitar, aguijonear; apresurar.—*to p. out*, empujar hacia afuera; echar, expulsar.—*vi.* empujar, dar un empujón, dar empellones; apresurarse; acometer. —*to p. forward*, adelantarse dando empujones; adelantar, avanzar.— *to p. further*, seguir adelante.—*to p. in*, entremeterse.—*to p. off*, (mar.) desatracar.—*s.* impulso; empuje, empujón; arremetida; apuro, aprieto; (fam.) energía, iniciativa; (mil.) ofensiva.— **cart** [púṣkart], *s.* carretilla de mano.— **er** [-æ(r)], *s.* persona emprendedora o agresiva.—

—ing [-iŋ], a. activo, emprendedor; agresivo.

pussy (cat) [púsi(kæt)], s. gatito, minino.

put [put], vti. poner; disponer, colocar; proponer, presentar; expresar, declarar; (dep.) lanzar (el peso).—to p. across, (fam.) realizar, llevar a cabo.—to p. after, poner detrás de (sitio); posponer a (tiempo).—to p. a question, hacer una pregunta.—to p. back, atrasar, retardar; devolver, reponer.—to p. by, guardar; arrinconar; desviar, apartar.—to p. down, poner (en el suelo, etc.); sofocar, reprimir; deprimir, abatir; depositar; anotar, apuntar; rebajar, disminuir; hacer callar.—to p. forward, adelantar; proponer como candidato. —to p. in, poner en, echar en o a, meter; poner, insertar, introducir, intercalar; presentar, hacer (reclamo, etc.); colocar (en un empleo, etc.); interponer (palabra, observación); (top., dib.) trazar (una curva, etc.); pasar o gastar (tiempo, haciendo algo).—to p. in a word for, interceder por, hablar en favor de.—to p. in gear, (aut.) hacer engranar.—to p. in print, imprimir.—to p. off, diferir, dilatar, aplazar; desechar, apartar; evadir, entretener (con promesas); quitarse, desprenderse de (ropa, etc.).—to p. on, poner sobre; ponerse (ropa, etc.); calzar (zapatos, etc.); echar, poner, dar, aplicar (vapor, el freno, etc.); instigar a; fingir, disimular; encender (las luces, el radio, etc.); (teat.) producir, representar, poner en escena.—to p. out, brotar, echar retoños; despedir, despachar, echar; apagar (la luz, el fuego); publicar; cegar; borrar, tachar; cortar, desconcertar; sacar de quicio; poner (dinero a interés), dar (a logro); extender, sacar, mostrar; enojar, irritar.—to p. out of order, descomponer, desordenar.—to p. to flight, poner en fuga, ahuyentar.—to p. together, juntar, acumular; (mec.) armar, montar; coordinar.—to p. to it, causar dificultad a, poner al parir.—to p. to shame, avergonzar.—to p. up, poner en su lugar, conservar; preparar, confeccionar; construir, erigir; (mec.) montar; presentar (como candidato); ofrecer, elevar; levantar (la mano); alojar, hospedar; envainar; ofrecer resistencia; (fam.) poner dinero en una apuesta; tramar, urdir.—to p. up to, incitar, instigar a; presentar o someter a; (fam.) dar instrucciones. —to p. up with, aguantar, soportar. —vi. (mar.) dirigirse, seguir rumbo.

—pret. y pp. de TO PUT.—s. acción del verbo TO PUT en cualquiera de sus acepciones.

putty [páti], s. masilla de aceite; cemento (esp. el de cal).—p. knife, espátula.—vti. [7] enmasillar, rellenar con masilla.

puzzle [pázl], s. acertijo, adivinanza, rompecabezas; enigma, misterio, (fam.) problema arduo.—vt. confundir, poner perplejo; enmarañar, embrollar.—to p. out, resolver, descifrar, desenredar.—vi. estar perplejo. —to p. over, tratar de resolver, hincarle el diente a, devanarse los sesos sobre.

pygmy [pígmi], s. pigmeo.

pyramid [píramid], s. pirámide.—vt. y vi. aumentar(se), acumular(se).

pyre [pair], s. pira, hoguera.

Q

quack [kwæk], vi. graznar; charlatanear; echárselas de médico; curar empíricamente o con sortilegios.—s. graznido del pato.—s. y a. charlatán. —s. curandero; medicucho, medicastro.— **ery** [kwǽkœri], s. charlatanismo; fraude.

quadrant [kwádrant], s. cuadrante.

quadroon [kwadrún], s. cuarterón.

quadruped [kwádruped], s. y a. cuadrúpedo.

quadruple [kwádrupl], a. cuádruple, cuádruplo.—vt. y vi. cuadruplicar(se). — **ts** [kwádruplits], s. pl. gemelos cuádruples.

quagmire [kwǽgmair], s. tremedal, cenagal; atolladero.

quail [kweil], s. codorniz; perdiz.—vi. acobardarse, decorazonarse; cejar.

quaint [kweint], a. singular, curioso; pintoresco; original, raro.- **ness** [kwéintnis], s. rareza, singularidad, pintorequismo.

quake [kweik], s. temblor.—vi. temblar, trepidar, estremecerse.

qualification [kwalifikéişon], s. calificación, requisito; c(u)alidad, capacidad, idoneidad; título, habilitación; atenuación, mitigación; limitación; salvedad.—without q., sin reservas o reparos.—**qualify** [kwalifai], vti. [7] capacitar, habilitar, hacer idóneo; calificar; modificar, limitar, restringir; templar, suavizar.—vii. prepararse, habilitarse; llenar los requisitos; (E.U.) prestar juramento antes de entrar en funciones.— **qualitative** [kwáliteitiv], a. cualitativo.—**quality** [kwáliti], s. c(u)alidad; clase, casta, jaez; propiedad, poder o virtud; categoría, distinción, alta posición social.

quantitative [kwántĭteĭtĭv], *a.* cuantitativo.—**quantity** [kwántĭtĭ], *s.* cantidad, cuantía, tanto; dosis; gran cantidad, gran número; (elec.) intensidad (de una corriente).

quarantine [kwárantĭn], *s.* cuarentena; estación de cuarentena.—*vt.* poner en cuarentena.

quarrel [kwárȩl], *s.* reyerta, pendencia, riña, disputa.—*vii.* [2] pelear, reñir, romper la amistad.— **some** [-sʌm], *a.* pendenciero.

quarry [kwari], *s.* cantera, pedrera; caza, presa; cuadrado, rombo (de vidrio, teja, etc.).—*vti.* [7] explotar (canteras).

quart [kwort], *s.* cuarto de galón (Ver Tabla); (mus.) cuarta.- —**er** [kwórtœ(r)], *s.* cuarto, cuarta parte; arroba (Ver Tabla); trimestre; cuarto de hora; moneda de 25 centavos; cuarto de luna, etc.; origen, procedencia; región, comarca, distrito; barrio, barriada, vecindad; (carp.) entrepaño; cuartel, merced, clemencia.—*pl.* domicilio vivienda, morada; (mil.) cuartel, alojamiento. —*a.* cuarto.—*vt.* descuartizar, hacer cuartos; dividir en cuatro partes iguales o en cuarteles; (mil.) acuartelar, acantonar; alojar, hospedar.- —**erly** [-œrlĭ], *a.* trimestral.—*q. payment*, trimestre.—*s.* publicación trimestral.—*adv.* trimestralmente; en cuartos, por cuartos. —**ermaster** [-œrmǣstœ(r)], *s.* (mil.) comisario; furriel.—*q. general*, intendente del ejército.- —**et(te)** [kwortét], *s.* cuatro personas o cosas de una misma clase; (mus. poét.) cuarteto.

quartz [kworts], *s.* cuarzo, sílice.

quash [kwaš], *vt.* sofocar, reprimir; anular, invalidar.

quatrain [kwátreĭn], *s.* cuarteta, redondilla.

quaver [kwéĭvœ(r)], *vi.* gorjear, trinar; temblar, vibrar.—*s.* gorjeo, trino; trémolo, vibración; (mus.) corchea.- —**ing** [-ĭŋ], *s.* gorgorito, trino, gorjeo.

quay [ki], *s.* muelle; (des)embarcadero.

Quechuan [kéchwan], *s.* y *a.* quechua.

queen [kwin], *s.* reina.

queer [kwĭr], *a.* extraño, raro; indispuesto, desfalleciente; (fam.) chiflado, excéntrico, estrafalario; (fam.) sospechoso, misterioso; (fam.) falso; (coll.) afeminado.—*s.* (fam.) moneda falsa.—*vt.* (fam.) comprometer, poner a uno en mal lugar; echar a perder; (fam.) ridiculizar.

quell [kwȩl], *vt.* reprimir, sofocar, domar, sojuzgar; calmar, mitigar (un dolor).

quench [kwȩnch], *vt.* apagar, matar (luz, fuego); calmar, apagar (la sed); ahogar, sofocar; sosegar; extinguir; templar (hierro).

query [kwĭri], *s.* pregunta; duda; (imp.) signo interrogante (?).—*vti.* [7] marcar con signo de interrogación; preguntar, indagar, pesquisar. —*vii.* expresar una duda; preguntar.

quest [kwest], *s.* pesquisa, averiguación; busca.—*vi.* y *vt.* averiguar, investigar; buscar.

question [kwéschȩn], *s.* pregunta, interrogación; cuestión, caso, asunto; problema; debate, controversia; proposición a discutir; objeción, discusión.—*beside the q.*, ajeno al asunto. —*beyond o without q.*, fuera de duda, indiscutible.—*out of q.*, sin duda, de veras.—*q.-begging*, de carácter de círculo vicioso.—*q. mark*, signo de interrogación.—*to ask a q.*, hacer una pregunta.—*to be out of q.*, ser indiscutible; no haber que pensar en.—*to put the q.*, interrogar; torturar; someter a votación.—*vt.* preguntar; dudar, poner en tela de juicio; desconfiar de; oponerse a, objetar; recusar.—*vi.* inquirir, preguntar, escudriñar.- —**able** [-abl], *a.* problemático, dudoso, discutible, sospechoso.- —**naire** [kweschȩnér], *s.* cuestionario, encuesta.

quick [kwĭk], *a.* rápido, veloz, ágil; ardiente, penetrante, fino; irritable, petulante; disponible, efectivo; vivo. —*s.* carne viva; lo más hondo o profundo (del alma, de la sensibilidad); lo más delicado.—*to cut (hurt, offend, etc.) to the q.*, herir en lo vivo, en el alma o profundamente.—*adv* con presteza, prontamente, velozmente.—*q.-sighted*, de vista aguda, penetrante.—*q.-tempered*, de genio vivo, irascible.—*q.-witted*, vivo de ingenio, listo, agudo, perspicaz.—*en* [kwĭkn], *vt.* vivificar, resucitar; avivar, urgir; excitar, aguzar, animar. —*vi.* avivarse, vivificarse, revivir; moverse más aprisa; ser más sensitivo.- —**lime** [-laĭm], *s.* cal viva.- —**ly** [-lĭ], *adv.* prontamente, pronto aprisa.- —**ness** [-nĭs], *s.* presteza, vivacidad, prontitud, celeridad; sagacidad, viveza, penetración.- —**sand** [-sænd], *s.* arena movediza.- —**silver** [-sĭlvœ(r)], *s.* azogue, mercurio.

quiet [kwáĭȩt], *a.* quieto, quedo; sereno, tranquilo; callado, silencioso; sencillo, modesto; apacible; (com.) inactivo (mercado, etc.).—*to be q.*, callarse; guardar silencio.—*s.* quietud; silencio; tranquilidad, calma. —*on the q.*, (fam.) a la chita callando. —*vt.* acallar, apaciguar; tranquilizar, calmar.—*vi.* aquietarse, apaciguarse.-

—ness [-nis], **s.** quietud, sosiego, tranquilidad, paz.

quill [kwil], **s.** pluma de ave; cañón de pluma; cañón o pluma para escribir; escritor; púa del puerco espín; devanador, canutillo; estría, pliegue de un rizado.—**vt.** desplumar; (cost.) rizar, hacer un encarrujado.

quilt [kwilt], **s.** colcha, cobertor acolchado, edredón.—**vt.** acolchar, acojinar.

quince [kwins], **s.** membrillo.

quinine [kwáinain], **s.** quinina.

quintessence [kwintésens], **s.** quintaesencia.

quintuple [kwíntiupl], **a.** y **s.** quíntuplo. —**vt.** y **vi.** quintuplicarse.

quip [kwip], **s.** pulla, escarnio, mofa. —**vii.** [1] echar pullas, mofarse.

quit [kwit], **vti.** [3] dejar, parar, cesar o desistir de; dejarse de, soltar, dejar ir, abandonar; renunciar; evacuar, desocupar; irse, salir o marcharse de.—**vii.** desistir; parar; cejar; irse, quitarse; abandonar (una empresa, una causa, a sus amigos, etc.), zafarse.—**pret.** y **pp.** de TO QUIT.—**a.** libre, descargado.—**to be quits**, estar en paz; quedar vengado; no deberse nada.—**to call it quits**, dar (algo) por terminado.

quite [kwait], **adv.** completamente, enteramente, absolutamente, del todo; verdadera, efectiva o justamente; (fam.) bastante, asaz, harto, más bien.—**q. a bit**, considerable, bastante.

quitter [kwítœ(r)], **s.** (metal.) escorias; el que se da fácilmente por vencido; desertor (de una causa, etc.).

quiver [kwívœ(r)], **s.** carcaj, aljaba; estremecimiento; temblor.—**vi.** temblar; estremecerse; palpitar.

quixotic [kwiksátik], **a.** quijotesco.

quiz [kwiz], **s.** examen o serie de preguntas; chanza, broma, guasa; zumbón, chancero, guasón.—**vti.** [1] examinar a un discípulo o clase; tomar a guasa, chancearse; mirar con aire burlón.

quota [kwóutə], **s.** cuota, cupo; prorrata.

quotation [kwoutéjšon], **s.** citación; cita; texto citado; (com.) cotización. —**q. marks**, comillas.—**quote** [kwout], **vt.** y **vi.** citar; repetir un texto; (com.) cotizar.—**s.** (fam.) cita.—**pl.** (fam.) comillas.

quotient [kwóušent], **s.** (mat.) cociente.

R

rabbi [rǽbai], **s.** rabí, rabino.— —**nical** [rǽbínikal], **a.** rabínico.

rabbit [rǽbit], **s.** conejo.—**r.** *hole*, conejera.

rabble [rǽbl], **s.** canalla, chusma, populacho.

rabid [rǽbid], **a.** (med.) rabioso; fanático, violento, feroz.—**rabies** [réjbiz], **s.** rabia, hidrofobia.

raccoon [rækún], **s.** mapache, oso lavador.

race [reis], **s.** raza; estirpe; carrera, corrida, regata.—**r.** *course* o *track*, pista de carreras; hipódromo.—**vt.** hacer competir en una carrera; hacer correr deprisa.—**vi.** correr deprisa; competir en una carrera.— —**r** [réisœ(r)], **s.** corredor; caballo de carrera; auto de carrera.

racial [réjšal], **a.** racial, étnico, de (la) raza o de (las) razas.

rack [ræk], **s.** percha, colgador; bastidor; potro del tormento; dolor, pena, angustia; (mec.) cremallera.—**r.** *bar*, cremallera.—**to be on the r.**, estar en angustias.—**vt.** atormentar; agobiar. —**to r. one's brains**, devanarse los sesos.

racket [rǽkit], **s.** raqueta; confusión, baraúnda; (fam.) parranda, franca-chela; (fam.) negocio turbio, trapisonda.—**vi.** meter bulla.— —**eer** [rækitír], **s.** bandido urbano que explota la extorsión, (Am., neol.) raquetero.—**vi.** extorsionar, extraer por la intimidación y la violencia.

racy [réisi], **a.** picante.

radar [réjda(r)], **s.** radar.

radial [réjdial], **a.** radial.

radiance [réjdians], **s.** brillo, resplandor, esplendor.—**radiant** [réjdiant], **a.** radiante; resplandeciente, brillante. —**radiate** [réjdieit], **vt.** emitir, irradiar.—**vi.** radiar, brillar.—**radiation** [reidiéišon], **s.** radiación, irradiación. —**radiator** [réjdieitø(r)], **s.** aparato de calefacción; (aut., etc.) radiador.

radical [rǽdikal], **a.** y **s.** radical.

radio [réjdiou], **s.** radio; radiocomunicación.—**by r.**, por radio, radiado.—**r.** *amateur*, *fan* o *ham*, radioaficionado. —**r.** *announcer*, locutor, anunciador. —**r.** *beacon*, radiofaro.—**r.** *frequency*, radiofrecuencia.—**r.** *listener*, radioyente, radioescucha.—**r.** *station*, (estación) emisora o difusora.—**vt.** y **vi.** radiar, radiodifundir.— —**active** [-æktiv], **a.** radioactivo.— —**activity** [-æktíviti], **s.** radioactividad.— —**logist** [-álodžist], **s.** radiólogo.

radish [rǽdiš], **s.** rábano.

radium [réjdiam], **s.** (quím.) radio.

radius [réjdias], **s.** (geom. y anat.) radio; alcance.

raffle [rǽfl], **vt.** (gen. con *off*) rifar, sortear.—**s.** rifa, sorteo.

raft [ræft], **s.** balsa, almadía.—**vt.**

transportar en balsa; pasar en balsa.

rafter [ráftœ(r)], *s.* viga (de techo).

rag [ræg], *s.* trapo, andrajo, harapo; persona andrajosa; (mús.) tiempo sincopado.—*r. doll*, muñeca de trapo. —*vti.* [1] rasgar; poner en música sincopada o musiquilla.—*vii.* tocar musiquilla o música sincopada.

ragamuffin [rǽgamʌfin], *s.* galopín, golfo; pelafustán, pelagatos.

rage [rejdž], *s.* rabia, furor, cólera; (fam.) boga, moda.—*vi.* rabiar, bramar, encolerizarse, enfurecerse.

ragged [rǽgid], *a.* roto, desharrapado, andrajoso, harapiento; mellado, áspero.

raging [rejdžiṇ], *a.* rabioso, furioso, bramador.—*r. fever*, calentura ardiente.

raid [rejd], *vt.* invadir; (fam.) entrar o apoderarse por fuerza legal; allanar. —*vi.* hacer una irrupción.—*s.* correría, irrupción, incursión; (fam.) invasión repentina.—*air r.*, ataque aéreo.

rail [rejl], *s.* pasamano, barandilla; antepecho; (f.c.) riel, rail, carril; ferrocarril.—*by r.*, por ferrocarril.— *vt.* (a veces con in u of) poner barandilla, barrera o verja.—*vi.* (con at o against) injuriar; protestar contra.— —*ing* [rejliṇ], *s.* baranda, barandilla, pasamano; cerca, verja, enrejado; (f.c.) rieles; material para rieles.

raillery [rejlœri], *s.* zumba, chocarrería.

railroad [rejlroud], *s.* ferrocarril, vía férrea.—*a.* ferroviario, de ferrocarril, para ferrocarriles.—*r. crossing*, paso a nivel.—*r. junction*, entronque.—*vt.* (fam.) apresurar; hacer aprobar (una ley, etc.) con precipitación; hacer encarcelar falsamente.

rain [rejn], *vi.* llover.—*r. or shine*, que llueva o no; con buen o mal tiempo.— *to r. cats and dogs*, llover a cántaros.— *s.* lluvia.—*r. water*, agua lluvia.— —*bow* [réjnbou], *s.* arco iris.—*coat* [-kout], *s.* impermeable, (Am.) capa de agua.—*drop* [-drap], *s.* gota de agua.— *fall* [-fɔl], *s.* aguacero; lluvias; cantidad de lluvia caída.— *y* [-i], *a.* lluvioso.—*for a r. day*, por lo que pueda tronar.

raise [rejz], *vt.* levantar, alzar, poner en pie; elevar; construir, erigir; aumentar, subir; promover, ascender; criar, cultivar; hacer brotar; reclutar, alistar; reunir, recoger o juntar (dinero); levantar (en la caza); fermentar (pan).—*to r. a point*, presentar una cuestión, hacer una observación.—*to r. Cain*, o *a racket*, o *a rumpus*, (fam.) armar un escándalo, un alboroto; armar un lío.—*s.* levantamiento, alzamiento; aumento (de sueldo); ascenso.

raisin [réjzin], *s.* pasa, uva seca.

rake [rejk], *s.* rastro, rastrillo; calavera, libertino, perdido.—*vt.* rastrillar; barrer; atizar (el fuego); (mil.) enfilar, barrer.—*to r. over the coals*, (fam.) despellejar, poner como un trapo.— *vi.* pasar el rastrillo; llevar una vida disoluta.

rally [réli], *vti.* [7] (mil.) reunir y reanimar.—*vii.* (mil.) reunirse, rehacerse; recobrar las fuerzas, revivir.— *s.* unión o reunión (de tropas dispersas o de gente); recuperación.

ram [ræm], *s.* carnero padre, morueco; (mec.) martinete, pisón; ariete hidráulico; (mar.) espolón.—*vti.* [1] apisonar; meter por la fuerza; atestar, henchir.

ramble [rǽmbl], *vi.* vagar, callejear; divagar, ir por las ramas; discurrir.— *s.* paseo.— *r* [rǽmblœ(r)], *s.* vagabundo, callejero; paseador.

ramp [ræmp], *s.* rampa, declive.

rampart [rǽmpart], *s.* (fort.) terraplén; muralla; baluarte.

ramrod [rǽmrad], *s.* baqueta.

ramshackle [rǽmšækl], *a.* desvencijado, destartalado, ruinoso.

ran [ræn], *pret.* de TO RUN.

ranch [rænch], *s.* (Am.) rancho, estancia; hacienda de ganado.—*vi.* tener hacienda de ganado.— *er* [rǽnchœ(r)], *s.* (Am.) ranchero; ganadero.

rancid [rǽnsid], *a.* rancio.

rancor [rǽŋkɔ(r)], *s.* rencor, encono, inquina.—*ous* [-ʌs], *a.* rencoroso.

random [rǽndəm], *a.* fortuito, casual, impensado; sin orden ni concierto.— *at r.*, a la ventura, al azar, a trochemoche.

rang [ræŋ], *pret.* de TO RING (tocar).

range [rejndž], *vt.* recorrer; poner en posición; poner en fila; (a veces con in) alinear; arreglar, clasificar.—*vi.* vagar; estar en línea; estar a la misma altura; variar, fluctuar; (arti.) tener alcance (un proyectil).—*s.* distancia; extensión, recorrido; alcance (de un arma o proyectil); pastizal; radio de acción; fila, hilera, clase, orden; cocina económica.—*at close r.*, a quema ropa.—*r. finder*, (arti.) telémetro.—*r. of mountains*, cadena de montañas, cordillera.—*to be within the r. of*, estar a tiro, al alcance de.— *r* [réjndžœ(r)], *s.* guardabosque; vigilante.

rank [ræŋk], *s.* rango, posición (social, etc.); (mil.) grado, graduación, categoría; línea, hilera; (mil.) fila.—*the ranks, the r. and file*, la tropa, los soldados de fila; las masas.—*vt.* clasificar, ordenar; colocar por grados; poner en fila.—*vi.* tener tal o cual grado o clasificación; ocupar (primero, segundo, etc.) lugar; (con with) estar al nivel (de); (con high, low) ocupar (alta, baja) posición.—*a.* rancio; lozano; espeso; grosero; completo; fétido.

rankle [ránkl], *vi.* enconarse, inflamarse; causar resentimiento o enojo.

ransom [ránsǫm], *s.* rescate.—*vt.* rescatar, redimir.

rap [ræp], *vti.* y *vii.* [1] golpear, dar un golpe seco; (fam.) criticar, zaherir.—*to r. at the door*, tocar o llamar a la puerta.—*s.* golpe seco; (fam.) crítica. —*I don't care a r.*, no me importa un bledo.—*to take the r. for*, (fam.) pagar los vidrios rotos.

rapacious [rapéišas], *a.* rapaz.

rape [reip], *s.* violación, estupro.—*vt.* violar; forzar.

rapid [rápid], *a.* rápido, veloz.—*s. pl.* rápidos (de un río), rabión.— —**ity** [rapíditi], *s.* rapidez, velocidad.

rapine [rápin], *s.* rapiña.

rapt [ræpt], *a.* arrebatado o extasiado. —*r. in thought*, absorto.— —**ure** [rápchū(r)], *s.* rapto, arrobamiento, embeleso, éxtasis.

rare [rer], *a.* raro; precioso; extraordinario; (coc.) poco pasado, a medio pasar.— —**ly** [rérli], *adv.* raramente, rara vez, por rareza; sólo de tarde en tarde; excelente o extremamente. —**rarity** [réríti], *s.* rareza; curiosidad; tenuidad.

rascal [ráskal], *s.* pícaro, bribón, bellaco, pillo.— —**ity** [ræskéliti], *s.* bribonería, bellaquería.

rash [ræš], *a.* temerario, imprudente, precipitado.—*s.* salpullido, erupción. — —**ness** [rášnis], *s.* temeridad, imprudencia, precipitación.

rasp [ræsp], *s.* chirrido, sonido estridente; ronquera; escofina, raspador. —*vt.* chirriar; escofinar; raspar.

raspberry [rázberi], *s.* (bot.) frambuesa; (fam.) trompetilla, sonido de mofa.—*r. bush*, frambueso.

rat [ræt], *s.* rata; (fam.) postizo para el pelo.—*r. trap*, ratonera.—*to smell a r.*, recelar, haber gato encerrado.

rate [reit], *s.* tarifa, precio o valor fijo; tipo (de interés, etc.); proporción, tanto (por ciento, por unidad, etc.); modo, manera; clase.—*at any r.*, de todos modos, sea como sea, en todo caso.—*at that r.*, en esa proporción, de ese modo; a ese paso.—*at the r. of*, a razón de.—*r. of exchange*, cambio, tipo del cambio.—*vt.* tasar, valuar; clasificar; considerar, justipreciar; fijar precio, tarifa, etc.—*vi.* ser considerado (como); estar clasificado (como).

rather [ráðœ(r)], *adv.* bastante, un poco, algo; más bien, mejor dicho; antes bien.—*(I) had r. o would r.*, preferiría, más bien quisiera.—*r. than*, más bien que, en vez de, mejor que.

ratification [rætijfkéišǫn], *s.* ratificación.—**ratify** [rátifai], *vti.* [7] ratificar, confirmar.

rating [réitiŋ], *s.* justiprecio; clasificación (de un buque, marinero, etc.); (mec.) capacidad o potencia normal; clase, rango.

ratio [réišiou], *s.* razón, relación, proporción.

ration [ráŝǫn, réišǫn], *s.* (mil.) ración.— *r. book o card*, cartilla o tarjeta de racionamiento.—*vt.* racionar.

rational [ráŝǫnal], *a.* racional.- —**ization** [ræŝǫnạlizéišǫn], *s.* explicación racional de acciones, creencias, etc. —**ize** [ráŝǫnalaiz], *vt.* interpretar racionalmente; buscar explicación racional o justificativa de.

rationing [ráŝǫniŋ, réišǫniŋ], *s.* racionamiento.

rattan [rætǽn], *s.* bejuco.

rattle [rátl], *vt.* hacer sonar como una matraca; batir o sacudir con ruido; (fam.) atolondrar, aturrullar; (con off) decir a la carrera.—*vi.* matraquear; parlotear.—*s.* cascabel (de crótalo); sonajero; (Am.) maruga (juguete); matraca; estertor.—*r.-brained, r.-headed*, ligero de cascos, casquivano.— —**snake** [-sneik], *s.* culebra o serpiente de cascabel.

raucous [rókas], *a.* ronco; bronco; estentóreo.

ravage [rávidž], *vt.* saquear, pillar, asolar, destruir.—*s.* ruina, estrago, destrucción; saqueo, pillaje.

rave [reiv], *vi.* delirar, desvariar; disparatar; bramar, salirse de sus casillas.—*to r. over o about*, entusiasmarse locamente por.

raven [réivn], *s.* cuervo.—*a.* negro brillante.

ravenous [rávenas], *a.* voraz, famélico; rapaz.

ravine [ravín], *s.* barranca, cañada, hondonada.

ravish [ráviš], *vt.* arrebatar, atraer, encantar; violar, estuprar.— —**ing** [-iŋ], *a.* embriagador, arrebatador.

raw [ro], *a.* crudo; pelado, despellejado; descarnado; desapacible; fresco, nuevo; novato, bisoño (recluta, etc.); vulgar.—*r.-boned*, huesudo.—*r. cotton (silk)*, algodón (seda) en rama.—*r. flesh*, en carne viva.—*r. material*, materia prima.— —**hide** [róhaid], *s.* de cuero sin curtir.—*s.* cuero crudo; látigo de cuero crudo.

ray [rei], *s.* rayo (de luz, calor, etc.); (ict.) raya.

rayon [réiạn], *s.* rayón.

raze [reiz], *vt.* arrasar, demoler, destruir.
razor [réizǫ(r)], *s.* navaja de afeitar.—
— *r. blade*, hoja o cuchilla de afeitar.
reach [rich], *vt.* llegar a o hasta; alcanzar, lograr, conseguir; penetrar.—*te* *r. out one's hand*, tender la mano.—
vi. extenderse, alcanzar.—*to r. into*, penetrar en.—*s.* alcance; extensión; poder.—*beyond one's r.*, fuera del alcance de uno.—*within one's r.*, al alcance de uno; dentro del poder de uno.
react [riǽkt], *vi.* reaccionar. —**ion** [riǽkšǫn], *s.* reacción.— —**ionary** [riǽkšǫneri], *a.* y *s.* reaccionario.
reactor [riǽktǫ(r)], *s.* (quím.) reactivo.
read [rid], *vti.* [9] leer; marcar, indicar. —*the thermometer reads* 20°, el termómetro marca 20°.—*to r. law*, estudiar derecho.—*to r. proofs*, corregir pruebas.—*vii.* leer.—[red], *pret.* y *pp.* de TO READ.— —**able** [rídabl], *a.* legible; ameno, entretenido.— —**er** [-œ(r)], *s.* lector; libro de lectura (de texto); corrector (de pruebas).
readily [rédili], *adv.* fácilmente; luego; con placer, de buena gana.—**readiness** [rédinis], *s.* disposición, buena voluntad; prontitud; facilidad.—*in r.*, listo, preparado.
reading [rídiṇ], *s.* lectura; conferencia, disertación; lectura de un proyecto de ley; apertura de un testamento.— *r. matter*, material de lectura; sección de lectura (de un periódico).—*r. room*, salón de lectura.
readjust [riadʒʌst], *vt.* ajustar de nuevo; readaptar.— —**ment** [-mǫnt], *s.* readaptación; reajuste.
ready [rédi], *a.* listo, pronto, preparado, dispuesto; inclinado, propenso; al alcance; útil, disponible.—*r.-made*, ya hecho; confeccionado.—*r. money*, dinero contante, dinero al contado.
reagent [riédʒǫnt], *s.* (quím.) reactivo.
real [ríal], *a.* real, verdadero, auténtico, genuino, legítimo.—*r. estate*, bienes raíces o inmuebles.—*adv.* (fam.) muy, bastante.— —**ism** [-izm], *s.* realismo.— —**ist** [-ist], *s.* realista.— —**ity** [riǽliti], *s.* realidad, verdad.—*in r.*, en realidad, de veras, efectivamente.— —**ization** [-izéišǫn], *s.* realización; comprensión.— —**ize** [-aiz], *vt.* realizar, efectuar; darse cuenta, hacerse cargo de; comprender; (com.) realizar.
realm [relm], *s.* reino; región, dominio.
realtor [ríaltǫ(r)], *s.* corredor de bienes raíces.
ream [rim], *s.* resma.—*vt.* escariar, agrandar un agujero.
reanimate [riǽnimeit], *vt.* reanimar, resucitar.
reap [rip], *vt.* segar; cosechar; obtener o sacar provecho de.— —**er** [rípœ(r)],

s. segador; segadora mecánica.— —**ing** [-iṇ], *s.* siega, cosecha.
reappear [riapír], *vi.* reaparecer.— —**ance** [-ans], *s.* reaparición.
rear [rir], *a.* de atrás, trasero, posterior; último, de más atrás.—*r. admiral*, contra(a)lmirante.—*r. guard*, retaguardia.—*s.* fondo; espalda, parte de atrás o posterior; trasero; cola.—*r. view mirror*, (aut.) espejo retrovisor. —*vt.* levantar, alzar; criar, educar.— *vi.* encabritarse (el caballo).
rearm [riárm], *vt.* rearmar.— —**ament** [-amǫnt], *s.* rearme.
rearrange [riaréindʒ], *vt.* volver a arreglar; cambiar el arreglo o el orden de; refundir.
reason [rízǫn], *s.* razón; causa, motivo, porqué; argumento.—*by r. of*, con motivo de, a causa de, en virtud de.— *in (all) r.*, con justicia, con razón.—*it stands to r.*, está puesto en razón.—*r. why*, el porqué.—*to bring to r.*, meter en razón.—*within r.*, con moderación; dentro de los términos de la razón.— *vi.* razonar; discurrir.— —**able** [-abl], *a.* razonable, justo; equitativo, módico; prudencial.— —**ableness** [-ablnis], *s.* racionalidad; razón; moderación; justicia.— —**ably** [-abli], *adv.* razonablemente; bastante.— —**ing** [-iṇ], *s.* razonamiento, raciocinio.
reassure [riašúr], *vt.* tranquilizar.
rebate [ríbeit], *vt.* y *vi.* rebajar, descontar.—*s.* rebaja, descuento.
rebel [rébǫl], *a.* y *s.* rebelde; faccioso, insurrecto.—*vii.* [1] [ribél], rebelarse, sublevarse.— —**lion** [ribélyǫn], *s.* rebelión, sublevación.— —**lious** [ribélyʌs], *a.* rebelde; insubordinado.— —**liousness** [ribélyʌsnis], *s.* rebeldía.
rebirth [ribérθ], *s.* renacimiento.
rebound [ribáund], *vi.* (re)botar; repercutir.—*s.* [ríbaund], (re)bote; repercusión.
rebuff [ribʌf], *s.* desaire, repulsa.—*vt.* desairar, rechazar.
rebuild [ribild], *vti.* [10] reedificar, reconstruir.—**rebuilt** [ribílt], *pret.* y *pp.* de TO REBUILD.
rebuke [ribiúk], *vt.* increpar, reprochar, reprender.—*s.* repulsa, reproche, increpación, reprensión, reprimenda.
recall [rikól], *vt.* revocar, anular; recordar, acordarse de.—*to r. an ambassador*, retirar a un embajador.—*s.* recordación; revocación; (mil.) toque o aviso de llamada.
recant [rikǽnt], *vt.* y *vi.* retractar(se); desdecirse, desmentirse.— —**ation** [rikæntéišǫn], *s.* retractación.
recast [rikǽst], *vti.* [9] volver a fundir; refundir, volver a escribir; volver a hacer; (teat.) volver a repartir (papeles).—*pret.* y *pp.* de TO RECAST.

recede [rɪsíd], *vi.* retroceder; retirarse, alejarse; desistir, volverse atrás; bajar (los precios).

receipt [rɪsít], *s.* recibo; carta de pago; receta, fórmula.—*pl.* ingresos, entradas.—*on r. of*, al recibo de.—*to acknowledge r.*, acusar recibo.—*vt.* y *vi.* firmar o extender recibo; poner el recibí.—**receive** [rɪsív], *vt.* recibir.—*received payment*, recibí.—**receiver** [rɪsívœ(r)], *s.* recibidor; destinatario; recipiente; (tlf.) auricular, receptor; radiorreceptor; (for.) depositario, síndico, administrador judicial.

recent [rísɛnt], *a.* reciente.— —**ly** [-lɪ], *adv.* recientemente.—*r. married*, recién casados.

receptacle [rɪséptakl], *s.* receptáculo, recipiente, vasija.—**reception** [rɪsépʂɒn], *s.* recepción, recibimiento, recibo; acogimiento, acogida.—*r. room*, gabinete, recibidor.—**receptionist** [rɪsépʂɒnɪst], *s.* recibidor, persona que atiende a las visitas en oficinas o empresas.

recess [rɪsés], *s.* nicho, hueco; tregua; recreo (escolar); retiro, lugar o cosa recónditos.—*vi.* suspender temporalmente, recesar.— —**ion** [rɪséʂɒn], *s.* receso, retirada; retracción; (com.) crisis o depresión temporal.

recharge [richárdʒ], *vt.* recargar.

recipe [résɪpi], *s.* receta (médica o de cocina); fórmula.

recipient [rɪsípɪɛnt], *a.* y *s.* que recibe, recipiente, recibidor.

reciprocal [rɪsíprɒkal], *a.* recíproco, mutuo.—**reciprocate** [rɪsíprɒkeit], *vt.* reciprocar, corresponder.—*vi.* estar a la recíproca.—**reciprocity** [resɪprásɪtɪ], *s.* reciprocidad.

recital [rɪsáital], *s.* recitación (mus.) recital; relación, narración.—**recitation** [resɪtéiʂɒn], *s.* recitación, declamación.—**recite** [rɪsáit], *vt.* y *vi.* narrar, relatar; recitar; declamar; dar o decir la lección.

reckless [réklɪs], *a.* imprudente, temerario; atolondrado.— —**ness** [-nɪs], *s.* temeridad; imprudencia; indiferencia, descuido.

reckon [rékɒn], *vt.* y *vi.* contar, enumerar; calcular; estimar; suponer, creer; (con **on** o **upon**) contar con, fiar en.—*to r. with*, tener en cuenta; habérselas con.— —**ing** [-ɪŋ], *s.* cuenta; cómputo, cálculo; ajuste de cuentas.—*day of r.*, día del juicio (final).

reclaim [rɪkléim], *vt.* (for.) reclamar (derechos, etc.); (rei)vindicar; mejorar y utilizar (tierras); utilizar (material usado).—**reclamation** [reklaméiʂɒn], *s.* reclamación; mejoramiento.

recline [rɪkláin], *vt.* y *vi.* reclinar(se), recostar(se).

recognition [rekɒgníʂɒn], *s.* reconocimiento.—**recognize** [rékɒgnaiz], *vt.* reconocer; confesar, admitir.

recoil [ríkɔil], *s.* rechazo, reculada; (arti.) retroceso, culatazo.—*vi.* [rɪkɔ́il], recular; retirarse; retroceder; culatear, patear (un arma de fuego).

recollect [rekɒlékt], *vt.* y *vi.* recordar; acordarse (de); [rɪkɒlékt], recoger, recolectar, reunir.— —**ion** [rekɒlékʂɒn], *s.* recuerdo, recordación.

recommend [rekɒménd], *vt.* recomendar.— —**ation** [-éiʂɒn], *s.* recomendación.

recompense [rékɒmpens], *vt.* recompensar.—*s.* recompensa.

reconcile [rékɒnsail], *vt.* reconciliar; ajustar, conciliar.—**reconciliation** [rekɒnsiliéiʂɒn], *s.* reconciliación, ajuste; conformidad.

recondition [rikɒndíʂɒn], *vt.* (mec.) reacondicionar; restaurar, reparar.

reconnaissance [rɪkánɪsans], *s.* reconocimiento.—**reconnoiter** [rɪkɒnɔ́itœ(r)], *vt.* reconocer, explorar, inspeccionar.—*vi.* practicar un reconocimiento.

record [rɪkɔ́rd], *vt.* registrar, inscribir; protocolizar (documentos); archivar; grabar (un disco, etc.).—*recorded music*, música en discos.—*s.* [rékɒrd], registro; partida, inscripción, anotación; acta; documento; crónica, historia; hoja de servicios, antecedentes de una persona; disco fonográfico; (for.) memorial, informe; testimonio; memoria; (dep.) marca. —*pl.* archivo, protocolo; actas, autos; memorias, datos.—*r. que consta (en el expediente, la escritura, etc.). —*off the r.*, confidencialmente, extraoficialmente.—*on r.*, registrado; de que hay o queda constancia.— —**er** [rɪkɔ́rdœ(r)], *s.* registrador, archivero; dulzaina, caramillo.—*r. of deeds*, registrador de la propiedad.—*tape r.*, grabadora de cinta magnetofónica.

recount [rɪkáunt], *vt.* contar, referir, relatar; [rikáunt], recontar, hacer un recuento.—*s.* [ríkáunt], recuento.

recoup [rɪkúp], *vt.* resarcir, recobrar; indemnizar; desquitarse de.

recourse [ríkors], *s.* recurso, remedio, auxilio, refugio; (for.) recurso.—*to have r. to*, recurrir a, apelar a, valerse de.—*without r.*, (com.) sin responsabilidad (de parte del endosante).

recover [rɪkávœ(r)], *vt.* recobrar, recuperar.—*vi.* recobrar la salud; reponerse, restablecerse.— —**y** [-i], *s.* recobro, recuperación; cobranza; restablecimiento; mejoría, convalecencia.

recreate [rékrieit], *vt.* y *vi.* recrear(se), divertir(se).—**recreation** [rekriéiʂɒn], *s.* recreación, recreo; diversión; esparcimiento.

recruit [rįkrút], *vt.* y *vi.* (mil.) alistar, reclutar.——*s.* (mil.) recluta; novicio, novato.——**ing** [-į̇n], *s.* reclutamiento.

rectangle [réktæŋgl], *s.* rectángulo.—**rectangular** [rektǽŋgyųlǎ(r)], *a.* rectangular.

rectification [rektįfįkéįṣọn], *s.* rectificación.—**rectify** [réktįfaį], *vti.* [7] rectificar.

rector [réktǫ(r)], *s.* rector (de universidad, orden religiosa); cura párroco.—**y** [-į], *s.* casa del párroco.

rectum [réktʌm], *s.* (anat.) recto.

recuperate [rįkjúpẹreįt], *vt.* recuperar, recobrar.—*vi.* recuperar la salud, reponerse.—**recuperation** [rįkjupẹréįṣọn], *s.* recuperación.

recur [rįkẹ́r], *vii.* [1] repetirse, volver a ocurrir; (med.) recaer.

red [red], *a.* rojo, encarnado, colorado; rojo (comunista).—*r. ball*, mingo (en el billar).—*r. (blood) cell*, hematíe, glóbulo rojo.—*r.-handed*, con las manos en la masa; en flagrante.—*r.-hot*, candente, enrojecido al fuego; acérrimo; muy entusiasta o enardecido; reciente (informe, noticia, etc.).—*r. tape*, expedienteo, burocratismo; formulismo dilatorio.—*r. wine*, vino tinto.—*s.* color rojo; (pol.) rojo, comunista.—*to see r.*, (fam.) enfurecerse.—**den** [rédn], *vt.* teñir de rojo.—*vi.* ponerse colorado; ruborizarse.—**dish** [-įṣ], *a.* rojizo.

redeem [rįdím], *vt.* redimir; desempeñar (un objeto); rescatar; cumplir (lo prometido).—**er** [-œ(r)], *s.* redentor.—*the R.*, el Redentor, el Salvador.—**redemption** [rįdémpṣọn], *s.* redención; rescate; desempeño; amortización de una deuda.

redness [rédnįs], *s.* rojez.

redouble [rįdʌ́bl], *vt.* redoblar; repetir.—*vi.* redoblarse.

redoubt [rįdáut], *s.* (fort.) reducto.

redound [rįdáund], *vi.* redundar (en), resultar (en), contribuir (a).

redraft [rídræft], *s.* nuevo dibujo, copia o borrador; (com.) resaca.—*vt.* [rįdrǽft], redactar, dibujar de nuevo.

redress [rįdrés], *vt.* enderezar; reparar, resarcir; remediar, compensar, desagraviar; hacer justicia.—*s.* [rídres], reparación, satisfacción, desagravio; remedio; compensación.

reduce [rįdjús], *vt.* someter.—*vt.* y *vi.* reducir(se); disminuir, aminorar, rebajar; mermar.—*vi.* adelgazar.—**reduction** [rįdʌ́kṣọn], *s.* reducción; rebaja, disminución.

redundance [rįdʌ́ndạns], *s.* redundancia.—**redundant** [rįdʌ́ndạnt], *a.* redundante.

redwood [rédwụd], *s.* secoya, pino gigantesco de California (árbol y madera).

reed [rid], *s.* caña, junquillo, (Am.) bejuco; (mús.) lengüeta; caramillo; cualquier instrumento de boquilla.

reef [rif], *s.* arrécife, escollo.

reek [rik], *vi.* (gen. con **of** o **with**) humear, exhalar, oler a; oler mal.—*s.* tufo; vaho; hedor.

reel [ril], *s.* carrete; carretel; broca; canilla; devanadera; rollo de cinta cinematográfica.—*vt.* aspar, enrollar, devanar.—*vi.* hacer eses, tambalear, bambolear.

reëlect [rįẹlékt], *vt.* reelegir.—**ion** [rįẹlékṣọn], *s.* reelección.

reëstablish [rięstǽblįṣ], *vt.* restablecer, instaurar.

refer [rįfẹ́r], *vti.* [1] referir, remitir; trasladar.—*vii.* referirse, remitirse, aludir; acudir; dar referencias.—*referred to*, mencionado; a que se hace referencia, a que uno se refiere.—**ee** [refẹrí], *s.* árbitro; juez de campo.—*vt.* y *vi.* arbitrar; servir de árbitro.—**ence** [réfẹrẹns], *s.* referencia; recomendación; alusión, mención; persona que sirve como referencia o fiador.—*in* o *with r. to*, respecto de, en cuanto a.—*a.* de referencias; de consulta (libro, etc.).—**endum** [refẹréndʌm], *s.* plebiscito, referendum.

refill [rifíl], *vt.* llenar de nuevo, rellenar, reenvasar; recambiar.—*s.* [rífįl], recambio, repuesto.

refine [rįfáįn], *vt.* y *vi.* refinar(se), purificar(se); perfeccionar(se).—**d** [-d], *a.* refino, refinado; fino, cortés.—**ment** [-mẹnt], *s.* refinamiento, cortesía; purificación, refinación.—**ry** [rįfáįnœrį], *s.* refinería.—**refining** [rįfáįnįŋ], *s.* refinación, depuración.

reflect [rįflékt], *vt.* reflejar; reflexionar.—*vi.* reflexionar, meditar; reflejar; *to r. on* o *upon*, desprestigiar; desdecir de.—**ion** [rįflékṣọn], *s.* reflexión; reflejo; reproche, tacha.—*on* o *upon r.*, después de pensarlo; bien pensado.—**or** [rįfléktǫ(r)], *s.* reflector.—

reflex [rífleks], *a.* reflejo.—*s.* acción refleja; reflejo, reverberación.—**reflexive** [rįfléksįv], *a.* (gram.) reflexivo, reflejo.

reform [rįfórm], *vt.* y *vi.* reformar(se), corregir(se), enmendar(se).—*s.* reforma, enmienda.—*r. school*, reformatorio para jóvenes.—**ation** [reforméįṣọn], *s.* reforma; (R. hist.) Reforma.—**er** [rįfórmœ(r)], *s.* reformador, reformista.

refrain [rįfréįn], *vi.* refrenarse, abstenerse de, contenerse.—*s.* (poét.) estribillo; (fam.) cantinela.

refresh [rịfréš], *vt.* refrescar, renovar; aliviar.—*vr.* refrescarse.— —ing [-ịŋ], *a.* refrescante; alentador, placentero.— —ment [-mẹnt], *s.* refrigerio, tentempié; refresco.

refrigerate [ɪịfrịdʒẹreịt], *vt.* refrigerar, enfriar.—**refrigeration** [rịfrịdʒẹréịšọn], *s.* refrigeración, enfriamiento.— **refrigerator** [rịfrịdʒẹreịtọ(r)], *s.* refrigerador, nevera; frigorífico; refrigerante.

refuel [rịfiúẹl], *vt.* y *vi.* reabastecer(se) de combustible.

refuge [réfiudʒ], *s.* refugio, amparo, asilo.— —e [refiudʒí], *s.* refugiado; asilado.

refund [rifʌnd], *s.* reembolso, restitución.—*vt.* [rịfʌnd], restituir, reintegrar, reembolsar; amortizar; consolidar una deuda.— —able [rịfʌndạbl], *a.* reembolsable.

refusal [rịfiúzạl], *s.* negativa, denegación; desaire; opción, exclusiva.— **refuse** [rịfiúz], *vt.* y *vi.* rehusar; rechazar; desechar; denegar; negarse a.—*s.* [réfius], desecho, basura, desperdicio; sobra.—*r. dump*, escombrera.—*a.* desechado, de desecho.

refute [rịfiút], *vt.* refutar, rebatir.

regain [rịgéịn], *vt.* recobrar, recuperar.

regal [rígạl], *a.* real, regio.

regale [rịgéịl], *vt.* regalar, agasajar, festejar; recrear, deleitar.—*vi.* regalarse.

regalia [rịgéịliạ], *s. pl.* regalía; insignias, distintivos; galas.—*in full r.*, (fig.) de punta en blanco; de gran gala.

regard [rịgárd], *vt.* observar, mirar; considerar, reputar, juzgar; tocar a, referirse a, concernir, relacionarse con.—*as regards*, tocante a, en cuanto a, por (o en) lo que respecta a.—*s.* miramiento, consideración; estimación, respeto; relación; mirada.—*pl.* memorias, afectos, recuerdos.—*in o with r. to*, (con) respecto a o de, tocante a.—*in this r.*, a este respecto.—*with (best, kind) regards*, con los mejores afectos; con saludos cariñosos.—*without (any) r. to*, sin miramientos por, sin hacer caso de.— —ing [-ịŋ], *prep.* en cuanto a, respecto de.— —less [-lịs], *a.* descuidado, desatento.—*r. of*, sin hacer caso de, haciendo caso omiso de; a pesar de.

regatta [rịgǽtạ], *s.* regata.

regency [rídʒẹnsị], *s.* regencia.

regent [rídʒẹnt], *a.* y *s.* regente.

regime [reịžím], *s.* régimen, gobierno, administración.

regimen [rédʒịmẹn], *s.* (med., gram.) régimen.

regiment [rédʒịmẹnt], *s.* regimiento.

region [rídʒọn], *s.* región.—*in the r. of*,

en las cercanías de.— —al [-ạl], *a.* regional.

register [rédʒịstœ(r)], *s.* registro, inscripción, matrícula; lista, archivo, protocolo; padrón, nómina; registrador; indicador, contador; (mús.) registro (de la voz y del órgano).— *vt.* registrar, inscribir, matricular; protocolar; marcar (según escala o graduación); certificar (una carta).— *vi.* inscribirse; matricularse.—**registrar** [rédʒịstrar], *s.* registrador, archivero.—**registration** [redʒịstréịšọn], *s.* asiento, registro; inscripción; matrícula.

regret [rịgrét], *s.* pena, pesar, sentimiento; remordimiento.—*pl.* excusa (que se envía para rehusar una invitación).—*vt.* [1] sentir, deplorar, lamentar.— —table [-ạbl], *a.* lamentable, sensible.

regular [régiụlạ(r)], *a.* regular, ordinario, normal, corriente; ordenado, metódico.—*s.* (mil.) soldado de línea; obrero permanente.— —ity [regiụlǽrịtị], *s.* regularidad.—**regulate** [régiụleịt], *vt.* regular(izar), reglamentar.—**regulation** [regiụléịšọn], *s.* regulación; orden, regla.—*pl.* reglamento.—*a.* reglamentario, de reglamento.—**regulator** [régiụleịtọ(r)], *s.* regulador (de una máquina, turbina, etc.); registro (de reloj).

rehearsal [rịhœ́rsạl], *s.* (teat.) ensayo. —**rehearse** [rịhœ́rs], *vt.* y *vi.* (teat.) ensayar; repasar; repetir.

reheat [rịhít], *vt.* recalentar; calentar de nuevo.

reign [reịn], *vi.* reinar; prevalecer, imperar, predominar.—*s.* reinado.— —ing [réịnịŋ], *a.* reinante, imperante.

reimburse [rịịmbœ́rs], *vt.* reembolsar, reintegrar.— —ment [-mẹnt], *s.* reembolso, reintegro.

rein [reịn], *s.* rienda; brida; (fig.) dirección; sujeción, freno.—*to give r. to*, dar rienda suelta a.—*vt.* gobernar, refrenar (un caballo); llevar las riendas de.

reindeer [réịndịr], *s.* reno.

reinforce [rịịnfórs], *vt.* reforzar, fortalecer.—*reinforced concrete*, hormigón armado.— —ment [-mẹnt], *s.* refuerzo.

reinsurance [rịịnšúrạns], *s.* reaseguro.— **reinsure** [rịịnšúr], *vt.* reasegurar.

reissue [rịíšu], *s.* reimpresión; nueva edición o emisión.—*vt.* volver a publicar o emitir.

reiterate [rịịtẹreịt], *vt.* reiterar.— **reiteration** [rịịtẹréịšọn], *s.* reiteración, repetición.

reject [rịdʒékt], *vt.* rechazar, rehusar; repeler; arrojar; desechar; descartar.— —ion [rịdʒékšọn], *s.* rechazo, desecho, exclusión, repudio.

rejoice [rịdʒóịs], vt. y vi. regocijar(se), alegrar(se).—**rejoicing** [rịdʒóịsịŋ], s. regocijo, júbilo.

rejoin [rịdʒóịn], vt. reunir con, volver a la compañia de.—vi. [rịdʒóịn], replicar.—**der** [rịdʒóịndœ(r)], s. respuesta, réplica.

relapse [rịlǽps], vi. recaer; reincidir (en un error, etc.).—s. recaída; reincidencia.

relate [rịléịt], vt. relatar, contar, narrar; relacionar; emparentar.—**d** [rịléịtịd], a. relacionado; afín; emparentado, allegado.—**relation** [rịléịʃǫn], s. relación; relato, narración; parentesco; pariente.—pl. parentela, parientes; tratos, comunicaciones.—in r. to, con relación a, con respecto a.—**relationship** [rịléịʃǫnʃịp], s. relación; parentesco.—**relative** [rélạtịv], a. relativo.—s. pariente, deudo, allegado; (gram.) relativo, pronombre relativo.

relax [rịlǽks], vt. relajar, aflojar; mitigar; causar languidez.—vi. aflojar, ceder; descansar, esparcirse.—**ation** [-éịʃǫn], s. aflojamiento, flojedad; descanso, reposo; solaz, recreo, distracción, esparcimiento; mitigación; relajación, relajamiento de nervios, músculos, etc.

relay [rịleị], s. relevo; (elec.) relevador.—r. race, (dep.) carrera de relevos o de equipos.—vt. retransmitir (un mensaje, etc.).

release [rịlís], vt. soltar; poner en libertad; relevar; renunciar a o abandonar; aliviar; poner en circulación.—s. liberación; exoneración; alivio; (m.v.) escape.

relegate [rélẹgeịt], vt. relegar.—**relegation** [relẹgéịʃǫn], s. relegación.

relent [rịlént], vi. aplacarse; ceder; ablandarse, enternecerse.—**less** [-lịs], a. implacable, inexorable.—**lessness** [-lịsnịs], s. inexorabilidad.

relevance [rélẹvạns], **relevancy** [rélẹvạnsị], s. pertinencia.—**relevant** [rélẹvạnt], a. pertinente, a propósito, apropiado; que hace o viene al caso.

reliability [rịlájạbịlịt], **reliableness** [rịlájạblnịs], s. confiabilidad; calidad de seguro o digno de confianza; formalidad; precisión; veracidad.—**reliable** [rịlájạbl], a. seguro, digno de confianza, confiable, fidedigno, formal.—**reliance** [rịlájạns], s. confianza, seguridad.—**reliant** [rịlájạnt], a. confiado (en sí mismo).

relic [rélịk], s. reliquia, vestigio.

relief [rịlíf], s. ayuda, auxilio; subsidio de paro forzoso; auxilio social; consuelo; socorro, limosna; descanso; (mil.) relevo; (b.a.) relieve, realce.—r. agencies, agencias de auxilio o de socorro.—r. valve, válvula de seguridad.—to be on r., recibir auxilio social.—**relieve** [rịlív], vt. relevar, socorrer, aliviar; mitigar; realzar, hacer resaltar; (mil.) relevar.

religion [rịlídʒǫn], s. religión.—**religious** [rịlídʒʌs], a. y s. religioso.—**religiousness** [rịlídʒʌsnịs], s. religiosidad.

relinquish [rịlíŋkwịʃ], vt. abandonar, dejar, ceder.—**ment** [-mạnt], s. abandono, dejación, renuncia.

reliquary [rélịkwerị], s. relicario.

relish [rélịʃ], s. buen gusto, sabor grato, dejo; sazón, condimento; entremés; goce, saboreo.—vt. saborear, paladear; gustar de; sazonar, condimentar.—vi. saber bien, ser sabroso; gustar.

reload [rịlóụd], vt. recargar; cargar de nuevo.

reluctance [rịlʌ́ktạns], s. repugnancia, renuencia, aversión, desgana, disgusto.—with r., de mala gana.—**reluctant** [rịlʌ́ktạnt], a. renuente, maldispuesto.—**reluctantly** [rịlʌ́ktạntlị], adv. de mala gana, a regañadientes.

rely [rịláị], vii. [7] (con on o upon) confiar o fiar en, fiarse de, contar con.

remade [rịméịd], pret. y pp. de TO REMAKE.

remain [rịméịn], vi. quedar(se), restar o faltar; sobrar; estarse, permanecer; continuar.—**der** [-dœ(r)], s. resto, restante, residuo, sobra(nte).—**s** [-z], s. pl. restos, sobras, despojos; reliquias; ruinas.

remake [rịméịk], vti. [10] rehacer.

remark [rịmárk], s. observación, advertencia, nota.—vt. hacer una observación, observar, notar, reparar.—**able** [-ạbl], a. notable, extraordinario, admirable, señalado.

remedy [rémẹdị], s. remedio, medicamento; cura.—vti. [7] curar, remediar.

remember [rịmémbœ(r)], vt. recordar, acordarse de.—vi. acordarse, hacer memoria.—**remembrance** [rịmémbrạns], s. memoria; recordación; recuerdo.

remind [rịmáịnd], vt. recordar.—**er** [-œ(r)], s. recordatorio; advertencia.

reminiscence [remịnísẹns], s. reminiscencia.—pl. memorias.—**reminiscent** [remịnísẹnt], a. evocador, rememorativo.

remiss [rịmís], a. remiso, descuidado.—**ion** [rịmíʃǫn], s. remisión, perdón; (com.) remesa.—**remit** [rịmít], vti. [1] (com.) remesar; remitir; perdonar, condonar; eximir; relajar.—vii. (com.) hacer remesas; girar.—**remittance** [rịmítạns], s. remesa, envío, giro.

remnant [rémnạnt], s. remanente, resto,

residuo; vestigio; **retazo.**—*r. sale,* saldo, baratillo.

remodel [rimádęl], *vt.* [2] modelar de nuevo; rehacer, reconstruir; renovar.

remora [rémŏrą̃], *s.* (ict.) rémora.

remorse [rįmórs], *s.* remordimiento, cargo de conciencia.— **—ful** [-fų̃l], *a.* arrepentido, con remordimientos.— **—less** [-lįs], *a.* sin remordimientos, cruel, despiadado.

remote [rįmóųt], *a.* remoto, apartado, lejano, distante.— **—ness** [-nįs], *s.* lejanía, gran distancia.

removable [rįmúvąbl], *a.* separable; amovible; de quita y pon.—**removal** [rįmúvąl], *s.* acción de quitar o levantar; remoción; deposición; eliminación; alejamiento; traslado, mudanza, cambio de domicilio.—**remove** [rįmúv], *vt.* remover; quitar; eliminar; alejar, mudar, cambiar, trasladar; destituir, deponer; apartar; sacar, extirpar.—*vi.* mudarse, trasladarse, alejarse; cambiar de sitio o domicilio.—**removed** [rįmúvd], *a.* apartado, alejado, distante; destituído.—**remover** [rįmúvœ(r)], *s.* removedor.

remunerate [rįmiúnęrẹit], *vt.* remunerar.—**remuneration** [rįmįunęréįṣǫn], *s.* remuneración.

renaissance [renęsáns], **renascence** [rįnǽsęns], *s.* renacimiento; (R.) Renacimiento.

rend [rend], *vti.* y *vii.* [10] rasgar(se), desgarrar(se); rajar(se).

render [réndœ(r)], *vt.* hacer; dar, prestar, rendir; (mus., teat.) interpretar, ejecutar; traducir; derretir; (com.) enviar, girar (una cuenta).—*to r. assistance,* prestar auxilio, auxiliar.— **—ing** [-įŋ], *s.* traducción; interpretación.—**rendition** [rendíṣǫn], *s.* versión o traducción; (mus., teat.) interpretación, ejecución; rendición, entrega.

renegade [rénįgẹid], *s.* renegado, desertor; apóstata.—*a.* renegado, falso, traidor.

renew [rįniú], *vt.* renovar; restaurar; reanudar; (com.) extender, prorrogar.— **—al** [-ąl], *s.* renovación; reanudación; (com.) prórroga.

renounce [rįnáųns], *vt.* renunciar.— **—ment** [-męnt], *s.* renuncia, renunciamiento.

renovate [rénovẹit], *vt.* renovar.

renown [rįnáųn], *s.* renombre.

rent [rent], *vt.* alquilar, arrendar, dar o tomar en arrendamiento.—*s.* renta, alquiler; arrendamiento; rasgadura; raja, grieta.—*for r.,* se alquila o arrienda.—*pret.* y *pp.* de TO REND.—

—al [réntąl], *s.* renta; arrendamiento, alquiler.

reopen [rióų̃pn], *vt.* y *vi.* reabrir(se), volver a abrir(se); reanudar (una discusión, etc.).— **—ing** [-įŋ], *s.* reapertura.

reorganization [riorgąnįzéįṣǫn], *s.* reorganización.—**reorganize** [riórgąnạiz], *vt.* reorganizar.

repaid [rįpéįd], *pret.* y *pp.* de TO REPAY.

repair [rįpér], *vt.* reparar, restaurar, componer; remendar.—*s.* reparo, reparación, restauración; compostura, remiendo.—*out of r.,* descompuesto, en mal estado.—**reparation** [repąréįṣǫn], *s.* reparación; satisfacción, desagravio.

repatriate [rípéįtrẹit], *vt.* repatriar.

repay [rįpéį], *vti.* [10] pagar, reembolsar; reintegrar; pagar en la misma moneda.— **—ment** [-męnt], *s.* pago, devolución, retorno.

repeal [rįpíl], *vt.* derogar, revocar, abrogar, abolir.—*s.* revocación, derogación, abrogación.

repeat [rįpít], *vt.* repetir.—*s.* repetición. — **—edly** [-įdlį], *adv.* repetidamente, repetidas veces, a menudo.

repel [rįpél], *vti.* [1] repeler, rechazar.— *vii.* ser repelente o repulsivo.— **—lent** [-ęnt], *a.* repelente.

repent [rįpént], *vt.* y *vi.* arrepentirse (de).— **—ance** [-ąns], *s.* arrepentimiento.— **—ant** [-ąnt], *a.* arrepentido, contrito.

repertory [répœrtorį], *s.* repertorio; depósito, colección; inventario, lista; almacén.

repetition [repįtíṣǫn], *s.* repetición.

replace [rįpléįs], *vt.* reemplazar; suplir; reponer.— **—able** [-ąbl], *a.* reemplazable; renovable.— **—ment** [-męnt], *s.* reemplazo, sustitución; reemplazante; pieza de repuesto; restitución, reposición.

replenish [rįplénįṣ], *vt.* rellenar; llenar o surtir nuevamente.—**replete** [rįplít], *a.* repleto; ahíto.

replica [réplįką̃], *s.* (b.a.) réplica; copia, reproducción; (mus.) repetición.

reply [rįpláį], *s.* respuesta; réplica.— *vti.* y *vii.* [7] contestar, responder; replicar.

report [rįpórt], *vt.* informar acerca de, dar parte de; denunciar; comunicar; relatar; redactar un informe o dictamen; reseñar.—*it is reported,* corre la voz, se dice.—*vi.* presentar informe o dictamen; servir como reportero; comparecer, personarse.—*s.* relato, parte, noticia; comunicado; reseña; informe, dictamen; voz, rumor; reportaje; detonación.—*by r.,* según se dice.— **—er** [-œ(r)], *s.* repórter, reportero; noticiero; relator.

repose [ripóṳz], *vt.* descansar, reclinar; poner (confianza o esperanza).—*vi.* reposar, descansar; tener confianza en.—*vr.* tenderse, reclinarse, recostarse.—*s.* reposo, descanso; tranquilidad, quietud.

repository [ripáziṭori], *s.* depósito, almacén, repositorio.

represent [reprizént], *vt.* representar; significar, exponer; [riprizént], presentar de nuevo.— —**ation** [reprizentéiṣọn], *s.* representación.— —**ative** [reprizéntaṭiv], *a.* representativo, típico; representante.—*s.* representante; símbolo, tipo, ejemplar; (R.) diputado, representante.

repress [riprés], *vt.* reprimir, contener.— —**ion** [ripréṣọn], *s.* represión.

reprieve [riprív], *vt.* aplazar la ejecución de; suspender; aliviar (un dolor). —*s.* aplazamiento de ejecución de sentencia; tregua; suspensión; alivio.

reprimand [réprimænd], *vt.* reprender, reconvenir, (fam.) sermonear.—*s.* reprimenda, regaño, censura.

reprint [riprínt], *vt.* reimprimir.—*s.* [ríprint], reimpresión; tirada aparte (de un artículo).

reprisal [ripráiẓạl], *s.* represalia.

reproach [ripróuch], *vt.* reprochar, increpar; vituperar, censurar.—*s.* reproche; vituperio; tacha, baldón.— *above r.*, sin tacha.

reprobate [réprọbeịt], *s.* réprobo, malvado.

reproduce [riprodiús], *vt.* reproducir; duplicar, copiar.—**reproduction** [riprọdʎkṣọn], *s.* reproducción; (b.a.) copia.

reproof [riprúf], *s.* reprobación, reproche, reprensión.—**reprove** [riprúv], *vt.* reprobar, culpar, censurar; acusar; condenar.

reptile [répṭil], *s.* y *a.* reptil; (fig.) bajo, rastrero.

republic [ripʎblik], *s.* república.— —**an** [-ạn], *a.* y *s.* republicano.

repudiate [ripiúdieịt], *vt.* repudiar, repeler; rechazar, renunciar; desconocer.

repugnance [ripʎgnạns], *s.* repugnancia; aversión.—**repugnant** [ripʎgnạnt], *a.* repugnante, repulsivo; antipático.

repulse [ripʎls], *s.* repulsa, repulsión; denegación.—*vt.* desechar, rechazar, repeler.—**repulsive** [ripʎlsiv], *a.* repulsivo, repugnante, repelente.

reputable [répʎṭabl], *a.* honroso, honrado, intachable; lícito.—**reputation** [repʎṭéiṣọn], *s.* reputación; crédito, estimación, prestigio.—**repute** [ripiút], *vt.* reputar, juzgar, tener por.—*s.* reputación, fama, crédito.

request [rikwést], *s.* súplica, ruego; petición, instancia, solicitud; (com.) demanda.—*at the r. of*, o *by r.*, a petición, a solicitud o instancia de.— *on r.*, en boga, muy solicitado, pedido o buscado.—*vt.* rogar, suplicar, solicitar.

require [rikwáir], *vt.* requerir, demandar, exigir, necesitar.— —**ment** [-mẹnt], *s.* demanda, requerimiento, exigencia; requisito, necesidad; formalidad; estipulación.—**requisite** [rékwizit], *a.* necesario, forzoso, indispensable.—*s.* requisito.—**requisition** [rekwizíṣọn], *s.* pedimento, petición, demanda; (mil.) requisa; necesidad, requisito, menester; (com.) demanda, solicitud; (for.) requisitoria.—*vt.* (mil.) requisar.

resale [ríseịl], *s.* reventa.

rescind [risínd], *vt.* rescindir, anular, abrogar.

rescue [réskiu], *vt.* rescatar, redimir; salvar, librar.—*s.* rescate, redención, salvación, libramiento, recobro; socorro.— —**r** [-œ(r)], *s.* salvador, libertador.

research [risœrch], *s.* investigación; búsqueda.—*vt.* investigar.

resell [risél], *vti.* y *vii.* [10] revender.

resemblance [rizémblạns], *s.* parecido, semejanza.—**resemble** [rizémbl], *vt.* (a)semejarse a, parecerse a; salir (uno) a (su padre, etc.).

resent [rizént], *vt.* (re)sentirse de, llevar a mal, ofenderse por.— —**ful** [-fʎl], *a.* resentido, ofendido.— —**ment** [-mẹnt], *s.* resentimiento, pique, enojo.

reservation [rezœrvéiṣọn], *s.* reservación; reserva, excepción, restricción (mental); pasaje (sitio, alojamiento, etc.) reservados de antemano.—**reserve** [rizœrv], *vt.* reservar, guardar, retener, conservar; exceptuar, excluir.—*s.* reserva.—**reservoir** [rézœrvwar], *s.* depósito; receptáculo; cubeta; (com.) surtido de reserva; alberca; cisterna, aljibe; depósito (de gas, petróleo, etc.).

reset [risét], *vti.* [9] montar de nuevo.— *pret.* y *pp.* de TO RESET.

reside [rizáid], *vi.* residir, vivir, habitar. — —**nce** [rézidẹns], *s.* residencia, domicilio; casa; estancia, mansión; quedada, permanencia.— —**nt** [rézidẹnt], *a.* residente.—*s.* habitante, vecino; (dipl.) ministro residente.

residual [rizídẓụạl], *a.* restante, remanente.—**residue** [rézidiu], *s.* residuo, resto, sobrante, remanente.

resign [rizáin], *vt.* dimitir, renunciar.— *vi.* presentar la dimisión.—*vr.* resignarse, rendirse, someterse, conformarse.— —**ation** [rezignéiṣọn], *s.*

dimisión, renuncia, dejación; resignación, conformidad.

resilience [rizíljęns], *s.* elasticidad, resorte, rebote; capacidad de recobrar la figura y el tamaño original después de deformación.—resilient [rizíljęnt], *a.* elástico; (fig.) alegre, animado.

resin [rézin], *s.* resina.

resist [rizíst], *vt.* y *vi.* resistir, rechazar; oponerse; impedir, negarse a; aguantar, soportar, hacer frente a.—**-ance** [-ans], *s.* resistencia; defensa, oposición, fuerza contraria; aguante.—**-ant** [-ant], *a.* resistente.

resold [risóuld], *pret.* y *pp.* de TO RESELL.

resole [risóul], *vt.* remontar (zapatos).

resolute [rézoljut], *a.* resuelto, determinado, firme, denodado.—**resolution** [rezoljúšǫn], *s.* resolución; determinación; propósito; acuerdo (de una junta o asamblea); disolución de un todo.—**resolve** [rizálv], *vt.* y *vi.* resolver(se); tomar acuerdo, determinar, decidir(se), solucionar; descomponer (una fuerza, etc.); disipar, desvanecer; (con into) transformarse en o reducirse a.—*s.* resolución, determinación, propósito, acuerdo.

resonance [rézǫnans], *s.* resonancia.—**resonant** [rézǫnant], *a.* resonante, retumbante; sonoro.

resort [rizórt], *vi.* (con to) acudir, recurrir, frecuentar; pasar a, recorrer a, hacer uso de, echar mano de.—*s.* concurso, concurrencia; punto de reunión; recurso, medio, expediente; lugar de temporada o muy frecuentado.

resound [rizáund], *vt.* repetir, repercutir el sonido; cantar, celebrar.—*vi.* resonar, retumbar; formar eco; tener resonancia; tener fama, ser celebrado.

resource [risórs], *s.* recurso, medio, expediente.—*pl.* fondos, recursos, riquezas, recursos naturales.—**-ful** [-ful], *a.* listo, ingenioso, dotado de inventiva.—**-fulness** [-fulnis], *s.* inventiva, iniciativa.

respect [rispékt], *vt.* respetar, venerar, estimar; acatar, observar, guardar; corresponder, tocar, concernir, atenerse a.—*s.* respeto, estimación; reverencia, veneración, culto; acatamiento, miramiento; honra, homenaje; respecto, asunto.—*pl.* memorias, recuerdos, respetos.—*in other respects*, por lo demás.—*in r. that*, puesto que.—*in some r.*, de algún modo, hasta cierto punto.—*out of r. for* o to, en obsequio de, por consideración a.—**-ability** [rispektǫbíliti], *s.* respectabilidad.—**-able** [rispéktǫbl], *a.* respetable, formal; estimable,

honroso; acreditado, autorizado; bastante bueno; considerable.—**-ful** [-ful], *a.* respetuoso.—**-ing** [-iŋ], *prep.* con respecto a, en cuanto a, por lo que toca a, (en lo) tocante a.—**-ive** [-iv], *a.* respectivo; particular, individual; sendos.

respiration [respiréišǫn], *s.* respiración, respiro.—**respire** [rispáir], *vt.* y *vi.* resollar, respirar; espirar, exhalar.

respite [réspit], *s.* tregua, espera, pausa; plazo, prórroga, respiro.

respond [rispánd], *vi.* responder, contestar; reaccionar; corresponder; obedecer, acudir; venir bien, ajustarse.—**response** [rispáns], *s.* respuesta, contestación.—**responsibility** [rispansibíliti], *s.* responsabilidad; obligación, deber; solvencia.—**responsible** [rispánsibl], *a.* responsable; solvente; autorizado; de responsabilidad.—*r. for*, responsable de; causa de; autor de; origen de.

responsory [rispánsǫri], *s.* (igl.) responso.

rest [rest], *s.* descanso, reposo; tregua, pausa; paz, quietud; apoyo, base; resto, residuo, sobra; (poét.) cesura; (con the) los demás, los otros; el resto.—*at r.*, en paz (apl. a los muertos).—*vi.* descansar, reposar; yacer, reposar en el seno de la muerte; cesar, parar; estar en paz, vivir tranquilo; posarse o asentarse; apoyarse (en), cargar (sobre); confiar (en), contar (con); depender (de); permanecer.—*to r. assured*, perder cuidado.—*vt.* y *vi.* descansar, proporcionar descanso; apoyar o asentar; (for.) terminar la presentación de pruebas.

restaurant [réstǫrant], *s.* restaurante, fonda.

restful [réstful], *a.* reposado, quieto, tranquilo.

restitution [restitjúšǫn], *s.* restitución, restablecimiento; devolución, reintegración; reparación, indemnización; recuperación, recobro; (fís.) elasticidad.

restless [réstlis], *a.* inquieto, impaciente; bullicioso, levantisco; insomne.—**-ness** [-nis], *s.* inquietud, impaciencia, desasosiego; insomnio.

restoration [restoréišǫn], *s.* restauración; reintegración, instauración, rehabilitación; restablecimiento.—**restore** [ristór], *vt.* restaurar, reconstruir; reintegrar, restablecer, instaurar; restituir, reponer.

restrain [ristréin], *vt.* refrenar, reprimir, cohibir; represar; moderar, limitar, coartar; (for.) prohibir o vedar a.—**-t** [-t], *s.* moderación; sujeción; restricción; coerción, prohibición.—

restrict [ristríkt], *vt.* restringir, coartar.—**restriction** [ristríkṣǫn], *s.* restricción, limitación, coartación.

result [rizÁlt], *vi.* resultar; inferirse; (con in) dar por resultado, venir a parar, acabar en, conducir a; causar. —*s.* resultado; conclusión, deducción.

resume [rizjúm], *vt.* reasumir; reanudar; recuperar; resumir, compendiar.—*vi.* tomar el hilo; empezar de nuevo.— **résumé** [rezƱméi], *s.* resumen, sumario.—**resumption** [rizÁmpṣǫn], *s.* reanudación; recobro.

resurrect [rezarÉkt], *vi.* resucitar, volver a la vida.—**resurrection** [rezaRÉkṣǫn], *s.* resurrección; renovación, restablecimiento.

resuscitate [risÁsiteit], *vt.* y *vi.* resucitar, reanimar, (hacer) revivir.

retail [ríteil], *vt.* vender al menudeo; detallar.—*s.* menudeo, venta (al) por menor; detalle.—*adv.* al por menor.— **er** [-œ(r)], *s.* comerciante al por menor, detallista, (Am.) minorista, tendero, revendedor.

retain [ritéin], *vt.* retener, guardar, conservar; represar, detener, contener; contratar.— **er** [-œ(r)], *s.* partidario; criado, dependiente; (for.) anticipo.

retake [ritéik], *vti.* [10] volver a tomar; reasumir, recoger; (fot. y cine) volver a fotografiar o filmar.—**retaken** [ritéik], *pp.* de TO RETAKE.

retaliate [ritǽlieit], *vi.* desquitarse, vengarse; tomar represalias.—**retaliation** [ritæliéiṣǫn], *s.* talión, desquite; represalia; desagravio; pago, retorno.

retard [ritárd], *vt.* retardar, retrasar, demorar; aplazar, diferir, dilatar.—*s.* retraso, atraso, dilación, demora.

reticence [rétisens], *s.* reticencia, reserva.—**reticent** [rétisent], *a.* reticente.

retina [rétinə], *s.* retina.

retinue [rétinju], *s.* tren, comitiva, séquito.

retiral [ritáirəl], *s.* retiro, retirada; (com.) recogida.—**retire** [ritáir], *vi.* retirarse, irse a acostar; retirarse de la vida activa, de un empleo, etc.; jubilarse; retraerse, retroceder, recogerse, apartarse, separarse.—*vt.* (com.) recoger, retirar de la circulación; jubilar.—**retirement** [ritáirment], *s.* retiro; retraimiento; recogida, recogimiento; lugar retirado; jubilación.

retook [ritúk], *pret.* de TO RETAKE.

retort [ritórt], *vt.* redargüir; devolver (un insulto); replicar.—*s.* réplica mordaz; retorta.

retouch [ritÁch], *vt.* retocar.—*s.* retoque.

retrace [ritréis], *vt.* desandar, volver atrás; buscar el origen de; repasar; volver a trazar.—*to r. one's steps,* volver sobre sus pasos.

retract [ritrǽkt], *vt.* retractar, retirar; retractarse de; retraer, encoger.—*vi.* retractarse, desdecirse; encogerse.

retreat [ritrít], *s.* retiro; soledad, retraimiento; refugio, asilo; (mil.) retirada; retreta.—*vi.* retirarse; retroceder, retraerse, refugiarse; cejar.

retribution [retribjúsǫn], *s.* retribución, pago; justo retorno, pena incurrida.

retrievable [ritrívəbl], *a.* recuperable, reparable.—**retrieve** [ritrív], *vt.* recuperar, recobrar; restaurar, remediar; cobrar (la caza).—*vi.* cobrar la caza. —**retriever** [ritrívœ(r)], *s.* perro cobrador, perdiguero.

retroactive [retroÁktiv], *a.* retroactivo.

retrospect [rétrospekt], *s.* mirada retrospectiva.—*in r.,* en retrospectiva.— **ive** [retrospÉktiv], *a.* retrospectivo.

return [ritœrn], *vt.* (de)volver; corresponder a, pagar, dar en cambio, recompensar; dar (gracias, fallo, respuesta, etc.); (pol.) elegir, enviar (al congreso, etc.).—*to r. a call,* pagar una visita.—*to r. a kindness,* corresponder a un favor.—*to r. a verdict,* dictar un fallo, dar un veredicto.—*vi.* volver, regresar; reaparecer; responder, replicar.—*vt.* y *vi.* volver otra vez; dar otra vuelta o doblez.—*s.* vuelta, regreso; correspondencia (a un favor, etc.), pago, recompensa; respuesta; devolución; reaparición; utilidad, rédito; cambio, trueque; informe o parte oficial; curva, vuelta; desviadero; (arq.) ala, vuelta de moldura, marco, etc.; (pol.) elección. —*pl.* resultado, cifras (de elecciones). —*by r. mail,* a vuelta de correo.— *happy returns,* felicidades en su cumpleaños.—*income tax r.,* declaración de ingresos.—*in r.,* en cambio, en pago, en recompensa.—*r. address,* señas del remitente.

reunion [riyúnyǫn], *s.* reunión; reconciliación; tertulia, junta.—**reunite** [riyunáit], *vt.* reunir, juntar; volver a unir; reconciliar.—*vi.* reunirse, reconciliarse.

reveal [rivíl], *vt.* revelar; dar a conocer.— **ing** [-iŋ], *a.* revelador; impúdico, sugestivo (vestido).

reveille [révɛli], *s.* (mil.) toque de diana.

revel [rével], *vii.* [2] jaranear, ir de parranda; gozarse (en).—*s.* algazara, jarana, parranda.

revelation [reveléiṣǫn], *s.* revelación; visión; (R.) Apocalipsis.

revelry [révelri], *s.* jarana, gresca, francachela, orgía, borrachera.

revenge [rivéndʒ], *vt.* y *vi.* vengar(se); desquitarse, satisfacerse o vengarse

de.—*s.* venganza, desquite.— —**ful**
[-fǔl], *a.* vengativo.
revenue [révęnju], *s.* rentas públicas;
(com.) renta; rédito; entrada, ingreso;
beneficio, recompensa.—*r. officer,*
aduanero; agente fiscal o del fisco.—
r. stamp, sello fiscal, sello de impuesto.
revere [rįvír], *vt.* reverenciar, venerar.-
—**nce** [révręns], *s.* reverencia, veneración; reverencia (saludo); (R., igl.)
Reverencia (tratamiento).—*to pay r.,*
rendir homenaje.—*vt.* reverenciar,
venerar.—**nd** [révręnd], *a.* reverendo, venerable; (R., igl.) Reverendo
(tratamiento).—*s.* (fam.) clérigo.-
—**nt** [révręnt], *a.* reverente.
reverie [révęrį], *s.* ensueño; embelesa-
miento, arrobamiento; (mus.) fantasía.
reversal [rįvǿrsạl], *s.* reversión; inversión; (for.) revocación; cambio (de
opinión, etc.).—**reverse** [rįvǿrs], *vt.*
trastocar, invertir; trastornar; (for.)
revocar.—*vi.* volver a un estado
anterior, invertirse.—*a.* reverso, invertido; opuesto, contrario; (mec.) de
inversión o contramarcha.—*s.* lo
contrario, lo opuesto, respaldo, dorso,
reverso; reversión, inversión; contratiempo, revés.—**revert** [rįvǿrt], *vi.*
retroceder, volver, resurtir; (biol.)
saltar atrás; (for.) revertir.—**re-
vertible** [rįvǿrtįbl], *a.* reversible.
review [rįvjú], *vt.* rever, remirar; repasar (estudios, etc.); revisar; censurar;
reseñar, criticar o analizar (un libro,
etc.); (mil.) revistar, pasar revista a.
—*vi.* reseñar, escribir para una
revista.—*s.* repaso; examen, análisis;
reseña; censura, juicio crítico; revista;
(for.) revisión.— —**er** [-œ(r)], *s.*
crítico, revistero (literario, teatral,
etc.).
revise [rįvájz], *vt.* revisar, releer,
repasar; corregir, enmendar.—**revi-
sion** [rįvížǫn], *s.* revisión, repaso;
enmienda; edición revisada.
revival [rįvájvạl], *s.* renacimiento, renovación, reavivamiento; (teat.) reposición o reestreno; despertamiento
religioso.—**revive** [rįvájv], *vt.* hacer
revivir, (re)avivar, resucitar; restablecer, restaurar; despertar; hacer
recordar.—*vi.* revivir; restablecerse,
reanimarse; volver en sí; renacer.
revocable [révǫkạbl], *a.* revocable.—
revoke [rįvóuk], *vt.* revocar, derogar.
—*vi.* (en los naipes) renunciar.
revolt [rįvóult], *vi.* rebelarse, sublevarse; sentir repugnancia o repulsión.
—*vt.* rebelar, sublevar; causar asco o
repulsión; indignar.—*s.* sublevación,
alzamiento, rebelión.— —**ing** [-įŋ], *a.*
odioso, repugnante, asqueroso.
revolution [revǫlúšǫn], *s.* revolución,

revuelta; (mec.) giro.— —**ary** [-erį],
a. y *s.* revolucionario.— —**ist** [-įst], *s.*
revolucionario.
revolve [rįválv], *vi.* girar, dar vueltas,
rodar; moverse en ciclos, suceder
periódicamente.—*vt.* voltear, hacer
girar o rodar; revolver (en la cabeza),
considerar bajo todos los aspectos,-
—**r** [-œ(r)], *s.* revólver (arma).—
revolving [-įŋ], *a.* giratorio.
reward [rįwórd], *vt.* premiar, recompensar.—*s.* recompensa, premio, galardón; hallazgo; merecido; gratificación, remuneración.
rhapsody [rǽpsǫdį], *s* rapsodia.
rhetoric [rétǫrįk], *s.* retórica.— —**al**
[rįtárįkạl], *a.* retórico.
rheumatism [rúmạtįzm], *s.* reumatismo.
rhinoceros [rajnásęrǫs], *s.* rinoceronte.
rhombus [rámbąs], *s.* rombo.
rhubarb [rįúbarb], *s.* ruibarbo.
rhyme [rajm], *s.* rima; verso; poesía.—
without r. or reason, sin ton ni son.—
vt. rimar, versificar; emplear como
consonante.—*vi.* rimar; corresponder,
armonizarse.
rhythm [ríðm], *s.* ritmo; armonía;
(med.) periodicidad.— —**ic(al)**
[ríðmįk(ạl)], *a.* rítmico, cadencioso,
armónico.
rib [rįb], *s.* costilla; (arq.) faja, listón,
nervio, nervadura; viga de tejado;
arco; saliente; varilla (de abanico o
paraguas); tirante; (mec.) pestaña,
reborde; (cost.) vivo; (bot.) nervadura de las hojas; (fam.) costilla,
esposa.—*vti.* [1] marcar con rayas,
listones o filetes; afianzar con re-
bordes o pestañas; (cost.) poner
vivos; (fam.) embromar, burlarse de.
ribbon [ríbǫn], *s.* cinta; tira, banda,
faja; galón.—*vt.* encintar.—*a.* hecho
de cinta; de forma de cinta.
rice [rajs], *s.* arroz.
rich [rįch], *a.* rico; costoso, precioso;
suntuoso, cuantioso; exquisito; vivo
(color, etc.); muy sazonado, dulce,
fuerte, etc.; fértil; (fam.) muy divertido; risible.—*to get r.,* enriquecerse.
—*s. pl.* riqueza(s); bienes; opulencia;
sazón, dulzura, suculencia.
rickety [ríkįtį], *a.* desvencijado, destartalado; (med.) raquítico.
rid [rįd], *vti.* [3] desembarazar, quitar
de encima, zafar.—*to be r. of,* estar
libre o exento de.—*pret. y pp.* de TO
RID.— —**dance** [rídạns], *s.* supresión,
liberación de una pejiguera o peligro.
ridden [rídn], *pp.* de TO RIDE.
riddle [rídl], *s.* acertijo, enigma, adivinanza, rompecabezas; (fam.) busilis,
quisicosa; misterio; criba.—*vt.* resolver, adivinar; acribillar.—*vi.* hablar
enigmáticamente.
ride [rajd], *vti.* [10] cabalgar, montar;

ir montado en o sobre; pasear o recorrer (a caballo, en automóvil, etc.).—*to r. down* u *over*, pasar por encima de, derribar y hollar; pisotear, atropellar; mandar con arrogancia.—*to r. out*, hacer frente a, resistir bien (el viento).—*vii.* cabalgar; pasear (a caballo o en un vehículo); ir en automóvil, coche, etc.; flotar; (mec.) rodar, tener juego, funcionar.—*s.* paseo (a caballo, en auto, etc.).—*r* [rájdœ(r)], *s.* jinete; amazona; persona que va en automóvil, bicicleta, etc.; picador, (Am.) amansador; cosa que va montada sobre otra; pesa corrediza (de una balanza); hojuela pegada a un documento; adición a un proyecto de ley.

ridge [ridž], *vt.* (agr.) formar camellones; acanalar, arrugar.—*vi.* tener camellones.—*s.* cerro, colina, cordillera, serranía; escollo, arrecife; arruga, costurón; camellón; caballete del tejado.—*r. roof*, tejado a dos vertientes o aguas.—*r. tile*, teja acanalada.

ridicule [rídikjul], *s.* ridículo, mofa, rechifla.—*vt.* ridiculizar, mofarse de, rechiflar.—**ridiculous** [ridíkyʊlʌs], *a.* ridículo, risible, grotesco.

riding [rájdiŋ], *s.* equitación.—*r. boots*, botas de montar.

riffraff [ríffræf], *s.* canalla, gentuza.

rifle [ráifl], *s.* rifle, fusil; espiral de rifle; piedra de afilar.—*vt.* robar, arrebatar. —**-man** [-mʌn], *s.* fusilero.

rig [rig], *vti.* [1] equipar, aparejar; enjarciar (un velero).—*to r. oneself up*, ataviarse, emperifollarse.—*s.* equipo, aparejo; traje, atavío; aparato.—**-ging** [rígiŋ], *s.* (mar.) aparejo, cordaje, jarcia; (mec.) aparejo (de poleas); equipo de arrastre (de trozas).

right [rajt], *a.* recto, justo, equitativo; propio, conveniente; correcto, exacto; cierto, real, genuino, legal, legítimo; derecho, directo; ordenado, ajustado; derecho (lado, mano); verdadero; derecho (contrario de revés).—*all r.*, bueno, conforme.—*it is r.*, está bien; es justo.—*r. and left*, a diestra y siniestra.—*r. angle*, ángulo recto. —*r. hand*, diestra; de la mano derecha.—*r.-hand man*, (fam.) hombre de confianza, brazo derecho.—*r. or wrong*, con razón o sin ella; bueno o malo.—*r. side*, lado derecho; lado de afuera, cara; haz (telas, etc.). —*to be r.*, tener razón.—*interj.* ¡bien! ¡bueno!—*adv.* rectamente, justamente; exactamente, perfectamente, precisamente; bien; correctamente, debidamente; derechamente; a la derecha.—*r. about face*, media vuelta.

—*r. now*, ahora mismo.—*r. there*, allí mismo.—*to go r. home*, ir derechito para la casa.—*s.* derecho; justicia; rectitud; propiedad, dominio, título; poder, autoridad; privilegio, prerrogativa; opción; (la) diestra, (la) derecha; (pol.) derecha(s).—*vt.* hacer justicia; enderezar. —*to r. a wrong*, enderezar un entuerto, corregir un abuso.—**-eous** [rájchʌs], *a.* justo, recto, equitativo; virtuoso, honrado, probo.— **-eousness** [rájchʌsnis], *s.* rectitud, virtud, honradez, probidad.—**-ful** [rájtfʊl], *a.* legítimo.— **-ist** [-ist], *s.* y *a.* (pol.) derechista.

rigid [rídžid], *a.* rígido, inflexible, yerto; austero, estricto, riguroso.—**-ity** [ridžíditi], *s.* rigidez.

rigor [rígo(r)], *s.* rigor; inclemencia; severidad, austeridad; tesón, terquedad; exactitud; (med.) escalofrío.—**-ous** [-ʌs], *a.* rigoroso o riguroso; recio (tiempo); estricto, severo.

rill [ril], *s.* riachuelo, arroyuelo.

rim [rim], *s.* canto, borde, margen, orilla; llanta, aro; cerco, reborde, pestaña; ceja.

rime [rajm], *s.* escarcha; = RHYME.

rind [rajnd], *s.* corteza, pellejo, cuero, hollejo.

ring [riŋ], *s.* anillo, argolla, anilla; (joy.) anillo, sortija; circo, arena, liza; cerco; corro o corrillo; ojera; campaneo, repique; juego de campanas; campanilleo; toque de timbre; sonido metálico.—*r. finger*, dedo anular.—*r. leader*, jefe, cabecilla.— *vt.* rodear, circundar; poner una anilla a; anillar, ensortijar.—*vi.* moverse en círculo o en espiral; formar círculo.—*vti.* [10] tocar, sonar, tañer, repicar (campanas), timbre, campanilla); repetir, reiterar.—*to r. up*, llamar (a uno) por teléfono; (teat.) levantar el telón.—*vii.* sonar, tañer; campanillear; retumbar, resonar; zumbar (los oídos).—*to r. off*, terminar (una conversación telefónica); (fam.) cesar de hablar.—*to r. true*, sonar bien (una moneda, etc.); sonar a verdad.—**-let** [ríŋlit], *s.* anillejo, círculo; sortija, bucle, rizo; (Am.) crespo.—**-worm** [-wœrm], *s.* tiña.

rink [riŋk], *s.* pista de patinar.

rinse [rins], *vt.* enjuagar; lavar; aclarar (la ropa).—*s.* enjuague.

riot [rájot], *s.* tumulto; alboroto; motín, asonada, desorden; borrachera.—*vi.* armar motines; alborotarse.— **-er** [-œ(r)], *s.* amotinado, alborotador.— **-ous** [-ʌs], *a.* amotinado, sedicioso, bullicioso, desenfrenado.

rip [rip], *vti.* y *vii.* [1] rasgar(se)

rajar(se), romper(se); descoser(se), soltar(se); arrancar(se).—*to r. off,* rasgar, arrancar; cortar.—*to r. out a seam,* descoser, desbaratar una costura.—*s.* laceración, rasgadura, rasgón; (fam.) persona, caballo o cosa que no vale nada.

ripe [raip], *a.* maduro; en sazón; hecho, acabado; preparado, a propósito; rosado, colorado; (agr.) espigado.— **—n** [ráipn], *vt.* y *vi.* madurar, sazonar(se).— **—ness** [-njs], *s.* madurez, sazón.

ripple [rípl], *vt.* rizar, ondear.—*vi.* agitarse, rizarse la superficie del agua; murmurar.—*s.* escarceo, onda, rizo (del agua); murmullo.

rise [raiz], *vii.* [10] ascender, subir, elevarse, remontarse; levantarse, ponerse en pie; levantarse (de la cama); alzarse, sublevarse; suspender una sesión; salir (el sol); nacer o brotar (las plantas o los manantiales); surgir, aparecer, presentarse; sobrevenir, suscitarse (una disputa); ascender, mejorar de posición; aumentar de volumen; subir de precio.—*to r. early,* madrugar.—*to r. to one's feet,* ponerse en pie, levantarse. —*s.* ascensión, elevación; levantamiento, insurrección; crecimiento o desarrollo; cuesta, subida; nacimiento (de un manantial); altura, eminencia; salida (de un astro); encarecimiento, alza de precios; crecimiento (de un río, etc.); origen, causa; ascenso; elevación de la voz. —*to give r. to,* dar origen a, ocasionar. —**risen** [rízn], *pp.* de TO RISE.

risk [risk], *s.* riesgo, peligro; contingencia; albur.—*vt.* arriesgar, aventurar, exponer.— **—y** [ríski], *a.* peligroso, arriesgado, aventurado; imprudente, temerario.

rite [rait], *s.* rito, ceremonia.—**ritual** [ríchual], *a.* y *s.* ritual, ceremonial.

rival [ráival], *s.* rival.—*a.* competidor, opuesto.—*vti.* [2] emular; competir con, rivalizar con.—*vii.* rivalizar.

river [rívœ(r)], *s.* río.— **—side** [-said], *s.* ladera, ribera u orilla de un río.

rivet [rívit], *s.* remache.—*vt.* remachar; (fig.) asegurar, afianzar.

rivulet [rívyolit], *s.* riachuelo, arroyuelo.

roach [rouch], *s.* cucaracha.

road [roud], *s.* camino, vía; carretera.— **—side** [róudsaid], *s.* orilla o borde del camino.— **—way** [-wei], *s.* carretera, calzada.

roam [roum], *vt.* y *vi.* vagar, andar errante.

roar [ror], *vi.* rugir, bramar.—*s.* rugido, bramido; estruendo, estrépito.

roast [roust], *vt.* asar; tostar; calcinar;

(fam.) hablar mal de; ridiculizar. —*a.* asado; tostado.—*s.* asado.— **—er** [róustœ(r)], *s.* asador; tostador.

rob [rab], *vti.* y *vii.* [1] robar; saltear; saquear.—*to r. one of,* robar, hurtar o quitarle a uno (el dinero, etc.).— **—ber** [rábœ(r)], *s.* ladrón; salteador, bandido; bandolero.— **—bery** [-œrj], *s.* robo, hurto, latrocinio.

robe [roub], *s.* manto; túnico o túnica; ropón, toga, traje talar; bata; corte de vestido; manta de coche.—*vt.* vestir de gala o de ceremonia; vestir, ataviar.—*vi.* vestirse; cubrirse.

robin [rábin], *s.* petirrojo.

robust [robást], *a.* robusto, vigoroso, fuerte.

rock [rak], *s.* roca, peña, peñasco; arrecife, escollo; (fig.) amparo, protección; diamante, moneda.—*on the rocks,* (bebidas) con hielo; arruinado, tronado.—*vt.* mecer, balancear; arrullar; sosegar.—*vi.* mecerse, bambolear, oscilar.— **—er** [rákœ(r)], *s.* cualquier cosa que mece o se mece; cuna; columpio; mecedora (silla); balancín.

rocket [rákit], *s.* cohete, volador.—*r. bomb,* (mil.) bomba cohete.—*r. plane,* avión cohete.—*vi.* volar o ascender verticalmente en el aire.

rocking [rákiŋ], *a.* mecedor; oscilante. —*s.* mecedura, balance, balanceo.

rocky [ráki], *a.* peñascoso, rocoso, pedregoso, duro, endurecido.

rod [rad], *s.* vara, varilla; cetro; bastón de mando; varilla de virtudes; caña de pescar; barra de cortina; vara de medir; (mec.) vástago, barra; azote; (fig.) disciplina, castigo; linaje.

rode [roud], *pret.* de TO RIDE.

rodent [róudent], *a.* y *s.* roedor.

roe [rou], *s.* hueva, ovas de pescado. —*r. deer,* corzo.

rogue [roug], *s.* bribón, pícaro, pillo, golfo, villano; (fam.) pilluelo, perillán.—*r.'s gallery,* galería de malhechores (colección policíaca de retratos).—**roguish** [róugiš], *a.* picaresco, (fam.) tuno, travieso.

role [roul], *s.* (teat.) papel, parte.

roll [roul], *vt.* hacer rodar; girar, voltear; enrollar, abarquillar; (fund.) laminar; alisar, emparejar con rodillo; apisonar (el césped); liar; envolver, fajar; redoblar (el tambor); hacer vibrar (lengua o voz); poner (los ojos) en blanco.—*to r. up,* enrollar; (fam.) acumular; revolver. —*vi.* rodar; agitarse (las olas); ondular, fluctuar; retumbar, retemblar; bambolearse, balancearse; arrollarse, abarquillarse; dar un redoble de tambores.—*to r. about,* rodar,

divagar, andar de acá para allá.
—*to r. down*, bajar rodando.—*to r. in
money*, nadar en la abundancia.—
to r. to a stop, seguir rodando hasta
pararse.—*s.* rollo; rol, lista, nómina,
matrícula, registro; bollo, panecillo;
(mec.) rodillo, cilindro de emparejar
allanar o laminar; laminador; maza
de trapiche; redoble (de tambores);
retumbo del trueno; balanceo, bamboleo; oleaje; (cir.) mecha.—*pl.*
archivos.—*r. call*, lista.— —er [róul-
œ(r)], *s.* rodillo, tambor, cilindro;
aplanadera; alisador; ola larga; (cir.)
venda, faja.—*r. coaster*, montaña
rusa.—*r. skate*, patín de ruedas.

rolling [róulị], *a.* rodante; ondulante.
—*s.* balanceo; revuelco.

Roman [róumạn], *a.* romano; católico
romano.—*R. nose*, nariz aquilina.—
s. romano.

romance [románs], *s.* romance; novela,
ficción, cuento, fábula; (mús.) ro-
manza; aventura, drama, episodio
extraño y conmovedor; (fam.) amorío, idilio.—*vi.* mentir; fingir fábulas;
hablar o pensar románticamente.—
a. (R.) romance; neolatino.—*R.
language*, lengua neolatina o romá-
nica.

Romanesque [roumạnésk], *a.* (arq.)
románico.

romantic [romántik], *a.* romántico,
novelesco; sentimental; fantástico.
—ism [romántịsịzm], *s.* romanti-
cismo.— —ist [romántịsịst], *s.* (escritor, músico, etc.) romántico.

romp [ramp], *vi.* juguetear, retozar.
—*s.* retozo.

roof [ruf], *s.* tejado, techo, azotea;
bóveda, cielo; cubierta; casa, hogar,
habitación.—*r. garden*, jardín de la
azotea; azotea de baile y diversión.
—*r. of the mouth*, bóveda palatina,
paladar.—*r. tile*, teja.—*vt.* techar;
abrigar, alojar.— —ing [rúfị], *s.*
techado, techumbre.

room [rum], *vi.* vivir, hospedarse, alojarse.—*s.* habitación, cuarto, aposento, sala, cámara, pieza; lugar,
espacio, puesto; paraje, sitio; causa,
motivo, razón; tiempo, ocasión,
oportunidad.— —er [rúmœ(r)], *s.*
huésped, inquilino.— —iness [-inịs],
s. espaciosidad, holgura, amplitud.—
—mate [-meịt], *s.* compañero de
cuarto.— —y [-i], *a.* espacioso, capaz,
amplio, holgado.

roost [rust], *s.* percha de gallinero;
lugar de descanso; sueño, descanso
(de la aves domésticas).—*vi.* dormir
o descansar (las aves) en una percha.-
—er [rústœ(r)], *s.* gallo.

root [rut], *s.* raíz.—*r. and branch*, por
completo.—*vi.* y *vt.* echar o criar

raíces, arraigar(se); hozar.—*to r. for*,
(fam.) aplaudir, alabar, vitorear.—
to r. up o *out*, arrancar de raíz,
desarraigar; extirpar.—*to take r.*,
radicar, arraigar(se).

rope [roup], *s.* soga; cuerda, cordel,
cabo; driza; reata; sarta, ristra,
trenza; hilera, fila.—*r. ladder*, escala
de cuerdas.—*r. sandal*, alpargata.—
vt. atar con una cuerda; rodear con
soga; coger con lazo.—*to r. in*,
(fam.) atraer, embaucar, engañar.—
to r. off, cercar con cuerdas.—*vi.*
hacer hebras o madeja.

rosary [róuzạri], *s.* rosario.—**rose**
[rouz], *s.* rosa; color de rosa.—*r.
tree*, rosal.—**rosebay** [róuzbei], *s.*
adelfa.—**rosebud** [róuzbʌd], *s.* pimpollo, botón o capullo de rosa; niña
adolescente.—**rosebush** [róuzbuş], *s.*
rosal.

rosemary [róuzmeri], *s.* (bot.) romero.

rosette [rouzét], *s.* rosa, roseta; esca-
rapela, moña; (arq.) rosetón, florón.

rosin [rázịn], *s.* resina.

rostrum [rástrʌm], *s.* tribuna; (zool.)
rostro, pico, hocico; (mar.) espolón.

rosy [róuzị], *a.* róseo, rosado; sonro-
sado; sonrojado; (fig.) agradable,
lisonjero; optimista.—*r. dream*, sueño
dorado.—*r.-hued*, rosado.

rot [rat], *vti.* y *vii.* [1] pudrir(se),
corromper(se).—*s.* putrefacción, podredumbre, podre.

rotary [róutạri], *a.* giratorio, rotativo,
rotatorio.—**rotate** [róuteit], *vi.* girar;
alternar(se).—*vt.* hacer girar, dar
vuelta(s) a; alternar; (agr.) sembrar
o cultivar en rotación.—**rotation**
[routéişạn], *s.* rotación, giro; turno;
alternativa.—*by r., in r.*, por turnos,
alternadamente; (agr.) en rotación.

rote [rout], *s.* lo que se aprende de
memoria.—*by r.*, de memoria o de
coro; mecánicamente.

rotten [rátn], *a.* podrido; (fam.)
malísimo; dañado, en mal estado.

rouge [ruʒ], *s.* colorete.—*a.* colorado,
encarnado.—*vt.* y *vr.* arrebolar(se),
pintar(se), dar(se) colorete.

rough [rʌf], *a.* áspero; tosco; fragoso,
escabroso; erizado; encrespado; desapacible; rudo, inculto; grosero,
brusco; tempestuoso, borrascoso,
agitado; chapucero; aproximativo,
general; preliminar, preparativo.—
as o at a r. guess, a ojo de buen cu-
bero.—*r. diamond*, diamante en
bruto; persona ruda pero de buen
fondo.—*r. draft*, boceto, bosquejo;
borrador.—*s.* matón, rufián.—*in the
r.*, en bruto, sin pulimento.—*vt.*
poner áspero, tosco, escabroso; labrar
toscamente; (fam.) molestar, irritar.
—*to r. it*, pasar trabajos, vivir sin

comodidades.— **—en** [rʌfn], *vt.* y *vi.* poner(se) áspero o tosco; picar, rascar.— **—ness** [-nje], *s.* aspereza, rudeza, tosquedad, escabrosidad; severidad, dureza; ordinariez, brusquedad; chapucería; tempestad, tormenta.

round [raund], *a.* redondo, circular, cilíndrico, esférico, orbicular; rollizo; rotundo; sonoro; cabal, grande, cuantioso; franco, llano, ingenuo; vivo, veloz; justo, honrado.—*r. numbers*, cifras globales.—*r. trip*, viaje de ida y vuelta.—*r. trip ticket*, billete de ida y vuelta.—*to go r. and r.*, dar vuelta tras vuelta.—*s.* círculo, esfera; círculo de personas o cosas; redondez; vuelta, giro, rotación; peldaño (de escala); listón o travesaño (de silla); rodaja de carne; (arq.) mediacaña; (mil.) ronda; andanada, salva, disparo, descarga; cartucho con bala; ruta, camino, circuito; rutina, serie (dep.) tanda, suerte, turno; (boxeo, etc.) asalto; (naipes) mano; (mus.) rondó; danza.—*adv.* alrededor, en derredor, por todos lados; a la redonda.— *all-r.*, completo, que sirve para todo; cabal.—*r. about*, por el lado opuesto; por todos lados, a la redonda.— *r.-shouldered*, cargado de espaldas. —*prep.* alrededor de; a la vuelta de.—*vt.* redondear, dar vuelta; doblar (un cabo, una esquina); acabar, perfeccionar.—*to r. up*, recoger, juntar, reunir; coger; recoger el ganado. —*vi.* redondearse; desarrollarse, perfeccionarse; dar vueltas; rondar.— *to r. out*, llenarse, redondearse.— **—about** [ráundəbaut], *a.* indirecto, vago; desviado.—*s.* chaqueta; tiovivo; rodeo.— **—ness** [-nje], *s.* redondez.— **—up** [-ʌp], *s.* rodeo de ganado; recogida, junta; apresuramiento, aprehensión.

rouse [rauz], *vt.* despertar, animar, excitar, suscitar; levantar (la caza); (mar.) halar.—*vi.* despertar(se), despabilarse, animarse, moverse.

route [rut, raut], *s.* ruta, vía; rumbo, derrotero; marcha, curso.—*vt.* encaminar, señalar ruta, pista, vía (a trenes, aviones, etc.).

routine [rutín], *a.* rutinario.—*s.* rutina; costumbre, hábito.

rove [rouv], *vi.* corretear, vagar, vagabundear.—*s.* correría, paseo.— **—r** [róuvœr], *s.* vagabundo; persona inconstante.

row [rou], *s.* hilera, fila; paseo en lancha o bote; remadura; [rau], camorra, trifulca.—*vt.* [rou], conducir remando. —*vi.* [rou], remar, bogar; [rau], armar camorra.— **—boat** [róubout],

s. bote de remos.— **—dy** [ráudi], *a.* alborotador, pendenciero.—*s.* rufián.— **—dyism** [ráudiizm], *s.* rufianismo.— **—er** [róuœr], *s.* remero.

royal [róiəl], *a.* real, regio, magnífico. —*to have a r. time*, divertirse en grande, o a cuerpo de rey.— **—ist** [-ist], *s.* (pol.) realista.— **—ty** [-ti], *s.* realeza.—*pl.* derechos de autor o de inventor.

rub [rʌb], *vti.* [1] estregar, frotar, friccionar; raspar, raer; incomodar, fastidiar.—*to r. away*, quitar frotando.—*to r. down*, dar un masaje; alisar frotando.—*to r. in*, hacer penetrar frotando; (fam.) machacar. —*to r. off*, quitar; limpiar frotando. —*to r. out*, borrar.—*to r. the wrong way*, frotar a contrapelo; irritar; incomodar.—*to r. up*, aguijonear, excitar; retocar, pulir.—*vii.* pasar raspando, rozar; ser desagradable o molesto; ir a contrapelo.—*s.* frotación, roce; tropiezo, dificultad; sarcasmo, denuesto.— **—ber** [rʌbœr], *a.* de caucho.—*r. band*, faja de goma, elástico, liga.—*r. eraser*, goma de borrar.—*r. stamp*, estampilla, sello o cuño de goma; (fig.) el que aprueba ciegamente.—*to r.-stamp*, estampar con un sello de goma; (fam.) aprobar ciegamente.—*s.* caucho, goma elástica; masajista; goma de borrar; estropajo; escofina; jugada decisiva. —*pl.* chanclos, zapatos de goma.

rubbish [rʌbiʃ], *s.* basura, desperdicio(s), desecho, escombro, cascajo, ripio; (fam.) tontería.

rubble [rʌbl], *s.* piedra en bruto o sin labrar; escombros; cascote, cascajo.

ruby [rúbi], *s.* rubí; carmín, color rojo vivo.—*a.* rojo.

rudder [rʌdœr], *s.* timón (de barco).

ruddiness [rʌdinjs], *s.* rojez, rubicundez.— **ruddy** [rʌdi], *a.* rojo, rojizo; rubicundo.

rude [rud], *a.* rudo, brusco, descortés; tosco, chabacano; inculto; fuerte, vigoroso.— **—ness** [rúdnjs], *s.* grosería; descortesía; rudeza, aspereza, rusticidad, crudeza.

rudiment [rúdimənt], *s.* rudimento; (biol.) embrión, germen.— **—ary** [rudiméntəri], *a.* rudimentario.

ruffian [rʌfiən], *a.* y *s.* rufián.

ruffle [rʌfl], *vt.* (cost.) fruncir un volante, rizar; ajar, arrugar, desordenar; encrespar; desazonar, enfadar; vejar; redoblar (el tambor).—*vi.* rizarse, arrugarse; desarreglarse; temblar; enojarse, incomodarse.—*s.* (cost.) volante fruncido; desazón, enojo; escarceo del agua; redoble de tambor.

rug [rag], *s.* alfombra.

rugged [rʌgid], *a.* áspero, escarpado,

abrupto; tosco, basto; inculto; desapacible; descomedido; arrugado; ceñudo, regañón; desgreñado; robusto, vigoroso; tempestuoso, borrascoso.—**—ness** [-nịs], *s.* escabrosidad; rudeza; robustez.

ruin [rúịn], *s.* ruina, bancarrota; estrago, destrucción; degradación, perdición.—*pl.* ruinas, escombros.—*vt.* arruinar, devastar; dar al traste con, echar a perder; desbaratar; estropear; seducir, perder (a una mujer).—*vi.* arruinarse; decaer.—**—ous** [-ʌs], *a.* ruinoso, desmantelado; desastroso, funesto.

rule [rul], *s.* regla; gobierno, mando, dominio; soberanía; régimen, reinado; estatuto, precepto; regularidad, buen orden; (fig.) norma, guía, modelo; (for.) auto, fallo; (impr.) pleca, filete; raya, línea trazada.—*as a r.*, por regla general.—*r. book*, reglamento.—*r. of thumb*, regla o método empírico.—*to be the r.*, ser la regla; ser de reglamento.—*vt.* gobernar, mandar, regir; reprimir; (for.) decidir, determinar, disponer; dirigir, guiar; arreglar, ordenar; rayar (papel).—*to r. out*, excluir; descartar.—*vi.* gobernar, mandar; establecer una regla, formular una decisión; prevalecer, estar en boga; (com.) mantenerse a un tipo.—*to r. over*, mandar, gobernar, dominar.—**r** [rúlœ(r)], *s.* soberano, príncipe; gobernador, gobernante; pauta, regla (para trazar líneas).—**ruling** [rúlịŋ], *s.* (for.) decisión, fallo, disposición; rayadura; rayado.—*a.* gobernante, imperante.—*r. price* (com.) precio predominante.

rum [rʌm], *s.* ron.

Rumanian [ruméịnịạn], *a.* y *s.* rumano (persona e idioma).

rumble [rʌmbl], *vi.* retumbar, rugir; avanzar con estruendo.—*vt.* hacer retumbar, etc.—*s.* rumor, ruido sordo y prolongado; estruendo.

ruminant [rúmịnạnt], *a.* y *s.* rumiante.—**ruminate** [rúmịnẹịt], *vt.* y *vi.* rumiar; considerar, reflexionar.

rumor [rúmọ(r)], *s.* rumor, ruarún.—*vt.* divulgar, propalar.—*it is rumored*, se dice, corre la voz.

rump [rʌmp], *s.* rabadilla de ave; anca o grupa de caballo, etc.; nalgas; cadera de vaca; resto, retazo.

rumple [rʌmpl], *vt.* arrugar, ajar.—*s.* arruga, doblez, estrujadura.

rumpus [rʌmpʌs], *s.* (fam.) batahola, zipizape.

run [rʌn], *vti.* [10] correr, hacer correr; mover, poner en movimiento; dejar correr o salir; meter, clavar, introducir; empujar, echar; cazar, perseguir; tirar, trazar (una línea, en el papel o el terreno); pasar (la vista); atravesar, cruzar; derramar, manar; correr (un peligro); fundir, moldear; (cost.) bastear; tener o proponer como candidato; mandar; dominar; manejar, dirigir (una máquina, institución, empresa).—*to r. a blockade*, violar o burlar un bloqueo.—*to r. a temperature*, tener fiebre.—*to r. down*, dar caza; (mar.) echar a pique; difamar, hablar mal de; quebrantar, postrar; gastar (la salud, etc.).—*to r. for office*, aspirar a un cargo electivo.—*to r. in*, recorrer; encerrar; (fam.) prender.—*to r. into the ground*, meter en la tierra; extender hasta más abajo del suelo; (fam.) llevar al exceso.—*to r. off*, desviar; desecar, vaciar; repetir, decir de coro; imprimir.—*to r. out*, agotar; desperdiciar; (fam.) echar.—*to r. over*, atropellar, pasar encima de; hojear, repasar, revisar de prisa.—*to r. through*, ver, examinar, presentar, etc. a la ligera; atravesar, pasar de parte a parte; traspasar; hojear, leer por encima; gastar, derrochar, malbaratar.—*to r. up*, (cost.) remendar, repasar; incurrir, hacer subir (una cuenta); sumar, hacer una suma; montar o edificar de prisa; (mar.) izar.—*vii.* correr; pasar, deslizarse; marchar, andar, funcionar, moverse (un buque, reloj, máquina, etc.); derretirse, fluir, gotear o chorrear; derramarse; correrse (un color); competir, lidiar; ser candidato, presentarse como tal; (med.) supurar; (teat.) representarse consecutivamente; extenderse, ir, llegar (hasta), correr, transcurrir; tener predilección; continuar, durar; rezar, decir; tener curso, circular; salirse, dejar fugar el agua, etc.; ir, andar (en manadas, etc.).—*to r. about*, andar de lugar en lugar; corretear.—*to r. across*, atravesar corriendo; hallar; dar o tropezar con.—*to r. against*, chocar, topar, dar contra; oponerse; ser contrario a.—*to r. ahead*, correr delante; llevar ventaja.—*to r. away*, huir, escapar, zafarse; desbocarse.—*to r. away with*, arrebatar; fugarse con; (fam.) llevarse la palma en, ser el protagonista en.—*a.* extraído; vaciado; derretido; (fam.) de contrabando.—*s.* corrida, carrera; curso, marcha; batida de caza; (mil.) marcha forzada; vuelta, viajecito, jornada; recorrido, trayecto; distancia; (mec.) marcha, movimiento, funcionamiento; serie, continuación; duración, vida; hilo (del discurso); (teat.) serie de representaciones consecutivas de una pieza; lo que sale o se saca cada vez (hornada, vaciado, etc.); mando, dirección; (béisbol) carrera; arribazón (de peces); clase, tipo; aspecto, carácter.—*in the long r.*, a la larga. —*the (common) r.*, el común de las gentes; lo común, lo corriente.— *pp.* de TO RUN.— **-away** [rΛnᵫwei], **s.** y **s.** fugitivo, desertor.—*s.* fuga; rapto, secuestro; desbocamiento; caballo desbocado.

rung [rΛŋ], *pp.* de TO RING (tocar).—*s.* peldaño de escalera, escalón; travesaño.

runner [rΛnœ(r)], *s.* corredor; andarín; pieza o parte giratoria o corrediza; mensajero; (fam.) correve(i)dile; fugitivo; contrabandista; agente, factor; alguacil; corredera; muela (de molino).

running [rΛnĭŋ], *s.* carrera, corrida; contrabando; funcionamiento.—*a.* que corre; que fluye o mana; que funciona.—*r. board*, estribo.—*r. expenses*, gastos corrientes.—*r. water*, agua corriente.

runt [rΛnt], *s.* enano; paloma.

runway [rΛnᵫei], *s.* lecho, madre, cauce; senda; rampa; (aer.) pista; vía (gen. de rieles).

rupture [rΛpchŭ(r)], *s.* rompimiento, rotura, fractura; reventazón; ruptura, desavenencia; hernia, quebradura.—*vt.* romper, fracturar; reventar.—*vi.* abrirse, romperse, rajarse, reventar.

rural [rúᵫal], *a.* rural.

rush [rΛsh], *s.* ímpetu, embestida, acometida; prisa, precipitación; torrente, tropel, agolpamiento, asedio; lucha, rebatiña; tierra rica en oro; (bot.) junco; friolera, bagatela.— *with a r.*, de golpe; de repente.—*vi.* lanzarse, abalanzarse, precipitarse; embestir, acometer; agolparse.—*to r. forward*, lanzarse.—*to r. in*, entrar de rondón.—*to r. in upon*, sorprender. —*to r. out*, salir con precipitación.— *to r. through*, lanzarse por entre o a través de.—*vt.* empujar o arrojar con violencia; activar.—*to r. through*, ejecutar deprisa.

Russian [rÁshᵫan], *a.* y *s.* ruso (persona o idioma).

rust [rΛst], *s.* herrumbre, orín, moho. —*vt.* y *vi.* enmohecer(se); entorpecer(se), embotar(se).

rustic [rΛstĭk], *a.* rústico, rural; agrario, agreste; campesino; sencillo; inculto. —*s.* rústico, campesino.

rustle [rΛsl], *vt.* y *vi.* susurrar, crujir (la seda), murmurar (las hojas); (fam.) hurtar ganado.—*s.* susurro, crujido, murmullo.

rusty [rΛsti], *a.* mohoso, herrumbroso; rojizo o amarillento; entorpecido, torpe por falta de práctica.

rut [rΛt], *vti.* [1] hacer rodadas o surcos.—*vii.* bramar (los venados, etc.), estar en celo.—*s.* rodada, surco, bache; rutina, costumbre; sendero trillado; brama, celo de los animales; mugido, bramido; ruido, batahola.

ruthless [rúθlĭs], *a.* cruel, inhumano; inexorable.— **-ness** [-nĭs], *s.* crueldad, empedernimiento.

rye [rai], *s.* centeno; whisky de centeno.

S

saber [séibœ(r)], *s.* sable.

sable [séibl], *s.* (zool.) marta cibelina.

sabot [sæbou], *s.* zueco.

sabotage [sæbotaʒ], *s.* sabotaje.—*vt.* cometer sabotaje (contra, en).

saccharin [sækᵫrin], *s.* sacarina.— **-e** [sækᵫrin], *a.* dulzón.

sack [sæk], *s.* saco, costal, talega; (mil.) saqueo, saco.—*vt.* saquear.— **-cloth** [sækklŏθ], *s.* arpillera.

sacrament [sækᵫmᵫnt], *s.* sacramento; eucaristía.— **-sacred** [séikrĭd], *a.* (con)sagrado, santo(santo).

sacrifice [sækᵫrifais], *vt.* y *vi.* sacrificar, inmolar.—*s.* sacrificio, inmolación.— *at a s.*, haciendo un sacrificio; perdiendo, con pérdida.

sacrilege [sækᵫrilĭdʒ], *s.* sacrilegio.— **sacrilegious** [sækᵫrilídʒΛs], *a.* sacrílego.

sacristan [sækᵫristᵫn], *s.* sacristán.— **sacristy** [sækᵫristi], *s.* sacristía.

sacrum [séikram], *s.* (anat.) sacro.

sad [sæd], *a.* triste, pesaroso; cariacontecido; aciago, nefasto.— **-den** [sædn], *vt.* y *vi.* entristecer(se).

saddle [sædl], *s.* silla de montar, montura; silla o sillín (de bicicleta o motocicleta).—*s. horse*, caballo de silla, cabalgadura.—*vt.* ensillar; enalbardar.—*to s. with*, hacer cargar con.— **-bag** [-bæg], *s.* alforja, jaque.— **-cloth** [-kloθ], *s.* mantilla (de silla).— **-r** [sædloœ(r)], *s.* talabartero.

sadism [sædizm], *s.* sadismo.— **sadistic** [sædĭstĭk], *a.* sádico, sadista.

sadness [sædnĭs], *s.* tristeza.

safe [seif], *a.* seguro; salvo, ileso; sin peligro; intacto; digno de confianza. —*s. and sound*, sano y salvo.—*s.conduct*, salvoconducto, salvaguardia. —*s. deposit box*, caja de seguridad (en el banco).—*s.* caja de caudales, caja fuerte.— **-guard** [séifgard], *s.* salvaguardia; resguardo; defensor, escolta; defensa, abrigo.—*vt.* salvaguardar, proteger; escoltar.— **-ty** [-ti], *s.* seguridad, protección; seguro de arma de fuego).—*a.* de seguridad.—

s. pin, imperdible.—*s. razor,* maquinilla de seguridad (de afeitarse).

saffron [sǽfrǫn], *s.* (bot.) azafrán.

sag [sæg], *vti.* [1] combar, pandear.—*vii.* combarse, pandearse; aflojarse; doblegarse; hundirse.—*s.* comba, pandeo.

sage [seidʒ], *s.* sabio; (bot.) salvia.—*a.* sabio; sagaz; cuerdo, prudente.

said [sed], *pret.* y *pp.* de TO SAY.—*a.* (el) mencionado o citado; (for.) dicho, antedicho.—*s. and dene,* dicho y hecho.

sail [seil], *s.* (mar.) vela; excursión o paseo en barco.—*pl.* velamen.—*under full s.,* a toda vela, a todo trapo.—*vi.* hacerse o darse a la vela; zarpar; salir (un buque); navegar.—*to s. before the wind,* navegar viento en popa.—*to s. close with the wind,* ceñir el viento, bolinear.—*vt.* navegar por, surcar.—**boat** [séilbout], *s.* barco de vela, balandro, velero.—**fish** [-fiŝ], *s.* aguja de mar, (Am.) pez vela, aguja de abanico.— **ing** [-iŋ], *s.* navegación (a vela); salida o partida de un barco.—*clear o plain s.,* coser y cantar.—**or** [-ǫ(r)], *s.* marinero; marino.

saint [seint], *s.* santo.—*s.'s day,* día del santo.—*a.* san, santo.—*vt.* canonizar. — **hood** [séinthud], *s.* santidad.— **liness** [-linis], *s.* santidad.— **ly** [-li], *a.* santo.

sake [seik], *s.* causa, motivo, fin, objeto, razón; amor, respeto, consideración. —*for God's s.,* por Dios, por el amor de Dios.—*for mercy's s.,* por piedad, por misericordia.—*for the s. of,* en consideración a.

salad [sǽlǎd], *s.* ensalada.—*s. bowl,* ensaladera.—*s. dressing,* aliño, aderezo para ensalada.

salamander [sǽlǎmændœ(r)], *s.* salamandra.

salami [salámi], *s.* salchichón.

salary [sǽlǎri], *s.* sueldo, salario, pago.

sale [seil], *s.* venta; liquidación; saldo; (com.) realización.—*sales tax,* impuesto sobre las ventas.—*for s.* u *on s.,* de venta, en venta.—**sman** [séilzman], *s.* vendedor; dependiente de tienda.— **swoman** [-zwụman], *s.* vendedora; dependienta de tienda.

saliva [salájvǎ], *s.* saliva.

sallow [sǽloụ], *a.* cetrino.

sally [sǽli], *vii.* [7] (a veces con forth) salir, hacer una salida.—*s.* salida.

salmon [sǽmǫn], *s.* salmón.

saloon [salún], *s.* salón; cámara de un vapor; (E.U.) taberna, cantina, tugurio.

salt [sǫlt], *s.* sal; agudeza, ingenio chispeante.—*old s.,* lobo de mar.—*pl.* sales medicinales; sal de higuera,

sulfato de magnesia.—*a.* salado; salobre; curado o conservado con sal. —*s. pork,* tocino salado.—*s. shaker,* salero (de mesa).—*vt.* salar; (fig.) sazonar.—*to s. away,* ahorrar.—**ed** [sǫ́ltid], *a.* salado.— **peter** [-pítœ(r)], *s.* nitro, salitre.— **y** [-i], *a.* salado; salobre.

salutation [sælyutéiʃǫn], *s.* salutación, saludo; bienvenida.—**salute** [saliút], *vt.* y *vi.* saludar; cuadrarse.—*s.* saludo.

Salvadoran [sælvǎdórǎn], **Salvadorian** [sælvǎdóriǎn], *s.* y *a.* salvadoreño.

salvage [sǽlvjdʒ], *s.* salvamento; objetos salvados.—**salvation** [sælvéiʃǫn], *s.* salvación.

salve [sæv, sav], *s.* ungüento, pomada; remedio.—*vt.* curar (una herida) con ungüentos; salvar; remediar.

salver [sǽlvœ(r)], *s.* salva, bandeja.

same [seim], *a.* y *pron.* mismo; igual, idéntico.—*all the s.,* a pesar de esto, a pesar de todo.—*it is all the s. to me,* me es igual, lo mismo me da.—*just the s.,* del mismo modo; a pesar de eso.—*much the s. as,* casi como.—*the s.,* lo mismo; el mismo, los mismos; otro tanto.

sample [sémpl], *s.* muestra, prueba; patrón.—*s. book,* muestrario.—*vt.* sacar una muestra; probar, catar.

sanctify [sǽŋktjfai], *vti.* [7] santificar, consagrar.—**sanctimonious** [sæŋktimóuniʌs], *a.* beato, mojigato.—**sanctimoniousness** [sænktjmóuɲjʌsnjs], *s.* beatería, mojigatería.

sanction [sǽŋkʃǫn], *s.* sanción, pena; sanción, ratificación.—*vt.* sancionar; autorizar, ratificar.

sanctity [sǽŋktjtj], *s.* santidad.—**sanctuary** [sǽŋkchueri], *s.* santuario.

sand [sænd], *s.* arena.—*s. bar,* barra, banco de arena.—*s. blasting,* limpiadura por chorro de arena.—*s. pit,* arenal.—*vt.* (en)arenar; (gen. con down) alisar con papel de lija.

sandal [séndal], *s.* sandalia.—*fiber s., rope s.,* alpargata.

sandpaper [séndpeipœ(r)], *s.* papel de lija.—*vt.* lijar.—**sandstone** [séndstoụn], *s.* piedra arenisca.—**sandstorm** [séndstorm], *s.* tempestad de arena.

sandwich [séndwjch], *vt.* colocar entre dos capas; intercalar, insertar.—*s.* emparedado, bocadito, bocadillo.

sandy [séndj], *a.* arenoso, arenisco.

sane [sein], *a.* cuerdo; sano.

sang [sæŋ], *pret.* de TO SING.

sanguinary [séŋgwineri], *a.* sanguinario. —**sanguine** [séŋgwin], *a.* confiado, lleno de esperanza; sanguíneo.

sanitarium [sænitériʌm], *s.* enfermería, sanatorio.—**sanitary** [séniteri], *a.* sanitario; higiénico.—**sanitation** [sæn-

itéi̯ṣon], *s.* saneamiento; sanidad.—
sanity [sǽnị̇tị̇], *s.* cordura; sensatez;
sanidad.

sank [sæŋk], *pret.* de TO SINK.

sap [sæp], *vti.* [1] zapar, minar.—*s.*
savia; (fort.) zapa; (fam.) tonto.

sapling [sǽplị̇ŋ], *s.* renuevo, vástago.

sapphire [sǽfaị̇r], *s.* zafiro.

Saracen [sǽrạṣen], *s.* sarraceno.

sarcasm [sárkæzm], *s.* sarcasmo.—**sar-
castic** [sarkǽstị̇k], *a.* sarcástico.

sardine [sardín], *s.* sardina.

sash [sæš], *s.* (mil.) faja, banda; cinturón, ceñidor; (carp.) bastidor o marco
de ventana.—*s. window,* ventana de
guillotina.

sat [sæt], *pret.* y *pp.* de TO SIT.

satanic [seị̇tǽnị̇k], *a.* satánico.

satchel [sǽchẹl], *s.* maletín; bolsa.

sate [seị̇t], *vt.* hartar, saciar; hastiar.

sateen [sætín], *s.* (tej.) satén, rasete.

satellite [sǽtẹlaị̇t], *s.* satélite.

satin [sǽtị̇n], *s.* (tej.) raso.

satire [sǽtaị̇r], *s.* sátira.—**satiric(al)**
[sạtị́rị̇k(ạl)], *a.* satírico.—**satirize**
[sǽtị̇raị̇z], *vt.* satirizar.

satisfaction [sætị̇sfǽkṣon], *s.* satisfacción.—**satisfactory** [sætị̇sfǽktọrị̇], *a.*
satisfactorio; suficiente.—*a.* satisfecho, contento.—**satisfy** [sǽtị̇sfaị̇],
vti. y *vii.* [7] satisfacer.—*to s. oneself
that,* convencerse de que.

saturate [sǽchọreị̇t], *vt.* saturar; empapar, impregnar.—**saturation** [sæch-
ọréị̇ṣon], *s.* saturación.

Saturday [sǽtœrdị̇], *s.* sábado.

satyr [séị̇tœ(r), sǽtœ(r)], *s.* sátiro

sauce [sos], *s.* salsa.—*vt.* condimentar;
sazonar.—**dish** [sóṣdị̇š], *s.* salsera.—
pan [-pæn], *s.* cacerola.—**r**
[sóscœ(r)], *s.* platillo.—**sauciness** [sósị̇-
nị̇s], *s.* insolencia.—**saucy** [sósị̇], *a.*
respondón, descarado, insolente.

sauerkraut [sáụrkraụt], *s.* col agria.

sausage [sósị̇dẓ], *s.* salchicha; embutido; chorizo; longaniza; morcilla.

savage [sǽvị̇dẓ], *a.* salvaje; bárbaro;
feroz; enfurecido.—*s.* salvaje.—**ry**
[-rị̇], *s.* salvajismo.

savanna(h) [ṣavǽnạ], *s.* (Am.) sabana.

save [seị̇v], *vt.* salvar; guardar, conservar; evitar; ahorrar, economizar.—
prep. salvo, excepto.—*conj.* sino, a
menos que, a no ser que.—**saving**
[iŋ], *a.* ahorrativo, frugal, económico;
salvador.—*s.* economía, ahorro; salvedad.—*pl.* ahorros.—*savings bank,*
caja de ahorros.—*prep.* con excepción
de, fuera de, excepto, salvo.—**savior**
[séị̇vyọ(r)], *s.* salvador.—*the Saviour*
[séị̇vyọ(r)], *s.* salvador, *the Saviour*,
el Salvador (Jesucristo).

saw [so], *s.* (carp.) sierra.—*vti.* [6]
serrar, aserrar.—*pret.* de TO SEE.—
buck [sóbʌk], *s.* caballete de aserrar, tijera; (fam.) billete de diez

pesos.— **dust** [-dʌst], *s.* (a)serrín.—
horse [-hors], *s.* = SAWBUCK.—
mill [-mị̇l], *s.* aserradero, aserrío.—
sawn [son], *pp.* de TO SAW.—*a.* ase-
rrado.— **pit** [-pị̇t], *s.* aserradero.

Saxon [sǽksọn], *a.* y *s.* sajón.

saxophone [sǽksofoụn], *s.* saxofón.

say [seị̇], *vti.* y *vii.* [10] decir.—*I s.!*
¡digo!—*it is said, they s.,* se dice,
dicen.—*s.!* ¡oiga!—*so to s.,* por decirlo
así.—*to s. good-bye,* despedirse, decir
adiós.—*to s. in one's sleeve,* decir para
su capote.—*to s. nothing of,* sin mencionar.—*to s. on,* continuar hablando.
—*that is to s.,* es decir, esto es.—
you don't s. (so)! ¡calle Ud.! ¡no es
posible!—*s.* uso de la palabra; expresión de opinión; afirmación.—*s.-so,*
(fam.) opinión o juicio personal; declaración autorizada.—**ing** [séị̇ị̇ŋ],
s. dicho; aserto; decir, refrán.—*as the
s. goes,* como dijo el otro, como dice
el refrán.

scab [skæb], *s.* (cir.) costra, escara.
—*vii.* [1] encostrar.

scabbard [skǽbạrd], *s.* vaina.

scabies [skéị̇bị̇z], *s.* sarna.

scaffold [skǽfoụld], *s.* andamio, tablado; cadalso, patíbulo.— **ing** [-ị̇ŋ],
s. andamiada, andamiaje; paral.

scald [skold], *vt.* escaldar; (coc.) escalfar.—*s.* quemadura, escaldadura.

scale [skeị̇l], *s.* escala; gama; platillo
de balanza; (gen. en *pl.*) balanza,
báscula; escama (de peces, reptiles);
(med.) costra; laminita, plancha, hojuela.—*to s.,* (dib.) según escala.—
vt. escamar o des(es)camar; cubrir con
escamas; incrustar o desincrustar; escalar; (con down) reducir según
escala; pesar.—*vi.* (a veces con off)
descostrarse; desconcharse, pelarse.

scallop [skǽlop], *s.* (molusco) vieira;
concha de peregrino; venera; (cost.)
festón, onda.—*vt.* festonear, ondear;
(coc.) asar ostras empanadas.

scalp [skælp], *s.* cuero cabelludo.—*vt.*
arrancar el cuero cabelludo; comprar
y revender (acciones, billetes de f.c.,
teatro, etc.) a precios extraoficiales.

scaly [skéị̇lị̇], *a.* escamoso; herrumbroso.

scan [skæn], *vti.* [1] escudriñar; hojear,
repasar; medir (versos).

scandal [skǽndạl], *s.* escándalo.— **ize**
[- aị̇z], *vt.* escandalizar.— **ous** [-ʌs],
a. escandaloso.

Scandinavian [skændị̇néị̇vị̇an], *a.* y *s.*
escandinavo.

scapular [skǽpyọlạ̈(r)], *s.* (igl.) escapulario; (cir.) escapulario, vendaje
para el hombro.

scar [skar], *s.* cicatriz; costurón.—*vti.*
[1] marcar con una cicatriz.

scarce [skers], *a.* raro, escaso, contado.

—**scarcity** [skérsiti], *s.* carestía, escasez; rareza.

scare [sker], *vt.* asustar, espantar; amedrentar, intimidar.—*to s. away*, espantar, ahuyentar.—*s.* susto, sobresalto, espanto.— **crow** [skérkrou], *s.* espantajo; (fam.) esperpento.

scarf [skarf], *s.* bufanda; chalina; tapete (de mesa).—*vt.* (carp.) acoplar.

scarlet [skárlit], *s.* escarlata, grana.— *a.* de color escarlata.—*s. fever*, escarlatina.

scary [skéri], *a.* (fam.) medroso, asustadizo.

scatter [skǽtœ(r)], *vt. y vi.* esparcir(se), diseminar(se),   desparramar(se), desperdigar(se);   dispersar(se).—*s.-brained*, atolondrado, ligero de cascos.

scene [sin], *s.* escena, vista; escenario; decoración.—*behind the scenes*, entre bastidores.—*to make a s.*, dar un escándalo.— **ry** [sínœri], *s.* vista, paisaje; (teat.) decoraciones, decorado.—**scenic** [sínjk], *a.* escénico; teatral; pintoresco.

scent [sɛnt], *s.* olfato; olor, perfume, fragancia; rastro, pista.—*to throw off the s.*, despistar.—*vt. y vi.* oler, olfatear, husmear, ventear; rastrear.

scepter [séptœ(r)], *s.* cetro.

sceptic [sképtjk], *s. y a.* = SKEPTIC.

schedule [skédžul], *vt.* inventariar, catalogar; fijar el tiempo para; establecer un itinerario.—*s.* cédula; horario (de f.c., etc.), itinerario; suplemento; plan, programa; lista; tarifa.

scheme [skim], *s.* plan, proyecto, programa; planta, esquema; diseño, bosquejo; ardid, treta, artificio.—*vt. y vi.* proyectar, trazar; urdir, tramar.

schism [sjzm], *s.* cisma; escisión.— **atic** [sjzmǽtjk], *a. y s.* cismático.

scholar [skálɚ(r)], *s.* escolar, estudiante, colegial; becario; hombre erudito, docto.— **ly** [lj], *a.* erudito, ilustrado, docto.—*adv.* eruditamente, doctamente.— **ship** [šjp], *s.* saber, erudición; beca.—**scholastic** [skolǽstjk], *a.* escolástico; escolar.—**school** [skul], *s.* escuela; colegio; facultad de universidad.—*boarding s.*, colegio de internos.—*s. of fishes*, banco de peces.—*s. year*, año escolar.—*a.* escolar; de escuela; para escuela.—*s. board*, junta de educación.—*s. desk*, pupitre.—*secondary s.*, instituto de segunda enseñanza.—*vt.* instruir, enseñar, aleccionar, adiestrar.— **schoolboy** [skúlboj], *s.* muchacho de escuela, colegial.—**schoolgirl** [skúlgœrl], *s.* niña de escuela, colegiala.— **schoolhouse** [skúlhaus], *s.* escuela (edificio).—**schooling** [skúljŋ], *s.* instrucción elemental; educación, en-

señanza.—**schoolmaster** [skúlmæstœ(r)], *s.* maestro de escuela.—**schoolmate** [skúlmejt], *s.* condiscípulo.— **schoolroom** [skúlrum], *s.* aula, sala de clase.—**schoolteacher** [skúltichœ(r)], *s.* = SCHOOLMASTER.

schooner [skúnœ(r)], *s.* goleta.

science [sájɛns], *s.* ciencia.—**scientific** [sajɛntíjfjk], *a.* científico.—**scientist** [sájɛntjst], *s.* científico u hombre de ciencia.

scissors [sízo(r)z], *s. pl.* tijeras.

scoff [skaf], *vi.* (con at) mofarse o burlarse de; befar.—*s.* mofa, escarnio, burla, befa.— **law** [skáflo], *s.* el que burla el cumplimiento de la ley.

scold [skould], *vt. y vi.* regañar, reñir, reprender.—*s.* regañón; mujer de lenguaje soez.— **ing** [skóuldjŋ], *s.* regaño, reprensión.—*a.* regañón.

scoop [skup], *s.* pala de mano; cuchara o cucharón de draga; paletada; (fam.) hallazgo, ganancia; noticia que publica un periódico antes que los demás.—*vt.* sacar con pala o cuchara; achicar; ahuecar, cavar, excavar.

scoot [skut], *vi.* (fam.) largarse, tomar las de Villadiego.— **er** [skútœ(r)], *s.* patinete, carriola; motoneta.

scope [skoup], *s.* alcance, extensión; campo, espacio o esfera de acción; (fig.) envergadura.

scorch [skorch], *vt.* chamuscar, rescaldar, tostar; quemar, abrasar, picar (el sol).—*vi.* quemarse, secarse; abrasarse (apl. a las plantas).—*s.* quemadura superficial, chamusquina.

score [skor], *s.* línea, raya; cuenta, tantos (en el juego); (dep.) anotación, punteo, tanteo; resultado final; (mús.) partitura; veintena.—*on that s.*, a ese respecto, en cuanto a eso.—*on the s. of*, con motivo de.—*s. keeper*, (dep.) anotador, tanteador.—*to settle a s.*, ajustar cuentas; saldar una cuenta.—*vt.* rayar; tantear, ganar tantos en un juego; (mús.) instrumentar.—*to s. a point*, (dep.) ganar un tanto; obtener un triunfo.—*vi.* marcar; llevar una cuenta; marcar los tantos en un juego; (fig.) recibir buena acogida, merecer aplausos.— **r** [skórœ(r)], *s.* marcador.

scorn [skorn], *vt. y vi.* despreciar, menospreciar, desdeñar.—*s.* desdén, menosprecio, desprecio.— **ful** [skórnful], *a.* desdeñoso, despreciativo.

scorpion [skórpjon], *s.* escorpión, alacrán.

scot [skat], *s.* escote; tasa, gravamen, contribución; (S.) escocés.—*s. free*, libre de gravámenes; sano y salvo; impune.—**Scotch** [skach], *a.* escocés. —*s.* pueblo escocés; lengua escocesa; (E.U.) whisky escocés.—**Scotchman**

[skáchman], s. escocés.—**Scottish** [skátiš], a. = SCOTCH.

scoundrel [skáųndrẹl], s. pícaro, bribón, truhán.

scour [skaụr], vt. y vi. fregar, restregar, limpiar; pulir, alisar; quitar restregando.—s. recorrida; limpiador (esp. de lana).— er [skáụrœ(r)], s. limpiador, desengrasador, asperón.

scourge [skœrdž], s. azote, flagelo; plaga.—vt. azotar, flagelar.

scout [skaụt], s. (mil.) explorador, batidor, escucha; niño explorador.—vt. y vi. (mil.) explorar; reconocer.—to s. at, burlarse de, escarnecer; rechazar con desdén.

scowl [skaụl], vi. fruncir el ceño o el entrecejo; enfurruñarse; tener mal cariz.—s. ceño, entrecejo; mal cariz.

scram [skræm], vii. [1] (fam.) irse de prisa.—interj. ¡largo! ¡fuera!

scramble [skrǽmbl], vt. recoger de prisa o confusamente; embrollar; (coc.) hacer un revoltillo.—scrambled eggs, revoltillo, huevos revueltos.—vi. (bot.) trepar; andar a la rebatiña, bregar.— s. contienda, rebatiña.

scrap [skræp], s. migaja, mendrugo; pedacillo, fragmento; sobras; material viejo o de deshecho; (fam.) riña, camorra.—s. iron, hierro viejo, chatarra.—vti. [1] echar a la basura; descartar; desbaratar, desmantelar (un buque).—vii. (fam.) reñir, armar camorra.—book [skrǽpbųk], s. álbum de recortes.

scrape [skreịp], vt. y vi. raspar, rozar; rasguñar, arañar; (a veces con up o together) recoger, amontonar poco a poco; tocar mal (un instrumento de cuerda); restregar los pies.—to s. acquaintance, trabar amistad.—to s. along, (fam.) ir tirando, ir escapando.—s. raspadura, rasguño, arañazo; enredo, lío, aprieto, apuro.— r [skréịpœ(r)], s. raspador, rascador; (fam.) rascatripas; (mar.) rasqueta.

scratch [skræch], vt. y vi. rascar, raspar; arañar; rasguñar; rayar (el vidrio); escribir mal, garrapatear; escarbar; borrar.—s. rasguño, arañazo; marca o raya; (dep.) línea de arrancada en una carrera.—s. paper o pad, papel o cuadernillo de apuntes.—to start from s., empezar sin nada, o de (la) nada; comenzar desde el principio.—up to s., en buenas o excelentes condiciones.

scrawl [skrol], vt. garrapatear, garabatear.—s. garabato, garrapato.

scream [skrim], vt. y vi. chillar; gritar.—s. grito, alarido, chillido; (fam.) cosa o persona jocosa.

screech [skrich], vi. chillar, ulular.—

s. chillido, alarido.— y [skríchị], a. chillón, agudo.

screen [skrin], s. biombo, mampara; pantalla; resguardo; criba, cedazo, tamiz.—s. star, (cine) estrella o astro de la pantalla.—the s., el cine, la celuloide,. la pantalla.—vt. cribar, cerner, tamizar; escudar, proteger; filmar; proyectar en la pantalla.

screw [skru], s. tornillo.—a. de tornillo.—s. bolt, perno roscado.—s. nut, rosca, hembra de tornillo.—s. plate, terraja o tarraja.—s. thread, rosca (de tornillo).—vt. atornillar, (Am.) tornillar; torcer, retorcer.—to s. off, des(a)tornillar.—driver [skrúdraịvœ(r)], s. destornillador.

scribble [skríbl], vt. y vi. escribir de prisa; garrapatear, garabatear, emborronar.—s. garabato, garabateo.

script [skrịpt], s. guión de película; (teat.) manuscrito; (rad.) libreto; letra cursiva; (for.) escritura; material escrito a máquina.—**Scripture** [skrípchụr], s. (Sagrada) Escritura.

scrofula [skráfyǫlǎ], s. escrófula, (Am.) lamparón.

scroll [skroul], s. rollo de papel o pergamino; rasgo, rúbrica; (arq.) cinta, voluta.—a. en espiral; de caracol.

scrub [skrʌb], vti. [1] fregar, estregar; restregar.—a. achaparrado, desmirriado; inferior.—s. team, (dep.) equipo de jugadores novicios o suplentes.—s. estropajo, escoba vieja; animal de raza mixta e inferior; persona mezquina o inferior.

scruff [skrʌf], s. nuca, pescuezo.

scruple [skrúpl], s. escrúpulo.—vi. tener escrúpulos.—**scrupulous** [skrúpyǫlǎs], a. escrupuloso; puntilloso.—**scrupulousness** [skrúpyǫlịsnịs], s. escrupulosidad.

scrutinize [skrútịnaịz], vt. escudriñar, escrutar.—**scrutiny** [skrútịnị], s. escrutinio.

sculptor [skálptǫ(r)], s. escultor.—**sculpture** [skálpchụ(r)], s. escultura.—vt. esculpir, cincelar.

scum [skʌm], s. espuma, nata; hez, escoria.—the s. of the people, la canalla.

scurvy [skœrvị], s. escorbuto.

scuttle [skátl], s. escotillón; trampa; barreno, agujero; carrera corta; cubo, balde (para carbón).—vt. barrenar, dar barreno a un barco; echar a pique.—vi. apretar a correr.

scythe [saịθ], s. guadaña.

sea [si], s. mar.—a. de mar, marino, marítimo.—beyond the s. o seas, allende el mar; fuera de aguas jurisdiccionales.—s. biscuit, galleta de barco.—s. breeze, brisa de mar, virazón.—s. chart, carta náutica o de marear.—s. food, pescado y mariscos comestibles.—*s.* green, verdemar, glauco.—*s.* gull. gaviota.—*s.* lion, foca, león marino.—*s.* power, potencia naval.— —board [síbord], *a.* costanero, litoral.—*s.* costa; litoral.— —coast [-koųst], *s.* costa, litoral.

seal [sil], *s.* sello; timbre; precinto; firma; (zool.) foca.—*under the hand and s. of,* firmado y sellado por.— *vt.* sellar, precintar; estampar; cerrar una carta o paquete (con goma o lacre).— —ing wax [síliŋ wæks], *s.* lacre.

seam [sim], *s.* costura, cosedura; sutura; cicatriz, marca; (min.) filón, veta; yacimiento; (mec.) junta, costura (de un tubo, una caldera, etc.).— *vt.* echar una costura, coser; marcar con cicatriz.

seaman [símạn], *s.* marinero, marino.

seamless [símlịs], *a.* sin costura.— seamstress [símstrịs], *s.* costurera; modistilla.—seamy [símị], *a.* con costuras.—*the s. side,* el lado malo.

seaplane [síplẹin], *s.* hidroavión.—seaport [síport], *s.* puerto de mar.

sear [sịr], *a.* seco, marchito.—*vt.* secar, marchitar; tostar, chamuscar; cauterizar.

search [sŏrch], *vt. y vi.* buscar, explorar, escudriñar; registrar (una casa); investigar, indagar.—*to s. after,* preguntar por; indagar, inquirir.—*to s. for,* buscar; solicitar, procurar.—*to s. out,* buscar hasta descubrir.—*s.* registro, reconocimiento; pesquisa, indagación o investigación; búsqueda, busca.—*in s. of,* en busca de.—*s. for arms,* cacheo.— —ing [sŏrchịŋ], *a.* penetrante, escrutador.— —light [-lạịt], *s.* reflector lumínico (orientable); luz proyectada por éste.

seashore [síshọr], *s.* playa, litoral, ribera, costa, orilla del mar.—seasick [sísịk], *a.* mareado.—*to get s.,* marearse.—seasickness [sísịknịs], *s.* mareo.—seaside [sísạjd], *s.* = SEASHORE.

season [sízọn], *s.* estación (del año); sazón; temporada.—*in s.,* en sazón; a su tiempo.—*vt.* (coc.) sazonar, condimentar, aliñar; aclimatar, habituar. *vi.* sazonarse, madurarse, habituarse.— —ing [-iŋ], *s.* (coc.) condimento, aliño, aderezo, sazón; salsa o sal (de un cuento, etc.); desecación, cura (de la madera).

seat [sit], *s.* asiento; silla; escaño; (teat.) localidad; (sast.) fondillo de los calzones; nalga; sede (de diócesis); sitio, paraje; mansión, quinta.—*s. of war,* teatro de la guerra.—*vt.* sentar, asentar; colocar en asientos; tener asientos o cabida para; ajustar (una válvula) en su asiento; poner asiento a (una silla, etc.); echar fondillos (a

un pantalón).—*vi.* asentar, ajustar en su asiento (una válvula, etc.).

seaweed [síwịd], *s.* alga marina.

secant [síkẹnt], *s.* (geom.) secante.

seclude [sịklíụd], *vt.* apartar, recluir.— *vi.* alejarse de otros.— —d [sịklíụdịd], *a.* alejado o apartado; retirado, solitario, recogido.—seclusion [sịklíụžọn], *s.* reclusión, aislamiento, soledad; retiro.

second [sékọnd], *a.* segundo, secundario; inferior.—*every s. day,* cada dos días; un día sí y otro no.—*on s. thought,* después de repensarlo; después de pensarlo bien.—*s. hand,* segundero (de reloj).—*s. rate,* de segunda clase o categoría, de pacotilla. —*s.* segundo; momento, instante; brazo derecho; ayudante; padrine (en un duelo); segundo (de tiempo).— *vt.* apoyar, apadrinar; secundar o apoyar (una proposición).— —*adv.* en segundo lugar.— —ary [-ẹrị], *a.* secundario.—*s. school,* escuela secundaria o de segunda enseñanza.— —hand [-hænd], *a.* de segunda mano, usado; indirecto, por conducto ajeno o de oídas.— —ly [-lị], *adv.* en segundo lugar.

secrecy [síkrẹsị], *s.* secreto, reserva; sigilo.—secret [síkrịt], *a.* secreto; escondido, oculto, recóndito.—*s.* secreto.—secretary [sékrẹtẹrị], *s.* secretario, secretaria.—secrete [sịkrít], *vt.* esconder, ocultar, encubrir; (fisiol.) secretar.—secretion [sịkríšọn], *s.* (fisiol.) secreción.—secretive [sịkrítịv], *a.* callado, reservado; secretorio.

section [sékšọn], *s.* sección, división; porción; tajada muy delgada; departamento, negociado; (dib.) corte, sección.—*vt.* seccionar, dividir en secciones.

secular [sékyựlạ(r)], *a. y s.* secular.

secure [sịkịúr], *a.* seguro; confiado; firme, fuerte.—*vt.* asegurar, resguardar; afianzar, fijar; garantizar; procurarse, obtener.—security [sịkịúrịtị], *s.* seguridad, seguro (social); protección o defensa; fianza, garantía, prenda; fiador.—*pl.* (com.) valores, obligaciones.—*public securities,* efectos públicos.—*securities in hand,* valores en cartera.

sedate [sịdéịt], *a.* sentado, sosegado, serio.—sedative [sédạtịv], *a. y s.* (med.) sedativo, sedante, calmante.

sedge [sedž], *s.* (bot.) junco.

sediment [sédịmẹnt], *s.* sedimento, borra.

sedition [sịdíšọn], *s.* sedición.—seditious [sịdíšạs], *a.* sedicioso.

seduce [sịdíụs], *vt.* seducir, deshonrar.— —r [-œ(r)], *s.* seductor, burlador. —seduction [sịdákšọn], *s.* seducción.

see [si], *vti.* y *vii.* [10] ver.—*s.?* (fam.)
¿comprende? ¿sabe?—*to s. about,*
pensar en; averiguar.—*to s. (a person)
home,* acompañar (a una persona) a
su casa.—*to s. (a person) off,* ir a
despedir (a una persona).—*to s. red,*
echar chispas, montar en cólera.—*to
s. through (a proposition),* comprender
(una proposición).—*to s. through (a
person),* (fig.) leer, adivinar el pensamiento (a una persona).—*to s. (a person) through,* ayudar (a una persona)
a salir del paso, o hasta lo último.—
to s. (a thing) through, llevar (una
cosa) hasta el cabo; estar (en una
cosa) hasta lo último.—*to s. to,* atender
a, tener cuidado de; cuidarse de.—
to s. to it that, atender a que, ver que,
hacer que.—*I see,* ¡ya! ya veo, com-
prendo.—*let me s.,* vamos a ver; dé-
jeme pensar.—*s.* (igl.) silla, sede.
seed [sid], *s.* semilla, simiente; grano;
pepita.—*s. plot,* semillero.—*to go o
run to s.,* granar; agotarse, envejecerse.—*vt.* sembrar; despepitar.—*vi.*
hacer la siembra.— *—ling* [sídliŋ], *s.*
planta de semilla; planta de semillero;
retoño, brote.— *—y* [-i], *a.* que tiene
muchas semillas; (fam.) andrajoso,
descamisado, zarrapastroso.
seeing [síiŋ], *s.* vista, visión.—*conj.—s.
that,* visto que, siendo así que, puesto
que, ya que.—*a.* vidente, que ve.
seek [sik], *vti.* y *vii.* [10] buscar; pedir,
procurar, solicitar, aspirar a.—*to s.
after,* buscar, tratar de obtener.—*to
s. for,* buscar.
seem [sim], *vi.* parecer; parecerle a uno.
—*it seems to me,* me parece.— *—ingly*
[símiŋli], *adv.* aparentemente, al parecer.
seen [sin], *pp.* de TO SEE.
seep [sip], *vi.* filtrar; colarse, rezumarse,
escurrirse.
seesaw [síso], *s.* vaivén, columpio.—
a. de vaivén, de balance.—*vi.* colum-
piarse.
seethe [sið], *vt.* remojar, empapar.—
vi. hervir, bullir; estar agitado; burbujear.
segment [ségment], *s.* segmento; sección.
segregate [ségregeit], *vt.* y *vi.* segre-
gar(se), separar(se).—*a.* segregado,
separado.—**segregation** [segregéisọn],
s. segregación, separación.
seismic [sáizmik], *a.* sísmico.—**seismo-
graph** [sáizmogræf], *s.* sismógrafo.
seize [siz], *vt.* asir, agarrar, coger; capturar, prender; apoderarse de; aprovecharse de; (for.) secuestrar, embargar, decomisar, incautarse de (bienes, etc.).—*to be seized of,* (for.)
obtener posesión de.—*to be seized
with,* sobrecogerse de.—*vi.* (gen con

on o **upon**) agarrar, coger; apoderarse de.—**seizure** [síʒ(r)], *s.* aprehensión, prisión; captura, presa; (mil.)
toma; (for.) embargo, secuestro, (de)-
comiso; (med.) ataque, acceso súbito
de una enfermedad.
seldom [séldọm], *adv.* raramente, rara
vez, por rareza.
select [sẹlékt], *vt.* seleccionar, escoger,
entresacar.—*a.* selecto, escogido.—
—ion [sẹléksọn], *s.* selección, elección.
self [self], *a.* uno mismo; se; sí mismo.
—*s.* uno mismo, sí mismo.—*s.-con-
scious,* consciente de sí mismo; afectado, falto de naturalidad.—*s.-con-
sistent,* consecuente consigo mismo.—
s.-control, continencia; imperio sobre
sí mismo.—*s.-defense,* defensa propia.
—*s.-possession,* sangre fría, serenidad,
aplomo.—*s.-respect,* pundonor, dignidad, decoro, respeto de sí mismo.—
s.-winding, de cuerda automática (apl.
a relojes).— *—ish* [sélfis], *a.* egoísta,
interesado.— *—ishness* [-ísnis], *s.*
egoísmo.— *—same* [-séim], *a.* idéntico, mismísimo.
sell [sel], *vti.* y *vii.* [10] vender(se).—
to s. on trust, fiar, vender al fiado o
al crédito.—*to s. out,* realizar, hacer
venta de realización; venderlo todo.—
—er [sélẹ(r)], *s.* vendedor.— *—ing*
[-iŋ], *s.* venta.
selves [selvz], *s. pl.* de SELF.
semen [símen], *s.* semen, esperma;
(bot.) simiente, semilla.
semester [sẹméstẹ(r)], *s.* semestre.
semicircle [sémisœrkl], *s.* semicírculo.
semicolon [sémikoulọn], *s.* punto y
coma (;).
seminary [séminẹri], *s.* seminario.
senate [sénit], *s.* senado.—**senator** [sén-
ạtọ(r)], *s.* senador.
send [send], *vti.* [10] enviar, despachar,
expedir; lanzar, arrojar.—*to s. away,*
despedir, poner en la calle.—*to s. back,*
devolver; enviar de vuelta.—*to s.
forth,* echar (retoños, etc.); emitir,
despedir (luz, vapores); enviar, despachar.—*to s. in,* hacer entrar; introducir.—*to s. off,* despachar, expedir.—
to s. one about one's business, enviar
a paseo.—*to s. up,* mandar subir;
(fam.) enviar a la cárcel.—*to s. word,*
mandar recado; avisar; enviar a decir.— *—er* [séndẹ(r)], *s.* remitente;
(elec.) transmisor.
senile [sínail], *a.* senil, caduco, chocho.
—**senility** [sẹníliti], *s.* senilidad,
senectud.
senior [sínyọ(r)], *a.* mayor, de mayor
edad; más antiguo.—*s.* señor mayor,
anciano; socio más antiguo o principal; (E.U.) escolar del último año;
(abreviado Sr.) padre.

sensation [sɛnséiʃǫn], *s.* sensación.—*to be a s.*, ser un exitazo.— —*al* [-ạl], *a.* sensacional; escandaloso; emocionante.—**sense** [sɛns], *s.* sentido; razón, juicio; sensación; sentimiento; significado, interpretación.—*in a s.*, hasta cierto punto.—*to be out of one's senses*, haber perdido el juicio, no estar en sus cabales.—*vt.* percibir por los sentidos; (fam.) sentir.—**senseless** [sɛ́nslịs], *a.* insensible, privado, sin conocimiento; sin sentido, absurdo; insensato, necio.—**sensibility** [sɛnsibílịti], *s.* sensibilidad.—**sensible** [sɛ́nsịbl], *a.* cuerdo, razonable; sensato; sensible; sensitivo.—**sensibly** [sɛ́nsịblị], *adv.* perceptiblemente, sensiblemente; con sensatez o sentido común. —**sensitive** [sɛ́nsịtịv], *a.* sensitivo; sensible, impresionable; susceptible; tierno; delicado; (fot.) sensibilizado. —**sensitiveness** [sɛ́nsịtịvnịs], *s.* sensibilidad; susceptibilidad; finura, delicadeza.

sensual [sɛ́nsụạl], *a.* sensual, lascivo, lujurioso; carnal.— —*ity* [sɛnsụélịti], *s.* sensualidad, lascivia; lujuria.

sent [sɛnt], *pret.* y *pp.* de TO SEND.

sentence [sɛ́ntɛns], *s.* (gram.) oración, cláusula; (for.) sentencia, fallo; condena (de presidio); máxima, sentencia o dicho.—*vt.* sentenciar, condenar.

sentiment [sɛ́ntịmɛnt], *s.* sentimiento; afecto, simpatía; opinión, sentir; sentido, significado.— —*al* [sɛntịméntạl], *a.* sentimental.— —*ality* [sɛntịmentǽlịti], *s.* sentimentalismo.

sentinel [sɛ́ntịnɛl], **sentry** [sɛ́ntrị], *s.* (mil.) centinela.—*s. box*, garita (de centinela).

separate [sɛ́pạrẹit], *vt.* y *vi.* separar(se); apartar(se).—*a.* [sɛ́pạrịt], separado, aparte, suelto; distinto, diferente.— **separation** [sɛpạréiʃǫn], *s.* separación.

September [sɛptémbœ(r)], *s.* septiembre.

sepulcher [sɛ́pʌlkœ(r)], *s.* sepulcro, sepultura.

sequel [síkwɛl], *s.* secuela, consecuencia, efecto; continuación.—**sequence** [síkwɛns], *s.* secuencia; serie, orden de sucesión; arreglo; encadenamiento, ilación; efecto; (en los naipes) runfla de un palo.

sequin [síkwịn], *s.* lentejuela.

sequoia [sịkwóịạ], *s.* abeto gigantesco de California, secoya.

serape [serápei], *s.* sarape.

Serb [sœrb], **Serbian** [sœ́rbịạn], *s.* y *a.* servio.

serenade [serẹnéjd], *s.* (mús.) serenata. —*vt.* dar serenata a.

serene [sẹrín], *a.* sereno, despejado; sosegado, tranquilo.—**serenity** [sẹrén-

iti], *s.* serenidad; tranquilidad, calma, quietud.

serge [sœrdʒ], *s.* estameña.

sergeant [sárdʒɛnt], *s.* (mil.) sargento.

serial [sírịạl], *a.* de o en serie; de orden (número, marca, etc.); consecutivo; formando serie; que se publica por entregas.—*s.* obra que se publica por entregas; película por episodios.—**series** [sírịz], *s.* serie; sucesión, cadena; ciclo.—*in s.*, (elec.) en serie.

serious [sírịʌs], *a.* serio; formal; grave, de peso.— —*ness* [-nịs], *s.* seriedad; formalidad; gravedad.

sermon [sœ́rmǫn], *s.* sermón.

serpent [sœ́rpɛnt], *s.* serpiente o sierpe.

serum [sírʌm], *s.* suero.

servant [sœ́rvạnt], *s.* criado, sirviente; servidor.—*pl.* servidumbre.—*s. girl*, *s. maid*, criada, sirvienta, doncella, (Am.) mucama.—**serve** [sœrv], *vt.* servir; manejar, hacer funcionar (un cañón, etc.); abastecer, surtir; cumplir (una condena).—*it serves you right*, (en tono de represión) te está bien empleado; bien se lo merece Ud.—*to s. an office*, desempeñar un cargo.—*to s. a warrant*, ejecutar un auto de prisión.—*to s. one a trick*, jugar a uno una mala partida.—*to s. notice (on)*, avisar o dar aviso, hacer saber, advertir, notificar.—*to s. time*, cumplir una condena en presidio. —*vi.* servir; bastar, ser suficiente o apto; (dep.) efectuar el saque, sacar. —*to s. for*, servir de; hacer oficio de. —*s.* (dep.) saque.—**server** [sœ́rvœ(r)], *s.* servidor.—**service** [sœ́rvịs], *s.* servicio; (dep.) saque; vajilla, servicio de mesa, juego (de café, etc.); entrega legal de una citación.—*at your s.*, a su disposición, a sus órdenes, servidor de Ud.—*it is of no s.*, no vale nada, de nada sirve.—*out of s.*, (mec.) que no funciona, descompuesto.—*s. station*, (aut.) estación de servicio, taller de reparaciones.—*vt.* atender a, suministrar lo necesario a o para.— **serviceable** [sœ́rvịsạbl], *a.* servicial, servible, útil; duradero.—**servile** [sœ́rvịl], *a.* servil, bajo, abyecto.—**servitude** [sœ́rvịtjud], *s.* servidumbre; esclavitud; vasallaje; (for.) servidumbre.

session [sɛ́ʃǫn], *s.* sesión; período escolar.

set [sɛt], *vti.* [9] poner; colocar, asentar; instalar, establecer; fijar, inmovilizar; señalar; engastar, montar (piedras preciosas); arreglar; regular, ajustar; establecer; componer (tipos de imprenta); poner en música; (med.) reducir (fracturas).—*to s. afire*, poner fuego a, incendiar.—*to s. ajar*, entornar, entreabrir.—*to s. an example*, dar ejemplo.—*to s. a price on*, fijar precio a; poner precio, ofrecer premio por.—*to s. aside*, poner aparte.—*to s. a trap*, armar una trampa.—*to s. back*, hacer retroceder; atrasar, retrasar.—*to s. eyes on*, ver; mirar; clavar los ojos en.—*to s. fire to*, poner o prender fuego a, incendiar; inflamar (las pasiones).—*to s. forth*, manifestar; exponer; publicar.—*to s. in*, (joy.) montar, engastar.—*to s. off*, poner aparte, separar; poner en relieve: disparar. —*to s. up the drinks*, (fam.) convidar (a beber).—*vii.* ponerse (un astro); cuajarse, solidificarse; endurecerse; fraguar (el hormigón, etc.); correr, moverse o fluir (una corriente); empollar (las aves); (fam.) ajustar, caer bien (una prenda de vestir).—*to s. forth*, avanzar, ponerse en marcha.— *to s. in*, comenzar, aparecer, sobrevenir; cerrar (la noche).—*to set off*, salir, partir.—*to s. on o upon*, salir, partir; emprender un viaje o un negocio.—*to s. to work*, poner manos a la obra; emprender el trabajo.—*to s. up*, establecerse; principiar.—*pret.* y *pp.* de to set.—*a.* resuelto; fijo, invariable; establecido; arreglado, ajustado; puesto, colocado; rígido; (mec.) armado; joy.) montado, engastado.— *to be all s. to*, estar listo o preparado. —*s.* juego, surtido, colección, serie, grupo, clase; equipo; aparato (de radio); (astr.) puesta; curso, dirección; (teat.) decoración; (dep.) partida; (danz.) tanda; fraguado (del cemento, etc.).—*s. of books*, colección de libros.—*s. of diamonds*, terno.— **back** [sétbæk], *s.* retroceso, revés, contracorriente.

settee [setí], *s.* canapé, diván.

setter [sétœ(r)], *s.* perro perdiguero.

setting [sétiŋ], *s.* puesta de un astro, ocaso; (teat.) puesta en escena, decoraciones; (joy.) engaste, montadura; (fam.) nidada.—*s. sun*, sol poniente. —*s. up*, establecimiento; (mec.) montaje.

settle [sétl], *vt.* asentar; fijar, asegurar; arreglar; establecer, estatuir; casar; colonizar, poblar; sosegar, calmar; resolver (dudas); solucionar (un problema); señalar, fijar; saldar, finiquitar, ajustar (cuentas); componer.—*to s. on o upon*, señalar, asignar, dar en dote.—*vi.* asentarse; establecerse; radicarse; instalarse, poner casa; calmar; determinarse; saldar una cuenta. —*to s. differences*, avenirse, hacer las paces.—*to s. down*, asentarse; posarse (un hidroavión o ave).— **ment** [-mênt], *s.* establecimiento; colonización; colonia; caserío, poblado; (for.) asiento, domicilio; dote; empleo, des-

tino; ajuste, arreglo; (com.) saldo, liquidación, finiquito, pago.—*s. house*, casa de beneficencia.—**r** [sétlœ(r)], *s.* poblador, colono; fundador.

sever [sévœ(r)], *vt.* separar, desunir, dividir; cortar, romper.—*vi.* separarse, desunirse; partirse.

several [sévœral], *a.* varios, diversos; distinto(s), respectivo(s).—*s.* varios, cada uno en particular.

severe [sevír], *a.* severo, riguroso; duro; rígido, estricto, austero; grave, serio; recio, fuerte.—**severity** [sevériti], *s.* severidad, rigor; rigidez, austeridad; seriedad, gravedad.

sew [soų], *vti.* y *vii.* [6] coser.

sewer [siúœ(r)], *s.* albañal, cloaca, alcantarilla.

sewing [sóųiŋ], *s.* costura.—*a.* de coser; para coser.—*s. machine*, máquina de coser.—**sewn** [soųn], *pp.* de to sew.

sex [seks], *s.* sexo.—*s. appeal*, atracción sexual.—*the fair s.*, el bello sexo.

sexagenarian [seksædženérįan], *a.* y *s.* sexagenario.

sexton [sékstǫn], *s.* sacristán.

sexual [sékšųal], *a.* sexual.—*s. intercourse*, comercio sexual.—**sexy** [séksi], *a.* sensual.

shabby [šæbi], *a.* usado, gastado, raído; andrajoso, zarrapastroso; ruin, vil.

shack [šæk], *s.* choza, casucha.

shackle [šækl], *vt.* encadenar; poner esposas o grilletes a; trabar; poner obstáculos, estorbar.—*s.* grillete, grillo, esposa; traba; impedimento.—*pl.* hierros, prisiones.

shade [šeįd], *s.* sombra; matiz, tinte; visillo, cortina; pantalla de lámpara; visera.—*vt.* sombrear, dar sombra; resguardar de la luz; matizar.—**shading** [šéįdiŋ], *s.* (b.a.) sombreado.— **shadow** [šædoų], *s.* sombra (proyectada por un objeto); oscuridad; imagen reflejada (en agua o espejo).— *vt.* oscurecer, sombrear; espiar, seguir a uno como su sombra; (b.a.) sombrear, matizar.—*vi.* oscurecerse; cambiar gradualmente de color.—**shady** [šéįdi], *a.* sombreado, sombrío; (fam.) sospechoso.—*to keep s.*, (fam.) guardar oculto.

shaft [šæft], *s.* pieza larga y estrecha o parte larga y estrecha de la misma (mango, cabo, etc. de un arma o herramienta); flecha o saeta; lanza, vara (de coche, carretón, etc.); fuste (de una columna o carruaje); (mec.) eje árbol; pozo, tiro (de mina, ascensor, etc.); cañón de chimenea.

shaggy [šægi], *a.* peludo, velludo, hirsuto; lanudo; áspero.

shake [šeįk], *vti.* [10] sacudir o menear, cimbrear; hacer temblar; hacer vacilar o flaquear; agitar.—*to s. hands*, estrecharse la mano.—*to s. one's head*, cabecear, mover la cabeza.—*to s. up*, sacudir; agitar; (fam.) regañar, sermonear.—*vii.* temblar; estremecerse; cimbrearse; vacilar, titubear; (fam.) dar(se) la mano.—*to s. in one's shoes* o *boots*, temblar de miedo.—*to s. with cold*, tiritar.—*to s. with laughter*, desternillarse o reventar de risa.—*s.* sacudida; sacudimiento; temblor; apretón de manos; instante; batido (de leche, fruta, chocolate, etc.).— **shaken** [šéikn], *pp.* de TO SHAKE.— **shaky** [šéiki], *a.* trémulo; vacilante, tambaleante; tembloroso; debilitado; incierto.

shall [šæl], *vai.* [11] (se usa para formar el futuro o para expresar obligación). —*they s. not pass*, no pasarán.—*you s. do it*, tiene Ud. que hacerlo.—(V. SHOULD).

shallow [šǽlou], *a.* bajo, poco profundo; superficial.—*s.-brained*, ligero de cascos.—*s.* (mar.) bajío, bajo.— *ness* [-nis], *s.* poca profundidad; superficialidad; frivolidad.

sham [šæm], *vti.* y *vii.* [1] simular, fingir.—*s.* fingimiento, ficción; (fam.) bambolla, farsa.—*a.* fingido, disimulado; falso, postizo.—*s. battle*, (mil.) simulacro.

shame [šeim], *s.* vergüenza; ignominia, deshonra; bochorno.—*for s.! s. on you!* ¡qué vergüenza!—*it is a s.*, es una vergüenza o una lástima.— *what a s.!* ¡qué lástima!—*vt.* avergonzar, abochornar; deshonrar.— —**ful** [šéimful], *a.* vergonzoso, escandaloso. — —**less** [-lis], *a.* desvergonzado, sin vergüenza, descarado.

shampoo [šæmpú], *s.* lavado de cabeza; champú.—*vt.* lavar la cabeza; dar champú.

shamrock [šǽmrak], *s.* trébol.

shank [šǽŋk], *s.* caña o canilla de la pierna; zanca; (mec.) asta o astil, mango, vástago, caña.

shanty [šǽnti], *s.* casucha, choza.

shape [šeip], *vt.* formar; dar forma a.— *vi.* (a veces con up) empezar a tomar, formar o mostrar progreso.—*s.* forma, figura, hechura (de una persona); estado, manera, modo.— —**less** [šéiplis], *a.* informe; disforme.

share [šer], *vt.* repartir; compartir; (con **in**) participar de, tener o tomar parte en.—*vi.* participar o tener parte.— *s.* parte, porción; (com.) acción; participación.—*to go shares*, ir a medias.— —**holder** [šérhouldœr(r)], *s.* (com.) accionista.

shark [šark], *s.* tiburón, escualo; (fig.) estafador; usurero; (fam.) perito, experto.

sharp [šarp], *a.* agudo; puntiagudo;

cortante, afilado; sagaz; vivo, astuto; incisivo, penetrante; acre, agrio; mordaz, sarcástico; distinto, claro, bien delineado o definido; (mús.) sostenido; punzante (dolor); abrupto, pronunciado (pendiente, curva, etc.).— *s. features*, facciones enjutas.—*s.* (mús.) sostenido; estafador, fullero. —*adv.* V. SHARPLY.—*at four o'clock s.*, (fam.) a las cuatro en punto.— *s.-edged*, afilado.—*s.-pointed*, puntiagudo.—*s.-witted*, penetrante, perspicaz.— —**en** [šárpn], *vt.* afilar; aguzar, sacar punta a, amolar.—*vi.* aguzarse; afilarse.— —**ener** [-œnœ(r)], *s.* afilador, aguzador.—*pencil s.*, sacapuntas.— —**er** [-œ(r)], *s.* tahur, fullero; estafador.— —**ly** [-li], *adv.* con filo; prontamente; brusca y mordazmente; agudamente, vivamente; sutil o ingeniosamente.— —**ness** [-nis], *s.* agudeza, sutileza, perspicacia; mordacidad; acidez; rigor; inclemencia.— —**shooter** [-šútœ(r)], *s.* tirador certero.

shatter [šǽtœ(r)], *vt.* destrozar, hacer pedazos o añicos; estrellar, romper; quebrantar (la salud).—*vi.* hacerse pedazos, quebrarse, romperse.—*s.* fragmento, pedazo.

shave [šeiv], *vti.* [6] rasurar o afeitar; rapar; (carp.) (a)cepillar; desbastar. —*vii.* rasurarse, afeitarse.—*s.* afeitado, (Am.) afeitada.—*to have a close s.*, salvarse en una tabla, escapar por casualidad.—**shaving** [šéiviŋ], *s.* afeitado, rasura(ción), (Am.) afeitada. —*pl.* virutas.

shawl [šol], *s.* chal, mantón, pañolón.— *Spanish s.*, mantón de Manila.

she [ši], *pron. pers.* ella; (delante de **who** o **that**) la que, aquella que.—*s. -cat* (*-goat*, *-ass*, etc.) gata (cabra, burra, etc.).

sheaf [šif], *s.* gavilla, haz; atado, manojo.—*vt.* agavillar.

shear [šir], *vti.* [6] rapar, esquilar, trasquilar; tonsurar; cortar (gen. con tijeras o cizallas).— —**er** [šírœ(r)], *s.* esquilador.— —**s** [-z], *s. pl.* tijeras grandes; (mec.) cizallas.

sheath [šiθ], *s.* vaina; funda, estuche, cubierta.— —**e** [šið], *vt.* envainar; poner vaina.

sheaves [šivz], *pl.* de SHEAF.

shed [šed], *vti.* [9] desprenderse de, largar; mudar; verter, derramar; esparcir.—*vii.* mudar (los cuernos, la piel, las plumas).—*s.* cobertizo; tejadillo.—*pret.* y *pp.* de TO SHED.

sheen [šin], *s.* lustre, viso.

sheep [šip], *s.* oveja, carnero; ovejas; ganado lanar; (fig.) rebaño, grey.— *s. dog*, perro de pastor.—*s. tick*, garrapata.— —**fold** [šípfould], *s.* redil, aprisco, majada.— —**ish** [-iš], *a.* avergonzado; tímido, pusilánime.—**—skin** [-skịn], *s.* badana.

sheet [šit], *s.* lámina (de metal); sábana; pliego u hoja (de papel); extensión de agua.—*s. lightning*, fucilazo(s), relampagueo.

shelf [šɛlf], *s.* anaquel, estante, repisa, tabla, entrepaño; saliente (de roca).

shell [šɛl], *s.* concha, carapacho; casco (de embarcación); cáscara (de nuez, huevo, etc.); vaina (de legumbres); cubierta, corteza; armazón (de edificio); (arti.) bomba, granada, proyectil; cápsula para cartuchos; bote o canoa para regatas.—*vt.* descascarar, desvainar, mondar, pelar; (arti.) bombardear.—*vi.* descascararse.—*to s. out,* (fam.) aflojar la mosca.

shellac [šɛlǽk], *s.* (goma) laca.—*vti.* [8] barnizar con laca.—**shellacked** [šɛlǽkt], *pret.* y *pp.* de TO SHELLAC.

shellfish [šɛlfiš], *s.* marisco(s).

shelter [šɛltœ(r)], *s.* resguardo; albergue, refugio, abrigo, asilo; protector.—*vt.* guarecer, abrigar, albergar, amparar, proteger.—*to take s.*, refugiarse, guarecerse.

shelve [šɛlv], *vt.* poner sobre un estante o anaquel; (fig.) poner a un lado, dar carpetazo, archivar, arrinconar.—**—s** [-z], *pl.* de SHELF.

shepherd [šépœrd], *s.* pastor; zagal; (fig.) párroco, cura.—*s. dog*, perro de pastor.—*s.'s hut*, tugurio.—**—ess** [-ịs], *s.* pastora; zagala.

sherbet [šœrbịt], *s.* sorbete, helado.

sheriff [šérịf], *s.* (E.U.) oficial de justicia; alguacil mayor.

sherry [šérị], *s.* vino de Jerez.

shield [šild], *s.* escudo; broquel, rodela; resguardo, defensa; protector.—*vt.* escudar, resguardar, proteger.

shift [šịft], *vt.* cambiar; desviar; trasladar; mudar la ropa; (teat.) cambiar de decoración.—*to s. about*, revolverse, girar.—*to s. for oneself*, ingeniarse, darse maña, componérselas.—*to s. gears*, (aut.) cambiar de marcha; *to s. into high*, (aut.) meter la directa.—*vi.* moverse; cambiar de puesto, mudarse; mudar, cambiar, variar.—*to s. for oneself*, ingeniarse, arreglárselas.—*s.* cambio; desviación; maña, subterfugio; turno o tanda de obreros.

shilling [šílịŋ], *s.* chelín.

shin [šịn], *s.* espinilla (de la pierna).—*s. bone*, tibia, canilla, caña.—*vti.* y *vii.* [1] trepar.

shine [šajn], *vii.* [10] (re)lucir, brillar, fulgurar, resplandecer; hacer sol o buen tiempo.—*vt.* pulir, bruñir; dar lustre (a los zapatos); limpiar (el calzado), (Méx.) embolar.—*s.* resplandor, lustre, brillo.

shingle [šíŋgl], *vt.* cubrir con ripia;

techar o entejar con tejamaniles; cortar (el pelo) corto y en declive.—*s.* pelo corto rebajado gradualmente; tabla de ripia o uralita; (Am.) tejamanil; (E.U.) letrero de oficina; china, cascajo.

shining [šájnịŋ], *a.* brillante, resplandeciente; (re)luciente.

shiny [šájnị], *a.* lustroso, brillante.

ship [šịp], *s.* barco, buque, nave, navío; dirigible; avión.—*s. boy*, grumete.—*s. carpenter*, carpintero de ribera.—*s. chandler*, proveedor de buques.—*vti.* [1] embarcar; (com.) enviar, despachar, remesar;—*vii.* ir a bordo, embarcar; enrolarse como marinero.—**—board** [šípbɔrd], *s.* (mar.) bordo; *on s.*, a bordo.—**—builder** [-bịldœ(r)], *s.* ingeniero naval, constructor de buques.—**—mate** [-mejt], *s.* compañero de a bordo.—**—ment** [-mẹnt], *s.* (com.) embarque; cargamento, partida; envío, despacho, consignación, remesa.—**—owner** [-oųnœ(r)], *s.* naviero, armador.—**—per** [-œ(r)], *s.* embarcador, fletador; expedidor, remitente.—**—ping** [-ịŋ], *s.* (com.) embarque; envío, despacho.—*a.* naval, marítimo, de marina mercante.—*s. agent*, consignatario de buques.—**—wreck** [-rɛk], *s.* naufragio.—*vt.* hacer naufragar o zozobrar, echar a pique.—*shipwrecked person*, naúfrago.—**—yard** [-yard], *s.* astillero, varadero.

shirk [šœrk], *vt.* y *vi.* evadir(se de); eludir, evitar.

shirt [šœrt], *s.* camisa; blusa.

shiver [šívœ(r)], *s.* temblor, (es)calofrío, estremecimiento.—*vi.* tiritar, temblar.

shoal [šoųl], *s.* bajo, bajío, banco de arena; banco de peces.—*a.* poco profundo, bajo.

shock [šak], *s.* choque; sacudida, sacudimiento; golpe; susto, sobresalto, emoción; ofensa; (med.) choque, postración nerviosa.—*s. absorber*, (mec. y aut.) amortiguador.—*s. dog*, perro de lanas.—*s. troops*, tropas (escogidas) de asalto.—*vt.* y *vi.* sacudir, dar una sacudida; chocar, ofender, disgustar; conmover; escandalizar, horrorizar; (agr.) hacinar.—**—ing** [šákịŋ], *a.* espantoso, horrible; chocante, ofensivo.

shod [šad], *pret.* y *pp.* de TO SHOE.

shoe [šu], *s.* zapato; herradura.—*s. blacking*, betún para zapatos, bola.—*s. lace*, cordón, lazo (de zapatos).—*s. polish*, lustre, betún, bola.—*s. store*, zapatería.—*to be in his* (their, etc.) *shoes*, estar en su pellejo.—*vti.* [10] herrar (un caballo); calzar (a una persona, el ancla).—**—horn** [šúhorn], *s.* calzador.—**—maker** [-mejkœ(r)], *s.*

zapatero.— —**string** [-striŋ], *s.* cordón, lazo (de zapato).

shone [śoun], *pret.* y *pp.* de TO SHINE.

shook [śuk], *pret.* de TO SHAKE.

shoot [śut], *vti.* [10] tirar, disparar; descargar; herir o matar con arma de fuego; fusilar, pasar por las armas; arrojar, lanzar; emitir (un rayo); rodar, filmar (una escena o película).— *to s. down*, tumbar a balazos.—*to s. off*, tirar, descargar (arma de fuego); llevarse.—*vii.* tirar, disparar armas de fuego; pasar o correr rápidamente; nacer, brotar, germinar; punzar (un dolor).—*to s. forth*, lanzarse o abalanzarse.— *to s. out*, brotar, germinar.— *to s. up*, nacer, crecer; madurar.— *s.* vástago, retoño.— —**er** [śutœ(r)], *s.* tirador.— —**ing** [-iŋ], *s.* tiroteo, tiro(s), descarga; (cine) filmación de una escena.—*s. star*, estrella fugaz.

shop [śap], *s.* tienda; taller.—*a.* de tienda; de taller.—*vii.* [1] ir de tiendas o de compras, hacer compras.— —**keeper** [śápkipœ(r)], *s.* tendero.— —**ping** [-iŋ], *s.* compras.—*to go s.*, ir de tiendas o de compras.— —**worn** [-worn], *a.* sobado, deslucido por el manoseo y trajín de la tienda.

shore [śor], *s.* costa, ribera, playa, orilla; litoral; (constr.) puntal.—*vt.* apuntalar, acodalar.

shorn [śorn], *pp.* de TO SHEAR.—*a.* mocho, chamorro.

short [śort], *a.* corto; bajo de estatura; diminuto, pequeño; falto, escaso; breve, conciso; próximo, cercano.— *in a o within a s. time o while*, en un rato; en poco tiempo; dentro de poco.—*in s. order*, prontamente.—*on s. notice*, prontamente, con poco tiempo de aviso.—*on s. term*, (com.) a corto plazo.—*s. circuit*, cortocircuito.—*s. cut*, atajo; método abreviado o corto.—*s. of this*, fuera de esto.—*s. sale*, venta de artículos que el vendedor no tiene aún.—*to be s.*, para abreviar.—*to be s. of*, estar lejos de; no responder a; estar escaso de.— *to cut s.*, interrumpir, abreviar.—*to fall s. of*, ser inferior a, no corresponder a, no alcanzar.—*to grow s.*, acortarse, disminuir.—*s.* resumen, (com.) déficit.—*for s.*, para abreviar. para mayor brevedad.—*in s.*, en resumidas cuentas.—*pl.* pantalones cortos; calzoncillos; (cine) películas cortas.—*adv.* brevemente.—*s.-handed*, escaso de personal.—*s.-tempered*, irascible.—*s.-winded*, asmático, corto de respiración.— —**age** [śrtidž], *s.* déficit; carestía, escasez, falta, merma.— —**cake** [-keik], *s.* (coc.) torta de frutas.- —**coming** [-kʌmiŋ], *s.* defecto; negligencia, descuido; falta.— —**en**

[-n], *vt.* y *vi.* acortar(se), abreviar(se), disminuir(se), encoger(se).— —**ening** [-eniŋ], *s.* acortamiento; abreviación; (coc.) manteca o grasa con que se hacen hojaldres, etc.— —**hand** [-hænd], *s.* taquigrafía, estenografía.—*a.* taquigráfico.— —**ly** [-li], *adv.* luego, al instante, dentro de poco; brevemente; en breve.—*s. after*, a poco de.—*s. afterward*, al poco rato.—*s. before*, poco antes.— —**ness** [-nis], *s.* cortedad; pequeñez; brevedad; deficiencia.- —**sighted** [-saitid], *a.* miope, cegato; falto de perspicacia.

shot [śat], *pret.* y *pp.* de TO SHOOT.— *vti.* [1] cargar con perdigones.—*s.* perdigón; munición, perdigones; bala, proyectil; tiro, disparo; escopetazo; balazo; alcance (de pistola, etc.); tirada, jugada (en el billar); inyección; (fam.) trago (de licor).—*a good s.*, un tirador certero.—*like a s.*, como un rayo; disparado.—*not by a long s.*, (fam.) ni por asomo, ni por pienso.— *to take a s. at*, hacer un tiro a; echar una púa, burla o indirecta a.— —**gun** [śatgʌn], *s.* escopeta.

should [śud], *vai.* [11] (se usa para formar el condicional o para expresar obligación).—*I said that I s. go*, dije que iría.—*you s. tell him*, Ud. debe (o debería) decírselo.—V. SHALL.

shoulder [śóuldœ(r)], *s.* hombro; encuentro (de un ave); pernil, cuarto delantero (de un cuadrúpedo); saliente o contenes (de carretera, camino, etc.).—*pl.* espalda(s), hombros. —*on one's shoulders*, a cuestas.—*s. blade*, omóplato u omoplato, paletilla.—*s. pad*, hombrera.—*s. to s.*, hombro con hombro; unidamente.— *to put one's s. to the wheel*, arrimar el hombro, echar una mano.—*vt.* echarse a la espalda, cargar al hombro, llevar a hombros; (fig.) cargar con, asumir. —*s. arms*, (mil.) armas al hombro.

shout [śaut], *vt.* y *vi.* vocear, gritar, vociferar; vitorear.—*s.* grito, alarido; aclamación.

shove [śʌv], *vt.* y *vi.* empujar, dar empujones o empellones.—*to s. away*, rechazar, alejar.—*to s. off*, echar afuera (una embarcación); alejarse de, dejar.—*to s. out*, empujar hacia afuera, hacer salir.—*s.* empellón, empujón, empuje.

shovel [śʌvel], *s.* pala.—*vti.* [2] traspalar, (Am.) palear.— —**ful** [-ful], *s.* palada.

show [śou], *vti.* [6] mostrar, enseñar; señalar; exhibir; indicar, probar, demostrar; poner en escena, representar (un drama); poner, proyectar (una película).—*to s. forth*, exponer, mostrar; publicar.—*to s. in*, introducir, hacer entrar (a una persona).—*to s. off*, hacer gala de.—*to s. one's cards o hand*, mostrar el juego; (fig.) dejarse ver (las intenciones).—*to s. up*, hacer subir (a una persona); denunciar, descubrir, arrancar la careta a.—*vii*. aparecer, mostrarse, asomarse.—*to s. off*, alardear; pavonearse.—*to s. through*, transparentarse; entrelucir.—*to s. up*, aparecer, presentarse.—*s*. exhibición, exposición; espectáculo público; (teat.) función; ostentación; apariencia; (fam. E.U.) oportunidad. —*s. bill*, cartel, cartelón, rótulo.— *s. window*, escaparate de tienda, vidriera.— —*case* [sóukeis], *s.* aparador, vitrina.— —*down* [-daun], *s*. acción perentoria o definitiva; hora de la verdad.

shower [sháʊœ(r)], *s*. chubasco, chaparrón; (baño de) ducha.—*heavy s.*, aguacero.—*vt*. llover, regar, derramar con abundancia.—*vi*. llover, caer un chubasco.

shown [soʊn], *pp.* de TO SHOW.—**showy** [sóui], *a*. ostentoso, vistoso, suntuoso, rimbombante; chillón, charro.

shrank [ʃræŋk], *pret*. de TO SHRINK.

shrapnel [ʃrǽpnəl], *s*. (arti.) metralla; granada de metralla.

shred [ʃred], *vti*. [3] picar, desmenuzar, hacer trizas o tiras.—*s*. triza, jirón, tira, retazo; fragmento, pizca.

shrew [ʃru], *s*. arpía, virago, mujer de mal genio; (zool.) musaraña.

shrewd [ʃrud], *a*. perspicaz, sagaz; astuto; agudo, cortante.— —*ness* [ʃrúdnis], *s*. sagacidad, astucia, sutileza.

shriek [ʃrik], *vi*. chillar, gritar.—*s*. chillido, grito agudo.

shrill [ʃril], *a*. chillón, estridente, agudo, penetrante.—*vt. y vi*. chillar.

shrimp [ʃrimp], *s*. (zool.) camarón, quisquilla; (fam.) enano.

shrine [ʃrain], *s*. santuario, capilla, templete.

shrink [ʃriŋk], *vii*. [10] encogerse, contraerse; disminuir, mermar; (con *from*) evadir, apartarse o huir de; retroceder.—*to s. back*, retirarse, retroceder.—*vti*. encoger, contraer.— —*age* [ʃríŋkidʒ], *s*. encogimiento o contracción; (com.) merma, pérdida.

shrivel [ʃrívəl], *vti*. [2] arrugar, fruncir, doblar, encoger; estrechar; marchitar. —*vii*. arrugarse, fruncirse, encogerse, deshincharse; marchitarse.

shroud [ʃraud], *s*. mortaja, sudario.— *vt*. amortajar; (fig.) cubrir, ocultar.

shrub [ʃrʌb], *s*. arbusto.— —*bery* [ʃrʌ́bœri], *s*. arbustos; grupo de arbustos; maleza.

shrug [ʃrʌg], *vii*. [1] encogerse de hombros.—*s*. encogimiento de hombros.

shrunk [ʃrʌŋk], *pret*. y *pp*. de TO SHRINK.—**shrunken** [ʃrʌ́ŋkən], *pp*. de TO SHRINK.

shudder [ʃʌ́dœ(r)], *vi*. estremecerse, temblar.—*s*. temblor, estremecimiento.

shuffle [ʃʌ́fl], *vt. y vi*. barajar (naipes); mezclar, revolver.—*to s. along*, arrastrar los pies, chancletear; ir tirando o pasando.—*s*. evasiva, salida; mezcla, confusión; restregamiento de los pies en el suelo, chancleteo.

shun [ʃʌn], *vti. y vii*. [1] huir, rehuir, esquivar, evitar.

shut [ʃʌt], *vti. y vii*. [9] cerrar(se).— *to s. down*, cesar en el trabajo, parar· —*to s. from*, excluir.—*to s. in*, encerrar, confinar.—*to s. off*, impedir la entrada, interceptar; cortar (el agua, etc.); interrumpir (a uno) en el teléfono, cortarle el circuito.—*to s. out*, cerrar la puerta (a uno); excluir.— *to s. up*, hacer callar; cerrar; acabar; tapar; encerrar; callarse.—*pret.* y *pp*. de TO SHUT.—*a*. cerrado.— —*down* [ʃʌ́tdaun], *s*. paro, cesación o suspensión de trabajo (en una fábrica, etc.).— —*ter* [-œ(r)], *s*. cerrador; persiana; contraventana; postigo; (foto.) obturador.

shuttle [ʃʌ́tl], *s*. (tej.) lanzadera; tren de traspaso (entre dos vías férreas); tren que va y viene entre dos lugares cercanos.—*vt. y vi*. mover(se) alternativamente de un lado a otro o de una parte a otra; ir y venir.

shy [ʃai], *a*. tímido; asustadizo; cauteloso; esquivo, arisco; vergonzoso; (fam.) ñoño.—*vii*. [7] (con *off*) hacer desviar, apartar; lanzar o arrojar.— *vii*. respingar (un caballo); asustarse.— —*ness* [ʃáinis], *s*. timidez; recato; esquivez; vergüenza, (fam.) ñoñez.

shyster [ʃáistœ(r)], *s*. (fam. E.U.) picapleitos, trapisondista, leguleyo.

Siamese [saiamíz], *s. y a*. siamés.

Sicilian [sisílyan], *a. y s*. siciliano.

sick [sik], *a*. enfermo; malo; nauseado; (con *of*) cansado, disgustado, fastidiado.—*s. leave*, licencia por enfermedad.—*s. room*, enfermería.—*to be s. to one's stomach*, tener náuseas.—*vt*. azuzar, excitar o incitar (a un perro).— —*en* [síkn], *vt*. enfermar; dar asco; debilitar, extenuar.—*vi*. enfermarse; nausear, tener asco.— —*ening* [-əniŋ], *a*. nauseabundo, repugnante.

sickle [síkl], *s*. hoz.

sickly [síkli], *a*. enfermizo, achacoso; enclenque; nauseabundo.—**sickness** [síknis], *s*. enfermedad, dolencia; náusea.

side [said], *s*. lado, costado; flanco; ladera, falda; facción, partido, bando; banda (de un barco).—*by the s.*, al lado de; cerca de.—*on all sides* u *on every s.*, por todos lados, por todas partes.—*on that s.*, a, de, en o por ese lado.—*on the other s.*, del o al otro lado; más allá; a la otra parte.— *on this s.*, a, de en o por este lado; más acá.—*s. by s.*, lado a lado; hombro a hombro, juntos.—*a.* lateral; de lado; oblicuo; secundario, incidental. —*s. arms*, armas blancas.—*s. glance*, mirada de soslayo.—*s. issue*, cuestión secundaria.—*s. light*, luz lateral; información o detalle incidental.—*s. line*, negocio o actividad incidentales; (dep.) línea o límite del terreno de juego.—*vt.* y *vi.* (con with) tomar parte por, declararse por, ser de la opinión de.—**board** [sáidbord], *s.* aparador.— **burns** [-bœrnz], *s. pl.* patillas.

sidesaddle [sáidsædl], *a.* sillón, silla de amazona.—**sideswipe** [sáidswaip], *vt.* (fam.) chocar o rozar oblicuamente. —*s.* choque o rozamiento oblicuo.— **sidetrack** [sáidtræk], *vt.* desviar; echar a un lado, arrinconar; (f.c.) meter en un desviadero.—**sidewalk** [sáidwɔk], *s.* acera, (Am.) banqueta; (Am.) vereda.—**sideways** [sáidweiz], *a.* y *adv.* de lado, lateral(mente), de soslayo, al través.—**siding** [sáidiŋ], *s.* (f.c.) apartadero, desviadero, vía muerta.

siege [sidʒ], *s.* sitio, asedio, cerco.— *to lay s.*, poner sitio o cerco.

sierra [siérɑ], *s.* sierra, cordillera.

siesta [siéstɑ], *s.* siesta, siestecilla.

sieve [siv], *s.* cedazo, tamiz, criba.— *vt.* = SIFT.—**sift** [sift], *vt.* cerner, cribar, tamizar.—*to s. out*, investigar.— *vi.* caer o pasar al través de un tamiz o cedazo.

sigh [sai], *vi.* suspirar.—*s.* suspiro.

sight [sait], *s.* vista; visión, perspectiva; escena, espectáculo; modo de ver; mira (de armas de fuego); agujero o abertura para mirar. *at s.*, a la vista (letra, giro, etc.); a primera vista; al ver, cuando se vea.—*thirty days after s.*, (com.) a treinta días vista.—*to be a s.*, (fam.) parecer o estar como un adefesio; ser extraordinario o extraño.—*a.* visual; (com.) a la vista.—*vt.* alcanzar con la vista, avistar, divisar.—*to s. land*, (mar.) recalar.—*vi.* apuntar; dirigir una visual.—**seeing** [sáitsiŋ], *s.* visita turística a lugares de interés.

sign [sain], *s.* signo; señal, seña; rastro, indicio; muestra, letrero, rótulo.—*vt.* firmar; rubricar; suscribir (un tratado, etc.); (con off o away) firmar la cesión o traspaso de.—*vi.* firmar.— **al** [sígnal], *a.* señalado, notable, memorable.—*s.* seña, señal.—*vti.* y *vii.* [2]

hacer señas, señalar, indicar.—**signatory** [sígnatori], *a.* y *s.* firmante, signatario.—**signature** [sígnachur], *s.* firma; rúbrica.— **signer** [sáinœ(r)], *s.* firmante, signatario.

signet [sígnit], *s.* sello; timbre, estampilla.

significance [signífikans], *s.* significación; significado.—**significant** [signífikant], *a.* significante, significativo.— **signify** [sígnifai], *vti.* y *vii.* [7] significar.

silence [sáilens], *s.* silencio.—*s. gives consent*, quien calla otorga.—*vt.* imponer silencio, mandar o hacer callar; sosegar, aquietar.—**silent** [sáilent], *a.* silencioso; taciturno; tácito.—*s. partner*, socio comanditario.

silhouette [siluét], *vt.* hacer aparecer en silueta; perfilar.—*s.* silueta.

silk [silk], *s.* seda.—*pl.* sedería, géneros de seda.—*a.* de seda.— **en** [sílkn], *a.* de seda; sedoso.— **worm** [-wœrm], *s.* gusano de seda.— **y** [-i], *a.* sedoso, sedeño; de seda.

sill [sil], *s.* umbral de puerta; solera, mesilla.—*window s.*, antepecho de ventana.

silliness [sílinis], *s.* necedad, tontería, simpleza.—**silly** [síli], *a.* necio, tonto, mentecato, bobo; simple; disparatado, ridículo.

silver [sílvœ(r)], *s.* plata; vajilla de plata o plateada.—*a.* de plata; plateado.—*vt.* platear; azogar (un espejo, etc.).— **smith** [-smiθ], *s.* platero, orfebre.— **ware** [-wer], *s.* vajilla de plata; artículos de plata.— **y** [-i], *a.* plateado; argentino, argentado.

simian [símian], *s.* simio, mono.

similar [símilɑ(r)], *a.* similar, semejante, análogo, parecido.— **ity** [similériti], *s.* semejanza, analogía, parecido.— **ly** [símilɑrli], *adv.* semejantemente, asimismo, de igual manera.—**simile** [símili], *s.* símil.— **similitude** [simílitjud], *s.* similitud, semejanza.

simmer [símœ(r)], *vi.* hervir a fuego lento.

simple [símpl], *a.* simple; sencillo; llano; ingenuo, cándido; mentecato, necio; insignificante, ordinario.— *s.-minded*, cándido, confiado, candoroso.—*s.-mindedness*, candor, sencillez.—*s.* simplón, gaznápiro, bobo; simple.— **ton** [-tɔn], *s.* bobalicón, simplón, papanatas, gaznápiro.— **simplicity** [simplísiti], *s.* sencillez, llaneza, simplicidad; simpleza, bobería.—**simplify** [símplifai], *vti.* [7] simplificar.

simulate [símjuleit], *vt.* simular, fingir.

simultaneity [saimʌltaníiti], *s.* simul-

taneidad.—**simultaneous** [sajmʌltéj-
nĭʌs], *a.* simultáneo.

sin [sĭn], *s.* pecado, culpa.—*vii.* [1]
pecar.

since [sĭns], *adv.* hace; desde entonces.
—*four days s.*, hace cuatro días.
—*not long s.*, no hace mucho, hace
poco.—*s. when? how long s.?* ¿de
cuándo acá? ¿desde cuándo?—*prep.*
desde, después de, a contar de.—
conj. desde que, después que; puesto
que, como, como quiera que, ya que,
en vista de que.

sincere [sĭnsír], *a.* sincero; serio.—
sincerity [sĭnsérĭti], *s.* sinceridad.

sine [sajn], *s.* (mat.) seno.

sinew [sínyu], *s.* tendón; fibra, nervio.

sinful [sínfμl], *a.* pecaminoso; pecador.

sing [sĭŋ], *vii.* y *vti.* [10] cantar.

singe [sĭndʒ], *vt.* chamuscar; quemar
(las puntas del pelo).—*s.* chamusquina.

singer [síŋœ(r)], *s.* cantante, cantor(a).
—**singing** [síŋĭŋ], *a.* cantante, de
canto; cantor.—*s. bird*, ave canora.

single [síŋgl], *a.* único, solo; particular,
individual; sencillo (no doble, etc.);
soltero.—*s. file*, hilera; en hilera,
uno tras otro.—*s.-handed*, solo, sin
ayuda.—*vt.* (gen. con **out**) singula-
rizar; particularizar; escoger.—*s.*
billete de un dólar.—*pl.* partido de
individuales (no parejas) (en el
tenis, etc.).—**singly** [síŋglĭ], *adv.*
individualmente, uno a uno, separadamente.

singsong [síŋsɔŋ], *s.* cadencia uniforme,
sonsonete.

singular [síŋgĭulə(r)ֽ], *a.* singular;
extraño, extraordinario, raro; único.
—*s.* (gram.) (número) singular.

sinister [sínĭstœ(r)], *a.* siniestro.

sink [sĭŋk], *vti.* [10] hundir, sumergir;
(mar.) echar a pique o a fondo;
sumir; cavar, abrir (un pozo); clavar,
enterrar.—*vii.* hundirse, sumirse;
(mar.) naufragar, zozobrar, irse a
pique.—*to s. on one's knees*, caer
de rodillas.—*s.* sumidero, vertedero;
fregadero.—*er* [síŋkœ(r)], *s.* plomada de pescar; el que o lo que se
hunde.—**ing** [-ĭŋ], *s.* hundimiento;
abertura (de un pozo, etc.); acción
de hundirse, echar a pique.—*a.* que
(se) hunde.

sir [sœr], *s.* señor, caballero.—*Dear S.*,
(en cartas) Muy Señor mío (nuestro).

sinner [sínœ(r)], *s.* pecador(a).

sinus [sájnʌs], *s.* cavidad, abertura;
(anat.) seno, cavidad ósea.

sip [sĭp], *vti.* [1] sorber, libar, chupar.
—*s.* sorbo.

siphon [sájfʌn], *s.* sifón.—*vt.* y *vi.* sacar
líquidos con sifón.

siren [sájrɛn], *s.* sirena.

sirloin [sœ́rlɔjn], *s.* solomillo, lomo.

sissy [sísĭ], *s.* y *a.* (fam.) marica,
afeminado.

sister [sístœ(r)], *s.* hermana; sor;
monja.—*s.-in-law*, cuñada.

sit [sĭt], *vti.* [10] sentar; dar asiento a;
tener capacidad o espacio para.—*vri.*
sentarse.—*vii.* sentarse; estar sentado; posarse; empollar (las aves);
reunirse, celebrar junta o sesión;
formar parte de un congreso, tribunal, etc.; sentar, caer bien o mal
(un vestido, etc.); descansar, apoyarse.—*to s. by*, sentarse o estar
sentado cerca de, junto o al lado de.
—*to s. down*, sentarse.—*to s. for*,
servir de modelo, posar.—*to s. still*,
estarse quieto, no moverse; no levantarse Ud.—*to s. tight*, (fam.) esperar
sin decir nada, tenerse firme.—*to s.
up*, incorporarse.—*e* [sajt], *s.* sitio,
situación, local; asiento.—**ting**
[sítĭŋ], *s.* acción o modo de sentarse;
sesión, junta; (a)sentada; nidada.

situate [síchμejt], *vt.* situar; fijar sitio
o lugar para.—*d* [síchμejtĭd], *a.*
situado, sito, ubicado.—**situation**
[síchμéjʃʌn], *s.* situación; ubicación,
posición; colocación, plaza, empleo.

sizable [sájzʌbl], *a.* de tamaño razonable, adecuado; considerable.—**size**
[sajz], *s.* tamaño, medida, dimensiones; diámetro (de un tubo, alambre, etc.); apresto, cola; talla,
estatura.—*vt.* clasificar o separar
según el tamaño o estatura; valuar,
justipreciar; aprestar, encolar.

sizzle [sízl], *vi.* chirriar (al freírse);
(fam.) estar muy caliente.—*s.* chirrido (al freírse).

skate [skejt], *vi.* patinar.—*s.* patín.—
r [skéjtœ(r)], *s.* patinador.—**skating** [skéjtĭŋ], *s.* patinaje.—*a.* de o
para patinar.—*s. rink*, pista o sala
de patinar.

skein [skejn], *s.* madeja.

skeleton [skélɛtʌn], *s.* esqueleto; armazón.—*s. key*, ganzúa, llave maestra.

skeptic [sképtĭk], *s.* y *a.* escéptico.—
al [-al], *a.* escéptico.

sketch [skech], *s.* diseño, bosquejo,
boceto, croquis; (teat.) pieza corta
o ligera; drama o cuadro dramático
de radio.—*vt.* diseñar, esbozar, de
linear, bosquejar, hacer un croquis de.

skewer [skjúœ(r)], *s.* pincho.—*vt.*
espetar.

ski [ski], *s.* esquí.—*vi.* esquiar.

skid [skĭd], *vii.* [1] deslizar; patinar
(una rueda); (aut.) patinar o resbalar
lateralmente.—*s.* patinazo.

skier [skíœ(r)], *s.* esquiador.

skiff [skĭf], *s.* esquife.

skill [skĭl], *s.* habilidad, destreza,
pericia, maña.—**ed** [skĭld], *a.*

práctico, instruido, experimentado, experto.

skillet [skílit], *s.* sartén; cacerola pequeña.

skillful [skílful], *a.* diestro, hábil, experto, ducho.

skim [skim], *vti.* [1] desnatar; espumar; examinar superficialmente, hojear (un libro).—*vii.* deslizarse o pasar rasando.—*to s. over*, resbalar, rozar.

skin [skin], *s.* piel (cutis, epidermis, tez); odre, pellejo; cuero; cáscara.—*vti.* [1] desollar, despellejar; pelar, mondar; (fam.) sacar dinero a, pelar.—*vii.* mudar la piel; (fam.) ser embaucador o engañador; (fam.) (gen. con out) escabullirse.—**flint** [skínflint], *s.* avaro.—**ny** [-i], *a.* flaco, descarnado; pellejudo.

skip [skip], *vti.* [1] saltar, omitir; saltar por encima de, pasar por alto.—*vii.* saltar, brincar.—*s.* cabriola, salto, brinco; omisión.—**per** [skípœ(r)], *s.* (mar.) patrón.

skirmish [skœrmiŝ], *s.* (mil.) escaramuza, refriega.—*vi.* (sos)tener una escaramuza.

skirt [skœrt], *s.* falda, faldellín, saya; orilla, margen, borde.—*pl.* (fam.) mujer, faldas.—*vt.* seguir la orilla de; costear; (cost.) orillar.—*vi.* (con **along, near**, etc.) ladear, (mar.) costear.

skittish [skítiŝ], *a.* espantadizo; tímido; retozón; caprichudo, voluble.

skull [skʌl], *s.* cráneo; calavera.—**cap** [skálkæp], *s.* bonete, solideo.

skunk [skʌŋk], *s.* mofeta, zorrillo; (fam.) canalla, persona ruin.

sky [skai], *s.* cielo, firmamento.—*s.-blue, s.-colored*, azul celeste, cerúleo.—*to praise to the skies*, poner en, o sobre, las nubes.— **lark** [skáilark], *s.* alondra, calandria.— **light** [-lait], *s.* claraboya, tragaluz.— **rocket** [-rakit], *s.* cohete, volador.—**scraper** [-skreipœ(r)], *s.* rascacielos.

slab [slæb], *s.* losa, baldosa; lonja, tajada gruesa; plancha, tablón; laja, lancha.

slack [slæk], *a.* flojo; poco firme, aflojado; remiso, tardo.—*s.* (mar.) seno de un cabo; flojedad; (com.) período de poca actividad; estación o tiempo muerto.—*pl.* pantalones ligeros de verano.—*s.*, **slacken** [slǽkn], *vt.* aflojar, relajar, desapretar; disminuir.—*vi.* aflojarse, relajarse; disminuir; retardarse; flojear.

slag [slæg], *s.* escoria (de metales o volcanes).

slain [slein], *pp.* de TO SLAY.

slake [sleik], *vt.* apagar (la cal, la sed); refrescar; desleír (la cal); moderar.—

slaked lime, cal muerta o apagada.—*vi.* apagarse (la cal).

slam [slæm], *vti.* [1] cerrar de golpe.—*vii.* cerrarse de golpe y con estrépito.—*s.* portazo; (fam.) crítica severa.—*s.-bang*, (fam.) de golpe y porrazo.

slander [slǽndœ(r)], *vt.* calumniar, difamar.—*s.* calumnia, difamación.—**ous** [-ʌs], *a.* calumnioso, difamatorio.

slang [slæŋ], *s.* vulgarismo; jerga, jerigonza, germanía.

slant [slænt], *vt. y vi.* sesgar(se), inclinar(se).—*s.* oblicuidad; inclinación; sesgo; declive; punto de vista.

slap [slæp], *vti.* [1] abofetear, acachetear.—*s.* bofetada, bofetón, manotada, manotazo.—*a s. in the face*, bofetada; insulto.—*adv.* de golpe y porrazo, de sopetón.—**dash** [slépdæŝ], *a. y adv.* descuidado, chapucero; de prisa, descuidadamente.

slash [slæŝ], *vt.* acuchillar, dar cuchilladas; cortar, hacer un corte largo en; rebajar, reducir radicalmente (sueldos, gastos, precios, etc.).—*vi.* tirar tajos y reveses.—*s.* cuchillada; corte, cortadura.

slat [slæt], *s.* tablilla (de madera o metal).

slate [sleit], *s.* pizarra; pizarra para escribir; (E.U. pol.) lista de candidatos; candidatura.

slaughter [slótœ(r)], *s.* carnicería, matanza, (fam.) degollina.—*vt.* matar, sacrificar (las reses); hacer una carnicería o matanza; destrozar.—**house** [-haus], *s.* matadero.

Slav [slav], *a. y s.* eslavo.

slave [sleiv], *s.* esclavo.—*vi.* trabajar como esclavo.

slaver [slévœ(r)], *s.* baba.—*vi.* babear.

slavery [sléivœri], *s.* esclavitud.

Slavic [slávik], *s.* lengua eslava.—*a.* eslavo.

slavish [sléiviŝ], *a.* servil, abyecto; esclavizado.

slay [slei], *vti.* [10] matar.— **er** [sléiœ(r)], *s.* matador; asesino.

sled [sled], *vti. y vii.* [1] ir o llevar en trineo.—*s.* trineo, rastra.—*s. hammer*, macho, mandarria.

sleek [slik], *a.* liso, bruñido, alisado; suave, zalamero.—*vt.* alisar, pulir, suavizar.

sleep [slip], *vti. y vii.* [10] dormir.—*to s. off*, curar durmiendo (un dolor de cabeza, etc.); dormirla (la borrachera, etc.).—*to s. on o upon*, descuidarse o no hacer caso de; consultar con la almohada.—*to s. out*, dormir fuera de casa; saciarse de dormir.—*to s. over*, consultar con la almohada.—*to s. soundly*, dormir profundamente **o a pierna suelta.**—*s.* sueño.— —er [slípœ(r)], *s.* persona dormida; (f.c.) coche dormitorio, coche cama; (f.c.) traviesa, (Am.) durmiente.— —ily [-ili], *adv.* con somnolencia o soñolencia.— —iness [-inis], *s.* soñolencia o somnolencia, sueño, modorra.— —ing [-iŋ], *a.* durmiente; dormido.—*s. car,* coche cama o coche dormitorio.— *s. partner,* socio comanditario.—*s. sickness,* encefalitis letárgica.— —less [-lis], *a.* desvelado, insomne.— —walker [-wɔkœ(r)], *s.* so(m)námbulo.— —y [-i], *a.* soñoliento, amodorrado.—*to be s.,* tener sueño.

sleet [slit], *s.* aguanieve.—*vi.* caer aguanieve.

sleeve [sliv], *s.* (sast.) manga.— —less [slívlis], *a.* sin mangas.

sleigh [slej], *s.* trineo.—*vi.* pasearse en trineo.

sleight [slajt], *s.* habilidad; ardid, estratagema.—*s. of hand,* juego de manos, prestidigitación.

slender [sléndœ(r)], *a.* delgado; esbelto; sutil; escaso; insuficiente.

slept [slept], *pret.* y *pp.* de TO SLEEP.

sleuth [sljuθ], *s.* detective; agente de policía secreta o investigador privado.

slew [slju], *pret.* de TO SLAY.

slice [slajs], *vt.* rebanar, cortar en tajadas; tajar, cortar.—*s.* rebanada, tajada, lonja.

slick [slik], *vt.* alisar, pulir.—*vi.* (gen. con **up**) (fam.) componerse, acicalarse.—*a.* liso, terso, lustroso; resbaladizo, aceitoso; meloso; (fam.) diestro, mañoso; (fam.) de primera.— —er [slíkœ(r)], *s.* impermeable flojo; (fam.) embaucador, farsante.

slid [slid], *pret.* y *pp.* de TO SLIDE.— **slidden** [slídn], *pp.* de TO SLIDE. — **slide** [slajd], *vii.* [10] resbalar(se), deslizarse, caer(se); patinar.—*vti.* hacer resbalar; (con let) dejar correr, no hacer caso de.—*s.* tapa corrediza; (foto.) diapositiva, transparencia; platina de microscopio; resbalón, resbaladura; resbaladero; (geol.) falla; desmoronamiento, alud; (mús.) ligado.—*a.* corredizo; de corredera. —*s. rule,* regla de cálculo.—**sliding** [slájdiŋ], *s.* deslizamiento, resbalo. —*a.* corredizo, deslizante.—*s. door,* puerta corredera.

slight [slajt], *a.* ligero, leve; pequeño, fútil, débil, delgado.—*s.* desaire, desatención, feo, desprecio.—*vt.* menospreciar, despreciar, desairar; desatender, descuidar.

slim [slim], *a.* delgado; baladí; delicado; escaso.

slime [slajm], *s.* limo, lama, cieno, fango, babaza.—*vt.* y *vi.* enfangar,

enlodar.—**slimy** [sláimi], *a.* viscoso, fangoso, limoso; mucoso.

sling [sliŋ], *s.* honda; (cir.) cabestrillo; (mar.) eslinga.—*vti.* [10] tirar con honda; tirar, arrojar; eslingar, izar.— —**shot** [slíŋšat], *s.* tirador, tiragomas, tiraflechas.

slink [sliŋk], *vii.* [10] escabullirse, escaparse, escurrirse.

slip [slip], *vti.* [1] deslizar; soltarse, zafarse, soltar, desatar; irse de (la memoria, etc.).—*to s. a cog,* equivocarse.—*to s. in,* introducir o meter (esp. secretamente).—*to s. off,* quitarse de encima, soltar.—*to s. on,* ponerse (vestido, etc.) de prisa.— *to s. one's arm around o through,* pasar el brazo por (la cintura, etc.). —*vii.* resbalar, deslizarse; salirse de su sitio; cometer un desliz; errar o equivocarse; olvidársele a uno. —*to s. into,* introducirse, entrometerse.—*to s. out,* salir sin ser observado; dislocarse un hueso.—*s.* resbalón; deslizamiento; tropiezo; traspié; desliz; resbaladero; declive; falta, error; descuido, lapso; (agr.) plantón; tira o pedazo (de papel); funda de almohada; combinación (de vestir); boleta, papeleta.—*s. cover,* funda (de muebles, etc.).—*s. of the tongue,* lapsus linguae.— —**knot,** [slípnat], *s.* lazo o nudo corredizo.— —**per** [slípœ(r)], *s.* pantufla, chancleta, babucha; zapatilla.— —**pery** [slípœri], *a.* resbaladizo, resbaloso; evasivo, zorro; voluble.— —**shod** [-šad], *a.* descuidado, desaliñado; tosco, mal hecho.

slit [slit], *vti.* [9] rajar, hender; cortar en tiras; rasgar (un vestido).—*s.* cortadura larga; hendedura, tajo; ranura, abertura.—*pret.* y *pp.* de TO SLIT.

slogan [slóugan], *s.* consigna; lema.

sloop [slup], *s.* balandro, chalupa.

slop [slap], *vti.* [1] derramar; ensuciar, enlodar.—*vii.* derramarse; chapalear (por el fango, agua nieve, etc.).—*s.* líquido derramado en el suelo; mojadura.—*pl.* agua sucia; aguachirle, lavazas; té o café flojo.

slope [sloup], *s.* (geol. y min.) inclinación; (f.c.) talud; declive, bajada; cuesta, falda, ladera; agua, vertiente (de tejado); (fort.) rampa.—*vt.* y *vi.* inclinar(se).

slot [slat], *s.* (mec.) muesca, ranura, abertura, hendedura.—*s. machine,* máquina tragamonedas o traganiqueles.—*vti.* [1] acanalar, hacer una ranura en.

sloth [sloθ], *s.* pereza, haraganería; (zool.) perezoso.

slough [slau], *s.* lodazal, cenagal,

cieno; estado de degradación; [slju], (E.U.) charca cenagosa; [slʌf], piel o camisa que muda la serpiente; (med.) tejido muerto.—*vi.* y *vt.* echar de sí tejido muerto o la piel.

Slovak [slóṷvæk], *a.* y *s.* eslovaco.

slovenliness [slʌ́vənlinis], *s.* desaliño, desaseo, abandono; suciedad, porquería.—**slovenly** [slʌ́vənli], *a.* desaliñado, puerco o sucio; dejado, descuidado.

slow [sloṷ], *vt.* y *vi.* (con **up** o **down**) retardar, aflojar el paso, ir más despacio.—*a.* lento, despacioso; tardo; atrasado (el reloj); calmoso, cachazudo; lerdo, estúpido.—*s. motion,* velocidad reducida; (cine) cámara lenta.—*adv.* despacio, lentamente.— **-ly** [slóṷli], *adv.* despacio, lentamente, pausadamente.— **-ness** [-nis], *s.* lentitud, retraso; cachaza; torpeza.

slug [slʌg], *s.* cualquier cosa, animal o persona de movimiento(s) lento(s); (zool.) babosa; (arti.) posta; bala; (impr.) lingote.—*vti.* [1] (arti.) cargar con posta; (fam.) aporrear.—**-gard** [slʌ́gərd], *s.* haragán, holgazán, pelmazo.

sluice [sljus], *s.* esclusa; compuerta; canal; (fig.) salida.—*s. gate,* compuerta.

slum [slʌm], *s.* vivienda miserable. —*pl.* arrabales, barrios bajos.—*vii.* [1] visitar los barrios bajos.—*to go slumming,* recorrer tugurios o lugares de mala vida.

slumber [slʌ́mbœ(r)], *vi.* dormitar; dormir; dormirse o descuidarse.—*s.* sueño ligero y tranquilo.

slump [slʌmp], *vi.* hundirse el pie en una materia blanda; aplastarse, rebajarse; caer, bajar.—*vt.* arrojar violentamente; hacer bajar (precios) súbitamente.—*s.* hundimiento; aplastamiento; disminución de actividad o vigor; (com.) baja repentina en los valores, bajón, desplome.

slung [slʌ̃g], *pret.* y *pp.* de TO SLING.

slunk [slʌ̃k], *pret.* y *pp.* de TO SLINK.

slur [slœr], *vti.* [1] menospreciar, rebajar; pasar por encima, suprimir; comerse sílabas o letras.—*s.* reparo, pulla; estigma; mancilla o mancha ligera en la reputación.

slush [slʌʃ], *s.* lodo blando, fango; aguanieve fangosa; desperdicios de cocina; (fam.) tonterías sentimentales.

slut [slʌt], *s.* mujerzuela, ramera; mujer sucia; perra.

sly [slaj], *a.* astuto, taimado, socarrón. —*on the s.,* a hurtadillas, a la chiticallando.— **-ness** [slájnis], *s.* socarronería, astucia, disimulo.

smack [smæk], *vt.* y *vi.* manotear, golpear; besar ruidosamente; hacer sonar o chasquear (un beso, golpe, latigazo, etc.); rechuparse, saborear; saborearse.—*vi.* (con **of**) saber (a), tener gusto, dejo (de); oler (a).—*s.* sabor, gusto, gustillo; beso sonado; rechupete; manotada; chasquido de látigo.

small [smɔl], *a.* pequeño, diminuto, chico; menor; bajo de estatura; corto; insignificante; despreciable, mezquino.— **-ness** [smɔ́lnis], *s.* pequeñez; bajeza, ruindad.— **-pox** [-paks], *s.* viruela(s).

smart [smart], *a.* vivo, listo, hábil; despabilado, astuto, ladino; inteligente, talentoso; agudo, sutil; punzante, mordaz; elegante, de buen tono.—*s.* escozor; dolor, aflicción. —*vi.* escocer, picar; requemar.— **-ness** [smártnis], *s.* agudeza, viveza, ingenio, talento; astucia; elegancia, buen tono.

smash [smæʃ], *vt.* y *vi.* romper, quebrar, aplastar, destrozar.—*s.* rotura, destrozo; fracaso; ruina, quiebra.—*to go to s.,* arruinarse; hacerse añicos.

smattering [smǽtəriŋ], *s.* tintura.

smear [smir], *vt.* untar, embarrar, tiznar, manchar.—*s.* embarradura, mancha.

smell [smel], *vti.* y *vii.* [4] oler.—*to s. a rat,* haber gato encerrado.—*to s. of,* oler a.—*s.* olfato; olor (bueno o malo).—**smelt** [smelt], *vt.* fundir o derretir (metales).—**smelter** [smélt-œ(r)], *s.* fundidor; alto horno.

smile [smajl], *vi.* sonreír(se).—*s.* sonrisa.—**smiling** [smájliŋ], *a.* risueño, sonriente.—**smilingly** [smájliŋli], *adv.* con cara risueña.

smirch [smœrch], *vt.* ensuciar, tiznar; mancillar, deslucir.—*s.* mancilla, tizne.

smith [smiθ], *s.* forjador, herrero.— **-y** [smiθi], *s.* fragua, forja; herrería.

smitten [smítn], *pp.* de TO SMITE.—*a.* profundamente afectado; muy conmovido; muy enamorado.

smock [smak], *s.* bata corta, blusa.

smoke [smoṷk], *s.* humo.—*to have a s.,* dar una fumada; fumar.—*vt.* fumar; curar al humo; sahumar; (con **out**) ahumar, ahogar con humo; hacer salir con humo.—*vi.* fumar; humear, echar humo.— **-less** [smóṷklis], *a.* sin humo.—*s. powder,* pólvora sin humo.— **-r** [smóṷkœ(r)], *s.* fumador; (f.c.) coche o salón de fumar; (fam.) tertulia en que se fuma.—**stack** [-stæk], *s.* chimenea.—**smoking** [smóṷkiŋ], *s.* acción de fumar.—*a.* humeante.—*s. car,* (f.c.) coche fumador.—*s.* *jacket,* batín.—*s.* *room,* cuarto o salón de fumar.—*smoky* [smóuki], *a.* humeante; humoso, ahumado.

smolder [smóuldœ(r)], *vi.* arder en rescoldo; estar latente.

smooth [smuð], *a.* liso, pulido; parejo, plano, igual; uniforme; suave; tranquilo (agua, etc.); cortés, afable. —*s.-shaven,* bien afeitado.—*s.-sliding,* que se desliza con suavidad e igualdad.—*vt.* allanar, alisar, suavizar; (gen. con *over*) zanjar, atenuar.— —*ness* [smúðnis], *s.* lisura, tersura, igualdad; suavidad, blandura; dulzura.

smote [smout], *pret.* de TO SMITE.

smother [smáðœ(r)], *vt.* y *vi.* ahogar(se), asfixiar(se); sofocar(se).

smoulder [smóuldœ(r)], *vi.* = SMOLDER.

smudge [smʌdʒ], *vt.* tiznar, ensuciar o manchar con tizne, tinta u hollín; fumigar, ahumar.—*s.* tiznajo, tiznadura, tiznón; fumigación o ahumadura.

smuggle [smágl], *vt.* pasar o meter de contrabando.—*vi.* hacer contrabando, contrabandear.— —r [smáglœ(r)], *s.* contrabandista.

smut [smʌt], *s.* tiznón, tiznadura, mancha; obscenidad, indecencia; (bot., agr.) tizón.—*vti.* [1] tiznar, manchar; (fig.) mancillar.—*ty* [-i], *a.* tiznado; indecente, verde.

snack [snæk], *s.* bocad(ill)o, refrigerio, (fam.) tente(e)mpié, piscolabis.

snag [snæg], *s.* nudo que sobresale en la madera; tocón o tronco sumergido; obstáculo oculto ignorado.— *vti.* [1] rasgar o dañar, chocando contra algo sumergido; impedir, obstruir; arrancar troncos o tocones (de un río).

snail [sneil], *s.* caracol.

snake [sneik], *s.* serpiente, culebra. —*vi.* serpentear, culebrear.—*snaky* [snéiki], *a.* tortuoso; solapado, astuto.

snap [snæp], *vti.* [1] chasquear, hacer estallar; dar, apretar o cerrar con golpe o estallido; romper con ruido y violencia; atrapar, arrebatar, echar la zarpa a; interrumpir; fotografiar instantáneamente.—*to s. one's fingers,* castañetear con los dedos.—*to s. up,* comprar, aceptar, etc. con avidez; cortar, interrumpir (a uno) con una réplica mordaz.—*vii.* chasquear, dar un chasquido; estallar, romperse con estallido; romperse una cosa tirante; chispear (los ojos); hablar fuerte; fallar un tiro.—*to s. at,* tirar mordiscos a, pegar una dentellada a; hablar mordazmente o con aspereza (a uno); aceptar una oferta con

entusiasmo y de prisa.—*to s. in two,* romperse en dos pedazos.—*to s. off,* soltarse, saltar, abrirse de golpe.—*s.* chasquido; castañeteo (con los dedos); estallido; cierre de resorte; dentellada, mordiscón; (fam.) vigor, energía; período corto (de frío); (fam.) ganga, cosa fácil.—*a.* hecho de repente, de golpe o instantáneamente.—*s. fastener,* cierre automático.— —**shot** [snépʃat], *s.* disparo rápido, sin apuntar; fotografía instantánea.— —**py** [-i], *a.* (fam.) vivo, enérgico; elegante, garboso; mordedor; enojadizo; acre, picante; chispeante.

snare [sner], *s.* trampa, lazo, cepo; garlito, celada, asechanza, artimaña, red; (cir.) lazo; cuerda de tripa (para tambor).—*vt.* enredar, tender trampas o lazos.—*vi.* cazar con trampas o lazos, cepos, etc.

snarl [snarl], *vi.* gruñir, regañar; refunfuñar; hacer fu (el gato).—*vt.* enredar, enmarañar; embutir, estampar (artículos huecos de metal). —*vi.* enredarse, enmarañarse.—*s.* gruñido, regaño; (fam.) riña; maraña, hilo enredado; complicación, enredo; nudo en la madera.

snatch [snæch], *vt.* arrebatar; (fam.) raptar.—*to s. off,* arrebatar.—*vi.* (con *at*) tratar de agarrar o arrebatar.—*s.* arrebatamiento; arrebatiña; (fam.) rapto; pedacito; ratito.—*by snatches,* a ratos.

sneak [snik], *vi.* (con *in*) entrarse a hurtadillas; (con *out* o *away*) salirse a hurtadillas, escurrir el bulto; obrar solapada o bajamente; arrastrarse. —*vt.* ratear, cometer ratería, hurtar. —*s.* (fam.) persona solapada.—*s.* *thief,* ratero.

sneer [snir], *vi.* hacer un gesto de desprecio; echar una mirada despectiva; mofarse de.—*vt.* expresar con un gesto de desprecio.—*s.* gesto, mirada o expresión de desprecio; mofa.

sneeze [sniz], *vi.* estornudar.—*not to be sneezed at,* no ser de despreciar, no ser un cualquiera.—*to s. at,* despreciar, menospreciar.—*s.* estornudo.

sniff [snif], *vt.* husmear, olfatear, oliscar; inspirar o aspirar audiblemente.— *vi.* resollar, oler; sorberse los mocos; (con *at*) desdeñar, mostrar desprecio con resoplidos.—*s.* olfateo; cosa olfateada.— —**le** [snifl], *vi.* sorber por las narices; moquear; lloriquear.—*s.* moquita; lloriqueo.

snip [snip], *vti.* [1] tijeretear; cortar con tijeras.—*to s. off,* cortar o recortar de un golpe.—*s.* tijeretada;

recorte, retazo, pedacito; parte; (fam.) persona pequeña o insignificante.

snipe [snaip], *vt.* y *vi.* disparar o hacer fuego desde un escondite o apostadero.— **—r** [snáipœ(r)], *s.* francotirador, paco.

snivel [snível], *vii.* [2] lloriquear, llorar como una criatura.—*s.* moco.

snob [snab], *s.* esnob, persona con pretensiones.— **—bery** [snáboeri], *s.* esnobismo, pretensiones.

snoop [snup], *s.* (fam.) entremetido; fisgón, curioso.—*vi.* entremeterse; husmear, fisgonear.

snooze [snuz], *vi.* (fam.) dormitar, descabezar el sueño.—*s.* (fam.) siestecita, sueño ligero.

snore [snɔr], *vi.* roncar.—*s.* ronquido.

snot [snat], *s.* moco.

snout [snaut], *s.* hocico, morro, jeta; trompa de elefante; cañón de un fuelle; lanza de manguera; embocadura de un cañón.

snort [snɔrt], *vt.* y *vi.* resoplar, bufar. —*s.* bufido, resoplido.

snow [snou], *s.* nieve; nevada.—*vi.* nevar.—*vt.* (con in, over, under o up) cubrir, obstruir, detener o aprisionar con nieve.—*to s. under*, derrotar por completo.— **—ball** [snóubɔl], *vt.* lanzar bolas de nieve a.—*s.* pelota de nieve.— **—drift** [-drift], *s.* ventisca, ventisquero.— **—fall** [-fɔl], *s.* nevada.— **—flake** [-fleik], *s.* copo de nieve.— **—plow** [-plau], *s.* (máquina) quitanieves.— **—storm** [-stɔrm], *s.* nevasca, tormenta de nieve.— **—y** [-i], *a.* níveo; puro, sin mancha; nevoso; cargado de nieve.

snub [snʌb], *vti.* [1] desairar, tratar con desprecio estudiado o afectada arrogancia; reprender; (con up) parar de repente.—*s.* desaire, repulsa; (fam.) nariz chata.—*a.* romo, chato.

snuff [snʌf], *s.* moco, pabilo o pavesa de candela o vela; tufo, olor; rapé. —*up to s.*, (fam.) despabilado.—*vt.* olfatear, oler, ventear; sorber por la nariz; despabilar (una vela).— *vi.* aspirar; tomar rapé.—*to s. it o out*, (fam.) morirse.— **—le** [snʌfl], *vi.* ganguear.—*s.* gangueo.—*pl.* catarro nasal, romadizo.

snug [snʌg], *a.* cómodo, abrigado; bien dispuesto; acomodado; apretado, ajustado.

so [sou], *adv.* y *pron.* así; de esta manera; pues bien, conque; tan; (fam.) muy, tan.—*how s.?* ¿cómo así? ¿cómo es eso?—*if s.*, si así es, si lo fuere, en tal caso.—*I hope s.*, I think *s.*, así lo espero, lo creo.—*is that s.?* ¿así? ¿de veras?—*just s.*, ni más ni menos; exactamente.—*not*

s., no es así, eso no es verdad.— *S.-and-S.*, Fulano de tal.—*s.* as to, para, a fin de.—*s. be it*, amén, así sea.—*s. big*, de este tamaño, así de grande.—*s.-called*, así llamado, llamado, según se llama.—*s. far*, hasta aquí, hasta ahí; hasta ahora; tan lejos.—*s. far as*, tan lejos como; hasta, hasta donde.—*s. forth*, etcétera; y así sucesivamente.—*s. long*, hasta luego, hasta más ver; hasta aquí (ahí).—*s. long as*, mientras que.—*s. many*, tantos.—*s. much*, tanto.—*s. much a*, tanto por.—*s. much as*, por mucho que; tanto como; siquiera.—*s. much for*, eso en cuanto a, eso basta en cuanto a.—*s. much s. o that*, tanto que.—*s. much the better*, tanto mejor.—*s. much the less*, tanto menos.—*s. much the worse*, tanto peor.—*s. or s.*, de un modo u otro.—*s.-s.*, así así, tal cual, regular, medianamente.—*s. that*, de suerte que, de modo que; para que, a fin de que.—*s. then*, así pues, conque, por tanto.—*s. to say o speak*, por decirlo así.—*conj.* con tal que; (fam.) para que; (fam.) por lo tanto; de modo que.

soak [souk], *vt.* empapar; remojar; (con in o up) embeber, absorber; (con through) calar, poner hecho una sopa; (fam.) cobrar precios exorbitantes (a uno); (fam.) beber con exceso.—*vi.* estar en remojo; (con in, to o through) remojarse, esponjarse, calarse; (fam.) empinar el codo.—*to be soaked to the skin*, estar calado hasta los huesos.—*s.* remojo, calada; (fam.) bebedor borracho; orgía.

soap [soup], *s.* jabón; (fam.) adulación; (fam.) dinero.—*vt.* enjabonar, lavar con jabón; (fam.) adular.— **—y** [sóupi], *a.* jabonoso.

soar [sɔr], *vi.* remontarse, cernerse; encumbrarse, aspirar; (aer.) planear horizontalmente sin motor.—*s.* vuelo o remonte.

sob [sab], *s.* sollozo.—*s. sister*, (fam.) escritora de sentimentalismo cursi. —*vii.* [1] sollozar.—*vti.* decir sollozando.

sober [sóubœ(r)], *a.* cuerdo; sobrio; sereno; templado, moderado; de sangre fría; sombrío; de color apagado.—*in s. earnest*, de veras, con seriedad, formalmente.—*s.-minded*, desapasionado.—*vt.* y *vi.* desemborrachar(se); poner(se) grave, serio o pensativo; volverse sobrio, cuerdo, moderado.—*to s. down*, serenar(se); hacer volver o volverse cuerdo; sosegar(se).— **—ness** [-nis], **sobriety** [sobráiēti], *s.* sobriedad, templanza,

moderación; cordura; seriedad;
calma.

sobriquet [sóụbrįkej], *s.* sobrenombre,
apodo.

soccer [sákœ(r)], *s.* fútbol.

sociable [sóụşabl], *a.* sociable, afable,
comunicativo.—**social** [sóụşạl], *a.*
social; sociable; (zool.) que vive en
comunidad; (bot.) que ocupa grandes
áreas; de agrupación densa.—*s.* tertulia, reunión informal.—**socialism**
[sóụşạlįzm], *s.* socialismo.—**socialist**
[sóụşạlįst], *a.* y *s.* socialista.—**society** [sọsáịẹty], *s.* sociedad; comunidad; asociación, gremio; consorcio;
círculos del buen tono; compañía,
conversación o trato amenos.—
sociology [sọşiálọḍʒi], *s.* sociología.

sock [sak], *s.* calcetín; escarpín; (fam.)
porrazo, golpe; zapato ligero.—*vt.*
(fam.) pegar, golpear con fuerza.

socket [sákįt], *s.* cuenca (del ojo);
casquillo; portalámpara; enchufe;
cualquier hueco donde encaja alguna
cosa.

sod [sad], *vti.* [1] cubrir de césped.—*s.*
césped; témpano de tierra vegetal.

soda [sóụḍạ], *s.* soda, sosa; gaseosa.

sodium [sóụḍịʌm], *s.* sodio.—*s. bicarbonate*, bicarbonato de sodio.

sodomy [sáḍọmį], *s.* sodomía.

sofa [sóụfạ], *s.* sofá.

soft [sɔft], *a.* blando; muelle; dúctil;
suave; liso; dulce, grato al oído;
fofo; tierno, delicado; mimoso; afeminado; apocado; de matices delicados o apagados.—*s.-boiled — eggs*,
huevos pasados por agua.— —**en**
[sɔ́fn], *vt.* ablandar; reblandecer;
mitigar, suavizar; enternecer; afe-
minar; amortiguar o apagar (colores).
—*vi.* ablandarse; reblandecerse; tem-
plarse; amansarse; enternecerse.—
—**ly** [sɔ́ftlį], *adv.* blandamente;
callando; suavemente, sin ruido;
lentamente.— —**ness** [-nįs], *s.* blandura; suavidad; pastosidad; malea-
bilidad; dulzura; ternura; morbidez.

soggy [sáǵị], *a.* empapado, mojado;
esponjoso.

soil [sɔjl], *vt.* y *vi.* manchar(se), ensu-
ciar(se), empañar(se).—*s.* terreno,
tierra vegetal, suelo; país; región; suciedad; mancha; abono;
pantano en que se refugia la caza.

solace [sálịs], *s.* solaz.—*vt.* solazar.

solar [sóụlạ(r)], *a.* solar.

sold [sọuld], *pret.* y *pp.* de TO SELL.
—*s. out*, (com.) agotado.—*to be s. on*,
(fam.) estar convencido de, o con-
vertido a.

solder [sádœ(r)], *vt.* soldar.—*s.* soldadura.— —**ing** [-įŋ], *s.* soldadura.—
s. iron, soldador.

soldier [sóụldʒœ(r)], *s.* soldado, militar.

—*pl.* tropa, fuerza.— —**ly** [-lį] *a.*
militar, marcial.— —**y** [-į], *s.* soldadesca.

sole [sọul], *vt.* echar suelas.—*s.* planta
del pie; suela; suelo; lenguado.—*a.*
único, solo; (for.) soltero; absoluto,
exclusivo.—*s. agency* o *right*, (com.)
exclusiva, exclusividad.—*s. agent*,
agente exclusivo.

solemn [sálẹm], *a.* solemne.— —**ity**
[solémnịtį], *s.* solemnidad; formalidad; pompa; rito, ceremonia.

solicit [solísịt], *vt.* solicitar.—*vi.* pretender, hacer una solicitud.— —**or**
[-ǫ(r)], *s.* agente, solicitador; pretendiente.— —**ous** [-ʌs], *a.* solícito,
cuidadoso.— —**ude** [-įud], *s.* solicitud,
cuidado, afán.

solid [sálịd], *s.* sólido.—*a.* sólido; puro
(oro, plata, etc.); macizo; cúbico;
unánime; (fam.) completo, verdadero.—*s. for*, unánimemente en favor
de.— —**arity** [sálịdárịti], *s.* solidari-
dad.—**solidify** [solídịfai], *vti.* y *vii.*
[7] solidificar(se).— —**ity** [solídịtį],
s. solidez.

soliloquy [solílokwị], *s.* soliloquio,
monólogo.—**solitaire** [sálịtẹr], *s.*
(joy., naipes) solitario.—**solitary** [sálị-
ịtẹrị], *a.* solitario; retirado; solo,
aislado; incomunicado.—*s.* solitario,
ermitaño.—**solitude** [sálịtjud], *s.* soledad; vida solitaria.—**solo** [sóụloụ],
s. (mús.) solo.—**soloist** [sóụloụịst], *s.*
(mús.) solista.

soluble [sályǫbl], *a.* soluble.—**solution**
[soljúšǫn], *s.* solución.

solve [salv], *vt.* resolver; solucionar,
desentrañar, desenredar, aclarar.

solvency [sálvẹnsį], *s.* solvencia.—
solvent [sálvẹnt], *a.* solvente.—*s.*
(quím.) disolvente.

somber [sámbœ(r)], *a.* sombrío, lóbrego, lúgubre, oscuro, tétrico.

some [sʌm], *a.* algo de, un poco; algún,
alguno; unos pocos, varios, ciertos;
algunos, unos.—*he is s. man*, (fam.)
es todo un hombre.—*s. difficulty*,
cierta dificultad.—*s. fine day*, el mejor
día, cuando menos se piensa.—*s.
house*, (fam.) gran casa.—*pron.* algunos; parte, una parte, una porción,
un poco, algo (de).—*adv.* (fam.)
cerca de, como, poco más o menos.—
—**body** [sámbadị], *s.* alguien, alguno;
un personaje.—*s. else*, algún otro.—
—**how** [-haụ], *adv.* de algún modo o
manera.—*s. or other*, de un modo u
otro.— —**one** [-wʌn], *pron.* alguien,
alguno.

somersault [sámœrsolt], *s.* salto mortal,
tumbo, voltereta.—*vt.* dar un salto
mortal.

something [sámθįŋ], *s.* alguna cosa,
algo.—*s. else*, otra cosa; alguna otra

cosa; algo más.—*adv.* algo, algún
tanto.—**sometime** [sámtajm], *adv.*
algún día, oportunamente, alguna
vez.—*s. last week*, durante la semana
pasada.—*s. soon*, un día de éstos,
en breve, sin tardar mucho.—**some-
times** [sámtajmz], *adv.* algunas veces,
a veces, de vez en cuando.—**some-
what** [sámhwat], *s.* alguna cosa,
algo; un poco.—*adv.* algo, algún
tanto, un poco.—**somewhere** [sám-
hwer], *adv.* en alguna parte.—*s. else*,
en alguna otra parte.

somnolence [sámnolęns], *s.* somnolencia.—**somnolent** [sámnolęnt], *a.*
soñoliento; soporífero.

son [san], *s.* hijo.—*s.-in-law*, yerno,
hijo político.

song [son], *s.* canción, canto, cantar,
copla; balada, poema lírico; poesía,
verso; bagatela, nimiedad, bicoca.—
-ster [sónstœr)], *s.* cantor, cantante, cancionista; pájaro cantor.

sonnet [sánit], *s.* soneto.

sonorous [sonóras], *a.* sonoro.

soon [sun], *adv.* pronto, prontamente;
de buena gana.—*as s. as*, tan pronto
como; así que, no bien.—*how s.?*
¿cuándo? ¿cuándo, a más tardar?—*s.
after*, poco después (de).

soot [sut], *s.* hollín, tizne.

soothe [suð], *vt.* calmar, sedar; consolar; desenfadar.—**soothing** [súðiŋ],
a. calmante, sedante.

soothsayer [súθsejœr)], *s.* adivino.

sooty [súti], *a.* tiznado, hollniente.

sop [sap], *s.* sopa (cosa empapada);
soborno, regalo para sobornar o
apaciguar a alguien.—*vti.* [1] ensopar,
empapar.—*to be sopping wet*, estar
hecho una sopa, estar calado hasta
los huesos.—*to s. up*, absorber.

sophism [sáfizm], *s.* sofisma.—**sophis-
ticate** [sofístikejt], *vt.* falsificar,
adulterar.—**sophisticated** [sofístikej-
tid], *a.* con experiencia, avezado al
mundo; afectado, artificial.—**sophis-
tication** [sofístikéjšon], *s.* mundani-
dad, experiencia; afectación.—**soph-
istry** [sáfistri], *s.* sofistería.—*pl.*
retóricas.

sophomore [sáfomor], *s.* estudiante de
segundo año.

soporific [soupqrífik], *a.* soporífero;
soñoliento.

soprano [sopránou], *s.* tiple, soprano.
—*a.* de soprano.

sorcerer [sórscœr)], *s.* hechicero,
brujo.—**sorceress** [sórscœris], *s.* bruja,
hechicera.—**sorcery** [sórscœri], *s.* sortilegio; brujería, hechicería.

sordid [sórdid], *a.* sórdido; vil, bajo;
interesado, mezquino.

sore [sœr], *s.* llaga, úlcera; lastimadura;
mal, dolor; matadura (del ganado);

encono; pena, espina, memoria
dolorosa; disgusto.—*a.* enconado,
dolorido, sensible; apenado, apesa-
rado; (fam.) enojado, sentido, picado;
doloroso, penoso; molesto; vehemente.—*s. throat*, mal de garganta;
carraspera.—*to be s. at*, estar enojado
con.—*to be sorely in need of*, necesitar
urgentemente.—*ness* [sórnis], *s.*
dolor, mal; calidad de dolorido,
enconado o sensible; amargura de
una pena.

sorrel [sáręl], *a.* alazán, roano.—*s.* color
alazán o roano; animal alazán.

sorrily [sárili], *adv.* mal, malamente,
lastimosamente.—**sorrow** [sárou], *s.*
pesar, dolor, pena; duelo, luto; desgracia, infortunio.—*s.-stricken*, afligido, agobiado de dolor.—*to my s.*,
con gran sentimiento mío.—*vi.*
afligirse, sentir pena.—**sorrowful**
[sárouful], *a.* afligido, angustiado;
triste, doloroso.—**sorry** [sári], *a.*
apesadumbrado; arrepentido; lamentable; malo, miserable, ruin, de
inferior calidad; despreciable, ridículo.—*I am s.*, lo siento, estoy
apenado.

sort [sort], *s.* clase, especie, suerte;
manera, modo, forma.—*after a s.*
o *in a s.*, de cierto modo, hasta
cierto punto.—*all sorts of*, toda clase
de.—*in like s.*, de modo análogo.—
of sorts, de varias clases; de mala
muerte.—*out of sorts*, indispuesto;
malhumorado; triste.—*they are a
bad s.*, son mala gente.—*vt.* (con
over) separar, dividir, distribuir en
grupos, clasificar; (con out) escoger,
seleccionar; colocar, arreglar.—*vi.*
corresponder, ajustar; estar de
acuerdo; rozarse; adaptarse.

sot [sat], *s.* borrachín.

sought [sot], *pret.* y *pp.* de TO SEEK.

soul [soul], *s.* alma; psiquis; (fig.)
corazón; esencia, virtud principal;
inspiración; personificación; individuo, persona; vecino, habitante.—
All Souls' Day, Día de Difuntos.
—*not a s.*, nadie, ni un alma.—*on* o
upon my s., por vida mía.— **-ful**
[sóulful], *a.* sentimental, espiritual.—
-less [-lis], *a.* desalmado, vil.

sound [saund], *a.* sano, bueno; sólido,
firme; ileso, incólume; puro, ortodoxo; cierto, justo; firme; cabal;
(com.) solvente.—*of s. mind*, en su
cabal juicio.—*safe and s.*, sano y
salvo.—*s. business*, negocio seguro.
—*s. sleep*, sueño profundo.—*adv.* sanamente, vigorosamente.—*s.* (geog.)
estrecho; (mar. y cir.) sonda; son,
sonido, tañido; ruido; vejiga nata-
toria (peces).—*vt.* sonar, tocar, tañer;
dar el toque de; entonar; proclamar;

celebrar; probar por el sonido; sondear; auscultar.—*to s. a note*, dar señal, avisar; formular, enunciar.—*vi.* sonar; resonar, divulgarse; dar toque de aviso e llamada.— **—ing** [sáundiŋ], *a.* sonante, resonante. **—high-s.**, retumbante.—*s.* sondeo, sondaje.— **—ly** [-lị], *adv.* sanamente.—*to sleep* s., dormir profundamente.— **—ness** [-nịs], *s.* sanidad, salud; **vigor;** firmeza, solidez, estabilidad; verdad, rectitud, pureza; fuerza, validez; rectitud, justicia; pureza de la fe, ortodoxia; (com.) solvencia.

soup [sup], *s.* sopa.—*in the s.*, (fam.) en apuros.

sour [sạụr], *a.* agrio; ácido, fermentado, rancio; desabrido, acre, huraño, malhumorado.—*vt.* agriar, cortar (la leche, etc.); irritar, indisponer (los ánimos); desagradar; hacer fermentar.—*vi.* agriarse, cortarse; fermentar; irritarse, enojarse; corromperse.

source [sors], *s.* fuente, nacimiento, origen, causa, procedencia, germen.

sourness [sáụrnịs], *s.* agrura, acedía, acidez; acritud, acrimenia.

south [sạụθ], *s.* sur o sud; comarca o región situada al sur.—*a.* meridional, austral.—*S. American*, sudamericano.—*adv.* hacia el sur; del sur (viento).— **—east** [-íst], *s.* y *a.* sudeste.— **—eastern** [-ístœrn], *a.* y *adv.* del sudeste.— **—ern** [sáðœrn], *a.* meridional, del sur.— **—erner** [sáðœrnœ(r)], *s.* habitante del sur.— **—ernmost** [sáðœrnmoụst], *a.* de más al sur, más meridional.— **—ward** [-wǎrd], *a.* situado hacia el sur.—*adv.* hacia el mediodía.— **—west** [-wést], *s.* y *a.* sudoeste.— **—western** [-wéstœrn], *a.* en, hacia e del sudoeste.

souvenir [súvẹnịr], *s.* memoria, prenda de recuerdo.

sovereign [sávrịn], *s.* soberane, monarca.—*a.* soberano, independiente; preeminente; eficacísimo.— **—ty** [-tị], *s.* soberanía; estado soberano.

soviet [sóųvịet], *s.* sóviet.—*a.* soviético.

sow [sạụ], *s.* (zool.) puerca, cerda, marrana.—*vti.* y *vii.* [6] [sou], (agr.) sembrar; desparramar, esparcir, diseminar.

soy [sọị], *s.* soja, soya; salsa de soja.— **—bean** [sóịbin], *s.* soja, soya.

space [speịs], *vt.* espaciar.—*s.* espacio; lugar, cabida; período, intervalo; rato; ocasión, oportunidad.— **—spacious** [spéịʃʌs], *a.* espacioso, amplio, extenso.— **—spaciousness** [spéịʃʌsnịs], *s.* espaciosidad, extensión.

spade [speịd], *s.* pala plana; (naipes) espadas; (mil.) zapa.—*to call a s. a s.*,

llamar al pan, pan y al vino, vino.—*vt.* remover o cavar con la azada.

spaghetti [spagéti], *s.* fideos largos; macarrones finos.

span [spæn], *s.* palme; lapse, espacio, trecho; (arq.) luz; (aer.) envergadura, dimensión máxima transversal; ojo, apertura de puente, arco o bóveda; pareja (de caballos).—*vti.* [1] medir a palmos; atravesar; abarcar, llegar de un lado a otro de; extenderse sobre; ligar, atar.

spangle [spæŋgl], *s.* lentejuela.

Spaniard [spænyǎrd], *s.* español (persona española).

spaniel [spænyẹl], *s.* perro de aguas.

Spanish [spænịʃ], *s.* español (idioma). —*a.* español (de España), hispánico, hispano.—*S. shawl*, mantón de Manila.

spank [spæŋk], *vt.* zurrar, dar palmadas o nalgadas.—*s.* nalgada, palmada.

spar [spạr], *s.* (mar.) mástil, palo; (min.) espato; pugilato; riña, pelea. —*vi.* boxear, pelear.

spare [sper], *vt.* ahorrar, economizar; escatimar; prescindir de, pasarse sin; conceder, dedicar (tiempo); perdonar; no abusar de, compadecer; evitar, ahorrar trabajo o molestia a; usar con moderación; eximir de.—*there's no time to s.*, no hay tiempo que perder.—*to have time to s.*, tener tiempo de sobra o libre.—*to s. oneself*, cuidarse de sí mismo, ahorrarse trabajo, molestia, etc.—*a.* disponible, sobrante; de reserva, de repuesto; enjuto; económico, mezquino; escaso; sobrio.

spark [spark], *s.* chispa; pizca; petimetre o pisaverde.—*pl.* (fam.) radiotelegrafista.— **—plug**, bujía (de un motor).—*vt.* (fam.) galantear, enamorar.—*vi.* echar chispas, centellear.— **—le** [spárkl], *s.* centelleo, destello, chispa.—*vi.* centellear, brillar, relampaguear; ser espumoso (vinos, etc.).— **—ling** [-lịŋ], *a.* centelleante; brillante; agudo, ingenioso; espumoso.

sparrow [spærọụ], *s.* gorrión, pardal. —*s. hawk*, esparaván, gavilán, cernícalo.—*s. shot*, mostacilla.

sparse [spars], *a.* esparcido, desparramado; claro, ralo.

spasm [spæzm], *s.* espasmo.

spat [spæt], *pret.* y *pp.* de **TO SPIT** (escupir).—*vti.* y *vii.* [1] (fam.) reñir, disputar ligeramente.—*s.* huevas de los mariscos; palmadita; manotada, sopapo, bofetada; riña, disputa.—*pl.* botines; polainas cortas.

spatula [spæchụlǎ], *s.* espátula.

spawn [spọn], *s.* huevas; pececillos. —*vt.* y *vi.* desovar.

speak [spik], *vti.* y *vii.* [10] hablar; decir; conversar; comunicar(se); recitar.—*so to s.*, por decirlo así.—*to s. about* u *of*, hablar o tratar de.—*to s. brokenly*, chapurr(e)ar.—*to s. daggers*, decir improperios, echar chispas.—*to s. for*, hablar en favor de; hablar en nombre de; ser recomendación para; solicitar.—*to s. out*, hablar claro.—*to s. to the point*, ir al grano.—*to s. up*, hablar en alta voz; interponer; decir claridades.— —**er** [spíkœ(r)], *s.* hablante, orador; presidente de un cuerpo legislativo; locutor; altavoz.

spear [spir], *s.* lanza; venablo; arpón de pesca; brizna, brote, retoño.—*vt.* alancear, herir con lanza.—*vi.* (bot.) brotar.— —**mint** [spírmint], *s.* (bot.) hierbabuena, menta verde.

special [spéʃəl], *a.* especial; extraordinario, peculiar; diferencial; hecho especialmente.—*s. delivery*, entrega inmediata (de correo).—*s. warrant*, orden de arresto.—*s.* persona o cosa (tren, etc.) especial; carta de entrega inmediata; (fam., com.) ganga. saldo. — —**ist** [-ist], *s.* y *a.* especialista, especializado.—**ize** [-aįz], *vt.* y *vi.* especializar(se); tener por especialidad.— —**ness** [-nįs], *s.* especialidad.— —**ity** [spɛʃiǽlįti], *s.* especialidad, peculiaridad, rasgo característico.

specie [spíʃi], *s.* efectivo, numerario.

species [spíʃiz], *s.* (biol., lóg.) especie; clase, género, suerte, variedad; forma, naturaleza.—**specific** [spisífįkį], *a.* específico, preciso; especificativo, determinado; peculiar.—*s.* (med.) específico.—**specify** [spésifai], *vti.* [7] especificar; estipular, prescribir.—**specimen** [spésimįn], *s.* espécimen, muestra; ejemplar.

speck(le) [spék(l)], *s.* manchita, mácula; motita; nube (en un ojo); lunar, señal; pizca, punto.—*vt.* manchar, motear.

spectacle [spéktąkl], *s.* espectáculo.—*pl.* espejuelos.—**spectacular** [spektǽkyȯlǫ(r)], *a.* espectacular; aparatoso.—**spectator** [spéktetǫ(r)], *s.* espectador, mirón.

specter [spéktœ(r)], *s.* espectro, visión.—**spectrum** [spéktram], *s.* (opt.) espectro.

speculate [spékyȯleįt], *vt.* y *vi.* especular.—**speculation** [spekyȯléjšǫɲ], *s.* especulación.—**speculative** [spékyȯleįtįv], *a.* especulativo; (com.) especulador.—**speculator** [spékyȯleįtǫ(r)], *s.* teórico; (com.) especulador; (teat.) revendedor de billetes.

sped [spɛd], *pret.* y *pp.* de TO SPEED.

speech [spich], *s.* palabra, lenguaje; idioma; voz; discurso, arenga, perorata; disertación; (teat.) parlamento. — —**less** [spíchlįs], *a.* mudo; callado.

speed [spid], *vti.* [4] ayudar, favorecer; acompañar, despedir; despachar, expedir; acelerar, apresurar, dar prisa, avivar.—*vii.* correr, apresurarse, darse prisa; andar o moverse con presteza; (aut.) exceder la velocidad permitida; adelantar, progresar.—*s.* velocidad; rapidez; presteza; progreso, buen éxito.—*s. gear*, (aut.) cambio de velocidades.—*s. limit*, velocidad máxima permitida; límite de velocidad.—*s. trap*, (aut.) aparato que registra automáticamente la velocidad de un vehículo y descubre a los infractores. — —**ily** [-ịlį], *adv.* rápidamente, de prisa; pronto.— —**ometer** [spidámętœ(r)], *s.* velocímetro, cuentaquilómetros, indicador de velocidad. — —**y** [-į], *a.* veloz, rápido, vivo.

spell [spel], *vti.* [4] deletrear; descifrar, leer con dificultad; indicar, significar; hechizar, encantar; (fam.) relevar, reemplazar.—*to s. the watch*, relevar a la guardia.—*vii.* deletrear; (fam.) descansar por un rato.—*s.* hechizo, encanto, ensalmo; fascinación; turno, tanda; (fam.) poco tiempo, rato, trecho.—*by spells*, por turnos; a ratos.—*under a s.*, fascinado.— —**bind** [spélbaịnd], *vti.* [10] fascinar, embelesar, hechizar.— —**bound** [spélbaụnd], *pret.* y *pp.* de TO SPELLBIND.—*a.* fascinado, embelesado, hechizado.— —**er** [spélœ(r)], *s.* silabario; libro de deletrear.— —**ing** [-įŋ], *s.* deletreo; ortografía, grafía.

spend [spend], *vti.* [10] gastar; consumir, agotar; pasar, emplear (tiempo, etc.).—*vii.* gastar dinero, hacer gastos; gastarse, consumirse; desovar.— —**thrift** [spéndθrįft], *s.* pródigo, derrochador, manirroto.—**spent** [spent], *pret.* y *pp.* de TO SPEND.—*a.* agotado, rendido.

sperm [spœrm], *s.* esperma, semen; aceite de ballena.—*s. whale*, cachalote.

sphere [sfir], *s.* esfera; orbe; astro; esfera o círculo de acción.—**spherical** [sférįkąl], *a.* esférico.

sphinx [sfįŋks], *s.* esfinge; persona misteriosa o enigmática.

spice [spaįs], *s.* especia; (poét.) aroma, fragancia.—*vt.* condimentar con especias.—**spicy** [spáįsį], *a.* que contiene o sabe a especias; aromático, especiado; (fig.) sabroso, picante.

spider [spáįdœ(r)], *s.* araña, arácnido; sartén; cubo y rayos (de una rueda).—*s. web, s's web*, telaraña.

spigot [spígǫt], *s.* espita; tapón de espita; llave, grifo; macho, espiga (de un tubo).

spike [spaɪk], *s.* (bot.) espiga; alcayata, escarpia, espigón, clavo largo, perno; pico.—*vt.* clavetear; empernar, enclavijar; anular, poner fin a.

spikenard [spáɪknard], *s.* (bot.) nardo.

spiky [spáɪkɪ], *a.* erizado, puntiagudo; armado de púas.

spill [spɪl], *s.* astilla; clavija; mecha; (fam.) vuelco, caída (del caballo o de un vehículo); derramamiento.—*vti.* [4] derramar, verter; desparramar, esparcir; (fam.) divulgar; volcar.—*vii.* derramarse, rebosar.

spin [spɪn], *vti.* [10] hilar; (mec.) tornear.—*to s. a yarn*, hilar; contar un cuento increíble.—*to s. out*, alargar, prolongar; retorcer, hacer bailar (un trompo).—*vii.* hilar; girar, rodar rápidamente; (aut.) girar sin avanzar (las ruedas); bailar (un trompo).—*s.* giro, vuelta; (fam.) paseo en coche o bicicleta; (aer.) barrena.

spinach [spínɪch], *s.* espinaca.

spinal [spáɪnal], *a.* (anat.) espinal.— *s. column*, columna vertebral o espina dorsal.—*s. cord*, médula espinal.

spindle [spíndl], *s.* huso; eje.

spine [spaɪn], *s.* espinazo, espina dorsal; (bot.) espina; (zool.) púa.— **—less** [spáɪnlɪs], *a.* sin espinazo; pusilánime; servil.

spinner [spínœ(r)], *s.* hilandero; hiladera, máquina de hilar; cebo artificial para pescar.—**spinning** [spíniŋ], *s.* hilandería, arte de hilar; (aut.) rotación estacionaria de las ruedas.

spinster [spínstœ(r)], *s.* soltera, solterona; hilandera.— **—hood** [-hʊd], *s.* soltería.

spiral [spáɪral], *s.* espiral; (aer.) vuelo en espiral.—*a.* espiral; en espiral; de caracol.—*vii.* [2] (aer.) volar en espiral; tomar forma o curso espiral.

spire [spaɪr], *s.* (arq.) aguja; brizna de hierba; cúspide, cima, ápice; espira, espiral, caracol.—*vi.* rematar en punta; (bot.) germinar.

spirit [spírɪt], *s.* espíritu; aparecido, espectro; inclinación, vocación; temple; intención; ánimo, brío, valor. —*pl.* espíritus, vapores; bebidas espirituosas; estado de ánimo.—*high spirits*, alegría, animación.—*vt.* (con **away**) arrebatar, hacer desaparecer (como por ensalmo).— **—ed** [-ɪd], *a.* vivo, brioso; animoso.— **—ual** [spírɪchʊal], *a.* espiritual; mental, intelectual; místico; piadoso, religioso; espiritualista.— **—ualism** [spírɪchʊalɪzm], *s.* espiritismo; espiritualismo.— **—uous** [spírɪchʊʌs], *a.* espirituoso, alcohólico; embriagador.

spit [spɪt], *vti.* [10] escupir, esputar. —*vii.* escupir; chisporrotear.—*pret.*

y *pp.* de TO SPIT.—*vti.* [1] espetar, ensartar.—*s.* saliva, salivazo, escupitajo; lengua de tierra; asador, espiche.—*the s. and image* o *the spitting image*, (fam.) el vivo retrato, la imagen viva.

spite [spaɪt], *s.* rencor, despecho, ojeriza.—*(in) s. of*, a pesar de, a despecho de, no obstante.—*vt.* mostrar resentimiento, mortificar.— **—ful** [spáɪtfʊl], *a.* rencoroso; malicioso, malévolo.

spitfire [spítfaɪr], *s.* fierabrás; mujer colérica.

spittle [spɪtl], *s.* saliva, escupitajo.— **spittoon** [spɪtún], *s.* escupidera.

splash [splæʃ], *vt.* salpicar, rociar, enlodar; chapotear, humedecer.—*vi.* chapotear.—*s.* salpicadura, rociada; chapoteo.— **—board** [splǽʃbɔrd], *s.* guardabarros, (Am.) guardafangos.

spleen [splin], *s.* bazo; mal humor; tristeza, esplín.

splendid [spléndɪd], *a.* espléndido; esplendente, brillante; ilustre, glorioso; excelente.—**splendor** [spléndo(r)], *s.* esplendor.

splice [splaɪs], *vt.* empalmar; empotrar; (fam.) casar.—*s.* junta o empalme.

splint [splɪnt], *vt.* (cir.) entablillar.—*s.* tira plana y delgada; astilla; (cir.) tablilla.— **—er** [splíntœ(r)], *vt.* astillar; (cir.) entablillar.—*vi.* hacerse pedazos, romperse en astillas.—*s.* astilla; esquirla (de hueso); brizna; astilla clavada en la carne.

split [splɪt], *vti.* [9] hender, partir; rajar, cuartear, separar; dividir, repartir; (quim.) escindir, desdoblar; descomponer.—*to s. off* o *up*, desunir, desamistar.—*vii.* henderse, escindirse, rajarse, romperse a lo largo, cuartearse, resquebrajarse; estallar, reventar; dividirse; (fam.) disentir; (fam.) ser traidor, revelar secretos. —*pret.* y *pp.* de TO SPLIT.—*s.* hendidura, grieta, rendija, cuarteadura; división, cisma, rompimiento.—*a.* hendido, partido, rajado, cuarteado; curado (pescado).

spoil [spɔɪl], *vti.* [4] echar a perder; estropear, desgraciar; inutilizar; viciar, corromper; malcriar, consentir; despojar, saquear.—*vii.* inutilizarse, estropearse; podrirse.—*s.* saqueo; botín.—*pl.* beneficios de un cargo público.—*spoils system*, premio de servicios políticos con empleos públicos. **—age** [spóɪlɪdʒ], *s.* desperdicio, daño, inutilización.

spoke [spoʊk], *s.* rayo, radio (de rueda).—*pret.* de TO SPEAK.—**spoken** [spóʊkn], *pp.* de TO SPEAK.— **—sman** [-sman], *s.* interlocutor; vocero, portavoz; el que lleva la palabra.

spoliation [spouliéiṣon], *s.* despojo, rapiña; (for.) expoliación.

sponge [spʌndʒ], *s.* esponja; (fam.) gorrón, parásito.—*s. cake,* bizcocho. —*vt.* lavar o mojar con esponja; esponjar.—*to s. up,* absorber, chupar; (fam.) comer de gorra, sablear; sacar (dinero, etc.).—*vi.* embeberse; (fam.) vivir o comer a expensas de otro, darle un sablazo a uno.——r [spʌndʒœ(r)], *s.* (fam.) gorrista, sablista, pegote.—**spongy** [spʌndʒi], *a.* esponjoso, esponjado.

sponsor [spʌnso(r)], *s.* fiador; patrocinador, patrón, patrono; (rad. y T.V.) entidad que patrocina un programa; padrino o madrina; defensor, apadrinador, fomentador.— *vt.* salir fiador de, ser responsable de; apadrinar, ser padrino de; promover, fomentar, patrocinar; (rad. y T.V.) costear o presentar un programa comercial.——**ship** [-ṣip], *s.* patrocinio.

spool [spul], *s.* carretel, bobina.—*vt.* devanar, ovillar.

spoon [spun], *s.* cuchara.—*vt.* sacar con cuchara.—*vi.* pescar con cuchara; (fam.) acariciarse, besarse.——**ful** [spúnful], *s.* cucharada, cucharadita.

sport [sport], *s.* deporte.—*pl.* deportismo.—*for o in s.,* de burlas, en broma.—*to be a good s.,* ser buen compañero; saber perder (en el juego).—*to make s of,* burlarse de. —*vt.* (fam.) hacer alarde de, lucir, ostentar.—*vi.* divertirse, jugar; bromear, chancearse.—*a.* deportivo.— —**s** [-s], *a.* deportivo; de o para deportes.——**sman** [spórtsmạn], *s.* deportista.

spot [spat], *s.* sitio, lugar, paraje, puesto, punto; mancha, borrón, tacha; grano; lunar.—*in spots,* (fam.) en algunos respectos; aquí y allí. —*on o upon the s.,* ahí mismo, allí mismo, en el acto, al punto, inmediatamente.—*to be on the s.,* (fam.) hallarse en un aprieto; estar en peligro de muerte; estar en el lugar de los hechos.—*a.* (com.) en existencia, listo para entregarse.—*s. cash,* dinero contante; pago al contado.—*vt.* [1] motear, manchar, macular; (fam.) observar, notar, distinguir.—*vi.* salir manchas; mancharse.——**less** [spátlis], *a.* inmaculado.——**light** [-lait], *s.* (teat., fot., aut., etc.) reflector (móvil).— **spotted** [spátid], *a.* manchado.

spouse [spaus], *s.* esposa, esposo; cónyuge.

spout [spaut], *s.* chorro, surtidor; caño, conducto; espita; (arq.) gárgola; cuello de vasija, pico de cafetera

o tetera.—*to go up the s.,* (fam.) fracasar.—*vt. y vi.* arrojar o echar (un líquido); surgir, brotar, correr a chorro; (fam.) recitar, declamar.

sprain [sprein], *vt.* torcer, producir un esguince.—*s.* (med.) torcedura, esguince.

sprang [spræŋ], *pret.* de TO SPRING.

sprawl [sprol], *vt. y vi.* tender(se); despatarrar(se); (agr.) desparramarse.

spray [sprei], *vt. y vi.* rociar, pulverizar un líquido.—*s.* rociada, rocío; espuma del mar; salpicadura; rociador, pulverizador; líquido de rociar; ramaje.

spread [spred], *vti. y vii.* [9] tender(se); extender(se), desplegar(se), desenvolver(se); desparramar(se), esparcir(se); divulgar(se); diseminar(se), propalar(se).—*to s. apart,* abrir(se), separar(se).—*to s. something (butter, etc.) on,* untar con; dar una capa de.—*to s. out the tablecloth,* extender el mantel.—*to s. with,* untar con; cubrir de.—*pret. y pp.* de TO SPREAD.—*a.* extendido, desparramado; (joy.) de poco brillo.—*s.* extensión, amplitud; propagación; diseminación; cobertor de cama; tapete de mesa, mantel; (fam.) festín, banquete, comilona; (com.) diferencia; anuncio con encabezamiento a través de dos páginas.

spree [spri], *s.* borrachera; juerga, parranda.—*to go on a s.,* ir (o andar) de juerga, parranda o farra.

sprig [sprig], *s.* ramita, renuevo, pimpollo.

sprightly [spráitli], *a.* alegre, vivo, garboso.

spring [spriŋ], *vti.* [10] soltar (un resorte o muelle); sacar o presentar de golpe; hacer volar (una mina); combar; rendir un palo o verga; (arq.) vaciar (un arco); insertar o meter doblando o forzando; saltar por encima de; pasar saltando; ojear (la caza); asegurar o montar con resortes o muelles.—*vii.* saltar, brincar; salir, brotar, manar (un líquido); dimanar, provenir; presentarse súbitamente; combarse, rendirse; nacer, crecer; levantarse, elevarse.—*to s. at,* abalanzarse sobre; saltar a.—*to s. away,* saltar a un lado; lanzarse de un salto.—*to s. forward,* abalanzarse, dispararse.— *to s. up,* nacer, brotar, desarrollarse; salir a luz; subir, engrandecerse.—*to s. upon,* abalanzarse sobre; saltar a.—*s.* muelle, resorte; elasticidad; salto, corcovo, bote; vuelta a su posición anterior; motivo, móvil; primavera; fuente, manantial; origen,

nacimiento; surtidor; combadura.—*a.*
primaveral; de manantial.

sprinkle [spríŋkl], *vt.* rociar; regar;
salpicar, polvorear.—*vi.* lloviznar.
—*s.* rocío, rociada; llovizna; una
pizca, un poquito.— —r [spríŋklœ(r)],
s. rociador, regadera; (igl.) hisopo,
aspersorio; carro de riego.—**sprin-
kling** [spríŋkliŋ], *s.* rociada, asper-
sión; pizca.

sprout [spraut], *vt.* hacer germinar o
brotar; (agr.) desbotonar.—*vi.* retoñar, echar botones o renuevos;
crecer; ramificarse.—*s.* renuevo, retoño, botón.—*Brussels sprouts,* coles
de Bruselas.

spruce [sprus], *a.* garboso, apuesto,
majo.—*s.* abeto.—*to s. up,* vestir(se)
con esmero, emperifollar(se), po-
ner(se) majo.

sprung [sprʌŋ], *pret.* **y** *pp.* de TO
SPRING.

spun [spʌn], *pret.* **y** *pp.* de TO SPIN.

spur [spœr], *s.* espuela, acicate; incentivo, estímulo; excitación; espolón
(del gallo); uña puntiaguda; pincho;
(geog.) estribación; (arq.) puntal.—
on the s. of the moment, sin pensarlo,
impulsivamente.—*vti.* **y** *vii.* [1]
espolear, acicatear, aguijonear; incitar, estimular; calzarse las espuelas;
apretar el paso.—*to s. on,* espolear,
estimular.

spurn [spœrn], *vt.* **y** *vi.* despreciar;
menospreciar; rechazar a puntapiés;
cocear.

spurt [spœrt], *vt.* **y** *vi.* arrojar o salir
un chorro o chorros; brotar, surgir;
hacer un esfuerzo supremo.—*s.* chorro; arrebato, esfuerzo supremo; rato,
momento.

sputter [spátœ(r)], *vt.* **y** *vi.* espurrear,
rociar con la boca; chisporrotear;
farfullar, barbotar.—*s.* chisporroteo,
chispeo de saliva; farfulla.

sputum [spjútʌm], *s.* saliva; (med.)
esputo.

spy [spai], *s.* espía.—*vti.* [7] atisbar,
divisar; espiar, observar; (con out)
explorar, reconocer un país.—*vii.*
espiar; ser espía.— —**glass** [spáiglæs],
s. anteojo de larga vista.

squab [skwab], *s.* (orn.) pichón; persona
gordiflona; cojín, otomana.

squabble [skwábl], *vt.* (imp.) empaste-
lar.—*vi.* reñir, disputar.—*s.* pendencia, riña, disputa.

squad [skwad], *s.* (mil.) escuadra,
patrulla, pelotón; partida; equipo.—
—**ron** [skwádrɒn], *s.* (mar.) escuadra, armada, flota; (mil.) escuadrón;
cuadro; soldados en formación;
(aer.) escuadrilla.

squalid [skwálid], *a.* escuálido; miserable, sucio, asqueroso.

squall [skwɔl], *vt.* **y** *vi.* chillar, berrear.
—*vi.* haber borrasca.—*s.* chillido,
berrido; borrasca; (mar.) racha,
turbonada, chubasco.

squalor [skwálɒ(r)], *s.* miseria; porquería, mugre.

squander [skwándœ(r)], *vt.* **y** *vi.*
malgastar, despilfarrar, desparramar,
disipar.— —er [-œ(r)], *s.* derrochador,
manirroto.

square [skwer], *a.* cuadrado; en cuadro;
rectangular; a escuadra; perfecto,
exacto, justo, cabal; íntegro, honrado,
equitativo; (fam.) completo, abundante; (com.) saldado, en paz; (mar.)
en cruz; (mat.) elevado al cuadrado.
—*s. dance,* baile de figuras.—*s.
deal(ing),* buena fe, equidad, justicia,
honradez, juego limpio.—*s.-shooter,*
(fam.) persona honrada.—*to get s.
with,* (fam.) desquitarse de, hacér-
selas pagar a.—*s.* cuadrado; cuadro;
plaza, plazoleta; casilla (de tablero
de damas, etc.); manzana de casas;
escuadra, cartabón; proporción debida, orden, exactitud; honradez,
equidad; (mil.) cuadro.—*on the s.,*
(fam.) honradamente, de buena fe;
a escuadra.—*out of s.,* fuera de
escuadra.—*vt.* cuadrar, formar un
cuadro; escuadrar; (mat.) cuadrar,
elevar al cuadrado; (b.a.) cuadricular;
(com.) saldar, ajustar, arreglar
(cuentas); pasar balance; justificar;
poner de acuerdo; medir superficies
en pies, metros, etc., cuadrados.—
to s. one's self, sincerarse, justificarse,
dar satisfacción.—*vi.* estar en ángulo
recto; cuadrar, encajar convenir
estar de acuerdo.

squash [skwaš], *s.* (bot.) alabaza.—
vt. aplastar, (fam.) despachurrar.

squat [skwat], *vi.* [1] agacharse
agazaparse, sentarse en cuclillas;
establecerse sin derecho en un local.
—*a.* agachado, puesto en cuclillas;
rechoncho.—*s.* posición del que está
en cuclillas.

squawk [skwɔk], *vi.* graznar; (fam.)
quejarse ruidosamente.—*s.* graznido;
(fam.) queja o protesta ruidosa.

squeak [skwik], *vi.* chirriar, rechinar;
(fam.) delatar.—*s.* chillido, chirrido.
—*to have a narrow s.,* escapar en
una tabla.—**squeal** [skwil], *vi.* chillar; (fam.) delatar.—*s.* chillido.

squeamish [skwímiš], *a.* remilgado,
delicado, escrupuloso.— —**ness** [-nis],
s. remilgo, escrúpulo; náusea.

squeeze [skwiz], *vt.* apretar, comprimir;
estrechar; estrujar, exprimir, prensar; acosar, agobiar; rebajar (jornales).—*to s. in,* hacer entrar apretando.
—*to s. through,* forzar al través de.—
vi. pasar, entrar o salir apretando.

—*s.* apretadura, apretón; abrazo fuerte.

squelch [skwelch], *vt.* aplastar; sofocar; (fam.) hacer callar, paralizar, (fig.) desconcertar.—*vi.* ser vencido, desconcertado; chapotear.

squid [skwịd], *s.* calamar.

squint [skwịnt], *s.* estrabismo; mirada bizca; mirada furtiva o de soslayo.—*vt.* y *vi.* mirar bizco, bizquear; mirar achicando los ojos; mirar de través o de soslayo.—*squint-eyed*, bizco, bisojo, estrábico; avieso; ambiguo.

squirm [skwœrm], *vi.* retorcerse, serpentear; trepar.—*to s. out of a difficulty*, esforzarse para vencer una dificultad o salir de un aprieto.—*s.* retorcimiento.

squirrel [skwœrẹl], *s.* ardilla.

squirt [skwœrt], *vt.* y *vi.* (hacer) salir a chorros; chorrear; jeringar.—*s.* chisguete, chorretada; (fam.) jeringazo.—*s. gun*, jeringa.

stab [stæb], *vti.* y *vii.* [1] herir con arma blanca, dar de puñaladas.—*s.* puñalada; estocada.

stability [stạbịlịti], *s.* estabilidad; firmeza, consistencia, solidez; asiento. —**stabilize** [stéjbịlajz], *vt.* estabilizar. —**stabilizer** [stéjbjalzœ(r)], *s.* estabilizador.—**stable** [stéjbl], *a.* estable. —*s.* establo, cuadra.—*vt.* y *vi.* poner o estar en establo.

stack [stæk], *s.* montón, pila, rimero; hacina (de heno); cañón de chimenea; (fam.) abundancia; (mil.) pabellón de fusiles.—*vt.* hacinar, apilar, amontonar; poner las armas en pabellón.

stadium [stéjdịʌm], *s.* estadio, campo deportivo; grado de progreso o adelanto.

staff [stæf], *s.* báculo, bordón, cayado; apoyo, sostén; vara, bastón de mando; pértiga; vara de medir; asta (de bandera o lanza); baliza, jalón de mira; estado mayor, plana mayor; personal; facultad; junta, cuerpo. —*vt.* proveer de personal, funcionarios u oficiales.

stag [stæg], *s.* venado, ciervo; (fam.) hombre, varón, macho.—*s. party*, (fam.) tertulia de hombres solos.

stage [stéjdʒ], *s.* (teat.) escenario, escena, tablas; (fig.) teatro (arte y profesión); escena de acción; tablado, entarimado, plataforma, estrado; andamio; etapa, jornada; grado, estado; período (de una enfermedad); platina (de microscopio); diligencia, ómnibus; (arq.) escalón, paso de escalera; (rad.) elemento, unidad; (mec.) grado.—*by short stages*, a pequeñas etapas, a cortas jornadas.

—*s. scenery* o *setting*, decoración, decorado.—*s.-struck*, fascinado por el teatro; que se muere por ser actor o actriz.—*vt.* preparar; ejecutar, efectuar; (teat.) poner en escena, montar, escenificar; (re)presentar.

stagecoach [stéjdʒkouch], *s.* diligencia, ómnibus.

stagger [stǽgœ(r)], *vi.* hacer eses, tambalear, bambolear; vacilar, titubear.—*vt.* causar vértigos o vahídos; asustar; hacer vacilar; hacer tambalear; disponer o arreglar (plantas, etc.) al tresbolillo; alternar; espaciar (horas de trabajo, etc.).—*s.* tambaleo, vacilación.

stagnant [stǽgnạnt], *a.* estancado.— **stagnate** [stǽgnejt], *vi.* estancarse, estacionarse.—**stagnation** [stægnéjšọn], *s.* estancamiento, paralización.

staid [stejd], *pret.* y *pp.* de TO STAY. —*a.* grave, serio, sosegado, formal.

stain [stejn], *vt.* y *vi.* manchar, macular; teñir; tiznar; mancillar, desdorar. —*stained glass*, vidrio de color.—*s.* mancha, mácula; tinte; solución colorante; borrón, estigma.—*less* [stéjnlịs], *a.* limpio; inmaculado; que no se mancha.—*s. steel*, acero inoxidable.

stair [ster], *s.* escalón, peldaño.—*pl.* escalera.— *—case* [stérkejs], *—way* [-wej], *s.* escalera; escalinata (exterior).

stake [stejk], *s.* estaca; (fig.) hoguera, pira; apuesta, posta o puesta; azar, riesgo; premio del vencedor; (com.) interés, ganancia o pérdida contingente.—*at s.*, en juego, envuelto, comprometido, en peligro.—*vt.* jugarse, apostar; aventurar, arriesgar; (fam.) establecer a uno en los negocios, etc.; darle o prestarle dinero.

stale [stejl], *a.* añejo; rancio, pasado; viciado (el aire); gastado, anticuado, trillado; improductivo.—*s. bread*, pan duro.—*s. wine*, vino picado.

stalk [stɔk], *vt.* cazar al acecho.—*vi.* taconear, andar con paso majestuoso. —*s.* tallo, pedúnculo, peciolo; troncho de hortalizas; pie de copa; paso majestuoso, taconeo.

stall [stɔl], *s.* pesebre, casilla de establo; casilla, puesto (en el mercado, etc.); tabla (de carnicero); (teat.) luneta o butaca; (igl.) sitial de coro; (min.) galería; (aer.) disminución de velocidad.—*vt.* meter en cuadra o establo; poner puestos o casillas; atascar, atollar; poner obstáculos.—*to s. off*, evitar, eludir, tener a raya.—*vi.* estar atascado; (aut.) pararse, ahogarse (el motor); (aer.) bajar de la velocidad mínima de vuelo.—*to s. for time*, (fam.) dar largas; demorar para ganar tiempo o no hacer una cosa.

stallion [stǽlyɘn], *s.* caballo semental.

stalwart [stɔ́lwɐrt], *a.* fornido, membrudo; (pol.) leal, firme, fiel.

stamina [stǽminɐ], *s.* nervio, fibra, vigor.

stammer [stǽmœ(r)], *vt.* y *vi.* tartamudear; balbucear.—*s.* tartamudeo; balbuceo.——**er** [-œ(r)], *s.* tartamudo, gago.

stamp [stæmp], *vt.* estampar; marcar, señalar; imprimir; sellar, estampillar; timbrar (papel, cartas); poner el sello (de correo); acuñar; patear (el suelo, etc.); estigmatizar.—*to s. out,* extirpar, suprimir.—*vi.* patalear; piafar.—*s.* sello, estampilla; timbre; impresión, marca, estampa; estampador; cuño, troquel; mano de mortero; (fig.) temple, suerte, clase; laya, calaña.—*s. duties,* derechos del timbre.—*s. duty,* impuesto del timbre.

stampede [stæmpíd], *vt.* y *vi.* espantar(se); dispersar(se) en desorden.—*s.* estampida; huida en tropel; determinación repentina y unánime.

stance [stæns], *s.* postura.

stanch [stænch], *vt.* restañar; estancar.—*a.* [stanch], firme, fiel, adicto.

stand [stænd], *vti.* [10] poner derecho, colocar o poner de pie; resistir, hacer frente a; aguantar, tolerar; sostener, defender; (fam.) sufragar. —*to s. one's ground,* resistir, defender su puesto o posición, mantenerse en su puesto.—*to s. treat,* (fam.) pagar la convidada.—*to s. up,* (fam.) dejar plantado a uno.—*vii.* estar, estar situado; ponerse o estar de pie; tenerse derecho; mantenerse, durar, perdurar; sostenerse; quedarse; pararse, detenerse; quedar suspenso; ponerse o estar en cierta posición; erguirse, enderezarse.—*to s. about,* rodear, cercar.—*to s. against,* hacer frente a.—*to s. aloof (from),* retraerse (de).—*to s. aside,* apartarse. —*to s. back,* retroceder; quedarse atrás.—*to s. by,* ser o permanecer fiel a; estar listo; sostener, favorecer; atenerse a; sostenerse en; someterse a; estar de mirón; estar cerca, quedarse allí; mantenerse listo.—*to s. fast,* no cejar o ceder.—*to s. for,* estar en lugar de; significar, querer decir; tolerar; aprobar, favorecer; solicitar, pretender; presentarse como candidato u opositor; sostener, defender; apadrinar; llevar rumbo hacia.—*to s. forth,* adelantarse, avanzar; presentarse.—*to s. in good stead,* servir, ser útil.—*to s. in line,* hacer cola.—*to s. in the way,* cerrar el paso; estorbar.—*to s. in with,* juntarse o estar aliado con; estar

en gracia de.—*to s. off,* mantenerse a distancia, apartarse; negar, denegar.—*to s. on o upon,* estar colocado sobre, estar en; adherirse a; interesar, concernir, pertenecer; estimar, valuar; fijarse en; picarse de, tener su orgullo en; insistir en.—*to s. on end,* erizarse; ponerse de punta; mantenerse derecho.—*to s. on one's own feet,* valerse a sí mismo.—*to s. on tiptoe,* ponerse o estar de puntillas.—*to s. out,* mantenerse firme; apartarse; denegar; resaltar, destacarse, estar en relieve.—*to s. over,* aplazar; plantarse al lado de para vigilar o apurar. —*to s. pat,* mantenerse en sus trece. —*to s. up,* levantarse, alzarse. —*s.* puesto, sitio, lugar, posición, estación; tarima, estrado, plataforma; tribuna, grada, galería (de espectadores); mostrador, puesto en un mercado; velador, mesita, pie, estante, pedestal, sostén, soporte; actitud, opinión; parada, pausa, alto; término; inactividad, estancamiento; oposición, resistencia.—*to make a s.,* pararse y resistir.

standard [stǽndɐrd], *s.* norma, tipo, pauta, patrón, modelo; (mec.) soporte, madrina, pie, montante, árbol; bandera, estandarte, pendón.—*s. of living,* nivel o norma de vida.—*a.* normal, de ley; patrón (vara, libra, etc.); clásico; *s.-bearer,* abanderado; cacique, jefe político.—*s. book o work,* obra de autoridad reconocida; obra clásica.—*s. equipment,* equipo regular o de uso corriente.—*s. gauge,* marca o medida que sirve de norma. —*s. pitch,* (mús.) diapasón normal. —**ization** [stændɐrdizéjʃɘn], *s.* uniformación, normalización, reducción a un patrón común. —**ize** [-ajz], *vt.* (Am.) estandarizar; normalizar.

standing [stǽndiŋ], *a.* derecho o en pie, levantado, de pie; erecto; con pedestal o pie; permanente, fijo, establecido; duradero, estable; parado; estancado, encharcado; (for.) vigente.—*s.* posición, reputación; categoría; puesto, sitio, paraje; duración, antigüedad; alto, parada. —*of long s.,* (que existe, dura etc.) desde hace mucho tiempo.—**standpoint** [stǽndpojnt], *s.* punto de vista.—**standstill** [stǽndstil], *s.* parada, detención, alto; pausa.

stank [stæŋk], *pret.* de TO STINK.

stanza [stǽnzɐ], *s.* estrofa.

staple [stéjpl], *s.* artículo o producto principal; renglón de comercio; elemento o asunto principal; materia prima o bruta; hembra de cerrojo, grapa, aro, argolla; grapa de alambre (para sujetar papeles)—*pl.* artículos de primera necesidad.—*a.* (com.) corriente, de consumo o uso general; principal, prominente; establecido, reconocido; vendible.—*vt.* asegurar (papeles, etc.) con grapas; coser con alambre; clasificar hebras textiles por su longitud.

star [star], *s.* estrella; cosa o persona principal; asterisco; mancha en la frente de un animal.—*shooting s.,* estrella fugaz.—*s.-spangled,* tachonado de estrellas.—*S.-Spangled Banner,* bandera estrellada (nombre dado a la bandera y al himno de E.U.A.). —*vti.* [1] adornar con estrellas; marcar con asterisco; (teat., cine) introducir como estrella.—*vii.* ser estrella (teat. cine, etc.).—*a.* sobresaliente, excelente.

starboard [stárbərd], *s.* (mar.) estribor.

starch [starch], *s.* almidón, fécula; (fig.) entereza, vigor; rigidez.—*vt.* almidonar.—*y* [stárchi], *a.* feculento; estirado, entonado.

stare [ster], *vt.* clavar o fijar la vista en o a; encararse con; mirar de hito en hito o descaradamente.—*vi.* abrir grandes ojos; mirar con fijeza, asombro o insolencia; saltar a la vista; ser muy vivo o chillón (un color); erizarse (el pelo).—*s.* mirada fija de hito en hito; encaro.

starfish [stárfiš], *s.* estrella de mar.

stark [stark], *a.* tieso, rígido; (fig.) inflexible, severo; completo, cabal; puro.

starling [stárliŋ], *s.* estornino.

starry [stári], *a.* estrellado; como estrellas, centelleante, rutilante.

start [start], *vt.* empezar, iniciar; poner en marcha; dar la señal de salida; levantar (la caza).—*to s. a row,* armar una gresca.—*vi.* comenzar; partir, salir; arrancar (un motor, etc.); sobresaltarse, asustarse; provenir, proceder de; aflojarse; descoyuntarse; combarse.—*to s. after,* salir tras o en busca de; seguir a.—*to s. back,* dar un respingo; emprender el viaje de regreso.—*to s. for,* ponerse en camino hacia; presentarse como candidato para.—*to s. off,* partir, ponerse en marcha.—*to s. out,* salir, partir; principiar a.—*to s. up,* levantarse precipitadamente; salir de repente; ponerse en movimiento, arrancar.—*s.* principio, comienzo; salida, partida; arranque; sobresalto, susto; respingo; ímpetu, arranque, pronto; ventaja, delantera; grieta, raja.—*at the s.,* al primer paso, al principio.—*by fits and starts,* a saltos y corcovos; a ratos.—*er* [stártœ(r)], *s.* iniciador; el que da la señal de partida; (dep.) juez de

salida; comienzo; cosa con que se principia; (aut.) arranque, mecanismo de arranque.

startle [startl], *vt. y vi.* espantar(se), dar(se) un susto; sobrecoger(se); alarmar(se).

starvation [starvéišən], *a.* que causa hambre o inanición.—*s.* hambre, inanición.—**starve** [starv], *vi.* morir de hambre; hallarse en la inopia.—*vt.* matar de hambre.

state [steit], *s.* estado; situación, condición; pompa, ceremonia.—*in a s. of nature,* desnudo; en pecado; indomado; incivilizado.—*in (great) s.,* con (gran) pompa, de (gran) ceremonia.—*in s. of o to,* en estado de.—*to lie in s.,* estar de cuerpo presente.—*a.* de estado; del estado; estatal; político, público; de lujo o gala; perteneciente a los estados o a cada estado.—*vt. y vi.* decir, expresar; consignar; rezar (un texto); formular (un principio, ley, etc.); enunciar, plantear.—*liness* [stéitlinis], *s.* majestad, dignidad.—*ly* [-li], *a.* augusto, majestuoso.—*ment* [-mənt], *s.* declaración, exposición; afirmación, aserto; manifestación, cuenta, estado de cuenta; relato, información, memoria; planteo, enunciado; proposición; (com.) balance.—*room* [-rum], *s.* (mar.) camarote; (f.c.) salón; salón de recepción de un palacio.—*sman* [-smən], *s.* estadista.

static [statik], *s.* (rad.) estática.—*estático.*—*s* [-s], *s.* (mec.) estática.

station [stéišən], *s.* estación (de f.c., radio, policía, vía crucis, etc.); sitio, puesto; rango o posición social; (mar.) apostadero; (mil.) puesto.—*s. master,* jefe de estación.—*vt.* estacionar, colocar, situar, apostar.—*ary* [-eri], *a.* estacionario, fijo.—*to remain in s.,* estacionarse, quedarse inmóvil.—*er* [-œ(r)], *s.* papelero.—*ery* [eri], *s.* papelería, objetos de escritorio; papel de cartas.

statistic(al) [statístik(al)], *a.* estadístico.—**statistics** [statístiks], *s.* estadística; datos estadísticos.

statuary [stáchueri], *s.* estatuaria; estatuario, escultor.—**statue** [stáchu], *s.* estatua.

stature [stáchü(r)], *s.* estatura, altura, tamaño; alzada; importancia.

statute [stáchut], *s.* estatuto, ley, reglamento.—*s. law,* derecho escrito.

staunch [stonch], *vt. y a.* = STANCH.

stave [steiv], *vti.* [4] desfondar, abrir boquete; poner duelas (a un barril). —*to s. off,* rechazar, parar; retardar, diferir.—*vii.* desfondarse, hacerse pedazos.—*s.* duela de barril; escalón, peldaño (de escala); (mus.) penta- grama; (poét.) estrofa.

stay [stej], *vti.* [4] parar, impedir; sostener, apoyar, reforzar; aplazar; (for.) sobreseer.—*vii.* quedarse, per- manecer; parar(se); tardar(se); alo- jarse.—*to s. away*, mantenerse ale- jado; no volver.—*to s. in*, quedarse en casa, no salir.—*to s. out*, quedarse fuera, no entrar.—*to s. put*, (fam.) estarse quieto o en un mismo sitio. —*to s. up*, velar, no acostarse.—*s.* estancia; residencia, permanencia; suspensión, espera, parada; (for.) sobreseimiento; impedimento, obs- táculo; refuerzo; sostén, soporte; ballena de corsé; estabilidad, fijeza.

stead [sted], *s.* (con in) lugar, sitio; utilidad; ayuda.—*in his (her) s.*, en su lugar.—*in s. of*, en lugar de, en vez de, haciendo las veces de.—*to stand in (good) s.*, ser útil o de provecho.— **—fast** [stédfæst], *a.* constante, inmutable; resuelto, de- terminado.— **—ily** [-ili], *adv.* cons- tantemente; de firme; regular o progresivamente.— **—iness** [-inis], *s.* estabilidad, firmeza, entereza; constancia.— **—y** [-i], *a.* firme, fijo, seguro; juicioso, formal; cons- tante, uniforme, continuo.—*s.-going*, metódico, constante.—*vti.* [7] refor- zar; impedir el movimiento de; calmar; fortalecer.

steak [stejk], *s.* biftec, bisté.

steal [stil], *vti.* y *vii.* [10] hurtar, robar; pasar furtivamente.—*s.* (fam.) hurto, robo.— **—th** [stelθ], *s.* cautela, reserva.—*by s.*, a hurtadillas.— **—thy** [stélθi], *a.* furtivo, escondido, clan- destino.

steam [stim], *s.* vapor; vaho.—*a.* de vapor; para vapor; por vapor.—*s. engine*, máquina de vapor.—*s. heat- (ing)*, calefacción por vapor.—*vt.* proveer de vapor; cocinar al vapor; limpiar con vapor.—*vi.* generar o emitir vapor; funcionar por vapor.— **—boat** [stímbout], **—ship** [stímʃip], *s.* buque de vapor.— **—er** [-œ(r)], *s.* buque o máquina de vapor; baño (de) María.

steed [stid], *s.* corcel.

steel [stil], *s.* acero.—*a.* de acero.—*vt.* acerar, revestir de acero; acorazar; fortalecer; hacer insensible.— **—y** [stíli], *a.* acerado, duro, inflexible.

steep [stip], *a.* empinado, pendiente, escarpado; (fam.) exorbitante.—*vt.* impregnar, remojar, macerar; poner en infusión.— **—le** [stípl], *s.* aguja, torre, campanario.— **—ness** [stípnis], *s.* calidad de empinado o pendiente; inclinación.

steer [stir], *s.* novillo.—*vt.* guiar,

dirigir, conducir; timonear; (mar.) patronear (un barco).—*vi.* navegar, timonear; gobernarse, conducirse; obedecer al timón.— **—ing** [stírin], *s.* dirección (automóvil), gobierno (buque).—*power s.*, (aut.) dirección hidráulica o movida por motor.—*a.* de dirección o gobierno.

stem [stém], *s.* (bot.) tallo, vástago; caña, varita; estirpe, linaje; (mec. y carp.) espiga, caña; pie (de copa); (gram.) raíz; (mar.) tajamar.—*vti.* [1] ir contra, hacer frente a; embestir con la proa; represar, contener; desgranar (uvas, etc.).—*vii.* dete- nerse, contenerse.

stench [stench], *s.* hedor, hediondez.

stencil [sténsil], *s.* estarcido.—*vti.* [2] estarcir.

stenographer [stenágrafœ(r)], *s.* es- tenógrafo, taquígrafo.—**stenography** [stenágrafi], *s.* estenografía.

step [step], *vti.* [1] plantar (el pie). —*to s. down*, reducir, disminuir; escalonar; hacer escaleras en.—*to s. off*, medir a pasos.—*to s. up*, acelerar (el paso); (elec.) elevar (la tensión de una corriente).—*vii.* dar un paso; pisar; andar, caminar.—*to s. after*, seguir o ir detrás.—*to s. aside*, apartarse, hacerse a un lado.—*to s. back*, retroceder.—*to s. down*, bajar, descender.—*to s. forth*, avanzar.— *to s. in*, entrar; intervenir; entrome- terse.—*to s. on*, poner el pie sobre; pisar; andar sobre.—*to s. on the gas*, (aut.) pisar el acelerador; (fam.) menearse, darse prisa.—*to s. out*, salir; apearse (de un vehículo); apre- tar el paso; (fam.) andar de parranda. —*to s. over*, atravesar.—*to s. up*, subir.—*s.* paso; escalón; grada, pel- daño; estribo; umbral (de la puerta de entrada); pisada, huella; com- portamiento; (mús.) intervalo; diente de una llave; (rad.) elemento, unidad. —*pl.* medios, pasos, gestiones; gra- dería; escalinata.—*s. by s.*, paso a paso; punto por punto.— **—brother** [stépbrɑðœ(r)], *s.* medio hermano, hermanastro.— **—child** [-chaild], *s.* hijastro, hijastra.— **—daughter** [-do- tœ(r)], *s.* hijastra.- **—father** [-fa- ðœ(r)], *s.* padrastro.— **—ladder** [-lædœ(r)], *s.* escala, escalera de mano.— **—mother** [-mʌðœ(r)], *s.* madrastra.

stepsister [stépsistœ(r)], *s.* media her- mana, hermanastra.—**stepson** [stép- sʌn], *s.* hijastro.

stereoscope [stérioskoup], *s.* estereos- copio.—**stereoscopic** [sterioskápik], *a.* estereoscópico.

stereotype [stériotaip], *vt.* estereotipar.

sterile [stéril], *a.* estéril.—**sterility**

[sterļliti], *s.* esterilidad.—**sterilization** [steriļizéjšǫn], *s.* esterilización.—**sterilize** [stériļaiz], *vt.* y *vi.* esterilizar.

sterling [stǽrliǫ], *a.* esterlina; genuino, de ley.

stern [stœrn], *a.* austero, severo; firme.—*s.* (mar.) popa; (fam.) rabo.—**ness** [stǽrnnis], *s.* severidad, rigor.

stethoscope [stéθoskoup], *s.* estetoscopio.

stevedore [stívędǝr], *s.* estibador.

stew [stju], *vt.* y *vi.* estofar; (fam.) inquietarse; achicharrarse.—*s.* estofado, guisado, puchero; (fam.) ansiedad; agitación mental.

steward [stjúwǝrd], *s.* administrador; mayordomo; despensero; camarero (en aviones, vapores, etc.).—*s.'s room*, despensa.——**ess** [-is], *s.* camarera (de buque o avión); aeromoza, azafata.

stick [stik], *s.* palo, estaca; garrote, porra; vara, bastón (de mando); varilla; palillo (de tambor); barra (de lacre, tinta china, etc.); batuta; estique de escultor; (mus.) arco de contrabajo; (mar.) verga; pinchazo; adhesión; parada, demora; escrúpulo; (teat.) mal actor.—*pl.* leña menuda.—*the sticks*, (fam.) las afueras, despoblado.—*vti.* [10] pegar, adherir; clavar, hincar; prender (con alfiler); fijar (con tachuelas, etc.); meter, introducir; matar o herir de una puñalada; picar, punzar; llenar de puntas; (fam.) aturrullar.—*to s. out*, sacar, asomar, mostrar; perseverar hasta el fin.—*to s. up*, (fam.) atracar, parar para robar.—*to s. up one's hands*, poner las manos arriba en señal de entrega.—*to s. up one's nose at*, hacer ascos, despreciar, hacer un gesto despreciativo.—*vii.* estar clavado o prendido o pegado; pegarse, adherirse; permanecer fijo; ser constante; vacilar; atollarse.—*to s. at*, detenerse, sentir escrúpulos de.—*to s. at it*, (fam.) persistir.—*to s. by*, sostener, apoyar; pegarse (a alguno).—*to s. close*, mantenerse juntos.—*to s. fast*, adherirse fuertemente.—*to s. out*, salir, sobresalir, proyectarse.—*to s. to one's guns*, seguir uno en sus trece; mantenerse firme.—*to s. up for*, (fam.) volver por; salir a la defensa de.—*a.* [-i], *a.* pegajoso, viscoso.

stiff [stif], *a.* tieso; duro, firme; embotado; yerto, aterido; rígido, inflexible; tenso; chabacano; ceremonioso, afectado; almidonado; espeso; terco; (fam.) peliagudo; bravo (viento, etc.); fuerte, cargado (bebidas, etc.); (com.) firme (mercado, precios);

(fam.) caro.—*s.* (fam.) cadáver.—**en** [stífn], *vt.* atiesar; endurecer; espesar; aterir; dificultar.—*vi.* atiesarse; endurecerse; enderezarse; espesarse; obstinarse; aterirse.—**ness** [-nis], *s.* tiesura; rigidez; aterimiento; (med.) rigor; obstinación; dureza de estilo; espesura.

stifle [stáifl], *vt.* sofocar, ahogar, asfixiar; apagar; suprimir, callar, ocultar.—*vi.* ahogarse, sofocarse, asfixiarse.

stigma [stigmǎ], *s.* estigma.——**tize** [stígmataiz], *vt.* estigmatizar.

stiletto [stilétou], *s.* estilete.

still [stil], *vt.* acallar, hacer callar; amortiguar; aquietar; detener; destilar.—*vi.* acallarse; aquietarse.—*adv.* todavía, aún; aun; no obstante, sin embargo, a pesar de eso.—*a.* inmóvil; tranquilo, silencioso; fijo; apacible; suave, sordo (ruido); no espumoso (vino); muerto, inanimado.—*s. life*, (pint.) naturaleza muerta.—*s.* silencio, quietud; alambique.——**ness** [stílnis], *s.* silencio, quietud, calma.

stilt [stilt], *s.* zanco; soporte; ave zancuda.——**ed** [stíltid], *a.* altisonante, pomposo.

stimulant [stímyǫlạnt], *a.* y *s.* estimulante.—**stimulate** [stímyǫleit], *vt.* estimular.—**stimulation** [stimyǫléišǫn], *s.* estímulo, excitación; (med.) estimulación.—**stimulus** [stímyǫlʌs], *s.* estímulo; incentivo; (med.) estimulante; (bot.) aguijón.

sting [stiǫ], *vti.* y *vii.* [10] picar; punzar, pinchar; estimular, aguijonear; herir, atormentar; remorder la conciencia.—*to s. to the quick*, herir en lo vivo.—*s.* aguijón; picada, picadura; picazón; (bot.) púa; remordimiento de conciencia; estímulo.

stinginess [stíndžinis], *s.* tacañería, mezquindad, avaricia.—**stingy** [stíndži], *a.* mezquino, tacaño, avaro; escaso, nimio.

stink [stiǫk], *vii.* [10] heder, apestar.—*s.* hedor, hediondez.——**er** [stínkœ(r)], *s.* cosa o persona hedionda; (fam.) sujeto vil o despreciable.

stint [stint], *vt.* restringir, escatimar; asignar una tarea.—*vi.* ser económico o parco; estrecharse.—*s.* cuota, tarea, límite, restricción.

stipend [stáipend], *s.* estipendio, sueldo.

stipple [stípl], *vt.* puntear, granear.—*s.* picado, punteado.

stipulate [stípyǫleit], *vt.* estipular, especificar.—**stipulation** [stipyǫléišǫn], *s.* estipulación, condición; convenio.

stir [stœr], *vti.* [1] agitar, menear, batir; hurgar, revolver; perturbar, excitar, incitar; conmover; ventilar, discutir.—*to s. up*, conmover, excitar;

aguijonear; poner en movimiento; revolver; suscitar (interés, etc.).—*vii.* moverse, menearse.—*s.* movimiento, conmoción, excitación, alboroto, revuelo.

stirrup [stírꞎp], *s.* estribo.—*s. bone,* (anat.) estribo, huesecillo del oído.

stitch [stịtch], *vt.* coser, hilvanar.—*to s. up,* remendar, (cir.) dar puntos.—*vi.* dar puntadas, coser.—*s.* puntada, punto; (med.) dolor punzante; (agr.) caballón, surco.

stock [stak], *s.* (bot. y hort.) tronco, cepa; patrón; injerto; linaje, estirpe; (com.) acciones, valores; capital comercial; surtido (de mercancías); mercancías almacenadas, existencias; (teat.) repertorio; enseres, muebles.—*in s.,* (com.) en existencia.—*out of s.,* (com.) agotado.—*s. company,* (com.) sociedad anónima; (teat.) compañía de repertorio.—*s. exchange,* bolsa; asociación de corredores de bolsa.—*s. in hand,* mercancías en almacén, existencias.—*to lay in a s.* (of), almacenar, proveerse (de).—*a.* perteneciente o relativo a la bolsa, la ganadería o el teatro de repertorio; normal, usual; muy usado; estereotipado; (com.) de surtido.—*vt.* poner o llevar en surtido; surtir; acumular, juntar, acopiar.— **—ade** [stakéjd], *vt.* empalizar.—*s.* empalizada; vallado.— **—broker** [stákbroukœ(r)], *s.* corredor de bolsa, bolsista.— **—holder** [-houldœ(r)], *s.* accionista, tenedor de títulos o acciones.

stocking [stákịŋ], *s.* media, calceta.

stocky [stákị], *a.* rechoncho, fornido.

stoic [stóụịk], *s.* y *a.* estoico.—**stoicism** [stóụịsịzm], *s.* estoicismo; estoicidad.

stoke [stouk], *vt.* y *vi.* atizar (el fuego); alimentar, cargar (un horno).— **—r** [stóụkœ(r)], *s.* fogonero.

stole [stoụl], *pret.* de TO STEAL.—*s.* estola.—**stolen** [stóụlẹn], *pp.* de TO STEAL.

stomach [stámạk], *s.* estómago.—*vt.* sufrir, aguantar, tolerar.

stone [stoụn], *s.* piedra; hueso (de las frutas).—*s.-blind,* enteramente ciego.—*s.-broke,* (fam.) tronado, arrancado.—*s.-dead,* muerto como una piedra.—*s.-deaf,* sordo como una tapia, enteramente sordo.—*s.-dumb,* enteramente mudo.—*s. mason,* albañil, cantero.—*s.'s cast, s.'s throw,* tiro de piedra, corta distancia.—*vt.* apedrear; deshuesar (frutas); (alb.) revestir de piedras.—*to s. to death,* matar a pedradas, lapidar.—**stony** [stóụnị], *a.* pedregoso; pétreo, de piedra; duro, insensible.

stood [stụd], *pret.* y *pp.* de TO STAND.

stool [stul], *s.* banquillo, taburete, escabel; banqueta; inodoro, bacín; (caza) señuelo.—*pl.* evacuación de vientre, deposiciones.—*s. pigeon,* (fam.) soplón, espía.—*vt.* atraer con añagazas o señuelos.—*vi.* echar tallos, retoños, etc.; evacuar (el vientre); atraer con señuelos; (fam.) actuar como soplón.

stoop [stup], *vi.* agacharse, doblar o inclinar el cuerpo; ir encorvado, ser cargado de espaldas; encorvarse; humillarse, rebajarse; condescender; arrojarse sobre la presa.—*vt.* rebajar, degradar.—*s.* inclinación de hombros, cargazón de espaldas; descenso, caída; abatimiento; gradería, escalinata de entrada.

stop [stap], *vti.* [1] parar; detener, atajar; suspender, paralizar; contener, reprimir; obstruir, tapar; estancar, represar.—*to s. short,* detener brusca o repentinamente.—*to s. up,* tapar, cerrar, tupir, obturar.—*vii.* parar(se); detenerse, hacer alto; demorarse; cesar; acabarse; (fam.) quedarse algún tiempo, alojarse.—*to s.* (working, etc.), cesar o dejar de (trabajar, etc.).—*s.* parada, detención; cesación; pausa, alto; interrupción; suspensión, paro (de trabajo); obstáculo, impedimento; represión; (gram.) punto; (mec.) retén; tope, lengüeta; seguro; (mús.) tecla; llave; traste (de guitarra); registro (de órgano).— **—over** [stápọuvœ(r)], *s.* parada temporal en un lugar.— **—page** [-ịdž], *s.* cesación, interrupción; paro (del trabajo); detención, interceptación, obstrucción, impedimento; represa; retención (sobre un pago); (med.) estrangulación.— **—per** [-œ(r)], *vt.* entaponar.—*s.* tapón; taco, tarugo.

storage [stórịdž], *s.* (derechos de) almacenaje.—*s. battery,* (elec.) acumulador.—*to keep in s.,* almacenar.

store [stọr], *s.* tienda; almacén, depósito; acopio.—*pl.* pertrechos, equipos; víveres, provisiones.—*vt.* proveer o abastecer; pertrechar; acumular; tener en reserva; almacenar.— **—house** [stórhạụs], *s.* almacén.— **—keeper** [-kipœ(r)], *s.* guardaalmacén; jefe de depósito; tendero, comerciante; (mar.) pañolero.— **—room** [-rum], *s.* despensa; bodega; almacén; (mar.) pañol de víveres.

stork [stọrk], *s.* (orn.) cigüeña.

storm [stọrm], *s.* tempestad, temporal, tormenta o borrasca; vendaval; arrebato, frenesí; tumulto; (mil.) ataque, asalto.—*s. troops,* tropas de asalto.—*vt.* (mil.) asaltar, tomar por asalto.—*vi.* haber tormenta; estallar de cólera.— —y [stórmi], a. tempestuoso, borrascoso; violento, turbulento.

story [stórį], s. cuento, historia, historieta; fábula, conseja, (fam.) cuento de viejas; hablilla, rumor; enredo, trama o argumento; (fam.) mentira, embuste; (fam.) artículo (escrito); (arq.) alto, piso, planta.

stout [staųt], a. fornido, forzudo; gordo, corpulento; fuerte, sólido, firme; resuelto, intrépido.—s. cerveza fuerte.

stove [stoųv], s. estufa, hornillo, cocina o fogón de hierro.—pret. y pp. de TO STAVE.

stow [stoų], vt. colocar, meter, alojar; esconder, ocultar; (mar.) estibar, acomodar la carga en el barco; rellenar.—to s. away on a ship, esconderse en un barco, embarcarse clandestinamente.— —away [stóų-ąwej], s. (mar.) polizón.

straggle [strǽgl], vi. extraviarse; rezagarse.— —r [-œ(r)], s. rezagado.

straight [streįt], a. derecho, recto; directo, en línea recta; lacio (pelo); erguido; equitativo; íntegro, honrado; exacto; sin estorbos; ininterrumpido.—s. face, cara seria.—s. line, línea recta.—s.-line, en línea recta; de movimiento en línea recta. —s.-out, sincero; intransigente.— adv. directamente, en línea recta; inmediatamente, al punto.—s. ahead, todo derecho; enfrente.—s. away, en seguida, inmediatamente.—s. off, sin vacilar, sin demora.—s. runfia de cinco naipes del mismo palo.— —en [stréįtn], vt. enderezar; poner en orden, arreglar.— —forward [-fórwąrd], a. recto, directo; íntegro, honrado, sincero.— —adv. de frente.— —ness [-nįs], s. derechura, calidad de recto o derecho; rectitud, probidad, honradez.— —way [-wej], adv. inmediatamente, en seguida.

strain [streįn], vt. hacer fuerza a; poner tirante; poner, consagrar (la atención, etc.); forzar (la vista, etc.); estirar; forzar; extremar; perjudicar por esfuerzo excesivo; colar, tamizar, cribar; apretar; agarrar; (mec.) deformar.—to s. a point, excederse; hacer una concesión; hacer violencia (a la lógica, la conciencia, etc.).—vi. esforzarse; estar sometido a esfuerzo; pasar o meterse por, infiltrarse.—to s. at, esforzarse por.—s. tensión, tirantez; esfuerzo violento; (med.) lesión por esfuerzo violento o excesivo; (mec.) esfuerzo; deformación; indicio; (mus.) aire, tonada; rasgo racial; parte distintiva de un poema; tono, modo de hablar; genio o disposición heredada.— —er [stréįnœ(r)], s. colador, filtro, tamiz.

strait(s) [streįt(s)], s. (geog.) estrecho; apuro, aprieto; estrechez.—strait jacket, camisa de fuerza.—strait-laced, estrecho, mojigato.

strand [strǽnd], vt. y vi. (mar.) encallar; dejar o quedarse desamparado; trenzar (un cordel).—s. costa, playa, ribera; cabo, hebra, hilo; sarta; ramal (de cable, etc.).

strange [streįndž], a. extraño, singular; forastero; ajeno; desconocido, reservado, esquivo.—s. to say, lo cual es extraño; (es) cosa extraña.— —ness [stréįndžnįs], s. extranjería; extrañeza, rareza; reserva, esquivez; maravilla.— —r [stréįndžœ(r)], s. extranjero, extraño, forastero; desconocido.

strangle [strǽngl], vt. estrangular; dar garrote; ahogar, sofocar.—vi. morir estrangulado, estrangularse.

strap [strǽp], s. correa; tira, faja, banda; abrazadera; precinta; (mec.) cabeza de biela.—vti. [1] atar con correas; precintar; asentar (navajas de afeitar).

stratagem [strǽtądžem], s. estratagema, artimaña.—**strategic(al)** [strątidžj-k(ąl)], a. estratégico.—**strategy** [strǽtįdžį], s. estrategia.

stratify [strǽtįfaj], vti. [7] estratificar.

straw [stro], s. paja.—not to care a s., no importarle a uno un comino.—the last s., el golpe de gracia, el acábose.—a. de paja; pajizo.

strawberry [stróberį], s. fresa.

stray [strej], vi. descarriarse, extraviarse; desmandarse (el ganado).—a. extraviado, descarriado.—s. persona o animal descarriado o perdido.

streak [strik], s. raya, lista, línea, faja, veta; rayo de luz; vena, rasgo de ingenio; traza, pizca; antojo, capricho.—like a s., veloz como un relámpago.—s. of luck, racha.—vt. rayar, listar; abigarrar.—vi. pasar o viajar con suma rapidez.— —y [stríkį], a. listado, rayado; entreverado.

stream [strim], s. corriente; arroyo, corriente de agua; flujo, chorro (de líquido, gas, luz, etc.); curso.—down s., agua abajo.—up s., agua arriba.—vt. y vi. correr, manar, fluir, brotar; salir a torrentes; derramar con abundancia; lavar en agua corriente; ondear, flotar, flamear, tremolar (una bandera); pasar dejando un rastro de luz.— —er [strím-œ(r)], s. banderola, gallardete; aurora boreal; cinta (que flota en el aire); serpentina.

street [strit], s. calle.— —car [strítkar],

s. tranvía.- —**walker** [-wɔkœ(r)], *s.* prostituta.

strength [streŋθ], *s.* fuerza, vigor; reciedumbre; pujanza; fuerza legal; (ing.) resistencia; aguante; solidez; intensidad; vehemencia; (quim.) concentración, grado de concentración; seguridad, confianza; (mil.) efectivos. —*on* o *upon the s. of,* fundándose en, confiando en.- —**en** [stréŋθn], *vt.* fortalecer, fortificar; consolidar; corroborar; reforzar; confortar, alentar.—*vi.* fortalecerse; reforzarse; arreciar(se).—**strenuous** [strényɥʌs], *a.* fuerte; activo, enérgico; acérrimo, tenaz.

stress [stres], *s.* fuerza, peso, importancia; (ing., mec.) esfuerzo; tensión; énfasis.—*vt.* someter a esfuerzo; recalcar, subrayar, poner de relieve.

stretch [strech], *vt.* extender, alargar, tender; estirar, atesar; ensanchar, dilatar; violentar, forzar; (fam.) exagerar, llevar al extremo.—*to s. a point,* excederse; ceder un poco.—*to s. forth,* alargar, extender.—*to s. oneself,* desperezarse.—*to s. out,* extender, estirar, alargar.—*vi.* alargarse, dar de sí, dilatarse; (fig.) esforzarse, exagerar.—*to s. out,* extenderse, llegar (hasta); echarse (en la cama, etc.).—*s.* alargamiento; dilatación; elasticidad; tirantez; violencia o interpretación forzada; alcance, trecho, distancia; lapso, tirada.—*at a s.,* de una vez, de un tirón.- —**er** [stréchœ(r)], *s.* estirador, dilatador, atesador; camilla, andas; ladrillo o losa (planos); (carp.) viga, madero largo, tirante; (pint.) bastidor.—*s.-bearer,* camillero.

strew [stru], *vti.* [6] regar, esparcir, derramar; rociar, salpicar.

striate [strájeit], *vt.* estriar.

stricken [stríkn], *pp.* de TO STRIKE.—*a.* herido (por un proyectil); atacado (por delencias); agobiado; afligido.

strict [strikt], *a.* estricto; exacto, riguroso, escrupuloso; estirado, tirante; (zool.) ceñido, limitado.

stridden [strídn], *pp.* de TO STRIDE. —**stride** [strajd], *vti.* [10] cruzar a grandes trancos; montar a horcajadas.—*vii.* andar a trancos.—*s.* paso largo, tranco, zancada.

strident [strájdent], *a.* estridente, chillón.

strife [strajf], *s.* contienda; rivalidad, porfía.

strike [strajk], *vti.* [10] golpear; percutir; batir, tocar, sonar; dar contra, chocar con; encender (un fósforo); acuñar (monedas).—*to s. off,* cortar, quitar, cercenar; cerrar (un trato). —*to s. oil,* encontrar petróleo; (fam.)

hacerse rico de pronto.—*to s. through,* traspasar, atravesar; calar.—*to s. up,* (mús.) tocar, tañer.—*to s. work,* hallar trabajo.—*vii.* golpear; dar golpes; sonar (una campana); encontrarse; ir delante, avanzar; brotar, estallar, manifestarse (una epidemia, etc.); declararse en huelga; rehusar, resistirse, plantarse; rendirse, arriar el pabellón; arraigar.—*to s. at,* acometer.—*to s. back,* dar golpe por golpe.—*to s. for,* (fam.) dirigirse hacia; acometer.—*to s. in,* meterse; juntarse, unirse; interrumpir; conformarse con.—*to s. into,* comenzar de repente; penetrar.—*to s. on,* dar contra; descubrir.—*to s. out,* tomar una resolución; arrojarse, lanzarse. —*s.* golpe; ataque rápido o inesperado; huelga, paro; (min.) descubrimiento.—*s. breaker,* obrero que reemplaza a los huelguistas.— —r [strájkœ(r)], *s.* huelguista; golpeador, percusor.—**striking** [strájkiŋ], *a.* sorprendente, notable; llamativo; vívido; que está en huelga; conspicuo.

string [striŋ], *s.* cuerda; cordel, bramante; ristra, sarta; hilera, fila; recua, fibra, nervio, tendón.—*pl.* (mus.) instrumentos de cuerda; (fam.) condiciones, estipulaciones.— *s. bean,* habichuela verde, judía verde, (Am.) poroto; alubia.—*to have on a s.,* (fam.) tener (a uno) en un puño.—*vti.* [10] encordar; templar (un instrumento); ensartar, enhebrar; encordelar, atar con cordel; tender (alambre, etc.); estirar, atesar; quitar las fibras.—*to s. (along),* (fam.) tomarle el pelo a uno; hacer esperar a uno.—*to s. out,* extender.—*to s. up,* (fam.) ahorcar.—*vii.* extenderse en línea.

strip [strip], *vti.* [1] desnudar; despojar, quitar; desguarnecer; robar; descortezar; ordeñar hasta agotar; desgarrar o cortar en tiras; desvenar, despalillar (tabaco); (mec.) desmontar.—*to s. off,* desnudar; deshojar.—*vii.* desnudarse, despojarse (de).—*s.* tira, faja, listón, lista; lonja (de carne).

stripe [strajp], *vt.* rayar.—*s.* raya, lista, banda, franja, tira; (mil.) galón, barra; cardenal (en el cuerpo); calaña, clase.— —**d** [-t], *a.* rayado, listado, a rayas.

strive [strajv], *vii.* [10] esforzarse, hacer lo posible; disputar; oponerse; contrarrestar.—**striven** [strívn], *pp.* de TO STRIVE.

strode [stroud], *pret.* de TO STRIDE.

stroke [strouk], *s.* golpe; toque; boga, remada; rasgo, trazo; (med.) ataque fulminante.—*at one s.,* de un golpe, de un tirón.—*at the s. of twelve,* al dar las doce.—*s. of a bell*, campanada.—*s. of a pen o brush*, plumazo, pincelada.—*s. ef the hand*, caricia. —*s. of wit*, rasgo de ingenio, chiste, gracia.—*vt.* pasar la mano por, acariciar; frotar suavemente; (cost.) alisar un plegado.

stroll [stroŭl], *vi.* vagar, callejear; pasearse.—*s.* paseo, vuelta.— —er [stroŭlœ(r)], *s.* vagabundo; paseante; cochecito de bebé; cómico de la legua.— —ing [stróŭliŋ], *a.* ambulante.

strong [stroŋ], *a.* fuerte; firme; recio, fornido; enérgico; vivo, subido (colores); (com.) con tendencia a la alza.

strop [strap], *vti.* [1] asentar (navajas). —*s.* asentador; (mar.) estrobo.

strove [stroŭv], *pret.* de TO STRIVE.

struck [strʌk], *pret. y pp.* de TO STRIKE.

structural [strʌ́kchŭṛal], *a.* estructural; de estructura; relativo a la estructura; (ing.) de construcción, de construcciones.—**structure** [strʌ́kchŭ(r)], *s.* construcción (edificio, puente, etc.); estructura; (fig.) textura, hechura.

struggle [strʌ́gl], *vi.* luchar, pugnar, bregar; esforzarse; contender; agitarse.—*s.* esfuerzo; disputa, contienda; pugna, forcejeo; lucha, conflicto.

strung [strʌŋ], *pret. y pp.* de TO STRING.

strut [strʌt], *vti.* [1] contonearse, pavonearse; ensoberbecerse, inflarse. —*vti.* (ing., etc.) apuntalar.—*s.* contoneo; poste, puntal; columna.

stub [stʌb], *s.* (agr.) tocón, cepa; zoquete; fragmento, resto; colilla (de cigarro, etc.); talón.—*vti.* [1] tropezar contra una cosa baja; (agr.) desarraigar; reducir a tocón.

stubble [stʌ́bl], *s.* (agr.) rastrojo; barba cerdosa.

stubborn [stʌ́bọrn], *a.* obstinado, terco, tesonero, contumaz; reñido; inquebrantable.— —ness [-ņs], *s.* obstinación, testarudez, contumacia.

stucco [stʌ́koŭ], *vt.* (alb.) estucar.—*s.* estuco.

stuck [stʌk], *pret. y pp.* de TO STICK.

stud [stʌd], *s.* (carp.) montante, pie derecho; perno, pasador; tachón, clavo de adorno; botón de camisa o cuello, gemelo de puño; caballeriza; yeguada, caballada; (elec.) tornillo de contacto.—*vti.* [1] tachonar.

student [stjúdẹnt], *s.* estudiante; alumno, escolar.—*s. body*, alumnado, estudiantado.—**studio** [stjúdjoŭ], *s.* estudio, taller; gabinete.—**studious** [stjúdjʌs], *a.* estudioso; aplicado; estudiado.—**study** [stʌ́dj], *s.* estudio; materia que se estudia; meditación profunda; despacho, gabinete.—*vti.*

[7] estudiar; cursar (una asignatura, etc.).—*to s. up*, considerar, meditar; proyectar.—*vii.* estudiar; meditar.

stuff [stʌf], *s.* material; materia, sustancia, elemento fundamental; cosa, objeto; cachivaches, baratijas; desechos, desperdicios; cosas, ideas o sentimientos sin valor; mejunje, pócima.—*vt.* henchir, llenar; rellenar (un pavo, etc.); hartar; atestar; disecar (un animal).—*vi. y vr.* atracarse, hartarse, engullir, tupirse.— —ing [stʌ́fiŋ], *s.* relleno; (mec.) empaquetado.— —y [-i], *a.* sofocante, mal ventilado; (fam.) estirado, afectado.

stumble [stʌ́mbl], *vi.* tropezar, dar un traspié.—*to s. on o upon*, encontrar o tropezar con.—*s.* traspié, tropezón; desliz; desatino.—*stumbling block*, obstáculo, tropiezo.

stump [stʌmp], *s.* tocón, cepa; muñón (de brazo o pierna); raigón (de una muela); poste; (b.a.) difumino; tope de cerradura; tribuna pública; arenga electoral; (fam.) desafío, reto.—*vt.* confundir, dejar patidifuso; cercenar, mutilar.—*to s. the country*, recorrer el país diciendo discursos políticos.—*vi.* renquear; (fam.) pronunciar discursos políticos.— —y [stʌ́mpi], *a.* lleno de tocones; rechoncho, cachigordete; (Am.) chaparro.

stun [stʌn], *vti.* [1] aturdir, atontar; pasmar, privar; atronar, ensordecer. —*s.* choque, golpe o sacudimiento (emotivos); aturdimiento.

stung [stʌŋ], *pret. y pp.* de TO STING. —*a.* (fam.) chasqueado, burlado, engañado.

stunk [stʌŋk], *pret. y pp.* de TO STINK.

stunning [stʌ́niŋ], *a.* (fam.) sorprendente; magnífico, excelente; elegante, hermoso.

stunt [stʌnt], *vt.* impedir el crecimiento o desarrollo de; no dejar medrar. —*vi.* (fam.) hacer ejercicicios malabares o gimnásticos; hacer suertes o maniobras sensacionales.—*s.* falta de crecimiento o desarrollo; animal o planta raquíticos; (fam.) suerte, ejercicio o acción de habilidad; maniobra sensacional (de aviación, etc.).—*s. flying*, vuelos acrobáticos.

stupefaction [stjupẹfǽkṣọn], *s.* estupefacción.—**stupefy** [stjúpẹfai], *vti.* [7] atontar, atolondrar.

stupid [stjúpid], *a.* estúpido; necio.— —ity [stjupídit̩i], *s.* estupidez; necedad; inepcia.

stupor [stjúpọ(r)], *s.* estupor; atontamiento.

sturdy [stœ́rdi], *a.* fuerte, robusto; tenaz, porfiado.

stutter [stʌ́tœ(r)], *vi.* tartamudear.—*s.*

tartamudeo.— —er [-œ(r)], s. tartamudo.— —ing [-ịŋ], s. tartamudeo.
—a. tartamudo, balbuciente.

sty [staị], s. pocilga, cuchitril; lupanar;
(también **stye** [staị]), (med.) orzuelo.

style [staịl], s. estilo; uso, moda;
género, escuela; (cir.) estilete.—to be
in s., estilarse, estar de moda.—vt.
(in)titular, nombrar, llamar.—styl-
ish [stáịlịš], a. elegante; a la moda.

subconscious [sʌbkánšʌs], a. subcons-
ciente.—s. subconsciencia.

subdivide [sʌbdịváịd], vt. subdividir.

subdue [sʌbdjú], vt. subyugar, sojuzgar,
dominar; domar o amansar; mejorar
(tierras); suavizar.

subject [sʌbdžékt], vt. sujetar; sojuzgar,
avasallar; exponer, presentar; supe-
ditar, subordinar.—a. [sábdžect],
sujeto; propenso; supeditado.—s. to,
sujeto · a, afecto a.—s. súbdito;
vasallo; materia, tópico; asignatura
(de estudios); (gram.) sujeto.—s.
matter, asunto, materia de que se
trata.— —ion [sʌbdžékšọn], s. sujeción, supeditación, dependencia; so-
metimiento; ligadura.— —ive [sʌb-
džéktịv], a. subjetivo.

subjugate [sábdžugeịt], vt. subyugar,
sojuzgar, someter.

subjunctive [sʌbdžʌ́ŋktịv], a. y s.
subjuntivo.

sublease [sáblis], s. subarriendo.—vt.
[sáblis], subarrendar.—**sublet** [sʌb-
lét], vti. [9] subarrendar.—pret. y
pp. de TO SUBLET.

sublimate [sáblịmeịt], vt. (quím.)
sublimar; (fig.) refinar, purificar.—
sublime [sʌbláịm], a. sublime.—s.
sublimidad, lo sublime.—vt. y vi.
sublimar, exaltar; (quím.) subli-
mar(se).

submarine [sábmarịn], s. y a. submarino.

submerge [sʌbmǽrdž], vt. y vi. su-
mergir(se), hundir(se).—**submersible**
[sʌbmǽrsịbl], a. sumergible.—**sub-
mersion** [sʌbmǽršọn], s. sumersión.

submission [sʌbmịšọn], s. sumisión.
—**submissive** [sʌbmịsịv], a. sumiso,
obediente, dócil.—**submit** [sʌbmịt],
vti. [1] someter; presentar, exponer,
proponer.—vri. y vii. someterse,
conformarse.

subordinate [sʌbórdịnịt], a. y s. subalterno, subordinado.—vt. [sʌbórdị-
neịt], subordinar.

suborn [sʌbórn], vt. (for.) sobornar,
cohechar.— —ation [sʌbornéịžọn], s.
soborno, cohecho.

subscribe [sʌbskráịb], vt. y vi. sus-
cribir(se); firmar; aprobar; abo-
nar(se).—to s. for, suscribirse a.—
to s. ten dollars, prometer una contribución de diez dólares (para una

colecta, etc.).— —r [sʌbskráịbœ(r)],
s. suscritor, abonado; firmante, el
que suscribe.—**subscription** [sʌb-
skrípšọn], s. suscripción, abono;
cantidad suscrita; firma.

subsequent [sʌ́bsịkwent], a. subse-
cuente, subsiguiente.—s. to, con
posterioridad a, después de.

subside [sʌbsáịd], vi. calmarse, ate-
nuarse; bajar (el nivel); disminuir;
irse al fondo, asentarse, (quim.)
precipitarse.

subsidize [sʌ́bsịdaịz], vt. subvencionar.
—**subsidy** [sʌ́bsịdị], s. subvención,
subsidio.

subsist [sʌbsíst], vi. subsistir; perdurar;
sustentarse, mantenerse.—vt. alimentar o mantener.

substance [sʌ́bstạns], s. sustancia.—
substantial [sʌbstǽnšạl], a. sólido,
fuerte, resistente; importante, valioso; considerable; seguro; responsable; existente, real; duradero; esencial; corpóreo, material; sustancial,
sustancioso.—s. realidad; parte esencial.—**substantive** [sʌ́bstạntịv], a. y
s. sustantivo.

substitute [sʌ́bstịtịut], vt. sustituir.—s.
sustituto.—a. sustitutivo.—**substitu-
tion** [sʌbstịtịúšọn], s. sustitución.

subterranean [sʌbtẹréịnịan], a. subterráneo.

subtle [sʌ́tl], a. sutil; perspicaz; apto;
ingenioso.— —ty [-tị], s. sutileza;
astucia.

subtract [sʌbtrǽkt], vt. y vi. sustraer,
quitar; (mat.) restar, sustraer.— —ion
[sʌbtrǽkšọn], s. sustracción; resta.

suburb [sʌ́bœrb], s. suburbio; barrio
residencial.— —an [sʌbǽrbạn], a. y
s. suburbano.

subversion [sʌbvǽržọn], s. subversión.
—**subversive** [sʌbvǽrsịv], a. sub-
versivo.—s. persona subversiva.—
subvert [sʌbvǽrt], vt. subvertir.

subway [sʌ́bweị], s. subterráneo;
ferrocarril subterráneo, metropolitano, (fam.) el metro, (Am.) el
subte.

succeed [sʌksíd], vt. suceder o seguir a.
—vi. salir bien, tener buen éxito.—
to s. in, lograr, conseguir.—**success**
[sʌksés], s. buen éxito, logro;
prosperidad; triunfo; persona o
asunto que tiene buen éxito.—
successful [sʌksésfụl], a. próspero,
afortunado; productivo, satisfactorio.
—**succession** [sʌksésọn], s. sucesión,
serie; continuación; descendencia;
herencia.—**successive** [sʌksésịv], a.
sucesivo.—**successor** [sʌksésọ(r)], s.
sucesor; heredero.

succumb [sʌkʌ́m], vi. sucumbir.

such [sʌch], a. tal; semejante; dicho,
mencionado.—no s. (a) thing, no

hay tal.—*s. α*, (fam.) tan.—*such α
bad man*, un hombre tan malo.—
s. α man, tal hombre, semejante
hombre.—*s. and s.*, o *s. or s.*, tal(es)
y tal(es), o *el* cual.—*s. as*, (tal) como.
—*there is s. a thing as*, hay algo que
se llama; hay casos en que.—*pron.*
tal.—*s. as*, los que, quienes.—*s. is
life*, tal (o así) es la vida.

suck [sʌk], *vt. y vi.* chupar, libar;
mamar; (mec.) aspirar.—*to s. in*,
embeber, absorber, chupar.—*to s. out
o up*, chupar, extraer por succión.—*s.*
succión; chupada.—*to give s.*, amamantar.— —**er** [sʌkœ(r)], *s.* lechón
o cochinillo que todavía mama;
chupador; mamador; mamón, chu-
pón; dulce que se chupa; primo,
persona fácil de engañar.- —**le**
[sʌkl], *vt.* amamantar, criar.—*vi.*
lactar, mamar.— —**ling** [-lɪŋ], *a. y s.*
mamón, recental.—*a.* de teta, de
cría.—**suction** [sʌkʃən], *s.* succión.

sudden [sʌdn], *a.* repentino, súbito;
apresurado; (med.) fulminante.—
—**ness** [-nɪs], *s.* calidad de repentino,
inesperado o imprevisto; brusquedad.

suds [sʌdz], *s. pl.* jabonaduras; espuma.

sue [sju], *vt. y vi.* (for.) demandar.—
to s. to, to s. for, rogar, pedir, tratar
de persuadir.

suet [sjúɪt], *s.* sebo en rama; grasa,
gordo.

suffer [sʌfœ(r)], *vt. y vi.* sufrir, padecer;
soportar, tolerar.—*to s. from*, adolecer
de.— —**er** [-œ(r)], *s.* paciente, sufri-
dor; víctima; perjudicado; el que
tolera tácitamente.- —**ing** [-ɪŋ], *s.*
sufrimiento, padecimiento, pena,
suplicio.—*a.* paciente, sufriente.

suffice [sʌfáɪs], *vt. y vi.* bastar, ser
suficiente.—*s. it to say*, basta decir.
—**sufficiency** [sʌfíʃ ̩ənsɪ], *s.* suficiencia; lo suficiente; eficacia; presunción.—**sufficient** [sʌfíʃ ̩ənt], *a.* suficiente, bastante.

suffix [sʌfɪks], *vt.* añadir como sufijo.
—*s.* [sʌfɪks], (gram.) sufijo, afijo.

suffocate [sʌfokeɪt], *vt.* sofocar, asfixiar,
ahogar; apagar (un fuego).—*vi.* sofocarse, asfixiarse, ahogarse.—**suffoca-
tion** [sʌfokéɪʃ ̩ən], *s.* sofocación,
asfixia, ahogo.

suffrage [sʌfrɪdʒ], *s.* sufragio, voto;
aprobación; (igl.) sufragio.- —**tte**
[sʌfrədʒét], *s.* mujer sufragista.

sugar [ʃúgə(r)], *s.* azúcar.—*lump of s.*,
terrón de azúcar.—*s. bowl*, azucarero,
azucarera.—*s. cane*, caña de azúcar.
—*s. making (season)*, zafra.—*vt.*
azucarar, endulzar.—*to s. coat*, confitar, garapiñar; (fig.) dorar la
píldora.—*vi.* cristalizarse (el almíbar), (Am.) azucararse.- —**plum**

[-plʌm], *s.* merengue, confite, dulce.
suggest [sʌgdʒést], *vt.* sugerir, insinuar;
evocar.- —**ion** [sʌgdʒéschən], *s.*
sugestión; sugerencia, insinuación.—
—**ive** [sʌgdʒéstɪv], *a.* sugestivo;
sugerente.

suicidal [sjuɪsáɪdəl], *a.* suicida.—**suicide**
[sjúɪsaɪd], *s.* suicidio; suicida.—*to
commit s.*, suicidarse.

suit [sjut], *s.* petición, súplica; galanteo;
(for.) pleito, juicio; colección, serie,
juego, surtido; (sast.) traje completo,
(Am.) flus; (naipes) palo.—*vt. y vi.*
convenir, acomodar, adaptar(se).—
to s. oneself, hacer uno lo que guste.
— —**able** [sjútəbl], *a.* adecuado,
satisfactorio, a propósito.— —**case**
[-keɪs], *s.* maleta.— —**e** [swit], *s.*
serie, juego; séquito, comitiva.—*s. of
rooms*, serie de departamentos o
habitaciones; habitación o pieza (gen.
muy lujosa).- —**or** [sjútə(r)], *s.*
(for.) demandante, parte actora;
pretendiente, novio; aspirante; postu-
lante.

sulfate [sʌlfeɪt], *s.* sulfato.—**sulfur**
[sʌlfœ(r)], *s.* azufre.

sullen [sʌlən], *a.* hosco, arisco; lento
(río); sombrío, tétrico.- —**ness** [-nɪs],
s. hosquedad.

sulphate [sʌlfeɪt], *s.* = SULFATE.—**sul-
phur** [sʌlfœ(r)], *s.* = SULFUR.

sultry [sʌltrɪ], *a.* bochornoso, sofocante
(verano, calor, etc.).

sum [sʌm], *s.* suma; cantidad; sustancia, esencia.—*in s.*, en esencia, suma
o resumen.—*s. total*, suma total,
monta o monto.—*vti. y vii.* [1]
sumar.—*to s. up*, recapitular, resumir, compendiar; (for.) presentar su
alegato.— —**marize** [sʌmᶕraɪz], *vt.*
resumir.— —**mary** [-ᶕrɪ], *s.* sumario,
resumen, recopilación, reseña (de un
libro).

summer [sʌmœ(r)], *a.* estival, vera-
niego.—*s.* verano, estío; (arq.) viga
maestra; dintel.—*s. boarder*, vera-
neante.—*vi.* veranear.

summit [sʌmɪt], *s.* cima, cumbre, cúspide, ápice.

summon [sʌmən], *vt.* (for.) citar,
apercibir; llamar, convocar; mandar,
requerir; (mil.) intimar.—*to s. up*,
evocar; despertar, excitar (valor,
fuerza, etc.).- —**s** [-z], *s.* (for.)
citación, apercibimiento; (mil.) inti-
mación (de rendición).

sumptuous [sʌmpchʊəs], *a.* suntuoso.
sun [sʌn], *s.* sol.—*vti.* [1] (a)solear.
—*to s. oneself*, tomar el sol.— —**burn**
[sʌnbœrn], *vti. y vii.* [4] quemar(se)
o tostar(se) con el sol.—*s.* quemadura
de sol.— —**burned** [sʌnbœrnd],
—**burnt** [sʌnbœrnt], *a.* quemado,
tostado o bronceado por el sol.

—*pret.* y *pp.* de TO **sunburn**. —**Sunday** [sándi], *s.* domingo.— —**dial** [-daiəl], *s.* reloj de sol, cuadrante solar.— **down** [-daṇn], *s.* puesta de sol.

sundries [sándriz], *s. pl.* (com.) géneros varios.—**sundry** [sándri], *a.* varios, diversos.—*all and s.*, todos y cada uno.

sunflower [sánflaυœ(r)], *s.* (bot.) girasol.

sung [saŋ], *pret.* y *pp.* de TO **sing**.

sunk [saŋk], *pret.* y *pp.* de TO **sink**.— **sunken** [sáŋkn], *a.* sumido, hundido. —*pp. de* TO **sink**.

sunless [sánlis], *a.* sombrío; sin luz; sin sol, nublado.—**sunlight** [sánlait], *s.* luz del sol.—**sunny** [sáni], *a.* de sol (día); asoleado; resplandeciente; alegre, risueño; halagüeño.— *s. side*, lado del sol; lado bueno, aspecto favorable.—*s. side up*, (huevos) fritos.—**sunrise** [sánraiz], *s.* salida del sol, amanecer; (poét.) Oriente.—**sunset** [sánset], *s.* puesta del sol, ocaso.—**sunshine** [sánšain], *s.* luz del sol, claridad del sol; día. —**sunstroke** [sánstroυk], *s.* (med.) insolación, (fam.) tabardillo.

sup [sap], *vti.* [1] sorber.—*vii.* cenar.

super [siúpœ(r)], *s.* (com.) cosa excelente; alta calidad; (abrev. fam.) de **superintendent.**—*a.* (fam.) excelente.

superb [siupœrb], *a.* soberbio, grandioso; (fam.) de primera.

supercargo [siupœrkárgoυ], *s.* (mar.) sobrecargo.

superficial [siupœrfíšəl], *a.* superficial, somero.

superfluous [supœrflυas], *a.* superfluo.

superheat [siupœrhít], *vt.* recalentar.

superhuman [siupœrhiúmən], *a.* sobrehumano.

superimpose [siupœrimpóυz], *vt.* superponer, sobreponer.

superintend [siupœrinténd], *vt.* estar encargado de, dirigir.— *ent* [-ənt], *s.* superintendente; inspector; capataz; encargado de un edificio de apartamentos.

superior [supíriο(r)], *a.* y *s.* superior.— *ity* [supiriáriti], *s.* superieridad.

superlative [supœrlativ], *a.* y *s.* superlativo.

superman [siúpœrmæn], *s.* superhombre.

supernatural [siupœrnǽchυṛəl], *a.* sobrenatural.—*s.* lo sobrenatural.

superposition [siupœrpọzíšọn], *s.* superposición.

supersede [siupœrsíd], *vt.* reemplazar; desalojar; invalidar; (for.) sobreseer.

superstition [siupœrstíšọn], *s.* supersti-

ción.—**superstitious** [siupœrstíšʌs], *a.* supersticioso.

supervise [siupœrváiz], *vt.* supervisar. —**supervision** [siupœrvíẓọn], *s.* supervisión.—**supervisor** [siupœrvái-zọ(r)], *s.* supervisor.

supper [sápœ(r)], *s.* cena.

supplant [saplǽnt], *vt.* suplantar.

supple [sápl], *a.* flexible; dócil, obediente; servil.

supplement [sápləmənt], *s.* suplemento; apéndice.—*vt.* [sáplement], suplementar.

suppli(c)ant [sáplị(k)ạnt], *s.* y *a.* suplicante.—**supplication** [saplikéišọn], *s.* súplica, ruego; (igl.) preces, rogativa.

supplier [saplái̧œ(r)], *s.* proveedor, abastecedor.—**supplies** [sapláiz], *s. pl.* (mil.) pertrechos; materiales, efectos; provisiones, víveres; enseres. —**supply** [saplái], *vti.* [7] abastecer, proveer (de); suministrar, habilitar; suplir, reemplazar.—*s.* suministro, provisión, abastecimiento; substituto, suplente; (com.) abasto, oferta; repuesto, surtido.

support [sapórt], *vt.* sostener, aguantar, apoyar; mantener (a una persona, etc.), proveer para; sostener (un trato o diálogo); resistir, tolerar; abogar por, defender; probar, confirmar; justificar.—*s.* sostén, soporte; puntal; sustentación, sostenimiento; ayuda, protección; sustento, manutención. —*er* [-œ(r)], *s.* mantenedor; defensor, partidario; sostén, soporte.

suppose [sapóυz], *vt.* suponer; dar por sentado o existente; poner por caso; creer, imaginar.—**supposition** [sapọzíšọn], *s.* suposición, supuesto, hipótesis.

suppository [sapázitọri], *s.* supositorio.

suppress [saprés], *vt.* suprimir, acabar con; reprimir, contener; eliminar.— *ion* [sapréšọn], *s.* supresión; (med.) suspensión.

suppurate [sápyụṛeit], *vi.* supurar.— **suppuration** [sapyụṛéišọn], *s.* supuración; pus.

supremacy [siuprémạsi], *s.* supremacía. —**supreme** [siuprím], *a.* supremo, sumo.—*S. Being,* Ser Supremo.

sure [šυr], *a.* seguro, cierto, infalible; firme; certero.—*be s. to come,* o *be s. and come,* no deje(n) de venir, venga(n) sin falta.—*for s.,* de fijo, con seguridad.—*adv.* (fam.) ciertamente, indudablemente.—*s. enough,* a buen seguro, con certeza; en efecto, en realidad de verdad.— *ty* [šúrti], *s.* (for. y com.) fiador; fianza, garantía; seguridad, certeza.—*of a s.,* de seguro, como cosa cierta.—*to be* o *go s. for,* ser fiador, salir garante de.

surf [sœrf], *s.* oleaje, resaca, marejada; espuma del mar.

surface [sœrfis], *s.* superficie.—*vt.* allanar, alisar; poner superficie a. —*vt.* y *vi.* (hacer) emerger, surgir o salir a la superficie.

surge [sœrdż], *s.* (mar.) oleaje; (fig.) ola, onda.—*vi.* agitarse o embravecerse (el mar); romper (las olas).— *vt.* hacer ondular; (mar.) largar.

surgeon [sœrdżọn], *s.* cirujano.

surgery [sœrdżeri], *s.* cirugía.—

surgical [sœrdżikạl], *a.* quirúrgico.

surly [sœrli], *a.* áspero, rudo, hosco.

surmise [sœrmáiz], *vt.* conjeturar, suponer, vislumbrar.—*s.* conjetura, suposición, vislumbre.

surmount [sœrmáunt], *vt.* vencer, superar, salvar; coronar, poner (algo) sobre.

surname [sœrneim], *s.* apellido; sobrenombre.—*vt.* apellidar, llamar.

surpass [sœrpǽs], *vt.* sobrepasar, superar, aventajar.

surplus [sœrplʌs], *s.* sobrante, excedente; (com.) superávit.—*a.* excedente, de sobra, sobrante.

surprise [sœrpráiz], *s.* sorpresa; novedad; extrañeza; asombro.—*by s.,* de sorpresa.—*vt.* sorprender.

surrender [sʌréndœ(r)], *vt.* rendir, entregar; ceder.—*vi.* rendirse, entregarse; (mil.) capitular.—*s.* rendición, entrega; (mil.) capitulación; (for.) cesión.—*s. value,* valor de rescate (de un seguro, etc.).

surround [sʌráund], *vt.* circundar, cercar, rodear, ceñir.— *—ing* [-iŋ], *a.* circunstante, circunvecino.—*s. pl.* alrededores, contornos, inmediaciones; medio, circunstancias que rodean (a una persona, hecho o lugar).

surtax [sœrtæks], *s.* recargo; impuesto adicional.

survey [sœrvéi], *vt.* inspeccionar, examinar, reconocer; medir o deslindar terrenos.—*vi.* ejecutar operaciones topográficas.—*s.* [sœrvei], examen, estudio; encuesta (de la opinión pública); medición o deslinde (de terrenos).— *—or* [sœrvéiọ(r)], *s.* topógrafo; agrimensor.

survival [sœrváivạl], *s.* supervivencia; sobreviviente; reliquia.—*s. of the fittest,* supervivencia del más apto. —**survive** [sœrváiv], *vt.* y *vi.* sobrevivir; salir o quedar vivo.—**survivor** [sœrváivọ(r)], *s.* sobreviviente, superviviente.

suspect [sʌspékt], *vt.* y *vi.* sospechar (de), desconfiar (de); maliciar.—*s.* [sʌspekt], persona sospechosa.—*a.* sospechoso.

suspend [sʌspénd], *vt.* suspender.— *—ers* [-œrz], *s. pl.* tirantes del

pantalón.—**suspense** [sʌspéns], *s.* suspensión; impaciencia; ansiedad; (for.) entredicho.—**suspension** [sʌspénsọn], *s.* suspensión.

suspicion [sʌspíšọn], *s.* sospecha, recelo. —**suspicious** [sʌspíšʌs], *a.* sospechoso; suspicaz.

sustain [sʌstéin], *vt.* sostener, aguantar; tener, mantener; sufrir (una desgracia, pérdida, etc.); (mus.) prolongar, sostener; apoyar; confortar; alimentar; defender; establecer, probar.—**sustenance** [sʌstenạns], *s.* sustento, mantenimiento, subsistencia; alimentos.

suture [sjúchǫ(r)], *vt.* (cir.) suturar.—*s.* sutura.

swagger [swǽgœ(r)], *vi.* fanfarronear; pavonearse.—*s.* jactancia, baladronada; pavoneo.

swallow [swálou], *vt.* y *vi.* tragar(se); engullir.—*to s. up,* tragar(se); absorber.—*s.* bocado, trago; deglución; (orn.) golondrina.

swam [swæm], *pret.* de TO SWIM.

swamp [swamp], *s.* pantano, ciénaga, fangal.—*vt.* empantanar, encharcar; abrumar, recargar; inundar.—*vi.* empantanarse; zozobrar.— *—y* [swámpi], *a.* pantanoso, cenagoso.

swan [swan], *s.* cisne.—*s. song,* canto del cisne; obra última.

swap [swap], *vti.* [1] cambiar, cambalachear, permutar.—*vii.* hacer trueques o cambalaches.—*s.* trueque, (fam.) cambalache.

swarm [sworm], *s.* enjambre; (fig.) hormiguero, multitud.—*vt.* y *vi.* enjambrar; pulular, bullir, hormiguear; (fam.) trepar.

swarthy [swórˀi], *a.* moreno, trigueño.

swath [swaˀ], *s.* ringla o ringlera de mies segada; guadañada.—*to cut a wide s.,* hacer alarde u ostentación.

sway [swei], *vt.* inclinar, ladear; influir en el ánimo de (alguno), inducir; blandir, cimbrar; gobernar, regir; (mar.) izar, guindar.—*vi.* ladearse, inclinarse; torcerse; oscilar, mecerse; ondular; flaquear, tambalear.—*s.* poder, predominio, influjo; vaivén, oscilación, ondulación, balanceo.—*to give full s. to,* dar ancho campo a.— *—backed* [swéibækt], *a.* derrengado.

swear [swer], *vti.* y *vii.* [10] jurar.

sweat [swet], *vti.* y *vii.* [4] sudar; trasudar; hacer sudar; trabajar duro; (fam.) hacer confesar a un preso mediante interrogatorio persistente; secar en horno.—*s.* sudor, exudación, trabajo.— *—er* [-œ(r)], *s.* el que suda; patrono explotador; suéter.

Swede [swid], *s.* sueco.—**Swedish** [swídiš], *a.* sueco.—*s.* idioma sueco.

sweep [swip], *vti*. [10] barrer; deshollinar (chimeneas); recorrer; pasar la vista por.—*to s. away*, robar sin dejar nada; arrastrar con todo.—*to s. the bottom*, dragar.—*vi*. barrer; pasar o deslizarse rápidamente; pasar arrasando; pasar con paso o ademán majestuosos.—*to s. down*, descender precipitadamente.—*s*. barredura, barrido; ojeada, vistazo; alcance, abarque, extensión— —er [swípœ(r)], *s*. barrendero; basurero; barredera, barredora.— —ing [-iŋ], *a*. que barre. —*s*. barrido.—*pl*. barreduras, basura.

sweet [swit], *a*. dulce; fragante; melodioso; bonito; lindo; agradable; amable, bondadoso; fresco; (mec.) suave y sin ruido; fértil (tierra).—*s. corn*, maíz tierno.—*s. herbs*, hierbas olorosas.—*s. pea*, guisante de olor. —*s. potato*, batata, boniato, (Am.) camote.—*s.-scented*, perfumado.—*s.-smelling*, fragante.—*s.-spoken*, melifluo.—*to have a s. tooth*, ser goloso.—*s*. dulzura; deleite; persona querida; golosina, dulce.—*pl*. dulces, golosinas.— —bread [swítbred], *s*. lechecilla o molleja de ternera.— —en [-n], *vt*. endulzar, dulcificar; (farm.) edulcorar; mitigar; hacer salubre. —*vi*. endulzarse.— —heart [-hart], *s*. novia, prometida; novio, prometido; persona querida, amante.—*a*. querido, cielo, vida.— —meat [-mit], *s*. dulce, confitura, golosina.— —ness [-njs], *s*. dulzura, melosidad, suavidad, delicadeza, bondad.

swell [swel], *vti*. y *vii*. [6] binchar(se), inflar(se), henchir(se); engreir(se).— *to s. out*, arrojar (el árbol) sus hojas; ampollarse; bufar.—*a*. elegante, de buen tono; magnífico.—*s*. hinchazón; oleada, marejada; prominencia; ondulación del terreno. —*ing* [swéljŋ], *s*. hinchazón; tumefacción, turgencia, abotagamiento; bulto, chichón, protuberancia.

swept [swept], *pret*. y *pp*. de TO SWEEP.

swerve [swœrv], *vt*. y *vi*. desviar(se), apartar(se), extraviar(se), virar(se), torcer(se).—*s*. desviación, viraje.

swift [swift], *a*. rápido, ligero, raudo; veloz, volador; vivo, diligente; sumarísimo; (mar.) velero.— —ness [swíftnjs], *s*. velocidad, rapidez, prontitud.

swim [swim], *vii*. [10] nadar; flotar; dejarse ir o llevar; deslizarse suavemente; tener la cabeza ida; tener mareo o vértigo; padecer vahídos. —*vti*. pasar a nado; hacer nadar o flotar.—*s*. natación; nadada; nadadera de pez; movimiento de deslizarse; mundo, corriente de las cosas; sociedad, vida social; clases influyentes.—*to be in the s*., estar en la corriente o marcha de las cosas.— *to take a s*., ir a nadar.- —mer [swímœ(r)], *s*. nadador.— —ming [-iŋ], *a*. que nada, natatorio; para nadar.—*s. pool*, piscina, (Am.) alberca, pileta.

swindle [swíndl], *vt*. estafar, timar.—*s*. estafa, timo.- —r [swíndlœ(r)], *s*. estafador, timador.

swine [swain], *s*. marrano(s), puerco(s), cerdo(s); persona soez.— —herd [swáinhœrd], *s*. porquero, porquerizo.

swing [swiŋ], *vti*. y *vii*. [10] columpiar(se), mecer(se); balancear(se), bambolear(se); girar, hacer girar.— *vti*. blandir.—*to s. about*, dar una vuelta.—*to s. clear*, evitar un choque. —*s*. oscilación, vaivén, balanceo; columpio, mecedor; libertad de acción, libre curso; autoridad, control; (mec.) juego, recorrido, alcance.— *in full s*., en plena operación, en su apogeo.

Swiss [swis], *a*. y *s*. suizo, helvético.

switch [swich], *s*. latiguillo, fusta; trenza postiza; fustazo; (f.c.) cambiavía, agujas; (elec.) interruptor, conmutador; acción de desviar, cambiar, conmutar (un tren, una corriente).—*s. engine*, locomotora de patio o de maniobras.—*vt*. fustigar, dar latigazos; (f.c.) desviar; (elec.) cambiar.—*to s. off*, desconectar, cortar (la corriente); apagar (las luces). —*to s. on*, conectar; encender (las luces).—*vi*. (off) desviarse, cambiarse.— —board [swíchbɔrd], *s*. (elec.) pizarra o cuadro de distribución; (tlf.) cuadro conmutador.

swollen [swóuln], *pp*. de TO SWELL.

swoon [swun], *vi*. desmayarse, desfallecer.—*s*. desmayo, síncope, desfallecimiento.

sword [sord], *s*. espada.

swore [swor], *pret*. de TO SWEAR.—

sworn [sworn], *pp*. de TO SWEAR.

swum [swam], *pp*. de TO SWIM.

swung [swaŋ], *pret*. y *pp*. de TO SWING.

syllable [sílabl], *s*. sílaba.

symbol [símbɔl], *s*. símbolo; emblema; (teol.) credo.— —ic(al) [simbáljk(al)], *a*. simbólico.— —ism [símbɔlizm], *s*. simbolismo.

symmetrical [simétrjkal], *a*. simétrico.— —symmetry [símjtri], *s*. simetría.

sympathetic(al) [simpaθétjk(al)], *a*. simpático; que simpatiza; afín; benévolo, compasivo.—**sympathize** [símpaθaiz], *vi*. simpatizar; compadecerse, condolerse; padecer por simpatía; congeniar.—**sympathy** [símpaθi], *s*. simpatía, afinidad; benevolencia; condolencia, lástima; pésame; (med.) simpatía.

symphony [símfoni], *s*. sinfonía.

symptom [símptǫm], *s.* síntoma.

synagogue [sínagag], *s.* sinagoga.

synchronization [siŋkrǫnjzéjšǫn], *s.* sincronización.— **synchronize** [síŋkrǫnajz], *vt.* y *vi.* sincronizar.

syndicate [síndjkejt], *vt.* y *vi.* (com.) sindicar(se).—*s.* [síndjkjt], (com.) sindicato.

synonym [sínǫnjm], *s.* sinónimo.— **synonymous** [sjnánjmʌs], *a.* sinónimo.

synopsis [sjnápsjs], *s.* sinopsis.

syntax [síntæks], *s.* sintaxis.

synthesis [sínθesjs], *s.* síntesis.— **synthetic** [sjnθétjk], *a.* sintético.

syphilis [sífjljs], *s.* sífilis.

syringe [sírjndž], *s.* (med.) jeringa.

syrup [sírʌp], *s.* jarabe; almíbar; sirope. — **—y** [-j], *a.* almibarado; meloso.

system [sístęm], *s.* sistema.— **-atic(al)** [sjstemǽtjk(ʌl)], *a.* sistemático.— **-atize** [sjstemątajz], *vt.* sistematizar.

T

tab [tæb], *s.* lengüeta (de zapato); (fam.) cuenta.

tabernacle [tǽbœrnækl], *s.* tabernáculo.

table [téjbl], *s.* mesa; tabla (matemática, de materias, etc.), cuadro; tablero; meseta.—*t. boarder,* pupilo, pensionista.—*t. cover,* tapete, cubremesa.—*t.-land,* altiplanicie, meseta.—*t. linen,* mantelería.—*t. set,* vajilla.—*vt.* y *vi.* poner sobre la mesa; formar una tabla o índice, catalogar; (carp.) ensamblar, acoplar.—*to t. a motion,* dar carpetazo a una moción, aplazar su discusión.— **—cloth** [-klᴏθ], *s.* mantel; tela para manteles.— **—spoon** [-spun], *s.* cuchara.— **—spoonful** [-spunful], *s.* cucharada.— **—t** [tǽbljt], *s.* tableta, pastilla; bloc de papel; plancha, lápida; tabla.— **—ware** [-wer], *s.* servicio de mesa, artículos para la mesa.

taboo [tabú], *a.* proscrito, prohibido. —*s.* tabú.—*vt.* declarar tabú; (fig.) prohibir, excluir.

tabor [téjbǫ(r)], *s.* tamboril.— **—et** [tæborét], *s.* taburete.

tabulate [tǽbyụlejt], *vt.* (neol.) tabular, catalogar en forma de tabla.— **tabulator** [tǽbyụlejtǫ(r)], *s.* tabulador.

tacit [tǽsjt], *a.* tácito.— **—urn** [-œrn], *a.* taciturno.

tack [tæk], *vt.* clavar con tachuelas; (mar.) cambiar de rumbo; (cost.) puntear, pegar, coser, hilvanar; unir, añadir.—*s.* tachuela, puntilla; hilván; cambio de política, nuevo plan de acción; (mar.) cambio de rumbo.

tackle [tǽkl], *vt.* agarrar, asir; atacar, abordar (un problema, etc.), luchar con; atajar a un adversario.—*s.* aparejo; (football) atajo, agarrada; atajador.—*fishing t.,* avíos de pescar.

tact [tækt], *s.* tacto; tino, tiento, ten con ten.— **—ful** [tǽktful], *a.* discreto, cauto, político.— **—ical** [-jkal], *a.* táctico.

tactics [tǽktjks], *s. pl.* táctica.

tactless [tǽktljs], *a.* falto de tacto o de tino, impolítico.

tadpole [tǽdpoụl], *s.* (zool.) renacuajo.

taffeta [tǽfjtą], *s.* tafetán.

tag [tæg], *s.* marbete, marca, rótulo; herrete; apéndice, rabito; pingajo; populacho, muchedumbre; cita, nota al pie.—*vti.* [1] marcar con marbete o rótulo; clavetear, poner herretes; pisar los talones, alcanzar y tocar.

tail [tejl], *s.* cola, rabo; cabo, extremidad; apéndice.—*pl.* frac.—*t. light,* farol trasero, luz de cola.—*t. spin,* (aer.) barrena.—*vt.* seguir de cerca, vigilar, espiar.

tailor [téjlǫ(r)], *s.* sastre.—*t.-made suit,* traje sastre.

taint [tejnt], *vt.* y *vi.* manchar(se), inficionar(se), corromper(se).— *tainted food,* alimentos pasados, echados a perder.—*s.* mácula, mancha, corrupción.

take [tejk], *vti.* [10] tomar; coger, asir, agarrar; recibir, aceptar; apropiarse, apoderarse de; percibir o cobrar; llevar, conducir, acompañar; restar, deducir; usar, emplear, adoptar; considerar, tener por; admitir; adaptarse o hacerse a; coger, contraer (una enfermedad); sacar (un retrato, una copia); dar (un salto, un paso, un paseo).—*to t. aback,* desconcertar. —*to t. advantage of,* aprovecharse de. —*to t. down,* bajar; descolgar; desmontar.—*to t. for granted,* dar por sentado; no apreciar.—*to t. heart,* animarse, cobrar valer.—*to t. hold of,* asir, agarrar; tomar posesión de; encargarse de.—*to t. in,* entrar; aceptar, recibir; comprender; engañar; abarcar.—*to t. into account,* tomar en consideración.—*to t. into consideration,* tener en cuenta.—*to t. offense,* ofenderse.—*to t. on,* emprender; contratar.—*to t. out,* sacar; llevar a pasear; extraer.—*to t. over,* tomar posesión de.—*to t. pains,* esmerarse.—*to t. pity on,* apiadarse, compadecerse de.—*to t. place,* celebrarse, verificarse.—*to t. the floor,* tomar la palabra.—*to t. the trouble to,* tomarse la molestia.—*to t. to heart,* tomar a pecho.—*to t. to task,* reprender.—*to t. up,* subir; dedicarse a; recoger.—*vii.* ser poseedor, adquirir propiedad; pegar bien, tener buen éxito, (fam.) cuajar; prender (la vacuna, el fuego, etc.); hacer su efecto, ser eficaz; (fam.) picar (el pez); sacar buen o mal retrato; pegar, adherirse; arraigar (las plantas).—*to t. after*, parecerse a, salir a; imitar a, seguir el ejemplo de; ser como.—*to t. ill*, caer enfermo.—*to t. off*, partir, salir; (aer.) despegar, hacerse al aire. —*to t. to*, aficionarse a; tomar cariño a; recurrir a; dedicarse a.—*s.* toma; cogida, redada; entrada, producto, ingresos (de una función, etc.).— *t.-in*, (fam.) fraude, engaño; estafador; entrada, ingresos.—*t.-off*, (fam.) sátira; caricatura, remedo; (aer.) despegue; (dep., gimn.) trampolín, raya de donde se salta.—taken [téjkn], *pp.* de TO TAKE.—*to be t. ill*, caer enfermo.—*to be t. off o away*, morir(se).—*to be t. with*, prendarse o estar prendado de.—taking [téjkiŋ], *a.* atractivo, seductor; (fam.) contagioso.—*s.* toma; (for.) embargo.—*t. for*, afición, inclinación, afecto; (fam.) arrebato, agitación.—*pl.* ingresos.

talcum [tǽlkam], *s.* talco.—*t. powder*, polvos de talco.

tale [tejl], *s.* cuento; narración, relato; fábula, conseja; embuste, filfa; habilla, chisme.— —bearer [téjlberœ(r)], *s.* chismoso, cuentista, (fam.) correve(i)dile, enredador, soplón.

talent [tǽlent], *s.* talento, ingenio; aptitud.— —ed [-jd], *a.* talentoso, de talento; hábil.

talisman [tǽljsman], *s.* talismán.

talk [tok], *vt.* y *vi.* hablar; charlar, conversar.—*to t. away*, malgastar el tiempo hablando; disipar con la palabra.—*to t. into*, convencer de, inducir a.—*to t. out of*, disuadir; sonsacar.—*to t. over*, discutir, conferenciar acerca de.—*to t. to*, hablar a; reprender.—*to t. to the purpose*, hablar al alma.—*to t. up*, alabar.—*s.* conversación, plática; habla; charla; tema de una conversación; discurso; comidilla (objeto de chismes, etc.).— —ative [tókatjv], *a.* locuaz, charlatán.— —ativeness [-atjvnjs], *s.* locuacidad.— —er [-œ(r)], *s.* conversador; decidor; orador; charlatán.

tall [tol], *a.* alto; (fam.) grande.—*six feet t.*, seis pies de alto o de altura.

tallow [tǽlou], *vt.* ensebar.—*s.* sebo.

tally [tǽlj], *s.* cuenta.—*t. sheet*, hoja de cuentas o apuntes.—*vti.* [7] llevar la cuenta.—*vii.* cuadrar, concordar, estar conforme.—*to t. up*, sumar, contar.

talon [tǽlon], *s.* garra.

tamale [tamálj], *s.* (Am.) tamal.

tambourine [tæmborín], *s.* pandero, pandereta.

tame [tejm], *a.* manso, domesticado; dócil, tratable; insustancial, insípido; (fam.) moderado.—*vt.* domar, amansar, domesticar; avasallar; suavizar; represar (un río).— —ness [téjmnjs], *s.* mansedumbre, docilidad.— —r [-œ(r)], *s.* domador.

tamp [tæmp], *vt.* apisonar.

tamper [tǽmpœ(r)], *vi.* (con with) meterse en o con; falsificar, adulterar; tocar lo que no se debe; sobornar.

tampon [tǽmpan], *s.* (cir.) tapón.—*vt.* taponar.

tan [tæn], *vti.* [1] curtir; zurrar; tostar, requemar.—*a.* tostado, de color de canela.—*s.* color de canela; tostadura del sol.

tang [tæŋ], *s.* dejo, gustillo, sabor.

tangent [tǽndžent], *a.* y *s.* tangente.— *to fly o go off on a t.*, salirse por la tangente.

tangerine [tǽndžerín], *s.* (naranja) tangerina o mandarina.

tangible [tǽndžjbl], *a.* tangible, palpable.

tangle [tǽŋgl], *vt.* y *vi.* enredar(se), enmarañar(se); confundir(se).—*to t. with*, venir a las manos (con).—*s.* enredo, embrollo; confusión; alga marina.

tank [tæŋk], *s.* tanque, depósito, cuba; aljibe; (mil.) tanque.

tanner [tǽnœ(r)], *s.* curtidor.—tannery [tǽnœrj], *s.* tenería, curtiduría.

tantalize [tǽntalajz], *vt.* torturar lentamente con lo inasequible.— tantalizing [tǽntalajziŋ], *a.* tentador e inasequible.

tantrum [tǽntrʌm], *s.* (fam.) berrinche, pataleta.

tap [tæp], *vti.* [1] perforar (un barril, etc. para sacar líquido) o sangrar (un árbol); unir o conectar con (para tomar agua, corriente, etc. o para interceptar o transmitir mensajes telefónicos, etc.); sacar de, tomar de; (cir.) sajar o punzar (un absceso, etc.); golpear ligeramente, dar una palmadita.—*vii.* tocar o golpear ligeramente.—*s.* espita; tapón o tarugo; (mec.) macho de terraja; toma (de agua, elec., etc.), derivación; golpecito, palmadita.—*beer on t.*, cerveza del barril o de sifón.— *t. dance*, zapateado, zapateo.—*t. room*, bar.

tape [tejp], *s.* cinta, cintilla; cinta de papel o de metal.—*adhesive t.*, tela o cinta adhesiva, esparadrapo.— *red t.*, burocratismo, formulismo dilatorio.—*t. measure*, cinta para medir, cinta métrica.—*t. recorder*, grabadora (de cinta magnetofónica).

—*vt.* atar o arrollar con cinta; vendar; medir con la cinta métrica; grabar en cinta magnetofónica.

taper [téjpœ(r)], *s.* velita, candela; cirio; ahusamiento de un objeto.—*vt.* afilar, adelgazar, ahusar.—*vi.* rematar en punta, tener forma ahusada; cesar poco a poco.

tapestry [tǽpįstrį], *s.* tapiz; tapicería, colgadura.

tapeworm [téjpwœrm], *s.* (lombriz) solitaria, tenia.

tapioca [tǽpįóu̞ḳǎ], *s.* tapioca.

tar [tar], *s.* alquitrán, brea o pez líquida; (fam.) marinero.—*vti.* [1] alquitranar, embrear, embetunar.

tardiness [tárdįnįs], *s.* tardanza, lentitud.—**tardy** [tárdį], *a.* tardío, moroso, lento.

tare [ter], *s.* (bot.) cizaña; (com.) tara.

target [tárg̣įt], *s.* blanco a que se tira.

tariff [tǽrįf], *s.* tarifa; arancel; impuesto.—*a.* arancelario, aduanero. —*vt.* tarifar; afectar por razón de impuestos.

tarnish [tárnįŝ], *vt.* deslustrar, empañar, deslucir; manchar, mancillar.—*vi.* deslustrarse; enmohecerse.—*s.* deslustre, mancha, empañadura.

tarpaulin [tarpólįn], *s.* lona embreada.

tarry [tǽrį], *vii.* [7] demorarse, tardar, entretenerse.

tart [tart], *a.* acre, ácido; agridulce; mordaz.—*s.* tarta; pastelillo de fruta.

task [tæsk], *s.* tarea, faena, labor.—*to take to t.*, amonestar, regañar.

tassel [tǽsȩl], *s.* borla.—*vti.* [2] adornar con borlas.

taste [tejst], *vt.* gustar; saborear, probar, catar.—*vi.* saber a, tener sabor o gusto.—*s.* gusto; sabor; (fig.) paladar; saboreo, paladeo; prueba, sorbo, trago, pedacito; muestra; gusto, discernimiento; afición.—*in bad t.*, de mal gusto.— *to have a t., for*, gustar de.- —**ful** [téjstfu̞l], *a.* elegante, de buen gusto.- —**less** [-lįs], *a.* insípido; desabrido; sin gracia; de mal gusto.—**tasty** [téjstį], *a.* sabroso, gustoso.

tatter [tǽtœ(r)], *s.* andrajo, harapo, guiñapo, jirón.- —**ed** [-d], *a.* andrajoso, harapiento.

tattle [tǽtl], *vi.* chismear, comadrear; descubrir o revelar secretos indiscretamente.—*s.* charla, cháchara; chismografía.- —**r** [-œ(r)], *s.* chismoso.

tattoo [tǽtú], *s.* tatuaje; (mil.) retreta. —*vt.* tatuar.

taught [tɔt], *pret.* y *pp.* de TO TEACH.

taunt [tɔnt], *vt.* vilipendiar, vituperar; mofarse de; reprender.—*s.* vituperio; dicterio; sarcasmo.

taut [tɔt], *a.* tirante, tenso; listo, preparado, en regla.

tavern [tǽvœrn], *s.* taberna; mesón, posada, figón.

tax [tæks], *s.* impuesto, tributo, contribución, gabela; carga, exacción. —*vt.* imponer contribuciones a; (for.) tasar; abusar de; reprender; reprobar; (fam.) pedir como precio. —*to t. with*, acusar, tachar, imputar.- —**ation** [-éjŝǝn], *s.* tributación; imposición de contribuciones.

taxi(cab) [tǽksį(kǽb)], *s.* auto de alquiler, taxímetro.

taxpayer [tǽkspejœ(r)], *s.* contribuyente, tributario.

tea [ti], *s.* te; reunión en que se sirve te; infusión, cocimiento.

teach [tich], *vti.* [10] enseñar, instruir; aleccionar.—*vii.* ser maestro, enseñar.- —**er** [tíchœ(r)], *s.* maestro.- —**ing** [-įŋ], *a.* docente, enseñador, aleccionador.—*s.* enseñanza, instrucción, docencia, magisterio; doctrina.

teacup [tíkʌp], *s.* taza para te.— **teakettle** [tíketl], *s.* marmita, olla de calentar agua.

team [tim], *s.* (dep.) equipo (de jugadores); conjunto de personas que trabaja coordinadamente; tronco, par, yunta (de animales de tiro).—*vt.* uncir, enganchar, enyugar.—*vi.* guiar un tronco o yunta.—*to t. up*, asociarse (con) para formar un equipo.- —**ster** [tímstœ(r)], *s.* tronquista; carretero; camionero.- —**work** [-wœrk], *s.* cooperación, esfuerzo coordinado de un equipo.

teapot [típat], *s.* tetera.

tear [tįr], *s.* lágrima.—*in tears*, llorando.—*t. bomb* (*gas*), bomba lacrimógena (gas lacrimógeno).—*vi.* llorar, derramar lágrimas.—*vti.* [10] [ter], desgarrar, rasgar.—*to t. asunder* separar con violencia.—*to t. away*, arrancar, desmembrar.—*to t. down*, derribar, demoler.—*to t. one's hair*, mesarse los cabellos.—*to t. out*, arrancar, separar con violencia.—*to t. up*, arrancar, desarraigar; deshacer, desbaratar.—*vii.* rasgarse; andar precipitadamente.—*s.* rasgadura, desgarradura; precipitación; (fam.) borrachera.- —**ful** [tírfu̞l], *a.* lloroso, lacrimoso.

tease [tiz], *vt.* molestar, atormentar; fastidiar; embromar, torear.—*s.* broma continua; (fam.) embromador.

teaspoon [tíspun], *s.* cucharita, cucharilla.- —**ful** [-fu̞l], *s.* cucharadita.

teat [tit], *s.* teta; tetilla; pezón; ubre.

technical [téknįḳal], *a.* técnico, tecnológico.—**technician** [tekníŝǝn], *s.* técnico, experto.—**technique** [tekník], *s.* técnica, ejecución.

tedious [tídiʌs], a. tedioso, fastidioso, pesado.— —ness [-nịs], tedium [tídiʌm], s. tedio.

teem [tim], vi. bullir, hormiguear.

teens [tíns], s. números de trece a diecinueve; edad de trece a diecinueve años.—teen-age, adolescencia, de trece a diecinueve años de edad.—teen-ager, adolescente, persona de trece a diecinueve años de edad.

teeth [tiθ], pl. de TOOTH.— —ing [tíθịŋ], s. dentición.—t. ring, chupete.

teetotaler [titóutalœ(r)], s. abstemio.

telegram [télẹgræm], s. telegrama.—telegraph [télẹgræf], vt. y vi. telegrafiar; enviar por telégrafo.—s. telégrafo.—telegraphic [telẹgrǽfịk], a. telegráfico.—telegraphy [telégræfị], s. telegrafía.

telepathy [telẹpaθị], s. telepatía.

telephone [télẹfoun], vt. y vi. telefonear.—s. teléfono.—t. booth, cabina o casilla de teléfonos.—t. directory, guía de teléfonos.—t. exchange, central telefónica.—t. operator, telefonista, operadora.

telescope [télẹskoup], s. telescopio.—vt. y vi. encajar(se), enchufar(se) un objeto en otro.—telescopic [telẹskápịk], a. telescópico; de enchufe.

televise [télẹvajz], vt. trasmitir por televisión.—television [telẹvíʒọn], s. televisión.

tell [tel], vti. y vii. [10] decir; contar; expresar; explicar; revelar, descubrir; adivinar, decidir, determinar.—to t. off, contar, recontar; (mil.) designar.—to t. on, descubrir, delatar a; dejarse ver en, afectar a.—to t. one (where to get) off, decir a uno cuántas son cinco, cantárselas claras, soltarle cuatro frescas.—to t. tales out of school, revelar secretos.—to t. volumes, ser muy significativo.— —er [télœ(r)], s. relator, narrador; escrutador de votos; pagador o cobrador de un banco.—t.'s window, taquilla.— —ing [-iŋ], a. eficaz, notable.—a t. argument, un argumento convincente.— —tale [-teịl], s. soplón, chismoso.—s. revelador.

temerity [tẹmérịtị], s. temeridad.

temper [témpœ(r)], vt. moderar, mitigar, calmar; (pint.) mezclar; modificar, ajustar; (a)temperar, ablandar; (metal) templar.—s. mal genio; índole, humor, disposición, genio, condición; calma, ecuanimidad; temple; punto (grado de densidad).—to lose one's t., perder la paciencia, enojarse.— —ament [témp(œ)rạmẹnt], s. temperamento; complexión, naturaleza; composición; disposición; temple.— —ance [témp(œ)rạns], s. templanza, temperancia, sobriedad.—

—ate [témp(œ)rịt], a. sobrio, abstemio; templado, benigno; moderado.

temperature [témp(œ)rạchū(r)], s. temperatura.—to have o run a t., tener fiebre o calentura.

tempest [témpịst], s. tempestad.—vt. agitar, conmover violentamente.— —uous [tẹmpéschụʌs], a. tempestuoso, borrascoso; impetuoso.

temple [témpl], s. templo; (anat.) sien.

temporal [témporạl], a. temporal.—s. hueso temporal.

temporary [témporerị], a. temporal, provisional; temporero.

tempt [tempt], vt. tentar, incitar, provocar; seducir, atraer; poner a prueba.— —ation [-éịʂọn], s. tentación; solicitación, prueba.

tenacious [tịnéịʂạs], a. tenaz; pegajoso; porfiado, terco; firme.—tenacity [tịnǽsịtị], s. tenacidad; tesón; terquedad; cohesión; adhesión.

tenant [ténạnt], s. arrendatario, inquilino.

tend [tend], vt. guardar, vigilar, cuidar; atender.—vi. tender, propender; dirigirse; atender.—to tend on, o upon, asistir, servir a.— —ency [téndẹnsị], s. tendencia, propensión; dirección.

tender [téndœ(r)], a. tierno; delicado; muelle; benigno, compasivo; sensible.—t.-hearted, de corazón tierno.—t. of u over, cuidadoso de, solícito de los sentimientos ajenos.—s. oferta, ofrecimiento, propuesta.—vt. ofrecer, presentar, proponer; enternecer, ablandar.—vi. hacer una oferta; enternecerse.— —loin [-loịn], s. filete.— —ness [-nịs], s. terneza, ternura; sensibilidad; delicadeza; benevolencia.

tendon [téndọn], s. tendón.

tendril [téndrịl], s. (bot.) zarcillo.

tenement [ténẹmẹnt], s. casa de vecindad; vivienda (barata).

tenet [ténịt], s. dogma, principio, credo.

tennis [ténịs], s. tenis.

tenor [ténọ(r)], s. (mus.) tenor; tendencia; texto, contenido.—a. (mus.) de tenor.

tense [tens], a. tenso, tirante.—s. (gram.) tiempo.—tension [ténʂọn], s. tensión, tirantez.

tent [tent], s. toldo; tienda de campaña, (Am.) carpa.

tentacle [téntạkl], s. tentáculo.

tentative [téntạtịv], a. tentativo de ensayo.—s. tentativa, ensayo, tanteo.

tenuous [tényụʌs], a. tenue, sutil; raro.

tenure [tényụ(r)], s. (for.) (per)tenencia, posesión.—t. right, o right of t., inmovilidad (de un cargo, etc.).

tepid [tépịd], a. tibio, templado.

term [tœrm], s. término, vocablo; trimestre escolar; plazo; término, período; sesión.—*pl.* condiciones, estipulaciones; obligaciones impuestas; relaciones mutuas; precio; (com.) facilidades de pago; palabras, expresiones.—*to be on good (bad) terms with,* llevarse bien (mal) con; estar en buenas (malas) relaciones con.—*to bring to terms,* imponer condiciones a, hacer arreglos con.—*to come to terms,* arreglarse, convenirse.—*vt.* nombrar, llamar, calificar de.— —inal [términal], *a.* terminal.—*s.* término, final; (f.c. y elec.) terminal.— —inate [-jneit], *vt.* y *vi.* terminar.— —ination [-jnéişən], *s.* terminación o fin; (gram.) desinencia.

termite [térmait], *s.* termita, comején.

tern [tœrn], *s.* golondrina de mar; terno.

terrace [térjs], *vt.* terraplenar.—*s.* terraplén; terraza; azotea; balcón, galería abierta.

terrain [teróin], *s.* terreno, campo.

terramycin [teramáisjn], *s.* terramicina.

terrible [téribl], *a.* terrible; (fam.) tremendo, extremado.

terrier [térjœ(r)], *s.* perro de busca; zorrero.

terrific [teríſjk], *a.* terrífico, espantoso; (fam.) excelente, tremendo, formidable.—terrify [téríſaj], *vti.* [7] aterrar, aterrorizar, espantar.

territory [térjtorj], *s.* territorio, región, distrito, comarca.

terror [térǫ(r)], *s.* espanto, terror.— —ism [-jzm], *s.* terrorismo.— —ist [-jst], *s.* terrorista.— —ize [-ajz], *vt.* aterrorizar.

test [test], *s.* prueba, ensayo, experimento; examen; comprobación; (quím.) análisis; resultado de un análisis, reacción, reactivo.—*t. flight,* (aer.) vuelo experimental o de prueba. —*t. tube,* probeta, tubo de ensayo. —*the acid t.,* la prueba suprema o decisiva.—*vt.* ensayar, comprobar, hacer la prueba de; someter a prueba; examinar (a un estudiante, etc.); (for.) atestiguar.

testament [téstament], *s.* testamento.

testicle [téstjkl], *s.* testículo.

testify [téstjfaj], *vti.* y *vii.* [7] testificar, atestiguar, atestar.— —testimonial [testjmóunjal], *s.* atestación; certificado; encomio; recomendación.— —testimony [testjmóunj], *s.* testimonio, declaración.—*in t. whereof,* en fe de lo cual.

tetanus [tétanas], *s.* tétano, tétanos.

text [tekst], *s.* texto.— —book [tékstbuk], *s.* libro de texto; libreto de ópera.

textile [tékstjl], *a.* textil, tejido; de tejer, de tejidos.—*s.* tejido; material textil.—texture [tékschur], *s.* textura, contextura; tejido.

Thai [tái, taj], *s.* lengua siamesa.—*a.* siamés.

than [ðæn], *conj.* que; de; del que, de la que, etc.—*fewer than ten,* menos de diez.—*I am taller than he,* soy más alto que él.—*less time than they expected,* menos tiempo del que esperaban.—*more than once,* más de una vez.

thank [θæɳk], *vt.* agradecer, dar gracias a.—*t. you,* gracias.— —fulness [θéɳkfulnjs], *s.* agradecimiento, gratitud.— —less [-ljs], *a.* desagradecido; ingrato.— —s [-s], *s.* gracias.—*t. to,* gracias a, merced a, debido a.— —sgiving [θæɳksgívjɳ], *s.* acción de gracias.—*Thanksgiving Day,* día de acción de gracias.

that [ðæt], *a.* ese, esa, aquel, aquella.—*t. way,* por aquel camino; por allí; de ese modo.—*pron.* ése, ésa, eso; aquél, aquélla, aquello; que, quien, el que, la que, lo que; el cual, la cual, lo cual.—*t. is (to say),* es decir.—*t. is how,* así es como se hace.—*t. is t.,* eso es lo que hay, no hay más que hablar, etc.—*t. of John,* el de Juan. —*t. of yesterday,* el o lo de ayer.—*t. which,* el que, la que, etc.—*conj.* que; para que, a fin de que, con el objeto de.—*in t.,* en que, a causa de que, por cuanto.—*not but t.,* no es decir que.—*save t.,* salvo que.—*so t.,* para que, con tal que; de modo que, de suerte que.—*adv.* tan.—*not t. far,* no tan lejos.—*t. large,* así de grande, de este tamaño.—*t. many,* tantos. —*t. much,* tanto.

thatch [θæch], *s.* paja (para techos).—*vt.* techar con paja.—*thatched roof,* techumbre de paja.

thaw [θɔ], *vt.* y *vi.* deshelar(se), derretir(se).—*to t. out,* hacer(se) más tratable, menos reservado o ceremonioso, abrirse.—*s.* deshielo, derretimiento.

the [ði, ðə], *art.* el, la, lo, los, las.—*adv.* cuanto, tanto, mientras más, etc. —*t. less you say, t. better,* cuanto menos diga, tanto mejor.—*t. more he spoke, t. more we admired him,* mientras más hablaba, más lo admirábamos.

theater, theatre [θíatœ(r)], *s.* teatro; arte dramático.—theatrical [θjátrjkal], *a.* teatral.—*s. pl.* funciones teatrales.

thee [ði], *pron.* (ant.) te, a ti.—*for t. o with t.,* para o por ti (contigo).

theft [θeft], *s.* hurto, robo, latrocinio.

their [ðer], *a.* su, sus, suyo(s), suya(s) (de ellos, de ellas).— —s [-z], *pron.* el suyo (de ellos), la suya (de ellas), los suyos (de ellos), las suyas (de ellas).

them [ðem], *pron.* los, las, les; ellos, ellas (precedidos de preposición).

theme [θim], *s.* tema, asunto.

themselves [ðemsélvz], *pron.* ellos mismos, ellas mismas; sí (mismos, mismas) (después de *prep.*); se (*refl.*). —*with t.*, consigo.—V. MIMSELF, HERSELF.

then [ðen], *adv.* entonces, en aquel tiempo, a la sazón; después, luego, en seguida; en otro tiempo; además; en tal caso; pues, conque; por consiguiente, por esta razón.—*but t.*, por otra parte, sin embargo; si bien es cierto que.—*by t.*, para entonces. —*now and t.*, de cuando en cuando; de vez en cuando.—*now t.*, ahora bien; tenemos pues.—*t. and there*, allí mismo, al punto.—*conj.* pues, en tal caso.

thence [ðens], *adv.* de allí, desde allí; desde entonces, desde aquel momento, de allí en adelante; de ahí, por eso, por esa razón o ese motivo.

theological [θioládʒikal], *a.* teológico, teologal.—**theology** [θiálodʒi], *s.* teología.

theorem [θíorem], *s.* teorema.—**theoretical** [θiorétikal], *a.* teórico, especulativo.—**theory** [θíori], *s.* teoría.

therapeutic [θerapiútik], *a.* terapéutico.— —*s* [-s], *s.* terapéutica.—**therapy** [θérapi], *s.* terapia.

there [ðer], *adv.* ahí, allí, allá; en eso, en cuanto a eso.—*down t.*, ahí (allí) abajo.—*over t.*, ahí.—*t. is, t. are*, hay.—*t. you are*, (fam.) eso es todo; ahí nos (me, etc.) tiene; ahí está el busilis.—*up t.*, ahí (allí) arriba. —**abouts** [ðerabáuts], *adv.* por ahí, por allí, cerca; acerca de eso; aproximadamente.— —**after** [ðeréftœ(r)], *adv.* después, después de eso; conforme.— —**by** [ðerbái], *adv.* con eso, con lo cual; de tal modo, así; allí, por allí cerca; acerca de eso.— —**for** [ðerfɔr], *adv.* por es(t)o; para es(t)o.— —**fore** [ðérfɔr], *adv.* por es(to), por (lo) tanto, po. ende, por consiguiente, en consecuencia, luego.— —**from** [ðerfrám], *adv.* de allí, de ahí; de eso.— —**in** [ðerín], *adv.* allí dentro; en este, en eso.— —**of** [ðeráv], *adv.* de esto, de eso.— —**on** [ðerán], *adv.* sobre o encima de él, ella, etc.; por encima; por lo tanto; luego, al punto.— —**upon** [ðerapán], *adv.* sobre o encima de él, ella, etc.; por lo tanto, por consiguiente; sobre lo cual, luego, al punto.— —**with** [ðerwíð], *adv.* con eso, con esto; en eso, entonces, luego, inmediatamente.

thermometer [θœrmámetœ(r)], *s.* termómetro.—**thermos** [θœrmos], *s.*

termo(s).—thermostat [θœrmostæt], *s.* termóstato.

these [ðiz], *a. pl.* de THIS: estos, estas. —*pron.* éstos, éstas.

thesis [θísis], *s.* tesis.

they [ðei], *pron. pl.* de HE, SHE, IT: ellos, ellas.—*t. say*, se dice, dicen.

thick [θik], *a.* grueso; espeso; tupido; denso; atestado, lleno; estúpido; apagado (voz, etc.); impenetrable; profundo (sombra, etc.); (fam.) íntimo.—*t.-and-thin*, cabal, a toda prueba.—*s.* grueso, espesor; lo más denso, nutrido, tupido o recio.—*adv.* frecuentemente, continuadamente; densa o tupidamente.—*t.-headed*, espeso, torpe.—*t.-lipped*, bezudo, (Am.) bembón.—*t.-set*, rechoncho. —*t.-skinned*, insensible, sinvergüenza. —*to lay it on t.*, exagerar.— —**en** [θíkn], *vt. y vi.* espesar(se), condensar(se), engrosar(se); reforzar(se); enturbiar(se); complicar(se).— —**et** [-it], *s.* maleza, espesura, matorral, broza.— —**ness** [-nis], *s.* espesor; densidad; grosor; cuerpo, consistencia; capa (superpuesta); (fam.) estupidez.

thief [θif], *s.* ladrón.—**thieve** [θiv], *vt. y vi.* hurtar, robar.—**thieves** [θivz], *s. pl.* de THIEF.

thigh [θai], *s.* muslo.—*t. bone*, fémur.

thimble [θímbl], *s.* dedal.

thin [θin], *a.* delgado, fino, tenue; flaco, descarnado; ligero, transparente; aguado; (mus.) débil, poco resonante; apagado (color); escaso; pequeño. —*vti. y vii.* [1] enrarecer(se); adelgazar(se); fluidificarse.—*to t. out*, aclarar, entresacar (el monte, etc.).

thine [ðain], *pron. y a.* (ant.) tuyo, el tuyo; tu, tus.

thing [θin], *s.* cosa, objeto; asunto, acontecimiento, hecho.

think [θink], *vti. y vii.* [10] pensar; proponerse; creer, juzgar, conjeturar. —*as you t. fit*, como a usted le parezca mejor, como Ud. quiera.—*to t. better of*, cambiar de opinión acerca de; formar mejor opinión de.—*to t. it over*, pensarlo, meditarlo.—*to t. nothing of*, mirar con desprecio, tener en poco; creer fácil, no dar importancia a.—*to t. on o upon*, acordarse de, recordar; pensar en; reflexionar acerca de; meditar, considerar.— —**able** [θíŋkabl], *a.* concebible.— —**er** [-œ(r)], *s.* pensador.— —**ing** [-iŋ], *s.* pensamiento, reflexión; concepto, juicio.—*to my t.*, en mi opinión.

thinness [θínnis], *s.* tenuidad, delgadez; poca consistencia; debilidad.

thirst [θœrst], *s.* sed; ansia, anhelo. —*vi.* tener o padecer sed; ansiar, anhelar.—*to t. for*, tener sed de; anhelar.— —*y* [θǿɛrsti], *a*. sediento. —*to be t.*, tener sed.

this [ðis], *a*. este, esta.—*pron*. éste, ésta, esto.—*t. way*, por aquí.

thistle [θísl], *s*. cardo, abrojo.—*t. bird, t. finch*, jilguero.

tho' [ðou], *conj*. = THOUGH.

thong [θaŋ], *s*. correa, tira de cuero, látigo.

thorax [θóræks], *s*. tórax, pecho.

thorn [θorn], *s*. (bot.) espina, púa; espino, abrojo; (fig.) pesadumbre, zozobra.— —*y* [θórni], *a*. espinoso; arduo.

thorough [θǿrou], *a*. cabal, completo, acabado, perfecto; cuidadoso, concienzudo.— —**bred** [-bred], *a*. de pura raza, casta o sangre; bien nacido. —*s*. (un) pura sangre (caballo, etc.).— —**fare** [-fer], *s*. vía pública; paso, tránsito.—*no t.*, no hay paso; calle cerrada.

those [ðouz], *a. pl*. de THAT: aquellos, aquellas; esos, esas.—*pron*. ésos, ésas; aquéllos, aquéllas.—*t. that, t. which, t. who*, los que, aquellos que, quienes.

thou [ðau], *pron*. (ant.) tú.

though [ðou], *conj*. aunque, bien que, si bien, aun cuando.—*as t.*, como si. —*adv*. (fam.) sin embargo; a pesar de eso.

thought [θot], *pret. y pp*. de TO THINK. —*s*. pensamiento; meditación, reflexión; idea; intención, propósito; recuerdo; cuidado, solicitud; poquito, pizca.—*to take t. for*, pensar en, proveer para.— —**ful** [θótful], *a*. pensativo; considerado; precavido.— —**fulness** [-fulnis], *s*. calidad de meditativo, precavido o considerado; consideración; cuidado, atención; previsión.— —**less** [-lis], *a*. atolondrado, descuidado; irreflexivo; inconsiderado.— —**lessness** [-lisnis], *s*. descuido o inadvertencia; falta de consideración; atolondramiento; indiscreción, ligereza.

thrash [θræš], *vt*. zurrar, apalear; (fam.) vencer decisivamente.—*vi*. arrojarse, agitarse.—*to t. out a matter*, ventilar un asunto.— —*ing* [θrǽšiŋ], *s*. trilla; paliza.

thread [θred], *s*. hilo; fibra, hebra, filamento.—*screw t.*, rosca (de un tornillo).—*t. lace*, encaje de hilo. —*vt*. enhebrar, enhilar, ensartar; colarse a través de, pasar por; (mec.) roscar, aterrajar.—*vi*. colarse en, llegar hasta.— —**bare** [θrédber], *a*. raído, gastado.

threat [θret], *s*. amenaza.— —**en** [θrétn], *vt. y vi*. amenazar, amagar.— —**ening** [θrétniŋ], *a*. amenazador.

threefold [θrífould], *a*. trino, triple; tres veces más.—*adv*. tres veces. —**threescore** [θrískór], *s*. tres veintenas, sesenta.

thresh [θreš], *vt*. (agr.) trillar, desgranar. —*vi*. trillar el grano.— —*ing* [θrǽšiŋ], *s*. trilla.—*t. floor*, era.— —**er** [-œ(r)], *s*. trillador; máquina trilladora.

threshold [θréšould], *s*. umbral; entrada; (fig.) comienzo.

threw [θru], *pret*. de TO THROW.

thrice [θrais], *adv*. tres veces.

thrift [θrift], *s*. economía, frugalidad; desarrollo vigoroso (de una planta, etc.).— —*y* [θrífti], *a*. frugal, económico.

thrill [θril], *vt*. emocionar vivamente, hacer estremecer.—*vi*. emocionarse, conmoverse.—*s*. emoción, estremecimiento.— —**er** [θrílœ(r)], *s*. novela o película melodramática.— —*ing* [-iŋ], *a*. emocionante, conmovedor.

thrive [θraiv], *vii*. [4] medrar, prosperar, tener buen éxito.

throat [θrout], *s*. garganta.

throb [θrab], *vii*. [1] latir, palpitar.—*s*. latido, pulsación, palpitación.

thrombosis [θrambósis], *s*. trombosis.

throne [θroun], *s*. trono; poder o dignidad soberanos.—*vt*. entronizar. —*vi*. ocupar el trono.

throng [θraŋ], *s*. tropel de gente, muchedumbre.—*vt*. llenar de bote en bote; estrujar.—*vi*. venir en tropel, amontonarse, apiñarse.

throstle [θrásl], *s*. zorzal, tordo; (tej.) telar continuo.

throttle [θrátl], *s*. regulador, obturador, válvula reguladora.—*t. valve*, válvula de estrangulación, válvula reguladora; (aut.) acelerador.—*vt*. ahogar, estrangular.—*vi*. ahogarse, asfixiarse.

through [θru], *a*. continuo, que va hasta el fin.—*t. ticket*, (f.c., etc.) billete, boleto o boletín directo.—*adv*. de al través, de parte a parte, de un lado a otro; desde el principio hasta el fin; enteramente, completamente.—*t. and t.*, enteramente; en todo; hasta los tuétanos.—*to be t.*, haber terminado; (fam.) no poder más.—*prep*. por; a través de; de un extremo (o lado) a otro de; por conducto o por medio de, mediante; por entre; por causa de, gracias a, por mediación de.— —**out** [-áut], *prep*. por todo, en todo; a lo largo de; durante todo.—*adv*. en todas partes; desde el principio hasta el fin; de parte a parte; en todo respecto.

throw [θrou], *vti. y vii*. [10] arrojar, tirar, disparar, lanzar; echar.—*to t. about*, esparcir.—*to t. aside*, desechar. —*to t. away*, arrojar; desperdiciar, malgastar; desechar, arrinconar.—

to t. back, rechazar, devolver.—*to t. out*, proferir, insinuar; expeler, excluir; esparcir, exhalar, emitir.—*to t. out of gear*, (mec.) desengranar, desconectar; (fig.) trastornar.—*to t. up*, echar al aire; elevar, levantar; renunciar a, abandonar; (fam.) vomitar.—*s.* tiro, tirada.—**thrown** [θroṷn], *pp.* de TO THROW.

thrush [θrʌʃ], *s.* tordo, zorzal; (med.) afta.

thrust [θrʌst], *vii.* [9] acometer, embestir (con espada, etc.); tirar una estocada (con); meterse, pasar abriéndose campo.—*vti.* meter; empujar; forzar; atravesar; clavar, hincar.—*to t. aside*, rechazar; empujar a un lado.—*to t. forward*, empujar, echar adelante.—*to t. in*, meter, introducir.—*to t. on*, incitar, empujar. —*to t. out*, echar fuera; sacar (la lengua, etc.).—*to t. through*, apuñalar, atravesar de parte a parte.—*to t. upon*, imponer.—*pret.* y *pp.* de TO THRUST. —*s.* empuje, empujón; estocada, cuchillada, lanzada, etc.; arremetida; derrumbe.

thud [θʌd], *s.* sonido apagado; golpe sordo.

thug [θʌg], *s.* asesino; ladrón, salteador.

thumb [θʌm], *s.* pulgar.—*under the t. of*, dominado por, bajo el talón de.—*vt.* hojear (un libro) con el pulgar; manosear con poca destreza; emporcar con los dedos.—**tack** [vʌmtæk], *s.* chinche (de dibujo).

thump [θʌmp], *s.* golpazo, porrazo; golpe sordo.—*vt.* y *vi.* aporrear, acachetear; latir con violencia (el corazón).

thunder [θʌndœ(r)], *s.* trueno, tronido; estruendo, estampido.—*vi.* tronar; retumbar.—*vt.* (fig.) tronar; fulminar. ——**bolt** [-boṷlt], *s.* rayo, centella.— —**ing** [-ɪŋ], —**ous** [-ʌs], *a.* atronador; fulminante.— —**storm** [-stɔrm], *s.* tronada.

Thursday [θœrzdi], *s.* jueves.

thus [ðʌs], *adv.* así, de este modo; por eso, por lo tanto; en estos términos; hasta ese punto, tanto, a ese grado; siendo así, en este caso.—*t. and so*, tal y tal cosa; de tal y tal modo. —*t. far*, hasta ahora; hasta aquí.

thwart [θwort], *vt.* impedir, desbaratar, frustrar.

thy [ðaj], *a.* (ant.) tu, tus.

thyme [tajm], *s.* (bot.) tomillo.

thyself [ðajsélf], *pron.* (ant.) tú mismo, ti mismo.

tibia [tíbịạ], (anat.) tibia; (ent.) cuarta articulación.

tick [tɪk], *s.* tictac; garrapata; funda de colchón; (fam.) crédito, fiado.—*vi.* hacer sonar produciendo tictac.—*vi.*

hacer sonido de tictac; batir, latir; (fam.) vender o comprar al fiado. —*to t. off*, marcar.

ticket [tíkit], *s.* billete, (Am.) boleto (de tren, teatro, etc.); rótulo, marbete; marca; candidatura de un partido político; papeleta o (Am.) balota (para votar).—*t. office*, taquilla o despacho de billetes.

tickle [tíkl], *vt.* hacer cosquillas a; halagar, lisonjear; divertir; agradar. —*vi.* hacer, tener o sentir cosquillas. —**tcklish** [tíklịʃ], *a.* cosquilloso; inseguro, incierto; arduo, delicado, difícil.

tide [tajd], *s.* marea; corriente; curso, marcha; flujo; tiempo, estación, sazón.—*tidal wave*, marejada, aguaje. —*vt.* llevar, conducir (la marea). —*vi.* navegar o flotar con la marea.

tidiness [tájdịnịs], *s.* limpieza, aseo; orden.

tidings [tájdịŋs], *s. pl.* nuevas, noticias.

tidy [tájdị], *a.* limpio, pulcro, ordenado; (fam.) considerable.—*s.* cubierta de respaldar.—*vti.* y *vii.* [7] asear, poner en orden.

tie [taj], *vt.* atar, amarrar, liar; unir, enlazar, encadenar, vincular; restringir, limitar; (pol., dep.) empatar.— *to t. the knot*, (fam.) casarse.—*to t. tight*, apretar.—*to t. up*, atar, amarrar, asegurar; recoger; impedir, obstruir, paralizar (el tránsito, la industria, etc.); envolver; vincular (con).—*vi.* liarse; relacionarse; empatarse.—*s.* lazo, nudo, ligadura; vínculo, conexión; apego, adhesión; (dep., etc.) empate; corbata; (mus.) ligadura.—*pl.* zapatos bajos.

tier [tɪr], *s.* fila, hilera, ringlera; (teat.) fila de palcos.

tiger [tájgœ(r)], *s.* tigre.

tight [tajt], *a.* bien cerrado, hermético; tirante, tieso; apretado, estrecho; compacto; (com.) escaso, difícil de obtener; (fam.) apurado, difícil, grave; tacaño; borracho.—*t.-fitting*, muy ajustado.—*t. squeeze*, (fam.) aprieto.— —**en** [tájtn], *vt.* y *vi.* estrechar(se), apretar(se); estirar(se), atesar(se).— —**ness** [-nịs], *s.* tensión, tirantez; estrechez; apretadura; impermeabilidad; (fam.) tacañería.— —**s** [-s], *s.* traje de malla, calzas.

tilde [tíldẹ], *s.* (gram.) tilde.

tile [tájl], *s.* azulejo, baldosa; teja; mosaico; bloque hueco; tubo de barro cocido.—*t. roof*, tejado, techo de tejas.—*vt.* tejar; embaldosar.

till [tɪl], *s.* gaveta o cajón para guardar dinero.—*prep.* hasta.—*conj.* hasta que.—*vt.* cultivar, labrar.— —**age** [tíljdʒ], *s.* labranza, labor, cultivo.

tilt [tɪlt], *s.* inclinación, declive; justa,

torneo; lanzada; toldo, tendal.—*vt.* y *vi.* ladear(se), inclinar(se).—*vt.* y *vi.* (over) volcar(se).

timber [tímbœ(r)], *s.* madera o materiales de construcción; palo, fuste; maderamen, maderaje; monte, bosque, árboles de monte; viga, madero; armazón; mango de madera; (fig.) cualidades.—*t. yard,* maderería, taller de maderas.—*vt.* enmaderar.

time [taim], *s.* tiempo; época; período, estación; hora; vez, turno; oportunidad, ocasión; (com.) prórroga; plazo; (mús.) compás.—*at a t., at the same t.,* a la vez, al mismo tiempo.—*at no t.,* nunca.—*at times,* a veces.—*behind the times,* atrasado de noticias; anticuado.—*behind t.,* atrasado, retardado.—*between times,* en los intervalos.—*for the t. being,* por ahora. —*from t. to t.,* de cuando en cuando. —*in good t.,* temprano.—*on t.,* a la hora debida; (com.) a plazos.—*to beat t.,* llevar el compás.—*to be on time,* ser puntual.—*to have a good t.,* pasar un buen rato; divertirse.—*what t. is it?* ¿qué hora es?—*vt.* adaptar al tiempo, hacer con oportunidad; regular, poner a la hora; contar o medir el tiempo de; (mús.) llevar el compás.— **—keeper** [tájmkipœ(r)], *s.* cronometrista. **—less** [-lịs], *a.* eterno.— **—liness** [-lịnịs], *s.* oportunidad.— **—ly** [-lị], *adv.* oportunamente; a tiempo.—*a.* oportuno, conveniente.— **—piece** [-pís], *s.* cronómetro, reloj.— **—table** [-tejbl], *s.* horario, itinerario.

timid [tímịd], *a.* tímido.— **—ity** [tịmíditị], *s.* timidez.—**timorous** [tímorʌs], *a.* miedoso, timorato; tímido.

tin [tịn], *s.* estaño; (hoja de) lata, hojalata; objeto de hojalatería; (fam.) dinero, moneda.—*t. can,* (recipiente de) lata.—*t. foil,* hoja de papel de estaño.—*vti.* [1] estañar, cubrir con estaño; enlatar.

tincture [tíŋkchŭ(r)], *s.* tintura; tinte. —*t. of iodine,* tintura de iodo.—*vt.* teñir; impregnar, imbuir.

tinder [tíndœ(r)], *s.* yesca; mecha.

tinge [tịndž], *vi.* y *vt.* colorar, teñir, matizar.—*s.* tinte, matiz; gustillo, dejo.

tingle [tíŋgl], *vi.* y *vt.* sentir o producir hormigueo o picazón; zumbar los oídos.—*s.* picazón, hormigueo, comezón; retintín.

tinkle [tíŋkl], *vt.* y *vi.* (hacer) tintinear. —*s.* tintineo; retintín.

tinsel [tínsel], *s.* oropel, relumbrón; talco; lentejuelas.—*a.* de oropel; de relumbrón.

tint [tịnt], *vt.* teñir, colorar, matizar.

—*s.* tinte, color, matiz; (b.a.) media tinta.

tiny [tájnị], *a.* diminuto, minúsculo.

tip [tịp], *s.* punta, extremidad, cabo; casquillo, regatón; yema del dedo; puntera (zapato); propina, gratificación; aviso confidencial; palmadita, golpecito.—*vti.* [1] ladear, inclinar, voltear; dar un golpecito a; dar propina a; informar confidencialmente; guarnecer.—*to t. off,* (fam.) advertir en confianza o en secreto.— *to t. over,* volcar(se).—*vii.* ladearse, inclinarse; dar propina.

tipsy [típsị], *a.* achispado; **vacilante;** ladeado.

tiptoe [típtou], *s.* punta del pie.—*on t.,* de o en puntillas; ansioso.—*vi.* andar de puntillas.

tiptop [típtap], *a.* (fam.) de primera, excelente.—*s.* cima, cumbre.

tire [tájr], *s.* llanta, neumático, goma. —*vt.* cansar, fatigar; aburrir, fastidiar.—*to t. out,* rendir de cansancio. —*vi.* cansarse; aburrirse, fastidiarse.— **—d** [-d], *a.* cansado, fatigado; aburrido; provisto de llantas.— **—less** [tájrlịs], *a.* infatigable, incansable; sin llanta.— **—some** [-sʌm], *a.* tedioso, cansado, aburrido.

tissue [tíšu], *s.* (biol.) tejido; gasa, tisú; (fig.) serie conexa, encadenamiento.—*t. paper,* papel de seda.—*vt.* entretejer.

tithe [tájð], *s.* diezmo; minucia; pizca.

title [tájtl], *s.* título.—*t. page,* portada.

to [tu], *adv.* hacia adelante.—*to and fro,* de un lado para otro; yendo y viniendo.—*to come to,* volver en sí. —*prep.* a, para; por; hasta; en; con; según; menos.—*five minutes to four,* las cuatro menos cinco.—*from house to house,* de casa en casa.—*he wishes to go,* desea ir.—*kind to her,* amable o bondadoso con ella.—*to a certain extent,* hasta cierto punto.—*to be or not to be,* ser o no ser.—*to my way of thinking,* según mi modo de pensar.

toad [tóud], *s.* sapo.

toast [toust], *vt.* tostar; brindar por. —*vi.* tostarse; calentarse; brindar, beber a la salud de.—*s.* tostada; brindis.— **—er** [tóustœ(r)], *s.* el que brinda; tostador; tostadera, parrilla.— **—master** [-mæstœ(r)], *s.* el que preside un banquete; maestro de ceremonias.

tobacco [tobǽkou], *s.* (bot.) tabaco.

today [tudéj], *s.* y *adv.* hoy; hoy en día.

toddle [tádl], *vi.* (del niño o viejo) titubear.— **—r** [-œ(r)], *s.* niño, niña.

toe [tou], *s.* dedo del pie; puntera, punta (del pie, de media, de zapato); pie, base (de un terraplén, etc.); (mec.) saliente, brazo.—*big t.,* dedo

gordo del pie.—*t.-in*, convergencia.
—*toes up*, muerto.—*vt.* tocar con
la punta del pie; dar un puntapié;
poner punteras.—*vi.* (con in) andar
con la punta de los pies hacia adentro;
(mec.) converger (una rueda).——nail
[tóu̯neı̯l], *s.* uña (de los dedos de los
pies).

together [tugéðœ(r)], *adv.* juntamente;
a un tiempo; sin interrupción.—*t.
with*, a una con, juntos; junto con.
—*a.* juntos.

toil [tou̯l], *vi.* afanarse, trabajar asidua-
mente; moverse con dificultad.—*vt.*
conseguir a duras penas.—*s.* faena,
trabajo; pena, afán; obra laboriosa.—
—er [tou̯lœ(r)], *s.* trabajador, el que
se afana.

toilet [tói̯lı̯t], *s.* vestido, tocado, atavío;
acto de vestirse; tocador; excusado,
retrete.—*t. case*, neceser.—*t. paper* o
tissue, papel higiénico.—*t. set*, juego
de tocador.

token [tóu̯kn], *s.* señal, muestra,
prueba; prenda, recuerdo; ficha,
disco metálico (usado en tranvías,
teléfonos, etc.).—*as a t. of*, en prenda
de.—*t. money*, moneda fraccionaria;
monedas inferiores al dólar.—*t. payment*, pago parcial (en señal de buena
fe y de adeudo).

told [tou̯ld], *pret.* y *pp.* de TO TELL.

tolerable [tálı̯rạbl], *a.* tolerable, sufrible; mediano, pasadero.—**tolerance**
[tálı̯rạns], *s.* tolerancia.—**tolerant**
[tálı̯rạnt], *a.* tolerante.—**tolerate**
[tálı̯reı̯t], *vt.* tolerar.—**toleration**
[talı̯réı̯šọn], *s.* tolerancia, indulgencia.

toll [tou̯l], *s.* peaje, portazgo, pontazgo;
(fig.) pérdida, número de víctimas
(en un siniestro, etc.); tañido o doble
de campanas.—*to take a heavy t.*,
(fig.) costar caro (en víctimas, etc.).
—*vt.* y *vi.* cobrar o pagar peaje o
portazgo; tañer o doblar (las campanas).—*to t. the hour*, dar la hora.

tomato [tọméı̯tọu̯], *s.* tomate.

tomb [tum], *s.* tumba, sepulcro.

tomboy [támbọı̯], *s.* muchacha traviesa.

tombstone [túmstọu̯n], *s.* losa, lápida
sepulcral.

tome [tóu̯m], *s.* tomo, volumen.

tommy-gun [támı̯ gʌn], *s.* ametralladora ligera.

tomorrow [tumárọu̯], *s.* y *adv.* mañana.
—*day after t.*, pasado mañana.
—*t. afternoon* (*morning, neon, night*),
mañana por la tarde (por la mañana,
al mediodía, por la noche).

ton [tʌn], *s.* tonelada.

tone [tọu̯n], *s.* tono; sonido, metal o
timbre de la voz.—*vt.* dar o modificar
el tono, entonar; templar, afinar.
—*to t. down*, (pint.) suavizar el tono;

(mus.) amortiguar el sonido; modificar la expresión.—*to t. up*, subir de
tono; vigorizar, robustecer; (med.)
entonar, tonificar.—*vi.* corresponder
en tono o matiz.

tongs [taŋz], *s. pl.* tenazas, tenacillas;
pinzas, alicates; mordazas.

tongue [tʌŋ], *s.* lengua; lengüeta;
badajo de campana.

tonic [tánı̯k], *a.* y *s.* tónico.

tonight [tunáı̯t], *adv.* y *s.* esta noche;
durante esta noche.

tonnage [tánı̯dž], *s.* tonelaje; (com.)
derechos de tonelaje.

tonsil [tánsı̯l], *s.* amígdala, tonsila.—
—itis [-áı̯tı̯s], *s.* (med.) tonsilitis,
amigdalitis.

too [tu], *adv.* también, además,
asimismo; demasiado.—(*it is*) *too bad*,
es lástima, es de sentirse.—*t. many*,
demasiados.—*t. much*, demasiado.

took [tuk], *pret.* de TO TAKE.

tool [tul], *s.* herramienta; utensilio o
instrumento.—*pl.* útiles, bártulos,
aperos.

tooth [tuθ], *s.* diente, muela.—*to have
a sweet t.*, ser muy goloso, gustar de
los dulces.—*t. and nail*, con todo
tesón, con empeño.—*t. decay*, caries
dental.——ache [túθeı̯k], *s.* dolor de
muelas o de diente.——brush [-brãš],
s. cepillo de dientes.——ed [-t], *a.*
dentado, serrado, dentellado.——less
[-lı̯s], *a.* desdentado.——paste [-peı̯st],
s. pasta de dientes.——pick [-pı̯k], *s.*
mondadientes, palillo.

top [tap], *s.* cima, cumbre, pico,
cúspide, vértice, cabeza, cresta (de
una montaña); ápice, punta, remate,
parte superior; superficie; cabeza
(de una página); tabla (de mesa);
coronilla (de la cabeza); copa (de
árbol); cielo (de un automóvil, etc.);
auge, apogeo; primer puesto, último
grado; tupé; trompo, peonza; (aut.)
capota, fuelle; cofa; tope.—*at o from
the t.*, por arriba.—*on t.*, con buen
éxito.—*on t. of*, encima de; además
de.—*t.-flight, t.-notch*, de primera fila,
sobresaliente.—*t. hat*, (fam.) sombrero de copa, chistera.—*vti.* [1]
desmochar (un árbol, etc.); cubrir,
coronar, rematar; llegar a la cima de,
coronar; aventajar, exceder.—*to t.
off*, rematar, terminar.—*vii.* erguirse,
ser eminente; predominar.—*to t. off
with*, terminar con.

topaz [tóu̯pæz], *s.* topacio.

topcoat [tápkou̯t], *s.* saco; sobretodo,
gabán.

toper [tóu̯pœ(r)], *s.* borrachín, (fam.)
cuba.

topic [tápı̯k], *s.* asunto, materia, tema.

topsy-turvy [tápsı̯ tœ́rvı̯], *adv.* y *a.*

trastornado, desbarajustado, patas arriba.

torch [torch], *s.* antorcha.

tore [tɔr], *pret.* de TO TEAR.

torment [tormént], *vt.* atormentar, torturar; afligir.—*s.* [tórment], tormento, suplicio, tortura; pena, angustia.

torn [torn], *pp.* de TO TEAR.

tornado [tornéidou], *s.* tornado, huracán.

torpedo [torpídou], *s.* torpedo.—*vt.* torpedear.

torpid [tórpid], *a.* torpe; entorpecido; adormecido, aletargado.—**torpor** [tórpɔ(r)], *s.* torpeza; entorpecimiento; adormecimiento; letargo, apatía.

torrent [tárent], *s.* torrente; raudal; agolpamiento.

torrid [tárid], *a.* tórrido; abrasador, ardiente.

tortoise [tórtis], *s.* tortuga, galápago; tortuga de tierra, (Am.) jicotea.

tortuous [tórchɐʌs], *a.* tortuoso, sinuoso.

torture [tórchŭ(r)], *s.* tortura, tormento, suplicio.—*vt.* torturar, dar tormento; tergiversar.— **r** [-œ(r)], *s.* atormentador, verdugo.

toss [tos], *vt.* tirar, lanzar al aire; menear, agitar, sacudir.—*to t. aside*, echar a un lado.—*to t. in a blanket*, mantear.—*to t. in o up the sponge*, darse por vencido; desistir.—*to t. off*, tragar de golpe; echar a un lado, no hacer caso de; hacer sin esfuerzo ni esmero.—*to t. out*, derrocar (un gobierno, etc.).—*vi.* corcovear; mecerse.—*to t. for*, *to t. up*, echar o jugar a cara o cruz.—*s.* meneo, sacudida; lanzamiento; ajetreo.

tot [tat], *s.* chiquitín, nene, nena.

total [tóutɐl], *a.* y *s.* total.— **itarian** [toutælitérian], *s.* y *a.* totalitario.— **itarianism** [toutælitérianizm], *s.* totalitarismo.— **ity** [toutǽliti], *s.* totalidad.

totter [tátœ(r)], *vi.* tambalear, temblar, vacilar.

touch [tʌch], *vt.* tocar; tentar, palpar, manosear; alcanzar, herir; conmover, enternecer; igualar, aproximarse a; (b.a.) delinear, esbozar; tratar (un asunto); concernir, importar; aludir a, tratar por encima; afectar.—*to t. for*, (fam.) dar un sablazo, pedir prestado a; robar a.—*to t. off*, descargar (arma); hacer o acabar de prisa; bosquejar.—*to t. up*, retocar; corregir.—*vi.* tocar(se); estar en contacto.—*to t. and go*, tratar de un asunto ligeramente.—*to t. on o upon*, tocar en; tratar ligeramente de; concernir; acercarse a.—*s.* tacto (sentido); toque; dolorcito, punzada;

indirecta; prueba, examen; corazonada; pincelada; dejo; (fam.) sablazo.—*t.-and-go*, montado al pelo; precario; ligero de cascos.— **iness** [táchinis], *s.* susceptibilidad, delicadeza.— **ing** [-iŋ], *prep.* tocante a, en cuanto a, acerca de.—*a.* patético, conmovedor.—*s.* toque; tacto; contacto.— **wood** [-wŭd], *s.* yesca.— **y** [-i], *a.* quisquilloso, susceptible.

tough [tʌf], *a.* correoso, duro; vigoroso, (fam.) de pelo en pecho; resistente; testarudo, tenaz; flexible y fuerte; (metal) trabajable; (fam.) difícil, penoso; rudo, vulgar.—*t. break*, *t. luck*, (fam.) mala pata o suerte.—*s.* villano, rufián.— **en** [tʌfn], *vt.* y *vi.* hacer(se) correoso; endurecer(se).— **ness** [-njs], *s.* tenacidad; endurecimiento; rigidez; flexibilidad; resistencia; rudeza.

toupee [tupéi], *s.* tupé, peluca.

tour [tur], *s.* viaje de turismo, excursión; jira de inspección; vuelta, circuito; turno.—*vt.* viajar por, recorrer.—*vi.* viajar por distracción.— **ist** [túrist], *a.* turístico, de turismo.—*s.* turista.— **ism** [-izm], *s.* turismo.

tournament [túrnament], *s.* (dep.) torneo; justa.

tourniquet [túrniket], *s.* (cir.) torniquete.

tow [tou], *s.* estopa; remolque; lo que va remolcado.—*vt.* remolcar.

toward(s) [tord(z), tuwórd(z)], *prep.* hacia; con, para con; cosa de, alrededor de; tocante a.

towel [tául], *s.* toalla.—*t. rack*, toallero.

tower [táuœ(r)], *s.* torre; (mil.) torreón.— **bell** *t.*, campanario.—*vi.* descollar, sobresalir, destacarse; remontarse.— **ing** [-iŋ], *a.* encumbrado; sobresaliente.—*t. rage*, furia violenta.

town [taun], *s.* ciudad; villa, pueblo, aldea; municipio; la ciudad, el pueblo.—*t. hall*, *t. house*, casa consistorial, concejo.—*t. planning*, urbanismo.

toxin [táksin], *s.* toxina.

toy [toi], *s.* juguete.—*a.* de juego; diminuto.—*vi.* jugar, juguetear, retozar.

trace [treis], *s.* rastro, huella, pisada, pista; vestigio, señal, indicio; una pizca, un ápice.—*vt.* trazar, delinear; calcar; rastrear, seguir la pista; plantear, indicar; reconstruir, determinar el origen de.

trachea [tréikiä], *s.* tráquea.

track [træk], *s.* vestigio, rastro, pista, huella, pisada; carril; rumbo, ruta; curso (de cometa, etc.); senda, vereda; (f.c.) vía, rieles o carriles; estera o banda (de tractor oruga); atletismo; pista (de atletismo, carreras, etc.).—*off the t.*, descarrilado; desviado,

extraviado.—*on the t.*, sobre la pista,
en el rastro.—*vt.* rastrear.—*to t. down*,
descubrir (el origen, escondite, etc.
de).

tract [trækt], *s.* trecho; región, comarca,
terreno; (anat.) área, canal, sistema;
opúsculo, panfleto.

traction [trǽkṣǫn], *s.* tracción; acarrea-
miento; (fisiol.) contracción.—**tractor**
[trǽktǫ(r)], *s.* tractor.

trade [treid], *s.* comercio; ramo o giro;
trueque, trato, negocio; movimiento
mercantil; oficio; gremio.—*t. agreement*, tratado comercial (entre
naciones); pacto entre patronos y
gremios obreros.—*t. mark*, marca de
fábrica.—*t. name*, razón social;
nombre comercial o de fábrica.
—*t. school*, escuela industrial o de
artes y oficios.—*t. union*, gremio,
sindicato.—*t. winds*, vientos alisios.
—*vt.* y *vi.* negociar, comerciar,
traficar; cambiar.—*to t. in*, negociar
en; entregar un objeto (auto, radio,
etc.) en pago total o parcial de otro.
—*to t. off*, cambalachear.—*to t. on*,
aprovecharse de.—*r* [tréidœ(r)], *s.*
negociante, comerciante, traficante,
mercader; buque mercante. —**sman**
[tréidzmǫn], *s.* tendero, mercader;
artesano, menestral.

tradition [trǫdíṣǫn], *s.* tradición.—**al**
[-ǫl], *a.* tradicional.

traffic [trǽfik], *s.* tráfico.—*vti.* y *vii.*
[8] traficar.—**trafficked** [trǽfikt],
pret. y *pp.* DE TO TRAFFIC.

tragedy [trǽdʒidi], *s.* tragedia.—
tragic(al) [trǽdʒik(ǫl)], *a.* trágico.

trail [treil], *vt.* arrastrar; remolcar;
traer, llevar (barro, etc.) en los pies,
zapatos, etc.; asentar (la yerba) con
el andar hasta formar vereda;
rastrear, seguir la pista; (f.c.) agregar
(vagones) a un tren.—*vi.* ir arras-
trando; dejar rastro; rezagarse; seguir
el rastro; arrastrarse, trepar (una
planta).—*s.* rastro, huella; cola (de
vestido, cometa, etc.); sendero,
vereda; carretera; indicio.—*er*
[tréilœ(r)], *s.* rastreador; carro o
coche remolcado; remolque.—*t. truck*,
camión con remolque.

train [trein], *vt.* adiestrar, entrenar;
apuntar (un arma); enfocar (un
anteojo).—*vi.* adiestrarse, entrenarse.
—*s.* tren; séquito, comitiva; cabal-
gata; recua; reguero de pólvora;
serie, sucesión, curso (de las ideas,
acontecimientos, etc.); cola (de ave,
vestido, cometa); (mec.) juego,
movimiento.—**ee** [treiní], *s.* persona
a quien se entrena o adiestra; (mil.)
soldado recluta.—**er** [tréinœ(r)], *s.*
entrenador; domador.—**ing** [-iŋ], *s.*
adiestramiento, entrenamiento, pre-

paración.—*a.* de entrenamiento, de
instrucción.

trait [treit], *s.* rasgo, característica,
cualidad; golpe, toque.

traitor [tréitǫ(r)], *s.* traidor.

trajectory [trǫdʒéktǫri], *s.* trayectoria.

tram [træm], *s.* (min.) vagoneta.

tramp [træmp], *vt.* y *vi.* pisar con fuerza;
caminar; vagabundear.—*s.* marcha
pesada; ruido de pisadas; caminata;
vagabundo.—**le** [trǽmpl], *vt.* hollar,
pisar, pisotear, conculcar.—*vi.* pisar
fuerte.—*to t. on*, atropellar, hollar,
pisotear.—*s.* pisoteo; atropello.

trance [træns], *s.* rapto, arrobamiento;
(med.) síncope, catalepsia; estado
hipnótico.

tranquil [trǽŋkwil], *a.* tranquilo, sereno.
—**lity** [træŋkwíliti], *s.* tranquilidad,
calma, serenidad, sosiego.—**lize**
[trǽŋkwilaiz], *vt.* y *vi.* tranquili-
zar(se).

transact [trænzǽkt], *vt.* transar,
negociar.—**ion** [trænzǽkṣǫn], *s.*
transacción, negociación.

transatlantic [trænzætlǽntik], *a.*
transatlántico.—*t. liner*, (vapor o
buque) transatlántico.

transcontinental [trænzkantinéntǫl], *a.*
transcontinental.

transcribe [trænskráib], *vt.* transcribir.
—**transcript** [trǽnskript], *s.* copia,
traslado.—**transcription** [trænskríp-
ṣǫn], *s.* transcripción.

transfer [trænsfœr], *vti.* [1] transferir,
pasar, trasladar; transbordar; (for.)
traspasar, ceder.—*s.* [trǽnsfœ(r)],
transferencia; traslado; transbordo;
(for.) traspaso, cesión.—*t. paper*,
papel de calcar.

transform [trænsfórm], *vt.* y *vi.*
transformar(se).—**able** [-ǫbl], *a.*
transformable.—**ation** [-éiṣǫn], *s.*
transformación.

transfusion [trænzfiúʒǫn], *s.* trans-
fusión.

transient [trǽnṣǫnt], *a.* pasajero,
transitorio; que está de paso o de
tránsito; transeúnte.—*s.* transeúnte.
—**transit** [trǽnsit], *s.* tránsito.—*in t.*,
en tránsito.—**transition** [trænzíṣǫn],
s. tránsito, paso; transición.—**transi-
tive** [trǽnsitiv], *a.* (gram.) transitivo.
—**transitory** [trǽnsitǫri], *a.* transitorio; provisional.

translate [trænsléit], *vt.* traducir;
descifrar; transformar.—*to t. from
Spanish to English*, traducir del
español al inglés.—**translation** [trænsl-
éiṣǫn], *s.* traducción; interpretación;
traslación, remoción.—**translator**
[trænsléitǫ(r)], *s.* traductor, intérprete.

transmission [trænsmíṣǫn], *s.* transmisión.—**transmit** [trænsmít], *vti.*

[1] transmitir.—**transmitter** [træns-mítœ(r)], *s.* remitente; transmisor.

transom [trǽnsǫm], *s.* montante, claraboya.

transparency [trænspǽrǫnsi], *s.* transparencia; (foto.) diapositiva.—**transparent** [trænspǽrǫnt], *a.* transparente, diáfano, hialino; (fig.) franco, sincero.

transplant [trænsplǽnt], *vt.* trasplantar.

transport [trænspórt], *vt.* transportar, acarrear; arrebatar, conmover.—*s.* [trǽnsport], transporte, transportación, acarreo; buque o avión transporte; rapto, arrobamiento; paroxismo, acceso.— **—ation** [trænsportéiʃǫn], *s.* transporte, acarreo; boleto, billete, pasaje; coste del transporte.

transpose [trænspoúz], *vt.* transponer; (mus.) transportar.

transverse [trænsvǿrs], *a.* transversal, transverso.

trap [træp], *s.* trampa, garlito, red, lazo.—*mouse t.*, ratonera.—*t. shooting*, tiro de pichón; tiro al vuelo a un blanco movible.—*vti.* [1] coger con trampa; atrapar; hacer caer en el garlito.—*vii.* armar lazos, trampas o asechanzas.— **—door** [trǽpdor], *s.* escotillón, trampa; (min.) puerta de ventilación.

trapeze [trapíz], *s.* trapecio (de gimnasia o circo).—**trapezium** [trapíziʌm], *s.* (geom.) trapecio.—**trapezoid** [trǽpǝzǫid], *s.* trapezoide.

trappings [trǽpiŋz], *s. pl.* arreos, aderezos, galas.

trash [trǽʃ], *s.* hojarasca, paja, basura, desperdicio, escombro, desecho; bagazo; cachivache, trasto; quídam, un cualquiera.— **—y** [trǽʃi], *a.* despreciable, baladí.

traumatic [tromǽtjk], *a.* traumático.

travel [trǽvǝl], *vti.* y *vii.* [2] viajar; recorrer.—*s.* viaje; excursión; jornada; (mec.) recorrido.—*pl.* correrías; relación de un viaje.—*t.-worn*, fatigado por el viaje.— **—er** [-œ(r)], *s.* viajero; viajante.—*traveling salesman*, viajante de comercio, agente viajero.

traverse [trǽvœrs], *a.* transversal.—*t. board*, rosa náutica o de los vientos.—*adv.* de través, en sentido transversal.—*s.* travesaño.—*vt.* atravesar, cruzar; mover transversalmente.—*vi.* atravesarse; moverse de un lado a otro.

tray [trej], *s.* bandeja; (Am.) batea; (foto.) cubeta; cualquier vasija casi plana o de bordes bajos.

treacherous [trécħœrʌs], *a.* traidor, traicionero.—**treachery** [trécħœri], *s.* traición, perfidia, deslealtad.

tread [tred], *vti.* y *vii.* [10] pisar, hollar; andar, caminar.—*s.* paso; pisada, huella; escalón; superficie de rodadura (de rueda, neumático, etc.); banda o cadena (de tractor oruga).— **—le** [trédl], *s.* (mec.) pedal.

treason [trízǫn], *s.* traición.—*high t.*, lesa patria; lesa majestad.— **—able** [-ǝbl], *a.* pérfido, desleal, traidor.

treasure [trézy(r)], *s.* tesoro.—*t.-trove*, tesoro hallado.—*vt.* atesorar; acumular riquezas; guardar como un tesoro.— **—r** [trézūrœ(r)], *s.* tesorero.—**treasury** [trézūri], *s.* tesorería; erario; (com.) caja; (T.) Ministerio de Hacienda o del Tesoro.

treat [trit], *vt.* y *vi.* tratar (bien o mal); curar; convidar, invitar.—*s.* placer; obsequio; convite.— **—ise** [trítjs], *s.* tratado (libro).— **—ment** [-mǝnt], *s.* tratamiento, trato; (med.) cura, cuidado.— **—y** [-i], *s.* tratado, pacto.

treble [trébl], *a.* triple; (mus.) atiplado.—*s.* (mus.) tiple.—*vt.* triplicar.—*vi.* triplicarse.

tree [tri], *s.* árbol.—*shoe t.*, horma de zapato.—*up a tree*, puesto entre la espada y la pared.— **—less** [tríljs], *a.* pelado, sin árboles.— **—top** [-tap], *s.* copa.

trellis [tréljs], *s.* enrejado; emparrado.

tremble [trémbl], *vi.* temblar; estremecerse; tiritar; trinar.—*s* temblor.

tremendous [triméndʌs], *a.* tremendo.

tremolo [trémolǫu], *s.* (mús.) trémolo.

tremor [trémǫ(r)], *s.* tremor, temblor, estremecimiento; vibración, trepidación.—**tremulous** [trémyǫlʌs], *a.* trémulo, tembloroso.

trench [trench], *vt.* y *vi.* surcar; hacer zanjas o fosos; (mil.) atrincherar.—*s.* foso, zanja; tajo; presa (de riego); trinchera.

trend [trend], *vi.* dirigirse, tender, inclinarse.—*s.* dirección, rumbo, curso, tendencia.

trespass [tréspǝs], *vi.* (con **on** o **upon**) violar, infringir; invadir, rebasar o traspasar los límites; (con **against**) pecar, faltar.—*s.* transgresión, translimitación; infracción, violación; culpa, pecado; deuda (en el padrenuestro).

tress [tres], *s.* trenza; rizo, bucle.—*pl.* cabellera.

trial [trájǝl], *s.* prueba, ensayo, tanteo, tentativa; desgracia, aflicción; (for.) proceso, juicio, vista.—*a.* de prueba; experimental.—*by t.*, al tanteo.—*on t.*, (com.) a prueba; (for.) enjuiciado.

triangle [trájæŋgl], *s.* triángulo.—**triangular** [trajæŋgyǫlǫ(r)], *a.* triangular.

tribal [trájbǝl], *a.* tribal, de tribu.—**tribe** [trajb], *s.* tribu.

tribulation [trȋbyŋléȷ̇s̹ŋ], *s.* tribulación.
tribunal [trȋbȷ̇únᶏl], *s.* (for.) sala, juzgado; tribunal; foro.
tributary [trȋbyŋteri], *a.* y *s.* tributario; subordinado, subalterno.—**tribute** [trȋbȷ̇ut], *s.* tributo; contribución, impuesto; homenaje.
trice [traȷ̇s], *s.* momento, instante. —*in a t.*, en un tris; en un abrir y cerrar de ojos.
trichina [trȋkáȷ̇nᶏ], *s.* triquina.
trick [trȋk], *s.* treta; ardid, truco; trampa; juego de manos; chasco, burla; travesura, jugarreta; destreza, maña; marrullería; (naipes) baza; (mar.) guardia del timonel.—*to do the t.*, resolver el problema, dar en el busilis.—*vt.* engañar, embaucar.—*to t. out*, ataviar, componer, asear.—*vi.* trampear, vivir de trampas.— —**ery** [trȋkœrȷ̇], *s.* ardid, engaño, astucia.
trickle [trȋkl], *vt.* y *vi.* (hacer) gotear; escurrir.—*s.* goteo.
tricky [trȋkȷ̇], *a.* falso, tramposo, marrullero; intrincado.
tricycle [tráȷ̇sȷ̇kl], *s.* triciclo.
trifle [tráȷ̇fᶅ], *s.* bagatela, fruslería, friolera, baratija, menudencia, chuchería.—*vt.* (con away) malgastar (el tiempo, etc.).—*vi.* bromear, chancearse; holgar(se).—*to t. with*, jugar con, tratar sin seriedad; burlarse de, engañar.—**trifling** [tráȷ̇flȷ̇ŋ], *a.* frívolo, trivial.
trigger [trȋgœ(r)], *s.* gatillo, disparador; calzo.
trigonometry [trȷ̇gonámetrȷ̇], *s.* trigonometría.
trill [trȋl], *s.* trino, gorjeo, (fam.) gorgorito; (fon.) vibración.—*vt.* vibrar (la r).—*vi.* trinar, gorjear; gotear.
trilogy [trȋlodȝ̇ȷ̇], *s.* trilogía.
trim [trȷ̇m], *a.* ajustado, bien acondicionado; ataviado, acicalado.—*vti.* [1] componer, arreglar, pulir, ajustar, adaptar; (carp.) desbastar, acepillar; (agr.) podar; recortar (cabellos, barba); (cost.) adornar, guarnecer, ribetear; (fam.) reprender, zurrar; (fam.) derrotar; sacar ventaja a.— *to t. off*, recortar; atusar.—*to t. up*, adornar, hermosear, componer.—*vti.* vacilar, titubear; nadar entre dos aguas.—*s.* atavío, adorno; traje, vestido; estilo; condición, estado; (cost.) franja, ribete, guarnición; (arq.) molduras.— —**ming** [trȷ̇mȷ̇ŋ], *s.* (cost.) guarnición, cenefa; ajuste, arreglo; (agr.) poda; recorte (del pelo, barba); (fam.) derrota.
trinity [trȷ̇nȷ̇tȷ̇], *s.* trinidad; (T.) Trinidad.
trinket [trȷ̇ŋkȷ̇t], *s.* baratija, chuchería.
trio [tríoȷ̇], *s.* terno; (mus.) trío.
trip [trȷ̇p], *vti.* [1] hacer caer a uno (con una zancadilla), hacer tropezar; armar un lazo o zancadilla; coger a uno en falta; (mec.) disparar, soltar; desatar; (mar.) zarpar, levar anclas. —*vii.* tropezar; equivocarse, cometer un desliz o descuido; (mar.) zarpar; correr, ir aprisa.—*s.* viaje corto, excursión; tropiezo, traspiés; paso falso, desliz; zancadilla; paso o movimiento ágil.
tripe [traȷ̇p], *s.* (coc.) callos, mondongo; (fam.) cosa sin valor, necedades.
triple [trȷ̇pl], *a.* triple.—*vt.* triplicar. —**tripod** [tráȷ̇pad], *s.* trípode.
trite [traȷ̇t], *a.* trillado, gastado; trivial, vulgar.- —**ness** [tráȷ̇tnȷ̇s], *s.* vulgaridad, trivialidad.
triumph [tráȷ̇amf], *s.* triunfo, victoria. —*vi.* triunfar; vencer, salir victorioso. - —**al** [traȷ̇Ámfᶅl], *a.* triunfal.— —**ant** [traȷ̇Ámfᶏnt], *a.* triunfante, victorioso.
trivial [trȷ̇vȷ̇ᶅl], *a.* trivial, frívolo, fútil.
trod [trad], *pret.* y *pp.* de TO TREAD. —**trodden** [trádn], *pp.* de TO TREAD.
trolley [trálȷ̇], *s.* (elec.) polea de trole; coche o tranvía de trole.—*t. car*, (coche de) tranvía.
trombone [trámboʊn], *s.* (mus.) trombón.
troop [trup], *s.* tropa; cuadrilla, grupo; compañía (de actores); (mil.) escuadrón de caballería.—*vi.* apiñarse, ir en tropel.
trophy [tróȷ̇fȷ̇], *s.* trofeo.
tropic [trápȷ̇k], *s.* trópico.- —**al** [-ᶅl] *a.* tropical.
trot [trat], *vti.* [1] hacer trotar.—*t. out* (fam.) sacar a exhibir.—*vii.* trotar, ir al trote.—*s.* trote.—*at a t.*, al trote.
troubador [trúbᶏdor], *s.* trovador.
trouble [trÁbl], *vt.* (per)turbar, disturbar; enturbiar; enfadar, hostigar; atribular, preocupar; molestar, importunar.—*to t. oneself*, tomarse la molestia; inquietarse.—*vi.* incomodarse, darse molestia, apurarse.—*s.* perturbación; disturbio, inquietud; enfermedad, mal; (mec.) avería; cuita, pena, congoja; disgusto, desavenencia; dificultad, molestia; impertinencia, engorro.—*to be in t.*, hallarse en dificultades.- —**maker** [-meȷ̇kœ(r)], *s.* perturbador, agitador. - —**some** [-sam], *a.* penoso, pesado; importuno; dificultoso, fastidioso, molesto; pendenciero.
trough [trof], *s.* artesa; comedero (para animales); abrevadero, bebedero; seno de dos olas; canal (artificial; canalón (del tejado); (meteor.) mínimo de presión.
trousers [tráʊzœrz], *s. pl.* pantalones.
trousseau [trúsoʊ], *s.* ajuar de novia.
trout [traʊt], *s.* trucha.

trowel [tráuęl], *s.* (alb.) llana, paleta, palustre, (Am.) cuchara.

truancy [trúansi], *s.* ausencia sin permiso de la escuela o del deber.— **truant** [trúant], *s.* novillero, que se ausenta de la escuela.—*to play t.*, hacer novillos, capear la escuela.

truce [trus], *s.* (mil.) tregua; suspensión, cesación.

truck [trʌk], *vt.* y *vi.* trocar, permutar, traficar; acarrear, transportar en camión o carretón.—*s.* camión; carretón; carretilla de mano; carreta; efectos para vender o trocar; hortalizas para el mercado; (fam.) cosas sin valor, basura; trueque; (fam.) trato.

trudge [trʌdž], *vi.* andar a pie; caminar con trabajo.—*s.* (fam.) caminata, paseo largo y difícil.

true [tru], *a.* verdadero, cierto, real, efectivo; ingenuo, sincero; exacto; justo, a plomo, a nivel, alineado, bien arreglado; legítimo, genuino; fiel, leal.—*t. to life*, verosímil; al natural.

truffle [trʌfl], *s.* trufa.

truism [trúizm], *s.* perogrullada.— **truly** [trúli], *adv.* verdaderamente, en verdad; realmente, exactamente; sinceramente, de buena fe.—*yours (very) t.*, su afectísimo, su seguro servidor.

trump [trʌmp], *s.* triunfo (naipes); (fam.) real mozo, excelente persona; (poét.) trompeta; trompetazo.—*vt.* (naipes) matar con triunfo; engañar. —*to t. up*, forjar; inventar.—*vi.* (naipes) jugar un triunfo, matar.

trumpet [trʌ́mpit], *s.* (mus.) trompa, trompeta, clarín (instrumento y músico); bocina, megáfono.—*vi.* trompetear.—*vt.* (fig.) divulgar.

truncate [trʌ́ŋkejt], *vt.* truncar.

truncheon [trʌ́nchọn], *s.* porra, tranca.

trunk [trʌŋk], *s.* tronco; baúl; trompa de elefante.—*pl.* calzones cortos para deportes.—*t. line*, línea principal (f.c., elec., telf., etc.).—*a.* troncal.

trust [trʌst], *s.* confianza, fe; creencia; (com.) crédito; (for.) fideicomiso, cargo, depósito; (com.) combinación monopolista.—*vt.* y *vi.* confiar (en), contar con; tener confianza en o hacer confianza de; encargar y fiar; fiarse (de); creer, dar crédito a; vender al fiado.— **ee** [trʌstí], *s.* síndico, fideicomisario, fiduciario, depositario; miembro de un patronato.— **ful** [trʌ́stfụl], *a.* confiado.— **worthy** [-wœrði], *a.* fiable, confiable; fidedigno.— **y** [-i], *a.* fiel; íntegro, confiable; firme, seguro.

truth [truθ], *s.* verdad, realidad; veracidad; exactitud.— **ful** [trúθfụl],

a. verídico; verdadero, exacto.— **fulness** [-fụlnis], *s.* veracidad; exactitud; realismo.

try [traj], *vti.* [7] probar, ensayar; procurar, tratar de, intentar; exasperar, cansar; comprobar, (for.) procesar; ver (una causa); (metal.) purificar, refinar.—*to t. on*, probarse (ropa).—*to t. one's hand*, hacer uno la prueba.—*to t. out*, probar, someter a prueba.—*vii.* probar, ensayar; procurar, hacer lo posible; (mar.) capear.—*s.* prueba, ensayo.— **ing** [trájiŋ], *a.* de prueba; molesto, exasperador, irritante; angustioso, penoso.

tub [tʌb], *s.* cuba; batea; tina; cubeta; bañera; (fam.) acto de bañarse.

tube [tjub], *s.* tubo; cámara de llanta o neumático; (rad.) válvula, bombillo, tubo.

tuber [tjúbœ(r)], *s.* (bot.) tubérculo; (anat.) tubérculo, hinchazón, prominencia.— **cle** [-kl], *s.* tubérculo.— **cular** [tjubœ́rkyụlạ(r)], *a.* tuberculoso, tísico.— **culosis** [tjubœrkyụlóụsis], *s.* tuberculosis.

tubing [tjúbiŋ], *s.* tubería.— **tubular** [tjúbyụlạ(r)], *a.* tubular.

tuck [tʌk], *s.* (cost.) alforza.—*vt.* alforzar; arropar; doblar, aprestar. —*to t. up*, arremangar.— **er** [tʌ́kœ(r)], *s.* (cost.) escote.—*vt.* (E.U., fam.) (a menudo con **out**) cansar, fatigar.

Tuesday [tjúzdj], *s.* martes.

tuft [tʌft], *s.* penacho, cresta; borla; manojo, ramillete; tupé, moño; macizo (de plantas).

tug [tʌg], *vti.* [1] tirar de, arrastrar; remolcar.—*vii.* esforzarse, tirar con fuerza.—*s.* tirón, estirón; (mar.) remolcador.

tuition [tjuíšọn], *s.* instrucción o enseñanza; precio de la enseñanza, matrícula (mensual, anual, etc.) que se paga por ella.

tulip [tjúlip], *s.* tulipán.

tulle [tul], *s.* tul.

tumble [tʌ́mbl], *vi.* caer, dar en tierra. —*to t. down*, desplomarse; voltear, rodar; dar saltos, brincar; revolcarse; (fam.) comprender, caer en ello.—*to t. out*, (fam.) levantarse.—*vt.* revolver; tirar, arrojar.—*to t. over o about*, tumbar, derribar; volcar; desarreglar, trastornar; ajar o arrugar (la ropa); cazar al vuelo; pulir por fricción.—*s.* caída, tumbo; vuelco, voltereta; desorden, confusión.— **r** [tʌ́mblœ(r)], *s.* vaso (de mesa); cubilete; acróbata, saltimbanqui, titiritero.

tumor [tjúmọ(r)], *s.* tumor.

tumult [tjúmʌlt], *s.* tumulto, escándalo;

agitación.- —uous [tjumʌlchɹʌs], *a.* tumultuoso, alborotado.

tun [tʌn], *s.* tonel, cuba.

tuna [túnǎ], *s.* (ict.) atún; (bot.) tuna; nopal.—*t. fish,* atún.

tune [tjun], *s.* (mús.) aire, tonada, son, melodía; afinación, concordancia, armonía.—*in t.,* templado, afinado. —*out of t.,* destemplado, desafinado, desentonado.—*to the t. of,* al son de, tocando o entonando.—*vt.* templar, afinar, entonar; ajustar, adaptar; (rad.) sintonizar.—*to t. up,* (mec.) poner a punto el motor.—*vi.* armonizar, modular.—*to t. in,* (rad.) sintonizar.— —*r* [tjúnœ(r)], *s.* afinador, templador; (rad.) sintonizador.

tungsten [tʌŋsten], *s.* (quím.) tungsteno.

tunic [tjúnɪk], *s.* túnica; (mil.) casaca, guerrera.

tuning [tjúnɪŋ], *s.* (mús.) acto de templar, afinación; (rad.) sintonización.—*t. fork,* (mús.) diapasón.

tunnel [tʌnɛl], *s.* túnel; (min.) socavón. —*vti.* y *vii.* [2] horadar; construir o abrir un túnel.

tunny [tʌnɪ], *s.* atún.—*striped t.,* bonito.

turban [tœrban], *s.* turbante.

turbid [tœrbɪd], *a.* turbio, espeso; turbulento.

turbine [tœrbɪn], *s.* turbina.

tureen [tjɹin], *s.* sopera, salsera.

turf [tœrf], *s.* césped; terrón (con césped); carreras de caballos, hipódromo.

Turk [tœrk], *s.* turco.

turkey [tœrkɪ], *s.* pavo.

Turkish [tœrkɪʃ], *a.* turco.—*s.* idioma turco.

turmoil [tœrmɔɪl], *s.* disturbio, tumulto, alboroto.

turn [tœrn], *vt.* voltear, hacer girar; transformar; (mec.) tornear; invertir (posición); revolver (en la mente); doblar (una esquina, etc.).—*to t. against,* predisponer en contra de; causar aversión a o contra.—*to t. around,* voltear, dar vuelta a.—*to t. aside,* desviar, hacer a un lado.— *to t. away,* despedir, echar; desviar. —*to t. back,* devolver, restituir; volver atrás.—*to t. down,* plegar, doblar; poner boca abajo: bajar, disminuir (intensidad de una llama, etc.); (fam.) abandonar; rechazar, rehusar.—*to t. from,* desviar o alejar de.—*to t. in,* replegar; doblar hacia adentro; entregar.—*to t. into,* convertir en, cambiar en.—*to t. off,* cortar (el agua, el vapor, etc.); cerrar (la llave del agua, etc.); desconectar o apagar (la luz, el radio, etc.); (mec.) tornear.—*to t. on,* abrir (la llave del agua, etc.); dar (vapor, etc.); conectar o encender (la luz, el radio, etc.); establecer el servicio de electricidad, etc.).—*to t. out,* echar, expeler, arrojar; sacar hacia afuera; apagar (la luz, etc.); producir; volver al revés; doblar, torcer; echar al campo (los animales).—*to t. over,* transferir, pasar, trasladar; invertir, volcar; revolver.—*to t. up,* voltear; levantar; cavar (el suelo); arremangar; subir (el cuello).—*vi.* girar, rodar, voltear; torcer, seguir otra dirección; voltearse; convertirse en; ponerse (pálido, colorado, etc.); mudar (de posición, opinión, etc.). —*my head turns* (round), se me va la cabeza.—*to t. about* o *around,* volverse; voltearse.—*to t. against,* volverse contra.—*to t. aside,* desviarse.—*to t. back,* retroceder; volverse.—*to t. down a street,* torcer por una calle.—*to t. in,* guarecerse; entrar; llegar a casa; (fam.) irse a la cama.—*to t. into,* entrar en; transformarse en.—*to t. off,* torcer, desviarse.—*to t. on,* depender de; volverse contra; acometer a.—*to t. out,* resultar; asistir, acudir; estar vuelto hacia afuera; (fam.) salir de casa; levantarse.—*to t. over,* revolverse, dar vueltas; volcarse (un auto, etc.).—*to t. short,* dar media vuelta. —*to t. to,* recurrir o acudir a; dirigirse hacia o a; convertirse en; redundar en.—*to t. up,* acontecer; aparecer; tirar hacia arriba (la nariz).—*to t. upon,* estribar, depender de; recaer sobre.—*s.* vuelta, giro; rodeo; recodo; turno, tanda; lance; ocasión; cambio, mudanza; torcedura; curso, dirección; fase, aspecto, cariz; proceder, procedimiento; partida o pasada (buena o mala) hecha a alguno; inclinación, propensión; giro de frase; vuelta, paseo corto; (teat.) pieza corta; (dep.) contienda, partido; (com.) transacción.—*a friendly t.,* un favor. —*at every t.,* a cada instante.— *to take another t.,* cambiar de aspecto, tomar otro sesgo o cariz.—*to take turns,* turnarse, alternar.

turnbuckle [tœrnbakl], *s.* (mec.) torniquete.—*turncoat* [tœrnkoɥt], *s.* desertor, renegado, tránsfuga.— *turner* [tœrnœ(r)], *s.* (mec.) tornero.

turnip [tœrnɪp], *s.* nabo.

turnover [tœrnoɥvœ(r)], *a.* doblado o vuelto hacia abajo.—*s.* vuelco, voltereta; (com.) movimiento de mercancías; ciclo de compra y venta; cambio (de personal); reorganización; empleo parcial turnado.

turnpike [tœrnpajk], *s.* camino o barrera de portazgo.

turnstile [tǽrnstajl], *s.* torniquete (en una entrada, etc.).—**turntable** [tǽrntejbl], *s.* placa giratoria; platillo del gramófono.

turpentine [tǽrpentajn], *s.* trementina; aguarrás.—*oil of t.*, aguarrás.

turquoise [tǽrkwɔjz], *s.* (min.) turquesa.

turret [tǽrit], *s.* torre(cilla); (fort.) roqueta; (mar. y aer.) torre blindada.

turtle [tǽrtl], *s.* tortuga de mar, carey.—**dove** [-dʌv], *s.* tórtola.

tusk [tʌsk], *s.* colmillo (de elefante, jabalí, etc.).

tussle [tʌsl], *s.* lucha, agarrada.—*vi.* forcejear, tener una agarrada.

tutor [tjútǫ(r)], *s.* tutor, ayo, preceptor; (for.) curador.—*vt.* enseñar, instruir.—**ing** [-iŋ], *s.* instrucción.

tuxedo [tʌksídǫu], *s.* "smoking", traje de media etiqueta.

tweed [twid], *s.* paño de lana de dos colores.—*a.* hecho de este paño.

tweezers [twízœrz], *s. pl.* tenacillas, pinzas.

Twelfth-night [twɛlfθ nájt], *s.* pascua, víspera del día de los Reyes.

twice [twajs], *adv.* dos veces; al doble.

twig [twig], *s.* (bot.) ramita, vástago; varilla.

twilight [twájlajt], *s.* crepúsculo.—*by t.*, entre dos luces.—*a.* oscuro, sombrío.

twin [twin], *s.* y *a.* gemelo, mellizo.

twine [twajn], *vt.* retorcer; enroscar.—*vi.* enroscarse; ensortijarse; caracolear.—*to t. about*, abrazar.—*s.* cuerda, cordel.

twinge [twindʒ], *vt.* y *vi.* causar o sentir un dolor agudo; atormentar; sufrir.—*s.* dolor agudo, punzada; remordimiento.

twinkle [twiŋkl], *vt.* y *vi.* destellar, (hacer) centellear, rutilar, titilar; (hacer) parpadear, pestañear.—*s.* destello, centelleo; pestañeo; guiño, guiñada; momento, instante.

twirl [twœrl], *vt.* y *vi.* (hacer) girar.—*s.* rotación, vuelta; zasgueo.

twist [twist], *vt.* (re)torcer, enroscar, entretejer, enrollar; doblar, doblegar; trenzar; ceñir.—*vi.* enroscarse, torcerse, envolverse; virar; ensortijarse; serpentear, caracolear.—*s.* torsión, torcedura; tirón, sacudida; cordoncillo; peculiaridad; contorsión, quiebro; rosca de pan, pan retorcido; efecto dado a la pelota (en baseball).

twitch [twich], *vt.* tirar o sacudir bruscamente.—*vi.* crisparse.—*s.* tirón, sacudida; contracción espasmódica.—**ing** [twíchiŋ], *s.* tic nervioso.

twitter [twítœ(r)], *vi.* gorjear (pájaros); temblar de agitación.—*s.* gorjeo; inquietud.

twofold [tufóuld], *a.* doble; duplicado;

de dos clases o aspectos.—*adv.* duplicadamente, al doble.

tycoon [tajkún], *s.* (E.U., fam.) magnate industrial.

type [tajp], *s.* tipo.—*vt.* y *vi.* mecanografiar.—**write** [-rajt], *vti.* y *vii.* [10] mecanografiar.—**writer** [tájprajtœ(r)], *s.* máquina de escribir.—**writing** [-rajtiŋ], *s.* mecanografía; trabajo de mecanógrafo.—**written** [tájpritn], *pp.* de TO TYPEWRITE.—*a.* mecanografiado.—**wrote** [tájprǫut], *pret.* de TO TYPEWRITE.

typhoid [tájfǫjd], *a.* (med.) tifoideo.—*s.* fiebre tifoidea.

typhoon [tajfún], *s.* tifón.

typhus [tájfʌs], *s.* (med.) tifus, (Am.) tifo.

typical [típikal], *a.* típico.—**typify** [típifaj], *vti.* [7] representar, ejemplificar, simbolizar.

typist [tájpist], *s.* mecanógrafo.

tyrannical [tirǽnikal], *a.* tiránico, tirano.—**tyranny** [tírani], *s.* tiranía.—**tyrant** [tájrant], *s.* tirano.

U

udder [ʌdœ(r)], *s.* ubre.

ugliness [Áglinjs], *s.* fealdad; fiereza.—**ugly** [Ágli], *a.* feo; repugnante; perverso; fiero; insolente, rudo; peligroso.

ulcer [Álsœ(r)], *s.* úlcera, llaga.—**ate** [-ejt], *vt.* y *vi.* ulcerar(se).

ulterior [Altírjǫ(r)], *a.* ulterior.—**ultimate** [Áltimjt], *a.* último, final; fundamental; primario.

ultrasonic [Altrasánjk], *a.* ultrasónico.—**ultraviolet** [Altravájǫljt], *a.* ultravioleta.

umbilical [Ambílikal], *a.* umbilical; central.

umbrella [Ambrélǎ], *s.* paraguas; sombrilla.

umpire [Ámpajr], *s.* árbitro; arbitrador.—*vt.* y *vi.* arbitrar.

unable [Anéjbl], *a.* inhábil, incapaz, impotente; imposibilitado.—*to be u.*, no poder, serle a uno imposible.

unabridged [Anabrídʒd], *a.* íntegro completo, sin abreviar.

unadulterated [Anadáltœreitjd], *a.* genuino, puro, sin mezcla.

unaffected [AnafÉktjd], *a.* inafectado; franco, natural; impasible.

unanimity [yunanímjtj], *s.* unanimidad.—**unanimous** [yunÉnjmʌs], *a.* unanime.

unanswerable [Anǽnsœrabl], *a.* incontestable, incontrovertible.

unarmed [Anármd], *a.* desarmado, indefenso, inerme.

unassuming [Anasjúmiŋ], *a.* modesto.

unattainable [ʌnatéinəbl], *a.* inasequible, irrealizable.

unattractive [ʌnatréktiv], *a.* desagradable, poco atractivo.

unauthorized [ʌnóθorajzd], *a.* sin autorización.

unavailable [ʌnavéilabl], *a.* inasequible. —**unavailing** [ʌnavéilin], *a.* inútil, vano, infructuoso.

unavoidable [ʌnavóidabl], *a.* inevitable, ineludible.

unaware [ʌnawér], *a.* ignorante o inconsciente de. ajeno a.

unbalanced [ʌnbǽlanst], *a.* desequilibrado; (fam.) chiflado; (com.) no balanceado.

unbearable [ʌnbérabl], *a.* intolerable, insufrible.

unbecoming [ʌnbikʌ́min], *a.* indecoroso; impropio, indigno; que sienta mal (vestido, etc.).

unbending [ʌnbéndiŋ], *a.* inflexible.

unbias(s)ed [ʌnbájast], *a.* imparcial.

unbound [ʌnbáund], *a.* no encuadernado, en rústica; suelto, desatado.

unbreakable [ʌnbréjkabl], *a.* irrompible; impenetrable.—**unbroken** [ʌnbróukn], *a.* intacto, entero; inviolado; continuo; invicto; indómito.

unbutton [ʌnbʌ́tn] *vt.* desabotonar, desabrochar.

uncanny [ʌnkǽni], *a.* misterioso, pavoroso.

unceasing [ʌnsísiŋ], *a.* incesante.— —**ly** [-li], *adv.* sin cesar.

uncertain [ʌnsǽrtan], *a.* incierto; perplejo, indeciso.— —**ty** [-ti], *s.* incertidumbre; (lo) incierto; irresolución; inseguridad.

unchangeable [ʌnchéindʒabl], *a.* inalterable, inmutable; igual.—**unchanged** [ʌnchéindʒd], *a.* inalterado.

uncharitable [ʌnchǽritabl], *a.* no caritativo, duro.

unchastity [ʌnchǽstiti], *s.* incontinencia, impureza.

unchecked [ʌnchékt], *a.* desenfrenado, sin control.

uncivil [ʌnsívil], *a.* incivil, descortés, grosero.— —**ized** [-ajzd], *a.* bárbaro, salvaje.

unclassifiable [ʌnklǽsifajabl], *a.* inclasificable.

uncle [ʌ́ŋkl], *s.* tío.

unclean [ʌnklín], *a.* sucio, desaseado, impuro; obsceno.

unclothe [ʌnklóuð], *vti.* [4] desnudar, quitar la ropa a.

uncoil [ʌnkóil], *vt.* desenrollar.

uncollectable [ʌnkoléktabl], *a.* incobrable.

uncombed [ʌnkóumd], *a.* despeinado.

uncomfortable [ʌnkʌ́mfortabl], *a.* incómodo, molesto; intranquilo; indispuesto, con malestar.

uncommon [ʌnkámon], *a.* poco común, raro, infrecuente.

unconcern [ʌnkonsǽrn], *s.* indiferencia, frialdad.

unconditional [ʌnkondíʃonəl], *a.* absoluto, incondicional; a discreción.

uncongenial [ʌnkondʒínial], *a.* antipático, incompatible.

unconnected [ʌnkonéktid], *a.* inconexo.

unconquerable [ʌnkáŋkœrabl], *a.* invencible, insuperable, inconquistable.

unconscious [ʌnkánʃʌs], *a.* inconsciente; privado, sin conocimiento; que ignora; desconocido, involuntario. —*the u.*, (psic.) lo inconsciente.— —**ness** [-nis], *s.* insensibilidad; inconsciencia.

unconstitutional [ʌnkanstitjúʃonəl], *a.* inconstitucional.— —**ity** [ʌnkanstitjuʃonǽliti], *s.* inconstitucionalidad.

unconventional [ʌnkonvénʃonəl], *a.* despreocupado, informal, libre.

uncork [ʌnkórk], *vt.* descorchar, destapar.

uncouth [ʌnkúθ], *a.* tosco, zafio, grosero.

uncover [ʌnkʌ́vœ(r)], *vt.* destapar, descubrir; desabrigar; poner al descubierto.—*vi.* descubrirse, desabrigarse.

unction [ʌ́ŋkʃon], *s.* unción, ungimiento; untura, untamiento; ungüento; (igl.) extremaunción; fervor; divina gracia; —**unctuous** [ʌ́ŋkchuʌs], *a.* untuoso, craso; zalamero.

uncultivated [ʌnkʌ́ltiveitid], *a.* yermo, inculto; rústico, grosero.

uncultured [ʌnkʌ́lchŭrd], *a.* inculto, ignorante.

uncut [ʌnkʌ́t], *a.* sin cortar; sin tallar, en bruto (gemas).

undamaged [ʌndǽmidʒd], *a.* ileso, indemne.

undaunted [ʌndóntid], *a.* denodado, impávido, intrépido.

undecided [ʌndisájdid], *a.* indeciso; irresoluto.

undecipherable [ʌndisájfœrabl], *a.* indescifrable.

undefinable [ʌndifájnabl], *a.* indefinible.

undeniable [ʌndinájabl], *a.* innegable.

under [ʌ́ndœ(r)], *a.* inferior, de abajo. —*u.-secretary*, subsecretario.—*adv.* debajo; más abajo; menos.—*prep.* debajo de, bajo; so; menos de o que; a; en; en tiempo de, en la época de; conforme a, según.—*to be u. an obligation*, deber favores, estar obligado.—*u. a cloud*, en aprietos. —*u. arms*, bajo las armas.—*u. color of*, so color de.—*u. consideration*, en consideración.—*u. contract*, bajo contrato; conforme al contrato.—*u.*

cover, al abrigo, a cubierto.—*u. fire*, en combate; bajo el fuego del enemigo; (fig.) atacado, criticado, en aprietos.—*u. steam*, al vapor.— *u. way*, en camino, en marcha; andando; principiando.—**brush** [-brʌʃ], *s.* maleza, broza.—**clothes** [-klouðz], **clothing** [-klouðiŋ], *s.* ropa interior.—**dog** [-dɔg], *s.* el que pierde; el más débil.—*the underdogs*, los de abajo.—**estimate** [-éstimeit], *vt.* menospreciar, subestimar.—**fed** [-féd], *a.* malnutrido.—**go** [-góu], *vti.* [10] sufrir, padecer; aguantar, sobrellevar; pasar por, ser sometido a; arrostrar.—**gone** [-gɔn], *pp.* de TO UNDERGO.—**graduate** [-grǽdʒuit], *s.* estudiante universitario no graduado (E.U.); estudiante preuniversitario o de bachillerato.— **ground** [-graund], *a.* subterráneo; secreto.—*u. movement*, organización clandestina de resistencia política o patriótica.—*adv.* bajo tierra; ocultamente.—**grown** [-groun], *a.* de pequeña estatura, de desarrollo incompleto.—**handed** [-héndid], *a.* disimulado, clandestino.—**line** [-láin], *vt.* subrayar.—**lying** [-láiiŋ], *a.* subyacente; fundamental.—**mine** [-máin], *vt.* socavar, minar, zapar; debilitar, arruinar subrepticiamente.— **neath** [-níθ], *adv.* debajo.—*prep.* debajo de, bajo.—**paid** [-péid], *pret.* y *pp.* de TO UNDERPAY.— **underpay** [ʌndœrpéi], *vti.* [10] pagar insuficientemente.—**rate** [-réit], *vt.* menospreciar, desestimar, rebajar. —**undersell** [-sél], *vti.* [10] malbaratar; vender a menor precio que.— **shirt** [-ʃœrt], *s.* camiseta.—**sign** [-sáin], *vt.* su(b)scribir.—*the undersigned*, el que firma, el infrascrito, el suscrito, el abajo firmado.—**sized** [-sáizd], *a.* de tamaño o estatura menor que lo normal.—**skirt** [-skœrt], *s.* enagua(s); refajo, sayuela.—**sold** [-sóuld], *pret.* y *pp.* de TO UNDERSELL.

understand [ʌndœrstǽnd], *vti.* y *vii.* [10] entender, comprender; saber, ser sabedor, hacerse cargo, tener conocimiento de, tener entendido (que); sobrentender.—**able** [-əbl], *a.* comprensible.—**ing** [-iŋ], *s.* entendimiento, inteligencia; modo de ver o entender; comprensión; acuerdo, arreglo; armonía, mutua comprensión. —*a.* entendedor, inteligente, comprensivo.—**understood** [ʌndœrstúd], *pret.* y *pp.* de TO UNDERSTAND. **understudy** [ʌndœrstádi], *s.* (teat.) actor suplente.

undertake [ʌndœrtéik], *vti.* y *vii.* [10] emprender, acometer, intentar;

comprometerse a, responder de, encargarse de.—**undertaken** [ʌndœrtéikn], *pp.* de TO UNDERTAKE.— **r** [ʌndœrtéikœ(r)], *s.* empresario de pompas fúnebres; contratista.— **undertaking** [ʌndœrtéikiŋ], *s.* empresa; contratación; empresa funeraria; (for.) compromiso, promesa; empeño o garantía.—**undertook** [ʌndœrtúk], *pret.* de TO UNDERTAKE. **undertow** [ʌndœrtou], *s.* resaca. **undervalue** [ʌndœrvǽlyu], *vt.* desestimar, menospreciar, despreciar; tasar en menos del valor real.
underwear [ʌndœrwer], *s.* ropa interior.
underwent [ʌndœrwént], *pret.* de TO UNDERGO.
underworld [ʌndœrwœrld], *s.* hampa, vida del vicio, bajos fondos de la sociedad; el mundo terrenal; antípodas; averno, infierno.
undeserved [ʌndizǽrvd], *a.* inmerecido. —**undeserving** [ʌndizǽrviŋ], *a.* indigno.
undesirable [ʌndizáirabl], *a.* indeseable; inconveniente, desventajoso; pernicioso.
undetermined [ʌnditœrmind], *a.* indeterminado.
undeveloped [ʌndivélopt], *a.* no desarrollado, rudimentario; inexplotado.
undid [ʌndíd], *pret.* de TO UNDO.
undignified [ʌndígnifaid], *a.* indecoroso, falto de dignidad.
undisciplined [ʌndísiplind], *a.* indisciplinado; falto de corrección; sin instrucción.
undisturbed [ʌndistœrbd], *a.* imperturbable, impasible; intacto, sin cambio.
undo [ʌndú], *vti.* [10] anular, desvirtuar, contrarrestar; reparar (un daño); arruinar, perder; causar pesadumbre a; deshacer; desatar; (mec.) desmontar.—**undone** [ʌndán], *pp.* de TO UNDO.—*a.* sin hacer; sin terminar; deshecho.—*to be u.*, estar perdido o arruinado.—*to come u.*, deshacerse, desatarse.—*to leave nothing u.*, no dejar nada por hacer.
undoubtedly [ʌndáutidli], *adv.* indudablemente.
undress [ʌndrés], *vt.* desnudar, desvestir; (cir.) desvendar.—*vi.* desnudarse.—*s.* paños menores; ropa de casa.
undue [ʌndú], *a.* indebido, desmedido; ilícito, injusto; (com.) por vencer.
undulate [ʌndjuleit], *vi.* ondular, ondear, fluctuar.—*vt.* hacer ondear. —*a.* [ʌndjulit], ondeado, ondulado.
unduly [ʌndúli], *adv.* indebidamente; irregularmente, ilícitamente.
undying [ʌndáiiŋ], *a.* imperecedero.

unearth [ʌnˈɛrθ], *vt.* desenterrar.

uneasily [ʌnˈiːzili], *adv.* inquietamente; incómodamente, penosamente.—

uneasiness [ʌnˈiːznis], *s.* inquietud, desasosiego, ansiedad; incomodidad, disgusto, malestar.—**uneasy** [ʌnˈiːzi], *a.* inquieto, ansioso; molesto, incómodo; desgarbado; difícil, pesado. —*to be u.*, no tenerlas todas consigo.

uneducated [ʌnˈɛdʒukeitid], *a.* falto de educación, indocto, ignorante.

unemployed [ʌnimplˈɔid], *a.* sin empleo, desocupado, cesante; ocioso.—

unemployment [ʌnimplˈɔimɛnt], *s.* desempleo, desocupación, cesantía, paro forzoso, ociosidad.

unequal [ʌnˈiːkwəl], *a.* desigual, dispar; ineficaz, insuficiente, inferior; desproporcionado; injusto, parcial; falto de uniformidad.—*to be u. to*, no tener fuerzas para, ser incapaz de.

unerring [ʌnˈɛriŋ], *a.* infalible.

uneven [ʌnˈiːvən], *a.* desigual; escabroso; irregular, poco uniforme; non, impar (número).— **-ness** [-nis], *s.* desigualdad; escabrosidad, aspereza; abolladura; desnivel; irregularidad.

unexpected [ʌnikspˈɛktid], *a.* inesperado, impensado; repentino.

unfailing [ʌnˈfeiliŋ], *a.* inagotable; indefectible; seguro, infalible.

unfair [ʌnˈfɛr], *a.* doble, falso, desleal; injusto; (for.) leonino.

unfaithful [ʌnˈfeiθful], *a.* infiel; desleal; inexacto.— **-ness** [-nis], *s.* infidelidad, deslealtad; inexactitud.

unfamiliar [ʌnfəmˈiljə(r)], *a.* poco familiar, poco común; no conocido; poco conocedor.

unfashionable [ʌnfˈæʃənəbl], *a.* pasado de moda.

unfasten [ʌnfˈæsn], *vt.* desatar, desabrochar, desenganchar, desprender; soltar, aflojar, zafar.

unfathomable [ʌnfˈæðəməbl], *a.* insondable; sin fondo; impenetrable.

unfavorable [ʌnfˈeivərəbl], *a.* desfavorable, contrario, adverso.

unfeeling [ʌnfˈiːliŋ], *a.* insensible, impasible, empedernido.

unfit [ʌnfˈit], *a.* inepto, incapaz, incompetente; impropio, inoportuno; inadaptable, inadecuado, inservible.

unfold [ʌnfˈould], *vt.* desplegar, desdoblar, desenvolver, desarrollar, abrir; extender; descifrar, poner en claro; manifestar, explicar.—*vi.* abrirse, desenvolverse, desarrollarse.

unforeseen [ʌnfərsˈiːn], *a.* imprevisto, impensado, inesperado.

unforgettable [ʌnfərgˈɛtəbl], *a.* inolvidable.

unforgivable [ʌnfərgˈivəbl], *a.* imperdonable.

unfortunate [ʌnfˈɔrtʃunit], *a.* desafor-

tunado, infeliz, desventurado; infausto, aciago.—*s.* desventurado, desgraciado.— **-ly** [-li], *adv.* por desgracia.

unfounded [ʌnfˈaundid], *a.* infundado; (for.) improcedente.

unfriendly [ʌnfrˈɛndli], *a.* poco amistoso; hostil, enemigo; desfavorable, perjudicial.—*an u. act*, un acto hostil.

unfurl [ʌnfˈɛrl], *vt.* desplegar, desarrollar, desdoblar, extender.

unfurnished [ʌnfˈɛrniʃt], *a.* desamueblado; desprovisto.

ungrateful [ʌngrˈeitful], *a.* desagradecido, ingrato; desagradable.

unguent [ˈʌŋgwɛnt], *s.* ungüento.

unhappiness [ʌnhˈæpinis], *s.* infelicidad, desgracia, desdicha.—**unhappy** [ʌnhˈæpi], *a.* infeliz, desgraciado, desdichado; infausto, aciago.

unharmed [ʌnhˈɑːrmd], *a.* ileso, incólume, sano y salvo; a salvo, sin daño.

unharness [ʌnhˈɑːrnis], *vt.* desguarnecer, desenganchar.

unhealthy [ʌnhˈɛlθi], *a.* enfermizo, achacoso; insalubre, malsano.

unheard [ʌnhˈɛrd], *a.* que no se ha oído. —*u. of*, inaudito, desconocido.

unhinge [ʌnhˈindʒ], *vt.* desquiciar, sacar de quicio; desequilibrar, trastornar (el juicio).

unhitch [ʌnhˈitʃ], *vt.* descolgar, desatar; desenganchar, desaparejar (bestias).

unhook [ʌnhˈuk], *vt.* desenganchar, desabrochar; descolgar.

unhurt [ʌnhˈɛrt], *a.* ileso, indemne.

uniform [ˈjuːnifɔrm], *a.* uniforme; semejante; acorde; constante.—*s.* uniforme.—*in full u.*, de gran uniforme, de gala.—*vt.* uniformar; hacer uniforme; vestir de uniforme.— **-ity** [juːnifˈɔrmiti], *s.* uniformidad, uniformación.—**unify** [ˈjuːnifai], *vti.* [7] unificar, unir.

unilateral [juːnilˈætərəl], *a.* unilateral.

unimaginable [ʌnimˈædʒinəbl], *a.* inimaginable.

unimportant [ʌnimpˈɔrtənt], *a.* de poca o ninguna importancia, insignificante.

uninhabitable [ʌninhˈæbitəbl], *a.* inhabitable.—**uninhabited** [ʌninhˈæbitid], *a.* deshabitado.

uninjured [ʌnˈindʒurd], *a.* ileso, incólume; sin daño.

unintelligible [ʌnintˈɛlidʒibl], *a.* ininteligible.

unintentional [ʌnintˈɛnʃənəl], *a.* involuntario; no intencional.

union [ˈjuːnjən], *s.* unión; conformidad, concordia; mancomunidad, fusión; (E.U.) las estrellas de la bandera nacional; sindicato, gremio.

unique [juːnˈiːk], *a.* único en su género, original.

unison [ˈjuːnisən], *s.* unisonancia; (fig.)

concordancia, armonía.—*in u.*, todos juntos, a una

unit [yúnịt], *s.* unidad.—*a.* individual; unitario.

Unitarian [yunịtérịan], *a.* y *s.* (igl.) unitario.

unite [yụnáịt], *vt.* unir, reunir; avenir, concordar.—*vi.* unirse; concertarse. —**unity** [yúnịtị], *s.* unidad; unión, concordia; (mat.) la unidad.

universal [yunịvœrsạl], *a.* universal. —**universe** [yúnịvœrs], *s.* universo. —**university** [yunịvœrsịtị], *s.* universidad.—*a.* universitario.

unjust [ʌndžȧst], *a.* injusto.— —**ifiable** [ʌndžȧstịfáịabl], *a.* injustificable.

unkempt [ʌnkémpt], *a.* desgreñado; desaseado; tosco.

unkind [ʌnkáịnd], *a.* duro, brutal, intratable.— —**ness** [-nịs], *s.* dureza, brutalidad, falta de amabilidad.

unknown [ʌnnóụn], *a.* desconocido, ignoto.—*u. quantity*, (mat.) incógnita. —*u. to one*, sin saberlo uno.—*s.* cosa o persona desconocida; (mat.) incógnita.

unless [ʌnlés], *conj.* a menos que, a no ser que, como no sea, no siendo; salvo, con excepción de que, excepto, si no, si no es que.

unlike [ʌnláịk], *a.* diferente, dispar. —*adv.* de otro modo; a diferencia de.— —**ly** [-lị], *adv.* improbablemente.—*a.* inverosímil, improbable, difícil.

unlimited [ʌnlḯmịtịd], *a.* ilimitado; sin restricción.

unload [ʌnlóụd], *vt.* descargar; exonerar, aligerar; (fam., com.) deshacerse de una mercancía.—*vi.* descargar.

unlock [ʌnlák], *vt.* abrir (una cerradura, cerrojo, etc.); dar libre acceso; revelar (secretos).

unlucky [ʌnlȧkị], *a.* de mala suerte; desgraciado; infausto, de mal agüero.

unmanageable [ʌnmǽnịdžạbl], *a.* inmanejable.

unmarried [ʌnmǽrịd], *a.* soltero.

unmerciful [ʌnmœrsịfụl], *a.* inclemente, despiadado; cruel.

unmerited [ʌnmérịtịd], *a.* inmerecido.

unmistakable [ʌnmịstéịkabl], *a.* inequívoco, inconfundible, evidente.

unmoved [ʌnmúvd], *a.* inmovible, fijo; inmutable; inflexible, inexorable.

unnatural [ʌnnǽchụrạl], *a.* forzado, artificial o afectado; contranatural, monstruoso; desnaturalizado.

unnecessary [ʌnnéseserị], *a.* innecesario, inútil, superfluo.

unnoticed [ʌnnóụtịst], *a.* inadvertido.

unoccupied [ʌnákịupaịd], *a.* desocupado o vacante.

unofficial [ʌnọfíšạl], *a.* oficioso, extraoficial.

unorthodox [ʌnórθọdaks], *a.* heterodoxo.

unpack [ʌnpǽk], *vt.* desempaquetar, desembalar.

unpaid [ʌnpéịd], *a.* no pagado o por pagar.

unparalleled [ʌnpǽralẹld], *a.* único, sin igual, sin paralelo.

unpardonable [ʌnpárdọnạbl], *a.* imperdonable.

unpatriotic [ʌnpeịtrịátịk], *a.* antipatriótico.

unpaved [ʌnpéịvd], *a.* sin pavimentar, desempedrado.

unpleasant [ʌnplézạnt], *a.* desagradable.— —**ness** [-nịs], *s.* calidad de desagradable; desagrado o desazón; (fam.) riña, desavenencia.

unpopular [ʌnpápyọlạ(r)], *a.* impopular.— —**ity** [ʌnpapyọlǽrịtị], *s.* impopularidad.

unprecedented [ʌnprésẹdentịd], *a.* sin precedente, inaudito, nunca visto.

unprepared [ʌnprịpérd], *a.* desprevenido, desapercibido.

unprincipled [ʌnprínsịpld], *a.* sin principios, sin conciencia.

unprofitable [ʌnpráfịtạbl], *a.* no lucrativo; inútil, vano.

unprotected [ʌnprọtéktịd], *a.* sin protección, sin defensa.

unpublished [ʌnpáblịšt], *a.* inédito, no publicado.

unqualified [ʌnkwálịfaịd], *a.* inepto; incompetente; sin títulos; sin reservas, incondicional; entero, completo.

unquestionable [ʌnkwéschọnạbl], *a.* incuestionable, indiscutible.

unravel [ʌnrǽvl], *vti.* [2] desenredar, desenmarañar; aclarar; descifrar. —*vii.* desenredarse; desenlazarse.

unreal [ʌnríạl], *a.* irreal, quimérico, ilusorio; inmaterial, incorpóreo; insincero.— —**ity** [ʌnrịǽlịtị], *s.* irrealidad.

unreasonable [ʌnrízọnạbl], *a.* fuera de razón, irrazonable; irracional; exorbitante.—**unreasoning** [ʌnrízọnịŋ], *a.* irracional.

unrecognizable [ʌnrékọgnaịzạbl], *a.* irreconocible; desconocido.

unrefined [ʌnrịfáịnd], *a.* no refinado, impuro, en bruto; inculto, grosero, ordinario.

unreliable [ʌnrịláịabl], *a.* indigno de confianza, informal.

unrepentant [ʌnrịpéntạnt], *a.* impenitente.

unrest [ʌnrést], *s.* inquietud, desasosiego.

unripe [ʌnráịp], *a.* verde, agraz; prematuro.

unrivaled [ʌnráịvạld], *a.* sin rival, sin par.

unroll [ʌnróul], *vt.* desarrollar, desenrollar, desenvolver, desplegar.—*vi.* abrirse, desarrollarse.

unruly [ʌnrúli], *a.* indócil, inmanejable, ingobernable, indómito; revoltoso; levantisco; intratable; desarreglado.

unsafe [ʌnséif], *a.* peligroso, inseguro.

unsalable [ʌnséilabl], *a.* invendible.

unsanitary [ʌnsǽnịteri], *a.* antihigiénico; insalubre.

unsatisfactory [ʌnsætjsfǽktori], *a.* insatisfactorio; malo, inaceptable.

unscrew [ʌnskrú], *vt.* des(a)tornillar, desenroscar.

unscrupulous [ʌnskrúpiulʌs], *a.* sin escrúpulos, desaprensivo.

unseasonable [ʌnsízọnabl], *a.* intempestivo; prematuro; indebido, inconveniente.—*at u. hours,* a deshora. —**unseasoned** [ʌnsízọnd], *a.* sin sazonar, insípido; verde (madera).

unseat [ʌnsít], *vt.* desarzonar; echar abajo (de un puesto).

unselfish [ʌnsélfiʃ], *a.* desinteresado, generoso, abnegado.— **ness** [-nịs], *s.* desinterés, generosidad, abnegación.

unserviceable [ʌnsérvịsabl], *a.* inútil, inservible.

unsettle [ʌnsétl], *vt.* perturbar, trastornar.— **d** [-d], *a.* inestable, variable, inconstante; desarreglado, descompuesto; no establecido, no instalado, sin residencia fija; indeciso; incierto; (com.) por pagar, no liquidado, pendiente; turbio, revuelto; inhabitado, despoblado; lunático.

unshaken [ʌnʃéjkn], *a.* firme, inmovible.

unsheltered [ʌnʃéltœrd], *a.* desamparado, desvalido.—**unsheltering** [ʌnʃéltœrịŋ], *a.* inhospitalario.

unsightly [ʌnsáitli], *a.* feo, repugnante.

unskilled [ʌnskíld], *a.* inexperto.— **unskillful** [ʌnskílful], *a.* inhábil, desmañado.

unsociable [ʌnsóuʃabl], *a.* insociable, huraño.

unsophisticated [ʌnsọfístịkeịtịd], *a.* sencillo, ingenuo.

unsound [ʌnsáund], *a.* defectuoso, erróneo, falso; poco firme, falto de fuerza.

unspeakable [ʌnspíkabl], *a.* indecible, inefable; atroz.

unstable [ʌnstéjbl], *a.* inestable.

unsteady [ʌnstédj], *a.* inestable, inseguro, no firme; vacilante, tambaleante; inconstante, veleidoso.

unsuccessful [ʌnsʌksésful], *a.* infructuoso, sin éxito; desafortunado.

unsuitable [ʌnsjútabl], *a.* inapropiado, inadaptable; incompetente.

unsuspected [ʌnsʌspéktịd], *a* insospechado.—**unsuspecting** [ʌnsʌspéktịŋ], *a.* cándido, confiado.

untamed [ʌntéjmd], *a.* **indómito**, bravío, cerrero.

untaught [ʌntót], *a.* indocto; no enseñado, sin instrucción, ignorante.

unthinkable [ʌnθíŋkabl], *a.* inimaginable.—**unthinking** [ʌnθíŋkịŋ], *a.* descuidado, irreflexivo.

untidy [ʌntájdị], *a.* desaliñado, desarreglado, falto de pulcritud.

untie [ʌntáj], *vt.* desatar, desligar; deshacer (un nudo); aflojar, soltar, zafar.

until [ʌntíl], *prep.* hasta.—*conj.* hasta que.—*not u.,* no antes que.

untimely [ʌntájmlị], *a.* intempestivo, inoportuno, prematuro.—*adv.* intempestivamente; a destiempo, prematuramente.

untiring [ʌntájrịŋ], *a.* infatigable.

untold [ʌntóuld], *a.* nunca dicho; indecible, incalculable.

untouchable [ʌntáchabl], *a.* intocable, intangible.—**untouched** [ʌntácht], *a.* intacto, ileso; insensible, impasible.

untoward [ʌntórd], *a.* adverso, desfavorable.

untrained [ʌntréjnd], *a.* indisciplinado; inexperto, imperito.

untranslatable [ʌntrænsléjtabl], *a.* intraducible.

untried [ʌntrájd], *a.* no probado o ensayado; no experimentado; novel.

untroubled [ʌntrʌ́bld], *a.* no molestado o perturbado; tranquilo; claro, transparente.

untrue [ʌntrú], *a.* falso; mendaz; engañoso.

untruth [ʌntrúθ], *s.* falsedad, mentira; infidelidad.— **ful** [-ful], *a.* falso, mentiroso.

unused [ʌnyúzd], *a.* inusitado, insólito; no usado, nuevo; desacostumbrado. —**unusual** [ʌnyúʒual], *a.* raro, extraordinario, extraño; excepcional; insólito, inusitado; desacostumbrado.

unveil [ʌnvéjl], *vt.* quitar el velo a, revelar, descubrir; inaugurar (un monumento).—*vi.* quitarse el velo, descubrirse.

unwary [ʌnwérị], *a.* incauto, imprudente, irreflexivo.

unwelcome [ʌnwélkʌm], *a.* mal recibido o acogido; desagradable, incómodo, importuno.

unwholesome [ʌnhóulsʌm], *a.* dañino, nocivo, malsano, insalubre.

unwieldy [ʌnwíldị], *a.* pesado, difícil de manejar.

unwilling [ʌnwílịŋ], *a.* renuente.— **ly** [-li], *adv.* de mala gana.— **ness** [-nịs], *s.* mala gana, repugnancia, renuencia.

unwise [ʌnwáiz], *a.* **imprudente**; ignorante.

unwittingly [ʌnwítiŋli], *adv.* sin saber, inconscientemente.

unworthiness [ʌnwɔ́ərðinis], *s.* indignidad, falta de mérito.—**unworthy** [ʌnwɔ́ərði], *a.* indigno, desmerecedor.

unwrap [ʌnrǽp], *vti.* [1] desenvolver.

unwritten [ʌnrítn], *a.* no escrito; en blanco; tradicional.—*u. law,* derecho consuetudinario; derecho natural.

unyielding [ʌnyíldiŋ], *a.* inflexible, inexorable, inconmovible, firme; reacio, terco.

up [ʌp], *a.* que va hacia arriba; levantado (de la cama); empinado; erecto; ascendente (tren, etc.).—*adv.* arriba, hacia arriba, para arriba; en pie, derecho; de pie, levantado; (fam.) bien enterado, competente, a la altura de; llegado, acabado, concluido; enteramente, totalmente, completamente.—*it is all u.,* todo se acabó.—*time is u.,* se ha cumplido el tiempo; ha expirado el plazo; ha llegado la hora.—*to be u. in* u *on,* estar al corriente de, al día de o versado en.—*to be u. to,* ser suficiente o competente para; estar a la altura de; estar haciendo o urdiendo, andar (en travesuras, intrigas, etc.).—*to be u. to one,* (fam.) depender de, ser asunto de, o tocarle a uno.—*u. above,* arriba, más arriba.—*u.-and-doing,* emprendedor, activo.—*u.-and-down,* vertical, de vaivén; (fam.) franco, claro.—*u. to,* hasta; capaz de; tramando; al corriente de, sabedor de.—*u. to date,* hasta la fecha.—*u.-to-date,* moderno, al día.—*what's u.?* ¿qué hay? ¿de qué se trata?—*prep.* hacia arriba de; a lo largo de; en lo alto de.—*u. one's sleeve,* en secreto, para sí.—*vti.* [1] subir, elevar; aumentar (precios, etc.).—*s.* prosperidad.—*ups and downs,* vaivenes, altibajos, vicisitudes.—*interj.* ¡arriba! ¡aúpa!

upbringing [ʌ́pb·iŋiŋ], *s.* crianza, educación.

upheaval [ʌphíval], *s.* solevantamiento, trastorno, cataclismo.

upheld [ʌphéld], *pret.* y *pp.* de TO UPHOLD.

uphill [ʌphíl], *adv.* cuesta arriba.—*a.* ascendente; penoso, dificultoso.

uphold [ʌphóuld], *vti.* [10] sostener, apoyar, defender.

upholster [ʌphóulstœ(r)], *vt.* rellenar y cubrir muebles; tapizar; poner colgaduras, cortinas, etc.— *y* [-i], *s.* tapicería.

upkeep [ʌ́pkip], *s.* conservación, mantenimiento.

uplift [ʌplíft], *vt.* elevar, levantar, alzar.—*s.* [ʌ́plift], levanatamiento, elevación.

upon [ʌpán], *prep.* en, sobre, encima de.

upper [ʌ́pœ(r)], *a.* superior, de encima o de arriba; (más) alto.—*s.* (fam.) litera alta.—*pl.* botines.—*on one's uppers,* (fam.) en aprietos, tronado, sin dinero.

upright [ʌ́prait], *a.* derecho, vertical, recto; probo, honrado.—*s.* montante, pieza vertical; soporte, apoyo.— **—ness** [-nis], *s.* calidad de vertical; rectitud, probidad.

uprising [ʌpráiziŋ], *s.* levantamiento (acto de levantar algo); levantamiento, insurrección; cuesta, pendiente.

uproar [ʌ́pror], *s.* grita, bulla, bullicio, conmoción; (fig.) rugido.— **—ious** [ʌprórias], *a.* ruidoso, tumultuoso; bullanguero.

uproot [ʌprút], *vt.* desarraigar.

upset [ʌpsét], *vti.* [9] trastornar, desbaratar; volcar, derribar; desconcertar, turbar; (mar.) zozobrar.—*vi.* volcarse; (mar.) zozobrar.—*pret.* y *pp.* de TO UPSET.—*a.* trastornado; volcado; turbado; erigido; fijo, determinado.—*u. price,* precio mínimo fijado en una subasta.—*s.* [ʌ́pset], vuelco; trastorno.

upside [ʌ́psaid], *s.* parte superior, lo de arriba.—*u. down,* lo de arriba abajo; al revés, invertido; (fam.) patas arriba; en confusión, trastornado.

upstairs [ʌ́pstérz], *adv.* arriba, en el piso de arriba.—*a.* alto (piso, etc.); de arriba (de las escaleras).

upstart [ʌ́pstart], *a.* y *s.* advenedizo; encumbrado, presuntuoso.

upturn [ʌ́ptœrn], *s.* vuelta hacia arriba; alza.—*vt.* [ʌptœrn], volver hacia arriba; trastornar; volcar.— **—ed** [ʌptœrnd], *a.* respingada (nariz).

upward [ʌ́pwǝrd], *a.* vuelto hacia arriba; ascendente.— **—(s)** [-(z)], *adv.* hacia arriba; más.—*from ten cents u.,* de diez centavos en adelante.

uranium [yuréiniʌm], *s.* uranio.

urban [œ́rbən], *a.* urbano.— **—e** [œrbéin], *a.* fino, cortés.— **—ity** [œrbǽniti], *s.* urbanidad.

urchin [œ́rchin], *s.* rapaz, granuja, pilluelo, golfillo; (zool.) erizo.

urge [œrdʒ], *vt.* urgir, apresurar, apremiar; incitar; acosar; solicitar; recomendar con ahinco.—*vi.* asurarse; estimular; presentar argumentos o pretensiones.—*s.* impulso, estímulo; ganas.— **—ncy** [œ́rdʒənsi], *s.* urgencia.— **—nt** [œ́rdʒənt], *a.* urgente, apremiante.

urinal [yúrinǝl], *s.* urinario.—**urinate** [yúrineit], *vt.* y *vi.* orinar.—**urine** [yúrin], *s.* orina, orines.

urn [œrn], *s.* urna; jarrón.

Uruguayan [yụrọgwéiạn, yụrọgwáiạn], *a.* y *s.* uruguayo.

us [ʌs], *pron.* nos; nosotros.

usage [yúsidʒ], *s.* trato, tratamiento; uso, usanza.—use [yus], *s.* uso; aprovechamiento; aplicación; servicio, utilidad, provecho; necesidad; ocasión de usar; costumbre, uso. —*no u.* (of) *talking*, es inútil discutirlo, eso no tiene discusión; sin duda, es claro que.—*to have no u. for*, no necesitar o no servirse de; (fam.) no tener muy buena opinión de, tener en poco.—*vt.* [yuz], usar, utilizar; hacer uso, servirse de; acostumbrar, soler.—*to u. up*, gastar, consumir, agotar; (fam.) rendir (de cansancio). —*vi.* soler, acostumbrar.—*he used to come every day*, el venía todos los días o acostumbraba venir todos los días.—*the city used to be smaller*, antes la ciudad era más pequeña. —useful [yúsfụl], *a.* útil, provechoso. —usefulness [yúsfụlnịs], *s.* utilidad. —useless [yúslịs], *a.* inútil; ocioso; inservible; inepto.—uselessness [yúslịsnịs], *s.* inutilidad.—user [yúzœ(r)], *s.* el que usa o utiliza; consumidor; comprador.

usher [ʌ́œ(r)], *s.* (teat., etc.) acomodador; ujier.—*vt.* introducir, acomodar, acompañar; anunciar.

usual [yúžụal], *a.* usual, acostumbrado, común.—*as u.*, como de costumbre, como siempre.

usufruct [yúzufrʌkt], *s.* usufructo.

usurer [yúžọrœ(r)], *s.* usurero.— usurious [yužúrịʌs], *a.* usurario.

usurp [yuzœ́rp], *vt.* usurpar; arrogarse.— —er [-œ(r)], *s.* usurpador.

usury [yúžọrị], *s.* usura.

utensil [yuténsịl], *s.* utensilio.—*pl.* útiles.

uterus [yútєrʌs], *s.* útero.

utilitarian [yutịlịtérịạn], *a.* utilitario. —utility [yutịlịtị], *s.* utilidad; servicio.—utilize [yútịlaịz], *vt.* utilizar, hacer uso de, aprovechar.

utmost [ʌ́tmoụst], *a.* extremo, sumo; mayor, más grande; más posible; más distante; último, postrero.—*to the u.*, lo sumo, lo mayor, lo más.—*the u.*, hasta no más.

utter [ʌ́tœ(r)], *a.* total, entero, cabal, completo; absoluto; terminante.—*vt.* proferir, pronunciar; decir, expresar; dar (un grito, etc.); descubrir, publicar, revelar; engañar, defraudar con (moneda falsa); hacer pasar fraudulentamente; emitir, poner en circulación.— —ance [-ạns], *s.* pronunciación; expresión; lenguaje; aserción, declaración.— —ly [-lị], *adv.* completamente, de remate.

uvula [yúvyụlạ̈], *s.* (anat.) campanilla, úvula, galillo.

V

vacancy [véịkạnsị], *s.* vacío; vacante; empleo vacante; local o cuarto desocupado.—vacant [véịkạnt], *a.* vacío, vacante; desocupado; libre. —vacate [véịkeịt], *vt.* evacuar, dejar vacío; desocupar; abandonar; dejar vacante; (for.) anular, rescindir, revocar.—*vi.* salir, irse, marcharse; desalojar; vacar; desocupar.—vacation [veịkéịṣọn], *s.* vacación, asueto; (for.) anulación, revocación.

vaccinate [vǽksịneịt], *vt.* vacunar.— vaccination [vǽksịnéịṣọn], *s.* vacunación, inoculación.—vaccine [vǽksin], *s.* vacuna.

vacillate [vǽsịleịt], *vi.* vacilar.—vacillation [vǽsịléịṣọn], *s.* vacilación.

vacuum [vǽkyụʌm], *s.* vacío.—*a.* de vacío; (mec.) aspirante.—*in a v.*, en el vacío.—*v. cleaner*, aspirador (de polvo), limpiador al vacío.

vagabond [vǽgạband], *a.* vagabundo, errante; fluctuante.—*s.* vago, (fam.) pelafustán.—vagrancy [véịgrạnsị], *s.* vagancia.—vagrant [véịgrạnt], *s.* y *a.* vago, vagabundo.

vague [veịg], *a.* vago, indefinido, impreciso; incierto, dudoso.- —ness [véịgnịs], *s.* vaguedad.

vain [veịn], *a.* vano, vanidoso; inútil; fútil, insustancial.—*in v.*, en vano.

valance [vǽlạns], *s.* cenefa, doselera.

Valencian [vạlénṣịạn], *s.* y *a.* valenciano.

valentine [vǽlạntaịn], *s.* misiva o regalo del día 14 de Feb. (San Valentín); misiva anónima, jocosa o satírica.

valiant [vǽlyạnt], *a.* valiente, valeroso, bravo; (fam.) de puños.

valid [vǽlịd], *a.* válido; valedero.- —ate [-eịt], *vt.* validar.- —ity [vạlídịtị], *s.* validez; fuerza legal.

valise [vạlís], *s.* maleta, valija, saco de viaje.

valley [vǽlị], *s.* valle.

valor [vǽlọr], *s.* valor, valentía, ánimo, fortaleza.- —ous [-ʌs], *a.* valeroso, valiente, intrépido.

valuable [vǽlyụabl], *a.* valioso; precioso, apreciable, preciado.—*s. pl.* joyas u otros objetos de valor.— valuation [vǽlyụéịṣọn], *s.* justiprecio, tasación, valoración.—value [vǽlyụ], *s.* mérito, valor; precio, valuación; aprecio, estimación; (mus.) valor de una nota.—*vt.* tasar, valorar; hacer caso de, tener en mucho; considerar.

valve [vǽlv], *s.* válvula; ventalla; valva.

vamp [vǽmp], *s.* (fam.) sirena, mujer peligrosa.- —ire [vǽmpaịr], *s.*

vampiro; estafador; aventurero (apl. esp. a mujeres).

van [væn], *s.* vehículo (camión, etc.) cubierto para transportar muebles, etc.

vane [vejn], *s.* veleta; aspa (de molino); paleta (de hélice).

vanguard [vǽngard], *s.* vanguardia.

vanilla [vænĵla], *s.* vainilla.

vanish [vǽnĵš], *vi.* desvanecerse, desaparecer, esfumarse.

vanity [vǽnĵtĵ], *s.* vanidad.—*v. box, v. case,* neceser para polvos, etc.

vanquish [vǽŋkwĵš], *vt. y vi.* vencer.

vapor [véjpǫ(r)], *s.* vapor; vaho; hálito.— *—ize* [-ajz], *vt. y vi.* evaporar(se).— *—izer* [-ajzœ(r)], *s.* vaporizador.

variable [vérĵabl], *s. y a.* variable.— **variance** [vérĵans], *s.* variación, cambio; desavenencia, discrepancia. *—to be at v.,* estar en desacuerdo (con).—**variation** [verĵéĵšǫn], *s.* variación; variedad; (gram.) flexión.

varicose [vérĵkous], *a.* varicoso.—*v. vein,* varice, várice.

varied [vérĵd], *a.* variado, vario; alterado, (zool., orn.) abigarrado, multicolor.—**variegated** [vérĵgejtĵd], *a.* abigarrado, jaspeado, veteado; diverso, diversificado.—**variety** [vǫrájetĵ], *s.* variedad, diversidad; surtido; tipo, clase, especie.—*v. show* (teat.) función de variedades.—**various** [vérĵʌs], *a.* varios, algunos, unos cuantos; desemejante, diferente; inconstante; veteado, abigarrado.

varnish [várnĵš], *s.* barniz.—*vt.* barnizar.

vary [vérĵ], *vti. y vii.* [7] variar, cambiar; diversificar(se); desviar(se).

vase [vejs], *s.* jarrón, vaso; florero, búcaro.

vaseline [vǽsǫlin], *s.* vaselina.

vast [væst], *a.* vasto; inmenso.

vat [væt], *s.* tina, tanque, cuba.

vaudeville [vóudvĵl], *s.* función de variedades.

vault [vɔlt], *s.* (arq.) bóveda, cúpula; cueva, bodega, subterráneo; tumba; (igl.) cripta; (fig.) cielo, firmamento; (dep.) volereta, salto con garrocha. *—vt.* (arq.) abovedar, voltear.—*vt. y vi.* (dep.) voltear, saltar (con garrocha o apoyando las manos).

veal [vil], *s.* (carne de) ternera.— *v. cutlet,* chuleta de ternera.

veer [vir], *vi.* desviarse; cambiar (el viento, etc.).—*vt. y vi.* (mar.) virar.

vegetable [védžtabl], *s.* vegetal, planta. *—pl.* verduras, hortalizas, legumbres. *—a.* vegetal; de hortalizas.—**vegetarian** [vedžǫtérĵan], *a. y s.* vegetariano.—**vegetate** [védžǫtejt],

vi. vegetar.—**vegetation** [vedžǫtéĵšǫn], *s.* vegetación.

vehemence [víhĵmǫns], *s.* vehemencia. *—vehement* [víhĵmǫnt], *a.* vehemente, impetuoso, extremoso.

vehicle [víhĵkl], *s.* vehículo; medio; (farm.) excipiente.

veil [vejl], *vt.* velar, cubrir con velo; encubrir, disimular, tapar.—*s.* velo.

vein [vejn], *s.* vena; veta; (fig.) humor, genio.— *—ed* [-d], *a.* venoso; veteado, jaspeado.

vellum [vélʌm], *s.* vitela, pergamino.

velocity [vĵlásĵtĵ], *s.* velocidad.

velum [vílʌm], *s.* cubierta membranosa; velo del paladar.

velvet [vélvĵt], *s.* terciopelo.—*a.* de terciopelo.— *—y* [-ĵ], *a.* aterciopelado.

vender [véndœ(r)], *s.* vendedor ambulante.—**vendor** [véndǫ(r)], *s.* (for.) vendedor, cedente.

veneer [vǫnír], *vt.* enchapar; revestir; ocultar, disfrazar.—*s.* material para enchapar, chapa; capa exterior, apariencia.

venerable [vénǫrabl], *a.* venerable; sagrado; antiguo.—**venerate** [vénǫrejt], *vt.* venerar, reverenciar.—**veneration** [venǫréĵšǫn], *s.* veneración.

venereal [vǫnírĵal], *a.* venéreo.

Venezuelan [venǫzwéĵlǫn], *a. y s.* venezolano.

vengeance [véndžǫns], *s.* venganza. *—with a v.,* con violencia, con toda su alma; con creces, extremadamente. *—vengeful* [véndžfʋl], *a.* vengativo.

venial [vínĵal], *a.* venial; perdonable.

venom [vénǫm], *s.* veneno; rencor, malignidad.— *—ous* [-ʌs], *a.* venenoso; dañoso; maligno.

venous [vínʌs], *a.* venoso; veteado.

vent [vent], *s.* respiradero, abertura, lumbrera; salida, paso; fogón de arma de fuego; (zool.) ano; emisión; desahogo.—*vt.* expresar, desahogar, (fam.) desembuchar.—*to v. one's spleen,* descargar uno la bilis.—**ilate** [véntĵlejt], *vt.* ventilar.— **ilation** [-ĵléĵšǫn], *s.* ventilación.— **ilator** [-ĵlejtǫ(r)], *s.* ventilador.

ventriloquist [ventrílokwĵst], *s.* ventrílocuo.

venture [vénchǫ(r)], *s.* riesgo, ventura, albur; (com.) pacotilla; operación o empresa arriesgada; especulación. *—vt.* arriesgar, aventurar.—*vi.* osar, atreverse; aventurarse, arriesgarse.

veranda [vĵrǽndǫ], *s.* pórtico, soportal, porche, mirador.

verb [vœrb], *s.* verbo.— *—al* [vœrbǫl], *a.* verbal; oral; literal.

verbena [vœrbínǫ], *s.* (bot.) verbena.

verdant [vœrdǫnt], *a.* verde, verdoso; inocente, sencillo.

verdict [vɜ́rdjkt], *s.* veredicto, fallo; opinión, dictamen.

verdigris [vɜ́rdjgris], *s.* verdín.— **verdure** [vɜ́rdʒųr], *s.* verde, verdor; frondas.

verge [vɜrdʒ], *s.* borde, margen; confín; (arq.) fuste; vara, báculo.—*on o upon the v. of,* al borde de; a punto de, al, a dos dedos de.—*vi.* acercarse a, tender.

verify [vérjfai], *vti.* [7] verificar, justificar, constatar, demostrar; cerciorarse de; cumplir (una promesa); (for.) afirmar bajo juramento; acreditar.

veritable [vérjtąbl], *a.* verdadero.— **verity** [vérjtj], *s.* verdad, realidad.

vermin [vɜ́rmjn], *s.* miseria, musaraña; bichos, piojos, chinches, ete.

vernacular [vɜrnékyǫlą̈(r)], *a.* vernáculo, nativo; (med.) local.—*s.* idioma vernáculo.

versatile [vɜ́rsątjl], *a.* versátil, de variados talentos o aptitudes; adaptable; voluble.—**versatility** [vɜrsątíljtj], *s.* versatilidad, adaptabilidad, variedad de talentos; veleidad.

verse [vɜrs], *s.* verso; (igl.) versículo.—**d** [-t], *a.* versado, perito.—**versicle** [vɜ́rsjkl], *s.* versículo.—**versification** [vɜrsjfjkéjṣǫn], *s.* versificación.—**version** [vɜ́rżǫn], *s.* versión; interpretación; (cir.) versión.

versus [vɜ́rsʌs], *prep.* contra.

vertebra [vɜ́rtębrą], *s.* (*pl.* **vertebrae** [vɜ́rtjbri]) vértebra.—**te** [vɜ́rtjbrejt], *a.* y *a.* vertebrado.

vertex [vɜ́rteks], *s.* (*pl.* **vertices** [vɜ́rtjsiz]) vértice; cima, cumbre, cúspide, ápice.

vertical [vɜ́rtjkąl], *a.* vertical.—**ity** [vɜrtjkáljtj], *s.* verticalidad.

vertigo [vɜ́rtjgou], *s.* (med.) vértigo, vahido.

vervain [vɜ́rvejn], *s.* (bot.) verbena.

very [vérj], *a.* mismo, propio, idéntico; verdadero, real; mismísimo.—*for that v. reason,* por lo mismo.—*the v. idea of doing it,* sólo la idea, o la mera idea de hacerlo.—*this v. day,* hoy mismo.—*adv.* muy, mucho, muchísimo.—*v. many,* muchísimos. —*v. much,* mucho, muchísimo; sumamente, muy.—*v. much so,* muy mucho, muchísimo, en sumo grado.

vesicle [vésjkl], *s.* vesícula.

vespers [véspœrz], *s.* vísperas.

vessel [vésęl], *s.* embarcación, barco, buque; vasija, vaso.

vest [vest], *s.* chaleco.—*vt.* investir (de autoridad), conferir; (for.) hacer entrega, dar posesión.—*to v. in,* revestir de, investir de, poner en posesión de.—*to v. with,* (re)vestir de. —*vi.* vestirse; ser válido.

vestibule [véstjbjul], *s.* vestíbulo; zaguán.

vestige [véstjdʒ], *s.* vestigio, huella, señal; reliquia; rudimento.

vestment [véstmęnt], *s.* prenda de vestir; ropa, vestidura; (igl.) vestimenta; sabanilla (de altar).

vestry [véstrj], *s.* vestuario, sacristía; junta que administra los asuntos de una iglesia episcopal protestante.

veteran [vétęrąn], *s.* y *a.* veterano.

veterinarian [vetęrinérjąn], *a.* y *s.* veterinario.

veto [vítou], *vt.* poner el veto; vedar, prohibir; rehusar la aprobación de, vetar.—*s.* veto.

vex [veks], *vt.* disgustar, irritar, enfadar. — **ation** [vekséjṣǫn], *s.* disgusto, irritación, enfado.

via [váją], *prep.* por (la vía de).—*s.* vía.— **duct** [vájądakt], *s.* viaducto.

vial [vájąl], *s.* redoma, frasco, ampolleta, pomo.

viand [vájąnd], *s.* vianda.—*pl.* comida, alimentos, provisiones.

vibrate [vájbrejt], *vt.* y *vi.* vibrar.— **vibration** [vajbréjṣǫn], *s.* vibración.

vice [vajs], *s.* vicio, inmoralidad; defecto, falta; resabio (caballo, etc.). —*prefijo* vice.—*v.-admiral,* vicealmirante.—*v.-president,* vicepresidente.—**roy** [vájsroj], *s.* virrey.

vicinity [visínjtj], *s.* vecindad, cercanía, inmediaciones, alrededores.

vicious [víṣʌs], *a.* vicioso, depravado; defectuoso, imperfecto; (fam.) maligno, rencoroso; dañino.—*v. dog,* perro bravo, que muerde.— **ness** [-njs], *s.* malignidad, depravación.

vicissitude [visísjtjud], *s.* vicisitud.

victim [víktjm], *s.* víctima; (for.) interfecto.

victor [víktǫ(r)], *s.* vencedor, triunfador.—**ious** [vjktórjʌs], *a.* victorioso. — **y** [víktorj], *s.* victoria, triunfo.

victuals [vítąlz], *s. pl.* (fam. o dial.) víveres, provisiones, comestibles.

vie [vaj], *vi.* competir, rivalizar, disputar(se).

view [vju], *vt.* mirar, ver; contemplar; examinar, inspeccionar, reconocer; considerar, especular.—*s.* vista, mirada; inspección; contemplación; visión; escena, panorama, paisaje, perspectiva; alcance de la vista; modo de ver, criterio; opinión, parecer; fase, aspecto; mira, intento, propósito.—*v. finder,* (foto.) visor.— **point** [vjúpǫjnt], *s.* punto de vista.

vigil [vídʒjl], *s.* vela, velación, vigilia, desvelo; vigilancia; (igl.) vigilia.— **ance** [-ąns], *s.* desvelo; vigilancia.— **ant** [-ąnt], *a.* vigilante.

vignette [vjnyét], *s.* (impr., foto.) viñeta; corto bosquejo literario.

vigor [vígọ(r)], *s.* vigor; fuerza, fortaleza; verdor, lozanía.— **—ous** [-ʌs], *a.* vigoroso, fuerte.

vile [vail], *a.* vil, bajo.— **—ness** [váilnịs], *s.* vileza, bajeza.

villa [vílạ̈], *s.* villa, quinta.— **—ge** [vílịdʒ̆], *s.* aldea, pueblo, caserío.— **—ger** [vílịdʒ̆œ(r)], *s.* aldeano.

villain [vílạ̈n], *s.* villano, malvado.— **—ous** [-ʌs], *a.* villano, malvado; asqueroso, repugnante.— **—y** [-i], *s.* villanía, vileza, infamia.

vim [vim], *s.* fuerza, vigor; energía, brío.

vindicate [víndịkeit], *vt.* vindicar.— **vindictive** [vindíktịv], *a.* vengativo.

vine [vain], *s.* (bot.) enredadera; vid, parra.— **—gar** [vínịgạ̈(r)], *s.* vinagre.— **—yard** [vínyạ̈rd], *s.* viña, viñedo. **—vintage** [víntịdʒ̆], *s.* vendimia.— *v.* wine, vino añejo.—**vintner** [vínt-nœ(r)], *s.* vinatero.

violate [vájoleit], *vt.* violar.—**violation** [vajoléịʃọn], *s.* violación.—**violence** [vájolẹns], *s.* violencia.—**violent** [vájolẹnt], *a.* violento.

violet [vájolịt], *s.* (bot.) violeta; color violado.—*a.* violado, violáceo.

violin [vajolín], *s.* violín; violinista.— **—ist** [-ịst], *s.* violinista.—**violoncello** [violanchélou], *s.* violoncelo.

viper [vájpœ(r)], *s.* víbora.— **—ish** [-ịʃ], *a.* viperino.

virgin [vœrdʒịn], *s.* virgen.— **—al** [-ạl], *a.* virginal.— **—ity** [vœrdʒínịti], *s.* virginidad.

virile [víril], *a.* viril.—**virility** [vịrílịti], *s.* virilidad.

virtual [vœrchụạl], *a.* virtual.

virtue [vœrchu], *s.* virtud.—**virtuoso** [vœrchúóṣouy], *s.* (mús.) virtuoso.— **virtuous** [vœrchụʌs], *a.* virtuoso.

virulence [vírọlẹns], *s.* virulencia; malignidad, acrimonia.—**virulent** [vírọlẹnt], *a.* virulento, ponzoñoso; maligno, cáustico.—**virus** [vájrạs], *s.* virus; virulencia, influencia maligna.

visa [víẓạ̈], *s.* visa, visado.

viscera [vísẹrạ̈], *s. pl.* vísceras, entrañas. — **—l** [vísẹrạl], *a.* visceral.

viscosity [vịskásịtị], *s.* viscosidad.

viscount [vájkạunt], *s.* vizconde.— **—ess** [-ịs], *s.* vizcondesa.

viscous [vískʌs], *a.* viscoso, pegajoso.

visibility [vịzịbílịti], *s.* visibilidad.— **visible** [vízịbl], *a.* visible.—**vision** [vízọn], *s.* visión, vista; clarividencia, perspicacia, previsión; fantasma; fantasía; revelación profética; (cine) representación de los pensamientos o sueños de un actor.—**visionary** [vízọnerị], *a.* y *s.* visionario.

visit [vízit], *vt.* visitar; hacer un reconocimiento o registro de.—*vi.*

visitarse; hacer visitas, ir de visita. —*s.* visita, visitación; reconocimiento, registro, inspección.— **—ation** [-éịʃọn], *s.* visitación, visita; inspección, registro, reconocimiento; gracia o castigo del cielo.— **—or** [-ọ(r)], *s.* visitante, visitador.

visor [vájzọ(r)], *s.* visera.

vista [vístạ̈], *s.* vista, perspectiva.

visual [vízụạl], *a.* visual.— **—ization** [vịẓụạlizéịʃọn], *s.* visualización (representación mental).

vital [vájtạl], *a.* vital, fundamental; fatal, mortal.— **—ity** [vajtælịti], *s.* vitalidad, energía vital.— **—ize** [vájtạlaiz], *vt.* vitalizar.

vitamin [vájtạmịn], *s.* vitamina.

vitiate [víʃieit], *vt.* viciar; inficionar, infectar, corromper; (for.) viciar, invalidar.

vitreous [vítrịʌs], *a.* vítreo, vidrioso.

vitriol [vítrịọl], *s.* vitriolo.— **—ic** [vịtrịálịk], *a.* ferozmente mordaz.

vivacious [vịvéịʃạs], *a.* vivo, vivaracho, vivaz.—**vivacity** [vịvǽsịti], *s.* vivacidad, viveza.—**vivid** [vívịd], *a.* vivo, vívido, gráfico; intenso; subido, brillante (color); animado, enérgico, activo.

vocabulary [vokǽbyụleri], *s.* vocabulario, léxico.

vocal [vóụkạl], *a.* vocal (rel. a la voz); oral; vocinglero, voceador.— **—ist** [-ịst], *s.* cantante.— **—ize** [-aịz], *vt.* y *vi.* vocalizar.

vocation [vokéịʃọn], *s.* oficio, profesión; vocación.— **—al** [-ạl], *a.* vocacional; práctico; de artes y oficios.

vogue [voụg], *s.* moda, boga.

voice [vois], *s.* voz; habla, palabra; el que habla en nombre de otro; opinión. —*with one v.*, por unanimidad.—*vt.* decir, expresar; interpretar; hacerse eco de; (mus.) escribir la parte vocal de; hacer sonoro.— **—less** [vójslịs], *a.* mudo; que no tiene voz ni voto; sordo, no sonoro.

void [void], *a.* vacío, desocupado, hueco; vacante; vano, ilusorio; (for.) nulo, inválido.—*v. of,* falto, privado, desprovisto de.—*s.* vacío; claro, laguna.—*vt.* (for.) anular, invalidar; vaciar, evacuar.—*vi.* vaciarse, evacuarse.

volatile [válạtil], *a.* volátil; sutil, fugaz; voluble, pasajero.—**volatilize** [válạtịlaiz], *vt.* y *vi.* volatilizar(se).

volcanic [valkénịk], *a.* volcánico.— **volcano** [valkéịnou], *s.* volcán.

volition [volíʃọn], *s.* voluntad; volición.

volley [válị], *s.* (mil.) descarga cerrada, andanada; salva; (dep.) voleo de la pelota.—*vt.* y *vi.* lanzar una descarga; (dep.) volear.

volt [voụlt], *s.* (elec.) volt, voltio;

(equit.) **vuelta.**— **—age** [vóųltįdž], *s.* voltaje, tensión.

volume [vályųm], *s.* tomo, volumen, obra; volumen, bulto; caudal de río; importe, suma, gran cantidad; (mat. y mus.) volumen; (fis.) masa.— **voluminous** [volįúmínʌs], *a.* voluminoso, abultado; prolijo, copioso.

voluntary [válʌnteri], *a.* voluntario.— *s.* voluntario; cualquier acción voluntaria.— **volunteer** [valʌntȷ̃r], *s.* voluntario.—*vt.* contribuir u ofrecer voluntariamente.—*vi.* ofrecerse o hacer algo; servir como voluntario.

volute [volįút], *s.* (arq.) voluta.

vomit [vámįt], *vt.* y *vi.* vomitar, arrojar. —*s.* vómito; vomitivo, emético.

voracious [voréȷ̃ʌs], *a.* voraz, devorador; rapaz o de rapiña.

vortex [vórteks], *s.* (*pl.* **vortices** [vórtȷ̃siz]) vórtice, vorágine; remolino, torbellino.

vote [voųt], *s.* voto; votación; sufragio. —*vt.* votar por; (fam.) dominar el voto de.—*to v. down*, rechazar por votación.—*vi.* votar, dar voto.— **—r** [vóųtœ(r)], *s.* votante, elector.— **voting** [vóųtįŋ], *s.* votación.

vouch [vaųch], *vt.* atestiguar, certificar, atestar, testificar; garantizar, responder de o por.—*vi.* salir fiador.—*to v. for*, avalar, responder por.— **—er** [váųchœ(r)], *s.* comprobante, recibo, documento justificativo; fiador.—*vt.* atestar, confirmar, certificar.

vow [vaų], *s.* voto, promesa solemne. —*vt.* hacer promesa solemne de, hacer voto de, jurar.—*vi.* hacer un voto.

vowel [váųęl], *s.* (gram.) vocal.—*a.* vocal, vocálico.

voyage [vóįįdž], *s.* viaje marítimo, travesía.—*vi.* viajar por mar.— **—r** [vóįįdžœ(r)], *s.* viajero.

vulcanization [vʌlkąnįzéȷ̃šǫn], *s.* vulcanización.— **vulcanize** [válkąnaįz], *vt.* vulcanizar.

vulgar [válgž(r)], *a.* vulgar, grosero, común; público, generalmente sabido; vernáculo.— **—ity** [vʌlgérįtį], *s.* vulgaridad, grosería.

vulnerable [válnęrąbl], *a.* vulnerable.

vulture [válchų(r)], *s.* buitre.

W

wad [wad], *s.* taco; bolita, pelotilla, rollo (de papeles, billetes de banco, etc.); material para rellenar muebles (guata, etc.); (fam.) dinero, dineral, ahorros.—*vti.* [1] (cost.) acolchar, enguatar; rellenar (muebles, colchones, etc.); (arti.) atacar.

waddle [wádl], *vi.* anadear, contonearse al andar.—*s.* anadeo, contoneo, meneo.

wade [weįd], *vt.* y *vi.* vadear; meterse en agua baja y andar en ella.—*to w. in* o *through*, andar con dificultad (en el lodo, etc.); terminar con dificultad o con tedio.—*to w. into*, (fam.) atacar resueltamente.

wafer [wéįfœ(r)], *s.* oblea; (igl.) hostia; (coc.) barquillo; (farm.) sello.

wag [wæg], *vti.* [1] sacudir, mover o menear ligeramente.—*to w. the tail*, mover la cola o rabo.—*vii.* oscilar, balancearse; ir pasando, deslizarse; (fam.) irse.—*s.* meneo; coleo; movimiento de cabeza; bromista, burlador.

wage [weįdž], *vt.* emprender, sostener; hacer (guerra), dar (batalla).—*s.* (gen. **wages**) salario, paga, jornal.— *w. earner*, jornalero, trabajador; asalariado.

wager [wéįdžœ(r)], *vt.* y *vi.* apostar. —*s.* apuesta.—*to lay a w.*, hacer una apuesta.

wagon [wǽgǫn], *s.* vagón, carro, carretón, carreta, carromato; furgón.

waif [weįf], *s.* niño, animalito u objeto extraviado o abandonado.

wail [weįl], *vt.* y *vi.* deplorar, llorar, lamentar(se).—*s.* lamentación, gemido.

waist [weįst], *s.* (anat.) cintura; talle; cinto, corpiño.— **—coat** [wéįstkoųt, wéskǫt], *s.* chaleco.— **—line** [-laįn], *s.* cintura.

wait [weįt], *vt.* esperar, aguardar.—*vi.* estar aguardando; atender; estar listo; servir; ser criado, sirviente o mozo (de fonda).—*to w. at table*, servir a la mesa.—*to w. for*, esperar. —*to w. on* o *upon*, ir a ver o presentar sus respetos a; servir a; atender a, despachar (en una tienda); (fam.) acompañar.—*s.* espera; (fam.) plantón; demora.—*in w.*, al o en acecho.— **—er** [wéįtœ(r)], *s.* mozo de café o restaurante, camarero.— **—ress** [-rįs], *s.* criada, moza, camarera.

waive [weįv], *vt.* renunciar a; desistir de; diferir, posponer; repudiar.— **—r** [wéįvœ(r)], *s.* renuncia (de un derecho, etc.); repudio.

wake [weįk], *vti.* y *vii.* [5] despertar(se). —*to w. up*, despertar(se), animar(se). —*s.* vel(at)orio; (mar.) estela.—*in the w. of*, tras; inmediatamente después de; a raíz de.— **—ful** [wéįkfųl], *a.* vigilante, en vela; desvelado.— **—n** [-n], *vt.* y *vi.* despertar(se).

wale [weįl], *s.* cardenal, verdugo, verdugón; (tej.) relieve.

walk [wɔk], *vi.* andar, caminar, ir a pie; pasear(se); (equit.) ir al paso; conducirse, portarse.—*to w. away*, irse, marcharse.—*to w. back*, regresar. —*to w. out*, salir, irse; declararse en huelga.—*to w. over*, ir al paso (caballo); (fam.) ganar fácilmente; abusar de.—*to w. up*, subir (a pie); acercarse.—*to w. up and down*, pasearse, ir y venir.—*vt.* hacer andar, (sacar a) pasear; recorrer, andar o pasar de una parte a otra de; andar por; hollar; llevar (un caballo) al paso.—*s.* paseo, caminata; modo de andar; paso del caballo; paseo, alameda; acera; carrera, oficio, empleo, estado, condición; método de vida, conducta, porte.

wall [wɔl], *s.* pared; tabique; muro o tapia; muralla.—*low mud w.*, tapia. —*to drive, push o thrust to the w.*, poner entre la espada y la pared; acosar.—*to go to the w.*, hallarse acosado; verse obligado a ceder; (com.) quebrar.—*vt.* emparedar, tapiar, murar.

wallet [wálit], *s.* cartera; bolsa de cuero; mochila; alforja.

wallflower [wólflauœ(r)], *s.* (bot.) al(h)elí; (fam.) mujer que en un baile "come pavo" o "plancha el asiento".

wallop [wálǫp], *vt.* (fam.) zurrar; vencer decisivamente.—*s.* (fam.) golpe rudo, bofetón; tunda; fuerza.

wallow [wálou], *vi.* revolcarse; chapotear (en el lodo); estar encenagado o sumido en el vicio.—*s.* revolcadura; revolcadero.

walnut [wólnʌt], *s.* (bot.) nuez; nogal.

walrus [wólrəs], *s.* morsa.

waltz [wolts], *vi.* valsar.—*s.* vals.

wan [wan], *a.* pálido, descolorido.

wand [wand], *s.* vara; varilla de virtudes; batuta.

wander [wándœ(r)], *vi.* errar, vagar; delirar; perderse, extraviarse; desviarse, apartarse.—*vt.* recorrer, andar por.— **er** [-œ(r)], *s.* vagabundo; transgresor.

wane [wein], *vi.* menguar, disminuir; decaer.—*s.* disminución; decadencia; menguante (de la luna); (carp.) bisel.

want [want], *vt.* necesitar; querer, desear; pedir con urgencia, exigir. —*vi.* estar necesitado, pasar necesidades; faltar.—*s.* necesidad, carencia; privación, indigencia; exigencia; solicitud, demanda.—*for w. of*, a o por falta de.—*to be in w.*, estar necesitado.— **ing** [wántiŋ], *a.* falto, defectuoso, deficiente; menguado; necesitado, escaso.—*to be w.*, faltar.

wanton [wántǫn], *a.* desenfrenado; protervo; (poét.) retozón, travieso; extravagante; libre; lascivo; desconsiderado; imperdonable; injustificable. —*s.* libertino; ramera; persona frívola.—*vt.* malgastar; echar a perder.—*vi.* retozar; hacer picardías; pasar el tiempo en liviandades.—

—**ness** [-nis], *s.* desenfreno, licencia; retozo.

war [wɔr], *s.* guerra; arte militar.—*a.* de o relativo a la guerra; bélico, marcial.—*vii.* [1] guerrear, estar en guerra.—*to w. on*, hacer la guerra a.

warble [wórbl], *vi.* trinar, gorjear; murmurar (un arroyo).—*s.* gorjeo, trino.— **r** [-œ(r)], *s.* ave cantora.

ward [wɔrd], *vt.* (off) resguardarse de; evitar, parar o desviar (un golpe). —*s.* pupilo o menor en tutela; barriada, barrio o distrito de ciudad; sala, división de hospital, etc.; tutela; protección; defensa, posición defensiva.— **en** [wórdɛn], *s.* custodio, celador, capataz; alcaide, carcelero; conserje; bedel.

wardrobe [wórdroub], *s.* guardarropa, ropero, armario; vestuario, ropa.

warehouse [wérhaus], *s.* almacén, depósito.—*vt.* almacenar.—**wares** [werz], *s. pl.* mercancías, efectos, géneros de comercio.

warfare [wórfer], *s.* guerra; arte militar; operaciones militares; lucha, combate.—**warlike** [wórlaik], *a.* bélico(so), marcial.

warm [wɔrm], *a.* caluroso, caliente, cálido; templado, tibio; acalorado; fogoso, violento; conmovido, apasionado; expresivo; afectuoso; (pint.) que tira a rojo o amarillo; reciente, fresco; (fam.) cercano al objeto buscado; molesto; peligroso.—*to be w.*, tener calor; estar o ser caliente (una cosa); (con por sujeto) hacer calor.—*vt.* calentar; caldear, abrigar; entusiasmar; (fam.) zurrar.—*to w. over o up*, calentar (comida fría). —*vi.* (con up) entusiasmarse; acalorarse; tomar bríos.—*to w. to(ward)*, simpatizar con; cobrar cariño o afición a.— **th** [-θ], *s.* calor (moderado); celo, entusiasmo; cordialidad; enojo.

warn [wɔrn], *vt.* avisar, prevenir, advertir, poner sobre aviso; aconsejar, amonestar; (for.) apercibir.—*vi.* servir de escarmiento.— **ing** [wórniŋ], *s.* aviso, advertencia; escarmiento.—*a.* de alarma.

warp [wɔrp], *s.* torcedura, comba; (tej.) urdimbre; (mar.) remolque, calabrote. —*w. and woof*, (tej.) trama y urdimbre.—*vt.* (re)torcer; encorvar, combar, alabear; prevenir el ánimo; (tej.) urdir; (mar.) remolcar.—*vi.* torcerse; combarse; desviarse, alejarse; (tej.) urdir; (mar.) ir a remolque.

warrant [wárant], *vt.* garantizar; responder por; aseverar, certificar; justificar; autorizar.—*s.* (for.) auto, mandamiento, orden, cédula; autorización, poder; documento justifica-

tivo; testimonio; sanción; motivo,
razón.— —y [-i], *s.* garantía;
seguridad; autorización.

warrior [wório(r)], *s.* guerrero.—
warship [wórṣip], *s.* navío o buque
de guerra.

wart [wort], *s.* verruga.

wartime [wórtaim], *s.* período o tiempo
de guerra.—*a.* relativo a dicho
período; de guerra.—**warworn** [wór-
worn], *a.* agotado por el servicio
militar.

wary [wéri], *a.* cauto, cauteloso,
prudente, precavido, prevenido.—*to
be w. of*, desconfiar de.

was [waz, wʌz], (*1a.* y *3a. pers. sing.*)
pret. de TO BE.

wash [waš], *vt.* lavar; fregar.—*to w.
away, off o out*, lavar, borrar, hacer
desaparecer; quitar lavando; llevarse
(el agua o un golpe de mar).—*vi.*
lavarse; lavar ropa; no perder el color
o no estropearse cuando se lava.—*s.*
lavado, lavadura; ropa lavada o para
lavar; lavatorio; lavazas, agua sucia.
—*w. basin*, palangana.—*w. stand*,
lavabo.—*w. tub*, tina.—*a.* de o para
lavar; lavable.— **—able** [wáṣǎbl], *a.*
lavable.— **—er** [-œ(r)], *s.* máquina de
lavar; lavador; (mec.) arandela.—
w. woman, lavandera.— **—ing** [-iŋ],
s. lavado, lavamiento; ropa lavada;
ropa sucia.—*w. machine*, lavadora,
máquina de lavar.

wasp [wasp], *s.* avispa.—*wasp's nest*,
avispero.

waste [weist], *vt.* malgastar, derrochar,
desperdiciar; gastar, consumir; desolar, talar.—*vi.* gastarse, consumirse;
desgastarse, dañarse.—*to w. away*,
demacrarse, consumirse; ir a menos,
menguar.—*a.* desechado, inútil;
yermo; desolado; arruinado; sobrante.—*to lay w.*, devastar, asolar.
—*s.* despilfarro; decadencia; merma,
pérdida; despojos, desperdicios; erial;
extensión, inmensidad; devastación;
escombros.— **—ful** [wéistful], *a.*
manirroto, pródigo; ruinoso, antieco-
nómico; destructivo.— **—fulness**
[-fulniṣ], *s.* prodigalidad, derroche.

watch [wach], *s.* reloj (de bolsillo);
vela, desvelo o vigilia; velorio;
vigilancia, cuidado, observación;
centinela, vigilante; cuarto, guardia,
turno de servicio.—*to be on the w.*,
estar alerta.—*to keep w. over*, vigilar a.
—*w. charm*, dije.—*wrist w.*, reloj de
pulsera.—*vt.* vigilar, observar; ver,
oír (T.V., radio, etc.); atisbar, espiar;
cuidar, guardar.—*to w. one's step*,
tener cuidado, andarse con tiento.
—*vi.* estar alerta; hacer guardia;
velar.—*to w. for*, esperar; buscar.
—*to w. out for*, tener cuidado con.—

to w. over, guardar, vigilar; velar por;
cuidar de; inspeccionar; estar a cargo
de.—*w. out!* ¡cuidado!— **—ful** [wách-
ful], *a.* despierto, vigilante, observador, que está alerta; desvelado.—
—man [-man], *s.* sereno, guardián.—
—tower [-tauœ(r)], *s.* atalaya;
mirador.— **—word** [-word], *s.* santo
y seña; lema.

water [wótœ(r)], *s.* agua; extensión de
agua (lago, río, etc.); marea; líquido
semejante al agua (lágrimas, etc.).
—*like w.*, en abundancia.—*w. closet*,
inodoro, excusado, retrete.—*w. color*,
acuarela; color para acuarela.—
w.-cooled, enfriado por agua.—
w. front, barrio de los muelles.—
w. main, cañería maestra (de agua).
—*vt.* regar; humedecer, mojar; aguar,
diluir, echar agua a; abrevar; dar
agua a (un barco, locomotora, etc.).
—*vi.* chorrear agua o humedad;
tomar agua (un barco, etc.); beber
agua (los animales).—*my eyes w.*,
me lloran los ojos.—*my mouth waters*,
se me hace la boca agua.— **—cress**
[-kres], *s.* berros.— **—fall** [-fol], *s.*
cascada, catarata, salto de agua.
—**melon** [-melon], *s.* sandía, melón de
agua.— **—proof** [-pruf], *a.* a prueba
de agua, impermeable.—*vt.* imperme-
abilizar.— **—spout** [-spaut], *s.* tromba;
remolino.— **—tight** [-tait], *a.* hermético.— **—way** [-wei], *s.* vía acuática
o fluvial; canal o río navegable.
—**y** [-i], *a.* acuoso, aguado; insípido,
soso; lloroso.

watt [wat], *s.* vatio.

wave [weiv], *s.* ola; onda, ondulación;
movimiento de la mano, ademán;
(tej. y joy.) aguas, visos.—*vt.* y *vi.*
(hacer) ondear o flamear, blandir(se);
ondular (el pelo, etc.); hacer señas o
señales.—*to w. good-bye*, agitar la
mano, el pañuelo, etc. en señal de
despedida.— **—r** [wéivœ(r)], *vi.*
ondear, oscilar; tambalear, balancearse; vacilar, titubear, fluctuar.
—**wavy** [wéivi], *a.* ondeado, rizado;
ondulante.

wax [wæks], *s.* cera; cerumen; parafina.
—*a.* de cera, ceroso; encerado.—*vt.*
encerar; encerotar (hilo).—*vi.* crecer
(la luna); hacerse, ponerse.

way [wei], *s.* vía; camino, senda;
conducto, paso; espacio recorrido;
rumbo, dirección; marcha, andar,
velocidad (de un buque, etc.); modo,
medio, manera; uso, costumbre.—
all the w., en todo el camino; del todo;
hasta el fin.—*a long w. off*, muy lejos.
—*by the w.*, a propósito, ya que viene
al caso; de paso.—*by w. of*, por la vía
de, pasando por; por vía de, a modo
de; a título de.—*every w.*, por todas

partes, de todos lados; de todos modos.—*no w.*, de ningún modo, de ninguna manera.—*on the w.*, de camino, de paso.—*on the w. to*, rumbo a, camino de.—*that w.*, por ahí, por allí; de ese modo, así.—*the other w. around*, al contrario, al revés.—*this w.*, por aquí; así, de este modo.—*to be in the w. of*, impedir, estorbar.—*to give w.*, ceder.—*to have one's (own) w.*, hacer uno lo que quiera; salirse con la suya.—*to make w.*, abrir paso.—*under w.*, en camino, en marcha; empezado, haciéndose.—*w. in*, entrada.—*w. out*, salida.—*w. through*, pasaje.—**waylaid** [wejléjd], *pret. y pp.* de TO WAYLAY.—**waylay** [wejléj], *vti.* [10] estar en acecho para asaltar o robar; asaltar; detener a alguien en su camino.—**-side** [wéjsajd], *s.* orilla o borde del camino.— **-ward** [wéjwǎrd], *a.* descarriado; díscolo, voluntarioso; vacilante.

we [wi], *pron.* nosotros, nosotras.

weak [wik], *a.* débil, enclenque, endeble, flaco; (com.) flojo (precio o mercado). **- -en** [wíkn], *vt.* debilitar; quebrantar; atenuar.—*vi.* debilitarse, flaquear, desfallecer, resentirse.— **-ly** [-lj], *adv.* débilmente.—*a.* enfermizo, achacoso, enclenque.— **-ness** [-njs], *s.* debilidad, debilitamiento; decaimiento; inconsistencia; fragilidad; flaqueza, desliz; (fam.) el flaco, el lado de montar.

wealth [welθ], *s.* riqueza, opulencia; lujo; caudal, abundancia.— **-y** [wélθj], *a.* rico, adinerado, acaudalado.

wean [win], *vt.* destetar; apartar poco a poco (de un hábito, de una amistad, etc.); enajenar el afecto de.

weapon [wépǫn], *s.* arma.—*pl.* medios de defensa (de animales y vegetales); armas.

wear [wer], *vti.* [10] llevar o traer puesto (un traje, etc.), usar, gastar (bigote, sombrero, etc. habitualmente); desgastar, deteriorar.—*to w. away*, gastar o consumir.—*to w. down*, (des)gastar (por rozamiento).—*vti.* gastarse, consumirse; durar, perdurar; pasar, correr (el tiempo).—*to w. away*, decaer; gastarse, consumirse.—*to w. off*, usarse, gastarse; borrarse; desaparecer.—*to w. well*, durar largo tiempo, ser duradero.—*s.* uso, gasto, deterioro; moda, boga; prendas de vestir; durabilidad.—*w. and tear*, uso; desgaste o deterioro natural (debido al uso).— **-iness** [wérjnjs], *s.* lasitud, cansancio; aburrimiento; fastidio.— **-ing** [wérjŋ], *s.* uso; desgaste.

deterioro; pérdida, decaimiento.— *a.* de uso; desgastador; agotador, fatigoso.—*w. apparel*, ropa, prendas de vestir.- **-isome** [wírjsǫm], *a.* fatigoso; tedioso, pesado.—**weary** [wíri], *vti.* [7] cansar, fatigar; hastiar, aburrir, molestar.—*to w. of*, agotar la paciencia.—*vii.* fatigarse, cansarse, aburrirse.—*a.* cansado; aburrido, hastiado; tedioso, fastidioso.

weasel [wízęl], *s.* comadreja.

weather [wéðœ(r)], *s.* tiempo (estado atmosférico).—*pl.* vicisitudes de la suerte.—*it is good (bad) weather*, hace buen (mal) tiempo.—*a.* del tiempo, relativo al tiempo.—*w.-beaten*, curtido por la intemperie.—*w.-bound*, detenido por el mal tiempo.—*w. bureau*, observatorio, oficina metereológica. —*w. forecast(ing)*, predicción o pronóstico del tiempo.—*w.-worn*, deteriorado por la intemperie o por los agentes atmosféricos.—*vt.* aguantar (el temporal); resistir a, sobrevivir (a la adversidad); orear, secar al aire; (mar.) doblar o montar (un cabo). —*to w. out*, vencer (obstáculos).—*vi.* curtirse en la intemperie.

weave [wiv], *vti.* [6] tejer, tramar; entrelazar, entretejer, trenzar; urdir, forjar (cuentos).—*vii.* tejer, trabajar en telar.—*s.* tejido; textura.- **-r** [wívœ(r)], *s.* tejedor; araña tejedora.

web [web], *s.* tela, tejido; bobina o rollo de papel; (orn.) membrana interdigital.—*spider's w.*, tela de araña.— **-bed** [-d], *a.* unido por una telilla o membrana; (orn.) palmípedo.

wed [wed], *vti.* [3] casarse con; casar. —*vii.* casarse.—*pp.* de TO WED.— **wedded** [wédjd], *a.* casado; conyugal. —*w. to*, (fig.) empeñado en, declarado por, aferrado en.— **-ding** [wédjŋ], *s.* boda, nupcias.—*pl.* casamiento; unión, enlace.—*a.* de boda, nupcial; de novia.

wedge [wedž], *s.* cuña, calzo; prisma triangular.—*entering w.*, cuña, entrada, medio de entrar; para abrir brecha.—*vt.* acuñar, meter cuñas, calzar.

wedlock [wédlak], *s.* matrimonio, vínculo matrimonial.

Wednesday [wénzdj], *s.* miércoles.

weed [wid], *s.* maleza, cizaña.—*vt.* desyerbar, arrancar las malas hierbas.

week [wik], *s.* semana.—*to w.-end*, pasar el fin de semana, ir a descansar durante el fin de semana.—*w.-end*, fin de semana.—*w.-ender*, el que sale de vacación durante el fin de semana. —*w. in w. out*, semana tras semana.— **-ly** [wiklj], *a.* semanal.—*adv.* semanalmente, por semana.—*s.* semanario.

weep [wip], *vti.* y *vii.* [10] llorar; lamentar, condolerse de.— **er** [wípœ(r)], *s.* plañidera, lloraduelos; llorón; señal de luto.—*pl.* velo de viuda; festón musgoso pendiente de algunos árboles.— **ing** [-iŋ], *s.* llanto, lloro.—*a.* plañidero llorón.— *w. willow,* sauce llorón.

weevil [wívįl], *s.* gorgojo, gusano del trigo.

weft [weft], *s.* (tej.) trama.

weigh [wej], *vt.* pesar; considerar, reflexionar acerca de.—*to w. anchor,* levar anclas.—*to w. down,* exceder en peso; sobrepujar; sobrecargar, agobiar, oprimir.—*to w. out,* pesar, clasificar por peso.—*vi.* pesar, ser pesado; ser importante.—*to w. down,* hundirse por su propio peso.—*to w. on,* gravar, ser gravoso; levar anclas, hacerse a la vela.— **t** [-t], *vt.* cargar, gravar; aumentar el peso de; poner un peso a.— **s.** peso; pesa; carga, gravamen; lastre; importancia, autoridad.— **ty** [wéjįi], *a.* de peso, pesado; grave, serio, importante.

weird [wįrd], *a.* misterioso, horripilante, sobrenatural, raro, fantástico.

welcome [wélkʌm], *a.* bienvenido; grato, agradable.—*you are w.,* (respuesta a "muchas gracias", etc.) de nada, no hay de que; sea usted bienvenido.—*you are w. to it,* está a su disposición; se lo doy o presto con gusto; (irónico) buen provecho le haga.— **s.** bienvenida, buena acogida. — *vt.* dar la bienvenida a, recibir con agrado.

weld [weld], *vt.* soldar, unir; unificar — *vi.* ser soldable, soldarse.— **s.** soldadura.— **er** [wéldœ(r)], *s.* soldador.— **ing** [-įŋ], *s.* soldadura.

welfare [wélfεr], *s.* bienestar, felicidad; prosperidad; beneficencia.

well [wel], *vi.* manar, brotar, fluir.— **s.** pozo; manantial, ojo de agua; aljibe, cisterna; origen; tintero.—*a.* bueno, en buena salud; salvo, sano; satisfactorio, conveniente; agradable, provechoso, ventajoso.—*it is just as w.,* menos mal.—*w. and good,* bien está, santo y muy bueno.—*w.-being,* bienandanza, felicidad, bienestar.— *w.-doer,* bienhechor.—*w.-doing,* benéfico; beneficencia.—*adv.* bien; muy; favorablemente; suficientemente; convenientemente; con propiedad, razonablemente; en sumo grado. —*as w.,* también.—*as w. as,* tanto como; además de.—*she is w. over forty,* anda por encima de los cuarenta años.—*w.-appointed,* bien provisto; bien equipado.— *w.-bred,* bien criado o educado.— *w.-thought of,* bien mirado.—*w.-timed,*

oportuno.—*w.-to-do,* acomodado.— *w.-worn,* usado, trillado, gastado. —*interj.* ¡vaya, vaya! ¡qué cosa!

Welsh [wεlʃ], *a.* galés.—*s.* idioma galés. — **man** [wεlʃman], *s.* galés.

welt [wεlt], *s.* roncha, verdugón; (cost.) ribete, vivo; (carp.) refuerzo; (fam.) costurón; azotaina, tunda.—*vt.* ribetear; (fam.) azotar levantando ronchas.

wen [wεn], *s.* lobanillo.

went [wεnt], *pret.* de TO GO.

wept [wεpt], *pret.* y *pp.* de TO WEEP.

were [wœr], *pret. sing.* de 2a pers. y *pl.* de *indic.* y *sing.* y *pl.* de *subj.* de TO BE.—*as it w.,* por decirlo así; como si fuese.—*if I w. you,* yo en su caso, si yo fuera usted.—*there w.,* había, hubo.

west [wεst], *s.* oeste, poniente, occidente, ocaso.—*a.* occidental, del oeste.—*W. Indian,* natural de las Antillas inglesas.—*adv.* a o hacia el poniente; hacia el occidente.— **ern** [wéstœrn], *a.* occidental.—*s.* novela o película del oeste o de vaqueros. — **erner** [-œrnœ(r)], *s.* natural o habitante del oeste.— **ward** [-wərd], *a.* que tiende o está al oeste.—*adv.* hacia el oeste.

wet [wet], *a.* mojado; húmedo; lluvioso. —*w. blanket,* aguafiestas.—*w. nurse,* nodriza.—*w. through,* empapado, hecho una sopa.—*s.* humedad; lluvia; antiprohibicionista (enemigo de la Ley Seca en E.U.).—*vti.* [3] mojar, humedecer.—*pret.* y *pp.* de TO WET. — **ness** [wétnįs], *s.* humedad.—

whack [hwæk], *vt.* (fam.) pegar, golpear. —*vi.* dar una tunda; ajustar cuentas; participar de.—*s.* (fam.) golpe; participación; porción; tentativa.

whale [hwejl], *s.* ballena; cachalote; algo enorme, descomunal o de magnífica calidad.—*vi.* dedicarse a la pesca de la ballena.—*vt.* vapulear, dar una tunda.

wharf [hwɔrf], *s.* muelle, (des)embarcadero, descargadero.

what [hwat], *pron., a.* y *adv.* qué; lo que; cuál; cómo; cualquiera.— *he knows w.'s w.,* sabe lo que se trae, sabe cuántas son cinco.—*w. a boy!* ¡qué muchacho!—*w. else?* ¿qué más? —*w. for?* ¿para qué? ¿por qué?—*w. of it?* ¿y qué? ¿y eso qué importa? —*w. people may say,* el qué dirán.— **(so)ever** [hwat(so)évœ(r)], *pron.* cuanto, cualquier cosa que, todo lo que; sea lo que fuere, que sea.—*a.* cualquier(a).—*w. you say,* diga Ud. lo que diga.

wheat [hwit], *s.* trigo.—*w. field,* trigal.

wheedle [hwídl], *vt.* y *vi.* engatusar, hacer zalamerías, halagar.

wheel [hwil], *s.* rueda; rodaja; torno; polea.—*steering w.*, volante (de automóvil); rueda del timón.—*vt.* (hacer) rodar; transportar sobre ruedas; (hacer) girar; poner ruedas. —*vi.* rodar, girar; (fam.) ir en bicicleta.—*to w. about o around*, cambiar de rumbo o de opinión.— **—barrow** [hwílbærou], *s.* carretilla.

whelp [hwelp], *s.* (zool.) cachorro; osezno (de oso).—*vi.* parir (la hembra de animal carnívoro).

when [hwen], *adv. y conj.* cuando, al tiempo que, mientras que; que, en que; en cuanto, así que, tan pronto como; y entonces.—*since w.?* ¿desde cuándo? ¿de cuándo acá?— **—ce** [-s], *adv.* de donde o desde donde, de que o quien; de qué causa; de ahí que, por eso es por lo que; por consiguiente. — **—(so)ever** [-(so)évœ(r)], *adv.* cuando quiera que, siempre que, en cualquier tiempo que sea, todas las veces que.

where [hwer], *adv.* donde, dónde; en donde, por donde; en dónde, por dónde; adonde, adónde.- **—abouts** [hwérabauts], *s.* paradero.—*adv.* donde, donde, en qué lugar.- **—as** [hweræz], *conj.* considerando; por cuanto, visto que, en vista de que, puesto que, siendo así que; mientras que, al paso que.- **—by** [hwerbái], *adv.* por lo cual, como lo cual, por donde, de que; por medio del cual; ¿por qué? ¿cómo?- **—fore** [hwérfor], *adv.* por lo cual; por eso.—*s.* porqué, causa, motivo.- **—in** [hwerín], *adv.* donde, en donde, en lo cual; en qué, (en) dónde.- **—of** [hweráv], *adv.* de lo cual, de (lo) que; cuyo; de qué, de quién.- **—on** [hwerán], *adv.* en que, sobre lo cual, sobre que; en qué.- **—upon** [hwerʌpán], *adv.* sobre lo cual, después de lo cual, con lo cual; entonces; en qué, sobre qué.- **—ver** [hwerévœ(r)], *adv.* dondequiera que o por dondequiera que, adondequiera que.- **—withal** [hwerwiðɔ́l], *adv.* con que, con lo cual, ¿con qué?—*s.* [hwérwiðɔl], dinero necesario.

whet [hwet], *vti.* [1] afilar, amolar; estimular, incitar; aguzar o abrir el apetito.

whether [hwéðœ(r)], *conj.* si; sea, sea que, ora, ya.—*w. you will or not*, que quieras que no quieras, tanto si quieres como si no quieres.

whetstone [hwétstoun], *s.* piedra de afilar, piedra de amolar.

whey [hwei], *s.* suero.

which [hwich], *pron. y a.* qué, cuál; el cual, la cual, lo cual, los cuales, las cuales; que; el que, la que, lo que, los que, las que.—*all of w., all w.*, todo lo cual.—*w. of them?* ¿cuál de ellos? —*w. way?* ¿por dónde? ¿por qué camino?— **—ever** [hwichévœ(r)], *pron. y a.* cualquiera (que); el que.

while [hwail], *s.* rato; lapso o espacio de tiempo.—*a (little) w. ago*, hace poco rato, no hace mucho.—*all this w.*, en todo este tiempo.—*for a w.*, por algún tiempo.—*to be worth w.*, valer la pena.—*conj.* mientras (que), en tanto que, al mismo tiempo que; aun cuando, si bien.—*to w. away*, pasar, entretener el tiempo.

whim [hwim], *s.* antojo, capricho; fantasía.

whimper [hwímpœ(r)], *vi.* sollozar; lloriquear, gimotear.—*vt.* decir lloriqueando.—*s.* quejido, lloriqueo, gimoteo.

whimsical [hwímzikal], *a.* caprichoso, fantástico.

whine [hwain], *vi.* gemir, quejarse, lamentarse; lloriquear, gimotear.—*s.* quejido, lamento; lloriqueo, gimoteo.

whip [hwip], *vti.* [3] azotar, fustigar, flagelar; zurrar; (fam.) vencer, ganar a; batir (leche, huevos, etc.); sobrecoser; envolver (una soga, etc.) con cuerdecilla.—*to w. away*, arrebatar, llevarse.—*to w. in*, meter con violencia; reunir, hacer juntar; mantener juntos.—*to w. off*, ahuyentar a latigazos; quitar de repente; despachar prontamente.— *to w. on*, ponerse rápidamente.— *to w. out*, arrebatar; sacar prontamente.—*to w. up*, coger de repente; preparar en el momento; batir.—*s.* azote; látigo; latigazo; movimiento circular de vaivén.

whir [hwœr], *vti. y vii.* [1] zumbar.—*s.* zumbido; aleteo.— **—l** [-l], *vt. y vi.* girar, rodar, voltejear, remolin(e)ar. —*s.* giro, vuelta, volteo, remolino. **—whirlpool** [hwœrlpul], *s.* vórtice, vorágine, remolino.—**whirlwind** [-wind], *s.* torbellino, remolino de viento.

whisk [hwisk], *s.* escobilla, cepillo; movimiento rápido.—*vt.* cepillar, barrer.—*vi.* menear la cola; marcharse deprisa.

whisker [hwískœ(r)], *s.* pelo de la barba.—*pl.* patillas; barba; bigotes del gato, de la rata, etc.

whiskey [hwíski], *s.* whiskey (bebida alcohólica).

whisper [hwíspœ(r)], *vt. y vi.* cuchichear, secretear; murmurar, susurrar; apuntar, soplar, sugerir.—*s.* cuchicheo, susurro, murmullo.

whistle [hwísl], *vt. y vi.* silbar; chiflar.— *to w. for*, llamar silbando; (fam.) buscar en vano.—*s.* silbo, silbido; silbato, pito; (fam.) gaznate.

whit [hwịt], *s.* ápice, pizca, jota, etc.

white [hwaịt], *a.* blanco; puro, inmaculado.—*w. feather*, (fig.) cobardía o señal de cobardía.—*w. lead*, albayalde.—*w. lie*, mentirilla, mentira blanca o venial.—*w. lily*, azucena.—*w.-livered*, pálido, débil; cobarde.—*w. slavery*, trata de blancas.—*s.* blanco (color); persona blanca; clara del huevo; esclerótica; (impr.) espacio en blanco.- —**n** [hwáịtn], *vt.* y *vi.* blanquear(se), emblanquecer(se).- —**ness** [-nịs], *s.* blancura, albura, albor; palidez; pureza, candor.- —**wash** [-waš], *s.* lechada, blanqueo.—*vt.* (alb.) blanquear, enlucir, encalar, dar lechada a; encubrir (las faltas de alguno).

whitish [hwáịtịš], *a.* blanquecino.

whittle [hwịtl], *vt.* mondar; sacar pedazos (a un trozo de madera); aguzar, sacar punta.—*to w. away* o *down*, cortar o reducir poco a poco.

whiz [hwịz], *vii.* [1] zumbar (por la gran velocidad); (fig.) pasar o ir muy deprisa.—*s.* zumbido (debido a la velocidad); (fam.) fenómeno, persona muy destacada, cosa muy buena.

who [hu], *pron.* quién, quiénes; quien, quienes; que; el, la, los, las que; el, la cual, los, las cuales.—*w. goes there?* ¿quién vive?- —**ever** [huévœ(r)], *pron.* quienquiera que, cualquiera que; quien, el que, la que, etc.

whole [houl], *a.* todo, entero, completo, total; íntegro, intacto; enterizo, continuo; sano; ileso.—*w.-hearted*, sincero; enérgico, activo.—*w.-heartedly*, de todo corazón; con tesón. —*s.* totalidad, todo, conjunto.—*as a w.*, en conjunto.—*on* o *upon the w.*, en conjunto, en general.- —**sale** [hóụlseịl], *a.* y *adv.* (com.) (al) por mayor; en grande.—*s.* venta o comercio (al) por mayor.—*vt.* y *vi.* vender (al) por mayor.- —**some** [-sam], *a.* sano, saludable, salutífero; edificante.—**wholly** [hóụlị], *adv.* totalmente, del todo, por completo.

whom [hum], *pron.* (a) quién. (a) quiénes; (a) quien, (a) quienes; que; al (a la, a los, a las) que; al (a la) cual, a los (a las) cuales.

whoop [hup], *s.* grito; alarido; estertor de la tosferina; chillido del buho. —*vt.* y *vi.* gritar, vocear.—*vi.* respirar ruidosamente (después de un paroxismo de tos).—*to w. it up*, armar una gritería.—*whooping cough*, tosferina, coqueluche.

whore [hor], *s.* prostituta, ramera, puta.

whose [huz], *pron.* cuyo, cuya, cuyos, cuyas; de quien, de quienes; de quién, de quiénes.

why [hwaị], *adv.* ¿por qué? ¿para qué?

¿a qué? por qué, por el cual, etc.— *the reason w.*, la razón por la cual. —*we don't know w.*, no sabemos por qué.—*s.* porqué, causa, razón, motivo.—*interj.* ¡cómo . . .! ¡pero . . .! ¡sí . . .!—*w., I just saw her!* pero sí la acabo de ver!

wick [wịk], *s.* mecha, pabilo, torcida.

wicked [wịkịd], *a.* malo, malvado, inicuo; travieso, picaresco.- —**ness** [-nịs], *s.* maldad, iniquidad.

wicker [wịkœ(r)], *a.* de mimbre, tejido de mimbres.—*s.* mimbre.

wicket [wịkịt], *s.* portillo, postigo, portezuela.

wide [waịd], *a.* ancho, anchuroso; holgado; vasto.—*five inches w.*, cinco pulgadas de ancho.—*adv.* lejos, a gran distancia; anchamente; extensamente; descaminadamente; fuera de lugar o del caso.—*far and w.*, por todas partes.—*w.-open*, abierto de par en par.- —**ly** [wáịdlị], *adv.* lejos, a gran distancia; extensivamente; muy, mucho; ancha u holgadamente. - —**n** [-n], *vt.* ensanchar, extender, ampliar, dilatar.—*vi.* ensancharse, dilatarse.- —**spread** [-spred], *a.* esparcido, diseminado; general, extenso.

widow [wịdou], *s.* viuda.- —**ed** [-d], *a* viudo; enviudado.- —**er** [-œ(r)], *s.* viudo.

width [wịdθ], *s.* anchura, ancho.

wield [wịld], *vt.* esgrimir; manejar; (fig.) empuñar (el cetro); mandar, gobernar.

wife [waịf], *s.* esposa, señora, mujer.

wig [wịg], *s.* peluca.

wiggle [wịgl], *vt.* y *vi.* menear(se) rápidamente; culebrear.—*s.* culebreo; meneo.

wild [waịld], *a.* salvaje, silvestre, selvático, montés; fiero, feroz, bravo; inculto, desierto, despoblado; turbulento, borrascoso; alocado, descabellado; desenfrenado; insensato; impetuoso, violento.—*w. boar*, jabalí. —*w.-goose chase*, empresa quimérica. —*w. oats*, excesos de la juventud.— —**cat** [wáịldkæt], *s.* gato montés; negocio arriesgado; pozo (de petróleo) de exploración; (fam.) locomotora sin vehículos.—*a.* atolondrado, sin fundamento; ilícito, no autorizado. —*w. strike*, huelga repentina, no autorizada por el sindicato.- —**erness** [wịldœrnịs], *s.* desierto, yermo; despoblado, soledad.- —**ness** [wáịldnịs], *s.* escabrosidad, fragosidad; tosquedad; rudeza, ferocidad; travesura; desvarío, locura.

wile [waịl], *vt.* engañar, sonsacar; (fam.) engatusar.—*to w. away*, pasar (el rato).—**s.** ardid, red, superchería, treta, fraude, engaño; astucia.

will [wil], **s.** voluntad; albedrío; decisión; intención; gana, inclinación; precepto, mandato; (for.) testamento. —*vt.* querer; legar.—*vai.* y *v.* defect. [11] (como auxiliar forma el futuro): *h*e *w.* speak, él hablará; (como defectivo se traduce en el presente por 'querer'): *w. you sit*¦ *down?* ¿quiere Ud. sentarse?

willful [wílfụl], **a.** voluntarioso, testarudo; premeditado, voluntario.- • **ness** [-nịs], **s.** testarudez; premeditación.—**willing** [wílịŋ], **a.** gustoso; complaciente; espontáneo. —**willingness** [wílịŋnịs], **s.** buena voluntad, gusto, complacencia.

will-o'-the-wisp [wil ọ δẹ wịsp], **s.** fuego fatuo.

willow [wílou], **s.** sauce.- —**y** [-i], **a.** esbelto, cimbreante.

wilt [wilt], **vt.** marchitar, ajar.—*vi.* agostarse, marchitarse, secarse; (fam.) amansarse; irse con el rabo entre las piernas.

wily [wáili], **a.** astuto, marrullero.

wimple [wímpl], **s.** toca.

win [win], **vti.** y **vii.** [10] ganar, vencer; lograr, conquistar; persuadir, atraer; prevalecer.—*to w. out*, triunfar, salir bien, lograr buen éxito.—**s.** (fam.) victoria.

wince [wịns], **vi.** retroceder, recular; respingar.—**s.** respingo.

winch [wịnch], **s.** montacargas, malacate, cabria, cabrestante; manubrio, cigüeña.

wind [wịnd], **s.** viento, aire; aliento; flatulencia; palabrería.—*pl.* (mús.) instrumentos de viento; los músicos que los tocan.—*between w. and water*, a flor de agua.—*to catch* o *get one's w.*, recobrar el aliento.—*to get w. of*, husmear, descubrir.—*w. aft*, viento en popa.—*vti.* [10] [wạịnd], quitar el resuello; olfatear; devanar, ovillar; enrollar; tejer; (re)torcer; dar cuerda a; manejar, dirigir, gobernar; perseguir, seguir las vueltas o los rodeos de. —*to w. off*, desenrollar.—*to w. out*, desenmarañar, desenredar, salir de un enredo.—*to w. up*, concluir; devanar, ovillar; dar cuerda (a un reloj).—*vii.* enrollar, arrollarse; (con **up**) enroscarse; culebrear; ir con rodeos; insinuarse; (re)torcerse, ensortijarse.—*to w. about*, enrollarse. —*to w. along*, serpentear, culebrear.— **bag** [wíndbæg], **s.** (fam.) charlatán; palabreo vano.- —**fall** [wíndfọl], **s.** fruta caída del árbol; ganga, ganancia inesperada, (fam.) chiripa.—**ing** [wáịndịŋ], **s.** vuelta, revuelta, giro, rodeo; recodo, recoveco, tortuosidad;

combadura; (elec., etc.) arrollamiento; (min.) extracción del mineral.—*w. up*, acto de dar cuerda (a un reloj); liquidación; conclusión, desenlace.—**a.** sinuoso; enrollado; en espiral.- —**lass** [wíndlạs], **s.** torno.- —**mill** [wíndmịl], **s.** molino de viento; (aer.) turbina de aire.

window [wíndou], **s.** ventana; ventanilla; vidriera, escaparate (de tienda). —*w. blind*, persiana, celosía (en el interior); postigo, contraventana, puertaventana (en el exterior).— *w. sill*, antepecho de ventana.— —**pane** [-peịn], **s.** cristal o vidrio de ventana.—**windpipe** [wíndpaịp], **s.** tráquea; gaznate.—**windshield** [wíndsịld], **s.** (aut.) parabrisa(s).—*w. wiper*, limpiavidrios del parabrisas.—**windy** [wíndị], **a.** ventoso; ventiscoso; borrascoso; expuesto al viento; pomposo; flatulento.—*it is w.*, hace viento.

wine [waịn], **s.** vino; color de vino, rojo oscuro.—*w. cellar*, bodega.—*w. skin*, bota o pellejo de vino.

wing [wịŋ], **s.** ala; flanco; lado; aspa (de molino); (teat.) bastidor; bambalina.

wink [wịŋk], **vi.** pestañear, parpadear; guiñar; centellear, dar luz trémula. —*to w. at*, hacer la vista gorda.—**s.** pestañeo, parpadeo; un abrir y cerrar de ojos; guiño, guiñada; siestecita.

winner [wíncẹ(r)], **s.** ganador, vencedor. —**winning** [wíniŋ], **s.** triunfo.—*pl.* ganancias.—**a.** victorioso, triunfante; ganancioso; atractivo; persuasivo.— *w. back*, desquite.—*w. manners*, don de gente.

winsome [wínsʌm], **a.** atractivo, simpático.

winter [wíntcẹ(r)], **s.** invierno.—**a.** hibernal, invernal.—*vi.* invernar.— **wintry** [wíntrị], **a.** invernal; como de invierno.

wipe [waịp], **vt.** limpiar frotando; enjugar; frotar, restregar.—*to w. away*, secar (frotando).—*to w. off*, borrar, cancelar; limpiar, lavar.— *to w. out*, borrar, cancelar, suprimir; destruir, extirpar, aniquilar, exterminar; agotar.

wire [waịr], **s.** alambre; (fam.) telegrama.—*barbed w.*, alambre de púas. —*w. gauze*, *w. screening*, tela metálica. —*w. tapping*, interceptación de mensajes telefónicos o telegráficos.— *vt.* poner alambres; atar con alambre; instalar conductores eléctricos.—*vt.* y *vi.* telegrafiar.- —**less** [wáịrlịs], **s.** radiocomunicación; telégrafo o teléfono sin hilos.—**a.** inalámbrico, sin hilos o alambres; de o por radiocomunicación.—**wiry** [-i], **a.** de alambre; como un alambre; tieso, tenso; flaco pero fuerte.

wisdom [wízdǫm], s. sabiduría, sapiencia; discernimiento, juicio, cordura; prudencia, sentido común; máxima, apotegma.—*w. tooth*, muela del juicio.—**wise** [wajz], a. sabio, docto, erudito; cuerdo, sensato, discreto; atinado; (fam.) vivo, listo.—*the three W. Men*, los tres Reyes Magos.—s. modo, manera.—*in any w.*, de cualquier modo.—*in no w.*, de ningún modo, absolutamente.- —**crack** [wájzkræk], s. (fam.) agudeza, chiste, dicho u observación agudos.—*vi.* (fam.) decir agudezas.

wish [wiš], vt. y vi. desear, querer; hacer votos por; pedir.—*to w. for*, apetecer, ansiar, anhelar, querer, hacer votos por.—s. deseo, anhelo; cosa deseada; voto; súplica.—*to make a w.*, pensar en algo que se desea.— —**bone** [wíšboṇ], s. espoleta de la pechuga de las aves, (fam.) hueso de la suerte.- —**ful** [-fǔl], a. deseoso; ávido, ansioso.

wistful [wístfǔl], a. anhelante, ansioso, ávido; pensativo, triste.

wit [wit], s. rasgo de ingenio, agudeza; ingenio; hombre de ingenio.—*pl.* juicio, sentido, razón; industria.— *to be at one's wits' end*, no saber uno qué hacer o decir; (fam.) perder la chaveta.—*to live by one's wits*, vivir de gorra, ser caballero de industria.

witch [wich], s. bruja; (fam.) mujer encantadora o fascinante; niña traviesa.- —**craft** [wíchkræft], s. brujería; sortilegio; fascinación.

with [wið], prep. con; para con; en compañía de.—*a man w. good sense*, un hombre de juicio.—*that country abounds w. oil*, ese país abunda en petróleo.—*the lady w. the camellias*, la dama de las camelias.—*to part w.*, separarse de.—*to struggle w.*, luchar contra.—*w. all speed*, a toda prisa, a toda velocidad.

withdraw [wiðdró], vti. [10] retirar; apartar, quitar, sacar, privar de; desdecirse de, retractar o retractarse de.—*vii.* retirarse, separarse; irse, salir.- —**al** [-al], s. retiro, retirada; recogida.—**withdrawn** [wiðdrón], pp. de TO WITHDRAW.—**withdrew** [wiðdrú], pret. de TO WITHDRAW

wither [wíðœ(r)], vt. marchitar, ajar, deslucir; debilitar; avergonzar, sonrojar.—*vi.* marchitarse, secarse.

withheld [wiðhéld], pret. y pp. de TO WITHHOLD.—**withhold** [wiðhóǔld], vti. [10] retener; negar, rehusar; apartar; detener, impedir.—*vii.* reprimirse, contenerse.—*to w. one's*

consent, negar la aprobación, no dar el consentimiento.

within [wiðín], prep. dentro de, en lo interior de, en el espacio de; a la distancia de; al alcance de; a poco de; casi a, cerca de.—*w. an inch*, pulgada más o menos; (fig.) a dos dedos (de). —*w. bounds*, a raya.—*w. hearing*, al alcance de la voz.—*adv.* dentro, adentro; dentro de uno; en casa, en la habitación.

without [wiðáut], prep. sin; falto de; fuera de, más allá de.—*to do w.*, pasarse sin, prescindir de.—*adv.* fuera, afuera, por fuera, hacia afuera, de la parte de afuera; exteriormente. —*conj.* (fam.) si no, a menos que.

witness [wítnis], s. testigo; espectador; testimonio.—*in w. whereof*, en fe de lo cual.—*vt.* presenciar; dar fe.

witty [wíti], a. satírico, sarcástico; ingenioso, agudo; gracioso, ocurrente.

wives [wajvz], s. pl. de WIFE.

wizard [wízård], a. hechicero, mágico. —s. hechicero, mago, brujo.- —**ry** [-ri], s. hechicería, magia.

wobble [wábl], vi. balancearse, tambalearse; (fam.) vacilar.—*vt.* hacer tambalear(se) o vacilar.—s. bamboleo, tambaleo.

woe [wou], s. infortunio, miseria, pesar, calamidad.—*w. is me!* ¡desgraciado de mí!

woke [wouk], pret. de TO WAKE.

wolf [wulf], s. lobo; (fam.) mujeriego, libertino.—*to cry w.*, dar falsa alarma. —*w. cub*, lobezno, lobato.—*vt.* (fam.) engullir, devorar.—**wolves** [wulvz], s. pl. de WOLF.

woman [wúmaṇ], s. mujer.—*w. hater*, misógino.—*w. voter*, electora.—*w. writer*, escritora.- —**hood** [-hud], s. estado o condición de mujer adulta; sexo femenino, las mujeres.- —**kind** [-kaind], s. las mujeres; el sexo femenino.- —**ly** [-li], a. mujeril, de mujer, femenino.—*adv.* mujerilmente; femenilmente.

womb [wum], s. útero, matriz; (fig.) madre; caverna; seno, entrañas.

women [wímin], s. pl. de WOMAN.

won [wan], pret. y pp. de TO WIN.

wonder [wándœ(r)], vt. desear saber; sorprenderse, maravillarse de; preguntarse.—*I w. what he means*, ¿qué querrá decir?—*vi.* admirarse. —*to w. at*, extrañar, maravillarse de. —s. admiración; maravilla, portento, milagro; enigma, cosa extraña o inexplicable.—*no w.*, no es extraño, no es mucho.- —**ful** [-fǔl], a. maravilloso, asombroso; admirable, excelente.

wont [want], a. acostumbrado.—*to*

be w., soler, tener la costumbre.—*s.* uso, costumbre, hábito.

won't [woʊnt], *contr.* de WILL NOT.

woo [wu], *vt.* y *vi.* cortejar, galantear, enamorar; pretender a una mujer; solicitar, importunar; esforzarse por obtener (fama, etc.).

wood [wʊd], *s.* madera; leña; madero. —*pl.* bosque, selva, monte.—*a.* de o para madera o para almacenarla, transportarla o labrarla; de monte, que vive o crece en la selva.—*to be out of the woods*, haber puesto una pica en Flandes; estar a salvo.— *w. carving*, talla en madera.—*w. engraving*, grabado en madera.— *w. screw*, tornillo tirafondo.- —cut [wʊdkʌt], *s.* grabado en madera.- —cutter [-kʌtœ(r)], *s.* leñador; grabador en madera.- —ed [-id], *a.* provisto de madera; arbolado; boscoso.- —en [-n], *a.* de palo o madera; grosero, rudo; estúpido, inexpresivo.— —land [-lænd], *s.* arbolado, monte, bosque, selva.—*a.* [-lænd], de bosque, selvático.- —(s)man [-(z)mæn], *s.* leñador, hachero.— —pecker [-pɛkœ(r)], *s.* pájaro carpintero, picaposte, picamaderos.- —work [wœrk], *s.* enmaderamiento, maderaje, maderamen; obra de carpintería; ebanistería.

woof [wuf], *s.* (tej.) trama, textura.

wool [wʊl], *s.* lana; pasa (cabello rizado en el negro).—*a.* lanar; de lana.— *w.-bearing*, lanar.- —(l)en [wʊljɪn], *a.* de lana; lanudo; lanero.—*w. yarn*, estambre.—*s.* paño o tejido de lana. —*pl.* ropa o prendas de lana.- —ly [-i], *a.* lanudo; lanar; de lana; crespo, pasudo (cabello); (b.a.) falto de detalles; aborregado (cielo).

word [wœrd], *s.* palabra; vocablo, voz; aviso, recado, mensaje; noticia(s); santo y seña; voz de mando, orden, mandato.—*pl.* contienda verbal; (mús.) letra (de una canción, etc.).— *by w. of mouth*, de palabra.—*in so many words*, en esas mismas palabras, textualmente; claramente, sin ambages.—*in the words of*, según las palabras de, como dice.—*on my w.*, bajo mi palabra, a fe mía.—*to have a w. with*, hablar con.—*to have words*, (fam.) tener unas palabras, disputar. —*to leave w.*, dejar dicho.—*vt.* expresar; redactar.- —iness [wœrd-jnɪs], *s.* verbosidad.- —ing [-jŋ], *s.* redacción, fraseología; expresión; términos.

wore [wɔr], *pret.* de TO WEAR.

work [wœrk], *vti.* [4] trabajar; laborar; explotar (una mina, etc.); fabricar, elaborar; obrar sobre, influir en; hacer trabajar o funcionar; manipu-

lar; surtir efecto; resolver (un problema).—*to w. one's way through*, abrirse camino por o en; pagar uno con su trabajo los gastos de.—*to w. through*, penetrar; atravesar a fuerza de trabajo.—*vii.* trabajar; funcionar; tener buen éxito, ser eficaz; ir (bien o mal); obrar u operar (un remedio). —*to w. at*, trabajar en; ocuparse en o de.—*to w. down*, bajarse.—*to w. free*, aflojarse o soltarse con el movimiento o el uso.—*to w. loose*, aflojarse, soltarse con el uso.—*to w. out*, tener buen éxito; surtir efecto; resultar.—*s.* trabajo; tarea, empresa; labor; obra; (cost.) labor.—*out of w.*, sin trabajo, cesante.—*(to be) at w.*, (estar) ocupado, trabajando o funcionando.—*to be hard at w.*, estar muy atareado.— —er [wœrkœ(r)], *s.* trabajador, obrero, operario; abeja u hormiga obrera.— —ing [jŋ], *s.* obra, trabajo; funcionamiento; laboreo, explotación; maniobra.—*a.* que trabaja, trabajador; de trabajo; fundamental.—*w. class*, clase obrera.—*w. day*, día de trabajo o laborable; jornada.—*w. theory*, postulado.- —ingman [-jŋmæn], *s.* obrero, jornalero, operario.— —man [-mæn], *s.* trabajador, obrero, operario.— —manship [-mænʃɪp], *s.* hechura, mano de obra; artificio; primor o destreza del artífice.— —shop [-ʃap], *s.* taller, obrador.

world [wœrld], *s.* mundo.—*W. War*, guerra mundial.—*w.-wide*, mundial, global, de alcance mundial.—*w. without end*, para siempre jamás; por los siglos de los siglos.- —ly [wœrldlj], *a.* mundano, mundanal, carnal, terreno, terrenal, terrestre; seglar, profano.—*adv.* mundanamente, profanamente.

worm [wœrm], *s.* gusano; lombriz; oruga; polilla, carcoma; gorgojo.— *w.-eaten*, carcomido, apolillado, picado o comido de gusanos.—*vt.* y *vi.* insinuarse, introducirse o arrastrarse (como un gusano).—*to w. from o out of*, arrancar un secreto; quitar gusanos o lombrices.—*vi.* trabajar u obrar lentamente y por bajo mano.

worn [wɔrn], *pp.* de TO WEAR.—*w.-out*, gastado, raído; estropeado; cansado; agotado.

worry [wœrj], *vti.* y *vii.* [7] preocupar(se), inquietar(se); apurar(se); afligir(se).—*s.* preocupación, inquietud, cuidado, apuro.

worse [wœrs], *a.* peor, más malo; inferior; en peor situación.—*to be w. off*, estar en peores circunstancias, o quedar peor.—*to get w.*, empeorar(se). —*to make o render w.*, empeorar.—

w. and w., de mal en peor; peor que nunca; cada vez peor.—*adv.* peor; menos.—*s.* menoscabo, detrimento; (lo) peor.—*to change for the w.*, empeorar(se).

worship [wǿrśip], *s.* culto, adoración; reverencia, respeto.—*your w.*, usía; vuestra merced.—*vti.* [2] adorar; reverenciar, honrar.—*vii.* adorar; profesar culto o religión.— —(p)per [-œ(r)], *s.* adorador, devoto.

worst [wœrst], *a.* pésimo, malísimo.— *the w.*, el, o la, o lo peor.—*adv.* del peor modo posible; pésimamente.—*vt.* vencer, rendir o derrotar a; triunfar de.

worsted [wústjd], *s.* estambre.

worth [wœrθ], *s.* mérito; consideración, importancia; valor, valía; monta, precio; nobleza, excelencia, dignidad. —*a.* que vale o posee; equivalente a; de precio o valor de; digno de, que vale la pena de.—*to be w.*, valer, costar; merecer; tener.—*to be w. -while*, valer la pena.— —less [wǿrθljs], *a.* inútil, inservible; sin valor; indigno, despreciable.— —y [wǿrðj], *a.* digno; apreciable, benemérito; merecedor.

would [wųd], *vai., pret.* de WILL (forma el modo condicional): *she said she w. come*, dijo que vendría.—*v. defect., pret.* de WILL.—*w. you sit down?* ¿querría Ud. sentarse?

wound [wąund], *pret. y pp.* de TO WIND (devanar).—*s.* [wund] herida; llaga, lesión; ofensa, golpe, daño.—*vt. y vi.* herir, lesionar, llagar, lastimar; ofender, agraviar.

wove [wouv], *pret. y pp.* de TO WEAVE. —woven [wóuvn], *pp.* de TO WEAVE.

wrangle [ræŋgl], *vi.* reñir; disputar.—*s.* pendencia, riña; disputa, altercado.

wrap [ræp], *vti.* [3] arrollar o enrollar; envolver.—*to w. up*, arrollar; envolver; arropar; embozar; cubrir, ocultar.—*vii.* arrollarse; envolverse. —*to w. up (in)*, envolverse (en).—*s.* bata; abrigo.—*pl.* abrigos y mantas (de viaje, etc.).— —per [ræpœ(r)], *s.* envoltura, cubierta; faja de periódicos; bata, peinador; pañal de niño.— —ping [ræpiŋ], *a.* de envolver, de estraza (papel).—*s.* envoltura, cubierta.

wrath [ræθ], *s.* ira, cólera.— —ful [ræθful], *a.* airado, colérico.

wreath [riθ], *s.* corona, guirnalda; festón; trenza; espiral.— —e [rið], *vt.* enroscar, entrelazar, tejer (coronas o guirnaldas); ceñir, rodear.—*vi.* enroscarse, ensortijarse.

wreck [rek], *s.* naufragio; destrozo, destrucción; buque naufragado, barco perdido; restos de un naufragio.—*vt.*

hacer naufragar; arruinar, echar a pique; demoler, desbaratar.—*vi.* naufragar, zozobrar, irse a pique; fracasar.

wrench [rench], *vt.* arrancar, arrebatar; (re)torcer; dislocar, sacar de quicio. —*to w. one's foot*, torcerse el pie.—*s.* arranque, tirón; torcedura; (mec.) llave de tuercas.—*monkey w.*, llave inglesa.

wrestle [résl], *vt.* luchar con; forcejear contra.—*vi.* luchar a brazo partido; esforzarse; disputar.— —r [réslœ(r)], *s.* luchador.—wrestling [résljŋ], *s.* (dep.) lucha grecorromana; lucha a brazo partido.

wretch [rech], *s.* infeliz, desventurado, miserable; ente vil, despreciable.— —ed [réchjd], *a.* infeliz, miserable; calamitoso; vil, despreciable; perverso; mezquino; malísimo, detestable.—wretchedness [réchjdnjs], *s.* miseria; desgracia; vileza.

wriggle [rígl], *vt.* menear, retorcer, hacer colear.—*vi.* colear, culebrear, undular; retorcerse.

wring [riŋ], *vti.* [10] torcer, retorcer; arrancar; estrujar, exprimir, escurrir; forzar; atormentar, aquejar.—*to w. out*, exprimir.

wrinkle [ríŋkl], *s.* arruga; surco, buche; (fam.) capricho, maña; artificio; idea, ocurrencia; indicio, insinuación.—*vt.* arrugar, fruncir.—*to w. up*, arrugar, plegar.—*vi.* arrugarse; encarrujarse.

wrist [rjst], *s.* (anat.) muñeca; (mec.) muñón.—*w. watch*, reloj de pulsera.

writ [rjt], *s.* (for.) escrito, orden, auto, mandamiento, decreto judicial.— Holy W., Sagrada Escritura.

write [rajt], *vti.* [10] escribir; describir. —*to w. after*, copiar de.—*to w. a good hand*, hacer o tener buena letra.— *to w. off*, (com.) cancelar, saldar. —*to w. out*, redactar; copiar, transcribir; escribir completo (sin abreviar).—*to w. up*, narrar, relatar; describir; (fam.) ensalzar por escrito; (com.) poner al día (el libro mayor); valorar en demasía una partida del activo.—*vii.* escribir, tener correspondencia; ser escritor o autor. —*to w. back*, contestar a una carta. —*to w. on*, continuar escribiendo; escribir acerca de.— —r [rájtœ(r)], *s.* escritor; literato, hombre de letras, autor.

writhe [rajð], *vt.* (re)torcer.—*vi.* retorcerse; contorcerse (por algún dolor).—writhing [rájðjŋ], *s.* retorcimiento, contorsión.

writing [rájtjŋ], *s.* escritura; letra; escrito; (el arte de) escribir.—*a.* de o para escribir.—*at the present w. o at this w.*, al tiempo que esto se escribe, ahora mismo.—(to put) in w., (poner) por escrito.—w. desk, escritorio.— w. pad, block de papel.—written [rítn], pp. de TO WRITE.

wreng [roŋ], s. injusticia, sinrazón, agravio; mal, daño, perjuicio; culpa; error; falsedad.—to be in the w., no tener razón.—to do w., obrar o hacer mal; hacer daño, perjudicar.—a. erróneo, desacertado; injusto; censurable; falso; irregular; equivocado; inconveniente; mal hecho, mal escrito, etc.—he took the w. book, cogió el libro que no era, o se equivocó de libro.—adv. mal, sin razón o causa; injustamente; al revés.—vt. causar perjuicio a; hacer mal a; ofender; agraviar; ser injusto con.

wrote [rout], pret. de TO WRITE.

wrought [rot], pret. y pp. de TO WORK. —a. forjado, labrado, trabajado.— w. iron, hierro forjado.—w.-up, (sobre)excitado, perturbado.

wrung [rʌŋ], pret. y pp. de TO WRING.

wry [rai], a. torcido, doblado, sesg(ad)o; pervertido, tergiversado.—w. face, gesto, visaje, mueca, mohín.

X

Xmas [krísmas], s. = CHRISTMAS.

X-rays [éks reiz], s. pl. rayos X, catódicos o Roentgen.

xylophone [záilofoun], s. xilófono; (Am.) especie de marimba.

Y

yacht [yat], s. yate.

Yankee [yǽŋki], a. y s. (fam.) yanqui (natural del Norte de los EE.UU.).

yard [yard], s. corral; patio; cercado; yarda (medida). Ver Tabla.— stick [yárdstik], s. yarda graduada de medir; patrón, modelo; criterio.

yarn [yarn], s. hilaza; hilo, hilado; estambre; (fam.) cuento chino, historia inverosímil.

yaw [yo], vi. y vt. (mar.) guiñar.—s. guiñada.

yawn [yon], vi. bostezar; quedarse con la boca abierta; anhelar; abrirse.—s. bostezo; abrimiento; abertura.

yea [yei], adv. sí, ciertamente; y aún, más aún, no solamente.—y. or nay, sí o no.—s. sí, voto afirmativo.— the yeas and nays, los votos en pro y en contra.

year [yir], s. año.—pl. años, edad; vejez.— book [yírbuk], s. anuario.— ly [-li], a. anual.—adv. anualmente; una vez al año; al año.

yearn [yœrn], vi. anhelar.—to y. for, suspirar por.— ing [yœrniŋ], s. anhelo.

yeast [yist], s. levadura, fermento.

yell [yel], vt. y vi. dar alaridos, vociferar; decir a gritos.—s. alarido, grito, aullido; grito salvaje o de guerra.

yellow [yélou], a. amarillo; sensacional, escandaloso (periódico, etc.); (fam.) cobarde, gallina.—y. fever, fiebre amarilla.—s. amarillo (color).—vi. ponerse amarillo, amarillear.- —ish [-iš], a. amarillento.

yelp [yelp], vi. (re)gañir (el perro).—s. gañido.

yeoman [yóuman], s. (pl. yeomen [yóumen]), (mar.) pañolero; (E.U.) subalterno de marina.—y. service, servicio leal o notable.

yes [yes], adv. sí.—y. indeed, sí por cierto, ya lo creo.—s. respuesta afirmativa o favorable.—y. man, hombre servil, que obedece ciegamente.

yesterday [yéstœrdi], s. y adv. ayer.— yesteryear [yéstœryir], adv. antaño.

yet [yet], conj. con todo, sin embargo, no obstante; mas, pero, empero; aun así.—adv. aún, todavía, hasta ahora; a lo menos; más, además, más que. —as y., hasta ahora, hasta aquí, todavía.—not y., todavía no, aún no.

yield [yild], vt. producir; redituar, rentar, dar, dejar; dar de sí, ceder; condescender; devolver, restituir; admitir, pasar por, conceder; otorgar. —to y. up, ceder, entregar; devolver; abandonar.—vi. producir; dar utilidad; ceder, someterse; consentir; flaquear.

yoke [youk], s. yugo.—pl. yunta de bueyes; pareja de animales de tiro. —vt. uncir; acoplar, unir.

yolk [youk], s. yema (de huevo).

yonder [yándœ(r)], adv. allí, allá, acullá.—a. aquel, aquella, aquellos, aquellas.

yore [yor], s.—in days of y., de otro tiempo; de antaño.

you [yu], pron. tú, usted, vosotros, ustedes; te, a ti, le, la, a usted, os, a vosotros, les, a ustedes; se, uno.

young [yʌŋ], a. joven; nuevo; tierno; fresco, reciente.—y. fellow, joven, mozo.—y. lady, muchacha, señorita, jovencita (joven).—y. man, muchacho, joven.—s. hijuelos, la cría de los animales.- —ster [yʌ́ŋstœ(r)], s. jovencito, mozalbete; niño, chiquillo, pequeñuelo.

your [yur], a. tu(s), vuestro(s), vuestra(s); su(s), de usted(es).- —s [-z], pron. el tuyo, la tuya, los tuyos, las tuyas; el vuestro, etc.; el, la, lo, los o las de usted(es); el suyo, etc.— y. affectionately, su afectísimo.- —self [-sélf], pron. tú mismo, tú misma; usted mismo, usted misma.- —selves

[-sélvz]. *s. pl.* vosotros, vosotras o ustedes mismos (mismas).

youth [yuθ], *s.* juventud. mocedad; mozalbete, joven; la juventud. los jóvenes.— **—ful** [yúθful]. *a.* juvenil; joven, mozo; fresco, vigoroso; juguetón.—*y. exploits,* mocedades.

Yugoslav [yúgosláv], *s.* yugoeslavo.— **—ian** [-iạn],— **—ic** [-ik], *a.* yugoeslavo.

Yuletide [yúltạid], *s.* Pascua de Navidad, natividad.

Z

zany [zéịnị], *a.* y *s.* cómico, bufo.

zeal [zil], *s.* celo, fervor, ahinco.— **—ot** [zélọt], *s.* entusiasta, fanático.— **—ous** [zélʌs], *a.* entusiasta, fervoroso.

zebra [zíbrạ], *s.* cebra.

zebu [zíbju], *s.* cebú.

zenith [zínịθ], *s.* cenit; (fig.) apogeo.

zephyr [zéfœ(r)], *s.* céfiro.

zero [zírọụ], *s.* cero.

zest [zεst], *s.* deleite, gusto; gusto, sabor.—*vt.* dar gusto o sabor.

zinc [zịŋk], *s.* cinc o zinc.

zipper [zípœ(r)], *s.* cierre de cremallera, automático o relámpago.

zodiac [zóụdjæk], *s.* zodíaco.

zone [zoụn], *s.* zona; distrito, sección, territorio; banda circular, faja.—*vt.* dividir en zonas o secciones.

zoo [zu], *s.* jardín o parque zoológico.— **—logic(al)** [zoụoládžịk(ạl)], *a.* zoológico.— **—logist** [zoụálodžịst], *s.* zoólogo.— **—logy** [zoụálodžị], *s.* zoología.

NOMBRES GEOGRAFICOS QUE DIFIEREN EN ESPAÑOL Y EN INGLES

A

Abyssinia [æbisíniǝ], Abisinia.
Adriatic [eidriǽtik], Adriático.
Ægean [idžíǝn], Egeo.
Afghanistan [æfgǽnistæn], Afgandistán.
Africa [ǽfrikǝ], Africa.
Alexandria [ælegzǽndriǝ], Alejandría.
Algeria [ældžíriǝ], Argelia.
Algiers [ældžírz], Argel.
Alps [ælps], Alpes.
Alsace-Lorraine [ælséis o ælsǽs / loréin], Alsacia Y Lorena.
Amazon [ǽmǝzan], (Río de las) Amazonas.
America [ǝmérikǝ], América.
Andalusia [ændǝlúžǝ], Andalucía.
Antilles [æntíliz], Antillas.
Antwerp [ǽntwœrp], Amberes.
Apennines [ǽpenainz], Apeninos.
Appalachians [æpǝléchiǝnz], (Montañas) Apalaches.
Asia Minor [éižǝ / máinǝ(r)], Asia Menor.
Assyria [ǝsíriǝ], Asiria.
Athens [ǽθinz], Atenas.
Atlantic [ætlǽntik], Atlántico.

B

Babylon [bǽbilǝn], Babilonia.
Balearic Islands [bæliǽrik], Islas Baleares.
Balkans [bólkǝnz], Balcanes.
Baltic [bóltik], Báltico.
Barbary [bárbǝri], Berbería.
Basel [bázǝl], Basilea.
Bavaria [bǝvériǝ], Baviera.
Belgium [béldž(j)ʌm], Bélgica.
Belgrade [belgréid], Belgrado.
Belize [belíz], Belice, Beliza.
Berlin [bœrlín], Berlín.
Bern [bœrn], Berna.
Bethlehem [béθli(h)em], Belén.
Biscay [bískei], Vizcaya.
Black Sea, Mar Negro.
Bologna [boulóunyǝ], Bolonia.
Bonn [ban], Bona.
Bordeaux [bordóu], Burdeos.
Bosporus [básporʌs], Bósforo.
Brazil [brǝzíl], Brasil.
Bretagne [bretány], **Brittany** [brítni], Bretaña.
British Columbia [brítiš kolʌ́mbiǝ], Columbia Británica.
British Honduras [handúrǝs], Belice, Honduras Británicas.
British Isles, Islas Británicas.
Brussels [brʌ́sǝlz], Bruselas.
Bucharest [bjukarést], Bucarest.
Burgundy [bǽrgǝndi], Borgoña.
Burma [bœ́rmǝ], Birmania.
Byzantium [bizǽnšiʌm], Bizancio.

C

Calcutta [kælkʌ́tǝ], Calcuta.
Cameroons [kæmǝrúnz], Camerún, Kamerún.

Canada

Canada [kǽnǝdǝ], Canadá.
Canary Islands, Canarias.
Cape Horn, Cabo de Hornos.
Cape of Good Hope, Cabo de Buena Esperanza.
Caribbean [kæribíǝn, kǝríbiǝn], Caribe.
Carthage [kárθidž], Cartago.
Caspian [kǽspiǝn], Caspio.
Castile [kæstíl], Castilla.
Catalonia [kætǝlóuniǝ], Cataluña.
Caucasus [kókǝsʌs], Cáucaso.
Cayenne [kaién, kaién], Cayena.
Ceylon [silán], Ceilán.
Chaldea [kældíǝ], Caldea.
Champagne [šæmpéin], Champaña.
Cologne [kǝlóun], Colonia.
Constantinople [kanstæntinóupl], Constantinopla.
Copenhagen [koupǝnhéigǝn], Copen(h)ague.
Corinth [kǝrínθ], Corinto.
Corsica [kórsikǝ], Córcega.
Crete [krit], Creta.
Croatia [kroéišǝ], Croacia.
Curaçao [kyurǝsóu], Curazao.
Cyprus [sáiprʌs], Chipre.
Czechoslovakia [chekoslovǽkiǝ], Checoslovaquia.

D

Dalmatia [dælméišǝ], Dalmacia.
Damascus [dǝmǽskʌs], Damasco.
Danube [dǽnjub], Danubio.
Dardanelles [dardǝnélz], Dardanelos.
Dead Sea, Mar Muerto.
Delphi [délfai], Delfos.
Denmark [dénmark], Dinamarca.
Douro River [dóury], Duero (Río).
Dover [dóuvœ (r)], Duvres.
Dresden [drézdǝn], Dresde.
Dunkirk [dʌ́nkœrk], Dunquerque.

E

East Indies [índiz], Indias Orientales.
Edinburgh [édinbœrou], Edimburgo.
Egypt [ídžipt], Egipto.
Elbe [élbǝ], Elba.
England [íŋglænd], Inglaterra.
English Channel, Canal de la Mancha, Paso de Calais.
Escurial [eskyúriǝl], Escorial.
Ethiopia [iθióupiǝ], Etiopía, Abisinia.
Euphrates [yufréitiz], Eufrates.
Europe [yúrǝp], Europa.

F

Finland [fínlǝnd], Finlandia.
Flanders [flǽndœrz], Flandes.
Florence [flɔ́rens], Florencia.
France [fræns], Francia.
Frankfort-on-the-Main [frǽŋkfɔrt], Francfort del Mein.

G

Galilee [gǽlili], Galilea.
Gascony [gǽskoni], Gascuña.

297

Gaul [gol], Galia.
Geneva [dʒenívǝ], Ginebra.
Genoa [dʒénowǝ], Génova.
Germany [dʒǿrmǝni], Alemania.
Ghent [gent], Gante.
Gold Coast [goʊld koʊst],
　Costa de Oro.
Great Britain [greit brítn],
　Gran Bretaña.
Greece [gris], Grecia.
Greenland [grínlǝnd], Groenlandia.
Guadeloupe [gwadǝlúp], Guadalupe.
Guam [gwam], Guaján, Guam.
Guiana [giǽnǝ, giánǝ], Guayana.

H

Hague [heig], (La) Haya.
Haiti [héiti], Haití, Isla Española.
Hamburg [hǽmbœrg], Hamburgo.
Havana [havǽnǝ], La Habana.
Hawaii [hawáii], Hawaí, Hauaí.
Hebrides [hébridiz], Hébridas.
Hindustan [hindustǽn], Indostán.
Hispaniola [hispǝnyóʊlǝ],
　La Española.
Holland [bálǝnd], Holanda.
Holy Land, Tierra Santa.
Hungary [hʌ́ŋgǝri], Hungría.

I

Iceland [áislǝnd], Islandia.
India [índiǝ], India, Indostán.
Indian Ocean, (Mar de las) Indias,
　(Océano) Índico.
Ionia [aióʊniǝ], Jonia.
Ireland [áirlǝnd], Irlanda.
Istanbul [istænbúl], Estambul.
Italy [ítǝli], Italia.
Ivory Coast, Costa del Marfil.
Izmir [ízmir], Esmirna.

J

Japan [dʒǝpǽn], Japón.
Jericho [dʒérikoʊ], Jericó.
Jerusalem [dʒirúsalem], Jerusalén.
Jugoslavia [yugoʊslávjǝ], = YUGOSLA-
　VIA.
Jutland [dʒʌ́tlǝnd], Jutlandia.

K

Kashmir [kæʃmír], Cachemira.
Khartoum [kartúm], Kartum.
Key West, Cayo Hueso.
Korea [koʊríǝ], Corea.
Kurdistan [kɜ́rdistæn], Kurdistán.

L

Labrador [lǽbrǝdɔr], Tierra del
　Labrador.
Lapland [lǽplǝnd], Laponia.
Lausanne [loʊzǽn], Lausana.
Lebanon [lébǝnǝn], Líbano.
Leghorn [lég̬hɔrn], Liorno.
Leningrad [léniŋgræd], Leningrado.
Lesser Antilles [lésœ(r) æntíliz],
　Las Pequeñas Antillas.
Lhasa [lásǝ], Lasa.
Libya [líbiǝ], Libia.
Liége [liéʒ, liéʒ], Lieja.
Lisbon [lízbǝn], Lisboa.
Lithuania [liθuéjniǝ], Lituania.
Lombardy [lámbǝrdi], Lombardia.
London [lándǝn], Londres.
Lorraine [loréin], Lorena.
Louisiana [luiziǽnǝ], Luisiana.

Low Countries, Países Bajos,
　Holanda.
Lower California [lóʊœ(r)
　kæliforniǝ], Baja California.
Lucerne [lusǿrn], Lucerna.
Luxemburg [láksembœrg],
　Luxemburgo.

M

Madeira [madírǝ], Madera.
Majorca [madʒórkǝ], Mallorca.
Malay [méjlei, maléi], Malaca.
Marseilles [marséi(l)z], Marsella.
Martinique [martiník], Martinica.
Mecca [mékǝ], Meca.
Mediterranean [mediterréiniǝn],
　Mediterráneo.
Memphis [mémfis], Menfis.
Mexico [méksikoʊ], México, Méjico.
Minorca [minórkǝ], Menorca.
Mississippi [misisípi], Misisipí.
Missouri [mizúri], Misurí.
Mobile [moʊbíl], Mobila.
Montpellier [mǝnpelyé], Mompellier.
Morocco [mǝrákoʊ], Marruecos.
Moscow [máskoʊ], Moscú.
Moselle [moʊzél], Mosela.
Musqat [mʌskǽt], Omán.

N

Naples [néiplz], Nápoles.
Navarre [navár], Navarra.
Nazareth [nǽzareθ, nǽzriθ], Nazaret.
Netherlands [néðœrlǝndz], Países
　Bajos, Holanda.
New Castile, Castilla la Nueva.
New England, Nueva Inglaterra.
Newfoundland [njúfʌndlænd],
　Terranova.
New Mexico, Nuevo México
　(o Méjico).
New Orleans [órljanz, orlínz],
　Nueva Orleáns.
New South Wales, Nueva Gales
　del Sur.
New York [yɔ́rk], Nueva York.
New Zealand [zílǝnd], Nueva
　Zelandia.
Nice [nis], Niza.
Nile [nail], Nilo.
Normandy [nórmǝndi], Normandía.
North America, América del Norte.
North Carolina [kærolájnǝ], Carolina
　del Norte.
North Dakota [dǝkóʊtǝ], Dakota del
　Norte.
Norway [nórwej], Norueza.
Nova Scotia [nóʊvǝ skóʊʃǝ],
　Nueva Escocia.
Nyasaland [nyásalænd], Niaslandia.

O

Oceania [oʊʃiǽniǝ], Oceanica
　[oʊʃiǽnikǝ], Oceanía.
Old Castile, Castilla la Vieja.
Olympus [oʊlímpʌs], Olimpo.
Ostend [asténd], Ostende.

P

Pacific [pǝsífik], Pacífico.
Palestine [pǽlestain], Palestina.
Panama [pǽnamǝ], Panamá.
Paris [pǽris], París.
Parnassus [parnǽsʌs], Parnaso.
Peking [pikíŋ], Pekin.

298

Peloponnesus [pelopanísʌs], Peloponeso.
Pennsylvania [pensilvéiniǎ], Pensilvania.
Persian Gulf [pɛ́rǯan], Golfo Pérsico.
Peru [pɛrú], Perú.
Philadelphia [fiḷadélfiǎ], Filadelfia.
Philippines [fílipinz], Filipinas.
Phoenicia [finíšǎ], Fenicia.
Poland [póuḷand], Polonia.
Polynesia [palíníšǎ], Polinesia.
Pompeii [pampéji], Pompeya.
Port-au-Prince [port o prins], Puerto Príncipe.
Porto Rico [pórtou ríkou], Puerto Rico.
Prague [prag], Praga.
Provence [prováns], Provenza.
Providence [právidɛns], Providencia.
Prussia [prʌ́šǎ], Prusia.
Pyrenees [píréniz], Pireneos.

R

Red Sea, Mar Rojo.
Rhine [rain], Rin o Rhin.
Rhineland [ráinlænd], Renania.
Rhodes [roudz], Rodas.
Rhodesia [roudíʒǎ], Rodesia.
Rhone [roun], Ródano.
Rocky Mountains, Montañas Rocosas o Rocallosas.
Rome [roum], Roma.
Rouen [ruán], Ruán.
Russia [rʌ́šǎ], Rusia.

S

Saragossa [særagásǎ], Zaragoza.
Sardinia [sardíniǎ], Cerdeña.
Saudi Arabia [saúdi ǎréibiǎ], Arabia Saudita.
Saxony [sǽksoni], Sajonia.
Scandinavia [skændinéiviǎ], Escandinavia.
Scotland [skátḷand], Escocia.
Seine [sein, sɛn], Sena.
Seoul [saúl], Seúl.
Serbia [sɛ́rbiǎ], Servia.
Seville [sɛvíl], Sevilla.
Sicily [sísili], Sicilia.
Sierra Leone [siɛ́rǎ lióun(i)], Sierra Leona.
Slavonia [slǎvóuniǎ], Eslavonia.
Slovakia [slovákiǎ], Eslovaquia.
Slovenia [slovíniǎ], Eslovenia.
South Africa, Sud-África.
South America, América del Sur, Sud-América, Sur-América.
South Carolina [kæroláinǎ], Carolina del Sur.
South Dakota [dǎkóutǎ], Dakota del Sur.
Soviet Union [sóuviet], Unión Soviética.
Spain [spein], España.
Spanish America, Hispano-América, América Española.
Sparta [spártǎ], Esparta.
Spoleto [spoléitou], Espoleto.

Stockholm [stákhou(l)m], Estocolmo.
Strait of Magellan [mǎdʒélǎn], Estrecho de Magallanes.
Sudan [sudǽn], Sudán.
Sweden [swídǎn], Suecia.
Switzerland [swítsœrḷand], Suiza.
Syracuse [sírakius], Siracusa.
Syria [síriǎ], Siria.

T

Tagus [téigʌs], Tajo.
Tahiti [tahíti], Tahití.
Tanganyika [tǽŋganyíkǎ], Tanganica.
Tangier [tændʒír], Tánger.
Texas [tɛ́ksas], Tejas.
Thailand [táiland], Thailandia.
Thames [tɛmz], Támesis.
Thebes [θibz], Tebas.
Thrace [θreis], Tracia.
Tobago [toubéigou], Tabago.
Tokyo [tóukiou], Tokio.
Toulouse [tulúz], Tolosa.
Trent [trɛnt], Trento.
Troy [trɔi], Troya.
Tunis(ia) [t(i)únis; t(i)unísǎ], Túnez (ciudad, país).
Turkey [tɛ́rki], Turquía.
Tuscany [tʌ́skani], Toscana.
Tyrol [tíral, tiróul], Tirol.

U

Ukraine [yúkrein, yukréin], Ucrania.
Union of South Africa, Unión Sudafricana.
United Kingdom, Reino Unido.
United States of America, Estados Unidos de América.
Upper Volta [vóulṭǎ], Alto Volta.
USSR [yu ɛs ɛs ar], URSS.

V

Venice [vénis], Venecia.
Versailles [vœrséilz, vɛrsáy], Versalles.
Vesuvius [vɛsúviʌs], Vesubio.
Vienna [viénǎ], Viena.
Virgin Islands, Islas Vírgenes.

W

Wales [weilz], Gales.
Warsaw [wɔ́rsɔ], Varsovia.
Watling Island [wátlin], Isla de San Salvador.
West Indies [índiz], Antillas.
West Virginia [vœrdʒíŋyǎ], Virginia Occidental.

Y

Yugoslavia [yugouslǎ́viǎ], Yugoeslavia.

Z

Zanzibar [zǽnzibar], Zanzíbar.
Zealand [zíland], Zelandia.
Zion [záion], Sion.
Zululand [zúlulænd], Zululandia.

NOMBRES PROPIOS DE PERSONAS Y DE PERSONAJES HISTORICOS, LITERARIOS Y MITOLOGICOS

(Sólo se incluyen los que difieren en ambas lenguas. Se excluyen los diminutivos y afectivos que se forman añadiendo "ito," "illo," etc., v.gr. Agustinito, Juanillo, Juanico, etc.)

A

Abelard [ǽbelard], Abelardo.
Abraham [éjbrahæm], Abrahán.
Achilles [akíliz], Aquiles.
Adam [ǽdam], Adán.
Æneas [inías], Eneas.
Æschylus [éskilas], Esquilo.
Æsop [ísop, ísap], Esopo.
Agatha [ǽgaθ̣ǝ], Agueda, Ágata.
Agnes [ǽgnis], Inés.
Alan [ǽlan], Alano.
Albert [ǽlbœrt], Alberto.
Alexander [ælígzændœ(r)], Alejandro.
Alfred [ǽlfrid], Alfredo.
Alice [ǽlis], Alicia.
Allan [ǽlan], Allen [ǽlen], Alano.
Alphonso [ælfánsou], Alfonso, Alonso, Ildefonso.
Andrew [ǽndru], Andrés.
Angel [éjndžel], Angel.
Anne [æn], Anna [ǽnǝ], Ana.
Anthony [ǽnθoni], Antonio.
Archimedes [arkímídiz], Arquímedes.
Aristophanes [æristáfaniz], Aristófanes.
Aristotle [ǽristatl], Aristóteles.
Arnold [árnold], Arnaldo, Arnoldo.
Arthur [árθœ(r)], Arturo.
Attila [ǽtilǝ], Atila.
Augustine [ɔ́gʌstin, ogʌ́stin], Agustín.
Augustus [ogʌ́stʌs], Augusto.

B

Bacchus [bǽkʌs], Baco.
Bartholomew [barθálomiu], Bartolomé.
Basil [bǽzil], Basilio.
Beatrice [bíatris], Beatriz.
Benedict [bénędikt], Benito.
Benedicta [benędíktǝ], Benita.
Benjamin [béndžamin], Benjamín.
Bernard [bœ́rnard, bernárd], Bernardo.
Bertha [bœ́rθǝ], Berta.
Bonaventura [bánavenchūrǝ], Buenaventura, Ventura.
Brutus [brútas], Bruto.
Buddha [búdǝ], Buda.

C

Caesar [sízǝ(r)], César.
Calvin [kǽlvin], Calvino.
Camille [kamíl], Camila.
Camillus [kamílas], Camilo.
Caroline [kǽrolain], Carolina.
Cassandra [kasǽndrǝ], Cassandra.
Catharine [kǽθarin], Catherine [kǽθerin], Catalina.
Cato [kéjtou], Catón.
Catullus [katʌ́lʌs], Catulo.

Cecile [sisíl], Cecilia.
Charlemagne [šárlemejn], Carlomagno.
Charles [charlz], Carlos.
Charlotte [šárlot], Carlota.
Christ [krajst], Cristo.
Christine [kristín], Cristina.
Christopher [krístofœ(r)], Cristóbal.
Cicero [síserou], Cicerón.
Claire, Clare [kler], Clara.
Claude [klɔd], Claudio.
Clement [klément], Clemente.
Clovis [klóuvis], Clodoveo.
Columbus [kǝlʌ́mbas], Colón.
Confucius [kǝnfiúšas], Confucio.
Constance [kánstǝns], Constanza, Constancia.
Constantine [kánstantajn], Constantino.
Cyrus [sájrʌs], Ciro.

D

Daisy [déjzi], Margarita.
Delilah [dilájlǝ], Dalila.
Demosthenes [dimásθeniz], Demóstenes.
Dennis [dénis], Dionisio.
Diogenes [dajádženiz], Diógenes.
Dionysius [dajonísjǝs], Dionisio.
Dominic [dáminik], Domingo.
Dorothy [dóroθi, dároθi], Dorotea.

E

Edith [ídiθ], Edita.
Edmund [édmʌnd], Edmundo.
Edward [édwǝrd], Eduardo.
Eleanor, Elinor [élinǝ(r)], Leonor.
Eliza [jlájzǝ], Elisa.
Elizabeth [jlízabeθ], Isabel.
Ellen [élen], Elena.
Eloise [élɔiz], Eloísa.
Em(m)anuel [imǽniuel], Manuel.
Emil [éjmil], Emilio.
Emily [émili], Emilia.
Emma [émǝ], Ema, Manuela.
Epicurus [epikiúrǝs], Epicuro.
Erasmus [irǽzmʌs], Erasmo.
Ernest [œ́rnjst], Ernesto.
Ernestine [œ́rnestin], Ernestina.
Esther [éstœ(r)], Ester.
Euclid [yúklid], Euclides.
Eugene [yudžin], Eugenio.
Eugénie [œžéní], Eugenia.
Eve [iv], Eva.

F

Felicia [filíšiǝ], Felisa, Felicia.
Ferdinand [fœ́rdinænd], Fernando.
Florence [flɔ́rens], Florencia.
Frances [frǽnsis], Francisca.
Francis [frǽnsis], Frank [frǽŋk], Francisco.

Frederica [frederíkə], Federica.
Frederick [fréderik], Federico.

G

Galen [géilen], Galeno.
George [dʒɔrdʒ], Jorge.
Geraldine [dʒéraldin], Gerarda.
Gerard [dʒirárd], Gerardo.
Gertrude [gœrtrud], Gertrudis.
Gilbert [gílbœrt], Gilberto.
Godfrey [gádfri], Godofredo.
Gracchus [grǽkʌs], Graco.
Grace [greis], Engracia.
Gregory [grégori], Gregorio.
Gustave [gástav], **Gustavus**
[gʌstéivʌs], Gustavo.

H

Hadrian [héidrian], Adriano.
Hannah [hǽnə], Ana.
Hannibal [hǽnibəl], Aníbal.
Harold [hǽrold], Haroldo.
Helen [hélin], Elena.
Henrietta [henriétə], Enriqueta.
Henry [hénri], Enrique.
Herbert [hœrbœrt], Heriberto.
Herman [hœrman], Arminio.
Herod [hérod], Herodes.
Herodotus [hirádotʌs], Herodoto.
Hezekiah [hezekáiə], Ezequías.
Hippocrates [hipákratiz], Hipócrates.
Homer [hóumœr], Homero.
Horace [hóris], Horacio.
Hortense [horténs], Hortensia.
Hubert [hjúbœrt], Huberto.
Humbert [hámbœrt], Humberto.
Humphrey [hámfri], Hunfredo.

I

Ignatius [ignéiʃʌs], Ignacio.
Inez [áinez, ínez], Inés.
Innocent [ínosent], Inocencio.
Isabella [izabélə], Isabel.
Isidore [ízidor], Isidro, Isidoro.

J

James [dʒeimz], Jaime, Jacobo,
Santiago.
Jane [dʒein], Juana.
Jasper [dʒǽspœr], Gaspar.
Jeffrey [dʒéfri], Geofredo.
Jehovah [dʒihóuvə], Jehová.
Jeremiah [dʒeremáiə], Jeremías.
Jerome [dʒiróum, dʒérom],
Jerónimo, Gerónimo.
Jesus Christ [dʒízʌs], Jesucristo.
Joachim [yóuakim], Joaquín.
Joan [dʒoun], Juana.
Joan of Arc [ark], Juana de Arco.
John [dʒan], Juan.
Jonathan [dʒánəθan], Jonatán,
Jonatás.
Joseph [dʒóuzef], José.
Josephine [dʒóuzefin], Josefina.
Joshua [dʒáʃuə], Josué.
Judith [dʒúdiθ], Judit.
Julian [dʒúlyan], Julián; Juliano
(emperador).
Juliet [dʒúlyet, dʒuliét], Julia,
Julieta.
Julius [dʒúlyʌs], Julio.
Justinian [dʒʌstínian], Justiniano.

K

Katharine [kǽθarin], **Katherine**
[kǽθerin], Catalina.

L

Laurence, Lawrence [lórens],
Lorenzo.
Lazarus [lǽzarʌs], Lázaro.
Lenore [linór], Lenora.
Leo [líou], León.
Leonard [lénərd], Leonardo.
Leonora [lionórə], Lenora.
Leopold [líopould], Leopoldo.
Lewis [lúis], Luis.
Livy [lívi], Livio.
Louis [lúis, lúi], Luis.
Louise [luíz], Luisa.
Lucan [lúkan], Lucano.
Lucian [lúʃan], Luciano.
Lucretia [lukríʃə], Lucrecia.
Lucretius [lukríʃʌs], Lucrecio.
Lucy [lúsi], Lucía.
Luke [luk], Lucas.
Luther [lúθœr], Lutero.

M

Magdalen [mǽgdalen], Magdalena.
Magellan [madʒélan], Magallanes.
Margaret [márgarit], Margarita.
Marian [mérian], **Marion** [mérion],
Mariana.
Marjorie [márdʒori], Margarita.
Mark [mark], Marco, Marcos.
Martha [márθə], Marta.
Mary [méri], María.
Matthew [mǽθju], Mateo.
Maurice [móris], Mauricio.
Messiah [mesáiə], Mesías.
Michael [máikel], Miguel.
Michelangelo [maikelǽndʒelou],
Miguel Angel.
Miriam [míriam], María.
Mohammed [mouhǽmid], Mahoma.
Moses [móuziz], Moisés.

N

Nathan [néiθan], Natán.
Nathaniel [naθǽnyel], Nataniel.
Nebuchadnezzar [nebyukadnézə(r)],
Nabucodonosor.
Nero [nírou], Nerón.
Nicholas [níkolas], Nicolás.
Noah [nóuə], Noé.

O

Octavius [aktéiviʌs], Octavio.
Oliver [álivœ(r)], Oliverio.
Otto [átou], Otón.
Ovid [ávid], Ovidio.

P

Patrick [pǽtrik], Patricio.
Paul [pol], Pablo.
Pauline [polín], Paula, Paulina.
Perseus [pœrsus], Perseo.
Peter [pitœ(r)], Pedro.
Philip [fílip], Felipe, Felipo
(de Macedonia).
Philippa [fílipə], Felipa.
Pilate [páilat], Pilatos.
Pindar [píndə(r)], Píndaro.
Pius [páiʌs], Pío.
Plato [pléitou], Platón.
Plautus [plótʌs], Plauto.
Pliny [plíni], Plinio.
Plutarch [plútark], Plutarco.
Prometheus [promíθus], Prometeo.
Ptolemy [tálemi], Tolomeo,
Ptolomeo.

301

Pythagoras [pɪθǽgọrạs], Pitágoras.

Susan [súzan], Susana.
Sylvester [sɪlvéstœ(r)], Silvestre.

Q

Quentin [kwéntɪn], Quintín.

T

Tacitus [tǽsịtʌs], Tácito.
Tamerlane [tǽmœrleịn], Tamerlán.
Terence [térẹns], Terencio.
Theodore [θíodor], Teodoro.
Theresa [tịrísạ], Teresa.
Thomas [támạs], Tomás.
Thucydides [θusídịdiz], Tucídides.
Tiberius [taịbírịạs], Tiberio.
Timothy [tímoθị], Timoteo.
Titian [tíʃạn], el Ticiano.
Tristram [trístrạm], Tristán.

R

Rachel [réịchẹl], Raquel.
Ralph [rælf], Rodolfo.
Randolph [réndalf], Randolfo.
Raphael [réịfịẹl], Rafael.
Raymond [réịmọnd], Raimundo, Ramón.
Rebecca [rịbékạ], Rebeca.
Reginald [rédʒịnạld], Reinaldo.
Reuben [rúbịn], Rubén.
Richard [ríchạrd], Ricardo.
Robert [rábœrt], Roberto.
Roderick [rádẹrịk], Rodrigo.
Roger [rádʒœ(r)], Rogelio, Rogerio.
Roland [róụlạnd], Rolando, Orlando.
Romulus [rámyụlʌs], Rómulo.
Ronald [ránạld], Renaldo.
Rosalie [róụzạlị], Rosalía.
Rosary [róụzạrị], Rosario.
Rose [roụz], Rosa.
Rubin [rúbịn], Rubén.
Rudolph [rúdalf], Rodolfo.

U

Ulysses [yulísiz], Ulises.
Urban [œ́rbạn], Urbano.

V

Valentine [vǽlẹntaịn], Valentín.
Vergil [vœ́rdʒịl], Virgilio.
Vespucci [vespútchi], Vespucio.
Vincent [vínsẹnt], Vicente.
Virgil [vœ́rdʒịl], Virgilio.
Vivian [vívịạn], Bibiana.

S

Saladin [sǽladịn], Saladino.
Salome [salóụmị], Salomé.
Samson [sǽmsọn], Sansón.
Sarah [sérạ], Sara.
Satan [séịtạn], Satanás.
Scipio [sípịoụ], Escipión.
Solomon [sálomọn], Salomón.
Sophia [sóụfị̃ạ], Sofía.
Sophocles [sáfokliz], Sófocles.
Stephen, Steven [stívẹn], Esteban.
Strabo [stréịboụ], Estrabón.
Stradivarius [strædịvérịʌs], Estradivario.
Suleiman [suleịmán], Solimán.

W

Walter [wóltœ(r)], Gualterio.
Wilhelmina [wịlhelmínạ], Guillermina.
William [wílyạm], Guillermo.

X

Xavier [zéịvịœ(r), zǽvịœ(r)], Javier.
Xenophon [zénofan], Jenofonte.
Xerxes [zœ́rksiz], Jerjes.

Z

Zachary [zǽkạrị], Zacarías.
Zeno [zínoụ], Zenón, Cenón.
Zoroaster [zóroæstœ(r)], Zoroastro.

ABREVIATURAS MAS USUALES EN INGLES

A

a., acre(s).
A.B., Bachelor of Arts.
abbr., abbreviation.
abr., abridgment, abridged.
A.C., alternating current; Air Corps.
acct., account.
Adm., admiral(ty).
Afr., Africa(n).
aft., afternoon.
agcy., agency.
agr(ic)., agriculture; agricultural.
agt., agent.
Ala., Alabama.
Alas., Alaska.
a.m., ante meridiem (before noon).
A.M., Master of Arts; before noon; amplitude modulation.

amp., ampere; amperage.
amt., amount.
anat., anatomy.
anon., anonymous.
ans., answer.
A.P., Associated Press.
app., appendix; appointed.
Apr., April.
apt., apartment.
Ar., Arabic; Aramaic.
arith., arithmetic(al).
Ariz., Arizona.
Ark., Arkansas.
assn., association.
assoc., association; associate.
asst., assistant.
att., attorney.
Att.Gen., Attorney General.
atty., attorney.

Aug., August.
ave., avenue.

B

b., base; book; born; brother.
B., British.
B.A., Bachelor of Arts.
bal., balance.
B.B.A., Bachelor of Business Administration.
B.C., before Christ.
bd., board; bond; bound.
b.e., B/E, bill of exchange.
bet., between.
Bibl., Biblical; bibliographical.
biog., biographical; biography.

302

biol., biological; biology.

bk., book.

b.l., **B/L**, bill of lading.

bldg., building.

blvd., boulevard.

b.p., bills payable; boiling point.

Br., British; Britain.

Bro(s)., brother(s).

b.s., balance sheet; bill of sale.

B.S(c)., Bachelor of Science.

bus., business.

bx., box.

C

c., cent; chapter; cubic; current; center.

C., Cape; Catholic; centigrade.

C.A., Central America; Chartered Accountant.

cal., calorie; caliber.

Cal(if)., California.

Can., Canada; Canadian.

cap., capital; capitalize(d); Chapter.

Capt., Captain.

Cath., Catholic.

cent., centigrade; central; century.

cert., certificate; certify.

cf., confer; compare.

C.F.I., cost, freight, and insurance.

C.G., Coast Guard.

Ch., Church.

chap., chapter.

chem., chemical, chemistry.

C.I.F., cost, insurance, and freight (c.i.f., o c.s.f. costo, seguro y flete).

c.o., **c/o.**, care of; carried over.

C.O., Commanding Officer.

Co., company; county.

C.O.D., collect (o cash) on delivery (cóbrese a la entrega).

Col., Colonel; Colorado.

Colo., Colorado.

com., commerce.

Com., Commander; Commission(er); Committee; Commodore.

comp., comparative; compare; compound.

con., conclusion; contra (against, opposing).

Cong., Congress(ional).

Conn., Connecticut.

cont., containing; contents; continent; continue(d).

cor., corrected; correction; corresponding corner.

Corp., Corporal; corporation.

cp., compare.

C.P.A., Certified Public Accountant.

Cpl., Corporal.

cr., credit(or).

C.S.A., Confederate States of America.

C.S.T., Central Standard Time.

ct., cent.

Ct., Connecticut.

cts., cents; certificates.

c.w.o., cash with order.

D

d., died; dime; dollar.

D.A., District Attorney.

Dan., Danish.

D.C., District of Columbia; direct current.

D.D., Doctor of Divinity.

D.D.S., Doctor of Dental Surgery.

Dec., December.

deg., degree(s).

Del., Delaware.

Dem., Democrat(ic).

dep., department; deputy.

dept., department.

der(iv)., derivation; derivative.

D.H.C., Doctor Honoris Causa.

dial., dialect(al).

diam., diameter.

diff., difference; different.

disc., discount; discovered.

dist., distance; district.

div., divided; dividend; division.

D.Lit., Doctor of Literature.

D.Litt., Doctor of Letters.

doz., dozen(s).

Dr., Doctor.

dup., duplicate.

D.V., Deo volente (God willing).

dz., dozen(s).

E

E., east(ern); English.

ea., each.

econ., economic(s); economy.

ed., edition; editor.

educ., education(al).

e.g., exempligratia (for example), v.g.

elec(t)., electric(al); electricity.

Eng., England; English.

esp(ec)., especially.

est., established.

E.S.T., Eastern Standard Time.

etc., et cetera (and so forth).

Eur., Europe(an).

ex., example; exception; executive.

exc., except(ed); exception.

exch., exchange.

exp., export(ed); express; expenses.

F

F., Fahrenheit; Father; French; Friday.

Fahr., Fahrenheit.

FBI, Federal Bureau of Investigation.

Feb., February.

Fed., Federal.

ff., following.

fin., financial.

Fla., Florida.

F.M., frequency modulation.

f.o.b., free on board (libre a bordo).

fol(l)., following.

fr., francs; from.

Fr., France; French.

Fri., Friday.

ft., foot, feet.

Ft., fort.

G

G., German.

Ga., Georgia.

gal(l)., **(pl., gals.),** gallon(s).

G.B., Great Britain.

Gen., General.

geog., geographic(al); geography.

Ger., German(y).

Gov., government; Governor.

Govt., government.

G.P.O., General Post Office.

Gt.Br(it)., Great Britain.

H

hdqrs., headquarters.

H.E., His Eminence; His Excellency.

H.H., His (o Her) Highness; His Holiness.

H.I., Hawaiian Islands.

H.M., His (o Her) Majesty.

H.M.S., His (o Her) Majesty's service, ship o steamer.

Hon., Honorable.

h.p., horse power; high pressure.

H.Q., headquarters.

H.R., House of Representatives.

hr(s)., hour(s).

ht., height; heat.

I

I., Island.

Ia., Iowa.

Ice(l)., Iceland(ic).

Id(a)., Idaho.

Ill., Illinois.

303

inc., incorporated; including; increase.

Ind., Indiana; India; Indian; Indies.

ins., insurance.

inst., instant; institute.

int., interest; international.

inv., invented; inventor; invoice.

I.O.U., I owe you.

I.Q., intelligence quotient.

Is(l)., Island(s); Isle(s).

It(al)., Italian; Italy.

ital., italic.

J

Jam., Jamaica.

Jan., January.

Jap., Japan(ese).

J.C., Jesus Christ; Julius Caesar.

J.P., Justice of the Peace.

Jr., Junior.

Jul., July.

Jun., June; Junior.

K

K., King; Knight(s).

Kan(s)., Kansas.

Ken., Kentucky.

Knt., Knight.

k.o., knockout.

kt., carat.

Kt., Knight.

Ky., Kentucky.

L

l., latitude; length; line.

L., lake; Latin.

La., Louisiana.

lat., latitude.

Lat., Latin.

Leg(is)., legislature; legislative.

Lieut., Lieutenant.

liq., liquid; liquor.

lon(g)., longitude.

Lt., Lieutenant.

Ltd., Limited.

M

M., Monday; member.

M.A., Master of Arts.

mag., magazine; magnetism.

Maj., Major.

Mar., March.

Mass., Massachusetts.

M.C., Master of Ceremonies; Member of Congress.

M.D., Medical Doctor.

Md., Maryland.

mdse., merchandise.

Me., Maine.

Mex., Mexican; Mexico.

mfg., manufacturing.

Mgr., manager.

Mich., Michigan.

Minn., Minnesota.

misc., miscellaneous; miscellany.

Miss., Mississippi.

Mo., Missouri; Monday.

mo(s)., month(s).

Mon., Monday.

Mont., Montana.

M.P., Member of Parliament; Military Police.

m.p.h., miles per hour.

Mr., Mister, Master.

Mrs., Mistress.

M.S(c)., Master of Science.

Mt(s)., Mount, Mountain(s).

N

N., North(ern).

N.A(m)., North America(n).

nat(l)., national.

NATO, North Atlantic Treaty Organization.

N.B., New Brunswick; nota bene (note well).

N.C., North Carolina.

N.Dak., North Dakota.

Neb(r)., Nebraska.

N.Eng., New England.

Neth., Netherlands.

Nev., Nevada.

n.g., (fam.) no good.

N.G., National Guard.

N.H., New Hampshire.

N.J., New Jersey.

N.M(ex)., New Mexico.

No. (*pl.,* **nos.**), number.

noncom., noncommissioned officer.

Norw., Norwegian; Norway.

Nov., November.

nt.wt., net weight.

N.Y., New York.

N.Y.C., New York City.

N.Z(eal)., New Zealand.

O

O., Ohio; Ontario; Ocean.

O.A.S., Organization of American States.

obs., observation; observatory; obsolete.

Oct., October.

O.K., all right; correct.

Okla., Oklahoma.

Ont., Ontario.

ord., order; ordinance.

Ore(g)., Oregon.

P

p., page; part; pint.

Pa., Pennsylvania.

Pac., Pacific.

payt., payment.

p.c., per cent; post card.

pd., paid.

Penn., Pennsylvania.

Ph.D., Doctor of Philosophy.

photog., photographic; photography.

phys., physician; physics.

P.I., Philippine Islands.

pkg(s)., package(s).

pl., place; plate; plural.

P.M., Postmaster; paymaster; post meridiem (after noon).

P.O.D., Post Office Department; pay on delivery.

pop., population.

pos., positive.

pp., pages.

P.R., Porto Rico *o* Puerto Rico.

pr., pair; price.

pres., present; presidency.

Pres., President.

prin., principal.

Prof., Professor.

Prot., Protestant.

pro tem., pro tempore (temporarily).

prov., province; provincial.

P.S., postscript.

pt., part; payment; point; pint; port.

pub., public; published; publisher.

P.X., (military) post exchange.

Q

Q., Quebec; Queen.

qt., quantity; quart.

qu., quart(er); queen; query; question.

Que., Quebec.

ques., question.

quot., quotation.

q.v., quod vide (which see).

qy., query.

R

R., Republican; river; Royal.

R.A., Rear Admiral; Royal Academy.

R.C., Roman Catholic; Red Cross.

Rd., Road.

rec., receipt.

rec'd., recd., received.

ref., reference; referred; reformed.

reg., registry; regular.

Reg(t)., regiment.

Rep., Representative; Republic(an).

Rev., Reverend.

R.I., Rhode Island.

R.I.P., rest in peace.

R.N., registered nurse.

r.p.m., revolutions per minute.

R.R., railroad.

R.S.V.P., Répondez, s'il vous plaît (please answer).

Ry., railway, railroad.

S

S., Saturday; Sunday; South(ern).

S.A., South America(n); South Africa;

304

South Australia; Salvation Army.
Sab., Sabbath.
S.Am., South America.
Sat., Saturday.
S.C., South Carolina; Supreme Court.
Scot., Scotch, Scottish; Scotland.
S.Dak., South Dakota.
SEATO, Southeast Asia Treaty Organization.
sec., second(ary); secretary; section.
Sen., Senate; Senator.
Sep(t)., September; Septuagint.
seq., sequel; the following.
Serg(t)., Sergeant.
serv(t)., servant.
Sgt., Sergeant.
S.I., Staten Island.
Soc., Society.
Sp., Spain; Spanish.
spt., seaport.
Sr., senior; sir.
S.S., steamship; Sunday School.
St., Saint; Street.
str., steamer.
sub., substitute; suburban.
Sun(d)., Sunday.
sup., superior.
Supp., Supplement.
Supt., superintendent.

T

tbs., tablespoon(s).
tel., telegram; telegraph; telephone.
teleg., telegram; telegraph.
Tenn., Tennessee.
Ter(r)., Territory.
Tex., Texas.
Th., Thur(s)., Thursday.
tp., township.

trans., translation; translated; transaction.
treas., treasurer; treasury.
tsp., teaspoon(s).
Tu(es)., Tuesday.

U

U., University.
U.K., United Kingdom.
ult., ultimate.
ult(o)., ultimo (the past month) (el mes pasado).
Univ., University.
U.P.I., United Press International.
U.S., United States.
U.S.A., United States of America; United States Army; Union of South Africa.
U.S.A.F., United States Air Force.
U.S.C.G., United States Coast Guard.
U.S.M., United States Mail.
U.S.M.C., United States Marine Corps.
U.S.N., United States Navy.
U.S.S., United States Ship; United States Senate.
U.S.S.R., USSR, Union of Soviet Socialist Republics.
usu., usual(ly).
Ut., Utah.

V

v., verse; versus; volume.
Va., Virginia.
V.A., Veterans' Administration.
var., variant; variation; variety; various.

vet., veteran; veterinary.
Vice Pres., Vice President.
vid., vide (see).
viz., videlicet (namely).
vocab., vocabulary.
vol., volume; volunteer.
V.P., Vice President.
vs., versus.
Vt., Vermont.

W

w., week; weight; with.
W., Wednesday; Welsh; west(ern).
Wash., Washington (estado).
Wed., Wednesday.
W.I., West Indian; West Indies.
Wis(c)., Wisconsin.
wk., week; work.
wt., weight.
W.Va., West Virginia.
Wy(o)., Wyoming.
wk., week; work.
wt., weight.
W.Va., West Virginia.
Wy(o)., Wyoming.

X

Xn., Xtian., Christian.

Y

Y., Young Men's Christian *o* Hebrew Association.
y., yard; year.
Y.M.C.A., Young Men's Christian Association.
Y.M.H.A., Young Men's Hebrew Association.
yr., year; your.

Z

Z., Zone.

TABLAS DE PESOS Y MEDIDAS
(TABLES OF WEIGHTS AND MEASURES)

Avoirdupois Weights
(Unidades comunes de peso)

1 ounce (oz.) = 28.35 gramos (g.)
1 pound (lb.) = 16 ounces = 435,59 gramos
1 hundredweight (cwt.) = 112 pounds = 50,8 kilogramos

Troy and Apothecaries' Weights
(Unidades de peso usadas en joyería y farmacia)

1 ounce = 31,10 gramos
1 pound = 12 ounces = 373,24 gramos

Liquid and Dry Measures
(Medidas de capacidad para líquidos y áridos)

Liquid (Líquidos)

1 pint (pt.) = 0,47 litros (l.)
1 quart (qt.) = 2 pints = 0,94 litros
1 gallon (gal.) = 4 quarts = 3,78 litros
1 barrel (b.) = 31.5 gallons = 119,07 litros

Dry (Áridos)

1 pint (pt.) = 0,55 litros
1 quart (qt.) = 2 pints = 1,1 litros
1 gallon (gal.) = 4 quarts = 4,40 litros
1 peck (pk.) = 2 gallons = 8.80 litros
1 bushel = 4 pecks = 35 litros

Linear Measures
(Medidas de longitud)

1 inch (in.) o 1″ = 2,54 centímetros (cm.)
1 foot (ft.) o 1′ = 12 inches = 30,48 centímetros
1 yard (yd.) = 3 feet = 91,44 centímetros
1 mile (m.) = 1,760 yards = 1,609 kilómetros (km.)

Square Measures
(Medidas de superficie)

1 square inch (sq.in.) = 6,45 centímetros cuadrados (cm.²)
1 square foot (sq.ft.) = 144 square inches = 0,93 metros cuadrados
1 square yard (sq.yd.) = 9 square feet = 0.836 metros cuadrados (m.²)
1 acre = 4,830 square yards = 40,468 hectáreas
1 square mile (sq.m.) = 640 acres = 2,59 kilómetros cuadrados (km.²)

TERMOMETRO

32° Fahrenheit (punto de congelación) = 0° centígrados
212° Fahrenheit (punto de ebullición) = 100° centígrados

Para reducir grados Fahrenheit a grados centígrados multiplíquese por 5/9 e réstense 32°.